Y0-CBO-980

1978
Art & Crafts Market

1978 Art & Crafts Market

Edited by
Lynne Lapin and Betsy Wones

A Writer's Digest Book
Cincinnati, Ohio

Acknowledgments

The editors would like to thank the following people for their contributions to this book:

Joe Bobbey, John Brady, William Brohaugh, Cathy Bruce, Cecelia Curee, Bruce Hillman, Ron Klett, Jane Koester, Jeff Lapin, Melissa Milar, Ed Nies, Betsy Parcell, Kirk Polking, Bob Rogers, Carol Rogers, Richard Rosenthal, Doug Sandhage, Jean Smith, Ruby Taylor, Budge Wallis and Jan Wolf.

Published by
Writer's Digest Books, 9933 Alliance Rd., Cincinnati, Ohio 45242

International Standard Serial Number 0147-2461
International Standard Book Number 0-911654-47-X

Printed and bound in the United States of America

Preface

Art & Crafts Market 1978 has one major purpose: to list places where you can sell your crafts and art. Places from New York City to Los Angeles and beyond. 4,498 places in all.

Besides names and addresses, each listing — which was OKed by the buyer cited — tells what the buyer wants in art or crafts, how much the pay is, and how work is to be submitted for approval. It's direct, accurate and up-dated information. Everything you need to help you sell your work is here.

Since last year's edition (then called *Artist's & Photographer's Market* — camera buffs now have our new *Photographer's Market*), we followed up every lead to obtain new listings for this book. The result: 1,000 brand new ones.

Most of these came in from craft dealers, craft galleries and craft competitions and exhibitions. Thus the name change to *Art & Crafts Market.*

To best use this book, read "How to Use This Book" and check out the contents pages. Then go through the listings till you find those asking for your kind of work. If you're looking for markets close to home, look at the index for local firms or publications you know about (some sections of the book are arranged by state locations to help you find those in your locale).

In addition to all the places listed here in the various sections and categories, there are thousands more that might consider freelance work if you ask them. Once you get an assignment from a firm or publication not listed in this book, let us know and we'll consider including its freelance requirements next year.

We've included a number of introductory articles (pages 1-22) that contain information to help you make sales. Don Jardine, editor of *The Illustrator* — Loretta Holz, author of *How to Sell Your Art and Crafts* — and Diane Cochrane, editor of the *American Artist Business Letter* — all offer solid advice. Also, note the pieces on selling crafts, and copyrighting and shipping your work.

Finally, the back of the book includes a list of agents available to do the selling for you (several agents use this book to find potential clients), foundations which offer grants to artists and craftsmen, subject-related publications of interest, and a handful of art colonies where you can get away from it all and just create.

It's one big book. And it's all yours. Happy sales.

— *Lynne Lapin* and *Betsy Wones*

Contents

Getting Started

How to Use This Book

Art & Crafts Market contains a wealth of information to help you become a successful freelance artist or craftsman. To utilize the book to its best capacity, here are a few directions:

- The book has been divided into 17 sections, each of which is listed in the Table of Contents. Most sections are further divided into categories. Depending on your interests, choose which sections and categories you'd like to look over.
- Within each section and category, markets are listed alphabetically. In the Competition/Exhibition, Craft Dealers and Exposition Space sections, however, markets are arranged according to state and then alphabetically. New Jersey artists, for example, can quickly locate shows in their area.
- Don't limit yourself to one section or category. For example, since many galleries exhibit crafts as well as art, the craftsman need not limit himself only to craft dealers. Similarly, many businesses other than advertising agencies, seek advertising art.
- Pay attention to specifications. If an editor requests b&w cartoons only, don't send color. Follow directions carefully.
- If you stumble across words with which you're not familiar, check the glossary for explanations.
- Listings not included in *Art & Crafts Market* are not necessarily bad markets. They may be omitted because they asked to be; they didn't return our questionnaire; or they don't buy freelance art.
- If one of our markets doesn't respond to your queries or fails to pay for accepted artwork — contact us. We don't necessarily endorse the listings in this book, although we do review them annually and remove those that accumulate numerous legitimate complaints. A complaint letter to us should include copies of letters you've sent in an attempt to settle the problem yourself and SASE. We'll photocopy the complaint letter and send it with a letter of our own to the publication or firm in question. If we don't get a response within three weeks, we'll consider deleting the listing from the next edition.

Here are some abbreviations and U.S. Postal Service's state codes you'll find commonly used throughout the book:

B.C.	British Columbia
B&W	Black & white
Circ	Circulation
Estab	Established
Ms(s)	Manuscript(s)
POP	Point-of-Purchase
SASE	Self-addressed stamped envelope

State Codes

AK	Alaska
AL	Alabama
AR	Arkansas
AZ	Arizona
CA	California
CO	Colorado
CT	Connecticut
DC	District of Columbia
DE	Delaware
FL	Florida
GA	Georgia
HI	Hawaii
IA	Iowa
ID	Idaho
IL	Illinois
IN	Indiana
KS	Kansas
KY	Kentucky
LA	Louisiana
MA	Massachusetts
MD	Maryland
ME	Maine
MI	Michigan
MN	Minnesota
MO	Missouri
MS	Mississippi
MT	Montana
NC	North Carolina
ND	North Dakota
NE	Nebraska
NH	New Hampshire
NJ	New Jersey
NM	New Mexico
NV	Nevada
NY	New York
OH	Ohio
OK	Oklahoma
OR	Oregon
PA	Pennsylvania
PR	Puerto Rico
RI	Rhode Island
SC	South Carolina
SD	South Dakota
TN	Tennessee
TX	Texas
UT	Utah
VA	Virginia
VI	Virgin Islands
VT	Vermont
WA	Washington
WI	Wisconsin
WV	West Virginia
WY	Wyoming

The Art of Successful Freelancing

By Don Jardine

Never has the need for art been so great. With the development of computer graphics, more and more illustrated books being published annually, fashions changing seasonally and thousands of art shows springing up across the country, the demand for art is phenomenal.

Everything produced by man, from the mundane to the magnificent, is in some way related to art. The countless styles and variations of the alphabet and numbers don't grow on trees. Artists design them. Design, packaging and marketing involve artists.

Opportunities are most frequently offered to artists on the basis of knowledge and abilities, rather than for diplomas, sex or ethnic background. Indeed, no length of study or specific curriculum is required by those who need your services or creations; but the more comprehensive and competent your abilities, the better your chances for selling your work.

You should study realistic and commercial drawing, perspective, color, lettering, design, composition, tools and terms, media and techniques, illustration, painting, cartooning, keylining, and sales and advertising psychology.

Commercial art classes generally include most, if not all, of the study areas mentioned. Art mediums are generally covered with a variety of techniques; tools are shown and demonstrated; and color, design, illustration and painting are sometimes included. Instruction on how artwork is processed to appear in print is also valuable. Reproduction processes instruction should include letterpress and offset lithography, color separations, screens, line, halftone and shading sheets.

If you are interested in acquiring specialized training, discuss your interests with working artists and investigate schools carefully. A good reference source is the *Art School Directory* (published by *American Artist*).

If you're not interested in schools, try to get on-the-job training and study art books and publications. Ralph Mayer's *Artist's Handbook of Materials and Techniques* (Viking Press) and John Snyder's *Commercial Artist's Handbook* (Watson-Guptill Publications) provide extensive information.

Once you have a firm grasp on your fine or commercial art skills, you can begin seeking markets for your talents, both locally and nationally.

Local Markets

Local markets have the advantage of enabling you to contact people you know, or who are at least acquainted with your work or are familiar with your references.

These markets also allow you to make personal contacts and personally present your work. Refer to the yellow pages for builders, decorators and other potential buyers and sales outlets in your area.

Don Jardine is associate educational director of the Art Instruction Schools, Inc., editor of The Illustrator *magazine and author of* How To Sell Your Artwork.

Out-of-Town Markets

You can supplement the markets in *Art & Crafts Market* by referring to the yellow pages for cities that interest you. Most major telephone company offices and some university libraries maintain collections of telephone books.

It is generally best to take a soft-sell approach to contacts outside your local area. Sending large amounts of art, especially heavy, bulky unsolicited shipments, is considered presumptuous. Doing so without making it possible for convenient postage or freight-paid return (SASE) is unforgivable.

As a rule, initial out-of-town contacts should be made by telephone or letter. Explain and describe what you have to sell, why the art buyer should deal with you, and ask if you can send samples of your artwork. Unless the subject is brought up by the contact, avoid discussing financial arrangements until your artwork has been examined.

Having your name or studio listed in a national publication or directory can also provide out-of-town markets revenue. The *Creative Black Book* (Friendly Publications, Inc.) offers free listings to commercial artists.

Fine Art Markets

Today, art is sold not only in museums and galleries but in banks, theaters, supermarkets, cafes, hotels, motels, furniture stores, hair stylist salons and many other businesses. Displaying art attracts customers and builds sales; therefore, businesses which display art often publicize displays and/or pay for advertising to attract patrons.

Businesses often enter into agreements with artists to show and promote the sale of artwork for a commission (percentage of the sale price). That percentage ranges from as little as ten percent (charged by businesses which are not art-oriented: beauty salons, cafes, furniture stores) to fifty percent (charged by galleries who frequently offer advertising, publicity, public relations and agent services). The prospect for volume business encourages their best sales efforts toward your mutual benefit.

Pet owners provide a good market if you are capable of doing likenesses of cats, dogs, horses and other animals. If that work appeals to you, visit horse shows, state fairs, rodeos and cat and dog shows. Display samples of your artwork at local kennels; advertise in specialized publications; send fliers to stockmen, ranchers and breeders; and contact owners of award-winning animals.

Businesses and institutions sometimes commission artists to paint portraits of founders, retiring executives and clients. Portraits might also be suggested as gifts for anniversaries, Christmas, birthdays and other special occasions. Sometimes families want paintings made from photographs of relatives.

Night clubs, country clubs, offices, hospitals, motels and nursing homes sometimes buy art for decoration. Exposure here can lead to impressed patrons contacting you with assignments.

Don't overlook rentals. Many artists rent their work for display in offices, businesses and in private homes. This brings in good, steady income. Sales often result when rental payments are credited to the sale price.

Display your art in shopping malls, sidewalk art shows and fairs. These attract crowds of individuals who normally might not be exposed to your work.

Commercial Art Markets

Analysis of advertising art in your local newspaper, store windows, displays and store fliers gives excellent clues to the commercial art being commissioned in your community. In addition, contacting businesses and industries may result in design commissions for letterheads and envelopes, business cards, brochures and advertisements. Those who already have these items may be interested in having them revised. Check every opportunity.

All newspapers, printers and publishers need artwork. Sometimes a portfolio containing samples similar to the art you know they use most will result in sales, commissions or employment. Art samples might include seasonal subjects, holiday art and art for special occasions.

Are any parades scheduled for your community? Consider designing and perhaps building floats for local sponsors: businesses, schools, churches and chambers of commerce. It's a lucrative job and one where the opportunities for repeat and increased business are excellent.

Can you do lettering? Many individuals and businesses need posters, banners, point-of-purchase signs and price cards. In addition, there are always certificates and documents requiring the insertion of names, awards, dates and other information. Even delivery vans and trucks are adorned with designs, scenes and cartoons in addition to lettering. You'll find many of these markets listed in the Exhibit, Display & Sign Firms category.

Remember that government agencies, at all levels, require the services of artists. Federal jobs usually require successful completion of civil service examinations, but state, county and local governments often employ artists with nothing more than the best and/or most appropriate portfolio of art samples.

Let it be known that you are looking for art and/or art-related opportunities. Don't dismiss any possibility for which you have only partial qualifications because your art background may well be better than that of other applicants and a great deal of training is usually given "on the job."

Approaching the Buyer — The Portfolio

Your portfolio should contain 12 to 20 samples of the artwork you are interested in doing. A variety of subject matter, mediums and techniques is desirable. Don't make it too fancy. Show predominately b&w art because the expense of color production usually dictates that color assignments be reserved for the most experienced artists.

Quality is far more desirable than quantity. You shouldn't have to apologize for quality or condition. If it isn't the best you are capable of, don't show it. If it is the best you can do, don't imply that you are capable of doing better. Be honest.

The Resume

As you read *Art & Crafts Market*, you'll discover that many markets require resumes from out-of-town artists. A resume is a fact sheet describing you and your qualifications. Include your name, address, telephone number, personal data, educational background, achievements, awards, art experience and perhaps the names and addresses of three or four reputable persons willing to supply references.

The resume should be neatly typed, as potential clients may keep it on file for future assignments.

Business Cards

A business card often makes a very favorable impression and can lead to business which might otherwise be lost. It is not uncommon for firms to maintain business card files. If your card is in such a file, chances of being contacted are substantially improved. Though it contains limited information (your name, address, telephone number, area of expertise), it is often more readily accessible than the more detailed resume. Also, it is simple for you to take a business card from your wallet, pocket or purse at a given opportunity — whereas you may not have a supply of the larger resume sheets immediately available when an unexpected opportunity arises.

Both business cards and resumes can be inexpensively reproduced in large quantities. Call local printers for estimates.

The Interview

Remember, the people you're calling on are busy, so if you waste their time, your chances for sales or commissions are practically nil. Research your prospect's needs before making an appointment, then telephone to schedule an interview.

Remember the importance of first impressions. Perhaps seventy-five percent of the impression you make will depend on how you look, so neatness and cleanliness are vital. If you don't have enough self-respect to be neat and clean, the client may question whether your work will be carefully done. Neatness is essential in commercial art because it is reproduced for either display or reproduction. Until the client gets to know you, the only way he has of judging your standards of neatness is by your personal appearance and the condition of your samples.

Punctuality is also extremely important. A friendly approach — introducing yourself as you hand over a business card and exhibiting self-confidence — always helps. Be brief and thorough. State your purpose for the meeting, show your samples, answer questions and indicate you have something on the ball.

The Studio

If you are successful in obtaining commissions, you should set up a studio. Keep it simple and practical; don't purchase "gadgets." What you need is a workshop, not a Hollywood movie set. The important thing is the work you do, not where it is done. Nevertheless, basic tools and supplies are necessary.

The essentials are a table, chair and good lighting. If possible, the working area should be devoted solely to artwork. Even if it is just a corner of a room, the idea is to have it "ready to go" at all times. Wall shelves, bookcases or small stands with one or more drawers are handy for storing supplies.

Supplies should include an 11x14" tracing paper pad and a layout pad. India ink, rubber cement, masking tape and clear cellulose tape should be in every studio. A mat knife with a supply of blades is useful for mat cutting, trimming, paste-up and cut-outs. A French curve is handy for drawing various curves with control. A T-square and triangle enable you to draw lines with accuracy and speed. Have a wide variety of pen points and a good ruling pen for drawing straight lines of variable widths.

Light blue pencils are used for any marking, sketching or notemaking on "camera-ready" copy since it will not reproduce when photographed.

Your art supply dealer can make paper recommendations if you describe the work you plan to do and the mediums you plan to use. Art suppliers are listed in the *Directory of Arts & Crafts Materials* (published by Syndicate Magazines, Inc.) and the *Creative Black Book*.

Pricing

One of the most common questions I hear is, "How much should I charge for my artwork?"

The value of artwork varies with the economics of different geographic areas. In addition, the competition in one area may force prices down, or the demand for artwork may escalate prices.

Charging too little may cause a client to question the quality and value of your work. And if you overprice your work, chances are the client will turn to your competitors.

Many art organizations (guilds, artists equity, associations) supply information and advice regarding pricing. The Graphic Artists Guild (3928 Grand Central Station, New York City 10017) publishes a booklet on this subject entitled *Pricing & Ethical Guidelines.*

Remember when starting out, an assignment has more value than the money you make. The experience you gain and having your "foot in the door" is of considerable value. Of even more value is the opportunity to include printed artwork in your portfolio, or to add buyers to your list of "collectors."

Getting started will seem strange and you should be concerned about approach, pricing and speed. Every artist goes through the same experiences and benefits from every job. Your speed, efficiency and capability will increase with experience. Make good use of *Art & Crafts Market.* Exercise initiative, practice often and always do your best.

The Craft of Successful Freelancing

By Lynne Lapin

Never has the interest in crafts been so great — and it's growing. The World Crafts Council says that the interest is growing at an annual rate of about 20 percent.

People are awaking to the fact that the inflationary prices paid for goods today no longer get us quality — yet there is quality in handcrafted items, says Julie Schafler of Julie: Artisan's Gallery, New York City.

"Crafts fulfill a need in each of us to personalize what comes into our lives. And as we become more and more industrialized, that need for handcrafted items will also increase," says Schafler.

Likewise, the markets for crafts are also increasing. Today crafts are becoming accepted into the once exclusive "art" galleries; department stores like Saks Fifth Avenue; florist shops; gift shops; interior design studios and the homes of art collectors.

And all of these, just like the listings in *Art & Crafts Market,* are in need of quality crafts.

Types of Craftsmen

There are two types of craftsmen: the designer craftsman and the production craftsman.

The designer craftsman specializes in one-of-a-kind designs. You'll find his work in galleries along with the fine art forms. Unfortunately, although the designer craftsman's work is being displayed along with fine art, it is not getting the same payment.

For example: during the Fifth International Craft Show (1977) in New York City, a gallery owner from an elite section of Michigan said the crafts in her gallery were of the same quality as the art. When asked the prices of the various work in her shop, however, she revealed that the lowest price on a piece of artwork was $950, while the lowest price on crafts was $95.

So although crafts are gaining recognition as art and are becoming collector's items, they are not yet receiving the price of art. The only way craft dealers believe this will come about is for the craftsman to work together with the dealer to educate and change the public's attitude. Although the craft dealer is often seen as the great robber baron, he too is suffering by the small income obtained from crafts — he too has overhead.

The production craftsman, on the other hand, probably never will receive the art-level price due to his repetition of designs. Although his work may be one-of-a-kind in that it was produced by hand, this type of craftsman is frequently thought of as an artisan.

Most craftsmen who try to make a living at crafts (be they artist or production craftsmen) realize that it takes some time to gain sufficient income and recognition. So, it's wise for even the designer craftsman to have at least one production-line (bread and butter) craft. For example, a designer craftsman who specializes in one-of-a-kind vases could produce several vases based on the same basic design.

Local Markets

If you're a beginning craftsman, your first sales will probably be on a local level. Aside from contacting the markets in this book, a good means of discovering new outlets in your area is to call local craft museums and councils. Contact the American Crafts Council (44 W. 53rd St., New York City 10019) for the address of your local crafts council.

Most local galleries and shops prefer a personal interview. As one gallery owner explains, "A photo or slide is fine for indicating what a particular piece is like, but nothing is better than actually seeing the piece in person." Not only should you have samples of the work, you should be able to talk about the pieces you've made. This adds interest and helps sell the work.

Call ahead to learn the best time to visit. Also ask how work should be presented, the best time to stop in, and whether they are buying. Remember, buying for a particular season is usually done months in advance — so plan ahead.

Don't ever leave anything with a dealer unless you obtain a receipt, and preferably some sort of contract or "letter-of-agreement." Although you'll find most dealers are reputable, this will protect you if a dealer loses his records, forgets agreements or claims your work was stolen or lost. (For a sample contract agreement, you may want to read *The Crafts Business Encyclopedia*, published by Harcourt Brace Jovanovich.)

Out-of-Town Markets

Most of the local markets' pitch also applies when dealing with out-of-town dealers. This type of work will most often be done by shipping. Most dealers agree the best agent for shipping (particularly breakable items) is the United Parcel Service (U.P.S.).

For craft dealers listed in this book, breakage is the most prevalent problem. Protect yourself by insuring any work you mail (U.P.S. automatically insures all packages for $100).

But, in order to keep yourself from having to claim this insurance, you should take steps to assure your work is properly packed. Packing should be lightweight to reduce overhead. For more advice on shipping, consult your yellow pages for a packing firm in your area (and, if possible, spend a day with them learning how to package your work); ask your local Post Office for advice; or send $3 to the American Crafts Council for a copy of *Packing/Shipping of Crafts*.

Never send unsolicited work to galleries. You're likely never to see it again as it could get lost or may be disregarded. Also, if the dealer doesn't want the piece, you're inconveniencing him by forcing him to repack and mail the piece — which he never asked for in the first place.

The best way to let an out-of-town gallery or craft dealer see what you have to offer is to send slides or photos. Be certain to take these photos against a plain background to avoid distracting from the piece. Take close-up (detail), front and back shots. If your work is wearable, take a slide of someone wearing it. More information on photographing your work may be obtained by reading *Photography for Artists & Craftsmen*, published by Van Nostrand Reinhold Company.

Breaking in and Passing the Word — The Resume

The resume is sometimes requested by craft outlets considering whether to carry your work. At other times, even when not specifically requested, it is a good idea to offer a resume. A resume tells the dealer about your qualifications and credits, which he may relay to the customers he deals with. Most customers (especially collectors) will ask for this information, so resumes can increase your salability. But, it is the actual craft — not resume — that sells.

Your resume should include information about your education; group or one-man shows you've participated in; awards; outlets where your work has appeared; a discussion of any interesting private collections your work may be in; publications that have included information about you; and possibly a paragraph on how you feel about your work. (The latter is particularly helpful for press releases the craft dealer might want to send out on you.)

Business Cards, Labeling and Signing Work

Work should be signed whenever possible; this is part of the value of the piece. It also serves as good advertising because others who see and like the piece will probably remember your name.

Another excellent way to tell potential buyers more about you and your creations is to attach labels to your work. But, beware of attaching labels with too much information — such as address and phone number. By supplying the customer with a means of contacting you directly, you are threatening to cut out the middle man — the gallery.

A label, if designed with a detachable address (as with a perforated line), can also serve as a business card. This can be left with outlets you are interested in dealing with. Contact local printers for estimates on various types of cards. (For more information on labeling, see "Advertise Yourself Through Labels" in the Craft Dealers section.)

Pricing

Whether your purpose for selling crafts is to acquire funds for additional craft supplies or to make a living, you must price your work high enough to cover costs and allow you to make a profit, yet low enough to attract customers.

For this reason, it is vital to keep good records (see "Art Is A Business, Too"). Your records should include labor, materials and overhead.

Labor (time spent on a piece) cannot be forgotten — your time is definitely worth money. But, the truth is that the payment for crafts, if determined on an hourly basis, is minimal. Ideally, the craftsman should be able to demand the pay other production jobs offer, but by doing so he would price himself out of the market. Therefore, in order to assure sells and earn a profit, it is best to place most of your emphasis on the cost of materials and overhead.

Materials should include everything it takes to make a piece, but not packing, boxes, labels and other overhead costs.

Overhead will include all costs that are not directly a part of your production efforts. This is the most complicated of the costs to estimate.

Many craftsmen produce their art in a portion of their home. You should determine what portion of your house, utilities, phone, insurance and other household costs involve your work. In addition, you should determine devaluation on equipment, repairs, packing costs, shipping fees and other nonproduction costs. By combining these three types of costs — labor, materials and overhead — and adding your profit, you should be able to determine what your wholesale cost should be.

A final and usually forgotten item that comes into play when considering cost is ego. It is important to remember that although your work may be of fine quality and merit a great deal of pride, it takes time to build a reputation at which you can demand high prices.

A general rule on pricing your work is that it is better to underprice your work as a beginner than to overprice. It is always easier to ease your public up to higher prices than to suddenly lower prices because your work won't sell at what you're asking.

It is also vital to keep abreast of what similar works in your area are selling for. If you price your work considerably higher than your competition's, you'll soon find that your competitor is making all the sales.

Remember to be consistent in pricing your work. Don't charge fees simply by having a base price and adding that to the gallery's commission. For example, don't say to yourself, "I want to make $50 on this piece, so I'll add $20 if the gallery wants 40%, or $25 if it wants 50%." If you do this, your prices will vary greatly from showing to showing. People who are following your work will be leery of such irregular pricing. And, this is something gallery and shop owners frown on.

Even the best of marketing advice, however, isn't enough to make you a selling craftsman. That's where the listings in this book come in. Check the Table of Contents for markets to help you make the most of your talent and marketing skills.

Art Is a Business, Too

By Diane Cochrane

The first thing the fledgling freelance artist or craftsman must learn is that he is also a businessperson. Aside from selling your work, this means keeping accurate, up-to-date records, paying business taxes, and protecting your work.

As you become more successful, and perhaps add others to your payroll, you will probably delegate the responsibilities of records and taxes to an accountant. Meanwhile, it's up to you to devise an efficient system that will keep bookkeeping to a minimum so you can spend more time creating and yet satisfy the requirements of the Internal Revenue Service.

What Records Should I Keep?

Keep two types of records. The first type includes information on how a piece of artwork is made and what happens to it after completion.

Buy yourself 3x5 index cards or a loose-leaf notebook. Then, when a new work is begun, assign a number to it and jot it down on the card along with the starting and completing dates. As the work progresses, record the costs of all materials that go into the piece, the hours you spend thinking about and working on the project, and the number of hours worked by assistants and their wages.

Later, when the work is finished, add the asking price, the price it actually sells for (in case you give a discount), the name and address of the purchaser, the rights you sell (or, if you sell only reproduction rights, the price for them), where the piece is exhibited or appears, the name of any galleries where it is consigned and the name and address of any new purchaser. In other words, write down any pertinent information you might need later.

These records should be accompanied by a photo of the work, which should also bear the code number assigned to the piece. If the piece is then lost, stolen or damaged, the photo proves its existence and condition for insurance purposes. If the work is illegally altered, the photo will demonstrate the extent to which it has been altered. And finally, of course, the photo is a must for publicity purposes.

By collecting this information, you can track down the work later, if necessary. This is especially important to the fine artist who may want to exhibit the work after its sale. Also, it takes pricing out of the realm of the educated guess. When you sell a piece of artwork, your price must cover costs at the least. You can't do this if you don't know what they are, and this is where your records prove invaluable.

The file cards record your direct costs for each work. They also tell you how much time you devoted to freelance work over one year. This, in turn, allows you to determine what your indirect costs are.

Suppose you worked 1,000 hours one year, according to your cards. Now suppose that during the year you bought $1,000 worth of equipment and tools

---

Diane Cochrane is editor of American Artist Business Letter; *author of an upcoming legal and financial handbook for artists; contributing editor of* American Artist *and lecturer on the business of art.*

(brushes, knives, paints) that can't be directly charged to a single piece of artwork. In addition, your selling expenses (travel, entertainment, postage, framing, publicity) come to $2,000, and your overhead (rent, utilities, upkeep) costs another $1,000. If you total these expenses and divide by the number of hours spent on artwork during the year, you find that indirect expenses cost you $4 an hour. (Records for these items will be explained in the section on tax substantiation records.)

Now you can figure out your costs for any one work. The $4 hourly cost is multiplied by the number of hours you work on a piece, and added to the direct costs for materials, outside labor and your labor. Your hourly wage can be calculated by what you think you would earn if you took a comparable job (for example, as an illustrator). And don't overestimate. If you're just starting out, $5 an hour might be about right.

Once you calculate all costs, you can price your work accordingly. This method may seem complicated, but it helps you avoid making a charitable contribution to your client because you didn't cover costs.

Now let's turn to the second type of records — those necessary to back up tax deductions.

The IRS requires two types of records: informal and formal. Informal records are those innumerable pieces of paper you collect every day in business — like sales receipts, stubs, cancelled checks, bank statements and invoices which are used to back up your formal recordkeeping. Some receipts aren't always available; nor does the IRS expect you to have receipts for such expenses as taxis between business appointments. But other receipts are a must, like hotel and restaurant bills over $25. These receipts must show the name of the hotel or restaurant, its address, the date and itemized charges.

An easy way to organize these informal records is to file them by month or by descriptions like "travel" and "entertainment."

When keeping formal records, you must maintain a separate checking account for your freelance work. This way you won't mix business and personal accounts. It's also wise to pay for all expenses by check rather than with cash because cancelled checks can serve as records. And when you're opening a separate checking account, order voucher checks. These provide spaces where you record the date and items bought.

Formal records include single-entry and double-entry records. Single-entry recordkeeping is the simplest method and the one recommended for most artists/craftsmen.

Single-entry systems are diaries or date books that record income and expenses on the day received or incurred. For example, if you travel on business you will record the amounts spent on taxis, meals and hotels each day you are away.

Notations for travel and entertainment must be more detailed than those describing more straightforward expenses. Explanations for these expenses should include the purpose of the business trip or entertainment, who you saw and what was discussed.

At the end of the year, a quick total of expenses and income payments, as recorded in your diary, will indicate the amount of profit or loss.

You'll want to use double-entry bookkeeping as your business grows. Under this system, business transactions are posted (usually monthly) to appropriate ledger accounts such as income, expenses, assets, liability and net worth. The main advantage of double-entry bookkeeping is that you end up with a balance sheet showing the financial position of the business in terms of assets, liabilities and net worth, at a given time.

But you probably don't need this system unless you're a craftsman or artist manufacturing large numbers of objects and maintaining inventories, or a commercial artist producing a large volume of work and employing others. Nevertheless, if you feel your business demands balance sheets and very formal records, ask an accountant to set up a double-entry system for you. Once this is done, you can probably do your own books.

What Expenses Can I Deduct?

Anything that relates to your business is deductible: rent, utilities and upkeep on a separate studio, or a portion of them or mortgage interest if your studio is in your home; annual depreciation and other expenses if you own your home; telephone bills (or a part of them); premiums on commercial property and casualty insurance; legal and accounting fees; supplies; postage; promotional expenses; travel; entertainment; books, journals and admission to theaters, films and museums related to your work.

Many of these items — like telephone bills, car expenses and bills connected with your studio — must be allocated by a little research on your part. For example, if you allocate your phone bills, analyze your calls for about four months to see what percentage are business calls. Then take the average of the four months. If business calls predominate, consider a separate phone which can be totally written off.

Allocating your studio is a bit more complicated. Let's suppose your studio is in your home and you own the home. Add up all bills for heat, electricity, water, cleaning services, general repairs and homeowner's insurance premiums. Now figure out the annual depreciation on your house.

There are several ways to depreciate your house, but here's the easiest one. Take the cost or purchase price of your home, subtract the land value (get this from your tax assessor), add the cost of major improvements (like a new furnace) and divide the results by useful life. Useful life is an estimate you can make based on how long you think you could continue to live in the house. Your estimate will take into consideration improvements and repairs, but the average life of a house is usually 30 to 40 years.

Once you've added up these costs, you can determine the tax-deductible portion in two ways; choose the one most advantageous to you. The first is based on the number of rooms. For a six-room house, one-sixth of the total home costs is eligible as a tax deduction. The second method is to compute the ratio of square feet in the studio to the total square feet in the house. Do not include cellars, utility and storage areas.

Remember, you can only deduct allocable expenses up to the point where they don't exceed your gross income derived from art minus mortgage interest and property taxes. In other words, if you sell $2,000 worth of art this year and your allocable mortgage interest and taxes come to $500, you can write off $1,500 for other allocable expenses related to your home/studio. But no more. If your expenses are $3,000, you'll just have to absorb the other $1,500 yourself.

Artists have also been worried about the provision in the Tax Provision Act of 1976 that says that home-studio deductions may be taken only if it "is used exclusively on a regular basis as the taxpayer's principal place of business." The question is this: if artists have another place of business that furnishes them with their primary income (like a school or a frame shop), is their home-studio a principal place of business?

Yes. It's the principal place of your art business, just as the school is the principal place of your commercial art business. But if you have a job as a commercial artist and bring home work during the evenings, forget about writing off your home-studio. This is not the principal place of your commercial art business.

Besides allocating certain expenses, you may have to depreciate others. Capital expenditures (i.e., items that have a useful life of longer than a year, like kilns, cameras and drawing boards) cannot be totally deducted in the year you buy them. They must be depreciated over a period of years.

The IRS publishes many helpful guides for self-employed people. Visit your local tax office at tax time as it can provide literature on the methods of determining depreciation.

How Do I Handle Sales Taxes?

Probably the most frequently asked question is this: what do I do about state sales taxes? The answer depends on whether you're concerned about collecting the tax or paying it.

If you are a retailer and your state has a sales tax, you must charge your customers a sales tax and remit it to the government. By a retailer, I mean that you sell directly to the person who plans to use the work and not resell it. You're a retailer if you're a craftsman or an artist selling your work directly to collectors (for instance, at a competition or exhibition). You're not a retailer if you sell work to a shop or consign work to a gallery. In these cases, the shop or gallery collects the tax.

These distinctions are straightforward, but the issue can get a little fuzzy for the commercial artist. In certain states, for example, it's unclear who's responsible for collecting the tax when an artist sells a work to an advertising agency that in turn "sells" it to its client. If you're confronted by such a situation, the wise course is for you to charge the tax. It's much easier than trying to collect it later.

Before you can collect the tax, you must register with your state tax department. It will issue you a resale number — which brings us to the opposite side of the sales tax coin.

If you have a resale number, you can avoid paying state tax on certain art supplies. Materials that compose an artwork are exempt from sales tax because they are considered goods bought for resale. When you buy canvas, paint, clay, etc., show your resale number to the clerk at your art supply store and he will eliminate the tax.

Caution: unless you're a professional artist with a fairly consistent sales record, the tax authorities may look askance at these exemptions, figuring you're a nonprofessional trying to avoid the tax. So, since the tax most artists pay is not great, you might consider paying it until you can fully justify its exemption.

How Can I Insure My Work?

Frankly, many fine artists and craftsmen can't. Insurance companies don't like to insure artists' work, because the security and construction of many artists' studios are poor and — more important — because it's difficult to assign values to works by an artist who doesn't have an established sales record.

So, even if you do find a company willing to insure your work, you'll have a problem establishing a value when the work is lost or damaged. Without a solid sales record, your word on how much an artwork is worth isn't going to mean much when it comes to a settlement.

On the other hand, if valuation is no problem, then you can insure against fire or other risks like theft, or even buy an all-risk fine arts policy. And you can insure art while it's in your studio or anywhere in the world, depending on what your needs are and how much you can afford — it *is* expensive. Rates can run as high as $2 or more per $100 of value for an artist working in a building that an insurance company considers undesirable.

So you may or may not want to insure work in your own studio. But you should take precautions when it leaves there. For example, not all galleries and art shows will insure work; therefore, the best way to safeguard yourself from loss is to buy your own insurance on exhibited work.

Commercial artists do not encounter the same difficulties in insuring work that a fine artist does, because the commercial value of their work can be readily established. Therefore, you can buy fire insurance or "valuable papers" insurance, to use the lingo of insurance brokers. The latter can also include "off premises" coverage to protect work in transit and at its destination, if you and your broker think you need such protection.

If work is not insured outside your studio, the question arises concerning its safety when it arrives at the office of an advertising agency, magazine or whatever. If you send work on speculation to a firm and it is lost, the firm is responsible for the loss of property — if you can prove gross negligence, a pretty tough thing to prove. But if a commissioned work is lost after it is received, the firm is liable for it even if it is guilty of only ordinary negligence, putting you in a far better position to sue for damages.

In either case, to prevent the firm from saying it never received the work, get a receipt if you take it in personally — or register it, if you send it by mail, and request a return receipt.

So much for the business of art. On with the creating.

The New Copyright Law: What You Need To Know

By Betsy Wones

Artist Robert Indiana forgot only one thing when he published his popular design, LOVE. Copyrighting it. Within no time, other artists copied LOVE as their own work. The result: money and recognition lost.

The moral of the story is to learn about copyright.

Though copyright is far from a simple subject, the important thing to remember about this area of the law is that owning copyright enables the artist/craftsman alone to profit from his work. Unless he gives permission in the form of rights purchased to a magazine, newspaper or other reproducer, the copyright owner has exclusive rights to reproduce, prepare derivatives of or distribute the work.

Under the new law (effective January 1, 1978), copyright ownership is automatic, from the moment of creation. However, to obtain some form of legal backing from the Copyright Office in the case of plagiarism, it's often a good idea to register the work with the Office.

You should register copyright when there's a good possibility that the work might be plagiarized. For example, the cartoonist submitting to a non-copyrighted newspaper should register his work. And, registration serves as a safety precaution when an artist/craftsman exhibits work at a public display, which is not considered "publication" but which attracts many viewers.

When contributing to a copyrighted publication, the cartoonist's or illustrator's work is not only protected by federal copyright (under the new law) but by the publication's general copyright notice. Under the old law, there was some dispute whether a publication's copyright notice protected contributions inside.

Also, in determining what to register, you should decide if the expense justifies the need. For example, registering each cartoon strip in a copyrighted publication is expensive and may not really be necessary for full protection. On the other hand, registering the prototype of that cartoon strip might be wise.

To register copyright for a work, send $10, a photo, slide or photocopy (one for unpublished, two for published work) and an application form (available on request) to the United States Copyright Office, Library of Congress, Washington D.C. 20540. One way to save some money is to register and obtain one copyright for a group of unpublished artworks — created by the same artist — as a collection.

Regardless of whether you register a work, you should attach the copyright symbol ©, "Copr" or "Copyright," the year of creation or publication and your name somewhere on the work. Your individual copyright notice can accompany contributions to any publications, and should definitely be present on work appearing in a non-copyrighted periodical.

Besides these updates on copyright, the new law also changes copyright term length and eliminates perpetual common law copyright and renewal.

New Copyright Term Length

All artworks created after January 1, 1978 and all unpublished and non-copyrighted (common law copyright) artworks created before January 1, 1978 are automatically protected by federal copyright for the artist/craftsman's life plus 50 years.

Under the old law, enacted in 1909, unpublished and non-copyrighted artworks were protected by common law copyright forever. Long after the deaths of an artist and his heirs, archivists and librarians could not copy or distribute an artwork for academic research or publication.

Renewal

Once 50 years has elapsed after the artist/craftsman's death, work eligible under the new law becomes public domain and can be reproduced and distributed by anyone.

For published artworks copyrighted under the old law, however, renewal is still in effect. If you want to retain protection, you must renew copyright early in the last year of the first 28-year term. The new law increases the second term to 47 years, rather than another 28-year term as mandated by the old law.

For further copyright information, write for the Copyright Office's Circular 1 "General Information on Copyright"; Circular 15a "Duration of Copyright Under the New Law"; Circular R99 "Highlights of the New Copyright Law"; and Circular 40 "Copyright for Pictorial, Graphic and Sculptural Works." A copy of the revised copyright statute is also available from the Copyright Office.

For those who don't relish tackling government literature, the February-March 1976 issue of *Art and the Law* (published by Volunteer Lawyers for the Arts) breaks the language barrier between legalese and plain English in its comprehensive coverage of the new law. Also useful is Barbara Ringer's article, "Finding Your Way Around the New Copyright Law" in the December 13, 1976 issue of *Publishers Weekly.*

Shipping Your Work

How to Pack Fragile Items for Shipping, Storage and Transport

- Wrap all fragile items individually in paper at least two layers thick.
- Place about 3" of paper on the bottom of the box or carton.
- Place larger and heavier items on the bottom of the carton.
- Cushion well between layers. Use about 2" of paper or cushioning material.
- Start packing by placing wrapped items at the outside edge of the box; continue by filling towards the center.
- Place bowls, plates, platters on edge; never place them flat.
- If only one item is being packed, place it in the center of the box with cushioning under, over and around it.
- Fill box to within 3" of the top, then finish by putting paper or cushioning material to fill the last few inches.
- Mark the outside of all boxes or cartons containing breakables: FRAGILE!

Reprinted with permission from the Crafts Report *(9-76)*

Crating Pictures for Shipping

Although claims for care exercised vary from carrier to carrier, the best insurance for an artwork's safe arrival is proper packing.

All works should be wrapped in plastic sheeting to prevent water damage. If polyethylene rolls are unavailable, cheap plastic drop cloths are a good substitute.

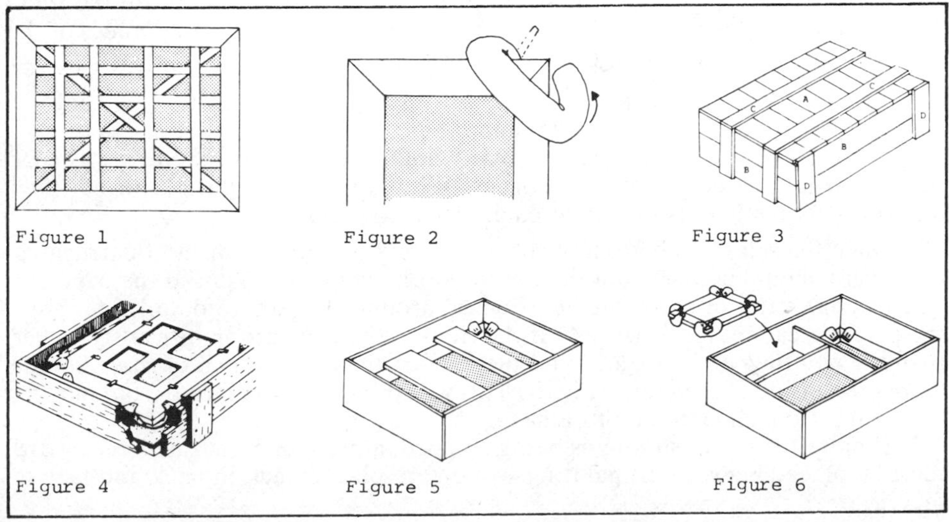

Figure 1 Figure 2 Figure 3

Figure 4 Figure 5 Figure 6

Framed works, especially those with carved or raised corners, should also be further protected. Newspaper, rolled up, is excellent for corner protection. (Fig. 1) The ends of the rolled paper should be stapled to the back of the frame.

Remember to remove screw eyes, picture light brackets and other protruding objects which might damage other works.

When pictures with glass are shipped, it is important to tape the glass so that in the event of breakage it does not damage work. Masking tape is strong enough to prevent pieces of glass from coming loose. Never use tape requiring water — it could damage the work.

First tape a large X on the glass. Then tape horizontal and vertical rows a couple of inches apart. (Fig. 2) Do not overlap the frame. Works framed with Plexiglas need no tape because it is unbreakable.

A wooden box makes the most reliable crate. The frame of the crate should be about 2" larger than the picture on all sides. The same size is not good, because a diagonal shock can break a corner of a frame.

To build a crate, stack the work to be packed on a table so that you can measure the height, width and length to determine size of lumber needed.

The top (a) and bottom of the crate must be able to resist puncture. Museums usually recommend ¾" to ⅞" thick pine, but cheap boards are as good as the more expensive grades. Plywood is best. Cheap construction grade sheathing also works well, as does paper-faced ply-score. Masonite which is brittle should be used with trepidation because it can be punctured, and in any case ⅛" Masonite should never be considered. Construction grade board is adequate for sides of crate.

Cut lumber for sides (b) to size allowing 2" all the way around work. Butt longer boards against shorter sides and nail together with 2½" rosin-coated box nails about 1½" apart.

Measure outside dimensions of frame sides and cut top and bottom. Nail bottom of crate to sides (1½" plaster board nails work well for this). The top of crate should be screwed on with either six or eight 1" flat head screws (Fig. 3).

If you wish to enforce corners of the crate, use 1x4" boards cut to width of two sides, top and bottom (c). These eight pieces should be nailed to board ends before crate assembly. Longer nails are required here — 3½" will do the trick. On the longer sides they should overlap enough to butt against the braces of the shorter sides which are flush to the end of the side.

Be careful not to leave nail heads protruding into the crate. Bend into U shape rather than just turn, and hammer into sides.

If a crate is to be made deeper than width of lumber available, use two or more boards for sides, joining at corners using above procedures and nail two additional brace boards (d) along each of the four sides.

Once the sides and bottom of the crate are assembled, a sheet of corrugated cardboard should be placed in the bottom of the crate. Next, put in the painting. Then wedge strips of corrugated cardboard around the picture on all sides until the painting cannot move. (Fig. 4) If the sides of the crate are significantly higher than the painting, add an additional piece of cardboard and two or three boards across the inside of the crate. (Fig. 5) This will prevent the painting from moving — the most common cause of damage.

If more than one painting is being shipped, a piece of corrugated cardboard must be placed between all paintings which are placed back to back and face to face.

If one or two small paintings are shipped along with large works, it is important to put the larger works in first and cushion them along the sides with strips of cardboard. Smaller works should be laid next to one another and stacked evenly. Cradling with board may be necessary to provide compartments for small pictures. (Fig. 6)

When unframed graphic work is included in the crate, be sure to mark it clearly. Work has occasionally been mistaken for packing and discarded.

Finally mark the box on at least two sides with appropriate cautions such as "Fine Art," "Fragile," "Handle with Care," "Glass."

The Markets

Advertising & Public Relations

More than $80 billion was spent in the U.S. on advertising between 1973 and 1975. This, coupled with the fact that the advertising industry has long been glamorously portrayed, has caused the advertising door to become the most frequently knocked on in the art field. And many of those knocking are freelance artists.

It's as Forbes Smith, freelancer and former art director of Keck Advertising Inc., says, "There's no shortage of freelancers here." So with all the competition, how do you break in?

First, a knowledge of production is important. The artist should know what happens to his artwork once he turns it over to the printers or platemakers. Many times the art buyer will require that the artist follow his art all the way through from conception to the press.

Second, know how to do realistic illustration. Abstract art is fine for galleries and other fine art outlets, but advertisers want drawings that look like their products — not interpretations of what they're trying to sell.

Third, prepare a portfolio. Almost all of the markets in this section require portfolio presentations. It is important that your portfolio be clean, professionally presented and representative of the type of work you're capable of doing. The portfolio is usually the determining factor as to whether you're chosen for an assignment.

"Submit enough graphics (in your portfolio) to indicate ability to work on the account in question," says Terence Smith, art director for Paul Silver Advertising, Inc. " 'Blue sky' graphics may be interesting, but the artist's ability to perform the job required is prime. Portfolios should show design, lettering, paste-up and the areas the freelancer feels he can adequately cover."

Ralph Bing, president/art director of Ralph Bing Advertising Company, says a portfolio should "contain basic samples with an approximation of time spent on each. It should clearly represent the artist's average work, but not necessarily all best work. Certainly no work accomplished at a school under supervision of instructors."

To rise above the mere basics of getting an ad job, and create a demand for your talents, you must learn the various aspects of the advertising business. Develop a distinctive style and keep abreast of what is happening in the industry. Art buyers in this section repeatedly indicate that the surest way to their hearts is to develop a distinctive style — something that will make their ads stand out from the thousands of others seen daily by the public.

The best way to keep up on what is currently happening in advertising is to read trade publications. *Communication Arts, Art Direction* and *Advertising Age* are three of the best. Also, it is wise to read a few trade journals relating to the type of account you want to work on.

For those with little or no experience, yet a desire to crack the illustration or graphic arts market, you'll find that keyline assignments (many of which are listed in the Studios, Art Service Firms & Printers category) are a good way to start out. They put money in your pocket and help you get your name at the beginning of files for future work.

Don't sit around waiting for advertising firms to call you. Most of them only report back if and when they find an assignment for you. Supplement the listings you find in this book by checking trade directories such as the *Standard Directory of Advertising Agencies* (National Register Publishing Co., Inc.) and *Public Relations Journal/Register* (Public Relations Society of America).

Once you've gotten your foot in the door, the possibilities for assignments in the advertising/public relations field are endless. There are thousands of markets for your work.

Advertising Agencies & Specialty Firms

There are three basic types of firms listed in this category: direct marketing companies, specialty firms and advertising agencies.

Direct marketing firms are, basically, advertising agencies that sell products and services through the mail. They frequently use artists to design and illustrate brochures and similar media. A complete brochure design is one of the highest paying assignments in the industry. Cooper Rand Corporation, for example, will pay a minimum of $500 for a direct mail brochure design.

Specialty advertising firms most often deal with items designed to carry the advertiser's name, address and advertising message to his target audience. These items (everything from key chains to desk accessories) are usually given away in order to provide the customer with two messages: "Thanks for your business" and "Keep us in mind in the future."

Advertising agencies cover an even broader range of advertising techniques, often incorporating specialty and direct mail methods into their marketing mix. You'll find there are freelance markets for everything from print ad layouts and illustrations to audiovisuals to architecture to even a few requests for craftwork.

The door for assignments is wide open to anyone with a good portfolio, ability to meet deadlines and talent. And, most of all, persistence. Don't give up just because the right assignment hasn't come your way. "Keep showing new work to prospective clients you've already seen. You're bound to hit the right moment for someone's needs if you keep reminding them you're around," says Art Nechamkin of Berger Nechamkin & Associates, Inc.

A&A ACCREDITED ADVERTISING, Division of Sound Advertising, 1 Ocean Ave., Massapequa NY 11758. Art Director: S. Chinkes. Annual billing: $200,000. Clients include food and electronics firms. Needs artists for layout, illustration, type spec, paste-up and retouching. Media used: newspapers, radio, consumer and trade magazines, collateral, direct mail and POP. Local artists only. Call for interview. Pays $25, rough or comprehensive layout; $5 per hour, paste-up.

ACKERMAN ADVERTISING COMMUNICATIONS, INC., 55 Northern Blvd., Greenvale NY 11548. Art/Creative Director: Skip Ackerman. Annual billing: $2,500,000. Uses local artists for layout, illustration, paste-up and retouching. Clients are food stores, shopping centers, banks and schools. Buys illustrations for newspapers, television, magazines, transit, billboards, collateral material, direct mail, and point-of-purchase. Arrange interview.

ADLER, SCHWARTZ & CONNES, INC., 140 Sylvan Ave., Englewood Cliffs NJ 07632. Estab: 1965. Creative Director: Peter Adler. Annual billing: $3 million. Clients are automotive, office equipment and building/construction equipment firms. Buys 50 illustrations annually for annual reports, billboards, print ads, letterheads, packaging, POP displays, posters and trademarks; especially needs line drawings and washes of people, cars and interiors. Also uses artists for color separations, layout, lettering, paste-up, retouching and type spec. Payment determined by project budget. Query with samples or call for interview. Reports in 2 weeks. SASE.

AD/MAN, 612 Executive Bldg., Cincinnati OH 45202. Art Buyer: Don Dickman. Buys advertising art; architectural and art renderings; building interiors; audiovisuals; signs; technical illustration; calligraphy; catalog illustrations and covers; advertising; and retouching work. "If there is one type of freelance service we need more than another, it is the more technical type of illustration — whether it's an architectural rendering or an exploded view for a parts catalog." Mail samples. Reports in 2 weeks. SASE.

ADMINISTRATIVE ASSOCIATES, INC., 1118 West St., Wilmington DE 19801. PR Director: Thomas R. Dew. Uses artists for direct mail brochures, manuals and other publications. Pays $10 minimum per hour; negotiates price. Query with printed samples.

ADVANTAGE ADVERTISING AGENCY, 4132 N. 12th St., Phoenix AZ 85014. (602)277-9751. Production Manager: Vincent Powers. Estab: 1972. Buys 20 illustrations annually for annual reports, billboards, catalogs, print ads, letterheads, packaging, POP displays, posters, TV ads and trademarks. Also uses artists for animation, layout and paste-up. Pays $100 minimum. Query with samples. Reports in 1 week. SASE.

ADVERTISING ASSOCIATES, INC., 416 Center St., Little Rock AR 72201. Creative Director: Larry Stone. Estab: 1975. Annual billing: $2 million. Financial clients. Buys 25-50 illustrations annually for annual reports, billboards, print ads, letterheads, POP displays, posters and television; especially needs b&w newspaper ads, trademarks and brochure designs. Also uses artists for layout, lettering, paste-up and retouching. Payment determined by complexity and/or quality. Pays $30-200 for b&w newspaper illustration. Submit artwork by mail. Reports in 1 week. SASE.

AHREND ASSOCIATES, INC., 64 University Place, New York NY 10003. (212)533-1640. Production Manager: Carmen Ossorio. Estab: 1951. Clients are publishers (book and magazine); industrial, direct response and mail order firms; financial institutions; and nonprofit organizations. Buys 100-200 illustrations annually for annual reports, catalogs, print ads, letterheads, brochures and mailing pieces. Also uses artists for layout, lettering, paste-up, retouching and type spec. Payment determined by complexity, number of illustrations and/or time spent. "In each instance, cost is agreed upon (specifically or within a range) before work is assigned." No payment for unsatisfactory assigned work; "if because of client's change of mind, full payment." Prefers local artists. Query or write for interview. Reports in 1 week.
To Break In: "Should have advertising, preferably direct response, experience. Must know basic requirements for submission to printers, platemakers, and others involved in production of promotional material (except for illustrations or spots which will be used as elements of a mechanical and are not the mechanicals themselves). A portfolio should offer proof that what you're showing is really your work."

ALOYSIUS BUTLER & CLARK, 1211 French St., Wilmington DE 19801. Art/Creative Director: Ken Wiggins. Annual billing: $1 million. Clients are State Lottery, hotels/motels, and insurance, banking and construction firms. Uses artists for layout, illustration, and paste-up. Media used: newspapers, television, radio, transit, magazines, billboards, collateral, direct mail, and POP. Minimum payment: $3 per hour, layouts/paste-up. Local artists only. Call for appointment.

AMERICAN ADVERTISING SERVICE, 121 Chestnut, Philadelphia PA 19106. Creative Director: Joseph Ball. Uses artists for advertising and billboard art, package design, graphic design, commercials, cover design, exhibits and art renderings. Prefers to deal with artist in person, but artist may mail layouts. Not responsible for layouts after submission. Will look at photostats. All jobs are by advance quotation. All rights bought. Original unpublished works only.

AMERICAN PAPER & WOODENWARE CO., Box 37385, Cincinnati OH 45222. (513)761-5600. Contact: Harold L. Sheff. Estab: 1906. Buys 15-25 illustrations annually for retail packaging; especially needs layout for printed paper and plastic bags. Also uses artists for paste-up. Payment determined by time spent on work. Pays $35-145, box layout; $25-130, bag layout. Original payment as promised for unused assigned illustrations. Local artists only. Mail artwork. Reports in 2 weeks. SASE.

ARNOLD, HINTON & HOFF, 1701 E. Woodfield Rd., Schaumburg IL 60172. Art Director: John F. Perkins. Clients are medical, chemical, food, electronics and security industries. Uses artists for advertising art, cartoons, lettering, displays, exhibits, retouching, spot drawings and technical illustrations. Query. No previously published work.

THE ART & DESIGN DEPARTMENT, Box 14481, Omaha NE 68124. Contact: Director. Clients in arts and entertainment fields. "We try to work with anyone who is promoting almost anything. Ideas come from us or our clients." Buys illustrations for billboards, print ads, letterheads, POP displays, posters and trademarks. Also uses artists for color preparations, layout, lettering and paste-up. "Interested in artists who are able to work with new and original ideas, are very experienced and able to meet tight deadlines." Payment determined by complexity, number of illustrations, time spent, where the work appears and/or how frequently it appears. Artist paid for time spent on unused assigned illustrations. Query with non-returnable samples for agency's files. "We contact the artist when work of his/her kind is needed."
To Break In: "Samples should be what the artist feels is his best work. By best we mean what they feel is the most artistic and would be most effective in a sales program. Be very confident of your own ideas, push them to buyers in a very professional way; let them know that you do things 'your own way'."

ASSOCIATED ADVERTISING AGENCY, Box 4, Roanoke VA 24001. Contact: J.W. Creasy. Annual billing: $1,000,000. Clients are financial institutions and furniture manufacturers. Uses artists for billboards, TV commercials, advertising layouts, direct mail promotions and point-of-purchase displays. Prefers local artists. Pays $10-15. Send photostats or tearsheets of work.
To Break In: "Work should have a creative look, good reproduction qualities and should be presented in a professional manner."

AURELIO AND FRIENDS, 11500 SW 81 Terrace, Miami FL 33173. President; Aurelio Sica. Vice President: Nancy Simons. Clients are retailers; restaurants; boating and real estate firms; and various media. Uses artists for illustration, layout, paste-up, retouching and lettering. Media used: newspapers, TV, radio, magazines, billboards, direct mail and collateral. Local artists only. Mail samples.

AYERDIRECT, Division of N.W. Ayer ABH International, 1345 Avenue of the Americas, New York NY 10019. (212)974-6290. Creative Director: Harvey Bacal.

BACHRACH KETCHUM, 55 Union St., San Francisco CA 94111. Art Buyer: John Helgeson. Clients are highly scientific and technical firms. Uses artists for technical illustration, direct mail brochures and package designs. Mail resume and arrange interview.

BAILEY, ORNER, MAKSTALLER, INC., 2754 Erie, Cincinnati OH 45208. (513)871-9006. Contact: Jim Makstaller. Estab: 1972. Clients are banks, insurance firms, restaurants, investment counselors, colleges and industry. Buys finished art and layouts for ads and brochures. Also uses artists for paste-up. Query with samples. Prefers "a person confident and consistent in style. We're interested in working with a number of illustrators with various techniques; must be dedicated to quality work, sensitive to suggestions, able to carry out ideas."
To Break In: "Try various styles and techniques and remain consistent with as many as possible. Flexibility is a good asset."

BALL ADVERTISING, INC., 1101 N. Fulton, Evansville IN 47710. Art Buyer: Ron Firebaugh. Clients are insurance companies, van lines, condominium developers and industrial firms. Uses artists for direct mail brochures, posters and folders. Payment determined by budget and complexity of assignment. Pays artists after client pays agency. Buys exclusive rights. Reports in 1 week.

BANNING COMPANY, 11818 Wilshire Blvd., Los Angeles CA 90025. (213)477-8517. Estab: 1963. Art Director: Orlando Lucia. Annual billing: $500,000. Variety of clients, mostly print. Buys 25 illustrations annually for annual reports, catalogs, print ads and POP displays. Also uses artists for layout, paste-up and retouching. Payment determined by artist's reputation, complexity and number of illustrations. Original payment as agreed for unused assigned illustrations. Call for interview. Reports in 1-2 weeks.
Crafts: Buys carved wooden signs.
To Break In: "Bring me samples of work and an idea of your prices. Work up samples that are not esoteric, but practical, usable commercial art."

BARD FUNKHOUSER ASSOCIATES, 680 Beach St., Suite 353, San Francisco CA 94109. Contact: Priscilla Funkhouser or Paula Bard. Clients are wineries, publishers, clothing manufacturers, retail stores and industrial firms. Specializes in visual/audiovisual communication. Uses artists for graphic design, illustration, package and product design, mechanical art, sculpture, architectural renderings and calligraphy. Submit slides and resume. Media used: direct mail brochures, posters, newspaper ads, programs and trade magazine ads.

BARICKMAN ADVERTISING, INC., 427 W. 12th St., Kansas City MO 64105. Art Director: Jerry L. Wanninger. Clients are food manufacturers. Uses artists for advertising art, animation, billboard art, catalogs, displays, graphic design, illustrations, lettering, package design, retouching and typography. Pays $15 per hour, paste-up; $20-30 per hour, layout. Mail artwork. Assignment made on "usually guaranteed" basis to artist whose style is liked.

TED BARKUS COMPANY, INC., 225 S. 15th St., Philadelphia PA 19102. President and Creative Director: Ted Barkus. Clients are consumer and industrial firms. Uses artists for illustrations and other finished art.

BARLOW/JOHNSON INC., 117 Highbridge St., Fayetteville NY 13066. Art Administrator: John M. Wright. Annual billing: $8,000,000. Clients are dairy and farm products, trucks, pharmaceuticals, banks, retail, paper making, hospitals, heavy machinery, clothing, bicycles, machine tools and housing firms. Uses artists for illustration, commercials and retouching. Media include newspapers, television and radio, magazines, billboards, direct mail, transit and point-of-purchase. Mail samples of art.

BARNHART ASSOCIATES INC., 302 Elmwood Blvd., York PA 17403. Uses artists for advertising art, design, illustrations, industrial design, layouts, lettering, promotional art, and retouching. Mail tearsheets or photostats or query in person. Of particular interest are "illustrations of an industrial or commercial situation." Reports in 10-20 days. Buys all reproduction rights, but occasionally one-time rights.

R. REECE BARRETT ASSOCIATES, INC., The Quadrangle Village of Cross Keys, Baltimore MD 21210. Creative Director: Harry Sprow. Uses artists for ad layouts, catalogs and sales promotion materials. Advertising is in business and trade publications. Submit tearsheets or photostats of published work. Negotiates payment. Pays on acceptance. Reports in 1 week.

TED BATES & COMPANY, INC., 1515 Broadway, New York NY 10036. Senior Vice President/Executive Creative Director: Irving Sonn.

BATTEN, BARTON, DURSTINE, & OSBORN, INC., 383 Madison Ave., New York NY 10017. Contact: Creative Director.

BB&W ADVERTISING, 1106 W. State St., Boise ID 83702. (208)343-2572. Art Director: Pete Wilson. Estab: 1963. Annual billing: $565,000. Clients are financial firms, food processors, auto dealers, real estate developers and agricultural firms. Buys 24 illustrations annually for annual reports, billboards, catalogs and newspaper ads; especially needs architectural line renderings, comic book illustrations and illustrations of people for billboards. Also uses artists for lettering and retouching. Payment determined by complexity of assignment and time spent. Pays $50 minimum. "Original payment as agreed for unused assigned illustrations where layout is followed and/or roughs are approved." Mail artwork. Reports in 1 week. SASE.

BENAUL ASSOCIATES ADVERTISING, 286 5th Ave., New York NY 10001. Art/Creative Director: Bernard Hoffman. Clients are fashion accessories, real estate and publishing firms. Uses artists for layout, illustration, technical art, paste-up and retouching. Media include newspaper, consumer and trade advertising, collateral material, direct mail and point-of-purchase material. Call for interview.

BENTON & BOWLES, INC., 909 3rd Ave., New York NY 10022. Executive Vice President/Director, Creative Services: Alvin Hampel.

BENTON & BOWLES UND PARTNER, 6 Frankfurt (Main), Freiherr-Vom-Stein-Str. 31, West Germany. Contact: Anthony Harrison/Ottilie Dietrich. Clients are car, cigarette, soft drink, beer, cosmetic, food and alcohol firms. Uses artists for illustration and lettering. Media used: newspapers, TV, radio, magazines, billboards and direct mail. Mail samples.

BERGER NECHAMKIN & ASSOCIATES, INC., 211 E. 43rd St., New York NY 10017. (212)986-1233. Contact: Art Nechamkin. Estab: 1973. Annual billing: $500,000. Clients are industrial and technical manufacturers, sports products firms and industries. Buys 30 illustrations annually for annual reports, catalogs, print ads, letterheads, packaging, POP displays and posters. Also uses artists for layout, lettering, paste-up and retouching. Payment determined by artist's reputation, complexity, number of illustrations and/or where work appears. Pays $50-1,500, illustrations; $25 minimum, retouching. Original payment as agreed for unused assigned illustrations. Local artists only. Query with samples or call for interview.
Crafts: Uses craftsmen for mock-up products and displays. Pays $100 minimum.
To Break In: "Keep showing new work to prospective clients you've already seen. You're bound to hit the right moment for someone's needs if you keep reminding them you're around."

ALAN BERNI CORPORATION, 666 Steamboat Rd., Greenwich CT 06830. (203)661-4747. Vice President: Stuart Berni. Estab: 1937. Clients are manufacturers and retailers of consumer products. Buys 25 illustrations annually for annual reports, catalogs, letterheads, POP displays and trademarks; especially needs packaging illustrations. Also uses artists for layout, lettering, paste-up, retouching and type spec. Payment determined by reputation of artist, complexity, number of illustrations, time spent and/or where the work appears. Pays $10 per hour minimum. Pays original payment as promised or percentage for unused assigned illustrations. Write for interview.

RALPH BING ADVERTISING COMPANY, 23215 Commerce Park Dr., Beachwood OH 44122. (216)464-3350. President/Art Director: Ralph S. Bing. Assistant Art Director: Earl Olson, Jr. Estab: 1946. Annual billing: $1 million. Industrial clients are primarily in steel and non-ferrous alloys, stamping, cranes, industrial warehousing, adhesives and glass. Consumer clients are in automotives, food and food products, hotels, motels and entertainment. Buys 25 freelance illustrations annually for annual reports, billboards, ads, catalogs, letterheads, packaging, POP displays, posters, trademarks and corporate ID's. Also uses artists for layout and retouching. Payment determined by number of illustrations, time spent and where the work appears. Pays $5-35 per hour. Original payment made for unused assigned illustrations; some exceptions as agreed. Local artists only. Query. Reports immediately.
To Break In: "Portfolio should contain basic samples with an approximation of time spent on each. It should clearly represent the artist's average work, not necessarily all best work. Certainly no work accomplished at school under supervision of instructors."

THOMAS H. BIRCH ADVERTISING, 4221 Hamilton Ave., Cincinnati OH 45223. (513)541-1441. Contact: Thomas H. Birch. Estab: 1960. Annual billing: $200,000. Clients are industrial, mail order and soft drink firms. Buys 10 illustrations annually for ads, letterheads, packaging, POP displays, television and trademarks; especially needs catalogs. Also uses artists for color separations, layout, lettering, paste-up, retouching and type spec. Payment determined by complexity of assignment and/or time spent. Minimum payment: $15 per hour, illustration; $10 per hour, layout; $6 per hour, paste-up. Original payment as promised for unused assigned illustrations or layouts. Local artists only. Call for interview. "After viewing portfolio, artists' names are placed in file for possible assignments. SASE." Prefers artist with "experience in knowing what will reproduce."

BYRON BOOTHE & ASSOCIATES, INC., 437 S. Hydraulic, Wichita KS 67211. Contact: Byron W. Boothe or Robert E. Peck. Clients are drug, financial, retail and co-op groups. Uses artists for advertising art, audiovisuals, direct mail, posters and TV commercials. Mail resume before sending samples.

JOHN BORDEN ADVERTISING AGENCY, 430 Oak Grove, Minneapolis MN 55403. Art Director: John Borden. Clients are financial, retail, architectural and medical firms. Uses artists for layout, illustrations, technical art, paste-up, retouching and lettering. Media include newspapers, magazines, radio, television, billboards, direct mail and posters. Pays $12-200, layout; $15-20, paste-up. "Some of those whose work I see are not as well trained as they should be."

BOZELL & JACOBS, 1 Dag Hammarskjold Plaza, New York NY 10017. Senior Vice President/Creative Director: Marce Mayhew.

R.C. BRETH INC., Box 929, Green Bay WI 54305. Annual billing: $303,000. Clients are industrial manufacturers, direct mail firms, farm implement producers, specialty firms, publishers (maps, books, etc.), and special service (leasing) firms. Uses artists for layout, illustrations, technical art, retouching, TV film, commercials and lettering. Media include newspapers, TV, radio, transit, magazines, billboards, displays and direct mail. Pays $20, layout; $7.50 per hour, paste-up. Query. "We look for the highest quality consistent with where art is to be used."

BROOKS-WESLEY ADVERTISING, Box 299, Topeka KS 66601. Art Director: F.L. Wielandy. Clients are manufacturers, publishers and insurance firms. Uses artists for layout, illustration, paste-up and retouching. Media used: newspapers, radio, magazines and direct mail. Pays $15-100, layout; $5-20 per hour, paste-up. Mail samples.

BUNTIN ADVERTISING, INC., 900 Division St., Nashville TN 37203. Contact: William Holley or Jack Pentzer. Clients are manufacturers, commercial banks, and coffee, shoe, sportswear, boat, retail automotive, dairy, chemical and retail firms. Uses artists for layout, illustration, type spec, paste-up, retouching and commercials. Media include newspapers, radio, TV, magazines and direct mail. Query before sending samples.

DAVID K. BURNAP ADVERTISING, 3480 Office Park Dr., Dayton OH 45439. (513)298-7380. Variety of clients. Buys 100 illustrations annually for print ads, annual reports, catalogs, letterheads, packaging, POP displays, posters and trademarks. Also uses artists for animation, keylines, layout, lettering, paste-up and retouching. Payment determined by artist's reputation, complexity of work and/or time spent. Pays $5-5,000 per retouching assignment or illustration. Original payment as promised for unused assigned illustrations. Query with samples. Reports in 4 weeks. No work returned. Prefers to work with "the best of each type of artist or the most efficient craftsman in any phase of graphic arts."

ED BURNETT, CONSULTANTS, INC., 176 Madison Ave., New York NY 10016. (212)679-0630. Contact: Donn Rappaport. Uses artists for direct mail promotion; advertising art and design; catalog illustrations and covers; convention exhibits; graphic design; letterheads; and posters. Most projects are related to direct response advertising. Pays $100 for direct mail brochure designs. Local artists only. Submit resume.

LEO BURNETT COMPANY, INC., Prudential Plaza, Chicago IL 60601. Administrative Manager/Creative Services Division: M.A. Hiller.

BUSINESS EXTENSION BUREAU, 4802 Travis, Houston TX 77002. (713)528-5568. Contact: R.L. Royall. Uses artists for direct mail promotion, advertising art and design, letterheads and lettering. Prefers local artists. Call for appointment.

BUTLER-TURNER ADVERTISING, 2001 9th Ave., Vero Beach FL 32960. Senior Art Director: Gary Veranich. Clients are real estate, banks, savings and loans, insurance, citrus products firms, a hospital and chambers of commerce. Uses artists for layout, illustration, technical art, type spec, paste-up and lettering. Media include newspapers, radio, TV, magazines, billboards and direct mail. Local artists only. Arrange interview. "We're always looking for outstanding and unique design and photo angles for our clients."

CAL-AD, 915 N. Hollywood Way, Burbank CA 91505. (213)984-2890. Art Director: Claude Lagardere. Estab: 1960. Annual billing: $650,000. Clients are manufacturers of arts and crafts, paneling and home hobbies. Buys illustrations for catalogs, letterheads, print ads, packaging, POP displays, posters and trademarks. Also uses artists for retouching and airbrush work. Payment determined by time spent. Original payment as promised for unused assigned illustrations. Local artists only. Query with samples. Reports in 1 week. SASE.

CAMPBELL AND CO., ADVERTISING AGENCY, 214 N. 8th St., Allentown PA 18102. (215)435-2110. Public Relations Director: Robert O. Campbell. Buys illustrations for direct mail brochures, annual reports, billboards, public service TV spots, print ads and collateral material. Query with samples of printed work.

CAMPBELL-MITHUN, INC., Northstar Center, Minneapolis MN 55402. Vice President/Creative Director: Al Olson.

CARGILL, WILSON & ACREE, INC., 2112 11th Ave. S., Suite 101, Birmingham AL 35202. Art Director: Steve Johnson. Uses artists for advertising art and design, illustrations, graphic design and retouching services. Mail samples or call for interview.

CASE & McGRATH, 445 Park Ave., New York NY 10022. (212)832-1800. Contact: Vince Ansaldi. Estab: 1969. Annual billing: $20 million. Clients are men's toiletries, food, stockings, liquor, wine, baby shampoo, bath oil and face cleanser firms. Buys 25-50 illustrations annually for print ads, packaging, POP displays and posters; 5-8 TV storyboard illustrations bought per month. Also uses artists for animation, lettering, paste-up and retouching. Pays $7-10 per hour, mechanicals; $20 per frame, TV storyboards. No payment for unsatisfactory assigned work; negotiates payment if unused but not artist's fault. Call for interview. Evaluates artist at interview.

THE CHARTMAKERS, INC., 25 W. 45th St., New York NY 10036. Contact: Larry LePeer. Specializes in promotions/management communications. Uses artists for audiovisuals, direct mail brochures, graphic design, lettering, sales promotion art, mechanicals and story boards.

CHERENSON, CARROLL & HOLZER, Box 508, Livingston NJ 07039. Creative Director: Mark Kupperman. Estab: 1956. Annual billing: $500,000. Clients are housing developers, financial institutions, sports facilities, realtors and retailers. Buys 100+ illustrations annually for annual reports, billboards, catalogs, letterheads, print ads, POP displays, posters and trademarks; especially needs artists to work on total advertising campaign design with copywriter. Also needs artists for color separations, layout, lettering, paste-up, type spec and design. Payment determined by complexity, number of illustrations and/or time spent. Pays $10-40 per hour, design; $8-12 per hour, mechanicals; $8-25 per hour, illustrations. Original payment as agreed for unused assigned illustrations. Local artists only. Query with samples. Reports in 1 week. SASE.

THE CHICAGO GROUP INC., Division of Resources for Marketing, 2123 N. Racine Ave., Chicago IL 60614. (312)248-4866. Contact: Lester Teichner. Estab: 1974. Annual billing: $2 million. Clients are electrical, chemical, machinery, architectural and construction producers. Uses artists for 10-15 major projects annually concerning annual reports, catalogs, letterheads, packaging, POP displays, posters, trade magazine ads and trademarks. Also uses artists for layout, lettering, paste-up and type spec. Payment determined by complexity, number of illustrations and time spent. Pays $100 minimum for illustrations/layouts. Original payment as agreed for unused assigned illustrations. Local artists only. Write for interview. Reports in 2 weeks. No samples returned.

GEORGE P. CLARKE ADVERTISING, INC., 420 Madison Ave., New York NY 10017. Creative Director: Dan Mollo. Clients are automotive aftermarket manufacturers, financial

"A simple, yet dramatic style" prompted Undercover Graphics to buy this architectural sketch from Stuart Jay Miller. Purchased for $100, the drawing was used as a book illustration. "We prefer avant-garde styles of 'new art,' " says L. A. Paul, creative director.

accounts and trade advertisers. Uses artists for layout, illustration and paste-up. Media include newspapers, television and radio, magazines and direct mail. Prefers local artists. Query with resume.

CLASSIFIED INTERNATIONAL ADVERTISING SERVICES, INC., 1345 E. 10th Ave., Hialeah FL 33010. Operations Manager: Margaret Tamosaitis. Senior Artist: Jennifer Thomson. Clients are auto dealers and real estate agencies. Uses artists for b&w line illustrations, cartoons and spot color. Mail samples or call for interview.

COMPTON ADVERTISING, INC., 625 Madison Ave., New York NY 10022. Executive Art Director: Rupert Witalis.

CONTI ADVERTISING AGENCY, INC., 210 Summit Ave., Montvale NJ 07645. Vice President: Richard Conti. Clients are industry and small package goods firms. Uses artists for layout, technical art, type spec, paste-up and retouching. Media include newspapers, trade magazines and direct mail. Call for interview or mail samples.

COOPER RAND CORPORATION, 127 E. 62nd St., New York NY 10021. Contact: Lynn Hassett. Uses artists for direct mail promotion. Pays $500 minimum for brochure design. Local artists only. Query with resume or call for interview.

COPY GROUP ADVERTISING, Box 311, Encino CA 91316. Art Buyer: Len Miller. Uses artists for cartoons and humorous sketches, for use in the areas of resort, vacation, travel and gambling. Also uses spot drawings and illustrations for direct mail customers. "Artists with experience in book publishing fields, advertising and greeting cards, would probably have the skills we're looking for." Reports in 3 days. Pays on acceptance.

CORBETT ADVERTISING, INC., 40 S. 3rd St., Columbus OH 43215. Art Director: James Mitchell. Clients are colleges, hospitals, insurance firms, shopping centers, banks and other manufacturers and institutions. Uses artists for layout, illustrations and TV commercials. Welcomes samples, "especially of new illustration techniques." Likes to have a file of dependable craftsmen. The job is explained to the artist who sets his fee. If mutually agreeable, the artist proceeds and is paid upon completion."

CORPORATE RESOURCES FOR MARKETING, 424 E. 52nd St., New York NY 10022. (212)421-0846. Contact: John Shea. Estab: 1972. Industrial clients. Buys up to 25 illustrations annually for annual reports, catalogs, letterheads, packaging, print ads, trademarks and POP displays. Also uses artists for layout, lettering, paste-up, retouching and type spec. Payment determined by complexity, number of illustrations and/or time spent. Pays $8-18 per hour, mechanicals; $30 per hour, art director. Original payment as agreed for unused assigned illustrations.
To Break In: "Get a rounded education in advertising, art, etc. Don't price yourself too high or too low. Artists wishing to work with us should have industrial materials as samples and should understand industrial products and the marketplace."

THE CORPORATION FOR CREATIVE COMMUNICATION, 56 Steele, Denver CO 80206. (303)399-4390. Art Director: Peter Szollosi. Estab: 1971. Annual billing: $2 million. Clients are developers, manufacturers, financial institutions, resorts and travel firms. Buys 25 illustrations annually for annual reports, billboards, print ads, packaging, POP displays, posters and TV ads. Also uses artists for animation, color separations, lettering and retouching. Pays $25, simple line drawing. Payment determined by artist's reputation, complexity, number of illustrations and time spent. No payment for unused assigned illustrations. Call for interview. Reports in 1 week.

CREAMER/FSR, 410 N. Michigan Ave., Chicago IL 60611. (312)467-6800. Estab: 1917. Annual billing: $6½ million. Clients are agricultural, industrial and heavy consumer firms. Buys illustrations for annual reports, billboards, catalogs, print ads, posters and trademarks. Also uses artists for layout, lettering, paste-up and retouching. Payment determined by reputation, number of illustrations and/or where work will appear. Query with samples.

CREATIVE HOUSE ADVERTISING, INC., 17621 James Couzens, Detroit MI 48235. Vice President/Creative Director: Robert G. Washburn. Annual billing: $1,500,000. Uses artists for layout, illustration, keyline, technical art, type spec, paste-up, retouching, commercials and lettering. Media include newspapers, magazines, TV, radio, transit, billboards, direct mail, point-of-purchase displays and collateral projects. Clients are home builders, furniture dealers, financial and insurance institutions, business supply manufacturers, outdoor power equipment manufacturers, and national consumer and retail accounts. Prefers local artists. Call for appointment. "We buy for the usual—i.e. quality, service and price. Learn as much as possible about one particular area of the profession, then practice professionalism and fair pricing. Rates here depend on the job."

CREATIVE PROFESSIONAL SERVICES, INC., 36 Montvale Ave., Stoneham MA 02180. (617)438-3838. President: John Bell. Uses artists for direct mail promotion. Local artists only. Query with resume and request interview. Reports in 2 weeks. SASE.

JOHN CROWE ADVERTISING AGENCY, 1104 S. 2nd St., Springfield IL 62704. (217) 528-1076. Contact: John Crowe. Estab: 1951. Annual billing: $100,000. Clients are industries, manufacturers, retailers, banks, publishers, insurance firms, packaging firms and state agencies on aviation and law enforcement. Buys 3,000 illustrations annually for ads, annual reports, billboards, catalogs, letterheads, packaging, POP displays, TV and trademarks; especially needs layout sketches, publishers' camera-ready art and photo retouching. Also uses artists for color separations, animation, lettering, paste-up and type spec. Payment determined by number of illustrations and/or time spent. Pays $10 per illustration/camera-ready art; $4-10 per sketch. No

payment for unused assigned illustrations. Mail artwork. Reports in 5 days. SASE. Prefers to work with experienced artists.
To Break In: "Include in your portfolio the following: sketches, layouts, pen & ink, camera-ready art (color separations) and design work."

CULTURAL COMMUNICATIONS ASSOCIATES, Box 328, Brookline MA 02146. Contact: Margaret May Meredith. Clients are in performing arts field. Uses artists for direct mail brochures, posters and newspaper ads.

CUMMINGS ADVERTISING AGENCY, INC., 3630 Wakeforest, Houston TX 77098. (713)528-5335. Estab: 1952. Creative Director: Denise Zwicker. Clients are industrial, financial, retail, chemical and agricultural firms. Buys 150 illustrations annually for annual reports, billboards, catalogs, print ads, letterheads, direct mail packages, posters and trademarks. Also uses artists for lettering, retouching and logo design. Payment determined by complexity of assignment, number of illustrations and/or time spent. Pays $10-30 per hour, design; $75-200, 8½ x 11 line drawing; $25-75, small cartoons. No payment for unsatisfactory work; original payment as agreed for unused assigned illustrations if not artist's fault. Local artists only. Query, or write or call for interview. Reports in 2 weeks. SASE.
Portfolio: "Samples should include technical illustrations, whimsical drawings and other examples of his/her work."

CUNDALL/WHITEHEAD/ASSOCIATES, 3000 Bridgeway, Sausalito CA 94965. (415)332-3625. Contact: Alan Cundall. Estab: 1976. Handles creative and promotional services for advertisers and agencies. Buys illustrations for annual reports, catalogs, print ads, letterheads, packaging and POP displays; especially needs spot drawings for collateral. Also uses artists for layout, lettering, paste-up and type spec. Payment determined by artist's reputation, complexity and time spent. Pays $10 per hour or $300, mechanicals for brochure; $50 each, spot drawings for brochure; $100, rough layout of magazine ad. Original payment as agreed for unused assigned illustrations. Write or call for interview. Reports in 1 day.
To Break In: "Seek the counsel of an agency art director as to the merits of your portfolio before seeing other agencies."

CUNNINGHAM & WALSH INC., 260 Madison Ave., New York NY 10016. Executive Vice President/Creative Director: Robert G. Minicus.

CUNNINGHAM, SLY AND ASSOCIATES, INC., Box 4503, Shreveport LA 71104. Art/Creative Director: Harold J. Sly. Clients are heavy industries, food service equipment manufacturers, banks, savings and loans, oil tools and electronic instruments firms. Uses artists for illustration, technical art, paste-up, retouching and commercials, Media include newspapers, TV, radio, magazines, billboards and direct mail. Mail samples of work.

DALTON & ASSOCIATES, Box 250, Troy OH 45373. President: Ralph W. Dalton. Clients are manufacturers and farm equipment firms. Uses artists for layout, illustration, technical art and retouching. Media include newspapers, direct mail and magazines. Mail samples of work.

DANCER-FITZGERALD-SAMPLE, INC., 347 Madison Ave., New York NY 10017. Vice President/Director of Art Services: Warren C. Krey. Clients are food, drug, hosiery, candy, beer, automobile and cigarette firms. Uses artists for illustration, layout, retouching and lettering. Media include newspapers, TV, radio, magazines, transit, billboards, POP displays and collateral projects. Mail samples.

D'ARCY-MacMANUS & MASIUS, INC., 437 Madison Ave., New York NY 10022. Contact: Creative Director.

DE BRUYN ADVERTISING, INC., 3707 Admiral, El Paso TX 79925. (915)592-4191. Art Director: Walter Henn. Estab: 1945. Annual billing: $2 million+. Local clients are banks, car dealers and race tracks. National clients are members of Western-wear industry. Buys 20-50 illustrations annually for catalogs, magazines, letterheads and POP displays. Payment determined by reputation of artist, complexity of work and/or number of illustrations. Pays $75 minimum. Original payment as agreed for unused assigned illustrations. Query with samples or call if in town. Reports in 3 weeks. SASE.
Crafts: Uses potters, silk screeners and other craftsmen for ad props and speciality gift items for clients. Pays $1 minimum.

RANDALL DE LEEUW/DESIGNER, 21 Prince St., New York NY 10012. Clients are museums, art galleries, book publishers, nonprofit public interest groups and corporate businesses. Uses artists for technical art retouching. "Work is usually assigned on a project basis and fee depends on the end client." Pays $10 to $50, retouching; $25 to $40, 4x5 transparency of artwork.

DE MARTINI ASSOCIATES, 414 4th Ave., Haddon Heights NJ 08035. (609)547-2800. Annual billing: $750,000. Uses artists for illustration. Media include newspapers, TV, radio, billboards, direct mail and magazines. Clients are frozen and fast food firms and plastic eating utensil companies. Pays $15-$50 per hour, layout; $10 per hour, paste-up. Pays per frame, audiovisuals and filmstrips. Mail samples.

DELTA DESIGN GROUP, INC., 518 Central Ave., Box 112, Greenville MS 38701. Art Director: Noel Workman. Clients are financial institutions, fertilizer manufacturers, chambers of commerce, trade associations, industrial foundations, and seed, farm machinery, grain storage, dental and architectural firms. Uses artists for layout, illustration, retouching, model building and exhibit design. Media include newspapers, TV, radio, magazines, billboards, collateral, direct mail and POP displays. Pays $100-300 for layout. Mail samples.

DENTSU ADVERTISING LTD., 1114 Avenue of the Americas, New York NY 10036. Contact: Creative Director.

DICKINSON ADVERTISING, 67 Federal Ave., Quincy MA 02169. Assistant Creative Supervisor: Jeff Christo. Uses local artists for layout, illustration, technical art, paste-up and lettering. "We are interested in people who can produce professional-looking finished roughs and comprehensives for client presentation and who live in the Boston area. Lettering and illustration a must." Clients are travel agencies, nonprofit organizations, manufacturers of industrial and consumer products, and commercial services. Send resume and samples.

DIRECT MAIL/MARKETING ASSOCIATES, 6 E. 43rd St., New York NY 10017. Contact: Ruth C. Troiani. Uses artists for direct mail promotion. New York City area artists only. Query with resume or call for interview.

DIRECT MARKETING CORPORATION OF AMERICA, 3700 Wilshire Blvd., Los Angeles CA 90010. Art Director: James Glass. Uses artists for direct mail and POP brochures. Prefers artists in Los Angeles, Malibu, Santa Monica, Beverly Hills and West Los Angeles. Requests initial letter of inquiry outlining professional credits, minimum rate schedule and printed samples of work.

LAWRENCE DOBROW & ASSOCIATES, INC., 5530 Wisconsin Ave., Chevy Chase MD 20015. Art Director/Vice President: John Fyock. Clients are in aircraft, food, sports and men's wear fields. Uses artists for illustration and technical art. Media include newspapers, magazines, radio, TV, billboards and direct mail. Mail samples.

DOE-ANDERSON ADVERTISING AGENCY, INC., 223 E. Broadway, Louisville KY 40202. Senior Art Director: Dan Hogan. Clients are financial, heating-air conditioning-ventilating, shipping, discount store, packaging systems, manufacturing, restaurant, industrial products, paints, insurance, newspaper, TV, radio, meat and food products, wood products, appliances, lighting, marine, sporting goods and liquor firms. Uses artists for advertising art, architectural renderings, catalog illustrations and covers, graphic design, letterheads, retouching and technical illustration.

W.B. DONER & CO., 26711 Northwestern Hwy., Southfield MI 48034. (313)354-9700. Associate Creative Director: Steve LaGattuta. Estab: 1937. Annual billing: $45 million. Clients are food companies, appliance and department stores, liquor companies, banks and supermarkets. Buys 75-100 freelance illustrations annually for TV and print ads. Also uses artists for animation, paste-up and retouching. Payment determined by complexity of assignment. Original payment as promised for unused assigned illustrations. Query with samples. SASE.

DALLAS C. DORT & COMPANY, 811 Citizens Bank Bldg., Flint MI 48502. (313)238-4677. Contact: Lucinda Cooke. Estab: 1972. Annual billing: $700,000. Clients are food processing, building supply, retail and travel services firms. Buys illustrations for print ads, billboards, catalogs, letterheads, packaging, POP displays, posters, TV ads and trademarks; especially needs newspaper layouts. Also uses artists for paste-up, retouching and type spec. Original payment as agreed for unused assigned illustrations. Mail artwork. SASE.

DOYLE DANE BERNBACH INC., 437 Madison Ave., New York NY 10022. Executive Vice President/Art Director: Robert Gage.

DOZIER-EASTMAN & CO., Box 11484, Santa Ana CA 92701. Art Buyer: Phil Richards. Uses artists for advertising design, audiovisuals, brochures, industrial design, newspaper editorial cartoons, advertising, posters, retouching and technical illustration. "We seek freelancers with a basic understanding of the needs of a salesman in the field. Most artists cannot relate to the needs of a 'product' selling effort. They need to get into the field and see how products and ideas relate to the people who need them . . . " Media include newspapers, TV, radio, magazines, billboards, direct mail, POP displays and merchandising. "We particularly need resources in agriculture background and experience for industrial or agricultural clients." Query with resume.

MORT DUFF AGENCY, Box 21447, Phoenix AZ 85036. Art Director: Elmo Sears. Clients are horse care products firms. Uses artists for POP display, product labels, direct mail and national advertising, including consumer and trade magazines. Mail samples.

J. DUNN & ASSOCIATES, INC., 221 Scott St., Suite 250, Wausau WI 54401. President/Creative Director: Jim Dunn. Uses artists for illustration and commercials. Media include newspapers, television, magazines and direct mail. Clients are banks, consumer goods and heavy industrial firms. Mail or deliver samples personally.

EDELSTEIN-NELSON ADVERTISING AGENCY, INC., 3335 Main St., Skokie IL 60076. (312)676-4350. Contact: Tom Turner. Estab: 1945. Annual billing: $1 million. Clients are book publishers, binderies, POP manufacturers, electronic and camera companies and industrial firms. Buys 50 illustrations annually for catalogs and consumer magazine ads. Also uses artists for retouching and paste-up. "We buy only specialized art that our present staff cannot handle or lacks experience in." Payment determined by time spent. Pays original payment as agreed for unused assigned illustrations. Query first. SASE.

EDGECOMBE MARKETING, INC., Box 1406, Tarboro NC 27886. (919)823-1177. Art Director: Jay C. Rose. Annual billing: $800,000. Clients are agricultural and construction equipment manufacturers and aircraft sales and service firms. Uses artists for layouts, illustration, technical art, type spec, paste-up and retouching. Media used: newspapers, TV, radio, magazines, collateral, direct mail and POP displays. Query with samples.

EGR COMMUNICATIONS, 275 Madison Ave., New York NY 10016. Associate Creative Director: John C. Lefton. Uses artists for illustrations (line-color, etc.), catalogs, displays, graphic design, layouts, package design and promotional art. Query with credits. Buys first rights. Some previously published work OK. Reports in 2 weeks. Payment for work made as stages completed.

ENGINEERED MARKETING OF FLORIDA, 2350 NE 135th St., Suite 1410, North Miami FL 33161. President: Richard E. Stember. Clients are financial, real estate, theatre, political, industrial, EDP, automotive and lighting firms. Uses artists for technical art, illustration and retouching. Media used: print and TV. Mail samples.

FRED A. EPSTEIN ADVERTISING, INC., 390 Commonwealth Ave., Boston MA 02215. Contact: Fred A. Epstein. Uses artists for layout and illustration. Clients are entertainment, restaurant-night clubs, retailers, schools, universities, clinical laboratories and manufacturing accounts. Media used: newspapers, TV, transit, radio, magazines, direct mail, POP, billboards and collateral. Call for interview.

WILLIAM ESTY COMPANY, INC., 100 E. 42nd St., New York NY 10017. Senior Vice President/Executive Art Director: Robert Forgione. Uses artists for illustration, layout, retouching and lettering. Media used: newspapers, TV, radio, transit, billboards and magazines.

MICHAEL FAIN ADVERTISING, 156 5th Ave., New York NY 10010. Art/Creative Director: Mike Fain. Clients are industrial and surgical firms. Uses artists for layout, paste-up and retouching. Media used: newspapers, magazines, and direct mail. Local artists only. Call for appointment.
To Break In: "One of the many qualities required by professional artists with whom we deal is a good understanding of copyfitting. An artist is given a layout with an indicated space for text and some artists are inclined to 'fake' it — whereas actually making sure the required type will fit the space is something that has to be done properly."

FARRAGHER MARKETING SERVICES, 7 Court St., Canfield OH 44406. (216)533-3347. Art/Creative Director: A.E. Canon. Clients are mall developers; financial firms; and manufacturers of scientific equipment, balances and scales, and steel buildings. Uses artists for layout, illustration, technical art, type spec and retouching. Media used: newspapers, TV, magazines and direct mail.

FELDMAN & MOSER, INC., 270 Farmington Ave., Farmington CT 06032. (203)677-9701. Creative Director: Bernard Feldman. President: George Moser. Estab: 1975. Annual billing: $750,000. Clients are banking, industrial and consumer product firms. Buys illustrations for billboards, catalogs, ads, packaging, POP displays, posters, TV and trademarks; especially needs illustrations for brochures, trade magazine and newspaper ads. Also uses artists for animation, layout, paste-up and retouching. Payment determined by complexity, number of illustrations and/or time spent. New England or New York artists only. Call for interview. Reports in 1 week. SASE.

G.M. FELDMAN & COMPANY, 180 N. Michigan Ave., Chicago IL 60601. Art Director: Jerry Beauchamp. Estab: 1967. Uses artists for layout, illustration, technical art, retouching and lettering. Payment determined by job. Clients are real estate, fast food firms, banks, automotive manufacturers and industries. Media used: TV, radio, newspapers, magazines, transit, billboards, collateral, POP and direct mail firms. Call for interview.

GEORGE FELDMAN ADVERTISING, 15 W. 38th St., New York NY 10018. (212)279-3660. Contact: George Feldman. Uses artists for direct mail promotion. Call for interview; no mailed samples.

FILLMAN ADVERTISING, INC. 304 W. Hill St., Champaign IL 61820. (217)352-0002. Clients are manufacturers of steel pouring valves, sludge and fertilizer applicators, snow plows, hoists, leaf collectors, aviation trainers, tank trucks, caskets and real estate development firms. Media used: trade magazines and direct mail. Uses artists for layout, illustration, paste-up and retouching. Mail samples; none returned unless arrangements made.
To Break In: "Make up a sample book (small and mailable) aimed at business-trade advertising."

FLAX ADVERTISING, 964 3rd Ave., New York NY 10022. (212)355-0700. Art/Creative Director: Mike Schlueter. Clients are women's fashions, children's wear, menswear, hospital equipment, computer software, financial, manufacturing, optical, clocks, greeting cards, fabrics, shoes and pen firms. Specializes in fashion. Uses artists for illustration, technical art, retouching and lettering. Media used: newspapers, magazines and direct mail. Local artists only. Call for interview.

FOLEY ADVERTISING, INC., 332 S. Michigan Ave., Chicago IL 60604. Contact: J.E. Foley. Industrial clients. Uses local artists for layout, illustration, technical art, paste-up and retouching. Media used: trade magazines and direct mail. "Since our accounts are primarily industrial, there's obviously very little use of illustrations with people in them. Our artwork is very down-to-earth, very representational." Call for interview.

FOOTE, CONE & BELDING COMMUNICATIONS, INC., 200 Park Ave., New York NY 10017. Graphics Director: Hector Robledo. Uses artists for illustration and paste-up. Media used: TV, radio, newspapers, transit, billboards, magazines, direct mail, POP displays and collateral. Prefers local artists. Call for appointment. Clients are cosmetics, fragrancies, hair care, fashion, tobacco products and food firms.

FOREST ADVERTISING CORP., 24 Forest St., Brockton MA 02402. Creative Director: Michael Jordan. Uses artists for illustration. Clients specialize in men's apparel. Mail samples.

PETER FORSTENZER, INC., 331 Madison Ave., New York NY 10017. Annual billing: $250,000. Uses artists for layout, illustration, technical art, paste-up and retouching. Clients are industry, publications and consumer goods producers. Media used: newspapers, magazines, collateral, direct mail and POP. Minimum payment: $10 per hour, layout; $8 per hour, paste-up. Call for interview.

ALAN FRANK & ASSOCIATES INC., 1524 S. 11th E., Salt Lake City UT 84105. (801)486-7455. Contact: John Hart. Estab: 1955. Annual billing: $3 million. Clients are fast food companies, resorts, commodities and entertainment firms. Buys illustrations for annual reports, billboards, ads, letterheads, TV and packaging. Also uses artists for animation and retouching. Payment determined by complexity and/or time spent. Minimum payment: $500, animation; $100, illustrations; $200, brochure layout. Pays percentage on speculation as previously determined for unused assigned illustrations. Mail artwork. Reports in 2 weeks. SASE.

CLINTON E. FRANK, INC., ADVERTISING, 120 S. Riverside Plaza, Chicago IL 60606. Senior Vice President/Director, Creative Services: Thomas W. Laughlin, Sr.

FRANK-THOMAS, 2145 Buechel Bank Rd., Louisville KY 40218. President/General Manager: Frank Boone. Clients include manufacturers of kitchen and bathroom cabinets; wood and metal finishes; buttons and snaps; and general industrial accounts. Uses artists for illustration, and kitchen and bathroom display design assignments. Media used: collateral material, trade magazines, direct mail and POP displays. Arrange interview.

LARRY FREDERICKS ASSOCIATES, 845 3rd Ave., 15th Floor, New York NY 10022. Contact: Larry Fredericks. Clients are book publishers, firms with quarterly house organs, retailers and others which require travel and product photography. Media used: consumer and trade magazines. Uses artists for layout, illustration, type spec, paste-up and retouching. Prefers local artists. Call for interview.

W. J. FRITSCHE CO., ADVERTISING, Box 627, 1551 Allentown Rd., Lima OH 45802. Art/Creative Director: W.J. Fritsche, Jr. Clients are mail order, and farm and industrial equipment firms. Uses artists for illustration, technical art, retouching and lettering. Media used: newspapers, consumer and trade magazines. Mail nonreturnable printed samples. Original work only on request.

RALPH D. GARDNER ADVERTISING, 745 5th Ave., New York NY 10022. Art/Creative Director: I.W. Wallack. Clients deal in art, gifts, typewriters, paint, foreign cars, engineering, foods, liquors, tea, candy, bakery goods, displays and exhibits. Uses artists for lettering. Media used: newspapers, TV, magazines, radio, and billboards. Payment determined by assignment. Prefers established professionals. Usually gives assignments to those who have previously worked with them. "Out-of-town and local artists should not waste time calling. Send a brochure, card, or even a memo stating what you do. A list of credits is not essential, but is helpful. It shows that others have used your work."

GEORGE, GIBBS, HAMMERMAN & MYERS ADVERTISING, 1515 N. Warson Rd., St. Louis MO 63132. Art/Creative Director: Louis Myers. Clients are shoe firms, ice cream companies, bowling proprietors, shopping centers, automobile dealers and metals, cosmetics, cryogenics, and clothing/sportswear firms, banks, food and food stores, decorating products companies, educational institutions and paint and discount stores. Uses artists for illustration, technical art, and commercials. Media include newspapers, TV, radio, magazines, billboards and direct mail. Mail samples.

GERO & BIERSTEIN, INC., 369 Broadway, Paterson NJ 07501. Art/Creative Director: Harry Cooney. Clients are real estate/land development, automobiles, banks, restaurants, electronics, consumer and furniture accounts. Uses artists for illustration, paste-up, retouching and architectural illustration (interior-exterior). Prefers local artists. Call for interview. "We look for quality and punctuality, but frequently the samples or portfolios we're shown by freelancers are beautiful — but the work delivered doesn't measure up." Media include newspapers, magazines, direct mail, billboards and radio.

GIARDINI/RUSSELL, 126 Jackson St., Cambridge MA 02140. (617)547-4747. Executive Design Director: Bruce Morgan. Estab: 1961. Annual billing: $5 million. Serves toy, game and craft clients. Buys 5,000 illustrations annually for annual reports, billboards, catalogs, print ads, letterheads, packaging, POP displays, posters, TV and trademarks; especially needs illustrations for toys, game and crafts packaging. Also uses artists for retouching, animation, color separations, layout, lettering, paste-up and type spec. Payment determined by complexity of assignment and number of illustrations. Pays $15-3,000, illustration. Mail samples. Reports in 1 week. No work returned. "We very rarely use inexperienced artists."

CLIFFORD GILL ADVERTISING, INC., 8730 Wilshire Blvd., Beverly Hills CA 90211. Contact: Dorothy Gill. Clients are residential, commercial and condominium subdivisions. Uses artists for layout, illustration, type spec, paste-up and retouching. Media include newspapers, magazines, billboards and direct mail. Prefers local artists. Mail samples or call for interview.

MICHAEL GLICK ADVERTISING, 25152 Lathrup Blvd., Southfield MI 48075. Art/Creative Director: Robert Plonka. Trade clients are pharmaceutical and building products firms; commercial clients are banks and service firms; retail clients include clothing, toys, children's furniture, realty, builders, gage companies, door manufacturers, electrical supply companies and jewelry manufacturers. Uses artists for layout, illustration and retouching. Media include newspapers, magazines, direct mail, billboards, TV and POP displays. Detroit area artists only. Call for appointment.
To Break In: "Think and do a job till it is completely satisfactory to yourself, but don't price yourself out of the market. Speculate on your own ability."

GLOBE ADVERTISING, 35075 Automation, Mt. Clemens MI 48043. (313)791-2801. Contact: Craig Tarbeck. Estab: 1914. Annual billing: $1 million+. Mail order clients. Buys several hundred illustrations annually for ads and catalogs; especially needs layout, catalog and magazine illustration, and lettering. Also uses artists for color separations, retouching and type spec. Payment determined by time spent. Minimum payment: $10, layout; $5, illustration. Original payment as agreed for unused assigned illustrations. Local artists only. Query or write for interview. Reports in 1 week. SASE. Prefers to work with "those experienced in ad layout and finished design — especially mail order/direct response advertising.

RUSSELL T. GRAY, INC., 233 N. Michigan, Chicago IL 60601. Vice President/Art Director: Charles R. Miner. Uses artists for illustration, technical art and retouching. Media include trade magazines, direct mail and technical catalogs/bulletins. Clients are metrology, earth-moving, chemical processing and food processing equipment firms, and humidification systems. Prefers local artists. Call for appointment. "We need freelancers who pay attention to detail."

MARTIN GREENFIELD ASSOCIATES, INC., 525 Northern Blvd., Great Neck NY 11021. (516)487-3700. Vice President/Creative Director: Thom Gleason. Estab: 1960. Variety of clients. Uses artists for layout, illustration, paste-up and retouching. Media used: newspapers, transit, radio, magazines, billboards, collateral, direct mail, and POP displays.

GREENMAN ADVERTISING ASSOCIATES, 307 S. 21st Ave., Hollywood FL 33020. Creative Director: Bernard S. Schreft. Clients are banks, home and car stereo, furniture, resort, land development and swimming pool firms. Uses artists for illustration, commercials, lettering and display design. Mail samples. "I am not interested in seeing samples of work that the artist is personally proud of. I only want to see his best. At the present time, we are buying art from the finest people in New York, Chicago, Pittsburgh, Cleveland, Detroit, Atlanta, and a few other places you've probably never heard of. I only need to see a sample of an artist's best work — then we'll take it from there." Media include newspapers, magazines, radio, TV, billboards and direct mail.

HERB GREENWALD ADVERTISING, 2133 Campus Rd., Beachwood OH 44122. (216)382-3946. President: Herbert Greenwald. Estab: 1967. Clients are shopping centers. Buys illustrations for catalog covers and layouts, advertising, direct mail and publicity brochures, displays, exhibit designs, newspaper ad layouts, firm publications, lettering, packaging, POP displays, posters, signage, technical charts and illustrations, trademarks and logos. Pays $20

minimum, layout; $5 minimum, art; $20-50, posters. Local artists only. Write for interview. Reports in 3 weeks. SASE.
Portfolio: Should include line and tone drawings adaptable to magazine and newspaper reproduction.

GREY ADVERTISING INC., 777 3rd Ave., New York NY 10017. Executive Vice President/Creative Services: Joel R. Wayne.

GRISWOLD-ESHLEMAN/CHICAGO, 875 N. Michigan Ave., Chicago IL 60611. (312)943-6464. Contact: Ben Ruiz. Clients produce paper products and appliances. Uses artists for illustration. Media used: newspapers, TV, radio, collateral, magazines and direct mail. Call for appointment.

GROVES & ASSOCIATES, INC., 105 Ridge Rd., Muncie IN 47304. Art Director: Dan Kieffer. Clients are industrial, banks, food chains, and religious publishers. Uses artists for layout, illustration, technical art and lettering. Media used: newspapers, TV, radio, magazines, direct mail, POP displays, collateral and billboards.

GRUBB, GRAHAM & WILDER, INC., Century 21 Plaza, Champaign IL 61820. Contact: Art Director. Clients are industrial and agricultural producers of wire, seedcorn and food. Uses artists for layout, illustration, technical art and retouching. Media used: newspapers, TV, radio, magazines, billboards and direct mail. Mail samples.

GUTMAN ADVERTISING AGENCY, Peoples Federal Bldg., Wheeling WV 26003. (304)233-4700. Clients are financial; industrial; TV stations; meat packers; and building products, concrete, machine, tool, glassware, paint and medical firms. Uses artists for illustration and retouching. Media used: newspapers, magazines, TV, radio, billboards and direct mail. Local artists only. Call for interview.

HEPWORTH ADVERTISING COMPANY, 3403 McKinney Ave., Dallas TX 75204. Art/Creative Director: S.W. Hepworth. Clients are financial, stock broker, bank and insurance accounts. Uses artists for layout, illustration, technical art, paste-up, retouching and lettering. Media used: newspapers, TV, radio, magazines, billboards and direct mail. Mail samples.

HERMAN & ASSOCIATES, INC., 555 Madison Ave., New York NY 10022. Vice President: Paula Herman. Clients are industrial and travel firms. Uses artists for illustration, paste-up and retouching. Media used: newspapers, magazines and direct mail. Mail samples or call for interview. "Artist should display creativity with capability to follow through on an assignment."

HILL, HOLLIDAY, CONNORS, COSMOPULOS, INC., 137 Newbury St., Boston MA 02116. Chairman/Co-Creative Director: Stavros Cosmopulos. Clients are financial, retail, packaged goods, fashion, food and industrial accounts. Media used: TV, radio, magazines, newspapers, outdoor advertising and collateral materials. Mail samples.

HOEFER/AMIDEI ASSOCIATES, 426 Pacific Ave., San Francisco CA 94133. President: Neal Amidei. Uses artists for advertising art, editorial illustrations and technical art. Submit resume and samples.

HENRY HOOK ADVERTISING, 38 W. Bethune, Detroit MI 48202. (313)871-5333. Contact: Henry Hook. Estab: 1955. Annual billing: $100,000. Clients are plumbing and hardware manufacturers. Buys 25 illustrations annually for ads, annual reports, catalogs and POP displays. Also uses artists for lettering and retouching. Payment determined by time spent. Pays $40-100, illustration; $25-100, retouching. Original payment as promised for unused assigned illustrations. Local artists only. Query. Reports in 2 weeks. SASE.

HOUCK ADVERTISING, Box 12487, Roanoke VA 24026. Art Director: Chris H. Jamison. Clients are industrial, food, home furnishings, travel, electronic manufacturing and installation accounts. Media include newspapers, TV, transit, radio, magazines, billboards, collateral, direct mail and POP. Uses artists for layout, illustration, technical art, paste-up and retouching. Mail samples. Minimum payment: $25, layout; $15-20 per hour, paste-up.
Special Needs: Needs storyboards and slides for Radio/TV Department.

HOUSTON/RITZ/COHEN/JAGODA, 5207 McKinney, Dallas TX 75205. Art/Creative Directors: Wayne Houston and Mike Steel. Clients are magazines, TV station, technical equipment, political candidates, health studio, hotel, fashions, cosmetics and dish manufacturing accounts. Uses artists for magazine editorial illustration (b&w and full-color), technical art, paste-up, retouching and lettering. Media used: newspapers, TV, radio, magazines, billboards and direct mail.

THE HOWARD GROUP (formerly Imageast, Inc.), 310 Madison Ave., New York NY 10017. Art/Creative Director: Martin Howard. Clients are manufacturers, wholesalers and publishers. Use artists for layout and illustration. Media include newspapers, magazines, direct mail, POP display, packaging and radio. Pays $50 per hour, paste-up. Prefers local artists. Call for appointment.

LLOYD S. HOWARD ASSOCIATES INC., Box N, Millwood NY 10546. Art/Creative Director: L. Howard. Clients are industrial, home furnishing, lighting and swimming pool firms. Uses artists for design, mechanicals and finished art. "We are interested in freelance services locally (northern Westchester County), especially from individuals working in creative New York City shops." Media include newspapers, magazines, catalogs and direct mail. Call for interview.

IMAGE INC., Box 113, Casper WY 82601. Art/Creative Director: Sylvia Arkebauer. Clients are consumer product firms, manufacturers, services and associations. Use artists for layout, illustration, technical art, type spec, paste-up, retouching and lettering. Media include newspapers, TV, magazines, billboards, radio and direct mail. Mail samples.

SAMUEL IRVING ADVERTISING ART & DESIGN, 1719 Walnut St., Philadelphia PA 19103. (215)563-7800. Art/Creative Director: Samuel Irving. Clients are real estate firms, industrial (machinery) builders, government agencies, beverage manufacturers, fund raising groups, mall and apartment developers, publishing houses, food distributors and art galleries. Buys 10 illustrations annually for billboards, ads, packaging and POP displays. Also uses artists for animation, paste-up and retouching. Payment determined by complexity. Original payment as agreed for unused assigned illustrations. Query with samples or call for interview. Reports in 1 week. SASE.

To Break In: "It is important for a freelancer to have a professional attitude. He/she should be experienced, reliable, fast, able to adjust to various assignments and deadlines, and have a grasp of the problems involved in advertising. The best way to impress me is to show me a professional looking portfolio and have a willingness to take advice and apply it."

JACOBY & COMPANY, 155 W. Congress St., Detroit MI 48226. President: Albert K. Jacoby. Clients are manufacturers, services, publishers, sports (racing), auction services, education, marine products, construction, banking and real estate accounts. Uses artists for layout, illustration, technical art, type spec, paste-up, retouching, and lettering. Media include newspapers, magazines, TV, billboards, sales meetings, conventions and seminars. Out-of-town artists should mail samples; local artists should make appointment.

JACOBY & COMPANY, 716 E. Atlantic Blvd., Pompano Beach FL 33060. Vice President: Chris Mullon. See above listing.

LLOYD G. JAKEWAY ADVERTISING & PUBLIC RELATIONS, Box 646, Houston TX 77001. President/Creative Director: Lloyd G. Jakeway. Clients are automobile dealers, banks and furniture firms. Uses artists for layout, illustration, technical art, type spec, paste-up, retouching, commercials and lettering. Contact agency with samples. Media include newspapers, TV, radio, magazines, billboards and direct mail.

To Break In: "And by all means," says Jakeway, "enclose a bio sheet that we can keep on file. In addition to telling us about your previous work experience, tell us about the kinds of work you lean to — do you prefer to do tight renderings; or loose, imaginative illustrations? What do you think you're best at? We don't want to waste your time and ours giving you an assignment which it will take you extra hours to do or you wind up farming out to someone else because it's not really your thing."

JANUZ DIRECT MARKETING CORPORATION, 3545 W. Peterson Ave., Chicago IL 60659. Contact: L.R. Januz. Works only with artists living 30-45 minutes from office. Submit resume and call 3-4 days later.

T.S. JENKINS & ASSOCIATES INC., 140 E. 2nd St., 1 Capitol Court, Flint MI 48502. (313)235-5654. Estab: 1935. Clients include a commercial and savings bank, educational accounts and automobile dealers. Buys 10-20 illustrations annually for annual reports, billboards, catalogs, ads, letterheads, packaging, POP displays, posters, TV and trademarks. Also uses artists for layout, lettering, paste-up, retouching and type spec. Payment determined by complexity of assignment, number of illustrations and time spent. Pays $4 minimum per hour, keyline/paste-up; $4 per hour, layout. No payment for unused assigned illustrations. Call for interview.
Portfolio: "Be honest in your capabilities and samples. Samples should include b&w illustrations of people; hard line items; some 2 and 4-color work; 1-color and multiple-color layouts and printed samples."

ELVING JOHNSON ADVERTISING, INC., 4020 W. 111th St., Oak Lawn IL 60453. Art/Creative Director: Michael Hudak. Estab: 1958. Annual billing: $750,000. Clients are industrial and consumer firms. Uses artists for layout, illustration, technical art, paste-up and retouching. Media used: magazines, newspapers, direct mail, POP displays, collateral and billboards. Local artists only. Call for interview.

GEORGE JOHNSON, ADVERTISING, 755 New Ballas Rd. S., St. Louis MO 63141. (314)569-3440. Contact: Susan Brauer. Estab: 1964. Clients are real estate, fast food, nursery, savings and loan, community development, automotive, pharmaceutical, sports equipment and insurance firms. Buys 50 illustrations annually for annual reports, billboards, catalogs, print ads, letterheads, packaging, POP displays, posters, TV and trademarks. Also uses artists for animation, illustration, layout, lettering, paste-up, retouching, type spec and concepts. Payment determined by time spent. No payment for unused assigned illustrations. Local artists only. Query with samples. Reports in 1 week. SASE.
To Break In: "An artist wishing to work with us should have a minimum of 1 year's experience, be able to say 'I don't know,' have definite opinions and yet not be a sheep. His portfolio should include works rejected by his former clients as well as accepted."

R.N. JOHNSON & ASSOCIATES, 102 N. Evergreen, Arlington Heights IL 60004. (312)392-4802. Art Director: Jan Johnson. Estab: 1951. Clients are microfilming equipment, electronic components, TV testing equipment, travel, construction equipment and medical equipment firms. Uses artists for illustration, technical art, paste-up and retouching. Media used: newspapers, collateral material, direct mail and POP displays. Pays $20 per page, layout; $8 per hour, paste-up. Local artists only.

WALTER L. JOHNSON ADVERTISING, INC., 9233 Ward Parkway Extension, Suite 290, Kansas City MO 64114. Clients are industrial and consumer accounts. Uses artists for layout, illustration, technical art and retouching. Media used: newspapers, radio, TV, magazines, billboards and direct mail. Local artists only. Mail samples or call for interview.

JONETHIS/LARSON ADVERTISING INC., 310 Fairmount Ave., Box 189, Jamestown NY 14701. Art/Creative Director: Terry N. Jonethis. Industrial clients. Uses artists for layout and paste-up. Media used: newspapers and magazines. "We occasionally have need of an experienced artist strong in creative layout in this area, which is growing to become a four-season vacationland." Mail samples.

JORDAN/TAMRAZ/CARUSO/ADVERTISING, INC., 625 N. Michigan Ave., Chicago IL 60605. Executive Art Director: Jo Ann Grace. Clients are industrial, auto, financial and retail accounts. Uses artists for layout, illustration and paste-up. Media used: newspapers, TV, radio, magazines, billboards and direct mail. Prefers local artists. Call for appointment.

JPR ASSOCIATES/PRODUCT DEVELOPERS, 6600 Boulevard E., 12K, West New York NJ 07093. (201)861-5730. Contact: John Kirvan. Clients are religious and educational publishers. Buys 200 illustrations annually for book jacket design and inside book illustrations. Pays $150 minimum for 2-color cover; $15 minimum for b&w inside illustration. Payment on publication. Call for interview.

KATZ, JACOBS & DOUGLAS, INC., 655 Madison Ave., New York NY 10021. Art/Creative Director: Mike Love. Uses artists for layout, illustration, technical art, paste-up, retouching, commercials and lettering. Mail samples. Media used: newspapers, magazines, TV, radio, billboards and direct mail. Clients are industrial, fashion, real estate, hard goods, service and travel accounts. "Like most agencies we sometimes work on quite tight deadlines, so there would be a problem in dealing by mail on assignments unless the artist had a special style we wanted and we could plan for in advance."

KECK ADVERTISING INC., Box 207, Oconomowoc WI 53066. (414)567-4467. Contact: Dick Keck. Estab: 1945. Clients are material handling firms (cheesemaking and food industry equipment, foods, dairy and brewing chemical manufacturers). Buys 10-20 illustrations annually for catalogs, print ads, letterheads, packaging, POP displays, and TV. Also uses artists for color separations, layout, paste-up and retouching. Pays $7-15, mechanicals; $10-20, layouts. Original payment as agreed or 75% of agreed payment for unused assigned illustrations. Local artists only. Query, or call or write for interview. Reports in 1 week.
To Break In: "Take your work seriously — be consistent and make a business out of it. Don't undercharge. Put whatever you do best in your portfolio (your specialty). Generalists should show a broad range of work, both original renderings and printed pieces."

KELLER HAVER, INC., 770 Lexington Ave., New York NY 10021. Art/Creative Directors: Stan Bier and G. Keller. Clients are liquor and travel firms. Prefers local artists. Call for appointment.

KELLER-CRESCENT CO., Box 3, Evansville IN 47701. Vice President/Creative Director: Jon Rigsby. Clients are industrial (drills to road graders), food, dairy products, and consumer appliances accounts. Uses artists for layout, illustration, technical art and retouching. Media used: newspapers, magazines, radio, TV, billboards and direct mail.
To Break In: "Too many are simply followers, rather than suggesting or adding to the quality of the work. Others lack professionalism or drawing ability (craftmanship). They need to develop themselves — draw! draw! draw! And they are too tied to hourly rates — they should think in terms of the whole package when setting fees."

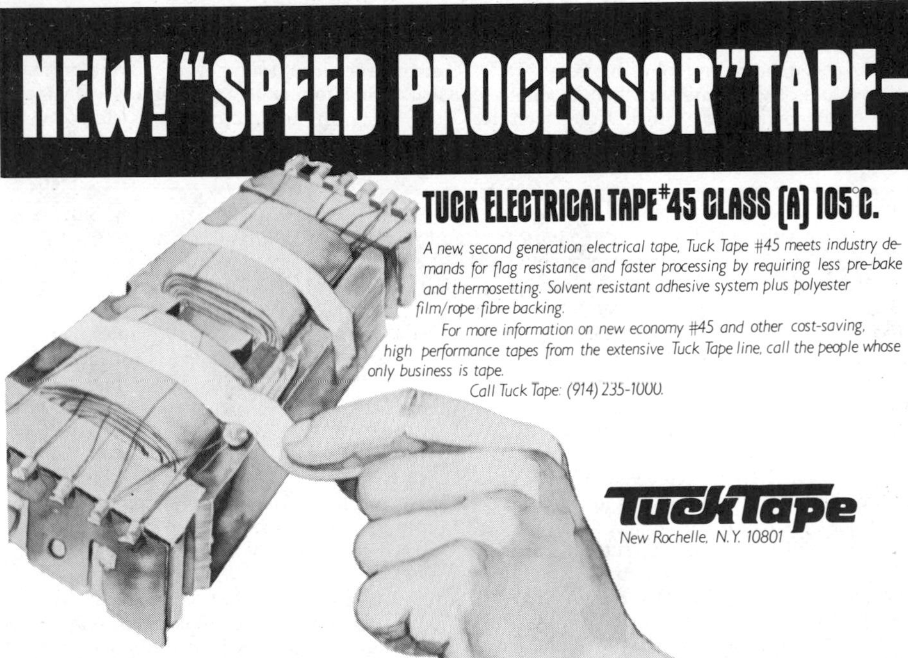

Berger Nechamkin & Associates, Inc. pays artists $50-1,500 for trade ad drawings for its industrial and technical manufacturing clients. For ad illustrations such as this one created by Howard Darden, the firm will provide the artist with specifications and notes.

KENYON & ECKHARDT ADVERTISING, INC., 200 Park Ave., New York NY 10017. Creative Director: Robert Fiore.

DUKE KERSTEIN ADVERTISING AGENCY, 3232 Candelaria NE, Albuquerque NM 87107. Art/Creative Director: H. Duke Kerstein. Uses artists for layout and retouching. Prefers local artists. Call for appointment. Media used: newspapers, TV, radio, magazines, billboards and direct mail.
To Break In: "Artist should be able to grasp understanding of the 'entire' project as related to the portion of work done. When that understanding is lacking, the portion is often overdone or underdone."

KETCHUM, MacLEOD & GROVE, INC., 4 Gateway Center, Pittsburgh PA 15222. Contact: Creative Director.

KINSLEY ADVERTISING, INC., Box 31, Worthington OH 43085. President: Gilman Calkins. Uses artists for advertising art, magazine layouts, newspaper advertising layouts, posters and sales catalogs. Prefers local artists. Query with resume and samples. SASE. Reports in 1 month.

KINZIE & GREEN INC., 128 Grand Ave., Wausau WI 54401. Executive Art Director: Bill Miller. Clients are heavy industrial and housing accounts. Uses artists for illustration. Media used: newspapers, TV, magazines and direct mail. Mail samples.

KIRCHER, HELTON & COLLETT, INC., Grant-Deneau Tower, 4th & Ludlow Sts., Dayton OH 45402. Art Director: Walter Strubczewski. Clients are banks, savings and loans, paper manufacturing, TV station, restaurant, manufacturing, caulking and paints and building accounts. Uses artists for layout, illustration, paste-up, retouching and lettering. Media used: newspapers, magazines, radio, TV, billboards and direct mail. Mail samples or call for interview.

KOEHLER COUNSELORS, 1119 Xenia Ave., Yellow Springs OH 45387. Contact: Karl Koehler. Uses artists for billboards, painted outdoor spectaculars and magazine/newspaper ad illustrations. Query with printed samples.

JOHN W. KOEHN COMPANY, Box 687, Adrian MI 49221. Contact: James W. Koehn. Clients include banks, savings and loans, fast food stores, malls, retail apparel and retail variety/specialty stores. Uses artists for illustration, technical art and retouching. Media include newspapers, TV, radio, consumer magazines, billboards, direct mail and POP displays. Mail samples.

JOSEPH A. KRUEGER & ASSOCIATES, Box 1470, San Rafael CA 94902. Annual billing: $1 million+. Uses artists for layout, illustration, paste-up, retouching, technical art and type spec. Clients are consumer, financial and industrial — "but we are primarily direct mail/direct marketing." Media used: newspapers, radio, TV, magazines and collateral.

LADDIN & COMPANY INC., 2 Park Ave., New York NY 10016. Executive Art Director: Richard Traeger. Uses artists for illustration, technical art and lettering. Clients are industrial and marine chemicals, retail, publishing, business machines, broadcast promotion, environmental systems, health foods, vitamins and pharmaceutical accounts.

LANE & LESLIE ADVERTISING AGENCY, INC., 1 N. Main, Box 978, Hutchinson KS 67501. Creative Director: W.E. Leslie. Clients are banks, savings and loans, and farm product manufacturers. Uses artists for retouching and illustration. Media used: newspapers, magazines, radio, TV, billboards and direct mail. Local artists only. Call for interview.

LANG ADVERTISING ASSOCIATES, INC., 108 S. East Ave., Vineland NJ 08360. President: Fred Lang. Clients include agricultural and industrial equipment manufacturers, educational institutions and industrial parks. Uses local artists for layout, illustration and retouching. "We're moving more strongly in the direction of illustration, particularly 4-color, using less photography." Media used: trade magazines, direct mail and billboards. Call for interview.

LASKY ADVERTISING, 48 Farrand St., Bloomfield NJ 07003. (201)748-0090. Contact: Karen Pfluger or Walter Gladowski. Estab: 1926. Annual billing: $5 million. Clients are financial, industrial and retail firms. Buys 20-30 illustrations annually for ads, annual reports, billboards, catalogs, letterheads, brochures and trademarks; especially needs illustrations, mechanicals and retouching. Also uses artists for layout, lettering and type spec. Payment determined by complexity of assignment, number of illustrations and/or time spent. Pays $15-125, retouching job; $35-50, spot illustration; $9-15 per hour, comps/layout; $7-10 per hour, paste-up. Full payment for unused assigned illustrations. Call or write for interview. Reports in 2 weeks. SASE. Prefers to work with "artists with at least 3-5 years experience in paste-up; must be fast, clean and accurate. Dedication to the art field and themselves is a must."

LAYMAN ASSOCIATES, INC., 708 Statler Bldg., Boston MA 02116. (617)542-8968. President: L.A. Layman. Annual billing: $300,000. Clients are industrial, commercial and service accounts; especially capital equipment manufacturers. Uses artists for technical illustration, type spec, layouts, retouching, paste-up and lettering. Media used: newspapers, trade magazines, direct mail, POP displays, collateral projects and exhibits. Pays $25 to $50, layout; $7.50-10 per hour, paste-up. Local artists should call for interview; others should mail work. Prefers local talent.

LENHART ADVERTISING, USA, 22 Chambers St., Princeton NJ 08540. (609)921-8888. Clients include restaurants, country clubs and large manufacturers. Uses artists for illustration, technical art and retouching. Media include newspapers, radio, magazines, billboards and direct mail. Send samples (no originals).

MERVIN N. LEVEY CO., The Hillcrest, 16th and Madison Sts., Toledo OH 43624. (419)243-4261 or 536-8186. President: M.N. Levey. Clients include manufacturers and distributors, land developers, and real estate, insurance, machinery, foods, baked goods, floor coverings, food processing and packing, automotive and pet foods firms, employment services, and educational facilities. Uses artists for original art, layout and paste-up. Media include newspapers, consumer and trade magazines, TV, direct mail and point of sale.

J.H. LEWIS ADVERTISING AGENCY, INC., Box 2024, Mobile AL 36601. (205)438-2507. Contact: John Lewis. Estab: 1951. Annual billing: $2,500,000. Clients are retail manufacturers, agricultural equipment companies and direct mail firms. Buys 15 illustrations annually for ads, annual reports, billboards, catalogs, letterheads, packaging, POP displays, posters, TV and trademarks; especially needs finished mechanicals. Payment determined by time spent. Pays $15-35, layout; $10-20, mechanicals. Original payment as promised for unused assigned illustrations. Prefers Southern artists, "who do neat, clean work and can adjust to the situation." Query. Reports in 5 days. SASE.

LINEAL ASSOCIATES, INC., 175 Great Neck Rd., Great Neck NY 11021. (516)482-1880. Art/Creative Director: Leonard Markman. Clients are educational, industrial and trade accounts. Uses artists for layout, illustration, technical art, paste-up, lettering and retouching. Media used: trade magazines and direct mail. Local artists only. Call for interview.

LITHOGRAPHICS, 600 N. Cotner (Box 5266 Station C), Lincoln NE 68505. (402)467-3492. Contact: J.C. Lambert or Phil Perry. Specializes in direct mail promotion. Uses artists for advertising art, billboard/advertising design, catalog illustrations, direct mail brochures, letterheads, magazine layout, hardware/software newspaper advertising layouts, package design and retail merchandise promotional art. Pays $4-30 an hour for direct mail brochure design. Mail samples. Artists wishing to show portfolio should query with resume. Roughs, finished and printed pieces should have notes on production detail. Reports in 3 weeks. SASE.

LIVING ARTS, 425 E. 79th St., New York NY 10021. Manager: Peter Klein. Estab: 1973. Clients are musicians and dance groups. Buys 10-15 illustrations annually for catalog layouts, posters and publicity brochures. Payment determined by time spent, degree of difficulty and/or reputation of artist. Pays $200 minimum, brochure design; $120 minimum, poster design. Query. Reports in 2 weeks. SASE.

LOWE & HALL ADVERTISING, INC., 501 E. North St., Box 1824, Greenville SC 29602. Art Director: Tom Hall. Uses artists for billboard art, direct mail, letterhead design, magazine layouts and retouching services. Send samples and resume.

WALTER P. LUEDKE & ASSOCIATES, 814 N. Main St., Rockford IL 61103. Clients include recreation vehicle components, restaurant equipment, tension control devices, hydraulic, cylinders and measuring and weighing accounts. Uses artists for layout, illustration, technical art, paste-up and retouching. Media used: newspapers, TV, radio, magazines, billboards, direct mail and POP display.

McANDREW ADVERTISING, 1541 Williamsbridge Rd., Bronx NY 10461. (212)792-1792. Art/Creative Director: Robert McAndrew. Client include technical and industrial firms. Uses artists for layout, illustration, technical art, paste-up and retouching. Media used: magazines and direct mail. Local artists only. Call for interview.

McCAFFREY AND McCALL, INC., 575 Lexington Ave., New York NY 10022. Vice President, Art: John Byrnes.

McCANN-ERICKSON WORLDWIDE, 485 Lexington Ave., New York NY 10017. Chairman/Chief Executive Officer: Eugene H. Kummel.

MACE ADVERTISING INC., 632 W. Jefferson, Morton IL 61550. (309)265-5371. Art Director: Charles Dill. Annual billing: $14,000,000. Uses artists for illustration, paste-up, retouching and lettering. Clients are banks, a brewery, industrial manufacturers, medical and dental accounts. Media used: newspapers, TV, transit, radio, billboards, collateral, trade magazines, direct mail and POP display. Pays $15 an hour for paste-up. Prefers local artists. Mail samples.

McFRANK & WILLIAMS ADVERTISING AGENCY, INC., 101 Park Ave., New York NY 10017. President: Michael Bruce. Uses artists for layout, illustration, type spec, and lettering for client help wanted-recruitment newspaper advertising. Artists must have all of the skills mentioned. Prefers local artists. Call for appointment.

MacLAREN ADVERTISING LIMITED, 415 Yonge St., Toronto, Ontario Canada M5B 2E6. Vice President/Manager, Creative Department: David Harrison.

MacMAHON ADVERTISING, INC., 600 S. Orlando Ave., Box 389, Maitland FL 32751. (305)644-4222. Art/Creative Director: William E. Ryerson. Clients are realtors (land, condominiums, single family homes, apartments), savings and loans, small aircraft corporations, photo labs, industrial complexes, industrial firms, restaurant chains, funeral homes, plant nurseries, motels, museums, a symphony and service clubs. Uses artists for layout, illustration, technical art, type spec, paste-up and retouching. Media used: newspapers, magazines, radio, TV, billboards and direct mail. Local artists only. Call for interview.

MAIL MARKETING SERVICES, 2442 Mary St., East St. Louis IL 62206. General Manager: Troy Atwood. Clients are manufacturing, industrial, business, syndicated direct mail, mail order promotion, book publishing and information service firms. Operates its own offset printing plant. Uses artists for direct mail promotion, advertising art and design, art renderings, book illustrations, book jacket design, syndicate cartoons, catalog illustrations and covers, direct mail brochures, graphic design, lettering, magazine covers and layout, newspaper advertising layouts in software and hardware, package design, posters, record album covers, retouching, sales promotion art, technical illustration, trademarks and TV commercials. Mail samples or query with resume. Pays on acceptance. Buys all rights. "Send only tearsheets or b&w copies of your work. No original art. Submit 4x5", 5x7" or 8x10" format. We file these as examples of your techniques and style for future reference." Reports in 4-6 weeks. SASE.

R. MALCOLM AND ASSOCIATES, INC., Box 304, Evansville IN 47702. Director: Robert W. Glascock. Uses artists for layout, illustration, technical art, retouching and commercials. Media used: newspapers, TV, magazines, radio, billboards and direct mail. Mail samples.

MANGAN RAINS GINNAVEN ASSOCIATES, Gaines Place/3rd & Gaines, Little Rock AR 72201. Contact: C. Stephen Mangan. Estab: 1972. Annual billing: $1 million. Variety of clients. Buys 26 illustrations annually for annual reports, billboards and print ads; especially needs print illustrations. Payment determined by ability. Original payment as agreed for unused assigned work. Write for interview. Reports in 2 weeks. SASE.

MARTIN D. MANN CO., INC., 540 Frontage Rd., Northfield IL 60093. Art Director: Delores Goodman. Clients are dental, medical, educational, office products and agri-marketing accounts. Uses artists for advertising design, art renderings, keyline, paste-up, slides, direct mail and collateral material. Call or write for appointment. No mailed samples. Minimum payment: $100 for collateral layouts. Buys artwork outright.

MAPLE CITY RUBBER CO., 55 Newton St., Norwalk OH 44857. Contact: M.B. Switzer. Toy balloon manufacturer interested in designs for advertising balloons. Send tearsheets, photostats or transparencies. Samples should be approximately 11x6". Previously published work OK. Pays on publication. Reports in 30 days.

MARKETAIDE, Box 1645, Salina KS 67401. (913)825-7161. Creative Director: Ray Beatty. Clients are midwestern agricultural/industrial advertisers and financial institutions. Uses artists for sales literature, publicity photographs, in-house publications, catalog covers/illustrations, exhibit designs and trade publication advertising. Pays $25-50 for b&w line art illustrations. Query with samples of work.

MARKETING SUPPORT, INC., 233 N. Michigan Ave., Chicago IL 60601. Art/Creative Director: Robert Becker. Clients handle office furniture, storage equipment, garbage disposals, humidifiers, valves, pumps, plumbing compounds, furniture hardware, pipe insulation, furnace filters and hobby goods. Uses artists for layout, illustration, type spec, paste-up and retouching. Media include trade magazines and direct mail. Local artists only. Call for appointment.

MARSTELLER INC., 866 3rd Ave., New York NY 10022. Vice President/Head Art Director: Joe Goldberg. Executive Art Director: Sonny Farese.

THE MATLIN COMPANY, INC., 170 S. Main St., Yardley PA 19067. Art/Creative Director: William A. Theodor. Clients are engineering and equipment, chemical, heavy industrial equipment, electrical, medical, surgical, rubber and ceramic accounts. Uses artists for illustration, technical art, paste-up and retouching. Media used: trade magazines and direct mail.

MDR, INC. ADVERTISING, 1770 St. James Place, #220, Houston TX 77056. (613)626-0922. Art Director: Don Willis. Estab: 1967. Annual billing: $960,000. Media used: newspapers, TV, radio, magazines, billboards, direct mail and POP display. Clients are oil, real estate and savings and loan accounts. Uses artists for layout, illustration, type spec, paste-up and retouching. Pays $30, layout; $20 per hour, paste-up.
Special Needs: Production department uses artists for paste-up and retouching.

MEDIAPRINT, 12 W. 18th St., New York NY 10011. President: S. Graham Silverstein. Clients are publishers and insurance firms. Uses artists for layout, illustration, type spec, paste-up and retouching. Prefers local artists. Media used: newspapers, magazines and direct mail. Call for appointment.

MELANSON ASSOCIATES, 77 Summer St., Boston MA 02110. (617)482-1967. Creative Director: Donya Melanson. Estab: 1968. Advertising agency and graphic design firm. Services include complete graphics and advertising. Clients are corporations, banks, publishers, associations and government. Uses artists for cartoons, charts, graphs, illustrations, lettering, logo design, paste-up, retouching and technical art. Previously published and simultaneous submissions OK. Assigns 15-20 freelance jobs annually. Pays $7-20 per hour, illustration/lettering/logo design; $3.50-12 per hour, paste-up. Payment determined by project. Write for interview. Submit photostats for files. No original art; slides are acceptable. Reports in 4 weeks. SASE.

MELTON ADVERTISING INC., 145 W. 45th St., New York NY 10036. (212)575-8877. President, Art/Creative Director: Melvin S. Glickman. Clients are industries producing printed plastic products, lighting, signs, displays, prints, paints, wallpaper, coin wrappers, advertising specialties, sales aids, books, films, apparel, lamps, furs, carpeting, giftwares, office products and candy. Uses artists for layout, illustration, technical art, type spec, paste-up and retouching. Media include newspapers, magazines, radio and direct mail. Call for interview.

THE MERCHANDISING FACTORY, 222 Front St., San Francisco CA 94111. (415)956-4990. Estab: 1972. Annual billing: $1,500,000. Clients are restaurants, food service firms and grocery store product companies. Buys 4-6 illustrations annually for catalogs, letterheads, packaging, POP displays, posters and trade magazine ads. Also uses artists for layout, lettering, paste-up, retouching and type spec. Payment determined by reputation of artist, complexity, time spent and/or where work appears. Pays $15-40 for art direction/cartoonist/illustrator. Original payment as promised for unused assigned illustrations. Local artists only. Query with samples or call for interview. Reports in 1-2 weeks. SASE. "Please, if you're just beginning in this field, don't make us your first stop."

THE MERRILL ANDERSON CO., INC., 100 Park Ave., New York NY 10017. Art Director: Louise Cuddihy. Specializes in financial advertising for banks. Uses artists for illustration, paste-up and retouching. Media used: newspaper, radio, trade magazine and direct mail advertising. Prefers local artists. Call for appointment. Pays $6 for mechanical paste-up.

MILICI/VALENTI ADVERTISING INC., 700 Bishop St., 12th Floor, Amfac Bldg., Honolulu HI 96813. (808)936-0881. Senior Vice President, Creative Director/Art: Jerry P. Huff. Clients are financial institutions, destination advertisers, packaged goods firms, realtors, development firms, corporations, steamship lines, insurance agencies, Blue Cross, hotels and resorts. Uses artists for illustration, retouching and lettering. Media used: newspapers, magazines, radio, TV and direct mail. Mail samples. SASE.

N.H. MILLER & CO., INC., 1127 Park Square Bldg., Boston MA 02116. Clients are eyeglass frame, leather, Early American furniture, plastic molding and housewares firms. Uses local artists for layout, illustration and paste-up. Media used: newspapers, trade magazines and direct mail. Call for interview.

HOWARD E. MITCHELL, JR., ADVERTISING, 301 S. Blanchard St., Findlay OH 45840. (419)423-0252. Creative Director: Howard E. Mitchell, Jr. Annual billing: $750,000. Clients are automotive, agricultural, industrial, financial, broadcast, publishing and consumer firms. Uses artists for illustration, technical art, paste-up and retouching. Media used: newspapers, magazines, TV, radio, billboards, direct mail and POP displays. Pays $15 per hour, layouts; $12 per hour, paste-up. Query with samples.

MOLNER & CO. ADVERTISING, 13815 W. Eight Mile Rd., Detroit MI 48235. (313)342-9944. President: Monroe "Bob" Molner. Estab: 1960. Annual billing: $600,000. Clients are clothing and furniture retailers, car dealers, financial firms and industrial companies. Buys 100-150 illustrations annually for print ads; especially needs TV storyboards, layouts, and fashion and furniture illustrations. Payment determined by complexity, number of illustrations and/or time spent. Pays $10-50, fashion or furniture illustration; $5-10 per hour, layout. Original payment as agreed for unused assigned illustrations. Local artists only. Query. Reports in 1 week. SASE.
Crafts: Occasionally uses craftsmen to create puppets for slide films to use on TV. Pays $100-200.

MORRIS COMMUNICATIONS CORP., 234 Valentine Lane, Yonkers NY 10705. Art/Creative Director: Rudy Michael. Estab: 1974. Annual billing: $500,000. Clients include recreation equipment, pharmaceuticals, film distribution and industrial firms. Uses local artists for layout, illustration, type spec, paste-up and retouching. Media include magazines, newspapers, radio, TV, transit, collateral, direct mail and POP displays. Call for interview.

RUTH MORRISON ASSOCIATES, 509 Madison Ave., New York NY 10022. Estab: 1972. Clients are food, home furnishing, restaurant and retail accounts. Buys illustrations for ads, catalogs, letterheads, packaging, POP displays and posters. Also uses artists for layout, lettering and paste-up. Payment determined by complexity of assignment. Original payment as promised for unused assigned illustrations. Call for interview. Reports in 3 weeks. SASE.

MARTIN S. MOSKOF & ASSOCIATES, INC., 159 W. 53rd St., New York NY 10019. (212)765-4810. Art Director: Martin Moskof. Estab: 1965. Annual billing: $250,000. Clients are museums, foundations, arts and crafts organizations, publishers, banks, financial firms and film companies. Buys 30-50 illustrations annually for annual reports, catalogs, packaging, posters and trade magazine ads; especially needs book cover illustrations. Also uses artists for layout, showroom design, interior design, lettering, paste-up and retouching. Payment determined by reputation of artist, complexity, number of illustrations and/or client's budget. Pays $100 minimum. Pays rejection fee (agreed upon) or full payment for unused assigned illustrations. Prefers local artists. Query or call for interview. Reports in 1 week maximum. SASE.

PAUL MUCHNICK CO., 1560 Saltair Ave., Los Angeles CA 90025. (213)826-0457. Art/Creative Director: Paul Muchnick. Clients are general consumer and mail order firms handling gifts, housewares, gadgets, household products, baby photos, fire alarms, restaurant supplies, drafting equipment and services. Uses artists for layouts, paste-up and retouching. Media used: newspapers, magazines and direct mail. Local artists only. Call for interview.

MURRAY & CHANEY ADVERTISING, (formerly Thomas Murray & Austin Chaney Advertising), 5 E. Main St., Hudson OH 44236. Contact: Mr. E.A. Schroeder. Estab: 1971. Clients are rubber, truck, meat, flower, automobile and airplane firms. Buys 12-24 illustrations annually for catalogs, posters, TV and print ads; especially needs technical drawings, TV animation, design art and color retouching. Also uses artists for layout, paste-up and retouching. Payment determined by reputation of artist, number of illustrations and/or where work will appear. Original payment as promised for unused assigned illustrations "if art satisfied the assignment and the client." Write or call for interview; bring stats and printed pieces for agency files. Reports in 1 week. SASE.

THEODORE READE NATHAN ADVERTISING, INC., 350 W. 57th St., New York NY 10019. (212)246-7954. Contact: Mary Ann Rispoli. Clients are hotels and resorts, schools, charity and religious groups, hospitals and employment and real estate agencies. Mail samples.
To Break In: "We look for the right synthesis of commercial and aesthetic values; so concentrate on creating this for 1 or 2 prospective account types or media."

NATIONAL ADVERTISING AND MARKETING ENTERPRISES, (N.A.M.E.), 1335 S. Flower St., Los Angeles CA 90015. Contact: J.A. Gatlin. Uses artists for graphic design, letterheads and direct mail brochures. Submit samples. May also wish to buy reproduction rights to already published designs and illustrations.
To Break In: "Make at least 2 sales calls daily to the type of user to whom you want to sell. Even if you can't sell it is good experience."

NEEDHAM, HARPER & STEERS ADVERTISING, INC., 909 3rd Ave., New York NY 10022. Executive Creative Director: Lois Korey. Associate Creative Director: Allen Kay.

RICHARD NEWMAN ASSOCIATES, INC., 702 Bloomington Rd., Champaign IL 61820. Art Director: Richard L. Burd. Clients are banks, tourism departments, and real estate, historic trails, restaurant and attraction accounts. Uses artists for illustration, retouching, commercials, lettering and cartooning. Media used: newspapers, magazines, radio, TV, billboards and direct mail. Mail samples.
To Break In: "Professionalism is lacking in about 70% of the portfolios we see. Specifically, lack of drawing ability, neatness and graphic reproduction knowledge are most common failures. Artists should get a good solid foundation of skills, and build from there. Get some good in-house experience before attempting to freelance."

NEWMARK'S ADVERTISING AGENCY, INC., 183 Madison Ave., New York NY 10016. Art/Creative Director: Al Wasserman. Annual billing: $2 million. Clients are manufacturing, industrial, banking and construction firms. Uses artists for illustration, cartoons, technical art, paste-up and retouching. Media used: newspapers, magazines, radio, TV, transit, billboards, direct mail, POP displays and collateral projects. Pays $8-10 per hour for paste-up. Mail samples or call for interview.

NORMAN, CRAIG & KUMMEL INC., 919 3rd Ave., New York NY 10022. Contact: Creative Director.

NORTHEAST ADVERTISING INC., 6 Benson Rd., Oxford CT 06483. Advertising/Sales Promotion Manager: Ron Phillips. Specializes in safety advertising and products including highway emergency and first aid kits. Uses artists for sales literature, catalog covers and illustrations, and displays. Query with samples.

NORTH-SOUTH ARTS, Box 10273, Winston-Salem NC 27108. Contact: Mary Nordstrom. Provides a booking and advertising service for artists, principally in the college and prep school market. Uses artists for newspaper and trade magazine ads, brochures, programs and posters. Mail resume. SASE.

THE NOTEWORTHY COMPANY, 100 Church St., Amsterdam NY 12010. (518)842-2660. Contact: Tom Constantino. Estab: 1954. Annual billing: $2 million. Clients are advertising specialty jobbers who in turn have clients in real estate, banks, chain stores, state parks, community service groups and other firms interested in advertising. Buys 20 illustrations annually for catalogs, packaging and litterbag designs. Pays $25 minimum for litterbag design. Query with samples. Reports in 2 weeks. No work returned.

OGILVY & MATHER INC., 2 E. 48th, New York NY 10017. Executive Art Director: Stan Smith. Clients are food, cosmetics, automobiles, household products, financial firms, insurance, credit cards and heavy industrial accounts. "We would be happy to have an advance inquiry by mail regarding a possible look at portfolios of good professionals in any discipline who honestly feel they have something fresh or unique to show us. While we have many people listed who can do excellent work in illustration, reportage, portraits, still life, etc., no artist, obviously, can cover all bases. Please write or call for an interview — but only if you have something outstanding."

OUTDOORS INC., Outdoors Bldg., Columbia MO 65201. Art/Creative Director: Lloyd E. Saulsbury. Estab: 1958. Clients are in the recreational and publications fields. Uses artists for layout, illustration and retouching. Media used: magazine, collateral, direct mail and POP advertising. Mail samples.

PAGE/SCHWESSINGER ADVERTISING, 2300 Mayfair Rd., Milwaukee WI 53226. Creative Director: Jess E. Maxwell. Clients are consumer financial, insurance, fashion, marine, food, home products, ski, snowmobile, automotive, industrial chemicals, electrical components, hard goods, motors, drives and automotive aftermarket accounts. Uses artists for illustrations, technical art, retouching, and commercials. Particularly interested in young artists. Media used: newspapers, magazines, radio, TV, outdoor and direct mail. Mail samples.

LARRY PAINTER & ASSOCIATES, LTD., Box 5007, Jackson MS 39216. Art/Creative Director: Daryl Ainsworth. Clients are banks, and agricultural chemical, communications and utilities firms. Uses artists for illustration, technical art, retouching, and interior and exterior architectural renderings. Media used: newspapers, magazines, radio, TV, billboards and direct mail. Mail samples.

CHARLES PALM & COMPANY, INC., 800 Cottage Grove Rd., Bloomfield CT 06002. (203)242-6258. Art Directors: John P. Vann and Raymond Dubel. Manufacturing and industrial clients. Uses artists for layout, illustration, technical art, paste-up, retouching, lettering and TV storyboards. Media used: newspapers, magazines, radio, TV, billboards, direct mail and collateral material. Submit samples or call for interview.

PARKER, WILLOX, FAIRCHILD & CAMPBELL ADVERTISING INC., 808 N. Michigan, Saginaw MI 48602. (517)755-8171. Art Director: Bob Lanka. Estab: 1969. Annual billing: $5 million. Consumer and industrial clients. Buys 25 full-color illustrations annually for ads, annual reports, billboards, catalogs, letterheads, packaging, POP displays, posters, TV and trademarks. Also uses artists for color separations, layout, lettering, paste-up, retouching and type spec. Payment determined by complexity of assignment, number of illustrations and/or time spent. Artist is asked to quote his price. Pays for work completed even if unused ("assignments are usually approved or disapproved at tissue stage"). Mail printed samples. Reports in 2 weeks. SASE.

PASTARNACK ASSOCIATES, INC., 235 E. 50th, New York NY 10022. (212)421-0140. President, Art/Creative Director: Irving J. Pastarnack. Industrial, travel, resort and school clients. Uses artists for layout, illustration, technical art, paste-up and retouching. Media used: newspapers, magazines and direct mail. Prefers local artists. Call for appointment.

BERNARD K. PAWLUS ASSOCIATES, 1306 Tri-State Bldg., Cincinnati OH 45202. (513)621-4030. Contact: Bernard Pawlus. Estab: 1968. Annual billing: $600,000. Customers are drug, housewares and furniture producers. Buys 20 illustrations annually for annual reports, catalogs, consumer magazine ads, packaging and TV. Also uses artists for magazine ad layout. Payment determined by complexity and/or time spent. Minimum payment: $7.50 per hour, rough layouts; $10 per hour or on assignment, concepts. Negotiates payment for unused assigned illustrations. Local artists who can create headlines or copy ideas only. Write for interview. Reports in 1 week.

PAUL PEASE ADVERTISING, INC., 151 University Ave., Palo Alto CA 94301. (415)327-4112. Art Director: Robert Fernandez. Clients are instrumentation, high technology and real estate firms. Uses local artists for design, comps, illustration, paste-up and retouching. Media used: newspapers, magazines and direct mail. Call for interview.

PENNY/OHLMANN/NEIMAN, INC., 1605 N. Main St., Dayton OH 45408. (513)278-0681. Art Buyer: Ralph Neiman. Uses artists for illustration, design, art renderings of building interiors, audiovisuals, billboard art, calligraphy, cartoons, catalog illustrations and covers, convention exhibits, magazine editorial decorative spots, direct mail brochures, letterheads, layout, posters and trademarks. Wants artists who are "creative, sensitive and innovative people with sound marketing knowledge." Call for interview. Accepts nothing by mail.

PERSUASIVE COMMUNICATIONS, 6677 N. Lincoln Ave., Lincolnwood IL 60645. Art/Creative Director: Mark Weinstein. Estab: 1974. Annual billing: $500,000. Clients are consumer products firms and specialized industrial markets. Local artists should make an appointment to discuss work. Uses artists for layout, paste-up, illustration, type spec and retouching. Member of DMMA and CADM. Media used: newspapers, magazines, direct mail and collateral material. Pays $20 per hour for paste-up.

PHILIP OFFICE ASSOCIATES, INC., 720 Harries Bldg., Dayton OH 45402. (513)461-1300. Vice President, Creative: Bob Killian. Clients are major and regional firms in telecommunications, electronic dictation equipment and the merchandise/travel industries. Uses artists for illustrations and layout. Media used: newspapers, magazines, direct mail, TV and collateral projects. Professionals only. Mail samples.

BURTON PINCUS, CONSULTANT, Box 194, Linwood NJ 08221. Art Buyer: Burton Pincus. Specializes in direct mail. Uses artists for advertising art, billboard art, advertising design and direct mail brochures.

POST KEYES GARDNER INC., 875 N. Michigan Ave., Chicago IL 60611. Manager of Creative Services: Charles C. Hatcher.

PRICE/McNABB, 400 Northwestern Bank Bldg., Asheville NC 28801. Contact: D. Belcher. Annual billing: $3 million. Clients are industrial manufacturers, resorts and tobacco processors. Uses artists for illustration, retouching, paste-up and sign lettering. Mail samples. Media used: newspapers, TV, radio, magazines, billboards, direct mail, POP displays and collateral projects. Reports in 6 weeks. Pays $25-100, layout; $3-5 per hour, paste-up.

PRO/CREATIVES CORP., 25 W. Burda, Spring Valley NY 10977. (212)679-4806 or (914)356-4623. Creative Director: David Rapp. Clients are radio stations, publications, restaurants, and packaged goods, sports, food, liquor, entertainment, health/beauty aids, retail and fashion firms. Uses artists for layout, illustration, type spec, paste-up and lettering. Media used: newspapers, magazines, TV, radio, POP display, direct mail and packaging. Query with resume and samples.

R/A ADVERTISING, INC., A subsidiary of Reiman Associates, 733 N. Van Buren, Milwaukee WI 53202. Art Director: Donald J. Lohr. Uses artists for illustration, technical art, paste-up, retouching and commercials. Media used: newspapers, magazines, TV, radio, billboards and direct mail. Clients are primarily agricultural: equipment, chemicals, seeds and magazines. Prefers local and regional artists. Call for appointment.

STAN RADLER/ASSOCIATES, INC., Pine Hill, Framingham MA 01701. (617)875-1007. Contact: Stan Radler. Estab: 1962. Annual billing: $500,000. Clients are electronics, computer equipment, food services and industrial equipment and services firms. Specializes in marketing and financial services. Uses local artists for layout, illustration, technical art, type spec, paste-up and retouching. Media used: newspapers, trade magazines, direct mail and collateral material. Call for interview.

GERALD RAFSHOON ADVERTISING, INC., 1422 W. Peachtree NW, Atlanta GA 30309. (404)872-3581. Art Director: Stephan M. Parks. Vice President, Creative Services: Susan Frasier. Annual billing: $6,500,000. Clients are tourism, jewelry, building materials, industrial machinery and finance firms. Uses artists for layout, illustration, paste-up, retouching and lettering. Media used: newspapers, TV, radio, magazines, billboards, collateral and direct mail. Pays $50-150 minimum, layout; $15 per hour minimum, paste-up. Mail samples.

RAINBOW ADVERTISING, 810 7th Ave., New York NY 10019. (212)582-6900. General Manager: Jude Lyons. Clients are rock concert promoters, rock clubs and record companies. Uses artists for illustration, retouching, lettering and design. Media used: newspapers, magazines, radio, TV, billboards and displays. Mail samples.
To Break In: "The freelance artist trying to get established should understand the needs of the client-company, be aware of the competition, and have a knowledge of the product line. Because our freelancers are so carefully chosen, we have few difficulties working with them. When we do have problems, it is in regard to reliability and the concept of time."

CHARLES J. REILLY CO., 761 E. Green St., Suite 5, Pasadena CA 91101. Contact: C.J. Reilly. Clients are educational and medical institutions and general corporate accounts. Local artists should query with resume and samples.

RESPONSE GROUP, INC., 39 Pine Dr., Park Ridge NJ 07656. (212)752-2320. Contact: Gloria Brager. Uses artists for direct mail promotion, design, catalog illustrations and covers, paste-up, calligraphy, convention exhibits, decorative spots, lettering, posters, technical illustration, theater programs, trademarks, envelopes, booklets and forms. Pays $200, direct mail brochure design; $25, spot illustration. Query with resume; no portfolios without approval. Calls artists as needs arise.

RESPONSE INDUSTRIES INC., 110 E. 59th St., New York NY 10024. President: D. Savage. Estab: 1973. Annual billing: $2 million. Specializes in direct response advertising with client products including clocks, books and records. Uses local artists for layout, technical art, paste-up and retouching. Media used: newspapers, consumer magazines and direct mail. Payment determined by job.

RFM ASSOCIATES, INC., 35 Atkins Ave., Trenton NJ 08610. President: Rodney F. Mortillaro. Estab: 1976. Annual billing: $250,000. Industrial, food, home furnishing, travel, real estate, record manufacturer and fashion clients. Buys 135-150 illustrations annually for billboards, catalogs, magazines, letterheads, newspapers, posters, trademarks and direct mail. Also uses artists for color separations, layout, paste-up and retouching. Pays $5-12 per hour for lettering, illustrations and color separations. No payment for unused assigned illustrations. Local artists only. Mail tearsheets or photocopies. Reports in 1 week. No work returned. "Be familiar with printing and press procedures."

"Show me a professional looking portfolio and have a willingness to take advice and apply it," says Samuel Irving of Samuel Irving Advertising Art & Design. Professionalism, and the art style desired, are the two elements that helped Michael Gary sell this logo to Irving.

RICHARD-LEWIS CORP., 455 Central Park Ave., Scarsdale NY 10583. Contact: Dick Byer. Clients are machinery and equipment, tool, book, business forms, office equipment, chemical, detergent, shortening, specialty papers, film, flavor, ink, printing supplies and press manufacturers. Uses artists for layout, paste-up and retouching. Media used: trade magazines and direct mail. Prefers local artists. Call for interview.

RICHARDSON, MYERS AND DONOFRIO, 10 E. Baltimore St., Baltimore MD 21202. Executive Art Director: John Burk. National consumer, commercial and industrial clients. Uses graphic artists for all advertising media.

RIEDL ASSOCIATES INC., 1200 Rte. 46, Clifton NJ 07013. Art Buyers: Lee Levy and Mike Erdek. Uses artists for ink, line drawings, washes, acrylics and finished art. Query with resume. Do not send samples without first mailing query. Buys all rights. Reports in 30 days maximum.

RONAN, HOWARD, ASSOCIATES, INC., 11 Buena Vista Ave., Spring Valley NY 10977. (914)356-6668. Estab: 1965. Advertising agency and public relations firm. Clients are mostly manufacturers. Uses artists for charts, graphs, illustrations, retouching, paste-up and technical art. Assigns 10-20 freelance jobs annually. Pays $25 per hour. Payment determined by time spent and job. Query. No work returned.

GORDON ROSHOLT & COMPANY, 2801 Wayzata Blvd., Minneapolis MN 55405. Art/Creative Director: Paul D. Shervey. Annual billing: $1 million. Estab: 1956. Clients are industrial, farm and electronics firms. Uses artists for illustration, technical art and lettering. Media used: magazines, direct mail, POP displays and collateral material. Mail samples.

ROSS ROY, INC., 2751 E. Jefferson Ave., Detroit MI 48207. Senior Vice President/Creative Director: Charles V. Hicks.

ROTSINGER TENNEY RICHARD INC., 3450 W. Central, Suite 336, Toledo OH 43606. Director: Jim Richard. Clients are industrial, automotive, political and dental accounts. Uses graphic artists for direct mail brochures, annual reports, billboards, public service TV spots, capability brochures and house organ illustrations. Mail samples. Minimum payment: $22.50 per hour, keylining; $27.50 per hour, illustration.

J.B. RUNDLE, INC., 15 E. 26th St., New York NY 10010. Art/Creative Director: Thomas R. Bowler. Clients are industrial basic metals, chemicals and rubber manufacturers, plastics firms, fabric mills, wood products and electronics firms. Artists/photographers may submit work samples by mail. Uses artists for layout, illustration, technical art, type spec, paste-up, retouching and lettering. Media used: newspapers, trade magazines and direct mail. Mail samples.

CHARLES RUPPMAN ADVERTISING, INC., 1909 E. Cornell St., Peoria IL 61604. Art/Creative Director: Steve Cripe. Uses artists for illustration. Media used: newspapers, magazines, radio, TV, billboards and direct mail. Clients are government, financial, marine and heavy equipment accounts. Mail samples.

SAWYER ADVERTISING, INC., Box O, Gainesville GA 30501. (404)532-6285. Art/Assistant Creative Director: Jack Waters. Uses artists for layout, illustration and camera ready mechanicals. Media used: magazines, direct mail, newspaper, TV and collateral material. Clients are agricultural, savings and loan and industrial accounts. Call for appointment.

SCHNEIDER, ALLEN, WALSH, INC., 180 Madison Ave., New York NY 10016. President/Creative Director: M. Barry Schneider. Uses artists for illustration, paste-up and retouching. Media used: newspapers, magazines, TV and direct mail. Clients are fashion (sportswear, men's, boys' and women's apparel and accessories, yarns); industrial (paint, lacquer, paper, metals, surgical products); resort; recreation; and real estate accounts. Prefers local artists. Call for appointment.

SCHWANBERG-BOLSTA ASSOCIATES, Box 1513, St. Cloud MN 56301. Contact: Glenn Schwanberg. Annual billing: $300,000. Clients are auto dealers, manufacturers, desk accessory, sign making kits and office supply aid accounts. Uses artists for direct mail, advertising, graphic illustrations, ad layout and lettering. Media used: newspapers, TV, radio, trade magazines and billboards. Reports in 3 weeks. Pays for final work on acceptance. "Most work is now being printed in 4-color process." Pays $500 minimum, direct mail brochure; $3 per hour, paste-up.

SCOTT ASSOCIATES, 30 Main St., Champaign IL 61820. Art/Creative Director: Bruce Casica. Clients are a water utility company, grain company, building products manufacturer, auto glass distributor and sports equipment manufacturer. Uses artists for layout, illustration, technical art, type spec, lettering, paste-up and retouching. Media used: newspapers, TV, radio, magazines, billboards and direct mail. Mail samples.

SHAILER DAVIDOFF ROGERS INC., Heritage Square, Fairfield CT 06430. Executive Vice President: Harold L. Rogers. Clients are financial, food products, condominium, insurance and retail firms. Uses local artists for layout, illustration, technical art, type spec, paste-up and retouching. Media used: newspapers, magazines, radio, TV, billboards and direct mail. Call for interview.

SHECTER & LEVIN ADVERTISING/PUBLIC RELATIONS, 1800 N. Charles St., Baltimore MD 21201. Art/Creative Director: Jack L. Levin. Clients are manufacturers, contractors, builders, institutions, organizations and retail store chains. Uses local artists for layout, paste-up and retail sale advertisements. Media used: newspapers, magazines, radio, TV, billboards and direct mail. Call for interview.

SHOREY & WALTER INC., (formerly Group Four, Inc.), 1617 E. North St., Greenville SC 29607. Creative Director: Philip Simmons. Clients are resort/land development, textile/industrial, insurance, architectural/engineering, hosiery, financial, food products and packaging firms. Uses artists for illustration, technical art and retouching. Media used: newspapers, magazines, radio, TV, billboards, direct mail, and collateral material. "Collateral" in this particular case refers chiefly to corporate/sales brochures. Mail samples.

PAUL SILVER ADVERTISING, INC., 2530 N. Calvert St., Baltimore MD 21218. (301)467-5200. Art Director: Terence Smith. Estab: 1955. Annual billing: approximately $2 million. Clients are the automotive aftermarket, vacation camps, kitchen designers, fund raising companies, inventors patenting services, psycotherapy clinics, model schools, and bottletop, record, appliance, travel, construction, window, insurance, ethical drug and cosmetic firms. Buys 300 illustrations annually for catalogs, print ads, letterheads, packaging, POP displays, posters, TV ads, and trademarks; especially needs art for collateral material. Also uses artists for color separations, layout, lettering, paste-up, retouching and type spec. Payment determined by complexity, number of illustrations, time spent, where work appears, and/or how frequently it appears. Pays $25-600 on assignment. Original payment as agreed for unused assigned illustrations. Query, or write or call for interview. Reports in 1 week. SASE.
Portfolio: "Submit enough graphics to indicate ability to work on the account in question. 'Blue sky' graphics may be interesting, but artist's ability to perform the job required is prime. Portfolios should show design, lettering, paste-up and the areas the freelancer feels he/she can adequately cover."

SMITH & DOUGLAS ADVERTISING, INC., 6033 Berkshire Lane, Dallas TX 75225. Art/Creative Director: Howard N. Smith. Clients are food, mining equipment, chemical, mail order, recruitment, store fixture, investigations and electronic supply firms. Uses local artists for layout, illustration, technical art, type spec, paste-up and retouching. Media used: newspapers, trade magazines, radio, TV, billboards and direct mail. Call for interview.

SMITH, DORIAN & BURMAN, INC., 589 New Park Ave., Hartford CT 06110. General Manager: Robert A. Canyock. Industrial clients. Annual billing: $2 million. Uses local artists for layout, illustration and retouching. Media used: trade magazines, collateral, direct mail and POP display. Call for appointment. Pays $50 minimum for layout.

MARC SMITH COMPANY, 570 Ritchie Hwy., Severna Park MD 21146. (301)647-2606. Art/Creative Director: Marc Smith. Clients are consumer and industrial products, sales services and public relations firms. Uses local artists for layout, illustration, lettering, technical art, type spec, paste-up and retouching. Media used: newspapers, magazines, radio, TV, billboards and direct mail. Mail samples or call for appointment.

SODERBERG & BELL ADVERTISING AGENCY, 221 1st Ave. W., Seattle WA 98119. Art/Creative Director: Michael G. Bell. Clients are banks, air freight, boats, skiing, industrial and recreational property. Uses artists for layout, illustration, type spec, paste-up, retouching and lettering. Media used: newspapers, magazines, radio, TV, billboards and direct mail. Mail samples.

ROBERT SOLOMON & ASSOCIATES ADVERTISING, INC., 3500 Book Bldg., Detroit MI 48226. Executive Art Director: Dean Adams. Clients are food chains, theaters, remodeling, furniture and travel firms. Uses local artists for layout, illustration, paste-up, retouching and lettering. Media used: newspapers, consumer magazines, radio, TV, billboards, direct mail, public relations and business cards. Mail samples.

SOUTHWARD & ASSOCIATES, INC., 20 N. Wacker Dr., Chicago IL 60606. Art/Creative Director: Don Kassel. Clients are resort, hotel, and financial firms. Uses artists for layout and illustration. Media used: newspapers, trade magazines, billboards and direct mail. Mail samples or call for interview.

J. J. SPECTOR & ASSOCIATES, 2900 NE 30th St., Ft. Lauderdale FL 33306. (305)563-4093. Contact: J.J. Spector. Estab: 1970. Annual billing: $1-2½ million. Clients are publishers, manufacturers, banks and commercial/industrial firms. Buys 10-15 illustrations annually for ads, annual reports, catalogs, letterheads, packaging and direct mail/mail order components; especially needs direct mail package design (includes outside carrier envelope, letterhead, brochures, and order card/reply elements). Also uses artists for color separations, layout, lettering, paste-up, retouching and type spec. Payment determined by reputation of artist, complexity of assignment, number of illustrations and/or time spent on work. Pays $200-350, package design; $50-175, paste-up/mechanicals; $20-50 per page, catalog layout. Original payment as promised for unused assigned illustrations. Query. Reports in 1 week. SASE.
To Break In: Collect direct mail packages received at home and redesign them more forcefully into alternative dummies for submission as samples.

SPITZ ADVERTISING AGENCY, 530 Oak St., Syracuse NY 13203. Contact: William Spitz or Nick Bibko. Clients are educational, institutional, retail, hotel, motel, bank and industrial accounts. Uses artists for illustrations, design, animated cartoons, technical art, billboard art, catalog illustrations and covers, direct mail material, graphic design, trademarks, layout, letterheads and retouching. Media used: newspapers, trade magazines, radio, TV and billboards. Mail samples.

SPOONER & COMPANY, 101 West St., Hillsdale NJ 07642. President: William B. Spooner III. Clients are mills, mixers, vacuum pumps, metals and ores, plastic blow molding machines and conveyor belting accounts. Uses artists for layout, illustration, technical art, type spec, paste-up, retouching and lettering. Media used: newspapers, trade magazines, direct mail, technical literature and trade shows. Mail samples.

LEODA STEINHEIMER ADVERTISING, 1106 Shell Bldg., 1221 Locust St., St. Louis MO 63103. Art/Creative Director: Leoda Steinheimer. Clients are retail fashion chain, home sewing products, misses and junior sleep/loungewear and orthodontic appliance firms. Uses local artists for layout, fashion illustration, paste-up and lettering. Media used: newspapers, magazines, direct mail, catalogs, packaging and displays. Artist must have ability to lay out catalogs covering fashion apparel for women. Call for interview.

THOMAS R. SUNDHEIM INCORPORATED, The Benson East, Jenkintown PA 19046. Art Director: Jim Stevenson. Clients are primarily industrial and technical accounts. Uses artists for layout, illustration, technical art, type spec, paste-up and retouching. Prefers local artists. Media used: trade magazines, direct mail and collateral literature. Call for interview.

SYNERGISTIC ASSOCIATES INTERNATIONAL, INC., 900 Dudley Ave., Cherry Hill NJ 08002. (609)665-8833. Art Buyer: Larry Solomon. Uses artists for advertising art and design, and direct mail brochures. Artist must have extensive experience with consumer mail order. Local artists only. Call for interview.

TATHAM-LAIRD & KUDNER, INC., 625 N. Michigan Ave., Chicago IL. 60611. Vice President/Executive Art Director: Jim Arthur.

TRAVIS-WALZ-LANE, INC., 5201 Johnson Dr., Suite 350, Mission KS 66205. Creative Director: Phelps D. Murdock, Jr. Estab: 1971. Electronics, food, finance, retailing, home maintenance and media clients. Uses artists for retouching and illustration. Media used: newspapers, magazines, TV, radio, transit, billboards, collateral material, direct mail, and POP display. Mail samples.

TRI-STATE ADVERTISING, 307 S. Buffalo, Warsaw IN 46580. Creative Director: Tweed Robinson. Clients are machine manufacturers, equipment, plastics, tableware and costume jewelry firms. Uses artists for layout, technical art, paste-up and retouching. Seeks professionals who can work with practical application, skill and speed. Media used: trade magazines and direct mail. Prefers local artists. Call for appointment.
To Break In: "Learn something about the graphic arts; ask a typical buyer for a hypothetical assignment and do it for a portfolio, instead of carrying school work."

TROXELL & ASSOCIATES, INC., 5757 Bellaire Blvd., Suite 100, Houston TX 77081. President/Art Creative Director: Richard K. Troxell. Hats, housing subdivisions, land development, office and industrial leasing, professional personnel consultants and art gallery accounts. Uses artists for layout, illustration and technical art. Media used: newspapers, radio, TV, magazines, direct mail and billboards. Prefers local artists. Mail samples.

UNDERCOVER GRAPHICS, 2402 Bush St., San Francisco CA 94115. (415)922-7242. Creative Director: L.A. Paul. Estab: 1973. Annual billing: $300,000. Clients are musical groups, producers, record companies and book publishers. Buys 10-12 illustrations annually for billboards, print ads, letterheads, packaging, POP displays, posters, TV ads, trademarks and logos; especially needs TV animation, cover artwork and illustrations. Also uses artists for animation, color separations, layout, lettering, paste-up, retouching and type spec. Payment determined by complexity, where work appears and/or how frequently it will appear. Pays $250-5,000, comprehensive layout and production; $10-25 per hour, creative services; $25-500, illustrations. Original payment as agreed for unused assigned illustrations. Query with samples. Reports in 4 weeks. SASE.
Crafts: Uses craftsmen for ambiance, background furnishings and 3-dimensional illustration. Payment determined by size, type and/or complexity. Pays $50 minimum.
Portfolio: "Show examples of published and nonpublished work representative of your range of abilities. These should include both assigned and self-generated work, conceptual art as well as production types."
To Break In: "To me, experience and efficiency is not as important as talent and style. At the same time, an artist should be highly original and very creative, technically competent, resourceful and conceptual. We prefer avant-garde styles of 'new art'. Get your work seen and used even if you're not paid. Advertise yourself with self-promotion mailings and knock on every door until you get a job."

UNIVERSAL TRAINING SYSTEMS COMPANY, 3201 Old Glenview Rd., Wilmette IL 60091. (312)251-8700. Production Manager: Ellen R. Skolnik. Estab: 1967. Clients are associations, manufacturers, retailers, service firms, publishers, bankers and financial institutions. Creates training programs for business and industry. Buys 250 illustrations annually for slide films, workbooks, training manuals, flipcharts, overhead transparencies and posters. Also uses artists for lettering, layout and paste-up. Payment determined by complexity, number of illustrations and time spent. Local artists only. Query. SASE.

UNIWORLD GROUP, INC., 101 Park Ave., New York NY 10017. Art/Creative Director: Bill Allen. Estab: 1970. Annual billing: $6 million. Cosmetics clients. Uses artists for illustration and lettering. Media used: consumer magazines, radio, TV, newspapers, transit, collateral material and billboards. Prefers local artists. Call for interview.

VICTOR van der LINDE CO., INC., 25 W. 43rd, New York NY 10036. Contact: Art Director. Uses artists for lettering. Media used: newspapers, magazines, radio, TV and direct mail. Prefers local artists. Call for interview.

VIDEODETICS ADVERTISING, 2121 S. Manchester Ave., Anaheim CA 92802. (714)634-2227. Uses artists for animation art and graphic and exhibit design. Pays $16 per hour. Buys all rights. Query with resume.

MICHAEL C. WALES & CO., 211 W. Madison St., Box 4123, South Bend IN 46634. (219)232-4200. Uses artists for advertising art, book jacket design, graphic/package design, magazine and newspaper publications and trademarks. Pays $100 average for direct mail brochure design. Mail samples. Reports in 2 weeks. SASE.

WALKER & ASSOCIATES, INC., 2605 Nonconnah Blvd., Memphis TN 38132. Clients are financial institutions, manufacturers and real estate developers. Uses artists for illustration, technical art and retouching. Prefers local artists. Media used: print, broadcast and outdoor. Call for appointment.

HERBERT S. WARMFLASH & ASSOCIATES, INC., 26 Washington St., East Orange NJ 07017. Art Director: B. Martin Grubman. Specializes in industrial accounts: weighing scales, conveyor systems, towline, switchcart and order picking systems. Uses artists for illustration. Prefers local artists. Media used: trade magazines, direct mail, POP display, transit and collateral. Call for interview.

WARREN, MULLER, DOLOBOWSKY, INC., 747 3rd Ave., New York NY 10017. (212)754-1571. Contact: David Perl. Estab: 1963. Annual billing: $25 million. Clients are drug products firms and variety of manufacturers. Buys 12-36 illustrations annually for ads, billboards, catalogs, packaging, POP displays, posters, television and trademarks; especially needs TV artwork and magazine ads. Also uses artists for layout, lettering, paste-up, retouching, costume/set/jewelry design and wardrobe. Payment determined by "what the budget will bear." Pays $1,000-5,000, 4-color magazine ad campaign or TV animation design; $250-1,000, b&w magazine ad campaign. Pays percentage of originally agreed payment for unused assignments/illustrations. Call for interview or mail photocopy of artwork. No work returned.
Crafts: Pays $25-250 for ad props and unusual, creative TV props.
To Break In: "Understand your client's needs and make that your objective; don't try to impress your client with technique if the concept is wrong."

WARWICK, WELSH & MILLER, INC., 375 Park Ave., New York NY 10022. Contact: Creative Director.

WASHINGTON INFORMATION SERVICES, INC., 4710 Auth Place SE, Suite 765, Washington DC 20023. Contact: George Petersen or Charlene Corbin. Uses artists for direct mail brochures, catalog illustrations and covers, letterheads and magazine layouts. Prefers local artists. Query with resume. Artist must have knowledge of direct mail design and be able to handle type selection with experience and confidence.

GORDON J. WEISBECK, INC., 5555 Main St., Buffalo NY 14221. Art Director: Edith Lausted. Clients are electronics, precious metals, solid waste disposal, special machinery and municipality firms. Uses artists for layout, illustration, technical art, type spec, paste-up, retouching, charts, presentations and displays. Call for interview.

WELBORN ADVERTISING, INC., 379 Morris Ave., Springfield NJ 07081. Art Director: Joe Napurano. Industrial clients. Uses artists for mechanicals, layout, illustration, technical art, lettering and retouching. Call for interview.

PAUL WELLS PRODUCTIONS, Rte. 1, Box 660, Auburndale FL 33823. Contact: P.J. Denneny. Uses artists for direct mail promotion, advertising art and design, audiovisuals, book illustrations and jacket design, calendar art, box and package design, direct mail brochures, film titles, graphic designs, letterheads, lettering, newspaper advertising layouts (hardware and software), sales promotion art and trademarks. Pays $125 minimum. Query or mail samples. Reports in 2 weeks. SASE.

WENDT ADVERTISING AGENCY, Box 1291, Great Falls MT 59403. Executive Art Director: Robert L. Lindborg. Annual billing: $2 million. Clients are financial, agricultural and general consumer accounts. Uses artists for "realistic" illustration. Media used: newspapers, radio, TV, magazines, billboards, direct mail, displays and audiovisual. Mail photocopied samples for files. Send no original art. SASE.

WENGER-MICHAEL, INC., 760 Market St., San Francisco CA 94102. Creative Director: Ben Wong. Clients are savings and loan associations, musical instrument manufacturers, hotels, real estate developers and radio stations. Uses artists for newspaper, magazine, TV, radio, billboards and direct mail art. "We're particularly interested in conceptually strong illustrators, as we make heavy use of full-color illustration in ads and posters." Mail samples or arrange to show portfolio.

THE WENK ORGANIZATION, INC., 377 Park Ave. S., New York NY 10016. Art/Creative Director: Joe Ognibene. Uses artists for illustration, technical art and paste-up. Media used: newspapers, magazines and direct mail. Mail samples.

WESTMARKETING GROUP LTD., 5 Broadway, Hawthorne NY 10532. Creative Director: R.C. Heyda. Clients are aviation, agriculture, financial and general accounts. Media used: newspapers, magazines, direct mail and collateral material. Uses artists for layout, illustration, paste-up and retouching. Prefers artists from Westchester County and surrounding area. Call for interview.

STAN WIENER & CO., INC., 19 W. 44th St., New York NY 10036. Clients are hard goods manufacturers, retailers and direct response firms. Call for appointment to show portfolio.

STUART WILLIAMS ASSOCIATES, 40 Signal Rd., Stamford CT 06902. (203)348-2621. Art Director: William Vollers. Clients are pharmaceutical companies. Uses artists for layout, illustration, technical art, and TV. Local artists only. Mail samples or call for interview.

WINARD ADVERTISING AGENCY, INC., 343 Pecks Rd., Pittsfield MA 01201. (413)445-5657. Art Director: William E. Dodge. Annual billing: $1 million. Clients are banking, paper machinery, paper, plastics, publishing, nuclear components, electronics, surveying, coffee makers, florists' material and wallpaper accounts. Uses local artists for illustration, technical artwork, layouts, paste-ups and retouching. Media used: newspapers, radio, magazines, billboards, direct mail, POP displays and collateral projects. Pays $7-10 per hour for mechanical paste-ups. Call for interview.

WINIUS-BRANDON/TEXAS, INC., 4710 Bellaire Blvd,. Suite 310, Bellaire TX 77401. (713)666-1765. Contact: Ed Kennard. Estab: 1965. Annual billing: $5 million+. Clients are furniture companies, auto dealers, restaurants, hotels, groceries, industrial equipment, banks, wholesale appliance distributors, TV and radio stations, jewelry store chains, savings and loans, women's and men's fashion stores and paper products manufacturers. Buys 50-100 illustrations annually for ads, billboards, catalogs, letterheads, POP displays, posters, TV and trademarks; especially needs brochure and print illustration. Also uses artists for layout, lettering, paste-up, retouching and type spec. Payment determined by complexity of assignment, number of illustrations, where the work will appear and/or how frequently work will appear. Pays $200-750, color illustration; $100-500, B&w newspaper illustration; $10-20 per hour, paste-up. Prefers local artists. Query. Reports in 2 weeks. Prefers to work with "reliable freelancer with clean work and strong concept abilities."

JACK WODELL ASSOCIATES, 582 Market St., San Francisco CA 94104. Vice President/Creative Director: Floyd Yost. Uses artists for illustration, retouching and design. Media used: newspapers, magazines, radio and outdoor. Arrange to show work.

WOOLF ADVERTISING, INC., 2252 W. Beverly Blvd., Los Angeles CA 90057. Art Director: Len Woolf. Uses Los Angeles artists for layout, illustration, type spec, retouching, paste-up and lettering. Clients are consumer and industrial accounts. Mail 8½x11" photocopy of work for consideration and agency file.

WYBLE ADVERTISING, 516 High St., Millville NJ 08332. (609)825-3403. Art Director: George F. Walter. Approximately 75% of clients are aviation oriented. Uses artists for aviation illustration and technical art. Largest portion of advertising is print media. Will review mailed samples. Prefers interview.

YOUNG & RUBICAM INC., 285 Madison Ave., New York NY 10017. Senior Vice President/Manager of Art: Don Egensteiner.

Exhibit, Display & Sign Firms

When the Point of Purchase Advertising Institute (POPAI) recently conducted a study of mass-merchandising stores in six areas of the nation, they found that 30% of shoppers made unplanned (impulse) purchases.

Impulse buying isn't something that just happens. It is something the artist, working with exhibit, display and sign firms, has a large influence on. An effective presentation creates a visual image that snags the eye of the consumer and then spurs him on to make a purchase.

Design and color both play a vital part in achieving this goal. In addition, artists wishing to work in this field should have a keen knowledge of lettering and illustration, and be familiar with human kinetics, theatrical design and lighting.

Firms listed in this category include department stores, manufacturers of store fixtures and props, exhibit design companies and sign firms. Additional markets can be found by consulting your yellow page directory, and by checking the Advertising Agencies & Specialty Firms and Businesses & Manufacturers categories in this book.

Magazines geared to this field include Signs of the Times *and* Visual Merchandising. *Each of these magazines sponsors trade competitions in which participation is an excellent way to achieve added recognition in your field — thus improving freelance sales.*

AAMES-WARNER CORP., 16320 S. Figueroa St., Gardena CA 90248. Contact: John Beccaria. Sign firm. Uses artists for advertising art; lettering; trademark, exhibit and display design; decorations; and cartoon theme stories. Mail transparencies or photos of work. Reports in 15 days. Payment determined by job or time spent.

ACE SIGN COMPANY OF GEORGIA, (formerly Anchor Sign Company of Georgia), 5500 Forge St., Tucker GA 30084. (404)939-5500. President: Ted Willis. Uses artists for lettering and trademark design. Payment determined by job. Mail samples or query with resume. Reports in 20 days.

ALLIED TREND SYSTEMS INC., (formerly Allied Display Materials Inc.), 300 W. 24th St., New York NY 10011. (212)243-0754. Contact: H. Hofman. Uses artists for exhibit and display design.

ANNIS-WAY SIGNS LIMITED, 595 West St. S., Orillia, Ontario Canada. Contact: Lloyd H. Annis. Uses artists for exhibit, trademark and display disign; sign redesign, and lettering.

APPLETON NEON SIGN CO., INC., Box 1152, Appleton WI 54910. Contact: Harold F. Hartzheim. Uses artists for advertising art, sign redesign, lettering and trademark design. Mail samples or arrange interview.

AUSTEN DISPLAY CORP., 139 W. 19th St., New York NY 10011. Art Buyer: A. David Scholder. Features store and display design. Uses artists for advertising art; architectural and art renderings; building interiors; decorations; graphic and industrial design; paper-goods decorations; sales promotion art; set and stage design; window displays; and store design. Seasonal need for Valentine's Day, Christmas, fall and spring. Pays $25-100 for artwork/designs to royalties of 7½% of selling price. Previously published work considered. Submit tearsheets, photostats or transparencies. Reports in 2 weeks.

BAUMGARTEN COMPANY OF WASHINGTON, 925 11th St., NW, Washington DC 20001. Contact: Edward J. Gramm. Sign company. "Most art requirements are for logos and layouts for plaques that are photoprinted on metal, or laminated to boards. Our needs are not large—the plaques are a small part of our sign engraving department—but we'd be interested to hear from local area artists and designers." Mail samples.

BEN'S INC., 4949 N. Western Ave., Chicago IL 60625. (312)784-7100. Contact: Lucie Sable. Uses artists for display design and decorations. Mail photos or transparencies.

BULLETIN & DIRECTORY BOARD MFG. CO., 2317 W. Pico, Los Angeles CA 90006. Manager: John Curtis. Estab: 1946. Exhibit/sign firm. Uses artists for brochures, display/trademark design, print media advertising, sign redesign, technical charts/illustrations and trade shows exhibit/design. Assigns 30 jobs annually. Pays $10 per hour minimum. All methods of contact OK. Reports in 1 week.

CARIBBEAN EXHIBITS, INC., Box 6806, Loiza Station, Santurce Puerto Rico 00914. (809)726-4630. Design Director: Franklin Sotomayor. Estab: 1971. Exhibit/display/sign firm. Uses artists for calligraphy, fine art, murals, neon signage and scale models. Assigns 15-25 freelance jobs annually. Especially needs artists from September-June. Pays $50-300, decoration rendering; $75-400, scenery; $50-500, exhibits. Payment determined by job. Call or write for interview. Reports in 2 weeks. SASE.

CENIT LETTERS, 7436 Varna Ave., North Hollywood CA 91605. (213)983-1234. Contact: Don Kurtz. Estab: 1964. Sign firm. Uses local artists for layout and gold leaf jobs. Assigns 25 freelance jobs annually. Pays $50 minimum for gold leaf. Payment determined by job. Query. Reports in 1 week. SASE. Recently assigned freelancer gold leafing of a corporate logo and lettering.

COLLINS-LACROSSE SIGN CORP., 222 Pine St., LaCrosse WI 54601. (608)784-8200. President/Manager: Charles C. Collins. Estab: 1917. Sign firm. Uses artists for billboards, display design, neon signage and sign redesign. Assigns 6-20 freelance jobs annually. Pays $7-50 for sketches. Payment determined by job and/or degree of difficulty. Mail photos of work or actual sketches. Reports in 3 days. Recently assigned artist to design 12x42' billboard.

CONSOLIDATED MOUNTING & FINISHING, 50-10 Kneeland St., Elmhurst NY 11373. Chief Designer: C. Sutnar. Estab: 1954. Display firm. Uses artists for POP displays and scale models. Assigns 60-100 freelance jobs annually. Pays $5-9 per hour for models. Query with samples or write for interview. Reports in 3 weeks. SASE.

CORONET ADVERTISING PRODUCTS, INC., Box 241, Flanders NJ 07836. Art Buyer: W.R. Gersch. Manufactures signs and displays. Interested in seeing designs for "small back bar illuminated signs for the beer and liquor industries, as well as window and wall signs with and without color motion. We also need designs for signs in the same categories which are not illuminated." Mail tearsheets, photostats or transparencies of work.

CREEGAN PRODUCTIONS COMPANY, 510 Washington St., Steubenville OH 43952. Contact: George Creegan. Display firm. Uses artists for sales promotion and window displays, advertising art, and direct mail. Mail design ideas.

DE NOVA ASSOCIATES LTD., 2820 Duchesne St., Ville St. Laurent, Montreal, Quebec Canada H4R 1J4. (514)336-3444. Contact: Terry Lapointe. Uses artists for exhibit design, POP displays, signs, displays and display design.

DECKEL & MONEYPENNY, INC., 615 Marret Ave., Louisville KY 40208. (502)636-5118. Contact: Bruce W. Deckel. Uses artists for advertising art; exhibit and display design; and scale model-making. Mail photos or transparencies of work.

DISCOVERIES, INC., 235 W. 1st St., Bayonne NJ 07002. Contact: Frank Latino. Buys original ideas for department store window and interior display props for spring, fall, Christmas and nonseasonal use. Submit ideas in August and September for spring or basic ideas; February and March for Christmas ideas. Pays 10% of sales for a display sold to individual store; 5% of sales for display purchased by chain. Payment made when idea is used. Payments range from $40-10,000 per design; on chain sales, $1,000-100,000. Submit tearsheets of previously published work. Reports in 2-3 weeks.

DISMAR CORP., NW Corner "A" and Clearfield Sts., Philadelphia PA 19134. Contact: Gerry Senker. Promotional sign and display company. Uses artists for advertising art, lettering, display design, decorations and poster design for retail stores. "We design, prepare and print promotional signing and displays for the retail industry." Payment determined by job and/or time spent. Mail photos or transparencies of work or arrange interview. Reports in 5 days.

THE DISPLAY HOUSE, INC., 1101 S. 20th St., Philadelphia PA 19146. (215)735-4448. Contact: B. Lewy. Estab: 1932. Exhibit/display firm. Uses local artists for brochures, display design, murals, POP displays and trade show and museum exhibits. Greatest time of need: January-June and September-November. Pays $75-1,000. Payment determined by job. Query or call for interview. SASE.

DISPLAY SALES INC., 5555 Fair Lane, Cincinnati OH 45227. Contact: Fred C. Pottschmidt. Uses artists for advertising art, exhibit design, scale model-making and murals. Arrange interview.

DUALITE, INC., Dualite Lane, Williamsburg OH 45176. (513)732-1500. Contact: W.A. Cobbe. Sign firm. Estab: 1947. Buys POP displays, print media advertising and sign redesigns. Assigns 25-50 freelance jobs annually. Pays $50-500. Payment determined by job and/or time spent. Query with samples, or write or call for interview. Samples should be actual artwork. Reports in 1 week. SASE. Looks for professional lettering and color combinations. Recently employed a freelance artist to develop a catalog page for a new indoor sign model.

DYECO STORE FIXTURE & DISPLAY MFG. CO., 1 Pines Plaza, Oregon IL 61061. (815)732-2411. Contact: D. Dean Dye. Estab: 1961. Exhibit/display firm. Assigns 12 jobs annually. Uses artists for catalog layouts, direct mail brochures and sketches of store fixtures, elevations and store interiors. Pays $20 per sketch. Send resume and sketches. Reports in 2 weeks. SASE.

EXHIBIT BUILDERS, INC., Box 226, Hwy. 17 N., Deland FL 32720. (904)734-3196. Contact: J.C. Burkhalter. Uses artists for exhibit and display design and scale model-making. Requires line drawings for blueprints and perspective color renderings of proposed exhibit or display.

EXHIBITS OF CALIFORNIA INC., 1877 Bay Rd., Palo Alto CA 94303. (415)323-7778. Design Director: Andy Beal. Estab: 1962. Exhibit firm. Uses local artists for scale models and trade show exhibit/design. Assigns 15-25 jobs annually. Payment by the hour and/or job. Query with photos or transparencies. No work returned.

GEORGE E. FERN CO., 1100 Gest St., Cincinnati OH 45203. (513)621-6111. General Manager: George J. Budig. Estab: 1909. Exposition service contractor/display firm. Uses local artists for backdrop displays, trade show exhibit/design, convention entrances and special room decorations. Assigns 6-10 freelance jobs annually. Pays $50-300 for sketch of exhibit. Payment determined by job or time spent. Query. Reports in 1 week. SASE.

FERROCRAFT, Box 55, Morganfield KY 42437. Contact: M.L. Meeder. Manufacturers of metal display and merchandising fixtures serving the retail and point-of-purchase fields. Uses outside design ideas for either decorative or functional fixtures. Payment negotiated. Usually pays 5% of sales when sold to a chain or POP account; 10% of sales when sold as stock display.

GERON ASSOCIATES LTD., 20 Progress Ave., Scarboro, Ontario Canada MIP 2Y4. Contact: G. Fattori. Exhibit/display/sign company. Uses artists for advertising art, exhibit design and scale model-making. Pays 5% of anticipated or estimated cost for exhibit design or scale model. Payment upon completion. Arrange interview or mail samples.

HUMAN FORM HANGER AND DISPLAY CORP., 35 Herkimer Place, Brooklyn NY 11216. Display fixture company. Uses artists for display fixtures and forms, garment hangers and metal fixtures trimming accessories executed in metal, plastics and wood. Submit line drawings of ideas. Reports in 1 week.

IMMCO INDUSTRIES INC., 58-01 Main St., Flushing NY 11355. Art Director: John Lukac. Estab: 1972. Display firm. Uses local artists for brochures, display design, scale models, technical charts/illustrations, POP and trademark design. Assigns 100+ freelance jobs annually. Pays $15-20 for marker comps and scale models. Payment by time spent and/or job. Write for interview. Reports in 1 week. Recently assigned freelancer to develop two 2-color mock-ups of finished art on corrugated floor bins.

Pop Off Light, Airy Designs for POP Sales

John Lukac

"A good POP sketch should express a POP's primary function, which is to separate the product from all other products and entice the customer to buy on instinct," says John Lukac, art director of Immco Industries, Inc. Immco has won the POPAI (Point of Purchase Advertising Institute) Award for its Dynamint, Chivas Regal and Seagram displays.

Lukac says artists wanting to break in to the area of POP design should: "First look into a variety of stores to see what POP advertisers are using. Then do some research and several comp sketches and arrange interviews with large firms.

"Your POP sketches should be light, airy and appealing. Make it look like it was done quickly, even though it wasn't. Avoid heavy, bold lines and colors. You're selling an idea, not an actual product. If you make your design look too finished, the prospective client may start saying things like 'Looks like it needs wires and screws here.' "

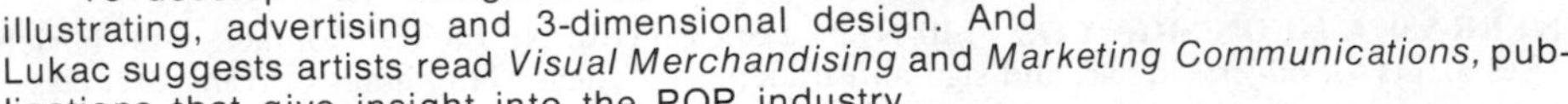

To develop POP design skills, artists should study illustrating, advertising and 3-dimensional design. And Lukac suggests artists read *Visual Merchandising* and *Marketing Communications*, publications that give insight into the POP industry.

INTERNATIONAL DESIGN CORP., 3441 W. Grand Ave., Chicago IL 60651. Contact: A. Stone. Display and furnishings company. Uses artists for convention exhibits, furniture and industrial design, window displays and sculpture. Payment by flat fee or 5% royalty. Query with samples. Reports in 3 months maximum.

JENTER EXHIBITS INC., 230 E. 8th St., Mt. Vernon NY 10550. Contact: Anthony Scaperotta or Carl Jenter. Estab: 1918. Exhibit/display firm. Uses artists for display and POP design, murals, neon signage, scale models, technical charts/illustrations and trade show exhibits/designs. Assigns 10-20 freelance jobs annually. Payment determined by time spent, job and/or degree of difficulty. Query with samples. Reports in 1 week. SASE.

MacFARLANE ENTERPRISES, 3714 Bladensburg Rd., Cottage City MD 20722. (301)864-4300. Creative Director: Stuart Andre. Estab: 1970. Display/sign firm. Uses local artists for technical charts/illustrations and transit signage. Assigns 25 freelance jobs annually. Pays $20-300, signs; $10-100, charts. Payment determined by job. Query. Reports in 2 weeks. No work returned.

MARKETECHS, INC., Rte. 5, York PA 17402. Contact: Caron Ehehalt. Exhibit/sales meeting firm. Uses freelance artists for advertising art, exhibit and display design and scale model-making. Artist must have thorough knowledge of exhibit graphics. Pays $300 for 15' exhibit. Arrange interview.

LOUIS W. MIAN, 18 Chestnut St., Winchester MA 01890. Produces murals in terrazzo and mosaic, terrazzo emblems and trademarks for industrial companies. Query with resume or send samples. SASE.

MISSOULA MERCANTILE, Box 8129, Missoula MT 59807. (406)543-7211. Visual Merchandising Manager: Kathy Solberg. Estab: 1865. Department store. Uses artists for display backdrops, POP displays, props and transit signage. Assigns 12 freelance jobs annually. Pays $60, seasonal props; $40, panel drops. Pay determined by job. Query with photos of work. Reports in 2 weeks. No work returned. Recently assigned freelancer to develop bunnies of wood and bark as Easter props.
Crafts: Pays $50, 3' pottery; $50-100, large ceramic vases.

MITTEN DESIGNER LETTERS, 85 5th Ave., New York NY 10003. Contact: Jessie S. Mitten. Produces 3-dimensional letters/signs/window displays. Always looking for more letter design. Submit line and wash rough drawings of letter designs and background designs for signs. Reports in 1 week.

JERRY MOSS, INC., 107 E. 31st St., New York NY 10016. Art Buyer: J. Bollbach. Display agency. Uses artists for floor display designs, merchandising displays, renderings of display designs, package designs, posters and brochures. Also needs Christmas liquor floor units. "Artists must have an awareness about production and be able to think in terms of dimensions." Pays $50 per design sketch on assignment. Buys rights for display purposes only. Submit photostats, tearsheets or transparencies of work. Will consider submissions previously published for a different purpose.

MULTIPLEX DISPLAY FIXTURE COMPANY, 1555 Larkin Williams Rd., Fenton MO 63026. Advertising Manager: K. Michael Brenizer. Manufacturers of display fixtures and audiovisual slide storage equipment. Occasionally uses artists for sales literature, catalog covers/illustrations, exhibit designs, displays and technical charts/illustrations.

NASHVILLE DISPLAY MFG. CO., 1415 Elm Hill Rd., Box 491, Nashville TN 37202. Contact: Scott Day. Continuous need for artwork and ideas for signs, ads, flyers and brochures. Pays $50-75, signs; $125, other artwork. Submit resume then arrange interview.

NEBRASKA NEON SIGN CO., 1140 N. 21st St., Lincoln NE 68503. Contact: John Pavich. Uses artists for advertising art and sign and trademark design. Mail photos or transparencies of work.

NORTON ADVERTISING, 5280 Kennedy Ave., Cincinnati OH 45213. (513)631-4864. Contact: Tom Norton. Estab: 1950. Sign firm. Uses local artists for billboards. Assigns 30-60 jobs annually. Pays $20 minimum, roughs; $75-100, finished sketch. Payment determined by job. Call for interview.

OBERLY & NEWELL, 488 Madison Ave., New York NY 10022. (212)421-3838. Contact: Marvin Zaro. Uses artists for advertising art, POP signs/displays, lettering, display design and scale model-making. Arrange interview.

PHASE FOUR PRODUCTS INC., 11-12 30 Drive Astoria, New York NY 11102. Creative Director: Mr. Small. Estab: 1958. Display/POP firm. Uses artists for POP display design. Assigns 400-500 freelance jobs annually. Pays $10+ per hour. Query with samples (samples may be photocopies, transparencies or photos of work). Reports in 1 week. SASE.

PRONTO PRINTING, 6231 Montgomery Rd., Cincinnati OH 45213. Contact: Phil Kabakoff. Sign company. Uses artists for advertising art, lettering and trademark design. Arrange interview or submit samples.

THE RAVENWARE COMPANY, INC., 360 Scholes St., Brooklyn NY 11206. (212)497-1232. Vice President: Richard G. Galef. Estab: 1950. Fixture manufacturer/display firm. Uses local artists for display/POP/fixture design, scale models and trade show exhibit/design. Assigns 200+ freelance jobs annually. Pays $40-150. Payment determined by job and/or degree of difficulty. Query. Reports in 1 week. No work returned.

BOB ROBINSON MARKETING, INC., 366 N. Broadway, Jericho NY 11753. (516)931-5900. President: Bob Robinson. Uses artists for display/POP design and scale models. Assigns 100 freelance jobs annually. Pays $25-75 per sketch, design of permanent displays; $200-300 per assignment. Payment determined by job and/or degree of difficulty. Call or write for interview (bring portfolio). Reports in 2 weeks. SASE.

ROGERS DISPLAY STUDIOS, INC., 1000 Wayside Rd., Cleveland OH 44110. Director of Design: Bernard Digman. Uses artists for trade shows, display designs, technical illustration and scale model-making. Submissions can be reproductions of previous work, or anything from thumbnail sketches in pencil to presentation comprehensive concepts of trade show exhibits (in pastel preferable). Felt pen and/or colored pencil designs also acceptable. Can be 8x10" to 20x30" on translucent tissue layout paper or illustration board.

SELEXOR DISPLAYS, 1916 Park Ave., New York NY 10037. (212)368-7791. Vice President: C.M. Kingsley. Estab: 1935. Exhibit/display/sign firm. Uses local artists for display backdrops, design, POP displays, scale models, sign redesign, technical charts/illustrations and trade show exhibit/design. Pays $100-300, exhibits; $100-250, POP displays; $150-500, scale models. Payment determined by job and/or time spent. Query with sketches or call or write for interview. Reports in 1 week. SASE.

SERVILIO ASSOCIATES, INC., 2 Prince St., Brooklyn NY 11201. Contact: Angelo Servilio. Uses artists for exhibit/display design, scale models and murals. Minimum payment: $150 per 17x20" comp; $250 per 1"-1' scale model. Mail photos of work or arrange interview.

SIMCO SIGN COMPANY, 2719 Maple, Box 68, Everett WA 98206. Contact: David Servine. Uses artists for advertising art, sign redesign and trademark design. Knowledge of sign readability requirements helpful as well as electric sign (or painted sign) manufacturing procedures/products. Pays $15-25, simple line drawings/"roughs;" $150-250, full-color illustrations/architectural renderings. Arrange interview.

W.H.B. SPANGENBERG STUDIOS, 1010 Central Ave., Metairie LA 70001. Contact: Walker Spangenberg. Uses artists for exhibit/display design, POP displays, signs, displays and scale model-making. Mail photos or transparencies of work.

TARGET COMMUNICATIONS INC., 44 Pittsburgh St., Boston MA 02210. Design Director: Joseph Ali. Occasionally uses artists/designers for exhibit/display design, scale model-making, graphic design and illustration. Pays $5-20 per hour for exhibit design/model buildings. Arrange interview. "We prefer to have direct contact on projects with designers and illustrators and for this reason usually work with people from the Boston area."

TEMPO COMMUNICATIONS, 4633 W. 16th St., Chicago IL 60650. Contact: Gordon S. Lundgren. Uses Chicago and Milwaukee artists for POP problems. Artists do finished work if job is sold. Submit felt pen sketches of displays or photos of previously produced designs. Reports in 2 weeks.

THALL PLASTICS AND METALS, INC., 76 Washington St., Brooklyn NY 11201. Contact: Chuck Rosenthal. Manufactures display fixtures. Uses artists for functional display equipment for fashion department stores. Interested in design ideas for floor, counter and ceiling fixtures made in plastic or metal. Pays $50-100 for designs. "For an idea of what is needed, take a look at fixtures used in new stores."

TRIM CORPORATION OF AMERICA, 10 W. 20th St., New York NY 10011. Contact: Sol Stern. Uses artists for advertising art, display design, scale model-making, murals and decorations. Pays $100, screen layouts; $50, renderings. Mail photos or transparencies of work.

UNICUBE CORP., 1290 Oak Point Ave., Bronx NY 10474. Contact: Robert J. Burg. Uses artists for advertising art and exhibit/display/store fixture design. Mail photos or transparencies of work.

VANADCO SIGN, INC., 200 W. Walnut St., Argos IN 46501. (219)892-5000. President: Bruce VanDerWeele. Estab: 1955. Sign firm. Uses out-of-town artists for plastic and neon signage, billboards, POP displays and sign redesign. Assigns 150 freelance jobs annually. "Payment determined when query is made." Reports in 1 week. "Any artist who can create new, fresh sign design will be given immediate attention."

Public Relations Firms

There is little difference between the type of artwork needed by advertising agencies and public relations firms. Ad agencies attempt to sell products or services; public relations firms sell images.

Most PR freelance assignments call for local artists, but there are some firms that are willing to work through the mail with talented artists.

Assignments range from developing brochures for beauty pageants to producing audiovisuals for the federal government. Other assignments include illustrating and developing charts for reports; designing booklets; working on in-house publications; developing advertisements; creating exhibits; and producing audiovisual materials for speeches. Payment ranges from a rock-bottom $5 for a logo to $1,000 for an artistic design.

Besides checking the markets listed in this book, consult the Public Relations Journal/Register *(Public Relations Society of America) for other potential markets; or, contact local firms with in-house public relations departments — they may have an opening for your work.* The Publicist *and* PR Aids' Party Line *are both good trade newsletters that the freelancer should subscribe to to get the latest news on PR developments.*

SOL ABRAMS ASSOCIATES INC., 331 Webster Dr., New Milford NJ 07646. Contact: Sol Abrams. Uses artists for sales and recruitment literature and school yearbook ads. Specializes in beauty pageants, entertainment, youth, food, publishing and fashion fields. Mail samples.

AG MEDIA SERVICES, Box 334, Johnson Creek WI 53038. (414)699-3767. Art Director: Dennis Bries. Estab: 1975. Agricultural clients. Buys 1-5 illustrations annually for annual reports; direct mail and publicity brochures; displays; lettering; trademarks; and logos. Pays $5-10 per logo and similar designs. No payment for unused assigned illustrations. Local artists only. Query. Reports in 60 days. SASE.

ALONSO Y ASOCIADOS, S.A., Public Relations Firm, Lancaster 17, Mexico D.F., 6. Director: Manuel Alonso. Uses artists for direct mail brochures, annual reports, billboards, interior design, posters and public service TV spots. Size: 8x10". Pays $100-1,000 for design. Query with printed samples. Will deal with artists by mail.

ARTS, INC., Box T, 4645 Van Nuys Blvd., Sherman Oaks CA 91413. Contact: Ken Frankel. Specializes in audience building for performing, visual and special arts. Uses artists for direct mail brochures, annual reports, billboards, interior design, posters, public service TV spots, newspaper ads and bus signs. Submit resume and printed samples of work. Will work with talented artists by mail. Minimum payment: $300, annual report; $450, direct mail brochure. "Please contact us on speculation with samples of your work. We are in constant need of new designs and print media art."

GENE BARTCZAK ASSOCIATES INC., Box E, North Bellmore NY 11710. (516)781-6230. Manager: Gordon Willson. Estab: 1954. Clients are technical industrial companies and related organizations. Buys 10-15 illustrations annually for ads and catalogs; especially needs design and mechanicals. Payment determined by complexity of assignment, number of illustrations and/or time spent on work. Pays $20 per page for design/layout and mechanical paste-up. Original payment as promised for unused assigned illustrations. Query. Reports in 2 weeks. SASE.

BELL PUBLICOM, INC., 1406 Third National Bldg., Dayton OH 45402. Art Director: Bill J. Evans. Uses local artists for direct mail brochures, annual reports, newsletters and bulletin graphics. Pays $5-10 minimum, keyline/mechanical art. Mail resume and printed samples.

ALEON BENNETT & ASSOCIATES, 8272 Sunset Blvd., Los Angeles CA 90046. Director: Aleon Bennett. Uses artists for direct mail brochures, annual reports, interior design and posters. Prefers local artists, but works with professionals by mail. Query with resume.

ERIK L. BURRO MARKETING & COMMUNICATIONS GROUP, Box 477, Willingboro NJ 08046. (609)877-3704. President: Erik L. Burro. Estab: 1972. Annual billing: $225,000. Clients are companies and organizations in the construction industry. Buys 35-80 illustrations annually for ads, annual reports, letterheads and trademarks; especially needs construction-oriented ad illustrations and audiovisuals. Also uses artists for color separations, layout, lettering, paste-up, retouching and type spec. Payment determined by complexity of assignment, time spent and/or where work appears. "We pay prevailing market price for work." Original payment as promised for unused assigned illustrations. Prefers Philadelphia and New Jersey

area artists. Query with resume and samples. Contacts artists as needs arise. SASE.
To Break In: Artist must have "understanding of printing, photography, relationship of copy and psychology of visuals. Skill without orientation in other areas is not effective."

C&S ASSOCIATES, 424 E. 52nd St., New York NY 10022. (212)421-0846. President: John E. Shea. Advertising/public relations/marketing firm. Uses artists for direct mail brochures, annual reports, interior design, copy writing/public relations and market research. Payment determined by job.

PATRICK CARR ASSOCIATES, INC., 147 E. 50th St., New York NY 10022. Contact: Annemarie Zinn. Uses artists for direct mail brochures and news releases. Query with resume and printed samples of work.

CCH ASSOCIATES, Box 535, Livingston NJ 07039. Public Relations Director: Lee Cherusen. Uses local artists to work on annual reports.

CLARK ASSOCIATES, 2 N. Riverside Plaza, Chicago IL 60606. Contact: Ray L. Clark. Uses artists for interior and exterior scenes for U.S. historic sites. Query with resume. Works with talented professionals by mail. Pays $30 per hour.

CONANT AND COMPANY, 30 E. 42nd St., New York NY 10017. Public Relations Director: Luther Conant. Clients are wine, food, jewelry and tourism accounts. Uses artists for brochures, interior design and posters. Prefers local artists. Submit resume and printed samples of work.

CRANFORD/JOHNSON/HUNT & ASSOCIATES, First National Bldg., Little Rock AR 72201. Creative Director: Jim Johnson. Clients are banks, utilities, thoroughbred racing interests and wineries. Uses artists for illustrations, direct mail brochures, annual reports, posters and public service TV spots. Mail resume with samples.

PATRICIA DOERING AND ASSOCIATES, Box 81702, San Diego CA 92138. Contact: Pat Doering. Uses artists for advertising, public relations, direct mail, posters and billboards. Pays $25 per hour average. Submit samples.

DICK DOTY AND ASSOCIATES, INC., Suite 200, 2727 E. Oakland Park Beach Blvd., Ft. Lauderdale FL 33306. Contact: Dick Doty. Clients are land developers, shopping centers, retailers and industries. Uses artists for direct mail brochures and annual reports. Submit resume and samples.

ALAN G. EISEN COMPANY, INC., 49 Titus Rd., Glen Cove NY 11542. President: Alan G. Eisen. Clients are school districts, insurance companies, luggage manufacturers, electronic firms, pharmaceutical companies, restaurants, real estate and financial firms. Uses artists for direct mail brochures, annual reports, posters and public service TV spots. Local artists only. Query with professional credits.

ETHOS INC., 216 W. Burton, Murfreesboro TN 37130. (615)896-1536. President: Paul Keckley. Estab: 1976. Clients are industry, schools, retailers, nonprofit associations and insurance companies. Buys 100 illustrations annually for annual reports, catalogs, print ads, direct mail brochures, displays, exhibit designs, company magazines, newsletters, POP displays, posters and trademarks. Also uses artists for animation, lettering and layout. Payment determined by project budget. Mail artwork. Reports in 4 weeks. SASE. Recently assigned freelancer to design an annual report for a bank.

FARBER & ASSOCIATES, Montmartre Bldg., Suite M5, 8600 Delmar Blvd., St. Louis MO 63142. Vice President: Thomas D. Widmar. Uses artists for direct mail brochures, annual reports, posters, general brochures, all types of printed literature, periodicals, logo creation and exhibits. Query with resume. Prefers local artists but sometimes works with out-of-town professionals.

FELTON GORDON ASSOCIATES, 3384 Peachtree Rd. NE, Suite 875, Atlanta GA 30326. Public Relations Director: Felton H. Gordon. Public relations counseling firm. Uses artists for direct mail brochures, annual reports and public service TV spots. Prefers local artists. Query with resume.

Resume Sheets Will Get You Filed

Alan G. Eisen

"When you're querying smaller public relations firms, send a one-page resume sheet with your name, address, credits and two or three different samples of your art styles. The samples should be printed on the resume," says Alan Eisen, president of the Alan G. Eisen Company, Inc.

"Freelance artists frequently waste time mailing art samples to smaller agencies because we simply don't have the filing space to keep all the artwork we receive for future reference. For this reason, they just get thrown away.

"On the other hand, we do have space to keep one-page resume sheets, and the artist can have a fair number of these printed inexpensively. Call local printers for estimates."

HARSHE-ROTMAN & DRUCK, INC., 444 N. Michigan Ave., Chicago IL 60611. Design Director: Don Levy. Uses artists from the Chicago area for financial, corporate, and stockholder publications; brochures; annual reports; and posters. Query with printed samples.

LESKO, INC., 3 Gateway Center, Pittsburgh PA 15222. Contact: George Lesko. Uses artists for direct mail brochures, annual reports, public service TV spots, posters and billboards. Send letter outlining credits.

PHILIP LESLY CO., 33 N. Dearborn St., Chicago IL 60602. Uses artists for direct mail brochures, annual reports, billboards, posters, public service TV spots, audiovisual presentations, cartoons and illustrated mats. Query with printed samples.

McCALL COMPANY PUBLIC RELATIONS, Brooks Towers, Suite 32-L, Denver CO 80202. (303)893-3303. Contact: John W. McCall. Estab: 1953. Clients are nonprofit educational institutions, health agencies, tourism firms and broadcasters. Buys 15 illustrations annually for annual reports, billboards, letterheads, print announcements, posters, TV, trademarks, professional journals and newsletters. Also uses artists for animation, color separations, layout, lettering, paste-up, retouching and type spec. Pays $25 per hour minimum. Does 90% of work with Denver artists; no in-house art department. Query. Contacts artists as needs arise. SASE.

McDADE PUBLIC RELATIONS, INC., 475 Colman Bldg., 811 1st. Ave., Seattle WA 98104. Director: Graham E. McDade. Uses artists for letterheads, direct mail brochures, annual reports, billboards, posters and public service TV spots. Prefers local talent. Submit resume and samples of work.

CAROL MOBERG, INC., 43 W. 61st St., New York NY 10023. Contact: Linda Taber. Uses artists for consumer booklets and brochures, educational filmstrips and related materials.

DICK MOORE AND ASSOCIATES, INC., 850 7th Ave., New York NY 10019. Public Relations Director: Dick Moore. Uses local artists for direct mail brochures and annual reports. Send resume and printed samples of work.

MYRICK-NEWMAN-DAHLBERG, INC., 5207 McKinney Ave., Dallas TX 75205. Public Relations Director: Walter G. Dahlberg. Uses artists for direct mail brochures and annual reports. Query with printed samples.

WILLIAM C. PFLAUM CO., INC., Reston International Center, Reston VA 22091. (703)620-3773. Uses local artists for direct mail brochures, annual reports and product spec sheets. Submit letter and samples.
To Break In: Versatility is very important — "sensitivity to a variety of clients and a variety of clients' needs are keys."

GERALD A. ROGOVIN/PUBLIC RELATIONS INC., 57 Shornecliffe Rd., Newton MA 02158. President: Gerald A. Rogovin. Estab: 1960. Clients are industrial manufacturers, nonprofit hospitals and schools, accounting firms and publishers. Buys 1-5 illustrations annually for annual reports, catalogs and letterheads; especially needs report design and illustration. Also uses artists for layout, paste-up, retouching and type spec. Payment determined by complexity, number of illustrations, time spent and artist's demands (contract). "Freelancers determine their own minimum payment. We respect individual needs and fees." Local artists only. Query. Reports in 2 weeks.

HORACE SADOWSKY & ASSOCIATES, 20 Jerusalem Ave., Hicksville, Long Island NY 11801. President/Creative Director: Horace Sadowsky. Clients include industrial machinery and hard goods firms. Uses local artists for layout, illustration, technical art, paste-up, and retouching. Media include magazines, direct mail, brochures, annual reports and corporated promotions. Arrange interview.

GERALD SCHWARTZ AGENCY, 420 Linclon Road Bldg., Suite 445, Miami Beach FL 33139. Public Relations Director: Felice P. Schwartz. Public relations/advertising/fund raising firm. Uses artists for direct mail brochures, posters, annual reports, public service TV spots and billboards. Submit resume and printed samples. Pays $15 minimum per hour.

SIMMONS PUBLIC RELATIONS, 500 Upland Rd., Louisville KY 40206. Contact: Raymond L. Simmons. Uses local artists for technical bulletins.

UNIVERSAL TRAINING SYSTEMS CO., 3201 Old Glenview Rd., Wilmette IL 60091. (312)251-8700. Contact: Richard Thorne. Uses artists for animation art. Query with resume before arranging interview.

JEANNE VINER ASSOCIATES, 2113 S St. NW, Washington DC 20008. (202)462-5200. Estab: 1960. Contact: Jeanne Viner. Clients are associations, government agencies, and real estate, financial and travel firms. Buys 5-50 illustrations annually for annual reports, catalogs, print ads, letterheads, packaging, POP displays, posters, TV ads and logos. Also uses artists for color separations, layout, lettering, paste-up, retouching and type spec. Payment determined by complexity, number of illustrations, time spent, budget and/or client. Pays "going rate." Negotiates payment for unused assigned illustrations. Local artists only. Query with samples. "Reporting time depends on work load and clients (usually very prompt)." SASE.

GLORIA ZIGNER & ASSOCIATES, INC., 328 N. Newport Blvd., Newport Beach CA 92663. (714)645-6300. Contact: Gloria Zigner. Estab: 1967. Clients are hotels, hospitals, restaurants, manufacturers, builders and developers. Buys 12-24 illustrations annually for ads and brochures. Also uses artists for color separations, layout, lettering, paste-up and type spec. Payment determined by reputation of artist, complexity of assignment, number of illustrations and/or time spent on work. Original payment as promised for unused assigned illustrations. Local artists only. Write for interview. Reports in 2 weeks. SASE.

Studios, Art Service Firms & Printers

Opportunities for jobs in this category are largely for those artists interested in the technical side of art. Among the assignments issued by art service firms, labs, studios and printers are retouching, layout, paste-up and other similar jobs.

As with most technical jobs in art, payment here is usually by the hour rather than by set fee. Most assignments in this field require that you work at the studio or printer's office.

Layout and paste-up jobs can be entry positions for more creative work. If the printer you are working for doesn't have regular work for you, he may have a client who is in the market for your art.

For more information on pricing, write for Pricing & Ethical Guidelines *from the Graphic Artists Guild, Box 3928, Grand Central Station, New York City 10017. More information on printing techniques can be found in* Lithographers' Handbook, *published by the Graphic Arts Technical Foundation.*

A/D ASSOCIATES, INC., 55 W. 42nd St., New York NY 10036. Art/Creative Director: Sal Terzo. Clients are ad agencies, apparel and soft and hard goods manufacturers. Uses artists for paste-up, retouching and package design. Media used: newspaper, magazine and direct mail advertising.

AD-CRAFT PRODUCTS CO., 3262 Guernsey Ave., Memphis TN 38112. Contact: S.J. La Vene. Uses artists to design art calendars, ceramic art, decals and imprinted custom items. Uses all types of seasonal designs as suited to the line produced. Query with resume. Submit nothing unless requested. Previously published work OK. Pays on publication.

ALFA COLOR LABS, INC., 535 W. 135th St., Gardina CA 90248. (213)532-2532. Vice President: Larry Glauber. Estab: 1965. Lab. Services include photo color processing and printing. Clients are professional photographers. Uses local artists for illustrations, lettering and retouching. Pays $3-6 per hour, color negative retouching. Needs thousands of negatives retouched annually. Write or call for interview. Reports in 2-3 weeks.

ALTON LITHO & GRAPHICS, 362 W. Garvey Ave., Monterey Park CA 91754. (213)288-8211. President/Creative Director: Mark Franklin. Estab: 1971. Art service firm and printer. Services include typesetting, layout, paste-up and printing. Clients are art studios, manufacturers and advertising agencies. Uses local artists for illustrations, layout and logo design. Previously published and simultaneous submissions OK. Assigns 3-4 freelance jobs annually. Payment for typesetting determined by time spent and job. Mail samples. Reports in 2 weeks. SASE.

AMBROSI & ASSOCIATES, INC., 75 E. Wacker Dr., Chicago IL 60601. (312)236-7262. Art/Creative Director: Nick Ambrosi. Uses artists for layout, illustration, technical art and paste-up. Submit samples or call for interview. Handles art services for retail and industrial clients in newspapers, magazines and direct mail.

LEE AMES & ZAK LTD., 6500 Jericho Turnpike, Commack NY 11725. Director: Lee J. Ames. Clients are major book and educational publishers, toy manufacturers and children's and technical books. Uses local artists for layouts, illustration, technical art, paste-up and cartoons. Query with samples.

ANCO/BOSTON, 80 Boylston St., Boston MA 02116. (617)482-9270. Graphic Director: Mathew Fortado. Services include art and writing. Clients are educational publishers, commercial and industrial clients. Uses local artists for charts, graphs, illustrations, technical art and paste-up. Arrange interview.

BARLENMIR HOUSE OF GRAPHICS, 413 City Island Ave., City Island NY 10464. (212)885-2120. Creative Director: Barry L. Mirenburg. Estab: 1972. Studio. Services include annual reports; form, poster and trademark design; and production and printing. Clients are manufacturers and service companies. Uses artists for cartoons, illustrations, paste-up and technical art. Previously published and simultaneous submissions OK. Assigns 10 freelance jobs annually. Payment determined by job. Query with small slides or prints. Reports in 2 weeks. SASE.

BASIC/BEDELL ADVERTISING SELLING IMPROVEMENT CORP., 2042 Alameda Padre Serra, Santa Barbara CA 93103. President: C. Barrie Bedell. Services include packaging advertising copy/layout suggestions, publishing advertising educational material and conducting seminars. Clients are national and international newspapers, publishers, direct response marketers, retail stores, hard lines manufacturers and trade associations. Uses artists for furniture/spot illustration and cartoons. Pays $15 for illustrations.

ROBERT BATOR AND ASSOCIATES, 40 Marion St., Chicopee MA 01013. Art Director: Robert Bator. Clients are newspapers, restaurants, small businesses and recording companies. Uses artists for illustration, lettering and record jackets. Pays $100-250, comprehensive layout; $8-12 per hour, lettering. Mail photos or photostats of work. All submissions kept on file.

MARY BEAVERS' STUDIO OF FINE ARTS, 827 N. Fairfax Ave., Unit 2, Los Angeles CA 90046. (213)651-0089. Creative Director: Mary Beavers. Estab: 1962. Art service firm and studio. Services include photo retouching, portrait painting, decor and restorations. Clients are actors, agents, columnists, businesses, public relations firms, political figures and publishers. Uses artists for cartoons, graphs, lettering and outside contracts. Previously published and simultaneous submissions OK. Assigns 100-150 freelance jobs annually. Payment determined by job. Reports in 10 days. SASE.

BECKWITH STUDIOS, 81 Columbia Heights, Brooklyn NY 11201. Creative Director: E.S. Beckwith. Clients are magazine and book publishers, public relations firms and advertising agencies. Handles art services for newspapers, magazines, direct mail, textbooks and trade books.

BENNETT STUDIOS, 310 Edgewood St., Bridgeville DE 19933. Uses artists for assistance in print finishing, color negative retouching and airbrush work. Pays $25 per hour.

ERIC BLAIR ASSOCIATES INC., 6 E. 39th St., New York NY 10016. (212)532-6455. Creative Director: Irwin Berson. Estab: 1964. Art service firm and studio. Services include layout, design and mechanicals for advertisements, brochures and packaging. Clients are manufacturers. Uses artists for cartoons, charts, illustrations, lettering, paste-up, retouching and technical art. Previously published and simultaneous submissions OK. Assigns 50 freelance jobs annually. Minimum payment: $15, design; $10, mechanicals. Payment determined by job or hour. Call for interview. Reports in 1 week. No work returned.

BOOK PRODUCTION SERVICES, INC., 5 Elm St., Danvers MA 01923. Contact: Dixie Clark. Uses Boston area artists for technical book design and illustrations. Send resume to be kept on file. No samples.

THE BOXANDALL COMPANY, 460 N. Main, Oshkosh WI 54901. Art Director: Pat Walter. Estab: 1926. Publishes business, career and trade technical school brochures. Specializes in illustrations for office situations and trade occupations. Uses artists for illustrations and designs. Buys 10+ annually. Pays $25-500, illustrations; $75-150, cover designs. Query with samples. Submit line drawings and color separations. Previously published work OK. No photocopied or simultaneous submissions. Buys all rights. SASE. Reports in 3 weeks.

MAX BRAININ STUDIO, 527 Madison Ave., New York NY 10022. Art/Creative Director: Max Brainin. Handles art services for consumer magazines and sales promotion catalogs for sewing companies. Uses artists for fashion illustration and lettering. Prefers local artists. Mail samples or call for appointment.

THE CHESTNUT HOUSE GROUP INC., 535 N. Michigan Ave., Chicago IL 60611. (312)822-9090. Creative Directors: Norman Baugher and Miles Zimmerman. Estab: 1968. Studio. Services include design and production of textbook programs and educational and promotional materials for industry. Clients are major educational publishers and advertisers. Uses artists for illustrations, layout and assembly. Assigns 20-50 freelance jobs annually. Payment determined by job. Contact for interview. "Letter inquiries are promptly answered. We do not want unsolicited samples."

COGENT COMMUNICATIONS CO., 401 15th Ave. N., South St. Paul MN 55075. Contact: James Reid. Uses artists for magazine design and illustration. Write with resume for more information. Payment determined by job.

THE CRANSTON MIRROR, 250 Auburn St., Cranston RI 02910. Contact: Malcolm L. Daniels. Publishes weekly newspaper; produces several monthly publications; does commercial printing. Uses artists for layout, illustration, technical art, paste-up, lettering and retouching. Needs freelancers year-round except July and August. Prefers local artists. Call for appointment to show portfolio. Minimum payment: booklet assignment, $175; illustrations, $15-75 each.

CREATIVE FREELANCERS, INC., 655 Madison Ave., New York NY 10022. Art/Creative Director: Marilyn Howard. Uses artists for layout, illustration, type spec, paste-up, retouching and lettering. Prefers local artists. Call for appointment. Handles art services for newspapers, magazines, direct mail and some TV.

CROW-QUILL STUDIOS, 706 Sansome St., San Francisco CA 94111. Art/Creative Director: Jaren Dahlstrom. Handles art services for magazines, direct mail, slide presentations and book design/illustration. Clients are publishers, real estate developers, insurance companies, financial institutions and transportation firms. Uses artists for illustration. Mail samples.

CWI, INC., 205 E. 42nd St., New York NY 10017. (212)679-4806. Art/Creative Director: Geoffrey Chaite. Clients are packaged goods, foods, tools, publishing, drugs, HBA, tobacco, banks and sports accounts. Uses artists for layout, illustration, technical art, type spec, paste-up, retouching and lettering. Media used: newspapers, magazines, billboards, direct mail, POP and collateral material.

ALEX D'AMATO GRAPHIC DESIGN, 32 Bayberry St., Bronxville NY 10708. (914)774-6264. Creative Director: Alex D'Amato. Estab: 1957. Art service firm and studio. Services include book, book jacket, box and record jacket design. Clients are publishers, audiovisual firms, manufacturers and trade advertisers. Uses local artists for lettering, paste-up, realistic illustrations and retouching. Payment determined by job. Assigns 12 freelance jobs annually. Write for interview.

DARBY PRINTING COMPANY, 715 W. Whitehall St. SW, Atlanta GA 30310. Contact: Lynn Hiller. Specializes in printing brochures, magazines, annual reports and law books. Uses artists for layout, illustration, type spec, and especially paste-up. "We want an artist experienced in preparing camera-ready art and able to work on our premises." Pays about $6.50 per hour.

DARI DESIGNS, Box 11, Newton Lower Falls MA 02162. Contact: C.R. Gordon. Clients are advertising agencies. Uses artists for catalog illustrations and covers, ceramic design, decorative spots (magazine editorial), fashion and graphic design, lettering, letterheads and trademarks. Prefers to see original, finished art. Buys all rights.

DAVIS GRAPHIC LTD., 468 Park Ave. S., New York NY 10016. (212)686-7128. Creative Director: A.N. Qureshi. Estab: 1967. Art service firm, printer and studio. Services include design art and printing of brochures, catalogs, books, book jackets, house organs and publication advertisements. Clients are publishers and manufacturers. Uses artists for charts, graphs, illustrations, lettering, paste-up, retouching and technical art. Payment determined by job and/or time spent. Assigns 100 freelance jobs annually. Call or write for interview.

THE DESIGN ELEMENT, 8624 Wonderland Ave., Los Angeles CA 90046. (213)656-3293. Creative Director: A. Marshall Licht. Handles art services for magazines, sales brochures, annual reports, book and trade publishers, public relations activities and industrial/documentary/training films. Uses artists for illustrations, cartoons and production. Query with samples or call for interview. SASE.

DESIGNERS 3, INC., 555 5th Ave., New York NY 10017. Contact: Jack Golden. Uses New York City area artists for layout, illustration, retouching and lettering. Handles newspaper, magazine and direct mail art services for clients in pharmaceutical, industrial, public relations, financial and printing fields.

DI FRANZA-WILLIAMSON INC., 1414 Avenue of the Americas, New York NY 10019. (212)832-2343. Creative Director: Seymour Augenbraun. Estab: 1955. Art service firm. Services include design art, mechanicals for packaging, sales promotion and advertising. Clients are manufacturers and advertising agencies. Uses local artists for illustrations, layout, lettering, paste-up and retouching. Assigns 200 freelance jobs annually. Pays $10-12 per hour, mechanicals; $12-15 per hour, layout. Payment determined by time spent. Call for interview. No work returned.

DIAMOND ART STUDIO LTD., 515 Madison Ave., New York NY 10023. (212)355-5444. Creative Director: Sam Diamond. Estab: 1945. Art service firm and studio. Complete graphic service. Clients are advertising agencies, manufacturers and publishers. Uses artists for cartoons, charts, graphs, illustrations, layout, lettering, logo design, paste-up, retouching, technical art and type spec. Assigns approximately 24 freelance assignments annually. Pays $10 minimum. Payment determined by time spent and budget. Write for interview. SASE.

DICKINSON ADVERTISING, 67 Federal Ave., Quincy MA 02169. Assistant Creative Supervisor: Jeff Christo. Art service firm. Clients are travel agencies, nonprofit organizations, industrial and commercial manufacturers and commercial services. Uses local artists for layout, illustration, technical art, paste-up and lettering. Media used: trade magazines, direct mail and custom printing. Send resume and samples.

DONATO & BERKLEY, INC., 370 Lexington Ave., New York NY 10017. (212)532-3884. Contact: Sy Berkley or Mike Donato. Clients are ad agencies, public relations firms, direct ad consumers and publishers. Uses artists for layout, illustration, technical art, type spec, paste-up, lettering and retouching. Media used: newspapers, magazines, billboards and direct mail. Arrange interview.

THE DRAWING BOARD, INC., 101 Park Ave., New York NY 10017. Contact: Stan Levy. Clients are major corporations. Media used: newspapers, magazines and direct mail. Uses artists for layout, illustration, paste-up, retouching and lettering.

ENGINEERED MARKETING OF LONG ISLAND, 80 Winfred Dr., North Merrick NY 11566. Manager: Frank C. Beckert. Prepares advertising in print and broadcast media for political, travel, industrial and lighting clients. Uses artists for technical art, illustration and retouching. Mail samples to: Engineered Marketing of Florida, Richard E. Stember, President, 2350 NE 135th St., North Miami FL 33161.

MEL ERIKSON ART SERVICE, 3180 Expressway Dr. S., Central Islip NY 11722. (516)234-1200. Creative Director: Mel Erikson. Estab: 1969. Art service firm and studio. Services include textbook and brochure production and complete art and composition service. Clients are publishers and electronic, toy and plastic manufacturers. Uses local artists for cartoons, illustrations, layout and paste-up. Assigns 25 freelance jobs annually. Pays $50 for mechanical production work. Payment determined by job. Query with 8½x11" photocopies of work. Reports in 2 weeks. No work returned.

FINN STUDIO LIMITED, 426 E. 73rd, New York NY 10021. (212)861-4574. Creative Director: Finn. Estab: 1969. Art service firm and studio. Services include logo design, T-shirts and illustrations. Clients are theatres, boutiques and magazines. Uses artists for illustrations, layout, lettering, logo design, paste-up and retouching. Assigns 500 freelance jobs annually. Pays $50-5,000, logo; $120-2,000, illustrations; $10-100, simple layout. Payment determined by job. Mail slides of work. Reports in 4 weeks. SASE.

JOHN D. FIRESTONE & ASSOCIATES, 119 W. Waterloo St., Canal Winchester OH 43110. (614)837-4680. Creative Director: Lois A. Firestone. Estab: 1969. Art service firm and studio. Services offered include design, artwork, photography, audiovisual and complete production. Clients are primarily publishers. Uses artists for cartoons, charts, graphs, illustrations, layout, logo design, paste-up, retouching, technical art and type spec. Assigns 300 freelance jobs annually. Pays $10-50, 1-color; $20-75, 2-color; $40-150, 4-color. Payment determined by job or hour. Query with 35mm slides of work. Reports in 2 weeks. SASE.

FIVE-P PROCESSING LABORATORIES INC., 7114 Bellfort, Houston TX 77017. (713)644-1716. Creative Director: Bob Shirley. Estab: 1958. Art service firm and lab. Services include complete color and b&w photographic laboratory work. Clients are businesses, advertising agencies and photographers. Uses local artists for cartoons, charts, graphs, illustrations, lettering, logo design, paste-up, technical art and type spec. Assigns 50 freelance jobs annually. Pays $5-10. Payment determined by hour and/or job. Call for interview. SASE.

Artists are used by Mary Beavers' Studio of Fine Arts for cartoons, graphs, lettering and to fulfill outside contracts for actors, columnists, businesses, public relations firms, political figures, publishers and other clients. Beavers assigns 100-150 jobs annually. This oil on canvas was commissioned from Lena Rea for $100.

FLEX, INC., (Free Lance Exchange, Inc.), 342 Madison Ave., New York NY 10017. (212)682-3042. Creative Director: Roslyn Friedman. Estab: 1968. Art service firm. Services include production and film. Clients are publications, TV, billboard and direct mail firms. Uses artists for cartoons, charts, graphs, illustrations, layout, lettering, logo design and mechanicals. Payment determined by hour or job. Mail resume and samples; "Say you saw the listing in *Art & Crafts Market*." SASE.

FOTO GRAPHIX, 3042 Fillmore St., San Francisco CA 94123. (415)922-6590. Art/Creative Director: Roger Mulkey. Clients are audiovisual firms, ad agencies, marketing and public relations firms and trade magazine publishers. Uses local artists for layout, illustration, technical art, type spec, paste-up, retouching and lettering. Pays $6 per hour, comprehensive layout; $4 per hour, paste-up. Call for interview.

G.P. COLOR LAB, 215 S. Oxford Ave., Los Angeles CA 90004. Contact: Jack Ward. Uses artists for print finishing, airbrush work, flexichrome dye work and retouching primarily June through January. Needs transparency retouching year-round. Write or call.

GAYNOR'S GRAPHICS, 1822 NW Park Place, Oklahoma City OK 73106. (405)524-7474. Creative Director: G. Gaynor Caperton. Estab: 1971. Art service firm and printer. Services include all artwork, logos, letterheads, business cards, brochures, POP displays, technical layout and calligraphy. Clients are manufacturers, medical clinics, law firms, jobbers and realtors. Uses artists for cartoons, illustrations, layout, lettering, technical art and type spec. Assigns 10-25 freelance jobs annually. Payment depends on space, intended use and complexity. Query with credits. Submit finished samples. Reports in 2 weeks. SASE.

GENOVESE/BOKER GRAPHICS, INC., 135 E. 55th St., New York NY 10022. Contact: Alfred Boker. Clients are food manufacturers, magazine publishers, can companies, stationery firms, battery companies, resort areas and liquor manufacturers. Uses artists for illustration and technical art, newspapers, magazines, direct mail and packaging. Mail samples.

DAVID GOULD STUDIO, 415 E. 52nd St., New York NY 10022. Uses artists for advertising art, retouching and technical illustration. Query with resume; then mail samples of original art. All assignments guaranteed. Pays on acceptance. No previously published work.

GRAPHIC ARTS INTERNATIONAL, 60 W. Main St., Bergenfield NJ 07621. (201)385-7676. Creative Director: Richard W. Stalzer. Estab: 1960. Art service firm and studio. Services include art/design. Clients are art directors, editors and production departments in major publishing houses. Uses artists for cartoons, charts, graphs, illustrations, layouts, logo design, paste-up, retouching and technical art. Previously published and simultaneous submissions OK. Assigns 40-60 freelance jobs annually. Pays $5-10 per hour for charts, graphs, paste-up; $7-12 per hour for technical art, layout, retouching; $5-75 per 1-color cartoon, illustration; $8.50-15 per hour for logo and book design. Payment determined by hour or job. Write or call for interview. Submit clean samples that can be photocopied. Work returned upon request.

GRAPHIC CONCERN, INC., 210 E. 53rd St., Suite 4-D, New York NY 10022. (212)759-8248. Art Director: Stanley'R. Konopka. Clients are primarily major book publishers and advertising agencies. Uses artists for layout, illustration, technical art, type spec and paste-up. Submit portfolio. Pays $10-12, comprehensive layout; $8-10 per hour, paste-up.

GRAPHIC DESIGN INC., 23800 Amber, Warren MI 48089. (313)758-0480. Art/Creative Director: Norah K. Gonyou. Clients are automotive manufacturers, large ad agencies and printers. Media used: TV, a magazine, direct mail and catalogs. Uses artists for layout, illustration, technical art, paste-up, lettering and retouching. Submit 4x5" samples of renderings, exploded views, retouching or layout. Minimum payment: $40-100, comprehensive layout; $4-5 per hour, paste-up; $3-6 per hour, typesetting. Arrange to show portfolio.

GRAPHIC PRESENTATION SERVICES INC., 150 Broad Hollow Rd., Melville NY 11746. (212)838-7520 or (516)421-3030. Creative Director: Peter Roccanova. Estab: 1945. Art service firm. Services include design, production, visuals, mechanicals and composition. Clients are publishers and industrial firms. Uses artists in the New York metropolitan area for cartoons, graphs, charts, illustrations, layout, lettering, logo design, paste-up, retouching, technical art and type spec. Previously published and simultaneous submissions OK.

Assigns 100-200 freelance jobs annually. Payment determined by hour or job. Submit tearsheets. SASE.

GRAPHICS INSTITUTE, INC., 42 W. 39th St., New York NY 10018. Art Director: Martin Miller. Design firm. Services include annual reports, booklets, slide shows and corporate identification campaigns. Clients are corporations, public relations firms, and government health and welfare agencies. Uses artists for illustration. Mail samples or arrange interview.

GRIFFITH & CUSTER INC., 38 W. 21st St., New York NY 10010. Contact: Marcia Laredo. Specializes in 4-color catalogs. Uses artists for layout, illustration, type spec, paste-up, lettering and retouching. Prefers local artists. Arrange to show portfolio.

HAMILTON DESIGN & ASSOCIATES, 2130 Arlington Ave., Columbus OH 43221. Contact: William Hamilton. Advertising design studio. Media used: print and direct mail. Uses artists for advertising art and design, container designs, direct mail brochures, graphic and package design, sales promotion art, trademarks and sculpture. Call for interview or mail slides with description or 1-2 original pieces. Pays $150-400 for direct mail brochure design. Reports in 2 weeks. SASE.

HARE PHOTOGRAPHS INC., 5 Johnson Park S., Buffalo NY 14201. (716)853-4114. Contact: William Blumreich. Uses artists for retouching and airbrush work. Mail resume.

HARSH-FINEGOLD INC., 14 E. 60th St., New York NY 10022. (212)752-3720. Creative Director: Rupert Finegold. Estab: 1961. Studio. Services include graphic and book jacket design, direct mail packages, advertisements, logos and mechanicals. Clients are manufacturers, magazines, newspapers, book publishers and service organizations. Uses artists for cartoons, illustrations, lettering, paste-up, retouching and technical art. Assigns 30-75 freelance jobs annually. Pays $25 minimum, spot illustration; $8-12 per hour, mechanicals. Payment determined by job or time spent. Call for interview.

BEN HARVEY GRAPHICS, 105 Havens Mill Rd., Freehold NJ 07728. Uses artists able to meet deadlines for realistic as well as fantasized illustrations for toys, games and general product advertising. Especially needs realistic artists able to draw women and men exceptionally well for cosmetic ads (mostly b&w; some color). Mail samples showing range of styles and techniques. Reports in 3 weeks.

IMAGE STUDIO, Main St., Stockbridge MA 01262. (413)298-5500. Creative Director: Clemens Kalischer. Estab: 1965. Studio. Services include graphic design for brochures, catalogs, posters, signs and exhibits. Clients are institutions, colleges, small businesses, resorts and organizations. Uses artists for illustration, layout, lettering, logo design, paste-up and type spec. Assigns 12-20 freelance jobs annually. Pays $4-6 per hour, mechanicals/paste-up; $5-10 per hour, layout/type spec/lettering; $15-200, illustration; $25-200, logo designs. Payment determined by job and time spent. Query. Reports in 4 weeks. SASE.

KARZEN AND ASSOCIATES, LTD., Suite 229, 2640 Golf Rd., Glenview IL 60025. (312)729-6013. Art/Creative Director: Max Karzen. Art service firm. Services include advertising for newspapers, magazines, billboards, direct mail and posters. Uses artists for layout, illustration, technical art, paste-up, retouching and lettering. Arrange interview.

WARREN A. KASS GRAPHICS, INC., 221 E. 50th St., New York NY 10002. Uses artists for contemporary graphic design, illustration and packaging. Submit resume and samples. Prefers original art but considers tearsheets of previously published work.

LARRY KERBS STUDIOS, INC., 225 E. 57th St., New York NY 10022. (212)759-1040. Contact: Larry Kerbs or Jim Lincoln. Art service firm. Clients are industrial, chemical, insurance and public relations firms. Handles art services for newspapers, trade magazines and direct mail. Uses artists in the New York, New Jersey and Connecticut areas for layout, illustration, technical art, paste-up and retouching. Pays $10-12 per hour, paste-up; $12-14, comprehensive layout. Mail samples or call for interview.

KOPPEL COLOR, 153 Central Ave., Hawthorne NJ 07506. (201)427-3151. Estab: 1952. Creative Director: Wesley Glass. Services include printing of brochures, postcards and related items. Clients are photographers, hotels, motels and small businesses. Uses local artists for cartoons, illustration, layout, lettering, logo design and paste-up. Pays $10 minimum. Payment determined by complexity of job. Call for interview. SASE.

LAWRENCE LEVY DESIGN/FILM, 1001 Maple Ave., Evanston IL 60202. Contact: Lawrence Levy. Clients are book/magazine publishers, and film, filmstrip and game accounts. Uses artists for editorial art for use in books and multimedia programs. Mail samples.

LEWAHL/KC GRAPHICS ADVERTISING, 40 W. 22nd St., New York NY 10010. Art/Creative Director: Hy Wahl. Handles cold typesetting and art services for newspapers, magazines, direct mail, brochures and catalogs for direct manufacturer and trade clients. Uses local artists for layout, illustration, technical art, type spec, paste-up, lettering and retouching. Call for interview.

JACK LUCEY/ART & DESIGN, 84 Crestwood Dr., San Rafael CA 94901. (415)453-3172. Creative Director: Jack Lucey. Estab: 1969. Art service firm and studio. Services include layout, camera-ready art, illustrations (pen and ink, wash, watercolor, oil or acrylic), client counseling, art direction and consumer research. Clients are newspapers, agencies, industry, publishers and printers. Uses artists for fashion illustrating and hand and specialized lettering. Reports in 2 days. SASE.

MARKOW PHOTOGRAPHY, INC., 2222 E. McDowell Rd., Phoenix AZ 85006. (602)273-1651. Contact: Robert Markow. Specializes in commercial, illustrative, public relations, aerial, portrait, advertising and industrial photography. Uses artists for negative retouching, print finishing, spotting and Flexichrome dye work. Submit resume and samples of work.

CHARLES MARTIGNETTE, ASSOCIATES, Box 9295, Boston MA 02114. (617)734-5400. Art Director: Dudley Winchester. Clients are regional and national corporations. Media used: newspapers, TV, radio and magazines. Uses artists for layout, illustration and retouching. Mail artwork. Not responsible for return.

MEISEL PHOTOCHROME CORPORATION, 1330 Conant, Dallas TX 75281. Vice President, Marketing: Dick Davies. Custom-color photography lab. Plants in Atlanta, Seattle and Kansas City. Uses artists for airbrush work, retouching, spotting, print finishing and dye work. Contact individual plants.

MELANSON ASSOCIATES, 77 Summer St., Boston MA 02110. (617)482-1967. Creative Director: Donya Melanson. Estab: 1968. Advertising agency and graphic design firm. Services include complete graphics and advertising. Clients are corporations, banks, publishers, associations and government. Uses artists for cartoons, charts, graphs, illustrations, lettering, logo design, paste-up, retouching and technical art. Previously published and simultaneous submissions OK. Assigns 15-20 freelance jobs annually. Pays $7-20 per hour for illustrations/lettering/logo design; $3.50-12 per hour, paste-up. Payment determined by project. Write for interview. Submit photocopies for file. No original art; slides OK. Reports in 4 weeks. SASE.

MILLER PRESS, 104 Jefferson St., Jacksonville FL 32204. Contact: Alfred Miller, Jr. Specializes in advertising printing. Uses artists for layout, illustration, type spec, technical art and retouching. Mail samples.

ALLEN MOORE DESIGNS, Suite 35C, 40 Harrison St., New York NY 10013. Handles art service for newspapers, TV, radio, magazines, direct mail and other print media. Uses artists for paste-up, layout and lettering. Prefers local artists. Mail samples or call for interview.

CLANCY MORALES AND ASSOCIATES, LTD., Box 9, Wyckoff NJ 07481. (201)891-0138. Art Director: Clancy Morales. Clients are record companies, music/book publishers, radio stations, ad agencies, record/tape manufacturers, album jacket printers and music publications. Pays $50, comprehensive layout; $300, jacket design; $4 per hour, paste-up. Submit photostats of artwork.

MURRAY HILL PRESS, 55 W. 42nd St., New York NY 11710. (212)563-0364. Contact: Ralph Ceisler. Services include "general production (occasionally design) of catalogs, brochures, mailing pieces, etc." Uses local artists for layout, illustration, type spec, paste-up, lettering and retouching. Pay $75 for illustrations. Call for interview.

MYRIAD PRODUCTIONS, 1314 N. Hayworth Ave., Suite 402, Los Angeles CA 90046. (213)851-1400. Executive Producer: Ed Harris. Clients are TV, film recording and concert production firms. Uses artists for layout, illustration, TV graphics and animation. Payment determined by production and distribution. Mail nonreturnable samples. "We are constantly looking for unique artwork in graphics. Artists with unusual work and/or interesting subjects may be considered as guests for television program productions. We are most interested in contemporary themes, and most materials submitted for consideration should reflect this interest."

PENPOINT STUDIOS, INC., 444 Park Ave. S. (The Penthouse), New York NY 10016. Art/Creative Director: Ed Rotkoff. Services include art for newspapers, trade magazines, direct mail and annual reports. Clients are industrial, financial, corporate and computer accounts. Uses local artists for layout, illustration, paste-up, retouching and lettering. Call for interview.

PENSACOLA ENGRAVING CO., 2101 W. Government St., Pensacola FL 32596. Services include printing brochures and publications. Uses artists for layout and illustration. Pays $50 for brochure layout. Mail samples.

HERBERT PINZKE DESIGN, INC., 505 N. Lakeshore Dr., Chicago IL 60611. Creative Director: Herbert Pinzke. Studio handles art services for magazines, manufacturers, real estate developers and movers. Uses artists for layout, illustration, package design, type spec, paste-up and retouching. Prefers local artists. Call for interview or mail samples.

PETER POTTER'S ARTEL STUDIO, 239 Dolan Ave., Gulfport MS 39501. (601)896-8186. Creative Director: Peter Potter. Estab: 1970. Art service, screen printer and textiles firm. Offers full art service for business and industry. Clients are manufacturers, graphics art houses, newspapers, advertising agencies and ad specialty houses. Uses artists for illustration, paste-up and mechanicals for screen-printed pieces. Assigns 20-30 freelance jobs annually. Pays $25-50, spot illustration; $10 per hour, paste-up; $25 minimum, mechanicals. Payment determined by time spent and job. Query with samples. Submit 8x10" b&w photoprints (no originals). Reports in 2 weeks. SASE.

THE PRINTER'S DEVIL, 4501 N. 18th Ave., Phoenix AZ 85015. (602)264-1552. Creative Director: Edd Welsh. Estab: 1973. Graphic arts research and analysis firm. Clients are printers (both commercial and in-plant shops) and related firms in the field of graphic arts: suppliers, commercial artists and agencies. Uses local artists for illustration and technical art. Emphasis is

Successful Selling Comes Through Self Advertising

Self advertising is the key to success in working with studios, says Mary Beavers, studio owner and 37-year art veteran.

"When you first start your career, you should spend a larger percentage of your income, 25% for example, on advertising. My first five years I ran ads continuously in various publications. But after that, I ran them only occasionally."

Another time you should advertise heavily, she adds, is when you're having a slump. "People tend to forget you."

Beavers concludes that the secret to successful freelance advertising work is finding publications — for your ads — that will reach the customers most interested in your type of work and prices. "If you're selling $1,000 paintings, you'd be wasting your money advertising in the free throwaway publications. The more elite publications would be better for that price range."

Mary Beavers

on the financial aspects of graphic arts with more work with charts, graphs and related technical illustrations. Previously published work or simultaneous submissions OK. Assigns 4-6 freelance jobs annually. Pays $15-75 for technical art; determined by job. Query. Reports in 4 weeks.

PROGRESSIVE GRAPHICS, 200 Washington St., Oregon IL 61061. Manager: Harold Goley. Uses artists for advertising art and magazine editorial illustrations.

PROMEDEUS ARTS, INC., 1776 Broadway, New York NY 10019. (212)586-3770. Art Director: Ron Parisi. Creative Director: Lew Morris. Services include art for newspapers, magazines, billboards, direct mail, sales promotion, POP displays and dealer incentives. Clients are record industry and music publishing firms. Uses artists for layout, illustration, type spec, paste-up, retouching and lettering. Call for interview or submit printed samples.

PROVIDENCE GRAVURE INC., Plant 99, W. River St., Providence RI 02904. Contact: Victor Beckerman. Specializes in unusual newspaper preprints and catalogs. "We are interested in conceptual layout people in various specialties. Send resume of credits but no samples until we specify the project." Payment determined by project.

PUBLISHERS' DESIGN AND PRODUCTION SERVICES, INC., 52 Roland St., Charlestown MA 02129. (617)628-9200. Design Director: Larry Taylor. Art services firm. Clients are consumer magazines, text and trade books. Uses artists for book and occasional magazine illustration. Submit tearsheets. Reports in 10 days.

RAPECIS, 17 E. 45th St., New York NY 10017. (212)697-1760. Contact: Robert Bothell. Uses artists for advertising, editorial, promotion and technical illustrations. Especially interested in professionals with medical subject experience.

REVIEW PRINTING COMPANY, 25 SW 2nd Ave., Miami FL 33101. Contact: Lee Ruwitch. Estab: 1926. Specialty is legal, business and financial newspapers. Uses artists for work in illustration and cartoons suitable for business and legal community. Artists may call in person or contact by mail. Payment for cartoons is $1-2.50.

RICHTER PHOTOGRAPHY, 402 NE 72nd St., Seattle WA 98115. (206)523-3734. Contact: Walt Richter. Specializes in advertising, architectural, industrial and illustrative photography. Uses artists for airbrush work and "oil painting portraits" of copy photographs.

S. ROSENTHAL & COMPANY, INC., 9933 Alliance Rd. Cincinnati OH 45242. (513)984-0710. Creative Director: Claire Schwarberg. Estab: 1868. Printing firm. Services offered include direct mail, magazines, catalogs and brochures. Clients are publishers, manufacturers, associations and schools. Uses local artists for illustration, layout and retouching. Assigns a mazimum of 20 freelance jobs annually. Payment maximum determined by job or hour. Query.

ROSS ADVERTISING ART, INC., 527 Madison Ave., New York NY 10022. Contact: Alex Ross. Services include art for magazines, direct mail, annual reports, brochures and sales promotion. Clients are retail chains, industrial firms, manufacturers, pharmaceutical companies and publishers. Uses local artists for layout, illustration, technical art, type spec, paste-up, lettering and retouching. Query.

THE ANDREW ROSS STUDIO, INC., 321 E. 48th St., New York NY 10017. Contact: Andrew Ross. Handles art services for a full range of clients (no fashion) in magazines and direct mail. Uses local artists for illustration, paste-up, lettering and retouching. Call for interview.

DELOS D. ROWE ASSOCIATES, 41 Union Square W., New York NY 10003. (212)929-1933. Creative Director: Delos D. Rowe. Estab: 1946. Art service firm and studio. Services include creative and mechanical art. Clients are book publishers. Uses artists for cartoons, charts, graphs, illustrations, layout, logo design, paste-up and technical art. Assigns 400-500 freelance jobs annually. Negotiates payment. Payment determined by job and/or hour. Query. Reports immediately "unless there is a reason to delay." SASE.

JACK SCHECTERSON ASSOCIATES INC., 6 E. 39th St., New York NY 10016. (212)889-3950. Creative Director: Jack Schecterson. Estab: 1967. Art service firm and studio. Services include product, package and graphic design. Clients are manufacturers. Uses local artists for cartoons, charts, POP/exhibit design, graphs, illustrations, layout, lettering, logo design, paste-up, product/package design, retouching and technical art. Payment determined by hour and/or job. Call for interview. SASE.

CARLA SCHROEDER, 40 Park Ave., New York NY 10016. Creative Director: Carla Schroeder. Estab: 1971. Art service firm. Services include package design and paste-up. Clients are manufacturers. Uses local artists for graphs, logo design, paste-up and technical art. Pays $6-10 per hour for paste-up. Assigns 15-30 freelance jobs annually. Call for interview. Reports in 3-4 days.

ROBERT SCHWARTZ AND ASSOCIATES, 14 E. 60th St., New York NY 10022. (212)935-1952. Creative Director: Robert Schwartz. Estab: 1950. Art service firm and studio. Services include print layouts, mechanicals and brochure design. Clients are publishers, agencies, financial institutions and travel firms. Uses artists for charts, graphs, illustrations, paste-up and technical art. Assigns 5-10 freelance jobs annually. Pays $8-12 per hour for mechanicals. Payment determined by job, hour and/or negotiations. Query. SASE

SHERRY ART, INC., 275 Madison Ave., New York NY 10016. Contact: Paul Sherry. Media used: magazines, direct mail and packaging. Uses local artists for layout, illustration, paste-up and lettering. Call for interview.

SIGNATURE GRAPHICS, 200 Administration Bldg., Rte. 3, Municipal Airport, Ames IA 50010. (515)232-5132. Contact: Art Harrison. Specializes in creative graphics for identity and communication. Uses artists for architectural renderings, landscape design, signs, graphic design and trademarks. Payment determined by job. Arrange interview. Reports in 7 days.

RICHARD SOLAY AND ASSOCIATES, 28 W. 44th St., New York NY 10036. (212)868-4270. Art Director: Susan Lyster. Studio handles art services for TV, magazines, direct mail and wholesale advertising. Clients are book publishers, towel and sheet manufacturers, business machine corporations, restaurants and cigarette companies. Uses artists for lettering, complete advertisements and posters. Query or mail samples.

THINK GROUP, INC., 1034 Lexington Ave., New York NY 10010. (212)988-8121. Art/Creative Director: Emil Dispenza. Handles art services for "*Fortune* 500" companies. Media used: newspapers, magazines, radio, TV, billboards, direct mail, corporate identity programs and annual reports. Uses artists for illustration, technical art and retouching. Call for interview.

TIMOTHY J. TOWNE STUDIO, Box R, Libertyville IL 60048. Contact: Tim Towne. Uses artists for advertising art, billboards, magazine layouts, sales promotion, TV commercials and technical illustration. Prefers Chicago Metropolitan area artists.

TRAFTON AND AUTRY PRINTERS, Box 9068, Amarillo TX 79105. (806)376-4347. Creative Director: Lorren Hallmark. Estab: 1973. Printing firm. Services include layout design through 4-color process printing. Clients are manufacturers and publishers. Uses local artists for illustration, layout, lettering, logo design and retouching. Assigns 20 freelance jobs annually. Pays $15 for layout and finished art. Payment determined by time spent. Call for interview. Submit original layouts or completed pieces. Reports in 2 weeks. SASE.

UNDERWOOD AND UNDERWOOD COLOR LAB, 30 S. Michigan Ave., Chicago IL 60603. Contact: Fred Yamaguchi. Uses artists for airbrush work, spotting, color negative retouching and dye work during September, October, November and December. Artists work at home or in own studios. Query with resume or call for interview.

VISUAL AID SERVICES, 866 United Nations Plaza, New York NY 10017. Uses artists for single and multi-panel cartoons, cartoon strips, displays, editorial cartoons and illustration, graphic designs, layouts, lettering, posters and technical illustration. All assignments guaranteed. Payment determined by budget for a particular project. Query with resume. Will request samples, if desired. Previously published work OK "only if artist accepts responsibility for any complications which might occur." Reports in 1 week.

VISUAL CONCEPTS, 212 E. 48th St., New York NY 10017. (212)935-9852. Contact: Barbara Patinkin. Advertising studio. Services include sales literature for publishers, manufacturers, direct mail firms, employment agencies, nonprofit organizations and other service companies. Media used: newspapers, trade magazines and direct mail. Uses local artists for design, layout, illustration and mechanicals. Pays $6-10 per hour. Payment determined by project.

JEROME VLOEBERGHS, 381 Bush St., Rm. 601, San Francisco CA 94104. (415)982-1287. Art Director: Jerome Vloeberghs. Estab: 1950. Photo retouching firm. Services include transparencies, airbrushing and dye transfer. Clients are advertising agencies and photographers. Uses local artists for illustration and retouching. Pays $20 per hour, retouching b&w; $25 per hour, retouching color. Payment determined by time spent. Query with samples.

DON ZUBALSKY AGENCY, 11284 Sunshine Terrace, Studio City CA 91604. Contact: Donald L. Zubalsky. Uses artists for illustration, paste-up, retouching and lettering.

Architecture

"Neither a five-year architectural education or an architectural license are prerequisites for working as a freelancer in the architectural field. More important is *talent,*" says Frank Adler, a Paramus, New Jersey architect. "There are various jobs for the freelance artist. He can be a freelance designer, freelance draftsman, freelance designer/draftsman, or a renderer. There's no limit."

For artists interested in fine art, calligraphy, cartography, stained glass and interior design, there are markets in the architectural field.

In addition to the places listed in this section, you can learn what projects are being developed in your area by visiting the library and following up on construction reports published by community building contractors' associations.

Once you obtain a list of the firms working in your area, call for an appointment or send a letter introducing yourself and your talents. Tell them why your work might be of interest to them and include photos or illustrations of your previous work.

The most impressive method of presenting photos and information on your experience to an architect or interior designer is to develop a brochure, says Scott Smitherman of Somdal Associates. "Every time I want to see an architect's art, I have to ask him to send samples, and then I have to send them back. Even with postage paid, this is a pain. With brochures I can keep them in my file and flick through them to find the work I like."

The cost of having brochures printed varies. Smitherman says 500 1-page fold-out color brochures cost approximately $250. (Exact estimates can be obtained from printers in your area.)

Response to a query letter or brochure is the exception, rather than the rule, when dealing with architectural firms. Most architects file material upon receipt until they have a specific need which they feel you can best fulfill.

When an assignment does come your way, keep the following points in mind:

"When working on renderings, the artist should make certain the assignment has been spelled out clearly. Then, he should make a layout and show it to whomever he is working with prior to working on the final rendering," says Adler.

Harold Van Niel of Seibert Worley Cady Kirk Partners Inc., adds that the artist should "be able to present drawings explaining his concepts so the client and architectural firm can understand his idea. It is important to have architectural sensitivity."

"When you're commissioned to do work, your primary function is to please your customer. Your work should also please you; but, remember your client is paying the bill. If you're on the ball though, you should be able to convince them that yours is the right way," concludes Adler.

More insight on the architectural field can be obtained by reading *Architectural Design.* Other trade publications of interest include *Lighting Design & Application, Residential Interiors, Interiors* and *Stained Glass.*

A BARREL N' CRATE INC., 200 Crandon Blvd., Key Biscayne FL 33149. (305)361-2098. Contact: Helyn L. Boyajian. Estab: 1963. Interior design and landscape firm. Uses artists for architectural renderings; building interiors; calligraphy; full-color renderings; graphic, interior, industrial and landscape design; murals; paintings; room sketches; sculpture; and signs. Commercial clients. Pays $100 minimum for renderings. Payment determined by job. Query first with photos. Reports in 1 week. SASE. Looks for efficiency and methods.

D. GAIL ABBEY & ASSOCIATES, Box 18010-A, Baton Rouge LA 70803. Landscape architecture firm. Uses artists for architectural renderings. Query with resume and photos or photocopies of work. Reports in 10 days.

HAROLD ABEL INTERIORS, 301 W. Hallandale Beach Blvd., Hallandale FL 33009. (305)927-9774. Contact: Suzanne L. Abel. Estab: 1968. Interior design firm. Uses artists for architectural and full-color renderings, building interiors, landscape design, murals, original art, paintings and wall art. Residential clients. Assigns 50-75 freelance jobs annually; local artists only. Payment determined by job. Send resume and photos of work for file and possible future assignments.

FRANK ADLER ARCHITECT, 54 Rte. 17, Paramus NJ 07652. (201)843-5248. Contact: Frank Adler. Estab: 1963. Architectural, interior design and landscape firm. Uses local artists for architectural, art and full-color renderings, graphic and interior design, and model buildings. Residential, commercial and industrial clients. Assigns 5 freelance jobs annually. Pays $250-500, renderings; $275-750, models. Payment determined by job. Query or call for interview. Contacts artists as needs arise.

ALFRED ALLEN ASSOCIATES, 331 W. 18th St., New York NY 10011. Contact: Allen Isaacs. Architectural interior design firm. Uses artists for architectural renderings and interior/landscape design. Arrange interview.

ALTMAN-SAICHEK ASSOCIATES, 300 W. Washington, Chicago IL 60606. Contact: S. Altman. Uses artists for architectural renderings. Will look at original art samples, tearsheets or photocopies of previously published work. Query with statement of professional credits and training. Artwork is usually casein or watercolor; 23x30" or 24x36". Assignments are guaranteed. Buys all rights. Pays on acceptance. Prefers to deal directly with artist.

ARCHITECTS TEAM ASSOCIATES, 425 E. 5th St., Cincinnati OH 45202. Uses artists for architectural renderings. Occasionally commissions fine art, sculpture and garden sculpture. Submit samples. SASE.

ARCHITECTS UNLIMITED, 9433 Montgomery Rd., Cincinnati OH 45243. Contact: Donald Pansiera. Uses artists for architectural renderings, building interiors and interior design. Payment determined by job. Arrange interview by sending resume and samples.

ART-IN-ARCHITECTURE PROGRAM, U.S. General Services Administration, 18th and F Sts. NW, Washington DC 20405. (202)566-0950. Director: Donald Thalacker. Estab: 1963. Uses artists to create works as an integral part of federal architecture, including murals, original art, sculpture and tapestries. Assigns an average of 20 freelance jobs annually. Pays $750-250,000 for original art. Payment determined by job. Mail nonreturnable 35mm slides and resume. Reports in 4 weeks. Recent freelance assignments include exterior sculpture by George Segal; oil on canvas murals by Jack Beal; and kinetic sculpture by George Rickey.
To Break In: "Getting exposure is usually the key to getting more exposure. Even if you're not selected for a commission, your work has at least been seen and studied. And once your work has been seen, somebody may remember it. If one panelist thinks your work is excellent and another says he's heard of you, your chances of being selected are improved. Don't waste time and money creating a design to submit to the panel. Send slides of completed work. And send quality slides. Even if your work is great, a poor slide won't sell it. On the other hand, if the work isn't really great, but it's photographed to advantage, it's possible to be accepted. Though many commissioned works have been done by big names like Alexander Calder and George Segal, there is plenty of room for locally and regionally-known artists. Of the 20 artists we accept annually from about 1,000 applications, there are as many local and regional artists as there are nationally-known people."

BOB BABA AND ASSOCIATES, 6101 N. Arlington Blvd., San Pablo CA 94806. Public Relations Director: Marjorie A. Nault. Uses artists for direct mail brochures, master plan transparencies, models and environmental impact reports. Payment negotiable, "dependent on the project budget." Query with samples.

BACKUS ASSOCIATES, INC., 370 Neeb Rd., Cincinnati OH 45238. Contact: Harry Backus. Uses local artists for room sketches and full-color renderings. Commercial clients. "One of the qualities we look for in artists with whom we work is the ability to provide renderings that will 'promote' the sale of the project!"

BARRY BANNETT ARCHITECT, 20 Kings Hwy. W., Haddonfield NJ 08033. Uses artists for architectural/art renderings, building interiors and interior/landscape design. Arrange interview.

BARBITTA, JAMES & ASSOCIATES, INC., 576 Diagonal Rd., Akron OH 44320. Uses artists for architectural renderings. Payment determined by job. Arrange interview or mail photos or transparencies of work.

HARLAND BARTHOLOMEW AND ASSOCIATES, 201 E. Cary St., Suite 301, Richmond VA 23219. Contact: Kenneth W. Poore. Uses artists for planning, engineering and landscape architecture. Query with resume and printed samples.

BARRY BENEPE, 24 W. 40th St., New York NY 10018. (212)868-2630. Contact: Barry Benepe. Estab: 1975. Architectural and planning firm. Uses artists for architectural and full-color renderings, graphic design and urban planning; especially needs completed and installed signs. Nonprofit and public clients. Assigns 1-4 freelance jobs annually. Pays $200-500, renderings; $50-200, graphics; $40-500+, signs (if installed). Payment determined by job and/or time spent. Query with photos, transparencies or printed graphics. Renderings should be guache on board with acetate covering or matting. Reports in 1 week or as assignments arise. Recently assigned freelancer a layout and finished drawing of market site plan (perspective layout and 4 renderings of market).

NATHAN BERNSTEIN ASSOCIATES, 1991 Lee Rd., Cleveland OH 44118. Contact: Nathan Bernstein. Architectural and engineering firm. Uses local artists for architectural and art renderings, building interiors, landscape design, room sketches and signs. Commercial and industrial clients. Assigns 20 freelance jobs annually. Payment determined by job and negotiation. Call for interview. Reports in 1 week.

JOAN BLUTTER/DESIGNS, 1343 Merchandise Mart, Chicago IL 60654. Interior design firm. Uses artists for art renderings, interior/landscaping/furniture/textile design, room sketches, full-color renderings and original art. Residential and commercial clients.

RICHARD L. BOWEN, AIA AND ASSOCIATES, 13124 Shaker Square, Cleveland OH 44120. Uses artists for architectural renderings, interior design, building interiors and urban planning materials. Query with resume or mail samples. Reports in 10 days.

IRVING BOWMAN & ASSOCIATES, 910 Quarrier St., Charleston WV 25327. Uses artists for architectural renderings, building interiors and landscape design. Payment determined by job. Submit resume and photos or transparencies of work. Reports in 10 days.
To Break In: "(1) We want to look at a rough-out of the perspective for approval prior to proceeding with the final rendering, in case we would like to change the viewpoint to emphasize one feature or another. (2) We like to have a cost estimate before authorizing the work. (3) We prefer shipment by United Parcel Service (for speed). (4) Generally we expect the final rendering within 2 weeks after approving the roughed-out sketch. (5) We send sample pieces of the brick, marble, wood or other important materials involved."

BRIDGERS, TROLLER ASSOCIATES, (formerly Bridgers Troller & Hazlett), 5336 Fountain Ave., Los Angeles CA 90029. Contact: Howard Troller. Uses artists for architectural renderings, graphic design, urban walls, landscape design, garden sculpture, trademarks, signs and site plans. Pays $10-20 per hour. Arrange interview. Works on personal basis.
To Break In: "We especially value an artist who can sketch quickly and cleanly in pencil, an idea given by the office, usually an outdoor scene. Sometimes we bring the artist in house to become part of the design process."

ANDREW DANIEL BRYANT AIA AND ASSOCIATES, 223 Missouri Ave. NW, Washington DC 20011. Uses artists for architectural renderings, landscape design and urban planning materials. Payment determined by job. Submit photos or transparencies of work.

BUCHER MEYERS & ASSOCIATES, INC., AIA, 8777 1st Ave., Silver Spring MD 20910. Contact: Alan R. Meyers. Uses artists for architectural renderings, interior/graphic design and original artwork. Works on commission basis. Payment determined by job. Mail photos or transparencies of work or query with resume.

BURKLEW DESIGN ASSOCIATES, INC., 4935 Wyaconda Rd., Rockville MD 20852. Contact: Vivian Pack. Estab: 1973. Uses local artists for room sketches, full-color renderings, wall art and murals. Commercial clients.

CADMAN, DROSTE & THOMAS, 405 Broadway, Troy NY 12180. Contact: B.M. Cadman. Architectural, engineering and planning firm. Uses artists for graphic and sculptural projects, interior design, building interiors, art and architectural renderings and model buildings. Public, housing and university clients. Negotiates payment. Query with resume, or mail photos or transparencies of work. Interview arranged "only when specific project is upcoming." Reports in 10 days. Seeks "sensitivity to architectural concepts" in artwork.

CHARLES CAPLINGER PLANNERS, 2609 Canal St., New Orleans LA 70119. Contact: Stephen Caplinger. Landscape architecture firm. "We are a small firm which engages mostly in urban design and park work—renovation of old neighborhoods and parks, new urban plazas and pedestrian ways." Uses artists for architectural renderings, urban walls, garden sculpture, signs and industrial sculpture. Mail photos or transparencies of work. Reports in 30 days.

S. FRED CARBONE, AIA & ASSOCIATES, 505 S. Lenola Rd., Moorestown NJ 08057. Uses artists for architectural renderings and building interior/landscape design. Prefers tempera renderings. Pays $350 for 2x3' rendering. Requires an ability to interpret architectural sketches and verbal descriptions. Commercial clients. Mail samples.

CARELLY SELEINE ASSOCIATES, INC., 7122½ Topanga Canyon Blvd., Canoga Park CA 91304. Uses artists for art renderings (interior and exterior); advertising, ceramic, cover, furniture, graphic, interior and landscape design; lettering; posters; spot drawings; signs; technical illustration; urban walls; exhibits; and window/door lettering. All work is contemporary. Previously published work OK. Pays for final work on acceptance. Query with resume. Buys all rights. Reports in 60 days.

CARMICHAEL-KEMP, ARCHITECTS, 2870 Los Feliz Place, Los Angeles CA 90039. (213)666-1265. Contact: Richard J. Kemp. Estab: 1959. Architectural firm. Uses artists for architectural renderings, model buildings, statuary, sculpture, graphic design, murals, mosaics and stained glass. Institutional clients. Assigns 2-10 freelance jobs annually. Pays $100-1,000+, architectural renderings; $300-2,500+, model-building; $25-60 per square foot standard fee, installed stained glass; $15-45 standard fee, installed mosaic work. Payment determined by job, degree of difficulty and/or size. Phone for interview; must have portfolio, brochure and samples of work (photos OK). Contacts freelancers as assignments arise. SASE. Recently assigned freelance architectural rendering, stained glass, statuary and sculpture work for a Roman Catholic church.
To Break In: "Have a well-organized portfolio and present it briefly."

THE CARRIAGE HOUSE INTERNATIONAL, 5800 State, Saginaw MI 48603. (517)799-1110. Contact: A. Van Vlaenderen. Estab: 1953. Interior design firm. Uses artists for interior design, graphics, paintings, room sketches, sculpture, signs and wall art. Residential, commercial and industrial clients. Assigns 12-15 freelance jobs annually. Payment determined by job and/or degree of difficulty. Mail photos of work. Reports in 3 weeks.

THOMAS PAUL CASTRONOVO, ARCHITECT, 1175 Main St., Akron OH 44310. Uses artists for architectural and art renderings, interior/landscape design, building interiors and model-building. Residential and commercial clients. Payment determined by job. Mail slides or b&w photos of work. Reports in 10 days.

CHATELAIN, SAMPERTON, AND CARCATERRA, 1625 K St. NW, Washington DC 20006. Contact: Leon Chatelain III. Uses artists for architectural renderings, models, artwork and interior design. Renders services for commercial projects (office buildings and banks), educational projects and public buildings for local, state and federal clients. Payment determined by job. Arrange interview or query with resume. Reports in 1 week.

WILLIAM A. CIOTTO & ASSOCIATES/ARCHITECTS, 309 S. 13th St., Philadelphia PA 19107. Contact: William A. Ciotti. Architectural firm. Uses artists for architectural renderings. Industrial clients. Assigns up to 2 freelance jobs annually. Pays $500 minimum. Payment determined by job. Query with photos of work. Reports immediately if artist contacts by phone or in person. SASE.

FREDERICK P. CLARK ASSOCIATES, 29 Locust Ave., Rye NY 10580. (914)967-6540. Contact: David J. Portman. Uses artists for architectural renderings, landscape design, urban planning materials, charts and maps. Mail photos or transparencies of work.

L. C. CLAY INTERIOR DECORATING AND REMODELING COMPANY, 3405 Venice Blvd., Los Angeles CA 90018. Uses artists for interior design.

COE & VAN LOO, 4550 N. 12th St., Phoenix AZ 85014. (602)264-6831. Contact: Dean F. Ashworth. Estab: 1956. Architectural, golf course architectural, landscape architectural and engineering firm. Uses artists for architectural/art renderings, building interiors, full-color renderings, graphic/landscape design, model buildings, site plans and urban planning materials. Residential and commercial clients. Assigns 1-10 freelance jobs annually. Pays $35-300, renderings; $100-1,000, models. Payment determined by job, time spent and/or contract. Query first (with or without transparencies of work). Reports in 2 weeks. SASE. Recently paid local artist $2,500 for Single-Tree-Ranch development, preparation of model and 6 renderings.

RAY COLLINS ASSOCIATES, 7520 Red Rd., Suite J, South Miami FL 33143. Contact: Ray Collins. Uses artists for architectural renderings, graphic design and garden sculpture. Payment determined by job. Submit samples or call for interview. Reports in 15 days.

DAVID FRANCIS COSTA, JR. & ASSOCIATES, 210 S. Ellsworth St., Albany OR 97321. (503)926-2263. Contact: David Francis Costa, Jr. Estab: 1958. Architectural firm. Uses out-of-town artists for architectural/full-color renderings, graphic/landscape design, model buildings, original art, paintings and sculpture. Commercial clients. Assigns minimum of 2 freelance jobs annually. Pays $275-600, architectural renderings; $100 minimum, original art; $1,000 minimum, sculpture. Payment determined by degree of difficulty. Query. Reports in 7 days. SASE.

COULTER ASSOCIATES, Box 912, Durham NC 27702. Contact: Ken Coulter or Will Hooker. Uses artists for architectural renderings, urban walls, garden sculpture and signs. "Our firm uses the concept of regionalism. For this reason we prefer local artists, or artists with a knowledge of this section of the country." Payment determined by job. Mail photos or transparencies of work.

CREATIVE DESIGNS, INC., 3829 N. 3rd St., Phoenix AZ 85012. Contact: Al Gustave. Interior design firm. Residential and commercial clients. Uses artists for producing wall art. Send resume and photos of work to keep on file for future assignments.

CUMMINGS BUCCI & ASSOCIATES, 758 E. Pico Blvd., Los Angeles CA 90021. Contact: Bob Bucci. Landscape architecture firm. Uses artists for architectural renderings and site plans. Payment determined by job. Mail samples. Reports in 10 days.

CURTIS-RASMUSSEN & ASSOCIATES, AIA, 122 Broad Blvd., Cuyahoga Falls OH 44224, or Quaker Square, 120 E. Mill St., Suite 408, Akron OH 44308. Contact: Ted Curtis. Uses artists for architectural renderings, building interiors and interior design. Query or submit photos or transparencies of work. Reports in 30 days.

DAFT-McCUNE-WALKER, INC., 300 E. Joppa Rd., Baltimore MD 21204. Contact: Bob Gallvin. Uses artists for architectural renderings. Pays $50 minimum for renderings. Mail samples.

DAVIS-SISKA & ASSOCIATES, 799 Roosevelt Road Bldg., Suite 305B, Glen Ellyn IL 60137. Contact: Dale E. Siska. Landscape architecture firm. Uses local artists for architectural renderings and calligraphy. Mail resume. Payments are usually by written contract from artists for specific job. Contract amount dependent on nature and scope of work for project.

A. DEWITT DAY & ASSOCIATES, 4566 Office Park Dr., Jackson MS 39206. Contact: A. Dewitt Day. Landscape architecture and planning firm. Uses artists for architectural renderings, graphic design and garden sculpture. Mail transparencies or photos of work. "We allow the artists to work directly with our clients. We approve space, size, color, etc. only. Clients also pay directly to the artist—we add nothing to the cost of the artist's work itself."

DERR & CORNACHIONE, ARCHITECTS, 2830 Copley Rd., Akron OH 44321. Contact: Paul Lorentzen. Uses artists for architectural renderings and building interiors. Payment determined by job. "Our office concentrates primarily in the commercial, industrial and religious areas, and generally on a medium size scale rather than high-rise or expansive projects." Most renderings are in tempera or opaque medium. Arrange interview.

DESIGN AND LIGHT, INC., 225 Madison Ave., Morristown NJ 07960. (201)377-6656. Contact: David C. Washington. Estab: 1965. Uses artists for room sketches, full-color renderings, wall art and murals. Mostly residential clients. "All work done on professional fee only."

THE DESIGN STUDIO, Petermann Office Bldg., Hwy. 44 E., Yazoo City MS 39194. (601)746-4804. Contact: Carolyn Perry Shipp ASID. Estab: 1976. Interior design firm. Uses artists for original art, paintings, sculpture, signs and wall art. Residential customers. Assigns 3-4 freelance jobs annually. Pays 25% of client's payment. Payment determined by the job and/or degree of difficulty. Mail photos of work. Reports in 3 weeks.

JOHN G. DIECKMANN (ASID), 2825 SW 81st Ave., Miami FL 33155. (305)264-6738. Contact: John Dieckmann. Estab: 1969. Architectural and interior design firm. Uses artists for interior design. Residential and commercial clients. Pays $100, renderings; $150, murals; $50-250, paintings/wall graphics. Payment determined by job and/or hour. Query with photos or transparencies. Reports in 2 weeks.

DOME—THE IMAGE DESIGN CONCEPTS, Box 69722, West Hollywood CA 90069. Contact: Angie Sheldon. Interior design firm. Uses artists for original art, full-color renderings, sculpture, wall art and custom design/execution of furniture or accessories. Prices for original art are up to $3,000. Firm also uses signed and numbered editions at more marketable prices in large quantities. Sculptures bring maximum $1,500 for originals. Somtimes needs large scale and outdoor works. Submit resume and photos of work to keep on file for future assignments.

WILLIAM DORSKY ASSOCIATES, 23200 Chagrin Blvd., Cleveland OH 44122. (216)464-8600. Contact: Curt Johnson. Estab: 1960. Architectural firm. Uses artists for architectural and full-color renderings, building interiors, graphics and landscape design, model buildings, murals, original art, paintings, sculpture, signs and wall art. Commercial clients. Call for interview (bring photos or transparencies of work).

DURYEA AND WILHELMI, PROFESSIONAL CORP., 1208 James St., Syracuse NY 13203. Contact: Henry P. Wilhelmi. Uses local artists for architectural renderings, graphic design, urban walls, trademarks, signs and industrial sculpture. Payment determined by job. Mail photos or transparencies. Samples promptly returned.

BETTY D. EASTIN, ASID, Bryan Station Pike, Rte. 9, Lexington KY 40505. Contact: Betty Eastin. Uses artists for original art. Residential customers.

EDAW, INC., 915 Fort St., Suite 410, Honolulu HI 96813. (808)536-1074. Contact: Richard Senelly. Estab: 1932. Landscape firm. Uses local artists for architectural renderings, original art, sculpture, signs and statuary. Commercial clients. Assigns maximum of 5 freelance jobs annually. Pays $100-500 for renderings. Payment determined by job. Query with 8x10" photos of work. Reports in 2 weeks. SASE.

RICHARD HENRY EISELT, 398 S. Grant Ave., Columbus OH 43215. (614)221-1013. Contact: Richard Henry Eiselt. Estab: 1920. Architectural and interior design firm. Uses artists for architectural and full-color renderings, graphic and interior design, paintings, sculpture, signs and wall art. Commercial clients. Payment determined by job, time spent and degree of difficulty. Mail photos or transparencies of work.

ELLERBE ARCHITECTS, 1660 L St. NW, Washington DC 20036. (202)293-4250. Contact: Mas Habashi. Estab: 1968. Architectural firm. Uses artists for architectural renderings, landscape design, signs and wall art. Commercial and institutional clients. Assigns 4-5 freelance jobs annually. Pays $30-650 for renderings. Payment determined by job. Query or write for interview. Reports in 2 weeks. SASE. Recently assigned freelancer to develop rendering for Oneology Center.

ENVIRONMENTAL IMPACT PLANNING CORP., 319 11th St., San Francisco CA 94103. (415)626-9034. Vice President: Russell Faure-Brac. Consultant firm engaged in environmental impact reporting. Mail samples of charts and maps (photos/transparencies). Pays $6.50 per hour.

ERNST, PAYER, AND ASSOCIATES, 1420 Keith Bldg., Cleveland OH 44115. Uses artists for architectural renderings or building interiors. Payment determined by job. Mail slides or photos of work.

FANNING & HOWEY, 540 E. Market St., Celina OH 45822. Contact: Al Siegfried. Uses artists for architectural renderings and graphic/landscape design. Payment determined by job. Mail photos or transparencies of work, or arrange interview. Reports in 3-4 days, "if there is a need for service on a current project."

FREE DESIGN INTERIORS, 209 Webster Ave., Yazoo City MS 39194. Contact: Carolyn Perry Shipp. Uses artists for creative art, wall sculpture and hangings for residential work. Also uses wall art, murals and statuary. Has paid $1,000 for original oil; $500 for wall hanging.

GALERIA MARIA LUISA, 320 S. Mission Dr., San Gabriel CA 91776. (213)282-5105 or 289-3729. Contact: Maria Luisa Ramirez. Estab: 1973. Interior design firm. Uses artists for murals, original art, paintings, sculpture, wall art and furniture design. "Uniqueness is important because I advertise every piece of work as one-of-a-kind." Residential customers. Assigns 16 freelance jobs annually. Pays $400 for framed oil on canvas. Payment determined by job. Mail photos of work. Reports in 3 weeks. SASE.

GEOMEGA PLANNING SERVICES, 13437 Ventura Blvd., Suite 101, Sherman Oaks CA 91423. (213)788-3981. Contact: Julian Montrose. Estab: 1974. Environmental planning firm. Uses artists for graphic design, mapping and urban planning exhibits. Residential and commercial clients. Assigns 3-5 freelance jobs annually; local artists only. Pays $5 per hour for mapping. Payment determined by degree of difficulty and/or time spent. Query. Reports in 2 weeks. SASE. Recently assigned stationery design and urban planning cartography to freelancers.

RUTH GLANTZ INTERIORS, 40 Sun Valley Way, Morris Plains NJ 07950. Contact: Ruth Glantz. Design firm. Estab: 1965. Uses local artists for room sketches, original art, full-color renderings, sculpture and statuary. Commercial and private clients. Pays $750 for renderings.

GLASER & MYERS AND ASSOCIATES, INC., 2753 Erie Ave., Cincinnati OH 45208. President: Russell C. Myers. Uses artists for architectural renderings, building interiors, interior/landscape design and urban planning graphics assignments. Model builders used consistently. Firm provides architectural service for institutional, commercial and industrial accounts, schools, office buildings, churches and retail buildings, Also constructs zoological displays; does master planning work. Prefers exterior renderings in tempera; interior renderings in tempera or watercolor. Payment determined by job. Pays $100-5,000. Query with resume and photos. Reports in 10 days.

GODWIN-BOHM-NBBJ, (formerly Nitschke-Godwin-Bohm, Planners, Architects & Graphic Designers), 505 S. High St., Columbus OH 43215. (614)224-7145. Contact: Howard McLean. Architectural, interior design and landscape firm. Uses artists for architectural/art/full-color renderings, building interiors, graphic/interior/landscape design, model buildings, original art, room sketches, signs, site plans, trademarks and urban planning materials. Payment negotiated; determined by hour and job. Call or write for interview. Reports in 1-2 weeks.

GOLLEHON SCHEMMER & ASSOCIATES, INC., 988 Woodcock Rd., Suite 220, Orlando FL 32803. Contact: L.W. Hughes. Estab: 1959. Architectural, landscape and engineering firm. Uses artists for architectural and full-color renderings, building interiors and model buildings. Commercial and industrial clients. Assigns 5 freelance jobs annually. Pays $150-350, renderings; $500-750, model buildings. Payment determined by job. Query with photos. Reports in 1 week. SASE.

W.A. GOULD AND ASSOCIATES, 1404 E. 9th St., Cleveland OH 44114. Architects and city planners. Uses artists for a full range of projects including maps, presentations, architectural models, interior design, street furniture, street signs for new communities and brochures. Payment determined by job. Submit resume and fee schedule.

THE WALTER HARRIS COMPANY, 506 E. Camelback Rd., Phoenix AZ 85012. Contact: Wayne Chaney. Interior design firm. Uses artists for full-color and ink renderings. Designs are for commercial applications. Prefers professionals in the immediate geographical area.

ERIC HILL ASSOCIATES, INC., 4124 Boulevard Center Dr., Jacksonville FL 32207. Vice President: Lewis L. Dismukes. Planning consultant firm. Uses Jacksonville area artists for the preparation of annual reports, architectural renderings and report charting. Pays $5 an hour minimum. Query with resume.

LAWRENCE. C. HILTON/ARCHITECTS, INC., 2761 Erie Ave., Cincinnati OH 45208. Uses artists for architectural renderings, interior design, building interiors and landscape design. Payment determined by job. Arrange interview.

RALPH A. HODGES, INTERIORS, 825 NE 28th St., Ft. Lauderdale FL 33308. Contact: Ralph A. Hodges. Uses artists for room sketches, original art, sculpture and wall art. Payment negotiated. Residential clients. Looks for "individual style."

JOHN HOLLOWELL & ASSOCIATES, 201 E. Liberty, Ann Arbor MI 48108. Contact: John Hollowell. Uses artists for graphic design and garden sculpture. Payment determined by job or time spent. Query with samples. Reports in 20 days.

THE HOUSE BY MARJORIE, 2631 Erie Ave., Cincinnati OH 45208. Contact: Marjorie Smith. Interior design firm. Uses local artists for room sketches and full-color renderings. Primarily residential clients.

HOWARD, NEEDLES, TAMMEN & BERGENDOFF, 1805 Grand Ave., Kansas City MO 64108. Art Director: Don Stevens. Specializes in commercial and industrial architectural projects. "Although we have in-house staff, we do need outside overload help on occasions." Architectural renderings preferred in tempera and watercolor, size 30x40". Payments range from $200-400. Occasionally uses local model builders and artists to superimpose architectural projects and highway projects on aerial photo mosaics. Freelance assignments would include interior design and architectural type delineations. Query with samples.

GEORGE R. HUNT & ASSOCIATES, 341 Birchwood Dr., Garland TX 75043. (214)270-4675. Contact: George R. Hunt. Estab: 1969. Landscape firm. Uses artists for graphic and landscape design, model buildings, sculpture, signs, statuary, fiber design and stitchery. Residential and commercial clients. Assigns 2-5 freelance jobs annually. Pays $200-5,000, sculpture. Payment determined by job, time spent and/or degree of difficulty. Query. Reports in 3 weeks. SASE. Recently assigned freelancer to develop model for land plan development; paid $400.
Special Needs: May require artists for downtown project in '78 (sculpture and fountains). "Also looking for craft guilds that would be interested in displaying in Dallas downtown convention area."

IGLEBURGER HENDERSON NOWAK, 1612 Prosser Ave., Dayton OH 45409. (513)294-3394. Contact: Igleburger, Henderson or Nowak. Estab: 1963. Architectural and landscape firm. Uses artists for architectural renderings, building interiors, full-color renderings and landscape design. Residential, commercial and industrial clients. Assigns 2-3 freelance jobs annually; out-of-town freelancers only. Pays $175-300 for color sketches. Payment determined by degree of difficulty and/or job. Submit photos or work by mail. Recently assigned color perspective of church.

IT'S A SMALL WORLD, (formerly Mary Jane Graham Interiors), 542 Linclon Ave., Winnetka IL 60093. (312)446-8399. Contact: Mary Jane Graham. Estab: 1972. Interior design firm. Uses artists for model buildings and rooms. Residential clients. Assigns 365 freelance jobs annually. Pays $1,200 maximum, miniature furniture and doll houses. Payment determined by degree of difficulty. Mail photos or designs. Reports in 3 weeks. SASE.

JAMES INTERIORS, INC., 2733 Riverland Rd., Ft. Lauderdale FL 33312. (305)581-8028. Contact: James R. James or Robert C. Barnes. Estab: 1956. Interior design firm. Uses artists for graphic and landscape design, murals, original art, paintings, sculpture, signs and wall art. Residential and commercial clients. Pays $15-3,000 for wall art; payment for other art "is totally dependent on the time, the service and the client." Query or call for personal interview. Reports in 1 week. SASE. Recently assigned 48 wall lithos for public areas.

JAMES M. JENNINGS ASSOCIATES, Box 5762, Columbus OH 43221. Contact: J.M Jennings. Estab: 1965. Planning and development firm. Uses local artists for architectural and full-color renderings, graphic and landscape design, model buildings, site plans, urban planning materials, brochures and reports. Commercial clients. Assigns 2-5 freelance jobs annually. Pays $200 minimum, illustrations. Payment determined by job. Query. Reports in 2 weeks. SASE. Looks for capability, dependability and ability to meet deadlines. Recently assigned artist to illustrate brochure for community report.

JAMES HALL JONES, 452 E. 5th St., Cincinnati OH 45202. Architect. Uses artists for architectural renderings and building interiors. Mail samples.

MARY K. INTERIORS, INC., 2400 Market St., Harrisburg PA 17105. (717)233-6575. Contact: Mary V. Knackstedt. Estab: 1958. Uses artists for room sketches, original art, full-color renderings, wall art, murals, sculpture and statuary. Residential and commercial clients.

GEROLD F. KESSLER & ASSOCIATES, INC., 2101 S. Clermont, Denver CO 80222. (303)756-1536. Contact: Art Buyer. Estab: 1962. Landscape architectural firm. Uses local freelancers for delineation model buildings, site plans and subdivision development layout. Residential and industrial clients. Assigns 3 freelance jobs annually. Pays $500-700, landscape and general site renderings; $600-1,000, subdivision land plan. Payment determined by job and/or time spent. Query with photos or brochures of work. Reports in 1 week. SASE.

BALLARD H.T. KIRK & ASSOCIATES, INC., 1392 King Ave., Columbus OH 43212. Contact: William N. Wilcox. Uses artists for architectural/art renderings, interior/landscaping design and graphics. Submit resume or arrange interview. Reports in 7 days.

Landscape, architectural and full-color renderings are all of interest to Land Design Associates. This marker rendering by Salvatore Coco earned the artist $200 from the firm. A Land Design customer ordered this rendering to demonstrate the style of architecture they were using for a planned unit development.

LEWIS D. KLEIN, AIA, 1508 N. Main St., Dayton OH 45405. Specializes in commercial, industrial and multi-family dwellings. Uses artists for architectural/art renderings and building interiors. Also uses model builders. Payment determined by job. Submit transparencies or b&w photos of work.
To Break In: "Freelance artists we use must be able to properly interpret working and/or architectural drawings."

DONALD R. KNOX INC., Box 3968, Greenville DE 19807. Landscape architect. Uses artists for architectural renderings, graphic/landscape design and signage systems. Payment determined by job. Submit resume and samples, or arrange interview. Reports in 14 days.

GEORGE J. KONTOGIANNIS & ASSOCIATES, 380 S. 5th St., Suite 1, Columbus OH 43215. Occasionally uses freelance artists for architectural renderings. Payment on a per job basis. Submit transparencies or photos of work. Reports in 30 days.

KORTE INTERIORS LTD., 36 W. Villard St., Dickinson ND 58601. (701)225-6317. Contact: Dick Korte. Estab: 1963. Occasionally uses artists for room sketches and full-color renderings. Residential and commercial clients.

LAND DESIGN ASSOCIATES, 91 Green St., Huntington NY 11743. Contact: Robert Manniello. Estab: 1971. Landscape architectural firm. Uses local artists for landscape, architectural and full-color renderings. Commercial clients. Assigns 10-15 freelance jobs annually. Pays $100-300 for renderings. Payment determined by job and/or time spent. Mail photos or work. Renderings should be pen and ink, pencil, or marker; 30x40" or 24x30". Reports in 1-2 weeks. SASE. Recently assigned freelancer perspective and interior sketches of regional shopping mall.

LAND SYSTEMS DESIGN, Box 322, Falls Church VA 22046. Contact: William Stanley. Landscape architecture firm. Uses artists for architectural renderings, landscape design, signs, graphic design, garden sculpture, site plans, engineering and structural elevations and scale models. "We plan where people live, so that means both private spaces (one to 12) and public spaces in the community (over 100). Shopping centers and parks are part of our 'people places'." Pays $150 for completed plan. Query with resume. Will review samples by mail, but prefers interview. Reports in 10 days.

PETER LENZ, CHIEF ARCHITECT, Stouffer Restaurants & Inns, 1375 Euclid Ave., Cleveland OH 44115. Works with hotels and restaurants. Estab: 1925. Uses artists for architectural renderings, building interiors, interior/landscape design, paintings and sculpture. Also uses model builders. "Interior perspective is a common need. A good representation of finished space with proper color and patterns but not literal hardline drawings is what's required, since renderings are often done prior to completion of design." Pays $250-380, architectural rendering; $100+, design; "fine art contemporary or traditional, from $100 to $2,500. Have paid as high as $600 for complex tempera rendering." Arrange interview.

McDONALD, CASSELL & BASSETT, 4707 N. High St., Columbus OH 43214. Contact: William McDonald. Uses artists for architectural renderings and landscape design. Payment determined by job. Query with resume, or submit photos or transparencies. Reports in 10 days.

JAMES A. MARTIS, JR., ARCHITECTS, #250, 28790 Chagrin Blvd., Cleveland OH 44122. (216)247-3255. Contact: James A. Martis, Jr., Estab: 1973. Architectural/interior design/construction management firm. Uses artists for architectural and full-color renderings, building interiors, graphic/interior/landscape design, model buildings, room sketches, signs and trademarks. Commercial and residential clients. Assigns 5-10 freelance jobs annually. Pays $150-750 for renderings. Payment determined by job, degree of difficulty and/or time spent. Mail samples. Reports in 2 weeks. SASE.

THE MARYLAND-NATIONAL CAPITAL PARK & PLANNING COMMISSION, 6600 Kenilworth Ave., Riverdale MD 20840. Chief Landscape Architect: Larry Hill. Uses artists for landscape design, architectural renderings, urban walls, supergraphics and site plans. Specifications are limited only by the nature of the officials or citizens to which the public presentation is made. Mail photos or transparencies. Reports in 10 days. Payment determined by job.

DANIEL T. MEEHAN, ARCHITECT, AND ASSOCIATES, 13 West Sharon Rd., Cincinnati OH 45246. Uses artists for architectural renderings, building interiors and interior design. Colored rendering must be done in colors that allow good colored photographic reproductions as well as good reproductions. Payment determined by job. Submit photos or transparencies of work and/or query with resume.

ELON MICKELS ASSOCIATES, 10641 W. McNichols, Detroit MI 48221. Urban planning and landscape design firm. Uses artists for design ideas for landscape and urban walls. Reports in 1 week. Pays in stages as work is completed.

MILLER WIHRY & LEE, Landward Court, 2147 Belcourt Ave., Nashville TN 37212. (615)298-5403. Contact: David O. Lose. Occasionally uses artists for architectural renderings and garden sculpture. Arrange interview.

WILTON FRANK MINCKLEY, ARCHITECT & URBAN AND REGIONAL PLANNER, 1421 Chandler Dr., Salt Lake City UT 84103. (801)531-0612. Uses artists for architectural renderings and urban planning materials. Pays $150-250 for architectural rendering. Payment determined by job. Mail photos or slides.

OLSAVSKY & INGLEDUE, ARCHITECTS, 312 N. Main St., Niles OH 44446. Uses artists for architectural and art renderings. Payment determined by job. Mail photos or transparencies of work.

OSSIPOFF, SNYDER, ROWLAND & GOETZ, 1210 Ward, Honolulu HI 96814. Contact: Sidney Snyder. Uses artists for architectural/art renderings and landscape design. Firm specializes in residential, governmental, medical and commercial projects. Payment determined by job. Call for interview. Reports in 10 days.

PAPESCH ASSOCIATES, ARCHITECTS AND PLANNERS, 128 Myrtle St., Boston MA 02114. (617)227-2869. Contact: Peter Papesch. Uses artists for architectural renderings, interior/landscape design, urban planning materials, charts and maps. Pays $250 for architectural rendering. Payment determined by job. Arrange interview.

PDT & COMPANY ARCHITECTS/PLANNERS, (formerly Pansiera Domme Tilsley & Co.), 7434 Montgomery Rd., Cincinnati OH 45236. Contact: John Bammerlin. Uses artists for architectural renderings. Mail samples of work (photos or transparencies). Payment determined by job.

THURMAN J. PEABODY, ARCHITECT, Box 565, Norwalk OH 44857. Uses artists for architectural renderings, interior design, art renderings and building interiors. Send photos or color transparencies of work. Payment determined by job. Pays $15 per hour minimum for renderings. Reports in 10 days.

PEP, INC., PROFESSIONAL ENGINEERS AND PLANNERS, 1612 Prosser Ave., Dayton OH 45409. (513)294-2422. Contact: Al Wahby. Uses artists for architectural and art renderings, landscape design, urban planning materials, charts and maps. Mail samples. Payment determined by job.

THE PLANNING CONSORTIUM, Box 32, Scotland PA 17254. Senior Partner: H. John Hall. Uses artists for posters, planning/development/community public relations brochures and annual reports. Pays $50, poster; $100, 3-4 ink sketches of urban landscape or buildings. Query.

POWERS-WILLIS & ASSOCIATES, 325 E. Washington St., Iowa City IA 52240. Director of Client Relations: J.L. Maynard. Uses local artists for architectural renderings and brochures. Query.

PPM DESIGN ASSOCIATES, INC., 2 Detroit St., Calumet City IL 60409. (312)264-3185. Contact: Bill Purvis. Estab: 1972. Interior design firm. Uses local artists for architectural and full-color renderings, building interiors, graphic design, model buildings, murals, original art, room sketches, paintings and signs. Residential and commercial clients. Pays $100-150 for renderings. Payment determined by job. Query. Reports in 1 week. SASE.

F.W. PRESSLER & ASSOCIATES, INC., 4939 Paddock Rd., Cincinnati OH 45237. Uses artists for architectural renderings and building interiors. Payment determined by job. Mail photos or transparencies of work. Reports in 10 days.

JOHN CREWS RAINEY ASSOCIATES, 310 E. 55th St., New York NY 10022. Contact: Mary Jane Norcross Tougas. Architectural firm. Uses artists for architectural renderings, interior design and building interiors.

LILLIAN RATHE INTERIORS, 340 E. 64th St., New York NY 10021. (212)294-5500. Contact: Lillian Rathe. Estab: 1938. Interior design firm and art gallery. Uses local artists for graphic design, original art, paintings and sculpture. Residential and commercial clients. Query with photo samples. Reports in 1 week. SASE.

REHLER, VAUGHN, BEATY & KOONE INC., 84 NE Loop 410 — 180 W., San Antonio TX 78216. (512)349-1106. Contact: George P. Vaughn. Estab: 1970. Architectural and interior design firm. Uses artists for architectural and full-color renderings, building interiors, graphic and landscape design, model buildings and signs. Commercial clients. Assigns 2-5 freelance jobs annually. Pays $500-1,000 for color renderings. Payment determined by job and/or degree of difficulty. Mail brochures of work. Reports in 2 weeks. SASE. Recently paid $500 for interior presentation for new savings and loan.

EDWARD H. RICHARDSON ASSOCIATES, INC., Box 675, Newark DE 19711. Contact: Thomas H. Kummer. Uses artists for architectural renderings, fine art, garden sculpture, signs, urban walls and related services. Payment determined by job or a negotiated time and material basis. Mail photos or transparencies, or query with resume. Reports in 10 days.

ROONEY, MUSSER & ASSOCIATES, INC., Hancock Savings Bldg., Findlay OH 45840. Contact: Jim Rooney. Uses artists for architectural/art renderings and building interiors. Payment determined by job. Submit photos or slides of work.

KENNETH H. ROSS ARCHITECT, 27 W. 53rd St., New York NY 10019. Contact: Kenneth Ross. Estab: 1967. Architectural firm. Uses local artists for architectural and full-color renderings, interior design, building interiors, graphic design and model buildings. Residential, commercial and industrial clients. Assigns 6 freelance jobs annually. Pays $150 for preliminary sketches. Payment determined by job. Write for interview. Reports in 2 weeks. Recently assigned freelancer to design showroom interior.

ROSSI & NICKERSON INC., ENGINEERS & ARCHITECTS, 970 S. Byrne Rd., Toledo OH 43609. Contact: M.F. Nickerson III. Uses artists for architectural renderings. Payment determined by job. Submit photos or transparencies of work and/or resume. Reports in 10 days.

SAGADENCKY & ASSOCIATES ARCHITECTS, INC., 2239 Front St., Cuyahoga Falls OH 44221. Contact: Trefon Sagadencky. Uses artists for architectural renderings and landscape design. Mail photos or transparencies. Payment determined by job.

SCHATZ ASSOCIATED ARCHITECTS, INC., 801 W. 8th St., Cincinnati OH 45203. Contact: Alan Schatz. Uses artists for architectural and art renderings, building interiors and landscape design. Arrange interview. Reports in 3 days. Payment determined by job.

SCHUYLER REID HAFELY, 2637 River Rd., Modesto CA 95351. Landscape architectural firm. Uses artists for landscape design and garden sculpture. "I am semi-retired and call on specialists as needed." Mail photos or transparencies. Payment determined by job and/or time spent.

SCHWARTZMAN & TUCCI CONSULTANTS, INC., (formerly Daniel Schwartzman, FAIA), 90 Park Ave., New York NY 10016. Architectural firm. Contact: F.M. Tucci. Uses artists for architectural and art renderings, interior design, building interiors and industrial/landscape design. Mail photos or transparencies and resume. Reports in 10 days. Payment determined by job.

SEIBERT WORLEY CADY KIRK PARTNERS INC., 2729 Prospect Ave., Cleveland OH 44115. (216)771-1845. Contact: Harold Van Niel. Estab: 1948. Architectural firm. Uses local

artists for architectural renderings, graphic/landscape design, murals, sculpture, signs and site plans. Commercial clients. Assigns 3 freelance jobs annually. Pays $100-800, architectural rendering; $1,500-4,500, landscape design; $300-1,500, murals; $150-5,000, sculpture. Payment determined by job. Query first. Reports in 1-3 weeks. SASE. Recently assigned a small fountain design for bank lobby.
To Break In: "Be able to present a drawing explaining your conception so the client and architectural firm can understand your idea. It is important to have architectural sensitivity."

RICHARD SEIDEN INTERIORS, 83 Rapple Dr., Albany NY 12205. (518)869-0762. Contact: Richard Seiden. Estab: 1974. Interior design firm. Uses artists for full-color renderings, interior design, original art, paintings, room sketches, statuary and wall art. Residential and commercial clients. Pays $150-1,800 for special original wall decor. Payment determined by job. Query. Reports in 1 week. SASE.

HARLAN E. SHERMAN, ARCHITECT, 13224 Shaker Square, Cleveland OH 44120. Uses artists for architectural/art renderings, building interiors and interior design. Payment determined by job or time spent. Mail photos or slides of work.

SMITH, CHATMAN-ROYCE ASSOCIATES, 101 E. King St., Malvern PA 19355. Contact: T. Chatman-Royce. Specializes in architecture, urban planning, landscape architecture and interior design. Arrange interview. Reports in 10 days on mailed samples.

SOMDAL ASSOCIATES, LBT-Milam Bldg., 316 Milam St., Shreveport LA 71101. (318)425-7721. Contact: G. Scott Smitherman. Estab: 1908. Architectural firm. Uses artists for architectural and full-color renderings. Commercial and institutional clients. Assigns 6-8 freelance jobs annually. Pays $350-1,000 for renderings. Payment determined by job. "We judge an artist's qualities as is illustrated in their brochures." Contacts artists as needs arise.
To Break In: "Develop a brochure with a list of your accomplishments and samples of your work."

MARK J. SORRENTINO, 210 S. Pine St., Langhorne PA 19047. Uses artists for architectural renderings, landscape design, garden sculpture, trademarks, signs and industrial sculpture. Payment determined by job. Mail photos or transparencies. Reports in 30 days.

THE SPINK CORPORATION, 720 F St., Sacramento CA 95814. (916)444-8170. Contact: Francis Koo. Uses artists for architectural/art renderings, interior/landscape design and urban planning materials. Payment determined by job and/or amount and nature of work. Mail photos or transparencies of work.

SSPF INC., 75 Second Ave., St. Charles IL 60157. Contact: J. Christopher Lannert. Uses artists for architectural renderings, signs and site plans. Payment determined by job. Query with resume, or mail photos or transparencies of work. Reports in 2 weeks.

STANLEY CONSULTANTS, INC., Stanley Bldg., Muscatine IA 52761. Marketing Communications Coordinator: Deane N. Haerer. International engineering, architecture, planning and management consulting firm. Deals with *Fortune* 500 clients; foreign governments; federal agencies; state, city and county governments. Uses artists for direct mail brochures, interior designs and posters. Query with resume and printed samples.

DUFFY B. STANLEY, ARCHITECTS, 308 Bassett Tower, El Paso TX 79901. Contact: Duffy Stanley. Uses artists for architectural renderings, urban planning materials, charts and maps. Payment determined by job. Submit photos or transparencies of work.

STATEN/PIERCE, LACEY INC., ARCHITECTS & PLANNERS, 4849 N. Mesa, Suite 101, El Paso TX 79912. (915)544-4444. Contact: George Staten, Jr. Architectural and interior design firm. Uses artists for architectural and full-color renderings, building interiors, landscape design, model buildings, original art, room sketches, sculpture, signs, site plans, urban planning and wall art. Residential, institutional and commercial clients. Assigns 6-8 freelance jobs annually. Pays $50-1,000+, architectural renderings; $25-400+, building interiors; $100-1,500, full-color renderings; $100 minimum, landscape design. Payment determined by job. Query or write for interview. Reports in 1 week. SASE. Recently assigned renderings of office park to freelancer.

JOHN V. TOWNSEND & ASSOCIATES, 604 Green Valley Rd., Greensboro NC 27408. Contact: John V. Townsend. Uses artists for graphic design, garden sculpture and signs. Payment determined by job. Call or write for interview, or query with resume. Reports in 10 days.

VITO J. TRICARICO, ARCHITECT, 3 E. 75th St., New York NY 10021. (212)421-9061. Uses artists for architectural renderings, interior design, building interiors and landscape design. Mail samples or arrange interview. Payment determined by job or time spent. Reports in 30 days.

TWELVE OAKS REGIONAL CONSERVATION CENTER, INC., 1922 South Rd., Baltimore MD 21209. (301)367-4380. Contact: Peter Michaels. Uses artists for restoring and conserving. Artists within a 500-mile radius only. Submit resume.

U.S. COAST GUARD, Department of Transportation, Box 3-5000, Juneau AK 99801. Contact: Contracting Officer. Uses artists for architectural and engineering services. Submit U.S. government Form SF 254.

URBAN ARCHITECTS/ABEND SINGLETON ASSOCIATES, 1016 Baltimore, Kansas City MO 64105. (816)221-5011. Contact: Steve Abend. Commercial and institutional clients. Uses artists for architectural renderings, model buildings and wall hangings.

VAN ARD DESIGN CORP., 150 Herricks Rd., Mineola NY 11501. (516)746-8111. Contact: Marvin J. Shervan. Estab: 1965. Interior design firm. Uses local artists for architectural, art and full-color renderings; interior design; and room sketches. Commercial clients. Assigns 25-35 freelance jobs annually. Pays $250-350 for restaurant and lobby renderings. Payment determined by job and going rate. Call or write for interview (bring actual renderings). Reports in 1 week. SASE. Recently assigned design of a New Jersey race track complex to freelancer.

VETERANS ADMINISTRATION HOSPITAL, American Lake, Tacoma WA 98493. Contact: G. Lane. Uses artists for architectural and engineering services. Send for file form 254.

VOGT SAGE & PFLUM CONSULTANTS, 222 E. Central Pkwy., Cincinnati OH 45202. (513)721-4477. Contact: Peter Wagner. Estab: 1967. Architectural, landscape and planning firm. Uses local freelancers for architectural renderings, graphic design, landscape design, model buildings and urban planning materials. Residential, commercial and industrial clients. Assigns 12 freelance jobs annually. Pays $750-2,500, graphic design. Payment determined by time spent. Query with photos. Reports in 3 weeks. Recently assigned freelancer a slide presentation for transit system.

VOGUE DECORATORS, 120 Post Rd., White Plains NY 10601. Interior design firm. Estab: 1936. Uses artists for room sketches, original art, full-color renderings, wall art and murals. Residential and commercial clients.

WADE NURSERIES, 24401 Peach Tree Rd., Clarksburg MD 20734. Contact: G. Wade Byerly. Landscape architectural firm. Uses artists for architectural renderings, landscape design and site plans. Payment determined by job. Query with resume or mail samples. Reports in 1 month.

WALLACE McHARG ROBERTS & TODD, 1737 Chestnut St., Philadelphia PA 19103. Contact: William Roberts or Thomas Todd. Architectural planning and landscape architectural firm. Occasionally uses artists for architectural renderings, models and graphic design. Payment determined by fixed fee. Query with resume or mail samples. Reports in 30 days.

WEIL INTERIORS, 3537 Section Rd., Cincinnati OH 45237. Contact: Ms. Burt Weil. Interior design firm. Uses local artists for original art, full-color renderings, sculpture, statuary and wall art. Residential and industrial clients.

WEISS WHELAN EDELBAUM WEBSTER, 555 Madison Ave., New York NY 10022. Contact: Donald V. Whelan. Architectural firm. Uses artists for art and architectural renderings and interior design. Payment determined by job. Query with resume or mail photos or transparencies of work. Reports in 10 days.

HELENE WEISSNER DESIGNS, INC., 3535 NE 2nd Ave., Miami FL 33137. Contact: J. Weissner. Interior design firm. Uses local artists for room sketches, original art, sculpture, statuary and wall art. Residential and commercial clients.

WILSEY & HAM, 1631 Huntington Dr., South Pasadena CA 91030. Public Relations Director: Daniel Boley. Uses artists for design, logos and architectural renderings. Query with resume and samples.

YUILL-THORNTON & LEVIKOW, 442 Post St., San Francisco CA 94102. Contact: John R. Levikow. Architectural firm. Specializes in hospitals, educational facilities, public works, interior renovations and some commercial projects. Uses artists for architectural renderings, interior design, model buildings, supergraphics and building interiors. Photos or transparencies of work and resume should be submitted for consideration. In hiring freelance artists and photographers, Levikow looks for "an ability to relate to the architectural essence of any project, to harmonize and not compete. We prefer b&w renderings on reproducible paper like 1000H for preliminary presentations." Reports in 10 days. Payment is usually by the job. Sample fee: $250 for sketches.

Audiovisual Firms & Record Companies

Thanks to the use of audiovisual tools in education and the popularity of music in this country, there is an ever-growing market in this field for artwork produced by freelance artists. Between 1963 and 1973, audiovisual investments increased a phenomenal 208%; also, manufacturers' sales of phonograph records and prerecorded tapes increased 7.5% during 1975, bringing sales to a high of $2.36 billion.

The sales for these "media of the senses" can be contributed in large part to the artist — creator of promotional catalogs, print ads and packaging. In addition to promotional needs, listings in this section also use artists for animation, storyboards, technical charts and mechanicals.

Most audiovisual firms are aimed toward educational markets. Audiences include business and industry, government, religious groups, medical organizations, community groups and schools. For this reason, "show samples that could apply to educational filmstrips, not artsy paintings," says the art buyer for Cinemakers, Inc.

Nat Bukar, president of Nat Bukar & Associates, says the artist should first write the audiovisual company saying what is unique about him, his work and his experience. "Why should I hire you over someone else?" he asks.

"An artist must have the ability to adapt artistic talents to the disciplines and needs of the media. Be on time with deliveries and stay within a budget," says Saul Taffet, producer/director of Telemated Motion Pictures.

Once you've acquired assignments, you'll need to "be able to translate written descriptions into visual images," says Musa Eubanks, president of Afro Audio-Visual Co.

Paul Snyder, production manager of Motivation Media, Inc., believes it helps to have a knowledge of film formats, color keys, gel applications and preparing art for top and bottom lighting on camera.

Artists interested in designing record jackets shouldn't limit themselves to the Record Companies category. Audiovisual firms also produce tapes and records to accompany filmstrips and similar media.

Assignments with firms listed in this section bring from $5 for a storyboard frame to a healthy $6,500 for animation art. Record jacket designs earn artists from $5-500.

Additional markets for audiovisual work are listed in the *Audiovisual Market Place,* published by R. R. Bowker Company.

Audiovisual Firms

ACADEMY FILM PRODUCTIONS, INC., 123 W. Chestnut St., Chicago IL 60610. (312)642-5877. President: Bernard Howard. Estab: 1950. Produces motion pictures, filmstrips and slides. Uses local artists for animation, technical charts/illustrations, slide and filmstrip artwork. Payment determined by job. Query or call for interview. Buys all rights.

ACADEMY FILM PRODUCTIONS, INC., 210 W. 29th St., Baltimore MD 21211. Contact: Randy or Marion Breer. Uses artists for set design. Arrange to show samples.

ADMASTER INC., 425 Park Ave. S., New York NY 10016. (212)679-1134. Art Director: Joe Pego. Estab: 1948. Produces industrial audiovisual material. Uses artists for animation, audiovisual art, technical charts/illustrations and type spec. Pays $6 per hour. Buys 250+ local freelance designs annually. Query or call. Reports in 1 week.

AERO PRODUCTS RESEARCH INC., 11201 Hindry Ave., Los Angeles CA 90045. Director of Public Relations: J. Parr. Publisher/audiovisual manufacturer. Artist "must be an experienced, rated pilot, and have excellent knowledge of the Federal Aviation Regulations." Produces silent and sound filmstrips, multimedia kits, overhead transparencies, slides, and study prints for grades K through 12 and college and aviation education courses. Project requirements differ. All material copyrighted. Local artists only. Query.

AFRO AUDIO-VISUAL CO., 141 Spencer St., Dorchester MA 02124. President: Musa Eubanks. Estab: 1969. Produces multimedia educational materials with emphasis on African-American images and people. Pays $10-25 for sketches. Payment determined by degree of difficulty and/or number of illustrations. Assigns 1-2 projects annually. Query. Buys all rights. Reports in 3 weeks. No work returned. Free brochure. Looks for "ability to translate written descriptions into visual images and consistency between people and faces in drawings."

AGRI-EDUCATION, INC., Rte. 2, Stratford IA 50249. (515)838-2785. President: Keith Carlson. Estab: 1968. Produces instructional charts, slides and transparencies for high schools and young farmers. Uses artists for multimedia kits. Pays $20-100, cover; $10-15, overhead transparency. Payment determined by time spent. Buys 10-20 freelance designs annually. Mail 8x10" pencil or ink sketches. Material copyrighted. Reports in 2 weeks. SASE. Free catalog. A farm background with knowledge of animals and machinery is helpful.

AIR FILMS, INC., 210 E. 47th St., New York NY 10017. Contact: Production Manager. Produces commercials, educational documentaries, slides, still photography, graphic design, animation art and set design. Query.

ANIMATED PRODUCTIONS, INC., 1600 Broadway, New York NY 10019. Contact: Al Stahl. Produces mail-order movies for photographers, film producers, ad agencies and artists. Uses artists for animation art and graphic design. Arrange interview to present samples.

ANIMATION ARTS ASSOCIATES, INC., 2225 Spring Garden St., Philadelphia PA 19130. (215)563-2520. President: Harry E. Ziegler. Estab: 1963. Produces 35/16mm films, sound/slide programs and filmstrips for government, industry, education and TV. Uses artists for animation. Pays $5-10 per hour for cartoon and technical animation. Call for interview. Material copyrighted. No work returned.

HAL MARC ARDEN AND CO., 240 Central Park S., New York NY 10019. President: Hal Marc Arden. Produces TV films, public relations packages and audiovisual programs for industry and education. Uses artists for animation, catalog covers/illustrations, direct mail brochures, layout and multimedia kits. Payment determined by job. Query with samples. Material copyrighted. SASE.

LINDA ARDIGO/CREATIVE WAYS FILMS, 48 W. 43rd St., New York NY 10028. Contact: Linda Ardigo. Uses artists for animation art; especially needs storyboard art. Pays $400-700 for 30-second spot artwork (approximately ten 7x14" frames). Arrange to show samples.

ARTSCOPE, LTD., 145 W. 96th, Suite A, New York NY 10025. (212)749-5567. President: A. Chaudhri. Estab: 1965. Uses artists for animation and catalog covers/illustrations. Pays $100 minimum. Payment determined by job. Buys 20 freelance designs annually. Query with samples. Material copyrighted. Reports in 2 weeks. SASE.

ASSOCIATED AUDIO-VISUAL CORPORATION, 2821 Central St., Evanston IL 60201. Contact: Ken Solomon or Don Ivener. Produces silent and sound filmstrips, 16/35mm motion pictures, multimedia kits, slides and visualized sales and business meetings. Clients are industrial and sales firms; most work is in intra-company communications; some is in education. Send resume and work samples with background information, rationale and treatment of project. Payment determined by time spent. Material not copyrighted.

AUDIO VISUAL PRODUCTIONS, INC., 1233 N. Ashland Ave., Chicago IL 60622. Contact: M. Rubel. Produces film loops, silent and sound filmstrips, 8/16mm motion pictures, overhead transparencies, slides and study prints for preschool, kindergarten and primary grades. Query with resume. Requests samples, if desired.

AUDITIONS BY SOUNDMASTERS, Box 8135, Chicago IL 60680. (312)787-8220. Executive Vice President: R.C. Hillsman. Estab: 1964. Produces radio/TV programs, commercials, jingles and records. Uses artists for animation; catalog covers/illustrations; layout and paste-up; multimedia kits; and record album design. Pays $500 minimum, animation; $100-350, record jackets; $50-225, layout; $35-165, paste-up. Payment determined by job. Buys 125-300 freelance designs annually. Mail 8x10" artwork. Material copyrighted. Reports in 3 weeks. SASE.

AURVID/VIDEO PRODUCTIONS, (formerly Videor/Aurvid Productions), Box 413, Philadelphia PA 19105. Executive Producer: F.O. Pease. Estab: 1945. Produces educational/news materials and jazz records. Uses artists for catalog covers/illustrations, direct mail brochures, magazine ads and record album design. Pays $100 minimum. Payment determined by job. Buys 30-35 freelance designs annually. Query. Buys all rights. Reports in 4 weeks. SASE.

A-V SCIENTIFIC AIDS, INC., 639 N. Fairfax Ave., Los Angeles CA 90036. Director of Production: John Rubin. Produces 16/35mm sound filmstrips for doctors, dentists and patients. Uses artists for 9x12" color artwork on cell or heavy poster board. Arrange to show portfolio.

AV/TV SYSTEMS, Box 179, Deerfield IL 60015. Contact: Libby Germaine. "Our primary interest for artists is those who have had extensive experience with projected graphics." Also uses artists for animation art, slides, graphic/exhibit design, industrial films and set design. Query with resume.

BACHNER PRODUCTIONS, INC., 501 Madison Ave., New York NY 10022. (212)688-2755. Producer/Director: A. Bachner. Estab: 1970. Produces industrial, educational and commercial films and videotapes. Uses artists for animation, films and videotapes. Pays $15 minimum per frame, storyboards; $200-1,000, title layout design. Payment determined by job. Buys 3-5 New York freelance designs annually. Query or write for interview. Buys all rights. Reports in 4 weeks. No work returned.

BAKER PRODUCTIONS, INC., 7 Bala Ave., Bala-Lynwyd PA 19004. (215)664-0991. President: Alan Baker. Estab: 1972. Produces TV commercials, documentaries and industrial films. Uses artists for storyboards and film graphics. Pays $5 per panel, storyboards; $10 per title card, titles. Payment determined by job. Buys approximately 100 local freelance designs annually. Write for interview. Buys all rights. Reports in 1 week "if prospect is pending." No work returned. Seeks artists with knowledge of TV requirements.

BANDELIER FILMS, INC., 2001 Gold SE, Albuquerque NM 87106. President: Allan Stevens. Produces submarine training film storyboards; public service TV spots for U.S. Forest Service; Navajo/English training films; and animated TV commercials. Uses artists for animation art and graphic design. Arrange to show samples.

BEAR FILMS, INC., 805 Smith St., Baldwin NY 11510. President: Frank Bear. Uses artists for graphic design. Query with resume.

BETZER PRODUCTIONS, INC., 450 E. Ohio St., Chicago IL 60611. President: Joseph G. Betzer. Uses artists for animation. Query with resume.

BILL BOAL PRODUCTIONS, INC., 43 5th Ave., New York NY 10003. (212)924-5040. Contact: Helene Berger. Produces sound filmstrips for elementary and junior high schools. Pays $15-25 for drawings. Payment determined by "art required and level of artist." Arrange to show work. Buys all rights.

NAT BUKAR & ASSOCIATES, 770 Lexington Ave., New York NY 10017. President: Nat Bukar. Estab: 1971. Produces sound slides, sound filmstrip programs, financial charts and slide presentations for management. Uses artists for catalog covers/illustrations, models, paste-up, technical charts/illustrations and presentation lettering. Pays $7-12 per hour, mechanics and assembly; $40-80 per hour, models; $25 minimum, illustration; $7-12 per hour, charts and lettering. Buys 25-50 local freelance projects annually. Query. Reports immediately. No work returned.

To Break In: "Tell us what is unique about you, your work, experience. Why should I hire you over someone else?"

CARLOCKE/LANGDEN, INC., Whitmark Associates, 4120 Main St., Suite 100, Dallas TX 75226. Creative Director: Margaret F. Murrell. Produces documentary/sales/industrial/motion pictures, public relations TV commercials, filmstrips and slide films. Uses artists for animation. Query with resume.

CAROUSEL FILMS, INC., 5646 La Mirada, Los Angeles CA 90038. Contact: Jack Strand. "We are primarily interested in catalog cover design for our 16mm educational film audiences. We'll be glad to send a catalog to any artist who works in the greater Los Angeles area." Pays on acceptance. Negotiates payment. Average payment: $250-350, catalog cover; $950-1,250, whole catalog.

CATHEDRAL TELEPRODUCTIONS, 2690 State Rd., Cuyahoga Falls OH 44223. Contact: Don Caminati. "We are a TV production house and are interested mostly in artists familiar with the medium. We deal primarily with advertising agencies on TV shows and commercials." Uses artists for set and graphic design. Query with resume.

THE CENTER FOR HUMANITIES, INC., 2 Holland Ave., White Plains NY 10603. Contact: Wilma Mann. Produces educational slide and tape programs. "We need creative artists. Images must be visually exciting. Each image is on the screen for a considerable amount of time and must have power to stand on its own. Artists' portfolios will be looked at in the office, but not kept here for any amount of time. We must have a written resume to keep on file." Negotiates payment. Payment determined by number of illustrations.

CENTER FOR MEDIA DEVELOPMENT, INC., Box 51, 300 Northern Blvd., Great Neck NY 11022. Director of Operations: Lynn Hyman. Estab: 1967. Produces educational books, kits, cassettes, records and filmstrips. Uses artists for layout, design, multimedia kits, paste-up, study prints, technical charts/illustrations, type spec and textbook illustrations. Payment for book illustration: $5-50, 1-color; $15-50, 2-color; $20+, 4-color. Payment determined by job. Buys 500-700 New York freelance designs annually. Query. Buys all rights. Reports in 3 weeks. SASE.

CHANNEL ONE, INC., 1727 Clifton Rd., Atlanta GA 30329. Contact: Peter Kontos. Uses artists for graphic and set design.

THE CHARTMAKERS, INC., 25 W. 45th St., New York NY 10036. Vice President/Creative Director: Joseph O'Hehir. Uses artists for miltimedia productions, graphic design, brochures and card presentations. Query with resume.

CINEMAKERS, INC., 200 W. 57th St., New York NY 10019. (212)765-1168. Contact: Art Buyer. Estab: 1965. Produces motion pictures, filmstrips, TV public service spots and teachers' guides for junior and senior high schools. Uses local artists for animation and filmstrip art (drawings and type). Pays $25-60 per filmstrip art frame. Payment determined by job. Buys 500 freelance designs annually. Write for interview; "send nonreturnable samples if possible." Buys all rights. Reports as needs arise.
To Break In: "Show samples that could apply to educational filmstrips, not 'artsy' paintings."

CIRSA PRODUCTIONS, 9 E. 37th St., New York NY 10016. (212)679-1101. Contact: Niki Patton. Uses artists for animation art and storybooks. Query with resume.

CLOSE PRODUCTIONS, INC., 2020 San Carlos Blvd., Fort Myers Beach FL 33931. Contact: E. Burt Close. Produces educational, business and industrial sound filmstrips, slide presentations, multimedia kits and prerecorded tapes and cassettes. Subjects include language arts, career guidance, medical, safety, fire-fighter training, salesmanship, loss prevention and management. Also produces its own advertising, sales promotion and publicity material. Uses artists for alyout design; simplified realistic pen and ink drawings overlaid with color; storyboards and cartoons. Buys art outright. Occasionally negotiates royalty arrangements.

COMMUNICATIONS PRODUCTIONS, 150 S. Forest Ave., Rockville Centre NY 11570. Executive Producer: Marilyn Fisher. Produces business and industrial filmstrips, slides, animation and multimedia kits; including display and printed materials. Mail samples or arrange interview.

THE COMMUNICATORS, Rte. 44, Pomfret Center CT 06259. (203)928-7766. Contact: Robert McDonell. Produces slide and industrial films. Pays $25 for 2-figure cartoons, flat background; and $75 for 8½x10" full-color illustration. Buys all rights. Query with resume.

CONTACT! VISUAL COMMUNICATIONS, INC., 1726½ Sherman Ave., Evanston IL 60201. (312)475-4656. Contact: Sidney H. Mayer, Jr. Occasionally uses artists with background in animation art, documentaries, industrial films, slides, and graphic and set design. Make appointment to present samples.

CONTEMPORARY DRAMA SERVICE, Box 457, Downers Grove IL 60515. Contact: Arthur Zapel. Produces silent and sound filmstrips, motion pictures (16mm), multimedia kits and slides. "We provide educational resource kits for churches and schools. The age level varies, but our primary interest is currently in the high school level. Most of our emphasis is on the communications arts — drama, literature, music and language arts. We are interested primarily in a unique positioning of an idea graphically but not so far-out that the communication is unclear or difficult. We like work with a sense of humor." Uses artists with ad agency and studio (commercial) experience in the applied arts. Fees negotiable with royalties from 5-10%, based on retail sales price. Single frames bring $25-45; projects up to $2,000. Catalog 25¢. SASE.

CORNHUSKER FILMS, 1817 Vinton St., Omaha NE 68108. (402)341-4290. Contact: Ernest Jones. Uses artists for industrial films and documentaries. Query with resume.

ROBERT CRANDALL ASSOCIATES, 306 E. 45th St., New York NY 10017. Contact: Marvin Saunders. Uses artists for animation art, slide films, graphic design and industrial films. Arrange interview.

CREATIVE ARTS STUDIO, INC., 2323 4th St. NE, Washington DC 20002. Contact: Edward C. Santelmann. Produces TV commercials, animation art, documentaries, industrial, educational and training films, slides, and graphic design. "We deal mostly with educational institutions and government." Query.

THE CREATIVE ESTABLISHMENT, 740 N. Rush St., Chicago IL 60611. Executive Vice President: Joan Beugen. Uses Chicago area artists. "We produce slides, films and multimedia presentations primarily for industry but also do some educational and government work in all areas of audiovisual materials. Our specialty is large sales and management meetings, using multi-screen slide projection. The slides we use range over every conceivable type and format, since we produce in the neighborhood of 2,000 slides a month. We use illustrators, cartoonists, designers, costume and set designers, sculptors, model-makers . . . you name it. I am most interested in hearing from artists and art directors who have experience in slides as opposed to print work. However, we do use illustrators occasionally and show them how to prepare their work for reproduction into slides." Submit tearsheets of work.

CREATIVE PRODUCTIONS, INC., 221 N. LaSalle St., Chicago IL 60601. Contact: Leo Cummins. Produces materials for manufacturers and associations. Uses artists for animation, slides, graphics, exhibits, and set design. Pays $5-35 per frame for finished art/pencils and uncolored inks on cells.

CREATIVE PRODUCTIONS, INC., 200 Main St., Orange NJ 07050. President: William E. Griffing. Vice President: Gus J. Nichols. Uses artists for educational, medical and industrial films, TV commercials, slides and artwork.
To Break In: "Artists should display some expertise in type and mechanicals, rather than design only."

CROCUS PRODUCTIONS, 926 Chicago Ave., Evanston IL 60202. Contact: Tedd Determan. Specializes in stop motion animation. Uses artists for animation art, industrial films, slides, filmstrips, graphics and exhibit/set design. Submit resume.

CRUNCH BIRD STUDIOS, INC., 20169 James Couzens, Detroit MI 48235. Contact: Ted Petok. Uses experienced artists for animation art. Arrange interview.

CRYSTAL PICTURES, INC., 1560 Broadway, New York NY 10036. (212)757-5130. Contact: S. Tager. Uses artists for film posters, press books, catalogs, paste-ups and mechanicals. "We can use a New York City artist who can do this type of work on a freelance, by-the-job basis." Query "indicating specific skills in relation to our requirements." Send nonreturnable samples.

CUSTOM FILMS, 11 Cob Dr., Westport CT 06880. Contact: Lester S. Becker. Uses animation art, graphic design and industrial films. Query with resume and list of credits.

DALMATIAN ENTERPRISES, INC., 161 W. 54th St., New York NY 10019. Contact: Phyllis Reed. Uses artists for production of animation art, documentaries, industrial films, and graphic/exhibit/set design. Query with resume. Dalmatian also operates an advertising agency and publishes Showfare theater programs.

DANREE PRODUCTIONS, 1624 N. Gower St., Hollywood CA 90028. Contact: Danny Rees. Produces 16mm motion pictures primarily for children, with some geared towards adults. "We do educational, show-how films." Material copyrighted.

ALFRED DE MARTINI EDUCATIONAL FILMS INC., 414 4th Ave., Haddon Heights NJ 08035. Art Director: Alfred De Martini. Produces educational filmstrips. Uses artists for layout, illustration and filmstrip art. Pays $15-25 per filmstrip frame. Filmstrips range from 30-80 frames. "No rushwork, no impossible deadlines." Mail samples.

DEFENSE PRODUCTS COMPANY, Audiovisual Division, 2016 Baltimore Rd., Suite I-32, Rockville MD 20815. (301)279-0608. Manager: Harry A. Carragher. Estab: 1958. Produces audiovisuals, distribution and laboratory services for industry, theater and government. Uses artists for animation, design, dioramas, direct mail brochures, layout, magazine ads, models, multimedia kits, motion picture production and TV spots. Pays $25 per hour. Payment determined by time spent, job, and/or contract. Buys 6 freelance designs annually. Call for interview. Material not copyrighted. Reports in 2 weeks. SASE. Free catalog.

DESIGN CENTER, INC., 11900 Parklawn Dr., Rockville MD 20852. Contact: Mel Emde. Send resume; company arranges interview.

D4 FILM STUDIOS, INC., 109 Highland Ave., Needham MA 02194. (617)444-0226. President: Stephen Dephoure. Estab: 1935. Produces 16mm motion pictures and complete post-production services for education, business, government and hospitals. Uses artists for animation, titles and lettering for logos. "We pay $25 to several hundred dollars, depending on job." Buys approximately 6 freelance designs annually. Query. Reports in 1 week.

HERB DIETZ ENTERPRISES, INC., 340 Sunset Dr., Ft. Lauderdale FL 33301. (315)463-1270. President: Herb Dietz. Estab: 1970. Produces motion pictures, TV spots, audiovisual presentations and filmstrips. Use artists for animation, multimedia kits and technical charts/illustrations. Pays $200-6,500 per job, animation; $15-100 per job, charts/illustrations. Buys 10+ freelance designs annually. Query. Buys all rights. Reports in 3 weeks. SASE.

DIRECTORS GROUP MOTION PICTURES, INC., 870 7th Ave., New York NY 10019. Contact: Nyles Gradus. Produces TV spots, animation art, documentaries, industrial films, set design and videotape shows. Query.

DISCOVERY PRODUCTIONS, 151 E. 50th St., New York NY 10022. Executive Producer: David Epstein. Uses artists for background in animation art, documentaries and industrial films. Clients are primarily educational and industrial. Arrange interview.

DMK FILMS, INC., 3632 Murphy Rd., Nashville TN 37209. Contact: Dennis Kostyk or Mike Castle. Uses artists for TV shows, documentaries, industrial films, slides, filmstrips and graphic/exhibit/set design. Query with resume.

DOLPHIN PRODUCTIONS, 140 E. 80th St., New York NY 10021. (212)628-5930. Contact: Allan Stanley. Uses artists for animation art and graphic design. Submit in the form of 16mm film or cassettes.

DONARS PRODUCTIONS, Box 24, Loveland CO 80537. (303)669-0586. Manager: Octavio Noda. Estab: 1971. Produces educational slide sets, filmstrips and single slides. Uses artists for catalog covers/illustrations, direct mail brochures, layout, magazine ads, multimedia kits and technical charts/illustrations.

E. I. DUPONT DE NEMOURS & CO., INC., Advertising Department, Wilmington DE 19898. Contact: William D. Davis. Audiovisual division produces charts, motion pictures (16mm), multimedia kits, overhead transparencies, prerecorded tapes, cassettes and slides. Market includes salesmen, schools (grades 9 to 12), colleges and career groups. "Before we assign a project we definitely want to see examples of the quality of work in given budget." Submit portfolio.

EDUCATION CORPORATION OF AMERICA, 984 Livernois Rd., Troy MI 48084. Contact: Jacqueline L. Lannin. Produces sound filmstrips for elementary and secondary schools. Uses artists for illustrations in acrylics. Query.

EDUCATIONAL DEVELOPMENT CORP., 4235 S. Memorial Dr., Tulsa OK 74145. (918)622-4522. Art Director: Stan Weir. Estab: 1965. Produces educational materials. Uses local artists for catalog covers/illustrations, direct mail brochures and technical charts/illustrations. Pays $50 minimum, illustration in ink; $100 minimum, 4-color illustration. Payment determined by job. Buys 50 designs annually. Write or call for interview. Material copyrighted. Reports in 2 weeks. SASE. Free catalog.

EDUCATIONAL MATERIALS AND EQUIPMENT COMPANY, Box 17, Pelham NY 10803. (914)576-1121. Contact: Thomas J. McMahon. Produces educational studies for elementary, secondary and college students. Experienced artists should submit typewritten frame descriptions and film commentary in conjunction with art submissions. Material is copyrighted. Buys all rights.

EMC CORPORATION, 180 E. 6th St., St. Paul MN 55101. (612)227-7366. General Manager: Wolfgang Kraft. Estab: 1954. Produces books, cassettes, charts and filmstrips for elementary and secondary schools. Uses local artists for books, catalogs, direct mail brochures, layout, multimedia kits, paste-up and type spec. Pays $15, filmstrip title frame; $500, wall chart. Payment determined by job. Buys 15-20 freelance designs annually. Write or call for interview. Material copyrighted. Free catalog.

RAY ENGEL PRODUCTIONS, 11627 Oxnard, North Hollywood CA 91606. (213)769-2200 or 769-2201. Contact: Ray Engel. Occasionally uses artists for graphic/exhibit design and advertising art. Content is primarily party invitations, flyers for concerts, movie premieres, fashion and trade shows, dances, beauty pageants and special events. Arrange interview.

DAVID W. EVANS, INC., 110 Social Hall Ave., Salt Lake City UT 84121. Contact: William Onyon. Uses artists for graphic/exhibit design and industrial films. Arrange interview; bring samples.

EYE GATE MEDIA, 146-01 Archer Ave., Jamaica NY 11435. (212)291-9100. Manager: Laurence Swinburne. Estab: 1917. Produces religious and educational filmstrips, audio cassettes, multimedia kits and educational charts. Uses artists for layout, paste-up, study prints, technical charts/illustrations and type spec. Pays $200 maximum, charts/studio prints; $7.50 per hour maximum, layout/paste-up/type spec. Payment determined by job. Buys New York freelance designs. Query. Buys all rights. Reports in 30 days. SASE. Free catalog.

FILM ASSOCIATES, INC., 4600 S. Dixie Hwy., Dayton OH 45439. (513)293-2164. President: Ray Arn. Estab: 1946. Produces motion picture services. Uses artists for animation art. Pays $7.50-$15 per hour. Buys up to 5 designs annually. Query with samples. Reports in 2 weeks. SASE.

FILM COMMUNICATORS, 11136 Weddington St., North Hollywood CA 91601. Contact: Ray Jewell. Produces motion pictures (16mm), slides, study prints, brochures, mailing pieces and advertisements. Audience composed of all educational levels and categories including fire service, police and industry. Assignments granted to qualified artists with sufficient background and experience in the particular area to be covered. Submission requirements include approval of rough and finished artwork.

FILM FACTORY, 151 E. 50th St., New York NY 10022. Contact: Arnie Levey. Produces live action and animation films. Arrange interview.

FILMS FIVE, INC., 42 Overlook Rd., Great Neck NY 10020. (516)487-5865. Contact: Walter Bergman. Uses artists with experience in documentaries and industrial films. Query with resume.

FILMS FOR THE HUMANITIES, Box 378, Princeton NJ 08540. Contact: M. Mantell. Produces sound filmstrips, 16mm motion pictures, multimedia kits and slides for schools (K through 12) and colleges. Particularly interested in experienced book and advertising designers. Material usually copyrighted. Catalog available.

Books, catalogs, direct mail brochures, multimedia kits and various mechanical work is assigned to artists by EMC Corporation. Approximately 15-20 designs are bought by the firm annually, with payment ranging from $15 for a filmstrip title frame to $500 for a wall chart. This illustration, by Scott W. Earle, is one of several used to illustrate *The Tongue of the Ocean*, a book by Eve Bunting.

FLETCHER-ROLLINS TELEVISION INC., (formerly Fletcher Films Limited), 73 Rivercourt Blvd., Toronto, Ontario Canada M4J 3A3. Contact: Howard D. Fletcher. Occasionally uses artists for animation art, slide/industrial films, documentaries and TV film series titles. Query with resume.

FOCAL POINT STUDIOS, 18107 Torrence Ave., Lansing IL 60438. (312)895-5120. Contact: Hugh M. Pieron. Estab: 1968. Produces slide presentations; creative, commercial and illustrative photography; 16mm and super 8mm motion pictures; trade meetings; and shows for commerce and industry. Uses artists for direct mail brochures, models, record album design, technical charts/illustrations and artwork for 35mm slides and filmstrips. Pays $20 minimum per slide frame. Payment determined by time spent or job. Buys 100+ freelance designs annually. Query or call for interview. Material not copyrighted. Reports in 2 weeks. SASE.

FURMAN FILMS, 3466 21st St., San Francisco CA 94110. President: Will Furman. Produces documentaries, industrial films and TV commercials. Arrange interview.

GIRL SCOUTS OF USA, Materials Production Section, 830 3rd Ave., New York NY 10022. (212)751-6900. Contact: Robert A. Elfers. Produces filmstrips concerned with Girl Scout programs and subjects of interest to girls and adults in Girl Scouting. "Some of our recent projects deal with the environment, Girl Scout activities in relation to community activities, and one of our Girl Scout national centers." Local artists should call for interview; others should send resume. "If I'm interested, I'll request more information and work samples." Catalog available.

JEFF GOLD PRODUCTIONS, INC., 300 E. 51st St., New York NY 10022. (212)759-8785. President: Jeff Gold. Estab: 1969. Produces TV shows, commercials and films. Uses artists for animation, documentaries, industrial films and graphic and set design. Payment determined by job. Mail samples.

GOLDSHOLL ASSOCIATES, 420 Frontage Rd., Northfield IL 60093. Contact: Morton Goldsholl. Uses artists for TV commercials, animation art, documentaries, industrial films, slides, graphic/exhibit design and multimedia. "Our work is varied and we serve corporations on a total basis as well as in package design specifically. A great deal of our package design is in food products. Our film work is quite broad — commercials as well as industrial and cultural films." Query with resume.

GRATTON ASSOCIATES, LTD., 1271 Avenue of the Americas, New York NY 10020. Contact: S. Douglas Gratton. Uses artists for videotape, industrial films and set design. Arrange interview.

THE GREAT SHOOTING GALLERY, INC., (formerly Hallmar Studios, Inc.), 1900 N. St. Paul, Dallas TX 75201. President: True Redd. Vice President: Jim Beresford. Occasionally uses artists with professional background in animation art, film production and set design. Query.

THE HABOUSH/STENGER COMPANY INC., 6611 Santa Monica Blvd., Hollywood CA 90038. Vice President: Richard Haboush. Uses artists experienced in animation art, commercials, documentaries, industrial films, slides and graphic/set design. Prefers to see portfolio or 16mm sample reels in person.

HARPER & ROW, PUBLISHERS, INC., 10 E. 53rd St., New York NY 10022. Associate Producer: Ellen Tweedy. Estab: 1970. Produces audio cassettes, sound filmstrips, 16mm motion pictures, multimedia kits and slides for college and political science markets. Mail artwork or arrange interview. Reports in 3 weeks. SASE. Free catalog.

HARWYN MEDICAL PHOTOGRAPHERS, 1001 City Ave., Suite 918 WB, Philadelphia PA 19151. (215)896-7137. Sales Manager: Barnett Steinsnyder. Estab: 1950. Produces 35mm color medical slides for colleges and hospitals. Uses artists for catalogs. Payment determined by job. Buys 10 freelance designs annually. Mail slides or illustrations. Material copyrighted. Reports in 15 days. SASE. Free catalog.

PAUL HAYES PRODUCTIONS, 2406 S. MacDill Ave., Tampa FL 33609. Producer: Paul Hayes. Produces TV commercials and industrial films. Uses artists for slide films. Buys all rights. Submit resume.

HAYES PUBLISHING CO., INC., 6304 Hamilton Ave., Cincinnati OH 45224. (513)681-7559. Office Manager: Mary Schneller. Estab: 1965. Produces educational books, brochures and audiovisuals on human sexuality and abortion. Uses artists for direct mail brochures. Payment determined by job. Mail samples. Material copyrighted. Reports in 4 weeks. SASE. Free catalog.

HESTER AND ASSOCIATES, INC., 11422 Hines Blvd., Dallas TX 75229. (214)241-4859. President: Stew Hester. Estab: 1965. Produces educational workbooks, games, filmstrips and cassette tapes. Uses artists for multimedia kits. Pays on royalty basis. Buys 12+ projects annually. Query. Material copyrighted. Reports in 2 weeks. SASE. Free catalog.

I. E. INCORPORATED, 736 S. Eddy St., South Bend IN 46615. Contact: Jim Baxter. Occasionally uses artists for animation art, motion picture documentaries, sound/slide presentations, filmstrips, graphic/exhibit design and industrial film production. Payment determined by job. Pays $40 per frame for filmstrip art. Arrange interview.

I. F. STUDIOS, INC., 328 E. 44th St., New York NY 10017. President: Ed Tricomi. Secretary/Treasurer: Lewis Cohen. Specializes in graphics for trailers, titles, animation, industrial films, documentaries, slides and exhibit design. Arrange interview.

IDEAL SCHOOL SUPPLY COMPANY, 11000 S. Lavergne, Oak Lawn IL 60453. Art Director: Dick Sendzik. Produces educational materials and advertising. Uses artists for catalog covers/illustrations, direct mail brochures, layout, magazine ads, multimedia kits, paste-up, technical charts/illustrations and packaging. Pays $10-50, small b&w illustrations; $100-250, large color illustration; $10-25 per page, paste-up. Payment determined by job. Buys 5-10 freelance designs annually. Mail 8½x11" printed or photocopied samples with price. Material copyrighted. Reports in 2 weeks. No work returned. Free catalog. "Must be able to render children in action."

INSGROUP, INC., 16052 Beach Blvd., Huntington Beach CA 92647. Contact: Joan Warner. Produces charts, film loops, sound filmstrips, multimedia kits, overhead transparencies, slides and illustrated syllabi. Audience includes adults and children in schools and colleges, and adults in industry, public schools and military. Artist's credentials must include "5 years of documented, cost-effective productivity." Fee arrangement is according to industry standards, with royalty versus advances preferred. "Instructional versus aesthetic considerations are primary." Material usually copyrighted. Submit portfolio.

INSTRUCTIONAL DYNAMICS, INC., 450 E. Ohio St., Chicago IL 60611. President: Dr. Philip Lewis. "Our audiovisual projects range from preschool through college level and include teacher inservice materials as well. Assignments vary depending upon the needs of our clients for whom we produce the materials. They involve all academic and technical areas." Submit resume. Contacts artists as assignments arise. Catalog available.

INSTRUCTIONAL MEDIA CENTER, University of Nebraska-Lincoln, 421 Nebraska Hall, Lincoln NE 68508. Contact: Dr. James Buterbaugh. Produces silent and sound filmstrips, 16mm motion pictures, multimedia kits, overhead transparencies and slides. Audience is educators, employees and employers, church groups and the general public. Uses artists with film production experience. Payment arranged on an individual basis. Query with resume.

INTERCULTURE ASSOCIATES, INC., Box 277, Thompson CT 06277. President: Dr. Henry Ferguson. Uses artists for multimedia kits, overhead transparencies, slides and study prints. Materials geared to all levels, K through graduate school and teacher education. "Normally the individual should have broad overseas experience or have worked among domestic ethnic minorities for some time. The key quality is to be able to represent a culture from the inside and not to appear as the omniscient Westerner looking at the exotic heathen. Will match our needs to artist's qualifications. Most assignments are previously scripted by our editorial staff." Payment made on a flat fee (usually by the hour for artwork), or royalty basis (ranging from 5-15% depending upon product.) Query.

INTERFILM CORP., Box 13955, Atlanta GA 30324. President: J. Hunter Todd. Produces animation art, documentaries, industrial films, slides and graphic/exhibit/set design. "Creativity, fair prices and on-time delivery" are points stressed. Query with resume.

INTERNATIONAL MOTION PICTURES, LTD., Box 3201, Erie PA 16509. Contact: Sales Manager. Estab: 1970. Produces motion pictures and exhibits. Uses artists for handcolored reproductions. Payment determined by job. Buys several hundred freelance designs annually. Query. Material copyrighted.

J. C. PRODUCTIONS, INC., 16 W. 46th St., New York NY 10037. (212)575-9611. Contact: Rosalie Klein or Joe Conforti. Occasionally uses artists experienced in animation art. Payment determined by time spent. Arrange interview.

JACOBY/STORM PRODUCTIONS, INC., 101 E. State St., Westport CT 06880. (203)227-2220. Vice President: Doris Storm. Produces sound filmstrips, slides and 16mm motion pictures for students, business firms and general audiences. Uses artists with strong line and color sense, whether realistic or graphic, historical accuracy and sense of drama and/or humor. Fees depend on complexity and extent of assignment. Query.

JEAN-GUY JACQUE ET COMPAGNIE, 633 N. LaBrea Ave., Los Angeles CA 90036. (213)936-7177. Contact: J. G. Jacque. Uses artists for animation art, graphic design and layout/design. Pays $1,000 for design for TV commercials. Query with resume.

JEPPESEN SANDERSON, 8065 E. 40th St., Denver CO 80207. (303)320-6070. Audiovisual Manager: George A. Beard. Produces Super 8mm film loops, sound filmstrips, videotapes, 8/16mm motion pictures and slides on aviation, scuba and skin diving and weather. Prefers Denver artists. Query with samples. Material copyrighted.

KAVIC HOUSE, INC., Box 308, Wellesley Hills MA 02181. Contact: Syd Green. Produces educational Super 8mm film loops, motion pictures, overhead transparencies and multimedia kits. Pays 8% minimum of net sales. Query with resume and portfolio or description of audiovisual project.

KEN-DEL PRODUCTIONS, INC., 111 Valley Rd., Richardson Park, Wilmington DE 19804. Contact: Edwin Kennedy. Produces 16mm film loops, silent and sound filmstrips, 16/35/Super 8mm motion pictures, overhead transparencies, and slides. Query with sample outline or storyboard.

RON KLEIN & COMPANY, 520 N. Michigan Ave., Chicago IL 60611. Contact: Ron Klein. Uses artists for animation art, industrial films and set design. Query.

DON B. KLUGMAN FILMS, 1446 N. Wells St., Chicago IL 60610. (312)642-8284. Contact: Don Klugman. Uses artists for animation art and set design. Payment determined by budget. Query with resume.

L.S.V. PRODUCTIONS, LTD., c/o Gold Eagle Productions, 70 E. 96th, New York NY 10028. Contact: Arthur Allan Seidelman. Uses artists experienced in advertising art/design/layout, animated cartoons, billboard art, film titles, fine art, lettering, posters and theater programs/posters. Requests initial submission of ink or line and wash; either rough or finished samples. Purchases "all rights necessary for the use of the work in motion pictures, posters for films or plays, or scene designs for films or theater." Maintains office in England.

ED LANG, INC., 73 Westpark Rd., Dayton OH 46459. (513)433-3133. Contact: Edward R. Lang. Uses artists experienced in animation art and graphic/set design. Arrange interview.

LARUE COMMUNICATIONS, INC., 708 N. Dearborn St., Chicago IL 60610. Art Director: Debra Ustanik. Produces educational films, filmstrips, slide programs and printed support material for the medical profession. Uses artists for animation, direct mail brochures, keyline/paste-up, magazine ads, multimedia kits, technical charts and slide art. Negotiates payment. Payment determined by personal capabilities and job. Assigns 50 freelance jobs annually. Send resume. Reports in 2 weeks.

LDA INC., (Lion's Den Associates, Inc.), 717 Main St., Woodbury CT 06798. (203)263-5669. Contact: Dorothea Bunting. Uses artists for animation art, slide films, filmstrips and graphic design. "Artists must be familiar with filmstrip and audiovisual formats. Most of our art is needed for the educational and commercial filmstrip market, in all subject areas." Pays $15-50 for each filmstrip frame. Filmstrip may contain as many as 40-80 frames; usually packaged in sets of 4 or 6. Buys all rights. Query with resume.

J.B. LIPPINCOTT COMPANY — MEDIA DEVELOPMENT/DIVISION OF HIGHER EDUCATION, E. Washington Square, Philadelphia PA 19105. (215)574-4235. Managing Editor: H. Michael Eisler. Estab: 1968. Produces educational materials for health and medical professions. Uses artists for animation. Pays $10-30 per frame of animation. Payment determined by job. Query. Material copyrighted. SASE. Free catalog.

M. C. PRODUCTIONS, 56-40 195th St., Fresh Meadows NY 11365. Contact: Martin Mauer. Uses artists for industrial films and set design. "All work we do is based on agency work which we bid on, so prices vary from one job to the next." Query with resume.

CAMERON McKAY PRODUCTIONS, 6850 Lexington Ave., Hollywood CA 90038. (213)463-6073. President: Cameron McKay. Estab: 1959. Produces motion pictures, educational filmstrips, cassettes, records, workbooks and art supplies for educators. Uses artists for animation, catalog covers/illustrations, multimedia kits, study prints, technical charts/illustrations and filmstrip art. Pays $50-85 for multiple pieces/filmstrip art. Payment determined by job. Buys 1,500+ freelance designs annually. Query or call for interview. Buys all rights. Reports in 1 week. SASE. Free catalog.

DONALD MANELLI & ASSOCIATES, INC., 307 N. Michigan Ave., Chicago IL 60601. Contact: Donald Manelli. Uses artists for graphic and exhibit design and print production. Query with resume.
To Break In: "In the development of coordinated communication programs involving several media, we often look for over-all program design, much like a corporate identification program."

ROBERT B. MANSOUR, LTD., 2250 Midland Ave., Unit #9, Scarborough, Ontario Canada. (416)291-2680. President: R. B. Mansour. Estab: 1973. Produces filmstrips and filmstrip/cassette combinations for kindergarten-8th grade. Uses artists for animation, multimedia kits and technical charts/illustrations. Payment determined by job; also pays advances and royalties. Buys approximately 350 freelance designs annually. Mail samples. Material copyrighted. Reports in 1-12 months. SASE. Free catalog. "We expect to expand or open offices in the U. S. in 1977 and will be producing new programs."

MARK XV/MARK DRUCK PRODUCTIONS, 300 E. 40th St., New York NY 10016. (212)682-5980. President: Mark Druck. Estab: 1972. Produces films and videotapes. Uses artists for animation, technical charts/illustrations and film and videotape production. Payment determined by job. Mail resumes.

A. MARVIN PRODUCTIONS, INC., 1224 N. Dearborn Pkwy., Chicago IL 60610. (312)649-0944. President: Marvin A. Gleicher. Estab: 1972. Produces ¾" and 2" videotapes and 16/35mm films for educational, commercial, PSA and record industry services. Uses artists for animation, catalog covers/illustrations, multimedia kits, record album design and technical services. Pays $75-2,000. Payment determined by job. Buys 20 freelance designs annually. Write for interview. Some material copyrighted. Buys all rights. Reports in 10 days. SASE.

ED MARZOLA & ASSOCIATES, 8831 Sunset Blvd., Suite 408, Hollywood CA 90069. (213)652-7481. Creative Director: John Randau. Estab: 1970. Produces educational (grades 5-12) shows, industrial sales training film and filmstrips and bilingual education programs. Uses artists for animation, direct mail brochures, layout, magazine ads, paste-up, technical charts/illustrations and type spec. Pays $10-30 per hour, animation, layout, and magazine ads; $10-15 per hour, direct mail brochures, paste-up, technical charts/illustrations and type spec. Buys approximately 50 freelance designs annually. Query. Material copyrighted. Reports in 10 days. SASE. "Be creative, professional and deliver on time."

MAYSLERS FILMS, INC., 1697 Broadway, New York NY 10019. Contact: Albert or David Maysles. Specializes in documentaries; also produces features and commercials.

MAZIN-WYCKOFF CO., INC., 2 W. 46th St., New York NY 10036. (212)586-2226. Creative Director: Edwin Brit Wyckoff. Estab: 1960. Produces motion pictures, filmstrips and slides. Uses artists for animation, multimedia kits and dimensional construction. Pays $5-10 per hour for dimensional construction. Query with samples or call for interview. Buys all rights. Reports in 2 weeks. SASE.

MEDICAL MULTIMEDIA CORPORATION, 211 E. 43rd St., New York NY 10017. (212)986-0180. Administrative Assistant: Susan Cotterall. Estab: 1973. Produces educational programs in health sciences for the medical profession. Uses artists for layout, multimedia kits, paste-up, technical charts and medical illustrations. Pays $7-12 per hour, mechanicals; $20-30 per hour, design. Payment determined by job. Buys 150-200 New York freelance designs annually. Call for interview. Buys all rights.

MEETING MAKERS INC., 18 E. 48 St., New York NY 10017. Contact: Sam Sugarman. Specializes in audiovisual presentations for industry. Uses artists with background in mechanicals and slide mounting. Query for interview.

ARTHUR MERIWETHER INC., Box 457, 921 Curtiss St., Downers Grove IL 60515. Creative Director: Art Zapel. Estab: 1966. Produces educational audiovisual projects. Uses artists for animation, dioramas, multimedia kits, paste-up, technical charts/illustrations and artwork for educational filmstrips. Pays $75-200, posters; $25-55 per frame for filmstrip art; $35-75, charts; $10-150, line art illustrations. Payment determined by time spent or job. Buys 75+ freelance designs annually. Query with small samples. Buys audiovisual or all rights. Reports in 3 weeks. SASE. Catalog 25¢.
To Break In: "Be interested in art concepts that can be adapted to filmstrips designed to teach communciation arts."

METCALFE FILMS, 3709 Locksley Dr., Birmingham AL 35223. Contact: Charles Metcalfe. Uses artists for animation art, documentaries, industrial films and slides. Query.

WARREN MILLER PRODUCTIONS, 505 Pier Ave., Hermosa CA 90254. (213)376-2494. Sales Manager: Bill Pennington. Estab: 1949. Produces sports documentaries. Use artists for direct mail brochures and magazine ads. Pays $100-200. Payment determined by job. Buys 6 freelance designs annually. Query with samples or write for interview. Buys nonexclusive rights. Reports in 2 weeks. SASE.

THE MISERY LOVES COMPANY, 1416 N. State Pkwy., Chicago IL 60610. Contact: Robert A. Levin. Uses artists for set design. Mail resume.

CLINT MOREHOUSE PHOTOGRAPHY, 3405 Crest Dr., Manhattan Beach CA 90266. (213)545-1837. Uses artists for animation art and graphic/exhibit/set design. Buys one-time only rights. Query with resume or arrange interview.

TOM MORRIS INC., 621 Devon, Park Ridge IL 60068. Contact: Tom Morris. Produces print media, charts, silent and sound filmstrips, motion pictures and slides for religious, commercial and industrial clients. Submit slides and resume.

MOSS COMMUNICATIONS INC., 160 E. 38th St., Suite 6A, New York NY 10016. (212)687-8640. Contact: Jack Moss. Produces animation art, slide films, graphic design, industrial films, multimedia and brochures. "Styles needed range from cartoon-type to sophisticated, realistic and designed. Requires 10-75 finished pieces." Pays $15, titles; $25-35, slide film art. Buys all rights. Query with resume; company then arranges interview.

MOTIVATION MEDIA, INC., 110 River Rd., Des Plaines IL 60016. (312)297-4740. Production Manager: Paul Snyder. Estab: 1969. Produces audiovisual programs. Uses local artists for animation, layout, paste-up, technical charts/illustrations, cartoons, acetate cell painting and set design. Pays $5-10 per hour, paste-up; $5-15 per hour, layout; $15-60 per frame, technical charts/illustrations; $20-40 per frame, cartoons. Call or write for interview. Present slides, photos and/or renderings. Reports at interview. SASE.
To Break In: "Knowledge of all film formats, color keys, gel applications, and preparing art for top and bottom lighting on camera are very important."

MRC FILMS, Division of McLaughlin Research Corp., 71 W. 23rd St., New York NY 10010. Contact: Larry Mollot. Produces motion pictures, sound filmstrips and slides. "Our market is a wide spectrum. Our audience may be business executives, white collar and blue collar workers, military personnel, children, general TV audiences, etc. We would like to know of competent animators and artists for future assignments. Write for an appointment. After we have reviewed samples of your work we can call you in for specific assignments." Fees are based on individual project requirements. "We're looking for professionals with experience, creativity and proficiency in their field of work."

MULTI IMAGE PRODUCTIONS, INC., Subsidiary of Fotomat Corp., 8849 Complex Dr., San Diego CA 92123. (714)560-8383. Contact: Fred W. Ashman. Uses artists for exhibit and set design. Pays $100-250 per day for crew members; $100-4,000, finished work. Query with resume. Buys all rights.

NATIONAL TEACHING AIDS, INC., 120 Fulton Ave., Garden City Park NY 11040. (516)248-5590. Contact: Aaron Becker. Produces silent filmstrips, models and slides for grades 3 through junior college. Will assign projects to qualified freelancers with evidence of talent and application. Experience in technical illustration, photomicroscopy and macrophotography is helpful. Rates negotiable. Material copyrighted. Will interview qualified local artists.

NEW WORLD PRODUCTIONS, 201 N. Rampart, Los Angeles CA 90026. President: Eric Reiner. Uses experienced artists for feature films, TV specials, industrial films and documentaries.

ONYX FILMS, INC., 361 Place Royale, Montreal, Quebec Canada. Contact: Betty-Ann Tutching. Uses artists for animation art, documentaries, industrial films, slides and graphic/exhibit/set design.

OUR SUNDAY VISITOR, INC., Audiovisual Department, Noll Plaza, Huntington IN 46750. Contact: Margaret Schultz or Rick Hawthorne. Produces sound filmstrips, overhead transparencies, slides for religion students in grades K through 12 and adult religious education groups and teacher training units. Artist must have comprehensive, realistic illustration talent and ability plus professional experience. Artwork may be purchased outright and/or receive a royalty of from 5-10% of price received, depending on the product and its market. Pays $30 for full-color, comprehensive (often multicharacter) artwork done in various styles in 8x12" format using acrylics, Magic Marker or designer colors. Query. Subjects range from the miracles and parables of Jesus to modern church history, liturgy and doctrine for all grade levels.

OUTDOOR PICTURES, Box 277, Anacortes WA 98221. (206)293-3200. President: Ernest Booth. Estab: 1958. Produces filmstrips, slides, motion pictures and mammal/fossil collections. Uses artists for filmstrip illustration. Pays 10% royalties on retail price. Query. Some material copyrighted. Reports in 1-3 days. Free catalog.

OVATION FILMS, INC., 33 W. 46th St., New York NY 10036. (212)581-4406. Contact: Art Petricone. Occasionally uses artists for exhibit/set design and animation art. Arrange interview.

PACE FILMS, INC., 411 E. 53rd St., New York NY 10022. (212)755-5486. Contact: R. Vanderbes. Produces documentaries, industrial/slide films, TV commercials and theatrical shorts. Query with resume.

PACIFIC PRODUCTIONS, Box 2881, Honolulu HI 96802. (808)531-1560. Manager: Bill Bennett. Estab: 1946. Produces educational, industrial and editorial audiovisual material. Use artists for layouts through finished art. Payment determined by job. Query. Buys all rights. Reports in 4 weeks. SASE.

PANORAMIC STUDIOS, 2243 W. Allegheny Ave., Philadelphia PA 19132. (215)228-2113. Contact: Leonard N. Abrams. Produces dioramas, models and exhibits. Assigns 10 freelance jobs annually. Uses artists for dioramas, models, cartography and technical charts/illustrations. Pays $5 per hour. Material copyrighted. Query. Reports in 3 weeks.

PARAGON PRODUCTIONS, Box 395, Oakton VA 22124. General Manager: Ron Dziekonski. "We've expanded our operations to include full media production: industrial, educational,

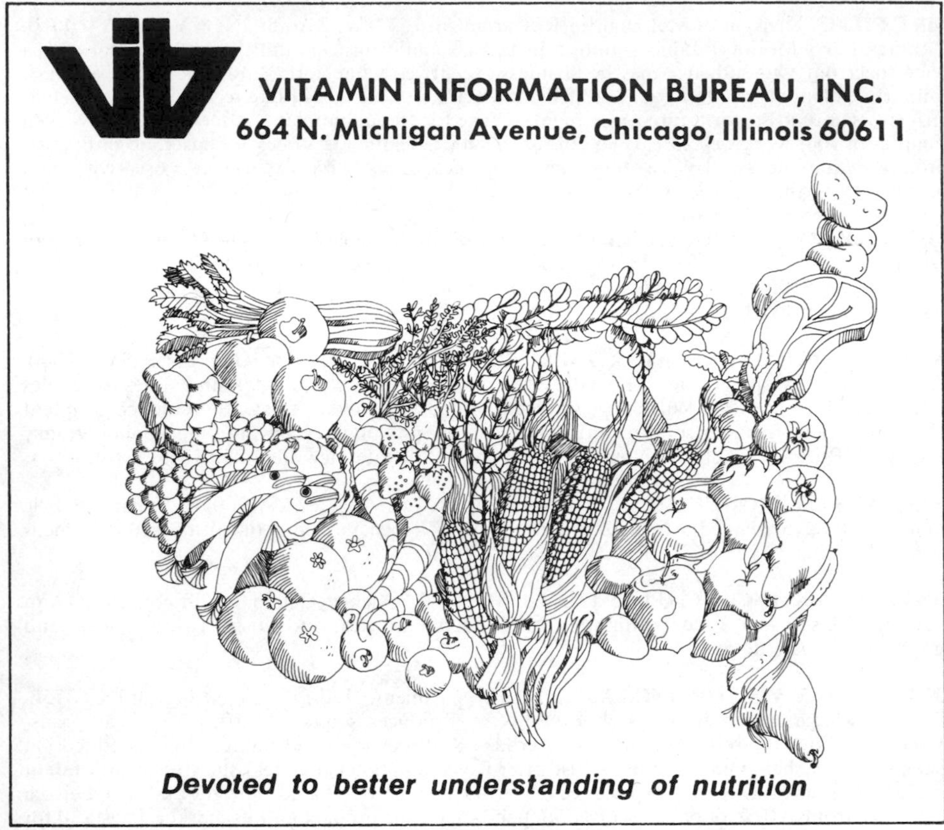

An "ability to appealingly represent nutrition in the U.S." helped George Naimark sell this drawing to Vitamin Information Bureau, Inc. Although the Bureau is usually in the market for wall charts, booklets, filmstrips and multimedia kits, this illustration was purchased for use on the cover of a reference folder and envelopes.

scientific and commercial motion pictures, audio and video tape, slides, filmstrips, graphic arts and publications. We use freelancers only on a per job basis, but we select from an active resume file of East Coast talent. We are particularly interested in storyboard artists and brochure/flyer designers. Our clients are trade associations, labor unions, professional societies, medical and public service agencies and private industry."

PERPETUAL MOTION PICTURES, INC., 18 E. 48th St., New York NY 10017. (212)759-7990. Contact: Karen or Vince. Estab: 1968. Produces animation for TV commercials and programs. Uses artists for animation. Pays $150 minimum for design and/or story. Payment determined by time spent and job. Buys 100 local freelance designs annually. Query. Buys all rights. SASE.

PHOENIX FILMS, INC., 470 Park Ave. S., New York NY 10016. (212)684-5910. Contact: H. Gelles. Produces educational materials. Uses artists for 16mm motion pictures, catalog sheets, mailing pieces and study guides. Payment determined by job.

PHOTOCOM PRODUCTIONS, Box 3135, Pismo Beach CA 93449. Contact: B. L. Pattison. Estab: 1976. Produces educational filmstrips. Uses artists for animation and multimedia kits. Pays $15-50 for filmstrip graphic art. Payment determined by job. Buys 100 freelance designs annually. Query. Buys all rights. Reports in 2 weeks. SASE.
To Break In: "We've recently found that work done with colored Zipatone is about the best for reproduction, but have used all media from cut paper to acrylics for illustrations."

PITTARO PRODUCTIONS, 137-73 70th Ave., Flushing NY 11367. Contact: Ernest M. Pittaro. Uses artists for animation art, slides, special effects, trick cinematography and construction of special props and models. Query with resume.

PLAYETTE CORPORATION, 301 E. Shore Rd., Great Neck NY 11023. President: Evans. Estab: 1940. Produces educational (ages 5-21) spoken records, books, slides, filmstrips, photos, posters and games. Uses artists for multimedia kits, study prints and technical charts/illustrations. Negotiates payment. Query. Material copyrighted. Reports in 4 weeks. No work returned. "Be familiar with foreign language and culture."

PUCK PRODUCTIONS/THE MIDLASH GROUP, 676 N. LaSalle St., Chicago IL 60610. Producer: Hank Puckhaber. "We produce in all media." Uses artists for animation art, slides, industrial films and graphic design. Submit resume.

PUNCH FILMS, INC., Box Q, New York NY 10011. Contact: Ms. F. Davis. Produces sound filmstrips and 16/35mm motion pictures in the language arts field from 6th grade to college level. Uses artists experienced in stop motion object animation. Submit resume.

LOU PUOPOLO INC., 381 Park Ave. S., New York NY 10016. Contact: Lou Puopolo. Uses artists for animation art, design and illustration. "Our clients are advertising agencies for whom we produce TV commercials. We would prefer to have samples sent to us for the rare occasions that we would use animation, illustration, etc."

Q-ED PRODUCTIONS, INC., 2921 W. Alameda Ave., Box 1608, Burbank CA 91507. Vice President of Production: Michael Halperin. Uses artists with previous experience in film and filmstrips. Produces audiovisual materials for public and private schools in grades K through 12. "Historically, we have leaned toward values and guidance materials. However, we are leaning toward curriculum-based programs. We are constantly looking for fresh concepts. Emphasis should be on the child's viewpoint (consistent with the target audience). We also like the photojournalistic approach to filmstrips with an eye to good continuity." Buys all rights. Will consider a distribution deal on projects produced and completed. Query with resume.

R.M.A. INC., 117 E. 30th St., New York NY 10016. (212)532-7083. President: R. J. Mechin, Jr. Estab: 1952. Produces audiovisual projection art for college level and above. Uses artists for catalog covers/illustrations, multimedia kits, paste-up, technical charts/illustrations and multiscreen-multimedia designers. Pays $8-10 per hour, mechanicals; $10-20 per hour, design and storyboards.

REACH PRODUCTIONS, 32 N. Main St., Suite 1301, Dayton OH 45402. Director of Visual Concepts: Austine Wood. Produces educational programs for cable TV which accompany community workshops. A project of the Dayton-Miami Valley Consortium of Colleges. Uses artists experienced in animation art and graphic/set design. Pays $5 an hour. "We would like to see the work of creative young cartoonists and animators who can interpret educational material—give it clarity and a sense of fun. We are not interested in slickness. We want work that reflects a real empathy with human beings and their daily struggles. We do not have a big budget, but we may be a good starting place for an innovative mind who would be interested in creating 'Seasame Street' type productions for adults. Reach programs are produced on 1 helical scan videotape in b&w. We would contract with an artist whose style of work we like. We would at that time detail the requirements for the particular job." Buys reproduction rights (repeat, but nonexclusive rights). Query with resume.

REEVES TELETAPE CORPORATION, 708 3rd Ave., New York NY 10017. (212)573-8600. Graphic Designer: David Palm. Estab: 1950. Produces TV training tapes, slides and collateral material ("Sesame St.," "Electric Co."). Uses artists for animation, calligraphy, direct mail brochures, layout, models, multimedia kits, paste-up, technical charts/illustrations and display. Pays $20 per hour maximum, design; $12 per hour maximum, paste-up. Buys New York freelance designs. Call for interview. Material copyrighted. No work returned.

RICHTER McBRIDE PRODUCTIONS INC., 1 E. 42nd St., New York NY 10017. President: Robert Richter. Estab: 1968. Produces motion pictures for TV, government, organizations, industries and schools. Uses local artists for animation and titles. Pays $500-3,000 per minute, animation; $75-1,500, titles. Payment determined by job. Buys 20-25 freelance designs annually. Query with 16mm sample reel. Buys all rights. Reports in 2 weeks. SASE.

LINFORD C. RICKARD, 5725 Lawton Dr., Sarasota FL 33581. Contact: Linford C. Rickard. Uses artists experienced in graphic and set design. Arrange interview.

RIVIERA PRODUCTIONS, 6610 Selma Ave., Hollywood CA 90028. Contact: Will Zens. Produces 16/35mm motion picture films, often for clients who want to get across a certain message in films that are offered free to groups. One film on the United Nations urged U. S. withdrawal from that group. Query with resume.

JOHN ROBERT PRODUCTIONS, 186 Francisco St., San Francisco CA 94133. Executive Producer: Henrietta Matta. Produces 16mm film for TV audiences. Uses artists for audiovisual projects. Payment determined by flat fee. Purchases rights to motion picture scripts.

ROCKET PICTURES, INC., 1150 W. Olive St., Burbank CA 91506. Contact: Dick Western. Produces animation art, documentaries, industrial films, slides and graphic/exhibit/set design. Query with resume.

F. K. ROCKETT PRODUCTIONS, INC., 10307 Glenbarr Ave., Los Angeles CA 90064. (213)985-1090. President: Tom Cole. Estab: 1924. Produces films. Uses artists for animation, direct mail brochures, models, multimedia kits and technical charts/illustrations. Pays $500-2,000. Payment determined by job. Buys approximately 10 freelance designs annually. Query. Buys all rights. "We never throw away a proposal, but as a practical matter anything over a year is dated."

PETER ROSEN PRODUCTIONS, INC., 19½ E. 62nd St., New York NY 10021. (212)751-7788. President: Peter Rosen. Estab: 1970. Produces motion picture films for government and TV. Uses artists for animation. Pays $5,000 per job; $200 minimum, animation shooting. Payment determined by job. Buys 1 local freelance design annually. Query with resume. SASE. Buys world-wide rights.

ROSS-GAFFNEY INC., 21 W. 46th St., New York NY 10036. (212)582-3744. Contact: Paul Burggraf. Uses artists for animation and graphic/exhibit/set design. Query with resume.

RUNNING PRODUCTIONS, 500 E. Birch St., Flagstaff AZ 86001. Contact: Yvonne Trostli or John Running. Produces 16mm films and 35mm filmstrips for the educational market, as well as promotional material for industry and organizations. Produces silent and sound filmstrips, motion pictures, slides and multimedia kits. "I'd like to see a portfolio of 20-60 slides (35mm) in 8½x11 sheets." Buys film or filmstrip rights. The fee arrangement is a flat fee basis depending upon the kind of work needed.

LEW SCHWARTZ, INC., 231 Waterway, New Seabury, Mashpee MA 02649. Contact: Lew Sayre Schwartz. Uses artists for animation art, slides and graphic/exhibit/set design. Query.

SERIOUS BUSINESS COMPANY, 1609 Jaynes St., Berkeley CA 94703. (415)527-6800. Contact: Ms. Freude Bartlett. Estab: 1969. Produces shorts. Uses artists for catalog covers/illustrations and paste-up. Pays "$10-300, depending on use and rights purchased." Payment determined by hour and/or job. Buys 6 freelance designs annually. Query. Usually buys one-time reproduction rights. Reports in 1 week. SASE. Sample catalog $2.

SKYLINE FILMS, INC., 160 E. 38th St., New York NY 10011. (212)490-1668. President: Joseph McDonough. Estab: 1963. Produces films, TV shows, comics, videotape and live shows. Uses artists for animation, multimedia kits, technical charts/illustrations, storyboards, art props and titles. Payment determined by job. SASE.

SLEEPING GIANT FILMS, INC., 3019 Dixwell Ave., Hamden CT 06518. Contact: Anthony Guarino, Jr. Produces slides, filmstrips, 16/35mm film loops, motion pictures and multimedia kits. Uses artists for audiovisuals.

THE SLIDE HOUSE, INC., 305 E. 47th St., New York NY 10017. Contact: Graphics Department. Designs and produces slide presentations and does phototypesetting. Clients are advertising agencies, major corporations, publishers, and graphic designers. Uses artists for mechanicals, paste-up art and decorative illustration. Submit resume. Portfolio showing by appointment.

KEN SNYDER INDUSTRIES, 2032 Alameda Padre Serra, Santa Barbara CA 93103. (805)962-8171. Project Director: Tish Gainey. Estab: 1962. Produces multimedia kits, 8/16/35mm films, presentations, videotapes, package designs, radio/TV advertising, public relations, exhibitions, and theme parks. Uses artists for animation, calligraphy, catalog covers/illustrations, dioramas, direct mail brochures, layout, magazine ads, models, multimedia kits, paste-up, study prints, technical charts/illustrations and type spec. Minimum payment: $5 per foot, 35mm animation; $150, posters. Payment determined by job. Buys 200 freelance designs annually. Query. Buys all rights. Reports in 2 weeks. SASE.

SOUNDLAB, INC., 4130 Aurora St., Coral Gables FL 33146. President: Eduardo More. Produces animation, art, slides, industrial films and documentaries.

STANART STUDIOS, 45 W. 45th St., New York NY 10036. Contact: Stan Popko. Specializes in creative animation for industrial films, including slides and graphic design. Query.

THE ROBERT STORY COMPANY, Box 8486, Universal City CA 91608. Contact: Mary Wilson. Uses artists for animated commercials, industrial films, documentaries and graphic/set design. Produces material for KNBC, KABC and "various advertising agencies." Query with resume.

BURT SUGARMAN, INC., 9000 Sunset Blvd., Los Angeles CA 90069. (213)278-8300. Contact: Jacques Andre. Uses artists experienced in animation art, documentaries, slide films, and graphic/exhibit/set design. Query. All material must be owned by artist.

SWANK MOTION PICTURES, INC., 201 S. Jefferson, St. Louis MO 63166. (314)534-6300. Creative Director: Fred T. Mirick. Estab: 1936. In-house production firm. Services include in-house direct mail. Uses artists for cartoons, illustrations, logo design and catalog/direct mail concept. Previously published work OK. Assigns 5-10 freelance jobs annually. Pays $75 for illustrations. Payment determined by job. Submit 8½x11" samples by mail. Reports in 3 weeks. SASE.

SYNTHAVISION, 3 Westchester Plaza, Elmsford NY 10523. President: Phillip S. Mittelman. Uses artists for preparation of storyboards and sketches for clients of the SynthaVision graphic process, a product of MAGI. "SynthaVision works on the principle of 'visual simulation.' You supply directions and descriptions of what you want on film, the objects and their movements, plus any other details. Then, the computer programmer takes over. SynthaVision generates realistic pictures of concepts by computer and brings them to life on film." Query with samples.

TALCO PRODUCTIONS, 279 E. 44th St., New York NY 10017. Contact: Alan Lawrence. Produces sound filmstrips, 16/35mm motion pictures and VTR (all formats). Needs vary, depending upon the project. Audiences range from elementary school to senior citizens. "We are in general production." Assigns projects to qualified artists if they "are very experienced." Occasionally uses inexperienced people if they show exceptional talent under close supervision. Payment determined by project. Material usually copyrighted. Send samples on request only. "We like to keep a file available of pros outside of New York. When a special need develops, we contact them to determine their competence for the job at hand. Our file contains only resumes and brochures — no samples."

TEL-AIR FILMS, 1755 NE 149 St., North Miami FL 33161. Contact: Charles Allen. Produces documentaries, industrial films, slides and graphic/exhibit/set design. Query.

TELEMATED MOTION PICTURES, 51 E. 42nd St., Room 1510, New York NY 10017. (212)682-3434. Producer/Director: Saul Taffet. Estab: 1947. Produces motion pictures, filmstrips, slides, animation and special effects. Uses artists for animation, layout and technical charts/illustrations. Payment determined by job. Buys all rights. SASE.
To Break In: "Have the ability to adapt artistic talent to the disciplines and needs of the medium. Be on time with deliveries and stay within budget."

DON TREVOR ASSOCIATES, INC., 20 E. 9th St., New York NY 10003. (212)260-2984. Producer/Director: Don Trevor. Uses artists for animation art, documentaries, film and tape commercials, sales training/industrial films and set design. Query with resume.

TROLL ASSOCIATES, 320 Rte. 17, Mahwah NJ 07430. Vice President, Production: Marian Schecter. Estab: 1968. Produces books, records, filmstrips and multimedia for schools. Uses local artists for catalog covers/illustrations, direct mail brochures, multimedia kits, record album designs and book illustrations. Payment determined by job. Buys approximately 50 designs annually. Query or write for interview. Buys all rights. Reports in 3 weeks. SASE.

UNIVERSAL PICTURES CO., 100 Universal City Plaza, Universal City CA 91608. Contact: Clark Ramsay. Interested in graphic designs, illustrations and complete concepts for motion picture advertising. Professionals with expertise and credits in these areas should arrange interview. Payment on an individual basis, per job. Buys all rights.

VARIS ASSOCIATES, 66 Bethpage Rd., Hicksville NY 11801. Contact: Mel Eisenberg. Produces materials for schools, grades K through 6. "We want people who make their living as artists — not teachers. But they should live in the area — either Long Island, Queens, Westchester or New York City." Arrange interview and/or do a 1-picture test.

VIDEO FILMS INC., 2211 E. Jefferson Ave., Detroit MI 48207. (313)393-0800. Production Manager: John M. Niskanen. Estab: 1947. Produces slide programs, filmstrips, motion pictures and videotapes. Uses artists for animation. Payment determined by job. Query. Material copyrighted.

THE VIDEO GROUP, INC., 77 W. Canfield, Detroit MI 48202. Production Manager: Rebecca Smith. Uses artists for animation art, documentaries, industrial films, slides and graphic/set design. "The majority of our work is in videotape; film fulfills approximately 10-20%." Query with resume.

VISCOUNT PRODUCTIONS, INC., 650 Miami Circle NE, Atlanta GA 30324. President: Charles Josey. Uses artists for animation art, documentaries, industrial films and slides. Query.

VITAMIN INFORMATION BUREAU, INC., 664 N. Michigan Ave., Chicago IL 60611. (312)751-2223. President: Caryl Wright. Estab: 1967. Produces wall charts, booklets, filmstrips and multimedia kits for schools and the medical profession. Uses artists for filmstrip frames, direct mail brochures, multimedia kits and technical charts/illustrations. Pays $1,500-3,000 for 50-frame filmstrips. Payment determined by job. Buys 1-2 Chicago freelance designs annually. Query, mail samples or write for interview. Buys all rights. Reports in 1-2 weeks. SASE. Free catalog.

VIVA PRODUCTIONS, INC., 4132 N. 12th St., Phoenix AZ 85014. (602)277-9751. Contact: Production Department. Estab: 1957. Produces motion pictures. Uses artists for animation and titles. Pays $100 minimum, titles; negotiates payment, animation. Payment determined by job. Buys 6 freelance designs annually. Mail samples. Material copyrighted. Buys motion picture rights. Reports in 1 month. SASE.

VOCATIONAL EDUCATION PRODUCTIONS, California Polytechnic State University, San Luis Obispo CA 93407. Acting Director: Steven C. LaMarine. Estab: 1968. Produces vocational agriculture instructional materials (filmstrips, slide sets, manuals) for high school. Uses artists for individual art frames, catalog covers/illustrations, direct mail brochures, layout, magazine ads, multimedia kits, paste-up and technical charts/illustrations. Pays $15-50, single art frames; $100 minimum, catalog covers; $200 minimum, brochures (price negotiated). Payment determined by job. Buys 200+ freelance designs annually. Query with 35mm slides (for film). Buys all rights. Reports in 2 weeks. SASE. Free catalog.

VOICE AND VISION PRODUCTIONS, INC., 1833 Kalorama Rd. NW, Washington DC 20009. Contact: Orlanzo Nunez. Uses artists experienced in animation art and slide films. Stresses quality. Buys world rights. Query with resume.

WAKEFOHD/ORLOFF, 29 E. 32nd St., New York NY 10016. (212)532-2850. Contact: Alice Mintzer. Uses artists for animation art, graphic/exhibit/set design, documentaries and slide/industrial films. Query with resume.

ROBERT WARNER PRODUCTIONS, 7 E. 78th St., New York NY 10021. Contact: Robert Warner. Uses artists for animation art and commercials. Query with resume.

LENNIE WEINRIB PRODUCTIONS, 9255 Sunset Blvd., Suite 515, Los Angeles CA 90069. (213)278-4831. Uses artists for animation art and children's, fiction and family films. Freelancers must have extensive experience in animation, storyboarding, set and movie composition frame design, and filmmaking. Interested in high integrity artistic achievement. Query with resume. "Top dollar salaries open for good qualified men or women."

BERNARD WEISS & ASSOCIATES, 500 Newfield Ave., Stamford CT 06905. (203)348-3719. President: Bernard Weiss. Estab: 1974. Produces multimedia materials for the health care industry and professions. Uses artists for catalog covers/illustrations, direct mail brochures, layout, multimedia kits, paste-up, anatomical drawings and type spec. Pays $500-1,200, brochure layout (including design, spec and paste-up); $50-500, anatomical illustrations. Payment determined by job. Buys 10-12 freelance designs annually. Query, or call or write for interview. Material usually copyrighted. Buys one-time and reprint rights. Reports in 1 week. SASE.

RUTH WHITE FILMS, Box 34485, Los Angeles CA 90034. Contact: Ruth White. Produces multimedia educational materials. Uses artists for animation art, slide films and graphic/book design. Pays $8-12 per filmstrip frame. Query with resume. Buys all rights.

WILDING INC., 500 N. Michigan Ave., Chicago IL 60611. Executive Producer: Donald K. Carlson. Uses artists for animation art, documentaries, industrial films, slides and graphic/exhibit/set design. Query.

JACK WILLIAMSON MOTION PICTURE PRODUCTION, 426 31st St., Newport Beach CA 92663. Contact: Jack Williamson. Produces sound and silent filmstrips, 16mm motion pictures and animation. "Our audience includes the broad spectrum of people sought out by the business community in promoting its wares, image and philosophy. Our audience is whomever our clients wish to reach with unique production — the public, the student, the consumer, the employee, willing or outraged. We work entirely with crews made up of freelancers chosen for each production according to their respective talents and the requirements of that particular film. We are willing to assign audiovisual projects to qualified artists outside our usual crew, but they must be superior to — not just as good as — the pool of people we now draw from, before we would offer an assignment. If you have a piece of film — no longer than ten minutes — which clearly demonstrates your talent with a paintbrush, we will look at it carefully, recognizing the expense it represents, and return it to you within 3 days. Do not bring it in or call to see if it's OK to bring it in; just send it to us." Pays $6-10 per hour for art. Buys all rights.

WORONER FILMS, INC., 1995 NE 150 St., North Miami FL 33161. President: Murry Woroner. "We produce educational and training films and documentaries." Uses artists for animation art, slides, graphic/set design, makeup and titles. Query with resume.

ZOUNDS!, 224 Bellevue Ave., Haddonfield NJ 08033. Contact: F. Knight. Uses artists for animation art, documentaries and industrial films.

Record Companies

ADVENT RECORDS, 4150 Mayfield Rd., Cleveland OH 44121. (216)381-9173. Producer: Robert Woods. Estab: 1961. Produces classical records. Uses artists for catalog covers/illustrations, direct mail brochures, layout, magazine ads and record album design. Pays $200-450, color record jacket. Payment determined by job. Buys 25-30 freelance designs annually. Query with samples. Buys all rights. Reports in 4-6 weeks. SASE.

ALLIGATOR RECORDS, Box 11741, Chicago IL 60611. (312)973-7736. President: Bruce Iglauer. Estab: 1971. Produces blues records. Uses artists for record album design. Payment determined by by job. Buys 1-2 local freelance designs annually. Mail samples. Material copyrighted. SASE. Free catalog.

BRIARMEADE RECORDS, 2008 S. 39th St., St. Louis MO 63110. President: Ken Keene. Estab: 1970. Produces country, rock, MOR and soul records. Uses artists for direct mail brochures, magazine ads and record album design. Pays $50 minimum, direct mail brochures;

$150 minimum, magazine ads; $150-500, record album design. Payment determined by job. Buys 10-25 freelance designs annually. Mail color slides, glossy color photos or original art. Buys all rights. Reports in 4 weeks. SASE.

BUDDAH RECORDS, 810 7th Ave., New York NY 10019. Vice President, Creative Services: Milton Sincoff. Specializes in soul and rhythm and blues. Uses artists for album cover designs. Query with resume or samples.

CHELSEA HOUSE FOLKLORE CENTER, Box 1057, Brattleboro VT 07301. (802)257-1482. Manager: Carol Levin. Estab: 1974. Produces folk music records, concerts and various folk music programs. Uses artists for direct mail brochures, layout, advertisements and record album design. Payment determined by job. Buys Vermont, New Hampshire, Massachusetts and sometimes New York freelance designs. Query with samples. Some material copyrighted. Often pays by giving artists tickets to concerts and dances or records. Occasionally pays in cash. SASE.

CHIMNEYVILLE RECORDS, Malaco Records, Box 9287, Jackson MS 39206. Contact: Tommy Couch. Uses record album cover designs. Submit resume and samples.

CREATIVE WORLD RECORDS, 1012 S. Robertson, Los Angeles CA 90035. Contact: Audree Coke. Uses artists for album cover designs. Also interested in original jazz-related art for the cover of *Creative World Magazine*. Write for sample copy. Pays $500 for finished art, including typesetting and paste-up. Buys all rights. Reports in 15 days.

DAWN PRODUCTS, Box 535, Belair MD 21014. (301)879-6633. President: Joey Welz. Estab: 1965. Produces rock records: Music City, Canadian American, Discgo Records. Uses artists for record album design. Payment determined by job. Buys 2 freelance designs annually. Query. SASE. Material copyrighted. Reports in 1 month.

DELMARK RECORDS, 4243 N. Lincoln, Chicago IL 60618. Contact: Steve Tomashefsky. Uses artists for album cover design and finished art. "Our records do not sell like hits, but remain in our catalog and active on the market for many years. We are therefore more interested in clean designs that do not date than in flashy covers. Most of the artists who work for us are interested in the music we issue: jazz and blues. We are especially interested in artists who can arrive at interesting multi-color designs based on black and white photographs." Pays $100, album design; $250, finished art. Buys nonexclusive rights; depending on fee paid. Query with resume.

DIVINE RECORDS, 140-11 Benchley Place, Bronx NY 10475. (212)671-4042. Vice President: Gilbert Northern. Estab: 1975. Produces black-oriented jazz records and posters. Uses local artists for layout, magazine ads, paste-up and record album design. Pays $200-400, record album design; $50-120, layout. Payment determined by job. Buys 2 freelance designs annually. Mail scale samples. Buys all rights. Reports in 3 weeks. SASE.

ECLIPSE/MARANTA RECORDS, INC. (Division of Maranta Music Entertainments, Inc.), Box 9, Wyckoff NJ 07481. Contact: Clancy Morales. Uses artists for album cover designs. "We would like to receive good pictures especially in colors (no slides), paintings, original art designs and comps, good lettering works (color keys will be fine) stats of good art and hand lettering (no cold type). Send copies or stats, no originals. Query with resume before sending samples. Pays $50, album design; $25, finished art; $50-300, album package with mechanicals and original art. Buys reproduction rights, but usually either leases or just uses art, most of which is returned to the artist after being used or printed. Reports in 15 days.

ESP DISK LTD., 290 W. End Ave., New York NY 10023. Contact: Bernard or Flavia Stollman. Underground record company. Requires strong, original statements by uncompromising artists. Welcome innovative ideas, whether in packaging, esthetics, materials or cartoons. Prefers to be outrageous, stimulating, provocative, in keeping with policy on recording. Query with resume. Sample materials should be submitted by personal presentation. Buys repro rights. Reports immediately on submissions.

FAMOUS DOOR RECORDS, 40-08 155th St., Flushing NY 11354. (212)463-6281. Contact: Harry Lim. Estab: 1974. Produces jazz records. Uses artists for record album design. Pays $50 minimum, jacket design. Payment determined by job. Buys 14 freelance designs annually. Material copyrighted. Reports in 3 weeks on solicited work.

FIDELITY SOUND RECORDINGS, 23 Don Court., Redwood City CA 94062. (415)366-3173. Contact: R. McGovern. Estab: 1953. Produces foreign and specialized material (catalog). Uses local artists for layout, paste-up and record album design. Pays $200-250, record album design and finish. Payment determined by job. Buys 4-10 freelance designs annually. Query. Material copyrighted. Reports in 2 weeks. Free catalog.

CARL FISCHER, INC., 62 Cooper Square, New York NY 10003. (212)777-0900. Director of Publications: John Boerner. Estab: 1872. Produces educational and religious books, music and records. Uses artists for direct mail brochures, paste-up, record album design and publication covers. Pays $70 minimum, covers/jackets; $25 (negotiable), illustrations. Payment determined by job. Buys 200 freelance designs annually. Write or call for interview. Buys all rights. Reports in 2-4 weeks. No work returned. Free catalog of listings.

KEN KEENE INTERNATIONAL 2008 S. 39th St., St. Louis MO 63110 President: Ken Keene. Estab: 1970. Produces country, rock, MOR and soul records. Uses artists for direct mail brochures, magazine ads and record album design. Pays $50 minimum, direct mail brochures; $150 minimum, magazine ads; $150-500, record album design. Payment determined by job.

Artists who can create interesting multi-color designs based on black & white photos are of special interest to Delmark Records. Since Delmark albums remain on the market for several years, the company is more interested in clear designs than flashy covers that date quickly. Designs, such as this by Andrew Epstein, earn artists a minimum of $100.

Buys 10-25 freelance designs annually. Mail color slides, glossy color photos or original art. Buys all rights. Reports in 4 weeks. SASE.

KICKING MULE RECORDS, Box 3233, Berkeley CA 94703. Manager: Ed Denson. Estab: 1973. Produces guitar and banjo records. Uses artists for layout and record album design. Pays $2.50 per page, layout of tab books; $75-250, album cover design; $25-75, album liner design. Payment determined by job. Buys 10-20 local freelance designs annually. Query with full-sized covers and/or actual layouts. Buys all rights. Reports in 2 weeks. SASE. Sample catalog 25¢.

SID KLEINER MUSIC ENTERPRISES, 4121 Gail Blvd., Naples FL 33942. (813)775-2545. Managing Director: Sid Kleiner. Estab: 1949. Produces folk, rock and country recordings; and nutritional, organic gardening and health audiovisuals. Uses artists for record album design, type spec and audiovisual assistance. Pays $50 minimum, covers and audiovisual work. Payment determined by job. Query. Material copyrighted. Reports in 4 weeks. SASE.

LA VAL RECORDS, 226 N. Burdick St., Kalamazoo MI 49006. Contact: Vic La Val. Uses artists for album cover designs. Submit resume and samples of work. Reports in 30 days. Buys all rights.

LE MANS RECORD CO., Box 24, Belle Mead NJ 08502. (201)359-5520. Contact: Bernard Goydish. Uses artists for album cover designs. Produces polka albums. All work should have a happy idea. Usually submits a theme to artist on assignment. Pays $10-25, album designs; $75-150, finished art. Reports in 5 days.

MALACO RECORDS, Box 9287, Jackson MS 39206. Contact: Tommy Couch. Uses record album cover designs. Submit resume and samples.

MARK CUSTOM RECORDING SERVICE, 10815 Bodine Rd., Clarence NY 14031. Contact: Vincent S. Morette. Uses artists for album cover designs. Pays $25 minimum for a design. Buys complete rights. Submit samples or resume. Reports in 60 days.

MARK RECORDS, 10815 Bodine Rd., Clarence NY 14031. (716)759-2600. Art Director: Bruce Marsh. Uses artists for illustration and retouching. Art services are for trade and consumer magazines, direct mail, record jackets and art relating to the music industry. Clients include groups from all musical areas and orchestral and choral societies. Pays $150 for color art comps. Buys all rights (U.S. and foreign). Needs "creative illustrative work that would lend itself to a 13x13" size suitable for record album covers; plates where possible when color is involved. Art with good contrast." Mail samples.

MELODY HOUSE PUBLISHING CO., 819 NW 92nd St., Oklahoma City OK 73114. (405)840-3383. Vice President, Marketing: A. B. Lecrone. Estab: 1969. Produces educational records, cassettes and filmstrips for preschool through elementary grades. Uses artist for catalog covers/illustrations, direct mail brochures, magazine ads and record album design. Pays $30-200, record jackets; $30-150, catalog covers; $25-75, brochures. Payment determined by job. Buys approximately 20 freelance designs annually. Query. Material copyrighted. Reports in 21 days. If samples are requested, SASE. Free catalog.

MUSIC MINUS ONE/CLASSIC JAZZ, INNER CITY/GUITAR WORLD, 43 W. 61st., New York NY 10023. Contact: Irv Kratka. Uses artists for record album cover designs. Submit resume, samples of style and record jacket layouts either printed, or typical work showing artist's particular style and concepts for drawing and typesetting. Reports in 5 days. "We work quickly and need work within 2 weeks of order. We buy all rights."

MYSTIC MUSIC CENTER INC. (Mystic Records—Mystic Sound Studios), 6277 Selma Ave., Hollywood CA 90038. (213)464-9667. President: Doug Moody. Estab: 1968. Produces TV and film music and records. Uses artists for record album design. Payment determined by album budget. Buys approximately 20 freelance designs annually.

NASHVILLE INTERNATIONAL, 20 Music Sq. W., Nashville TN 37203. (615)256-2885. Production Manager: Ron Coats. Designs and prints record album jackets. Uses local artists for layout, illustration, type spec, paste-up and lettering.

NATURAL GROOVE RECORDS, INC., 3588 Big Tree Cove, Memphis TN 38128. (901)382-2094. Secretary: Gwendolyn Greene. Estab: 1973. Produces modern and jazz records. Uses artists for record album design, promotions, posters and T-shirts. Pays $50 minimum. Payment determined by job. Buys 5 freelance designs annually. Mail samples. Buys all rights. Reports in 4 weeks. SASE.

REBEL RECORDING CO., INC., Rte. 12, Ashbury WV 24916. (304)645-6650. President: Charles R. Freeland. Estab: 1959. Produces bluegrass records and tapes. Uses artists for layout, magazine ads and record album design. Pays $100 minimum. Payment determined by job. Query. Buys all rights. Reports in 3 weeks. SASE. Free catalog.

RHYTHMS PRODUCTIONS, Whitney Bldg., Box 34485, Los Angeles CA 90034. (213)836-4678. President: R. S. White. Estab: 1955. Produces educational records, books and multimedia materials for schools. Uses artists for catalog covers/illustrations, direct mail brochures, layout, magazine ads, multimedia kits, paste-up and record album design. Pays $150 minimum for record jackets. Payment determined by job. Buys 3-4 California freelance designs annually. Query with samples. Buys all rights. Reports in 3 weeks.

ROUNDER RECORDS, 186 Willow Ave., Somerville MA 02144. (617)396-8400. Contact: Bill Nowlin. Estab: 1970. Produces American folk records. Uses artists for catalog covers/illustrations and record album design. Pays $100-125, record album design. Payment determined by job. Buys 35 local freelance designs annually. Write or call for interview. Material copyrighted. Free catalog.

SPEBSQSA, INC., (Society for the Preservation and Encouragement of Barber Shop Quartet Singing in America), Box 575, 6315 3rd Ave., Kenosha WI 53140. Marketing Director: Margaret York. Uses local artists for direct mail brochures, catalog design, album covers and advertising layouts. Album cover design pays $425. Call for appointment.

STASH RECORDS, INC., 10 Fieldstone Lane, Lake Success NY 11020. (516)482-1309. Contact: Bernard Brightman. Estab: 1975. Produces erotic, drug-oriented and jazz records. Uses artists for catalog covers/illustration, layout, record album design and engineering. Pays $100-300, cover. Payment determined by job. Buys 4-5 freelance designs annually. Mail small samples. "All designs, covers, etc., belong to Stash and are copyrighted." Reports in 2 weeks. Free catalog.

STEADY RECORDS, AND ARTOGRAPHY, 846 7th Ave., New York NY 10019. Contact: Art Department. Uses artists for album cover designs.

THE VANTAGE RECORDING COMPANY, Box 212, Pottstown PA 19464. Contact: A. A. Botto. Uses artists for album cover designs. Submit resume or produced or manufactured applications of previous art design projects. Personal interview/presentation desirable. Buys partial and/or complete rights. Payment depends on total project and respective budget allocations. Reports in 10 days. Also interested in artists with strong backgrounds in advertising and/or sales motivating promotion campaigns and bank/financial art designs and promotions.

WORLD RECORDS, 484 Waterloo Court, Oshawa, Ontario Canada L1H 3X1. (416)576-0250. General Manager: Bob Stone. Estab: 1969. Produces spoken word, classical, instructional foreign language and folk records; charts and print folios for record and educational (ages 5-16) markets. Uses artists for animation, catalog covers/illustrations, layout, magazine ads, models, multimedia kits, record album design and technical charts/illustrations. Pays $200 minimum, record albums. Payment determined by job. Buys 35 freelance designs annually. Query. Buys all rights. Reports in 2 weeks. SASE. Free catalog.

Book Publishers

A 15% employment drop in the book publishing industry — from 1973 to 1976 — seems to paint a grim picture for the freelance artist looking for assignments. But just the opposite has occurred. Fewer full-time staffers has led to smaller in-house art departments thus increasing the need for freelance help.

But just walking in off the street and asking for a job won't do. As with most other jobs, experience plays a major role. Art directors at book publishing firms want the artist to have a thorough knowledge of publishing terminology, printing and reproduction techniques.

Diane Zimmerman, production editor at Mott Media, says one way to learn about the basic publishing industry is to "visit printers' businesses and become acquainted with the various camera procedures and press capabilities." Marvin R. Warshaw, art director for Prentice-Hall, Inc., says to "Get a beginner staff job and learn from the bottom up, particularly about type."

With experience and knowledge under the belt, Liz Shaw, art director of Drake Publishing, Inc., advises artists to demonstrate their knowledge of book publishing by showing work from comp to finish in their portfolios. The portfolio is the *key* to getting into most book publishing offices.

"Any information sent to a publisher (such as a portfolio) should be made really easy to return to the artist. An SASE is a must, plus some form of convenient reply card," says Harold Pallatz, editor of Ideal World Publishing Company.

For the artist who has not had any previous assignments in the book industry, publishers suggest that he review several of their books and do a few illustrations to show a point of view. This will give the art buyer an idea of the type of work the artist is capable of doing.

Assignments from book publishers come basically in four forms: complete book design, cover design, inside illustrations or promotion. When arranging an assignment with a publisher, the Graphic Artists Guild suggests an analysis of the work be made in order to prepare a design brief. The brief can be prepared by either the artist or publisher and should include a copy of the manuscript; a summary of typographical problems; an outline of the publisher's manufacturing program (paper stock, binder, method of binding, composition method, etc.); and a description of the trim size, page length, list price, number to be printed and whether a particular artistic style is needed.

Every book publishing company has a particular style and expectations in relationship to art. It is important that the artist recognizes the publisher's needs.

Robert Alberti of Impact Publishers, Inc., says "the biggest single problem we have in dealing with freelance artists is their resistance to accommodating the client's requests and needs. We sincerely want originality and creativity, but we also know what our specific needs are.

"Many artists develop a design and then insist that it be used exactly as they designed it. The freelancer should be receptive to the specific requests of the publisher," adds Alberti.

Artists who don't understand an assignment or don't know what style is desired, are advised to ask questions. Time and money are both wasted when assignments are done in the wrong way.

"Artists too frequently fail to ask questions and communicate thoroughly with their clients," says Marcie Heil, manager of art and design services at Augsburg Publishing House. She advises artists to avoid the practice of 'dropping in' on the client without an appointment.

Molly Hindman, production manager of the University of Pennsylvania Press, concludes that the freelance artist should study "the *New York Review of Books, Book Forum* and *The New York Times* to learn what the competition is doing." She adds that such reading material gives the artist a sense of insight on what kind of books are being produced, their appearance and a look at the type of artwork used for promotion.

ABC-CLIO, Riviera Campus, 2040 APS, Box 4397, Santa Barbara CA 93103. Contact: S. Lowenkopf or M. Leimer. Publishes academic, reference and supplemental texts. "We use simple graphic designs for 1-color reproduction in contemporary mode. We have very limited illustrative requirements; but do need book jacket design; inside typographic page formats and advertising layouts from time to time. Pay is commensurate with assignment." Arrange interview.

ABERDEEN PRESS, 95 Morton St., New York NY 10014. Art Buyer: M. Greenberg. Publishes texts and professional books on drug abuse, urban problems and psychiatry/psychoanalysis. Uses artists from the New York metropolitan area for jacket design, direct mail promotion brochures and book design. Query.

ACROPOLIS BOOKS LTD., 2400 17th St. NW, Washington DC 20009. Production Manager: Lloyd Greene. Publishes political, Americana, humor and poetry. Uses artists for book jacket designs and advertising layouts. Pays $5-6 per hour, paste-up. Query.

ADDISON-WESLEY, Reading MA 01867. Art Buyers: Herbert Boes, college texts; Will Winslow, juvenile trade books. Educational and juvenile trade book publishing company. Uses artists for jacket design, inside book illustrations and book design. Submit photocopies or transparencies. Artists should take an existing story (fairy tale, etc.) and do 2-3 illustrations to show point of view.

ADVANCE HOUSE, INC., Box 334, Ardmore PA 19003. Contact: Dr. Worth Wade. Publishes business, science, patents and patent law books. Uses artists for jacket designs. Pays $50 minimum for 1-sheet cover design. Query with resume.

ALBION PUBLISHING COMPANY, 1736 Stockton St., San Francisco CA 94133. College textbook publisher. Uses artists for jacket designs and inside book illustrations. Query.

ALLYN & BACON, 470 Atlantic Ave., Boston MA 02110. Art Buyer: George McLean. Textbook publishing company. Uses artists for inside book illustrations and jacket designs. Send photocopies or transparencies. Pays minimum $12-25 for 1-color spot drawings; $20-100 for 4-color illustrative art; $50-200 for cover designs.

AMERICAN ASSOCIATION OF COMMUNITY AND JUNIOR COLLEGES, 1 Dupont Circle NW, Washington DC 20036. Art Buyers: W.A. Harper or D. Nordh. Book publishing division uses freelance artists for paperback book cover design and advertising layouts. Query.

AMERICAN UNIVERSITIES FIELD STAFF, 3 Lebanon St., Hanover NH 03755. Art Buyer: Mrs. Manon Spitzer. Uses freelance artists for direct mail promotion, brochures, advertising layouts. "We do not have a large promotion budget, but we would like to get in touch with a number of freelancers for those few items (2 or 3 per year) with which we do require help." Will look at photocopies or transparencies. Pays $100 for direct mail design and $50 for new magazine layout suggestions.

AMPHOTO, (American Photographic Book Publishing Co.), 750 Zeckendorf Blvd., Garden City NY 11530. Art Buyer: Richard Lieu. Publishers hardcover and paperback originals. Uses artists for book jacket design, inside book illustrations, direct mail promotion brochures, advertising layouts and complete illustrated book design. Query. Payment determined by job.

AMSCO SCHOOL PUBLICATIONS, 315 Hudson St., New York NY 10013. Art Buyer: Lawrence Weisburg. Textbook publishing company (all high school subjects). Uses artists for book cover design and inside book illustrations. Pays $175, paperback cover. Query.

ANTHELION PRESS, INC., 101 Townsend, 3rd Floor, San Francisco CA 94107. (415)957-1277. Art Director: LaDonna Hart. Publishes hardbound and paperback historical,

photography and juvenile books. Published 32 titles and bought 14 designs in 1976. Query with samples or contact by agent. Submit finished art. Pays on publication. Negotiates payment for unused assigned illustrations. Buys all rights. Reports in 2-4 weeks. SASE. Catalog 25c.
Jacket Design: B&w line drawings, halftones and color-separated art OK. Pays $35-75, b&w; $50-100, color.
Inside Book Illustrations: B&w line drawings, halftones and color-separated art OK. Pays $5-20, b&w; $10-50, color.
Special Needs: "We intend to emphasize more and more illustration in both our fiction and nonfiction books."

THE AQUARIAN PRESS, Denington Estate, Wellingborough, Northants NN82RQ England. Art Buyer: D.J. Young. Publishes hardcover and paperback books on astrology, magic, witchcraft, palmistry and other occult subjects. Uses artists for book jacket design. Send samples with International Postal Reply coupons.

ARCO PUBLISHING CO., INC., 219 Park Ave., S., New York NY 10003. Art Buyer: Edward Turner. Reviews portfolios. Uses artists for book illustrations, jacket designs, direct mail and advertising layouts. Query with resume.

ARES PUBLISHERS, INC., 612 N. Michigan Ave., Suite 216, Chicago IL 60611. (312)642-7850. Vice President: A. Barozzi. Estab: 1973. Publishes scholarly reference books; particularly ancient history, archaeology, history of ancient art, classics, Byzantium, Mediterranean studies and research. Uses artists for book jacket design, inside book illustrations, direct mail brochures, advertising, layouts, art, maps and plans of archaeological sites.

ARTISTS & WRITERS PUBLICATIONS, 305 Mission Ave., Suite 6, San Rafael CA 94901. (415)456-1213. Publisher: Owen S. Haddock. Publishes premium and gourmet consumer demand books. Uses artists for book jacket designs, inside book illustrations, direct mail brochures, and advertising layouts/art. Query with photocopies or transparencies. SASE.

ART'S INC., 32 E. 58 St., New York NY 10022. Art Buyer: B. Vanos. Uses artists for jacket design, inside book illustrations and advertising layouts. Query. Indicate minimum fee in query.

William C. Brown Co., Publishers purchase 50 designs from freelance artists in 1976, including this textbook cover design from Zdenek Pivcka. Art director David Corona pays $175-450 per cover design.

ASI, 127 Madison Ave., New York NY 10016. Art Buyer: Barbara Somerfield. Publishes astrology books. Query. New York area artists only.
Book Jacket Design: Pays $75 minimum. Work must deal with astrological symbolism, yoga or acupuncture. Artist must be familiar with metaphysical thought.

THE ATHLETIC PRESS, Box 2314-D, Pasadena CA 91105. Contact: Donald Duke. Publishes sports training and conditioning books. "We are looking for line art of sport movements, anatomical drawings, etc." Query.

AUGSBURG PUBLISHING HOUSE, 426 S. 5th St., Minneapolis MN 55415. (612)332-4561. Manager, Art/Design Services: Marcie Heil. Publishes mainly paperback books on Protestant/Lutheran subjects (all areas and ages). Published 40 titles in 1976. Query or phone. Submit photocopies or slides of art styles. Reports in 3 weeks. SASE.
Jacket Design: All media OK. Pays $150-250 standard fee. Payment determined prior to assignment.
Inside Book Illustrations: B&w line drawings, halftones and washes OK. Payment determined in preliminary discussions with artists.

Direct Mail Brochures and Advertising Art: Uses artists for layout, design and illustrations. All media OK. Payment discussed prior to assignment.
To Break In: "Artists too frequently fail to ask questions and communicate thoroughly with their clients. It's important to be neat in your work, be familiar with production procedures and be prompt. One thing beginning artists should try to avoid is the practice of 'dropping in' on the client without an appointment."

AVE MARIE PRESS, Notre Dame IN 46556. Production Manager: Robert L. Mutchler. Uses artists for jacket designs and inside book illustrations. "We are Catholic publishers specializing in religious education at all levels, publishing books for the general Catholic market, with some crossover into other denominations, especially in the area of Charismatic Renewal books. We also publish a few filmstrips for which we sometimes need slides, and a number of cassettes requiring jacket designs. Since our demands for the work of artists are small, we recommend that artists examine our publications before submitting work. Most Catholic bookstores carry a representative range of our publications." Will look at photocopies or transparencies (any standard size may be submitted) of artist's work.

AVON BOOKS, 959 8th Ave., New York NY 10019. (212)262-6243. Art Director: Barbara Bertoli. Publishes paperback books. Publishes 20-25 titles monthly and buys 250 designs annually. Drop off portfolio on Tuesday; pick it up Wednesday morning. Pays on acceptance. Buys first and reprint rights. Reports in 2-4 weeks. SASE. Artist's guidelines available. Uses artists for cover illustration. Reflective 4-color art OK. Pays $700 minimum.

BALLANTINE BOOKS, 201 E. 50th St., New York NY 10022. (212)572-2251. Art Director: Ian. Publishes paperback fiction and nonfiction mass market books. Published 400 titles in 1976. All artwork assigned. Query with samples or write for personal interview. Submit roughs. Pays on acceptance. For unused assigned illustrations, pays 50% contracted fee at sketch phase and 100% at completion. Buys world rights. SASE. "Whimsical illustrations are not often used."
Book Jacket Design: Full-color paintings OK. Pays $600-1,500. Payment determined by reputation of artist and/or budget based on projected sales.

BANTAM BOOKS, INC., 666 5th Ave., New York NY 10019. Art Director: Leonard Leone. Uses artists for paperback covers. Drop off portfolio or call on the first of the month for interview.

BARLENMIR HOUSE OF GRAPHICS, 413 City Island Ave., New York NY 10064. Creative Director: Leonard Steffan. Uses artists for jacket design, inside book illustrations, direct mail brochures, advertising layouts/art, hand lettering, calligraphy, display and package design and posters. Publishes art, fiction, nonfiction, poetry, children's literature and humanities books. Send photocopies, photos or transparencies with resume. SASE.

BARRE PUBLISHING, (Division of Clarkson N. Potter Inc.), 1 Park Ave., New York NY 10016. (212)532-9200. Editor: Carolyn Hart. Publishes hardbound and paperback books on Americana, antiques, art, cooking and photography. Published 30 titles in 1976; buying 50-75% of the designs. Query with photocopied samples of finished art. Pays on acceptance. Buys all book rights. Reports in 2 weeks "if we like samples." SASE. Free sample catalog.
Jacket Design: All media OK. Pays $250-300. "Jacket designers usually work with art from book; they don't create art."
Inside Book Illustrations: All media OK. Pays $10-25, spot illustrations; $50 minimum, full-page illustration; determined by degree of difficulty, number of illustrations and/or reputation of artist.

WILLIAM L. BAUHAN, PUBLISHER, Dublin NH 03444. Art Director: W. L. Bauhan. Publishes hardbound and paperback books on New England. Published 7 titles and bought 6 designs in 1976. Query. Pays on publication. Reports in 4 weeks. SASE.
Inside Book Illustrations: B&w line drawings OK. Artist should state his price. Payment determined by degree of difficulty, number of illustrations and/or reputation of artist.

BERKLEY PUBLISHING CORP., 200 Madison Ave., New York NY 10016. Contact: Don Longabucco. Uses artists for jacket designs for trade and mass market paperbacks. Send photocopies or transparencies of artist's work. Query with resume.

BLACK LETTER PRESS, 663 Bridge, NW, Grand Rapids MI 49504. Contact: Donald D. Teets. "Most of our books are of a historical nature, so we need someone who has this type of skill." Examples of types of books published by this firm are Cook, *History of Drummond Island;* Ingles, *Handbook for Travelers,* 1898; and Butterfield, *Brule's Discoveries.* Uses artists for direct mail/advertising layouts and inside and cover designs. Pays $25, small cover layout/mailing brochure.

BOWMAR PUBLISHING CORP., 622 Rodier Dr., Glendale CA 91201. Art Director: Paul Taylor. Publishes educational books for grades K-12. Also produces audiovisual materials. Send samples of work in jacket design, book illustrations, direct mail brochures and filmstrips. Pays $1,500 for full-color filmstrip; $4,000 for a full-color 48-page book.

BOXWOOD PRESS, 183 Ocean View Blvd., Pacific Grove CA 93950. Contact: Ralph Buchsbaum. Publishes science and natural history books. Query with resume. Uses artists for book jacket design and illustrations. Pen and ink art only.

BROADMAN PRESS, 127 9th Ave., N., Nashville TN 37234. Contact: Tom Seale. Specializes in religious material. Uses artists for jacket designs, inside book illustrations, direct mail brochures, advertising layouts, music and recording covers, church supply designs and filmstrip art. Pays $200, book jackets.

WILLIAM C. BROWN CO., PUBLISHERS, 2460 Kerper Blvd., Dubuque IA 52001. (319)588-1451. Art Director: David Corona. Publishes hardbound and paperback college textbooks. Published 200+ titles and bought 50+ designs in 1976. Query with finished 11x14" or smaller (transparencies if larger) art samples or call for interview. Payment determined by degree of difficulty, number of illustrations, priority and/or quality. Half contract paid for unused assigned work. Buys all rights. Reports in 4 weeks. SASE.
Book Jacket Design: B&w line drawing, halftones, washes and color-separated art OK. Pays $175-450.
Inside Book Illustrations: B&w line drawing, halftones and washes OK. Pays $35-200.
Direct Mail Brochures: Uses artists for layout and illustrations. B&w line drawings, halftones, washes, color-separated artwork OK. Pays $35-200.
Advertising Art: Uses artists for illustrations. B&w line drawings, halftones, and washes OK. Pays $35-200.

CAHNERS BOOKS, 221 Columbus Ave., Boston MA 02116. Production Manager: Gary Conger. Advertising Director: John Kallmann. Publishes architecture, food-service and business management books. Uses local artists for jacket design, direct mail brochures and advertising layouts/art. Query with resume.

JOHN W. CALER CORP., 7506 Clybourn Ave., Sun Valley CA 91352. Publishes aviation and general books. Uses artists for jacket design, advertising/book layouts, inside book illustrations and direct mail promotion brochures. Submit photocopies or transparencies. SASE.

CAMERAREADY CORPORATION, Box 5812, Pasadena CA 91104. President: Kenneth Caird. Publishes instruction manuals on the mechanics of producing technical documents; primarily offset. Prefers Los Angeles area artists. Query. Pays $5 minimum, sketch. Pays on acceptance. Reports in 1 day.

THE CHILD'S WORLD, INC., Box 681, Elgin IL 60120. Product Director: Jane Buerger. Juvenile book firm specializing in educating young children. Special use of "study print and other teaching aid illustrations." Uses artists for jacket design, book illustration and brochure/layout advertising copy. Royalties sometimes shared with authors on picture books. Send resume.

CHILTON BOOK COMPANY, 201 King of Prussia Rd., Radnor PA 19089. (215)687-8200. Art Director: Edna H. Jones. Publishes hardbound and paperback arts and crafts, trade and automotive books. Published 80 titles and bought 120 designs in 1976. Query. "I prefer to deal in person rather than through the mail." Submit roughs. Pays on acceptance. Full payment for unused assigned illustrations. Buys first serial, book club and reprint rights. Reports in 3 weeks. No work returned.
Jacket Design: B&w line drawings, halftones, washes and color-separated art OK. Pays $50-

150, b&w; $200-400, color. Payment determined by degree of difficulty and/or number of illustrations.
Inside Book Illustrations: B&w line drawings, halftones and washes OK. Pays $50-150, b&w. Payment determined by degree of difficulty and/or number of illustrations.

CLIFFS NOTES, INC., Box 80728, Lincoln NE 68501. Contact: Harry Kaste. Publishes educational and trade (Centennial Press) books. Uses artists for book cover/jacket art; especially needs technical illustrators experienced in precision drafting.

COLORADO ASSOCIATED UNIVERSITY PRESS, University of Colorado, 1424 15th St., Boulder CO 80302. Publishes hardbound and paperback scholarly books. Published 10 titles and bought 3 designs in 1976. Uses artists for color jacket design. Query. Submit roughs. Payment on acceptance. No payment for unused assigned illustrations. Reports in 1 week. SASE.

CONSOLIDATED BOOK PUBLISHERS, 1727 S. Indiana, Chicago IL 60616. (312)922-9467. Art Director: Charles Bozett. Publishes hardbound and paperback cookbooks, dictionaries and children's Bible stories. Published 6 cookbooks in 1976; assigned 1 artist per book. Write or call for interview or query with samples. Payment on publication. Pays $25 for unused assigned work. Buys all rights. Reports only in interested. "I'll call the same day I get the samples."
Jacket Design, Direct Mail Brochures and Advertising Art: Uses artists for layout. Pays $75-150 per semi-comp (between rough and finished) layout.
Inside Book Illustrations: 2-color art OK. Pays $25 minimum.

DAVID C. COOK PUBLISHING COMPANY, 850 N. Grove Ave., Elgin IL 60120. Art Director: Edmund G. Elsner, Jr. Uses artists for jacket design and book illustrations. Pays $350 maximum for complete finished art or color transparency design for jacket. Specializes in paperbacks of interest to adults, children, Christian educators and laymen.

R.D. CORTINA CO., INC., 136 W. 52nd St., New York NY 10019. Contact: Robert E. Livesey. Publishes language teaching material. Interested in photocopies of comprehensives or published samples from professional artists with background in jacket design, direct mail promotion and advertising art. Pays minimum $500, illustrations of books; $150, book jacket comps plus mechanicals.

CRAFTSMAN BOOK COMPANY, 542 Stevens Ave., Solana Beach CA 92075. Art Buyer: Gary Moselle. Publishes technical books for builders and engineers. "Drawings are required to illustrate a particular point or portion of the text. Isometric drawings and technical illustrations are used mostly." Will consider spot drawings, cartoons and cover designs of subject matter appropriate to the magazine; line drawings illustrating various aspects of building construction and continuous tone prints of buildings under construction. Spot illustrations used occasionally to provide a theme. Pen and ink preferred. Buys exclusive rights. Query. Reports in 10 days. Pays on acceptance.

CRESCENT PUBLICATIONS, INC., 5410 Wilshire Blvd., Suite 400, Los Angeles CA 90036. Editor: Joseph Lawrence. Uses artists for jacket designs, inside book illustrations, direct mail brochures and advertising layouts for general interest books. Payment determined by amount of work involved; fees arranged with artist in advance. Query. Catalog available.

CUSTOM BOOK COMPANY, Drawer 32, San Angelo TX 76901. Contact: John Yount. Produces books "of every nature except porno." Uses artists for book design and illustration. Query.

CUSTOM COMMUNICATIONS SYSTEMS, INC., 30 Ruta Court, S., Hackensack NJ 07606. (201)440-1020. Contact: Art Director. Uses artists for direct mail brochures, advertising layouts/art. Submit photocopies or transparencies.

JONATHAN DAVID PUBLISHERS INC., 68-22 Eliot Ave., Middle Village NY 11379. Contact: Alfred J. Kolatch. Uses artists for jacket designs and inside book illustrations. Pays $100 minimum, jacket design/mechanical. Publishes mass appeal nonfiction books. Some recent titles include *They Wouldn't Let Us Die — The Prisoners of War Tell Their Story; The World of Terrariums; The Shirley Temple Scrapbook*. Submit samples. SASE. "We prefer to be able to keep something on file which will show the style of the artist."

DELL PUBLISHING CO., INC., 1 Dag Hammarskjold Plaza, New York NY 10017. Contact: Ann Spinelli. Delacorte Press, a division of Dell Publishing, uses artists for trade jacket design and inside book illustrations for juvenile and adult books. "I see people (artists' reps, and individual artists) on Thursday afternoons between 2:30 and 5:00, but please call first for an appointment!" Bring photocopies and/or transparencies.

DIANA PRESS, INC., 4400 Market St., Oakland CA 94608. (415)444-7666. Art Director: Casey Czarnik. Publishes feminist paperback books. Published 9 titles and bought 8 designs in 1976. Query with photocopies of finished art. Payment determined by hour, difficulty, number of illustrations, reputation of artist and/or budget. Pays on publication. Buys first serial, book club, second serial, reprint and translation and foreign publication rights. Reports in 3 months. SASE. Free catalog.
Book Jacket Design: B&w line drawings, halftones and washes OK. Pays $50 minimum, b&w; $250 minimum, color.
Inside Book Illustrations: B&w line drawings, halftones, and washes OK. Pays $15 minimum per b&w illustration.
To Break In: "Every piece of art must be pro-woman and aimed at building women's consciousness and a women's movement."

DICKENSON PUBLISHING CO., 16250 Ventura Blvd., Encino CA 91436. Contact: Jack Reid. Publishes college textbooks. Uses artists for cover designs and inside book illustrations. Pays $300, cover designs. Mail photocopies or transparencies.

DIMENSION BOOKS, Box 811, Danville NJ 07834. (201)627-4334. Art Director: Thomas P. Coffey. Publishes religious and psychological hardbound and paperback books. Published 40 titles and bought 17 designs in 1976. Query with samples. Submit roughs. Pays on acceptance. Buys book rights. Reports in 1 week. SASE.
Jacket Design: B&w line drawings and halftones OK. Pays $50-150. Payment determined by job.
Direct Mail Brochures: B&w line drawings OK. Pays $50-150. Payment determined by job.
Advertising Art: Uses artists for illustration and layout. Pays $50-150. Payment determined by job.

DODD, MEAD & COMPANY, INC., 79 Madison Ave., New York NY 10016. Uses artists for book jacket designs and inside book illustrations. Publishes general interest and juvenile books.

DOUBLEDAY AND COMPANY, INC., 245 Park Ave., New York NY 10017. Art Director: Alex Gotfryd. Publishes general adult, juvenile, western, science fiction, mystery, religious and special interest titles. Uses artists for jackets, inside book illustrations, advertising and sales promotion material. Call for appointment.

DRAKE PUBLISHERS, INC., 801 2nd Ave., New York NY 10017. (212)679-4500. Art Director: Liz Shaw. Publishes hardbound and paperback how-to crafts books. Published 50 titles and bought 40 designs in 1976. Query with samples or call for interview. Submit finished art. Pays on publication. Buys reprint rights. SASE.
Jacket Design: B&w line drawings, halftones, washes and color-separated art OK. Pays $100-250, b&w; $150-350, color. Payment determined by degree of difficulty.
Inside Book Illustrations: B&w line drawings and halftones OK. Pays $20-75, b&w. Payment determined by time spent, degree of difficulty and/or number of illustrations.
To Break In: "Folios should demonstrate knowledge of typography and progression from comp to finish."

DRAMA BOOK SPECIALISTS, 150 W. 52nd St., New York NY 10019. (212)582-1475. Editor-in-Chief: Ralph Pine. Estab: 1967. Publishes books on the performing arts. Published 30 titles in 1976. Uses artists for book jacket design, inside book illustration, direct mail brochures and advertising layouts. Mail photocopies or transparencies of artwork.

DUNELLEN PUBLISHING CO., INC., 386 Park Ave., S., New York NY 10028. Contact: R. Nicholas or E.H. Nellen. Publishes scholarly books. Uses artists for jacket designs, direct mail brochures and advertising layouts. "Since we are a short-run scholarly house, our demands are minimal. Therefore we do not pay the top rate." Pays $60 for jacket design; $100 for catalog layout. Send photocopies or transparencies.

EDMUND-BRADLEY PUBLISHING COMPANY, 707 Stratford Rd., Stratford CT 06497. Art Buyer: Guido Paluchi. Uses artists for book jacket design. Publishes nonfiction art books on specific artists, and antique and hobby books. Query.

JOHN EDWARDS PUBLISHING CO., Box 836, Stratford CT 06497. Contact: Bernard Rosenfeld. Publishes antiques, hobby and photography books. Submit samples.

The style and execution of this illustration prompted Consolidated Book Publishers to buy this 2-color drawing from Justin Wager for use in *The Complete Book of Creative Crepes*, one of the publishing firm's "Adventure in Cooking" series. Consolidated pays a minimum of $25 for inside book illustrations.

ETC PUBLICATIONS, Drawer 1627-A, Palm Springs CA 92262. Art Director: Leeona S Hostrop. Publishes hardbound and paperback nonfiction books including southern California regional works. Published 12 titles and bought 6 cover designs in 1976. Query with finished samples on first assignment. Payment determined by degree of difficulty. Pays on acceptance. Pays half of originally agreed payment for unused assigned work. Buys all rights. Reports in 4 weeks. SASE.
Jacket and Cover Design: B&w line drawings, halftones, washes, color-separated artwork and veloxes OK. Pays $50-100, b&w; $75-200, color.
To Break In: "Prefer to see imaginative examples using 2 colors; though not mandatory."

FAIRCHILD BOOKS AND VISUALS, 7 E. 12th St., New York NY 10003. Promotion Director: Ken Handel. Publishes educational, commercial, careers and fashion books. Uses artists for cover designs, inside book illustrations, direct mail brochures, advertising layouts, paste-up and inside book design. Pays minimum $20 for b&w illustrations. Query.

FAR EASTERN RESEARCH & PUBLICATIONS CENTER, Box 31151, Washington DC 20031. Contact: Editor-in-Chief. Uses artists for jacket designs and inside book illustrations. Publishes reference books on Far Eastern subjects. Query.

FARNSWORTH PUBLISHING CO., INC., 78 Randall Ave., Rockville Centre NY 11570. Manager: Rosalie Campadonico. Publishes business, finance, insurance and consumer books. Uses artists for jacket design, direct mail promotion and advertising layouts. Pays minimum $200 for jacket design through mechanical; $75-$100 for advertising layouts.

FARRAR, STRAUS & GIROUX, INC., 19 Union Square W., New York NY 10003. Contact: Dorris Janowitz. Uses artists for jacket designs and inside book illustrations. Publishes general fiction, nonfiction (including biography) and juveniles. Pays $285 for a preseparated 3-color book jacket. Send samples.

FAWCETT WORLD LIBRARY, 1515 Broadway, New York NY 10036. Art Director: Dale Phillips. Uses artists for paperback cover illustrations. Publishes Crest, Gold Medal and Premier Books. Call for appointment; usually held Tuesdays or Thursdays.

FEARON PUBLISHERS, INC., 6 Davis Dr., Belmont CA 94002. Art Director: Richard Kharibian. Uses artists for inside textbook illustrations, special education and teacher-aid books. Majority of books are 1 and 2 colors. Payment determined by contract or fee. Query.

FIESTA PUBLISHING COMPANY, 6360 NE 4th Court, Miami FL 33138. Contact: W. Allan Sandler. Uses artists for paperback book cover designs for its sexy novels, mysteries and other action books published in Spanish. Pays $50 for book cover. Payment on publication. Buys all rights. Submit samples. Covers assigned after approval of "rough" in 4½x7" size. Reports in 30 days.

FITZHENRY & WHITESIDE LTD., 150 Lesmill Rd., Don Mills, Ontario Canada M3B 2T5. Editor-in-Chief: Robert W. Read. Publishes educational material and some general trade publishing. Educational publications consist of hard and soft cover books, study prints and filmstrips. Uses artists for jacket designs, cover and inside illustrations, promotion/advertising layout design and graphic material for study prints. Pays up to $100 for 1 or 2-color illustrations, up to $300 for single 4-color illustrations. Often illustration contracts are given for complete books (100-200 illustrations). Pays up to $3,000 for total book design. Submit samples. Prefers Canadian designers and illustrators.

FLORHAM PARK PRESS, INC., Box 303, Florham Park NJ 07932. Art Buyer: V. V. Mott. Specializes in college textbooks and scholarly works. Uses artists for hand lettering, mechanical drawings, graphs and charts. Pays minimum $10, chart; $20, mechanical drawing. Submit resume.

FODOR'S MODERN GUIDES, 750 3rd Ave., New York NY 10017. (212)949-1469. Editor: Robert C. Fisher. Associate Editor: Leslie Brown. Publishes hardbound and paperback travel guides. Published 35 titles and bought 120 designs in 1976. Query with samples. Submit finished art. Pays on acceptance. Full payment for unused assigned illustrations. Buys all rights. SASE. Prefers not to see "heavy black areas in drawings."
Jacket Design: B&w line drawings, color-separated art and veloxes OK. Pays minimum $200, b&w; $250, color.
Inside Book Illustrations: B&w line drawings only. Pays $15 minimum.

FOUR WINDS PRESS, 50 W. 44th St., New York NY 10036. (212)867-7700. Art Director: Lucy Bitzer. Publishes hardbound and paperback books for juveniles and young adults. Published 40 titles and bought 2 designs in 1976. Call for interview. Submit roughs. Pays on acceptance. Payment varies for unused assigned illustrations. Buys first serial rights. Reports in 1 month.
Book Jacket Design: B&w line drawings, halftones, washes and color-separated art OK. Pays $250 minimum.
Inside Book Illustrations: B&w line drawings, halftones, washes and color-separated art OK.

FREE PRESS, Division of Macmillan Publishing Co., Inc., 866 3rd Ave., New York NY 10022. Art Buyer: W. Weiss. Publishes college texts, professional reference and trade nonfiction in social sciences and humanities. Uses artists for book jacket design. Query. Pays approximately $150, interior and binding design; $200, jacket or cover design/mechanicals.

GOLDEN WEST BOOKS, Box 8136, San Marino CA 91108. Contact: Donald Duke. Publishes railroad, steamship and transportation Americana history books. Uses artists for book jacket design. Buys first printing rights. Pays $250 minimum. Catalog available.

GOODYEAR PUBLISHING CO., INC., 1640 5th St., Santa Monica CA 90401. (213)393-6731. Art Manager: Robert Hollander. Publishes hardbound and paperback college texts on business management, economics, education, mathematics, social science and vocational technology; business and professional books; and trade books. Published 57 titles and bought 50 designs in 1976. Query with samples, or write or call for interview. Submit roughs. Payment determined by hour, degree of difficulty, number of illustrations and/or reputation of artist. Pays on acceptance. Payment for unused assigned work "as agreed." Buys first serial, book club, second serial, reprint, translation and foreign publication rights. SASE.
Book Jacket Design: All media OK. Pays minimum $225.
Inside Book Illustrations: B&w line drawings, halftones, washes, color-separated artwork and veloxes OK. Payment determined by complexity.
Direct Mail Brochures and Advertising Art: Uses artists for layout and illustrations. B&w, halftones, washes, color-separated art and veloxes OK.
General Art Direction: "All art direction and major book design is done off-staff."

GOSPEL LIGHT PUBLICATIONS, 110 W. Broadway, Glendale CA 91204. Art Director: Joyce Thimsen. "We publish books: paperback, softcover, hardcover; curriculum materials for every age level. Includes a 32-40 page book for the student; a 64-page book for the teacher; teaching resources such as large pictures, posters, games for the teacher to use in class. A package like this comes out once very 3 months, for each age level. We also have miscellaneous items — posters, material for summer clubs, maps pacs, puppets, *Family Life Today* magazine, and take-home papers for use every Sunday. We have all kinds of needs: cover designs, line drawings, 4-color art, tone art, any medium. Nearly all of the art we use contains people and children of all ages. All of our art is done on assignment basis. We prepare roughs of what we want and buy the finished art from freelance people. I like to look at an artist's portfolio to determine his ability. Payment for spot drawings is $5-80 depending on job and color; cover design in 4 colors, finished art $200-300 including paste-up of cover 1 and 4. Payment is made in 3 weeks of acceptance. Buys all rights. Reports in 2-4 weeks.

H. M. GOUSHA COMPANY, Box 6227, San Jose CA 95150. Art Buyer: Ralph J. Butterworth. Occasionally uses artists for book illustrations, magazine cartoons, catalog illustrations/covers, decorative spots, graphic designs, magazine covers, magazine editorial layouts, magazine illustrations and technical illustrations. "Except for cartoons, the artist should always contact us before submitting anything. Cartoons may be submitted in rough form for consideration. If acceptable we will notify artist to proceed with finish. All cartoons must be travel-oriented since we are, basically, a travel publication company. Automotive maintenance also is a major subject category for our publications. If an artist does not query us first in the case of all artwork except cartoons, we cannot guarantee the return of his materials. In most cases, illustrations are purchased outright." Payment on acceptance. Reports in 2 weeks. "If longer, we would notify the artist."

GREAT OUTDOORS PUBLISHING CO., 4747 28th St. N., St. Petersburg FL 33714. Contact: Patricia Pope. Uses artists for jacket designs and inside book illustrations. Specializes in books on Florida outdoor life: fishing, shells, reptiles, gardening, cooking. "We prefer to deal locally, so we can be more exact with our requirements for a particular piece of art. Unsolicited art samples should include return postage." Pays minimum $10, b&w spot art; $100, 4-color cover art. Query.

THE STEPHEN GREENE PRESS, Box 1000, Brattleboro VT 05301. (802)257-7757. Managing Editor: Orion M. Barber. Publishes nonfiction hardbound and paperback books on Americana, regional (New England), occasional belles lettres, biography, self-help, sports (horse and individual outdoor), humor, technology, popular history, food, cooking, nature, environment, how-to and self-reliance. Published 19 titlesa an ought 27 designs in 1976. Query with h samtel . U aually solicit artwork by assignment. Submit roughs. Pays on acceptance. Unused assigned work is returned to artist. Buys world publishing rights in English, first and second serial, book club and reprint rights. Reports on commissioned submissions immediately. SASE. Free catalogs.

Book Jacket Design: B&w line drawings, halftones, washes, color-separated art and type design for combination with photos OK. Pays $150 minimum, b&w; $250 minimum, color. Payment determined by difficulty, scope of project and/or budget.
Inside Book Illustrations: B&w line drawings, halftones, and washes OK. Pays $15-35, b&w. Payment determined by degree of difficulty, number of illustrations, reputation of artist and/or announced budget.

HAESSNER PUBLISHING, INC., Drawer B, Newfoundland NJ 07435. (201)687-3773. Contact: Bob Retlaw. Uses artists for jacket design, inside book illustrations and total book design. Specializes in books on travel, automotive (historical and how-to), boating (sailing, cruising, historical and reference), hobby models and airplanes. Pays $75-150, cover art. Query.

HAGSTROM COMPANY, INC., 450 W. 33rd St., New York NY 10001. Contact: Martin Holmes. Uses artists for "cartography, color separations work, Leroy lettering and penline work — very detailed work in small areas. We also need draftsmen who can do very fine work with a pen on street maps, and craftsmen who can strip negatives. We prefer to deal with New York area professionals who may telephone for an in-person interview." Payment determined by job and/or time spent. Pays $50-1,500, cartography.

HARLEQUIN ENTERPRISES LTD., 240 Duncan Mill Rd., Toronto, Ontario Canada M3B 1Z4. Art Director: Charles Kadin. Publishes hardbound and paperback historical and suspense romance novels. Published 144 titles and bought 6 designs in 1976. Query with samples. Pays on acceptance. Pays half of originally agreed payment for unused assigned work. Reports in 2 weeks. No work returned. Artist's guidelines available. "Artist must have strong ability to render anatomy and portraiture, and paint with straightforward color application."
Book Jacket Design: Full-color paintings OK. Pays $250 minimum. Payment determined by reputation of artist.
Inside Book Illustrations: B&w line drawings, halftones and washes OK. Pays $65 minimum, b&w. Payment determined by artist's reputation.

HARVARD UNIVERSITY PRESS, 79 Garden St., Cambridge MA 02138. Contact: Nicholas Bromell. Publishes scholarly works. Uses artists for jacket designs and direct mail brochures. Pays $125 minimum for jacket design. Query with resume.

HARVEST HOUSE LTD., 4795 St. Catherine St. W., Montreal, Quebec Canada H3Z 2B9. Art Buyer: Maynard Gertler. Publishes hardbound and paperback books. Uses local artists for book jackets and book design (page layout and typography). Submit samples of previously published work.

HARVEY HOUSE, PUBLISHERS, 20 Waterside Plaza, New York NY 10010. Art Director: L.F. Reeves. Publishes hardbound juvenile books. Query with samples or write for interview. Submit finished art. Buys all rights. Reports in 3 weeks. SASE.
Jacket Design: Color-separated or full-color illustrations OK. Pays $150 minimum for single-color illustration. Payment determined by degree of difficulty, number of illustrations and/or reputation of artist.
Inside Book Illustration: B&w line drawings, washes and color-separated art OK. Pays $400-1,500 and frequently royalties. Payment determined by degree of difficulty, number of illustrations and/or reputation of artist.

HAYDEN BOOK COMPANY, INC., 50 Essex St., Rochelle Park NJ 07662. Contact: A. Victor Schwarz. Uses artists for book jacket design, inside book illustrations (electronics, technology, graphs — 1 color), direct mail brochures and advertising layouts. Publishes books for secondary courses in English language and social studies; books on computer technology and theory; and books on electronics for technical school and home study. Pays minimum $150 for cover design, plus mechanicals and art costs; $10 per figure for electronics home study books (includes 75 figures).

HEALTH SCIENCES PUBLISHING, CORP., 451 Greenwich St., New York NY 10013. Contact: R. Halporn. "Many of our book titles deal with death. This is very difficult for many people to handle." Uses artists for book design and illustration. Pays $125 for book jacket mechanical.

Book Jacket Design Calls for Research

"Show an art director that you've done a little research and have an idea of what's needed. Be familiar with books. Watch book displays and talk to bookstore owners," says Larry Cooke, art director of the University Press of Hawaii.

"It helps to understand the marketing function of a book jacket. A good jacket makes a book stand out on a shelf. It gets people's attention. Warm colors, such as reds, yellows and oranges, for example, have more appeal than cooler ones. And phosphorescent colors are difficult to ignore.

"Moreover, the right people must notice the jacket. Know a book publisher's audience. Jacket color and design vary greatly according to whom the publisher is appealing."

Larry Cooke

D.C. HEATH AND CO., Division of Raytheon, 125 Spring St., Lexington MA 02173. Contact: School Division/College Division Art Dept. Publishes elementary, secondary and college textbooks. Elementary/secondary textbooks are primarily language arts, math, science and foreign languages. The college division publishes nearly all subjects. Uses artists for inside book illustrations and book cover designs. Payment determined by importance and difficulty of project. Submit samples.

HERALD PRESS, 616 Walnut Ave., Scottdale PA 15683. Book Editor: Paul M. Schrock. Publishes hardbound and paperback inspirational, historical, juvenile, theological, biographical, fiction and nonfiction books. Published 26 titles in 1976. "All designs for books were assigned, some as the result of queries." Query with samples. Submit roughs. Pays on acceptance. Token payment for unused assigned illustrations. Buys all rights and shares half the subsidiary income with artist. Reports in 2 weeks. SASE. Catalog of current books available.
Jacket Designs: All media OK. Pays $75 minimum, b&w; $125 minimum, color. Payment determined by degree of difficulty.
Inside Book Illustrations: B&w line drawings, halftones and washes OK. Pays $50 minimum, b&w. Payment determined by degree of difficulty.

HERMAN PUBLISHING, INC., 45 Newbury St., Boston MA 02116. Contact: S.M. Herman. Publishes professional, reference and general nonfiction books. Uses Boston artists for book jacket design, inside book illustrations, direct mail brochures and advertising layouts. Pays $150 for book jacket design and mechanicals. General nonfiction titles include *Creating a Luxury Garden* and *Job Hunting Guide.*

HOLBROOK PRESS, INC., 470 Atlantic Ave., Boston MA 02210. (617)482-9220. Production Manager: Elydia P. Siegel. Publishes hardbound and paperback college and junior college textbooks. Published 20 titles in 1976. Query. Submit roughs or finished art. Pays on acceptance or publication, "depending on circumstances." No payment for unused assigned illustrations.
Book Jacket Design: B&w line drawings and halftones OK. Pays $75-125.
Inside Book Illustrations: B&w line drawings and halftones OK. Pays $20-75.

IDEAL WORLD PUBLISHING COMPANY, Box 1237-EG, Melbourne FL 32935. (305)254-6003. Editor: Harold Pallatz. Publishes hardbound and paperback books. Specializes in books on health, nutrition, vitamins, herbs, gold prospecting, treasure finding and ghost towns. Published 3 titles in 1976. Query. Pays on acceptance. "No pay for unused assigned sketches or roughs; full payment for unused assigned illustrations backed by our written order." Buys all rights. Reports in 4 weeks. SASE.
Book Jacket Design and Inside Illustrations: B&w line drawings and halftones OK. Pays minimum $5. Payment determined by time spent and/or degree of difficulty.

Direct Mail Brochures and Advertising Art: Uses artists for layout and illustrations. B&w line drawings and halftones OK. Pays minimum $5. Payment determined by time spent and/or degree of difficulty.
To Break In: "Any information sent to a publisher should be made really easy to return to artist; SASE a must, plus some form of convenient reply card."

IMPACT PUBLISHERS, INC., Box 1094, San Luis Obispo CA 93406. President: Robert Alberti. Publishes hardbound and paperback behavioral psychology books. Published 6 titles and bought 2 designs in 1976. Mail artwork. Submit roughs or finished art. Pays on publication. Negotiates payment for unused assigned work. Buys reprint rights. Reports in 3 weeks. SASE. Free catalog.
Book Jacket Design: All media OK. Pays approximately $100. Payment negotiable. Payment determined by time spent and/or number of illustrations.
Inside Book Illustrations: B&w line drawings and color-separated art OK. Negotiates payment. Payment determined by time spent, degree of difficulty and/or number of illustrations.
Advertising Art: Uses artists for illustrations. B&w line drawings and color-separated art OK. Negotiates payment. Payment determined by time spent and number of illustrations.
To Break In: "The biggest single problem we have in dealing with freelance artists is their resistance to accommodating the clients requests and needs. We sincerely want originality and creativity, but we also know what our specific needs are. Many artists develop a design and then insist that it be used exactly as they designed it. The freelancer should be receptive to the specific requests of the publisher."

INDIANA UNIVERSITY PRESS, 10th and Morton Sts., Bloomington IN 47401. Contact: John Vint. Uses artists for jacket designs. Publishes general interest and scholarly books. Titles include Colette, *Looking Backwards;* Jacobs, *The UFO Controversy in America;* and Berry, *The Alaska Pipeline.* Pays minimum $150 for simple 2-color book jacket design; $200 for illustrated, 3-color jacket design (plus cost of type).

INSCAPE CORP., 1629 K St. NW, Washington DC 20006. Art Director: Roger Brown. Publishes fiction and nonfiction books under 3 imprints: Black Orpheus Press, New Perspectives and Inscape Books. Uses artists for book jacket design, direct mail and advertising layout. Catalog available. Pays $250. Buys world rights. "We are interested in innovative jacket designs to complement the kind of innovative books we produce."

INTERNATIONAL MARINE PUBLISHING COMPANY, 21 Elm St., Camden ME 04843. Editor: Peter Spectre. Uses artists for jacket designs and inside book illustrations. Publishes books on the marine field. Query.

JUDSON PRESS, Valley Forge PA 19481. (215)768-2154. Contact: Art Dept. Publishes American Baptist books. Published 36 titles in 1976. Uses artists for jacket design and inside book illustration. Pays $150 for 5½x8½" book cover. Submit photos or transparencies.

KEATS PUBLISHING, INC., 36 Grove St., New Canaan CT 06840. Contact: Nathan Keats. Publishes health, inspirational and business-sponsored books. Uses artists for book illustration and advertising layout. Query with resume.

B. KLEIN PUBLICATIONS, INC., Box 8503, Coral Springs FL 33065. Editor: Bernard Klein. Publishes reference books, such as the *Guide to American Directories.* Uses artists for book jacket design and direct mail brochures. Pays $50-$300. Submit samples and resume.

ROBERT KNAPP, Box 7234, San Diego CA 92107. Publishes scholarly nonfiction; especially in the social sciences, psychology, education and statistics. Uses artists for jacket design, direct mail and advertising.

LE CERCLE DU LIVRE DE FRANCE, 8955 St. Laurent, Montreal, Quebec, Canada. Contact: Francois Tisseyre. Uses artists for book jacket designs. Publishes paperback novels in French. Pays $100 minimum for jacket design.

LIBRA PUBLISHERS, INC., Box 165, Roslyn Heights, Long Island NY 11577. Contact: William Kroll. General book publishing firm. Uses artists for jacket designs and inside book illustrations. Pays minimum $10, book illustration; $35-50, jacket designs. Submit samples and resume. Reports in 1 week.

LLEWELLYN PUBLICATIONS, Box 3383, St. Paul MN 55765. Art Editor: Jackie Urbanovic. Publishes occult astrology and witchcraft books. Buys b&w drawings and color art for book covers. Pays $100, b&w covers; $200, color covers. Previously published work OK. Reports in 8 weeks.

LOGOS INTERNATIONAL, 201 Church St., Plainfield NJ 07060. (201)754-0745. Contact: Dave Tommasino. Publishes religious books. Uses artists for jacket designs, inside book illustrations, direct mail brochures and advertising layouts. Pays $250, full-color book jackets.
Special Needs: Uses art for *Logos Journal* magazine covers. Pays $125 for 2-color illustration.

ROBERT B. LUCE, INC., 2000 N. St. NW, Washington DC 20036. Contact: Allison C. Gilbert. Publishes general science, public affairs, biography, history and how-to books. Uses artists for book jacket design and direct mail brochures. Query with photos or transparencies.

McGRAW HILL PUBLISHING, College Division, 1221 6th Ave., New York NY 10020. Art Director, College and University Division: Merrill Haber. Uses artists for book and jacket design; technical, medical, biological illustrations; and cartography. Submit samples. Reports in 3 weeks.

MacMILLAN PUBLISHING CORP., 866 3rd Ave., New York NY 10003. Macmillan Educational Division: Zelda Haber. Published 6 titles and revisions of 2 multi-volume encyclopedias; and bought 150 designs in 1976. Publishes hardbound encyclopedias and dictionaries. Query. Submit finished printed samples that have been reproduced. Pays on acceptance. Full payment for unused assigned work unless work has not fulfilled the stated requirements. Buys first reproduction rights. Reports in 2 weeks. SASE.
Inside Book Illustrations: B&w line drawings, halftones, washes and color-separated artwork OK. Pays $65 minimum, b&w; $75 minimum color. Payment determined by degree of difficulty, number of illustrations and/or reputation of artist.

MAJOR BOOKS, 21335 Roscoe Blvd., Canoga Park CA 91304. Art Director: Jerome Pecoraro. Publishes Western, gothic, mystery and educational books. Uses artists for inside book illustrations and book jacket designs. Illustrators for covers "must have a realistic approach." Reviews photocopies or transparencies of artists' work for future assignments. Query. Suggests that 3 sketches be submitted from assignment, with final art 150% larger than the original cover size.

THE MAKEPEACE COLONY, INC., Box 111, Stevens Point WI 54481. (715)344-2636. Art Director: James Murat. Publishes hardbound books. Query. Reports in 3-4 weeks. SASE.
Jacket Design: B&w line drawings and color-separated art OK. Pays $100 minimum,. Payment determined by degree of difficulty and/or quality.
Inside Book Illustrations: B&w line drawings and color-separated art OK. Payment determined by degree of difficulty, number of illustrations and/or quality of work.

MANYLAND BOOKS, INC., 84-39 90th St., Woodhaven NY 11421. Contact: Stepas Zobarskas. Uses artists for jacket design and inside book illustrations. Pays $25 minimum, inside illustration; $85, jacket design. Submit photocopies of work. SASE.

MEMPHIS STATE UNIVERSITY PRESS, Memphis State University, Memphis TN 38152. (901)454-2752. Director: James D. Simmons. Uses artists for jacket designs and inside book illustrations. Pays $125 for final jacket art with type in place. Mail samples. Specializes in history books, literary criticism and philosophy. Published 8 books in 1976.

JULIAN MESSNER, (Simon & Schuster Division of Gulf & Western Corp.), 1230 Avenue of the Americas, New York NY 10020. Executive Editor: Lee M. Hoffman. Uses artists for book jacket designs, and inside book illustrations (b&w only, no color). Specializes in nonfiction children's books for ages 8-12; also nonfiction teenage books (but these seldom include illustrations except those provided by the author). Query with resume.

MIMIR PUBLISHERS, INC., Box 5011, Madison WI 53705. Contact: Editor. Specializes in social sciences, texts and references in hardback. Uses artists for jacket design, inside book illustrations and advertising and promotion layouts. Pays minimum $50, jacket; $30, promotion flyer design.

MOJAVE BOOKS, 7040 Darby Ave., Reseda CA 91535. (213)342-3403. Art Director: Zvi Evez. Publishes hardbound and paperback books. Published 40 titles and bought 10-15 designs in 1976. Query. Submit roughs. Pays on acceptance. Full payment for unused assigned illustrations. Buys first serial rights. Reports in 3 weeks. SASE.
Jacket Design: B&w line drawings, halftones, washes and color-separated art OK. Pays $100 minimum, 1-color design; $100+, multi-color designs.

MOTT MEDIA, Box 236, Milford MI 48042. Production Editor: Diane Zimmerman. Publishes hardbound and paperback Christian books and textbooks. Published 20 titles and bought 150-175 art spots and 15 cover illustrations in 1976. Query with samples or contact by agent. Submit roughs. Pays on acceptance. Buys all rights. Reports in 1 month. SASE. Free catalog.
Jacket Design: B&w line drawings OK. Pays $150 minimum, b&w or color. Payment determined by degree of difficulty and/or reputation of artist.
Inside Book Illustrations: Washes OK. Pays $25 minimum, b&w; $30 minimum, color. Payment determined by degree of difficulty, number of illustrations and/or reputation of artist.
To Break In: "Visit printers' businesses and become acquainted with the various camera procedures and press capabilities."

FREDERICK MULLER, LTD., Victoria Works, Edgware Rd., London England NW2 6LE. Publishing Manager: Anne Williams. Uses artists for illustrations. Pays $75 for simple jacket designs. Payment determined by complexity. Artists sending unsolicited material should enclose International Postal Reply coupons.

THOMAS NELSON INC., 30 E. 42nd St., New York NY 10017. (212)697-5573. Art Director: Deborah Daly. Publishes juvenile, adult fiction and trade books. Published 70 titles; bought 60 designs in 1976. "We work only on assignment." Query with samples. Submit roughs. Pays on acceptance. Pays "1/3 of finished cost or $100, whichever is less," for unused assigned work. Buys all rights. Reports as assignments occur. SASE. Sample catalog/artist's guidelines available if artist provides SASE.
Jacket Design: All media, except veloxes, OK. Pays $150 minimum, b&w; $200 minimum, color. Payment determined by degree of difficulty.
Production Needs: Query Thomas Nelson, Inc., 407 7th Ave. S., Nashville TN 37202.

NELSON-HALL INC., 325 W. Jackson Blvd., Chicago IL 60606. Vice President: Stephen A. Ferrara. Uses artists for book jacket designs and technical illustration. Submit resume and photocopies of previously published work. Designers who are given assignments are usually asked to prepare colored sketches for approval and then color-separated camera-ready finished art. Pays $175, jacket design plus type. Pays on acceptance. Buys all rights. Catalog available on request.

THE NEW AMERICAN LIBRARY, INC., 1301 Avenue of the Americas, New York NY 10019. Art Director: James Plumeri. Paperback and hardcover publishing firm. Paperback titles carry the Signet, Mentor and other trade names. Artists may leave portfolios for review and subsequent pick-up. Query for details.

NORTHWOODS PRESS, INC., Rte. 1, Meadows of Dan VA 24120. (703)952-2388. Art Director: R. Olmsted. Publishes hardbound and paperback books. Published 9 titles and bought 3 designs in 1976. Query with samples. Pays on acceptance. Buys all rights, "except by arrangement." Reports in 4 weeks. SASE.
Jacket Design: B&w line drawings and occasionally halftones OK. Pays $5 minimum, b&w.
Inside Book Illustrations: B&w line drawings and halftones OK. Pays $5 minimum for b&w line drawing.

NOYES PRESS, 118 Mill Rd., Park Ridge NJ 07656. Contact: Gloria Weiss. Academic and technical book publishing firm. Uses artists for jacket design. Books published include chemistry, chemical engineering, food, environment, finance, archaeology and classical studies. Pays $250 minimum, camera-ready art in 2 colors.

ODDO PUBLISHING, INC., Storybook Acres, Box 68, Fayetteville GA 30214. (404)461-7627. Art Director: Paul C. Oddo. Publishes hardbound juvenile books. "We published no titles in 1976 because the tornado hit us. I hope to publish 4 titles and buy 128 designs in '78." Query. Submit finished art. Pays on publication. Full payment for unused assigned illustrations.

Buys all rights. Reports in 1 month. SASE. Sample catalog/artist's guidelines available.
Cover Design and Inside Illustrations: 2-color and full-color OK. Pays $250-1,500, book cover and inside illustration design. Payment determined by degree of difficulty and/or reputation of artist.
Direct Mail Brochures: Uses artists for illustrations. Pays $150 minimum, (or as agreed upon) b&w and color brochure.

OMEN COMMUNICATIONS, Box 12457, Tucson AZ 85732. Contact: Walter Bowart. Uses artists for jacket design, advertising and direct mail promotion. "We consider our graphics very important and would like to see queries on specific ideas for books." Pays $65, b&w art; $100, color covers. "We have at the present time 2 lines. Our main line is metaphysical/philosophical and "New Age" books. Our subsidiary line, Apocrypha Books, consists of controversial/avant-garde quality paperbacks featuring collaged anthologies on popular topics. These we think of as recycled print." Examples: male chauvinist reading matter — *Women's Lip;* marijuana reading matter — *Pot Art;* avaricious reading matter — *The Get Rich Catalog.*

OPEN COURT PUBLISHING COMPANY, Box 599, LaSalle IL 61301. Design Supervisor: John Grandits. Specializes in children's textbooks, grades K through 6. Buys jacket design, inside book illustrations and book design. Pays $125, full-color full page; $75, full-color half page.

OUTDOOR EMPIRE PUBLISHING, INC., 511 Eastlake Ave. E., Box C-19000, Seattle WA 98109. Art Director: Fay Ainsworth. Publishes paperback outdoor and how-to books. Published 6 new and 40 reprint titles; bought 20 designs in 1976. Write or call for interview or mail artwork. Submit proofs, slides or finished art. Pays on publication. Gives minimum payment for unused assigned illustrations. Buys all rights. Reports in 3 weeks. SASE.
Jacket Design: B&w line drawings, halftones, washes, color-separated art and full-color paintings OK. Pays $50 minimum, b&w or color.
Inside Book Illustrations: All media, including color paintings, OK. Minimum payments: $10, b&w; $15, color.
Direct Mail Brochure: Uses artists for layout and illustrations. All media OK. Minimum payments: $10, b&w; $15, color.
Advertising Art: Uses artists for layout and illustration. All media, including color paintings, OK. Minimum payments: $15, b&w; $20, color.

OXMOOR HOUSE, Box 2262, Birmingham AL 35202. Vice President: Leslie Adams. Director, Advertising: Betty Jones. Director, Editorial: Ann Harvey. Specializes in art books (deluxe hardcover) and the Family Guidebook Series (softcover). Query.

PACIFIC BOOKS, Box 558, Palo Alto CA 94302. (415)323-5529. Art Director: Henry Penleithner. Publishes hardbound and paperback general and scholarly nonfiction, professional and technical reference books and educational texts. Published 6 titles and bought 6 designs in 1976. Call for interview. "Artists should know typography and printing processes. Bring samples of previous book work." Buys all rights. SASE.
Book Jacket Design: Pays $150 minimum. Payment determined by nature of assignment.
Inside Book Illustrations: Payment determined by nature of assignment.
Direct Mail Brochures: Uses artists for layout and illustrations. Payment determined by nature of assignment.

PADRE PRODUCTIONS, Box 1275, San Luis Obispo CA 93406. Editor/Publisher: Lachlan P. MacDonald. Uses artists for original finished art samples of line drawings of western America. "We are only interested in camera-ready books, collections of drawings by a single artist dealing with a single topic or area, or occasional freelance assignments for line drawings." Query. Reports in 10 days. Will deal directly with artist or through artist's representative. Interested in artists and writers of county or area guidebooks, especially in California.

PARENTS' MAGAZINE PRESS, 52 Vanderbilt Ave., New York NY 10017. Art Director: Mildred Kantorowitz. Uses artists for inside book illustrations. "We prefer to see a varied portfolio of children's book artists with work from artists specializing in the picture book (Parents' Magazine Press publishes picture books for 4-8 year olds) and who have had some previous experience in working out a dummy for a given text." Query.

PAULIST PRESS, 1865 Broadway, New York NY 10023. Art Director: John Kirvan. Publishes religious and educational books, both hardcover and paperback, popular and scholarly. Uses artists for jacket design, book illustrations, direct mail brochures and advertising layouts. Pays $10 to $20, inside page; $150+, cover. Query.

PAWNEE PUBLISHING CO., INC., Box 3435, Boulder CO 80303. (303)666-6594. President: Ernest W. Schafer. Estab: 1972. Publishes educational books (grades 1-12; mathematics and science) and adult books (how-to series). Uses artists for jacket design, inside book illustrations, direct mail brochures and advertising. Pays $12, simple line drawing.

PEACE PRESS, INC., 3828 Willar Ave., Culver City CA 90230. (213)838-7387. Art Director: Harold Moskovitz. Publishes hardbound and paperback juvenile, political science and ecological books. Published 5 titles and bought 3 designs in 1976. Query with samples. Submit roughs. Pays on acceptance. Buys all rights. Reports in 4 weeks. SASE.
Jacket Design and Inside Illustrations: B&w line drawings, halftones, washes (book jacket only) and color-separated art OK. Pays $50 minimum. Payment determined by time spent, degree of difficulty and/or number of illustrations.
Direct Mail Brochures: Uses artists for layout and illustrations. B&w line drawings, halftones and washes OK. Pays $100 minimum, b&w. Payment determined by time spent, degree of difficulty and/or number of illustrations.

PEACOCK, Bantom Books, Rte. 212, Bearsville NY 12409. Contact: Betty Ballantine. Specialize in art books with 4-color reproduction. Pays artists an advance against royalties. Query.

THE PERFECTION FORM COMPANY, 8350 Hickman Rd., Des Moines IA 50322. Contact: Wayne F. DeMouth. Specializes in workbooks, posters, and filmstrips for use in secondary English and social studies courses; professional books for educators and some reprints. Uses artists for inside book illustrations, some covers and camera-ready art for posters. Query. Will look at samples or photocopies for possible future assignments. "Write for our catalog to get an idea of our product direction. We've found, too, that it's often easier to work with artists who live in our area."

PERGAMON PRESS, INC., Fairview Park, Elmsford NY 10523. (914)592-7700. Vice President: Albert Henderson. Estab: 1950. Specializes in scientific, technical, scholarly, educational, professional and business books. Uses artists for jacket designs and direct mail brochures. One and 2-color work only. Call for appointment.

S. G. PHILLIPS, INC., 305 W. 86th St., New York NY 10024. Contact: Sidney Phillips. Uses artists for jacket design, book illustrations and direct mail promotion design. "Since we are primarily publishers of books for young people, we are most interested in seeing work pertaining to this field." Check samples of books produced by this firm at the library and catalog information in *Publisher's Trade List Annual.*

PJD PUBLICATIONS, Box 966, Westbury NY 11590. Contact: Art Director. Publishes hardbound and paperback college and biomedical texts and journals. Published 27 titles in 1976. Query with samples. Payment determined by degree of difficulty and/or number of illustrations.
Book Jacket Design: Color-separated art OK. Pays $100 average.
Direct Mail Brochures: Uses artists for illustration. Color-separated art OK. Pays $100-300.
Advertising Art: Uses artists for illustrations. B&w line drawings and color-separated art OK.

PLATT & MUNK PUBLISHERS, 1055 Bronx River Ave., Bronx NY 10472. Art Buyer: Leslie McGuire. Specializes in hard cover picture books for children, ages 4-8. "Our style is standard mass market art, not school and library art. We use 4-color illustrations. Media and size of drawings depend on the assignment." Send photocopies. "If I am interested I will contact them. I will ask to see their color work before giving an assignment." Pays $3,500, 72-page book (approximately 72 illustrations).
To Break In: "The advantage of an agent for the beginning freelancer is that the agent knows where to go with the artist's work. If the artist can do this himself, that's fine. I often prefer to deal directly with the artist, although I will call an agent if after going through my files I can't find someone who does what I am looking for."

PLAYBOY PRESS PAPERBACKS, 919 N. Michigan Ave., 3rd Flr., Chicago IL 60611. (312)751-8000. Art Director: Robb Pawlak. Publishes paperbacks. Published 84 titles and

bought 10 designs in 1976. Write or call for interview. Submit finished art. Pays on acceptance. Buys all rights. SASE.
Book Jacket Design: B&w line drawings, washes and color-separated art OK. Pays $250-500.
Outside Cover Art and Inside Book Illustrations: B&w line drawings, washes and color-separated art OK. Pays $200-350, b&w; $550-750, color.

PLAYMORE INC., PUBLISHERS, 200 5th Ave., New York NY 10010. (212)924-7447. Art Director: Bob Horwich. Publishes adult and juvenile coloring, story and educational books. Published 24 titles and bought 24 designs in 1976. Query with samples. Pays on publication. Buys all rights.

POCKET BOOKS, 630 5th Ave., New York NY 10020. Vice President: Milton Charles. Paperback publishing firm. Uses artists for cover illustrations. Most cover design is done in house. Deliver portfolios for review and later pick-up; no mailed work.

POPULAR LIBRARY PUBLISHERS, 600 3rd Ave., New York NY 10016. Art Buyer: Christie Hadley. Adult general fiction and nonfiction publisher. Uses artists for jacket design. Pays $200, standard jacket design; $400, "realistic, 4-color painting for a mass market paperback." Query. SASE.

CLARKSON N. POTTER, INC., 1 Park Ave., New York NY 10016. (212)532-9200. Editor: Carolyn Hart. Publishes hardbound and paperback books on Americana, antiques, art, cooking and photography. Published 30 titles in 1976; buying 50-75% of the designs. Query with photocopied samples of finished art. Pays on acceptance. Buys all book rights. Reports in 2 weeks "if we like samples." SASE. Free sample catalog.
Jacket Design: All media OK. Pays $250-300. "Jacket designers usually work with art from book; they don't create art."
Inside Book Illustrations: All media OK. Pays $10-25, spot illustrations; $50 minimum, full-page illustration; determined by degree of difficulty, number of illustrations and/or reputation of artist.

PRENTICE-HALL, INC., Englewood Cliffs NJ 07632. (201)592-2294. Art Director: Marvin R. Warshaw. Publishes hardbound and paperback college textbooks. Published 400+ titles and bought "several text designs and hundreds of book jackets" in 1976. Query. Submit roughs. Payment on acceptance. Pays half contracted fee for unused assigned illustrations. Buys all rights, but will negotiate. Reports in 2 weeks. SASE.
Jacket Design and Inside Illustrations: All media OK. Pays $10-250, b&w; $25-500, color. Payment determined by degree of difficulty, number of illustrations and/or reputation of artist.
Special Needs: Pays $250 minimum, text design; $1 per page minimum, book dummying; 75¢ per page minimum camera copy preparation.
To Break In: "Get a beginner staff job and learn from the bottom up, particularly about type."

PRUETT PUBLISHING COMPANY, 3235-F Prairie Ave., Boulder CO 80301. (303)449-4919. Contact: Editor. Specializes in books on Americana, railroad histories and intermountain regional subjects. "We do not directly contract artwork. Authors of our titles supply their own art; however, we maintain a file of artist's brochures, query letters, etc. for the use of our authors in need of such services. No calls, please."

PULSE-FINGER PRESS, Box 16697, Philadelphia PA 19139. Contact: O. Roche or Raphael Farnesi. Publishes hardbound and paperback fiction, poetry and drama. Published 5 titles and bought 5 designs in 1976. Query. "We don't want anything unsolicited." Payment determined by degree of difficulty. Pays on acceptance. Buys first serial and reprint rights. Reports in 4 weeks. SASE.
Book Jacket Design: B&w line drawings and halftones OK. Pays $25-100.
Advertising Art: Uses artists for layout and illustrations for trade magazine ads. Pays minimum $25.

G.P. PUTNAM'S SONS, Coward, McCann & Goeghegan, Inc., 200 Madison Ave., New York NY 10016. (212)576-8918. Art Director, Children's Books: Aileen Friedman. Publishes hardbound juvenile books. Published 100+ titles and bought 30-35 jacket designs in 1976. Query by phone. Submit finished art usually with complete mechanical. Payment determined by degree of difficulty. Pays on acceptance. Small rejection fee for unused assigned work. Buys all

rights unless otherwise specified. Free catalog. Artist's guidelines with assignment.
Book Jacket Design: "Most techniques acceptable, preseparated work most common." Pays $225-250, preseparated color art; $250-300, full color.
To Break In: "For inside book illustration, artist should contact the editors of each (Putnam, Coward) juvenile books department. Contact Lynn Hollyn (Art Director) for adult book jacket illustration and design."

R.V.K. PUBLISHING COMPANY, Box 264, Menomonee Falls WI 53051. Art Buyer: S. P. Stavrakis. Uses artists for semiannual, copyrighted poetry books. Media include b&w art, India ink and color cover designs suitable for offset. Buys one-time rights. Will consider material published elsewhere for a different purpose. Reports in 2 months. Pays $5 to $30 (up to $50 for a cover design). Back issues available for $4 post paid.

RANDOM HOUSE, Education Division, 201 E. 50th St., New York NY 10022. Contact Stanley Wheatman. Uses artists for jacket design, inside book illustrations, direct mail brochures, advertising layout/art/photos and book design. Specializes in educational books. Send photocopies or transparencies. Pays $200-500, cover design; $200-500, book design.

READER'S DIGEST ASSOCIATION LTD., 215 Redfern Ave., Montreal, Quebec Canada M32 2V9. (514)934-0751. Managing Art Director (Books): James Hayes. Promotion Art Director (Direct Mail etc.): Ronald Durepos. Publishes hardbound books on cooking, reference, how-to, Canadian history, travel, anthology, nature and condensed novels. Bought 500 illustrations in 1976. Query or call for interview. Pays on acceptance. Full payment for unused assigned art if it meets requirements. Buys first Canadian (English and French) rights plus Canadian reprint and adaptation rights. Reports in 4 weeks.
Inside Book Illustrations: B&w line drawings, halftones, washes, color separated artwork OK. Pays $35-200, b&w; $35 minimum, color. Payment determined by degree of difficulty and/or number of illustrations.
Direct Mail Brochures: Uses artists for illustrations. B&w line drawings and color OK. Pays $35-200, b&w; $50-850, color. Payment determined by degree of difficulty.
Advertising Art: Uses artists for illustrations. B&w line drawings, washes and color OK. Pays $50-200, b&w; $75-850, color. Payment determined by degree of difficulty.
To Break In: "We work primarily with Canadian illustrators, preferably those who can travel easily to Montreal."

REDGRAVE PUBLISHING CO., 430 Manville Rd., Pleasantville NY 10570. (914)769-3629. Publisher: S. Wolf. Publishes academic journals and educational workbooks for libraries, college teachers and the medical profession. Published 9 titles and bought 30 local designs in 1976. Query. Payment determined by hour and/or job.
Direct Mail Brochures: Pays $100 minimum, brochure; $3.50-6 per hour, paste-up.

REED ENTERPRISES, 3511 Camino Del Rio S., San Diego CA 92120. Art Director: Mr. Bonfils. Paperback book publishing firm. Seeks "artists capable of painting attractive sexy females along with good design and background typical of today's paperback covers." Send photocopies or transparencies. Pays $100, spot full-color drawings, $150, full-color cover drawings. Buys all rights.

RICHARDS ROSEN PRESS, INC., 29 E. 21st St., New York NY 10010. (212)777-3017. Art Director: Roger Forrester. Publishes hardbound juvenile books. Published 36 titles; bought 4 designs in 1976. Query with samples. Submit roughs. Pays on acceptance. Full payment for unused assigned illustrations. Buys first serial rights. Reports in 10 days. SASE.
Jacket Design: Minimum payment: $35, 2-color; $50, full-color.
Inside Book Illustrations: B&w line drawings OK. Pays $15 minimum.
Direct Mail Brochures: Uses artists for layout and illustrations. Minimum payments: $10 per page for layout; $15, b&w illustration; $50, color illustration.

THE WARD RITCHIE PRESS, 474 S. Arroyo Pkwy., Pasadena CA 91105. Editor: William Chleboun. Uses artists for jacket design and inside book illustrations. Publishes general fiction, nonfiction and Western Americana books. Query.

RUTGERS UNIVERSITY PRESS, 30 College Ave., New Brunswick NJ 08903. Marketing Manager: Phyllis Lanz. Managing Editor: Gary F. Pugh. Uses artists for jacket design and inside book illustration. Publishes scholarly books and New Jersey regional books. Send photocopies or transparencies. Pays $100 minimum, jacket design.

SCHOLASTIC BOOK SERVICES, 50 West 44th St., New York NY 10036. Promotion Art Director, General Book Publishing Division: Carol Gildar. Publishes book promotions for trade and consumer material. Uses freelance illustrators and designers for book publications, direct mail brochures, advertising, layout and display. Prefers artists contact for an appointment or send sample for files.

SCHOLIUM INTERNATIONAL, INC., 130-30 31st Ave., Flushing NY 11354. (212)445-8700. President: A. L. Candido. Estab: 1970. Specializes in scientific and technical books. Uses artists for jacket designs, direct mail brochures, advertising layouts/art. Send photocopies or transparencies.

R. C. SCHUETTGE BOOK PRODUCTIONS, Scrimshaw Press, 6040 Claremont Ave., Oakland CA 94618. (415)658-2325. Art Director: R. C. Schuettge. Publishes hardbound and paperback picture books on architecture and lifestyle. Published 8 titles in 1976. Write or call for interview. Submit finished art. Pays on publication. No payment for unused assigned illustrations (rarely not used). Buys various rights. Reports in 2 weeks. SASE. "Most art is in the form of complete book concepts."
Jacket Design: B&w line drawings, washes and color separated art OK. Pays $250-500, color. Payment determined by degree of difficulty. Often pays percent of cover price. Royalty of 1% included with payment.
Inside Book Illustrations: Color transparencies and b&w flat reflective art OK. "Submit rough complete book ideas first." Pays 8% of cover price, paperback; 10% of cover price, hardbound. Payment determined by degree of difficulty.

SCIENTIFIC RESEARCH SERVICES, 839 N. Highland Ave., Hollywood CA 90038. Advertising Director: Ronn Dickinson. Uses local artists for jacket design, direct mail promotion brochures, advertising layouts and product preparation. Query. Pays $500, book jacket. Do not call; send brochure or resume.

SCOTT, FORESMAN AND COMPANY, 1900 E. Lake Ave., Glenview IL 60025. Advertising Design Buyer: Ghia Brenner. Art Director: Hal Kearney. Publishes textbooks and instructional material. Write or phone queries in advance, before submitting photocopies or transparencies for assignments. SASE. Uses artists in all aspects of illustration. About 15% of book design is freelanced; 50% of advertising design.

CHARLES SCRIBNER'S SONS, 597 5th Ave., New York NY 10017. Contact: D. Hrisinko. Uses artists for book jacket designs and inside book illustrations. Call for appointment.

E.A. SEEMANN PUBLISHING INC., Box K, Miami FL 33156. (305)233-5852. Contact: Ernest A. Seemann. Uses artists for jacket design, inside book illustrations, direct mail brochures, advertising layouts/art. Specializes in pictorial histories, popular natural history, Americana and handcrafts. Send photocopies or transparencies, or query.

SERENDIPITY PRESS, 3801 Kennett Pike, Suite 2, Wilmington DE 19807. Publishes and markets by mail. Book list is small. Uses local artists for design of direct mail flyers, book interiors, posters, book end sheets and dust jackets. Query with samples. Work is often interpretive and may require on-the-spot consultation. Pays $250, direct mail flyer; $500, book design, including original art.

SHEED, ANDREWS AND McMEEL, INC., 6700 Squibb Rd., Mission KS 66202. Contact: Tom Thornton. Specializes in nonfiction books. Uses artists for jackets, inside illustrations, advertising layouts and promotional brochures. Query with samples. "Our deadlines are tight and our art committee is critical." Pays $150, jacket art; $130, advertising layouts.

GEORGE SHUMWAY PUBLISHER, Rte. 7, York PA 17402. (717)755-1196. Publishes scholarly books on antique art, Americana and antique firearms. Estab: 1962. Uses artists for detailed technical drawings of antique firearms and scale drawings of early wagons.

SIERRA CLUB BOOKS, 530 Bush St., San Francisco CA 94108. Contact: Jon Beckmann or

Wendy Goldwyn. Publishes books on natural history and science, ecology, alternate technology and conservation issues; also produces calendars and guides. Uses artists for book and jacket designs. Query with resume.

SIGNPOST PUBLICATIONS, 16812 36th Ave. W., Lynnwood WA 98036. (206)743-3947. Contact: General Manager or Editor. Publishes paperback backpacking, canoeing, climbing and hiking books. Published 4 titles and bought 2 designs in 1976. Query with photocopies. Submit finished art. Pays on publication. Payment determined by degree of difficulty and/or number of illustrations. Full payment for unused assigned art. Buys first serial and translation and foreign publication rights. Reports in 1 month. SASE. Sample catalog and artist's guidelines available. Prefers not to see "violations of current outdoor activity ethics: washing dishes in a stream, building fires at base of tree or in alpine areas."
Book Jacket Design: All media OK. Minimum payments: $25, b&w; $50, color.
Inside Book Illustrations: B&w line drawings and halftones OK. Pays $10 minimum.
Direct Mail Brochures: Uses artists for layout and illustrations. B&w line drawings, halftones and washes OK. Pays $15 minimum, b&w.
Advertising Art: Uses artists for layout and illustrations. B&w line drawings, halftones and washes OK. Pays $10 minimum, b&w.

SILVER BURDETT COMPANY, 250 James St., Morristown NJ 07960. Contact: Douglas R. Steinbauer. Publishes textbooks and other education materials for pre-school through college levels. Submit samples.

SIMON & SCHUSTER, INC., 630 5th Ave., New York NY 10020. Art Director: Frank Metz. Publishes general adult fiction and nonfiction books. Uses artists for jackets and inside book illustrations. Leave portfolios for review and subsequent pick up.

SOUTHERN PUBLISHING ASSOCIATION, Box 59, Nashville TN 37202. Director of Book Design: Dean Tucker. Publishes juvenile and adult inspirational biographies, nature stories and religiously-oriented books. Uses artists for jacket designs, book illustrations and advertising layouts. Pays $40, full-page 1-color book illustration; $300-600, full-color book cover painting. Negotiates payment.

SOUTH-WESTERN PUBLISHING CO., 5101 Madison Rd., Cincinnati OH 45227. (513)271-8811. Art Director: E.H. Swillinger. Publishes hardbound and paperback business and economic textbooks. Published 50 titles in 1976 and bought 50-60% of designs from freelancers. Write or call for interview. Submit roughs or finished art. Buys all rights. No work returned.
Cover Design: B&w line drawings, halftones, washes and color separated art OK. Pays $150-400, b&w; $250 minimum, color.
Inside Book Illustrations: B&w line drawings, halftones and washes OK. Pays $15-30, charts and graphs.
To Break In: "Learn the basics! Know publishing terminology, printing, keyline and reproduction techniques."

STANDARD PUBLISHING, 8121 Hamilton Ave., Cincinnati OH 45231. Advertising Manager: John Weidner. Art Directors: Frank Sutton/Steve Clark. Publishes religious, self help and children's books. Uses artists for advertising art/design, book illustrations/design, catalog illustrations/covers, convention exhibits, decorative spots, direct mail brochures, letterheads, magazine covers, magazine editorial illustrations/layouts, package design and posters. Query with samples. Reports in 2 weeks. SASE. Pays $100, direct mail brochure design. Buys complete rights.

CLAUDE STARK & COMPANY, PUBLISHERS, Box 431, W. Dennis, Cape Cod MA 02670. General Manager: J.J. Liebermann. Specializes in "practical works of enduring beauty": The God Series, Africana Series, New Age Series and a philosophy series. Uses artists for jacket designs. Query. Also uses art related to book publishing, book design, graphics and display ads. Media include pen and ink, pastels, line drawings, prints and screens. A sample of the type of book published in The God Series is *God of All: Sri Ramakrishna's Approach to Religious Plurality.* Prefers to see original art aimed at this company's publications. Catalog available.

STEIN AND DAY, Scarborough House, Briarcliff Manor NY 10510. Art Director: Martin Cook. Publishes hardbound and paperback books on general trade subjects; fiction and nonfiction. Published 100+ titles in 1976. Query with samples. Submit roughs. Pays on publication. Payment for unused assigned work negotiated (usually ¼-½ full fee). Buys reproduction rights for copyright life. Reports in 2 weeks. SASE.
Jacket Design: All media OK. Pays $175 minimum, color.
Inside Book Illustrations: B&w line drawings, halftones, washes and veloxes OK.

STRUCTURES PUBLISHING COMPANY, Box 423, Farmington MI 48024. Editor: Shirley M. Horowitz. Publishes books that are construction related; reference and consumer type. Interested in artists with experience in book jacket and layout design.

LYLE STUART, INC., Citadel Press, 120 Enterprise Ave., Secaucus NJ 07094. Contact: David Robbins. Uses artists for jackets for adult trade fiction and nonfiction. "We cannot return samples of work submitted by artists." Pays $175, finished art for a quality size paperback cover; $175-250, hardcover book jacket including flaps; pays up to $300 maximum, large format designs. Pays extra to artists who do own color separations.

SWEET PUBLISHING CO., Box 4055, Austin TX 78765. (512)455-4171. Art Director: T.M. Williams. Specializes in religious books, classroom literature for Churches of Christ and vacation Bible school courses. Uses artists for inside book illustration. "We buy very little outside art; we have in-house art facilities. We do buy speciality art. We're especially interested in children's illustrations of Bible stories and life-application illustration." Transparencies should be 4x5 and b&w photos, 8x10. Send photocopies.

SYRACUSE UNIVERSITY PRESS, 1011 E. Water St., Syracuse NY 13210. Manager, Design/Production: Sally Eddy. Uses artists for jacket design, inside book illustrations, typographic design and direct mail brochures. Inside book illustrations usually supplied by individual authors. Publishes Adirondack series, Iroquois series, New York State Studies; foreign language bibliographies, history, geography, ecology — "almost any type for both trade and short discount in nonfiction." Also publishes some technical books. Published 23 books in 1976. Send photocopies or transparencies.

TANDEM PRESS, Tannersville PA 18372. (717)629-2250. Contact: Judith Keith. Publishes hardbound and paperback books. Bought 3 freelance designs in 1976. Query with resume. Prefers not to receive unsolicited samples. Pays on acceptance. Buys no rights. Reports in 1 week. Resumes kept on file and artist contacted for assignments.
Jacket Design: 4-color art OK. Pays $350 minimum. Average payment: $600 for 4-color design, including mechanicals.
Direct Mail Brochures: B&w and color OK.

TEACHERS COLLEGE PRESS, 1234 Amsterdam Ave., New York NY 10027. (212)678-3926. Art Director: Woody Finder. Publishes hardbound and paperback books on educational subjects. Published 12 titles; bought 8 designs in 1976. Query with samples. Submit roughs. Pays on acceptance. Buys all rights. Reports as assignments occur.
Jacket Design: B&w line drawings, halftones, color separated art and veloxes OK. Pays $250-300. Payment determined by degree of difficulty and/or set policy.
Inside Book Illustrations: B&w line drawings, halftones, color separated art and veloxes OK. Pays $25-35. Payment determined by degree of difficulty.
Promotional Needs: Contact: Marketing Department.

TEXAS WESTERN PRESS, The University of Texas at El Paso, El Paso TX 79968. Contact: Director. Publishes books on Southwestern history. Uses artists for jacket designs and inside illustrations. Query. Pays $100, jacket design.

TIME-LIFE BOOKS INC., 777 Duke St., Alexandria VA 22314. Art Directors: Tom Suzuki/Arnold C. Holeywell. Publishes hardback books on boating, home repair, World War II, gardening, nature, science, sports, cooking, history and photography. Write or call for interview; "definitely no artwork by mail." Pays on acceptance. Buys all rights. Contacts artists as assignments arise. SASE.

Inside Book Illustrations: Art medium assigned. Pays $30-80, b&w; $80-1,000, color. Payment determined by degree of difficulty.

TRANSACTION, INC., Rutgers University, New Brunswick NJ 08903. Art Buyer: Barbara Ciletti. Publishes social science books. Buys cover designs. Pays $100. Buys one-time rights. Pays on publication. Submit published samples. Reports in 4 month.

TROUBADOR PRESS, 385 Fremont, San Francisco CA 94105. (415)397-3717. Art Director: M.K. Whyte. Publishes hardbound and paperback books on art, activity, nature, self-help, games, cookbooks and entertainment. Published 11 titles and bought approximately 20 illustrated pages per book in 1976. Query with photocopied samples. Payment determined by degree of difficulty and/or budget. Pays on acceptance. Buys all rights. Reports in 2 weeks. SASE. Free catalog.
Jacket Design and Inside Illustration: B&w line drawings, halftones and washes OK. Pays $100-300, jacket; $25-75, inside illustrations.
Direct Mail Brochures: Uses artists for layout.

TRUCHA PUBLICATIONS, INC., Box 5223, Lubbock TX 79417. (806)763-3729. Art Editor: Hector F. DeLeon. Publishes bilingual and bicultural literature. Uses artists for jacket designs and inside book illustrations. Send photocopies or transparencies. Pays $5-50. "We prefer art to have meaning, depth and message of struggle and liberation."

UNITY PRESS, 113 New St., Santa Cruz CA 95060. (408)427-2020. Art Director: Craig Caughlan. Publishes hardbound and paperback general trade books. Published 4 titles and bought 15 designs in 1976. Query with samples. Submit roughs. Pays on acceptance. Payment determined by degree of difficulty. Buys all rights. Reports in 3 weeks. Pays7.50 per hour, mechanicals.
Book Jacket Design: B&w line drawings, washes and color-separated art OK. Pays $75-150, b&w; $125-250, color.
Inside Book Illustrations: B&w line drawings, halftones and washes OK. Pays $20-50, b&w.
Direct Mail Brochures: B&w line drawings, halftones, washes and color-separated art OK. Pays $50-150, b&w; $100-250, color.
Advertising Art: B&w line drawings, halftones and washes OK. Pays $25-75, b&w.

UNIVERSITY OF IOWA PRESS, Graphic Services Bldg., University of Iowa, Iowa City IA 52242. Managing Editor: Norman Sage. Uses artists experienced in jacket and book design. Specializes in scholarly works and poetry translation and short fiction series in connection with an award competition. Query. Pays minimum $350, book design; $150, jacket.

UNIVERSITY OF MASSACHUSETTS PRESS, Box 429, Amherst MA 01002. Contact: M. Mendell. Uses artists for book illustration and cover designs. Publishes books in philosophy, history, black studies, biography, science, poetry, art and studies of regional interest. Query with resume and samples. Pays $75 for jacket designs (not including type).

UNIVERSITY OF NEBRASKA PRESS, 901 N. 17th St., Lincoln NE 68588. Art Director: Thomas E. Sheahan. Publishes hardbound and paperback books on western and literary history. Published 55 titles; bought 6 designs in 1976. Query with samples. Submit roughs. Pays on acceptance. Negotiates payment for unused assigned illustrations. Buys first serial rights. Reports in 3 weeks. SASE. "No cowboy/Indian stereotypes."
Jacket Design: B&w line drawings, halftones, washes and color-separated art OK. Pays $70-120, b&w; $120-170, color. Payment determined by degree of difficulty.
Inside Book Illustrations: B&w line drawings and veloxes OK. Pays $30-60, b&w; $100-150, color. Payment determined by degree of difficulty, number of illustrations and/or reputation of artist.

UNIVERSITY OF NOTRE DAME PRESS, Notre Dame IN 46656. Editor: Ann Rice. Uses artists for jacket design, inside book illustrations and direct mail promotion brochures. Mail photocopies or transparencies. SASE. "Our inside book illustrations consist primarily of maps, graphs and charts. Jackets are 2-3 color." Requires completed camera-ready artwork. Pays $175-200 for book jacket design; $75 for front cover design of promotion piece.

UNIVERSITY OF PENNSYLVANIA PRESS, 3933 Walnut St., Philadelphia PA 19174.

Production Manager: Molly Hindman. Promotion Manager: Warren Slesinger. Publishes hardbound and paperback academic and scholarly books. Published 20 titles and bought 30 designs in 1976. Query with samples. Submit roughs. Pays on acceptance. Negotiates payment for unused assigned work. SASE. Free catalog.

Book Jacket Design: All media OK. Pays $50-85, design; $75-115, mechanicals.

Direct Mail Brochures and Advertising Art: Uses artists for layout and illustrations. B&w line drawings and halftones OK. Pays $75-250. Payment determined by time spent, degree of difficulty and/or number of illustrations.

To Break In: "Study the *New York Review of Books, Book Forum* and *The New York Times* to learn what the competition is doing."

Bob Chronister's combination of realism and fantasy was the secret selling ingredient for this book jacket, bought by Thomas Nelson Inc. Nelson holds artist's samples for future assignment consideration. "Our needs vary and we may have no use for the artist's style one year, but can use it another," says Deborah Daley, art director.

THE UNIVERSITY OF WISCONSIN PRESS, Box 1379, Madison WI 53701. (608)262-4978. Production Manager: Gardner R. Wills. Publishes scholarly hardbound and paperback books. Published 27 titles and bought 20 designs in 1976. Query. Submit roughs or finished art. Payment determined by degree of difficulty and/or cost of purchased materials. Pays on completion of project. Buys all rights. Reports in 2 weeks. SASE.
Jacket and Text Design: B&w line drawings, halftones, washes, color-separated artwork and veloxes OK. Pays $100-300, rough through finished mechanical.

THE UNIVERSITY PRESS OF HAWAII, 2840 Kolowalu St., Honolulu HI 96822. (808)948-8275. Art Director: Larry J. Cooke. Publishes hardbound and paperback books on scholarly work in Pacific anthropology, linguistics, Asian art and Hawaiian culture. Published 52 titles in 1976; bought approximately 25% of the designs. Write for interview. Submit roughs. Pays on acceptance. Negotiates payment for unused assigned work and rights. Contacts artists as needs arise.
Jacket Design: All media OK. Pays $100 minimum, b&w; payment negotiated before assignment made.
Direct Mail Brochures and Advertising Art: Uses artists for layout and illustrations. Write for specifics.

THE UNIVERSITY SOCIETY, INC., 25 Cottage St., Midland Park NJ 07432. Editor-in-Chief: George W. Cooke. Estab: 1897. "We specialize in music books — specifically high-quality anthologies and collections, some with full-color 9x12" cover illustrations. Our needs are specialized and extremely limited. Most of our work is supplied by local paste-up artists and illustrators." Uses artists for book jacket design, inside book illustrations, direct mail brochures, and advertising layout/art. Pays $150, detailed schematic diagram; $1,000, exceptional cover painting.

VALKYRIE PRESS, INC., 2135 1st Ave. S., St. Petersburg FL 33712. Editor/Publisher: Marjorie Schuck. "We publish approximately 10 books per year, both hardcover and paperback, mainly for adults; a few children's books. We use many kinds of art and art themes (such as animals, environmental) to illustrate and/or decorate our books. A special need is for b&w sketches or line drawings of faces of famous personalities throughout history." Needs include b&w drawings (line), cover designs, design ideas and finished cartoons (slightly less than 6x9"). Most books are copyrighted. Buys reprint rights for cartoons. Mail artwork and design ideas. Reports in 2-4 weeks. Pays $10 for spot drawings; $300 for full-color illustration; $125 for cover design in 1 or 2 colors. Payment on acceptance.
Special Needs: Commercial printing plant uses artists for design and format.

VANGUARD PRESS, INC., 424 Madison Ave., New York NY 10017. Contact: Thomas Woll/Evelyn Shrifte. Publishes general interest books. Uses artists for jacket designs and inside book illustrations. "We don't publish any gothic novels, textbooks or photography books, although photographs are used at times on our book jackets. We use a very, very small number of freelance artists and illustrators. If possible, work should be sent in by mail rather than presented in person. No one will be seen without an appointment. Portfolios should be neat and professional in appearance."

VISAGE PRESS INC., 3409 Wisconsin Ave. NW, Washington DC 20016. (202)686-5302. Art Director: Sherry Icenhower. Publishes hardbound and paperback books. Published 5 titles; bought 5 designs in 1976. Query with samples. Submit roughs or finished art. Payment determined by degree of difficulty. Pays on publication. Buys all rights. Reports in 1 month. SASE. Sample catalog/artist's guidelines available with SASE.
Jacket Design: B&w line drawings, halftones, color separated art and veloxes OK. Pays $50 minimum.
Direct Mail Brochures and Advertising Art: Uses artists for layout and illustrations. B&w line drawings, halftones, color separated art and veloxes OK. Pays $50 minimum.

WARNER BOOKS, INC., 75 Rockefeller Plaza, New York NY 10019. Art Director: Gene Light. Uses artists for jacket illustrations. Pays $400, book cover illustration. Query with resume. Will review portfolios of artists by representative or in person.

WATSON-GUPTILL PUBLICATIONS, 1515 Broadway, New York NY 10036. (212)764-7300. Art Director: Jim Craig. Publishes hardbound books on art instruction, needlecrafts,

architecture, crafts, interior design and communication arts. Published 75 titles in 1976. Query. Pays on acceptance. Buys book club rights. Reports immediately. Sample catalog/artist's guidelines available.
Direct Mail Brochures: Uses artists for illustrations. B&w line drawings OK. Pays $100 minimum; determined by job and time spent.

WESTERN PUBLISHING COMPANY, INC., 1220 Mound Ave., Racine WI 53404. Contact: Art Director. Publishes juvenile picture and story books. Works with an established list of artists and agents. Firm produces Golden Books, Whitman Tell-a-Tale books and cloth books for very small children.

WILLIAM-FREDERICK PRESS, 55 E. 86th St., New York NY 10028. (212)722-7272. Contact: T. Reed. Uses artists for spot drawings and book jackets. Pay $6 minimum. Custom book printing firm. Local artists should arrange interview; out-of-towners should submit resume and samples of work. Standard jacket assignment is for 6x9 or 8½x11 drawings.
To Break In: Reed suggests that the young artist attempting to establish him or herself become aware of the business aspect of book publishing. "Too often artists do not realize the budget allowances for artwork and tend to price themselves out of our range."

WINCHESTER PRESS, 205 E. 42nd St., New York NY 10017. Director, Production and Design: Josh Furman. Uses artists for book jacket designs and inside book illustrations. Send photocopies or transparencies. Query with resume. Publishes books on hunting, fishing, camping and other outdoor activities. "Our books are not mass-market; consequently, our rates are lower than many publishers."

WOODBRIDGE PRESS, Box 6189, Santa Barbara CA 93111. Contact: Howard Weeks. Specializes in how-to books on personal health, well being, gardening and cooking. Pays $15-30, simple inside illustrations; $150-350, finished jacket art. Buys all rights. Query.

BRIGHAM YOUNG UNIVERSITY PRESS, 221 UPB, Provo UT 84602. Contact: McRay Magleby. Uses artists for jacket design/illustrations, direct mail brochures and other advertising art. Pays $70 for b&w inside book illustrations; $250 for full-color cover art.

ZONDERVAN, 1415 Lake Drive SE, Grand Rapids MI 49506. Contact: Art Director. Uses artists for jacket design, book illustration, direct mail brochures and advertising. Pays $250 for jacket design. Query. Fiction and nonfiction books are primarily Christian oriented.

Competitions & Exhibitions

A successful artist is a well-known artist, and the best way to become well-known is to get as much exposure as possible in front of the people who will most likely become your customers. The best way to do this is to enter competitions and exhibitions.

Besides exposure, there's money to be made at such shows. Consider:

The 1976 Boston Mills Invitational Art Festival (Peninsula, Ohio) was only five years old, but 12,000 people attended, buying $110,000 worth of art in three days.

During the same year, the Frederick Craft Fair (Frederick, Maryland) attracted 50,000 people and each exhibitor averaged $1,100 in wholesale orders and $550 retail.

These two shows only hint at the promise listings in this section hold for the artist/craftsman. The real secret to making the most of entry into competitions and exhibitions is to know which shows best serve your interests and how to get accepted as an exhibitor.

Don Getz, exhibit director of the Boston Mills Invitational Art Festival and Artisan Fair, says the best method of learning about the merit of various shows is to "contact friends and ask about their personal experience on particular shows. This was my guide during the more than 20 years I participated in shows. And, I found that what I was told about shows usually was correct."

One-person juried competitions are more risky to enter than those judged by three or more persons, unless the juror's preferences are the same as yours. If you are a watercolor painter, for example, your work is more likely to be looked at favorably by a watercolor artist.

It is possible to enter shows outside your state or local area, but if entry fees are high and/or participation would involve expensive shipping or a costly trip, consider looking elsewhere — unless the show offers excellent exposure.

Enter as many competitions/exhibitions as possible. You'll find most reputable shows attract gallery and shop owners who will be looking for work for their businesses.

There are two types of shows listed in this section: Competitions — offering cash, purchase prizes, ribbons, certificates or other prizes for outstanding art; and exhibitions — offering only exposure and sales.

One certain way to increase sales at competitions or exhibitions is to demonstrate your art. "We encourage on-the-spot demonstrations, as they heighten the interest of the crowd and increase profits of artists/craftsmen," says Bob Quinlan, chairman of the Pawtuxet (Rhode Island) Village Arts & Crafts Festival.

"We encourage demonstrations because this allows the buyer to see how a craftsman does his work. Many times a viewer will stay until the craftsman is done because they want to buy what they saw produced," says Getz.

"Demonstrations also add an air of quality to the craftsman's ability. The customer can see the technical ability the craftsman applies. Demonstrations always draw a crowd, no matter what medium is being demonstrated. And, when you're attracting attention, you'll improve sales," he adds.

Although there are a few shows that are completely nonprofit, most seek a profit in one of four ways: by an entry fee, commission, entry fee plus commission, or by asking artists to donate a piece of artwork to the show.

When an entry fee is particularly high, carefully check into the show prior to registering. Have previous sales at the show been high for artists/craftsmen working in your medium? What has attendance been? What will you get for the money you've paid to register — promotion? a show catalog containing reproductions of your work?

Sandi Bianco, publicist of Theatre By the Sea Street Fair in New Hampshire, stresses the importance of providing shows with promotional material on you and your work: "It is helpful for our promotional purposes to receive clippings, resumes and other information on the participating artists for use in our releases. Descriptive pieces on the process used is also of considerable interest for feature items." Some shows ask for publicity photographs. These should be 8x10 black & white glossies, preferably showing the artist/craftsman at work. By supplying photos when show sponsors request them, you will increase your exposure and sales by preshow publicity. You can also use these shots for promotion when working with galleries or craft dealers.

Most of the listings in this section will send you a prospectus (a letter or brochure containing additional information and show dates) if you write to them.

Some shows are restricted to members only. For these, information is generally included in the listings on how you can become a member. When the information is not provided, you should ask about requirements when writing for a prospectus.

Always include a self-addressed stamped envelope (SASE) when writing for more information or submitting slides you would like returned. For more specific information on shipping artwork and crafts, read "Shipping Your Work."

Artists should consult the Art Competitions, Art Exhibitions and Show Sponsors categories for shows in their medium. Craftsmen will find shows for their work among the Craft Competitions, Craft Exhibitions and Show Sponsors listings. Occasionally, art shows will also accept crafts.

For more information on upcoming shows, artists/craftsmen should read art and crafts publications. The *Crafts Report* (monthly) and *Artweek* (weekly), for example, both have sections listing upcoming shows.

Art Competitions

Alabama

ART & CRAFTS FAIR, Fine Arts Museum of the South, Box 8404, Mobile AL 36608. (205)342-4642. Registration Chairman: Martina Roser. Sponsors: Mobile Art Association Inc. and Art Patrons League of Mobile. Estab: 1965. Annual outdoor show held the last weekend in September. Average attendance: 50,000+. Closing date for entry: 10 weeks before show. Entry fee: $5 jury fee; $30 per 12x6' display area. Maximum 1 artist per space. Prejudging by 3 slides; $30 refunded for refused work. Art must be offered for sale. Artist must attend show; demonstrations encouraged. Registration limit: 300 artists/craftsmen. Sponsor provides wire if requested. Considers all art.
Awards: Presents $1,000 purchase award; twenty $100 prizes; ribbons.

ART ON THE LAKE, 1500 Gunter Ave., Guntersville AL 35976. (205)582-4392. Chairman: Mrs. Robert Haden. Sponsor: Twentieth Century Club. Estab: 1962. Annual indoor/outdoor show held fourth Sunday in April. Average attendance: 1,500. Entries accepted until show. Entry fee: $5 per display area. Art may be offered for sale; no commission. Artist or representative must attend show; demonstrations OK. Considers all art except erotica.
Awards: Grants first, second and third place ribbons in 3 categories.

ART ON THE ROCKS, Box 973, Gadsden AL 35902. Sponsor: Gadsden Art Association. Annual outdoor show held the first Sunday in May. Closing date for entry: 1 week before show. No entry fee. Awards $75 first and $35 second prizes. Prejudging. Art may be offered for sale; 15% commission. Artist must attend show. Considers drawings, paintings, pastels and sculpture. Two-dimensional art must be framed and wired.

CHALAKA ARTS AND CRAFTS FESTIVAL, 1705 Springhill Rd., Sylacauga AL 35150. Chairman: Betty Anne Aldag. Sponsor: Sylacauga Area Council on Arts and Humanities. Estab: 1968. Annual outdoor show held 2 days in June. Average attendance: 100-150. Closing date for entry: 1 week before show. Entry fee: $15 per entry. Awards approximately $650 in prizes. Prejudging; entry fee refunded for refused work. Art may be offered for sale; 10% commission. Artist must attend show. Considers all art.

DIXIE ANNUAL, Montgomery Museum of Fine Arts, 440 S. McDonough St., Montgomery AL 36104. Assistant Director: Theodore James. Estab: 1960. Annual indoor show held 1 month in early spring. Average attendance: 5,600. Closing date for entries: 5-6 weeks before show. Entry fee: $5 per artist. Maximum 3 entries per artist. Awards are in the form of museum

purchases. Prejudging; no entry fees refunded for refused work. Art may be offered for sale; 10% commission. Open to Southern artists. Sponsor provides display equipment, insurance for exhibited work and return shipping. "Damaged cartons will be returned unopened." Prospectus available after December 1.
Acceptable Work: Considers all 2-dimensional work on paper. Maximum size: 60x60". "Only works that are matted, firmly backed and wrapped with a protective acetate covering will be accepted."

EXHIBITION SOUTH, Box 474, Tuscumbia AL 35674. (205)383-0533. Contact: Chairman. Sponsor: Tennessee Valley Authority. Estab: 1972. Annual indoor show held 3 weeks in October. Average attendance: 400. Closing date for entries: 1 week before show. Entry fee: $5 per work. Awards 1,000 in cash prizes and first, second and third place ribbons. Prejudging; no entry fees refunded for refused work. Art may be offered for sale; 33½% commission. Sponsor provides display equipment. Considers calligraphy, drawings, paintings, pastels and prints.

FIRST MONDAY'S ART SUNDAY, 601 Scott St., Scottsboro AL 35768. (205)259-5848. Chairman: Linda Kitchens. Sponsor: 3-Arts Club and Jackson County Arts Council. Estab: 1972. Annual outdoor show held Sunday during Labor Day weekend. Average attendance: 1,000. Closing date for entries: 1 week before show. Entry fee: $5 per entry. Art may be offered for sale; no commission. Artist must attend show; demonstrations encouraged.
Acceptable Work: Considers drawings, paintings and sculpture. Paintings must be framed. No erotica.
Awards: Grants $650 in cash prizes. Judge for each category is from an area college or museum.

KENTUCK ARTS & CRAFTS FESTIVAL, Box 127, Northport AL 35476. Contact: Alfred L. Knight. Sponsor: Northport Chamber of Commerce. Annual outdoor show held the first or second weekend in September. Entry fee: $10 for 10x10' space. Limit 2 exhibitors per space. Clubs or groups may obtain 15x15' display area for $15. No commission. Considers paintings and handmade objects.
Awards: Grants $150 purchase award, $25 display award, $100, $50 and $25 for art winners.

MARION MILITARY INSTITUTE ART SHOW, The Marion Military Institute, Baer Memorial Library, Marion AL 36756. Annual show held in April. Entry fee: $5 per person. No entry fee for students grade 9 or older. Art may be offered for sale; 10% commission. All entries must be original, completed within the past 2 years and not previously exhibited at Marion Institute shows.
Awards: Cash prizes and ribbons are awarded in all four categories — painting, drawing and sketching, mixed media and three dimensional. Also awarded are Best in Show and Popular Favorite. Prizes are cash, $50 maximum.

MOBILE'S ANNUAL OUTDOOR ART AND CRAFTS FAIR, Martina Roser, Box 8404, Mobile AL 36608. Sponsor: Mobile Art Association, Inc. and Art Patron's League. Exhibitor is responsible for setting up and manning his own booth. Open to artists over 18. Awards include 25 "Best of Show Winners," first prize of $300, second prize of $200 and third prize of $100. Best display booth wins $25 award.

WEST MOBILE ARTS & CRAFTS SHOW, Box 16243, Mobile AL 36616. (205)344-3750. Contact: Raymond McCoy. Sponsor: Mobile Federal Savings and Loan Association. Estab: 1973. Annual outdoor show held 2 days in May. Closing date for entry: 1 week before show. Awards cash prizes and ribbons. Art may be offered for sale; no commission. Artist must attend show; demonstrations OK. "We don't accept mailed artwork." Considers calligraphy, drawings, mobiles, pastels, pen and inks, paintings and sculpture.

Alaska

TANANA VALLEY STATE FAIR FINE ARTS SHOW, Box 188, Fairbanks AK 99707. (907)452-3750. Manager: Janet Baird. Annual indoor show held in August. Average attendance: 76,000. Entries accepted until show date. No entry fee. Maximum 1 entry per lot per artist. Awards cash prizes. Art may not be offered for sale. Considers all art "not previously shown for prizes."

Arizona

INDIAN ARTISTS AND CRAFTSMEN OF NORTH AMERICA, 22 E. Monte Vista, Phoenix

AZ 85004. Sponsored by Heard Museum Guild. Contact: Arts & Crafts Chairman. Annual show. November closing date. No entry fee. Size limits are 54x54" for paintings and 200 pounds for sculpture. Considers paintings, sculpture, crafts and jewelry. Art must relate to North American Indian heritage. Ship items prepaid to museum or hand deliver.

I-40 ART EXPO, Box 641, Winslow AZ 86047. (602)289-3540. Chairman: Stella Pitts. Sponsor: Winslow Arts Association. Estab: 1961. Annual indoor show held 52 days in June-August. Average attendance: 2,500. Entry fee: $4. Maximum 3 entries per classification, 10 total. Awards $1,130 in cash prizes; ribbons; and plaques. Prejudging; no entry fees refunded for refused work. Art may be offered for sale; 10% commission. Demonstrations by arrangements. Sponsor provides display panels. Considers all art.

SCOTTSDALE ARTS FESTIVAL ART EXHIBIT, Scottsdale Fine Arts Commission, 3839 N. Civic Center Plaza, Scottsdale AZ 85251. Fine Arts Director: Mrs. Pat Hartwell. Art may be offered for sale; 20% commission. Entry fee: $5. Maximum 3 entries. Awards two $100 prizes; two $50 prizes; 2 or more $25 prizes, merit awards and purchase prizes.

TWO FLAGS INTERNATIONAL FESTIVAL OF THE ARTS, Box 256, Douglas AZ 85607. Contact: Two Flags Committee. Annual show and festival held in May. Entry fee: $3 per item. Maximum 2 works per artist. Size limit: 48" overall, including frame. Art may be offered for sale; 20% commission. Open to citizens of the U.S. and Mexico. Grants cash awards of $1,000 and purchase awards.

Arkansas

NATIONAL INVITATIONAL ARTS/CRAFTS SHOW, c/o Jim Smith, Box 5, Dogpatch AR 72648. Sponsored by the Marble Falls Resort and Dogpatch U.S.A. Semiannual indoor/outdoor show held in May and October. Closing dates for entries: spring show, May 1; fall show, October 1. Entry fees, depending on booth size and location, are as follows: booth size 8x6' — $20 indoor on main floor; $10 outdoor. Booth size 16x6' — $35 indoor on main floor; $15 outdoor. Work may be offered for sale; no commission. Artist must attend show; demonstrations OK. Average number of exhibits is 150. Motel and campground accommodations available. Considers all art and crafts.
Awards: Cash awards total $300. First and second purchase awards given in art and crafts. Ribbons awarded in ten places.

California

AFFAIRE IN THE GARDENS, 450 N. Crescent Dr., Beverly Hills CA 90210. (213)550-4864. Contact: Michele Merrill. Sponsor: Beverly Hills Recreation Department Cultural Services. Estab: 1976. Annual outdoor show held 2 days in the fall. Average attendance: 3,000-5,000. Closing date for entry: 4 weeks before show. Entry fee: $35 per entry. Prejudging; entry fee less $3 for processing is refunded for refused work. Art may be offered for sale; no commission. "We give preference to those demonstrating." Registration limit: 200 artists/craftsmen.
Acceptable Work: Considers drawings, calligraphy, mobiles, paintings, pastels, prints and sculpture. Paintings must be framed and sculpture must have stands.
Awards: Presents prize ribbons. Judging panel consists of local university staff and art professionals.

ART & SCULPTURE SHOW, 1685 Main St., Santa Monica CA 90401. (213)393-9975 ext. 276. Contact: Frances Kreuz. Sponsor: Santa Monica Recreation and Parks Dept. Annual outdoor show held 2 days in August. Average attendance: 2,000. Closing date for entry: 2 weeks before show. Entry fee: $15 per artist. Awards up to $500 in cash prizes, ribbons and best of show award. Prejudging; entry fee refunded for refused work. Art may be offered for sale; no commission. Artist must attend show; demonstrations OK. Considers drawings, mobiles, paintings, pastels, mixed media, prints and sculpture. Work must be framed or have attractive base.
Profile: "This is the only outdoor show in the area that does not accept crafts. It gives painters, sculptors and other fine artists a chance to sell work without crafts competition."

ART IN ALL MEDIA, Del Mar Fairgrounds, Del Mar CA 92014. (714)755-1161. Director: J. Milford Ellison. Sponsor: Southern California Exposition. Estab: 1882. Annual indoor show

held 2 weeks in June/July. Average attendance: 250,000. Closing date for entry: 4 weeks before show. Entry fee: $3 per entry. Prejudging; no entry fees refunded for refused work. Art may be offered for sale; 25% commission. Open to Southern California residents only. Sponsor furnishes display equipment. "Deliver art personally or by Bruggers Fine Art Transfer Co., Inc. (Los Angeles) or by Cart and Crate (Los Angeles)."
Acceptable Work: Considers oils, watercolors, acrylics, mixed media, drawings and prints. No dimensions over 6' including frame. Paintings must be framed. Watercolors and graphics must have glass or a good protective covering. All work must be suitable for family viewing. No student work.
Awards: Grants $1,700 in cash prizes in paintings/graphics; $1,300, sculpture/crafts. Two-dimensional jury panel consists of a watercolor artist, oil painter and printmaker or drawing expert. Three-dimensional jury panel consists of a sculptor, craftsman and a ceramist.

ART IN THE REDWOODS, Gualala Arts, Inc., Box 297, Gualala CA 95445. Chairperson: Evelyn C. McGinn. Annual show held the last weekend in August. Entry fee: $2 per item ($1 for members). Fees due Friday the week before the show. Awards cash. Maximum 2 entries per artist; 27x36" size limitation. Art may be offered for sale; 20% commission. Display panels furnished. All pieces to be hung must have suitable hardware attached.

ART-A-FAIR, INC., SUMMER SHOW, Box 547, Laguna Beach CA 92652. Contact: Chairman. Annual show. Jury fees are $5 for first medium; $3 for each additional medium. Art may be offered for sale; 10% commission. Southern California artists only. Acceptable media include traditional art, finished drys and framed work. Crafts must also be finished.

ARTS, CRAFTS AND INDOOR PLANT SHOW, 10992 Ashton Ave., Los Angeles CA 90024. (213)479-7055. Director: Glen Beckman. Estab: 1977. Semiannual indoor show held in the Bonaventure Hotel 6 days in January and July. Average attendance: 12,000-16,000. Entries accepted until show date. Entry fee: $195 per 8x10' display area. Awards ribbons. Art may be offered for sale; no commission. Artist must attend show. Registration limit: 140 artists/craftsmen. Considers all art. Artists should bring his own promotional material and price lists to give to wholesale buyers.

ATASCADERO SPRING ART MART, Box 28, Atascadero CA 93422. Contact: Treasurer. Annual outdoor show. Sponsored by Atascadero Art Club, Inc. Entry fee: $4. Entries accepted until show date. Selling artists must have a permit from the State Board of Equalization. Artist handles sales tax; 10% commission. The club also sponsors a fall art festival. Entry fee is $6.50. Some cash prizes and ribbons are awarded. Write for details.

CALIFORNIA STATE FAIR ART SHOW, Box 15649, Sacramento CA 95813. (916)641-2391. Contact: William Keefer. Sponsor: California. Estab: 1948. Annual indoor show held 20 days in August-September. Average attendance: 400,000. Closing date for entry: 4 weeks before show. No entry fee. Maximum 2 entries per artist. Awards $15,000 in cash prizes. Prejudging. Art may be offered for sale; no commission. Open to California residents. Demonstrations OK. Sponsor provides display equipment. Shipping shared by artist and sponsor. Considers all art.

CATALINA FESTIVAL OF ART, Box 161, Avalon CA 90704. Contact: Festival Committee Chairman. Annual show held in September. Sponsor: Catalina Art Association. "Work must be brought to Avalon by the artists or they must arrange for someone they may know here to handle it." The festival consists of 3 categories: the Invitational Exhibit; the Street Show, which includes a nonjuried painting section, preregistered photography division and young artists section; and a preregistered craft show.
To Break In: "Some artists do not realize the exhibit area is family oriented (open free to the public) and so they include occasional works not suitable for a general audience, i.e., graphic nudes, which must be pulled. Also that is a 'traditionalist' show and is judged accordingly. Abstract, pop, surrealist, etc. rarely are in the award winning list."

CELEBRATION OF THE ARTS, 20600 Roscoe Blvd., Canoga Park CA 91306. (213)341-6434. Contact: Chairman. Sponsor: St. John's in the Valley United Methodist Church. Estab: 1970. Annual indoor/outdoor show held 2 days in May. Average attendance: 2,000. Closing date for entry: 1 week before show. Entry fee: $10 per 10x12' display area. Awards $50 best of show in youth and adult divisions and first, second and third place ribbons. Art may be offered for sale; 10% commission. Artist must attend show; demonstrations encouraged. Registration limit: 120 artists/craftsmen. Considers all art. Paintings and drawings must be framed.

COMMUNICATION ARTS MAGAZINE, Box 10300, 410 Sherman Ave., Palo Alto CA 94303. Annual competition. Closing date for entries: July. Entry fee: $5 each, single units; $10 each, print campaign series/TV commercials/radio commercials; $15, TV and radio series. Categories include Consumer Magazine Advertising, Consumer Newspaper Advertising, Trade/Business Advertising, Poster, Record Jacket, Packaging/Labeling, Trademark,

Two-dimensional works on paper by Southern artists are eligible for entry in the spring Dixie Annual, sponsored by the Montgomery Museum of Fine Arts (Montgomery, Alabama). This charcoal illustration, by Ronald Milhoan, is an example of the type of artwork awarded purchase prizes during the 1975 show.

Letterhead, Company Literature, Self-Promotion, Book, Editorial, TV Advertising, Radio Advertising and Miscellaneous (greeting cards, display, signage, interiors, anything not covered in other categories). Work must be produced within preceding year. May originate from any country (English translations may be helpful to the judges). Winning entries are reproduced (most in color) in the CA-78 Annual, a 240-page special issue of *Communication Arts* published in December. Circulation of the Annual is 37,000. Winners are also given an "Award of Excellence" certificate.

CROCKER-KINGSLEY ANNUAL, E.B. Crocker Art Gallery, 216 O St., Sacramento CA 95814. Annual spring show. Entry fee: $4 per item. Maximum 2 entries per artist. Art may be offered for sale; 15% commission. Entries must be original work not previously shown at this gallery. Entries may not exceed 100 pounds in weight. Open to residents of central and northern California. Money received in entry fees awarded in equal share to artists admitted to show. Purchase awards for permanent collection of gallery are also made. Contact gallery for additional information and copy of prospectus with entry cards.

EHRMAN MANSION ART SHOW & FAIR, Box 126, Carnelian Bay CA 95711. (916)583-6208 or 587-6446. Chairman: Joanna Gillis. Sponsors: North Tahoe Art Guild, North Lake Tahoe Federated Women's Club, Lake Tahoe State Park Advisory Committee and Chamber of Commerce. Estab: 1967. Annual indoor show held the second week in August. Average attendance: 5,000-6,000. Entries accepted until show date. Entry fee: $5 per entry. Maximum 3 entries per artist. Prejudging; entry fees refunded for refused work. Art may be offered for sale; 10% commission. Considers all art.
Awards: Presents cash prizes. Judges are professional artists experienced in the various media.

INLAND EXHIBITION, Box 2272, San Bernadino CA 92406. (714)882-2054. Contact: Harriett Ginland. Sponsor: San Bernadino Art Association. Estab: 1964. Annual indoor show held 3 weeks in October. Average attendance: 2,000. Closing date for entry: 10 days before show. Entry fee: $3 per entry. Maximum 3 entries per artist. Awards $700 in cash prizes; $300, purchase awards; 10 ribbons. Prejudging; no entry fees refunded for refused work. Art may be offered for sale; 30% commission. Open to California residents. Sponsor provides display equipment and panels. Deliver work by hand or ship by Bruggers in Los Angeles.
Acceptable Work: Considers original art. Maximum size: 51x51". Paintings must be framed and wired.

LODI ART ANNUAL, Lodi Art Center, 14½ W. Pine St., Lodi CA 95240. Contact: Art Annual Chairman. Annual show held 3 days in mid-May. Entry fee: $2.50 per entry. Maximum 4 entries per artist. Awards $4,000-5,000 cash and purchase prizes. Art may be offered for sale; 20% commission for members and 30% for nonmembers. Considers oils, acrylics, watercolors, graphics, mixed media and sculpture. Work must be fully framed or self-framed ready to hang; watercolors must be glassed. Entries must be hand delivered by artist or agent.

MARIN COUNTY FAIR JURIED ART COMPETITION, Civic Center Fairgrounds, San Rafael CA 94903. Manager: Marcelle McCoy. Entry fee: $2 per item. Maximum 2 entries. Art may be offered for sale; 20% commission. Considers paintings, graphics, weaving and sculpture. Entrants must be residents of California. Awards include $1,050 in cash, 1 trophy and 5 certificates. Work must be hand-delivered and of a size as to be handled without mechanical assistance.

MARYSVILLE MALL, CALIFORNIA, ART & CRAFT & FLOWER SHOW, 3608 Cinnabar Ave., Carson City NV 89701. (702)883-0968. Director: Bea Griffin. Sponsor: Creative Artists Group. Estab: 1962. Annual indoor show held 4 days in May in Marysville. Average attendance: 50,000. Entries accepted until show date. Entry fee: $25 per 10x10' display area. Awards cash prizes. Art may be offered for sale; 10% commission. Artist must attend show; demonstrations OK. Sponsor pays insurance. Considers mobiles, paintings, pastels, prints and sculpture. Maximum height 5'. Publicity needs: pays $700 for advertising art.

MOORPARK COLLEGE FESTIVAL OF THE ARTS, 7075 Campus Rd., Moorpark CA 93021. (805)529-2321. Contact: Betty Sullivan. Sponsor: Community Services. Estab: 1972. Annual indoor show held the month of May (also sponsors a 1-day unjuried show at this time). Average attendance: 1,000, first day; 5,000 during the month. Entries accepted until show date. Entry fee: $4 per entry for those accepted 1 week prior to show; $3 for those accepted before

that time. "We are a small gallery and can only hold 20-30 works." Art may be offered for sale; no commission. Sponsor furnishes display equipment and insurance on exhibited work. Categories include painting, ceramics, sculpture, photography and graphics.
Awards: Presents $100 first prize and possibly cash awards for second and third places and $500 purchase prize. Judges are "outstanding southern California artists, applying current artistic standards of judgement."

NATIONAL WATERCOLOR SOCIETY EXHIBITION, 1530 Greenfield Ave., Los Angeles CA 90025. Contact: Juliet Lavee. Estab: 1920. Annual indoor show held in Northridge during November. Average attendance: 4,000. Closing date for entry: September. Entry fee: $10 per nonmember; $4 per painting. Maximum 3 entries per artist; 2 entries per member. Awards $2,000, cash prizes; $3,500, purchase awards; merchandise awards. Slides due for prejudging in September. Sponsor provides display equipment and insurance for exhibited work. Considers acrylics and watercolors.

PASADENA ARTIST ASSOCIATES AIR FAIR, Box 307-M, Pasadena CA 91102. Annual outdoor show. Entry fees: $5, members (plus membership fee); $15, nonmembers. Fees are subject to change without notice. Artists/craftsmen must attend show. Sponsor provides 4x8' display panels. Cash awards.

JAMES D. PHELAN AWARDS IN ART, The San Francisco Foundation Awards Office, 425 California St., Suite 1602, San Francisco CA 94104. Coordinator: Margaret Cummings. The Phelan Awards co-sponsors an annual, conducted by one of the museums in the San Francisco Bay Area, each year. Until plans are finalized in January of each year, it is not possible to say in which medium the $2,000 in Phelan Awards will be offered. In the past, they have been offered for paintings, prints, drawings, photography and sculpture. Only persons born in California, ages 20-40, are eligible for the award. Write for competition and application information.

REDLANDS ART ASSOCIATION, MANY MEDIA MINI SHOW, 12 E. Vine St., Redlands CA 92373. Annual show usually held in October. Entry fee: $3 per item. Maximum 3 entries per artist. Considers art in any media — sculpture, ceramics, paintings, mobiles, constructions, graphics, drawings. Maximum size: 15" square including base or frame. Open to artists residing in California and Arizona. Art may be offered for sale; 20% commission.
Awards: Presents $200 first, $100 second, $50 third; $50 honorable mention; $50 juror's special award. Purchase prizes to be announced.

RICHMOND ART CENTER RENTAL GALLERY COMPETITION, 25th and Barrett Ave., Richmond CA 94804. Rental Gallery Director: Patience Rogge. Annual competition. No entry fee; 25% commission. Maximum 3 works per artist. Media include paintings, prints and drawings. Artists compete for entrance in the Rental Gallery. Works are retained 1 year for rental and sale. Hand deliver art. Artist must be Richmond Art Center member. No dimension less than 18" or larger than 48".

RIVERSIDE COUNTY SUMMER OUTDOOR ART SHOW, Riverside County Art and Culture Center, Cherry Valley CA 92223. (714)845-2626. Annual outdoor show held in mid-June. Media include watercolors, oils, acrylics, ceramics, creative crafts, sculpture and graphics. California artists only. Entry fee: $5. Artist must attend show. No commission. Cash awards.

SACRAMENTO FESTIVAL OF THE ARTS, 515 L St., Sacramento CA 95814. Sponsor: Sacramento Regional Arts Council. Annual show held 2 days in September. Entry fee: $10 for-10x5' display area. No commission. Original art and crafts only.

SAN JOAQUIN COUNTY FAIR & LODI GRAPE FESTIVAL AND NATIONAL WINE SHOW, Box 848, Lodi CA 95240. (209)369-2771. Contact: Devon "Dan" Lee. Estab: 1936. Annual indoor show held 4 days in September. Closing date for entry: 3 weeks before show. No entry fee. Maximum 2 entries per artist. Awards $100, $40 and $20 cash prizes; and first, second, third and honorable mention ribbons. Prejudging. Art may be offered for sale; 10% office charge. Open to California artists. No mailed or shipped entries.
Acceptable Work: Considers oils, pastels and watercolors. Maximum size: 48" wide; 20 lbs. (including frame). Watercolors must have glass covering.

SAN MATEO COUNTY FAIR ARTS, Box 1027, San Mateo CA 94403. (415)345-3541. Contact: Lois Kelley. Sponsor: San Mateo County Fair Arts Committee, Inc. Annual indoor show held 13 days in July. Closing date fore entry: 2 weeks before show. Entry fee: $5 per entry. Prejudging; no entry fees refunded. Art may be offered for sale; no commission. Sponsor provides display panels and equipment.
Acceptable Work: Considers drawings, paintings, pastels and prints. Maximum size: 70x70". Also considers mobiles and sculpture. Maximum size: 12x3x3'. Artist must provide frames and/or pedestals. No erotica.
Awards: Presents $11,000 in cash, scholarships and merchandise services.

SANTA MONICA ART SHOW, 200 Santa Monica Blvd., Santa Monica CA 90401. (213)393-9825. Contact: Nell Tupper. Sponsor: Cultural Arts Committee of the Chamber of Commerce. Estab: 1967. Annual outdoor show held the third weekend in October. Closing date for entry: October 1. Entry fee: $35 per 8x16' minimum display area. Prejudging; $32 refunded for refused work. Art may be offered for sale; no commission. Artist must attend show; demonstrations OK. Registration limit: 284 artists/craftsmen. Considers all art. Exhibits must be dismantled each night.
Awards: Presents $100, best of show; $50 first, $30 second and $20 third place cash prizes; and 1 ribbon in each category.

SEASIDE ANNUAL ART COMPETITION, 1962 Mariposa St., Seaside CA 93955. Contact: C.Y. Lee. Sponsor: Seaside Art Commission. Annual show. Entry fee: $1 per painting. Maximum 2 entries. Cash awards. Maximum size: 3x5'. Artists must live in Seaside, Del Rey Oaks, Sand City, Ft. Ord or Marina, California. No shipping allowed, delivery and pickup from Seaside City Hall.

SIERRA MADRE ART FAIR, Box 334, Sierra Madre CA 91024. Sponsored by: The Friends of Sierra Madre Library. Contact: Patricia Hofer. Annual show held the third weekend of May. Closing date: April 30. Entry fee: $10 per 10x10' display area. Art may be offered for sale; 15% commission. Considers paintings, ceramics, drawings, prints, leather and fiber arts. Interested participants should submit 3-5 photos of their work. Registration limit: 180-200 artists/craftsmen. "Interested artists should apply for review before April, since popular categories fill rapidly."

SOUTHLAND ARTISTS SHOW, Box 115, 29 Palms CA 92277. (714)367-9633. Contact: Lee Pickering. Sponsor: 29 Palms Artists Guild. Estab: 1962. Annual indoor show held 3 weeks in November. Average attendance: 400. Closing date for entry: 1 week before show. Entry fee: $2 per entry. Maximum 3 entries per artist. Awards 20 first, 10 second and 5 third place cash prizes. Prejudging; no entry fees refunded for refused work. Art may be offered for sale; 25% commission. Demonstrations welcome. Prefers work delivered by hand.
Acceptable Work: Considers all art. Maximum size: 45". Paintings must be wired and framed.

SPRING FLING ART & CRAFT SHOW, 200 Santa Monica Blvd., Santa Monica CA 90401. (213)393-9825. Contact: Nell Tupper. Sponsor: Cultural Arts Committee of the Santa Monica Chamber of Commerce. Estab: 1967. Annual outdoor show held the third weekend in April. Closing date for entry: April 1. Entry fee: $35 per 8x16' minimum display area. Prejudging; $32 refunded for refused work. Art may be offered for sale; no commission. Artist must attend show; demonstrations OK. Registration limit: 284 artists/craftsmen. Considers all art. Exhibits must be dismantled each night.
Awards: Presents $100, best of show; $50 first, $30 second and $20 third place cash prizes; and 1 ribbon in each category.

THOUSAND OAKS ART ASSOCIATION JURIED ART EXHIBITION, 255 Green Meadow Dr., Thousand Oaks CA 91360. (805)498-8488. Contact: Association Exhibitions Director: Sponsor: Arts Council of Conejo Valley. Estab: 1969. Annual indoor show held 1 month in fall. Average attendance: 200-400. Closing date for entry: 1 week before show (if prejudging instituted this year, slides will be due sooner). Entry fee: $3 per association member; $4 per nonmember. Maximum 3 entries per artist. No entry fees refunded for refused work. Art may be offered for sale; 20% commission. Open to southern California residents. Registration limit: 75-80 artists/craftsmen. Write for prospectus.
Acceptable Work: Considers all art created within last 2 years. Maximum size: 2-dimensional, 76x76", 25 lbs.; 3-dimensional, 48"x48"x6', 150 lbs. Coordinated display stand or base recommended.

Awards: Presents $750, cash prizes; first, second and honorable mention ribbons. Judging panel consists of 1 association member and 2 nonmember artists, gallery owners, art historians or instructors.

Colorado

ARTISTS ALPINE HOLIDAY, Box 149, Ouray CO 81427. (303)325-4487 or 325-4766. Secretary: Ramona Radcliff. Sponsor: Ouray County Arts Association. Estab: 1960. Annual indoor show held 1 week in August. Average attendance: 2,000. Closing date for entry: 2 days before show. Entry fee: $4 per item. Maximum 3 entries per artist. Prejudging; no entry fees refunded for refused work. Art must be offered for sale; 15% commission. Demonstrations arranged. Sponsor provides display equipment and insurance for exhibited work. Considers all art. Maximum size: 36' square. Must be framed and wired for hanging.
Awards: Presents $100 best of show, $50 first, $35 second and $20 third cash prizes; $375 purchase awards; and ribbons.

DENVER ART MUSEUM, 100 W. 14th Avenue Pkwy., Denver CO 80204. (303)297-2793. Director of Public Relations: Patricia Stocker. Sponsors annual competition for Colorado artists. Write for more information.

ROCKY MOUNTAIN NATIONAL WATERMEDIA EXHIBITION, 809 15th St., Golden CO 80401. (303)279-3922. Director: Marian Metsopoulos. Sponsor: Foothills Art Center, Inc. Estab: 1973. Annual indoor show held from mid-August to late September. Average attendance: 7,000. Closing date for entry: 2 months before show. Entry fee: $7.50 per slide. Maximum 2 entries per artist. Awards $9,000 in cash prizes. Prejudging by slides; no entry fees refunded for refused work. Art may be offered for sale; 25% commission. Registration limit: 130 paintings. Sponsor pays insurance ($50 deductible) for exhibited work. Considers acrylics, pastels and watercolors on paper. Work must be framed and wired.

Connecticut

CRAFT & ART SHOW, American Crafts Expositions, Box 274 Farmington CT 06032. Contact: Rudy Kowalczyk. Biennial indoor/outdoor competition. Entry fee: $60, inside space; $50, outside space. Prejudging by slides or photos of work. Artwork exhibited in tents limited to 8x10'; outside art may be 12x12'. Cash awards.

DANBURY AMATEUR ART SHOW, Greater Danbury Chamber of Commerce, 20 West St., Danbury CT 06810. (203)743-5565. Executive Assistant: William McGee. Annual indoor show held 4 days in October-November. Entry fee: $2 per entry. Maximum 3 entries per artist. Awards best of show, first and second place ribbons in each medium. Art must be offered for sale; 20% commission goes toward art scholarship for 1 high school senior.
Acceptable Work: Considers drawings, paintings and sculpture. Maximum size: 2-dimensional, 36x36"; sculpture, 18x25x60". All paintings and drawings must be framed or mounted.

EXHIBITION OF WORK BY CONNECTICUT ARTISTS, Slater Memorial Museum, Norwich Free Academy, 108 Crescent St., Norwich CT 06360. (203)887-2506. Director: Joseph Gualtieri. Estab: 1943. Annual indoor show held in April. Average attendance: 5,500. Closing date for entry: 1 week before show. Entry fee: $4 per entry. Maximum 2 entries per artist. Awards $250 first, $100 second, $75 third and $50 fourth prizes. Prejudging; no entry fees refunded for refused work. Art may be offered for sale; 20% commission. Open to Connecticut residents. Sponsor provides display equipment. Hand-deliver work.
Acceptable Work: Considers calligraphy, drawings, paintings, pastels, prints and sculpture. Maximum size: 200 lbs. Work must be framed or matted.

THE GREAT DANBURY STATE ARTS & CRAFTS FAIR, 130 White St., Danbury CT 06810. (203)748-3535. Contact: Jack Stetson. Sponsor: Danbury Fair, Inc. Estab: 1975. Annual indoor/outdoor show held 3 days in July. Average attendance: 30,000. Closing date for entry: 4 weeks before show. Entry fee: $20 per indoor/$15 per outdoor display area. Awards $1,000 in prizes and ribbons. Prejudging; entry fee refunded for refused work. Art may be offered for sale; no commission. Artist must attend show; demonstrations OK. Registration limit: 100 artists. Sponsor furnishes some hanging fences. Considers all art. Entrants with large items should arrive early to facilitate unloading and set-up.

GREATER HARTFORD CIVIC & ARTS FESTIVAL, 15 Lewis St., Hartford CT 06103. Contact: Sandra K. Hamer. Annual festival held first week in June is a free, outdoor exposition of visual and performing arts. Average attendance: 150,000. More than 2,000 works on display including paintings, sculptures, photos, graphics and crafts. Prizes total $6,000.

GREENWICH ART SOCIETY ANNUAL SIDEWALK SHOW, Western Greenwich Civic Center, 449 Pemberwick Ave., Greenwich CT 06830. (203)531-4010. Director: Elaine Huyer. Estab: 1954. Annual outdoor show held the first weekend in June. Average attendance: 2,000. Closing date for entry: 1 week before show. No entry fee for Society members; $5 per non-member. Maximum 3 entries per artist. Prejudging. Art must be offered for sale; 25% commission. Registration limit: 250 artists/craftsmen. Sponsor provides display equipment. Hand-deliver art.
Acceptable Work: Considers drawings, paintings, pastels, prints and sculpture. Art must be framed and ready for hanging or securely attached to pedestal.
Awards: Presents $600 in cash prizes. Judge is usually a museum director, art historian or nationally-known artist.

MUM FESTIVAL ART SHOW, Bristol Art League, 316 King St., Bristol CT 06010. Co-chairman: Ann Cornell. Annual show held the first week in October. Entry fee: $2 per item or $5 for 2 items. Considers oils, watercolors, polymer, mixed media, graphics, drawings and sculpture with pedestal. Closing date for entries: 1 month before show date. Art may be offered for sale; 15% commission. Open to anyone over 18. Work must be original, completed within the past 2 years, and not previously shown in the Mum Show. Committee reserves the right to reject work it deems objectionable. There will be no crating or uncrating.
Awards. Presents 1st, 2nd and 3rd prizes of $100, $75 and $25; 6, $25 category awards; $15 mixed media and $10 viewer award.

MYSTIC OUTDOOR ART FESTIVAL, Box 300, Mystic CT 06355. (203)536-8559. Director: John Lazarek. Sponsor: Chamber of Commerce. Estab: 1958. Annual show held 2 days in August. Average attendance: 75,000. Application requests due May 1; applications due May 21. Entry fee: $20 per entry. Prejudging; entry fee refunded for refused work. Art may be offered for sale; no commission. Artist must attend show; pastel and charcoal artists may demonstrate. Registration limit: 430 artists. Considers drawings, paintings, pastels, graphics and sculpture. Artist supplies display equipment.
Awards: Presents $500, best in show; $50 first prizes in various categories; and medals.

NCAA JURIED SHOW, (formerly Northwestern Connecticut Art Association Juried Show), c/o NCCC, Park Place, Winsted CT 06098. (203)379-8543. Contact: Elaine Reeve. Sponsor: Northwestern Connecticut Art Association. Estab: 1971. Annual indoor show held 2 weeks in June-July. Average attendance: 500+. Closing date for entry: 1 week before show. Entry fee: $6-7 per entry. Maximum 2 entries per artist. Awards $700, cash prizes; $500, purchase awards. Prejudging; no entry fees refunded for refused work. Art may be offered for sale; no commission. Open to artists living in the New York City area or New England. Registration limit: approximately 125 works.
Acceptable Work: Considers all art. Maximum size: 48" long; 200 lbs. Work must be framed and wired.

NEW ENGLAND EXHIBITION OF PAINTING & SCULPTURE, 1037 Silvermine Rd., New Canaan CT 06840. (203)966-5617. Gallery Director: Dee Robinson. Sponsor: Silvermine Guild of Artists. Estab: 1949. Annual indoor/outdoor show held 4 weeks during June-July. Average attendance: 5,000. Closing date for entry: May 14-15. Entry fee: $10 per entry. Awards $6,000-7,000 in cash prizes. Prejudging; no entry fees refunded for refused work. Art may be offered for sale; 33-1/3% commission. Open to New England, New York, New Jersey and Pennsylvania residents. Registration limit: 200 works.
Acceptable Work: Considers acrylics, airbrush, oils, pastels, watercolors and sculpture. Maximum size: paintings, 50x72"; sculpture, 16' square, 100 lbs. No wires or screws.

NIANTIC ART SHOW, 14 Parker Dr., East Lyme CT 06333. (203)739-0662. Chairman: Margaret Dexter. Sponsor: East Lyme Arts Council. Estab: 1962. Annual outdoor show held 2 days in early July. Average attendance: 2,500. Entries accepted until show date. Entry fee: $15 per 10' display area. Awards $50, $25 and $15 cash prizes; ribbons. Art may be offered for sale; no commission. Artist must attend show; demonstrations OK. Registration limit: 250 artists.

Sponsor provides fencing on request. No shipped art. Considers oils, watercolors, graphics and sculpture.

NORWICH ROSE ARTS FESTIVAL AND ARTS AND CRAFTS TENT SHOW, 407 Washington St., Norwich CT 06360. Sponsor: The Friends of the Slater Memorial Museum. Contact: J. Richard Salzer. Annual outdoor show held in June or July. Entry fee: $10 for 15 linear ft. Presents cash awards, purchase awards, ribbons and 2 one-man show awards. No commission. Artist's attendance desired. Open to all media except crafts and fine art.

OAK ROOM EXHIBITION, Fairfield Chamber of Commerce, 1597 Post Rd., Fairfield CT 06430. (203)255-1011. Estab: 1963. Executive Director: Harold B. Harris. Annual indoor show held 3 days in June. Average attendance: 400. Closing date for entry: 1 week before show. Entry fee: $7.50 per entry. Prejudging; entry fee refunded for refused art. Artist may offer work for sale; 25% commission. Registration limit: 200 artists/craftsmen.
Acceptable Work: Considers acrylics, airbrush, calligraphy, drawings, oils, pastels, prints, watercolors and sculpture. Maximum size: 50x50" or 75 lbs. Paintings should be framed and suitable for hanging.
Awards: Presents over $3,000 in cash (including purchase awards). Also gives medallions to first prize winners.

OLD SAYBROOK CHAMBER OF COMMERCE ART SHOW, Box 625, Old Saybrook CT 06475. (203)388-3266. Executive Director: A.G. McCausand. Estab: 1964. Annual outdoor show held the last weekend in July. Closing date for entry: 2 weeks before show. Entry fee: $15 per artist. Awards cash prizes; and first, second and third ribbons in each category. Art may be offered for sale; no commission. Artist must attend show; demonstrations OK. Registration limit: 175 artists. Sponsor provides display equipment. Considers all art.

"ON THE GREEN" FALL ART SHOW AND SALE, Box 304, Glastonbury CT 06033. (203)643-4034. Contact: Harriet Pfeifer. Sponsor: Glastonbury Art Guild. Estab: 1962. Annual outdoor show held 2 days in September. Average attendance: 15,000. Closing date for entry: mid-August. Entry fee: $20, Guild member; $25, nonmember. Awards $190 in cash prizes. Art may be offered for sale; 15% commission on non-judged work. Artist or representative must attend show; demonstrations encouraged. Registration limit: 250 artists/craftsmen. Sponsor furnishes snow fence. Considers all art. No painted rocks.

OUTDOOR ARTS AND CRAFTS FAIR, Temple Beth El, Roxbury Rd., Stamford CT 06903. Sponsored by Temple Beth El Sisterhood. Contact: Alex J. Goldman. Entry fee: $20 per 8' space. Ribbons and awards given. Considers all media.

PUTNAM AREA CHAMBER OF COMMERCE ART EXHIBIT, Box 489, Putnam CT 06260. (203)928-3407. Contact: Gregory King. Estab: 1964. Annual outdoor show held 1 day in May. Average attendance: 2,000-5,000. Closing date for entries: 2 weeks before show. Entry fee: $12 adults; $1 students under 16 years. Art may be offered for sale; no commission. Artist must attend show; demonstrations encouraged; advance notice requested. Considers all art.
Awards: Grants $50, first prize; $25, second; $10, third; and ribbons to all cash winners.

SLATER MEMORIAL MUSEUM, 108 Crescent St., Norwich CT 06360. (203)887-2505, ext. 218. Museum Director: Joseph P. Gualtieri. Annual show held in April. Entry fee: $4 per item. Friends of the museum may submit 1 piece free. Maximum 2 entries per artist. Open to residents of Connecticut. Cash awards: $250, $100, $75 and $50. Sales commission: 20%. Sculpture not to exceed 200 lbs. Entries must be hand delivered. Considers paintings, sculpture, drawings and prints.

YAAF EXHIBITION OF FINE ART, 18 Reef Rd., Fairfield CT 06430. Contact: Jack Farkas or Paul Strauss. Sponsor: Young Artist Association of Fairfield. Annual show. Entry fee: $7.50. Awards cash and purchase awards. Work may be offered for sale; 25% sales commission. Sponsor provides display equipment, but sculptures must be equipped with stands, paintings must be framed and wired for hanging. Considers all fine art. Maximum size: 36x36" on 2-dimensional pieces.

Florida

ART HARVEST, Box 593, Dunedin FL 33528. (813)733-0004 or 447-6256. Contact: Peggy

Mateer or Beverly Skinner. Sponsor: Dunedin Junior Service League. Estab: 1964. Annual outdoor show held 1 day in November. Average attendance: 30,000+. Closing date for entry: 2 weeks before show. Entry fee: $15 per entry. Awards $3,275 in prizes. Art may be offered for sale; no commission. Artist must attend show; some demonstrations OK. Registration limit: 225 artists/craftsmen. Artist provides 12x12" white card with name, space, number and category. Sponsor provides 10x12' display area. Considers all art except velvet paintings.

ART IN THE SUN, (formerly Pompano Beach Annual Arts & Crafts Festival), 2200 E. Atlantic Blvd., Pompano Beach FL 33062. (305)941-2940. Contact: Carole Simpson. Sponsor: Greater Pompano Beach Chamber of Commerce. Estab: 1974. Annual outdoor show held 2 days during the end of February or beginning of March. Average attendance: 10,000. Closing date for entry: 3 weeks before show. Entry fee: $25 per entry. Prejudging; entry fee refunded for refused work. Art may be offered for sale; no commission. Registration limit: 250-350 artists/craftsmen. Sponsor pays insurance on exhibited work. Considers all art.
Awards: Presents $800 in cash prizes, purchase awards and 24 ribbons. Judging by a panel of 6-9 individuals with experience in each area.

BACK TO YBOR CITY SHOW, (formerly Tampa Fine Arts Competition) 1509 8th Ave., Tampa FL 33605. (813)248-3712. Contact: Oscar Aguaye. Estab: 1972. Annual outdoor show held in October. Average attendance: 15,000. Entries accepted until show date. Art may be offered for sale; no commission. Artist must attend show. Considers all art.

BOYNTON BEACH ANNUAL FESTIVAL OF THE ARTS, Boynton Beach Recreation Dept., 128 E. Ocean Ave., Boynton Beach FL 33435. (305)732-2636. Recreation Supervisor: Patricia A. Shelley. Estab: 1975. Annual outdoor show held 2 days in March/April. Average attendance: 10,000-15,000. Closing date for entry: 2 weeks before show. Entry fee: $12 plus judging fee for Professional Division (subject to change). Maximum 3 entries for judging in Professional Division, 1 per category for judging in Amateur Division and no limit on general displaying. Awards $75 in cash prizes for paintings, graphics, sculpture and watercolors in Professional division; and $300 best of show. Also awards first and second place winners in Professional and Amateur divisions. Prejudging by 3 slides; entry fee refunded to those refused. Art may be offered for sale; no commission. Artist must attend show; demonstrations OK. Registration limit: 200 artists/craftsmen. Artist supplies display equipment.
Acceptable Work: Considers watercolors, acrylics, airbrush, calligraphy, drawings, oils, pastels and prints. Artists must provide easels for paintings. Paintings must be framed and drawings must be matted.

CAPE CORAL ANNUAL ART EXHIBITION, 5321 Bayshore Ave., Cape Coral FL 33904. Contact: Mary Chase. Sponsor: Edison Community College. Held in January. Entries accepted through October. Entry fee: $10 per 3 entries. Awards $1,000 in prizes. Prejudging. Considers paintings, prints, drawings, collage and sculpture. Write for prospectus.

CAROL CITY CENTER MERCHANTS ASSOCIATION, ANNUAL ART AND CRAFT SHOW, Office 207, 2734 NW 183rd St., Miami FL 33054. Contact: Evelyne Durgerian. Sponsor: Merchants Association. Annual show held along a covered sidewalk of the shopping center. Entry fee: $5 for 12 feet of space. Maximum 2 entries per artist, but number is unlimited for display in exhibit space. In addition to ribbons, prizes of $50, $25 and $15 will be awarded first, second and third place winners in both the arts and crafts competition. Also, 3 honorable mention awards of $5 will be made in each category. All artists have a chance to win in a drawing, held after the official judging, but which has nothing to do with the judging. Artists must attend show.

COCOA VILLAGE AUTUMN ART FESTIVAL, Box 1967, Cocoa FL 32922. (305)636-5946. Contact: Bette Marshall. Annual show held in the fall. Average attendance: 30,000-40,000. Entry fee; $25. For all media; all categories. No commission. Presents $5,000 in prizes; $4,000 in purchase awards.

COLLEGE PARK SIDEWALK ART FESTIVAL, Box 7744, Orlando FL 32804. Coordinator: Rita Diamond. Sponsor: College Park Merchants & Professional Association. Estab: 1968. Annual outdoor show held 2 days in the spring. Average attendance: 75,000-100,000. Closing date for entry: 1 week before show. Entry fee: $25 per 10x12' display area. Awards $1,500, cash prizes; ribbons. Art may be offered for sale; no commission. Artist must attend show; demonstrations OK. Registration limit: 250 artists/craftsmen. Considers all art.

CRYSTAL RIVER LIONS ART SHOW, Box 1706, Crystal River FL 32629. Contact: Colonel Thomas J. Street (Retired). Annual competition. Closing date for entries: October. Entry fee: $10 for preregistration, $12 for late registration. Maximum 5 entries per artists for competition; unlimited number for exhibition. Must be recent original work. Awards include cash in excess of $1,300 and ribbons. Considers all art and crafts.

DELAND OUTDOOR ART FESTIVAL, Rte. 2, Box 674F, Deland FL 32720. Contact: Joyce N. Campbell. Annual competition. Sponsor: West Volusia Artist, Inc. and Deland Chamber of Commerce. Entry fee: $10 per display area. Only 1 artist per space. Awards include approximately $1,245 in cash prizes. Art may be offered for sale; no commission. Considers drawings, woodcuts and lithographs. Categories are oils; acrylics and mixed media; watercolors; sculpture; graphics and photography; and creative crafts.

EXHIBITION OF CONTEMPORARY AMERICAN PAINTINGS, Society of the Four Arts, Four Arts Plaza, Palm Beach FL 33480. (305)655-7226. Estab: 1939. Annual indoor show held in December. Average attendance: 7,000. Entry forms due 7 weeks before show. Closing date for entry: 5 weeks before show. Entry fee: $3 per 1-2 entries. Maximum 2 entries per artist. Prejudging; entry fee refunded for accepted work only. Art may be offered for sale; 10% commission. Registration limit: 80-90 works. Sponsor pays return shipping for accepted work.
Acceptable Work: Considers acrylics, drawings, oils, pastels and watercolors. No graphics. Maximum size: 72x72". Drawings and watercolors must be matted and/or framed (ship without glass). No screw-eyes and wires.
Awards: Presents one $2,000 and two $1,500 cash prizes. Juror is from nationally-known museum: Art Institute of Chicago, Whitney and Guggenheim in the past.

FIESTA DAY ARTS AND CRAFTS SHOW, (formerly Tampa Fine Arts Competition), 1509 8th Ave., Tampa FL 33605. (813)248-3712. Contact: Oscar Aguaye. Sponsor: Ybor City Chamber of Commerce. Estab: 1970. Annual outdoor show held 1-2 days in mid-February. Entries accepted until show date. Entry fee: $7.50 minimum. Awards $600. Art may be offered for sale; no commission. Artist must attend show; demonstrations OK. Considers all art.

GASPARILLA SIDEWALK ART FESTIVAL, Box 10591, Tampa FL 33679. Contact: Chairman GSAF Committee. Annual outdoor show. Entry fee: $30 per 8x12' booth. No sales commission. Prejudging by 3 slides or photos. Cash awards total $8,200.

GREAT GULFCOAST FESTIVAL, Box 12710, Pensacola FL 32574. Chairman: Connie Thomas. Sponsors: Pensacola Arts Council and *Pensacola News-Journal.* Estab: 1973. Annual outdoor show held 2 days in November. Average attendance: 60,000. Closing date for entry: 6 weeks before show. Entry fee: $25 per entry. Awards $1,000 in cash prizes. Prejudging by slides; $20 refunded for refused work. Art may be offered for sale; no commission. Artist must attend show; demonstrations OK. Registration limit: 17 entries each per 10 categories. Considers all art. Work should be framed.

GREATER DADE CITY ARTS & CRAFTS FESTIVAL, Meridian at 7th St., Dade City FL 33025. (904)567-3769. Director: Patricia Burdick. Sponsor: Greater Dade City Chamber of Commerce. Estab: 1975. Annual outdoor show held 2 days in spring. Average attendance: 20,000. Closing date for entry: 2 weeks before show. Entry fee: $15 per 10x10' display area. Prejudging; no entry fees refunded. Art may be offered for sale; no commission. Artist must attend show; demonstrations OK. Registration limit: 200. Sponsor pays insurance on exhibited work. Considers all art.
Awards: Grants $1,750, cash prizes; and first, second place and honorable mention ribbons in 5 categories.

HALIFAX ART FESTIVAL, Box 504, Ormond Beach FL 32014. (904)255-0285. Contact: Director. Sponsor: Guild of the Museum of Arts and Sciences. Estab: 1963. Annual outdoor show (under porch) held the first weekend in November. Average attendance: 50,000. Closing date for entry: mid-August. Entry fee: $25 per entry. Prejudging by slides; $20 refunded for refused work. Art may be offered for sale; no commission. Artist must attend show; demonstrations OK. Registration limit: 200 artists/craftsmen. Sponsor pays insurance for exhibited work.
Acceptable Work: Considers calligraphy, drawings, paintings, pastels, prints, mobiles and sculpture. Paintings must be framed.
Awards: Presents $500 best of show purchase prize; seven $250 prizes; three $50 merit awards.

Cash prizes and ribbons are awarded to winners in three categories at the Marion Military Institute Art Show. The competition is open to fine artists, with the gallery reserving the right to prescreen entries. This piece by John Henry Heard, Jr. won first place in the 1977 show's "Three Dimensional Works" category.

HALLANDALE FALL ART FESTIVAL, c/o Chamber of Commerce, Box 249, Hallandale FL 33009. Chairman: Joseph H. Hanff, Jr. Annual outdoor show held Thanksgiving weekend at Gulfstream Race Track, U.S. #1, in Hallandale. Entry fee: $25. Artists provide own means of display, sturdy enough to withstand weather and crowds. No sales commission. Cash awards and ribbons awarded.

HOLLYWOOD FASHION CENTER ANNUAL ART SHOW, Hollywood Fashion Center, Joy Rubin's Art Emporium, Hollywood FL 33023. Contact: Ivan Rubin. Annual, juried show for professional artists held in March. Sponsor: Hollywood Fashion Center Merchants Association. Closing date: 7 weeks before show. Entry fee: $45 for 8x10' space. Pegboard walls, tables and electricity extra. Exhibitor may rent any number of spaces. No sales commission. Artist must be present.

IMAGES — A FESTIVAL OF THE ARTS, Box 2051, New Smyrna Beach FL 32069. (904)428-2239 or 427-5450. Chairman: Holly Bivins. Sponsor: New Smyrna Beach Recreation Dept. Estab: 1977. Annual outdoor show held the last weekend in February. Average attendance: 60,000-70,000. Closing date for entry: December 1. Entry fee: $5 non-refundable screening fee; $20 per 12x12' display area. Prejudging of three 35mm slides per category; $20 refunded for refused work. Art may be offered for sale; no commission. Artist must attend show; demonstrations OK. Registration limit: 210 artists/craftsmen. Sponsor furnishes electric outlets.
Acceptable Work: Considers drawings, mobiles, paintings, pastels, prints and sculpture. Paintings and graphics must be framed or matted. All work for sale must be priced.
Awards: Grants $6,000+, cash prizes; $1,000, purchase awards; 32 ribbons. Screening panel consists of a well-known painter, sculptor, photographer and craftsman. The 2 judges are nationally known.

KEY BISCAYNE ART FESTIVAL, 150 W. McIntire St., Key Biscayne FL 33149. Contact: Tim Hammonds. Annual show. Sponsor: Key Biscayne Community School. All media eligible. Entry fee: $40 for 10x10' display area. No sales commission. Awards cash prizes and ribbons.

LAKE WALES SIDEWALK ART SHOW, 1117 Yarnell Ave., Lake Wales FL 33853. Registrar: Gwen Burr. Sponsor: AAUW Arts Council. Estab: 1971. Annual outdoor show held 1 day in spring. Average attendance: 1,000. Entry fee: $10 per 12x12' display area. Art may be offered for sale; no commission. Artist must attend show. Considers drawings, mobiles, paintings, pastels, prints and sculpture.
Awards: Grants $100 first prizes in 6 categories; seven $50 prizes; $400 in purchase awards; $150, best of show; $100, judge's award; 10 ribbons.

LAS OLAS ART FESTIVAL, Box 2211, Fort Lauderdale FL 33303. Contact: Las Olas Art Festival Committee. Sponsor: Fort Lauderdale Museum of the Arts. Estab: 1969. Annual outdoor show held the fourth weekend in March. Closing date for entry: mid-November. Entry fee: $5 per item; $50 per 10x10' display area. Prejudging of 5 slides maximum; display fee refunded for refused work. Art may be offered for sale; no commission. Artist must attend show; demonstrations OK. Registration limit: 239 artists/craftsmen.
Acceptable Work: Considers calligraphy, drawings, mobiles, paintings and sculpture. "All hanging work must be framed; all work must be marked with price or NFS; portfolios permitted." No painting on rocks or velvet.
Awards: Presents $3,300, cash prizes; purchase awards; and 21 + ribbons. These include 6 best of shows and 15 awards of merit. Judges are usually 2 teaching artists from Florida colleges.

MIAMI BEACH FESTIVAL OF THE ARTS, Bin 39000, Miami Beach FL 33139. Contact: Pearl Kipnis. Annual outdoor show held in February at Miami Beach Convention Center. Sponsor: Fine Arts Board of the City of Miami Beach. Entry fee: $5 application fee, $15 per category entered. Cash awards over $4,000. Art may be offered for sale; no commission. Categories include painting, graphics, drawings, sculpture and crafts.

NEW SMYRNA SIDEWALK ART FIESTA, Box 2438, New Smyrna Beach FL 32069. (305)428-9530. Chairman: Arthur Vos. Sponsor: City of New Smyrna Beach. Estab: 1962. Annual outdoor show held 2 days in February or March. Closing date for entry: 2 weeks before show. Entry fee: $10 per entry. Art may be offered for sale; no commission. Artist must attend show; demonstrations OK. Registration limit: 200 artists/craftsmen. Considers drawings, paintings, pastels, prints and sculpture.
Awards: Presents $150, best of show; $100 first, $75 second, $35 third and two $10 honorable mention prizes in 2-dimensional categories; $75 first, $50 second and $25 third prizes for sculpture.

OLD ISLAND DAYS SIDEWALK ART FESTIVAL, Key West Art Center, 301 Front St., Key West FL 33040. (305)294-1241. Director: Florence Recher. Estab: 1964. Annual outdoor show held 3 days in February. Average attendance: 2,000-3,000. Closing date for entry: 5 days before show. Entry fee: $15 per art center member; $20 per nonmember. Art may be offered for sale; no commission. Artist must attend show; demonstrations OK. Considers paintings, pastels, prints and sculpture.
Awards: Presents $150, cash prizes in each category; $1,500-2,000, purchase awards; ribbons. Judges are gallery or museum directors and college art instructors.

"ON THE GREEN" ANNUAL ART FESTIVAL, Helen Hodges, Box 1562, Fort Pierce FL 33450. Annual exhibition sponsored by the Fort Pierce Art Club. Entry fee: $15 per 15' space. Maximum 2 spaces per artist. Artist must attend show. Considers oils, acrylics, mixed media, watercolors, graphics, drawings, pastels, sculpture and creative crafts. Work must be framed or matted.
Awards: Presents $100 best of show; first, second and third prizes ranging from $15-200 in each category.

PURPLE ISLES ANNUAL ARTS & CRAFTS SHOW, c/o John Stormont, 163 Coconut Row, Tavernier FL 33070. Annual show held in late February or early March. Entry fee: $5. Awards ribbons. Maximum 3 works per artist. Prejudging. Art may be offered for sale; 10% commission. Size range: 12-40".

RED AND SUNSET SHOW, Box 430585, South Miami FL 33143. (305)661-1621. Contact: Rhoda Protko. Sponsor: Chamber of Commerce. Estab: 1972. Annual outdoor show held 2 days in the fall. Closing date for entry: 2 weeks before show. Entry fee: $50 per artist. Maximum 2 entries per artist. Prejudging; entry fee refunded for refused work. Artist must attend show. Registration limit: 200 artists/craftsmen. Considers all 2-dimensional art. Grants $3,500 in cash prizes and ribbons.

RINGLING MUSEUMS MEMBERS COUNCIL CRAFTS FESTIVAL, Box 1838, Sarasota FL 33578. (813)355-5101. Chairman: Mrs. J. Kent Bartruff. Estab: 1972. Annual outdoor show held 3 days in mid-November. Average attendance: 5,000. Closing date for entry: 2 months before show. Entry fee: $5 jury fee; $25 per artist. Prejudging by slides; no entry fees refunded for refused work. Art may be offered for sale; no commission. Open to Florida residents. Demonstrations encouraged. Considers mobiles and sculpture.
Awards: Presents $500, best in show; 4, $200 merit awards; 2, $100 honorable mentions; $50, best presentation.

SARASOTA AND BRADENTON ARTS AND CRAFTS SHOWS, 1435 Burning Tree St., Sarasota FL 33580. Contact: "Uncle Milt" Kelly. "These are comparatively small shows that appeal to tourists and vacationers traveling US-41 along Florida's west coast. Long-distance travelers may find these shows suitable as 'fill-ins' between larger shows." Only quality, finished work is acceptable. No new applications from jewelry craftsmen accepted. All shows are sponsored by merchant associations. Awards are minimal. Registration fees vary from $8-15 a single space, $12-30 double. No sales commission. Query with SASE for more information.

SEAS NATIONAL, (formerly Southeastern Art Exhibit), Municipal Auditorium, Panama City FL 32401. (904)763-4696. Auditorium Manager: Cecil Koon. Annual indoor show held 1 month in the spring. Estab: 1964. Closing date for entry: 2 weeks before show. Entry fee: $8 per item. Maximum number of entries: 6. Art may be offered for sale; 20% commission. No demonstrations. Entry fee covers shipping. "Seas is not responsible for works of exhibitors at any time."
2-Dimensional Work: Considers oils, acrylics, calligraphy, drawings, pastels and watercolors. Watercolors, pastels and oils should be properly framed. Maximum size: 55" square. No controversial works.
3-Dimensional Work: Considers mobiles and sculpture. Artist must provide stands for sculpture and hanging equipment for mobiles. "We want original works of art (no copies of the masters' work)." Maximum size: 4' square.
Awards: Presents bonds, purchase prizes, ribbons, art boxes with brass plates, trophies and plaques.

7 LIVELY ARTS FESTIVAL, Hollywood Fashion Center, Joy Rubin's Art Emporium, Hollywood FL 33023. Contact: Ivan Rubin. Annual show held in November for professional artists and craftsmen. Closing date for entry: 6 weeks before show. Entry fee: $45 per 6x15' space. Awards $2,500 in prizes. Artist must attend show.

SHRIMPBOAT FESTIVAL SIDEWALK ART SHOW, c/o Amelia Island Arts & Crafts Association, Box 1251, Fernandina Beach FL 32034. Annual show held in May. Entry fee: $20 per 10x10' space, maximum 2 spaces. Prejudging by 3 slides. Awards cash and purchase prizes over $6,000. No sales commission.

SOCIETY OF THE ARTS AND THE CITY OF NORTH MIAMI, 1365 NE 139th St., North Miami FL 33161. Contact: Patricia Baurquin. Annual outdoor show. Considers all media and limited crafts. Entry fee: $15 for 12x6' space. Maximum 8 entries per classification. Prejudging. Presents cash awards to $2,500. No sales commission.

SOUTH MIAMI ART AND CRAFT FESTIVAL, Box 430585, South Miami FL 33143. (305)661-1621. Contact: Rhoda Protko. Sponsor: Chamber of Commerce. Estab: 1972. Annual outdoor show held 2 days in the spring. Average attendance: 2,000. Closing date for entry: 2 weeks before show. Entry fee: $50 per artist. Prejudging; entry fee refunded for refused work. Art may be offered for sale; no commission. Artist must attend show. Registration limit: 200 artists/craftsmen. Considers all 2-dimensional art. Awards $3,500 in cash prizes and ribbons.

SPRING ARTS FESTIVAL, Drawer 1187, Gainesville FL 32602. (904)372-1976. Director:

Karen Beach. Sponsors: Santa Fe Community College, Chamber of Commerce and City of Gainesville. Estab: 1970. Annual outdoor show held 2 days in April. Average attendance: 60,000. Closing date for entry: 6 weeks before show. Entry fee: $5 application fee; $15 per 10x12' display area. Minimum 4 entries per artist per category. Prejudging; no application fees refunded. Art may be offered for sale; no commission. Artist must attend show; demonstrations OK. Registration limit: 250 artists/craftsmen.
Acceptable Work: Considers drawings, graphics, mobiles, paintings, prints and sculpture. "Anything unframed must be in portfolio."
Awards: Presents $3,750, cash prizes; $3,000, purchase awards. Must be 10 artists minimum per category for awarding. Jurying by a panel of community experts in each category.

SPRING FESTIVAL ARTS AND CRAFTS SIDEWALK ART SHOW, (formerly Tampa Fine Arts Competition), 1509 8th Ave., Tampa FL 33605. (813)248-3712. Executive Director: Oscar Aguaye. Sponsor: Ybor City Chamber of Commerce. Estab: 1977. Annual outdoor show held 2 days in May. Average attendance: 40,000. Entry fee: $12 per artist. Awards $800 including $300 best of show. Art may be offered for sale; no commission. Artist must attend show. Registration limit: 200 artists/craftsmen. Considers all art.

SUNSHINE ART FESTIVAL, Box 831, Winter Haven FL 33880. Contact: E.C. Hill. Sponsor: Cypress Gardens Sertoma Club. Annual show held in March or April. Open to all media, fine arts and limited crafts. Entry fee: $20 per 10x10' area. Prejudging by slides or photos. Presents cash awards totaling $2,000 and ribbons. No sales commission.

TITUSVILLE ART LEAGUE ANNUAL SHOW, Box 6133, Titusville FL 32780. Contact: Chairman. Estab: 1964. Annual indoor show held 1 week in spring. Entries accepted until show date. Entry fee: $3 per item. Maximum 5 entries per artist. Prejudging; no entry fees refunded. Art may be offered for sale; no commission. Demonstrations on Art League's approval. Sponsor furnishes display panels and 4x6' display area. Unusual display needs are artist's responsibility. Considers calligraphy, drawings, pastels, paintings, prints and sculpture.
Awards: Presents $1,200+ in assorted cash prizes and 38 ribbons.

WINTER PARK MALL MERCHANTS ASSOCIATION ART FESTIVAL, 560 N. Orlando Ave., Winter Park FL 32789. Promotion Director: Sonja Unger. Annual show. Entry fee: $15. Cash awards total $1,200.

WINTER PARK SIDEWALK ART FESTIVAL, Box 597, Winter Park FL 32790. Annual outdoor show held in March. Entry fee: $30. Prejudging by slides. Registration limit: 300 artists/craftsmen. Presents 40 awards totaling more than $8,000. Considers all media. Write for application.

Georgia

ALBANY ARTS FESTIVAL, Box 571, Albany GA 31702. Contact: Mrs. Parks Jones. Sponsor: Southwest Georgia Art Association. Estab: 10 years. Annual indoor/outdoor show held 2 days in April. Closing date for entry: 6 weeks before show. Entry fee: $25 per artist. Minimum 4 entries per artist. Prejudging; entry fee refunded for refused work. Art may be offered for sale; no commission. Artist must attend show; demonstrations encouraged. Sponsor provides display panels and equipment; tables/chairs at cost; "S" hooks for sale.
Acceptable Work: Considers all art. All work shown must be original and completed no earlier than 1973. All paintings/drawings must be suitably mounted, framed or matted.
Awards: Presents $1,000, cash prizes; $1,000 purchase awards; 9 $100 merit awards.

GEORGIA JUBILEE, A FESTIVAL OF THE ARTS, 195 Holt Ave., Macon GA 31201. Contact: Gail Gunn. Artists may enter show in juried or non-juried division. Entry fee: $30, juried show; $20 nonjuried show. Purchase awards total $5,500. Prejudging by three 2x2 slides. Work must have been completed in the last 3 years and not previously shown in the Festival. All media accepted.

GOLDEN ISLES ARTS CRAFTS FESTIVAL, c/o Glynn Art Association, Box 673, St. Simons Island GA 31522. (912)638-8770. Contact: Mrs. William Hendrix. Estab: 1969. Annual outdoor show held 2 days in October. Average attendance: 15,000-20,000. Closing date for entry: 4 weeks before show. Entry fee: $40 per display area. Awards approximately $1,500, cash prizes; $500, purchase awards; ribbons. Prejudging by slides; entry fee refunded for refused work. Art may be offered for sale; no commission. Artist or representative must attend show; demonstrations encouraged. Registration limit: 160 artists/craftsmen. Considers all art. Two-dimensional art must be ready for hanging.

SAVANNAH ARTS FESTIVAL, c/o Savannah Art Association, 119 Jefferson St., Savannah GA 31401. Annual show held outdoors in historic section of Savannah, usually in May. Sponsor: Savannah Art Association and Chamber of Commerce with the joint support of the Georgia Council for the Arts and the National Endowment for the Arts. All artists/craftsmen age 18 and over eligible. Fees: table space 4x8', $30; additional space, $15; painting display panels 4x8', $15; additional panels, $5. Sales commission 25% for paintings. No commission for crafts. Awards include best of show; purchase awards of $600 cash; 3 awards of $200 each; and 4 merit awards of $100 each.

Idaho

"ART ON THE GREEN", (formerly Coeur d'Alene Arts & Crafts Festival), Box 901, Coeur d'Alene ID 83814. (208)664-9052. Contact: Opal Brooten. Sponsor: Citizens Council for the Arts. Estab: 1969. Annual outdoor (booths available) show held 3 days in August. Average attendance: 6,000. Closing date for entry: 1 week before show; booth applications must be in 6 weeks before show. Entry fee: $3 per entry; $15 per 8x8' display area. Maximum 2 entries per category per artist; maximum 2 artists per booth. Prejudging; no entry fees refunded for refused work. Art may be offered for sale; 20% commission. Artist must attend show; demonstrating artists given preference. Advance application must be made for demonstrations. Mailing addresses vary for different methods of shipping (U.S. Mail, Greyhound or hand-delivery).
Acceptable Work: Considers all art created within last 2 years. Maximum size: 55"; 150 lbs. Entries not framed, wired or otherwise ready for exhibiting will be disqualified.
Awards: Grants $800 in cash prizes, $200 in purchase awards and ribbons for 2-dimensional art; $400 in cash prizes and ribbons for 3-dimensional art. Judging panel consists of 3 professional artists or art teachers.

Illinois

ANDERSONVILLE MIDSUMMER FESTIVAL ART FAIR, 5344 N. Clark St., Chicago IL 60640. (312)769-0222. Art Director: David Cheesman. Sponsor: Andersonville Chamber of Commerce. Estab: 1965. Annual outdoor show held 2 days in June. Average attendance: 10,000-15,000. Closing date for entry: 4 weeks before show; "entries may be accepted after deadline, but may not be printed in program folders." Entry fee: $15 per 8' display area. Awards medals and ribbons. Prejudging by slides or photos; entry fee refunded for refused work. Art may be offered for sale; no commission. Artist must attend show; "demonstrating helps sell work." Considers all art.

ART AND CRAFT FAIR, 308 S. Malta Rd., Malta IL 60150. Contact: Anita L. Rogers. Sponsor: Kishwaukee Art League. Annual competition held in June. Closing date: May 1. Entry fee: $10 for 6x12' space for 2 days. Ribbons awarded in oils, watercolors, pen and ink, pottery, sculpture, crafts, jewelry and weaving. Also a best of show.

ART FAIR ON THE VILLAGE GREEN, 9226 N. Kedvale Ave., Skokie IL 60076. (312)674-0088. Contact: Alan Friedlander. Sponsor: Skokie Art Guild. Annual outdoor show held 2 days in June. Closing date for entries: mid-May. Entry fee: $20 per nonmember; $15 per member. Awards $500-700 in cash prizes; and ribbons. Prejudging. Art may be offered for sale; no commission. Artist must attend show; demonstrations OK. Considers all art.

ARTS IN THE STREET, (formerly Bond County Art and Cultural Association, Inc.), Box 352, Greenville IL 62246. Contact: Mrs. F.V. Davis. Annual show held the first Saturday in May. Entry fee: $5. Jurors select the work to be awarded purchase prizes, but all original work submitted is accepted. The Association also sponsors a 3-day craft show at the Bond County Fair in August, specializing in crafts of the pioneers.

BEVERLY ART CENTER ART FAIR & FESTIVAL, 2153 W. 111th, Chicago IL 60643. (312)445-3838. Contact: Pat Murphy. Sponsor: Beverly Art Center. Estab: 1969. Annual indoor/outdoor show held 2 days in June (tent space available). Average attendance: 2,000. Slides due for prejudging March 1. Slide entry fee: $5. Entry fee if accepted: $15. Maximum 5 slides per category per artist. Prejudging by panel of 5 artists and art historians. Entry fee

refunded for refused work. Art may be offered for sale; no commission. Artist must attend show; demonstrations OK. Registration limit: 150 artists/craftsmen. Sponsor provides nightguards; 8-12' display area. Considers all original art.
Awards: Presents $2,400 in cash prizes. Awards panel consists of 3 museum curators.

DES PLAINES ART GUILD FALL OUTDOOR ART FAIR, 885 Prairie Ave., Des Plaines IL 60016. Director: Thelma C. Spain. Closing date for entry: August. No molds or other non-original material permitted. No sales commission. Presents purchase, cash and ribbon awards. Guild is a nonprofit organization.

ELMHURST ANNUAL OUTDOOR ART FAIR, Box 263, Elmhurst IL 60126. Contact: Mrs. A. R. Harmon. Sponsors: Elmhurst Artists' Guild and Elmhurst Chamber of Commerce. Estab: 1961. Annual show held 2 days in July or August. Average attendance: 10,000. Entries accepted until show date. Show usually full by May 15. Entry fee: $15 per 4x10' display area. Prejudging of 5 photos or slides. Art may be offered for sale; no commission. Artist must attend show; demonstrations OK. Registration limit: 250 artists/craftsmen. Considers all art. Portfolios permitted. Art must be properly framed.
Awards: Grants ten $50 first prizes; 10 first and 20 second place ribbons; some special awards.
Promotion: "We ask out-of-town exhibitors to provide their own local publicity. For convenience, we use local exhibitors for local publicity."

FELICIAN ART FESTIVAL, 9476 Harding Ave., Surfside FL 33154. Director: Iris Klein. Sponsor: Felician College. Estab: 1972. Annual outdoor show held 1 day in Chicago in July. Average attendance: 5,000. Prejudging by slides or photos (with b&w mugshot and SASE) conducted 4 weeks before show. Entry fee: $12; refunded for refused work. Maximum 1 work per artist. Awards $200 in purchase prizes. Art may be offered for sale; no commission. Artist must attend show; demonstrations OK. Registration limit: 125 artists/craftsmen. Considers all original art. No erotica.

FOREST PARK ART FAIR, Park District of Forest Park, 7501 W. Harrison St., Forest Park IL 60130. Contact: Alice Conway. Annual outdoor show held in August. Estab: 1972. Average attendance: 1,500. Entry fee: $10 per artist for 10x10' display unit. Acceptable media include oils, acrylics, watercolors, graphics, drawings, sculpture, mixed media, photography and crafts. Prejudging by slides or photos of original-design crafts conducted in advance. Awards include $150 for best of show and 2 awards ($75 and $25) each in 4 categories: oils, watercolors, other media and 3-dimensional art. Artist or his representative must attend show. Mailed art not accepted. Fair proceeds used for scholarships for 2 college art students.

FOUR LAKES VILLAGE ART FAIR, Box 430, Lisle IL 60532. (312)964-6800. Contact: Linda Ross. Sponsor: Four Lakes Village Apartments. Estab: 1968. Annual outdoor show held 2 days in August. Entry fee: $25 per display area. Maximum 5 entries per artist. Prejudging by slides or photos; entry fee refunded for refused work. Art may be offered for sale; no commission. Artist must attend show; demonstrations encouraged. Considers all art.
Awards: Presents $650, cash prizes; $2,000, purchase awards; ribbons. Judging panel consists of professional artists.

GLENVIEW ART FAIR, 2122 Dewes St., Glenview IL 60025. Sponsor: Glenview Art League. Annual outdoor show. Average attendance: 10,000. Exhibition by invitation only. Submit 5 slides for jurying by June 1. Acceptable media are oils, acrylics, watercolors, graphics, drawings, sculpture, mixed media and photography. Cash awards total $900 and purchase awards $600. No commission. Artist must attend and handle display panels and insurance. Sponsor provides 10' display area.

GREENWICH VILLAGE ART FAIR, 737 N. Main St., Rockford IL 61103. (815)965-3131. Contact: Cheryl Nauert. Sponsor: Rockford Art Association. Estab: 1947. Annual outdoor show held 2 days in mid-September. Average attendance: 20,000. Submit 5 slides (with SASE) for prejudging by August 1. Entry fee: $2 per square foot; due after jurying. Awards $1,300 in cash prizes. Art must be offered for sale; no commission. Artist must attend show; demonstrations contracted. Registration limit: 180 artists/craftsmen. Sponsor furnishes snow fencing. Considers all original art.

HARVARD ART LEAGUE ARTS AND CRAFTS FAIR, c/o 20817 Bunker Hill, Marengo IL 60152. Contact: Alberta Dodson. Annual show held the last Sunday in July. Acceptable media include oils, acrylics, watercolors, graphics, sculpture and crafts not previously shown in Harvard. Entry fee: $5 per 3 paintings or crafts. Identification labels, frames and wiring required on all work. $50 cash award for art only. No sales commission. Sponsor provides 10' display area.

HOUBY ARTS & CRAFTS FAIR, 2130 S. 61st Court, Cicero IL 60650. (312)863-8979 or 2104. Executive Director: Norm Scaman. Estab: 1969. Annual outdoor show held 2 days in fall. Closing date for entry: September 30. Entry fee: $15 per 2 days. Awards ribbons. Art may be offered for sale; no commission. Considers all art.

JEFFERSON SQUARE ART FAIR, c/o Sylvia Krygowski, PMA, 18127 William St., Lansing IL 60438. Sponsor: Jefferson Square Mall Merchants Association. Semiannual indoor show held at Jefferson Square Mall in Joliet, Illinois. Photos must be submitted. Acceptable media include oils, acrylics, watercolors, graphics, drawings, sculpture, mixed media, photography and selected crafts. Entry fee: $18 per artist; $22 per craftsman. Artist must attend show. Each artist brings his work the day of the fair. No shipments accepted. Cash awards total $100; no commission on works offered for sale. Sponsor provides 8x8' display area. Write for entry blank.

LINCOLN SQUARE ART FAIR, 4800 N. Western Ave., Chicago IL 60625. Chairman: David R. Cheesman. Annual show sponsored by Lincoln Square Chamber of Commerce and Swedish Artists of Chicago. Entry fee: $15 per 6' display area. Artist must attend show. Media include fine arts, graphic arts, photography and original crafts. Awards gold, silver and bronze medals, citation certificates and cash prizes.

LINCOLNWOOD FESTIVAL OF ART, 6807 N. Kedvale Ave., Lincolnwood IL 60646. Contact: Natalie Immergluck. Outdoor show. Entry fee: $18 per 10' display area. Cash and purchase awards total $1,000. Art may be offered for sale; no commission. Artist may send glossy b&w photo of himself and/or work with short resume for publicity. Considers original art and selected crafts. Write for more information.

METRO '78 ART & CRAFT FESTIVAL, c/o Constance L. Barger, 2006 N. North St., Peoria IL 61604. Annual outdoor show (spaces available on sidewalk under canopy) held 3 days at Metro Centre. Entry fee: $25 per 7x10' display area. Limit 1 artist per space. Art must be offered for sale; no commission. Cash awards given on basis of public vote.

MORTON GROVE ART GUILD FAIR, Box 391, Morton Grove IL 60053. (312)966-4264. Chairman: Opal Schrader. Sponsor: Morton Grove Art Guild. Estab: 1965. Annual outdoor show held 1 day in June. Closing date for entry: 4 weeks before show. Entry fee: $7 per Guild member, $12 per nonmember. Presents purchase awards. Art may be offered for sale; no commission. Artist must attend show; demonstrations OK. Registration limit: 100 artists/craftsmen. Sponsor furnishes 10x10' display area. Considers all art.

MOUNT PROSPECT ANNUAL ART FAIR, 1058 Mt. Prospect Plaza, Mt. Prospect IL 60056. Contact: Adele Jeschke. Annual show sponsored by Mt. Prospect Plaza Merchants Association, Inc. Artist must be present. Entry fee: $15. Awards ribbons and prizes. All work for sale (items should be priced); no commission. Registration limit: 100 artists/craftsmen. Acceptable media include all arts and crafts.

OAK PARK VILLAGE ART FAIR, Box 483, Oak Park IL 60303. President: Robert Ransom. Annual outdoor show held the first Sunday after Labor Day. Average attendance: 15,000. Rain date is the following Sunday. Closing date is June 15. Entry fee: $10 per 6x12' display unit. Awards $450, cash prizes; $1,000, purchase prizes. No limit on entries. Art may be offered for sale; no commission. All media acceptable. No "paint by number types."

PARK FOREST ART FAIR, 410 Lakewood Blvd., Park Forest IL 60466. (312)748-3377. Chairman: Robert Wolf. Sponsors: Park Forest Art Center and Star-Tribune Publications. Estab: 1955. Annual outdoor show held 2 days in September. Average attendance: 30,000-40,000. Closing date for entry: 1 month before show. Entry fee: $15 per 12x12' display area. Prejudging by 5 slides; entry fee refunded for refused work. Art must be offered for sale; no commission. Open to artists ages 18+. Artist must attend show; demonstrations with prior arrangement OK. Sponsor pays insurance for exhibited work. Considers all art.
Awards: Grants $1,100, cash prizes; $2,400, purchase awards; ribbons with cash prizes.

RANDHURST AUTUMN ART FESTIVAL, 9476 Harding Ave., Surfside FL 33154. Director: Iris Klein. Sponsor: Randhurst Corp. Estab: 1962. Annual indoor show held 3 days in Mt. Prospect in October. Average attendance: 20,000-25,000. Closing date for entry: September. Entry fee: $30 per 4x16' display area. One entry per artist. Awards $1,000; cash prizes; ribbons. Prejudging; entry fee refunded for refused work. Art may be offered for sale; no commission. Artist must attend show; portrait sketching demonstrations OK. Registration limit: 140 artists. Sponsor furnishes display panels.
Acceptable Work: Considers batik, drawings, calligraphy, metal sculpture, paintings, pastels and prints. Two-dimensional art must be framed and wired for hanging. Pedestals or bases must be provided for sculpture.

RIDGE ART ASSOCIATION ART EXHIBIT, (formerly Ridge Art Fair), 2325 W. 113th Place, Chicago IL 60643. (312)233-1998 or 779-3913. Director: Mr. C. Taylor. Estab: 1955. Semiannual indoor show held 2 days in February and June. Closing date for entry: 1 week before show. Entry fee: $15 per entry. Awards cash prizes and ribbons. Prejudging; "if you don't live nearby, 5 slides are acceptable; if you live in the area, however, we require that you appear in person for jurying." Entry fee refunded for refused work. Art may be offered for sale; no commission. Artist must attend show; demonstrations encouraged. Considers fine art.

URBANA SIDEWALK ART FAIR, Box 459, Urbana IL 61801. (217)328-3465. Chairman: Juanita Gammon. Sponsor: Chamber of Commerce. Estab: 1958. Annual outdoor show held 1 day in late June. Average attendance: 2,000. Entry fee: $20 per 8x10' display area. Prejudging. Art may be offered for sale; no commission. Artist must attend show; demonstrations OK. Considers drawings, paintings, prints and sculpture.
Awards: Grants $465 in cash prizes. Judges are professional artists in exhibited categories.

WESTERN EXHIBITION OF WORKS OF ART ON PAPER, Western Illinois University, Art Department, Macomb IL 61455. Juror: Diane Kelder. Entry fee: $8 for 1-2 entries. Maximum 2 entries per artist. Size limit: 84" length and girth combined. $2,500 purchase awards. No sales commission. Ship work by Parcel Post or U.S. Mail only. Sponsor pays insurance for exhibited work.

Indiana

BALL STATE UNIVERSITY, ANNUAL DRAWING AND SMALL SCULPTURE SHOW, Art Gallery, Ball State University, Muncie IN 47306. Contact: Chairman.

CRAFTS FAIR AT RIVERFRONT, 1101 N. Fulton Ave., Evansville IN 47710. (812)422-2111. Contact: Jane Moore. Sponsor: Evansville Arts and Education Council. Estab: 1969. Annual outdoor show held 2 days in May. Average attendance: 12,000. Closing date for entry: 4 weeks before show. Entry fee: $5 jury fee; $20 exhibition fee. Maximum 3 entries per artist. Awards $500 in cash. Prejudging. Art may be offered for sale; 10% commission. Artist must attend show; demonstrations encouraged. Registration limit: 50 artists/craftsmen. Considers sculpture and mobiles.

EAGLE CREEK ARTS & FOLK MUSIC FESTIVAL, 5901 DeLong Rd., Indianapolis IN 46254. (317)293-4827. Coordinator: Bill Taylor. Sponsor: Indianapolis Dept. of Parks. Estab: 1974. Annual outdoor show held 2 days in July. Average attendance: 12,000-14,000. Closing date for entry: 4 weeks before show. Entry fee: $10 per 10x10' display area. Awards three $50 purchase awards. Prejudging of new entrants by 5 slides (include SASE); entry fee refunded for refused work. Art may be offered for sale; no commission. Open to professional artists ages 18+. Artist must attend show; demonstrations encouraged. Registration limit: 75 artists/craftsmen. Considers all art. Work must be ready to hang or have base.

FAIR-ON-THE-SQUARE, Box 14, Columbus IN 47201. Contact: Jane Gillis. Sponsor: Columbus Arts Guild, Art Division. Semiannual outdoor show and sale held in spring and fall. Entries accepted until show is filled. Media include watercolor, sculpture, stitchery, woodcarving, leathercraft, weaving, tempera, prints, candles, ceramics, drawing, acrylics and oils. 10' limit on size of exhibit. Entry fee: $5 for 10' space. Cash awards total $125. No sales commission. Art to be hand-delivered only. Artist must attend show.

FIESTA, 101 S. 9th St., Lafayette IN 47901. (317)742-4470. Director: Suzanne Stafford. Sponsors: Lafayette Art League and Lafayette Art Association. Estab: 1970. Annual outdoor show held first Saturday in September. Closing date for entry: 3 weeks before show. Entry fee: $20 per 10x10' display area. Presents $500 in cash prizes; merit awards. Prejudging; no entry fees refunded for refused work. Art may be offered for sale; no commission. Artist must attend show; demonstrations OK. Registration limit: 100 artists/craftsmen. Considers all art. Pays $200 minimum for publicity help/design.

LEEPER PARK ART FAIR, 333 Manchester Dr., South Bend IN 46615. Contact: Millie Sjoquist. Sponsor: St. Joe Valley Watercolor Society. Estab: 1964. Annual outdoor show held the fourth weekend in June. Average attendance: 2,000. Closing date for entry: 4 weeks before show. Entry fee: $15 per 14x14' display area. Awards best of show, ribbons and cash prizes. Art must be offered for sale; no commission. Open to artists age 18+. Artist must attend show. Registration limit: 120 artists. Considers original drawings, paintings, pastels, handthrown pottery, prints and sculpture.

LOWELL ARTS AND CRAFTS FESTIVAL, 333 Woodland Court, Lowell IN 46356. Contact: Mrs. Robert Wheeler. Annual show held in July with June deadline. Work must be original, quality pieces. Entry fee: $10 per 8x10' space. Registration limit: 75 artists/craftsmen. Show is well-advertised. Cash awards given.

MADISON CHAUTAUQUA OF THE ARTS, Green Hills Pottery, 1119 W. Main St., Madison IN 47250. Contact: Dixie McDonough. Annual outdoor show, sponsored by the Chautauqua Committee, held last weekend in September. Entry fee: amateurs, $10; professionals, $15. No limit on size or number of entries. Awards cash prizes. Artist must attend show. No sales commission. All media accepted.

MICHIANA REGIONAL ART SHOW, South Bend Art Center, 121 N. Lafayette Blvd., South Bend IN 46601. Director: Vincenzo Mangione. Sponsor: South Bend Art Center. Semiannual show open to all artists residing in Indiana and Michigan. Supported by donations from community. Average attendance: 2,500. Entry fee: $7 per artist with 20% sales commission requested. Awards over $1,600. Considers painting, drawing, photography, prints, craft and sculpture categories. Minimum of 2 entries. Center provides display panels, locked cases for small objects, panels and sculpture stands. Art insured on premises. Art should be sent pre-paid and insured.

MICHIGAN CITY ART FAIR, Box 923, Michigan City IN 46360. Contact: Toni Clem. Sponsor: Michigan City Art League. Annual show held in November. Average attendance: 10,000. Closing date in September. Entry fee: $18 per artist for 9x9' space. Most media acceptable. Cash awards total $500. No commission. Artist must be present.

MID-STATES ART EXHIBITION, c/o Evansville Museum of Arts and Sciences, 411 SE Riverside Dr., Evansville IN 47713. (812)425-2406. Contact: Art Committee. Estab: 1948. Annual indoor show held 4 weeks in November-December. Average attendance: 10,000. Entries accepted September 28-October 8. Entry fee: $5 per entry; $8 per 2 entries. Maximum 2 entries per artist. Awards $3,800, purchase prizes; $400, merit awards. Prejudging; no entry fees refunded for refused work. Art may be offered for sale; 20% commission. Open to Indiana residents and artists living within 200-mile radius of Evansville. "No work previously exhibited in this show." Brochure available September 1.
Acceptable Work: Considers all art created within last 3 years. Paintings must be framed; graphics must be matted.

OBJECTS & CRAFTS, 1200 W. 38th St., Indianapolis IN 46208. Sponsor: Indianapolis Museum of Art. Entry fee: $5. Limit 2 entries per artist. Indiana artists or former residents eligible. Awards $1,800+ in cash prizes.

TIPPECANOE REGIONAL COMPETITION, 101 S. 9th St., Lafayette IN 47901. Contact: Suzanne Stafford. Sponsor: Lafayette Art Association. Estab: 1959. Semiannual show open to artists living in Indiana. Average attendance: 3,000-5,000. Acceptable media are oils, acrylics, watercolors, graphics, drawings, sculpture, mixed media and photography. Entry fee: $5. Maximum 2 works per artist. Size limit: 60x60"; sculpture 50 lbs. Works insured while on display in gallery. Cash and purchase prizes awarded totaling $1,000. 25% sales commission.

WABASH VALLEY EXHIBITION, 25 S. 7th St., Terre Haute IN 47807. (812)238-1676.

Contact: Director. Sponsor: Sheldon Swope Art Gallery. Estab: 1943. Annual indoor show held 1 month in early spring. Average attendance: 3,000. Closing date for entry: early February. Entry fee: $4 per first entry; $3 per second and third entries. Maximum 3 entries per artist. Awards $6,000 in prizes. Prejudging; no entry fees refunded for refused work. Art may be offered for sale; 20% commission. Open to artists living within 160-mile radius of Terre Haute. Sponsor provides display equipment.
Acceptable Work: Considers all art. Maximum size: 72" in any direction. Work must be framed or suitable for hanging.

WICKER PARK ART FAIR, 5448 Hohman Ave., Hammond IN 46320. (219)93[illegible]8 or (312)891-2199. Executive Director: Arnold Feingold. Sponsor: Northern Indiana Arts Association. Estab: 1970. Annual outdoor show held 2 days in May. Average attendance: 7,000-10,000. Closing date for entry: 6 weeks before show. Entry fee: $20 per display area. Awards ribbons and prize money. Prejudging by 2-5 slides; $15 refunded for refused work. Art may be offered for sale; no commission. Artist must attend show; demonstrations OK. Registration limit: 120 artists. Artist provides backdrop for hanging work. Considers all art.

WOODLAND PARK ART FAIR, 3336 Brown St., Portage IN 46368. (219)762-9280. Chairman: Valerie Simcox. Sponsor: Portage Junior Women's Club. Estab: 1976. Annual outdoor show held 2 days in July. Average attendance: 5,000. Closing date for entry: 4 weeks before show. Entry fee: $15 per 12x12' display area. Prejudging by 3 slides; entry fee refunded for refused work. Art may be offered for sale; no commission. Artist or representative must attend show; demonstrations encouraged. Registration limit: 75 artists/craftsmen. Considers all art.
Awards: Presents $300+ in cash prizes; purchase awards; and ribbons. Judges are artists and craftsmen.

Iowa

CLAY & PAPER SHOW, (formerly The Octagon Annual Clay and Paper Show), 232½ Main St., Ames IA 50010. (515)232-5331. Director: Martha Benson. Sponsor: The Octagon Art Center. Estab: 1966. Biennial indoor show held 4-6 weeks in January and February. Closing date for entry: 2 weeks before show. Entry fee: $5 per entry. Maximum 3 entries per artist. Awards $300 in cash prizes. Prejudging; no entry fees refunded. Art may be offered for sale; 25% commission. Artist must live within 500-mile radius of Ames and be over 18-years-old. Sponsor supplies display equipment and insurance on exhibited work. Considers drawings, prints, watercolors and photography.

NATIONAL ROSEMALING EXHIBITION, 502 W. Water St., Decorah IA 52101. (319)382-3856. Contact: Betty Seegmiller. Sponsor: Norwegian-American Museum. Estab: 1967. Annual indoor show held 3 days in July. Average attendance: 15,000. Closing date for entry: 1 week before show. Entry fee: $2 per entry. Maximum 2 entries per artist. Prejudging; entry fee refunded for refused work. Art may be offered for sale; 20% commission. Sponsor furnishes display equipment and pays insurance and shipping to artist.
Acceptable Work: Considers rosemaling on wood. "Works must measure at least 8" in one direction and contain enough decoration to reveal artist's technical skill and design ability. It is not necessary for the artist to make the article; only the painting must be original."
Awards: Presents $125-150 in cash prizes; ribbons; Medal of Honor.

SIOUX CITY ART CENTER FALL SHOW, 513 Nebraska St., Sioux City IA 51101. (712)279-6272. Director: Peggy Parris. Sponsors: local financial institutions. Estab: 1938. Annual indoor show held 6 weeks during November-December. Average attendance: 2,500-3,000. Entry fee: $5 per artist. Maximum 3 entries per artist. Awards $1,200 in purchase awards. Slides due for prejudging 5 weeks before show; no entry fees refunded for refused work. Art may be offered for sale; 30% commission. Open to artists working in Iowa, Nebraska, Minnesota and South Dakota. Sponsor pays insurance for exhibited work.
Acceptable Work: Considers paintings. Maximum size: 250 lbs. Work must be framed and ready to hang.

Kansas

NORTHWEST KANSAS AREA ART SHOW & SALE, c/o Mrs. Duane Aase, 606 S. Broadway, Oberlin KS 67749. Sponsor: Sappa Valley Arts Club. Estab: 1970. Annual indoor show held 4 days in late September. Average attendance: 2,000. Entries accepted until show

date. Entry fee: $1 per artist. Maximum 3 entries per artist. Awards cash prizes to first 3 winners in 6 divisions; and ribbons. Art may be offered for sale; 10% commission. Open to artists living within 200-mile radius of Oberlin. Demonstrations encouraged. Address shipped items to Decatur County Extension Office, Court House, Oberlin, Kansas 67749.
Acceptable Work: Considers acrylics, drawings, oils, pastels and watercolors. Maximum size: 36x36".

PARSONS, OUTDOOR ART & CRAFTS FAIR, Parsons Chamber of Commerce Office, Box 737, Parsons KS 67357. Contact: D.D. Lemmond. Sponsors: Parsons Chamber of Commerce and Citizens and Patrons of the Community. Annual show. Entry fee: adults, $5; teenagers, $3. Fee entitles entrant to one 4x8' pegboard or 1 table for crafts. Awards $5-$75 in all categories; $100 for best of show; $300 in purchase awards. Open to artists, craftsmen and photographers. Original work only. Artist must attend show. Paintings must be matted and/or framed and wired for hanging. Sponsor provides display equipment and overnight storage facilities.

Kentucky

ART & CRAFTS FESTIVAL, TVA's Land Between the Lakes, Golden Pond KY 42231. (502)924-5602. Sponsor: Murray Art Guild. Estab: 1969. Annual outdoor show held the last weekend in June. Average attendance: 30,000-35,000. Entries accepted until show date. Entry fee: $8 per artist; plus $2 per entry in juried section. Art may be offered for sale; no commission. Artist must attend show; demonstrations encouraged. Considers all original art.

COCA COLA BOTTLING COMPANY ART SHOW, 808 Paddy Court, Elizabethtown KY 42701. (502)769-1292. Chairman: Linda Weis. Sponsor: Elizabethtown Junior Woman's Club. Annual indoor show held 2 days in May. Average attendance: 3,000. Closing date for entry: 3 weeks before show. Entry fee: $10 per 2 entries. Maximum 2 entries per artist. Grants $1,000 in cash prizes. Art may be offered for sale; 20% commission. Sponsor provides display equipment. Contact Weis on demonstrations. Also needs advertising art. Considers all art. Maximum size: 4x7'. No kits.

8-STATE ANNUAL, J.B. Speed Art Museum, Box 8345, Louisville KY 40208. (502)636-2893. Director: A.F. Page. Estab: 1973. Annual indoor show held the month of September. Average attendance: 6,000. Closing date for entry: 5 weeks before show. No entry fee. Awards $5,000 in purchase prizes. Maximum 2 entries per artist. Prejudging. Art may be offered for sale; no commission. Artists from Kentucky, Indiana, Illinois, Ohio, Virginia, West Virginia, Tennessee and Missouri only. Considers all art.

GATEWAY ART FESTIVAL, c/o White Elephant, Washington KY 41096. Annual show sponsored by Gateway Art Association. Entry fee: $5. Awards $50, best in show; $25, local artist; $25, first and $15, second prizes. Considers oils, acrylics, watercolors, pastels, drawings, creative crafts, sculpture, etchings, prints and photography. Sponsor provides 10' booth space.

LIONS BLUE GRASS FAIR, Box 4335, Lexington KY 40504. (606)276-3556. Manager: Don C. Sullivan. Sponsor: central Kentucky Lions Clubs. Annual outdoor show held in July (tent space available). Average attendance: 200,000. Closing date for entry: 4 weeks before show. No entry fee. Awards first and second place ribbons in each category. Art may be offered for sale; no commission. "We prefer to have Kentucky artists/craftsmen." Registration limit: 200 artists/craftsmen. Sponsor provides easels.
Acceptable Work: Considers calligraphy, drawings, metal sculpture, paintings and prints. Maximum size: 3x4'. Paintings must be framed. No obscenity.

THE PALETTE CLUB, INC., 310 Ridgeway Ave., Louisville KY 40207. (502)895-5285. Contact: Mrs. Robert Weisman. Estab: 1973. Semiannual indoor show held 3-7 days in spring and fall. Closing date for entry: 1 week before show. No entry fee. Maximum 2 entries per artist. Awards ribbons. Prejudging. Art may be offered for sale; 10% commission. Open to Palette Club members. Sponsor provides display panels. Considers all art. Two-dimensional art must be framed and wired.

Louisiana

LOUISIANA STATE ART EXHIBITION FOR NON-PROFESSIONALS AND/OR ART STUDENTS, Jay R. Broussard Memorial Galleries, Old State Capitol, Baton Rouge LA 70801.

Exhibits Director: Charles Ford. Sponsor: Louisiana State Art, Historical and Cultural Preservation Agency. Annual show held in spring. Open to Louisiana residents. No entry fee. Maximum 2 entries per artist. Awards 10 engraved bowls. All media accepted. No size limitation. No sales commission.

LOUISIANA STATE ART EXHIBITION FOR PROFESSIONAL ARTISTS, Old State Capitol Bldg., Baton Rouge LA 70801. Exhibits Director: Charles Ford. Sponsor: Louisiana State Art, Historical and Cultural Preservation Agency. Annual show held in the fall. Open to professional artists residing in Louisiana. No entry fee. Maximum 2 entries per artist. Awards five $100 prizes. All media accepted. No sales commission.

LOUISIANA WATERCOLOR SOCIETY, 3917 Jurgens St., Metaire LA 70002. Contact: Martha Guthrie. Annual international show exclusively for watercolor artists. Sponsors: Louisiana Watercolor Society and Louisiana Art Commission. Work must be original and executed within the last 3 years. Entry fee: $3 per entry. Awards cash prizes. Closing date for entries usually in October. Overall mat size no larger than 30x40"; no frames. Ship entries prepaid with return postage enclosed.

NEW ORLEANS MUSEUM OF ART, ARTISTS BIENNIAL, Box 19123, City Park, New Orleans LA 70179. Contact: William A. Fagaly. Open to artists living and working in Kentucky, Tennessee, West Virginia, Virginia, North and South Carolina, Georgia, Florida, Alabama, Mississippi, Arkansas, Louisiana and Texas. Media include painting, sculpture, print, drawing, ceramics, photography, videotape, fiber and conceptual works. No entry fee. Do not send original works for jurying. Artist may submit 3 separate works. Submit 2-dimensional works with one, 2x2" slide of each work. Submit three-dimensional works with three 2x2" slides of each work, or three 8x10" b&w photos of each work. Only paper documentation, typewritten proposals, and/or 8x10" b&w photos accepted for conceptual pieces. Museum reserves the right to retain any/all slides for archives of regional contemporary artists. Juror recommends artists for one-person exhibitions the next year. No sales commission. 10% purchase discount to Museum members only.

SHREVEPORT ART GUILD, Meadows Museum of Art, 2911 Centenary Blvd., Shreveport LA 71104. Annual show held in November. Works must be original and completed within last 2 years. Paintings in all media as well as drawings, prints and sculpture eligible. Entry fee: $10, first 3 entries; $1, each additional entry. Awards $3,000. Artists should send 2x2" color slides of work for jurying; sculptors submit three 2x2" slides of each work. Slides due in August usually. 10% sales commission.

SHREVEPORT NATIONAL ART EXHIBITION, Barnwell Garden and Art Center, 501 Clyde Fant Pkwy., Shreveport LA 71101. Contact: Gwen Norsworthy. Sponsor: Shreveport Parks and Recreation Department. Open to artists ages 18+. Entries must be original, by living artists, done without supervision and completed in the last 2 years. No entries eligible if previously shown in competitive exhibitions in Shreveport. All media considered. Must be of size to pass through ordinary doorway and be handled by 2 workmen. Initial submission of work must be by 35mm color slides. Entry fee: $10, first 3 entries; $1, each additional entry. Cash merit awards total $2,500. 20% commission. Barnwell Center reserves the right to reproduce works in the exhibition catalog and press.

Maine

ARTHRITIS ART COMMITTEE, Box 333, Bath ME 04530. One or 2 shows sponsored annually by the Maine Chapter, Arthritis Foundation. Closing date for entry: 15 days before show. Entry fee: $10, first work; $6, each additional work. Maximum 5 entries per artist. Requires art be framable. Size limit is 3x5'. Awards five $10 first prizes, ribbons and certificates. Commission is 25%.

BRIDGTON ART SHOW, Box 236 A & C, Bridgton ME 04009. (207)647-3472. Contact: Sandra Libby. Sponsor: Chamber of Commerce. Estab: 1971. Annual indoor show held Columbus Day weekend. Average attendance: 2,000-3,000. Closing date for entry: 1 week before show. Entry fee: $20 per 2 entries. Maximum 2 entries per artist. Prejudging; no entry fees refunded for refused work. Art may be offered for sale; 20% commission. Sponsor provides display equipment and insurance for exhibited work. Considers all art. Work must be ready for hanging or display.

Awards: Presents two $1,000 best in show prizes; $250 popular prize chosen by spectators; several $400 and $100 purchase awards. Judging usually done by director of prominent art museum.

KITTERY ART ASSOCIATION'S ART & CRAFT EXHIBIT, c/o Thelma Mandeville, 13 Foyes Lane, Kittery Point ME 03905. Annual show. Entry fee: $5 for 15' of snowfencing. Artist chooses 1 painting for competition. Cash awards and ribbons given. No sales commission. Original works only. Artist or representative must be present.

OGUNQUIT SIDEWALK ART SHOW, Ogunquit Chamber of Commerce, Box 637, Ogunquit ME 03907. Contact: Hilda Wallace. Annual show. All media accepted. No crafts. No entry fee. Ribbons awarded. No sales commission. Artist must be present and provide racks. Registration between 9-10 a.m. day of show.

WCSH TELEVISION SIDEWALK ART FESTIVAL, Congress Square, Portland ME 04101. (201)772-0181. Art Director: Art Hahn. Estab: 1966. Annual outdoor show held the third Saturday in August. Average attendance: 25,000-45,000. Entry forms available after January 1; show usually filled by mid-May. Entry fee: $20 per display area. Art may be offered for sale; no commission. Artist must attend show; demonstrations OK. Registration limit: 300-325 artists.
Acceptable Work: Considers all art. No serigraphy, lithography, etchings or work generally considered graphic or multiple copy. Work must be framed and ready for hanging.
Awards: Presents ten $50 merit awards; $750 first, $500 second, $350 third and thirty $200 purchase awards; ribbons. Judges are 3 recognized artists or associates of the arts.

Maryland

ACADEMY OF THE ARTS, South and Harrison Sts. (Box 605), Easton MD 21601. Curator: Robert Seyffert. Annual show. Eligible media include prints, multimedia, collage, paintings, oils, acrylics, ceramics, photography and metal and wood sculpture (plastics). Sculpture may not be impermanent material. Submit only original work completed in last 2 years. No wet canvases. No title may be changed after submission of entry card. Closing date for entry: 1 week before show. No entry fee. Artists born in Maryland, residents of the state and Maryland students may participate. 20% sales commission. Awards $1,000 in prizes. Size limit: 62x62", 2-dimensional; 14' in total dimension; 150 lbs. Material must be shipped in crates so it can be returned. $7,500 insurance release pro rata provided.

CUMBERLAND VALLEY EXHIBITION, Box 423, Hagerstown MD 21740. (301)739-5727. Director: H. Paul Kotun. Sponsor: Washington County Museum of Fine Arts. Estab: 1932. Annual indoor show held during June. Average attendance: 5,200. Closing date for entry: 2-3 weeks before show. Entry fee: $10 per artist. Maximum 2 entries per artist. Art may be offered for sale; 20% commission. Open to residents and former residents of the Cumberland Valley region.
Acceptable Work: Considers all art. Maximum size: 2-dimensional, 72x72". Two-dimensional work must be framed.
Awards: Presents $800 in cash prizes and $600 in purchase awards, 2-dimensional art; $200 in cash prizes and $100 in purchase awards, 3-dimensional art.

HAVRE DE GRACE ART SHOW, 131 S. Union Ave., Havre de Grace MD 21078. Contact: Dr. Gunther Hirsch or Edna Hirsch. Annual show sponsored by the Havre de Grace Parks and Recreation Department in Millard E. Tydings Park. Average attendance: 18,000. No entry fee. Contribution appreciated. All media accepted. No size limitation. 10% sales commission charged on crafts. Prizes awarded according to category: professional and amateur. Artist must attend show.

PREAKNESS FESTIVAL, c/o Art & Craft Education Inc., 475 Blackshire Rd., Severna Park MD 21146. Contact: Eunice Swann. Annual show held at Hopkins Hospital. Open to artists/craftsmen in all media. Entry fee: $25. Original work only. Artists/craftsmen must wear Colonial costumes. Limited to 200 entries. Presents awards and ribbons. No commission.

Massachusetts

ANDOVER ART IN THE PARK, 36 Bartlet St., Andover MA 01810. Sponsor: Andover Artist Guild/Recreation/Community Schools Dept., Stowe School. Contact: Gary C. Ralph. Estab: 1975. Outdoor show. Average attendance: 4,000-5,000. Entry fee: $10 per artist for

Good Showmanship Helps Sell Art/Crafts

Photo courtesy of Charles Scribner's Sons

One method of increasing show sales is to attract customers to your booth with an attractive, eye-catching display. Here the craftsman displays her dolls and sachets inexpensively using a ladder and net bag. A good display is not necessarily an expensive display.

Eye-catching displays and demonstrations are the best ways to attract customers to your booth.

Some items sell better shown against one background, while others are best against another. Experiment. You needn't buy expensive professional display materials. Use inexpensive items such as bricks, wood, fabric, baskets, boxes, chests, small bookcases, A-frames and standing pieces of pegboard.

Your display should include a variety of work, but not so many pieces that your presentation looks cluttered. Keep duplicates hidden under the table and replace items as they're sold.

Label each piece with its price. Customers who have to continually ask for prices may get discouraged and leave before finding items in their price range. And many will assume the price is high, if it's not on the work, and won't even bother to ask.

Give outstanding items a special place as the show pieces in your display. Use the most room for your best and most expensive work, while grouping your less expensive items together.

If possible, demonstrate your art or craft at your booth. Customers will gather to watch and, hopefully, buy.

Finally, evaluate each show according to customer response and your performance. Check your inventory sheet to see what sold well. And ask: "What did I learn at this show to make future sales efforts more effective?"

— Loretta Holz

15x6' display space. Acceptable media include oils, acrylics, watercolors, graphics, drawings, sculpture and mixed media. Awards include $150 for first place, $75 for second and $50 for third; honorable mentions and consumer purchase awards. 15% commission donated to art scholarship fund.

BOSTON PRINTMAKERS ANNUAL, Box 161, Lexington MA 02173. Estab: 1948. Annual indoor show held 1-2 months in the spring. Closing date for entry: 5-6 weeks before show. Entry fee: $6 for 2 prints. Maximum number of entries per artist: 2. Awards $2,500 in purchase prizes. Prejudging; no entry fees refunded. Art may be offered for sale; 33 1/3% commission. Sponsor supplies display panels. Ship art in cardboard cartons only; no crates.
Acceptable Work: Considers prints only. Work must be on white mats.

FALL RIVER ART ASSOCIATION REGIONAL EXHIBITION, Fall River Art Association, 80 Belmont St., Fall River MA 02720. (617)673-7212. Open to New England and New York state artists and potters. Entry fee: $5 per work. Maximum 4 entries per artist. Maximum size: 6' in any dimension. A total of $1,200 awarded. Commission is 20%. Artwork should be shipped UPS or parcel post.

NATIONAL AMATEUR ART FESTIVAL, Box 67, Rockport MA 01996. Executive Director: Sumner G. Ropper. Annual show held Columbus Day weekend. Entry fee: $2. Limit of 1 entry. No selling permitted. Media include oils, acrylics, watercolors, graphics, drawing, sculpture and ceramics. Maximum size: 4x3'. Certificate awards for best in show, first, second, third places and honorable mention. Popular vote determines recipient of a weekend in Rockport or lessons from an artist of the winner's choice.

PEMBROKE ARTS FESTIVAL, 363 Oldham St., Pembroke MA 02359. Contact: Brooks Kelly. Entry fee: $3 per entry. Awards $150, $100 and $50 prizes; $100 purchase prize; $50 popular prize. Media include oils, acrylics, casein, tempera, watercolor, prints, drawings and sculpture. Original work only. Two-dimensional works must be framed and ready to hang. 30% sales commission. Open to New England artists.

PROVINCETOWN ART ASSOCIATION, 460 Commercial St., Provincetown MA 02657. (617)487-1750. Director: Sheila Miles. Annual show held in summer. Open to members ($10 annual fee). 30% sales commission.

SOUTHBRIDGE ART ASSOCIATION FESTIVAL, c/o Christine O'Brien, 274 Marcy St., Southbridge MA 01550. Annual outdoor show and sale held Columbus Day weekend. Entry fee: $5. Considers oils, acrylics, watercolors, graphics, pastels and photography. No limits on size. Cash and ribbon awards given in adult and youth divisions in 6 categories. Artist or representative must be present. No sales commission.

SPRINGFIELD ART LEAGUE, NATIONAL EXHIBITION, Springfield Art League, c/o George Walter Vincent Smith Art Museum, 222 State St., Springfield MA 01103. Contact: Exhibition Chairman. Annual indoor show held in April. Closing date for entries: March. Entry fee: $8 per artist; maximum 1 entry. Media include oils, acrylics, watercolors, graphics, drawings, sculpture and mixed media. Maximum size: 52" in any dimension; 175 lbs., sculpture. Awards approximately $2,000. No commission. Write for additional details and entry blank.

Michigan

ARTS & CRAFTS SHOW, 520 Oak St., Dundee MI 48131. Contact: Mrs. Roger La Voy. Sponsor: Dundee Arts and Crafts Club. Estab: 1962. Annual outdoor show held 1 day in July. Average attendance: 2,000. Entries accepted until show date. Entry fee: $6 per 4x8' display area. Awards ribbons. Art may be offered for sale; no commission. Artist must attend show; demonstrations OK.
Acceptable Work: Considers acrylics, airbrush, calligraphy, drawings, oils, pastels, watercolors and sculpture. Paintings must be framed.

DANISH FESTIVAL ARTS & CRAFTS SHOW, Danish Festival, Inc., 302 S. Lafayette St., Greenville MI 48838. (616)754-6369. Managing Director: Mrs. Bart Fries. Estab: 1968. Annual outdoor show held third weekend in August. Average attendance: 50,000. Closing date for entry: 4 weeks before show. Entry fee: based on 10x10' display area. Prejudging; entry fee refunded for refused work. Art may be offered for sale; no commission. Artist must attend show; demonstrations OK. Registration limit: 130 artists/craftsmen. Sponsor pays insurance on exhibited work. Write for further information. Considers all quality art.

FLINT ART FAIR, Flint Institute of Arts, 1120 E. Kearsley St., Flint MI 48503. (313)234-1695. Assistant Director: Tom Kayser. Sponsor: Friends of Modern Art. Estab: 1966. Annual outdoor show held the second weekend in June. Average attendance: 10,000-15,000. Closing date for entry: mid-March. Entry fee: $30 per 15x5' display area; due after jury day. Requires 6 entries per artist. Awards $100 each and plaque to 10 best artists. Prejudging by 35mm slides. Art must be offered for sale; no commission. Artist must attend show; demonstrations encouraged. Registration limit: 125 artists/craftsmen. Sponsor furnishes scaffolding. Considers all art. "Label slides clearly as to top, media and artist's name. Please print."

HARTLAND ART SHOW, Box 126, Hartland MI 48029. (313)632-7481. Contact: Michael Van Wormer. Sponsor: Hartland Art Council. Estab: 1966. Annual indoor show held during the 3rd week in June. Average attendance: 2,000. Closing date for entries: 1 week before show. Entry fee: $3 per entry. Awards $225, cash prizes; three $300 and one $75 purchase prizes; and Awards of Excellence ribbons. Prejudging; no entry fees refunded for refused work. Art may be offered for sale; 10% commission. Sponsor provides display equipment.
Acceptable Work: Considers paintings, drawings, graphics and sculpture.

MIDWEST ARTS & CRAFTS SHOW, 1114 Grant St., Iron Mountain MI 49801. (906)774-0128. Chairman: Mrs. William Strand. Sponsor: Dickinson County Council for the Arts. Estab: 1967. Annual indoor/outdoor (artist may choose) show held 2 days in June. Average attendance: 3,000. Closing date for entry: 2 weeks before show. Entry fee: $10 per display area. Maximum 2 spaces per artist. Awards $250 in cash prizes; ribbons. Art may be offered for sale; no commission. Artist or representative must attend show; demonstrations encouraged. "Those who demonstrate generally seem to sell more." Sponsor provides pegboard on tables if requested. Considers all art. "Entries to be judged must include 3x5" card with title, media and artist's name."

PONTIAC ANNUAL ART FAIR — HERITAGE FESTIVAL, 47 Williams St., Pontiac MI 48053. (313)333-7849. Contact: Ian Lyons. Sponsor: Widetrack Festival Committee. Estab: 1975. Annual outdoor show held 3 days in June (tent space available). Average attendance: 2,000. Closing date for entry: 1 week before show. Entry fee: $10 per entry. Prejudging by slides (send before second week in June); entry fee refunded for refused work. Art may be offered for sale; 15% commission. Artist must attend show; demonstrations OK. Sponsor provides display panels. Considers all art.
Awards: Presents two $100 first prizes; five $50 honorable mentions. Judging panel consists of the Detroit Institute of Arts curator, Pontiac Arts Center director and 1 artist.

REGIONAL ART COMPETITION, Hackley Art Museum, Muskegon MI 49440. (616)722-6954. Contact: Ann Archambault. Estab: 1926. Annual indoor show held 6 weeks in winter. Average attendance: 3,000-4,000. Closing date for entry: 1 week before show. Entry fee: $1 per entry. Maximum 2 entries per artist. Awards $1,000 in cash prizes. Art may be offered for sale; no commission. Open to western Michigan residents. Registration limit: approximately 200 artists/craftsmen. Sponsor pays insurance for exhibited work. Considers all art. Paintings must be framed and ready to hang.

ST. CLAIR ART FAIR, Box 222, St. Clair MI 48079. (313)329-2803. Chairman: Mary Ann Garman. Sponsor: St. Clair Art Association. Estab: 1971. Annual outdoor (covered mall) show held 3 days in late June. Average attendance: 5,000-6,000. Closing date for entry: mid-March. Entry fee: $15 per 8x8' or 8x10' display area. Prejudging. Art must be offered for sale; 10% commission. Artist must attend show; demonstrations OK. Registration limit: 65 artists/craftsmen. Considers all art.

SAUGATUCK-DOUGLAS ANNUAL VILLAGE SQUARE ART FAIRS, Saugatuck MI 49453. (616)857-4707. President: Cathie Moore. Estab: 1950. Semiannual outdoor show held 2 days in July. Average attendance: 2,000-3,000. Closing date for entry: 2 weeks before show. Entry fee for non-members: $10 per 1 show; $15 per 2 shows. Art may be offered for sale; no commission. Registration limit: 250 artists/craftsmen. Sponsor pays insurance during exhibit period. Considers all art.

TAWAS BAY WATERFRONT ART FAIR, 1115 Bay Dr., Tawas City MI 48763. (517)362-3198. Art Director: Paula Peterson. Sponsor: Tawas Bay Arts Council. Estab: 1960. Annual indoor/outdoor show held the first weekend in August. Average attendance: 5,000. Entry fee: $10 per artist. Awards ribbons and cash prizes. Applications and photos due for prejudging July 1. Entry fees refunded for refused work. Art may be offered for sale; no commission. Artist must attend show; demonstrations OK. Registration limit: 225 artists/craftsmen. Considers drawings, mobiles, paintings, pastels and sculpture.

TRAVERSE BAY OUTDOOR ART FAIR, c/o Terry Tarnow, 3545 Orchard View, Traverse City MI 49684. Sponsor: Northwestern Michigan Artists and Craftsmen. Average attendance: 20,000. Annual show held last Saturday in July. Acceptable media include oils, acrylics, watercolors, pottery, sculpture, artistic leathercraft, weaving and macrame. Entry fee: $7.50 for 15x15' booth. Awards cash prizes. No sales commission. Artist must be present.

Minnesota

ARROWHEAD ART EXHIBIT, Depot Art Center, 506 W. Michigan St., Duluth MN 55802. Sponsor: Art Institute at the Depot. Biennial show held in spring. 20% commission. Considers prints and graphics. Awards $300, best in show; $150, second place; purchase prizes.

NORTH SHORE ART FAIR, Box 57, Lutsen MN 55612. (218)663-7533. Contact: Joan Maw. Sponsor: North Shore Arts Association. Estab: 1968. Annual indoor/outdoor show held the second weekend in July. Average attendance: 2,000. Entries accepted until show date. Awards cash prizes and ribbons. Art may be offered for sale; 15% commission. Sponsor furnishes display equipment. Considers drawings, paintings, pastels and sculpture. Art must be ready for hanging.

U.S. HOCKEY HALL OF FAME ART COMPETITION, Box 657, Eveleth MN 55734. (218)749-5167. Executive Director: Roger Godin. Estab: 1974. Annual indoor show held during summer. Closing date for entry: May 10. No entry fee. Maximum 3 entries per artist. Awards $250 first place prize. Prejudging.
Acceptable Work: Considers drawings, paintings, pastels and prints. Work must be framed for hanging. Back of each entry must include title, medium, artist's name and address. "Entries must have some aspect of hockey as a theme. This may include action other than on the ice, such as locker room, press box, etc."

Mississippi

CROSSTIE ARTS FESTIVAL, Crosstie Arts Council, Box 1064, Cleveland MS 38732. Contact: Lallah M. Perry. Annual show. Entry fee: $5. Awards $300, best of show, $100 first, $75 second and $50 third prizes in each category. Categories are painting, sculpture, ceramics/glass, jewelry/metalsmithing, fibers and prints/graphics. No sales commission.

GUM TREE FESTIVAL, Box 1146, Tupelo MS 38801. (601)842-1052. Co-Chairman: Bill Ford. Sponsor: Community Development Foundation. Estab: 1972. Annual outdoor show held 2 days in mid-May. Average attendance: 10,000-12,000. Closing date for entry: 3 weeks before show. Entry fee: $5 jury fee; $20 per 12x4' display area; $20 for each additional space. Prejudging by slides or photos; no jury fees refunded for refused work. Art may be offered for sale; no commission. Artist must attend show; demonstrations encouraged. Registration limit: 170 artists/craftsmen.
Acceptable Work: Considers all art. Paintings, drawings and prints must be matted or framed; other unframed work may be displayed in a portfolio; hanging pieces must be ready to hang.
Awards: Presents $500, best in show; $150 first, $75 second and $50 third prizes in 6 categories; $3,250, purchase awards; ribbons. (Total awards: $5,400.)

Missouri

DUCKS UNLIMITED MIDWEST WILDLIFE ART SHOW, 1900 Swift Ave., North Kansas City MO 64116. (816)471-3414. Chairman: David Wells. Estab: 1972. Annual indoor benefit show held 1½ days in March. Average attendance: 3,000. Closing date for entry: December. Entry fee: 1 original donated work. Maximum 15 entries per artist. Awards ribbons. Prejudging; donation refunded for refused work. Art may be offered for sale; no commission. Artist must attend show; demonstrations OK. Registration limit: 90 artists.
Acceptable Work: Considers acrylics, oils, pastels, watercolors and wood and decoy carving. Paintings must be framed and wired. Emphasis placed on realism. Artist should bring paintings of various subjects, sizes and prices.

FINE ARTS FALL SHOW, 101 Battlefield Mall, Springfield MO 65804. (417)883-8444. Promotion Director: Nancy Dillard. Estab: 1970. Annual indoor show held 3 days in September-October. Average attendance: 35,000. Closing date for entry: 2 weeks before show. Entry

fee: $40 per 10x20' display area. Prejudging by slides or photos; entry fee refunded for refused work. Art may be offered for sale; no commission. Artist must attend show; demonstrations arranged.
Acceptable Work: Considers calligraphy, drawings, paintings, pastels, pottery, prints, sculpture, weavings and woodcrafting. "Nudes are acceptable, if nothing too erotic."
Awards: Presents $50 cash prizes for first place in each category; second and third place ribbons. Judging by local college and art museum personnel.

NAMA ADVERTISING AWARDS, 800 W. 47th St., Kansas City MO 64112. (816)931-5934. Executive Director: Ernest Marshall. Sponsor: National Agri-Marketing Association. Annual indoor show held 3 days in April or May. Average attendance: 1,500-2,000. Closing date for entries to local chapters: January. Entry fee: $20 per artist. Maximum 1 entry per artist. Awards trophies. Prejudging; no entry fees refunded for refused work. Sponsor provides display equipment.
Acceptable Work: Considers prints and outdoor posters. Entries should be mounted on 13x6" folders which open to 26x16". Folders should be hinged together.

Montana

J. K. RALSTON MUSEUM & ART CENTER JURIED EXHIBIT, Box 50, Sidney MT 59270. (406)482-3500. Director: Linda K. Mann. Sponsor: Mon-Dak Historical & Arts Society. Estab: 1975. Annual indoor show held the month of October. Average attendance: 200. Closing date for entry: 1 week before show. Entry fee: $3 per artist. Maximum 2 entries per artist. Prejudging; entry fee refunded for refused work. Art may be offered for sale; 25% commission. No demonstrations. Work must have been done within 2 years prior to show. Sponsor provides display equipment. Art should be shipped prepaid; will be returned C.O.D. Considers all art except mobiles. Maximum size: 6x4' or 3 lbs.
Awards: Presents cash awards and ribbons for best of show, honorable mention and most popular work.

Nebraska

COUNTRYSIDE VILLAGE ART FAIR, 8715 Countryside Plaza, Omaha NE 68114. (402)391-2200. Contact: Jim Chase. Sponsor: Countryside Village Merchants Association. Estab: 1970. Annual outdoor show held the first weekend in June. Average attendance: 20,000. Closing date for entry: 4 weeks before show. Entry fee: $30 per 8-14' display area; due after jury day. Awards $100 first, $50 second and $25 third prizes. Prejudging. Art may be offered for sale; no commission. Artist must attend show; demonstrations OK. Registration limit: 160 artists/craftsmen. Considers all art.

MIDWEST BIENNIAL, 2200 Dodge St., Omaha NE 68112. (402)342-3996. Contact: Exhibition Dept. Sponsor: Joslyn Art Museum. Estab: 1930. Indoor show held 6 weeks in April-May. Closing date for entry: January 15. No entry fee. Maximum 2 entries per artist. Prejudging by 35mm color slides. Art may be offered for sale; 20% commission. Open to artists working in Nebraska, Arkansas, Colorado, Illinois, Iowa, Kansas, Louisiana, Minnesota, Missouri, Montana, New Mexico, North and South Dakota, Texas, Oklahoma and Wyoming.
Acceptable Work: Considers graphics, paintings, prints and sculpture. Maximum size: 2-dimensional art, 84x84"; sculpture, 48x84". "Prints and drawings may be framed or mounted in double-hinged mats with strong cardboard backing. Work mounted in mats must be covered with heavy acetate. Framed graphics must be covered with Plexiglas."
Awards: Presents $1,000 purchase award for best in show; $200, best painting; $200, best sculpture; $200, best graphic.

New Jersey

THE ART CENTRE OF THE ORANGES, Annual Regional Exhibition and Sale, 16 Washington St., East Orange NJ 07017. Contact: Ethel I. Brehm. Annual indoor show held in fall. Maximum 2 entries per artist. Open to residents of New Jersey, New York, Connecticut and Pennsylvania. Oils, acrylics, pastels, watercolors, graphics, drawings, sculpture and mixed media are acceptable. Size limit: 40x40"; sculptures, 24x24"; 50 lbs. Work must be recent and original. Work sent by express or mail not accepted. Awards including both cash and purchase prizes total about $2,000. 25% commission.

ART ON THE AVENUE, West Essex Art Association, 469 Fairview Ave., Cedar Grove NJ 07009. Contact: Vitalia Hodgetts. Annual outdoor show for all media (no crafts) held the first

Sunday in May (rain date if necessary). Closing date for entry: 2 weeks before show. Entry fee: $7 for 8-16' display area. Open to state residents only. Presents cash prizes of over $2,000 plus purchase awards. No commission.

BOARDWALK ART SHOW, 409 Westly Ave., Ocean City NJ 08226. (609)399-7628. Director: Frances Taylor. Sponsors: Ocean City Cultural Arts Center and Ocean City. Estab: 1962. Annual outdoor show held 2 days in August. Average attendance: 200,000. Slides (with SASE) due for prejudging 3 weeks before show. Entry fee: $5 per 12' boardwalk railing; due after jurying. Awards $3,000, cash prizes; ribbons. Art may be offered for sale; 20% commission. Artist must attend show. Considers all art. Base or stand must be provided for sculpture. "For new exhibitors without racks, pegboard sheets may be wired to boardwalk railing."

CAPE MAY COUNTY ART LEAGUE BOARDWALK ART SHOW, 1050 Washington St., Cape May NJ 08204. Contact: Helen Dilday or Winifred Fothergill. Charges entry fee. Awards prizes. No sales commission. Sponsor provides 10' display area. Acceptable media are oil, acrylic, pastel, casein, watercolor and handcrafts.

DEPTFORD MALL PATRIOTS ART BRIGADE, 131 Paradise Dr., Berlin NJ 08009. (609)767-3228. Director: Barbara Reeder and Dory Mann. Estab: 1968. Indoor show held 4 days in April, June and November. Average attendance: 10,000. Closing date for entries: 2 weeks before show. Entry fee: $40 per 12x4' display area. Awards ribbons; judging by a panel of 3 college professors, professional artists and craftsmen. Prejudging by slides. Art may be offered for sale; no commission. Demonstrations OK. Registration limit: 100 artists/craftsmen. Considers all art. Maximum height: 6'. Two-dimensional works must be matted or framed.

EAST BRUNSWICK OUTDOOR ART FESTIVAL, c/o Rosalind Herstein, 4 Phyllis Place, Milltown NJ 08850. Annual show held in September. Sponsor: East Brunswick Arts Council. Entry fee: $10 per 10' display space. Awards $1,000 in prizes. No sales commission. Artist must attend show. Original work only. Judging day of the show.

FORT DIX OUTDOOR ARTS AND CRAFTS SHOW, 15 Grace Rd., East Brunswick NJ 08816. (201)238-0680. Director: Helene Roth. Sponsor: Garden State Cultural Council, Inc. Estab: 1976. Annual outdoor show held 1 day in June (indoor arena available in case of rain). Entries accepted until show date. Entry fee: $10 per 10' display area. Art may be offered for sale; no commission. Artist must attend show; demonstrations OK. Registration limit: 200 artists/craftsmen. Sponsor pays insurance for exhibited work. Considers all art.
Awards: Presents cash prizes for first place and honorable mention ribbons.

HUNTERDON ART CENTER, c/o A. S. Marsh, 7 Center St., Clinton NJ 08809. Chairman: A. S. Marsh. Estab: 1957. Annual indoor show held in March (show also tours for 4 months). Closing date for entry: 3 weeks before show. Entry fee: $9 per 2 entries. Maximum 2 entries per artist. Awards $500 in purchase prizes. Prejudging; no entry fees refunded for refused work. Art may be offered for sale; 25% commission. Registration limit: 100-150 artists. Sponsor pays insurance for exhibited work and return shipping.
Acceptable Work: Considers prints. Maximum size: 36x36". Work must have acetate or plastic covering and be on white hinged mats.

INDIAN SUMMER ART & CRAFT SHOW, 205 N. Montpelier Ave., Atlantic City NJ 08401. Director: Florence Miller. Annual 2-day show held on the boardwalk. Sponsors: Atlantic City Art Center and City of Atlantic City. Entry fee: $20 per 15' display area. Presents $3,000 in cash awards.

M.A.S. NATIONAL MINIATURE ART EXHIBITION, 200 Chestnut St., Nutley NJ 07110. (201)661-2280. Contact: Vivian Fikus. Sponsor: M.A.S. of New Jersey. Estab: 1969. Annual indoor show held 2 weeks in spring. Average attendance: 1,600. Closing date for entry: 2 months before show. Prejudging; entry fee not refunded for refused work. Art may be offered for sale; 30% commission. Open to artists ages 18+. Sponsor provides display panels and equipment. Considers all art. Paintings must be framed in wood or matted with ¼" plywood backing. No erotica. Maximum size: 10x10".

NATIONAL BOARDWALK PROFESSIONAL ART SHOW, 205 N. Montpelier Ave., Atlantic City NJ 08401. Director: Florence Miller. Annual 2-day show held on Father's Day

Weekend on the boardwalk. Sponsors: City of Atlantic City and the Boardwalk Division, Chamber of Commerce. Entry fee: $20 per 15' display area. Awards $3,000 in cash prizes. Considers all media (no crafts).

NEW JERSEY STATE ART EXHIBITION, 18 Claremont Rd., Bernardsville NJ 07924. Exhibition Chairman: Rita Fritz. Sponsor: Somerset Art Association. Open to New Jersey artists. Categories include oils, watercolors, mixed media, graphics, sculpture and portraits. Maximum Size: 48"x7'; 75 lbs. Entry fee: $6. Maximum 2 entries per artist. Awards $1,500 in cash prizes. 15% sales commission.

POINT PLEASANT SUMMER ART FESTIVAL, 517 Arnold Ave., Point Pleasant NJ 08742. Sponsors: Greater Point Pleasant Area Chamber of Commerce and the Borough of Point Pleasant Beach, New Jersey. Categories: 1. Oil, Acrylic treated as oil. 2. Watercolor, Acrylic treated as watercolor. 3. Drawing and Graphics: pen and ink, charcoal, print making, photography. 4. Mixed Media. Original work only. Entry fee: $10 per 10' display area. Maximum 1 artist per area. Presents cash awards and ribbons; 1 award per artist.

WEST NEW YORK RIVERSIDE ART SHOW, 425 60th St., West New York NJ 07093. (201)861-7000. Director: John Montrone. Sponsor: Mayor's Cultural Council. Estab: 1972. Annual outdoor show held 1 day in June. Average attendance: 7,000. Closing date for entry: 2 weeks before show. Entry fee: $10 per 10x10' display area. Art may be offered for sale; no commission. Open to artists ages 18+. Artist must attend show; no demonstrations. Registration limit: 200 artists/craftsmen. Sponsor furnishes fence and insurance for exhibited work. Considers calligraphy, drawings, paintings, pastels, prints and sculpture.
Awards: Presents $150, first place; $100, second place; $50, third place; $250, best in show; ribbons.

New Mexico

ARTS AND CRAFTS FAIR OF THE SOUTHWEST, Box 122, Roswell NM 88201. Exhibitor Chairman: Bettie Lou Cheney. Sponsor: Roswell Jaycees. Annual outdoor show held in May. Closing date for entry: February. Booth rates (including pegboard): 8x8', $35; 8x16', $70. Acceptable work includes painting, graphics, sculpture, mosaics, photography, textiles, metals, jewelry, ceramics, wood, glass, leather, plastic, custom dolls and musical instruments. Artist must attend show. No commission. Entry forms must be accompanied by at least three 35mm color slides or 3 color photos of work per category. SASE. Awards cash prizes for first, second and third places.

NATIONAL ARTS & CRAFTS BENEFIT, 3529 Constitution NE, Albuquerque NM 87106. (505)262-0672. Contact: Tom W. Thomason. Sponsor: Council for Exceptional Children. Estab: 1976. Annual indoor show held 3 days in early May. Average attendance: 10,000. Closing date for entry: 8 weeks before show. Entry fee: $55 per 8x8' display area. Prejudging by 3 slides; entry fee refunded for refused work. Art may be offered for sale; no commission. Artist must attend show; demonstrations OK. Registration limit: 150 artists/craftsmen. Sponsor provides display panels.
Acceptable Work: Considers all art. Maximum size: 8x8'. Artist supplies hanging or display materials.
Awards: Presents cash prizes and ribbons. Judging panel consists of noted artists and craftsmen.

NEW MEXICO ARTS & CRAFTS FAIR, Box 30044, Albuquerque NM 87110. (505)265-3171. Manager: Vicki Macaulay. Estab: 1962. Annual outdoor (booths available) show held the last weekend in June. Average attendance: 100,000. Entry fee: $7.50 jury fee; $60 per booth. Awards $1,000 in purchase prizes; ribbons. Samples due for prejudging in February; no jury fees refunded for refused work. Art must be offered for sale; no commission. Open to New Mexico residents ages 18+. Artist must attend show. Sponsor provides lighting. Considers all art.

NEW MEXICO FINE ARTS BIENNIAL, Box 2087, Santa Fe NM 87501. Division Director: Don Strel. Sponsor: Museum of New Mexico. Estab: 1960. Next show held in 1979. Average attendance: 40,000. No entry fee. Maximum 1 entry per artist. Presents cash and purchase awards. 25% sales commission. Open to New Mexico residents only. All media acceptable. Size limitation: 10x10' and/or 200 lbs. Museum staff hangs and installs all entries. Insurance handled by sponsor.

SMALL PAINTING EXHIBITION (formerly Old Town Gallery), 3401 Juan Tabo NE, Albuquerque NM 87111. (505)293-5034. Director: Jean Rosenburg. Sponsor: New Mexico Art League. Estab: 1970. Annual indoor show held in February. Closing date for entry: 2 weeks before show. Entry fee: $6 per entry. Maximum 2 entries per artist. Awards $2,000 in prizes. Art may be offered for sale; 30% commission.
Acceptable Work: Considers calligraphy, drawings, paintings, pastels and prints. Minimum size (not including frame): 8x10"; Maximum size (including frame): 17x21". Work must be ready to hang.

SOUTHWEST FINE ARTS BIENNIAL, Box 2087, Santa Fe NM 87501. Division Director: Donald O. Strel. Biennial show next held in 1979. No entry fee. Awards cash and purchase prizes. 25% sales commission. Open to residents of New Mexico, Arizona, Texas, Oklahoma, Colorado and Utah ages 18+. Considers all media. Ship works prepaid to Fine Arts Bldg., 107 W. Palace Ave., Santa Fe NM 87501. Works returned to artists collect.

JOHN F. AND ANNA LEE STACEY SCHOLARSHIP, Box 2, Quemado NM 87892. Contact: Stacey Committee. Annual art show. Awards up to $4,000 in cash prizes. Open to artists ages 18-35. Categories: drawing and painting in conservative mode. Submit b&w photos of work for judging.

New York

AD DIRECTIONS, 19 W. 44th St., New York NY 10036. (212)986-4930. Contact: Ray Morrison. Sponsor: Bardo Publications, Inc. Annual indoor show held 3 days in October. Average attendance: 15,000-20,000. Closing date for entry: June. Entry fee: $3.50-20 per entry. Awards certificates of distinction. Prejudging. Sponsor provides display panels, equipment and insurance during exhibit period. Considers advertising art and design.

ALL MEDIA, Burgoyne Rd., #6, Saratoga NY 12866. (518)584-3663. Contact: Kate Brown. Annual indoor/outdoor show held the second Sunday in August. Entry fee: $3 per artist. No limit on size or number of entries exhibited. Awards ribbons and cash. Artist must be present at show. No mailed entries accepted. Considers all media. Paintings should be framed and ready for hanging.

ALLIED ARTISTS OF AMERICA EXHIBITION, 1083 5th Ave., New York NY 10028. (203)355-1013. Public Relations Chairman: Dorothy Stewart. Estab: 1913. Annual indoor show held 2 weeks during October-November. Average attendance: 2,000. Closing date for entry: 2 weeks before show. Entry fee: $8 per artist. Maximum 1 entry per artist. Prejudging; no entry fees refunded for refused work. Art may be offered for sale; 20% commission. "All work must be delivered and unpacked by the artist or an agent." Out-of-town exhibitors should send their entries at an early date to agents W.S. Budworth & Son, or Berkeley Express & Moving Co. (write Stewart for addresses).
Acceptable Work: Considers acrylics, oils, pastels, watercolors and sculpture. Maximum size: 2-dimensional: 60x60"; sculpture: 24x34x80"; reliefs: 40x60". "Oils may be framed, or have stripping or be on stretchers and neatly taped around the edges. No wires or screw eyes. Watercolors may be framed under glass or plastic or matted with strong backing and 2 rings."
Awards: Presents approximately $3,125 in cash prizes, 2-dimensional art; approximately $900 in cash prizes, sculpture; medals.

AMERICAN WATERCOLOR SOCIETY EXHIBITION, 1083 5th Ave., New York NY 10028. Annual show held in April. Acceptable media are acrylics (must be under glass or plastic) and watercolors (must be on paper). Maximum 1 entry per artist. Submit one 35mm slide with label. Nonmembers must also send file card and handling fee. Accepted slides kept for A.W.S. permanent slide collection. Painting, frame included, should not exceed 34x42". Oversized works and unusual renderings may be accepted at the discretion of the jury. Artists residing more than 100 miles from New York City may submit matted picture without frame. Mat must be 24x30" or 28x36". Nonmembers charged $8 handling fee for label to accompany entry. All paintings for sale unless otherwise listed. 20% sales commission. Awards approximately $12,000. In addition, 2 insured exhibitions of 50 paintings each selected by jury for nationwide travel. One exhibition is framed, the other uniformly matted. For information, write Edmond J. FitzGerald, Traveling Exhibition Chariman, A.W.S.

ANDY AWARDS, 23 Park Ave., New York NY 10016. Contact: Janet Musil-Rahtz. Sponsor: Advertising Club of New York. Annual show with closing date for entries in December. No size limits. Entry fee: $10 for print single; $15 for TV/radio single; $45 for campaigns. Entry must have been initially published, displayed or broadcasted during the calendar year submitted.

ART DIRECTORS CLUB EXHIBITION (formerly The One Show), 488 Madison Ave., New York NY 10022. (212)838-8140. Executive Administrator: Jeanne Sarcone. Sponsor: Art Directors Club. Estab: 1921. Annual indoor show held 2 weeks in spring. Average attendance: 1,000. Closing date for entry: 4 weeks before show. Write for awards information. Prejudging; no entry fees refunded for refused work. Open to works published or exhibited the previous year. Considers advertising, editorial and TV art and design.

ASID INTERNATIONAL EXPOSITION OF DESIGNER SOURCES, 730 5th Ave., New York NY 10019. (212)586-7111. Coordinator: Ed Gips. Sponsor: American Society of Interior Designers. Estab: 1971. Annual indoor show held 4 days in July. Average attendance: 2,000. Closing date for entry: 2 weeks before show. Charges entry fee for 8x10' display area. Awards ribbons. Prejudging; no entry fees refunded. Considers calligraphy, drawings, mobiles, paintings, prints and sculpture.

AUDUBON ARTISTS ANNUAL EXHIBITION, Audubon Artists, Inc., 1083 5th Ave., New York NY 10028. Contact: Secretary. Annual show held January-February at the National Academy Galleries. Comprehensive exhibition of contemporary work in all media, regardless of school, style or technique. Considers original paintings, sculpture and graphic arts in any medium, never before shown in an Audubon Annual. Prefers previously unexhibited work. Maximum 1 entry per artist. Audubon Artists' active members in good standing are jury-exempt in their elected class. Nonmembers pay handling fee of $8 (nonrefundable). Send original work; no photos. Sales promoted; 20% commission. Write for prospectus (available in October or early November) containing specific instructions and entry card.
Awards: Presents $3,000 in cash prizes; gold, silver and bronze medals; certificates of awards; honorable mentions. Unpriced work not eligible for purchase awards.

CHAUTAUQUA EXHIBITION OF AMERICAN ART, Chautauqua Art Association Gallery, c/o Director: Myron G. Johnson Jr., Box 23107, Cincinnati OH 45223. Annual show held in Chautauqua, New York.

COOPERSTOWN ANNUAL NATIONAL ART EXHIBITION, Cooperstown Art Association, 22 Main St., Cooperstown NY 13326. Director: Olga Welch. Annual show with 3 categories: painting, sculpture and crafts. "All works must be original and recent." Maximum size: 60" wide, 40 lbs., hanging objects; 48" in any dimension, 200 lbs., free-standing objects. Entry fee: $7.50. Maximum 1 entry per artist. Awards $3,000. 20% sales commission. No work will be listed POR. Ship works prepaid. Do not ship work by air freight or bus. All shipped entries returned collect.

CORTLAND ART LEAGUE, INC., PARK ART FESTIVAL, 39 N. Church St., Cortland NY 13045. President: Jane Zogg. Annual art show and sale. Non-Competitive Section: Entry fee: $3 for Art League members; $5 for non-members, for each 10' of fencing (limit 30'). Considers only original handcrafted work by exhibiting artist. No sales commission; artist responsible for collection of sales tax. Competitive Section: Entry fee: $5 per 1-2 works (paintings or graphics). No work entered should be priced lower than $100 as this is the amount of prizes offered. The Cortland Art League also sponsors an annual craft show.

CURBSTONE ART FESTIVAL, 55 St. Paul St., Rochester NY 14604. (716)454-2220. Director: Jim O'Brien. Sponsor: Downtown Promotion Council of the Rochester Area Chamber of Commerce, Inc. Estab: 1964. Annual outdoor show (some overhangs on stores) held 3 days in July. Closing date for entry: 2-3 weeks before show. Entry fee $20 plus rack charge per 10x8' display area. Prejudging; entry fee refunded for refused work. Art may be offered for sale; no commission. Artist must attend show; demonstrations encouraged. Registration limit: 250 artists/craftsmen. "Artist is required to use our displays where possible." Considers all art except mobiles.
Awards: Presents $1,000 in cash prizes; and first, second, third and best of show ribbons.

FESTIVAL OF THE ARTS, Upper Catskill Community Council of the Arts, Rm. 101A, Old Milne Library, State University College, Oneonta NY 13820. (607)432-2070. Contact: Leonard or Dorothy Ryndos. Estab: 1970. Annual indoor/outdoor show held 1 day in June. Average attendance: 25,000. Closing date for entry: 2 weeks before show. No entry fee. Prejudging. Art may be offered for sale; 5% commission on $50+ items. Open to regional artists. Artist must attend show; demonstrations preferred unless dangerous. Registration limit: 400-500 artists/craftsmen. Considers all art.

THE FLUSHING ART LEAGUE OUTDOOR EXHIBITION, Box 325, Flushing NY 11358. (212)358-0388. Contact: Anna Kraus. Estab: 1957. Semiannual outdoor show held 4 days in May and September. Entries accepted until show date. Entry fee: $15 per display area. Art may be offered for sale; no commission. Artist must attend show. Considers drawings, paintings, mobiles, pastels, prints and sculpture.
Awards: Presents $600, cash prizes; 25 ribbons. Judging panel consists of 3 artists and college department heads.

FRANKLIN TYPOGRAPHERS' PRIZE, Franklin Typographers Inc., 225 W. 39th St., New York NY 10018. Contact: Reuben Friedman. No entry fee. No entry or size limitations. Open to college students. Prize is 4 weeks work with leading designer.

GALLERY IN THE PARK, Cross Pond Rd., Pound Ridge NY 10576. (914)763-5241. Director: Ms. Dru Raley. Sponsor: Pound Ridge Elementary School Association. Estab: 1970. Annual outdoor show held 2 days in May. Average attendance: 5,000. Closing date for entry: 4 weeks before show. Entry fee: $15 per 1 day or $25 per 2 days. Maximum 1 entry per artist. Prejudging by slides; entry fee refunded for refused work. Art may be offered for sale; no commission. Artist must attend show; demonstrations OK. Registration limit: 120 artists/craftsmen. Sponsor furnishes chain-link and snow fence. Considers all art.
Awards: Presents $250, cash prizes; ribbons. Judging by a panel of 3 in related fields.

GALLERY NORTH OUTDOOR ART SHOW, N. Country Rd., Setauket NY 11733. Contact: Sharon Cowles or Marjorie Bishop. Sponsor: Gallery North. Estab: 1965. Annual outdoor show held 2 days in July. Entry fee: $20 per 10' display area. Awards $1,000 in cash prizes. Art may be offered for sale; no commission. Artist must attend show; demonstrations OK. Registration limit: 225 artists/craftsmen.
Acceptable Work: Considers acrylics, airbrush, drawings, oils, pastels, prints and watercolors.

THE HUDSON VALLEY ART ASSOCIATION, INC., c/o Rayma Spaulding, 15 Minivale Rd., Stamford CT 06907. Annual show held first Sunday in May at White Plains. Closing date for entries: 8 days before show. Paid membership includes exhibition fee for 1 exhibit. Fee for non-members is $10. Maximum 1 entry per artist. Considers original oils, watercolors, acrylics, sculpture and graphics not previously exhibited in County Center. Only works done in realistic manner. Maximum width: 60" including frame. 10% sales commission. Exhibitors outside the area may have work handled by transfer agent who will submit work for $25 fee.
Awards: Hudson Valley Art Association Gold Medal of Honor for oil, watercolor, sculpture and graphics; over $1,800 in cash awards; honorable mention in all classes.

NATIONAL SCULPTURE SOCIETY, 777 3rd Ave., New York NY 10017. Executive Director: Claire Stein. No entry fee or size limits. Presents $1,200 in prizes; 3 medals; 2 bronze casting awards. Maximum 1 entry per artist. Open to U.S. residents. 20% sales commission. Considers sculpture.

NEW YORK STATE FAIR, Syracuse NY 13209. (315)487-7741. Contact: Elizabeth Crowley. Sponsor: New York state. Estab: 1950. Annual indoor show held 1 week in August-September. Average attendance: 250,000. Closing date for entry: 3 weeks before show. Entry fee: $3 per 1 fine arts entry. Maximum 6 entries per artist. Awards $1,300 in cash prizes; $500, purchase awards; first, second and third place ribbons. Prejudging; no entry fees refunded for refused work. Art may be offered for sale; no commission. Sponsor provides display equipment.
Acceptable Work: Considers drawings, paintings, pastels, prints and sculpture. Maximum width: 50".

THE POPULATION INSTITUTE, 777 United Nations Plaza, New York NY 10017. Contact: Beth Blossom. Competition concerned with the population problem and related issues affecting the quality of life and human survival. Artists may submit not more than 3 published cartoons or comic strips for consideration. Categories include editorial, magazine and comic strip/panel. Closing date for entry: April 15 for cartoons published between April 1 and March 31 of previous year. Entry forms must be accompanied by the original drawing or photocopy, and a tearsheet of the cartoon or comic strip as it appeared in at least 1 publication. Average participation is 300-350. Cash prizes awarded total $4,100.

ROOSEVELT FIELD MALL ART EXPO, (formerly Woodwill Corp.), 349 Ridgefield Rd., Hauppauge NY 11787. (516)234-4183. Contact: Julianne Williams. Sponsor: Woodwill Corp. Annual show held in Garden City, Long Island in October. Entry fee: $70 for 11 days; $40 each weekend. Original work only. Photos of all exhibited work required with registration. Photos kept on file; no slides. No crafts, velvets, imports, dealers, string graphics, decoupage, plaques or painting on glass. Approximately 10' exhibit space assigned on first-come-first-serve basis on receipt of registration fee. Six portrait artists accepted by special arrangement with the mall through Woodwill.

SALON OF THE 50 STATES, c/o Ligoa Duncan, 1046 Madison Ave., New York NY 10021. Sponsor: Akademia Raymond Duncan. Estab: 1958. Monthly show (October-May) held 2 weeks in New York. "The purpose of the competition is to put together an annual exhibition in Paris covering the great variety of current artistic activity in America. And equally important, it gives every American artist an opportunity to exhibit his work in New York." Works are judged by artists and critics. Those artists awarded the Prix de Paris are subsequently given an exhibition in Paris at the Galleries Raymond Duncan, the largest gallery on the Left Bank. Judges try to include a wide variety of styles in their selection of prize-winners. Pictures may not exceed 28x36", except by special arrangement. Oils only may have taped edges or simple strip edging; watercolors should be protected by thin plexiglas or acetate. Art photography accepted. Entry fee: $15 for 1 or $20 for 2 paintings. Only 2 works may be entered in any 1 salon, but artists may enter as many salons as they wish. No additional expense to winners for the exhibition in Paris unless work is heavier than 2 lbs. 33⅓% sales commission. Entries accepted Tuesday through Saturday, 11 a.m.-5 p.m. at the Ligoa Duncan Gallery. Out-of-town work accepted in cartons only from REA Prepaid Air Express or United Parcel Service or from the NYC art handlers. Work returned collect the same way as received. If sent by parcel post, allow for rewrapping, and enclose return postage, plus $5 handling charges. Categories are amateurs, students and professionals. Sculpture can also be submitted through photos. Send SASE for entry form.

SARATOGA ART FAIR, 126 Woodlawn Ave., Saratoga Springs NY 12866. (518)584-4651. Contact: Nat Oppenheim. Sponsor: Saratoga Springs Arts Council. Estab: 1954. Annual indoor/outdoor show held 1 week in July. Average attendance: 3,500. Entries accepted until show date. Entry fee: $7.50 per 3 entries. Maximum 3 entries per artist. Awards $800 in cash prizes. Art may be offered for sale; no commission. Artist must attend show. Sponsor provides display panels and insurance for exhibited work. Considers all art.

SCHOLASTIC MAGAZINES' NATIONAL HIGH SCHOOL ART AWARDS, 50 W. 44th St., New York NY 10036. Director Scholastic Art Awards: Frank Cass. Artists chosen from regional competitions conducted by schools through sponsors in participating areas.

SOCIETY OF AMERICAN GRAPHIC ARTISTS, INC., 1083 5th Ave., New York NY 10027. Open to all graphic media except monotype. Charges entry fee for non-members. Awards over $3,000.

SOCIETY OF ILLUSTRATORS, 128 E. 63rd St., New York NY 10021. Annual competition usually held in the fall in various categories: advertising, editorial, institutional, book and TV.

SOCIETY OF PUBLICATION DESIGNERS, 23 Park Ave., New York NY 10016. Executive Director: Marie J. Archer. Annual competitions for publications in a variety of design, illustration and photography categories.

TICONDEROGA ARTS AND CRAFTS FESTIVAL, Ticonderoga Area Chamber of Commerce, Community Building, Ticonderoga NY 12883. Contact: Ed Kroner. Annual show usually held in August. Entry fee: $3.50 per 5x10' space. Closing date for entry: 1 week before show. Presents awards. 10% sales commission. Hand-deliver entries. Original work only.

VILLAGE ARTISTS & CRAFTSMEN ART & CRAFT FAIR, Box 292, Hamilton NY 13346. (315)824-1343. Contact: Phyllis Charles. Sponsor: Village Artists & Craftsmen. Estab: 1975. Annual outdoor show held 2 days in September (tent space available). Average attendance: 6,000-7,000. Closing date for entry: 4 weeks before show. Entry fee: $30 per 8x10' display area. Presents 5 ribbons. Prejudging by 5 slides; prejudging panel consists of 1 painter and 3 craftsmen. Entry fee refunded for refused work. Art may be offered for sale; no commission. Artist must attend show; demonstrations on sponsor's invitation only. Registration limit: 80 artists/craftsmen. Considers all art.

North Carolina

ASHEVILLE ART MUSEUM REGIONAL COLLEGE AND UNIVERSITY INSTRUCTORS' (AND STUDENTS') EXHIBITION, Asheville Art Museum, Haywood St., Asheville NC 28801. Contact: F. Thomas Gilmartin. Sponsors 2 annual regional college and university shows: 1 for instructors, 1 for students. Held in April, May and June. Closing date for entry: 10 days before show. Entry fee: $3 maximum per exhibit. Usual number of entries: 3-6 per artist. Awards cash and purchase prizes. 25% commission. Works should be shipped prepaid or hand-delivered. Works insured while in the museum's possession.

DAVIDSON NATIONAL PRINT & DRAWING COMPETITION, Box 2495, Davidson NC 28036. Contact: Herb Jackson. Entry fee: $5. Maximum 1 entry per artist. No size limitation. Entries must be from U.S. address; restricted to living artists. Entries accepted from dealers. Cash awards over $8,000; also an Impressions Workshop Publication Award. 20% sales commission. Artwork may be shipped by any carrier; will be returned per artist's instructions. Sponsor pays insurance for exhibited work.

DURHAM ART GUILD ANNUAL JURIED EXHIBIT, 810 W. Proctor St., Durham NC 27707. Contact: James C. McIntyre. Annual show held in February. Closing date for entry: January 31. Entry fee: $5. Maximum 2 entries per artist. Awards $1,700 cash and $1,000 purchase prizes. Paintings, prints, drawings and sculpture only. No work requiring special display devices accepted. 30% commission on work offered for sale. Crated works must be sent prepaid express. Parcel post entries not accepted.

NATIONAL STUDENT PRINTMAKERS' EXHIBITION, William Hayes Ackland Memorial Art Center, University of North Carolina at Chapel Hill, Chapel Hill NC 27514. Contact: Associate Director. Biennial exhibition held in January 1979. Deadline for entry: mid-October. No entry fee. Awards five $100 purchase prizes. No sales commission. Entrants must be students at an American college or university. Maximum 2 entries shipped in one shipping container by art department. Shipping expenses paid by Ackland Art Center.

NORTH CAROLINA ARTISTS EXHIBITION, North Carolina Museum of Art, Raleigh NC 27611. (919)733-7568. Head, Collections Care and Preparation: Ben F. Williams. Sponsors: Museum and the North Carolina Art Society. Estab: 1937. Annual indoor show held 1 month in late fall. Average attendance: 10,000. Closing date for entry: 8 weeks before show. Entry fee: $5 per artist. Maximum 2 entries per artist. "Three jurors from the art world (artists, critics, etc.) and from museum top-level administrative posts evaluate each work from personal esthetic viewpoints. A consensus is reached on each piece accepted or declined." Art may be offered for sale: 30% commission. Open to residents of North Carolina or non-residents who have lived in the state for at least 5 years. No demonstrations. Sponsor provides display equipment and insurance while work is on location at the museum or on tour.
Acceptable Work: Considers all art. Avoid special installation requirements. No screws, eyes or hanging wire. Paintings must be dry and framed; drawings and prints must be matted and may be framed. Maximum size: 80" square.
Awards: Presents 3 honorable mentions and gold, silver and bronze medals. "Approximately $4,000 in art is usually purchased by 3 organizations which commit specified amounts in advance. Purchases are at the total discretion of the organization and are necessarily award-winning works."

North Dakota

ALL NORTH DAKOTA ART EXHIBITION, Box 325, Linha Art Gallery, Minot ND 58701. (701)838-4445. Director: Galen Willert. Sponsor: Minot Art Association. Estab: 1976. Annual indoor show held month of March. Closing date for entry: 1 week before show. Entry fee: $3 per 2 entries. Maximum 2 entries per artist. Awards cash or purchase prizes. Prejudging; no entry fees refunded. Art may be offered for sale; 30% commission. Open to Minot Art Association members. Considers all art.

Art-in-action, such as this demonstration by a potter at the Three Rivers Art Festival, Pittsburgh, is a sure way to increase sales, according to show sponsors. The Three Rivers show encourages demonstrations in all crafts, from ikebana (Japanese flower arranging) to metal sculpture.

NATIONAL PRINT & DRAWINGS EXHIBITION, c/o Art Dept., Minot State College, Minot ND 58701. (701)852-3100 ext. 363. Director: C. Robert Schwieger. Estab: 1969. Annual indoor show held in February. Closing date for entry: 1 week before show. Entry fee: $5 per 2 entries. Maximum 2 entries per artist. Awards $1,500 minimum in prizes. Slides for prejudging due 6 weeks before show; no entry fees refunded for refused work. Art may be offered for sale; no commission. Registration limit: 75-80 works. Sponsor provides display panels and insurance for exhibited work.
Acceptable Work: Considers prints and drawings. Maximum size: 30x40". Work must be matted or mounted. Recommends acetate covering.

Ohio

ARTS & CRAFTS EXHIBITION, 620 Military Rd., Zanesville OH 43701. (614)452-0741. Director: Charles Dietz. Sponsor: Zanesville Art Center. Annual indoor show held in May. Average attendance: 1,200. Closing date for entry: 3 weeks before show. No entry fee. Maximum 6 entries per artist: Awards $35-40 cash prizes and ribbons. Art may be offered for sale; no commission. Open to artists from Zanesville and within 75-mile radius. Demonstrations OK.
Acceptable Work: Considers calligraphy, drawings, mobiles, paintings, prints and sculpture. Maximum size: 10x8', 100 lbs.

BEAUX ARTS/CRAFTSMAN, Columbus Gallery of Fine Arts, 480 E. Broad St., Columbus OH 43215. Contact: Ann Adams. Sponsor: Columbus Gallery of Fine Arts. Biennial contemporary crafts exhibition held in September and October of odd-numbered years. Closing date for entry: mid-June; date varies from show to show, depending on the Gallery schedule. Entry fee: $8 per 1-3 entries; maximum 3. Awards $7,000 in various media. Open to designer/craftsmen ages 18+ living or residing in Illinois, Indiana, Iowa, Michigan, Minnesota, Missouri, Ohio, Pennsylvania, Kentucky, West Virginia and Wisconsin. Submit slides for judging. 20% sales commission.

BOSTON MILLS INVITATIONAL ART FESTIVAL, Box 173, Peninsula OH 44264. Exhibit Director: Don Getz. Sponsors: Akron Society of Artists and the *Cleveland Plain Dealer*. Artists invited to show for the first time must submit five 35mm color slides. Accepted works include paintings, sculpture, silver and goldsmithing, leather, macrame, drawings, serigraphs, weaving and photography. No handicrafts or reproductions. Closing date: mid-May. Festival limited to 200 exhibitors. Entries mailed in April. Entry fee: $10 for 4x8' pegboard panel — limit 6 panels, minimum 2; 4x4' tables, $20 — limit 3; open lawn spaces, 10x10', $25 — limit 2; open tent spaces, 10x10', $35 — limit 2. Artist must attend; demonstrations welcome. No commission.
Awards: Participating exhibitors select best artist and craftsman in the exhibit. Presents certificate for best of show; first in category; 5 judges' choices in each category; purchase awards.

DAYTON ART INSTITUTE, Box 941, Dayton OH 45401. Biennial show, open to graphics and photography. Only work recently done and not shown previously in the Dayton area can be exhibited. Gives purchase awards. 10% sales commission. Open to Ohio residents. Work accepted will be returned prepaid by the Institute; work not accepted will be returned via express collect. Exhibited work insured by the Dayton Art Institute. Contact Registrar for further details.

INDIAN SUMMER FESTIVAL, Marietta College Art Department, Marietta College, Marietta OH 45750. Art Department Director: Arthur Howard Winer. Sponsor: Marietta Area Art & Crafts League. Annual show open to artists/craftsmen ages 18+. Charges entry fee for 10x10' space. No sales commission. Awards $500 cash and prizes in 2 categories.

LIMA ART ASSOCIATION, 129 N. Metcalf St., Lima OH 45801. Contact: Director. Annual show open to artists living within 75-mile radius of Lima, Ohio. No size limits. Entry fee: $4, students: $5, Lima Art Association members; $6, non-members. Maximum 3 entries. No sales commission.
Awards: Presents $100, best of show; $60, best 2-dimensional; $60, best 3-dimensional; three $30 prizes.

MAINSTREAM '78, Marietta College, Marietta OH 45750. (614)373-4643. Director: William Gerhold. Sponsor: Marietta College Art Department. Estab: 1968. Annual indoor show held 7 weeks in spring. Average attendance: 10,000. Closing date for entry: 4 weeks before show. Entry fee: $10 per artist. Maximum 5 entries per artist. Awards $4,000 in purchase prizes. Prejudging; no entry fees refunded for refused work. Art may be offered for sale; 25% commission. Sponsor pays insurance for exhibited work. Considers acrylics, oils, watercolors, pastels and sculpture.

THE MASSILLON MUSEUM OHIO ARTISTS AND CRAFTSMEN SHOW, 212 Lincoln Way E., Massillon OH 44646. (216)833-4061. Director: Mary M. Merwin. Biennial indoor show held in July and August. Average attendance: 3,000+. Closing date for entry: 3 weeks before show. Entry fee: $3 per artist. Awards $1,500 in cash and purchase prizes. Maximum 4 entries per artist. Prejudging; no entry fees refunded for refused work. Art may be offered for sale; 10% commission. Restricted to residents or former residents of Ohio (must be work not previously shown at the museum). Museum hangs and arranges show, and pays insurance on exhibited work. Considers recent and original drawings and prints. These must be matted or framed and ready for hanging.

MONTGOMERY KIWANIS SIDEWALK ART SHOW, 9399 Shelly Lane, Cincinnati OH 45242. (513)793-4390. Chairman: Harry Henderly. Sponsor: Montgomery Kiwanis Club. Estab: 1955. Annual outdoor show held 1 Sunday in September. Average attendance: 5,000-10,000. Entries accepted until show date. Entry fee: $10 per adult entry; $1 per youth entry. Art may be offered for sale; no commission. Artist must attend show; demonstrations OK. Considers all art.
Awards: Presents $485, cash prizes; $300, youth scholarship; $100 bicycle; 3 grand prizes and 60+ first, second, third and honorable mention ribbons. Judges are local artists and art teachers.

NATIONAL MIDYEAR SHOW, 524 Wick Ave., Youngstown OH 44502. (216)743-1711. Contact: Secretary. Sponsor: Butler Institute of American Art. Estab: 1919. Annual indoor show held July-August. Average attendance: 25,000. Closing date for entry: 4 weeks before show. Entry fee: $8 per 1-2 entries; $4 per shipped crate or box. Maximum 2 entries (only 1 can be hung) per artist. Prejudging; no entry fees refunded for refused work. Art may be offered for sale; 10% commission. Considers airbrush, acrylic, oil and watercolor paintings.
Awards: Presents $7,500 maximum, purchase awards; $1,000, cash prizes and medals for first, second and third places; $200 Strathmore Award for outstanding painting. Purchase prize jury consists of Butler Institute directors.

SALT FORK ARTS AND CRAFTS FESTIVAL, 910 Wheeling Ave., Cambridge OH 43725. (614)432-3943. Chairman: Grant Hafley. Sponsor: Ohio Arts and Crafts Foundation. Estab: 1969. Annual outdoor show held 3 days in August (pavilion and tent space provided). Average attendance: 65,000. Closing date for entry: mid-May. Entry fee: $32 per 10x10' outdoor display or 8' indoor table. Prejudging; entry fee due after jurying. Awards $400 in cash prizes. Art may be offered for sale; no commission. Open to Ohio artists/craftsmen. Artist must attend show; 3 daily demonstrations required. Registration limit: 200 artists/craftsmen. Sponsor furnishes snow fencing and pegboard. Considers all art.

SUMMERFAIR, INC., 999 Hill St., Cincinnati OH 45202. Contact: Director. Annual outdoor exhibit held the first weekend in June. Closing date in March. Entry fee: $20 per display area. Awards approximately $1,000 in prizes distributed among all categories. No sales commission. Prejudging by slides. Considers variety of media.

TOLEDO AREA ARTISTS ANNUAL EXHIBITION, The Toledo Museum of Art, Box 1013, Toledo OH 43697. Sponsor: Toledo Federation of Art Societies, Inc. Residents of the following Ohio and Michigan counties eligible: Ohio — Allen, Defiance, Fulton, Hancock, Henry, Lucas, Ottawa, Paulding, Putnam, Sandusky, Seneca, Van Wert, Williams, Wood and Wyandot; Michigan — Lenawee and Monroe. Original work completed within 2 years only. Work accepted in previous TAA exhibition not eligible. Acceptable media include oils, synthetics, mixed media, watercolors, gouache, drawings, prints, sculpture, mosaic tile, pottery, porcelain, jewelry, textiles, metalwork, enameling, woodwork and glass. Sales managed by Federation Sales Committee. 15% commission; no commission on purchase awards. Entry fee: $5 per artist. 3 entries accepted regardless of medium.
Awards: 4 first awards ($200); 4 second awards ($100); and 4 third awards ($50); $100 award

for outstanding painting; a medal for best painting, graphic or sculpture; a medal for best craft; purchase awards for the permanent Collection of the Toledo Federation of Art Societies administered by the Toledo Museum of Art.

TOLEDO FESTIVAL OF THE ARTS, 5403 Elmer Dr., Toledo OH 43560. (419)536-8365. Coordinator: Barbara States. Sponsors: Crosby Gardens Board, Toledo Artists Club, Garden Club Forum, Greater Toledo Arts Commission and Toledo's Forestry Division. Estab: 1965. Annual outdoor show held 2 days in June (covered booths provided). Average attendance: 40,000. Closing date for entry: 1 week before show. Entry fee: $40 per booth; $10 per table or easel. Prejudging by "slides or photos acceptable; presentation by the artist preferred." Entry fee refunded for refused work. Art may be offered for sale; no commission. Artist must attend show; demonstrations encouraged. Registration limit: 350 artists/craftsmen. Considers all art. Easels and tables must be draped.
Awards: Presents ten $25 first prizes; $500 purchase award; 10 second place; 10 third place and 10 honorable mention ribbons. Jurying done by 1 member of each sponsor.

WESTERVILLE MUSIC & ARTS FESTIVAL, 5 W. College Ave., Westerville OH 43081. (614)882-8917. Chairman: Doris Hoffman. Sponsor: Chamber of Commerce. Estab: 1974. Annual outdoor show held 1 Sunday in July. Average attendance: 25,000. Closing date for entry: 2 weeks before show. Entry fee: $8 per amateur entry; $10 per professional entry. Awards $1,000+, cash prizes; $700+, purchase awards; ribbons. Prejudging; entry fee refunded for refused work. Art may be offered for sale; no commission. Artist must attend show; demonstrations encouraged. Registration limit: 200 artists/craftsmen. Considers all art.

WESTLAND ARTS AND CRAFTS SHOW, 4273 Westland Mall, Columbus OH 43228. Contact: Dennis Adams. Annual show sponsored by the Westland Shopping Center. Entry fee: $20. Awards $750 in prizes. Space provided each exhibitor is two 5x7' panels of the 6 sides of an art rack. Additional space available at $20. One artist per space. Original work only. No sales commission.

Oklahoma

OKLAHOMA CITY FESTIVAL OF THE ARTS, 3014 Paseo, Oklahoma City OK 73103. (405)521-1426. Staff Festival Coordinator: Jackie Jones. Sponsor: Arts Council of Oklahoma City, Inc. Estab: 1967. Annual 6-day April show held in tents. Average attendance: 200,000. "Jurying of work occurs in January prior to the show." Entry fee: $50 per 6x8' panel or $200 per 8x8' tent. Awards purchase prizes. Maximum 10 slides for prejudging. Art must be offered for sale; 20% commission (with entry fee used as offset). Artist must attend show; demonstrations encouraged. "The only requirement we have on demonstrations is that the safety of the audience is considered. For instance, provide a protective shield if you're working with metal sculpture." Sponsor provides 184 visual arts panels, 24 tents and approximately 80 spaces at a street market. Display panels are provided for visual arts panels and tents; not for street market. Considers all art. "Since this is a family, community arts council, work should be acceptable in that environment."

Oregon

ALBANY SPRING ARTS FESTIVAL, Box 841, Albany OR 97321. (503)928-2815. Director: Terri Hopkins. Sponsor: Creative Arts Guild. Estab: 1969. Annual indoor/outdoor show held 2 days in early May. Average attendance: 20,000. Closing date for entry: 1 week before show. No entry fee. Maximum 2 entries per artist. Awards ribbons. Art may be offered for sale; 20% commission. Open to residents of Mid Wilamette Valley.
Acceptable Work: Two-dimensional art must be framed and wired. "Please specify 'which end is up' on paintings and sculpture if not obvious."

NOVEMBER ART SHOW, 515 Market Ave., Coos Bay OR 97420. (503)267-3901. Director: Maggie Karl. Sponsor: Coos Art Museum. Estab: 1966. Annual indoor show held the month of November. Average attendance: 5,000. Closing date for entry: 4 weeks before show. Entry fee: $7.50 per person. Maximum 2 entries per artist. Awards ten $100 cash prizes. Prejudging; no entry fees refunded for refused work. Art may be offered for sale; 25% commission. Considers all art created within the last year.

Pennsylvania

ALLENTOWN ART MUSEUM JURIED EXHIBITION, Box 117, Allentown PA 18105. (215)432-4333. Director: Richard N. Gregg. Estab: 1963. Annual indoor show held 6 weeks in May-June. Average attendance: 25,000. Closing date for entry: early April. Entry fee: $15 per entry. Maximum 2 entries per artist. Awards winner with one-man show. Prejudging; no entry fees refunded for refused work. Art may be offered for sale; 10% commission. Open to museum members. Sponsor furnishes display equipment. Considers all art. Maximum size: 6x6', 500 lbs.

CENTRE SQUARE ART FAIR, Downtown Improvement Group, Alpha Bldg., Easton PA 18042. (215)258-2881. Director: Liz John. Estab: 1965. Annual outdoor show held 1 Saturday in September. Average attendance: 5,000. Closing date for entries: 2 weeks before show. Entry fee: $7 per 10' display area. Awards: $500+ and ribbons. Art may be offered for sale. Artist must attend show; demonstrations encouraged. Registration limit: 200 artists/craftsmen. Considers all art.

HAZLETON CREATIVE ARTS FESTIVAL, Greater Hazleton Fine Arts Council, Northeast Bank Bldg., Hazleton PA 18201. (717)454-4049. Contact: Alice Laputka. Estab: 1965. Annual indoor show held Mother's Day weekend. Average attendance: 5,000. Closing date for entry: 2 weeks before show. Entry fee: $5 per 2 entries. Maximum 2 entries per artist. Prejudging; no entry fees refunded for refused work. Art may be offered for sale; no commission. Work must have been created within last 18 months and not previously entered. Sponsor provides pedestals and pins. Also sponsors Sidewalk Sale.
Acceptable Work: Considers all art. Maximum size: 4x5'. Two-dimensional work must be wired and framed.
Awards: Presents $255, cash prizes; $200, purchase award; merchandise awards if donated. Judges are professional artists and craftsmen.

LEWISBURG CRAFT FAIR, Box 532, Lewisburg PA 17837. (717)524-7006. Director: David Bussard. Estab: 1973. Annual indoor show held 3 days in October. Average attendance: 8,000. Closing date for entry: June. Entry fee: $45 per 9x7' display area. Awards $50 in cash prizes. Prejudging; entry fee refunded for refused work. Art may be offered for sale; no commission. Artist must attend show; demonstrations encouraged. Registration limit: 75 artists/craftsmen. Considers all art.

POCONO ART & CRAFTS FESTIVAL, Box 476, East Stroudsburg PA 18301. Chairman: Robert Gibson. Sponsors: Notre Dame and St. Matthews school PTA. Estab: 1975. Annual indoor/outdoor show held 3 days in September. Average attendance: 6,000. Closing date for entry: 4 weeks before show. Entry fee: $25 per outdoor/$30 per indoor 8x10' display area. Awards $1,200 in cash prizes; ribbons. Prejudging; entry fee refunded for refused work. Art must be offered for sale; no commission. Artist must attend show; demonstrations OK. Registration limit: 75-100 artists/craftsmen. Considers all art.

THE PRINT CLUB, 1614 Latimer St., Philadelphia PA 19103. Contact: Nancy Boylen. Annual Members Juried Exhibition held in December. Open to members of Print Club ($12.50 annual fee). No entry fee. Maximum 2 entries per artist; no size limit. All fine print media except monotypes eligible. Awards $50-500 in purchase prizes. 33 1/3% sales commission. All work insured while on exhibit.

REGIONAL ART EXHIBITION, 438 W. Broad St., Hazleton PA 18201. (717)454-5333. Chairman: E. Ruth Howe. Sponsor: Hazleton Art League. Estab: 1954. Annual indoor show held 2 weeks in April. Average attendance: 600. Closing date for entry: 2 weeks before show. Entry fee: $7 per 1 entry; $3 per additional entry. Awards cash, purchase prizes and ribbons. Maximum 3 entries per artist. Prejudging; no entry fees refunded for refused work. Art may be offered for sale; 20% commission. Open to artists living within 100-mile radius of Hazleton. Sponsor provides display panels and insurance (up to $300 per entry) for shipping to show and exhibited work. Hand-deliver work.
Acceptable Work: Considers paintings, sculpture, drawings and graphics. Maximum size: 45"x6'; 50 lbs. Work must be framed or have base. "In order to create a balanced show with a variety of media, subject matter and styles, sometimes good work will be rejected."

SUMMER ARTS AND CRAFTS FESTIVAL-SUSQUEHANNA, c/o Jeanne Rodriguez, Lanesboro PA 18827. (717)853-4625. Sponsor: Susquehanna Junior Club. Estab: 1969.

Annual outdoor show held 1 day in July. Average attendance: 8,000. Entries accepted until show date. Entry fee: $6 preregistration fee; $5 per 10x4' display area. Awards cash and ribbons. Art may be offered for sale. Artist must attend show; demonstrations encouraged. Considers all art.

THREE RIVERS ARTS FESTIVAL, 4400 Forbes Ave., Pittsburgh PA 15213. (412)687-7014. Contact: Barbara Widdoes or Paula Atlas. Sponsor: Carnegie Institute. Estab: 1960. Annual outdoor show held 10 days in May-June (limited covering available for paintings and prints). Average attendance: 200,000. Closing date for entry: April 1. Entry fee: $6 per entry. Awards cash and purchase prizes. Prejudging by slides; no entry fees refunded for refused work. Art must be offered for sale; 25% commission. Open to artists ages 18+. Demonstrations OK. Sponsor furnishes 7x4' display panels. Artist must deliver work personally.
Acceptable Work: Considers all art "not previously exhibited at the Festival." Two-dimensional work must be framed and ready for hanging. Sculpture must have stand or base. Hand-pulled prints only.

WASHINGTON & JEFFERSON NATIONAL PAINTING SHOW, Washington and Jefferson College, Washington PA 15301. (412)222-4400. Chairman: Paul Edwards. Sponsor: Arts Festival Committee. Estab: 1968. Annual indoor show held in March or April. Average attendance: 3,000. Slides due for prejudging in January. Entry fee: $3 per 1-2 entries. Maximum 2 entries per artist. Awards $1,500 in cash or purchase awards (judge decides); $250, purchase awards. No entry fees refunded for refused work. Art may be offered for sale; 10% commission. Open to artists ages 18+. Sponsor provides display equipment, insurance for exhibited work and shipping to artist.
Acceptable Work: Considers paintings in any permanent media. Maximum size: 54x72". Work must be framed; no glass.

Rhode Island

PROVIDENCE ART CLUB EXHIBITIONS, 11 Thomas St., Providence RI 02903. Contact: Marjory Dalenius. Usually sponsors 3 shows a season — September to July. Open to New England artists. Other exhibitions for members only.

SOUTH COUNTY ART ANNUAL, 1319 Kingstown Rd., Kingston RI 02881. Contact: Helme House. Sponsor: South County Art Association. Annual indoor show held the second and third weeks in April. Entry fee: $3 per item. Maximum 3 entries per artist. No size limit. 15% sales commission. Cash awards total $275. Insurance provided by the Art Association. Considers oils, acrylics, watercolors, graphics, drawings, sculpture, mixed media and photography.

WESTERLY ART FESTIVAL, 159 Main St., Westerly RI 02891. (401)596-7761. Contact: Diane Howard. Sponsor: Greater Westerly-Pawcatuck Area Chamber of Commerce. Estab: 1967. Annual outdoor show held 2 days in July. Average attendance: 3,000+. Closing date for entry: 2 weeks before show. Entry fee: $12 per adult entry; $1 per youth entry; $5 late charge. Art may be offered for sale; no commission. Artist or representative must attend show; demonstrations OK. "We do not accept shipping." Consider hanging batik, calligraphy, drawings, paintings, pastels, prints and sculpture.
Awards: Presents $25, $15 and $10 prizes to adults in 8 categories. Awards $15, $10 and $5 to youth in 3 categories.

South Carolina

FALL FESTIVAL OF CRAFTS, 7737 Nellview Dr., Charleston SC 29405. (803)552-3973. President: Pearl Marangelli. Sponsor: Coastal Crafters, Inc. Estab: 1974. Semiannual indoor show held 2 days in spring and fall. Average attendance: 3,000+. Entries accepted until show date. Entry fee: $37 per 10x10' display area. Awards cash prizes and ribbons. Prejudging; entry fee refunded for refused work. Art may be offered for sale; no commission. Artist must attend show; demonstrations encouraged. Registration limit: 100 artists/craftsmen. Sponsor furnishes table, 2 chairs and insurance for exhibited work. Considers all art. "Framed work sells better."

SOUTH CAROLINA ARTS COMMISSION EXHIBITION, 829 Richland St., Columbia SC 29201. (803)758-3442. Contact: Coordinator. Annual indoor show held 3-4 weeks in spring. Closing date for entry: 1 week before show. No entry fee. Maximum 2 entries per artist. Awards

$5,000 in purchase prizes. Art may be offered for sale; no commission. Open to South Carolina residents or artists having lived at least 1 year in the state. Considers all art. Two-dimensional work must be framed and wired.

SPRINGS ART SHOW, Springs Mills, Inc., Box 70, Fort Mill SC 29715. Director: Stephen R. McCrae. Annual show held in October and open to artists residing in North or South Carolina. Closing date for entry: September. Maximum 1 entry per artist in 1 of 5 categories. Awards $6,000 in prizes. Limited to original works completed in the last 2 years.

South Dakota

BROOKINGS SUMMER FESTIVAL, Box 555, Chamber of Commerce, Brookings SD 57006. (605)692-7171. Chairman: Perry Vining. Estab: 1971. Annual indoor show held the second weekend in July. Average attendance: 15,000. Entries accepted until show date. Entry fee: $1 per entry. Maximum 3 entries per artist. Awards $300 in cash prizes. Art may be offered for sale; no commission. Demonstrations encouraged. Considers all art. Two-dimensional art must be framed and ready for hanging.

RED CLOUD INDIAN ART SHOW, Red Cloud Indian School, Pine Ridge SD 57770. (605)867-5491. Director: Brother C.M. Simon. Sponsor: Red Cloud Indian School. Estab: 1969. Annual indoor show held 2 months in summer. Average attendance: 3,000+. Closing date for entry: 3 weeks before show. No entry fee. Maximum 3 entries per artist per category. Awards $1,150, cash prizes; $1,500, purchase awards. Prejudging. Art must be offered for sale; no commission. Open to Indian artists ages 18+. Sponsor provides display equipment and insurance for exhibited work. Ship by UPS or air freight.
Acceptable Work: Considers drawings, paintings, pastels and sculpture. Oils must be framed. "We judge on good, quality art, need not be Indian in theme; can be modern, transitional or traditional."

Tennessee

DAVID CROCKETT ARTS AND CRAFTS FESTIVAL, Lawrence County Arts Commission, Box 611, Lawrenceburg TN 38464. Contact: Ardythe Craig. Annual show held third weekend in August. Entries accepted until show date. Entry fee: $6, outside; $12, inside. Awards cash, purchase prizes and ribbons. No sales commission. Considers original paintings, sculpture, ceramics, leathercraft, needlecraft, metalcraft, jewelry and lapidary.

EASTGATE COLORAMA, 633 Courtney Lane, Chattanooga TN 37415. Contact: Pat Adams. Annual indoor show sponsored by the Civic Arts League. Entry fee: $10 per artist. Eastgate Merchants Association presents ribbons and cash awards. Commission is 10%. Considers oils, acrylics, watercolors, pastels, graphics, mixed media, abstracts and sculpture. Accepts portfolios.

TUCKALEECHEE COVE ARTS, CRAFTS AND MUSIC FESTIVAL, Box 176, Townsend TN 37882. Chairman: Jean Pullon. Sponsor: Townsend Chamber of Commerce. Annual show held in September. Closing date for entry: September. Entry fee: $25 and $35. Awards ribbons. No sales commission. All art and limited crafts eligible; no crackle art, decoupage, dip flowers, dimensional art, marble figures, plaster art or kit-made items.

Texas

ARTS IN ACTION, Amarillo Chamber of Commerce, Amarillo Bldg., Amarillo TX 79101. (806)374-5238. Assistant Manager: F. LeRoy Tillery. Sponsors: Chamber of Commerce and Fine Arts Council. Estab: 1970. Annual indoor show held 2 days in November. Average attendance: 5,000. Closing date for entry: 3 weeks before show. Entry fee: $50, space with table and chairs; $65, booth with pegboard. Prejudging; entry fee refunded for refused work. Art may be offered for sale; no commission. Artist must attend show; demonstrations encouraged. Registration limit: 150 spaces. Sponsor provides 8' table, pegboard and 6x10x6' booth. Considers all art.

FRONTIER FAIR & ART SHOW, Box 386, Brackettville TX 78832. (512)563-2466. Secretary: Laura Latham. Sponsor: Chamber of Commerce. Estab: 1968. Annual indoor show held 3 days in May. Average attendance: 3,000. Entries accepted until show date. Entry fee: $1 per entry. Awards $100 in cash prizes and ribbons. Art may be offered for sale; 15% commission. Demonstrations OK.

Acceptable Work: Considers calligraphy, drawings, paintings, pastels and prints. Work must be framed and wired.

NATIONAL DRAWING & SMALL SCULPTURE SHOW, Art Dept., Del Mar College, Corpus Christi TX 78404. (512)882-6231. Chairman: Joseph Cain. Estab: 1966. Annual indoor show held in May. Average attendance: 2,500-3,000. Closing date for illustration entry: 4 weeks before show. Entry fee: $5 per entry. Slides for sculpture prejudging due 6 weeks before show; no entry fees refunded for refused work. Art may be offered for sale; no commission.
Acceptable Work: Considers drawings in any media and sculpture. Maximum size: sculpture, 48x48x48" 150 lbs. Drawings must be matted, backed and covered with acetate (no frames).
Awards: Presents $100-250, cash prizes; 150 $100 purchase awards; one-man shows for top award winners in sculpture and drawing.

SALADO ART FAIR, Box 444, Salado TX 76571. Chairman: Gretchen Jackson. Sponsor: Chamber of Commerce. Estab: 1967. Annual outdoor show held 2 days in September. Average attendance: 10,000+. Closing date for entry: 6 weeks before show. Entry fee: $35 per artist per 10x10' display area; $50 if shared. Awards $3,000 in purchase prizes and ribbons. Prejudging. Art may be offered for sale; no commission. Artist must attend show; demonstrations OK. Registration limit: 150-175 artists/craftsmen. Sponsor provides 6x8' rack. Considers all art.

SPRING FLING REGIONAL ARTS & CRAFTS FAIR, Wichita Falls Museum and Art Center, #2 Eureka Circle, Wichita Falls TX 76308. (817)692-0923. Contact: Artist Selection Committee. Sponsor: Guild of the Museum and Art Center. Estab: 1971. Annual outdoor show held last full weekend in April (booths have roofs). Average attendance: 10,000. Closing date for entry: mid-February. Entry fee: $50 per artist or $35 per 2 artists sharing booth. Awards five $100 cash prizes; $500 purchase awards. Prejudging by slides or prints; entry fee refunded for refused work. Art may be offered for sale; no commission. Artist must attend show. Registration limit: 90 artists/craftsmen. Sponsor provides 8x8' display area and pegboard panels. Considers drawings, paintings, graphics, collage, and sculpture. No erotica.

STEPHENVILLE ART SHOW, 1187 Azalea Lane, Stephenville TX 76401. (817)968-8774. Treasurer: Mrs. T.H. Birdsong, III. Estab: 1964. Annual indoor show held 2 days the first weekend in October. Average attendance: 300-500. "Entries must be in by 7 p.m. the day before the opening, so they can be hung and judged by 1 p.m. the following day." Entry fee: $1 per entry (50c per entry in Children's Open section). Maximum 6 entries per artist. Art may be offered for sale; 10% commission. Work must have been completed within 2 years of the show date. Sponsor furnishes display equipment. Watchman hired for the show's duration.
Acceptable Work: Considers all fine art. Paintings must be wired and framed for hanging.
Awards: Presents cash prizes of $105; and best of show, second best and third best ribbons. Other entrants also win ribbons. Judging is handled "by an outstanding artist (non-local) and a professional. At times we have had the head of art departments from universities such as Southern Methodist in Dallas and Texas Christian."

TEXAS FINE ARTS ASSOCIATION, Box 5023, Austin TX 78763. Executive Director: Mrs. John D. Haltom. Annual show held at Laguna Gloria Art Museum. Entry fee: $3 per member; $6 per non-member. Sculpture: 3 views considered 1 entry. Prejudging by 2x2" slides. 30% sales commission. Works must be original and not done under supervision. All media eligible. Paintings must be framed. Size limit: 50" in any dimension. Fragile media (watercolor, drawings, pastels) must be framed under glass. Sculpture maximum 65" including base.
Awards: Presents prizes, cash and purchase awards to $5,000. Also selection of work for Traveling Exhibition Tour.

TEXAS SOCIETY OF SCULPTORS, INTERNATIONAL, 4203 Farhills Dr., Austin TX 78731. Contact: Chairman Membership Committee. Two sculpture exhibits held annually. No entry fee. Open to professional members of the society. Original work only; no student work. Submit resume and minimum of five 8x10" b&w photos for judging. Membership open to professional sculptors. Membership fee: $20 annually.

UNIVERSITY OF TEXAS AT ARLINGTON ART ACQUISITION COMMITTEE, c/o R. Wiseman, Box 19007, Arlington TX 76019. Annual show. All media accepted. Submit slides for judging. Entry fee: $5 per slide, with 3 views for sculpture. Awards $4,000 in purchase prizes. Works accepted prepaid, returned collect.

Utah

NATIONAL APRIL ART EXHIBIT, 126 E. 400 S., Springville UT 84663. (801)489-7305. Director: L. Ross Johnson. Sponsor: Springville Museum of Art. Estab: 1924. Annual indoor show held during April. Average attendance: 10,000. Closing date for entry: 2 weeks before show. Entry fee: $2 per entry. Awards up to $3,000 in cash and purchase prizes. Optional prejudging by slides; no entry fees refunded for refused work. Art may be offered for sale; 20% commission. Sponsor pays insurance for exhibited work. Considers all art.

PARK CITY ART FESTIVAL, Box 758, Park City UT 84060. (801)649-8899. Sponsor: Chamber of Commerce. Annual outdoor show held in mid-August. Closing date for entry: 4-5 weeks before show. Entry fee: $15. Art may be offered for sale; 10% commission on gross sales. Artist must attend show. Sponsor provides display equipment.

PEACH DAY ART FESTIVAL, 24 N. 3rd W., Brigham City UT 84302. Director: Phyllis K. Owen. Annual show sponsored by the Brigham City Museum-Gallery. Entrants must be local residents. Entry fee: $2. Maximum 2 works per artist. Paintings (all media) and photography eligible. Awards $200 in cash and ribbons. 20% sales commission. Deliver work personally.

UTAH OPEN '78, 609 E. South Temple St., Salt Lake City UT 84102. (801)533-5303. Coordinator: Arley Curtz. Sponsors: Utah State Division of Fine Arts and Utah Museum of Fine Arts. Estab: 1899. Annual indoor show held during the summer. Average attendance: 6,000-8,000. Closing date for entry: 2 weeks before show. No entry fee. Maximum 2 entries per artist per category. Awards $5,000+ in all categories. Art should be offered for sale; no commission. Open to Utah residents. Sponsor provides display equipment and insurance for exhibited work. Hand-deliver art. Considers all art.

Vermont

SUMMER FESTIVAL AT FROG HOLLOW, Vermont State Craft Center at Frog Hollow, Middlebury VT 05753. (802)388-4871. Gallery Director: Susan Veguez. Sponsor: Frog Hollow Craft Association. Estab: 1973. Annual indoor show held the month of August. Average attendance: 10,000-14,000. Closing date for entry: 2 weeks before show. No entry fee. Call to arrange interview and screening of works. Art must be offered for sale: 30% commission. Open to Vermont residents (6 months minimum). Write to arrange demonstrations. Sponsor pays insurance on exhibited work. "Frog Hollow sets up complete gallery, displaying all items taken by jurying."
Acceptable Work: Considers oils, prints and watercolors in limited quantities. Must be ready for display.
Awards: Selected works win purchase awards and are placed in the Permanent Collection of Vermont Crafts. Judging panel includes craft center director and 3-5 art-related people from Vermont and other states.

Virginia

BOARDWALK ART SHOW, Box 884, Virginia Beach VA 23451. (804)428-9294. Contact: Chairman. Sponsor: Virginia Beach Arts Center. Estab: 1955. Annual outdoor show held 5 days in late June. Closing date for entry: mid-April. Entry fee: $5 jury fee; $26 per 7x4x3' rail space; $36 per 7x7x4' lawn space. Maximum 2 entries per artist. Prejudging by 3 slides per entry; display area fee refunded for refused work. Art may be offered for sale; no commission. Artist must attend show; sketching demonstrations only. Registration limit: approximately 700 spaces. Sponsor provides chicken wire. Considers all art.
Awards: Presents $1,500, best in show; $200 first, $150 second and $100 third prizes in 6 categories.

LANDMARK ART SHOW "On the Green", Samuels Public Library, 101 Chester St., Front Royal VA 22630. Annual show held 2 days in October in conjunction with "Festival of Leaves." Entry fee: $5 for 8' of snow fence. Awards cash prizes and ribbons. No sales commission. Open to artists ages 18+. Considers oils, acrylics, watercolors, pastels, mixed media, collage and graphics.

PORTSMOUTH NATIONAL SEAWALL ART SHOW, c/o Parks and Recreation Dept., 430 High St., Portsmouth VA 23704. (804)393-8481. Director: Katherine Kitterman. Sponsors: Parks and Recreation Dept. and Chamber of Commerce. Estab: 1970. Annual outdoor show held Memorial Day weekend. Average attendance: 20,000. Closing date for entry: 4 weeks

before show. Entry fee: $13 per 6x8' display area; $17 with wire fencing. Maximum 3 spaces per artist. Art may be offered for sale; no commission. Artist or representative must attend show; demonstrations encouraged. Registration limit: 350 artists/craftsmen. No artwork accepted in advance. Considers all art.
Awards: Presents $2,500, cash prizes; $2,000+, purchase awards; 35 ribbons. Judging done by 3 well-known East Coast artists or art educators.
Special Needs: "Cover Contest" award usually given to an artist who captures the atmosphere of the show in some medium there on the Seawall.

SUMI-E SOCIETY OF AMERICA, INCORPORATED, EXHIBITION, c/o Ann O'Connell, 1341 Woodside Dr., McLean VA 22101. Contact: Ann O'Connell. Estab: 1962. Annual indoor show held 3 weeks in May. Closing date for entry: 4 weeks before show. Entry fee: $7.50 per 2 entries. Maximum 2 entries per artist. Prejudging; no entry fees refunded for refused work. Art may be offered for sale; 20% commission. Mail by UPS, registered, certified or insured mail.
Acceptable Work: Considers Oriental brush paintings on rice paper or silk. Maximum size: 66x66" (includes frame); scrolls, 25x60". Work (except scrolls) must be wired, matted, mounted or framed. No glass unless hand-delivered. No erotica.
Awards: Presents Consul General of Japan Cup; $300+, cash prizes; honorable mention ribbons.

SUMMER ART SHOW, 2302 Pershing Ave., Norfolk VA. Contact: Bessie Schmidt. Sponsor: Chesapeake Bay Art Show. Annual outdoor show held third weekend in June. Average attendance: 5,000-8,000. Closing date: June 12. Entry fee: $10 per 6x10' display unit. Oils, acrylics, watercolors, graphics, drawings, sculpture and mixed media accepted. Cash and purchase awards given. No commission. Artist must attend show. Sponsor furnishes A-frames.

Washington

ANACORTES ARTS & CRAFTS FESTIVAL, Box 6, Anacortes WA 98221. Annual show held first weekend in August and sponsored by the Anacortes Arts & Crafts Festival Board. Entry fee: $3 per category; $2 for ages 12-18. A total of $1,500 awarded in prizes. 20% commission. The festival includes booth exhibits, sales, fine art show/sale, antique show/sale, featured art exhibit, legitimate theatre and music, poetry, and children's activities. Categories in the fine arts show include painting, sculpture, prints, drawings, crafts and photography. For prospectus, write the Anacortes Chamber of Commerce.

EDMONDS ART FESTIVAL, Box 212, Edmonds WA 98020. (206)776-3350. President: Donald Schroeder. Sponsor: Edmonds Art Festival. Estab: 1957. Annual indoor/outdoor show held 3 days in June. Average attendance: 50,000. Closing date for entry: 1 week before show. Entry fee: $3 for 2 entries. Maximum 2 entries per artist per category. Art may be offered for sale; 25% commission. Sponsor provides display equipment and insurance. Artist must deliver and pick up work in person. Considers all art.
Awards: Presents $4,750 in cash prizes. Judging is by professionals in each area.

EVERETT WATERFRONT ART SHOW, Box 2937, Everett WA 98203. President: Pamela Moore. Sponsor: Creative Arts Association. Estab: 1967. Annual outdoor (covered balcony) show held 2 days in July. Average attendance: 4,000. Closing date for entry: 1 week before show. Entry fee: $3 per entry. Awards $2,000 in cash prizes. Prejudging; no entry fees refunded for refused work. Art must be offered for sale; 25% commission. Work must have been created within last 2 years and not previously entered. Demonstrations OK.
Acceptable Work: Considers calligraphy, drawings, mobiles, sculpture, paintings and pastels. Two-dimensional work must be framed and wired.

LAKEWOOD ARTISTS SUMMER ARTS AND CRAFTS FAIR, 5114 N. 45th St., Tacoma WA 98407. Sponsor: Lakewood Artists. Contact: Philip G. Thomas. Annual show held third weekend in July. Average attendance: 100,000. Entry fee: $3 per artist for 2 entries. Size limit: 48x72". Considers oils, acrylics, watercolors, graphics, drawings, sculpture and mixed media. Cash awards total $1,200. Art must be offered for sale; 20% commission. Sponsor provides 10x10' display unit, panels and insurance. Hand-deliver art.

PACIFIC NORTHWEST ARTS & CRAFTS FAIR, 10310 NE 4th, Bellevue WA 98004. Contact: Yvonne Miller. Annual show held last full weekend in July and sponsored by Pacific

Northwest Arts & Crafts Association. Attendance: 150,000. Sales: $275,000. Entry fee: $1.50 per work. Awards $10,000+ in prizes. Work must be original, less than 2 years old and for sale. 20% sales commission. Media include professional paintings, drawings, prints and sculpture; non-professional paintings, sculpture, drawings and prints; film festival for independent film makers; professional photography; junior arts and crafts; craft mall and artists in action. Space for craft mall, $6; artists in action $4.

SIDEWALK SHOW, 89 Lee Blvd., Richland WA 99352. (509)943-9815. Chairman: Jack Hess. Sponsor: Allied Arts Association. Estab: 1956. Annual outdoor show held 2 days in July. Closing date for entry: 2 weeks before show. Entry fee: $15 per artist. Awards display ribbons. Art may be offered for sale; 15% commission. "Items $200 or less sell very well." Artist must attend show; demonstrations encouraged. Registration limit: 200 artists/craftsmen. Sponsor furnishes 10x10' display area, electricity (if pre-requested) and security. Artist supplies easels and tables. Considers all art.

WESTERN WASHINGTON FAIR ART SHOW, Box 430, Puyallup WA 98371. Contact: Dwight Paulhamus. Annual show. Entry fee: $3. Limit of 2 entries. Awards $750 in prizes. 25% sales commission. Original work only, completed within the past 2 years, not previously shown in the area. Open to Washington artists ages 18+. All media eligible; no sculpture. Size limit: maximum, 6x7'; minimum, 8x12". Watercolors, prints and drawings must be under glass.

Washington, D.C.

BIENNIAL AWARDS FOR DESIGN EXCELLENCE, U.S. Department of Housing and Urban Development, Washington DC 20410. Contact: Urban Design Program Officer. Categories: Project Design, Urban Design Concepts and Management Approaches (innovative approaches in use of design process as a management tool). Entries judged on design quality as related to man-made and natural environments, user and community benefits and the physical, social and economic development of the metropolitan area, the central city and the neighborhood. Emphasis also placed on how people organize to solve problems. Publications illustrating award-winning designs may be obtained from the Superintendent of Documents, Government Printing Office, Washington DC 20402. Open to design professionals, builders and developers, local governments, public agencies and community groups participating in HUD-assisted plans and projects.

DUCK STAMP DESIGN CONTEST, c/o Audio Visual Public Affairs, U.S. Fish and Wildlife Service, Dept. of the Interior, Washington DC 20240. The annual contest is conducted for the purpose of selecting a new design for the Migratory Bird Hunting Stamp. The stamp is issued annually and is a requirement for everyone ages 16+ who hunts migratory waterfowl. Eligible media include pen and ink, oil, watercolor, etching or pencil. Design may be b&w or full color; 7x5". Awards an album containing a sheet of the stamps and the winning design is produced by the Bureau of Engraving and Printing of the Treasury Dept. Write for detailed contest rules.

West Virginia

EXHIBITION 280, Huntington Galleries, Park Hills, Huntington WV 25701. (304)529-2701. Contact: Registrar. Estab: 1952. Annual indoor show held 6 weeks in fall. Average attendance: 6,000. Closing date for entry: 3 weeks before show. Entry fee: $5 per artist. Maximum 3 entries per artist. Awards $1,500, cash prizes; $2,500 purchase awards. Prejudging; no entry fees refunded for refused work. Art may be offered for sale; no commission. Open to residents within 280-mile radius of Huntington. Considers drawings and prints. Write for prospectus in summer.

OGLEBAY INSTITUTE UPPER OHIO VALLEY ART SHOW, Oglebay Institute, Oglebay Park, Wheeling WV 26003. (304)242-7700. Art Specialist: Ken Morgan. Estab: 1964. Annual indoor show held 1 month in fall. Average attendance: 1,000. Closing date for entry: 1 week before show. Entry fee: $3, Institute member entry; $4, non-member entry. Maximum 2 entries per artist. Art may be offered for sale; 20% commission. Open to West Virginia artists and those living within 75-mile radius of Wheeling. For insurance purposes, work must be delivered by the artist or an agent.

Acceptable Work: Considers all art. Two-dimensional work must be framed and wired; base must be provided for sculpture. Prefers not to see "extremely fragile items not properly prepared for safe exhibition."

Awards: Presents $1,000 in cash prizes; 12 merit and some honorable mention ribbons. Judging panel consists of college art instructors or professional artists.

RHODODENDRON STATE OUTDOOR ART & CRAFT FESTIVAL, 3804 Noyes Ave., SE, Charleston WV 25304. Director: Eleanor Chandler. Annual outdoor festival held on the West Virginia State Capitol grounds, third Sunday in May. Entry fee: $5 per 6x10' display area. Prejudging. Awards $3,000 in cash; purchase prizes. Artist must attend show. Work must be original, designed and executed by exhibitor.

WEST VIRGINIA STRAWBERRY FESTIVAL ARTS & CRAFTS SHOW, Box 117, Buckhannon WV 26201. (304)472-3020. Contact: H. Gene Starr. Estab: 1970. Annual indoor show held 3 days in June. Average attendance: 7,000-10,000. Closing date for entry: 4 weeks before show. Entry fee: $5. Awards $40 first, $20 second and $10 third prizes; ribbons. Prejudging; no entry fees refunded for refused work. Art may be offered for sale; 15% commission. Prefers West Virginia artists. Sponsor provides display equipment and insurance for exhibited work. Considers all art.

Wisconsin

AAUW ART FAIR ON THE GREEN, Rte. 1, Stoddard WI 54658. (608)788-5356. Chairman: Sharon DeCicco. Sponsor: American Association of University Women. Estab: 1958. Annual outdoor show held last weekend in July. Average attendance: 2,000. Entries or 5 slides due for prejudging April 28. Entry fee: $15 per entry; due after jurying. Art may be offered for sale; no commission. Artist must attend show. Registration limit: 60 artists/craftsmen. Considers all original art.
Awards: Presents $800, cash prizes; $3,500, purchase awards. Jurying by a panel of 3 from area art institutes and university campuses.

ARTS & CRAFTS FAIR, Forest Mall, 835 W. Johnson St., Fond DuLac WI 54935. Contact: Lois Frank. Sponsor: Forest Mall Merchants Association. Estab: 1974. Annual indoor show held 3 days in October. Average attendance: 6,000-10,000. Closing date for entry: 2-3 weeks before show. Entry fee: $12-15 per 10x10' tent display area. Prejudging; entry fee refunded for refused work. Art may be offered for sale; 10% commission donated to charity. Artist must attend show. Registration limit: 70-75 artists/craftsmen. Considers all art.
Awards: Presents 1 best of show; first, second and third place ribbons in 3 categories.

BELOIT & VICINITY EXHIBITION, Wright Art Center, Beloit College, Beloit WI 53511. (608)365-3391. Director: Mary Lou S. Williams. Sponsor: Wright Art Center and Beloit Art League. Estab: 1957. Annual indoor show held 4 weeks in May-June. Average attendance: 800-1,000. Closing date for entry: 3 weeks before show. Entry free: $7 per entry. Maximum 1 entry per artist. Awards $2,000, cash prizes; $250, purchase awards. Prejudging; no entry fees refunded. Art may be offered for sale; 15% commission. Open to artists/craftsmen within driving distance of Beloit. Sponsor furnishes display equipment. Deliver art in person.
Acceptable Work: Considers all art. Maximum size: 8x8'. No student work. Art must be ready for installation. No brackets.

CEDAR CREEK FESTIVAL OF ARTS AND CRAFTS, Box 205, Cedarburg WI 53012. Contact: Kathleen Duerr. Sponsor: Cedarburg Junior Women's Club. Annual art and craft sale/exhibition for Midwest artists/craftsmen. All media accepted. Fine arts and crafts only. Entry fee: $15 per 10x12' booth. Awards $1,000 in prizes. No commission. Write for more information.

HOLLAND DAY ART FAIR "ON THE GREEN", Cedar Grove WI 53013. Contact: Mrs. Robert Klein or Mrs. Carl Winkelhorst. Annual art fair held last Saturday in July. Average attendance: 10,000. Closing date for entry: July 23. All media acceptable. Entry fee: $8, for 10x10' outdoor area. Artist must be present. No sales commission. Trophies and ribbons awarded.

INDIAN HEAD ART FAIR, Wisconsin Indian Head Country, Inc., 3015 E. Clairemont Ave., Eau Claire WI 54701. Show Director: Jean Johnson. Annual show held in March. Entry fee: $15 per 12x5' space; limit, 2 spaces per artist. 10% commission charged on total gross sales exceeding $100. Closing date for entry: previous exhibitors, January; new exhibitors, February. Purchase awards made by local/area firms. Considers paintings (oil, watercolor, acrylic), woodcuts, jewelry (gold, silver, copper, semi-precious stones), graphics, serigraphy, lithography, wood carving and wood turning, batik, leather, pottery and sculpture (metal, wood, clay). Work may be demonstrated. New exhibitors must submit representation of work and current resume to Art Committee. Also sponsors annual Indian Head Craft Show.

KENOSHA ART FAIR, Kenosha Public Museum, 5608 10th Ave., Kenosha WI 53140. Annual art fair sponsored by Friends of the Kenosha Public Museum. Entry fee: $8 per 12' fencing. Art must be offered for sale; no commission. Considers fine arts and crafts; no reproductions, craft kits, or painted bisque ware from dealers.
Awards: $500 in cash prizes; "Kady Faulkner Honorary Awards"; $150 museum purchase prize, purchase pledges, and pledger's choice award.

LAKEFRONT FESTIVAL OF ARTS, Milwaukee Art Center, 750 N. Lincoln Memorial Dr., Milwaukee WI 53202. Artist Coordinator: Barbara Coffman. Sponsor: Friends of Art of Milwaukee Art Center and Schlitz Brewing Co. Annual festival. Media include painting, sculpture, graphics and crafts in fiber, clay and metal. Entry fee: $5 jury fee; $35-50 per space. Awards $5,000 in cash; purchase prize for Schlitz Collection. Prejudging by slides. No sales commission.

MONUMENT SQUARE ART FAIR, 223 6th St., Racine WI 53403. Contact: Helen Hackl. Annual indoor/outdoor show held the second week in June. Closing date for entry: mid-April or when spaces filled. Entry fee: $25 per 5x12' display area. Awards $1,000, cash prizes; purchase awards; ribbons. Slides or samples of work due for prejudging in January. Art may be offered for sale; no commission. Registration limit: 145 artists/craftsmen. Sponsor provides snow fence. Considers graphics, prints and sculpture.

MUSCODA ARTS & CRAFTS SHOW & SALE, 124 N. 5th, Muscoda WI 53573. (608)739-3738. Contact: Barb Thomas. Sponsor: Muscoda Arts and Crafts Committee. Estab: 1972. Annual indoor/outdoor show held 2 days in August. Average attendance: 4,000-5,000. Entries accepted until show date ($1 extra charge if 1 week before show). Entry fee: $5 per booth. Awards first, second and third place ribbons. Art may be offered for sale; no commission. Artist must attend show; demonstrations OK. Registration limit: 60 artists/craftsmen. To register, write after April.
Acceptable Work: Considers all art. "If art is tall enough to block view, please request wall space." Judging by area people knowledgeable in various arts.

NORTHEASTERN WISCONSIN ART ANNUAL, 129 S. Jefferson St., Green Bay WI 54301. Curator of Art, Neville Public Museum: James W. Kreiter. Annual show usually held in late fall. Entry fee: $2 per entry. Maximum 5 entries per artist. Awards two $200 purchase prizes; ribbons; 4-person exhibition. Open to residents (ages 18+) of the following Wisconsin counties: Brown, Calumet, Door, Fond du Lac, Kewaunee, Manitowoc, Marinette, Oconto, Outagamie, Shawano, Sheboygan, Waupaca and Winnebago. All media acceptable. Work must be for sale, under $400. No sales commission. Work must be delivered. Exhibited items insured for 2/3 of the sale price. No 2-dimensional work over 5x5'; no 3-dimensional work over 150 lbs.

OUTDOOR ARTS FESTIVAL, Box 204, Watertown WI 53094. Corresponding Secretary: Sandra Pirkel. Estab: 1965. Annual outdoor show held 1 day in August. Entries accepted up until show date. Entry fee: $5 per display area. Awards $600 in purchase prizes and ribbons. Art may be offered for sale; 10% commission. Artist must attend show; demonstrations encouraged. Considers all original art.

PARK PLAZA ART FAIR, Box 234, Oshkosh WI 54901. (414)233-5050. Promotion Director: Ellen Dillon. Sponsor: Park Plaza Merchant Association. Estab: 1971. Semiannual indoor show held 3 days in fall and spring. Average attendance: 12,000-15,000. Closing date for entry: 2 weeks before show. Entry fee: $15 per 6x15' display area. Awards $500-600 in cash prizes. Art may be offered for sale; no commission. Artist must attend show; demonstrations encouraged. Registration limit: 100 artists/craftsmen. All work must be delivered by artist at time of show. Considers all art.

SHAWANO ARTS FAIR, Box 213, Shawano WI 54166. (715)526-6783. Contact: Sharon Romberg. Sponsor: Shawano County Arts Council. Estab: 1969. Annual outdoor show held 1 day in July. Average attendance: 2,000. Closing date for entry: 2 weeks before show. Entry fee: $10 per 12x6' display area. Art may be offered for sale; no commission. Artist or representative must attend show; demonstrations encouraged. Registration limit: 130 artists/craftsmen. Sponsor provides snow fence. Considers all art.
Awards: Present $100, best of show; $100, palette award; $75, first grand prize; $50, second grand prize; ten $25 and five $10 cash awards. Judge is usually an art professor or museum official.

WAUNAKEE ARTS COUNCIL FESTIVAL OF ARTS, 306 7th St., Waunakee WI 53597. (608)849-5079. Contact: Colette Koltes. Estab: 1975. Annual outdoor show held 1 day in late July. Average attendance: 3,000. Entries accepted until show date. Entry fee: $5 per entry. Awards purchase prizes. Art may be offered for sale; 10% commission. Demonstrations OK. Considers all art.

WISCONSIN FESTIVAL OF ARTS, 1655 S. 68th St., West Allis WI 53214. Director: Dennis R. Hill. Estab: 1969. Semiannual indoor show held in the State Fair Park Exhibition Center. Average attendance: 10,000-15,000. Entry fee: $50 per 10x10' display area. Awards $3,000 in cash. No sales commission. Artist must attend show. Acceptable media includes oils, acrylics, watercolors, mixed media, graphics, drawings, sculpture, photography and crafts. Pegboard display stands provided.

Wyoming

NATIONAL MINIATURE ART SHOW, 1054 Alta Vista, Laramie WY 82070. Contact: Linda Budge. Sponsor: Laramie Art Guild. Annual show. Closing date for entry: August. Entry fee: $4 per entry. Awards $2,000. 30% sales commission. Wide range of acceptable media. Maximum size: 10x12" including frame. Postage and carrier insurance must accompany work to be returned.

ROCK SPRINGS NATIONAL ART EXHIBIT, 1306 Kimberly, Rock Springs WY 82901. Contact: Mrs. Glenda Borzea. Sponsors: Rock Springs Art Guild and Fine Arts Center. Annual show. Entry fee: $4 per entry or 3 entries for $10. 20% sales commission. Prizes include best of show award, purchase award, various cash prizes and rosettes. Considers any original fine art.

SOUTHEASTERN WYOMING ART ASSOCIATION ANNUAL ART ROUNDUP, Box 212, Torrington WY 82240. Contact: Mrs. David Morey. Annual show for painting, sculpture and pottery. Entry fee: $3. No maximum number of entries. Judges award ribbons. Entry fees divided proportionately. 20% sales commission. Maximum size: 240" in perimeter including frame; 150 lbs.

WIND RIVER VALLEY NATIONAL SHOW, Box 26, Dubois WY 82513. Estab: 1948. Annual indoor show held the first week of August. Average attendance: 1,500. Closing date for entry: 3 weeks before show. Entry fee: $5 per 3 entries. Maximum 3 entries per artist. Art may be offered for sale; no commission.
Acceptable Work: Considers drawings, paintings, pastels and sculpture. Work should be ready for hanging or equipped with pedestal.
Awards: Presents $2,000, cash prizes; $500, purchase awards; $250 library award; sweepstakes; and first, second, third and honorable mention ribbons.

Craft Competitions

Alabama

ART & CRAFTS FAIR, Fine Arts Museum of the South, Box 8404, Mobile AL 36608. (205)342-4642. Registration Chairman: Martina Roser. Sponsors: Mobile Art Association Inc. and Art Patrons League of Mobile. Estab: 1965. Annual outdoor show held the last weekend in September. Average attendance: 50,000+. Closing date for entry: 10 weeks before show. Entry fee: $5 jury fee; $30 per 12x6' display area. Maximum 1 entry per craftsman. Prejudging by 3 slides; $30 refunded for refused work. Crafts must be offered for sale. Craftsman must attend show; demonstrations encouraged. Registration limit: 300 artists/craftsmen. Sponsor provides wire if requested. Considers all original crafts.
Awards: Presents $1,000 purchase prize; 20, $100 cash prizes; and ribbons.

ART ON THE LAKE, 1500 Gunter Ave., Guntersville AL 35976. (205)582-4392. Chairman: Mrs. Robert Haden. Sponsor: Twentieth Century Club. Estab: 1962. Annual indoor/outdoor show held fourth Sunday in April. Average attendance: 1,500. Entries accepted until show date. Entry fee: $5 per artist. Crafts may be offered for sale; no commission. Craftsman or representative must attend show; demonstrations OK. Considers all crafts.

ART ON THE ROCKS, Box 973, Gadsden AL 35902. Sponsor: Gadsden Art Association. Annual outdoor show held the first Sunday in May. Closing date for entry: 1 week before show. No entry fee. Awards $25 first and $15 second prizes. Prejudging. Crafts may be offered for sale; 15% commission. Craftsman must attend show.
Acceptable Work: Considers batik, candlemaking, dollmaking, glass art, jewelry, leatherworking, metalsmithing, needlecrafts, pottery, soft sculpture, tole painting, weavings, wall hangings and woodcrafting. Work must be framed or matted.

CHALAKA ARTS AND CRAFTS FESTIVAL, 1705 Springhill Rd., Sylacauga AL 35150. Chairman: Betty Anne Aldag. Sponsor: Sylacauga Area Council on Arts and Humanities. Estab: 1968. Annual outdoor show held 2 days in June. Average attendance 100-150. Closing date for entry: 1 week before show. Entry fee: $15 per entry. Awards $175 in cash prizes and ribbons. Prejudging; entry fee refunded for refused work. Crafts may be offered for sale; 10% commission. Craftsman must attend show. Considers all crafts.

FIRST MONDAY'S ART SUNDAY, 601 Scott St., Scottsboro AL 35768. (205)259-5848. Chairman: Linda Kitchens. Sponsor: 3-Arts Club and Jackson County Arts Council. Estab: 1972. Annual outdoor show held Sunday of Labor Day weekend. Average attendance: 1,000. Closing date for entry: 1 week before show. Entry fee: $5 per entry. Crafts may be offered for sale; no commission. Craftsman must attend show; demonstrations encouraged.
Acceptable Work: Considers batik, ceramics, leatherworking, needlecrafts, pottery, tole painting, weavings, wall hangings and woodcrafting.
Awards: Presents $650 in cash prizes. Judge for each category is from an area college or museum.

HORSE PENS 40, Rte. 1, Box 379, Steele AL 35987. (205)538-5159. Contact: the Musgrove family. Estab: 1962. Semiannual outdoor show held 2 days in May and October. Average attendance: 6,000. Slides or photos due for prejudging 6 months before show. No entry fee. Crafts may be offered for sale; 10% commission. Open to craftsmen whose work is known to the Musgroves. Craftsman must attend show. Registration limit: 100 artists/craftsmen.
Acceptable Work: Considers bonnet-making, mountain candy-making, quilting and woodcrafting. Maximum quilt size: full double bed.
Awards: Presents $100 cash prizes for 3 best quilts. Judging by a craft editor, quiltmaker and 1 Musgrove member.

WEST MOBILE ARTS & CRAFTS SHOW, Box 16243, Mobile AL 36616. (205)344-3750. Contact: Raymond McCoy. Sponsor: Mobile Federal Savings and Loan Association. Estab: 1973. Annual outdoor show held 2 days in May. Closing date for entry: 1 week before show. Entry fee: $15 per 10x10' space. Awards $1,650 in cash prizes; ribbons. Crafts may be offered for sale; no commission. Craftsman must attend show; demonstrations OK.
Acceptable Work: Considers batik, candlemaking, ceramics, glass art, jewelry, leatherworking, metalsmithing, pottery, soft sculpture, tole painting and woodcrafting. "All craftsmen must send photo of work before they will be accepted".

Alaska

TANANA VALLEY STATE FAIR FINE ARTS SHOW, Box 188, Fairbanks AK 99707. (907)452-3750. Manager: Janet Baird. Annual indoor show held in August. Average attendance: 76,000. Entries accepted until show date. No entry fee. Maximum 1 entry per lot per craftsman. Awards cash prizes. Crafts may not be offered for sale. Considers all crafts not shown previously anywhere for prizes.

Arizona

FOUNTAIN FESTIVAL, Box 18318, Fountain Hills AZ 85268. (602)837-1466. Chairman: Mary Read. Sponsor: Chamber of Commerce. Estab: 1975. Annual outdoor show held 2-3 days in November. Average attendance: 5,000. Closing date for entry: 2 weeks before show. Entry fee: $20 per 6x10' booth; $50 per 10x10' tent. Awards $900 in purchase prizes. Prejudging of jewelry by slides/photos; no entry fees refunded for refused work. Crafts may be offered for sale; no commission. Craftsman must attend show; demonstrations encouraged. Registration limit: 130 booths. Considers all crafts.

California

AFFAIRE IN THE GARDENS, 450 N. Crescent Dr., Beverly Hills CA 90210. (213)550-4864. Contact: Michele Merrill. Sponsor: Beverly Hills Recreation Department Cultural

Services. Estab: 1976. Annual outdoor show held 2 days in fall. Average attendance: 3,000-5,000. Closing date for entry: 4 weeks before show. Entry fee: $35 per entry. Prejudging; $32 refunded for refused work. Crafts may be offered for sale; no commission. "We give preference to those demonstrating." Registration limit: 200 artists/craftsmen.
Acceptable Work: Considers batik, ceramics, dollmaking, glass art, jewelry, metalsmithing, pottery, soft sculpture, tole painting, weavings and woodcrafting. All original works; no furniture, clothing or leather belts.
Awards: Presents ribbons. Judging panel consists of local university staff and art professionals.

ART IN ALL MEDIA, Del Mar Fairgrounds, Del Mar CA 92014. (714)755-1161. Director: J. Milford Ellison. Sponsor: Southern California Exposition. Estab: 1882. Annual indoor show held 2 weeks in June-July. Average attendance: 250,000. Closing date for entry: 4 weeks before show. Entry fee: $3 per entry. Prejudging; no entry fees refunded for refused work. Crafts may be offered for sale; 25% commission. Open to southern California residents only. Sponsor provides display equipment. "Deliver art personally or by Bruggers Fine Art Forwarding Service (Los Angeles)."
Acceptable Work: Considers batik, ceramics, glass art, jewelry, metalsmithing, needlecrafts, pottery, soft sculpture, weavings, wall hangings and woodcrafting. No student work. Maximum size: 6x8', 250 lbs.
Awards: Presents $1,300 in cash prizes. Two-dimensional jury panel consists of a watercolor artist, oil painter and printmaker or drawing expert. Three-dimensional jury panel consists of a sculptor, craftsman and ceramist.

ARTS, CRAFTS & INDOOR PLANT SHOW, 10992 Ashton Ave., Los Angeles CA 90024. (213)479-7055. Director: Glen Beckman. Estab: 1977. Semiannual indoor show held in the Bonaventure Hotel 6 days in January and July. Average attendance: 12,000-16,000. Entries accepted until show date. Entry fee: $195 per 8x10' display area. Awards ribbons. Crafts may be offered for sale; no commission. Craftsman must attend show. Registration limit: 140 artists/craftsmen. Considers all crafts. Craftsman should bring his own promotional material and price lists to give to wholesale buyers.

BROCKMAN GALLERY CHRISTMAS CRAFTS SHOW, 4334 Degnan Blvd., Los Angeles CA 90008. (213)294-3766. Program Coordinator: Pat Johnson. Sponsor: Brockman Gallery Productions. Estab: 1968. Annual indoor/outdoor show held 4 days in December. Average attendance: 700-800. Closing date for entry: 2 weeks before show. Prejudging. Crafts may be offered for sale; 40% commission. Registration limit: 100 artists/craftsmen. Sponsor provides inside display equipment and pays insurance on exhibited work.
Acceptable Work: Considers batik, ceramics, dollmaking, glass art, jewelry, leatherworking, metalsmithing, pottery, soft sculpture, weavings, wall hangings and woodcrafting.

CALIFORNIA STATE FAIR ART SHOW, Box 15649, Sacramento CA 95813. (916)641-2391. Contact: William Keefer. Sponsor: California state. Estab: 1948. Annual indoor show held 20 days in August-September. Average attendance: 400,000. Closing date for entry: 4 weeks before show. No entry fee. Maximum 2 entries per craftsman. Awards $15,000 in cash prizes. Prejudging. Crafts may be offered for sale; no commission. Open to California residents. Demonstrations OK. Sponsor provides display equipment. Shipping costs shared by craftsman and sponsor.
Acceptable Work: Considers batik, ceramics, decoupage, glass art, jewelry, leatherworking, metalsmithing, needlecrafts, pottery, soft sculpture, tole painting, weavings, wall hangings and woodcrafting.

CELEBRATION OF THE ARTS, 20600 Roscoe Blvd., Canoga Park CA 91306. (213)341-6434. Contact: Chairman. Sponsor: St. John's in the Valley United Methodist Church. Estab: 1970. Annual indoor/outdoor show held 2 days in May. Average attendance: 2,000. Closing date for entry: 1 week before show. Entry fee: $10 per 10x12' display area. Awards $50 best of show in youth and adult divisions; and first, second and third place ribbons. Crafts may be offered for sale; 10% commission. Craftsman must attend show; demonstrations encouraged. Registration limit: 120 artists/craftsmen. Consider all crafts. Needlework must be framed.

DESIGNER-CRAFTSMAN '78, Richmond Art Center, 25th and Barrett Aves., Richmond CA 94804. (415)234-2397. Curator: J. T. Soult. Estab: 1955. Annual indoor show held 1 month in fall. Average attendance: 3,000. Closing date for entry: 3 weeks before show. Entry fee: $2.50

per entry. Maximum 2 entries per craftsman. Prejudging; no entry fees refunded for refused work. Crafts may be offered for sale; 25% commission. Work must be hand-delivered.
Acceptable Work: Considers batik, ceramics, dollmaking, glass art, jewelry, metalsmithing, needlecrafts, pottery, small and soft sculpture, weavings, wall hangings and woodcrafting. Work must pass through 3x7' door and be easily handled by 2 men. Two-dimensional work must be ready for hanging.
Awards: Presents $1,000 in cash prizes. Judging panel changes annually and consists of 3-5 craftsmen, museum personnel and university professors.

DOWNTOWN CHRISTMAS CRAFTS SHOW, Box 3727, Chico CA 95927. (916)345-6633. Contact: Robert J. Calvert. Sponsor: R. J. Calvert Antiques. Estab: 1976. Annual indoor/outdoor show held 13 days during the Christmas season. Average attendance: 40,000. Entries accepted until show date. Entry fee: $20 per craftsman. Maximum 2 entries per craftsman. Prejudging; entry fee refunded for refused work. Crafts may be offered for sale; 10% commission. Craftsman may rent tables and chairs. Sponsor pays insurance on exhibited work. Considers all crafts.

EHRMAN MANSION ART SHOW & FAIR, Box 126, Carnelian Bay CA 95711. (916)583-6208 or 587-6446. Chairman: Joanna Gillis. Sponsors: North Tahoe Art Guild, North Lake Tahoe Chamber of Commerce and Lake Tahoe State Park Advisory Committee. Estab: 1967. Annual outdoor show held the second week in August. Average attendance: 5,000-6,000. Entries accepted until show date. Entry fee: $5. Crafts may be offered for sale; 10% commission. Demonstrations OK. Considers all crafts.

INLAND EXHIBITION 13 (formerly San Bernadino Art Association), Box 2272, San Bernadino CA 92406. (714)882-2054. Contact: Harriett Ginland. Estab: 1964. Annual indoor show held 3 weeks in October. Average attendance: 2,000. Closing date for entry: 10 days before show. Entry fee: $3 per entry. Maximum 3 entries per craftsman. Awards $700 in cash prizes; $250, purchase awards; 10 ribbons. Prejudging; no entry fees refunded for refused work. Crafts may be offered for sale; 30% commission. Open to California residents. Sponsor provides display equipment and panels. Deliver work by hand or ship by Bruggers in Los Angeles. Considers original batik, needlecrafts, weavings and wall hangings.

MARYSVILLE MALL ART & CRAFT & FLOWER SHOW, 3608 Cinnabar Ave., Carson City NV 89701. (702)883-0968. Director: Bea Griffin. Sponsor: Creative Artists Group. Estab: 1962. Annual indoor show held 4 days in May in Marysville, California. Average attendance: 50,000. Entries accepted until show date. Entry fee: $25 per 10x10' display area. Awards cash prizes. Crafts may be offered for sale; 10% commission. Craftsman must attend show; demonstrations OK. Sponsor pays insurance. Publicity needs: pays $700 for advertising art.
Acceptable Work: Considers batik, candlemaking, ceramics, decoupage, dollmaking, glass art, leatherworking, metalsmithing, needlecrafts, pottery, soft sculpture, tole painting, weavings, wall hangings, woodcrafting and all sculpture.

SAN MATEO COUNTY FAIR CRAFTS EXHIBITION, Box 1027, San Mateo CA 94403. (415)345-3541. Contact: Lois Kelley. Sponsor: San Mateo County Fair Arts Committee, Inc. Annual indoor show held 13 days in July. Closing date for entry: 2 weeks before show. Entry fee: $5 per entry. Prejudging; no entry fees refunded. Crafts may be offered for sale; no commission. Sponsor provides display panels and equipment.
Acceptable Work: Considers original batik, ceramics, glass art, jewelry, metalsmithing, pottery, soft sculpture, weavings and woodcrafting.
Awards: Presents $11,000 in cash scholarships, cash and merchandise or services.

SANTA MONICA ART SHOW, 200 Santa Monica Blvd., Santa Monica CA 90401. (213)393-9825. Contact: Nell Tupper. Sponsor: Cultural Arts Committee of the Chamber of Commerce. Estab: 1967. Annual outdoor show held the third weekend in October. Closing date for entry: October 1. Entry fee: $35 per 8x16' minimum display area. Prejudging; $32 refunded for refused work. Crafts may be offered for sale; no commission. Craftsman must attend show; demonstrations OK. Registration limit: 284 artists/craftsmen. Considers all crafts. Exhibits must be dismantled each night.
Awards: Presents $100, best of show; $50 first, $30 second and $20 third place cash prizes; and 1 ribbon in each catetory.

SOUTHLAND ARTISTS SHOW, Box 115, 29 Palms CA 92277. (714)367-9633. Contact: Lee Pickering. Sponsor: 29 Palms Artists Guild. Estab: 1962. Annual indoor show held 3 weeks in November. Average attendance: 400. Closing date for entry: 1 week before show. Entry fee: $2 per entry. Maximum 3 entries per craftsman. Awards 20 first, 10 second and 5 third place cash prizes. Prejudging; no entry fees refunded for refused work. Crafts may be offered for sale; 25% commission. Demonstrations welcome. Prefers work delivered by hand. Considers all crafts.

SPRING FLING ART & CRAFT SHOW, 200 Santa Monica Blvd., Santa Monica CA 90401. (213)393-9825. Contact: Nell Tupper. Sponsor: Cultural Arts Committee of the Chamber of Commerce. Estab: 1967. Annual outdoor show held the third weekend in April. Closing date for entry: April 1. Entry fee: $35 per 8x16' minimum display area. Prejudging; $32 refunded for refused work. Crafts may be offered for sale; no commission. Craftsman must attend show; demonstrations OK. Registration limit: 284 artists/craftsmen. Considers all crafts. Exhibits must be taken down each night.
Awards: Presents $100 best of show; $50 first, $30 second and $20 third place cash prizes; and 1 ribbon in each category.

THOUSAND OAKS ART ASSOCIATION JURIED ART EXHIBITION, 255 Green Meadow Dr., Thousand Oaks CA 91360. (805)498-8488. Contact: Association Exhibitions Director. Sponsor: Arts Council of Conejo Valley. Estab: 1969. Annual indoor show held 1 month in fall. Average attendance: 200-400. Closing date for entry: 1 week before show (if prejudging instituted this year, slides will be due sooner). Entry fee: $3 per association member; $4 per non-member. Maximum 3 entries per craftsman. No entry fees refunded for refused work. Crafts may be offered for sale; 20% commission. Open to southern California residents. Registration limit: 75-80 artists/craftsmen. Write for prospectus.
Acceptable Work: Considers ceramics and fiberworks created within last 2 years. Maximum size: 2-dimensional, 76x76", 25 lbs.; 3-dimensional, 48"x48"x6', 150 lbs. Coordinated display stand or base recommended.
Awards: Presents $750, cash prizes; purchase awards; first, second and honorable mention ribbons. Judging panel consists of 1 association member and 2 non-member artists, gallery owners, art historians or instructors.

Colorado

THREADS UNLIMITED, 809 15th St., Golden CO 80401. (303)279-3922. Director: Marian Metsoponlos. Sponsor: Foothills Art Center, Inc. Estab: 1975. Annual indoor show held 1 month in June. Average attendance: 3,000. Entry fee: $4 per entry. Maximum 3 entries per craftsman. Prejudging; no entry fees refunded for refused work. Crafts may be offered for sale; 25% commission. Write for awards information. Sponsor provides display panels, equipment and insurance during exhibit period.
Acceptable Work: Considers needlecrafts, soft sculpture, weavings, wall hangings and all fiber arts where fiber is the predominate material. Needlework must be framed; hooks must be provided for wall hangings.

Connecticut

GREAT DANBURY STATE ARTS & CRAFTS FAIR, 130 White St., Danbury CT 06810. (203)748-3535. Contact: Jack Stetson. Sponsor: Danbury Fair, Inc. Estab: 1975. Annual indoor/outdoor show held 3 days in July. Average attendance: 30,000. Closing date for entry: 4 weeks before show. Entry fee: $50 per outdoor/$60 per indoor display area. Awards $1,000 cash prizes and ribbons. Prejudging; entry fee refunded for refused work. Crafts may be offered for sale; no commission. Craftsman must attend show; demonstrations encouraged. Registration limit: 200 artists/craftsmen. Some hanging fence available. Craftsman must exhibit all 3 days.
Acceptable Work: Considers batik, candlemaking, dollmaking, glass art, jewelry, leatherworking, metalsmithing, needlecrafts, pottery, soft sculpture, weavings, wall hangings and woodcrafting.

GREENWICH ART SOCIETY ANNUAL SIDEWALK SHOW, Western Greenwich Civic Center, 449 Pemberwick Ave., Greenwich CT 06830. (203)531-4010. Director: Elaine Huyer. Estab: 1954. Annual outdoor show held first weekend in June. Average attendance: 2,000. Closing date for entry: 1 week before show. No entry fee for Society members; $5 per non-member entry. Maximum 3 entries per craftsman. Crafts may be offered for sale; 25% commission. Registration limit: 250 artists/craftsmen. Sponsor provides display equipment. Deliver crafts by hand.

Acceptable Work: Considers batik, ceramic sculpture, needlecrafts, soft sculpture, weavings and wall hangings. Work must be equipped with screw eyes and wire and be properly framed.
Awards: Presents $600 in cash prizes. Judge is usually a museum director, art historian or nationally-known artist.

NEW ENGLAND CRAFTS EXHIBITION, Slater Memorial Museum, Norwich Free Academy, 108 Crescent St., Norwich CT 06360. (203)887-2506. Director: Joseph Gualtieri. Sponsor: Katherine Forest Crafts Trust. Estab: 1976. Biennial indoor show held in October. Average attendance: 5,000. Closing date for entry: 1 week before show. No entry fee. Maximum 2 entries per craftsman. Awards $1,000 in purchase prizes. Prejudging. Crafts may be offered for sale; no commission. Open to New England and New York state residents. Sponsor provides display equipment. Work must be hand-delivered.
Acceptable Work: Considers batik, candlemaking, ceramics, glass art, jewelry, leatherworking, metalsmithing, needlecrafts, pottery, soft sculpture, tole painting, weavings, wall hangings and woodcrafting. Needlework must be framed.

ON THE GREEN FALL ART SHOW & SALE, Glastonbury Art Guild, Box 304, Glastonbury CT 06033. (203)643-4034. Chairman: Harriett Pfeifer. Estab: 1962. Annual outdoor show held 2 days in September. Average attendance: 10,000. Closing date for entry: early August. Entry fee: $15. Awards $1,000 in cash prizes and ribbons. Crafts may be offered for sale; 15% commission on unjudged work. Craftsman must attend show; demonstrations encouraged. Registration limit: 250 artists/craftsmen. Sponsor provides 12' snow fence per craftsman. Considers all original crafts.

PUTNAM AREA CHAMBER OF COMMERCE ART EXHIBIT, Box 489, Putnam CT 06260. Contact: Gregory King. Estab: 1964. Annual outdoor show held 1 day in May. Average attendance: 2,000-5,000. Closing date for entry: 2 weeks before show. Entry fee: $12, adults; $1, students under 16 years. Crafts may be offered for sale; no commission. Craftsman must attend show; demonstrations encouraged; advance notice requested. Considers all crafts except batik and decoupage.

Florida

ART HARVEST, Box 593, Dunedin FL 33528. (813)733-0004 or 447-6256. Contact: Peggy Mateer or Beverly Skinner. Sponsor: Junior Service League of Dunedin, Inc. Estab: 1964. Annual outdoor show held 1 day in November. Average attendance: 30,000+. Closing date for entry: 2 weeks before show. Entry fee: $15 per entry. Crafts may be offered for sale; no commission. Craftsman must attend show; limited demonstrations. Registration limit: 225 artists/craftsmen. Craftsman provides 12x12" white card with name, space number and category. Sponsor provides 10x12" display area.
Acceptable Work: Considers batik, glass art, metalsmithing, pottery, soft sculpture, tole painting, weavings, wall hangings and woodcrafting. No kits, tile, beads, shell work, velvet painting, knitting, crocheting, furniture, candles, feather work, plants or reproduced work.
Awards: Presents $600, best of show; $300, best in category; $125, honorable mention; $125, people's choice; first place ribbons.

ART IN THE SUN, 2200 E. Atlantic Blvd., Pompano Beach FL 33062. (305)941-2940. Contact: Carole Simpson. Sponsor: Greater Pompano Beach Chamber of Commerce. Estab: 1974. Annual outdoor show held 2 days during the end of February or beginning of March. Average attendance: 15,000. Closing date for entry: 3 weeks before show. Entry fee: $25 per entry. Prejudging; entry fee refunded for refused work. Crafts may be offered for sale; no commission. Registration limit: 250 artists/craftsmen. Sponsor pays insurance on exhibited work.
Acceptable Work: Considers all crafts. No plastic, beads, feathers, kit art or castings from wax or metal molds.
Awards: Present $1,600 in cash prizes, purchase awards and 24 ribbons. Judging by a panel of 6-9 individuals with experience in each area.

BOYNTON BEACH ANNUAL FESTIVAL OF THE ARTS, Boynton Beach Recreation Dept., 128 E. Ocean Ave., Boynton Beach FL 33435. (305)732-2636. Recreation Supervisor: Patricia A. Shelley. Estab: 1975. Annual outdoor show held 2 days in March-April. Average attendance: 10,000-15,000. Closing date for entry: 2 weeks before show. Entry fee: $12 entry fee plus judging fee for Professional Division (subject to change). Maximum 3 entries for

judging in Professional Division, 1 per category for judging in Amateur Division and no limit on general displaying. Prejudging by 3 slides; entry fee refunded to those refused. Crafts may be offered for sale; no commission. Craftsman must attend show; demonstrations OK. Registration limit: 200 artists/craftsmen. Considers all crafts.
Awards: Presents $300, best of show; $225, crafts (jewelry, ceramics, mixed media). Also awards first and second place in Professional and Amateur divisions.

COLLEGE PARK SIDEWALK ART FESTIVAL, Box 7744, Orlando FL 32804. (305)843-4084. Coordinator: Rita Diamond. Sponsor: College Park Merchants and Professional Association. Estab: 1968. Annual outdoor show held 2 days in spring. Average attendance: 75,000-100,000. Closing date for entry: 3 weeks before show. Entry fee: $25 per 10x12' display area. Awards $1,500, cash prizes; ribbons. Crafts may be offered for sale; no commission. Craftsman must attend show; demonstrations OK. Registration limit: 250 artists/craftsmen. Considers all crafts.

DELAND OUTDOOR ART FESTIVAL, Rte. 2, Box 674F, Deland FL 32720. Contact: Joyce N. Campbell. Annual show. Sponsors: West Volusia Artist, Inc. and Deland Chamber of Commerce. Entry fee: $10 per display area. Maximum 1 craftsman per space. Awards include approximately $1,245 in cash prizes. Crafts may be offered for sale; no commission.
Acceptable Work: Considers mosaics, ceramics, weaving, creative stitchery, batik, enameled metal, decoupage, eggery glass, jewelry, leather, shell craft and painted stones.

GREAT GULFCOAST FESTIVAL, Box 12710, Pensacola FL 32574. Chairman: Connie Thomas. Sponsors: Pensacola Arts Council and *Pensacola News-Journal*. Estab: 1973. Annual outdoor show held 2 days in November. Average attendance: 60,000. Closing date for entry: 6 weeks before show. Entry fee: $25 per entry. Awards $1,000 in cash prizes. Prejudging by slides; $20 refunded for refused work. Crafts may be offered for sale; no commission. Craftsman must attend show; demonstrations OK.
Acceptable Work: Considers batik, dollmaking, glass art, jewelry, leatherworking, metalsmithing, needlecrafts, pottery, soft sculpture, weavings, wall hangings and woodcrafting. No general carpentry or any work deemed not original in content or design.

GREATER DADE CITY ARTS & CRAFTS FESTIVAL, Meridian at 7th St., Dade City FL 33025. (904)567-3769. Director: Patricia Burdick. Sponsor: Chamber of Commerce. Estab: 1975. Annual outdoor show held 2 days in spring. Average attendance: 20,000. Closing date for entry: 2 weeks before show. Entry fee: $15 per 10x10' display area. Prejudging; no entry fees refunded. Crafts may be offered for sale; no commission. Craftsman must attend show; demonstrations OK. Registration limit: 200 artists/craftsmen. Sponsor pays insurance on exhibited work.
Acceptable Work: Considers batik, candlemaking, ceramics, decoupage, dollmaking, glass art, jewelry, leatherworking, metalsmithing, needlecrafts, pottery, tole painting, weaving, wall hangings and woodcrafting.
Awards: Presents $1,750, cash prizes; ribbons for first and second place, honorable mention and best of show.

HALIFAX ART FESTIVAL, Box 504, Ormond Beach FL 32074. Contact: Director. (904)255-0285. Sponsor: Guild of the Museum of Arts and Sciences. Estab: 1963. Annual outdoor show (under porch) held first weekend in November. Average attendance: 50,000. Closing date for entry: mid-August. Entry fee: $25 per entry. Prejudging by slides; $20 refunded for refused work. Crafts may be offered for sale; no commission. Craftsman must attend show; demonstrations OK. Registration limit: $200 artists/craftsmen. Sponsor pays insurance for exhibited work.
Acceptable Work: Considers batik, ceramics, glass art, jewelry, leatherworking, metalsmithing, pottery, soft sculpture, tole painting, weavings, wall hangings and woodcrafting. No dollmaking, decoupage or needlecrafts.
Awards: Presents $500 best of show purchase prize; seven $250 prizes; thirty $50 merit awards.

IMAGES — A FESTIVAL OF THE ARTS, Box 2051, New Smyrna Beach FL 32069. (904)428-2570 or 427-5450. Chairman: Holly Bivins. Sponsor: New Smyrna Beach Recreation Dept. Estab: 1977. Annual outdoor show held last weekend in February. Average attendance: 60,000-70,000. Closing date for entry: December 1. Entry fee: $5 non-refundable screening fee; $20 per 12x12' display area. Prejudging by three 35mm slides per category; $20 refunded

for refused work. Screening panel consists of a well-known painter, sculptor, photographer and craftsman. Crafts may be offered for sale; no commission. Craftsman must attend show; demonstrations OK. Registration limit: 210 artists/craftsmen. Sponsor provides electric outlets.
Acceptable Work: Considers batik, ceramics, glass art, jewelry, leatherworking, metalsmithing, needlecrafts, pottery, soft sculpture, weavings, wall hangings, woodcrafting, macrame and copper enameling. No commercially molded ceramics, kit objects, candles, decoupage, beadwork or shell craft.
Awards: Presents $6,000+, cash prizes; $1,000, purchase awards; 32 ribbons. The 2 judges are nationally known.

KEY WEST SIDEWALK CRAFT SHOW, Key West Craft Center, 520 Front St., Key West FL 33040. Contact: Malcolm C. Ross. Annual show held last weekend in February. Entry fee: $15. Awards $1,200 in cash prizes. Prejudging by slides. No sales commission. Considers 3-dimensional wood, metal, glass, fiber, ceramics and leather crafts.

LAKE WALES SIDEWALK ART SHOW, 1117 Yarnell Ave., Lake Wales FL 33853. Registrar: Gwen Burr. Sponsor: AAUW Arts Council. Estab: 1971. Annual outdoor show held 1 day in spring. Average attendance: 1,000. Entry fee: $10 per 12x12' display area. Crafts may be offered for sale; no commission. Craftsman must attend show.
Acceptable Work: Considers batik, candlemaking, ceramics, jewelry, metalsmithing, pottery, weavings and woodcrafting.
Awards: Presents $100 first prizes in 6 categories; seven $50 prizes; $400 in purchase awards; $150, best of show; $100, judge's award; 10 ribbons.

LAS OLAS ART FESTIVAL, Box 2211, Fort Lauderdale FL 33303. Contact: Las Olas Art Festival Committee. Sponsor: Fort Lauderdale Museum of the Arts. Estab: 1969. Annual outdoor show held the fourth weekend in March. Closing date for entry: mid-November. Entry fee: $5 per entry; $50 per 10x10' display area. Prejudging by 5 slides maximum; display fee refunded for refused work. Crafts may be offered for sale; no commission. Craftsman must attend show; demonstrations OK. Registration limit: 239 artists/craftsmen.
Acceptable Work: Considers batik, ceramics, glass art, jewelry, leatherworking, metalsmithing, pottery, woodcrafting, fiber, graphics and mixed media.
Awards: Presents $3,300, cash prizes; purchase awards; 21 ribbons. Judges are usually 2 teaching artists from Florida colleges.

NEW SMYRNA SIDEWALK ART FIESTA, Box 2438, New Smyrna Beach FL 32069. (305)428-9530. Chairman: Arthur Vos. Sponsor: City of New Smyrna Beach. Estab: 1962. Annual outdoor show held 2 days in February or March. Closing date for entry: 2 weeks before show. Entry fee: $10 per entry. Crafts may be offered for sale, no commission. Craftsman must attend show; demonstrations OK. Registration limit: 200 artists/craftsmen. Considers ceramics, glass art, pottery and soft sculpture.
Awards: Presents $150, best of show; $100 first, $75 second, $35 third and two $10 honorable mention prizes for crafts; $75 first, $50 second and $25 third prizes for sculpture.

RED AND SUNSET SHOW, Box 430585, South Miami FL 33143. (305)661-1621. Contact: Rhoda Protko. Sponsor: Chamber of Commerce. Estab: 1972. Annual outdoor show held 2 days in the fall. Closing date for entry: 2 weeks before show. Entry fee: $50 per craftsman. Awards $3,500 in prizes and ribbons. Maximum 2 entries per craftsman. Prejudging; entry fee refunded for refused work. Craftsman must attend show. Registration limit: 200 artists/craftsmen.
Acceptable Work: Considers batik, ceramics, decoupage, glass art, jewelry, leatherworking, metalsmithing, pottery, weavings, wall hangings, woodcrafting, candlemaking, knitting, crocheting and velvet painting.

RINGLING MUSEUMS MEMBERS COUNCIL CRAFTS FESTIVAL, Box 1838, Sarasota FL 33578. (813)355-5101. Chairman: Mrs. J. Kent Bartruff. Estab: 1972. Annual outdoor show held 3 days in mid-November. Average attendance: 5,000. Closing date for entry: 2 months before show. Entry fee: $5 jury fee; $25 per artist. Prejudging by slides; no jury fees refunded for refused work. Crafts may be offered for sale; no commission. Open to Florida residents. Demonstrations encouraged. Considers all crafts.
Awards: Presents $500, best in show; four $200 merit awards; two $100 honorable mentions; $50, best presentation.

7 LIVELY ARTS FESTIVAL, Hollywood Fashion Center, Joy Rubin's Art Emporium, Hollywood FL 33023. Contact: Ivan Rubin. Annual show held in November. Entry fee: $45 per 6x15' space. Closing date for entry: 6 weeks before show. Craftsman must attend show. Awards $2,500 in prizes.

SPRING ARTS FESTIVAL, Drawer 1187, Gainesville FL 32602. (904)372-1976. Director: Karen Beach. Sponsors: Sante Fe Community College, Chamber of Commerce and City of Gainesville. Estab: 1970. Annual outdoor show held 2 days in April. Average attendance: 60,000. Closing date for entry: 6 weeks before show. Entry fee: $5 application fee; $15 per 10x12' display area. Minimum 4 entries per craftsman per category. Prejudging; no application fees refunded. Crafts may be offered for sale; no commission. Craftsman must attend show; demonstrations OK. Registration limit: 200 artists/craftsmen.
Acceptable Work: Considers batik, ceramics, dollmaking, glass art, jewelry, leatherworking, metalsmithing, needlecrafts, pottery, soft sculpture, tole painting, weavings, wall hangings and woodcrafting.
Awards: Presents $3,750, cash prizes; $3,000, purchase awards. Must be 10 craftsmen minimum per category for awarding. Jurying by a panel of community experts in each category.

TITUSVILLE ART LEAGUE ANNUAL SHOW, Box 6133, Titusville FL 32780. Contact: Chairman. Estab: 1964. Annual indoor show held 1 week in spring. Entries accepted until show date. Entry fee: $3 per entry. Maximum 5 entries per craftsman. Prejudging; no entry fees refunded. Crafts may be offered for sale; no commission. Demonstrations on approval. Sponsor provides display panels and 4x6' display area. Craftsman provides display stand for unusual-size work.
Acceptable Work: Considers batik, ceramics, glass art, jewelry, leatherworking, metalsmithing, pottery, soft sculpture, weavings, wall hangings and woodcrafting.
Awards: Presents $300, best in show; five $100 first place; ten $50 merit awards; $1,200, purchase awards; and 38 ribbons. Judges are professional artists.

Georgia

ALBANY ARTS FESTIVAL, Box 471, Albany GA 31702. Contact: Mrs. Parks Jones. Sponsor: Southwest Georgia Art Association. Estab: 10 years. Annual outdoor show held 2 days in April. Closing date for entries: 6 weeks before show. Entry fee: $25 per craftsman per display area. Minimum 4 entries per craftsman. Prejudging; entry fee refunded for refused work. Crafts may be offered for sale; no commission. Craftsman must attend show; demonstrations encouraged. Sponsor provides display panels and equipment; tables/chairs at cost; and "S" hooks for sale.
Acceptable Works: Considers all crafts. All work shown must be original and completed no earlier than 5 years prior to show.
Awards: Grants $1,000, cash prizes; $1,000 purchase awards; nine $100 merit awards.

GOLDEN ISLES ARTS CRAFTS FESTIVAL, c/o Glynn Art Association, Box 673, St. Simons Island GA 31522. (912)638-8770. Contact: Mrs. William Hendrix. Estab: 1969. Annual outdoor show held 2 days in October. Average attendance: 15,000-20,000. Closing date for entry: 4 weeks before show. Entry fee: $20 per 8x10' display area. Awards $1,500, cash prizes; $500, purchase awards; ribbons. Prejudging by slides; entry fee refunded for refused work. Crafts may be offered for sale; no commission. Craftsman or representative must attend show; demonstrations encouraged. Registration limit: 160 artists/craftsmen. Sponsor provides display panels. Considers all crafts.

Idaho

"ART ON THE GREEN," Box 901, Coeur d'Alene ID 83814. (208)664-9052. Contact: Opal Brooten. Sponsor: Citizens Council for the Arts. Estab: 1969. Annual outdoor (booths available) show held 3 days in August. Average attendance: 6,000. Closing date for entry: 1 week before show; booth applications must be in 6 weeks before show. Entry fee: $3 per entry; $15 per 8x8' display area. Maximum 2 entries per category per craftsman; maximum 2 craftsmen per booth. Prejudging; no entry fees refunded for refused work. Crafts may be offered for sale; 20% commission. Craftsman must attend show; demonstrating craftsmen given preference. Mailing addresses vary for different methods of shipping (U.S. Mail, Greyhound or hand-delivery).
Acceptable Work: Considers all crafts (except decoupage) created within the last 2 years.

Maximum weight: 150 lbs. No fragile items such as unfired ceramic or plaster. Entries not equipped for exhibiting will be disqualified.
Awards: Presents $2,000 in cash prizes; ribbons. Judging panel consists of 3 professional artists or art teachers.

ARTS & CRAFTS FESTIVAL, Box 1505, Julia Davis Park, Boise ID 83701. (208)348-8330. Acting Director: Beth Sellars. Sponsor: Boise Gallery of Art. Estab: 1954. Annual outdoor show held 3 days in September. Average attendance: 30,000. Closing date for entry: 1 week before show. Entry fee: $15 per 10x20' display area. Crafts must be offered for sale; 30% commission. Craftsman must attend show; demonstrations encouraged. Sponsor provides picnic bench and liability insurance. Considers all crafts.

Illinois

ANDERSONVILLE MIDSUMMER FESTIVAL ART FAIR, 5344 N. Clark St., Chicago IL 60640. (312)769-0222. Art Director: David Cheesman. Sponsor: Andersonville Chamber of Commerce. Estab: 1965. Annual outdoor show held 2 days in June. Average attendance: 10,000-15,000. Closing date for entry: 4 weeks before show; "entries may be accepted after deadline, but may not be printed in program folders." Entry fee: $15 per 8' display area. Awards medals and ribbons. Prejudging by slides or photos; entry fee refunded for refused work. Crafts may be offered for sale; no commission. Craftsman must attend show; "demonstrating helps sell work."
Acceptable Work: Considers candlemaking, ceramics, decoupage, glass art, jewelry, leatherworking, metalsmithing, needlecrafts, pottery, soft sculpture, tole painting, weavings, wall hangings and woodcrafting.

ART FAIR ON THE VILLAGE GREEN, 9226 N. Kedvale Ave., Skokie IL 60076. (312)674-0088. Contact: Alan Friedlander. Sponsor: Skokie Art Guild. Annual outdoor show held 2 days in June. Closing date for entry: mid-May. Entry fee: $20 per non-member; $15 per member. Awards $500-700 in cash prizes; ribbons. Prejudging; entry fees refunded for refused work. Crafts may be offered for sale; no commission. Craftsman must attend show; demonstrations OK. Considers all crafts.

BEVERLY ART CENTER ART FAIR AND FESTIVAL, 2153 W. 111th, Chicago IL 60643. (312)445-3838. Contact: Pat Murphy. Estab: 1969. Annual indoor/outdoor show held 2 days in June (tent space available). Average attendance: 2,000. Slides due for prejudging May 1st. Slide entry fee: $5. Entry fee if accepted: $15. Maximum 5 slides per craftsman per category. Entry fee refunded for refused work. Crafts may be offered for sale; no commission. Craftsman must attend show; demonstrations OK. Registration limit: 150 artists/craftsmen. Sponsor provides nightguards; 8x12' display area.
Acceptable Work: Considers batik, ceramics, glass art, jewelry, leatherworking, metalsmithing, needlecrafts, pottery, soft sculpture, weavings, wall hangings and woodcrafting.
Awards: Presents $2,400 in cash prizes. Awards panel consists of 3 museum curators.

ELMHURST ANNUAL OUTDOOR ART FAIR, Box 263, Elmhurst IL 60126. Contact: Mrs. A.R. Harmon. Sponsors: Elmhurst Artists' Guild and Elmhurst Chamber of Commerce. Estab: 1961. Annual show held 2 days in July or August. Average attendance: 10,000. Entries accepted until show date. Show usually full by May 15. Entry fee: $15 per 4x10' display area. Prejudging of 5 photos or slides. Crafts may be offered for sale; no commission. Craftsman must attend show; demonstrations OK. Registration limit: 250 artists/craftsmen. Considers all crafts. No kits.
Awards: Grants ten $50 first prizes; 10 first and 20 second place ribbons; and some special awards.
Promotion: "We ask out-of-town exhibitors to provide their own local publicity. For convenience, we use local exhibitors for local publicity."

FELICIAN ART FESTIVAL, 9476 Harding Ave., Surfside FL 33154. Director: Iris Klein. Sponsor: Felician College. Estab: 1972. Annual outdoor show held 1 day in July in Chicago. Average attendance: 5,000. Prejudging by slides or photos (with b&w mugshot and SASE) conducted 4 weeks before show. Entry fee: $12; refunded for refused work. Maximum 1 work per craftsman. Awards $200 in purchase prizes. Crafts may be offered for sale; no commission. Craftsman must attend show; demonstrations OK. Registration limit: 125 artists/craftsmen. Considers all original crafts.

FOUR LAKES VILLAGE ART FAIR, Box 430, Lisle IL 60532. (312)964-6800. Contact: Linda Ross. Sponsor: Four Lakes Village Apartments. Estab: 1968. Annual outdoor show held 2 days in August. Entry fee: $25 per display area. Maximum 5 entries per craftsman. Prejudging of slides or photos; entry fee refunded for refused work. Crafts may be offered for sale; no commission. Craftsman must attend show; demonstrations encouraged. Considers all crafts.
Awards: Grants $650, cash prizes; $2,000, purchase awards; and ribbons. Judging panel consists of professional artists.

GOLF MILL CRAFT FAIR, 3735 Lindenwood, Glenview IL 60025. (312)724-3773. Coordinator: Georgia Collett. Sponsor: Golf Mill Merchants Association. Annual outdoor show held 2 days in early June. Average attendance: 100,000+. Closing date for entry: mid-May. Entry fee: $20 per entry. Awards $250 in cash prizes; ribbons. Prejudging; entry fees refunded for refused work. Crafts may be offered for sale; no commission. Craftsman must attend show.
Acceptable Work: Considers batik, ceramics, glass art, jewelry, leatherworking, metalsmithing, pottery, soft sculpture, tole painting, weavings, wall hangings and woodcrafting.

GREENWICH VILLAGE ART FAIR, 737 N. Main St., Rockford IL 61103. (815)965-3131. Contact: Cheryl Nauert. Sponsor: Rockford Art Association. Estab: 1947. Annual outdoor show held 2 days in mid-September. Average attendance: 20,000. Prejudging by 5 slides and SASE conducted August 1. Entry fee: $2 per square foot; due after jury. Awards $1,300 in cash prizes. Crafts must be offered for sale; no commission. Craftsman must attend show; demonstrations are contracted. Registration limit: 180 artists/craftsmen. Sponsor provides snow fencing.
Acceptable Work: Considers batik, candlemaking, ceramics, glass art, jewelry, leatherworking, metalsmithing, needlecrafts, pottery, soft sculpture, tole painting, weavings, wall hangings and woodcrafting.

KING RICHARD'S CHICAGO FAIRE, Box 432, Lake Forrest IL 60045. (312)689-2800. General Manager: Robert Rogers. Sponsor: Greathall of Illinois, Ltd. Estab: 1973. Annual outdoor show held for 6 consecutive weekends beginning in July. Average attendance: 125,000. Closing date for entry: 4 weeks before show. Entry fee: $110 per 30x30' display area. Prejudging; entry fee refunded for refused work. Crafts may be offered for sale; no commission. Craftsman or representative must attend show; demonstrations OK. Work must be hand-delivered. Considers all crafts except tole painting, but "show is a Renaissance period event and all exhibits must fit into that period of history." Craftsman or representative must also dress to that period.

MORTON GROVE ART GUILD FAIR, Box 391, Morton Grove IL 60053. (312)966-4264. Chairman: Opal Schrader. Sponsor: Morton Grove Art Guild. Estab: 1965. Annual outdoor show held 1 day in June. Closing date for entry: 4 weeks before show. Entry fee: $7 per Guild member; $12 per non-member. May award purchase prizes. Crafts may be offered for sale; no commission. Craftsman must attend show; demonstrations OK. Registration limit: 100 artists/craftsmen. Sponsor provides 10x10' display area.
Acceptable Work: Considers hand-wrought jewelry, metalsmithing, pottery and some woodcrafting.

PARK FOREST ART FAIR, 410 Lakewood Blvd., Park Forest IL 60466. (312)748-3377. Chairman: Robert Wolf. Sponsors: Park Forest Art Center and Star-Tribune Publications. Estab: 1955. Annual outdoor show held 2 days in September. Average attendance: 30,000-40,000. Closing date for entry: 1 month before show. Entry fee: $15 per 12x12' display area. Prejudging by 5 slides; entry fee refunded for refused work. Crafts must be offered for sale; no commission. Open to artists ages 18+. Craftsman must attend show; demonstrations OK with prior approval. Sponsors pays insurance for exhibited work.
Acceptable Work: Considers batik, ceramics, glass art, jewelry, metalsmithing, pottery, soft sculpture, weavings, wall hangings, woodcrafting and other fine crafts.
Awards: Presents $1,100, cash prizes; $2,400, purchase awards; ribbons with all prizes.

RIDGE ART ASSOCIATION ART EXHIBIT (formerly Ridge Art Fair), 2325 W. 113th Place, Chicago IL 60643. (312)233-1998 or 832-7382. Director: Mr. C. Taylor. Estab: 1955. Semiannual indoor show held 2 days in February and June. Closing date for entry: 1 week before show. Entry fee: $15 per entry. Awards cash prizes and 20 ribbons. Prejudging; "if you don't live nearby, 5 slides are acceptable; if you live in the area, however, we require that you appear in person for jurying." Entry fee refunded for refused work. Crafts may be offered for sale; no commission. Craftsman must attend show; demonstrations encouraged. Considers batik and pottery.

STARVING ARTISTS ARTS & CRAFTS FAIR, Oakton Community College, 7900 Nagle, Morton Grove IL 60201. (312)967-5120. Director: Jay Wollin. Estab: 1970. Annual outdoor show held 2 days during Memorial Day weekend. Average attendance: 18,000. Closing date for entry: 6 weeks before show. Entry fee: $20 per display area with 10' minimum frontage. Prejudging by 5 slides. Crafts may be sold for under $25; no commission. Committee of non-college jurors awards 5-6 purchase prizes to use as door prizes. Craftsman or representative must attend show; electricity and equipment provided for demonstrations. Registration limit: 125-150 artists/craftsmen. College has liability insurance and provides security guards.
Acceptable Work: Considers batik, candlemaking, ceramics, decoupage, glass art, jewelry, leatherworking, metalsmithing, pottery, soft sculpture, weavings, wall hangings and woodcrafting.

URBANA SIDEWALK ART FAIR, Box 459, 1212 S. Race, Urbana IL 61801. (217)328-3465. Chairman: Juanita Gammon. Sponsor: Chamber of Commerce. Estab: 1958. Annual outdoor show held 1 day in late June. Average attendance: 2,000. Entry fee: $20 per 8x10' display area. Prejudging. Crafts may be offered for sale; no commission. Craftsman must attend show; demonstrations OK.
Acceptable Work: Considers ceramics, glass art, jewelry, leatherworking, metalsmithing, pottery, weavings and woodcrafting.
Awards: Presents $465 in cash prizes. Judges are professional craftsmen in exhibited categories.

Indiana

CHRISTMAS GIFT & HOBBY SHOW, Box 20189, Indianapolis IN 46220. (317)255-4151. Contact: Thelma B. Schoenberger. Estab: 1950. Annual indoor show held 9 days in November. Average attendance: 100,000. "Show is usually full by September 1." Entry fee: $130 per 10x10' display area. Crafts may be offered for sale; no commission. Craftsman must attend show; demonstrations OK. Considers all crafts.

CRAFTS FAIR AT RIVERFRONT, 1101 N. Fulton Ave., Evansville IN 47710. (812)422-2111. Contact: Jane Moore. Sponsor: Evansville Arts & Education Council. Annual outdoor show held 2 days in spring. Average attendance: 6,000-10,000. Closing date for entry: 2 months before show. Entry fee: $5 per entry; $20 per display area. Awards $500 in cash prizes. Prejudging by slides/photos; no entry fees refunded for refused work. Crafts may be offered for sale; 10% commission. Craftsman must attend show; demonstrations OK.
Acceptable Work: Considers batik, candlemaking, ceramics, dollmaking, glass art, jewelry, leatherworking, metalsmithing, pottery, soft sculpture and weavings.

EAGLE CREEK ARTS & FOLK MUSIC FESTIVAL, 5901 DeLong Rd., Indianapolis IN 46254. (317)293-4827. Coordinator: Bill Taylor. Sponsor: Indianapolis Department of Parks. Estab: 1974. Annual outdoor show held 2 days in July. Average attendance: 12,000-14,000. Closing date for entry: early July. Entry fee: $10 per 10x10' display area. Awards three $50+ purchase prizes. Prejudging of new entrants by 5 slides (include SASE); entry fee refunded for refused work. Crafts may be offered for sale; no commission. Open to professional craftsmen ages 18+. Craftsman must attend show; demonstrations encouraged. Registration limit: 75 artists/craftsmen.
Acceptable Work: Considers batik, candlemaking, ceramics, stained glass art, leatherworking, jewelry, metalsmithing, pottery, soft sculpture, weavings, wall hangings and woodcrafting. Pottery must be hand-built or hand-thrown. No bent bottles, cloth flowers, paper flowers, plastic dipped flowers, molds, manufactured items, kits, imports or agents.

FIESTA, 101 S. 9th St., Lafayette IN 47901. (317)742-4470. Director: Suzanne Stafford. Sponsors: Lafayette Art League and Lafayette Art Association. Estab: 1974. Annual outdoor show held 1 day in September. Closing date for entry: 4 weeks before show. Entry fee: $20 per 10x10' display area. Awards $350 in cash prizes. Prejudging; entry fee refunded for refused work. Crafts may be offered for sale; no commission. Craftsman must attend show; demonstrations encouraged. Registration limit: 60-100 artists/craftsmen.
Acceptable Work: Considers batik, ceramics, jewelry, leatherworking, metalsmithing, pottery, soft sculpture, weavings, wall hangings and woodcrafting.

MID-STATES CRAFT EXHIBITION, c/o Evansville Museum of Arts and Sciences, 411 SE Riverside Dr., Evansville IN 47713. (812)425-2406. Contact: Craft Committee. Estab: 1961. Annual indoor show held 4 weeks in February-March. Average attendance: 10,000. Entries accepted January 6-15. Entry fee: $5 per 1-3 entries. Maximum 3 entries per craftsman. Awards $550, purchase prizes; $375, merit awards. Prejudging; no entry fees refunded for refused work. Crafts may be offered for sale; 20% commission. Open to Indiana residents and craftsmen living within 200-mile radius of Evansville. "No work previously exhibited in this show." Brochure available in December.
Acceptable Work: Considers original batik, ceramics, glass art, jewelry, metalsmithing, soft sculpture, weavings, wall hangings, woodcrafting, stitchery and enameling.

OHIO RIVER ARTS FESTIVAL, c/o Evansville Arts & Education Council, Inc., 1101 N. Fulton Ave., Evansville IN 47710. Executive Secretary: Jane Moore. Show held in April. Closing date for entry: early March. Charges entry fee and sales commission. Awards $200 first, $100 second and $50 third prizes.

WABASH VALLEY EXHIBITION, 25 S. 7th St., Terre Haute IN 47807. (812)238-1676. Contact: Director. Sponsor: Sheldon Swope Art Gallery. Estab: 1943. Annual indoor show held 1 month in early spring. Average attendance: 3,000. Closing date for entry: early February. Entry fee (may change): $4 per first entry; $3 per second and third entries. Maximum 3 entries per craftsman. Awards $6,000 in prizes. Prejudging; no entry fees refunded for refused work. Crafts may be offered for sale; 20% commission. Open to craftsmen living within 160-mile radius of Terre Haute. Sponsor provides display equipment.
Acceptable Work: Considers all media. Maximum size: 72" in any direction. Work must be framed or suitable for hanging.

WOODLAND PARK ART FAIR, 3336 Brown St., Portage IN 46368. (219)762-9280. Chairman: Valerie Simcox. Sponsor: Portage Junior Women's Club. Estab: 1976. Annual outdoor show held 2 days in July. Average attendance: 5,000. Closing date for entry: 4 weeks before show. Entry fee: $15 per 12x12' display area. Prejudging by 3 slides; entry fee refunded for refused work. Crafts may be offered for sale; no commission. Craftsman or representative must attend show; demonstrations encouraged. Registration limit: 75 artists/craftsmen.
Acceptable Work: Considers batik, candlemaking, ceramics, dollmaking, glass art, jewelry, leatherworking, metalsmithing, pottery, soft sculpture, weavings, wall hangings, woodcrafting and macrame.
Awards: Presents $300 in cash prizes and ribbons. Judges are artists and craftsmen.

Kansas

KANSAS DESIGNER CRAFTSMAN EXHIBIT, University of Kansas, Department of Design, Lawrence KS 66045. Contact: William Bracker. Estab: 1949. Annual indoor show held 1 month in fall. Closing date for entry: 1 week before show. Entry fee: $5 per entry. Maximum 1 entry per craftsman. Awards cash and purchase prizes. Crafts may be offered for sale; 20% commission. Craftsman must be resident or past resident of Kansas. Sponsor provides display panels, equipment and insurance on exhibited work. Considers all crafts.

NATIONAL CONE BOX SHOW, Department of Design, University of Kansas, Lawrence KS 66045. Contact: William Bracker. Sponsor: Edward Orton Jr., Foundation. Estab: 1975. Biennial indoor show. Closing date for entry: 2 weeks before show. Entry fee: $5 per entry. Maximum 1 entry per craftsman. Awards cash and purchase prizes. Crafts may be offered for sale; no commission. Registration limit: 250 works. Sponsor provides display panels and equipment, insurance on exhibited work and return shipping to craftsman. Next show scheduled for 1979.
Acceptable Work: Considers ceramics. "Ceramics are limited to 3x3x6" and must fit into a cone box of approximately the same size."

NORTHWEST KANSAS AREA ART SHOW & SALE, c/o Mrs. Duane Aase, 606 S. Broadway, Oberlin KS 67749. Sponsor: Sappa Valley Arts Club. Estab: 1970. Annual indoor show held 4 days in late September. Average attendance: 2,000. Entries accepted until show date. Entry fee: $1 per craftsman. Maximum 3 entries per craftsman. Awards cash prizes to first 3 winners in 6 divisions; ribbons. Crafts may be offered for sale; 10% commission. Open to craftsmen living within 200-mile radius of Oberlin. Demonstrations encouraged. Address shipped items to Decatur County Extension Office, Court House, Oberlin KS 67749. Considers batik.

Kentucky

COCA COLA BOTTLING COMPANY ART SHOW, 808 Paddy Court, Elizabethtown KY 42701. (502)769-1292. Chairman: Linda Weis. Sponsor: Elizabethtown Junior Woman's Club. Annual indoor show held 2 days in May. Average attendance: 3,000. Closing date for entry: 3 weeks before show. Entry fee: $10 per 2 entries. Maximum 2 entries per craftsman. Awards $1,000 in cash prizes. Crafts may be offered for sale; 20% commission. Sponsor provides display equipment. Contact Weis on demonstrations. Considers batik, soft sculpture and sculpture. Maximum size: 4x7'. Also needs advertising art.

LIONS BLUE GRASS FAIR, Box 4335, Lexington KY 40504. (606)276-3556. Manager: Don C. Sullivan. Sponsor: central Kentucky Lions Clubs. Annual outdoor show held in July (tent space available). Average attendance: 200,000. Closing date for entry: 4 weeks before show. No entry fee. Awards first and second place ribbons in each category. Crafts may be offered for sale; no commission. "We prefer to have Kentucky artist/craftsmen." Registration limit: 200 artists/craftsmen. Sponsor provides easels.
Acceptable Work: Considers candlemaking, ceramics, decoupage, glass art, metalsmithing, needlecrafts, pottery, soft sculpture, tole painting, weaving, wall hangings and woodcrafting.

Batik, candlemaking, ceramics, glass art, jewelry, leatherworking, metalsmithing, pottery, soft sculpture, weavings, wall hangings and woodcrafting are all eligible for entry into the Artisan Fair, Boston Mills (Peninsula, Ohio). Certificates are awarded to the best of the 250 craftsmen in the show.

Maine

BRIDGTON ART SHOW, Box 236 A & C, Bridgton ME 04009. (207)647-3472. Contact: Sandra Libby. Sponsor: Chamber of Commerce. Estab: 1971. Annual indoor show held Columbus Day weekend. Average attendance: 2,000-3,000. Closing date for entry: 1 week before show. Entry fee: $20 per 2 entries. Maximum 2 entries per craftsman. Prejudging; no entry fees refunded for refused work. Crafts may be offered for sale; 20% commission. Sponsor provides display equipment and insurance for exhibited work. Considers weavings, wall hangings, woodcrafting and sculpture. Work must be ready for hanging or display.
Awards: Presents two $1,000 best in show prizes; $250 popular prize chosen by spectators; several $400 and $100 purchase awards. Judging usually done by director of prominent art museum.

CHRISTMAS CRAFT FAIR, Box 257, Mt. Vernon ME 04352. (207)293-3816. Chairman: Martha Thornton. Sponsor: Kennebec Valley YMCA. Estab: 1974. Annual indoor show held the first weekend in December. Closing date for entry: November 1. Entry fee: $20 per 8x8' display area. Maximum 2 display areas per craftsman. Awards $100+ in cash prizes. Five slides due for prejudging after September 1; entry fee refunded for refused work. Crafts may be offered for sale; no commission. Craftsman must attend show. Registration limit: 70 spaces. "Craftsmen having exhibited previously whose work continues to be acceptable are invited first; remaining spaces are offered by invitation after September 1."
Acceptable Work: Considers batik, candlemaking, dollmaking, jewelry, leatherworking, metalsmithing, needlecrafts, pottery, soft sculpture, weavings, wall hangings and woodcrafting.

Massachusetts

CRAFT ADVENTURE (formerly Eastern States Exposition), 1305 Memorial Ave., West Springfield MA 01089. (413)732-2361. Director: Helen Bardwell. Sponsor: Eastern States Exposition. Annual indoor show held 1 day in September. Average attendance: 600 per day. Closing date for entry: 3 weeks before show. No entry fee. Maximum 2 entries per craftsman. Demonstrations OK. Sponsor pays insurance for exhibited work.
Acceptable Work: Considers crewel, needlepoint, certain rugs, quilts and macrame not previously entered in show.
Awards: Presents $10 first, $7 second and $5 third prizes; best of show rosette and ribbons in each category. "Prize winning entries displayed throughout Eastern States Exposition (1-2 weeks in September)."

Michigan

ARTS & CRAFTS SHOW, 520 Oak St., Dundee MI 48131. Contact: Mrs. Roger La Voy. Sponsor: Dundee Art & Crafts Club. Estab: 1962. Annual outdoor show held 1 day in July. Average attendance: 2,000. Entries accepted up until show date. Entry fee: $6 per 4x8' display area. Awards ribbons. Crafts may be offered for sale; no commission. Craftsman must attend show; demonstrations OK. Considers all crafts (needlework must be framed).

DANISH FESTIVAL ARTS & CRAFTS SHOW, Danish Festival, Inc., 302 S. Lafayette St., Greenville MI 48838. (616)754-6369. Managing Director: Mrs. Bart Fries. Estab: 1968. Annual outdoor show held third weekend in August. Average attendance: 50,000. Closing date for entry: 4 weeks before show. Entry fee: based on 10x10' display area. Prejudging; entry fee refunded for refused work. Crafts may be offered for sale; no commission. Craftsman must attend show; demonstrations OK. Registration limit: 130 artists/craftsmen. Sponsor pays insurance on exhibited work. Write for more information.
Acceptable Work: Considers all quality crafts. "Kits and some needlework would be better suited to display at our flea market."

FLINT ART FAIR, FLINT INSTITUTE OF ARTS, 1120 E. Kearsley St., Flint MI 48503. (313)234-1695. Assistant Director: Tom Kayser. Sponsor: Friends of Modern Art. Estab: 1966. Annual outdoor show held second weekend in June. Average attendance: 10,000-15,000. Closing date for entry: March 15. Entry fee: $30 per 15x5' display area; due after jurying. Requires 6 entries per craftsman. Awards $100 each and plaque to 10 best artists/craftsmen. Prejudging by 35mm slides. Crafts must be offered for sale; no commission. Craftsman must attend show; demonstrations encouraged. Registration limit: 125 artists/craftsmen. Sponsor provides scaffolding. Considers all crafts. "Label slides clearly as to top, media and artist's name. Please print."

HARTLAND ART SHOW, Box 126, Hartland MI 48029. (313)632-7481. Contact: Michael Van Wormer. Sponsor: Hartland Art Council. Estab: 1966. Annual indoor show held during

the 3rd week in June. Average attendance: 2,000. Closing date for entries: 1 week before show. Entry fee: $3 per entry. Awards $225, cash prizes; three $300 and one $75 purchase prizes; and Awards of Excellence ribbons. Prejudging; no entry fees refunded for refused work. Crafts may be offered for sale; 10% commission. Sponsor provides display equipment.
Acceptable Work: Considers ceramics, wallhangings and glass art.

MIDWEST ARTS & CRAFTS SHOW, 1114 Grant St., Iron Mountain MI 49801. (906)774-0128. Chairman: Mrs. William Strand. Sponsor: Dickinson County Council for the Arts. Estab: 1967. Annual indoor/outdoor (craftsman may choose) show held 2 days in June. Average attendance: 3,000. Closing date for entry: 2 weeks before show. Entry fee: $10 per display area. Maximum 2 spaces per craftsman. Awards $250 in cash prizes; ribbons. Crafts may be offered for sale; no commission. Craftsman or representative must attend show; demonstrations encouraged. "Those who demonstrate generally seem to sell more." Sponsor provides pegboard on tables if requested. Considers all crafts. Ceramics must be made from craftsman's own original molds, and nothing made from printed instructions or kits allowed. "Entries to be judged must include 3x5" card with title, media and craftsman's name."

PONTIAC ANNUAL ART FAIR-HERITAGE FESTIVAL, 47 Williams St., Pontiac MI 48053. (313)333-7849. Contact: Ian Lyons. Sponsor: Widetrack Festival Committee. Estab: 1975. Annual outdoor show held 3 days in June (tent space available). Average attendance: 2,000. Closing date for entry: 1 week before show. Entry fee: $10 per entry. Prejudging by slides (send before second week in June); entry fee refunded for refused work. Crafts may be offered for sale; 15% commission. Craftsman must attend show; demonstrations OK. Sponsor provides display panels. Considers all original crafts.
Awards: Presents $100 first prizes; five $50 honorable mentions. Judging panel consists of the Detroit Institute of Arts curator, Pontiac Arts Center director and 1 artist.

REGIONAL ART COMPETITION (formerly Hackley Art Museum), Muskegon MI 49440. (616)722-6954. Contact: Ann Archambault. Estab: 1926. Annual indoor show held 6 weeks in winter. Average attendance: 3,000-4,000. Closing date for entry: 1 week before show. Entry fee: $1 per entry. Maximum 2 entries per craftsman. Awards $1,000 in cash prizes. Crafts may be offered for sale; no commission. Open to western Michigan residents. Registration limit: 200 artists/craftsmen. Sponsor pays insurance for exhibited work. Considers all original crafts.

SAUGATUCK-DOUGLAS ANNUAL VILLAGE SQUARE ART FAIRS, Saugatuck MI 49453. (616)857-4707. President: Cathie Moore. Estab: 1950. Semiannual outdoor show held 2 Saturdays in July. Average attendance: 2,000-3,000. Closing date for entry: 2 weeks before show. Entry fee for non-members: $10 for 1 show; $15 for 2 shows. Crafts may be offered for sale; no commission. Registration limit: 250 artists/craftsmen. Sponsor provides insurance during exhibit period. Considers all crafts. No "T-shirt" art or imported Indian jewelry.

TAWAS BAY WATERFRONT ART FAIR, 1115 Bay Dr., Tawas City MI 48763. (517)362-3198. Art Director: Paula Peterson. Sponsor: Tawas Bay Arts Council. Estab: 1960. Annual indoor/outdoor show held the first weekend in August. Average attendance: 5,000. Entry fee: $10 per craftsman. Awards ribbons and cash prizes. Applications and photos due for prejudging July 1. Entry fees refunded for refused work. Craft may be offered for sale; no commission. Craftsman must attend show; demonstrations OK. Registration limit: 225 artists/craftsmen.
Acceptable Works: Considers batik, candlemaking, ceramics, glass art, jewelry, leatherworking, metalsmithing, pottery, weavings and woodcrafting. No kits, paint by number, prefab jewelry, artificial flowers, ceramics or candles from molds, knitting, crocheting, decals on wood, paper tole, ecology boxes or dough art.

Minnesota

NORTH SHORE ART FAIR, Box 57, Lutsen MN 55612. (218)663-7533. Contact: Joan Maw. Sponsor: North Shore Arts Association. Estab: 1968. Annual indoor/outdoor show held the second weekend in July. Average attendance: 2,000. Entries accepted until show date. Awards cash prizes and ribbons. Crafts may be offered for sale; 15% commission.
Acceptable Work: Considers original wood, metal or clay sculpture, pottery, needlework, weaving, textiles, jewelry and crafts.

Mississippi

GUM TREE FESTIVAL, Box 1146, Tupelo MS 38801. (601)842-1052. Co-Chairman: Bill Ford. Sponsor: Community Development Foundation. Estab: 1972. Annual outdoor show held

2 days in mid-May. Average attendance: 10,000-12,000. Closing date for entry: 3 weeks before show. Entry fee: $5 jury fee; $20 per 12x4' display area. Prejudging by slides or photos; no jury fees refunded for refused work. Crafts may be offered for sale; no commission. Craftsman must attend show; demonstrations encouraged. Registration limit: 170 artists/craftsmen.
Acceptable Work: Considers original batik, candlemaking, dollmaking, glass art, jewelry, leatherworking, metalsmithing, pottery, weavings, wallhangings and woodcrafting.
Awards: Presents $500, best in show; $150 first, $75 second and $50 third prizes in 6 categories; $3,250, purchase awards; ribbons. (Total prizes: $5,400.)

Montana

J.K. RALSTON MUSEUM & ART CENTER JURIED EXHIBIT, Box 50, Sidney MT 59270. (406)482-3500. Director: Linda K. Mann. Sponsor: Mon-Dak Historical & Arts Society. Estab: 1975. Annual indoor show held the month of October. Average attendance: 200. Closing date for entry: 1 week before show. Entry fee: $3 per craftsman. Maximum 2 entries per craftsman. Prejudging; entry fee refunded for refused work. Crafts may be offered for sale; 25% commission. No demonstrations. Work must have been done within 2 years prior to show. Sponsor provides display equipment. Crafts should be shipped prepaid; will be returned C.O.D.
Acceptable Work: Considers ceramics, metalsmithing and soft sculpture. Maximum size: 6x4' depth; ½x1' or 5 lbs.
Awards: Presents cash awards and ribbons for best of show, honorable mention and most popular work.

Nebraska

COUNTRYSIDE VILLAGE ART FAIR, 8715 Countryside Plaza, Omaha NE 68114. (402)391-2200. Contact: Jim Chase. Sponsor: Countryside Village Merchants Association. Estab: 1970. Annual outdoor show held the first weekend in June. Average attendance: 20,000. Closing date for entry: 4 weeks before show. Entry fee: $30 per 8x14' display area; due after jurying. Awards $100 first, $50 second and $25 third prizes. Prejudging. Crafts may be offered for sale; no commission. Craftsman must attend show; demonstrations OK. Registration limit: 160 artists/craftsmen.
Acceptable Work: Considers batik, pottery, wood, glass, metal, clay and stone sculpture and silver/gold jewelry.

ROCKBROOK VILLAGE ART FAIR, 11042 Elm St., Omaha NE 68144. (402)391-4874. Contact: Gloria Mathews. Sponsor: Rockbrook Merchants Association. Estab: 1973. Annual outdoor (some tent space available) show held the second weekend in September. Average attendance: 30,000. Closing date for entries: 2 weeks before show. Entry fee: $25 per entry. Craft may be offered for sale; no commission. Craftsman must attend show; demonstrations OK. Registration limit: 185 artists/craftsmen. Considers all crafts. No kits or mold painted crafts.

New Hampshire

CRAFTSMEN'S FAIR, 205 N. Main St., Concord NH 03301. (603)224-3375. Director: Merle D. Walker. Sponsor: League of New Hampshire Craftsmen. Annual outdoor show held 6 days in August. Average attendance: 30,000. Considers all crafts. "Participants must meet residency requirements."

New Jersey

DEPTFORD MALL PATRIOTS ART BRIGADE, 131 Paradise Dr., Berlin NJ 08009. (609)767-3228. Director: Barbara Reeder and Dory Mann. Estab: 1968. Indoor show held 4 days in April, June and November. Average attendance: 10,000. Closing date for entry: 2 weeks before show. Entry fee: $40 per 12x4' display area. Crafts may be offered for sale; no commission. Demonstrations OK. Registration limit: 100 artists/craftsmen.
Acceptable Work: Considers batik, candlemaking, dollmaking, glass art, metalsmithing, needlecrafts, pottery, soft sculpture, tole painting, weavings, wall hangings, woodcrafting, ceramics, jewelry, leather by invitation only and handmade miniature toys. No poured ceramics.
Awards: Presents ribbons. Judging by a panel of 3 college professors, professional artists and craftsmen.

FORT DIX OUTDOOR ARTS & CRAFTS SHOW, 15 Grace Rd., East Brunswick NJ 08816. (201)238-0680. Director: Helene Roth. Sponsor: Garden State Cultural Council, Inc. Estab: 1976. Annual outdoor show held 1 day in June (indoor arena available in case of rain). Entries accepted until show date. Entry fee: $10 per 10' display area. Crafts may be offered for sale; no

commission. Craftsman must attend show; demonstrations OK. Registration limit: 200 artists/craftsmen. Sponsor pays insurance for exhibited work.
Acceptable Works: Considers batik, candlemaking, ceramics, decoupage, dollmaking, glass art, jewelry, leatherworking, metalsmithing, needlecrafts, pottery, soft sculpture, weavings, wall hangings, woodcrafting and puppet-making.
Awards: Presents cash prizes; first, second, third, fourth, fifth and honorable mention ribbons in 5 categories.

WEST NEW YORK RIVERSIDE ART SHOW, Municipal Bldg., Mayor's Office, West New York NJ 07093. (201)861-7000. Director: John Montrone. Sponsor: Mayor's Cultural Council. Estab: 1972. Annual outdoor show held 1 day in June. Average attendance: 7,000. Closing date for entry: 2 weeks before show. Entry fee: $10 per 10x10' display area. Crafts may be offered for sale; no commission. Open to craftsmen ages 18+. Craftsman must attend show; no demonstrations. Registration limit: 200 artists/craftsmen. Sponsor provides fence and insurance for exhibited work. Considers batik, decoupage and metalsmithing.
Awards: Presents $250 best in show; $150 first, $100 second and $50 third prizes in each category.

New Mexico

NATIONAL ARTS & CRAFTS BENEFIT, 3529 Constitution NE, Albuquerque NM 87106. (505)262-0672. Contact: Tom W. Thomason. Sponsor: Council for Exceptional Children. Estab: 1976. Annual indoor show held 3 days in early May. Average attendance: 10,000. Closing date for entry: 8 weeks before show. Entry fee: $55 per 8x8' display area. Prejudging by 3 slides; entry fee refunded for refused work. Crafts may be offered for sale; no commission. Craftsman must attend show; demonstrations OK. Registration limit: 150 artists/craftsmen. Sponsor provides display panels. Considers all original crafts under 8x8'.
Awards: Presents cash prizes and ribbons. Judging panel consists of noted artists and craftsmen.

NEW MEXICO ARTS & CRAFTS FAIR, Box 30044, Albuquerque NM 87110. (505)265-3171. Manager: Vicki Macaulay. Estab: 1962. Annual outdoor (booths available) show held the last Friday, Saturday and Sunday in June. Average attendance: 100,000. Closing date for entry: February. Entry fee: $7.50 jury fee; $60 per booth. Awards $1,000 in purchase prizes; ribbons. Samples due for prejudging in February; no jury fees refunded for refused work. Crafts must be offered for sale; no commission. Open to New Mexico residents, ages 18+. Craftsman must attend show and use booths; demonstrations required. Sponsor provides lighting. Considers all crafts.

New York

ASID INTERNATIONAL EXPOSITION OF DESIGNER SOURCES, 730 5th Ave., New York NY 10019. (212)586-7111. Coordinator: Ed Gips. Sponsor: American Society of Interior Designers. Estab: 1971. Annual indoor show held 4 days in July. Average attendance: 2,000. Closing date for entry: 2 weeks before show. Charges entry fee for 8x10' display area. Awards ribbons. Prejudging; no entry fees refunded. Considers all crafts.

CRAFT FAIR ITHACA, New York State Craftsmen Inc., 27 W. 53rd St., New York NY 10019. Contact: Harry Dennis. Annual exhibition. Entry fee: $10 per 50 pieces. Maximum 150 entries per craftsman. Awards prizes. 30% sales commission. Open to state residents. Considers weaving, ceramics, jewelry, glassblowing, leatherwork and stained glass.

CURBSTONE CRAFT FESTIVAL, 55 St. Paul St., Rochester NY 14604. (716)454-2220 ext. 17. Director: Jim O'Brien. Sponsor: Downtown Promotion Council of the Rochester Area Chamber of Commerce, Inc. Estab: 1971. Annual outdoor show (some overhangs on stores) held 3 days in June. Closing date for entry: 2-3 weeks before show. Entry fee $20 plus equipment charge per 10x8' display area. Prejudging; entry refunded for refused work. Crafts may be offered for sale; no commission. Craftsman must attend show; demonstrations encouraged. Registration limit: 250 artists/craftsmen. Sponsor provides display equipment for rent. Considers all crafts except decoupage.
Awards: Presents $1,000 in cash prizes; and first, second, third and best of show ribbons.

FESTIVAL OF THE ARTS, Upper Catskill Community Council of the Arts, Rm. 101A, Old Milne Library, State University College, Oneonta NY 13820. (607)432-2070. Contact: Leonard or Dorothy Ryndos. Estb: 1970. Annual indoor/outdoor show held 1 day in June. Average attendance: 25,000. Closing date for entry: 2 weeks before show. No entry fee. Prejudging. Crafts may be offered for sale; 5% commission on $50+ items. Open to regional craftsmen. Craftsman must attend show; prefers demonstrations unless dangerous. Registration limit: 400-500 artists/craftsmen. Considers all handmade crafts.

THE FLUSHING ART LEAGUE OUTDOOR EXHIBITION, 43-24 160th St., Flushing NY 11358. (212)358-0388. Contact: Anna Kraus. Estab: 1957. Semiannual outdoor show held 4 days in May and September. Average attendance: 1,200-1,500. Entries accepted until show date. Entry fee: $15 per display area. Crafts may be offered for sale; no commission. Craftsman must attend show.
Acceptable Work: Considers candlemaking, ceramics, decoupage, dollmaking, glass art, jewelry, leatherworking, metalsmithing, pottery, soft sculpture, tole painting and woodworking.
Awards: Presents $600, cash prizes; 20-30 ribbons. Judging panel consists of 3 artists and college department heads.

GALLERY IN THE PARK, Cross Pond Rd., Pound Ridge NY 10576. (914)763-5241. Director: Ms. Dru Raley. Sponsor: Pound Ridge Elementary School Association. Estab: 1970. Annual outdoor show held 2 days in May. Average attendance: 5,000. Closing date for entry: 4 weeks before show. Entry fee: $15 per 1 day or $25 per 2 days. Maximum 1 entry (for cash awards) per craftsman. Prejudging by slides; entry fee refunded for refused work. Crafts may be offered for sale; no commission. Craftsman must attend show; demonstrations OK. Registration limit: 120 artists/craftsmen. Sponsor provides chain-link and snow fence. Considers all crafts.
Awards: Presents $250 in cash prizes; second and honorable mention ribbons. Judging by a panel of 3 in related fields.

GALLERY NORTH OUTDOOR ART SHOW, N. Country Rd., Setauket NY 11733. Contact: Sharon Cowles or Marjorie Bishop. Sponsor: Gallery North. Estab: 1965. Annual outdoor show held 2 days in July. Entry fee: $20 per 10' display area. Awards $1,000 in cash prizes. Crafts may be offered for sale; no commission. Craftsman must attend show; demonstrations OK. Registration limit: 225 artists/craftsmen.
Acceptable Work: Considers batik, ceramics, glass art, jewelry, leatherworking, metalsmithing, pottery, weavings, wall hangings, woodcrafting, graphics and sculpture.

HARVEST CRAFT FESTIVAL & RENAISSANCE MARKETPLACE, c/o Creative Faires, Ltd., 65 Main St., Westhampton Beach NY 11978. (516)288-4263. Directors: Barbara Hope/Don Gaiti. Estab: 1974. Annual indoor show held 3 days in November-December. Average attendance: 28,000. Closing date for entry: 4 weeks before show. Entry fee: $175-200 per 10x10' display area. Prejudging; entry fee refunded for refused work. Crafts may be offered for sale; no commission. Craftsman must attend show; demonstrations encouraged. Considers all crafts.

NEW YORK STATE FAIR, Syracuse NY 13209. (315)487-7741. Contact: Elizabeth Crowley. Sponsor: New York state. Estab: 1900. Annual indoor show held 1 week in August-September. Average attendance: 250,000. Closing date for entry: 3 weeks before show. Entry fee: $5 per 10 entries. Awards $1,770, cash prizes; first, second and third place ribbons. Prejudging; no entry fees refunded for refused work. Crafts may be offered for sale; no commission. Sponsor provides display equipment.
Acceptable Work: Considers batik, glass art, jewelry, leatherworking, pottery, weavings, wall hangings and woodcrafting.

VILLAGE ARTISTS & CRAFTSMEN ART & CRAFT FAIR, Box 292, Hamilton NY 13346. (315)824-1343. Contact: Phyllis Charles. Sponsor: Village Artists & Craftsmen. Estab: 1975. Annual outdoor show held 2 days in September (tent space available). Average attendance: 6,000-7,000. Closing date for entry: 4 weeks before show. Entry fee: $30 per 8x10' display area. Awards 5 ribbons. Prejudging by 5 slides; entry fee refunded for refused work. Prejudging by 1 painter and 3 craftsmen. Crafts may be offerded for sale; no commission. Craftsman must attend show; demonstration on invitation only. Registration limit: 80 artists/craftsmen. Considers all crafts. No unoriginal designs or "domestic crafts".

North Carolina

MT. MITCHELL CRAFTS FAIR, Yancey County Chamber of Commerce, Burnsville NC 28714. Contact: Jerry Newton. Annual show. Entry fee: $10 per out-of-county craftsman. Awards purchase prizes. 10% sales commission. Craftsman must attend show. Sponsor provides 10x8' booth with canopy. No shipments received.

NORTH CAROLINA ARTISTS EXHIBITION, North Carolina Museum of Art, Raleigh NC 27611. (919)733-7568. Head, Collections Care and Preparation: Ben F. Williams. Sponsors: Museum and the North Carolina Art Society. Estab: 1937. Annual indoor show held 1 month in late fall. Average attendance: 10,000. Closing date for entry: 8 weeks before show. Entry fee: $5 per craftsman. "Three jurors from the art world (artists, critics, etc.) and from the museum top-level administrative posts evaluate each work from their personal esthetic viewpoints. A concensus is reached on each piece." Crafts may be offered for sale; 30% commission. Open to residents of North Carolina or non-residents who have lived in the state for at least 5 years. No demonstration. Sponsor provides display equipment and insurance while work is on exhibit at the museum or on tour.
Acceptable Work: Considers all crafts. "Avoid special installation requirements. No screws, eyes or hanging wires." Maximum size: 80".
Awards: Presents 3 honorable mentions; and gold, silver and bronze medals. "Approximately $4,000 in art/crafts is usually purchased by 3 organizations who commit specified amounts in advance. Purchases are at the total discretion of the organization and are not necessarily award-winning works."

PIEDMONT CRAFTS EXHIBITION, Box 6011, Charlotte NC 28207. (704)334-9723. Curator of Exhibitions: Jerald Melberg. Sponsor: Mint Museum of Art. Estab: 1976. Biennial indoor show held 6 weeks in early spring. Closing date for entry: 5 weeks before show. Entry fee: $5 per 2 entries. Maximum 2 entries per craftsman. Awards approximately $4,500 in cash and purchase prizes. Prejudging; no entry fees refunded for refused work. Crafts may be offered for sale; 30% commission. Open to residents of Alabama, Florida, Georgia, Kentucky, Louisiana, Mississippi, North and South Carolina, Tennessee, Virginia and West Virginia. Considers all crafts.

North Dakota

ALL NORTH DAKOTA ART EXHIBITION, Box 325, Linha Art Gallery, Minot ND 58701. (701)838-4445. Director: Galen Willert. Sponsor: Minot Art Association. Estab: 1976. Annual indoor show held the month of March. Average attendance: 1,000. Closing date for entry: 1 week before show. Entry fee: $3 per 2 entries. Awards cash and purchase prizes. Maximum 2 entries per craftsman. Prejudging; no entry fees refunded. Crafts may be offered for sale; 30% commission. Open to North Dakota craftsmen and Minot Art Association members. Registration limit: 50 artists/craftsmen. Considers all original crafts.

Ohio

ARTISAN FAIR, BOSTON MILLS (formerly Boston Mills Invitational Art Festival), Box 173, Peninsula OH 44264. (216)657-2807. Exhibit Director: Don Getz. Sponsor: *Cleveland Plain Dealer* Charities. Estab: 1976. Annual indoor/outdoor show (tent and small canopy space) held Labor Day weekend. Average attendance: 10,000. Closing date for entry: 6 weeks before show. Entry fee: $25-75 per display area. Awards certificates. Prejudging by 5 slides; entry fee refunded for refused work. Crafts must be offered for sale; no commission. Craftsman must attend show; demonstrations encouraged. Registration limit: 250 craftsmen.
Acceptable Work: Considers batik, candlemaking, ceramics, glass art, jewelry, leatherworking, metalsmithing, pottery, soft sculpture, weavings, wall hangings and woodcrafting.

ARTS & CRAFTS EXHIBITION, 620 Military Rd., Zanesville OH 43701. (614)452-0741. Director: Charles Dietz. Sponsor: Zanesville Art Center. Annual indoor show held the month of May. Average attendance: 1,200. Closing dates for entry: 3 weeks before show. No entry fee. Awards $35-40, cash prizes; ribbons. Maximum 6 entries per craftsman. Crafts may be offered for sale; no commission. Open to craftsmen from Zanesville or living within 75-mile radius. Demonstrations OK.
Acceptable Work: Considers batik, ceramics, glass art, jewelry, leatherworking, metalsmithing, needlecrafts, pottery, soft sculpture, weavings, wall hangings, woodcrafting, paintings, drawings, prints and sculpture. Maximum size: 10x8', 100 lbs.

BEAUX ARTS/CRAFTSMAN, Columbus Gallery of Fine Arts, 480 E. Broad St., Columbus OH 43215. Contact: Ann Adams. Sponsor: Columbus Gallery of Fine Arts. Biennial contemporary craft exhibition held in September and October of odd-numbered years. Closing date for entry: mid-June; date varies from show to show, depending on the Gallery schedule. Entry fee: $8 per 1-3 entries; maximum 3. Awards $7,000 in various media. Open to designer/

craftsmen ages 18+ living or residing in Illinois, Indiana, Iowa, Michigan, Minnesota, Missouri, Ohio, Pennsylvania, Kentucky, West Virginia and Wisconsin. Submit slides for judging. 20% sales commission.

CERAMIC & SCULPTURE EXHIBITION, Butler Institute of American Art, 542 Wick Ave., Youngstown OH 44502. (216)743-1107. Contact: Lorinda T. Butler. Estab: 1948. Annual indoor show held 7 weeks in January-February. Average attendance: approximately 7,500. Deliver entries from November 1 to second week in December. Entry fee: $2 per work. Awards purchase prizes. No entry fees refunded for refused work. Crafts may be offered for sale; 10% commission. Craftsman must be resident or former resident of Ohio. Sponsor handles display.
Acceptable Work: Considers ceramics, glass art, jewelry, metalsmithing, pottery, soft sculpture, weavings, wall hangings and woodcrafting.
Shipping Tips: "Please be sure to save all mailing slips. Breakable objects should be packed with special care. If need be, attach instructions on unpacking or repacking of work to crate."

CRAFT SHOW (formerly Cincinnati Craft Show), 933 Avondale Ave., Cincinnati OH 45229. (513)281-8042. Newsletter Editor: Mrs. Kline. Sponsor: Craft Guild of Greater Cincinnati. Estab: 1966. Annual indoor show held 4 weeks in spring. Average attendance: 2,000. Closing date for entry: 1 week before show. Entry fee: $8 for 3 items. Maximum 3 entries per craftsman. Awards cash prizes. Prejudging by scoring system; no entry fees refunded for refused work. Crafts may be offered for sale; no commission. Craftsman must live within 50-mile radius of Cincinnati. Sponsor provides display equipment. Considers all crafts.

MARIETTA COLLEGE CRAFTS NATIONAL, c/o Art Dept., Marietta College, Marietta OH 45750. (614)373-4643 ext. 275. Director: Arthur Winer. Estab: 1972. Annual indoor show held in November. Average attendance: 10,000. Closing date for slide entry: September 10. Entry fee: $10 per 3 entries. Maximum 3 entries per craftsman. Awards $5,000 in cash prizes and purchase awards. Prejudging; no entry fees refunded for refused work. Crafts may be offered for sale; 25% commission. Sponsor provides display equipment and insurance for exhibited work. Considers mobiles, sculpture, ceramics, glass, jewelry, leather, metal, textiles and wood.

MIDWEST WEAVERS CONFERENCE, 2126 Skyline Dr., Bartlesville OK 74003. Contact: Marjorie O'Shaughnessy. Annual show held in a different state each year. 1978 show in Cincinnati. Presents cash and suppliers awards. Open to Conference members; $2 lifetime membership. Weavings may be shipped, but must be picked up in person at end of conference. Weavings are insured.

OHIO ARTISTS & CRAFTSMEN, 212 Lincoln Way E., Massillon OH 44646. (216)833-4061. Director: Mary Merwin. Sponsor: Massillon Museum. Estab: 1937. Biennial indoor show held in July and August. Average attendance: 3,500. Closing date for entry: 4 weeks before show. Entry fee: $3 per craftsman. Maximum 6 entries per craftsman. Awards $1,500 in prizes. Prejudging; no entry fees refunded for refused work. Crafts may be offered for sale; 10% commission. Open to Ohioans and former residents. Sponsor provides display equipment and insurance for exhibited work.
Acceptable Work: Considers batik, ceramics, glass art, jewelry, metalsmithing, pottery, weavings, wall hangings, sculpture, drawings and prints.

SALT FORK ARTS & CRAFTS FESTIVAL, 910 Wheeling Ave., Cambridge OH 43725. (614)432-3943. Chairman: Grant Hafley. Sponsor: Ohio Arts and Crafts Foundation. Estab: 1969. Annual outdoor show held 3 days in August (pavilion and tent space provided). Average attendance: 65,000. Closing date for entry: May 15. Entry fee: $32 per 10x10' outdoor display or 8' indoor table. Prejudging; entry fee due after jurying. Awards $400 in cash prizes. Crafts may be offered for sale; no commission. Open to Ohio craftsmen. Craftsman must attend show; 3 daily demonstrations required. Registration limit: 200 artists/craftsmen. Sponsor provides snow fencing and pegboard.
Acceptable Work: Considers batik, candlemaking, ceramics, decoupage, glass art, jewelry, leatherworking, metalsmithing, pottery, tole painting, weavings, wall hangings and woodcrafting.

SUMMERFAIR, INC., 999 Hill St., Cincinnati OH 45229. Contact: Director. Estab: 1965. Annual outdoor show held first weekend in June. Average attendance: 125,000. Closing date for entry applications: mid-March. Entry fee: $20 per display area. Awards $1,000 in cash prizes. Prejudging; entry fee refunded for refused work. Crafts may be offered for sale; no commission. Demonstrations OK. Registration limit: 350 artists/craftsmen. Considers all crafts. No kits.

TOLEDO FESTIVAL OF THE ARTS, 5403 Elmer Dr., Toledo OH 43560. (419)536-8365. Coordinator: Barbara States. Sponsors: Crosby Gardens Board, Toledo Artists Club, Garden Club Forum, Greater Toledo Arts Commission and Toledo's Forestry Division. Estab: 1965. Annual outdoor show held 2 days in June (covered booth provided). Average attendance: 40,000. Closing date for entry: 1 week before show. Entry fee: $40 per booth; $10 per table or easel. Prejudging by "slides or photos acceptable; presentation by the craftsman preferred." Entry fee refunded for refused work. Crafts may be offered for sale; no commission. Craftsman must attend show; demonstrations encouraged. Registration limit: 350 artists/craftsmen.
Acceptable Work: Considers original batik, ceramics, glass art, jewelry, leatherworking, metalsmithing, pottery, soft sculpture, weavings, wall hangings and woodcrafting. Easels and tables must be draped.
Awards: Presents ten $25 first prizes; $500 purchase award; 10 second, 10 third and 10 honorable mention ribbons. Jurying by 1 member of each sponsor.

WESTERVILLE MUSIC & ARTS FESTIVAL, 5 W. College Ave., Westerville OH 43081. (614)882-8917. Chairman: Doris Hoffman. Sponsor: Chamber of Commerce. Estab: 1973. Annual outdoor show held 1 day in July. Average attendance: 25,000. Closing date for entry: 2 weeks before show. Entry fee: $8 per amateur entry; $10 per professional entry. Awards $1,000+, cash prizes; $1,500, purchase awards; 25 ribbons. Prejudging; entry fee refunded for refused work. Crafts may be offered for sale; no commission. Craftsman must attend show; demonstrations OK. Registration limit: 200 artists/craftsmen.
Acceptable Work: Considers batik, candlemaking, glass art, jewelry, leatherworking, metalsmithing, pottery, soft sculpture, tole painting, weavings, wall hangings and woodcrafting. "All crafts must be at least 70% handcrafted."

Oregon

ALBANY SPRING ARTS FESTIVAL, Box 841, Albany OR 97321. (503)928-2815. Director: Terri Hopkins. Sponsor: Creative Arts Guild. Estab: 1969. Annual indoor/outdoor show held 2 days in early May. Average attendance: 20,000. Closing date for entry: 1 week before show. No entry fee: Maximum 2 entries per craftsman. Awards ribbons. Crafts may be offered for sale; 20% commission. Demonstrations OK. Open to residents of mid-Wilamette Valley. Considers all crafts.

COOS ART MUSEUM JURIED CRAFT EXHIBITION, 515 Market Ave., Coos Bay OR 97420. (503)267-3901. Contact: Marian Slack. Annual show. Charges entry fee. Awards ten $100 prizes. 25% sales commission. Sponsor pays insurance for exhibited work. Considers pottery, weaving, stitchery, jewelry, basketry, leatherwork, toy-makers, furniture, silversmithing, macrame, woodcrafting and blown and leaded glass. Utilitarian crafts only.

JULY CRAFT SHOW, 515 Market Ave., Coos Bay OR 97420. (503)267-3901. Director: Maggie Karl. Sponsor: Coos Art Museum. Estab: 1976. Annual indoor show held 4 weeks in July. Average attendance: 5,000. Closing date for entries: 4 weeks before show. Entry fee: $7.50 per person. Maximum 2 entries per craftsman. Prejudging; no entry fee refunded for refused work. Crafts may be offered for sale; 25% commission. Considers all crafts created within the past year. All works should be ready to hang or display.
Awards: Presents one $500 and ten $50 cash awards; and purchase awards, purchased for permanent collection.

Pennsylvania

ALLENTOWN ART MUSEUM JURIED EXHIBITION, Box 117, Allentown PA 18105. (215)432-4333. Director: Richard N. Gregg. Sponsor: Allentown Art Museum. Estab: 1963. Annual indoor show held 6 weeks in May-June. Average attendance: 25,000. Closing date for entry: early April. Entry fee: $15 per entry. Maximum 2 entries per craftsman. Awards winner with one-man show. Prejudging; no entry fees refunded for refused work. Crafts may be offered for sale; 10% commission. Open to museum members. Sponsor provides display equipment. Considers batik, ceramics, glass art, metalsmithing, needlecrafts, weavings and wall hangings.

CENTRE SQUARE ART FAIR, Downtown Improvement Group, Easton PA 18042. (215)258-2881. Director: Liz John. Estab: 1965. Annual outdoor show held 1 Saturday in September. Closing date for entry: 2 weeks before show. Entry fee: $7 per 10' display area. Awards $100, cash prizes; first, second and third place ribbons. Crafts may be offered for sale. Craftsman must attend show; demonstrations encouraged. Considers all original crafts.

EGGORAMA, Egg Shell Craft, 66 E. Union Blvd., Bethlehem PA 18018. Contact: Mary Ellen Ellington or Peter Evans. Indoor exhibition. Entry fee: craftsman, $25 per table; dealer, $40 per table (6' table). Entries accepted until show date if space available. Awards best of show and ribbons in each category. No sales commission. Craftsman or representative must attend show. Considers all media in egg shell decoration.

HAZLETON CREATIVE ARTS FESTIVAL, Greater Hazleton Fine Arts Council, Northeast Bank Bldg., Hazleton PA 18201. (717)455-1508. Contact: Alice Laputka. Estab: 1965. Annual indoor show held Mother's Day weekend. Average attendance: 5,000. Closing date for entry: 2 weeks before show. Entry fee: $5 per 2 entries. Maximum 2 entries per craftsman. Prejuding; no entry fees refunded for refused work. Crafts may be offered for sale; no commission. Work must have been created within last 18 months and not previously entered. Sponsor provides pedestals and pins. Considers all crafts.
Awards: Presents $255, cash prizes; $200, purchase award; merchandise awards if donated. Judges are professional artists and craftsmen.

JURIED CRAFTS EXHIBITION OF THE CENTRAL PENNSYLVANIA FESTIVAL OF THE ARTS, Box 1023, State College PA 16801. Managing Director: Marilyn Keat. Estab: 1966. Annual indoor show held 1 month in the summer. Average attendance: 9,000. Closing date for entry: 2 weeks before show. Entry fee: $7 per 1-2 entries. Maximum 2 entries per craftsman. Awards $3,000 in cash prizes. Prejudging; no entry fees refunded. Crafts may be offered for sale. Show is hung in the museum by the staff of the Museum of Art, Pennsylvania State University. Sponsors pays insurance for exhibited work. Considers ceramics, glass, metals, fibers and wood.

LEWISBURG CRAFT FAIR, Box 532, Lewisburg Pa 17837. (717)524-7006. Director David Bussard. Estab: 1973. Annual indoor show. Average attendance: 8,000. Entry fee: $45 per 9x7' display area. Awards $50 in cash prizes. Prejudging; entry fee refunded for refused work. Crafts may be offered for sale; no commission. Craftsman must attend show; demonstrations encouraged. Registration limit: 75 artists/craftsmen.
Acceptable Work: Considers batik, candlemaking, dollmaking, glass art, jewelry, leatherworking, metalsmithing, pottery, soft sculpture, tole painting, weavings, wall hangings and woodcrafting.

THE MANNINGS NATIONAL HANDWEAVERS JURIED SHOW, Rte. 2, East Berlin PA 17316. (717)624-2223. Sponsor: The Mannings Handweaving School and Weavers Supply Center. Estab: 1973. Annual indoor show held 3 weeks in April-May. Average attendance: 1,000-2,000. Closing date for entry: 2 weeks before show. Entry fee: $4 per entry. Maximum 1 entry per craftsman. Crafts may be offered for sale; 20% commission. Sponsor provides insurance on exhibited work.
Acceptable Work: Considers weaving, basketry, macrame and woven off-loom constructions created within the year of show. If work is to be hung, hanging device must be provided.
Awards: Presents approximately $2,500 in cash; merchandise prize; autographed copies of books from authors in weaving field.
Shipping Tips: All packages must be marked "Juried Show" and packed in a reusable container including entry forms and display tags. Fee must accompany entry.

POCONO ART & CRAFTS FESTIVAL, Box 476, East Stroudsburg PA 18301. Chairman: Robert Gibson. Sponsors: Notre Dame and St. Matthews School PTA. Estab: 1975. Annual indoor/outdoor show held 3 days in September. Average attendance: 6,000. Closing date for entry: 4 weeks before show. Entry fee: $25 per outdoor/$30 per indoor 8x10' display area. Awards $1,200 in cash prizes; ribbons. Prejudging; entry fee refunded for refused work. Crafts must be offered for sale; no commission. Craftsman must attend show; demonstrations OK. Registration limit: 75-100 artists/craftsmen.
Acceptable Work: Considers batik, candlemaking, ceramics, dollmaking, glass art, jewelry, leatherworking, metalsmithing, needlecrafts, pottery, weavings, wall hangings and woodcrafting.

STITCHERY, Arts & Crafts Center, 5th and Shady Aves., Pittsburgh PA 15232. Sponsor: Embroiderers' Guild. Estab: 1969. Biennial indoor show held for 3 weeks. Next show held in late 1978 or early 1979. Closing date for entry: 2½-3 months before show. Entry fee: $10 per entry. Maximum 3 entries per craftsman. Awards $770 in cash and merchandise prizes. Prejudging by slides; no entry fees refunded for refused work. Crafts may be offered for sale; 30% commission. Registration limit: 100-120 works. Sponsor provides display panels, equipment and insurance during exhibit period. Work must be mounted and complete with rods.
Acceptable Work: Considers crafts original in design and execution and created with a threaded needle (hand or machine).

SUMMER ARTS & CRAFTS FESTIVAL-SUSQUEHANNA, Lanesboro PA 18827. (717)853-4625. Chairman: Jeanne Rodriquez. Sponsor: Susquehanna Junior Club. Estab: 1969. Annual outdoor show held 1 day in July. Average attendance: 8,000. Entries accepted up until show date. Entry fee: $6 pre-registration fee; $5 per 10x4' display area. Awards cash prizes and ribbons. Crafts may be offered for sale. Craftsman must attend show; demonstrations encouraged. Considers all crafts.

THREE RIVERS ARTS FESTIVAL, 4400 Forbes Ave., Pittsburgh PA 15213. (412)687-7014. Contact: Barbara Widdoes or Paula Atlas. Sponsor: Carnegie Institute. Estab: 1960. Annual outdoor show held 10 days in May-June (limited covering available for paintings and prints). Average attendance: 200,000. Closing date for entry: April 1. Awards $3,000, cash prizes; $2,000, purchase awards. Prejudging by slides; no entry fees refunded for refused work. Crafts must be offered for sale; charges sales commission. Open to craftsmen ages 18+. Demonstrations OK. Sponsor provides 8x4' display area. Craftsman must deliver work personally. Accepts all original crafts not previously exhibited at the Festival.

South Carolina

FESTIVAL OF CRAFTS, 7737 Nellview Dr., Charleston SC 29405. (803)552-3973. President: Pearl Marangelli. Sponsor: Coastal Crafters, Inc. Estab: 1974. Semiannual indoor show held 2 days in spring and fall. Average attendance: 3,000+. Entries accepted until show date. Entry fee: $37 per 10x10' display area. Awards cash prizes and ribbons. Prejudging; entry fee refunded for refused work. Crafts may be offered for sale; no commission. Craftsman must attend show; demonstrations encouraged. Registration limit: 100 artists/craftsmen. Sponsor provides table, 2 chairs and insurance for exhibited work. Considers all crafts.

SOUTH CAROLINA ARTS COMMISSION EXHIBITION, 829 Richland St., Columbia SC 29201. (803)758-3442. Contact: Coordinator. Annual indoor show held 3-4 weeks in spring. Closing date for entry: 1 week before show. No entry fee. Maximum 2 entries per craftsman. Awards $5,000 in purchase awards. Crafts may be offered for sale; no commission. Open to South Carolina residents or craftsmen having lived at least 1 year in the state.
Acceptable Work: Considers batik, ceramics, glass art, jewelry, needlecrafts, pottery, soft sculpture, weavings, wall hangings and woodcrafting. "Works of professional quality are desired since those purchased will become works in the state's art collection; therefore simple hobby crafts are not acceptable."

South Dakota

BROOKINGS SUMMER FESTIVAL, Box 555, Chamber of Commerce, Brookings SD 57006. (605)692-7171. Chairman: Perry Vining. Estab: 1971. Annual outdoor show held second weekend in July. Average attendance: 15,000. Entries accepted until show date. Entry fee: $1 per entry. Maximum 3 entries per craftsman. Awards $300 in cash prizes. Crafts may be offered for sale; no commission. Demonstrations encouraged. Considers all crafts. Two-dimensional crafts must be framed and ready for hanging.

RED CLOUD INDIAN ART SHOW, Red Cloud Indian School, Pine Ridge SD 57770. (605)867-5491. Director: Brother C.N. Simon. Sponsor: Red Cloud Indian School. Estab: 1969. Annual indoor show held 2 months in summer. Average attendance: 3,000+. Closing date for entry: 3 weeks before show. No entry fee. Maximum 3 entries per category per craftsman. Awards $1,150, cash prizes; $1,500, purchase awards. Prejudging. Crafts may be offered for sale; no commission. Open to Indian craftsmen ages 18+. Sponsor provides display equipment and insurance for exhibited work. Ship by UPS or air freight. Considers original work by Indians including ceramics, paintings, graphics and sculpture.

Tennessee

MISSISSIPPI RIVER CRAFT SHOW, Brooks Memorial Art Gallery, Overton Park, Memphis TN 38112. Biennial show open to craftsmen residing in a state bordering on the Mississippi River. Next show held in 1978.

Texas

ARTS IN ACTION, Amarillo Chamber of Commerce, Amarillo Bldg., Amarillo TX 79101. (806)374-5238. Assistant Manager: F. LeRoy Tillery. Sponsor: Chamber of Commerce and Fine Arts Council. Estab: 1970. Annual indoor show held 2 days in November. Average attendance: 5,000. Closing date for entry: 3 weeks before show. Entry fee: $50 per space with table and chairs; $65 per booth with pegboard. Prejudging; entry fee refunded for refused work. Crafts may be offered for sale; no commission. Craftsman must attend show; demonstrations encouraged. Registration limit: 150 spaces. Sponsor provides 8' table, pegboard and 6x10x6' booth. Considers all crafts.

NATIONAL DRAWING & SMALL SCULPTURE SHOW, Art Dept., Del Mar College, Corpus Christi TX 78404. (512)882-6231. Chairman: Joseph Cain. Estab: 1966. Annual indoor show held in May. Average attendance: 2,500-3,000. Entry fee: $5 per entry. Slides for sculpture prejudging due 6 weeks before show; no entry fees refunded for refused work. Crafts may be offered for sale; no commission. Considers glass art and soft sculpture.
Awards: Presents $100-250, cash prizes; $700, $500 and $250 purchase awards.

SALADO ART FAIR, Box 444, Salado TX 76571. Chairman: Gretchen Jackson. Sponsor: Chamber of Commerce. Estab: 1967. Annual outdoor show held 2 days in September. Average attendance: 10,000+. Closing date for entry: 6 weeks before show. Entry fee: $35 per craftsman per 10x10' display area; $50 if shared. Awards $3,000 in purchase prizes and ribbons. Prejudging. Crafts may be offered for sale; no commission. Craftsman must attend show; demonstrations OK. Registration limit: 150-175 artists/craftsmen. Sponsor provides 6x8' rack. Considers all crafts.

SPRING FLING REGIONAL ARTS & CRAFTS FAIR, Wichita Falls Museum and Art Center, # 2 Eureka Circle, Wichita Falls TX 76308. (817)692-0923. Contact: Artists Selection Committee. Sponsor: Guild of the Museum and Art Center. Estab: 1971. Annual outdoor show held last full weekend in April. Average attendance: 10,000. Closing date for entry: February 15. Entry fee: $50 per craftsman or $35 per 2 craftsmen sharing booth. Awards five $100 cash prizes; $500 purchase awards. Prejudging by slides or prints; entry fee refunded for refused work. Crafts may be offered for sale; no commission. Craftsman must attend show. Registration limit: 90 artists/craftsmen. Sponsor provides 8x8' covered display area and pegboard panels.
Acceptable Work: Considers original pottery, fiberwork, glass art, jewelry, leatherworking, metalsmithing, toys, knives, musical instruments and woodcrafting.

Vermont

SUMMER FESTIVAL AT FROG HOLLOW, Vermont State Craft Center at Frog Hollow, Middlebury VT 05753. (802)388-4871. Gallery Director: Susan Veguez. Sponsor: Frog Hollow Craft Association. Estab: 1973. Annual indoor show held the month of August. Average attendance: 10,000-14,000. Closing date for entry: 2 weeks before show. No entry fee. Awards purchase prizes. Call to arrange interview and screening of works. Craftsman must offer work for sale; 30% commission. Open to Vermont residents (6 months minimum). Write to arrange demonstrations. Sponsor pays insurance on exhibited work. "Frog Hollow sets up complete gallery, displaying all items taken in by jurying. The Vermont State Craft Center is operated as a service to Vermont's craftsmen by exhibiting and selling what is considered the best of Vermont crafts."
Acceptable Work: Considers batik, ceramics, glass art, jewelry, leatherworking, metalsmithing, pottery, quilts, soft sculpture, weavings, wall hangings and woodcrafting. Work must be of original design and ready for display.

Virginia

BOARDWALK ART SHOW, Box 884, Virginia Beach VA 23451. (804)428-9294. Contact: Chairman. Sponsor: Virginia Beach Arts Center. Estab: 1955. Annual outdoor show held 5 days in late June. Closing date for entry: mid-April. Entry fee: $5 jury fee; $26 per 7x4x3' rail space; $36 per 7x7x4' lawn space. Maximum 2 entries per craftsman. Prejudging by 3 slides per entry;

display area fee refunded for refused work. Crafts may be offered for sale; no commission. Craftsman must attend show; sketching demonstrations only. Registration limit: 700 spaces. Sponsor provides chicken wire.
Acceptable Work: Considers batik, ceramics, glass art, jewelry, metalsmithing, needlecrafts, pottery, soft sculpture, weavings, wall hangings and woodcrafting.
Awards: Presents $1,500, best of show; $200 first, $150 second and $100 third prizes in 6 categories.

PORTSMOUTH NATIONAL SEAWALL ART SHOW, c/o Parks and Recreation Dept., 430 High St., Portsmouth VA 23704. (804)393-8481. Director: Katherine Kitterman. Sponsors: Parks and Recreation Dept. and Chamber of Commerce. Estab: 1970. Annual outdoor show held Memorial Day weekend. Average attendance: 20,000. Closing date for entry: 4 weeks before show. Entry fee: $13 per 6x8' display area; $17 with wire fencing. Maximum 3 spaces per craftsman. Crafts may be offered for sale; no commission. Craftsman or representative must attend show; demonstrations encouraged. Registration limit: 350 artists/craftsmen. No crafts accepted in advance. Considers all original crafts.
Awards: Presents $2,500, cash prizes; $2,000+, purchase awards; 35 ribbons. Judging done by 3 well-known East Coast artists or art educators.
Special Needs: "Cover Contest" award usually given to an artist who captures the atmosphere of the show in some medium there on the Seawall.

Washington

EDMONDS ART FESTIVAL, Box 212, Edmonds WA 98020. (206)776-3350. President: Donald Schroeder. Estab: 1957. Annual indoor/outdoor show held 3 days in June. Average attendance: 50,000. Closing date for entry: 1 week before show. Entry fee: $3 for 2 entries. Maximum 2 entries per category per craftsman. Crafts must be offered for sale; 25% commission. Sponsor provides display equipment and insurance. Deliver and pick up work in person.
Acceptable Work: Considers batik, ceramics, dollmaking, glass art, jewelry, leatherworking, metalsmithing, needlecrafts, pottery, soft sculpture, weavings, wall hangings and woodcrafting.
Awards: Presents $4,750 in cash prizes. Judging is by professionals in each area.

EVERETT WATERFRONT ART SHOW, Box 2938, Everett WA 98203. President: Pamela Moore. Sponsor: Creative Arts Association. Estab: 1967. Annual outdoor (covered balcony) show held 2 days in July. Average attendance: 4,000. Closing date for entry: 1 week before show. Entry fee: $3 per entry. Awards $2,000 in cash prizes. Prejudging; no entry fees refunded for refused work. Crafts may be offered for sale; 25% commission. Work must have been created within last 2 years and not previously entered. Demonstrations OK.
Acceptable Work: Considers batik, ceramics, glass art, jewelry, leatherworking, metalsmithing, needlecrafts, pottery, soft sculpture, weavings, wall hangings and woodcrafting.

West Virginia

EXHIBITION 280, Huntington Galleries, Park Hills, Huntington WV 25701. (304)529-2701. Contact: Registrar. Estab: 1952. Annual indoor show held 6 weeks in fall. Average attendance: 6,000. Closing date for entry: 3 weeks before show. Entry fee: $5 per craftsman. Maximum 3 entries per craftsman. Awards $1,500, cash prizes; $2,500, purchase prizes. Prejudging; no entry fees refunded for refused work. Crafts may be offered for sale; no commission. Open to residents within 280-mile radius of Huntington. Considers all crafts. Write for prospectus in summer.

OGLEBAY INSTITUTE UPPER OHIO VALLEY ART SHOW, Oglebay Institute, Oglebay Park, Wheeling WV 26003. (304)242-7700. Art Specialist: Ken Morgan. Estab: 1964. Annual indoor show held 1 month in fall. Average attendance: 1,000. Closing date for entry: 1 week before show. Entry fee: $3, Institute member entry; $4, non-member entry. Maximum 2 entries per craftsman. Crafts may be offered for sale; 20% commission. Open to West Virginia craftsmen and those living within 75-mile radius of Wheeling. For insurance purposes, work must be delivered by the craftsman or an agent.
Acceptable Work: Considers batik, glass art, leatherworking, metalsmithing, pottery, soft sculpture, weavings, wall hangings, and woodcrafting.
Awards: Presents $1,000 in cash prizes; 12 merit and some honorable mention ribbons. Judging panel consists of college art instructors or professional artists.

RHODODENDRON STATE OUTDOOR ART & CRAFT FESTIVAL, 3804 Noyes Ave. SE, Charleston WV 25304. (304)925-3364. President: Eleanor Chandler. Annual outdoor show held 1 day in spring. Average attendance: 10,000. Entries accepted until show date. Entry fee: $5 per 7x9' display area. Awards $3,000, cash prizes; purchase awards. Crafts may be offered for sale; no commission. Craftsman must attend show. Registration limit: 400-450 artists/craftsmen. Considers all crafts.

STONEWALL JACKSON JUBILEE, Box 956, Weston WV 26452. (304)269-4660. Director: William Frye. Sponsor: Stonewall Jackson Heritage Arts & Crafts Inc. Estab: 1974. Annual indoor show held 3 days in September. Closing date for entry: 3 weeks before show. Craftsman must provide samples. No entry fee. Crafts may be offered for sale; 15% commission. Craftsman must attend show; requires demonstrations. Registration limit: 100 artists/craftsmen. Sponsor provides tables.
Acceptable Work: Considers Appalachian candlemaking, dollmaking, glass art, jewelry, leatherworking, metalsmithing, needlecrafts, pottery, tole painting, weavings and woodcrafting.

WEST VIRGINIA STRAWBERRY FESTIVAL ARTS & CRAFTS SHOW, Box 117, Buckhannon WV 26201. (304)472-3020. Contact: H. Gene Starr. Estab: 1970. Annual indoor show held 3 days in June. Average attendance: 7,000-10,000. Closing date for entry: 4 weeks before show. Entry fee: $15. Awards $40 first, $20 second and $10 third prizes; and ribbons. Prejudging; no entry fees refunded for refused work. Crafts may be offered for sale; 15% commission. Prefers West Virginia craftsmen. Sponsor provides display equipment and insurance for exhibited work. Considers all crafts.

Wisconsin

AAUW ART FAIR ON THE GREEN, Rte. 1, Stoddard WI 54658. (608)788-5356. Chairman: Sharon DeCicco. Sponsor: American Association of University Women. Estab: 1958. Annual outdoor show held last weekend in July. Average attendance: 2,000. Entries or 5 slides due for prejudging April 28. Entry fee: $15 per entry; due after jurying. Crafts may be offered for sale; no commission. Craftsman must attend show. Registration limit: 60 artists/craftsmen.
Acceptable Work: Considers batik, ceramics, glass art, jewelry, leatherworking, metalsmithing, pottery, soft sculpture, weavings and woodcrafting.
Awards: Presents $800, cash prizes; $3,500, purchase awards. Jurying by a panel of 3 from area art institutes and university campuses.

BELOIT & VICINITY EXHIBITION, Wright Art Center, Beloit College, Beloit WI 53511. (608)365-3391. Director: Marylou S. Williams. Sponsor: Wright Art Center and Beloit Art League. Estab: 1957. Annual indoor show held 4 weeks in May-June. Average attendance: 800-1,000. Closing date for entry: 3 weeks before show. Entry fee: $7 per entry. Maximum 1 entry per craftsman. Awards $2,000, cash prizes; $250, purchase awards. Prejudging; no entry fees refunded. Crafts may be offered for sale; 15% commission. Open to artists/craftsmen within driving distance of Beloit. Sponsor provides display equipment. Deliver crafts in person.
Acceptable Work: Considers batik, ceramics, glass art, soft sculpture, weavings and wall hangings. No student work. Crafts must be ready for installation. No brackets.

FOREST MALL ARTS & CRAFTS FAIR, 835 W. Johnson St., Fond DuLac WI 54935. Contact: Lois Frank. Sponsor: Forest Mall Merchants Association. Estab: 1974. Annual indoor show held 3 days in October. Average attendance: 6,000-10,000. Closing date for entry: 2-3 weeks before show. Entry fee: $12-15 per 10x10' tent display area. Prejudging; entry fee refunded for refused work. Crafts may be offered for sale; 10% commission donated to charity. Craftsman must attend show. Registration limit: 70-75 artists/craftsmen.
Acceptable work: Considers batik, candlemaking, ceramics, glass art (no glass blowing), leatherworking, metal sculpture, stitchery, pottery, weavings, wall hangings and woodcrafting.
Awards: Presents 1 best of show; first, second and third place and honorable mention ribbons in 3 categories.

LAKEFRONT FESTIVAL OF ARTS, Milwaukee Art Center, 750 N. Lincoln Memorial Dr., Milwaukee WI 53202. (414)271-9508. Coordinator: Barbara Coffman. Sponsor: Friends of Art of MAC. Estab: 1961. Annual outdoor show held 3 days in June (tent space available). Average attendance: 200,000. Prospectus available February 1; slides due for prejudging in early March. Entry fee: $5 jury fee; $35 per outdoor/$50 per tent display area. Maximum 6 slides per craftsman. No entry fees refunded for refused work. Crafts may be offered for sale; no commission.

Craftsman must attend show; demonstrations are contracted. Registration limit: 175 artists/craftsmen. Sponsor provides fencing.
Acceptable Work: Considers original batik, candlemaking, ceramics, glass art, jewelry, leatherworking, metalsmithing, needlecrafts, pottery, soft sculpture, weavings, wall hangings and woodcrafting.
Awards: Presents $5,000 in cash prizes. Jurying panel consists of art center curators, outside university art professors and artists from the past year's show.
To Break In: Mark slides carefully and include SASE. Slides must cover work to be shown. "Judging is based on originality, craftsmanship and strongly on consistency."

MONUMENT SQUARE ART FAIR, 223 6th St., Racine WI 53403. Contact: Helen Hackl. Annual indoor/outdoor show held the second weekend in June. Closing date for entry: mid-April or when spaces filled. Entry fee: $25 per 5x12' display area. Awards $1,000, cash prizes; $12,100, purchase awards; ribbons. Slides or samples of work due for prejudging in January. Crafts must be offered for sale; no commission. Registration limit: 145 artists/craftsmen. Sponsor provides snow fence. Considers ceramics, jewelry, textiles, glass, enamels and batik.

MUSCODA ARTS & CRAFTS SHOW & SALE, 124 N. 5th, Muscoda WI 53573. (608)739-3738. Contact: Barb Thomas. Sponsor: Muscoda Arts and Crafts Committee. Estab: 1972. Annual indoor/outdoor show held 2 days in August. Average attendance: 4,000-5,000. Entries accepted until show date ($1 extra charge if 1 week before show). Entry fee: $5 per booth. Awards first, second and third place ribbons. Crafts may be offered for sale; no commission. Craftsman must attend show; demonstrations OK. Registration limit: 60 artists/craftsmen. To register, write after April. Considers all crafts.

OUTDOOR ARTS FESTIVAL, Box 204, Watertown WI 53094. Corresponding Secretary: Sandra Pirkel. Estab: 1965. Annual outdoor show held 1 day in August. Entries accepted until show date. Entry fee: $5 per display area. Awards $600 in purchase prizes and ribbons. Crafts may be offered for sale; 10% commission. Craftsman must attend show; demonstrations encouraged. Considers all original, fine crafts.

PARK PLAZA ART FAIR, Box 234, Oshkosh WI 54901. (414)233-5050. Promotion Director: Ellen Dillon. Sponsor: Park Plaza Merchant Association. Estab: 1971. Semiannual indoor show held 3 days in fall and spring. Average attendance: 15,000-20,000. Closing date for entry: 2 weeks before show. Entry fee: $15 per 6x15' display area. Awards $500-600 in cash prizes. Craftsman must attend show; demonstrations encouraged. Registration limit: 100 artists/craftsmen. All work must be delivered by craftsman at time of show. Considers batik, ceramics, pottery and weavings.

SHAWANO ARTS FAIR, Box 213, Shawano WI 54166. (715)526-6783. Contact: Sharon Romberg. Sponsor: Shawano County Arts Council. Estab: 1969. Annual outdoor show held 1 day in July. Average attendance: 2,000. Closing date for entry: 2 weeks before show. Entry fee: $10 per 12x6' display area. Crafts may be offered for sale; no commission. Craftsman or representative must attend show; demonstrations encouraged. Registration limit: 130 artists/craftsmen. Sponsor provides snow fence. Considers all crafts.
Awards: Presents $100, best of show; $100, palette award; $75, first grand prize; $50, second grand prize; ten $25 and five $10 cash awards. Judge is usually an art professor or museum official.

WAUNAKEE ARTS COUNCIL FESTIVAL OF ARTS, 306 7th St., Waunakee WI 53597. (608)849-5079. Contact: Colette Koltes. Estab: 1975. Annual outdoor show held 1 day in late July. Average attendance: 3,000. Entries accepted until show date. Entry fee: $5 per entry. Awards purchase prizes. Crafts may be offered for sale; 10% commission. Demonstrations OK. Considers all crafts. No molds.

Art Exhibitions

Alabama

THE CRAFT SHOW, Port City Craftsmen, Box U-1028, University of Southern Alabama, Mobile AL 36688. Estab: 1974. Semiannual indoor show held 2 days in spring and fall. Average attendance: 15,000-20,000. Closing date for entry: 4 weeks before show. Entry fee:

$15 per 10x10' display area. Art may be offered for sale; no commission. Artist must attend show; demonstrations encouraged. Registration limit: 170 spaces. Tables may be rented; sponsor provides chairs.
Acceptable Work: Considers paintings, sculpture and mobiles. "We reserve the right to refuse anything we consider in poor taste for a family-type show. No items can be hung from the gym ceiling or walls."

CREN-CREEK VILLAGE, C.C.A. School, Box 6, Luverne AL 36049. Contact: Josie M. Smith. Annual outdoor show. Entries accepted until show. Entry fee: $5 per day. Best display receives $25 award. No limit on entries. All media acceptable but no large antiques. Maximum size: 10x10'. Display panels, frames and tables available for $2.

HORSE PENS 40, Rte. 1, Box 379, Steele AL 35987. (205)538-5159. Contact: the Musgrove family. Estab: 1962. Semiannual outdoor show held 2 days in May and October. Average attendance: 6,000. Slides or photos due for prejudging 6 months before show. No entry fee. Art must be offered for sale; 10% commission. Open to artists whose work is known to the Musgroves. Artist must attend show. Registration limit: 100 artists/craftsmen. Considers drawings, paintings, prints, mobiles and sculpture.

RIVERFRONT MARKET DAY, Box 586, Selma AL 36701. Sponsor: Selma-Dallas County Historic Preservation Society. Contact: Sam O'Hara. Annual show held in fall. Average attendance: 20,000-30,000. Entry fee: $15 for street space; $25 for covered space. No limit on number or size of entries. Paintings, graphics, drawings, sculpture, mixed media, crafts and antiques acceptable. No commission. Artist must be present.

RUMBLING WATERS ARTS AND CRAFT SHOW, Box 456, Wetumpka AL 36092. (205)567-6289. Exhibitor Chairman: Gail Bass. Sponsor: Rumbling Waters Arts Club. Estab: 1970. Annual outdoor show held the first Saturday in October. Average attendance: 5,000. Entries accepted until show date. Entry fee: $7.50 per artist. Art may be offered for sale; no commission. Artist must attend show; demonstrations encouraged. Registration limit: 200 artists/craftsmen. Considers all art "that is in good taste and acceptable to the general public."

WHITE PLAINS COUNTRY FAIR, 404 W. Point St., Roanoke AL 36274. Contact: Mrs. W. E. Montgomery, Jr. Sponsor: Roanoke Junior Service League. Annual outdoor fair held in October. Average attendance: 3,000. Closing date for entry: September. Entry fee: $10 per display unit. No sales commission. Artist must attend show.

Arizona

ART IN THE PARK, Box 769, Sierra Vista AZ 85635. Sponsor: Huachuca Art Association. Annual outdoor show held in October. Average attendance: 5,000. Closing date for entry: August. Entry fee: $15. No limit on number or size of entries. Most media acceptable. No commission. Artist must be present. Insurance handled by sponsor.

FESTIVAL ARTS & CRAFTS FAIR, 8 W. Paseo Redondo, Tucson AZ 85705. (602)622-6911. Director: Jarvis Harriman. Sponsor: Tucson Festival Society, Inc. Estab: 1951. Annual outdoor show held 3 days in April. Average attendance: 50,000. Closing date for entry: 6 weeks before show. Entry fee: $75 per 8x8' booth. Art may be offered for sale; no commission. Artist must attend show; demonstrations OK. Registration limit: 140 artists/craftsmen. Considers all art.

Arkansas

ARKANSAS RIVER VALLEY ARTS & CRAFTS FAIR & SALE, Box 1122, Russellville AR 72801. (501)968-1552. Contact: Lois Griffin. Estab: 1970. Annual indoor show held 3 days in November. Average attendance: 20,000. Entries accepted until spaces filled; space granted in order of application. Entry fee: $15 per 6x8' display area. Art must be offered for sale; no commission. Artist must attend show; demonstrations encouraged. Registration limit: 167 artists/craftsmen. Considers handmade art.

BELLA VISTA ARTS & CRAFTS FESTIVAL, Kingsdale Recreation Center, Bella Vista AR 72712. (501)855-1443. Contact: Larry or Pam Collins. Sponsor: Village Art Club. Estab: 1966. Annual outdoor show with tents held 3 days in mid-October. Average attendance: 100,000. Closing date for entry: 2 weeks before show. Entry fee: $12.50 per 6x8' display area. Art must be offered for sale; 10% commission. Artist must attend show. "Exhibitors who demonstrate during the show have the best sales." Sponsor provides lattice-wire backing support in tents and pays insurance on exhibited work. Considers all art.

GRAND PRAIRIE FESTIVAL OF ARTS, Box 65, Stuttgart AR 72160. Annual show usually held in September. Categories include art, crafts, hobbies, music, prose and poetry.

NEWTON COUNTY GUILD ARTS & CRAFTS FAIR, Box 119, Limestone AR 72646. (501)428-5257. Secretary: Beverley Butler. Estab: 1970. Semiannual indoor show held 3 days in April and October. Closing date for entry: 2 weeks before show. Entry fee: $10 per 6x8' display area. Art may be offered for sale; no commission. Artist must attend show; demonstrations OK. "We want all booths and participants to be neat and orderly. No half-booths or part-time booths. We expect participants to be there Friday at 9 a.m. and not to pull their exhibit until closing at 6 p.m. Sunday." Considers all art.

SIDEWALK ARTS AND CRAFTS SHOW, c/o Chamber of Commerce, Auditorium Bldg., Eureka Springs AR 72632. (501)253-8737. Contact: Jim Emmons. Annual outdoor show held 2 days in spring. Entries accepted until show date. Entry fee: $15-25. Prejudging by slides or photos of work; entry fee refunded for refused work. Art may be offered for sale; no commission. Artist must attend show and is urged to work in his booth. Sponsor provides park benches for display. Considers all art.

California

APPLE SMORGY DAYS ARTS & CRAFTS FESTIVAL, 3170 Hassler Rd., Camino CA 95709. (916)626-0128. Show Director: Mike Visman. Sponsor: El Dorado Orchards. Estab: 1969. Annual outdoor show held each weekend during Apple Hills Festival in October. Average attendance: 25,000-35,000. Entries accepted until show date. Entry fee: $20 per weekend or $50 for the month. Art may be offered for sale; no commission. Artist or representative must attend; demonstrations OK. Registration limit: 3 artists per art category per weekend. Considers all art.

ART IN THE PARK TRADE FAIR, 14170 N. Highway 59, Merced CA 95340. (209)563-6519. Chairman: Eleanor Elkins. Sponsor: Merced River School Parents Club. Estab: 1973. Annual outdoor show held 1 day in May. Average attendance: 6,000. Closing date for entry: 2 weeks before show. Entry fee: $10 per picnic table display area. Art may be offered for sale; no commission. Demonstrations OK. Registration limit: 100 artists/craftsmen. Sponsor provides insurance for exhibited work. Considers all art.

BROCKMAN GALLERY CHRISTMAS CRAFTS SHOW, 4334 Degnaw Blvd., Los Angeles CA 90008. (213)294-3766. Program Coordinator: Pat Johnson. Sponsor: Brockman Gallery Productions. Estab: 1968. Annual show held 2 days outdoors and 2 weeks indoors in December. Average attendance: 500-600. Closing date for entry: 2 weeks before show. Prejudging. Art may be offered for sale; 40% commission. Registration limit: 50-60 artists/craftsmen. Sponsor provides inside display equipment and pays insurance on exhibited work. Considers all art.

CALICO ART FESTIVAL, 9484 Excelsior Ave., Hanford CA 93230. Contact: Dianne Vierra. Sponsor: Kings River Parents and Teachers Association. Annual outdoor show held in September. Average attendance: 2,000. Entry fee: $10 plus donation of 1 craft. No commission. Registration limit: 50 artists/craftsmen. Artist must attend show. Sponsor provides 10x15' display area. Considers most media. No size limit.

COUNTRY ARTS AND CRAFTS SHOW, c/o Graton Park Inc., 412 S. Brush St., Graton CA 95444. Contact: Lebo. Outdoor show held in conjunction with annual 4th of July Festival. Average attendance: 7,000. Entry fee: $5 per 10x10' display area. Considers all media.

DOWNTOWN CHRISTMAS CRAFTS SHOW, Box 3727, Chico CA 95927. (916)345-6633. Contact: Robert J. Calvert. Sponsor: R. J. Calvert Antiques. Estab: 1976. Annual indoor/outdoor show held 13 days during the Christmas season. Average attendance: 40,000. Entries accepted until show date. Entry fee: $20 per artist. Maximum 2 entries per artist. Prejudging; entry fee refunded for refused work. Art may be offered for sale; 10% commission. Artist may rent tables and chairs. Sponsor pays insurance on exhibited work. Considers all art.

FESTIVAL OF THE ARTS, Sacramento Regional Arts Council, 1930 T Street, Sacramento CA 95814. Chairman: Al Hellenthal. Annual open-air mall show held last weekend in September. Entry fee: $8 per display area. No sales commission. Artist or representative must be present at exhibit at all times. Considers original work only. No size limit.

FIESTA DEL ARTES, Box 404, Hermosa Beach CA 90254. (213)376-0951. Executive Manager: Charles A. Pinney. Sponsor: Chamber of Commerce. Estab: 1970. Semiannual outdoor show held 2 days during Memorial Day and Labor Day weekends. Average attendance: 5,000. Closing date for entry: 3 weeks before show. Entry fee: $45 per 10x10' display area. Prejudging; entry fee refunded for refused work. Art may be offered for sale; no commission. Registration limit: 275 artists/craftsmen. Considers all art.

FIRST SUNDAY IN THE PARK, Box 99, Ventura CA 93001. Program Coordinator: Cheryl M. Collart. Sponsor: City of Ventura, Parks and Recreation Dept. Estab: 1975. Outdoor show held the first Sunday of each month except January and October. Average attendance: 5,000-8,000. Closing date for entry: 1 week before show. Entry fee: $5 per artist. Prejudging by photos; entry fee refunded for refused work. Art may be offered for sale; no commission. Artist must attend show; demonstrations OK. Registration limit: 100 artists/craftsmen. Considers all art.

4TH OF JULY, 7246 Fair Oaks Blvd., Carmichael CA 95608. Contact: Chamber of Commerce. Annual indoor/outdoor show held July 4. Average attendance: 45,000. Closing date for entry: early June. Entry fee: $25. Crafts may be offered for sale; no commission. Craftsman or representative should attend show "if he has a sales or display booth." Considers all art.

HOLIDAY FAIRE, Muckenthaler Cultural Center, 1201 W. Malvern, Fullerton CA 92633. Contact: Dale Raoul. Estab: 1969. Annual show held from late November to the day before Christmas. Average attendance: 5,000. Closing date for entry: about October 15. 25% sales commission. Insurance handled by the cultural center. The center sets up displays. Considers all art; especially needs crafts.

INDEPENDENCE DAY VILLAGE FAIRE, Box 1058, Weaverville CA 96093. Contact: Bud Maddalena. Sponsor: Chamber of Commerce and Trinity Players. Average attendance: 2,500. Closing date for entry: June 15th. Entry fee: $15 per 10x10' booth. Maximum 1 booth per artist. Annual outdoor fair held 4th of July weekend. Media include oils, acrylics, watercolors, graphics, drawings, sculpture, mixed media and handcrafted items. Also a flea market open to all items. No sales commission. Artist or representative must attend show.

LOLA MONTEZ-LOTTA CRABTREE EXTRAVAGANZA, 128 Banner Rd., Nevada City CA 95959. (916)273-9389. Co-Chairman: Kathleen L. Coleman. Sponsor: Sunflower School. Estab: 1973. Annual outdoor show held 2 days in June. Average attendance: 2,000+. Closing date for entry: 4 weeks before show. Entry fee: $10 per 10x10' space. Prejudging by photos; entry fee refunded for refused work. Art may be offered for sale; 10% commission. Artist must attend show; demonstrations encouraged. Registration limit: 30-35 artists/craftsmen. Considers sculpture.

MONTEREY COUNTY ART COMPETITION, 559 Pacific St., Monterey CA 93940. Director: June Braucht. Sponsor: Monterey Peninsula Museum of Art. Annual show held in March. Open to residents of Monterey County. Acceptable media include paintings, sculpture and graphics.

MOUNTAIN AIRE, Box 4698, Modesto CA 95352. (209)521-6310. Sponsor: Rock 'N Chair Productions. Estab: 1974. Annual outdoor show held 2 days in June in conjunction with large music festival. Average attendance: 12,000 per day. Closing date for entry: 1 week before show. Write for entry fee. Prejudging; entry fee refunded for refused work. Art may be offered for sale; no commission. "Wares directed toward ages 15-35 sell best." Demonstrations OK. Registration limit: 75 artists/craftsmen. Considers all art.

SOUTH LAKE FESTIVAL OF THE ARTS, 492 S. Lake Ave., Pasadena CA 91101. (213)792-4417. Coordinator: Ray Leier. Sponsor: South Lake Business Association. Estab: 1974. Semiannual outdoor show held 2 days in early spring and late fall. "Located in well-shopped retail area." Closing date for entry: 2 weeks before show. Entry fee: $25 per 12x4' display area.

Prejudging by photos; entry fee refunded for refused work. Art may be offered for sale; no commission. Artist must attend show; demonstrations OK. Considers all art.

WOMEN'S ARTS AND CRAFTS FAIR, Box 7024, Berkeley CA 94704. Sponsor: East Bay National Organization for Women. Annual show held in late May or early June. Closing date for entry: late April or early May. Entry fee: $15 per 10x10' display unit. Open to women or a woman-man team. "Quite open" on media acceptable. No commission. Artist must attend show. Describe or submit slides of work.

Colorado

OWN YOUR OWN ART SHOW, c/o Art Dept., University of Southern Colorado, Pueblo CO 81001. (303)549-2552. Chairmen: Ed Sajbel/Bob Wands. Sponsors: University of Southern Colorado Art Dept. and Pueblo Service League. Estab: 1962. Annual indoor show held 2 weeks in November. Average attendance: 10,000. Closing date for entry: 1 week before show. Entry fee: $4 per artist. Prejudging; no entry fees refunded for refused work. Art may be offered for sale; 25% commission for art scholarships. Open to residents of Colorado, Idaho, Arizona, Montana, Nevada, New Mexico, Utah and Wyoming. Students may demonstrate. Registration limit: 900-1,000 artists/craftsmen. Considers all art. Maximum size: 12'x80".

ROCKY MOUNTAIN NATIONAL CRAFT FAIR, National Crafts Ltd., Gapland MD 21736. (301)432-8438. Director: Noel Clark. Estab: 1977. Annual indoor show held in the Adams County Fairgrounds in Denver 2-3 days in July. Average attendance: 40,000. Closing date for applications: 3-4 months before show. Entry fee: $90. Prejudging by 5 color slides; entry fee refunded for refused work. Art may be offered for sale; no commission. Artist must attend show. Registration limit: 400 artists/craftsmen. Considers printmaking.

WILDLIFE ART SHOWS, 1420 E. 91st Ave., Thornton CO 80229. (303)288-1144. Contact: David or C. Holly Merrifield. Sponsors: Colorado Wildlife Federation, Wilderness Society and the Audubon Society. Estab: 1974. Indoor/outdoor show held once a month for 3 days. Entries accepted year-round. Entry fee: $10 per artist; $5 prejudging fee. Art may be offered for sale; 15% commission. Artist must attend show; prefers demonstrations. Registration limit: 25-30 artists/craftsmen. Considers all art.
Acceptable Work: Work must pertain to wildlife. Art must be framed; bin work must be matted. No chicken wire screen displays; pegboard only. If wood-framed, must be painted in earth tones. Prefers sculpture displayed on pedestals.

Connecticut

AMERICRAFT CRAFTS EXPO, Box 370, Farmington CT 06032. (202)224-8388. Director: Ruby Kowalczyk. Sponsor: American Crafts Expositions. Estab: 1969. Annual indoor/outdoor show held in Berlin 3 days in August. Average attendance: 20,000+. Closing date for entry: 4 weeks before show. Entry fee: $50-60 per booth. Prejudging; entry fee refunded for refused work. Art may be offered for sale; no commission. Artist must attend show; demonstrations OK. Registration limit: 200 artists/craftsmen. Considers all art.

ANNUAL GUEST SPRING EXHIBITION, Couturier Galerie, 1814 Newfield Ave., Stamford CT 06903. (203)322-2405. Director: Marion Couturier. Annual show held in spring. Closing date for entry: December. No entry fee. Maximum 3 entries per artist. 40% commission. Gallery insures exhibited work. Considers oils, acrylics, watercolors, mixed media and graphics.

CHRISTMAS CRAFTS EXPO, Box 370, Farmington CT 06032. (202)224-8388. Director: Rudy Kowalczyk. Sponsor: American Crafts Expositions. Estab: 1973. Annual indoor show held at the Hartford Civic Center 3 days in December. Average attendance: 25,000+. Closing date for entry: 4 weeks before show. Entry fee: $100, 10x10' display area; $140, 10x15' display area; $180, 10x20' display area. Prejudging; entry fee refunded for refused work. Art may be offered for sale; no commission. Artist must attend show; demonstrations OK. Registration limit: 250 artists/craftsmen. Considers all art.

FARMINGTON CRAFTS EXPO, Box 370, Farmington CT 06032. (202)224-8388. Director: Rudy Kowalczyk. Sponsor: American Crafts Expositions. Estab: 1972. Annual outdoor show held 3 days in June (tent space available). Average attendance: 20,000+. Closing date for entry: 4 weeks before show. Entry fee: $60, outside; $70, tent. Prejudging; entry fee refunded for refused work. Art may be offered for sale; no commission. Artist must attend show; demonstrations OK. Registration limit: 200 artists/craftsmen. Considers all art.

GALLERY ON THE GREEN, Box 421, Litchfield CT 06759. Contact: Maureen Samuels. Sponsor: Junior Women's Club of Litchfield. Annual outdoor show. Entry fee: $10 (nonrefundable) per artist. Sponsor provides 10x12' display area and limited snow fencing. All media accepted. Write for application form.

GREATER VERNON JAYCEES ARTS & CRAFTS FAIR, Greater Vernon Jaycees, Box 119, Rockville CT 06066. Chairman: Joe Lieberman. Estab: 1974. Annual outdoor show held 2 days in late fall. Closing date for entry: 16 weeks before show. Entry fee: $2.50 per linear foot. Prejudging by photos; entry fee refunded for refused work. Art may be offered for sale; no commission. Artist must attend show; demonstrations OK. Sponsor pays insurance for exhibited work. Considers all art.

MEET THE ARTISTS, 41 Green St., Milford CT 06460. (203)874-5672. Contact: Director. Sponsor: Denise Morris Curt. Estab: 1963. Annual indoor/outdoor show held in Bridgeport, Connecticut 1-3 days in May. Entry fee: $10 per day. Prejudging by slides or photos; entry fee refunded for refused work. Art may be offered for sale; no commission. Artist must attend show; demonstrations OK. Considers all art.

MEET THE ARTISTS, 41 Green St., Milford CT 06460. (203)874-5672. Contact: Director. Sponsor: Denise Morris Curt. Estab: 1963. Semiannual indoor/outdoor show held at Chapel Square Mall in New Haven, Connecticut 1-3 days in June and November. Entry fee: $10 per day. Prejudging by slides or photos; entry fee refunded for refused work. Art may be offered for sale; no commission. Artist must attend show; demonstrations OK. Considers all art.

MEET THE ARTISTS, 41 Green St., Milford CT 06460. (203)874-5672. Contact: Director. Sponsor: Denise Morris Curt. Estab: 1963. Semiannual indoor/outdoor show held in Meriden Square 4 days in September and October. Entry fee: $10 per day. Prejudging by slides or photos; entry fee refunded for refused work. Art may be offered for sale; no commission. Artist must attend show; demonstrations OK. Considers all art.

SIDEWALK ART SHOW, Fairfield Chamber of Commerce, 1597 Post Rd., Fairfield CT 06430. (203)255-1011. Executive Director: Harold B. Harris. Annual outdoor show held 1 day in June. Closing date for entry: 1 week before show. Entry fee: $10 per display area. Art may be offered for sale; no commission. Artist must attend show.
Acceptable Work: Considers acrylics, airbrush, calligraphy, drawings, oils, pastels, prints, watercolors and sculpture. Art must be framed and suitable for hanging.

SISTERHOOD B'NAI ABRAHAM ARTS AND CRAFTS SHOW, Temple B'Nai Abraham, 127 E. Main St., Meriden CT 06450. Contact: Ms. Wallace Seidon. Annual show held in September. Entry fee: $12 per 5x10' space. Maximum 2 entries per artist. No commission. Artist must attend show. Sponsor provides insurance for exhibited work. Acceptable media include oils, acrylics, watercolors, graphics, drawings, sculpture, mixed media and crafts.

YAAF ARTS AND CRAFTS SALE, 18 Reef Rd., Fairfield CT 06430. Contact: Jack Farkas or Paul Strauss. Sponsor: Young Artist Association of Fairfield. Annual outdoor show. Average attendance: 250,000. Entry fee: $20 per 12' display area. No limit on number of entries. Prejudging. No commission. Registration limit: 100 artists/craftsmen. All media accepted.

Delaware

BRANDYWINE ARTS FESTIVAL, 1307 Orange St., Wilmington DE 19801. Director: George Sargisson. Estab: 1961. Annual outdoor show held 2 days in September. Average attendance: 15,000 per day. Closing date for entry: 4 weeks before show. Entry fee: $8 per 10' fence. Art must be offered for sale; 20% commission on daily sales. Artist must attend show. Considers drawings, pastels, paintings and prints.

Florida

ALTAMONTE MALL, 2918 Martel Dr., Dayton OH 45420. (513)254-2900. Director: Clarence Freeland. Annual indoor show held in Altamonte, Florida 1 week. Closing date for entry: 1 week before show. Charges entry fee: due after jurying. Prejudging. Art may be offered for sale; no commission. Artist must attend show; demonstrations OK. Sponsor provides 10x10' display area. Considers all art.

BEAUX ARTS CLOTHESLINE SALE, c/o Lowe Art Museum, 1301 Miller Dr., Coral Gables FL 33146. Contact: Mrs. William N. Taylor. Entry fee: $42 per 10x10' display space. Agents pay fee of $58. No sales commission. Considers oils, acrylics, mixed media, watercolors, graphics, drawings, ceramics, sculpture and crafts.

EASTLAKE SQUARE MALL, 2918 Martel Dr., Dayton OH 45420. (513)254-2900. Director: Clarence Freeland. Annual indoor show held in Tampa 1 week. Closing date for entry: 1 week before show. Entry fee due after jurying. Prejudging. Art may be offered for sale; no commission. Artist must attend show; demonstrations OK. Sponsor provides 10x10' display area. Considers all art.

FLORIDA FOREST FESTIVAL ARTS & CRAFTS SHOW & SALE, Box 892, Perry FL 32347. (904)584-5366. Chairman: Nadine O. Loughridge. Sponsor: Perry-Taylor County Chamber of Commerce. Estab: 1971. Annual outdoor show held 1 day the fourth weekend in October. Average attendance: 30,000. Closing date for entry: 1 week before show. Entry fee: $3 per 9x9' display area. Art may be offered for sale; 10% commission. Artist must attend show; demonstrations encouraged. Sponsor provides 24 canopies for rent and pays liability insurance. Considers all art.

LEE SIDEWALK ARTS & CRAFTS SHOW, Lee County Bank, Box 711, c/o Special Services, Fort Myers FL 33902. (813)334-1171 ext. 373. Vice President: Burnett Bloodworth. Estab: 1974. Annual outdoor show held 1 day in January. Average attendance: 12,000. Closing date for entry: 4 weeks before show. Entry fee: $10 per 10x10' display area. Art may be offered for sale; no commission. Demonstrations OK. Considers all art.

SPRING ARTS FESTIVAL, Drawer 1187, Gainesville FL 32602. (904)372-1976. Director: Karen Beach. Sponsors: Santa Fe Community College and Gainesville Chamber of Commerce. Estab: 1970. Annual outdoor show held 2 days in April. Average attendance: 60,000. Closing date for entry: 6 weeks before show or until spaces filled. Entry fee: $5 application fee. Prejudging; no entry fees refunded. Art may be offered for sale; no commission. Open to Alachua and Bradford counties residents. Artist must attend show; demonstrations OK. Registration limit: 250 artists/craftsmen.
Acceptable Work: Considers paintings, graphics, drawings, prints and sculpture.

TALLAHASSEE JUNIOR MUSEUM MARKET DAYS, c/o Frankie Mack, 2211 Orleans Dr., Tallahassee FL 32303. Annual indoor show for original oils, acrylics, watercolors, graphics, drawings, sculpture, mixed media and crafts. Entry fee: $15 per 10x13' display unit. Artist must attend show. 10% commission. Write for entry blank.

Georgia

ATLANTA CRAFT FAIR, National Crafts Ltd., Gapland MD 21736. (301)432-8438. Director: Noel Clark. Estab: 1977. Annual indoor show held in the Atlanta Civic Center 2-3 days in November. Average attendance: 40,000. Closing date for applications: 3-4 months before show. Entry fee: $90. Prejudging by 5 color slides; entry fee refunded for refused work. Art may be offered for sale; no commission. Artist must attend show. Registration limit: 400 artists/craftsmen. Considers printmaking.

BROWN'S CROSSING CRAFTSMEN FAIR, Brown's Crossing Craftsmen, Rte. 2, Box 271, Brown's Crossing, Milledgeville GA 31061. Contact: Carole S. Sirmans. Estab: 1970. Annual show held the third weekend in October. Average attendance: 12,000. Media accepted include watercolors, oils, acrylics, pottery, weaving, woodcarving, graphics, glass, leather, candles, needlework and macrame. Slides necessary for new exhibitors. Demonstrations are well received. Only 125 of the "best quality" exhibitors are accepted and evenly divided between craftsmen and 2-dimensional artists. No commission charged on works offered for sale. Sponsor provides 8x10' display area.

MILLION PINES ARTS & CRAFTS FESTIVAL, Box 238, Soperton GA 30457. (912)529-4524. Chairman: Jack Pournelle. Sponsor: City of Soperton. Estab: 1973. Annual outdoor show held 2 days in November. Closing date for entry: 4 weeks before show. Entry fee: $25. Maximum 2 entries per artist. Art may be offered for sale; no commission. Artist must attend show; demonstrations encouraged. Registration limit: 25 artists/craftsmen. Sponsor provides 10x12' display area. Considers all art.

THE PRATER'S MILL COUNTRY FAIR, 216 Riderwood Dr., Dalton GA 30720. Contact: Judy Alderman or Jane Harrell. Estab: 1970. Semiannual outdoor show held 2 days in May and October. Average attendance: 25,000 per show. Closing date for entry: 8 weeks before show date. Entry fee: $15 per artist. Send photo of work and SASE. Art may be offered for sale; no commission. Artist must attend show; demonstrations encouraged. Registration limit: 135-145 artists/craftsmen. Considers all art.

SOUTHEASTERN ARTS & CRAFTS FESTIVAL, Box 397, Roberta GA 31078. Contact: Dot Booth. Sponsor: Southeastern Arts and Crafts Committee. Annual show usually held in November. Entry fee: $35 per 6x10' display area. Prejudging by slides. Acceptable media include paintings, graphics, sculpture, ceramics and fine crafts.

VALDOSTA'S "CHRISTMAS SPECTACULAR" ARTS & CRAFTS FESTIVAL, Box 2043, Valdosta GA 31601. Contact: Diane Smith. Sponsor: Valdosta Junior Service League. Annual show held in December. Entry fee: $25. Open to all original media.

VIDALIA FESTIVAL OF THE ARTS, Vidalia Women's Club and Lions Club, Rte. 2, Box 74, Vidalia GA 30474. Annual show. Entry fee: $15 per 4x16' booth. Considers original art and crafts. Ten $100 bills awarded to visitors to spend on the work of their choice.

Idaho

ARTS & CRAFTS FESTIVAL, Box 1505, Julia Davis Park, Boise ID 83701. (208)348-8330. Acting Director: Beth Sellars. Sponsor: Boise Gallery of Art. Estab: 1954. Annual outdoor show held 3 days in September. Average attendance: 30,000. Closing date for entry: 1 week before show. Entry fee: $15 per 10x20' display area. Art may be offered for sale; 30% commission. Artist must attend show; demonstrations encouraged. Sponsor provides picnic bench and liability insurance. Considers all art.

BLAINE COUNTY ARTS FESTIVAL, Box 100A, Hailey ID 83333. Secretary: Roberta McKercher. Sponsor: Special Committee of Hailey Chamber of Commerce. Annual outdoor festival held in conjunction with "Days of the Old West" celebration on July 4. Average attendance: 2,500. Entry fee: $10 per artist. Accepts oils, acrylics, watercolors, graphics, drawings, sculpture, mixed media, leatherwork and jewelry. 15% commission. $50 cash award best display.

WESTGATE SHOPPING CENTER, Westgate Merchants Association, 7930 Fairview Ave., Boise ID 83704. Promotion Director: Donita Smith. "We are interested in all manner of displays, audience involvement and/or demonstrations. Artisans are welcome to display, take orders and, under some circumstances, sell their work during Association-sanctioned events."

Illinois

A DAY IN THE COUNTRY, Rte. 1, Box 194A, Pecatonica IL 61063. Chairman: Sandra Schoonmaker. Sponsor: Pecatonica Junior Woman's Club. Estab: 1971. Annual indoor show held 1 day in October. Average attendance: 3,000+. Closing date for entry: 4 weeks before show. Entry fee: $12 per entry. Art may be offered for sale; no commission. Artist must attend show; demonstrations encouraged. Limited number of spaces available. Sponsor provides electrical outlets and 10x10' display area. Considers all art.

BELVIDERE MALL STARVING ARTIST'S SHOW, Rte. 1, 146 Park Dr., Barrington IL 60010. (312)639-5665. Show Director: Irene Partridge. Sponsor: Belvidere Mall Merchants Association. Estab: 1964. Annual indoor show held 2 days in winter. Closing date for entry: 10 days before show. Entry fee: $20 per artist. Prejudging by 5 slides (send resume and SASE); entry fee refunded for refused work. Art may be offered for sale; no commission. Artist must attend show; demonstrations OK. Registration limit: 80-100 artists/craftsmen. Considers all art.

BLOWN GLASS II, 1521 Sherman Ave., Evanston IL 60201. (312)864-2660. Director: R. Isaacson. Sponsor: Mindscape Gallery & Studio. Estab: 1976. Annual indoor show held the month of April. Average attendance: 2,000. Closing date for entry: January 1. Entry fee: $5 per entry. Prejudging by slides; no entry fees refunded for refused work. Art must be offered for sale; 33 1/3% commission. Demonstrations pre-arranged. Registration limit: 24-30 artists/craftsmen. Sponsor provides insurance during exhibit period. Write for application.

CROSS COUNTY MALL SHOW, Box 61, Rome IL 61562. (309)274-3001. Contact: Judy Kelley. Estab: 1976. Semiannual indoor show held in Mattoon 3 days in spring and fall. Closing date for entry: 2 weeks before show. Entry fee: $30 per 6x12' display area; no personal checks. Prejudging by slides; entry fee refunded for refused work. Art may be offered for sale; no commission. Artist must attend show; prefers demonstrations. Registration limit: 50 artists/craftsmen. Artist may rent display table for $5. Considers all art.

CRYSTAL POINT MALL ART & CRAFT SHOW, Box 61, Rome IL 61562. (309)274-3001. Coordinator: Judy Kelley. Estab: 1977. Semiannual indoor show held in Crystal Lake 3 days in May and November. Closing date for entry: 2 weeks before show. Entry fee: $30 per entry; $5 late fee. Prejudging by slides; entry fee refunded for refused work. Art may be offered for sale; no commission. Artist must attend show; demonstrations OK. Registration limit: 40 artists/craftsmen. Considers all art. Work must be framed or on pedestal/base.

DEERFIELD COMMONS ARTS & SELECTED CRAFTS FESTIVAL, Rte. 1, 146 Park Dr., Barrington IL 60010. (312)639-5665. Director: Irene "Rae" Partridge. Sponsor: Deerfield Commons Merchants Association. Estab: 1971. Annual outdoor show held 1 day in September. Closing date for entry: 10 days before show. Entry fee: $18 per entry. Prejudging by slides; entry fee refunded for refused work. Artist must attend show; demonstrations encouraged. Registration limit: 63-65 artists/craftsmen. Considers all art. Maximum size: 10x6x5".

EDENS PLAZA ARTS & CRAFT FAIR, 9476 Harding Ave., Surfside FL 33154. Contact: Iris G. Klein. Sponsor: Edens Plaza Merchants Association. Estab: 1956. Annual outdoor show held in Wilmette, Illinois 2 days in June. Average attendance: 10,000-15,000. Closing date for entry: late May. Entry fee: $30 per 8x8' display area. Maximum 2 entries per artist. Prejudging by slides or photos (send resume and SASE). Art may be offered for sale; no commission. Registration limit: 225 artists/craftsmen. Artist must attend show; demonstrations OK. Considers all art. Paintings must be hung on display board; not set on ground. Send b&w glossies and resume for newspaper publicity.

GOLD COAST ART FAIR, 26 E. Huron St., Chicago IL 60611. Sponsors: Gold Coast Association and *Near North News*. Estab: 1958. Annual outdoor show held 3 days in August. Average attendance: 600,000. Entry fee: $25 per display area. Art may be offered for sale; no commission. Artist must attend show; demonstrations OK. Sponsor pays insurance for exhibited work. Considers calligraphy, drawings, paintings, pastels, prints and sculpture.

GROUP SHOWING OF AMERICAN ARTISTS, 9476 Harding Ave., Surfside FL 33154. Contact: Iris G. Klein. Sponsor: House of Fine Art, Inc. Annual show held in Skokie, Illinois from late fall-early winter. No entry fee. Maximum 5 entries per artist. 30% sales commission. Sponsor provides display boards. Considers all media. Maximum size: 4x8'.

HILLSIDE CENTER SELECTED CRAFTS FESTIVAL, Rte. 1, 146 Park Dr., Barrington IL 60010. (312)639-5665. Director: Irene "Rae" Partridge. Sponsor: Hillside Center Merchants Association. Estab: 1966. Annual outdoor show held in Hillside 2 days in spring. Closing date for entry: 10 days before show. Entry fee: $25 per entry. Prejudging by 5 slides or photos (include resume and SASE); entry fee refunded for refused work. Art may be offered for sale; no commission. Artist must attend show; demonstrations encouraged. Registration limit: 100-125 artists/craftsmen. Considers all art. Maximum size: 10x6x8'. "Keep packing out of sight; tables must be draped to floor on all sides; cartons should be removed."

HILLSIDE STARVING ARTIST'S SHOW, Rte. 1, 146 Park Dr., Barrington IL 60010. (312)639-5665. Show Director: Irene Partridge. Sponsor: Hillside Center Merchants Association. Estab: 1966. Annual indoor show held in Hillside 2 days during the winter. Closing date for entry: 10 days before show. Entry fee: $20 per artist. Prejudging by 5 slides or photos (send resume and SASE); entry fee refunded for refused work. Art may be offered for sale; no commission. Artist must attend show; demonstrations OK. Registration limit: 100-125 artists/craftsmen. Considers all art.

HOWARD-WESTERN CRAFT & SCULPTURE FAIR, 9476 Harding Ave., Surfside FL 33154. Art Director: Iris G. Klein. Sponsor: Howard-Western Merchants Association. Estab: 1970. Annual outdoor show held in Chicago 2 days in September. Average attendance: 2,000-

3,000. Closing date for entry: 4 weeks before show. Entry fee: $15. Maximum 2 entries per artist. Art may be offered for sale; no commission. Artist must attend show; demonstrations by caricaturists only. Registration limit: 75 artists/craftsmen. Considers mobiles and sculpture.

KISHWAUKEE VALLEY ART LEAGUE ANNUAL SPRING ART AND CRAFT FAIR, c/o Anita L. Rogers, 308 S. Malta Rd., Malta IL 60150. Held on Dekalb County Court House lawn, Rtes. 23 and 64.

MARKET PLACE MALL ART & CRAFT SHOW, Box 61, Rome IL 61562. (309)274-3001. Coordinator: Judy Kelley. Estab: 1976. Semiannual indoor show held in Champaign 3 days in spring and fall. Closing date for entry: 2 weeks before show. Entry fee: $40 per 6x12' display area. "No personal checks." Prejudging by 2 slides (include SASE); entry fee refunded for refused work. Art may be offered for sale; no commission. Artist must attend show. Registration limit: 80-100 artists/craftsmen. Considers all art.

NORTHPOINT CENTER ARTS & SELECTED CRAFTS FESTIVAL, Rte. 1, 146 Park Dr. Barrington IL 60010. (312)639-5665. Director: Irene "Rae" Partridge. Sponsor: Northpoint Merchants Association. Estab: 1971. Semiannual outdoor show held 1 day in July and September. Closing date for entry: 10 days before show. Entry fee: $15 per entry. Prejudging by 5 slides or photos (include resume and SASE); entry fee refunded for refused work. Art may be offered for sale; no commission. Artist must attend show; demonstrations encouraged. Registration limit: 125-150 artists/craftsmen. Considers all art. Maximum size: 10x6x8'.

NORTHWOODS FINE ARTS SHOW, 4501 War Memorial Dr., Peoria IL 61613. Call (309)688-0445 weekdays only from 9 a.m. to 5 p.m. Contact: Mrs. Lynda Michael. Sponsor: Northwoods Merchants' Association. Estab: 1975. Annual indoor show. Closing date for entry: 2 weeks before show. Entry fee: $25 per approximately 9x5' display area. Prejudging; entry free refunded for refused work. Art may be offered for sale; no commission. Open to artists ages 18+. Artist must attend show; demonstrations OK. Entrant must sign "Hold Harmless" form. Considers all art. No nudes. Send written request or call to be added to mailing list.

OLD CANAL DAYS ARTS AND CRAFTS SHOW, 1109 Garfield St., Lockport IL 60441. (815)838-7316. Acting Chairman: Louise Lamb. Sponsor: Old Canal Days Committee. Estab: 1973. Annual outdoor show held 2 days in June. Average attendance: 40,000. Closing date for entry: 4 weeks before show. Entry fee: $10 per entry. Art may be offered for sale; no commission. Demonstrations encouraged. Registration limit: 250 artists/craftsmen. Sponsor provides 3x8' display area.
Acceptable Work: Considers calligraphy, drawings, oils, pastels, prints, watercolors, mobiles and sculpture.

SANDBURG MALL ART & CRAFT SHOW, Box 61, Rome IL 61562. (309)274-3001. Contact: Judy Kelley. Estab: 1975. Semiannual indoor show held 3 days in spring and fall. Closing date for entry: 2 weeks before show. Entry fee: $35 per 6x12' display area. Prejudging by 2 slides (send SASE); no entry fees refunded. Art may be offered for sale; no commission. Artist must attend show. Considers all art.

SHERIDAN VILLAGE SHOPPING CENTER, c/o Constance L. Barger, 2006 N. North St., Peoria IL 61604. Annual sidewalk show held 3 days under a canopy. Entry fee: $25 per 7x10' display area. Art must be offered for sale; no commission. Cash awards given for best display voted by public. Small crafts will be limited and edited.

SPRING ARTS & CRAFTS, 2130 S. 61st Court, Cicero IL 60650. (312)863-8979 or 863-2104. Executive Director: Norm Scaman. Sponsor: Cermak Road Business Association. Estab: 1973. Annual outdoor show held 2 days in the spring. Closing date for entry: 1 week before show. Entry fee: $10 per artist. Art may be offered for sale; no commission. Artist or representative must attend show; demonstrations OK. Considers all art.

STARVING ARTISTS ARTS & CRAFTS FAIR, Oakton Community College, 7900 Nagle, Morton Grove IL 60053. (312)967-5120. Director: Jay Wollin. Estab: 1970. Annual outdoor show held 2 days during Memorial Day weekend. Average attendance: 18,000. Closing date for entry: 6 weeks before show. Entry fee: $20 per display area with 10' minimum frontage. Prejudging by 5 slides. Art may be sold for under $25; no commission. Committee of non-

college jurors awards 5-6 purchase prizes to use as door prizes. Artist or representative must attend show; electricity and equipment provided for demonstrations. Registration limit: 125-150 artists/craftsmen. College has liability insurance and provides security guards.
Acceptable Work: Considers acrylics, mobiles, sculpture, airbrush, calligraphy, drawings, oils, pastels, prints and watercolors.

VILLA OAKS STARVING ARTIST'S FAIR, Rte. 1, 146 Park Dr., Barrington IL 60010. Show Director: Irene Partridge. Sponsor: Villa Oaks Merchants Association. Estab: 1971. Annual outdoor show held in Villa Park 1 day during August. Closing date for entry: 10 days before show. Entry fee: $15 per artist. Prejudging by 5 slides or photos (send resume and SASE); entry fee refunded for refused work. Art may be offered for sale; no commission. Artist must attend show; demonstrations encouraged. Registration limit: 125-150 artists/craftsmen. Considers all art.

VILLAGE MALL ART & CRAFT SHOW, Box 61, Rome IL 61562. (309)274-3001. Contact: Judy Kelley. Estab: 1975. Semiannual indoor show held 3 days in spring and fall. Closing date for entry: 2 weeks before show. Entry fee: $30 per 6x12' display area. Prejudging by 2 slides (send SASE); entry fee refunded for refused work. Art may be offered for sale; no commission. Artist must attend show. Registration limit: 50 artists/craftsmen. Considers all art.

WATER TOWER ART & CRAFT FESTIVAL, American Society of Artists, 700 N. Michigan, Chicago IL 60611. (312)751-2500. President: Nancy Fregin. Estab: 1972. Annual outdoor show held 3 days in June. Closing date for entry: April. Entry fee: $17 per non-member. Prejudging by 3-5 slides or photos (send resume); entry fee refunded for refused work. Art may be offered for sale; no commission. Artist must attend show. Registration limit: 300 artists/craftsmen. Considers all art.

WOODFIELD COMMONS ANNUAL SUMMER ARTS AND SELECTED CRAFTS FESTIVAL, Rte. 1, 146 Park Ave., Barrington IL 60010. Contact: Irene Partridge. Annual outdoor show held in August (covers available). Entry fee: $15. Most media may be exhibited but crafts are limited. No sales commission. Artist or representative must attend show. Submit 5 slides or photos of what is representative of work to be exhibited, along with resume and SASE. "This is the open mall directly west of the large enclosed Woodfield Mall and should not be confused with the big mall."

Indiana

ASSOCIATION OF ARTISTS & CRAFTSMEN OF PORTER COUNTY, Box 783, Chesterton IN 46304. Contact: Barbara or Robert Funke. Annual fair held the first Saturday and Sunday in August. Entry fee: $20. Considers oils, acrylics, watercolors, fabrics, woven pieces, batik, silkscreen, pottery, glass, leather, jewelry, woodcarving and metal sculpture. Submit slides of work according to letter of instruction available on request. No sales commission.

BOULEVARD MALL ART & CRAFT SHOW, Box 61, Rome IL 61562. (309)274-3001. Contact: Judy Kelley. Estab: 1974. Annual indoor show held 3 days in South Crawfordsville in spring. Closing date for entry: 2 weeks before show. Entry fee: $30 per 6x12' display area. Prejudging by 2 slides or photos; entry fee refunded for refused work. Art may be offered for sale; no commission. Artist must attend show. Registration limit: 40 artists/craftsmen. Considers all art.

CHRISTMAS GIFT & HOBBY SHOW, Box 20189, Indianapolis IN 46220. (317)255-4151. Exhibit Sales Director: Thelma Schoenberger. Estab: 1950. Annual indoor show held 9 days in November. Average attendance: 100,000. "We're always full 2 months before show." Entry fee: $140 per 10x10' booth. Art may be offered for sale; no commission. Artist must attend show; demonstrations encouraged. Considers all art.

CREATIVE ARTS AND CRAFTS, INC., Rte. 5, Box 101, Bloomington IN 47401. (812)332-8076. Contact: Richard Taylor. Nonprofit, tax exempt public foundation seeking to "promote and encourage community interest and participation in various fields of art and crafts." Sponsors 3 art and crafts shows annually. Entry fee: $11.50, June show; $16.50, September show; $30, December show. Entry fees refunded to 2 best booths. Sponsor provides 6x8' display area. Considers only handmade crafts and original work. Plants may only be sold in hand-decorated pots and/or with handmade hangers. Beads may not be sold separately. Tables must be skirted. Write for entry form.

DAVIESS MARTIN COUNTY ART FESTIVAL, Box 245, Loogootee IN 47553. (812)295-3421. Park Superintendent: David L. Watson. Sponsor: West Boggs Park. Estab: 1975. Annual show held 2 days in August in 12x12' tents. Average attendance: 6,000. Entries accepted until show. Entry fee: $10 ($5 refunded on artist's arrival). Art may be offered for sale; no commission. Artist must attend show. "We recommend that artists demonstrate their talents as it helps promote sales." First 30 entries are given a 12x12' tent, table and 2 chairs. Considers all art.

DOWNTOWN FESTIVAL DAYS, Box 91, Connersville IN 47331. (317)825-7140. Contact: Carson McQueen. Sponsor: Connersville Jaycees. Estab: 1976. Annual outdoor show held 2 days in early May. Average attendance: 10,000-15,000. Entries accepted until show date. Entry fee: $8 per 10x15' display area; $15 per vehicle space. Art may be offered for sale; no commission. Demonstrations OK. Considers all art.

INDIANA ARTISTS, 1200 W. 38th St., Indianapolis IN 46208. Sponsor: Indianapolis Museum of Art. Entry fee: $5. Maximum 2 entries per artist. Open to past or present Indiana residents.

KAMM'S BREWERY ANNUAL ARTS & CRAFTS FESTIVAL, Box 806, Mishawaka IN 46544. (219)259-7861. Contact: William Strong. Sponsor: 100 Center Development Co. Average attendance: 30,000. Annual 2-day outdoor festival held the third weekend in July. Closing date for entry: June. Entry fee: $15 per 10x10' space. Artist must be present at booth. No commission. All media acceptable.

LA PORTE JAYCEES ART SHOW, 1510 Hillcrest St., La Porte IN 46350. Contact: Rolland Hardesty. Sponsor: La Porte Jaycees. Annual show held in July. Considers original paintings, pottery, jewelry, sculpture and crafts. Adult exhibitors only. Artist must attend; encourages demonstrations. Entry fee: $10 per artist (non-refundable). Write for application blank. Enter early as spaces are limited. Applications will be screened as to variety. No commission. Show publicized extensively along with the annual Jaycees July 4 week-long celebration through area radio, TV and newspapers.

LOGANSPORT MALL SHOW, Box 61, Rome IL 61562. (309)274-3001. Contact: Judy Kelley. Estab: 1976. Semiannual indoor show held in Logansport, Indiana 3 days in April and October. Closing date for entry: 2 weeks before show. Entry fee: $30 per 6x12' display area.

All original art is eligible for entry into the June Rose Festival Fine Arts & Selected Crafts show (Clarklake, Michigan). Among the entries in the 1976 show was this oil color by Leland Beaman, freelance artist and teacher.

Prejudging by 2 slides; entry fee refunded for refused work. SASE. Art may be offered for sale; no commission. Sponsor provides panels. Considers all art.

RICHMOND SQUARE MALL SUMMER ARTS & CRAFTS SHOW, c/o John Gromosiak, 1937 Wilene Dr., Dayton OH 45432. Entry fee: $50 for 10x10' booth. No sales commission. Considers all art and crafts. No imports.

TIPPECANOE BATTLEFIELD ARTS & CRAFTS FESTIVAL, Box 225, Battle Ground IN 47920. (317)567-2147. Director: D. Clarke Evans. Sponsor: Battle Ground Historical Corp. Estab: 1974. Annual outdoor show held 2 days in August. Average attendance: 4,000. Entries accepted until show date; "but to be in program, entries must be in by July." Entry fee: $15 per 8x14' display area. Art may be offered for sale; no commission. Artist must attend show. Considers all art.

WASHINGTON SQUARE MALL, 1937 Wilene Dr., Dayton OH 45432. Director: John Gromosiak. Annual show held in Indianapolis in April. Largest mall in Indiana. All media and crafts eligible. No agents. No sales commission. Although liability insurance is carried by the show director, it is recommended that artists arrange for their own insurance.

Iowa

ART IN THE PARK, Box 132, Clinton IA 52732. (319)242-9635 or 243-7476. Chairman: Bill Ross. Sponsors: Clinton Art Association and Lyons Retail Bureau. Estab: 1968. Annual outdoor show held 2 days in May. Average attendance: 3,000. Closing date for entry: 1 week before show. Entry fee: $10 per entry; due after jurying. Art may be offered for sale; no commission. Artist must attend show. Considers all art. No erotica.

SNAKE ALLEY ART FAIR, Box 5, Burlington IA 52601. Chairman: Jerry Rigdon. Sponsor: Burlington Art Guild. Estab: 1967. Annual outdoor show held 1 day in June. Average attendance: 2,500. Entries accepted until show date or until spaces filled. Entry fee: $10 per entry. Awards several $25 "best display of work" prizes. Prejudging; entry fee refunded for refused work. Art may be offered for sale; no commission. Artist must attend show; pastel portrait demonstrations OK. Registration limit: 100 artists/craftsmen. Sponsor provides some snow fence. Considers all art.

Kentucky

SUE BENNETT FOLK FESTIVAL, Sue Bennett College, London KY 40741. (606)864-9714. Chairman: Madge Chesnut. Estab: 1974. Annual indoor show held 3 days in April. Average attendance: 3,500. Closing date for entry: 3 weeks before show. No entry fee. Maximum 1 display area per artist. Prejudging. Art may be offered for sale; no commission. Artist must attend show; demonstrations OK. Registration limit: 50 exhibits. Sponsor provides 1 long table and 2 chairs. Considers all art.

CAPITAL EXPO, A KENTUCKY FOLKLIFE FESTIVAL, Capital Plaza, Box 496, Frankfort KY 40601. Show held in early June. Open to Kentucky artists. Send 3 color slides showing 3 different works. Some artists are invited to demonstrate their art or craft and are paid for this service. Considers only original work.

KAINTUCK TERRITORY, Rte. 7, Benton KY 42025. Contact: Walter F. Sill, Jr. Two shows held annually. Estab: 1971. Average attendance: 20,000. Frontier Days & Bluegrass Festival in April and October Fair 1880's. Acceptable media include paintings, graphics, drawings, sculpture and crafts. No entry fee. No commission. Artist must attend show. No shipments accepted. Write for booth rental information.

MOUNTAIN PARKWAY ART EXHIBIT, Rte. 1, Box 182, Stanton KY 40380. (606)663-4708. Contact: Dena Shepard. Sponsor: Powell County Art Club. Estab: 1966. Semiannual outdoor show held 1 day in August and October. Average attendance: 800-1,000+. Bring work the morning of show. Entry fee: $2 per display area. Art may be offered for sale; no commission. Demonstrations OK. Considers all art. Work should be framed, wired or have base.

Maine

ARTS & CRAFTS SHOW (formerly Zonta's Annual Arts and Crafts Show), Rockland ME 04841. Chairman: Enid Monaghan. Sponsor: Zonta Club of Rockland Area. Estab: 1975.

Annual outdoor show held 1 day in July. Closing date for entry: 1 week before show. Entry fee: $10 per entry. Art may be offered for sale; no commission. Artist must attend show; demonstrations encouraged. Considers all art.

BAR HARBOR VILLAGE GREEN ART EXHIBIT, c/o 29 W. Main St., Ellsworth ME 04605. Contact: Elise R. Witham. Annual show held in August. No entry fee. 10% commission. Artist must attend show. Acceptable media include oils, acrylics, watercolors, graphics and drawings. Write for additional details. SASE.

CLOTHESLINE ART EXHIBIT, Cottage St., Chamber of Commerce, Bar Harbor ME 04609. (207)288-5103. Secretary: Virginia Farnsworth. Annual outdoor show held 2 days in August. Entries accepted until show date. No entry fee. Art may be offered for sale; 10% commission. Artist must attend show. Considers all art. No crafts.

Maryland

JEWISH COMMUNITY CENTER CRAFTS SALE, 5700 Park Heights Ave., Baltimore MD 21215. (301)542-4900. Fine Arts Director: Freda Friedman. Estab: 1973. Annual indoor show held 2 days in early October. Average attendance: 4,000-6,000. Closing date for entry: 3 weeks before show. Entry fee: $45 per 12' display area. Prejudging by slides; entry fee refunded for refused work. Art must be offered for sale; no commission. Artist or representative must attend show; demonstrations encouraged. Registration limit: 80 artists/craftsmen. Sponsor provides display panels. Considers mobiles and sculpture.

MILLION DOLLAR MILE ART SHOW, Box 174, Havre de Grace MD 21078. (301)939-2329 or 4060. Contact: Marge Thompson or Ilse Seville. Annual outdoor show held in August. Closing date for entry: mid-July. Entry fee: $35 per artist. Considers all art.

NATIONAL CRAFT FAIR, National Crafts Ltd., Gapland MD 21736. (301)432-8438. Director: Noel Clark. Estab: 1977. Annual indoor show held in Gaithersburg 2-3 days in September. Average attendance: 40,000. Closing date for applications: 3-4 months before show. Entry fee: $90. Prejudging by 5 color slides; entry fee refunded for refused work. Art may be offered for sale; no commission. Artist must attend show. Registration limit: 400 artists/craftsmen. Considers printmaking.

Massachusetts

NEW ENGLAND'S CRAFTS EXPO, Box 370, Farmington CT 06032. (202)224-8388. Director: Rudy Kowalczyk. Sponsor: American Crafts Expositions. Estab: 1977. Annual indoor/outdoor show held at the Topsfield fairgrounds 3 days in July. Average attendance: 20,000. Closing date for entry: 4 weeks before show. Entry fee: $50-60 per booth (10x10', indoors; 14x14', outdoors). Prejudging; entry fee refunded for refused work. Art may be offered for sale; no commission. Artist must attend show; demonstrations OK. Registration limit: 200 artists/craftsmen. Considers all art.

Michigan

ALMA HIGHLAND FESTIVAL ART FAIR & SALE, 219 Fleming Dr., Alma MI 48801. Chairman: Tim Evans. Sponsor: Chamber of Commerce. Annual outdoor show held in May. Closing date: April 15. Entry fee: $7.50 per 6x10'-15' space. Acceptable media include oils, acrylics, watercolors, graphics, sculpture, mixed media, crafts, pottery, textiles and jewelry. Held inside if raining. Submit 3 slides or representative color photos. No sales commission. Artist must attend show.

THE ANN ARBOR STREET ART FAIR INC., Box 1352, Ann Arbor MI 48106. Annual show held 4 days in July. 250 artists/craftsmen will be invited to participate. All work exhibited at the fair is evaluated daily as a basis for issuance of invitations for the following year. Accepted artists are mailed an invitation to participate, which includes a registration form and special instructions. Registration form and fee due in February. Artist must share 10x10' booth. Prejudging by 3-5 color slides.

ANN ARBOR WINTER ART FAIR, 1725 Weldon, Ann Arbor MI 48103. Director: Audree Levy. Estab: 1974. Annual indoor show held 3 days in November. Average attendance: 50,000-60,000. Closing date for entry: 8 weeks before show. Entry fee: $110 per 10x12' display area.

Prejudging by 3 slides or photos (send resume and SASE). Art may be offered for sale; no sales commission. Artist must attend show; demonstrations OK.
Acceptable Work: Considers acrylics, airbrush, drawings, oils, pastels, watercolors, sculpture and mobiles.

CHARLEVOIX WATERFRONT ART FAIR, Box 296, Charlevoix MI 49720. (616)547-4204. Director: Suzi Reis. Sponsor: Chamber of Commerce. Estab: 1958. Annual outdoor show held the second Saturday in August (indoors if inclement weather). Average attendance: 10,000. Closing date for entry: May. Entry fee: $20 per 10x10' display area; $30 per 2 artists, 1 space; $40 per double space. Prejudging by slides; entry fee refunded for refused work. Art must be offered for sale; no commission. Artist must attend show; demonstrations OK. Registration limit: 175 artists/craftsmen. Sponsor pays insurance on exhibited work. Considers all art.

DOWNTOWN BAY CITY SIDEWALK DAYS, 409 Bay City Bank Bldg., Bay City MI 48706. Contact: Tillie Zimmerman. Sponsor: Downtown Bay City, Inc. Estab: 1962. Outdoor show usually held in July. Average attendance: 75,000. Arts and crafts displays open to amateurs only; all arts and crafts accepted. Artist must attend the show.

FRANKENMUTH BAVARIAN FESTIVAL, 635 S. Main St., Frankenmuth MI 48734. (517)652-6106. Contact: Chamber of Commerce. Sponsor: Frankenmuth Civic Events Council. Estab: 1959. Annual outdoor show held the second week in June. Average attendance: 250,000-300,000. Closing date for entry: March 31. Entry fee: $60 per 12x10' display area. Maximum 1 display area per artist. Prejudging by slides or photos; entry fee refunded for refused work. Art may be offered for sale; no commission. Open to demonstrating artists. Registration limit: 50 artists/craftsmen. Considers all art.
To Break In: "Demonstration is the key to selection. We like prices that are fair for work done. List basic price list on application. Apply before March; you'll be contacted in April."

HOLLAND FINE ARTS SHOW, Holland Civic Center, 150 W. 8th St., Holland MI 49423. President: John Kim Oudman. Sponsor: Holland Friends of Art and Holland Recreation Dept. Estab: 1963. Annual indoor show held in May. Average attendance: 2,000-4,000. Closing date for entry: April 1. Entry fee: $7-$14 per 6x8x10' display unit. Acceptable media include oils, acrylics, watercolors, graphics, drawings and sculpture. Artist must be present during show. Show provides heavy burlap-covered walls and 4x8' pegboard panels for display. Also sponsors outdoor art and crafts show in August.

LUDINGTON ARTS & CRAFTS FAIR, 1499 Betty Ave., C8, Ludington MI 49431. (616)843-3522. Director: Mildred Pirtle. Sponsor: West Shore Art League. Annual outdoor show held 2 days in July. Average attendance: 5,000+. Closing date for entry: 1 week before show. Entry fee: $5 per entry. Prejudging; entry fee refunded for refused work. Art may be offered for sale; no commission. Artist must attend show; demonstrations welcome. Registration limit: $300 artists/craftsmen. Considers drawings, paintings, pastels, mobiles and sculpture. "If we have seen a work before and know the quality, it won't be prejudged again."

NORTHMINSTER ART & CRAFT SHOW, 3633 W. Big Beaver, Troy MI 48084. Sponsor: Northminster Presbyterian Church. Estab: 1973. Annual indoor show held 2 days in fall. Average attendance: 1,200. Closing date for entry: 1 month before show. Entry fee: $3 per display area. Prejudging; no entry fees refunded for refused work. Art may be offered for sale; 10% commission if artist mans own booth or 20% if artist is not present. Demonstrations encouraged. Registration limit: 70 artists/craftsmen. Sponsor provides display equipment. Considers all art.

PENTWATER VILLAGE ART FAIR, Box 357, Pentwater MI 49449. Contact: Lawrence Spaulding. Sponsor: Chamber of Commerce. Annual outdoor fair held 2 days in summer. Entry fee: $4. Limited to 100 exhibitors. Space on first come, first served basis. Acceptable media include oils, acrylics, watercolors, graphics, drawings, sculpture, mixed media and crafts. No candles or leather goods. No commission. Artist must be present.

ROSE FESTIVAL FINE ARTS & SELECTED CRAFTS, 6250 W. Lake Rd., Clarklake MI 49234. (517)529-9144 or 784-4934. Contact: Grace McCourtie or Jean Boyers. Sponsor: Brooklyn Artists. Estab: 1973. Annual outdor show held 1 day in June. Average attendance: 10,000. Entries accepted until show date. Entry fee: $7 per artist before May 15; $10 after

May 15. Art may be offered for sale; no commission. Prefers that artist attends show. "We highly encourage demonstrations; they are a great attraction to your display and help in advertising." Registration limit: 100 display spaces. Sponsor provides display equipment and 15' display areas in rose garden area. Considers all original art.

ROYAL OAK OUTDOOR ART FAIR, 211 Williams, Royal Oak MI 48068. (313)546-0900. Coordinator: Susan Wedley. Sponsor: Parks and Recreation Dept. Estab: 1971. Annual outdoor show held first Sunday in August. Average attendance: 3,000. Closing date for entry: April. Entry fee: $20 per artist. Prejudging; entry fee refunded for refused work. Art may be offered for sale; no commission. Artist must attend show; demonstrations OK. Registration limit: 78 spaces. Considers all original art.

ST. CLAIR ART FAIR, Box 222, St. Clair MI 48079. (313)329-2803. Chairman: Mary Ann Garman. Sponsor: St. Clair Art Association. Estab: 1971. Annual outdoor (covered mall) show held 3 days in late June. Average attendance: 5,000-6,000. Closing date for entries: mid-March. Entry fee: $15 per 8x8' or 8x10' display area. Prejudging. Art must be offered for sale; 10% commission. Artist must attend show; demonstrations OK. Registration limit: 65 fine artists. Considers all art.

ST. JOSEPH ART ASSOCIATION'S OUTDOOR ART FAIR, 600 State St., St. Joseph MI 49085. (616)983-0271. Contact: St. Joseph Art Center. Estab: 1962. Annual outdoor show held 1 day in July. Average attendance: 35,000-40,000. Closing date for entries: 8 weeks before show. Entry fee: $25 per 20x20' display area. Prejudging; entry fee refunded for refused work. Art may be offered for sale; no commission. Artist must attend show; demonstrations OK. Registration limit: 150 artists/craftsmen. Considers all art "suitable for children's viewing."

TRAVERSE BAY ART FAIR, 718 Duell Rd., Traverse City MI 49684. Contact: Rose Blodgett. Sponsor: Northwestern Michigan Artists & Craftsmen. Annual outdoor show held 1 day in late July. Average attendance: 10,000. Applications due May 1. Entry fee: $15 per 15x20' booth; $20 if shared. Prejudging; entry fee refunded for refused work. Art may be offered for sale; no commission. Open to artists ages 18+. Artist must attend show; "we love demonstrations." Registration limit: 150 artists/craftsmen. Considers all art.

WESTWOOD MALL FINE ARTS FAIR, 4211 Alden Dr., Jackson MI 49201. Contact: Marion Brinker. Semiannual indoor exhibition. Entry fee: $15 per 8x12' space. Prejudging by slides. No sales commission. Artist must attend show. Eligible media include oils, acrylics, watercolors, graphics, drawings, sculpture, mixed media, pottery, hand formed clay, hand carved candles, block prints, batik, silkscreen, silversmithing and lapidary.

Minnesota

CROSSROADS MALL, 2918 Martel Dr., Dayton OH 45420. (513)254-2900. Director: Clarence Freeland. Annual indoor show held 1 week in St. Cloud, Minnesota. Closing date for entry: 1 week before show. Entry fee due after jurying. Prejudging. Art may be offered for sale; no commission. Artist must attend show; demonstrations OK. Sponsor provides 10x10' display area. Considers all art.

MIDWEST ART SHOW & SALE, Reiter Promotions, Inc., Box 321, Chanhassen MN 55317. (612)445-1998. Manager: Arthur Reiter. Sponsor: Miller Hill Mall Merchants' Association. Estab: 1974. Annual indoor show held in Duluth 2 days in November. Average attendance: 15,000. Closing date for entry: 1 week before show. Entry fee: $25 per 12x6' display area. Prejudging: entry fee refunded for refused work. Art may be offered for sale; no commission. Artist must attend show; demonstrations OK. Registration limit: 70 artists/craftsmen.
Acceptable Work: Considers original calligraphy, drawings, mobiles, paintings, prints and sculpture.

NORTH STAR ARTS & CRAFTS FESTIVAL, Rte. 2, Park Rapids MN 56470. Contact: Mrs. V. Cookson. Estab: 1972. Annual indoor show held in August. Charges entry fee. Acceptable media include oils, acrylics, watercolors, graphics, drawings, sculpture, mixed media and crafts. Artist must be present for show. Sponsor provides 8x12x16' display area.

NORTHBROOK ARTS & CRAFTS SHOW & SALE, Reiter Promotions, Inc., Box 321, Chanhassen MN 55317. (612)445-1998. Show Manager: Arthur Reiter. Sponsor: Northbrook

Shopping Center Businessmen's Association. Estab: 1974. Annual outdoor show on covered walks held 3 days in August, rain or shine. Closing date for entry: 1 week before show. Entry fee: $20 per 10x6' display area. Entry fee refunded for refused work. Art may be offered for sale; no commission. Artist must attend show; demonstrations OK. Considers original art.

SOUTHDALE FINE ARTS FAIR, 10 Southdale Center, Minneapolis MN 55435. Contact: Lisa Bonneville. Sponsor: Southdale Center Merchants Association. Annual show held in September. Closing date for entry: mid-August. Entry fee: $50 per 8x10' indoor booth. No commission. Artist must attend show. Considers paintings, graphics, drawings, sculpture, mixed media, serigraphy, lithography, thrown pottery (stoneware) and jewelry (metal with semi-precious, natural stone). "We are the oldest enclosed mall in the U.S. and the largest in Minnesota. All advertising is handled by the Promotion Department, and programs for the show and name signs for each exhibitor are provided." Write for entry blank.

UPTOWN ART FAIR, 7201 Shannon Dr., Edina MN 55435. Administrative Director: E. A. Nieland. Estab: 1964. Exhibition held annually the second weekend in August. Average attendance: 10,000+. Closing date for entry: June. Entry fee: $22.50 per 4x22' sidewalk space or 12x12' mall grass area. Maximum 1 space per artist. No sales commission. Artist must attend show. Applications mailed mid-May. Acceptable media include oils, acrylics, watercolors, mixed media, drawings, graphics, sculpture and crafts. Artist must display at least 1 fine art or craft form before others are acceptable.

Missouri

BLUE RIDGE MALL EXHIBITION SHOW & SALE, #55 Blue Ridge Mall, 4200 Blue Ridge Blvd., Kansas City MO 64133. Contact: Perry Wilcox. Sponsor: Blue Ridge Mall Merchants Association. Estab: 1961. Annual show held in May. Entry fee: $9 per 6x8' display unit. Maximum 3 display areas per artist. Considers oils, acrylics, watercolors and drawings. No commission. Artist must attend show.

Montana

CARBON COUNTY ARTS GUILD ANNUAL CHRISTMAS SALE & SHOW, Box 585, Red Lodge MT 59068. (406)446-1370. Director: Carol Orr. Estab: 1974. Annual indoor show held from the day after Thanksgiving to the first Sunday in December. Average attendance: 1,000 Christmas shoppers. Write for applications in October. Closing date for entry: 1 week before show. No entry fee. Maximum 10 entries per artist. Art must be offered for sale; 15% commission. Bestsellers: items under $500. Area artists only. No demonstrations. "Art displays are set up in vacant store fronts. The store is decorated and the display is hung by a committee." Sponsor pays insurance for exhibited work. Considers all art.
Promotion: "Work offered for sale is photographed for publicity purposes at least 2 weeks before the sale. TV publicity is also done at that time. Work that arrives early is used for publicity unless it cannot be easily transported to the TV station."
Shipping Tips: "If an artist is shipping artwork, he should be sure that the box or crate is reusable so the work can be easily returned in that packaging."

Nebraska

ART FAIR, Box 62, Scottsbluff NE 69361. (308)632-2226. Executive Director: Robert S. Hill. Sponsor: West Nebraska Arts Center. Estab: 1967. Annual outdoor show held 3 days in August. Closing date for entry: 4 weeks before show. Entry fee: $10 per table; $15 per table in tent. Art may be offered for sale; no commission. Artist or representative must attend show; demonstrations encouraged. Sponsor pays insurance during exhibit period. Considers all art.

ARTS FESTIVAL ON THE MALL, Studio 1, Aquila Court, 1615 Howard, Omaha NE 68102. (402)345-5401. Director: Vic Gutman. Sponsor: Pratt School Events Fund. Estab: 1975. Annual outdoor show held 3 days in June. Average attendance: 70,000. Closing date for entry: 2 weeks before show. Entry fee: $25 per 10x10' display area. Maximum 1 entry per artist. Art may be offered for sale; no commission. Demonstrations encouraged. Registration limit: 200 artists/craftsmen. Display equipment may be rented. "Displays must be sturdy enough to hold up in case of stiff winds." Considers all art.

ROCKBROOK VILLAGE ART FAIR, 11042 Elm St., Omaha NE 68144. (402)391-4874. Contact: Gloria Mathews. Sponsor: Rockbrook Merchants Association. Estab: 1973. Annual outdoor (some tent space available) show held the second weekend in September. Average attendance: 30,000. Closing date for entries: 2 weeks before show. Entry fee: $25 per entry. Art may be offered for sale; no commission. Artist must attend show; demonstrations OK. Registration limit: 185 artists/craftsmen. Considers all art.

Nevada

CREATIVE ARTISTS GROUP, 3608 Cinnabar Ave., Carson City NV 89701. (702)883-0968. Director: Bea Griffin. Estab: 1976. Annual outdoor show held 4 days in June. Entries accepted until show date. Entry fee: $15 per entry. Art may be offered for sale; 10% commission. Artist must attend show; demonstrations OK. Considers all art. Maximum height: 5'.

GOLD HILL ART FESTIVAL, Box 510, Virginia City NV 89440. (702)847-0737. Director: Diane Gordon. Sponsor: Gold Hill Pottery and Art Gallery. Estab: 1974. Annual outdoor show held 3 days during Memorial Day weekend. Closing date for entry: March 31. Entry fee: $15 per display area. "We provide whatever amount of space an artist/craftsman requires (a very large space would necessitate an additional fee)." Prejudging; entry fee refunded for refused work. Art may be offered for sale; no commission. Artist must attend show. " 'Art in Action' is strongly encouraged — it is an education for the public." Registration limit: 40 artists/craftsmen. Considers all art.

WAGON TRAIN DAYS, 3432 Tourmaline Dr., Carson City NV 89701. Contact: Bea Griffin. Annual show held at Round Hill Shopping Center. Entry fee: $15. 10% sales commission. Artist must attend show. Acceptable media include watercolors, graphics, drawings, sculpture, mixed media and crafts. Insurance handled by sponsor.

New Hampshire

CHRISTMAS PROFESSIONAL ART & CRAFT SHOW, c/o J & R Productions, Box 46 X, East Kingston NH 03827. (603)642-5073. Contact: Ron or June Richardson. Average attendance: 7,000. Professional artists/craftsmen may submit slides or photos of work. All media acceptable. No commission. Entry fee: $95-$145 for spaces from 8x10'-10x15'. Sponsor handles insurance but advises exhibitors to carry personal policy as well. Write or call for more information.

THEATRE BY THE SEA STREET FAIR, 91 Market St., Portsmouth NH 03801. (603)431-5846. Publicist: Sandi Bianco. Sponsor: Theatre by the Sea Board of Trustees. Estab: 1966. Annual outdoor show held 1 day in July. Average attendance: 6,000. Closing date for entry: 3 weeks before show or until spaces filled. Entry fee: $15 per 6' long display area. Art may be offered for sale; no commission. Artist or representative must attend show. Considers all art.
Profile: "The Theatre by the Sea Street Fair is a fundraising event which features the work of atists and craftspeople. The entire length of Ceres Street, along the Portsmouth waterfront, is closed for the day and the Theatre provides games, food, children's booths, films, activities tables and turn-of-the-century atmosphere."
Promotion: "It is helpful for our promotional purposes to receive clippings, resumes and other information on the participating artists for use in our releases. Photos, although not always printed, are indeed welcome. Descriptive pieces on the process used is also of considerable interest for feature items."

New Jersey

LIVINGSTON ART EXPO, Woodwill Corp., 349 Ridgefield Rd., Hauppauge NY 11787. (516)234-4183. Semiannual show held in spring and fall at Livingston Mall in Livingston, New Jersey. Entry fee: $60 per 10 days; $35 per weekend. No sales commission. Registration limit: 300 artists. Heavy advertising conducted before event. Submit photos of work exhibited. Original work only; no crafts.

New Mexico

ARTS & CRAFTS FAIR OF THE SOUTHWEST, Box 122, Roswell NM 88201. Contact: Exhibitors' Chairman. Sponsor: Roswell Jaycees. Estab: 1973. Annual indoor show held 2 days in May. Average attendance: 3,500. Closing date for entry: March 1. Entry fee: $35 per booth with 8x8' pegboard; $15 per additional artist. Prejudging; entry fee refunded for refused work. Art may be offered for sale; no commission. Open to artists ages 18+. Artist must attend show; demonstrations encouraged. Registration limit: 100 booths. Considers all art.

New York

ARTISTS OF CENTRAL NEW YORK EXHIBITION, 310 Genesee St., Utica NY 13502. Contact: Joseph S. Trovato. Sponsor: Museum of Art and Munson-Williams-Proctor Institute. Annual show held in fall with entries accepted in September. Charges entry fee. Maximum 1 entry per artist. No sales commission. Open to artists ages 18+ residing within 100 miles of Utica. Work which cannot be delivered in person should be shipped via Express prepaid and will be returned via Express collect.

BEDFORD VILLAGE HARVEST FESTIVAL ART SHOW, R.D. 1, Box 218, Bedford Village NY 10506. (914)234-3704. Director: Lydia Ward. Sponsor: Northern Westchester Chapter of Cancer Care, Inc. Estab: 1968. Annual outdoor show held third weekend in October. Average Attendance: 10,000. Closing date for entry: 4 weeks before show; usually full by August 1. Entry fee: $30 per 10x4' display area. Prejudging by slides; entry fee refunded for refused work. Art may be offered for sale; no commission. Artist must attend show; demonstrations OK. Registration limit: 185 artists. Considers all art. Maximum size: 2 spaces.

BRUSH & PALETTE CLUB'S ANNUAL LABOR DAY WEEKEND ARTS & CRAFTS SHOW, 85 Chestnut St., Cooperstown NY 13326. (607)547-5134. Show Director: Bettye Yanchisin. Estab: 1965. Annual outdoor show held 3 days during Labor Day weekend. Applications mailed after May 1. Closing date for entry: 4 weeks before show. Entry fee: $15 per 10x5' display area. Prejudging. Art may be offered for sale; no commission. Artist must attend show; demonstrations OK. Considers all art.

CHAUTAUQUA MALL, 2918 Martel Dr., Dayton OH 45420. (513)254-2900. Director: Clarence Freeland. Annual indoor show held 1 week in Jamestown, New York. Closing date for entry: 1 week before show. Entry fee due after jurying. Prejudging. Art may be offered for sale; no commission. Artist must attend show; demonstrations OK. Sponsor provides 10x10' display area. Considers all art.

MONTAUK ART & CRAFTS SHOW, Box 18, Montauk NY 11954. Contact: David A. Webb. Sponsor: Montauk Lions Club. Annual show held Labor Day weekend. Entry fee: $15 per day.

NIAGARA FALLS SUMMIT PARK MALL, c/o John Gromosiak, 1937 Wilene Dr., Dayton OH 45432. Show held in Niagara Falls, New York. Entry fee: $60 per 10x10' booth. No sales commission. Although the director carries liability insurance, he recommends that artists arrange for their own insurance.

ROBERSON HOLIDAY & ARTS FESTIVAL, 30 Front St., Binghamton NY 13905. (607)772-0660. Coordinator: Ms. Terry Kuehnemund. Sponsor: Roberson Center for the Arts and Sciences. Estab: 1955. Annual outdoor show held 2 days in September. Average attendance: 40,000. Closing date for entry: 4 weeks before show. Entry fee: $15 per 8x6' display area. Maximum 2 display areas per artist. Art may be offered for sale; 10% commission. Artist or agent must attend show; demonstrations encouraged. Registration limit: 300 artists/craftsmen. Sponsor provides fence or tables; electricity available. No advance deliveries accepted. Considers all art.

SENIOR CITIZENS ARTS & CRAFTS SHOW & SALE, 168 S. Clinton Ave., Rochester NY 14604. (716)454-3224. Contact: Gloria Harrington. Sponsors: Genesee Conference of Senior Citizens Directors, Inc. and Retired Senior Volunteer Program. Estab: 1974. Annual indoor show held 3 days in April. Average attendance: 3,000. Closing date for entry: 2 weeks before show. No entry fee. Prejudging. Art may be offered for sale; 10% commission. Open to artists ages 60+. Demonstrations by invitation. Consider all art.

North Carolina

BODYCRAFT GALLERIES SHOWS, 409 W. End Blvd., Winston-Salem NC 27101. (919)722-4396. Contact: Doug or Bonnie Barger. Estab: 1976. Indoor show held every 4-6 weeks. Average attendance: 1,000. Closing date for entry: 1 week before show. No entry fee. Maximum 5 entries per artist. Prejudging. Art may be offered for sale; 40% commission. Sponsor provides display equipment, insurance for exhibited work and pays return shipping. Considers all wearable art. "Care instructions must be included on a detachable card."
To Break In: "It really helps if the item can be cleaned, even if it's difficult. Masks are a good area for sculptural skills."

BROOKSTOWN ARTS & CRAFTS FESTIVAL, Box 10507, Winston-Salem NC 27108. (919)723-4800. President: Elizabeth Place. Sponsor: North Carolina League of Creative Arts & Crafts Inc. Estab: 1976. Annual indoor/outdoor show held 2 days in July. Entries accepted until show date. Entry fee: $30 for first person in booth; $10 for second person. Maximum 2 artists per 8x10' display area. Art may be offered for sale; no commission. Artist must attend show. Registration limit: 60-100 artists/craftsmen. Considers all original art.

MRS. JOHN FORREST MEMORIAL SIDEWALK ART SHOW, Box 489, Hendersonville NC 28739. (704)692-1413. General Manager: G. Ray Cantrell. Sponsors: Hendersonville Woman's Club, Chamber of Commerce and Artists League of Henderson County. Estab: 1959. Annual outdoor show held 2 days in early August. Average attendance: 4,000-4,500. Entries accepted until show date. Entry fee: $5. Art may be offered for sale; no commission. Artist or representative must attend show. Considers drawings, paintings and pastels.

SOUTHEASTERN FINE ARTS FESTIVAL, 778 Faircloth Dr., Winston-Salem NC 27106. Director: Mary Goslen. Sponsor: Southeastern Art Shows. Held annually at Benton Convention Center, downtown Winston-Salem, in early March. Closing date for entry: October 1. Entry fee: $125 per 8x10' booth. Maximum 3 spaces per artist. All fine arts media acceptable: canvas paintings, watercolors, collages, drawings, sculpture and original prints. 100 spaces available. Artist must attend show. No sales commission. Invitational show; new exhibitors qualify by submitting 6 slides or photos of type of work to be exhibited.

VILLAGE ART & CRAFT FAIR, New Morning Gallery, 3½ Kitchen Place, Asheville NC 28803. (704)274-2831. Contact: John Cram. Sponsor: New Morning Gallery. Estab: 1972. Annual outdoor show held the first weekend in August. Average attendance: 10,000. Closing date for entries: 4 weeks before show. Entry fee: $50 per 8x10' display area. Prejudging by color slides (include SASE) or actual work; entry fees refunded for refused work. Art may be offered for sale; no commission. Artist must attend show; demonstrations OK. Registration limit: 150 artists/craftsmen. Considers all art.

North Dakota

LINHA GALLERY ARTFEST, Box 325, Linha Art Gallery, Minot ND 58701. (701)838-4445. Director: Galen Willert. Sponsor: Friends of the Linha Art Gallery. Estab: 1976. Annual indoor show held 3 days in March. Closing date for entry: 1 week before show. Entry fee: $20 per 12x12' display area. Art may be offered for sale; no commission. Artist must attend show; demonstrations OK. Considers all art.

MINOT ART ASSOCIATION ART FAIR, Box 325, Linha Art Gallery, Minot ND 58701. (701)838-4445. Director: Galen R. Willert. Sponsor: Minot Art Association. Estab: 1975. Annual outdoor show held 1 day in the fall. Closing date for entry: 1 week before show. Entry fee: $10 per 6x12' display area. Art may be offered for sale; no commission. Artist must attend show; demonstrations OK. Considers all original art.

Ohio

ART IN THE PARK, 142 Riverbend Dr., Dayton OH 45405. (513)225-5433. Director: Pat Shoop. Sponsor: City of Dayton, Division of Recreation and Riverbend Arts Council. Estab: 1967. Annual outdoor show held 2 days during Memorial Day weekend. Average attendance: 25,000-30,000. Closing date for entry: 2 weeks before show. Entry fee: $15 per artist. "If an application appears questionable, artist is asked to bring work to center to be previewed." Entry fee refunded for refused work. Art must be offered for sale; no commission. "Out-of-state artists do exhibit in our show, but we prefer to promote area artists and we do call some artists from the previous year who had interesting exhibits." Artist must attend show. "Demonstrating is stressed as it makes for a more interesting show. We usually have 1-2 caricaturists working." Registration limit: 150 artists/craftsmen.
Acceptable Work: Considers all art except oil on velvet. "An exhibitor could be asked to remove a particular work of art if the arts council found it objectionable."

CEDAR POINT'S CRAFTS SHOW, Cedar Point, Merchandise Dept., Sandusky OH 44870. (419)626-0830. Crafts Manager: Jeff Savage. Estab: 1974. Annual outdoor show held 5 days in July-August. Closing date for entry: 2 weeks before show. No entry fee. Prejudging by slides. Art must be offered for sale; 20-30% commission. Artist must attend show; demonstrations required. Registration limit: 60-70 artists/craftsmen. Sponsor provides booth and work area. Hand-deliver work. Considers sculpture and mobiles.

COLUMBUS SPRING ART FAIR, 1725 Weldon, Ann Arbor MI 48103. Show Director: Audree Levy. Estab: 1977. Annual indoor show held in Columbus, Ohio 3 days in May. Closing date for entry: 8 weeks before show. Entry fee: $120 per 12x15' display area. Prejudging conducted in March; send 3 slides, resume and SASE after December. Art may be offered for sale; no commission. Artist must attend show; demonstrations OK.
Acceptable Work: Considers acrylics, airbrush, drawings, oils, pastels, watercolors, mobiles and sculpture.

DAYTON MALL, c/o John Gromosiak, 1937 Wilene Dr., Dayton OH 45432. Several arts and crafts shows held at this mall. Charges entry fee. No sales commission. No agents. Sponsor provides 10x10' display area.

GREAT LAKES MALL, 2918 Martel Dr., Dayton OH 45420. (513)254-2900. Director: Clarence Freeland. Annual indoor show held in Mentor (near Cleveland) 1 week in June. Closing date for entry: 1 week before show. Entry fee: $90. Prejudging. Art may be offered for sale; no commission. Artist must attend show; demonstrations OK. Sponsor provides 10x10' display area. Considers all art.

INDIAN SUMMER ARTS & CRAFTS FESTIVAL, c/o Marietta College, Marietta OH 45750. Director: Arthur Winer. Sponsor: Marietta Art League. Estab: 1955. Annual outdoor (tents and booths available) show held 3 days in fall. Average attendance: 12,000. Entry fee: $25 per entry. Slides due for prejudging in early July (entries accepted after July in event of cancellations); entry fee refunded for refused work. "Slides for jurying must include 3 separate views for 3-dimensional work (front, back and side) or enough views of the work to show what the piece looks like." Art may be offered for sale; no commission. Open to artists ages 18+. Artist must attend show; demonstrations encouraged. Registration limit: 100 artists/craftsmen. Sponsor provides booths and pegboard. Maximum 3 media per 1 booth. Considers all art.

RICHMOND MALL, 2918 Martel Dr., Dayton OH 45420. (513)254-2900. Director: Clarence Freeland. Annual indoor show held in Cleveland 1 week in April-May. Closing date for entry: 1 week before show. Entry fee: $75. Prejudging. Art may be offered for sale; no commission. Artist must attend show; demonstrations OK. Sponsor provides 10x10' display area. Considers all art.

SOUTHERN PARK MALL, 2918 Martel Dr , Dayton OH 45420. (513)254-2900. Director: Clarence Freeland. Indoor show held in Youngstown 1 week in April and June. Closing date for entry: 1 week before show. Entry fee: $65. Prejudging. Art may be offered for sale; no commission. Artist must attend show; demonstrations OK. Sponsor provides 10x10' display area. Considers all art.

SUMMIT MALL, 2918 Martel Dr., Dayton OH 45420. (513)254-2900. Director: Clarence Freeland. Annual indoor show held in Akron 1 week in May. Closing date for entry: 1 week before show. Entry fee: $60. Prejudging. Art may be offered for sale; no commission. Artist must attend show; demonstrations OK. Sponsor provides 10x10' display area. Considers all art.

WOODVILLE MALL, 2918 Martel Dr., Dayton OH 45420. (513)254-2900. Director: Clarence Freeland. Annual indoor show held in Toledo 1 week in May. Closing date for entry: 1 week before show. Entry fee: $50. Prejudging. Art may be offered for sale; no commission. Artist must attend show; demonstrations OK. Sponsor provides 10x10' display area. Considers all art.

Oklahoma

GREEN COUNTRY ART ASSOCIATION ANNUAL FINE ART SHOW, 1825 E. 15th St., Tulsa OK 74105. Contact: Dick Schellstede. Fine art exhibition and sale featuring paintings and sculpture. Artists limited to 4x8' panels or tables. Additional show fee for non-members required for first show with Green Country; thereafter, artist eligible for membership. Requests photos or slides of work. 20% sales commission.

INTERNATIONAL EXPOSITION OF PETROLEUM ART SHOW, Green Country Art Association, 1825 E. 15th St., Tulsa OK 74136. Contact: Dick Schellstede. Held last weekend of August preceding Labor Day weekend. Entry fee: $150. Maximum 5-10 entries per artist. Art must be offered for sale; 25% commission. Send photos or slides of work. Media include painting and sculpture. Size limit on paintings: 40x28" outside frame. Art on display is insured.

LAWTON FORT SILL ANNUAL ART SHOW, Lawton Fort Sill Art Council, 1601 NW 75th St., Lawton OK 73505. Contact: Barbara Ainsworth. Annual art exhibition for all media. No sales commission. Artist must hand-deliver entries.

Oregon

ALBANY SPRING ARTS FESTIVAL, Box 841, Albany OR 97321. (503)928-2815. Director: Terri Hopkins. Sponsor: Creative Arts Guild. Estab: 1969. Annual indoor/outdoor show held 2 days in early May. Average attendance: 20,000. Entries accepted until show date. Entry fee: $7 per weekend. Art may be offered for sale; no commission. Open to all artists, but mid-Wilamette artists given preference. Demonstrations OK. Sponsor provides 8x8' booth.
Acceptable Work: Considers all art. Two-dimensional art must be framed and wired. "Please specify 'which end is up' on sculpture if not obvious."

NEWPORT SUMMER FESTIVAL OF ARTS & CRAFTS, 5724 Aetna St. SE, Salem OR 97301. (503)585-1263. Manager: Vaughn L. Hayden. Sponsor: Capital Promotions. Estab: 1976. Annual indoor show held in Newport 2 days in June. Attendance: 3,000. Entries accepted until show date. Entry fee: $25 per 8x8' display area. Art may be offered for sale; no commmission. Demonstrations encouraged. Registration limit: 50 artists/craftsmen. Sponsor provides tables, chairs and liability insurance.
Acceptable Work: Considers all handcrafted items and supplies for artists. "Items not handcrafted will be excluded from the show and no refunds will be made on fees after 10 days prior to show."
Promotion: "News releases about artisans are welcomed and used. We advertise extensively. Applicants with the better items will be given special consideration."

SALEM ARTS & CRAFTS SHOW, 5724 Aetna St. SE, Salem OR 97301. (503)585-1263. Manager: Vaughn L. Hayden. Sponsor: Capital Promotions. Estab: 1975. Annual show held at Salem Armory Auditorium 3 days in November. Entries accepted until show date. Entry fee: $27.50-32.50 per 9x9' display area. Art may be offered for sale; no commission. Demonstrations encouraged. Registration limit: 106 artists/craftsmen. Sponsor provides tables, chairs and liability insurance. Considers all fine art.
Promotion: "News releases about artisans are welcomed and used. We advertise extensively. Applicants with the better items will be given special consideration."

SATURDAY MARKET, Box 427, Eugene OR 97401. (503)686-8885. Contact: Manager. Estab: 1970. Outdoor market held every Saturday during April-December. Average attendance: 1,000. Entries accepted anytime. Entry fee: $3 per artist the first time; $3-9 thereafter. Art may be offered for sale; no commission. Artist must attend market; demonstrations OK. Registration limit: 250 artists/craftsmen.
Acceptable Work: Considers all art. "Nothing is to be sold unless it's made by the salesperson or immediate family member. Also, nothing can be brought in from other stores and resold."

Pennsylvania

APPLE HARVEST FESTIVAL, Box 38, Biglerville PA 17307. (717)624-7623 or 677-7820. Contact: Nina Dillman. Sponsor: Upper Adams Jaycees. Estab: 1964. Annual indoor/outdoor show held 2 weekends in October. Average attendance: 12,000 per day. Closing date for entry: 3 weeks before show. Entry fee: $25 for 10x10' display area per weekend. Art may be offered for sale; no commission. Artist must attend show; demonstrations encouraged. Registration limit: 100 artists/craftsmen. Sponsor provides liability insurance during exhibit period. Considers all art.

CENTRAL PENNSYLVANIA FESTIVAL OF THE ARTS, Box 1023, State College PA 16801. Managing Director: Marilyn Keat. Estab: 1966. Annual outdoor show held 4 days in July. Average attendance: 150,000. Closing date for entry: 10 weeks before show. Entry fee: $3 jury fee; $40 per 10x4' booth. Prejudging. Art may be offered for sale; no commission. Artist must attend show; demonstrations OK. Registration limit: 450 artists/craftsmen. Sponsor provides snow fencing. Considers all art.

MILLCREEK MALL, 2918 Martel Dr., Dayton OH 45420. (513)254-2900. Director: Clarence Freeland. Annual indoor show held in Erie, Pennsylvania 1 week in April. Closing date for entry: 1 week before show. Entry fee: $75. Prejudging. Art may be offered for sale; no commission. Artist must attend show; demonstrations OK. Sponsor provides 10x10' display area. Considers all art.

SHADYSIDE SUMMER ART FESTIVAL, 5520 Walnut St., Pittsburgh PA 15232. (412)681-3494. Contact: Gregory G. lusi. Annual show held in August. Entry fee: $60. Prejudging by slides or photos. SASE. Artist or representative must attend show.

SUPERMUD — CERAMIC EXHIBITION, Dept. of Art, 102 Visual Arts Bldg., University Park PA 16802. (814)865-0444. Contact: David DonTigny, Jim Stephenson or Ron Gallas. Annual indoor show held 2 weeks in November. Estab: 1966. Average attendance: 5,000. Closing date for entry: 1 week before show. No entry fee. Maximum 3 entries per artist. Art may be offered for sale; 15% commission. Sponsor provides display equipment and pays insurance on exhibited work and shipping to artist. Considers ceramic statues.
Packing Tips: "Items must be packed to withstand truck freight. We suggest good packing in fiber drums; no cardboard boxes."

Rhode Island

PAWTUXET VILLAGE ARTS & CRAFTS FESTIVAL, 40 Elmbrook Dr., Warwick RI 02889. (401)738-9554. Committee Chairman: Bob Quinlan. Sponsor: Gaspee Day Committee. Estab: 1966. Annual outdoor show held 2 days the first weekend in June. Average attendance: 25,000-40,000. Entries accepted until show date. Entry fee: $15 per 15' long sidewalk display. Artists limited to 1 type of art or craft. Prejudging; entry fee refunded for refused work. Art may be offered for sale; no commission. Artist must attend show. "We encourage on-the-spot demonstrations, as they heighten the interest of the crowd and increase profits of artists/craftsmen." Registration limit: 300 artists/craftsmen (preference given to fine arts and previous participants). Considers all art.

WICKFORD ART FESTIVAL, Box 321, North Kingstown RI 02852. (401)295-5944. Chairman: Ella Rex. Sponsor: Wickford Art Association. Estab: 1960. Annual outdoor show held 3 days in July. Closing date for entry: 4 weeks before show. Entry fee: $25 for 1-3 days. Maximum 25 entries per artist. Art may be offered for sale; no commission. Artist must attend show; demonstrations OK. Considers most art. No mobiles.

All artwork is eligible for entry into the Jewish Community Center Crafts Sale (Baltimore), held annually in October. All entries must be received three weeks before the show, with only 80 artists accepted.

South Carolina

CHRISTMAS CRAFT & ART SHOW (formerly December Arts and Crafts Show), Box 1177, Aiken SC 29801. Contact: M. F. Facciolo. Sponsor: Aiken Recreation Dept. Estab: 1970. Annual indoor show held in December. Average attendance: 7,000. Entry fee: $10. Display unit is 5x8'. All media acceptable. No sales commission. Artist must be present during show.

Tennessee

ARTS & CRAFTS MART, Standards Committee, Box 5187, Kingsport TN 37663. Sponsor: Metropolitan Sertoma Club. Annual indoor show held in spring. Average attendance: 3,500. Closing date 2 months prior to show for previous entries. Write for entry blank and closing date information for new entries. Entry fee: $50 and $100 per artist for 8x8' and 8x16' display units. Send 3-5 slides, resume and price list. Registration limit: 44 artists/craftsmen. Artist must attend show. No sales commission. Acceptable media include oils, watercolors, mixed media, acrylics, graphics, drawings, sculpture and crafts. Display panels and equipment furnished (pegboard 8x2'x6" table; electricity if required).

BENLEE ART SHOWS, 915 Allen Ave., Cookeville TN 38501. Contact: Reba Bacon. Semiannual exhibitions held in June and October. Closing date for entry: 60 days before show. No entry fee. 20% commission. Artist must attend show. Acceptable media are oils, acrylics, watercolors, drawings, sculpture, mixed media and crafts. When writing for information, please state the type of arts or crafts you wish to exhibit.

BENTON COUNTY ARTS & CRAFT SHOW, Box 428, Camden TN 38320. (901)584-4601. Extension Agent: Wileva Mullins. Sponsor: Benton County Home Demonstration Clubs. Estab: 1970. Annual indoor show held 3 days in November. Closing date for entry: 1 week before show. Entry fee: $5 per 8x8' display area. Art may be offered for sale; commission is less than 5% (to be decided). Artist must attend show; demonstrations OK. Considers all art, but "our people do not accept nudes too well."

COTTON PICKIN' COUNTRY MUSIC CRAFTS JUBILEE, 722 S. Highland St., Memphis TN 38111. (901)458-8753. Promoter: Richard West. Sponsors: Memphis Chamber of Commerce, Memphis in May Society and Knudson Leather & Silver Shop. Estab: 1976. Annual indoor/outdoor show held 3 days in May. Average attendance: 30,000. Entries accepted until show date. Entry fee: $50 per outdoor space; $70 per tent space. Maximum 8 entries per artist. Art may be offered for sale; no commission. Demonstrations OK. Registration limit: 200 artists/craftsmen. Considers all art. Send brief resume and 2-3 captioned b&w glossies for publicity.

GERMANTOWN FESTIVAL'S RENAISSANCE FAIR, 722 S. Highland St., Memphis TN 38111. Promoter: Richard West. Estab: 1971. Annual outdoor show held 2 days the second weekend in September. Average attendance: 80,000. Entries accepted until show date. Entry fee: $50 per outdoor space; $70 per tent space. Art may be offered for sale; no commission. Considers all art.

GREATER KINGSPORT COMPETITIVE ART SHOW, Box 889, Kingsport TN 37662. Contact: Lillian Guenther. Sponsor: First National Bank of Sullivan County and Kingsport Art Guild. Annual show usually held in February.

GRINDERS SWITCH ARTS & CRAFTS FAIR, 107 Huddleston St., Centerville TN 37033. (615)729-3054. Chairman: Martha Chessor. Sponsor: Hickman County Art Guild. Estab: 1974. Annual outdoor show held 2 days in June. Average attendance: 8,000. Entries accepted until show date. Entry fee: $10 per 12x30' display area. Art may be offered for sale; no commission. Artist must attend show; demonstrations encouraged. Considers all art.
Profile: "Displays are set up in wooded camping sites and vehicles may be kept at exhibitor's site without distraction. Overnight camping, a bath house and showers are available at $3 per night."

NASHVILLE HOBBY & CRAFT CHRISTMAS MARKET, Box 155-D, Fairview TN 37062. (615)799-0084. Producer: Fred Hicks. Estab: 1974. Annual indoor show held first weekend in December. Closing date for entry: 4 weeks before show. Entry fee: $35 per 10x10' display area. Permits 2-3 artists to set up in 1 space. Maximum 2 booths per artist. Prejudging of new entrants by slides or photos; entry fee refunded for refused work. Art may be offered for sale; no commission. Artist must attend show. Registration limit: 225 artists/craftsmen. Sponsor provides 1 table and 2 chairs with each space. Security force on duty during show. Considers all art.

SIGNAL MOUNTAIN FALL FESTIVAL OF ARTS & CRAFTS, Rte. 1, Walker Rd., Signal Mountain TN 37377. (615)886-3584. Contact: Jake Hinds. Estab: 1972. Annual outdoor show held first weekend in October. Average attendance: 8,000-10,000. Closing date for entry: 2 weeks before show. Entry fee: $12.50 per entry. Art may be offered for sale; no commission. Artist must attend show; demonstrations OK. Considers all art.

Texas

BLACK-EYED PEA JAMBOREE ARTS & CRAFTS SHOW, Box 608, Athens TX 75751. Contact: Sherry Brasher. Sponsor: Chamber of Commerce. Annual outdoor show held 3 days in July. Average attendance: 10,000. Closing date for entries: 2 weeks before show. Entry fee: $15-25 per 10x12' space. Art may be offered for sale; no commission. Artist or representative must attend show. Wide variety of media acceptable — any crafts or artwork. Display panels furnished.

BORGER FINE ARTS FESTIVAL, 600 N. Deahl, Borger TX 79007. (806)274-2211. Contact: Wanda Guinn. Sponsor: Women's Division, Chamber of Commerce. Annual indoor show held 3 days in October. Average attendance: 6,000. Closing date for entry: 2 weeks before show. Prejudging; entry fee refunded for refused work. Art may be offered for sale; 10% commission. Artist must attend show; demonstrations encouraged. "We do not accept shipped items." Considers all art.

THE CRAFT EXPERIENCE, 300 Augusta St., San Antonio TX 78205. (512)224-1848. Executive Director: Marcia Baer Larsen. Sponsor: Southwest Craft Center. Estab: 1974. Annual outdoor show held 2 days in June. Average attendance: 10,000. Closing date for entry: 3 weeks before show. Entry fee: $50 per artist. Maximum 1 booth per artist. Prejudging by 35mm slides. Art may be offered for sale; no commission. Artist must attend show; demonstrations OK. Registration limit: 75 artists/craftsmen.
Acceptable Work: Considers calligraphy, drawings, prints, watercolors and sculpture.

GREAT ART EXTRAVANGANZA, 1515 College Dr., #114, Waco TX 76708. Contact: Kendal Lovett. Semiannual art and crafts show. Average attendance: 4,000. Entry fee: $50 for 10x10' display unit. No sales commission.

HOUSTON CRAFT FAIR, National Crafts Ltd., Gapland MD 21736. (301)432-8438. Director: Noel Clark. Estab: 1977. Annual indoor show held in the Houston Civic Center 2-3 days in December. Average attendance: 40,000. Closing date for applications: 3-4 months before show. Entry fee: $90. Prejudging by 5 color slides; entry fee refunded for refused work. Art may be offered for sale; no commission. Artist must attend show. Registration limit: 400 artists/craftsmen. Considers printmaking.

INTERNATIONAL ART FESTIVAL, Box 1388, McAllen TX 78501. Director: Vivian Thacker. Sponsor: Vivian Thacker Originals. Annual show held Friday evening, Saturday and Sunday after Thanksgiving. Entry fee: $30 per 8x10' booth for 3-day exhibit. No sales commission. Sponsor provides 8' table and 2 chairs.

INTERNATIONAL SCULPTURE SYMPOSIUM, Box 255, Liberty Hill TX 78642. Contact: Mel Fowler. Sponsor: Liberty Hill Cultural Affairs Council. Biennial outdoor show held in October-November. Closing date for entry: late May. No entry fee. Maximum 1 entry per artist. Provides room and board. Submit two 8x10" b&w photos for press release. Considers limestone, granite and concrete sculpture.

KALEIDOSCOPE CREATIVE ARTS & CRAFTS FESTIVAL, 1111 9th St., Beaumont TX 77702. (713)832-3432. Director: Betty W. Hirsch. Sponsor: Beaumont Art Museum. Estab: 1974. Annual outdoor (tent-covered booths available) show held second weekend in May. Average attendance: 16,000. Closing date for entry: 12 weeks before show. Entry fee: $60 per 8x10' display area; $35 per artist if shared. Prejudging by slides or samples of work; entry fee refunded for refused work. Art may be offered for sale; no commission. Artist must attend show; demonstrations OK. Registration limit: 72 booths. Considers all art. Work must be framed.

KERMEZAAR, El Paso Museum of Art, 1211 Montana Ave., El Paso TX 79902. Contact: Artist Registration Chairman. Annual festival usually held in late October. Average attendance: 15,000. Closing date July 1. Entry fee: $100 per 8x16' booth. Exibitors must be 18 or older. Submit 35mm slides or 5x7 photos of work for judging. Acceptable media include oils, acrylics, watercolors, drawings, sculpture, mixed media, textiles, ceramics, jewelry, leather, wood and glass. No commission. Artist must be present at show. Sponsor provides display panels. Security guards on 24-hour duty for show.

LUBBOCK GARDEN & ARTS CENTER "FIESTA", 4215 University Ave., Lubbock TX 79413. (806)762-6411. Contact: Georgia Booker. Estab: 1967. Annual outdoor show held 1 day in September. Average attendance: 5,000-6,000. Entry fee: $35 per 8x8x6' booth. Artist/craftsman must attend show; demonstrations encouraged. Registration limit: 100 booths. Considers all art.

OLD GEORGETOWN MARKET, Box 863, Georgetown TX 78626. Contact: Carol Paul. Sponsor: Chamber of Commerce. Estab: 1974. Show held every third Saturday in April-August. Average attendance: 4,000. Considers paintings, drawings, graphics, sculpture, handwork, needlework and jewelry. Chamber of Commerce reserves the right to restrict any merchandise judged unacceptable for public display. Closing date: day before the show. Entry fee: $10 per 20x30' outdoor display space; $40 for season pass for all 5 shows. Reservations on a first-come, first-served basis. No refunds. Each show limited to 150 exhibitors. Advertising for the show is statewide. No sales commission.

OLD SETTLERS VILLAGE ARTS & CRAFTS SHOW, 4200 Ansley Lane, Denison TX 75020. Contact: Mrs. John R. Summers. Sponsor: Old Settlers Pioneer Village of Grayson County. Most media acceptable; original work only. No sales commission. Artist must attend show. Proceeds used for construction on the Pioneer Village.

RIO GRANDE VALLEY ARTS & CRAFTS EXPOSITION, 1485 Acacia Lake Rd., Brownsville TX 78521. (512)542-8968. Contact: Anna Dailey. Sponsor: Brownsville Art League. Estab: 1971. Annual indoor show held 4 days in November. Entries accepted until show date. Entry fee: $25 per 9x10' display area, table and chairs. Art may be offered for sale; no commission. Artist must attend show; demonstrations encouraged. Considers all art.

RIVERSIDE ART SHOW, c/o Victoria Women's Club, Box 3201, Victoria TX 77901. Contact: Mrs. Jim Casey. Annual show held third Sunday in September. Average attendance: 3,000-4,000. Entry fee: $5 due 1 month before show; $7.50 late fee. All arts and crafts acceptable. Art must be for sale; 10% commission. Sponsor provides 6x12' or 8x8' booths.

SANTA'S TREASURE HOUSE ARTS & CRAFTS BAZAAR, Box 746, Raymondville TX 78580. (512)689-3171. Manager: Lucy Prater. Sponsor: Chamber of Commerce. Estab: 1971. Annual indoor show held the first Saturday in December. Average attendance: 500. Entries accepted until show date. Entry fee: $10 per 8x8' display area. Maximum 43 entries per artist. Art may be offered for sale; no commission. Sponsor provides chairs and tables on a first come, first served basis. Considers all art.

TEXAS RENAISSANCE FESTIVALS, INC., 12727 Memorial Dr., Houston TX 77024. Annual outdoor show usually held in October. Entry fee: $100.

TOWN PLAZA MALL SHOW & SALE, Box 4122, Victoria TX 77901. Contact: Betty Albrecht. Sponsor: American Business Women's Association. Semiannual indoor art and crafts market held in March and November. Entry fee: $10 per 8x12' display area. 10% commission. All media accepted. Write for more information.

WESTBURY SQUARE SIDEWALK ART FESTIVAL, Westbury Square Company, 542 Westbury Square, Houston TX 77035. (713)723-2550. Outdoor art show held 4 times annually. Entry fee: $25 per 1 artist/$40 per 2 for 10x10' display area. Fees may change. Closing date for entry: last Saturday before show. Acceptable media include painting, drawing, graphics, sculpture and selected crafts. Submit 3 photos (2 will be returned in SASE), resume, list of all media to be exhibited, and specifications of display apparatus for approval by jury committee. Work must be original. Entries and space preferences handled on a first come, first served basis.

WESTHEIMER COLONY ART FESTIVAL, 908 Westheimer Rd., Houston TX 77006. (713)521-0133. Contact: Arnold Bennitt. Sponsor: Westheimer Colony Association. Estab: 1970. Semiannual sidewalk show held 2 days in April and October. Average attendance: 200,000-300,000. Closing date for submitting photos and resumes: 6 weeks before show. Entry fee: $60 per 10x10' display area; $80 if shared. Art may be offered for sale; no commission. Registration limit: 300 artists/craftsmen. Considers calligraphy, drawings, paintings and prints. **Special Needs:** Present cash award before show for poster which best depicts show.

Utah

PARK CITY INVITATIONAL ART SHOW, Box 141, Park City UT 84060. Sponsor: Chamber of Commerce. Held annually. Entry fee: $25. Prejudging by slides.

Vermont

BROMLEY MOUNTAIN SHOW, Box 92, Readsboro VT 05350. Director: Riki Moss. Sponsor: Craftproducers Inc. Annual indoor show held in Peru, Vermont 2 days in October. Average attendance: 8,000-10,000. Closing date for entry: May 1. Entry fee: $60. Prejudging by 5 slides; entry fee refunded for refused work. Art may be offered for sale; no commission. Registration limit: 50 exhibitors. Demonstrations OK. Sponsor/artist share insurance for exhibited work. Considers graphics.

MOUNT SNOW FAIR, Box 92, Readsboro VT 05350. Director: Riki Moss. Sponsor: Craftproducers Inc. Annual indoor show held in West Dover 3 days the first week in August. Average attendance: 8,000-10,000. Closing date for entry: May 1. Entry fee: $70. Prejudging by 5 slides; entry fee refunded for refused work. Art may be offered for sale; no commission. Registration limit: 70 exhibits. Demonstrations OK. Sponsor/artist share insurance for exhibited work. Considers graphics.

MOUNT SNOW FALL FESTIVAL OF CRAFT, Box 92, Readsboro VT 05350. Director: Riki Moss. Sponsor: Craftproducers Inc. Annual indoor show held in West Dover 4 days during Columbus Day weekend. Average attendance: 8,000-10,000. Closing date for entry: May 1. Entry fee: $75. Prejudging by 5 slides; entry fee refunded for refused work. Art may be offered for sale; no commission. Registration limit: 70 exhibitors. Demonstrations OK. Sponsor/artist share insurance for exhibited work. Considers graphics.

STRATTON ARTS FESTIVAL, Stratton Mountain VT 05155. Sponsor: Vermont Council of the Arts. Annual indoor show usually held from mid-September to mid-October. No entry fee. Craftsmen only may enter more than 3 works. Art must be offered for sale; 30% commission. Open to Vermont residents. All media acceptable. Plywood display panels provided. Sponsor's insurance is $200 deductible, minus commission. Ship entries UPS or deliver in person by appointment.

Virginia

ARTS IN THE PARK, 1112 Sunset Ave., Richmond VA 23221. (804)353-8198. Chairman: Mrs. R. S. Lovelace. Sponsor: Carillon Civic Association. Estab: 1971. Annual indoor/outdoor show held 2 days in April-May. Average attendance: 50,000. Closing date for entry: 2 weeks before show. Entry fee: $15 per outdoor/$25 per indoor display areas. Art may be offered for sale; no commission. Artist must attend show; demonstrations encouraged. Considers all art.

FESTIVAL OF LEAVES, Box 1314, Front Royal VA 22630. (703)635-3637. Chairman: Prudence Matheaus. Sponsor: Warren Heritage Society. Estab: 1971. Annual show held 2 days in October. Average attendance: 3,000. Closing date for entry: 3 weeks before show. Prejudging. Art may be offered for sale; 15% commission. Artist must attend show. Registration limit: 60 artists/craftsmen. Sponsor provides display equipment and pays insurance on exhibited work. Considers all art.

GREENWOOD ARTS & CRAFTS FAIR, Greenwood Community Center, Greenwood VA 22943. (403)456-6447. Contact: Sally Wedvick. Annual indoor show held 2 days in September. Average attendance: 6,000. Closing date for entry: 4 weeks before show. Entry fee: $20, $30 or $40 per entry. Art may be offered for sale; no commission. Artist must attend show; demonstrations encouraged. Registration limit: 100 artists/craftsmen. Considers all art.

Washington

FAIR ART FESTIVAL INVITATIONAL, 4210 Terrace Heights Rd., Yakima WA 98901. (509)453-3379. Director: Ruth Wyman Reese. Sponsor: Central Washington Fair. Estab: 1973. Annual outdoor show held 9 days in early October. Average attendance: 180,000. Closing date for entry: September. Entry fee: $85-100 per 10x10' display area. Prejudging by photos or samples of work by artists whose work is unknown to this fair; SASE. Art may be offered for sale; 10% commission. Artist must attend show; demonstrations encouraged. Registration limit: 50 artists/craftsmen. Considers all art.
To Break In: "Much time and money is wasted by artists who do not send pictures and information. This year their letters will not be answered unless they comply with our request for pictures, information and an SASE."

THE SIDEWALK SHOW, Allied Arts Association, 89 Lee Blvd., Richland WA 99352. Chairman: Bette Szulinski. Annual outdoor show. Estab: 1950. 15% maximum sales commission. Artist must attend show. Acceptable media include oils, watercolors, acrylics, mixed media, graphics, drawings, sculpture, metalcraft, leather, candles, woodcraft, handwoven items and quilting. Demonstrations welcomed. 3 small cash awards given for best display. Size limit: 10x10'.

SILVERDALE'S WHALING DAYS, Box 1218, Silverdale WA 98383. Sponsor: Central Kitsap Chamber of Commerce. Contact: Gerri Mus. Show held in August. Average attendance: 5,000. Closing date for entry: 1 week before show. Entry fee: $5. Size limit is 10x10'. A variety of media accepted. Artist must attend show.

WHISTLIN' JACK LODGE FESTIVAL, 4210 Terrace Heights Rd., Yakima WA 98901. (509)453-3379. Director: Ruth Wyman Reese. Sponsor: Whistlin' Jack Lodge. Estab: 1976. Semiannual outdoor show held 3 days in September and July. Average attendance: 2,000-4,000. Closing date for entry: 2 weeks before show. Entry fee: $15 per 10x10' display area. Prejudging by photos or samples of work. SASE. Art must be offered for sale; 15% commission. Artist must attend show; demonstrations encouraged. Registration limit: 30 artists/craftsmen. Considers all art.

West Virginia

ALDERSON-BROADDUS COLLEGE ARTS & CRAFTS FAIR, Box 1397, A-B College, Philippi WV 26416. (304)457-1700 ext. 235. Director of Student Activities: Carl Hatfield. Estab: 1974. Annual indoor show held 1 day in October. Average attendance: 1,000. Closing date for entry: 2 weeks before show. No entry fee. Maximum 1 entry per artist. Art may be offered for sale; no commission. Primarily West Virginia artists. Artist must attend show; demonstrations OK. Registration limit: 40 artists/craftsmen. Sponsor provides tables. Considers all art.

CAPITAL CITY ART & CRAFT SHOW, 3820 N. Crede Dr., Charleston WV 25302. (304)346-3427. Contact: Bill Lanyi. Sponsor: Kanawha City Lions Club. Estab: 1971. Annual indoor show held 3 days in November. Average attendance: 13,000. Closing date for entry: 2 weeks before show. Entry fee: $17.50 per 10x10' display area. Artist limited to 2 booths. Prejudging by photos. Art must be offered for sale; 15% commission (sales for 2½-day show in 1976 were $48,500). Artist must attend show; prefers demonstrations. Sponsor provides display equipment and pays insurance on exhibited work. Considers all art except mobiles.

JOHN HENRY FOLK FESTIVAL, Box 135, Princeton WV 24740. (304)487-1148. Director: Edward J. Cabbell. Sponsor: John Henry Memorial Foundation, Inc. Estab: 1973. Annual outdoor show with tents held 3 days in late August. Closing date for entry: 2 months before show. No entry fee. Prejudging by photos or slides and resume conducted by panel of Appalachian artists/craftsmen. Art may be offered for sale; 10% commission. Artist must be from an Appalachian state or region and must attend show. Demonstrations OK. Sponsor provides display panels. Considers all art (at least 1 work must be related to John Henry folk legend).
Special Needs: "We buy artwork for newspaper ads and brochures." Pays $15-50 on acceptance.

MOUNTAIN STATE ART & CRAFT FAIR, Cedar Lakes, Ripley WV 25271. Contact: Fair Coordinator. Sponsors: West Virginia Depts. of Agriculture, Commerce, Education, Natural

Resources, University Extension Service, and Artists and Craftsmen Guild. Annual fair held in summer. No entry fee. 15% commission. Open to West Virginia residents.

PARKERSBURG COMMUNITY COLLEGE HERITAGE DAYS, Box 167A, Parkersburg WV 26101. (304)424-8000. Chairman: Nancy Pansing. Sponsor: Parkersburg Community College. Estab: 1974. Annual show held in tents and main halls of college 3 days in April. Average attendance: 10,000. Invitations to enter show sent in November and again in December. Closing date for entry: 6 weeks before show. No entry fee. Prejudging. Art may be offered for sale; no commission. Artist must attend show. Registration limit: 1-3 artists/craftsmen. Sponsor provides tables, chairs, platforms and other display equipment. Considers drawings, oils and watercolors. Artist should write for application. Panel then decides if type of art is suitable and not repetitious of other entries. Those artists not sent invitations for that particular year are kept in the exhibition files for following years.

STONEWALL JACKSON JUBILEE, Box 956, Weston WV 26452. (304)269-4660. Director: William Frye. Sponsor: Stonewall Jackson Heritage Arts & Crafts Inc. Estab: 1974. Annual indoor show held 3 days in September. Closing date for entry: 3 weeks before show. No entry fee. Art may be offered for sale; 15% commission. Artists must provide samples of each art or craft and attend show; demonstrations required. Registration limit: 100 artists/craftsmen. Sponsor provides tables. Considers Appalachian-oriented drawings, oils, watercolors and statues.

Wisconsin

APPLE BLOSSOM ART & CRAFTS FAIR, Rte. 2, Gay Mills WI 54631. Contact: Beverly Gaynor. Annual show. Entry fee: $10. All media acceptable; original work only. Artist must be present during show. Sponsor provides 10x4' display area and insurance for exhibited work.

ART FAIR, 1904 Washington St., New Holstein WI 53061. Contact: Warren Hollenbeck. Sponsor: Friends of the Library. Annual show. Entry fee: $5 per artist for display space approximately 15'. All media acceptable unless objection expressed at registration. No commission. Write for more information.

BLACKHAWK INDIAN VALLEY, Box 61, Rome IL 61562. (309)274-3001. Contact: Judy Kelley. Estab: 1973. Indoor show held 3 times annually in Janesville for 3 days in March, August and November. Closing date for entry: 2 weeks before show. Entry fee: $30-35 per 6x12' display area. Prejudging by 2 slides (send SASE); entry fee refunded for refused work. Art may be offered for sale; no commission. Artist must attend show. Registration limit: 80-100 artists/craftsmen. Artist may rent 8' tables at $5 each and chairs at 50¢. Considers all art. Artist should submit b&w glossies and resume for promotion.

FOREST MALL ARTS & CRAFTS FAIR, 835 W. Johnson St., Fond DuLac WI 54935. Contact: Lois Frank. Sponsor: Forest Mall Merchants Association. Estab: 1974. Annual indoor show held 3 days in April. Average attendance: 6,000-10,000. Closing date for entry: 2-3 weeks before show. Entry fee: $12-15 per 10x10' tent display area. Prejudging; entry fee refunded for refused work. Art may be offered for sale; 10% commission donated to charity. Artist must attend show. Registration limit: 70-75 artists/craftsmen. Considers all art.

FORT FEST ARTS & CRAFTS FAIR, Rte. 1, Box 49B, Fort Atkinson WI 53538. (414)563-8777. Chairman: Joy Wentz. Sponsor: Fort Fest, Inc. Estab: 1970. Annual outdoor show held 1 day in August. Closing date for entry: 3 weeks before show. Entry fee: $10 per artist. Art may be offered for sale; no commission. Artist must attend show; demonstrations encouraged. Considers all original art.

GAYS MILLS PACE CLUB ARTS & CRAFTS FAIR, Pace Club, Gays Mills WI 54631. Contact: Mrs. Richard Gainor. Semiannual show held 1 day in May (indoor) and September (outdoor). Average attendance: 1,000+. Entries accepted until spaces filled. Entry fee: $10 per 10x4' display area. Art may be offered for sale; no commission. Artist must attend show; demonstrations encouraged. Registration limit: 75-100 artists/craftsmen. Considers all art.

HOMESPUN HOLIDAY ARTS AND CRAFTS FAIR, c/o Rte. 1, Avalon WI 53525. Contact: Pat Beals. Sponsor: Clinton Jr. Women's Club. Annual fair held in late November in Clinton. Entry fee: $15 per 10x10' display unit. Exhibitors must be present. Acceptable media include oils, acrylics, watercolors, graphics, drawings, sculpture, mixed media and crafts. Everything displayed must be handcrafted by exhibitor. No commission.

MOUNT MARY STARVING ARTISTS SHOW, 17160 Deer Park Dr., Brookfield WI 53005. (414)782-7862. Registration Director: Laura Nesemann. Sponsor: Mount Mary College Alumnae Association. Estab: 1969. Annual outdoor show held 1 day in September. Average attendance: 20,000. Closing date for entry: March 1. Entry fee: $30 per artist. Prejudging by photos or slides; entry fee refunded for refused work. Art may be sold for under $35; no sales commission. Artist must attend show; no demonstrations. Registration limit: 195 artists/craftsmen. Sponsor provides snow fencing; 15x18' display area.
Acceptable Work: Considers acrylics, drawings, oils, pastels, prints, mobiles, sculpture and watercolors. No erotica.

RACINE CHRISTMAS GIFT MARKET, 422 Main St., Racine WI 53403. (414)637-4471. Director: Daniel Thekan. Estab: 1973. Annual indoor show held the second Sunday in December. Average attendance: 1,500-2,000. Entries accepted until show date. "Show is usually sold out 1 month ahead of time." Entry fee: $15 per entry. Prejudging; entry fee refunded for refused work. Art may be offered for sale; no commission. Prefers demonstrations. Registration limit: 140 artists/craftsmen. Sponsor provides tables and chairs. Considers all art. "Priority given to work that will make good Christmas gifts."

Craft Exhibitions

Alabama

CAMM (CRAFTS, ART, MUSIC AND MOVIES), Box 442, University Station, Birmingham AL 35294. Chairman: H. Jackson Wills. Sponsor: Birmingham Festival of Arts. Estab: 1970. Annual indoor show held 3 days in March. Entries accepted until show date. No entry fee. Work may not be offered for sale. "Demonstrations are the main feature." Craftsman must attend show. Sponsor provides display equipment and insurance for exhibited work. Considers all crafts.

THE CRAFT SHOW, Port City Craftsmen, Box U-1028, University of South Alabama, Mobile AL 36688. Co-sponsor: Recreation Club. Estab: 1974. Semiannual indoor show held 2 days in spring and fall. Average attendance: 15,000-20,000. Closing date for entry: 4 weeks before show. Entry fee: $15 per 10x10' display area. Crafts may be offered for sale; no commission. Craftsman must attend show; demonstrations encouraged. Registration limit: 170 spaces. Tables may be rented; sponsor provides chairs. Considers all crafts. "We reserve the right to refuse anything we consider in poor taste for a family-type show. No items can be hung from the gym ceiling or walls."

RIVERFRONT MARKET DAY, Box 586, Selma AL 36701. (205)872-8265. Coordinator: Sam H. O'Hara. Sponsor: Selma and Dallas County Historical Preservation Society. Estab: 1971. Annual outdoor show held 1 day in fall. Average attendance: 20,000-30,000. Closing date for entry: 1 week before show. Entry fee: $15 per uncovered/$25 per covered display area. Crafts may be offered for sale; no commission. Craftsman must attend show. Registration limit: 250 artists/craftsmen. Sponsor provides electrical outlets. Considers all crafts.

RUMBLING WATERS ARTS & CRAFT SHOW, Box 456, Wetumpka AL 36092. (205) 567-6289. Exhibitor Chairman: Gail Bass. Sponsor: Rumbling Waters Arts Club. Estab: 1970. Annual outdoor show held the first Saturday in October. Average attendance: 5,000. Entries accepted until show date. Entry fee: $7.50 per craftsman. Crafts may be offered for sale; no commission. Craftsman must attend show; demonstrations encouraged. Registration limit: 200 artists/craftsmen. Considers all crafts.

Arizona

FESTIVAL ARTS & CRAFTS FAIR, 8 W. Paseo Redondo, Tucson AZ 85705. (602)622-6911. Director: Jarvis Harriman. Sponsor: Tucson Festival Society, Inc. Estab: 1951. Annual outdoor show held 3 days in April. Average attendance: 50,000. Closing date for entry: 6 weeks before show. Entry fee: $75 per 8x8' booth. Crafts may be offered for sale; no commission. Craftsman must attend show; demonstrations OK. Registration limit: 140 artists/craftsmen. Considers all crafts.

Arkansas

ARKANSAS RIVER VALLEY ARTS & CRAFTS FAIR & SALE, Box 1122, Russellville AR 72801. (501)968-1552. Contact: Lois Griffin. Estab: 1970. Annual indoor show held 3 days in November. Average attendance: 20,000. Entries accepted until spaces filled; space granted in order of application. Entry fee: $15 per 6x8' display area. Crafts must be offered for sale: no commission. Craftsman must attend show; demonstrations encouraged. Rgistration limit: 167 artists/craftsmen. Considers handmade crafts.

BELLA VISTA ARTS & CRAFTS FESTIVAL, Kingsdale Recreation Center, Bella Vista AR 72712. (501)855-1443. Contact: Larry or Pam Collins. Sponsor: Village Art Club. Estab: 1966. Annual outdoor show held 3 days in mid-October (tents available). Average attendance: 100,000. Closing date for entry: 2 weeks before show. Entry fee: $12.50 per 6x8' display area. Crafts must be offered for sale; 10% commission. Craftsman must attend show. "Exhibitors who demonstrate during the show have the best sales." Sponsor provides lattice-wire backing support in tents and pays insurance on exhibited work. Considers all crafts. Jewelry must be handmade.

NEWTON COUNTY GUILD ARTS & CRAFTS FAIR, Box 119, Limestone AR 72646. (501)428-5257. Secretary: Beverley Butler. Estab: 1970. Semiannual indoor show held 3 days in April and October. Closing date for entry: 2 weeks before show. Entry fee: $10 per 6x8' display area. Crafts may be offered for sale; no commission. Craftsman must attend show; demonstrations OK. "We want all booths ready and participants there Friday morning at 9 and we don't want them to pull their exhibits until closing at 6 p.m. Sunday." Considers all crafts.

SIDEWALK ARTS & CRAFTS SHOW, c/o Chamber of Commerce, Auditorium Bldg., Eureka Springs AR 72632. (501)253-8737. Contact: Jim Emmons. Annual outdoor show held 2 days in spring. Entries accepted until show date. Entry fee: $15-25. Prejudging by slides or photos of work; entry fee refunded for refused work. Crafts may be offered for sale; no commission. Craftsman must attend show and is urged to work in his booth. Sponsor provides park benches for display. Considers all crafts.

California

APPLE SMORGY DAYS ARTS & CRAFTS FESTIVAL, 3170 Hassler Rd., Camino CA 95709. (916)626-0128. Show Director: Mike Visman. Sponsor: El Dorado Orchards. Estab: 1969. Annual outdoor show held during Apple Hill's Festival each weekend during October. Average attendance: 25,000-35,000. Entries accepted until show date. Entry fee: $20 per weekend or $50 for the month. Crafts may be offered for sale; no commission. Craftsman or representative must attend; demonstrations OK. Registration limit: 3 craftsmen per category (type of craft) per weekend. Considers all crafts.

ART IN THE PARK TRADE FAIR, 14170 N. Highway 59, Merced CA 95340. (209)563-6519. Chairman: Eleanor Elkins. Sponsor: Merced River School Parents Club. Estab: 1973. Annual outdoor show held 1 day in May. Average attendance: 6,000. Closing date for entry: 2 weeks before show. Entry fee: $10 per picnic table display area. Crafts may be offered for sale; no commission. Demonstrations OK. Registration limit: 100 artists/craftsmen. Sponsor provides insurance for exhibited work. Considers all crafts.

CALIFORNIA CRAFTS, E.B. Crocker Art Gallery, 216 O St., Sacramento CA 95814. Sponsor: Creative Arts League of Sacramento. Biennial crafts exhibition.

FIESTA DEL ARTES, Box 404, Hermosa Beach CA 90254. (213)376-0951. Show Chairman: Ben Wasserman. Sponsor: Chamber of Commerce. Estab: 1970. Semiannual outdoor show held 2 days during Labor Day and Memorial Day weekends. Average attendance: 5,000. Closing date for entry: 4 weeks before show. Entry fee: $47.50 per 10x10' display area. Prejudging; entry fee refunded for refused work. Crafts may be offered for sale; no commission. Demonstrations OK. Registration limit: 277 spaces. Considers all crafts.

FIRST SUNDAY IN THE PARK, Box 99, Ventura CA 93001. Program Coordinator: Cheryl M. Collart. Sponsor: City of Ventura, Parks and Recreation Dept. Estab: 1975. Outdoor show held the first Sunday of each month except January and October. Average attendance: 5,000-8,000. Closing date for entry: 1 week before show. Entry fee: $5 per craftsman. Prejudging by photos; entry fee refunded for refused work. Crafts may be offered for sale; no commission. Craftsman must attend show; demonstrations OK. Registration limit: 100 artists/craftsmen. Considers all crafts.

LOLA MONTEZ-LOTTA CRABTREE EXTRAVAGANZA, 128 Banner Rd., Nevada City CA 95959. (916)273-9389. Co-Chairman: Kathleen L. Coleman. Sponsor: Sunflower School. Estab: 1973. Annual outdoor show held 2 days in June. Average attendance: 2,000+. Closing date for entry: 4 weeks before show. Entry fee: $10 per 10x10' space. Prejudging by photos; display area fee refunded for refused work. Crafts may be offered for sale; 10% commission. Craftsman must attend show; demonstrations encouraged. Registration limit: 30-35 artists/craftsmen. Considers all crafts except decoupage, needlecrafts and tole painting.

MOUNTAIN AIRE, Box 4698, Modesto CA 95352. (209)521-6310. Sponsor: Rock 'N Chair Productions. Estab: 1974. Annual outdoor show held in conjunction with Music Festival 2 days in June. Average attendance: 12,000 per day. Closing date for entry: 1 week before show. Write for entry fee. Prejudging; entry fee refunded for refused work. Crafts may be offered for sale; no commission. "Wares directed toward ages 15-35 sell best." Demonstrations OK. Registration limit: 75 artists/craftsmen. Considers all handmade crafts.

OJAI CRAFTS FESTIVAL, Box 331, Ojai CA 93023. (805)646-2769. Director: Nancy Oatway. Sponsor: Ojai Valley Art Center. Estab: 1974. Annual indoor/outdoor show held second weekend in December. Average attendance: 3,000-5,000. Closing date for entry: 6 weeks before show. Entry fee: $15-20 per 6x10′ display area. Maximum 1 entry per craftsman. Prejudging by 3 slides. Crafts may be offered for sale; 10-20% commission. Craftsman must attend show; demonstrations encouraged. Registration limit: 60 craftsmen. Considers all crafts.

SIERRA NEVADA FOLK ARTS FESTIVAL, Box 926, Arnold CA 95223. (209)795-2593. Contact: Candace Hendricks. Sponsor: After the Gold Rush. Estab: 1974. Annual outdoor show held 2 days in July. Average attendance: 3,000. Closing date for entry: 4 weeks before show. Entry fee: $20 per display area. Prejudging by 3 photos; entry fee refunded for refused work. Crafts may be offered for sale; no commission. Craftsman must attend show; demonstrations encouraged. Registration limit: 60 booths. Considers all crafts.

SOUTH LAKE FESTIVAL OF THE ARTS, 492 S. Lake Ave., Pasadena CA 91101. (213)792-4417. Coordinator: Ray Leier. Sponsor: South Lake Business Association. Estab: 1974. Semiannual outdoor show held 2 days in early spring and late fall. "Located in well-shopped retail area." Closing date for entries: 2 weeks before show. Entry fee: $25 per 12x4' display area. Prejudging by photos; entry fee refunded for refused work. Crafts may be offered for sale; no commission. Craftsman must attend show; demonstrations OK. Considers all crafts; no kits.

Colorado

OWN YOUR OWN ART SHOW, c/o Art Dept., University of Southern Colorado, Pueblo CO 81001. (303)549-2552. Chairmen: Ed Sajbel/Bob Wands. Sponsors: University of Southern Colorado Art Dept. and Pueblo Service League. Estab: 1962. Annual indoor show held 2 weeks in November. Average attendance: 10,000. Closing date for entry: 1 week before show. Entry fee: $4 per craftsman. Prejudging; no entry fees refunded for refused work. Crafts may be offered for sale; 25% commission for art scholarships. Open to residents of Colorado, Idaho, Arizona, Montana, Nevada, New Mexico, Utah and Wyoming. Students may demonstrate. Registration limit: 900-1,000 artists/craftsmen.
Acceptable Work: Considers batik, ceramics, glass art, jewelry, leatherworking, metalsmithing, pottery, sculpture, weavings, wall hangings, woodcrafting and mixed media. Maximum size: 3x4x6'8", 300 lbs.

ROCKY MOUNTAIN NATIONAL CRAFT FAIR, National Crafts Ltd., Gapland MD 21736. (301)432-8438. Director: Noel Clark. Estab: 1977. Annual indoor show held in the Adams County Fairgrounds in Denver 2-3 days in July. Average attendance: 40,000. Closing date for applications: 3-4 months before show. Entry fee: $90. Prejudging by 5 color slides; entry fee refunded for refused work. Crafts may be offered for sale; no commission. Craftsman must attend show. Registration limit: 400 artists/craftsmen. Considers all crafts.

WILDLIFE ART SHOWS, 1420 E. 91st Ave., Thornton CO 80229. (303)288-1144. Contact: David or C. Holly Merrifield. Sponsors: Colorado Wildlife Federation, Wilderness Society and Audubon Society. Estab: 1974. Indoor/outdoor show held once a month for 3 days. Entries accepted year-round. Entry fee: $10; prejudging fee: $5 per artist. Crafts may be offered for sale; 15% commission. Craftsman must attend show; prefers demonstrations. Registration limit: 25-30 artists/craftsmen.

Acceptable Work: Considers batik; must be framed; bin work must be matted. No chickenwire screen displays; pegboard only. If wood-framed, must be painted in earth tones. Work must pertain to wildlife.

Connecticut

AMERICRAFT CRAFTS EXPO, Box 370, Farmington CT 06032. (203)224-8388. Director: Rudy Kowalczyk. Sponsor: American Crafts Expositions. Estab: 1969. Annual indoor/outdoor show held in Berlin 3 days in August. Average attendance: 20,000+. Closing date for entry: 4 weeks before show. Entry fee: $50-60 per booth. Prejudging; entry fee refunded for refused work. Crafts may be offered for sale; no commission. Craftsman must attend show; demonstrations OK. Registration limit: 200 artists/craftsmen.
Acceptable Work: Considers batik, candlemaking, ceramics, dollmaking, glass art, jewelry, leatherworking, metalsmithing, needlecrafts, pottery, soft sculpture, weaving, wall hangings and woodcrafting.

ANNUAL GUEST CHRISTMAS SHOW, Couturier Galerie, 1814 Newfield Ave., Stamford CT 06903. (203)322-2405. Director: Marion Couturier. Annual show held in December. Closing date for entry: August. No entry fee. Maximum 3 entries per craftsman. 40% commission. Gallery insures exhibited work. Considers handcrafted jewelry, pottery, weaving and other crafts.

ARTS & CRAFTS SHOW, 3 Cyrus Lane, Bloomfield CT 06002. Contact: Shirley Cohen. Sponsors: Connecticut River Valley Region, Women's American O.R.T. Held annually in May with closing date of April 30. Considers handcrafts and art. $15 entry fee. No commission on sales. "All items must be handcrafted by the exhibitor. No imports allowed."

BRISTOL MUM FESTIVAL CRAFT FAIR, 93 Divinity St., Bristol CT 06010. Contact: Ruth B. Johnson. Sponsor: Women's College Club of Bristol. Annual indoor show with September closing date. Average attendance: 5,000. Craftsman may pay $20 or $5 plus 20% commission on sales. Craftsman must attend. Sponsor provides 6x8' display area, table and 2 chairs. Considers crafts only.

CHRISTMAS CRAFTS EXPO, Box 370, Farmington CT 06032. (203)224-8388. Director: Rudy Kowalczyk. Sponsor: American Crafts Expositions. Estab: 1973. Annual indoor show held at the Hartford Civic Center 3 days in December. Average attendance: 25,000+. Closing date for entry: 4 weeks before show. Entry fee: $100, 10x10' display area; $140, 10x15' display area; $180, 10x20' display area. Prejudging; entry fee refunded for refused work. Crafts may be offered for sale; no commission. Craftsman must attend show; demonstrations OK. Registration limit: 250 artists/craftsmen.
Acceptable Work: Considers batik, candlemaking, ceramics, dollmaking, glass art, jewelry, leatherworking, metalsmithing, needlecrafts, pottery, soft sculpture, weaving, wall hangings and woodcrafting.

CRAFT FAIR, 21 Arvid Rd., Portland CT 06480. (203)342-2641. Chairman: Elaine Moss. Sponsor: Middletown Chapter of Hadassah. Estab: 1972. Annual outdoor show held 1 day in September. Average attendance: 10,000. Closing date for entry: show date or until 184 capacity is reached. Entry fee: $15 per 10x16' display area. Maximum 1 booth per craftsman. Crafts may be offered for sale; no commission. Craftsman or representative must attend show. Registration limit: 184 craftsmen. Considers all crafts.

FARMINGTON CRAFTS EXPO, Box 370, Farmington CT 06032. (202)224-8388. Director: Rudy Kowalczyk. Sponsor: American Crafts Expositions. Estab: 1972. Annual indoor/outdoor show held in Farmington 3 days in June. Average attendance: 20,000+. Closing date for entry: 4 weeks before show. Entry fee: $60 per outdoor display; $70 per tent. Prejudging; entry fee refunded for refused work. Crafts may be offered for sale; no commission. Craftsman must attend show; demonstrations OK. Registration limit: 200 artists/craftsmen.
Acceptable Work: Considers batik, candlemaking, ceramics, dollmaking, glass art, jewelry, leatherworking, metalsmithing, needlecrafts, pottery, soft sculpture, weaving, wall hangings and woodcrafting.

GREATER VERNON JAYCEES ARTS & CRAFTS FAIR, Greater Vernon Jaycees, Box 119, Rockville CT 06066. Chairman: Joe Lieberman. Estab: 1974. Annual outdoor show held 2 days in late fall. Closing date for entry: 16 weeks before show. Entry fee: $2.50 per linear foot. Prejudging by photos; entry fee refunded for refused work. Crafts may be offered for sale; no commission. Craftsman must attend show; demonstrations OK. Sponsor pays insurance for exhibited work. Considers all original crafts.

MEET THE ARTISTS (formerly Denise Morris Curt's Meet), 41 Green St., Milford CT 06460. (203)874-5672. Contact: Director. Sponsor: Denise Morris Curt. Estab: 1963. Annual indoor/outdoor show held in Bridgeport, Connecticut, 1-3 days in May. Entry fee: $10 per day. Entry fee refunded for refused work. Crafts may be offered for sale; no commission. Craftsman must attend show; demonstrations OK. Considers all crafts.

MEET THE ARTISTS (formerly Denise Morris Curt's Meet), 41 Green St., Milford CT 06460. (203)874-5672. Contact: Director. Sponsor: Denise Morris Curt. Estab: 1963. Semiannual indoor show held at Chapel Square Mall in New Haven 1-3 days in June and November. Closing date for entry: 1 week before show. Entry fee: $10 per day. Prejudging by slides or photos; entry fee refunded for refused work. Crafts may be offered for sale; no commission. Craftsman must attend show; demonstrations OK. Considers batik, metalsmithing and soft sculpture.

MEET THE ARTISTS (formerly Denise Morris Curt's Meet), 41 Green St., Milford CT 06460. (203)874-5672. Contact: Director. Sponsor: Denise Morris Curt. Estab: 1963. Semiannual indoor/outdoor show held in Meridan Square 4 days in September and October. Closing date for entry: 1 week before show. Entry fee: $10 per day. Prejudging by slides or photos; entry fee refunded for refused work. Crafts may be offered for sale; no commission. Craftsman must attend show; demonstrations OK. Considers batik, metalsmithing and soft sculpture.

NEW ENGLAND CRAFT FAIR, First Congregational Church, Granby CT 06035. Annual indoor show held 2 days in October. Average attendance: 1,400. Entry fee: $5 per 1/$7.50 per 2 days. 15% commission. Registration limit: 50-55 exhibits. Craftsman must attend show. Sponsor provides 8' table. Considers all media; mostly crafts.

SUMMER CRAFT SHOW & BAZAAR, First Church of Christ, Town St., East Haddam CT 06423. Chairman: Dr. Karl Stofko. Estab: 1968. Annual outdoor show held 1 day in July. Entries accepted until show date. Entry fee: $3 per 15' display area. Crafts may be offered for sale; 10% commission. Prefers Connecticut craftsmen. Craftsman must attend show; demonstrations encouraged. "We will not accept shipped work." Considers all crafts.

WESLEYAN POTTERS INCORPORATED, ANNUAL EXHIBIT & SALE, 350 S. Main St., Middletown CT 06457. Estab: 1956. Annual show held in late fall. Average attendance: 10,000. Submit work samples to jury. Crafts may be offered for sale; 30% commission. Graphics and crafts eligible.

WESTPORT CREATIVE ARTS FESTIVAL, 44 Imperial Ave., Westport CT 06880. Contact: Festival Chairman. Sponsor: Westport Young Woman's League. Annual indoor show held 2 days in mid-November. Closing date for entry: August 1. Entry fee: $15 per entry. Prejudging by slides or photos; entry fee refunded for refused work. Crafts may be offered for sale; 15% commission. Craftsman must attend show. Registration limit: 65 craftsmen. Considers all crafts.

WESTPORT HANDCRAFTS FAIR, 552 Hoydens Hill Rd., Fairfield CT 06430. Chairman: Nancy Jackson. Sponsor: Westport/Weston Cooperative Nursery School. Estab: 1965. Annual outdoor show held Memorial Day weekend. Entry fee: $15 per display area; due after jurying. Prejudging (when possible, best to send samples of work in addition to slides or photos); conducted in February. Crafts may be offered for sale; 15% commission. Craftsman must attend show; demonstrations encouraged. Registration limit: 85-90 craftsmen. Hand-deliver work only. Considers all crafts.

YAAF ARTS AND CRAFTS SALE, 18 Reef Rd., Fairfield CT 06430. Contact: Jack Farkas or Paul Strauss. Sponsor: Young Artist Association of Fairfield. Annual outdoor show. Average attendance: 250,000. Entry fee: $20 per 12' display area. No limit on number of entries. Prejudging. No commission. Registration limit: 100 artists/craftsmen. All media accepted.

Delaware

BRANDYWINE ARTS FESTIVAL, 1307 Orange St., Wilmington DE 19801. Director: George Sargisson. Estab: 1961. Annual outdoor show held 2 days in September. Average attendance: 15,000 per day. Closing date for entry: 4 weeks before show. Entry fee: $40 per 10x10' space. Crafts must be offered for sale; no commission. Craftsman must attend show. Considers all crafts except ceramics, metalsmithing and soft sculpture.

Florida

ALTAMONTE MALL, 2918 Martel Dr., Dayton OH 45420. (513)254-2900. Director: Clarence Freeland. Annual indoor show held in Altamonte, Florida, 1 week in January. Closing date for entry: 1 week before show. Entry fee: $75. Prejudging. Crafts may be offered for sale; no commission. Craftsman must attend show; demonstrations OK. Sponsor provides 10x10' display area. Considers all crafts.

FLORIDA FOREST FESTIVAL ARTS & CRAFTS SHOW & SALE, Box 892, Perry FL 32347. (904)584-5366. Chairman: Nadine O. Loughridge. Sponsor: Perry-Taylor County Chamber of Commerce. Estab: 1971. Annual outdoor show held 1 day the fourth weekend in October. Average attendance: 30,000. Closing date for entry: 1 week before show. Entry fee: $3 per 9x9' display area. Crafts may be offered for sale; 10% commission. Craftsman must attend show; demonstrations encouraged. Sponsor provides 24 canopies for rent and pays liability insurance. Considers all crafts.

LEE SIDEWALK ARTS & CRAFTS SHOW, Lee County Bank, Box 711, c/o Special Services, Fort Myers FL 33902. (813)334-1171 ext. 373. Vice President: Burnett Bloodworth. Estab: 1974. Annual outdoor show held 1 day in January. Average attendance: 12,000. Closing date for entry: 4 weeks before show. Entry fee: $10 per 10x10' display area. Demonstrations OK. Crafts may be offered for sale; no commission. Considers all original crafts.

SPRING ARTS FESTIVAL, Drawer 1187, Gainesville FL 32602. (904)372-1976. Director: Karen Beach. Sponsors: Santa Fe Community College and Gainesville Chamber of Commerce. Estab: 1970. Annual outdoor show held 2 days in April. Average attendance: 60,000. Closing date for entry: 6 weeks before show. Entry fee: $5 application fee. Prejudging; no entry fees refunded. Crafts may be offered for sale; no commission. Open to Alachua and Bradford counties residents. Craftsman must attend show; demonstrations OK. Registration limit: 100 artists/craftsmen.

Acceptable Work: Considers batik, ceramics, dollmaking, glass art, jewelry, leather, metalsmithing, needlecrafts, pottery, soft sculpture, tole painting, weavings, wall hangings and woodcrafting.

WINTER PARK MALL ANNUAL CRAFTS SHOW, 560 N. Orlando Ave., Winter Park FL 32789. Annual show held in May. Entry fee: $20. Prejudging by slides or photos.

Georgia

ATLANTA CRAFT FAIR, National Crafts Ltd., Gapland MD 21736. (301)432-8438. Director: Noel Clark. Estab: 1977. Annual indoor show held in the Atlanta Civic Center 2-3 days in November. Average attendance: 40,000. Closing date for applications: 3-4 months before show. Entry fee: $90. Prejudging by 5 color slides; entry fee refunded for refused work. Crafts may be offered for sale; no commission. Craftsman must attend show. Registration limit: 400 artists/craftsmen. Considers printmaking.

MILLION PINES ARTS & CRAFTS FESTIVAL, Box 238, Soperton GA 30457. (912) 529-4524. Chairman: Jack Pournelle. Sponsor: City of Soperton. Estab: 1973. Annual outdoor show held 2 days in November. Closing date for entry: 4 weeks before show. Entry fee: $25. Maximum 2 entries per craftsman. Crafts may be offered for sale; no commission. Craftsman must attend show; demonstrations encouraged. Registration limit: 125 artists/craftsmen. Sponsor provides 10x12' display area. Considers all crafts.

PRATER'S MILL COUNTRY FAIR, 216 Riderwood Dr., Dalton GA 30720. Director: Judy Alderman. Estab: 1971. Semiannual outdoor show held 2 days in May and October. Average attendance: 20,000-25,000. Closing date for entry: 8 weeks before show. Entry fee: $15 per 15x15' display area. Prejudging; entry fee refunded for refused work. Crafts may be offered for sale; no commission. Craftsman must attend show; demonstrations encouraged. Registration limit: 135 artists/craftsmen.

Acceptable Work: Considers batik, candlemaking, dollmaking, glass art, jewelry, leatherworking, metalsmithing, needlecrafts, pottery, soft sculpture, tole painting, weavings, wall hangings, woodcrafting and plants. All crafts must be handmade of natural materials by the craftsman exhibiting them.

Illinois

A DAY IN THE COUNTRY, Rte. 1, Box 194A, Pecatonica IL 61063. Chairman: Sandra Schoonmaker. Sponsor: Pecatonica Junior Woman's Club. Estab: 1971. Annual indoor show held 1 day in October. Average attendance: 3,000+. Closing date for entry: 4 weeks before show. Entry fee: $12 per entry. Crafts may be offered for sale; no commission. Craftsman must attend show; demonstrations encouraged. Sponsor provides electrical outlets and 10x10' display area. Considers all original crafts.

BELVIDERE MALL STARVING ARTIST'S SHOW, Rte. 1, 146 Park Dr., Barrington IL 60010. (312)639-5665. Show Director: Irene Partridge. Sponsor: Belvidere Mall Merchants Association. Estab: 1964. Annual indoor show held 2 days in winter. Closing date for entry: 10 days prior to show. Entry fee: $20 per craftsman. Prejudging by 5 slides (send resume and SASE); entry fee refunded for refused work. Crafts may be offered for sale; no commission. Craftsman must attend show; demonstrations OK. Registration limit: 80-100 artists/craftsmen. Considers all crafts.

BLOWN GLASS II, 1521 Sherman Ave., Evanston IL 60201. (312)864-2660. Director: R. Isaacson. Sponsor: Mindscape Gallery & Studio. Estab: 1975. Annual indoor show held 1 month in April. Average attendance: 2,000. Closing date for entry: mid-January. Entry fee: $5 per entry. Prejudging by slides; no entry fees refunded for refused work. Crafts must be offered for sale; 33 1/3% commission. Demonstrations pre-arranged. Registration limit: 24-30 artists/craftsmen. Sponsor provides insurance during exhibit period.

BOULEVARD MALL ART & CRAFT SHOW, Box 61, Rome IL 61562. (309)274-3001. Contact: Judy Kelley. Estab: 1974. Semiannual indoor show held 3 days in spring and fall. Closing date for entry: 2 weeks before show. Entry fee: $30 per 6x12' display area. Prejudging by 2 slides or photos; entry fee refunded for refused work. Crafts may be offered for sale; no commission. Craftsman must attend show. Registration limit: 40 artists/craftsmen.
Acceptable Work: Considers candlemaking, ceramics, glass art, jewelry, leatherworking, metalsmithing, pottery, tole painting, wall hangings and woodcrafting.

"CRITTERS & COHORTS," 1521 Sherman Ave., Evanston IL 60201. (312)864-2660. Director: Ron Isaacson. Sponsor: Mindscape Gallery & Studio. Estab: 1977. Annual indoor show held for the month of October. Closing date for entry: August 1. Entry fee: $5 per artist. Prejudging; entry fee refunded for refused work. Crafts must be offered for sale; 33 1/3% commission. Demonstrations may be arranged. Registration limit: 24-30 craftsmen. Sponsor provides all props and pays insurance for exhibit period.
Acceptable Work: Considers batik, ceramics, glass art, jewelry, metalsmithing, pottery, soft sculpture, woodworking and mobiles. Finished, one-of-a-kind items only. "We consider contemporary art forms using traditional or non-traditional media."
Promotion: "Send photos 30 days prior to show opening along with a resume and statement by the artist of his relationship to his media."

CROSS COUNTY MALL SHOW, Box 61, Rome IL 61562. (309)274-3001. Contact: Judy Kelley. Estab: 1976. Semiannual indoor show held in Mattoon 3 days in spring and fall. Closing date for entry: 2 weeks before show. Entry fee: $30 per 6x12' display area; no personal checks. Prejudging by slides; entry fee refunded for refused work. Crafts may be offered for sale; no commission. Craftsman must attend show; prefers demonstrations. Registration limit: 50 artists/craftsmen. Sponsor provides display table for $5.
Acceptable Work: Considers candlemaking, ceramics, jewelry, metalsmithing, pottery, tole painting, wall hangings and woodcrafting. No crochet, knitting or clothing.

CRYSTAL POINT MALL SPRING ART & CRAFT SHOW, Box 61, Rome IL 61562. (309)274-3001. Coordinator: Judy Kelley. Estab: 1977. Semiannual indoor show held in Crystal Lake 3 days in May and November. Closing date for entry: 2 weeks before show. Entry fee: $30 per entry; $5 late fee. Prejudging by slides; entry fee refunded for refused work. Crafts may be offered for sale; no commission. Craftsman must attend show; demonstrations OK. Registration limit: 40 artists/craftsmen.

Acceptable Work: Considers batik, candlemaking, ceramics, metalsmithing, pottery, tole painting, weavings, wall hangings and woodcrafting.

DEERFIELD COMMONS ARTS & SELECTED CRAFTS FESTIVAL, Rte. 1, 146 Park Dr., Barrington IL 60010. (312)639-5665. Director: Irene "Rae" Partridge. Sponsor: Deerfield Commons Merchants Association. Estab: 1971. Annual outdoor show held 1 day in September. Closing date for entry: 10 days before show. Entry fee: $18 per entry. Prejudging by slides; entry fee refunded for refused work. Craftsman must attend show; demonstrations encouraged. Registration limit: 63-65 artists/craftsmen. Considers all crafts. Maximum size: 10x6x5".

EDENS PLAZA ARTS & CRAFT FAIR, 9476 Harding Ave., Surfside FL 33154. Contact: Iris G. Klein. Sponsor: Edens Plaza Merchants Association. Estab: 1956. Annual outdoor show held in Wilmette, Illinois, 2 days in June. Average attendance: 10,000-15,000. Entry fee: $20 per 8x8' display area. Maximum 2 entries per craftsman. Prejudging by slides or photos (send resume and SASE). Crafts may be offered for sale; no commission. Craftsman must attend show; demonstrations OK. Considers all crafts. Submit b&w glossies and resume for newspaper publicity.

HILLSIDE CENTER SELECTED CRAFTS FESTIVAL, Rte. 1, 146 Park Dr., Barrington IL 60010. (312)639-5665. Director: Irene "Rae" Partridge. Sponsor: Hillside Center Merchants Association. Estab: 1966. Annual outdoor show held 2 days in spring. Closing date for entry: 10 days before show. Entry fee: $25 per entry. Prejudging by 5 slides or photos (send resume and SASE); entry fee refunded for refused work. Crafts may be offered for sale; no commission. Craftsman must attend show; demonstrations encouraged. Registration limit: 100-125 artists/craftsmen. Considers all handmade crafts. "Keep packing out of sight; tables must be draped to floor on all sides; cartons should be removed."

HILLSIDE STARVING ARTIST'S SHOW, Rte. 1, 146 Park Dr., Barrington IL 60010. (312)639-5665. Show Director: Irene Partridge. Sponsor: Hillside Center Merchants Association. Estab: 1966. Annual indoor show held in Hillside 2 days during winter. Closing date for entry: 10 days before show. Entry fee: $25 per craftsman. Prejudging by 5 slides or photos (send resume and SASE); entry fee refunded for refused work. Crafts may be offered for sale; no commission. Craftsman must attend show; demonstrations OK. Registration limit: 100-125 artists/craftsmen. Considers all crafts.

HOWARD-WESTERN CRAFT & SCULPTURE FAIR, 9476 Harding Ave., Surfside FL 33154. Art Director: Iris G. Klein. Sponsor: Howard-Western Merchants Association. Estab: 1970. Annual outdoor show held 2 days in September in Chicago. Average attendance: 2,000-3,000. Entries accepted until 4 weeks before show. Entry fcc: $15. Maximum 2 entries per artist. Art may be offered for sale; no commission. Artist must attend show; demonstrations by caricaturists only. Registration limit: 75 artists/craftsmen. Considers original crafts.

MARKET PLACE MALL ART & CRAFT SHOW, Box 61, Rome IL 61562. (309)274-3001. Coordinator: Judy Kelley. Estab: 1976. Semiannual indoor show held in Champaign 3 days in spring and fall. Closing date for entry: 2 weeks before show. Entry fee: $40 per 6x12' display area; no personal checks. Prejudging by 2 slides (send SASE); entry fee refunded for refused work. Crafts may be offered for sale; no commission. Craftsman must attend show. Registration limit: 80-100 artists/craftsmen.
Acceptable Work: Considers candlemaking, glass art, leatherworking, metalsmithing, pottery, tole painting, wall hangings and woodcrafting.

NORTHPOINT CENTER ARTS & SELECTED CRAFTS FESTIVAL, Rte. 1, 146 Park Dr., Barrington IL 60010. (312)639-5665. Director: Irene "Rae" Partridge. Sponsor: Northpoint Merchants Association. Estab: 1971. Semiannual outdoor show held 1 day in July and September. Closing date for entry: 10 days before show. Entry fee: $18 per entry. Prejudging by 5 slides or photos (send resume and SASE); entry fee refunded for refused work. Crafts may be offered for sale; no commission. Craftsman must attend show; demonstrations encouraged. Registration limit: 125-150 artists/craftsmen. Considers all handmade crafts. Maximum size: 10x8x6'.

NORTHWOODS FINE ARTS SHOW, 4501 War Memorial Dr., Peoria IL 61613. Call (309)688-0445 weekdays only from 9 a.m.-5 p.m. Contact: Mrs. Lynda Michael. Sponsor:

Northwoods Merchants' Association. Estab: 1975. Annual indoor show held 2 days in the fall. Closing date for entry: 2 weeks before show. Entry fee: $25 per approximately 9x5' display area. Prejudging; entry fee refunded for refused work. Crafts may be offered for sale; no commission. Open to craftsmen ages 18+. Craftsman must attend show; demonstrations OK. Entrants must sign "Hold Harmless" form.
Acceptable Work: Considers batik, glass art, soft sculpture, weavings, wall hangings (no plaques) and metal sculpture.

OLD CANAL DAYS ARTS & CRAFTS SHOW, 1109 Garfield St., Lockport IL 60441. (815)838-7316. Acting Chairman: Louise Lamb. Sponsor: Old Canal Days Committee. Estab: 1973. Annual outdoor show held 2 days in June. Average attendance: 40,000. Closing date for entry: 4 weeks before show. Entry fee: $10 per entry. Crafts may be offered for sale; no commission. Demonstrations encouraged. Registration limit: 250 artists/craftsmen. Sponsor provides 3x8' display area.
Acceptable Work: "We accept almost any type of craft, but no kits and other types of crafts that are only commercial exploitations of the crafts interest."

More than 20,000 persons visit the annual Rotary Crafts Festival in Portland, Maine, during the second Saturday in July. The only restriction on entry into the show is that items to be exhibited must be handmade crafts.

SANDBURG MALL ART & CRAFT SHOW, Box 61, Rome IL 61562. (309)274-3001. Contact: Judy Kelley. Estab: 1975. Semiannual indoor show held 3 days in spring and fall. Closing date for entry: 2 weeks before show. Entry fee: $35 per 6x12' display area. Prejudging by 2 slides (send SASE); no entry fees refunded. Crafts may be offered for sale; no commission. Craftsman must attend show.
Acceptable Work: Considers candlemaking, metalsmithing, pottery, wall hangings and woodcrafting. No crochet, knitting, clothing or commercial jewelry.

SPRING ARTS & CRAFTS FAIR, 2130 S. 61st Court, Cicero IL 60650. (312)863-2104 or 8979. Executive Director: Norm Scaman. Sponsor: Cermak Road Business Association. Estab: 1974. Annual outdoor show held 2 days in May. Closing date for entry: mid-May. Entry fee: $10 per craftsman. Crafts may be offered for sale; no commission. Considers all crafts.

VILLA OAKS STARVING ARTIST'S FAIR, Rte. 1, 146 Park Dr., Barrington IL 60010. Show Director: Irene Partridge. Sponsor: Villa Oaks Merchants Association. Estab: 1971. Annual outdoor show held in Villa Park 1 day in August. Closing date for entry: 10 days before show. Entry fee: $15 per craftsman. Prejudging by 5 slides or photos (send resume and SASE); entry fee refunded for refused work. Crafts may be offered for sale; no commission. Craftsman must attend show; demonstrations encouraged. Registration limit: 125-150 artists/craftsmen. Considers all crafts.

VILLAGE MALL ART & CRAFT SHOW, Box 61, Rome IL 61562. (309)274-3001. Contact: Judy Kelley. Estab: 1975. Semiannual indoor show held 3 days in spring and fall. Closing date for entry: 2 weeks before show. Entry fee: $30 per 6x12' display area. Prejudging by 2 slides (send SASE); entry fee refunded for refused work. Crafts may be offered for sale; no commission. Craftsman must attend show. Registration limit: 50 artists/craftsmen. Considers candlemaking, metalsmithing, pottery, tole painting, weavings and woodcrafting.

WATER TOWER ART & CRAFT FESTIVAL, American Society of Artists, 700 N. Michigan, Chicago IL 60611. (312)751-2500. President: Nancy Fregin. Estab: 1972. Annual outdoor show held 3 days in June. Closing date for entry: April. Entry fee: $20 per non-member. Prejudging by 3-5 slides or photos; entry fee refunded for refused work. Crafts may be offered for sale; no commission. Craftsman must attend show. Registration limit: 300 artists/craftsmen.
Acceptable Work: Considers batik, candlemaking, sand-cast, glass art, jewelry, leatherworking, metalsmithing, needlecrafts, pottery, soft sculpture, tole painting, weavings, wall hangings and woodcrafting.

Indiana

CHRISTMAS GIFT & HOBBY SHOW, Box 20189, Indianapolis IN 46220. (317)255-4151. Exhibit Sales Director: Thelma Schoenberger. Estab: 1950. Annual indoor show held 9 days in November. Average attendance: 100,000. "We're always full 2 months before show." Entry fee: $140 per 10x10' booth. Crafts may be offered for sale; no commission. Craftsman must attend show; demonstrations encouraged. Considers all crafts.

DAVIESS MARTIN COUNTY ART FESTIVAL, Box 245, Loogootee IN 47553. (812)295-3421. Park Superintendent: David L. Watson. Sponsor: West Boggs Park. Estab: 1975. Annual show held 2 days in August in 12x12' tents. Average attendance: 6,000. Entries accepted until show date. Entry fee: $10 ($5 refunded on craftsman's arrival). Crafts may be offered for sale; no commission. Craftsman must attend show. "We recommend that craftsmen demonstrate their talents as it helps promote sales." First 30 entries are given a 12x12' tent, table and 2 chairs. Considers all original crafts.

DOWNTOWN FESTIVAL DAYS, Box 91, Connersville IN 47331. (317)825-7140. Contact: Carson McQueen. Sponsor: Connersville Jaycees. Estab: 1976. Annual outdoor show held 2 days in early May. Average attendance: 10,000-15,000. Entries accepted until show date. Entry fee: $8 per 10x15' display area; $15 per vehicle space. Crafts may be offered for sale; no commission. Demonstrations OK. Considers all crafts.

HISTORIC HOOSIER HILLS GUILD ANTIQUE & CRAFT FESTIVAL, 2242 Cragmont, Madison IN 47250. (812)273-1697. Chairman: Helen Gourley. Estab: 1967. Semiannual outdoor show held 4 days in May, 3 days in September. Average attendance: 20,000. Closing date for entry: 2 weeks before show. Entry fee: $5 per day. Crafts may be offered for sale; no commission. Craftsman must attend show. Registration limit: approximately 90 display areas. Considers all original crafts.

LOGANSPORT MALL SHOW, Box 61, Rome IL 61562. (309)274-3001. Contact: Judy Kelley. Estab: 1976. Semiannual indoor show held in Logansport, Indiana, 3 days in April and September. Closing date for entry: 2 weeks before show. Entry fee: $30 per 6x12' display area; no personal checks. Prejudging by 2 slides (send SASE); entry fee refunded for refused work. Crafts may be offered for sale; no commission. Sponsor provides panels.
Acceptable Work: Considers candlemaking, ceramics, jewelry, leatherworking, metalsmithing, pottery, tole painting, weavings, wall hangings and woodcrafting. No crochet, knitting, clothing or commercial jewelry.

TALBOT STREET ART FAIR, 2823 W. 52nd St., Indianapolis IN 46208. (317)264-7711 or 297-1632. Chairman: Joe Lehman. Sponsor: Indiana Artist-Craftsmen, Inc. Estab: 1956. Annual outdoor show held 2 days in June. Average attendance: 30,000-38,000. Closing date for entry: 6 weeks before show. Entry fee: $10 per entry, IAC member; $20 per entry, non-member. Prejudging by slides; entry fee refunded for refused work. Crafts may be offered for sale; no commission. Craftsman must attend show. "We like demonstrations, but can't supply electricity or water." Registration limit: 175-200 artists/craftsmen. Sponsor provides 10x6' display area.
Acceptable Work: Considers batik, candlemaking, ceramics, dollmaking, enameling, glass art, jewelry, leatherworking, metalsmithing, pottery, soft sculpture, stitchery, weavings, wall hangings and woodcrafting.

TIPPECANOE BATTLEFIELD ARTS & CRAFTS FESTIVAL, Box 225, Battle Ground IN 47920. (317)567-2147. Director: D. Clarke Evans. Sponsor: Battle Ground Historical Corp. Estab: 1974. Annual outdoor show held 2 days in August. Average attendance: 4,000. Entries accepted until show date. Entry fee: $15 per 8x14' display area. Crafts may be offered for sale; no commission. Craftsman must attend show. Considers all crafts.

Iowa

NEEDLEWORK FESTIVAL, c/o Mrs. James E. Dunn, 1828 80th St., Des Moines IA 50322. Show held in spring. Considers original canvas work, crewel, surface stitchery, counted and metal threads.

SNAKE ALLEY ART FAIR, Box 5, Burlington IA 52601. Chairman: Jerry Rigdon. Sponsor: Burlington Art Guild. Estab: 1967. Annual outdoor show held 1 day in June. Average attendance: 2,500. Entries accepted until show date or until spaces filled. Entry fee: $10 per entry. Awards several $25 "best display of work" prizes. Prejudging; entry fee refunded for refused work. Crafts may be offered for sale; no commission. Craftsman must attend show; pastel portrait demonstrations OK. Registration limit: 100 artists/craftsmen. Sponsor provides some snow fence.
Acceptable Work: Considers batik, ceramics, glass art, jewelry, leatherworking, metalsmithing, pottery, soft sculpture, weavings and woodcrafting.

Kentucky

SUE BENNETT FOLK FESTIVAL, Sue Bennett College, London KY 40741. (606)864-9714. Chairman: Madge Chesnut. Estab: 1974. Annual indoor show held 3 days in April. Average attendance: 3,500. Closing date for entry: 3 weeks before show. No entry fee. Limited to 1 exhibit area per person. Prejudging. Crafts may be offered for sale; no commission. Craftsman must attend show; demonstrations OK. Registration limit: 50 exhibits. Sponsor provides 1 long table and 2 chairs. Considers all crafts.

KINGDOM COME SWAPPIN' MEETIN', Southeast Community College, Cumberland KY 40823. (606)589-8145. Coordinator: W. Bruce Ayers. Annual indoor/outdoor show held 1 day in October. Average attendance: 3,000. Entries accepted until show date. Entry fee: $5. Crafts may be offered for sale; no commission. Maximum 3 entries per craftsman. Registration limit: 100 craftsmen. Demonstrations encouraged. Considers all crafts.

MOUNTAIN PARKWAY ART EXHIBIT, Rte. 1, Box 182, Stanton KY 40380. (606)663-4708. Contact: Dena Shepard. Sponsor: Powell County Art Club. Estab: 1966. Annual outdoor show held 1 day in October. Average attendance: 1,000-5,000. Craftsman should bring work the morning of show. Entry fee: $2 per display area. Crafts may be offered for sale; no commission. Demonstrations OK. Considers all crafts.

Maine

ARTS & CRAFTS SHOW (formerly Zonta's Annual Art and Craft Show), Rockland ME 04841. Chairman: Enid Monaghan. Sponsor: Zonta Club of Rockland Area. Estab: 1975. Annual outdoor show held 1 day in July. Closing date for entry: 1 week before show. Entry fee: $10 per entry. Crafts may be offered for sale; no commission. Craftsman must attend show; demonstrations encouraged. Considers all crafts.

ROTARY CRAFTS FESTIVAL, 157 High St., Portland ME 04101. (207)773-7157. Chairman: Mark Stimson. Sponsor: Rotary Club of Portland. Estab: 1975. Annual outdoor show held the second Saturday in July. Average attendance: 20,000+. Closing date for entry: mid-May. Entry fee: $20 per 10' display area. Crafts may be offered for sale; no commission. Craftsman must attend show. Sponsor provides 30x96" table and liability insurance. Considers all crafts.

SEACOASTS CRAFTS FAIR, Box 25, York ME 03909. (207)363-2397. Director: Rachel Grieg. Estab: 1967. Annual indoor show held the last week in August. Closing date for entry: early June. Entry fee: $15. Prejudging by photos or transparencies; entry fee refunded for refused work. Crafts may be offered for sale; no commission. Open to New England craftsmen. Registration limit: 75 craftsmen. Craftsman must attend show. Sponsor provides insurance for exhibited work. Considers all crafts.

Maryland

FREDERICK CRAFT FAIR, c/o Noel Clark, National Crafts Ltd., Gapland MD 21736. Wholesale/retail fair held in Frederick in spring for professional craftsmen. Average attendance: approximately 50,000. Offers about 500 craftsmen, printmakers and photographers an opportunity to present work to the public in the Washington-Baltimore area.

MILLION DOLLAR MILE ART SHOW, Box 174, Havre de Grace MD 21078. (301)939-2329 or 4060. Contact: Marge Thompson or Ilse Seville. Annual outdoor show held in August. Closing date for entry: mid-July. Write for entry fee. Crafts may be offered for sale; no commission. Considers all crafts.

NATIONAL CRAFT FAIR, National Crafts Ltd., Gapland MD 21736. (301)432-8438. Director: Noel Clark. Estab: 1977. Annual indoor show held in Gaithersburg 2-3 days in September. Average attendance: 40,000. Closing date for applications: 3-4 months before show. Entry fee: $60-90. Prejudging by 5 color slides; entry fee refunded for refused work. Crafts may be offered for sale; no commission. Craftsman must attend show. Registration limit: 400 artists/craftsmen. Considers printmaking.

WINTER MARKET OF AMERICAN CRAFTS, Box 10, New Paltz NY 12561. (914)255-0039. Contact: Carol Sedestrom. Sponsor: Northeast Craft Fair, Ltd. Annual indoor show held in Baltimore's Civic Center 4 days in February or March. Average attendance: 25,000+. Closing date for entry: 5 months before show. Entry fee: $5 jury fee; $96 or $160 per display area. Prejudging; no entry fees refunded for refused work. Crafts must be offered for sale; no commission. Open to American Crafts Council members living east of the Mississippi River. Craftsman must attend show. Registration limit: 300-350 craftsmen. Considers all crafts.

Massachusetts

ANDOVER CRAFTS-IN-THE-PARK, Stowe School, 36 Bartlet St., Andover MA 01810. (617)475-5045. Director: Gary C. Ralph. Sponsor: Recreation/Community Schools Dept. and American Field Service. Estab: 1976. Annual outdoor show held in June. Average attendance: 2,500-3,000. Entries accepted until show date. Entry fee: $15 per 8x8' display area. Crafts may be offered for sale; no commission. Craftsman must attend show; demonstrations OK. Considers all crafts.

NEW ENGLAND'S CRAFTS EXPO, Box 370, Farmington CT 06032. (202)224-8388. Director: Rudy Kowalczyk. Sponsor: American Crafts Expositions. Estab: 1977. Annual indoor/outdoor show held in the Topsfield fairgrounds 3 days in July. Average attendance: 20,000. Closing date for entry: 4 weeks before show. Entry fee: $50-60 per booth (10x10', indoors; 14x14', outdoors). Prejudging; entry fee refunded for refused work. Crafts may be offered for sale; no commission. Craftsman must attend show; demonstrations OK. Registration limit: 200 artists/craftsmen.
Acceptable Work: Considers batik, candlemaking, ceramics, dollmaking, glass art, jewelry, leatherworking, metalsmithing, needlecrafts, pottery, soft sculpture, weaving, wall hangings and woodcrafting.

Michigan

THE ANN ARBOR STREET ART FAIR, Box 1352, Ann Arbor MI 48106. Estab: 1959. Annual outdoor show with plastic roofing held 4 days in July. Closing date for slides: April 2. Charges registration and jury fees. Prejudging; no entry fees refunded for refused work. Crafts

must be offered for sale; demonstrations by invited participating craftsmen. Registration limit: 250 artists/craftsmen.
Acceptable Work: Considers batik, ceramics, glass art, jewelry, leatherworking, metalsmithing, pottery, soft sculpture, weavings, wall hangings and woodcrafting. Acceptable work subject to change.

ANN ARBOR WINTER ART FAIR, 1725 Weldon, Ann Arbor MI 48103. Director: Audree Levy. Estab: 1974. Annual indoor show held 3 days in November. Average attendance: 30,000-60,000. Closing date for entry: 8 weeks before show. Entry fee: $110 per 10x12' display area; due after jurying. Prejudging by 3 slides or photos conducted in September (send resume and SASE); entry fee refunded for refused work. Crafts may be offered for sale; no commission. Craftsman must attend show; demonstrations OK.
Acceptable Work: Considers original batik, candlemaking, ceramics, dollmaking, glass art, jewelry, leatherworking, metalsmithing, pottery, soft sculpture, weavings, wall hangings and woodcrafting.

CHARLEVOIX WATERFRONT ART FAIR, Box 296, Charlevoix MI 49720. (616)547-4204. Director: Suzi Reis. Sponsor: Chamber of Commerce. Estab: 1958. Annual outdoor show held the second Saturday in August (indoors if inclement weather). Average attendance: 10,000. Closing date for entry: May. Entry fee: $20 per 10x10' display area; $30 per 1 space, 2 craftsmen; $40 per double space. Prejudging by slides; entry fee refunded for refused work. Crafts may be offered for sale; no commission. Craftsman must attend show; demonstrations OK. Registration limit: 175 artists/craftsmen. Sponsor pays insurance on exhibited work.
Acceptable Work: Considers batik, ceramics, glass art, jewelry, pottery, soft sculpture, weavings and wall hangings.

DOWNTOWN BAY CITY SIDEWALK DAYS, 409 Bay City Bank Bldg., Bay City MI 48706. (517)893-3573. Contact: Mrs. Tillie Zimmerman. Estab: 1964. Annual outdoor show held 3 days in July. Average attendance: 150,000-200,000. Entries accepted until 1 week before show. No entry fee. Maximum 1 entry per craftsman. Crafts may be offered for sale; no commission. Craftsman must attend show. Considers all crafts.

FRANKENMUTH BAVARIAN FESTIVAL, 635 S. Main St., Frankenmuth MI 48734. (517)652-6106. Contact: Chamber of Commerce. Sponsor: Frankenmuth Civic Events Council. Estab: 1959. Annual outdoor show held the second week in June. Average attendance: 250,000-300,000. Closing date for entry: March 31. Entry fee: $60 per 12x10' display area. Maximum 1 display area per craftsman. Prejudging by slides or photos; entry fee refunded for refused work. Crafts may be offered for sale; no commission. Open to demonstrating craftsmen. Registration limit: 50 craftsmen. Considers all crafts.
To Break In: "Demonstration is the key to selection. We like prices that are fair for work done. List basic price list on application. Apply before March; you'll be contacted in April."

LUDINGTON ARTS & CRAFTS FAIR, 1499 Betty Ave., C8, Ludington MI 49431. (616)843-3522. Director: Mildred Pirtle. Sponsor: West Shore Art League. Annual outdoor show held 2 days in July. Average attendance: 5,000+. Prejudging; entry fee refunded for refused work. Crafts may be offered for sale; no commission. Craftsman must attend show; demonstrations welcome. Registration limit: 300 artists/craftsmen.
Acceptable Work: Considers batik, dollmaking, glass art, limited jewelry, limited leatherwork, metalsmithing, pottery, soft sculpture, weavings, wall hangings and workcrafting. "If we have seen a work before and know the quality, it needn't be prejudged again."

NORTHMINSTER ART & CRAFT SHOW, 3633 W. Big Beaver, Troy MI 48084. Sponsor: Northminster Presbyterian Church. Estab: 1973. Annual indoor show held 2 days in the fall. Average attendance: 1,200. Closing date for entry: 1 month before show. Entry fee: $3 per display area. Prejudging; no entry fees refunded for refused work. Crafts may be offered for sale; 10% commission if craftsman mans own booth; 20% if craftsman is not present. Demonstrations encouraged. Registration limit: 70 artists/craftsmen. Sponsor provides display equipment.
Acceptable Work: Considers batik, ceramics, glass art, jewelry, leatherworking, metalsmithing, pottery, soft sculpture, weavings, wall hangings, woodcrafting, stained glass and sculpture. Only fine art media.

ROSE FESTIVAL FINE ARTS & SELECTED CRAFTS, 6250 N. Lake Rd., Clarklake MI 49234. (517)529-9144 or 784-4934. Contact: Grace McCourtie or Jean Boyers. Sponsor: Brooklyn Artists. Estab: 1973. Annual outdoor show held 1 day in June. Average attendance: 10,000. Entries accepted until show date. Entry fee: $7 per craftsman before May 15; $10 after May 15. Crafts may be offered for sale; no commission. Prefers craftsman attend show. "We highly encourage demonstrations; they are a great attraction to your display and help in advertising." Registration limit: 100 exhibits. Sponsor provides display equipment and 15' display area in rose garden area.
Acceptable Work: Considers batik, candlemaking, glass art, jewelry, leatherworking, metalsmithing, pottery, weavings, woodcrafting and wall hangings.

ROYAL OAK OUTDOOR ART FAIR, 211 Williams, Royal Oak MI 48068. (313)546-0900. Coordinator: Susan Wedley. Sponsor: Parks and Recreation Dept. Estab: 1971. Annual outdoor show held first Sunday in August. Average attendance: 3,000. Closing date for entry: April. Entry fee: $20 per craftsman. Prejudging; entry fee refunded for refused work. Crafts may be offered for sale; no commission. Craftsman must attend show; demonstrations OK. Registration limit: 78 spaces.
Acceptable Work: Considers batik, ceramics, glass art, jewelry, leatherworking, metalsmithing, pottery, weavings and woodcrafting.

ST. CLAIR ART FAIR, Box 222, St. Clair MI 48079. (313)329-2803. Chairman: Mary Ann Garman. Sponsor: St. Clair Art Association. Estab: 1971. Annual outdoor (covered mall) show held 3 days in late June. Average attendance: 5,000-6,000. Closing date for entry: mid-March. Entry fee: $15 per 8x8' or 8x10' display area. Prejudging. Crafts must be offered for sale; 10% commission. Craftsman must attend show; demonstrations OK. Registration limit: 65 artists/craftsmen. Considers batik, ceramics, glass art, jewelry, some leatherworking, metalsmithing, pottery, soft sculpture, weavings, wall hangings and some woodcrafting.

ST. JOSEPH ART ASSOCIATION'S OUTDOOR ART FAIR, 600 State St., St. Joseph MI 49085. (616)983-0271. Contact: St. Joseph Art Center. Estab: 1962. Annual outdoor show held 1 day in July. Average attendance: 35,000-40,000. Closing date for entry: 8 weeks before show. Entry fee: $25 per 20x20' display area. Prejudging; entry fee refunded for refused work. Crafts may be offered for sale; no commission. Craftsman must attend show; demonstrations OK. Registration limit: 150 artists/craftsmen.
Acceptable Work: Considers batik, ceramics, glass art, jewelry, leatherworking, metalsmithing, pottery, soft sculpture, weavings, wall hangings and woodcrafting. No kits, decoupage or sand sculpture.

TRAVERSE BAY ART FAIR, 718 Duell Rd., Traverse City MI 49684. Contact: Rose Blodgett. Sponsor: Northwestern Michigan Artists & Craftsmen. Annual outdoor show held 1 day in July. Average attendance: 10,000. Applications due May 1. Entry fee: $15 per 15x20' booth; $20 if shared. Prejudging; entry fee refunded for refused work. Crafts may be offered for sale; no commission. Open to craftsmen ages 18+. Craftsman must attend show; "we love demonstrations." Registration limit: 150 artists/craftsmen.
Acceptable Work: Considers batik, candlemaking, ceramics, dollmaking, glass art, jewelry, leatherworking, metalsmithing, needlecrafts, pottery, soft sculpture, weavings, wall hangings and woodcrafting.

Y'S OWL CRAFT MART, 3405 E. Midland Rd., Bay City MI 48706. Contact: Marjorie Anderson. Sponsor: YWCA of Bay County. Annual show held the third weekend in October. Average attendance: 2,500. Entry deadline is August 1. Entry fee: $12-15. Craftsman must attend show. Registration limit: 80 booths. Sponsor provides 8' table and 2 chairs. Considers crafts. Maximum size: 10x4'.

Minnesota

CROSSROADS MALL, 2918 Martel Dr., Dayton OH 45420. (513)254-2900. Director: Clarence Freeland. Annual indoor show held in St. Cloud, Minnesota, 1 week in June-July. Closing date for entry: 1 week before show. Entry fee: $65. Prejudging. Crafts may be offered for sale; no commission. Craftsman must attend show; demonstrations OK. Sponsor provides 10x10' display area. Considers all crafts.

MINNESOTA RENAISSANCE FESTIVAL, Rte. 1, Box 125, Chaska MN 55318. (612)448-5465. Contact: Jeff Siegel. Festival is a re-creation of 16th century Mayfaire and marketplace. Entry fee: $100 per 13 days ($125 late entry). Awards prizes for booth/costume/sign design, hawking and participation. No commission. Eligibility requirements: handcrafted wares only; shop of Renaissance design; Renaissance-style costume; Renaissance feeling through exhibitors' presentations and participations; demonstration if possible. Sponsor provides 15x20' booth.

NORTHBROOK ARTS & CRAFTS SHOW & SALE, Reiter Promotions, Inc., Box 321, Chanhassen MN 55317. (612)445-1998. Show Manager: Arthur Reiter. Sponsor: Northbrook Shopping Center Businessmen's Association. Estab: 1974. Annual outdoor show on covered walks held 3 days in August, rain or shine. Closing date for entry: 1 week before show. Entry fee: $20 per 10x6' display area. Entries must meet entry form requirements; entry fee refunded for refused work. Crafts may be offered for sale; no commission. Craftsman must attend show; demonstrations OK. Considers all original crafts.

SOUTHDALE CRAFT SHOW, 10 Southdale Center, Minneapolis MN 55435. Contact: Lisa Bonneville. Annual show held in March at an enclosed mall. Closing date for entry: mid-February. Entry fee: $40 per 6x8' booth. Crafts may be offered for sale; no commission. Acceptable media include jewelry, pottery and molded figurines (original molds only). "We are the oldest enclosed mall in the U.S. and the largest in Minnesota. All advertising is handled by the promotion department and programs for the show and the name signs for each exhibitor are provided." Write for entry blank.

VICTORIAN CRAFT FESTIVAL, 265 S. Exchange St., St. Paul MN 55102. (612)222-5717. Contact: Edna Reasoner. Sponsor: Minnesota Historical Society. Estab: 1971. Annual outdoor show held in July. Average attendance: 1,000-2,000. Entries accepted until show date. No entry fee. Crafts may be offered for sale; no commission. Craftsman must attend show; craft demonstrations only. Considers all Victorian period crafts.

Mississippi

GREAT RIVER ROADS CRAFT FAIR, Box Elder Lane, Natchez MS 39120. Contact: Sarah G. Tillman. Estab: 1974. Average attendance: 10,000. Entry fee: $50. Prejudging by slides or b&w photos. No commission. Categories include needlecrafts, rugs, tapestries, brooms, baskets and glass blowing.

Montana

CARBON COUNTY ARTS GUILD ANNUAL CHRISTMAS SALE & SHOW, Box 585, Red Lodge MT 59068. (406)446-1370. Director: Carol Orr. Estab: 1974. Annual indoor show held from the day after Thanksgiving to the first Sunday in December. Average attendance: 1,000 Christmas shoppers. Write for applications in October. Closing date for entry: 1 week before show. No entry fee. Maximum 10 entries per craftsman. Crafts must be offered for sale; 15% commission. Area craftsmen only. No demonstrations. "Art displays are set up in vacant store fronts. The front is decorated and the display is hung by a committee." Sponsor pays insurance for exhibited work. Considers all original crafts.
Promotion: "Work offered for sale is photographed for publicity purposes at least 2 weeks prior to the sale. TV publicity is also done at that time. Work that arrives early is used for publicity unless it cannot be easily transported to the TV station."
Shipping Tips: "If an artist is shipping artwork, he should be sure that the box or crate is reuseable so the unsold work can be easily returned in that packaging."

Nebraska

ART FAIR, Box 62, Scottsbluff NE 69361. (308)632-2226. Executive Director: Robert S. Hill. Sponsor: West Nebraska Arts Center. Estab: 1967. Annual outdoor show held 3 days in August. Closing date for entry: 4 weeks before show. Entry fee: $10 per table; $15 per table in tent. Prejudging by slides; no entry fees refunded for refused work. Crafts may be offered for sale; no commission. Craftsman or representative must attend show; demonstrations encouraged. Sponsor provides insurance during exhibit period. Considers all crafts.

ARTS FESTIVAL ON THE MALL, Studio 1, Aquila Court, 1615 Howard, Omaha NE 68102. (402)345-5401. Director: Vic Gutman. Sponsor: Pratt School Events Fund. Estab: 1975. Annual outdoor show held 3 days in June. Average attendance: 70,000. Closing date for entry: 2 weeks before show. Entry fee: $25 per 10x10' display area. Maximum 1 entry per craftsman. Crafts may be offered for sale; no commission. Demonstrations encouraged. Registration limit:

200 artists/craftsmen. Display equipment may be rented. "Displays must be sturdy enough to hold up in case of stiff winds." Considers all crafts. "Register early for crafts, especially pottery as there is a limit to the number of various artisans in any one media that will be accepted."

Nevada

CREATIVE ARTISTS GROUP, 3608 Cinnabar Ave., Carson City NV 89701. (702)883-0968. Director: Bea Griffin. Estab: 1976. Annual outdoor show held 4 days in June. Entries accepted until show date. Entry fee: $15 per entry. Crafts may be offered for sale; 10% commission. Craftsman must attend show; demonstrations OK. Considers all crafts. Maximum 4 entries of a kind in jewelry.

GOLD HILL ART FESTIVAL, Box 510, Virginia City NV 89440. (702)847-0737. Director: Diane Gordon. Sponsor: Gold Hill Pottery and Art Gallery. Estab: 1974. Annual outdoor show held 3 days during Memorial Day weekend. Closing date for entry: March 31. Entry fee: $15 per display area. "We provide whatever amount of space an artist/craftsman requires (a very large space would necessitate an additional fee)." Prejudging; entry fee refunded for refused work. Crafts may be offered for sale; no commission. Craftsman must attend show. "Demonstrations strongly encouraged — it is an education for the public." Registration limit: 40 artists/craftsmen.
Acceptable Work: Considers batik, candlemaking, ceramics, decoupage, dollmaking, glass art, jewelry, leatherworking, macrame, metalsmithing, pottery, soft sculpture, weavings, wall hangings and woodcrafting.

New Hampshire

BUYERS' MARKET PLACE, 205 N. Main St., Concord NH 03301. (603)224-3375. Merchandiser: Peter M. Solomon. Sponsor: League of New Hampshire Craftsmen. Estab: 1977. Annual indoor wholesale show held 3 days in March. "Applications will be available in early August and accepted until late October." Entry fee: $80-100 per 8x8' or 10x10' display area. Prejudging by 5 slides; no entry fees refunded. Work must be offered for sale; no commission. Open to residents of New Hampshire, Maine, Massachusetts and Vermont. Craftsman must attend show. Registration limit: 125 artists/craftsmen.
Acceptable Work: Considers batik, candlemaking, ceramics, dollmaking, glass art, jewelry, leatherworking, metalsmithing, needlecrafts, pottery, prints, sculpture, weavings, wall hangings and woodcrafting.
To Break In: "We prefer to see craftsmen who are committed to production and are willing and able to do business on a wholesale level. They should be familiar with wholesale pricing, shipping, production and capacity. One-of-a-kind and gallery-type items also accepted. Those involved in this type of work should be familiar with wholesaling their work."

THEATRE BY THE SEA STREET FAIR, 91 Market St., Portsmouth NH 03801. (603)431-5846. Publicist: Sandi Bianco. Sponsor: Theatre by the Sea Board of Trustees. Estab: 1966. Annual outdoor show held 1 day in the summer. Average attendance: 6,000. Closing date for entry: 3 weeks before show. Entry fee: $15 per 10' long display area (limit 1 space per artist). Crafts may be offered for sale; no commission. Craftsman or representative must attend show. Considers all crafts.
Profile: "The Theatre by the Sea Street Fair is a fund-raising event which features the work of artists and craftspeople. The entire length of Ceres Street, along the Portsmouth waterfront, is closed for the day and the Theatre provides games, food, children's booth, films, activities tables and turn-of-the-century atmosphere."
Promotion: "It is helpful for our promotional purposes to receive clippings, resumes and other information on the participating artists for use in our releases. Photos, although not always printed, are indeed welcome. Descriptive pieces on the process used is also of considerable interest for feature items."

New Jersey

ANNUAL CRAFTS FAIR & SALE, 409 Westley Ave., Ocean City NJ 08226. (609)399-7628. Director: Frances Taylor. Sponsors: Ocean City Cultural Arts Center and Ocean City. Estab: 1972. Annual indoor show held 2 days in September. Average attendance: 20,000. Slides (with SASE) due for prejudging 3 weeks before show. Entry fee: $15 per 12' table space; due after jurying. Crafts may be offered for sale. Craftsman must attend show.
Acceptable Work: Considers batik, dollmaking, leatherworking, metalsmithing, pottery, soft sculpture, weavings and woodcrafting. Jewelry accepted only if totally hand-made.

INVITATIONAL CRAFTS FAIR ON THE MUSIC PIER, 409 Wesley Ave., Ocean City NJ 08226. Contact: Chairman, Craft Show & Sale. Sponsor: Cultural Arts Center. Annual show held 2 days in September. Average attendance: 18,000. Closing date for entry: August 15. Entry fee: $15. Submit slides or photos to jury to receive invitation. No sales commission. Craftsman must attend show.

New Mexico

ARTS & CRAFTS FAIR OF THE SOUTHWEST, Box 122, Roswell NM 88201. Contact: Exhibitors' Chairman. Sponsor: Roswell Jaycees. Estab: 1973. Annual indoor show held 2 days in May. Average attendance: 3,500. Closing date for entry: March 1. Entry fee: $35 per booth with 8x8' pegboard; $15 per additional craftsman. Prejudging; entry fee refunded for refused work. Crafts may be offered for sale; no commission. Open to craftsmen ages 18+. Craftsman must attend show; demonstrations encouraged. Registration limit: 100 booths.
Acceptable Work: Considers batik, candlemaking, ceramics, dollmaking, glass art, jewelry, leatherworking, metalsmithing, needlecrafts, pottery, soft sculpture, tole painting, weavings, wall hangings, woodcrafting and mosaics. Only safety catches on jewelry are accepted as manufactured.

New York

BRUSH & PALETTE CLUB'S ANNUAL LABOR DAY WEEKEND ARTS & CRAFTS SHOW, 85 Chestnut St., Cooperstown NY 13326. (607)547-5134. Show Director: Bettye Yanchisin. Estab: 1965. Annual outdoor show held 3 days during Labor Day weekend. Closing date for entry: 4 weeks before show. Entry fee: $15 per 10x5' display area. Prejudging. Crafts may be offered for sale; no commission. Craftsman must attend show; demonstrations OK. Considers all crafts. Applications sent out after May 1.

CHAUTAUQUA MALL, 2918 Martel Dr., Dayton OH 45420. (513)254-2900. Director: Clarence Freeland. Annual indoor show held in Jamestown, New York, 1 week in August. Closing date for entry: 1 week before show. Entry fee: $50. Prejudging. Crafts may be offered for sale; no commission. Craftsman must attend show; demonstrations OK. Sponsor provides 10x10' display area. Considers all crafts.

CRAFT DAYS, 435 Main St., Oneida NY 13421. (315)363-4136. Director: David L. Parke, Jr. Sponsor: Madison County Historical Society. Estab: 1965. Annual outdoor show held the second weekend in September. Average attendance: 8,000. Closing date for entry: July 15. No entry fee. Crafts may be offered for sale; no commission. Craftsman must attend show. Considers traditional nature crafts.

THE FLUSHING ART LEAGUE OUTDOOR EXHIBITION, Box 325, Flushing NY 11358. (212)358-0388. Contact: Anna Draus. Estab: 1957. Semiannual outdoor show held 4 days in May and September. Entries accepted until show date. Entry fee: $15 per display area. Crafts may be offered for sale; no commission. Craftsman must attend show.
Acceptable Work: Considers candlemaking, ceramics, decoupage, dollmaking, glass art, jewelry, leatherworking, metalsmithing, pottery, soft sculpture, tole painting and woodworking. Maximum size: 9½x6'.

NORTHEAST CRAFT FAIR, Box 10, New Paltz NY 12561. (914)255-0039. Contact: Carol Sedestrom. Sponsor: Northeast Craft Fair, Ltd. Estab: 1965. Annual indoor/outdoor show held in Rhinebeck 1 week in June. Average attendance: 50,000-75,000. Closing date for entry: 6 months before show. Entry fee: $5 jury fee; $90 per indoor display area; $75 per tent; $60 per outdoor area. Prejudging by 5 slides; no entry fees refunded for refused work. Crafts must be offered for sale; no commission. Open to American Crafts Council members living in northeastern states. Craftsman must attend show. Registration limit: 500 craftsmen. Considers all crafts.

ROBERSON HOLIDAY & ARTS FESTIVAL, 30 Front St., Binghamton NY 13905. (607)772-0660. Coordinator: Ms. Terry Kuehnemund. Sponsor: Roberson Center for the Arts and Sciences. Estab: 1955. Annual outdoor show held 2 days in September. Average attendance: 40,000. Closing date for entry: 4 weeks before show. Entry fee: $15 per 8x6' display area. Maximum 2 display areas per craftsman. Crafts may be offered for sale; 10% commission. Craftsman or agent must attend show; demonstrations encouraged. Registration limit: 300 artists/craftsmen. Sponsor provides snow fence or table; electricity available. No advance deliveries accepted.

Close-Up Slides Best Show Your Work

The most common dilemma faced by artists/craftsmen entering a prejudged art or craft show is how to present their artwork in slide form.

Don Getz, exhibit director of the Boston Mills Invitational Art Festival and Artisan Fair (Ohio), a competing artist for more than 20 years, and a show sponsor for five, says "One of the biggest problems with slides occurs when the artist or craftsman gets too far away from his subject. For example, when you have a slide of a ring that is taken from a distance, you can't see the detail. This is of particular concern when we project a slide on the screen for judging, because the detail in jewelry is very important. On the other hand, art shouldn't be shot so close that you're cropping the edges of your picture."

He adds that background should make your artwork stand out. For example, he suggests showing silver against a flat black background.

The best color reproduction on slides is obtained by using natural light, rather than a flash. "Flash has a tendency to burn out vital detail as well as color value," says Getz.

"Naturally, another problem with slides is that they are often poor technically. I recommend that if you don't have a good 35mm camera, ask a friend to take slides for you, or even pay someone. In many cases, the photographer may be willing to trade his services for some of your work."

Photo by John J. Kucharchuk

"Never use pocket cameras to take slides of your work, as the actual viewing area on these slides is too small to show the work when it's projected," says Don Getz, exhibit director of two Ohio Shows.

Acceptable Work: Considers batik, candlemaking, ceramics, dollmaking, glass art, jewelry, leatherworking, metalsmithing, needlecrafts (needlepoint and crewel), pottery, soft sculpture, weavings, wall hangings, woodcrafting, scrimshaw, macrame, basketry, spinning and dyeing, patchwork and quilting.

SARATOGA CRAFT FAIR, 34 Circular St., Saratoga Springs NY 12866. (518)587-7507. Director: Joseph Levy. Sponsor: Saratoga Arts Workshop. Estab: 1974. Annual outdoor show held 2 days in July (cover provided in case of rain). Average attendance: 10,000 per day. Closing date for entry: May 30. Entry fee: $30 per 8x10' display area plus $2 per entry. Prejudging by 5 prints or slides of work; no entry fees refunded for refused work. "The Craft Fair Committee (jury) is composed of members of the Board of Directors of the Saratoga Workshop, each a professional artist or craftsman. Quality and imagination of work samples submitted are the prime criteria." Crafts may be offered for sale; no commission. Craftsman must attend show; demonstrations encouraged (electricity provided). Sponsors pays insurance on exhibited work.

Acceptable Work: Considers batik, candlemaking, ceramics, decoupage, dollmaking, glass art, jewelry, leatherworking, metalsmithing, needlecrafts, pottery, tole painting, weavings, wall hangings, woodcrafting, furniture-making, bookbinding, toolmaking and other useful handcrafted items.

To Break In: "Given a selection of crafts of equal quality to choose from, success at the fair is often a function of how imaginative and attractive the booth or display itself is."

SENIOR CITIZENS ARTS & CRAFTS SHOW & SALE, 168 S. Clinton Ave., Rochester NY 14604. (716)454-3224. Contact: Gloria Harrington. Sponsors: Genesee Conference of Senior Citizen Directors, Inc. and Retired Senior Volunteer Program. Estab: 1974. Annual indoor show held 3 days in April. Average attendance: 3,000. Closing date for entry: 2 weeks before show. No entry fee. Prejudging. Crafts may be offered for sale; 10% commission. Open to craftsmen ages 60+. Demonstrations by invitation. Considers all crafts.

North Carolina

BODYCRAFT GALLERIES SHOWS, 409 W. End Blvd., Winston-Salem NC 27101. (919)722-4396. Contact: Doug or Bonnie Barger. Estab: 1976. Indoor show held every 4-6 weeks. Average attendance: 1,000. Closing date for entry: 1 week before show. No entry fee. Maximum 5 entries per craftsman. Prejudging. Crafts may be offered for sale; 33 1/3% commission. Sponsor provides display equipment, insurance for exhibited work and pays return shipping.

Acceptable Work: Considers all wearable crafts. "Care instructions must be included on a detachable card. It really helps if the item can be cleaned, even if it's difficult. We have no objection to craftsmen using Vogue, McCall, etc. for basic garment patterns provided the item is unique in its treatment. Garments made from hand-woven cloth, for instance, are not disqualified by use of a professional pattern.

BROOKSTOWN ARTS & CRAFTS FESTIVAL, Box 10507, Winston-Salem NC 27108. (919)723-4800. President: Elizabeth Place. Sponsor: North Carolina League of Creative Arts & Crafts Inc. Estab: 1976. Annual indoor/outdoor show held 2 days in July. Entries accepted until show. Entry fee: $30 for first person in booth; $10 for second person. Maximum 2 craftsmen per 8x10' display area. Crafts may be offered for sale; no commission. Craftsman must attend show. Registration limit: 60-100 artists/craftsmen.

Acceptable Work: Considers original crafts; must be ready for hanging.

CRAFTSMAN'S FAIR OF THE SOUTHERN HIGHLANDS, Box 9145, Asheville NC 28805. (704)298-7928. Coordinator: Alex Miller. Sponsor: Southern Highlands Handicraft Guild. Estab: 1948. Semiannual indoor show held 5 days in July and October. Average attendance: 25,000. Open to Guild members. No entry fee. Prejudging. Crafts may be offered for sale; no commission. Craftsman must attend show. Sponsor provides display panels and equipment. Considers all crafts.

PIEDMONT CRAFTS FAIR, 936 W. 4th St., Winston-Salem NC 27101. Contact: Lida M. Lowrey. Annual indoor craft fair established in 1963 with average attendance of 15,000. Open to members of Piedmont Craftsmen, Inc., a nonprofit educational organization. Craftsmen from Alabama, Georgia, South and North Carolina, Maryland or Virginia eligible for membership. Membership jury date: April 1.

SOUTHEASTERN FINE ARTS FESTIVAL, 778 Faircloth Dr., Winston-Salem NC 27106. (919)768-4021. Director: Mary Goslen. Sponsor: Southeastern Art Shows. Estab: 1975. Annual indoor show held 3 days in March. Average attendance: 12,000. Closing date for entry: 3-6 months before show. Entry fee: $50-125 per 10x10' display area. Maximum 3 areas per craftsman. Prejudging; entry fee refunded for refused work. Crafts may be offered for sale; no commission. Craftsman must attend show; demonstrations OK. Registration limit: 90 artists/craftsmen. Considers batik, painting, printmaking and sculpture. No kits, copies of old masters or widely circulated photos. Work must be framed, matted or provided with base. Send resume and slides or photos for publicity.

VILLAGE ART & CRAFT FAIR, New Morning Gallery, 3½ Kitchen Place, Asheville NC 28803. (704)274-2831. Contact: John Cram. Sponsor: New Morning Gallery. Estab: 1972. Annual outdoor show held the first weekend in August. Average attendance: 10,000. Closing date for entries: 4 weeks before show. Entry fee: $50 per 8x10' display area. Prejudging by color slides (include SASE) or actual work; entry fees refunded for refused work. Crafts may be offered for sale; no commission. Craftsman must attend show; demonstrations OK. Registration limit: 150 artists/craftsmen. Considers all crafts except decoupage. Accepts work of only nal design and execution. Positively no commercial molds.

North Dakota

LINHA GALLERY ARTFEST, Box 325, Linha Art Gallery, Minot ND 58701. (701)838-4445. Director: Galen Willert. Sponsor: Friends of the Linha Art Gallery. Estab: 1976. Annual indoor show held 3 days in March. Closing date for entry: 1 week before show. Entry fee: $20 per 12x12' display area. Crafts may be offered for sale; no commission. Craftsman must attend show; demonstrations OK. Considers all crafts.

MINOT ART ASSOCIATION ART FAIR, Box 325, Linha Art Gallery, Minot ND 58701. (701)838-4445. Director: Galen R. Willert. Sponsor: Minot Art Association. Estab: 1975. Annual outdoor show held 1 day in the fall. Closing date for entry: 1 week before show. Entry fee: $10 per 6x12' display area. Crafts may be offered for sale; no commission. Craftsman must attend show; demonstrations OK. Considers all original crafts.

Ohio

ART IN THE PARK, 142 Riverbend Dr., Dayton OH 45405. (513)225-5433. Director: Pat Shoop. Sponsor: City of Dayton Division of Recreation and Riverbend Arts Council. Estab: 1967. Annual outdoor show held 2 days during Memorial Day weekend. Average attendance: 25,000-30,000. Closing date for entry: 2 weeks before show. Entry fee: $15 per craftsman. "If an application appears questionable, artist is asked to bring work to center to be previewed." Entry fee refunded for refused work. Crafts must be offered for sale; no commission. "Out-of-state artists do exhibit in our show, but we prefer to promote area artists and we call some artists from the previous year who had interesting exhibits." Craftsman must attend show. "Demonstrating is stressed as it makes for a more interesting show. We usually have 1-2 caricaturists working." Registration limit: 150 artists/craftsmen.
Acceptable Work: Considers batik, leatherworking, metalsmithing, pottery, weavings, wall hangings, woodcrafting, handmade jewelry and sculpture using casting or construction methods, enameling, lapidary, macrame, stained glass, and handmade instruments such as dulcimers. "We strive for a fine arts or fine arts type craft show. One-of-a-kind items."

CEDAR POINT'S CRAFTS SHOW, Cedar Point, Merchandise Dept., Sandusky OH 44870. (419)626-0830. Crafts Manager: Jeff Savage. Estab: 1974. Annual outdoor show held 5 days in July-August. Closing date for entry: 2 weeks before show. No entry fee. Prejudging by slides. Crafts must be offered for sale; 20-30% commission. Craftsman must attend show; demonstrations required. Registration limit: 60-70 artists/craftsmen. Sponsor provides booth and work area. Hand-deliver work.
Acceptable Work: Considers candlemaking, ceramics, decoupage, dollmaking, jewelry, leatherworking, metalsmithing, needlecrafts, pottery, weavings, wall hangings and woodcrafting. Maximum size: 12x12x12', 50 lbs.

COLUMBUS SPRING ART FAIR, 1725 Weldon, Ann Arbor MI 48103. Show Director: Audree Levy. Estab: 1977. Annual indoor show held in Columbus, Ohio, 3 days in May. Closing date for entry: 8 weeks before show. Entry fee: $120 per 12x15' display area. Prejudging by 3 slides (send resume and SASE). Crafts may be offered for sale; no commission. Craftsman must attend show; demonstrations OK.
Acceptable Work: Considers original batik, candlemaking, ceramics, dollmaking, glass art, jewelry, leatherworking, metalsmithing, pottery, soft sculpture, weavings, wall hangings and woodcrafting.

GREAT LAKES MALL, 2918 Martel Dr., Dayton OH 45420. (513)254-2900. Director: Clarence Freeland. Annual indoor show held in Mentor (near Cleveland) 1 week in October-November. Closing date for entry: 1 week before show. Entry fee: $90. Prejudging. Crafts may be offered for sale; no commission. Craftsman must attend show; demonstrations OK. Sponsor provides 10x10' display area. Considers all crafts.

INDIAN SUMMER ARTS & CRAFTS FESTIVAL, c/o Marietta College, Marietta OH 45750. Director: Arthur Winer. Sponsor: Marietta Art League. Estab: 1955. Annual outdoor (tents and booths available) show held 3 days in the fall. Average attendance: 12,000. Entry fee: $25 per entry. Slides due for prejudging in early July (entries accepted after July in event of cancellations); entry fee refunded for refused work. Crafts may be offered for sale; no commission. Open to craftsmen ages 18+. Craftsman must attend show; demonstrations encouraged. Registration limit: 100 artists/craftsmen. Sponsor provides booths and pegboard. Considers all crafts. Maximum 3 media per booth.

RICHMOND MALL, 2918 Martel Dr., Dayton OH 45420. (513)254-2900. Director: Clarence Freeland. Annual indoor show held in Cleveland 1 week in October. Closing date for entry: 1 week before show. Entry fee: $75. Prejudging. Crafts may be offered for sale; no commission. Craftsman must attend show; demonstrations OK. Sponsor provides 10x10' display area. Considers all crafts.

SOUTHERN PARK MALL, 2918 Martel Dr., Dayton OH 45420. (513)254-2900. Director: Clarence Freeland. Indoor show held in Youngstown 1 week in September. Closing date for entry: 1 week before show. Entry fee: $65. Prejudging. Crafts may be offered for sale; no commission. Craftsman must attend show; demonstrations OK. Sponsor provides 10x10' display area. Considers all crafts.

SUMMIT MALL, 2918 Martel Dr., Dayton OH 45420. (513)254-2900. Director: Clarence Freeland. Annual indoor show held in Akron 1 week in October. Closing date for entry: 1 week before show. Entry fee: $60. Prejudging. Crafts may be offered for sale; no commission. Craftsman must attend show; demonstrations OK. Sponsor provides 10x10' display area. Considers all crafts.

WOODVILLE MALL, 2918 Martel Dr., Dayton OH 45420. (513)254-2900. Director: Clarence Freeland. Annual indoor show held in Toledo 1 week in October. Closing date for entry: 1 week before show. Entry fee: $50. Prejudging. Crafts may be offered for sale; no commission. Craftsman must attend show; demonstrations OK. Sponsor provides 10x10' display area. Considers all crafts.

YANKEE PEDDLER FESTIVAL, 2174 Lewis Dr., Lakewood OH 44107. (216)221-1808. Vice President: Betty Cajka. Estab: 1973. Outdoor show held 2 weekends in September. Average attendance: 38,000. Closing date for entry: 4 weeks before show. Entry fee: approximately $40 per entry. Prejudging by photos; entry fee refunded for refused work. Crafts may be offered for sale; no commission. Craftsman must attend show; must demonstrate 50% of the time. Registration limit: 130 entries. Considers all 1776-1825 crafts.

Oklahoma

OKLAHOMA CITY FESTIVAL OF THE ARTS, 3014 Paseo, Oklahoma City OK 73103. (405)521-1426. Staff Festival Coordinator: Jackie Jones. Sponsor: Arts Council of Oklahoma City, Inc. Estab: 1967. Annual 2-day April show. "Entries accepted on a first-come basis until full." Entry fee: $60 per craftsman. Crafts must be offered for sale; no commission. Craftsman must attend show; demonstrations encouraged. "The only requirement we have on demonstrations is that the safety of the audience is considered. For instance, provide a protective shield if you're working with metal sculpture." Sponsor provides 184 visual arts panels and 24 tents; approximately 80 spaces at street market.
Acceptable Work: Considers batik, candlemaking, ceramics, dollmaking, glass art, jewelry, leatherworking, metalsmithing, needlecrafts, pottery, soft sculpture, weavings, wall hangings and woodcrafting. "Since this is a family, community arts council, work should be acceptable in that environment."

Oregon

ALBANY SPRING ARTS FESTIVAL, Box 841, Albany OR 97321. (503)928-2815. Director: Terri Hopkins. Sponsor: Creative Arts Guild. Estab: 1969. Annual indoor/outdoor show held 2 days in early May. Average attendance: 20,000. Entries accepted until show date. Entry fee: $7 per weekend. Crafts may be offered for sale; no commission. Open to all craftsmen, but mid-Wilamette Valley craftsmen given preference. Demonstrations OK. Sponsor provides 8x8' booth. Considers all crafts.

NEWPORT SUMMER FESTIVAL OF ARTS & CRAFTS, 5724 Aetna St. SE, Salem OR 97301. (503)585-1263. Manager: Vaughn L. Hayden. Sponsor: Capital Promotions. Estab: 1976. Annual indoor show held at Newport 2 days in July. Attendance: 3,000. Entries accepted until show date. Entry fee: $25 per 8x8' display area. Crafts may be offered for sale; no commission. Demonstrations encouraged. Registration limit: 50 artists/craftsmen. Sponsor provides tables, chairs and liability insurance.
Acceptable Work: Considers all handcrafted items and supplies for artists. "Items not handcrafted will be excluded from the show and no refunds will be made on fees after 10 days prior to show."
Promotion: "News releases about artisans are welcomed and used. We advertise extensively. Applicants with the better items will be given special consideration."

SALEM ARTS & CRAFTS SHOW, 5724 Aetna St. SE, Salem OR 97301. (503)585-1263. Manager: Vaughn L. Hayden. Sponsor: Capital Promotions. Estab: 1975. Annual show held at Salem Armory Auditorium 3 days in November. Entries accepted until show date. Entry fee: $27.50-32.50 per 9x9' display area. Crafts may be offered for sale; no commission. Demonstrations encouraged. Registration limit: 106 artists/craftsmen. Sponsor provides tables, chairs and liability insurance.
Acceptable Work: Considers all handcrafted items and supplies for artists. "Items not handcrafted will be excluded from the show and no refunds will be made on fees after 10 days prior to show."
Promotion: "News releases about artisans are welcomed and used. We advertise extensively. Applicants with the better items will be given special consideration."

SATURDAY MARKET, Box 427, Eugene OR 97401. (503)686-8885. Contact: Manager. Estab: 1971. Outdoor market held every Saturday during April-December. Average attendance: 1,000. Entries accepted until show date. Entry fee: $3 per craftsman the first time; $3-9 thereafter. Crafts may be offered for sale; no commission. Craftsman must attend market; demonstrations OK. Registration limit: 227 artists/craftsmen.
Acceptable Work: Considers all crafts. "Nothing is to be sold unless it's made by the salesperson or immediate family member. Also, nothing can be brought in from other stores and resold."

Pennsylvania

APPLE HARVEST FESTIVAL, Box 38, Biglerville PA 17307. (717)624-7623 or 677-6720. Contact: Nina Dillman. Sponsor: Upper Adams Jaycees. Estab: 1964. Indoor/outdoor show held 2 weekends in October. Average attendance: 12,000 per day. Closing date for entry: 3 weeks before show. Entry fee: $25 per 10x10' display area per weekend. Crafts may be offered for sale; no commission. Craftsman must attend show; demonstrations encouraged. Registration limit: 100 artists/craftsmen. Sponsor provides liability insurance during exhibit period. Considers all crafts including old-time crafts such as broom-making, soap-making, spinning, etc.

CENTRAL PENNSYLVANIA FESTIVAL OF THE ARTS, Box 1023, State College PA 16801. Managing Director: Marilyn Keat. Estab: 1966. Annual outdoor show held 4 days in July. Average attendance: 150,000. Closing date for entry: 10 weeks before show. Entry fee: $40 per 10x4' booth. Prejudging; $3 jurying fee. Crafts may be offered for sale; no commission. Craftsman must attend show; demonstrations OK. Registration limit: 450 artists/craftsmen. Sponsor provides snow fencing. Considers all crafts.

MILLCREEK MALL, 2918 Martel Dr., Dayton OH 45420. (513)254-2900. Director: Clarence Freeland. Annual indoor show held in Erie 1 week in August-September. Closing date for entry: 1 week before show. Entry fee: $75. Prejudging. Crafts may be offered for sale; no commission. Craftsman must attend show; demonstrations OK. Sponsor provides 10x10' display area. Considers all crafts.

SUPERMUD — CERAMIC CONFERENCE & EXHIBITION, Dept. of Art, 102 Visual Arts Bldg., University Park PA 16802. (814)865-0444. Contact: David Don Tigny, Jim Stephenson or Ron Gallas. Annual indoor show held 2 weeks in October-November. Estab: 1966. Average attendance: 5,000. Closing date for entry: 1 week before show. No entry fee. Maximum 3 entries per craftsman. Crafts may be offered for sale; 15% commission. Sponsor furnishes display equipment and pays insurance on exhibited work and shipping to craftsman. Considers ceramics, glass art and pottery.
Packing Tips: "Items must be packed to withstand truck freight. We suggest good packing in fiber drums; no cardboard boxes."

Rhode Island

PAWTUXET VILLAGE ARTS & CRAFTS FESTIVAL, 40 Elmbrook Dr., Warwick RI 02889. (401)738-9554. Committee Chairman: Bob Quinlan. Sponsor: Gaspee Day Committee. Estab: 1966. Annual outdoor show held 2 days the first weekend in June. Average attendance: 25,000-40,000. Entries accepted until show date. Entry fee: $15 per 15' sidewalk display. Craftsman limited to 1 type of art or craft. Prejudging; entry fee refunded for refused work. Crafts may be offered for sale; no commission. Craftsman must attend show. "We encourage on-the-spot demonstrations, as they heighten the interest of the crowd and increase profits of artists/craftsmen." Registration limit: 300 artists/craftsmen (preference given to fine arts and previous participants). Considers all handmade crafts.

WESTERLY ART FESTIVAL, 159 Main St., Westerly RI 02891. (401)596-7761. Contact: Diane Howard. Sponsor: Greater Westerly-Pawcatuck Area Chamber of Commerce. Estab: 1967. Annual outdoor show held 2 days in July. Average attendance: 3,000+. Closing date for entry: 2 weeks before show. Entry fee: $20 per entry. Prejudging; entry fee refunded for refused work. Crafts may be offered for sale; no commission. Craftsman or representative must attend show; demonstrations OK. Registration limit: 50 artists/craftsmen. "We do not accept shipping."
Acceptable Work: Consider batik, ceramics, dollmaking, glass art, handmade jewelry, leatherworking, metalsmithing, pottery, soft sculpture, tole painting, weavings, wall hangings and woodcrafting.

South Carolina

HILL SKILLS 307, INC., 627 Pelham Rd., Greenville SC 29607. Director: Mrs. C. C. McKaughan. Estab: 1969. Annual indoor show held 5 days in October. Average attendance: 15,000+. Closing date for entry: mid-February. Entry fee: $60 per craftsman. Crafts may be offered for sale; no commission. Craftsman must attend show. Registration limit: 150 craftsmen. Sponsor provides curtains, signage, electrical outlets, shopping bags and pre-advertising posters. Considers all crafts.

Tennessee

BENTON COUNTY ARTS & CRAFT SHOW, Box 428, Camden TN 38320. (901)584-4601. Extension Agent: Wileva Mullins. Sponsor: Benton County Home Demonstration Clubs. Estab: 1970. Annual indoor show held 3 days in November. Closing date for entry: 2 weeks before show. Entry fee: $5 per 8x8' display area. Crafts may be offered for sale; 1% commission. Craftsman must attend show; demonstrations OK. Considers all handmade crafts.

COTTON PICKIN' COUNTRY MUSIC CRAFTS JUBILEE, 722 S. Highland St., Memphis TN 38111. (901)458-8753. Promoter: Richard West. Sponsors: Memphis Chamber of Commerce, Memphis in May Society and Knudson Leather & Silver Shop. Estab: 1976. Annual indoor/outdoor show held 3 days during Memorial Day weekend. Entries accepted until show date. Entry fee: $50 per outdoor space; $70 per tent space. Maximum 8 entries per craftsman. Crafts may be offered for sale; no commission. Demonstrations OK. Registration limit: 200 artists/craftsmen. Considers all crafts. No items from molds or kits. Send brief resume and 2-3 captioned b&w glossies for publicity.

GERMANTOWN FESTIVAL'S RENAISSANCE FAIR, 722 S. Highland St., Memphis TN 38111. Promoter: Richard West. Estab: 1971. Annual outdoor show held 2 days the second weekend in September. Average attendance: 80,000. Entries accepted until show date. Entry fee: $50 per outdoor space; $70 per tent space. Crafts may be offered for sale; no commission. Considers all crafts.

GRINDERS SWITCH ARTS & CRAFTS FAIR, 107 Huddleston St., Centerville TN 37033. (615)729-3054. Chairman: Martha Chessor. Sponsor: Hickman County Art Guild. Estab: 1974. Annual outdoor show held 2 days in June. Average attendance: 8,000. Entries accepted until show date. Entry fee: $10 per 12x30' display area. Crafts must be offered for sale; no commission. Craftsman must attend show; demonstrations encouraged. Considers all crafts.
Profile: "Displays are set up in wooded camping sites and vehicles may be kept at exhibitor's site without distraction. Overnight camping, a bath house and showers are available at $3 per night."

LIONS CLUB SPRING ARTS & CRAFT SHOW, Box 141, Murfreesboro TN 37130. (615)893-1646. Co-Chairman: W. H. Duncan. Semiannual indoor/outdoor show held 2 days in April and November. Average attendance: 10,000. Closing date for entry: approximately 30 days before show. Entry fee: $10 per 8x10' display area. Prejudging; display area fee refunded for refused work. Crafts must be offered for sale; 10% commission. Craftsman must attend show. Registration limit: 58 booths, fall; 88 booths, spring. Sponsor provides insurance during exhibit period. Considers all crafts.

NASHVILLE HOBBY & CRAFT CHRISTMAS MARKET, Box 155-D, Fairview TN 37062. (615)799-0084. Producer: Fred Hicks. Estab: 1974. Annual indoor show held 2 days in December. Closing date for entry: 4 weeks before show. Entry fee: $35 per 10x10' display area. Permits 2-3 artists to set up in 1 space. Maximum 2 booths per craftsman. Prejudging of new entrants by slides or photos; entry fee refunded for refused work. Crafts may be offered for sale; no commission. Craftsman must attend show. "Craftspeople that do demonstrations are given corner locations as space is available." Registration limit: 225 artists/craftsmen. Sponsor provides table and 2 chairs with each space. Security force on duty during show. Accepts all crafts, but limited jewelry.

SIGNAL MOUNTAIN FALL FESTIVAL OF ARTS & CRAFTS, Rte. 1, Walker Rd., Signal Mountain TN 37377. (615)886-3584. Contact: Jake Hinds. Estab: 1972. Annual outdoor show held the first weekend in October. Average attendance: 8,000-10,000. Closing date for entry: 2 weeks before show. Entry fee: $12.50 per entry. Crafts may be offered for sale; no commission. Craftsman must attend show; demonstrations OK. Considers all crafts.

Texas

BLACK-EYED PEA JAMBOREE, Box 608, Athens TX 75751. Contact: Sherry Brasher. Sponsor: Athens Chamber of Commerce. Estab: 1971. Annual outdoor show held 3 days in July. Closing date for entries: 2 weeks before show. Entry fee: $14 per display area. Crafts may be offered for sale; no commission. Craftsman or representative must attend show; no demonstrations. Sponsor provides 6' chain link fence (for additional $5) and 10x12' display area. Considers all handmade crafts.

BORGER FINE ARTS FESTIVAL, 600 N. Deahl, Borger TX 79007. (806)274-2211. Contact: Wanda Guinn. Sponsor: Women's Division, Chamber of Commerce. Annual indoor show held 3 days in October. Average attendance: 6,000. Closing date for entry: 2 weeks before show. Write for entry fee. Prejudging; entry fee refunded for refused work. Crafts may be offered for sale; 10% commission. Craftsman must attend show; demonstrations encouraged. "We do not accept shipped items." Considers all handmade crafts.

THE CRAFT EXPERIENCE, 300 Augusta St., San Antonio TX 78205. (512)224-1848. Executive Director: Marcia Baer Larsen. Sponsor: Southwest Craft Center. Estab: 1974. Annual outdoor show held 2 days in June. Average attendance: 10,000. Closing date for entry: 3 weeks before show. Entry fee: $50 per craftsman. Maximum 1 booth per craftsman. Prejudging by 35mm slides. Crafts may be offered for sale; no commission. Craftsman must attend show. "Selected craftsmen who will give demonstrations receive 20% discount on booth fee." Registration limit: 75 artists/craftsmen. Sponsor pays insurance on exhibited work.
Acceptable Work: Considers batik, glass art, jewelry, leatherworking, metalsmithing, needlecrafts, pottery, soft sculpture, weavings, wall hangings and woodcrafting.

HOUSTON CRAFT FAIR, National Crafts Ltd., Gapland MD 21736. (301)432-8438. Director: Noel Clark. Estab: 1977. Annual indoor show held in the Houston Civic Center 2-3 days in December. Average attendance: 40,000. Closing date for applications: 3-4 months before show. Entry fee: $90. Prejudging by 5 color slides; entry fee refunded for refused work. Crafts may be offered for sale; no commission. Craftsman must attend show. Registration limit: 400 artists/craftsmen. Considers printmaking.

KALEIDOSCOPE CREATIVE ARTS & CRAFTS FESTIVAL, 1111 9th St., Beaumont TX 77702. (713)832-3432. Director: Betty W. Hirsch. Sponsor: Beaumont Art Museum. Estab: 1974. Annual outdoor (tent-covered booths available) show held the second weekend in May. Average attendance: 16,000. Closing date for entry: 12 weeks before show. Entry fee: $60 per 8x10' display area; $35 per craftsman if shared. Prejudging by slides or samples of work; entry fee refunded for refused work. Crafts may be offered for sale; no commission. Craftsman must attend show; demonstrations OK. Registration limit: 72 booths. Considers all original crafts.

LUBBOCK GARDEN & ARTS CENTER "FIESTA", 4215 University Ave., Lubbock TX 79413. (806)762-6411. Contact: Georgia Booker. Estab: 1967. Annual outdoor show held 1 day in September. Average attendance: 5,000-6,000. Entry fee: $35 per 8x8x6' booth. Artists/craftsmen must attend show; demonstrations encouraged. Registration limit: 100 booths. Considers all crafts.

RIO GRANDE VALLEY ARTS & CRAFTS EXPOSITION, 1485 Acacia Lake Rd., Brownsville TX 78521. Contact: Anna L. Dailey. Sponsor: Brownsville Art League. Estab: 1971. Annual indoor show held 4 days in November. Entries accepted until show date. Entry fee: $25 per 9x10' display area, 1 table and chairs (more tables available at $5 each). Art may be offered for sale; no commission. Artist must attend show; demonstrations encouraged.

In addition to being acclaimed by East Coast craft dealers as one of the best places to go to buy crafts for their shops, the Frederick Craft Fair (Frederick, Maryland) also attracts a large retail audience. The show is open to 500 craftsmen, regardless of organizational affiliation or geographical backgrounds.

SANTA'S TREASURE HOUSE ARTS & CRAFTS BAZAAR, Box 746, Raymondville TX 78580. (512)689-3171. Manager: Lucy Prater. Sponsor: Chamber of Commerce. Estab: 1971. Annual indoor show held the first Saturday in December. Average attendance: 500. Entries accepted until show date. Entry fee: $10 per 8x8' display area. Maximum 43 entries per craftsman. Crafts may be offered for sale; no commission. Sponsor provides chairs and tables on a first-come, first-serve basis. Considers all crafts.

WESTHEIMER COLONY ART FESTIVAL, 908 Westheimer Rd., Houston TX 77006. (713)521-0133. Contact: Arnold Bennitt. Sponsor: Westheimer Colony Association. Estab: 1970. Semiannual sidewalk show held 2 days in April and October. Average attendance: 200,000-300,000. Closing date for photos and resumes: 6 weeks before show. Entry fee: $60 per 10x10' display area; $80 if shared. Crafts may be offered for sale; no commission. Craftsman must attend show. Registration limit: 300 artists/craftsmen. Considers all crafts.

Utah

GREAT WEST FAIR, Utah State University, Logan UT 84322. Contact: Steve Black. Sponsor: Festival of the American West. Attendance: 50,000-75,000. Outdoor show under canopies. Closing date for entry: 2 weeks before show. No entry fee. Most craftsmen paid $25 per day for participating. Demonstrations and exhibits of pioneer and Indian arts and crafts: quilting, pottery, leatherworking, blacksmithing, soap and candle making, weaving and wood carving. Quality workmanship of early West crafts stressed. Some commercial arts and crafts of the era admitted. Tables furnished. Write for prospectus.

PARK CITY ART FESTIVAL, Box 758, Park City UT 84060. (801)649-8899. Sponsor: Chamber of Commerce. Annual outdoor show held in mid-August. Closing date for entry: 4-5 weeks before show. Entry fee: $15. Crafts may be offered for sale: 10% commission on gross sales. Craftsman must attend show. Sponsor provides display equipment. Show criteria for crafts varies each year. Information brochure available.

Vermont

BROMLEY MOUNTAIN SHOW, Box 92, Readsboro VT 05350. Director: Riki Moss. Sponsor: Craftproducers Inc. Annual indoor show held in Peru, Vermont, 2 days the first week in October. Average attendance: 8,000-10,000. Closing date for entry: May 1. Entry fee: $60. Prejudging by 5 slides; entry fee refunded for refused work. Crafts may be offered for sale; no commission. Registration limit: 50 exhibitors. Demonstrations OK. Sponsor/craftsman share insurance for exhibited work. Considers graphics.

GREEN MOUNTAIN CRAFT FAIR, R.D. 1, Arlington VT 05250. (802)375-6981. Directors: Bill and Holly Patrick. Estab: 1976. Annual indoor/outdoor show held 4 days Columbus Day weekend. Average attendance: 12,000. Closing date for entry: 12 weeks before show. Entry fee: $1 application fee; $40-60 per 10x10' display area. Prejudging by slides. Craftsman must attend show; demonstrations pre-arranged. Registration limit: 250 craftsmen. Sponsor pays insurance for exhibit period. Considers all crafts.

MOUNT SNOW FAIR, Box 92, Readsboro VT 05350. Director: Riki Moss. Sponsor: Craftproducers Inc. Annual indoor show held in West Dover 3 days in August. Average attendance: 8,000-10,000. Closing date for entry: May 1. Entry fee: $70. Prejudging by 5 slides; entry fee refunded for refused work. Crafts may be offered for sale; no commission. Registration limit: 70 exhibitors. Demonstrations OK. Sponsor/craftsman share insurance for exhibited work. Considers graphics.

MOUNT SNOW FALL FESTIVAL OF CRAFT, Box 92, Readsboro VT 05350. Director: Riki Moss. Sponsor: Craftproducers Inc. Annual indoor show held in West Dover 4 days during Columbus Day weekend. Average attendance: 8,000-10,000. Closing date for entry: May 1. Entry fee: $75. Prejudging by 5 slides; entry fee refunded for refused work. Crafts may be offered for sale; no commission. Registration limit: 70 exhibitors. Demonstrations OK. Sponsor/craftsman share insurance for exhibited work. Considers graphics.

STOWE CRAFT SHOW & SALE, Rte. 2, Stowe VT 05672. Contact: Jane Roberts. Exhibition of handcrafts. Entry fee: $45 per 6x9' space. No sales commission. Wood block prints acceptable. Original work only.

Virginia

ARTS IN THE PARK, 1112 Sunset Ave., Richmond VA 23221. (804)353-8198. Chairman: Mrs. R. S. Lovelace. Sponsor: Carillon Civic Association. Estab: 1971. Annual indoor/outdoor show held 2 days in April-May. Average attendance: 50,000. Closing date for entry: 2 weeks before show. Entry fee: $15 per outdoor/$25 per indoor display area. Crafts may be offered for sale; no commission. Craftsman must attend show; demonstrations encouraged. Considers all crafts.

FESTIVAL OF LEAVES, Box 1314, Front Royal VA 22630. (703)635-3637. Chairman: Prudence Matheaus. Sponsor: Warren Heritage Society. Estab: 1970. Annual show held 2 days in October. Average attendance: 3,000. Closing date for entry: 3 weeks before show. No entry fee. Prejudging. Art may be offered for sale; 15% commission. Craftsman must attend show. Registration limit: 50 artists/craftsmen. Sponsor provides display equipment and pays insurance on exhibited work. Considers all crafts.

GREENWOOD ARTS & CRAFTS FAIR, Greenwood Community Center, Greenwood VA 22943. (703)456-6447. Contact: Sally Wedvick. Annual indoor show held 2 days in September. Average attendance: 6,000. Closing date for entry: July. Entry fee: $20, $30 or $40 per entry. Crafts may be offered for sale; no commission. Craftsman must attend show; demonstrations encouraged. Registration limit: 100 artists/craftsmen. Considers all handmade crafts.

ROANOKE CRAFT FESTIVAL, Box 8161, Roanoke VA 24015. Contact: Coordinator. Estab: 1971. Annual indoor show held 3 days in November. Average attendance: 10,000-11,000. Closing date for entry: early June. Entry fee: $55 per 8x6' display area. Prejudging by slides. Crafts may be offered for sale; no commission. Craftsman must attend show; demonstrations encouraged. Sponsor provides display panels and continuous security. Considers all original crafts.

Washington

NORTHWEST CRAFTS EXHIBITION, Henry Gallery, University of Washington, Seattle WA 98195. Contact: Director. Estab: 1953. Regional, biennial Northwest competition next held in 1979. No entry fee. Maximum 3 entries per craftsman. Several solo exhibitions given. 20% sales commission.

SIDEWALK SHOW, 89 Lee Blvd., Richland WA 99352. (509)943-9815. Chairman: Jack Hess. Sponsor: Allied Arts Association. Estab: 1950. Annual outdoor show held 2 days in July. Average attendance: 10,000-15,000. Closing (postmark) date for entry: 2 weeks before show. Entry fee: $10 per craftsman. Awards $50 for best display. Crafts may be offered for sale; 15% commission. "Items $200 or less sell very well." Craftsman must attend show; demonstrations encouraged. Registration limit: approximately 200 artists/craftsmen. Sponsor provides 10x10' display area, some electricity (if pre-requested) and security. Considers all crafts. No decoupage. Write for prospectus in mid-May.

WHISTLIN' JACK LODGE FESTIVAL, 4210 Terrace Heights Rd., Yakima WA 98901. (509)453-3379. Director: Ruth Wyman Reese. Sponsor: Whistlin' Jack Lodge. Estab: 1976. Semiannual outdoor show held 3 days in September and July. Average attendance: 2,000-4,000. Closing date for entry: 2 weeks before show. Entry fee: $15 per 10x10' display area. Prejudging by photos or samples of work. SASE. Crafts must be offered for sale; 15% commission. Craftsman must attend show; demonstrations encouraged. Registration limit: 30 artists/craftsmen. Considers all crafts. No kits or stamped work.

West Virginia

ALDERSON-BROADDUS COLLEGE ARTS & CRAFTS FAIR, Box 1397, A-B College, Philippi WV 26416. (304)457-1700 ext. 235. Director of Student Activities: Carl Hatfield. Estab: 1974. Annual indoor show held 1 day in October. Average attendance: 1,000. Closing date for entry: 2 weeks before show. No entry fee. Maximum 1 entry per craftsman. Crafts may be offered for sale; no commission. Considers primarily West Virginia craftsmen. Craftsman must attend show; demonstrations OK. Registration limit: 40 artists/craftsmen. Sponsor provides tables. Considers all crafts. Maximum size: 12x12'.

APPALACHIAN FESTIVAL, Morris Harvey College, Charleston WV 25304. (304)346-9471. Director: William Plumley. Estab: 1970. Annual indoor show held 3 days in April. Average attendance: 8,000. Closing date for entry: January. Entry fee: $20-25 per 8x2½' or 5x3' table. Prejudging; entry fee refunded for refused work. Crafts may be offered for sale; no commission. Craftsman must attend show. Registration limit: 50-60 exhibits. Considers Appalachian crafts only.

CAPITAL CITY ART & CRAFT SHOW, 3820 N. Crede Dr., Charleston WV 25302. (304)346-3427. Contact: Bill Lanyi. Sponsor: Kanawha City Lions Club. Estab: 1971. Annual indoor show held 3 days in November. Average attendance: 13,000. Closing date for entry: 2 weeks before show. Entry fee: $17.50 per 10x10' display area. Craftsman limited to 2 booths. Prejudging by photos. Crafts must be offered for sale; 15% commission (sales for 2½-day show in 1976 were $48,500). Craftsman must attend show; demonstrations preferred. Sponsor supplies display equipment and pays insurance on exhibited work. Considers all crafts.

JOHN HENRY FOLK FESTIVAL, Box 135, Princeton WV 24740. (304)487-1148. Director: Edward J. Cabbell. Sponsor: John Henry Memorial Foundation, Inc. Estab: 1973. Annual outdoor show with tents held 3 days in late August. Closing date for entry: 2 months before show. No entry fee. Prejudging by photos or slides (send resume) conducted by panel of Appalachian artists/craftsmen. Crafts may be offered for sale; 10% commission. Craftsman must be from an Appalachian state or region and must attend show. Demonstrations OK. Sponsor provides display panels. Considers all traditional Appalachian crafts (at least 1 work must be related to John Henry folk legend).

PARKERSBURG COMMUNITY COLLEGE HERITAGE DAYS, Box 167A, Parkersburg WV 26101. (304)424-8000. Chairman: Nancy Pansing. Sponsor: Parkersburg Community College. Estab: 1974. Annual indoor show held 3 days in April. Average attendance: 10,000. Invitations to enter show sent in November and again in December. Closing date for entry: 6 weeks before show. No entry fee. Prejudging. Crafts may be offered for sale; no commission. Craftsman must attend show. Registration limit: 50 artists/craftsmen. Sponsor provides tables, chairs, platforms and other display equipment.
Acceptable Work: Considers candlemaking, dollmaking, glass art, jewelry, leatherworking, metalsmithing, needlecrafts, pottery, tole painting, weavings, quilting, whittling, furniture-making, book display, lacemaking, basketmaking, dulcimer-making, guitar-making, dollhouses and clock-making. Craftsman expected to demonstrate frequently and answer questions.
To Break In: Write for application. Panel then decides if type of craft is suitable and not repetitious of other entries. Those craftsmen not sent invitations for that particular year are kept in the exhibition files for following years.

Wisconsin

BLACKHAWK INDIAN VALLEY, Box 61, Rome IL 61562. (309)274-3001. Contact: Judy Kelley. Estab: 1973. Indoor show held in Janesville, Wisconsin, 3 days in March, August and November. Closing date for entry: 2 weeks before show. Entry fee: $30 per 6x12' display area. Prejudging by 2 slides (send SASE); entry fee refunded for refused work. Crafts may be offered for sale; no commission. Craftsman must attend show. Registration limit: 80-100 artists/craftsmen. Craftsman may rent 8' tables at $5 each and chairs at 50¢.
Acceptable Work: Considers candlemaking, ceramics, leatherworking, metalsmithing, pottery, tole painting, wall hangings and woodcrafting. No crochet, knitting or commercial items.

FOREST MALL ARTS & CRAFTS FAIR, 835 W. Johnson St., Fond Du Lac WI 54935. Contact: Lois Frank. Sponsor: Forest Mall Merchants Association. Estab: 1974. Annual indoor show held 3 days in April. Average attendance: 6,000-10,000. Closing date for entry: 2-3 weeks before show. Entry fee: $12-15 per 10x10' tent display area. Prejudging; entry fee refunded for refused work. Crafts may be offered for sale; 10% commission donated to charity. Craftsman must attend show. Registration limit: 70-75 artists/craftsmen.
Acceptable Work: Considers batik, candlemaking, ceramics, glass art (no glass blowing), leatherworking, metal sculpture, creative stitchery, pottery, weavings, wall hangings and woodcrafting.

FORT FEST ARTS & CRAFTS FAIR, Rte. 1, Box 49B, Fort Atkinson WI 53538. (414)563-8777. Chairman: Joy Wentz. Sponsor: Fort Fest, Inc. Estab: 1970. Annual outdoor show held 1 day in August. Closing date for entry: 3 weeks before show. Entry fee: $10 per craftsman. Crafts may be offered for sale; no commission. Craftsman must attend show; demonstrations encouraged. Considers all original crafts.

GAYS MILLS PACE CLUB ARTS & CRAFTS FAIR, Pace Club, Gays Mills WI 54631. Contact: Mrs. Richard Gainor. Semiannual indoor/outdoor show held 1 day in May and September. Average attendance: 1,000+. Entries accepted until spaces filled. Entry fee: $10 per 10x4' display area. Crafts may be offered for sale; no commission. Craftsman must attend show; demonstrations encouraged. Registration limit: 75-100 artists/craftsmen. Considers all crafts.

GREATER MILWAUKEE CRAFT FAIR, 1655 S. 68th St., West Allis WI 53214. Craft Fair Director: Dennis R. Hill. Invitational exhibition for Midwest craftsmen held in November. Average attendance: 10,000-15,000. All original crafts eligible. Held at Wisconsin State Fair Park. Open to craftsmen ages 18+.

HANDICAPPED CRAFT FAIR, W237 N478 Oakridge Dr., Waukesha WI 53186. Sponsors: Ruth and Robert Hoss. Estab: 1970. No entry fee. Registration limit: 40 craftsmen. Craftsmen should sell their own crafts when possible. No sales commission. Only handicapped people from Wisconsin are eligible (doctor's statement must be furnished).

MOUNT MARY STARVING ARTISTS SHOW, 17160 Deer Park Dr., Brookfield WI 53005. (414)782-7862. Registration Director: Laura Nesemann. Sponsor: Mount Mary College Alumnae Association. Estab: 1969. Annual outdoor show held 1 day in September. Average attendance: 20,000. Closing date for entry: March 1. Entry fee: $30 per craftsman. Prejudging by photos or slides; entry fee refunded for refused work. Crafts may be sold for under $35; no sales commission. Craftsman must attend show; no demonstrations. Registration limit: 195 artists/craftsmen. Sponsor provides snow fencing; 15x18' display area.
Acceptable Work: Considers batik, ceramics, jewelry, leatherworking, metalsmithing, pottery, weavings, wall hangings and woodcrafting. "Nothing too craftsy."

RACINE CHRISTMAS GIFT MARKET, 422 Main St., Racine WI 53403. (414)637-4471. Director: Daniel Thekan. Estab: 1973. Annual indoor show held the second Sunday in December. Average attendance: 1,500-2,000. Entries accepted until show date. "Show usually sold out 1 month ahead of time." Entry fee: $15 per entry. Prejudging; entry fee refunded for refused work. Crafts may be offered for sale; no commission. Prefers demonstrations. Registration limit: 140 artists/craftsmen. Sponsor provides tables and chairs. Considers all crafts. "Priority given to work that will make good Christmas gifts."

SUMMERFEST, 120 N. Harbor Dr., Milwaukee WI 53202. Contact: Kathy Kranstover. Estab: 1968. Annual outdoor show held 11 days in July. Average attendance: 600,000. Closing date for entry: May 1. Entry fee: $500 per entry. Crafts may be offered for sale; no commission. Registration limit: 22 craftsmen. Sponsor pays insurance during exhibit period. Considers all crafts.

Show Sponsors

AMERICAN FAIRS, INC., 2131 Union St., San Francisco CA 94123. (415)346-6800. Contact: Michael J. Warfield or Sybil Douglas. Estab: 1970. Sponsors arts and crafts shows in California, Arizona, Utah, Nevada and Oregon; 70 annually. Entry fee: $20-25; 10% sales commission. Write for more information. "Send photos of craft and display unit with SASE."

AMERICAN INSTITUTE OF GRAPHIC ARTS, 1059 3rd Ave., New York NY 10021. (212)752-0813. Coordinator: Nathan Gluck. Sponsors 10-12 fine art print shows in New York City. Entry fee: $5-10; no sales commission.

ART ENTERPRISE, 3294 Desertwood Lane, San Jose CA 95132. (408)262-6606. Contact: Manfred P. Schiedeck or Charles W. Woodhead. Estab: 1969. Sponsors art and craft shows in the Midwest; 52 annually. Entry fee: $15-100; 10% sales commission. Write with resume for more information. SASE.

ART-CRAFT ASSOCIATES, Millside Manor Arcade, Delran NJ 08075. (609)764-1600. Contact: Gordon T. Gattone. Estab: 1971. Sponsors fine art, craft, sculpture, painting and miniature doll shows in the East, South, Midwest and New England; 50 annually. Entry fee: $30-100; no sales commission. Write for more information.

ARTISTS CO-OP, Box 7112, South Lake Tahoe CA 95731. (916)544-4696 or (213)355-3766. Contact: Wayne Denney. Estab: 1972. Sponsors arts and crafts fairs, Renaissance festivals and Western fairs in southern California and Lake Tahoe; 25 annually. Entries prejudged. Entry fee: $15-75; maximum 15% sales commission. Write for more information. SASE.

ARTS UNLIMITED, 149 Kalb Ave., Green Bay WI 54301. (414)437-5849. Contact: Nancy Hacker. Estab: 1974. Sponsors art and craft shows in Green Bay area. Entry fee: $10; no sales commission. Write with slides and resume for more information.

BETTY BALDWIN ARTIST'S SHOWPLACE, 18415 North Dr., Southfield MI 48076. (313)642-7905. Contact: Nate Baker. Estab: 1959. Sponsors craft and painting shows in Michigan and Ohio; 16 annually. Entries prejudged. Entry fee: $25; 20% sales commission. Write for more information.

CONSTANCE L. BARGER, 2006 N. North St., Peoria IL 61604. Sponsors arts and crafts shows in Illinois. Entry fee: approximately $25; no sales commission. New entrants should send short resume and photos of work.

BOSTON MARKETPLACE, 29 Newbury St., Boston MA 02116. (617)536-0300. Contact: Brenda Metrano. Estab: 1971. Sponsors antiques and craft shows in Boston and Ohio; 33 annually. Entries prejudged. Entry fee: $20-185; no sales commission. Write for more information.

CAREER ART PROMOTIONS (formerly Colorado Art Shows, Inc.), 1420 E. 91st Ave., Thornton CO 80229. (303)288-1144. Promoter: David and C. Holly Merrifield. Estab: 1970. Sponsors sculpture, painting and occasionally craft shows in Colorado; 25-30 annually. Entries prejudged. Entry fee: $10-20; 10% sales commission. Write for more information.

CERMAK ROAD BUSINESS ASSOCIATION, 2130 S. 61st Court, Cicero IL 60650. (312)863-2104. Contact: Norm Scaman. Estab: 1915. Sponsors crafts and painting shows in Berwyn and Cicero, Illinois. No prejudging. Entry fee: $15; no sales commission. Write for more information.

COLORADO WILDLIFE FEDERATION, 1420 E. 91st Ave., Thornton CO 80229. Contact: Holly Merrifield, Gallery East. Sponsors shows held in malls throughout Colorado; 12 annually. Show theme is conservation. Entries must depict wildlife or close-ups of nature; no scenic paintings. Entry fee: $5 jury fee; $8-10 per entry. 15% sales commission. Acceptable media include oils, acrylics, watercolors, graphics, drawings, sculpture and mixed media.

DENISE MORRIS CURT'S MEET THE ARTISTS, 41 Green St., Milford CT 06460. Sponsors art and limited crafts shows; 6 annually. Prejudging by slides or photos. Charges entry fee; no sales commission. SASE.

THE FIREBIRD ARTISTS, THE FIREBIRD CRAFTSMEN, 4501 W. Acoma Dr., Glendale AZ 85306. (602)938-4597 or 934-5800. Contact: Candice C. Collmar. Sponsors art and craft shows in Arizona.

FREELANDS NATIONAL ARTS & CRAFTS SHOWS, 2918 Martel Dr., Dayton OH 45420. (513)254-2900. Director: Clarence Freeland. Estab: 1970. Sponsors arts and crafts shows in Ohio, Florida, Pennsylvania and New York; 35 annually. Entries sometimes prejudged. Entry fee: $50-90; no sales commission. Write for entry blank. SASE. "Describe your art or craft."

FULL SAIL PRODUCTIONS LTD., 65 Main St., Westhampton Beach NY 11978. (516)288-4263. Directors: Barbara Hope and Don Gaiti. Estab: 1974. Sponsors craft shows in New York City and Long Island. Entries prejudged. Entry fee: $135-215; no sales commission. Write or call for more information.

LEE GILPIN'S ARTISTS EXPO, 9612 Glenbrook St., Cypress CA 90630. (714)821-1244 or 826-9386. Contact: Lee Gilpin. Estab: 1973. Sponsors fine arts and crafts shows in California and Arizona; 50+ annually. Entry fee: $12-20; 10% sales commission. Write with slides and/or photos for more information. SASE.

GRAND CANYON INC., 6930 N. Grand Dr., Boca Raton FL 33433. (305)368-1027. President: Larry Burdgick. Estab: 1974. Sponsors arts and crafts shows in Coconut Grove, Florida; 4 annually. Entries prejudged. Entry fee: $40 minimum; no sales commission. Write for information. SASE.

GREATHALL CORPORATION RENAISSANCE FAIRES, 1624 Harmon Place, Minneapolis MN 55403. Estab: 1973. Contact: Richard N. Olmsted. Sponsors oil, watercolor, drawing, sculpture, mixed media and craft shows with Renaissance themes in Chicago and Dallas. Entry fee: $35 plus $10 deposit; no sales commission.

BEA GRIFFIN CREATIVE ARTISTS GROUP, 3608 Cinnabar Ave., Carson City NV 89701. (707)883-0968. Contact: Bea Griffin. Estab: 1944. Sponsors crafts, sculpture and painting shows in the California Bay area, Lake Tahoe and Nevada; 50 annually. Entry fee: $15-30; 10% sales commission.

JINX HARRIS SHOWS, INC., RFD #1, Box 153J, Auburn NH 03032. (603)483-2742. Director: Jinx Harris. Estab: 1959. Sponsors arts, sculpture, crafts, fiber and wood shows in New Jersey, Pennsylvania, New Hampshire, Massachusetts and Maryland; 68 annually. Entries prejudged. Entry fee: $30-60; no sales commission. Send slides/photos for application.

HERBIE PRODUCTIONS, Box 5567, South Lake Tahoe CA 95729. (916)541-8717. Contact: Herb Gorden or Ronnie Marr. Estab: 1975. Sponsors national crafts, painting and sculpture shows; 40 annually. Entries prejudged. Entry fee: $25; 10% sales commission. Write or call for more information.

IDAHO FALLS ART GUILD, 1525 Claire View Lane, Idaho Falls ID 83401. Contact: LaReine Feltman. Sponsors art shows for Guild members. No entry fee; 10% sales commission.

J & R PRODUCTIONS, Box 46X, East Kingston NH 03827. (603)642-5073. Directors: Ron and June Richardson. Estab: 1974. Sponsors arts and crafts shows in New England; 10-20 annually. Entries prejudged. Entry fee: $35; no sales commission. Write for applications and rules.

KARAMAC PRODUCTIONS, Rte. 2, Box 341B, New Braunfels TX 78130. (512)629-2285. Contact: Sam or Mary Lou Machotka. Estab: 1975. Sponsors art and craft shows in south central states; 12 annually. Jewelry prejudged. Entry fee: $40-50; no sales commission. Write for brochure.

KENT ART ASSOCIATION, INC., Kent CT 06757. Contact: Jayne McGarvey. Estab: 1923. Sponsors oil, watercolor, graphics, acrylic and small sculpture shows; 3 annually. Entry fee: $5 per 1-2 works; 20% sales commission. Awards $600 in prizes.

IRIS G. KLEIN, 9476 Harding Ave., Surfside FL 33154. Estab: 1961. Sponsors art and craft shows in Florida, Chicago and suburbs. Entries prejudged. Entry fee: $12-30; 40% sales commission on gallery items only. Write with slides and/or photos for more information.

KREGGER SHOWS, Box 433, Orangevale CA 95662. Coordinator: Sally Jo Kregger. Sponsors annual fine art and art and crafts shows. Entry fee: $10 minimum; 10% sales commission. Prejudging by slides or photos. SASE.

LA PLAZA MALL ART PROMOTION COUNSELORS, Box 776, Alamo TX 78516. (512)787-6996. Contact: Lauretta Worstell. Estab: 1973. Sponsors art and craft shows in Texas; 6 annually. Entries prejudged. Entry fee: $17.50, 10% sales commission; $45, no sales commission. Write for more information.

LOS ANGELES ART ASSOCIATION & GALLERIES, 825 N. La Cienega Blvd., Los Angeles CA 90069. (213)652-8272. Estab: 1926. Sponsors fine art shows in Los Angeles; 12 monthly. Open to southern California artists. Entries prejudged. No entry fee; 33 1/3% sales commission.

NANCY McGUIRE ART SHOWS, 11 Doris St., Unionville CT 06085. (203)673-5527. Directors: Nancy McGuire. Sponsors arts and crafts shows in Connecticut, Massachusetts, New Hampshire, New Jersey, New York and Rhode Island; approximately 40 annually. Entries prejudged. Entry fee: $30; no sales commission.

MERIDIAN MUSEUM OF ART, Box 5773, Meridian MS 39301. (601)693-1501. Contact: William M. Watkins III. Original works of art may be purchased, exhibited and/or entered in annual competitions. 10% commission. Cash awards. Write for information.

MIDWEST ARTISTS ASSOCIATION, Box 454, Palos Heights IL 60463. (312) 448-0334 or 448-8995. Contact: John Basso or Amy Doherty. Estab: 1969. Sponsors arts and crafts, fine art and antiques shows in Chicago and suburbs; 12 seasonally. Entry fee: $15 minimum; no sales commission. Write for more information.

NATIONAL ARTISTS TOUR, 18060 3rd St., Fountain Valley CA 92708. (714)963-2560. Contact: Robert E. Downs. Estab: 1974. Sponsors national art and craft shows; 30 annually. Entries prejudged. Entry fee: $5 per day; 10% sales commission. Write for more information.

IRENE "RAE" PARTRIDGE, Rte. 1, 146 Park Dr., Barrington IL 60010. (312)639-5665. Contact: Irene "Rae" Partridge. Estab: 1966. Sponsors fine arts and selected craft shows in Chicago; 7-10 annually. Entries prejudged. Entry fee: $18-25; no sales commission. Write for more information.

PROVIDENCE ART CLUB EXHIBITIONS, 11 Thomas St., Providence RI 02903. Contact: Marjory Dalenius. Sponsors shows for New England artists; 3 seasonally (September-July). Some member-only shows.

R & S ASSOCIATES, Box 97, Bloomsbury NJ 08804. (201)454-3737. Contact: Raymond Roe. Estab: 1973. Sponsors arts, crafts, collectables, stamp and coin shows on the East Coast; mall shows weekly. Entries prejudged. Entry fee: $30-100; no sales commission. Write for more information.

REITER PROMOTIONS, INC., Box 321, Chanhassen MN 55317. (612)445-1998. Contact: Arthur Reiter. Estab: 1973. Sponsors art, craft and fine art shows in Rochester and Duluth. Entry fee: $20-25; no sales commission. Write for more information.

SHANOAH ART FAIRS, 4 W. Shady Lane, Houston TX 77063. (713)781-1565. Director: Lewis Steinberg. Estab: 1973. Sponsors art and craft shows in Houston, Little Rock, Arkansas, and Louisiana; 12-15 annually. Entries prejudged. Entry fee: $40-50; no sales commission. Write or call for more information.

SOUTHERN SHOWS, INC., 2500 E. Independence Blvd., Charlotte NC 28205. (704)334-3086. Contact: Robert E. Zimmerman. Estab: 1960. Sponsors trade and consumer shows in the South; 5 annually. Entries prejudged. Entry fee: $150-200 per booth; no sales commission. Write for more information.

SPECTRA PRODUCTIONS INC., Box 333, Eagle ID 83616. (208)939-6426. Manager: Doug Fitzgerald. Estab: 1970. Sponsors arts and crafts shows in the Northwest; 13 annually. Entry fee: $5-135; no sales commission. Write for more information.

SPRINGFIELD ART ASSOCIATION, 700 N. 4th, Springfield IL 62704. (217)523-0093. Contact: William Bealmer. Estab: 1933. Sponsors invitational fiber, fabric and watercolor shows in Springfield; 9 annually. Entries prejudged. No entry fee; 25% sales commission. Write for more information.

TOR ENTERPRISES, 615 S. H St., Lakeworth FL 33460. (305)582-6133. Director: Jim Readey. Estab: 1974. Sponsors art and craft shows in Florida, Georgia and Tennessee; approximately 40 annually. Entry fee: $15-100; no sales commission.

UNCLE MILT SHOWS, 1435 Burning Tree St., Sarasota FL 33580. Contact: "Uncle Milt" Kelly. Estab: 1974. Sponsors arts and crafts shows in Sarasota and Manatee counties; 7-8 annually. Entry fee: $9-15; no sales commission. Send detailed description of work to be exhibited with SASE.

JAY VIETS — CREATIVE PROMOTIONS, 5702 Lubao Ave., Woodland Hills CA 91367. (213)348-0540. Contact: Peggy or Jay Viets. Estab: 1975. Sponsors crafts, sculpture and painting shows in Texas, Mississippi, Louisiana, Arizona, New Mexico, California, Oregon,

Montana, Washington, Idaho and Oklahoma; 52 annually. Entry fee: $20; 10% sales commission. Write for more information.

VIRGINIA MUSEUM, Boulevard & Grove Ave., Richmond VA 23220. (804)786-6386. Contact: Charlotte Minor. Estab: 1936. Sponsors biennial painting, scultpure, crafts, photography, graphic design and printmaking shows in Virginia. Open to Virginia residents, those born in the state or having minimum 3-year residency. Charges entry fee; 20% sales commission. Write for more information.

WORLD SHOWS, Box 339, Stanton CA 90680. (714)995-7509. Contact: Don Palmer. Estab: 1967. Sponsors painting shows in the U.S. and Canada; 60 annually. Entry fee: $15-20; 10% sales commission.

Craft Dealers

In 1976, the craft industry reported a record $600 million business. And of all the full-time craftsmen, five percent reported incomes exceeding $25,000.

As a full or part-time craftsman, you can make money selling your crafts in one of three ways: direct selling (see Competitions & Exhibitions), wholesaling or selling through retailers.

The markets in this section are retailers — both craft shops and galleries. Before approaching either one, the craftsman should know the differences between the two. Charles Evans, owner of Incorporated Galleries (New York City), defines them this way: "In a gallery, work is shown for a designated period of time. Purchases made during that time remain until the end of the show. These pieces are displayed with integrity, cleanness of space and are exclusive to the public in that area. Galleries deal on consignment only.

"A (craft) shop contains a collection of work that is dispersed as it is sold. Shops can have the clean look of a gallery; but, they have more control over inventory, whereas galleries are tied to particular show times. Shops can sell outright or on consignment."

Common to craft shops and galleries is their benefit to the craftsman. Adds Evans: "The shop or gallery is a functionary plant that goes on while the artist continues to do his work." The craftsman can spend more time producing and less time selling.

Retailers usually ask for a commission on sales. In addition to the obvious benefit of helping the retailer pay his bills, some of the commission money may also be used for publicity purposes. Other shops buy outright and then double the wholesale price to arrive at their retail cost.

The percentage of commission charged by retailers on sales varies greatly, generally ranging from 30-60%. But, according to many craft retailers attending the 1977 International Crafts Show (New York City), the trend for the future calls for even higher commissions and consistent percentages between shops and galleries.

Initial contact with craft dealers can usually be made either in person or by sending slides or photos of your work through the mail. The listings in this section indicate the method the dealer prefers. For example, Caroline Riddle, of the Arrowcraft Shop (Gatlinburg, Indiana) says she prefers to personally review work. "The best way for me to truly judge the work of a craftsman is to see the actual product. On wood, for example, it is the best way to see the finish, detail and workmanship. This also helps people doing the selling by letting them know about the person who made the work they are buying. Actually, in a sense, we're hiring the craftsman and are depending on him to be reliable, so we essentially interview him for the job."
reliable, so we essentially interview him for the job."

Whether your approach is by mail or in person, presentation has much to do with whether your work is accepted by the retailer. "When considering crafts for our gallery, we give the most complete presentations top priority. Give us samples that clearly show and represent your work," says William Tanguay, president of Wonderful Things Inc. (Great Barrington, Massachusetts).

A complete resume should be a part of your presentation as it tells the retailer something about you and your work, so he can answer any customer questions. But, "never send unsolicited work to galleries (and craft shops). If you do, you're likely never to see it again. Also, this inconveniences the gallery because they have to wrap it up and return it," says Julie Schafler of Julie: Artisans' Gallery (New York City).

When your work is accepted by a gallery or shop, most dealers suggest sending it by United Parcel Service (UPS). Packing, particularly for breakable items, should be done with care. Read "How to Pack Fragile Items for Shipping, Storage and Transport" for packing tips.

Always draw up a letter of agreement with the dealer prior to submitting any work. The letter should include the title of the show (when applicable), arrival and pick-up dates, who's responsible for what (insurance, equipment, etc.) and the percentage on sales you'll receive when your work's sold.

According to many retailers attending the 1977 International Craft Show, the most frequent problem they encounter is craftsmen who break contracts prior to an announced show. This is both unprofessional and a sure way to get yourself on the black list of dealers in your area.

In addition to the markets listed in this section, there are other ways to sell your crafts: through competitions and exhibitions; supplying department stores like Saks Fifth Avenue; and direct sales from your home or studio. Or, you can let customers find you through a listing — complete with illustrations of your work — in the *Goodfellow Catalog of Wonderful Things* (Box 4520, Berkeley, California 94704). And, don't overlook the market possibilities in your own community. Many florists, gift boutiques, antique shops and other businesses are supplementing their present lines with handcrafted items.

More information on markets and other craft-related happenings can be found by reading *The Crafts Report, Goodfellow Review of Crafts,* and *Working Craftsman,* plus a host of other craft publications.

Alabama

WINDWARD CRAFTS, Rte. 1, Mentone AL 35894. (205)634-3819. Contact: Mildred Moerlins or Jill Howard. Estab: 1975. Represents 15-20 craftsmen. Considers batik, candlemaking, dollmaking, glass art, jewelry, leatherworking, metalsmithing, needlecrafts, pottery, quilting, soft sculpture, wall hangings, weavings and woodcrafting. Finished, one-of-a-kind or handmade production items OK; utilitarian and/or decorative. Price range: $1-300; bestsellers: $2-20. Works on consignment and occasionally buys outright; 30% commission. Craftsman sets retail price. Write or query with color transparencies or b&w prints of work. Reports in 2 weeks. Artist pays shipping to shop and in-transit insurance; dealer pays shipping from shop and insurance for exhibited work.

Profile: "Windward Crafts is an old 2-story log house which was originally a small inn for summer tourists. We are open only in the summer, with all items displayed all summer. Customers are a wide variety of people vacationing in the area."

Alaska

ALASKA NATIVE ARTS & CRAFTS, 425 "D" St., Anchorage AK 99501. (907)274-2932. Contact: Susan Fair. Estab: 1937. Represents hundreds of local craftsmen. Native art only. One-of-a-kind, primitive and finished items OK; utilitarian and/or decorative. Price range: $1.50-4,500; bestsellers: $40-110. Buys outright or on consignment; 20% commission. Retail price set by joint agreement. Heaviest wholesale buying time: winter; best selling time: summer. Shop is a native co-op. Customers buy crafts for their artistic value and as an investment.

KAILL FINE CRAFTS, 4 Marine Way, Merchants Wharf, Juneau AK 99801. (907)586-2880. Contact: Anne Kaill. Estab: 1976. Represents 75 craftsmen. Considers batik, candlemaking, ceramics, dollmaking, glass art, jewelry, leatherworking, metalsmithing, pottery, quilting, soft sculpture, toys, wall hangings, weavings and woodcrafting. Finished one-of-a-kind items OK; utilitarian and/or decorative. Price range: 65¢-$2,000; bestsellers: $10-20 and $40-80. Buys outright or on consignment; 33 1/3% commission. Retail price set by joint agreement. Requires exclusive area representation. All methods of contact OK. Reports in 2 weeks. "In Alaska, U.S. Mail or air freight is our only means of shipment." Dealer pays insurance for exhibited work; negotiates shipping and in-transit insurance.

Profile: "I rotate items and change the gallery weekly." Best selling time: Christmas.

Special Needs: Unusual, not necessarily expensive items, including kites, musical instruments, cards, prints, quilts and dolls.

Arizona

COB-WEB HALL, Box 2035, Prescott AZ 86301. (602)445-2262. Contact: Dick Jorgensen. Estab: 1962. Represents 40-50 craftsmen. Considers batik, ceramics, glass art, jewelry, leatherworking, metalsmithing, needlecrafts, soft sculpture and woodcrafting. Finished handmade items OK; utilitarian and/or decorative. Price range: $2-300; bestsellers: under $100. "We prefer to consign, as most of our craftsmen prefer it that way, but we do on occasion by out-

right." 33⅓% commission. Craftsman sets retail price. Requires exclusive area representation. Write. Reports in 6 weeks. Artist pays shipping to shop and insurance; dealer pays shipping from shop.
Profile: "Although we rotate work, customers are allowed in storage area so work is always available for sale." Heaviest wholesale buying time: pre-Christmas season; best selling time: Christmas. "Prescott has a large retirement population of individuals of means. Also has an active college."

COLORADO RIVER INDIAN TRIBES MUSEUM, Rte. 1, Box 23-B, Parker AZ 85344. (602)669-9211. Director: Charles A. Lamb. Estab: 1965. Represents 40 local craftsmen. Considers beadworking, leatherworking, pottery, wall hangings, weavings, woodcrafting and silversmithing. Traditional, finished or one-of-a-kind items OK; utilitarian, decorative and/or ceremonial. Price range: $4-900; bestsellers: under $20. Buys outright or on consignment; 20% commission. Retail price set by joint agreement. Shop is tribally-owned and operated. Best selling time: holidays, especially pre-Christmas.

GRA WUN JEWELERS, LTD., 7122 5th Ave., Scottsdale AZ 85251. Contact: Margaret Graves. Considers ceramics, jewelry, metalsmithing and glass art. Price range: $14-75. Buys outright. Craftsman determines fee. Requires exclusive area representation. Send transparencies or b&w photos (12x12x24" or smaller) of work. Items displayed one week minimum.

THE HAND AND THE SPIRIT CRAFTS GALLERY, 4200 N. Marshall Way, Scottsdale AZ 85251. Contact: Joanne Rapp. Estab: 1973. Represents 100 craftsmen. Considers ceramics, dollmaking, glass art, jewelry and quilting; especially needs "crafts geared toward children and men." Finished handmade production-line items OK; utilitarian. Price range: $5-3,500; bestsellers: $20-100. Buys outright or on consignment; 40% commission. Requires exclusive area representation. Send resume, slides and SASE. Reports in 1 month. Artist pays shipping to shop and insurance; dealer pays shipping from shop.
Profile: Items displayed on museum-like pedestals, "given breathing room." Heaviest wholesale buying time: winter.

HOPI ARTS & CRAFTS COOPERATIVE GUILD, Box 37, Second Mesa AZ 86043. (602)734-2463. Co-Managers: Mark Lormayestewa/Michael Kabotic. Estab: 1949. Represents 280 local craftsmen. Considers basketweaving, dollmaking, jewelry, painting, pottery and weaving. Finished, one-of-a-kind and handmade production-line items OK; utilitarian and/or decorative. Price range: $5-3,000; bestsellers: $7-150. Buys outright; 40% commission. Retail price set by joint agreement. Requires exclusive area representation. Reports in 2 weeks. Dealer pays shipping from shop and insurance. Best selling time: summer. Customers ages 50-60; they buy crafts for artistic value and gifts.

MUSEUM OF NORTHERN ARIZONA, Rte. 4, Box 720, Flagstaff AZ 86001. (602)774-5211. Exhibits Coordinator: David Cross. Gift shop considers Navajo rugs, jewelry and pottery (all Indian). Price range: $1-5,000. Buys outright. Sponsors 3 annual art competitions: Junior Indian Art; Hopi Craftsmen; Navajo Craftsmen.
Special Needs: Uses graphic artists for *Plateau* magazine and exhibits.

THE PENDLETON SHOP, 407 Jordan Rd., Sedona AZ 86336. (602)282-3671. Contact: Mary Pendleton. Estab: 1958. Represents 5 craftsmen. Considers candlemaking, jewelry, leatherworking, needlecrafts, pottery, wall hangings, weavings, woodcrafting and hand-painted or embroidered clothing. Finished, one-of-a-kind and handmade production-line items OK; utilitarian and/or decorative. Price range: $2-300; bestsellers: $15-50. Buys outright or on consignment; 60% commission. Retail price set by joint agreement. Requires exclusive area representation. Write. Reports in 2 weeks.

YUMA FINE ARTS ASSOCIATION, INC., RENTAL SALES GALLERY, Box 1471, Yuma AZ 85364. (602)782-9261. Represents Arizona and some southern California craftsmen. Considers prints, cards and crafts. Price range: 75¢-$200. 33⅓% commission. Also sponsors 2 annual art competitions: Yuma area artists/craftsmen show and the Southwest Invitational. Reviews portfolios from Arizona artists throughout the year.

Arkansas

THE DULCIMER SHOPPE, Drawer E, Hwy. 14 N., Mountain View AR 72560. (501)269-8639. Contact: Lynn McSpadden. Estab: 1962. Represents 10-12 craftsmen. Considers doll-

making, dried arrangements, jewelry, pottery, shuckery, white oak baskets and woodcrafting. Finished, one-of-a-kind and handmade production-line items OK; utilitarian and/or decorative. Price range: $1-200; bestsellers: $1-125. Buys outright. Shop sets retail price, usually twice wholesale. Prefers exclusive area representation. Query. Reports in 2-3 weeks. Dealer pays shipping to shop and in-transit insurance.
Profile: "We do woodcarving where visitors can watch." Heaviest wholesale buying time: March-August. Tourist customers.

THE OZARK FOLK CENTER SALES SHOP, General Delivery, Mountain View AR 72560. (501)269-3851. Contact: Kay Blair. Estab: 1973. Represents 60 Ozark area craftsmen. Considers candlemaking, dollmaking, leatherworking, needlecrafts, pottery, quilting, wall hangings, weavings and woodcrafting. Primitive and finished, one-of-a-kind and handmade production-line items OK; utilitarian and/or decorative. Price range: 35¢-$500; bestsellers: 35¢-$20. Buys outright. Gallery sets retail price. Query with transparencies or photos. Reports in 3 weeks.
Profile: "The period we are interested in is 1820-1920 Ozark. The merchandise is displayed in period settings at times and also on well-lighted display shelves or rustic 'islands'. Located in state park." Heaviest wholesale buying time: winter; best selling time: August and October.

TRAIL OF TEARS CRAFTS CENTER, Blue Spring Rd., Eureka Springs AR 72632. Contact: W. Lowell Baker. Estab: 1972. Represents 10 local craftsmen. Considers glass art, jewelry, wall hangings and weavings. One-of-a-kind and handmade production-line items OK; utilitarian and/or decorative. Price range: $1.50-200. Buys outright. Gallery sets retail price. Call for interview. Reports in 2 weeks. Dealer pays shipping to shop and insurance. Items displayed continuously. Buys and sells most crafts in summer. Customers buy for artistic value and gifts.

WILDWOOD CARVERS, Drawer E, Hwy. 14 N., Mountain View AR 72560. (501)269-8237. Contact: Jon Thompson. Estab: 1976. Represents 15-20 craftsmen. Considers dollmaking, dried arrangements, wooden jewelry, shuckery, white oak baskets and woodcarving. Finished, one-of-a-kind and handmade production-line items OK; utilitarian and/or decorative. Price range: $1-600; bestsellers: $1-125. Buys outright. Shop sets retail price, usually twice wholesale. Prefers exclusive area representation. Query with transparencies or photos. Reports in 1 week.
Profile: "We do woodcarving where visitors can watch." Heaviest wholesale buying time: March-August. Tourist customers. Prefers Ozark craftsmen.

California

THE ARTIFACTRIE, 1329 N. Main, Walnut Creek CA 94596. (415)938-8666. Contact: Valerie Adams. Estab: 1967. Represents 2,000 craftsmen. Considers batik, candlemaking, ceramics, dollmaking, glass art, jewelry, leatherworking, needlecrafts, pottery, wall hangings, weavings and woodcrafting. Finished, one-of-a-kind and handmade production-line items OK; utilitarian and/or decorative. Price range: 10¢-$5,000; best-sellers: $3-100. Buys outright or on consignment; 40% commission. Retail price set by joint agreement. Write. Reports in 1 week. Dealer pays insurance on exhibited work.
Profile: Each craftsman's work displayed as a unit on redwood and glass fixtures. Displays rotated weekly. Heaviest wholesale buying time: fall; best selling time: holidays and summer. Customers are upper-middle class from a fairly intellectual community. They buy crafts for appreciation of handmade goods.

THE ARTIFACTRIE, 2120 Vine, Berkeley CA 94709. (415)843-9440. Contact: Valerie Adams. See The Artifactrie (Walnut Creek).

THE ARTIFACTRIE, 277 Arlington, Kensington CA 94708. (415)526-5821. Contact: Valerie Adams. See The Artifactrie (Walnut Creek).

ARTISANS' ALLEY, 9858 Garden Grove Blvd., Garden Grove CA 92644. Contact: Vivian Dearing. Represents over 150 craftsmen. Considers candles, stained glass, men's clothing items, wood toys, tapestries, weaving, metal sculpture, silkscreen, turquoise jewelry, scrimshaw, woodcarving and hand-drawn or painted stationery/greeting cards. No macrame, hydracal statuary or dried flowers. Price range: $1-2,500. Works on consignment: 35% commission. Craftsman sets retail price. Send transparencies or photos of work. "We carry an all-risk floater policy which covers virtually everything (except shoplifting)." Shipping paid by artist.

BROCKMAN GALLERY PRODUCTIONS, 4334 Degnan Blvd., Los Angeles CA 90008. (213)294-3766. Program Coordinator: Ms. Pat Johnson. Exhibits batik, ceramics, drawings,

dollmaking, jewelry, leatherworking, metalsmithing, mobiles, pottery, prints, sculpture, wall hangings, watercolors, weavings and woodcrafting; 3 weeks exposure. Maximum size: 5x7'. Paintings must be ready to hang. Art may be offered for sale. Works on consignment; 40% commission. Price range: $10-1,500; bestsellers: $15-75. Retail price set by joint agreement. Send slides or photos or call or write for interview. SASE. Gallery pays shipping from gallery and insurance for exhibited work.
Promotional Needs: Uses artists for catalogs, posters and graphic work relating to the gallery's activities. Negotiates payment.

CALIFORNIA ARTISTS AND CRAFTSMEN'S GUILD, 1131 State St., Santa Barbara CA 93101. (805)963-2424. Contact: Fran Doll. Estab: 1971. Represents 60 craftsmen. Co-op interested in consignment or booth space rental. Price range: $3-600; bestsellers: $20-100. 40% commission. Craftsman sets retail price. Requires exclusive area representation. Write. Reports in 1 week. Best selling time: summer. Customers are young college students and married couples with good incomes.

CARMEL WORK CENTER SHOP, Box 3547, Carmel by the Sea CA 93921. (408)624-6990. Contact: Wes or Fritzie Bonenberger. Estab: 1955. Represents 30 California craftsmen. Considers ceramics, glass art, pottery, wall hangings, weavings, woodcrafting and small sculpture; especially needs inexpensive hand-blown glass, raku and salt glazes. Finished, one-of-a-kind and handmade production-line items OK; utilitarian and/or decorative. Price range: $2-150; bestsellers: $5-25. Buys outright or on consignment; 40% commission. Retail price set by joint agreement. Requires exclusive area representation. Dealer pays shipping and in-transit insurance to shop.
Profile: Displays changed frequently and special shows held to introduce craftsmen and their work. Heaviest buying and selling time: summer and fall. "We try to have a large selection from many different craftsmen because the public is becoming more educated to good design and workmanship. Customers are local residents, tourists and foreign visitors."

CATHEXIS, 3927 24th St., San Francisco CA 94114. Contact: Peggy Burge. Estab: 1971. Represents 100 craftsmen from west of the Mississippi only. Considers candlemaking, ceramics, glass art, leatherworking, needlecrafts, pottery, quilting, soft sculpture, cards and stationery. Finished, handmade production-line items OK; utilitarian only. Price range: 25¢-$100; bestsellers: $2-30. Buys outright or on consignment; 33⅓% commission. Gallery sets retail price. Query with transparencies or photos. Reports in 4 weeks. Dealer pays shipping and insurance.
Profile: Items displayed in front window for 2 weeks, or given special attention in floor displays using antique furniture and plants. Heaviest wholesale buying time: fall and winter; best selling time: summer through Christmas. Customers are 20-40 year-old craftspeople, artists and students with average incomes.

COUNTERPANE, 800 San Anselmo Ave., San Anselmo CA 94960. Contact: Susan Melvin. Considers fabric hangings (no weaving), contemporary quilts and soft sculpture. Maximum size: 10x10'. Works on consignment; 35% commission. Requires exclusive area representation. Commission charged on crafts sold through gallery after exclusive representation. Retail price set by joint agreement. Craftsman pays shipping to gallery; gallery pays return shipping and insurance for exhibited work.
Special Needs: Uses artists for show announcement design. Occasionally uses freelance artists for show announcements design.

PETER CRANE ASSOCIATES, Box 561, San Clemente CA 92672. Director: Peter D. Crane. "My major interest is in original handcrafted dolls, woodcarving, weaving and toys." Also considers needlecrafts and leather. Price range: $5-900. Negotiates commission, price and insurance. Retail price set by joint agreement. Requires exclusive area representation. Send transparencies or photos. Items displayed 4 weeks minimum. "We have outlet in Laguna Beach, which is a high-traffic area."

BETH & BILL ETGEN FINE JEWELRY, 3600 Whitney Ave., Sacramento CA 95821. (916)481-3912. Contact: Bill Etgen. Estab: 1970. Represents 6 craftsmen. Considers jewelry (wax models and cut fine stones). Finished, one-of-a-kind and handmade production-line items OK; utilitarian and/or decorative. Price range: $21-1,600; bestsellers: $35-800. Buys on consignment or outright; 25% commission. Retail price set by joint agreement. Craftsmen

Kaill Fine Crafts, Alaska, is looking for unusual, but not necessarily expensive, items. Prices range from 65¢ to $2,000 but the bestsellers go for $10-80. Anne Kaill, owner of the shop, says she's especially interested in kites, musical instruments, cars, quilts, dolls and prints.

should write. Reports in 1 week. Craftsman pays shipping to shop and in-transit insurance; Etgen pays shipping from shop and insurance for exhibited works.

Profile: Previous customers ($35+) receive monthly newsletter showing latest styles and featuring certain stones and artist/designer. Items displayed 3 months. Heaviest wholesale buying time: Christmas and May. "We offer top quality for almost wholesale prices. 93% of business is customer referral." Customers, ages 25-40, are professionals with $25,000+ income; they buy jewelry for gifts and for individuality.

Seasonal Needs: Heavy need for wedding ring styles (his and hers) in November and May.

FIBERWORKS, 1940 Bonita Ave., Berkeley CA 94704. Contact: Gallery Committee. Estab: 1973. Considers experimental artwork, prints, graphics, drawings, sketches, sculpture and textile arts. The gallery is fiber-related, but not restricted to that area. Price range: $50-1,000 or more. Works on consignment; 30% commission. Craftsman sets minimum price. Send resume with slides or photos of work. Items displayed 2 weeks minimum. Mailings sent 6 times annually, with extra mailings for special shows. List includes about 9,000 names.

FLETCHER SILVERSMITHS, 12744 Ventura Blvd., Studio City CA 91604. Contact: Patrick Fletcher. "We are interested in original jewelry designs, preferably bracelets, for men and women. The designs can range from classical to avant garde." Gallery pays return shipping.

GALLERY 8, International Center, Q-018, University of California at San Diego, La Jolla CA 92093. (714)452-3732. Co-Director: Ruth Newmark. Estab: 1973. Represents over 25 craftsmen. Considers batik, ceramics, dollmaking, glass art, jewelry, leatherworking, needlecrafts, pottery, quilting, soft sculpture, wall hangings, weavings, woodcrafting and baskets. Primitive and finished, one-of-a-kind and handmade production-line items OK; utilitarian and/or decorative. Price range: $1-600; bestsellers: $15-30. Buys outright or on consignment; 33⅓% commission. Retail price set by gallery or joint agreement. Write. Reports in 2 weeks. Dealer pays shipping from shop and insurance for exhibited work.

Profile: Heaviest wholesale buying time: fall; best selling time: October-December. Primarily middle-aged, upper middle-class customers, some students and university staff; they buy crafts for artistic value or gifts.

GRAPH VISUAL, 55 Colton St., San Francisco CA 94103. Contact: Raymond Howell. Considers pottery, crafts, painting, sculpture, prints and drawings. Price range: $50-500. 40% commission. Requires exclusive area representation; charges commission on art sold in area after show. Send transparencies or photos. Shipping costs shared. Exhibited work insured.

IRIS, 1894 Solano Ave., Berkeley CA 94707. (415)525-1043. Contact: Ira or Susan Klein. Estab: 1976. Represents 120 craftsmen. Considers batik, ceramics, glass art, jewelry, leatherworking, metalsmithing, needlecrafts, pottery, wall hangings, original handmade clothing, weavings and woodcrafting. Finished, one-of-a-kind or handmade production-line items OK; utilitarian and/or decorative. Price range: 40¢-$480; bestsellers: 40¢-$20. Works on consignment; 20-40% commission. Retail price set by joint agreement. Query with color transparencies or b&w prints of work. Reports in 1 week. Accepts personally-delivered work only. Dealer insures exhibited work.
Profile: Crafts displayed 6 months maximum. Best work placed in window. Heaviest wholesale buying season: Christmas. Customers average age 32; $25,000 median income.
Special Needs: Candles, handblown stemware and ornaments.

JUBILEE GALLERY, 15024 Ventura Blvd., Sherman Oaks CA 91403. Contact: Robin Steckler. Considers ceramics, jewelry, metalsmithing, needlecraft, glass, leather and outdoor-related crafts. "We generally work on consignment till we see how the crafts sell." 35-40% commission. Retail price set by joint agreement. Send transparencies or photos of work. Artist pays shipping. Gallery pays insurance for exhibited work.

KEFFELER'S JUBILANT JEWELRY, 9 Strawflower Center, Half Moon Bay CA 94019. (415)726-4223. Contact: Boyd or Toni Keffeler. Estab: 1975. Represents 15 craftsmen. Considers candlemaking, ceramics, glass art, leatherworking, metalsmithing, pottery and woodcrafting; specialty is jewelry. Finished, one-of-a-kind or production-line items OK; utilitarian and/or decorative. Price range: $1.75-$400; bestsellers: $5-40. Works on consignment; 40% commission. Retail price set by joint agreement. Query with color transparencies or b&w prints of work, or mail artwork. Reports in 2 weeks. Artist pays shipping to shop and insurance; dealer pays shipping from shop.
Profile: Limited display area; 60-day minimum without selling. All cases and displays handcrafted by owners. "Only shop devoted to crafts in this area. Customers include a mix of local people and tourists. While we accept all crafts listed, we are more concerned to receive jewelry."

ESTHER LEWITTES DESIGN GALLERY, 8344 Melrose Ave., Los Angeles CA 90009. (213)655-7112. Contact: Esther Lewittes. Represents 12 craftsmen. Considers ceramics, enamels, glass art, metalsmithing, pottery, wall hangings, weavings and woodcrafting. Finished one-of-a-kind items OK; decorative. Price range: $15-800; bestsellers: $10-750. Buys outright or occasionally on consignment; 40% commission. Gallery sets retail price. Requires exclusive area representation. Query with transparencies or photos. Reports in 2 weeks. Artist pays shipping to shop and in-transit insurance; dealer pays shipping from shop and insurance for exhibited work. Heaviest wholesale buying time: spring and early summer. Middle-class customers; they buy crafts for artistic value and gifts.

THE LIGHT OPERA, 900 Northpoint St., #102, San Francisco CA 94109. (415)775-7665. Contact: Gwyneth Welch. Estab: 1970. Represents 50 craftsmen. Considers glass art. Finished, one-of-a-kind and handmade production-line items OK; utilitarian and/or decorative. Price range: $5-10,000; bestsellers: $50-500. Buys outright. Retail price set by joint agreement. Call for interview. Reports in 1 week. Dealer pays insurance for exhibited work; negotiates shipping and in-transit insurance. Heaviest wholesale buying time: January-July. Best selling time: September-December. Young to middle-age professional customers; they buy crafts for artistic value.

MY HOUSE GALLERY, 168 Glendale Galleria, Glendale CA 90210. (213)247-3173. Contact: Barry Axelrod. Estab: 1976. Represents 90 craftsmen. Considers all crafts. Finished, one-of-a-kind and handmade production-line items OK; utilitarian and/or decorative. Price

range: $1.25-400; bestsellers: $1.99-45. "We lease space to craftsmen." Craftsman sets retail price. Call or write. Reports in 2 weeks. Artist pays shipping to gallery and in-transit insurance.
Profile: "Each craftsman builds and stocks his own display. It is similar to a co-op, but we take all the responsibility for running it as a retail store." Best selling time: Christmas, Mother's Day and graduation.

PACIFIC BASIN TEXTILE ARTS, 1659 San Pablo Ave., Berkeley CA 94702. (415)526-9836. Contact: Director: Considers batik, soft sculpture, weavings and other fiber media; 5-6 weeks exposure. Craftsman supplies and installs any special lights, stands or other special installation accessories. Works on consignment; 25% commission. Bestsellers: $25-300. Craftsman sets retail price. Write for interview. Gallery sponsors reception.
Publicity: Exhibit is listed on the Pacific Basin calendar and on the gallery's brochure distributed in the community; press release is sent to all local papers and mailing list publications.

THE PLEBIAN, 834 Kline St., La Jolla CA 92037. (714)454-1888. Contact: David and Marji Nightingale. Estab: 1968. Represents 30 craftsmen. Considers primarily metalsmithing and contemporary jewelry; especially needs silver or gold jewelry and other functional metal items. Finished, one-of-a-kind items OK; utilitarian and/or decorative. Price range: $4-1,500; bestsellers: $20-75. Buys outright or on consignment; 30% commission. Retail price set by joint agreement. Write or query with transparencies or photos. Reports in 2 weeks. Dealer pays insurance on exhibited work.
Profile: "When we have a group of items made by 1 craftsman, we feature it separately — usually for 1-6 months — in locked, glass showcases." Buys and sells most crafts in summer and winter. Customers are 16-30 with above average incomes.

WAYNE RED-HORSE, 106-K St., Suite 1, Sacramento CA 95814. Contact: Wayne Red-Horse. Estab: 1972. Represents 10 Indian craftsmen. Considers all Indian-made crafts. Finished one-of-a-kind items OK; utilitarian and/or decorative. Price range: $1-500; bestsellers: $3-90. Buys outright or on consignment; 33 1/3% commission. Craftsman sets retail price. Write. Reports in 2 weeks. Artist pays shipping to shop and in-transit insurance; dealer pays shipping from shop and insurance for exhibited work.
Profile: Heaviest wholesale buying time: summer. "We do custom orders and repairs." Tourist customers; they buy crafts for gifts.

THE SANDALMAKERS, 50 University Ave., Los Gatos CA 95030. Contact: Peter Rundberg. "We are a custom and retail leather shop, dealing in custom-made sandals, bags, belts, wallets and the like. Only the highest quality and marketable price range will be considered." Price range: $1 key rings; $80 briefcases; $40-150, leather clothing. Send slides or b&w photos of work.

SANTA BARBARA MUSEUM OF ART SHOP, 1124 State St., Santa Barbara CA 93101. (805)963-4364. Manager: Douglas Bartoli. Considers contemporary ceramics, dollmaking, glass art, jewelry, leatherworking, metalsmithing, mobiles, needlecrafts, pottery, soft sculpture, tole paintings, wall hangings, weavings and woodcrafting. Price range: 50¢-$1,000; bestsellers: 50¢-$100. Buys outright or on consignment; 100% mark-up on consigned items. Gallery sets retail price. Requires exclusive area representation. Call or write for interview or send photos. Artist pays shipping to shop and in-transit insurance; dealer pays shipping from shop and insurance for exhibited work. Items displayed 6-8 weeks.
Special Needs: Shop uses art for membership literature, catalogs and public service TV announcements.

THE SEA, 525 N. Harbor Blvd., San Pedro CA 90731. (213)831-1694. Contact: Mr. Ponce or Mrs. Williams. Considers crafts with sea themes making use of seashells and other sea items. Artist and gallery decide how work is bought, depending on item and price. Price range: $1-100 with commission depending on item.

THE SHOP, Box 133, Amador City CA 95601. (209)267-5438. Contact: Harold Dickey. Estab: 1968. Represents 7 craftsmen. Considers pottery, weaving, wood and leather that is not tooled or stamped. Price range: $2-600; bestsellers: $4-125. Works on consignment; 40% commission. Requires exclusive area representation. Write. Reports in 1 week. Dealer usually pays shipping from shop. Negotiates in-transit insurance. Related items are segregated. Best selling time: October-April.

CYNTHIA SNOW ART GALLERY, 3255 Sacramento St., San Francisco CA 94115. Contact: Wayne K. Steele. Considers ceramics, sculpture, rugs, tapestry and glass. Prices up to $1,000. 40% commission. Send transparencies or photos. Gallery pays insurance for exhibited work. Items displayed 4 weeks minimum.

SOURCE GALLERY, 1099 Folsom St., San Francisco CA 94103. (415)621-0545. Considers acrylics, airbrush, oils, pastels, prints, sculpture, soft sculpture, wall hangings, watercolors and weavings; 6 weeks minimum exposure. Works on consignment; 50% commission. Price range: $200-2,000, paintings; $500 minimum, fiberworks; $75-350, prints. Retail price set by joint agreement. Requires exclusive area representation. "Visit gallery to see if artwork is appropriate and compatible," then, query or call for interview; if out-of-town, send resume and slides. SASE. Gallery pays insurance on exhibited work and shipping from gallery unless work is specifically requested by artist at an earlier date.

THE STUDIO, 214 W. Ridgecrest Blvd., Ridgecrest CA 93555. (714)375-7970. Contact: Barbara Battles or Allene Archibald. Estab: 1976. Represents 70+ craftsmen. Considers batik, decoupage, fabric and apple dollmaking, glass art, jewelry, needlecrafts, pottery, quilting, tole painting, wall hangings, weavings and woodcrafting. Finished, one-of-a-kind and handmade production-line items OK; utilitarian and/or decorative. Price range: $1-125; bestsellers: $1-25. Works on consignment; 34% commission. Retail price set by joint agreement. Write. Reports in 2 weeks. Artist pays shipping to shop and in-transit insurance; dealer pays insurance on exhibited work; negotiates payment for shipping from shop.
Profile: Craftsmen get prime display space on a revolving basis. Seasonal items only kept during use time. Heaviest wholesale buying time: late summer, early fall; best selling time: November-December. Customers are mostly middle to high-income women.
Special Needs: Quilted, not tied, quilts; silver jewelry; and gold rings.

THE TAMARIND TREE, 35 Miller Ave., Mill Valley CA 94941. (415)388-6066. Contact: Catherine Todhunter. Estab: 1971. Represents 50 craftsmen. Considers batik, candlemaking, ceramics, dollmaking, glass art, jewelry, leatherworking, metalsmithing, pottery, wall hangings, weavings, woodcrafting and functional sculpture. Primitive and finished, one-of-a-kind and handmade production-line items OK; utilitarian and/or decorative. Price range: 50¢-$2; bestsellers: $5-20. Buys outright or on consignment; 40% commission. Retail price set by joint agreement. Requires exclusive area representation. Write or query with transparencies or photos. Reports in 2 weeks. Negotiates payment for shipping and insurance. Best selling and wholesale buying time: fall. Customers are ages 20-40.

UPPER ECHELON, 777 Bridgeway, Sausalito CA 94965. (415)332-4664. Contact: Bette Weideman. Estab: 1961. Represents 50 craftsmen. Considers candlemaking, ceramics, glass art, jewelry, leatherworking, metalsmithing, pottery, wall hangings, weavings and woodcraftings; especially needs serigraphs, ceramic plaques and small paintings. Finished, one-of-a-kind and handmade production-line items OK; utilitarian and/or decorative. Price range: 60¢-$250; bestsellers: 60¢-$150. Buys outright or on consignment; 33 1/3% commission. Craftsman sets retail price. Requires exclusive area representation.
Profile: Heaviest wholesale buying time: March, April and September. Shop tries to provide customers with a resume on craftsmen they are buying from. Customers are mostly professionals.

WESTWOOD CERAMIC SUPPLY COMPANY GALLERY, 14400 Lomitas Ave., City of Industry CA 91744. (213)330-0631. Director: Darrel Trzeciak. Considers glass art, pottery and sculpture; especially needs ceramics. 4 weeks maximum exposure. Maximum size: 8x4'. Price range: $15-500, ceramics. Works on consignment; 20% commission. Craftsman sets retail price. Query or send slides or photos of work. SASE.

WHOLLY COW, 813 State St., Santa Barbara CA 93101. (805)964-8884. Contact: Gina Lestrade. Estab: 1976. Represents 9 craftsmen. Considers leatherworking. Finished, one-of-a-kind and handmade production-line items OK; utilitarian and/or decorative. Price range: $1-125; bestsellers: $20-60. Buys outright or on consignment; 35% commission. Retail price set by joint agreement. Query with transparencies or photos. Reports in 2 weeks. Artist pays shipping from shop; dealer pays shipping to shop and insurance.
Profile: Items displayed in groups and rearranged weekly. Heaviest wholesale buying time: spring-Christmas; best selling time: Christmas. Customers buy crafts for artistic value.

Colorado

DENVER ART MUSEUM, 100 W. 14th Avenue Pkwy., Denver CO 80204. (303)297-2793. Contact: Director of Public Relations. Considers American Indian jewelry, museum replicas and crafts. Buys outright; 40-50% commission. Price range: $1-150.

THE GOLD AND SILVERSMITHS OF VAIL, Box 385, Vail CO 81657. Contact: Dan Telleen. Considers ceramics, jewelry and metalsmithing. "Looking especially for fine earrings of original design." Price range: $15-500. 40% commission. Retail price set by joint agreement. Requires exclusive area representation. Send transparencies or photos.

TAPESTRY, 2859 E. 3rd Ave., Denver CO 80206. (303)322-2441. Contact: Carolyn Fineran. Estab: 1973. Represents 50 craftsmen. Considers fiberwork, wall hangings and weavings; especially needs sophisticated and/or humorous soft sculpture, jewelry, glass art and pottery. Finished, one-of-a-kind and handmade production-line items OK; utilitarian and/or decorative. Price range: $15-3,000; bestsellers: $20-500. Buys outright or on consignment; 40-60% commission. Retail price set by joint agreement. Requires exclusive area representation. Query with color transparencies or b&w prints. SASE. Reports in 4 weeks. Artist pays shipping to shop. Dealer pays shipping from shop and insurance for exhibited work. Shipper pays in-transit insurance.
Profile: Displays crafts 6-12 weeks with lighting. Heaviest wholesale buying time: fall through Christmas. Customers are well-educated, middle to upper class.

THE TOM THUMB GALLERY, Box 57, 200 S. Mill, Aspen CO 81611. Contact: Mary-Helen Cattell. Considers sculpture, jewelry, metalsmithing, pewter and mobiles. Also needs a production enamelist to execute designs. Buys outright.

THE UNIQUE, 21½ E. Bijou St., Colorado Springs CO 80903. (303)473-9406. Contact: Zita Miller. Estab: 1966. Represents 50 craftsmen. Considers batik, ceramics, glass art, needlecrafts, pottery, tole painting, wall hangings and weavings. Considers all media. Primitive and finished, one-of-a-kind and handmade production-line items OK; utilitarian and/or decorative. Price range: $2-300; bestsellers: $5-40. Buys outright or on consignment; 40% commission. Retail price set by joint agreement. Write or query with transparencies or photos. Reports in 1 week. Dealer pays insurance for exhibited work.
Profile: Consigns items for 90 days minimum. After that, artist may choose to leave work or have it returned. Best selling time: tourist season and Christmas.

URIAH HEEPS, Box 1362, Aspen CO 81611. Contact: Tukey Koffend. "We are always looking for new jewelry — silver preferably. Price range: $10-2,000. 33% commission. Retail price set by joint agreement. Prefers exclusive area representation. Send transparencies or photos. Dealer pays insurance for exhibited work; shipping costs shared. Openings sponsored and items displayed 6 weeks minimum.

WHICKERBILL CONTEMPORARY, 212 N. Tejon, Colorado Springs CO 80903. (303)633-0518. Contact: John Eastham. Estab: 1957. Represents 40 craftsmen. Considers candlemaking, ceramics, glass art, jewelry, pottery and woodcrafting; especially needs candleholders, banks and large pottery bowls. Finished, one-of-a-kind and handmade production-line items OK; utilitarian and/or decorative. Price range: $3-75; bestsellers: $8.95-24.50. Buys outright. Shop sets retail price. Requires exclusive area representation. Query with color transparencies or b&w prints of work. Reports in 2 weeks. Artist pays shipping to shop. Dealer pays shipping from shop and in-transit insurance.

Connecticut

ALENA JEWELRY GALLERY, 20 W. Putnam Ave., Greenwich CT 06830. (203)869-0934. Contact: Alena Zinn. Estab: 1974. Represents 10 craftsmen. Considers sterling, karat gold and fine enamel jewelry. Finished, one-of-a-kind and handmade production-line items OK. Price range: $15-2,000; bestsellers: $25-80. Buys outright; occasionally on consignment; 40% commission. Retail price set by joint agreement. Requires exclusive area representation. Query with transparencies or photos. Reports in 1 week. Dealer pays return shipping on consigned items.
Profile: Items displayed in locked cases, windows or counters, and are rotated frequently. Heaviest wholesale buying time: Christmas. Customers are fairly conservative and like well-finished, simple designs.

APPALACHIAN HOUSE, 1591 Post Rd., Fairfield CT 06430. (203)259-6149. Manager: John Potterton. Estab: 1974. Represents 300+ Appalachian craftsmen. Considers all crafts. Primitive and finished, one-of-a-kind and handmade production-line items OK; utilitarian and/or decorative. Price range: 75¢-$250; bestsellers: $2.25-15. Buys outright. Shop sets retail price. Write. Reports in 2 weeks. Artist pays in-transit insurance; dealer pays shipping and insurance for exhibited work.
Profile: Items displayed on rustic shelves and handmade wood units. Heaviest wholesale buying time: fall and spring. Best selling time: November-December. "Our retail mark-up is lower than average thanks to our volunteer staff, which keeps down overhead." Women customers age 20-55 with middle to upper-middle income.

THE ARGYLE CRAFT GALLERY, 40 Post Rd. E., West Port CT 06880. (203)226-1334. Contact: Helenita Mathias. Estab: 1975. Represents 35-50 craftsmen. Considers candlemaking, ceramics, glass art, metalsmithing, pottery, soft sculpture, wall hangings and weavings; especially needs flameware. Finished, one-of-a-kind and handmade production-line items OK; utilitarian and/or decorative. Price range: $5-300; bestsellers: $5-75. Buys outright or on consignment; 33% commission. Retail price set by joint agreement. Requires exclusive area representation. Query with transparencies or photos, or mail artwork. Reports in 2 weeks. Dealer pays all shipping and insurance for exhibited artwork. Heaviest wholesale buying time: fall and spring; best selling time: winter and summer. Affluent customers.

BITTERSWEET FARM, 777 E. Main St., Branford CT 06405. (203)488-9126. Contact: Bob Wallace. Estab: 1973. Leases space to 38 artists/craftsmen. Considers batik, glass art, jewelry, lead sculpture, leatherworking, metalsmithing, needlecrafts, painting, pottery, quilting, silk screening and woodcrafting. Studio prices: $50, 10x10'; $75-100, 200-300' square. Utilities included. Write. Reports in 2 weeks.

COLLECTION CRAFT GALLERY, Mill Lane, Farmington CT 06032. (203)677-4474. Contact: Ginger Tayntor. Considers sculpture, jewelry, metalsmithing, needlecraft (quilts), glass, leather, pewter, individualized crafts and unique toys. Price range: $1-300. Works on consignment; 33⅓% commission. Buys proven items. Requires exclusive area representation. Send transparencies or photos. Items displayed 6 weeks minimum.

CURRENT CRAFTS, 3208 Whitney Ave., Mt. Carmel CT 06518. (203)288-9868. Contact: Robert L. Evans. Estab: 1961. Represents 300 craftsmen. Considers candlemaking, glass art, jewelry, leatherworking, metalsmithing, pottery, wall hangings and woodcrafting. Finished, one-of-a-kind and handmade production-line items OK; utilitarian and/or decorative. Price range: $1-200; bestsellers: $5-50. Buys outright. Shop sets retail price. Query with transparencies or photos. Reports in 30 days. Artist pays in-transit insurance; dealer pays shipping to shop and insurance for exhibited work. Heaviest wholesale buying time: spring and summer. Best selling time: winter.

THE GALLERY SHOP, 80 Audubon St., New Haven CT 06511. (203)562-2329. Manager: Marjorie Shutkin. Estab: 1974. Represents 60 craftsmen. Considers batik, ceramics, glass art, jewelry, metalsmithing, pewter, pottery, wall hangings and weavings; especially needs leatherworking and quilting. Finished, one-of-a-kind and handmade production-line items OK; utilitarian and/or decorative. Price range: $1.75-175; bestsellers: $2-90. Buys outright or on consignment; 30% commission. Craftsman sets retail price. Write. Reports in 1 week. Dealer pays shipping from shop and insurance for exhibited work; negotiates shipping to shop and in-transit insurance. Heaviest wholesale buying time: January-May.

LUTA STUDIOS, Rte. 9A, Deep River CT 06417. (203)526-5812. Contact: Nancy Mazzoni. Estab: 1971. Represents 3-6 craftsmen. Considers all crafts. Finished, one-of-a-kind and production-line, handmade items OK; utilitarian and/or decorative. Price range: $1.50-350; bestsellers: $3.50-35. Works on consignment; 25% commission. Artist sets retail price. Write.
Profile: "Items displayed 8-12 weeks in gallery setting with spot lighting. Items moved after several weeks for optimum attention." Heaviest wholesale buying time: fall and spring. Best selling time: Christmas and summer. "High quality, well-displayed crafts; not like a hodge-podge gift shop." Customers age 25-35 with $18-35,000 income; they buy crafts for artistic value.

SOCIETY OF CONNECTICUT CRAFTSMEN, Box 37, Rte. 9A, Deep River CT 06417. (203)526-5812. Contact: Nancy Mazzoni. Estab: 1935. Represents about 250 member craftsmen. Contact SCC for membership details. Considers batik, candlemaking, ceramics, dollmaking, glass art, leatherworking, metalsmithing, mobiles, needlecrafts, pottery, sculpture, tole paintings, wall hangings, weavings and woodcrafting. Price range: $1.50-unlimited; bestsellers: $1.50-35. Takes 25% commission. Craftsman sets retail price. Reports on jury review in spring and fall in *SCC Newsletter*. Artist pays shipping and insurance.

THE WOODEN AWL, 6 Hartford Rd., Weatogue CT 06089. Contact: Frank L. Magee III. Considers ceramics, jewelry, metalsmithing, glass, leather and anything in functional art. "We buy outright from proven areas, and like to work with the artist in setting prices." Price range: $5-400. Takes 25-33% commission. Prefers exclusive area representation. Send transparencies or photos. Dealer pays insurance for exhibited work.

Florida

BOUNTY SHOP, 219 Atlantic Blvd., Atlantic Beach FL 32233. Contact: Connie McManus. Considers ceramics, sculpture, jewelry, metalsmithing, glass, leather, tie dying and batik. Price range: $5-200. Retail price set by joint agreement. Send transparencies or photos.

FORT LAUDERDALE MUSEUM OF THE ARTS GIFT SHOP, 426 E. Las Olas Blvd., Ft. Lauderdale FL 33301. (305)463-5184. Buys original art and crafts outright or on consignment; 33⅓ minimum commission. Price range: 50¢-$100 for such items as small booklets to African/pre-Columbian artifacts. Museum holds Annual Hortt Memorial Competition & Exhibition, with residents of Broward, Dade, Monroe and Palm Beach Counties invited.

GROVE HOUSE, INC., 3496 Main Hwy., Miami FL 33133. (305)444-0659. Director: Thyrza Jacocks. Estab: 1960. Represents 400 Florida craftsmen. Considers batik, ceramics, dollmaking, glass art, jewelry, metalsmithing, needlecrafts, pottery, quilting, soft sculpture, wall hangings, weavings and woodcrafting. Finished, one-of-a-kind and handmade production-line items OK. Price range: $3-1,000; bestsellers: $20-50. Works on consignment; 35% commission. Craftsman sets retail price. Query with transparencies or photos. Reports in 10 days. Dealer pays insurance for exhibited work.
Profile: Items displayed 90 days. Heaviest wholesale buying time: winter. Gallery is non-profit state artists' co-op.

JACKSONVILLE ART MUSEUM SHOP, 4160 Boulevard Center Dr., Jacksonville FL 32207. (904)398-8336. Contact: Ruth Hall. Estab: 1968. Considers most crafts; especially interested in well-made ceramic work. Primitive and finished, one-of-a-kind and handmade production-line items OK; utilitarian and/or decorative. Price range: $2.50-$75; bestsellers: $5-15. Buys outright or on consignment; 30% commission. Craftsman sets retail price. Write. Tries to report within 10 days. Dealer pays shipping from shop and insurance for exhibited work.
Profile: Best selling time: November-December. "We are a museum shop in a teaching institution and we seek items to stimulate classroom discussion."

LAMOUREUX DESIGNS, 191 NW 71st St., Miami FL 33150. Contact: E. Lamoureux. Estab: 1969. Represents 12 craftsmen. Considers crafts for mail order, stuffed toys, quilted items and patterns. Price range: $10-100; bestsellers: $25+. Buys outright. Retail price set by joint agreement. Query. Reports in 10 days.

MUSEUM OF ARTS AND SCIENCES, 1040 Museum Blvd., Daytona Beach FL 32014. (904)255-0285. Contact: Sharon Whempner. Museum offers rental gallery service, and members only exhibit every 2 years. No commission. Public relations department occasionally uses artists for catalogs and posters. Gift shop buys crafts outright or on consignment. Prices in shop range from $1-$30. No commission. Also sponsors annual festival.

ROOFTOP GALLERY, Harbor House, Key West FL 33040. Contact: Barbara Doremus. Considers ceramics, sculpture, jewelry, rugs, tapestries, leather, wood and prints. Price range: $5-500. Works on consignment; 40% commission. Retail price set by joint agreement. Requires exclusive area representation. No commission charged on crafts sold in area after exclusive representation. Send transparencies or photos.

Georgia

MARK OF THE POTTER, INC., Rte. 3, Clarkesville GA 30523. (404)947-3440. Contact: Glen or John LaRowe. Estab: 1968. Represents 30-40 craftsmen. Considers glass art, jewelry, pottery, some wall hangings, weavings and woodcrafting. Finished, one-of-a-kind and handmade production-line items OK; utilitarian and/or decorative. Price range: $2-300; bestsellers: $2-30. Buys outright. Retail price set by craftsman or joint agreement. Requires exclusive area representation. Query with transparencies or photos. Reports in 3 weeks. Dealer pays shipping from shop. Heaviest wholesale buying time: spring and late summer. Shop located in converted grist mill.

WESTVILLE HISTORIC HANDICRAFTS, INC., Box 1850, Lumpkin GA 31815. Contact: Ron Slusarchuk. Considers ceramics, woodwork, metalsmithing, graphics, glass, needlecrafts and leather. "I am interested only in traditional items, particularly those patterned after mid-19th century American — rural or primitive." Price range: $5-150. 30% commission. Items displayed 6 weeks minimum.

Hawaii

FOLLOWING SEA, 1441 Kapiolani Blvd., Honolulu HI 96814. Contact: Michael Gibson. Represents about 250 craftsmen from 35 states. Considers ceramics, jewelry, metal, glass, leather, batik, wood and weaving. Price range: $1-1,500. Buys mostly outright. 35-50% commission. Craftsman sets retail price. Send transparencies or photos. Gallery pays shipping. From early spring through fall, features 1-man and group shows. Craftsmen juried year-round and selected works are offered for display and sale through 4-week show periods. Show schedule available. "We are endeavoring to develop one of the finest representations of contemporary American craftsmanship in the country, and a truly valid representation of each craft medium and each area of the country."

Illinois

THE ARTISAN SHOP, 1515 Sheridan Rd., Plaza del Lago, Wilmette IL 60091. (312)251-3775. Contact: Lila Goddard. Estab: 1968. Represents 350 craftsmen. Considers batik, ceramics, glass art, jewelry, quilting, soft sculpture, wall hangings and weavings. Finished, one-of-a-kind and handmade production-line items OK; utilitarian and/or decorative. Price range: $5-1,000; bestsellers: $20-65. Buys outright or on consignment. 40% commission. Retail price set by joint agreement. Write or query with transparencies or photos. Reports in 15-30 days. Negotiates payment for shipping. Dealer pays insurance for exhibited work. Heaviest wholesale buying time: March-October.

THE CLAY PEOPLE, 3345 N. Halsted, Chicago IL 60657. Contact: Bruce Jacobson or Sam Burns. Considers ceramics and sculpture. Price range: $3-1,000. Works on consignment; 30% commission. Craftsman sets retail price. Send slides or photos. Items displayed 4 weeks minimum.

THE COMSTOCK LODE, 450 Duane St., Glen Ellyn IL 60137. (312)858-3230. Contact: Jean Weliver. Estab: 1974. Represents 60 craftsmen. Considers jewelry: rings, stud earrings, bracelets and pendants. Finished one-of-a-kind items OK. Price range: $2-400; bestsellers: $10-40. Works mostly on consignment; some outright purchases; 25% commission. Retail price set by joint agreement. Query with transparencies or photos. Reports in 1 week. Dealer pays shipping from shop. Half of artist's price is insured by shop.
Profile: Items displayed 3 months minimum. Best selling time: winter and spring.

CREATIVELY YOURS STUDIO, 1313 E. State St., Rockford IL 61108. (815)962-1313. Buyer: Liz Hill. Estab: 1974. Represents 100+ craftsmen. Considers candlemaking, ceramics, glass art, jewelry, leatherworking, macrame, metalsmithing, needlecrafts, pottery, quilting, tole painting, wall hangings, weavings and woodcrafting. Finished, one-of-a-kind and handmade production-line items OK; utilitarian and/or decorative. Price range: $3-250; bestsellers: $3-50. Works on consignment; 40% commission. Retail price set by joint agreement. Prefers exclusive area representation. Write or send transparencies or photos. Reports in 3 weeks. Artist pays shipping to shop and insurance; negotiates shipping from shop.
Profile: Items displayed 3 months maximum, unless prior agreement arranged. Heaviest wholesale buying time: fall-Christmas. Customers are women with middle to upper-middle-class incomes; they buy crafts for artistic value and gifts.

D. DEAN DYE CO. (formerly Dyeco.), 1 Pines Plaza, Oregon IL 61061. (815)732-2411. Contact: D. Dean Dye. Estab: 1961. Considers candlemaking, ceramics, decoupage, dollmaking, glass art, jewelry, leatherworking, metalsmithing, needlecrafts, pottery, quilting, soft sculpture, tole painting, wall hangings, weavings and woodcrafting. Primitive and finished, one-of-a-kind and handmade production-line items OK; utilitarian and/or decorative. Price range: $3-200; bestsellers: $5-20. Buys outright. Gallery sets retail price. Mail artwork. Reports in 2 weeks. Dealer pays shipping and insurance for exhibited work. Customers average age 35 with average income $16,000.

GIRAFFE, 212 W. Green, Urbana IL 61801. (217)344-7802. Contact: William Makris. Estab: 1970. Represents 10 craftsmen. Considers candlemaking, jewelry, leatherworking and pottery. Finished, one-of-a-kind and handmade production-line items OK; utilitarian and/or decorative. Price range: $2-140; bestsellers: $10-50. Buys outright. Seller sets retail price. Requires exclusive area representation. Write. Reports in 2 weeks. Dealer pays shipping from shop. Heaviest wholesale buying time: fall; best selling time: August-December. Customers are college students; they buy crafts for artistic value.

MINDSCAPE GALLERY AND STUDIO, INC., 1521 Sherman Ave., Evanston IL 60201. (312)864-2660. Director: Ron Isaacson. Estab: 1974. Represents 200 designer/craftsmen. Considers batik, ceramics, glass art, jewelry, leatherworking, pottery, soft sculpture, wall hangings, weavings and woodcrafting. Finished one-of-a-kind items only; utilitarian and/or decorative. Price range: $5-2,000; bestsellers: $25-150. Works mainly on consignment; 40% commission. Retail price set by joint agreement. Requires exclusive area representation. Query with resume and slides. Artist pays shipping; dealer pays insurance for exhibited work; artist and dealer pay in-transit insurance.
Profile: Artist's item(s) gets its own display area. Heaviest wholesale buying time: fall. Juried shop with national coverage on special shows. Upper-middle to upper-class customers; they buy crafts for artistic value.

PRAIRIE HOUSE, 213 S. 6th, Springfield IL 62701. (217)544-2094. Contact: Edith Myers. Considers only "superior crafts . . . no 'craftsy' types." Price range: $5-1,000. Buys production-line items outright. Works on consignment with one-of-a-kind items; 40% commission. Craftsman sets retail price. Requires exclusive Springfield representation. Shop pays return shipping and insurance for exhibited work.

THE RED OAK, Bishop Hill IL 61419. (309)927-3539. Contact: Jan Arter. Estab: 1970. Represents 75 craftsmen. Considers decoupage, dollmaking, jewelry, leatherworking, metalsmithing, needlecrafts, pottery, quilting, tole painting, wall hangings, weaving and woodcrafting. Primitive and finished, one-of-a-kind and handmade production-line items OK; utilitarian and/or decorative. Price range: 75¢-$150; bestsellers: $5-30. Buys outright or on consignment; 34% commission. Retail price set by joint agreement. Requires exclusive area representation. Query with transparencies or photos. Reports in 1 week. Dealer pays shipping from shop and insurance for exhibited work. Best selling time: Christmas. Shop is in state park with tourist customers.

THE SIDE STREET, 434 Franklin St., Waukegan IL 60085. (312)623-5155. Contact: Arva L. Wallace. Estab: 1971. Represents 225-250 craftsmen. Senior citizen craftsmen especially welcome. Considers all crafts; especially needs pottery, crewel pillows and crafts for use by men and boys. One-of-a-kind, primitive and finished items OK; utilitarian and/or decorative. Price range: 50¢-$210; bestsellers: $2-25. Works on consignment; 40% commission. Craftsman sets retail price. Requires exclusive area representation. Write or call. Reports in 1 week. Dealer pays shipping from shop.
Profile: Shop located in neighborhood of antique stores. Best selling time: October-December and April-May. Middle-income customers; they buy crafts for gifts.

SUSIE SELLS CRAFTS, 330 W. State St., Sycamore IL 60178. (815)895-3331. Contact: Sue Sells. Estab: 1970. Represents 10 craftsmen. Considers all crafts. Primitive or finished, one-of-a-kind and handmade production-line items OK; utilitarian and/or decorative. Price range: 50¢-$80. Buys outright or on consignment; 50% commission. Retail price set by joint agreement. Query with color transparencies or b&w photos. Reports in 1 week. Dealer pays shipping to shop.

WEAVING WORKSHOP, 3352 N. Halsted, Chicago IL 60657. (312)929-5776. Contact: Barbara diMauro. Estab: 1970. Represents 10 craftsmen. Considers glass art, leatherwork, rugs and tapestries; especially needs utilitarian crafts. Finished, one-of-a-kind items OK; utilitarian

Advertise Your Work Through Labels

The most *inexpensive* form of advertising for the craftsman is the label attached to his work.

Design your label so it is distinctive and attractive, and choose a style that agrees with your work both in appearance and quality. Let the copy tell your story and reflect your personality, but be concise. Include what is most interesting and unique about you, your craft and your materials.

Recall the questions customers frequently ask about your work and answer them on the label. Impress them with the quality and value of your craft, but don't make exaggerated claims. And finally, add an appropriate design to enhance the text.

Fabric labels, which can be sewn in an inconspicuous place, should be used for soft items. Use a small card or folder of heavy paper for all other pieces. The latter can be attached to your work by string or glue. First timers at labeling may want to try silkscreening their cards or drawing them individually. But, once you begin selling many items, it's best to have the labels printed professionally.

For added benefits, plan your label to double as your business card. Add your phone number and address if you want customers to contact you directly; but place these so they can be cut off if the shop manager doesn't want to have this information on the label.

—*Loretta Holz, author of* How to Sell Your Art and Crafts

Penny's owls combine the art of nature with the art of man. As in nature, no piece is ever duplicated and each is the artist's rendition of an authentic specie from around the world. The owls of North America are favored, with the Snowy being a striking specialty.

Stones are selected along the New England coast with great attention given their shape, so when complete the very life and breath of the owl is captured. Driftwood is collected from the New Jersey shore for an appropriate perch. A final touch of lichen, gathered atop the Adirondack Mountains, is often added to further enhance the realism and overall design.

Each piece is then signed and labeled as to specie. Some say, if you listen very carefully, you may even hear a faint whoo... But only at night!

Owls created by Penny Preuss

Photo courtesy of Charles Scribner's Sons

A label attached to your work says it is a special and personal gift— *not* one made by machine, but by a person who cares enough about his work to put his name on it.

and/or decorative. Price range: $5-1,000; bestsellers: $5-150. Works on consignment; 25% commission. Retail price set by joint agreement. Write. Reports in 3 weeks. Dealer pays shipping from shop and insurance for exhibited work.
Profile: Heaviest wholesale buying time: fall. Customers, ages 25-40, buy crafts for unusual gifts.

Indiana

ARROWCRAFT SHOP, Box 567, Parkway, Gatlinburg IN 37738. (615)436-4604. Contact: Caroline Riddle. Estab: 1925. Represents 50 Appalachian craftsmen. Considers jewelry, pottery and woodcrafting; especially needs off-loom weavings and small batik or woven wall hangings. Finished, one-of-a-kind and handmade production-line items OK; utilitarian and/or decorative. Price range: $5-100; bestsellers: $10-15. Buys outright. Craftsman sets retail price; occasionally shop does. Prefers exclusive area representation. "Call on shop so we can see your work." Reports in 2 weeks. Artist pays shipping to shop (unless ordered by shop) and in-transit insurance. Heaviest wholesale buying time: spring and summer.

COMMON PLACE, 302 Washington St., Columbus IN 47201. Contact: Peggy Leach. Estab: 1974. Represents 175 craftsmen. Finished one-of-a-kind items OK. Price range: 75¢-$200; bestsellers: $2-40. Works on consignment; 30% commission. Retail price set by joint agreement. Write. Reports in 2 weeks. Dealer pays insurance for exhibited work.
Profile: Items displayed in museum-type plastic cubes for 90 days. Best selling time: September-December. Items in the shop may be viewed 24 hours a day. Shop also serves as a mini-museum; it is non-profit and all income supports community projects. Customers buy crafts for artistic value, to use as gifts or to support artists and other community projects.

FLOYD COUNTY MUSEUM, 201 E. Spring St., New Albany IN 47150. (812)944-7336. Contact: Carol Tobe. Estab: 1971. Represents 10 craftsmen. Considers ceramics, jewelry and some textiles. Works on consignment; 25% commission. Craftsman sets retail price. Call or write.

GOURLEY'S OLDE SHOPPE, 2242 Cragmont, Madison IN 47250. (812)273-1697. Contact: Helen Gourley. Estab: 1968. Represents 20 local craftsmen. Especially needs weavings, wooden items and dolls. Finished, one-of-a-kind and handmade production-line items OK; utilitarian and/or decorative. Price range: $1-50; bestsellers: $10. Works on consignment; 20% commission. Craftsman sets retail price. Requires exclusive area representation. Write. Reports in 2 weeks.
Profile: Items displayed 3 months. Best selling time: summer. Shop has antiques and displays many old-time skills. Customers buy crafts for their usefulness.

NICHOLS ASSOCIATES, INC., 402 N. Calvert, Muncie IN 47303. (317)284-1878. Contact: Alice W. Nichols. Considers ceramics and sculpture. Price range: $2-100. Buys outright or on consignment; 33½% commission on consignment; 50% on purchase. Artist usually sets price. Dealer pays shipping costs.

Iowa

CORNERHOUSE GALLERY AND FRAME, 2753 1st Ave. SE, Cedar Rapids IA 52402. (319)365-4348. Director: Janelle McClain. Estab: 1976. Represents 50 craftsmen. Considers glass art, jewelry, pottery and wall hangings. Finished, one-of-a-kind and handmade production-line items OK; utilitarian and/or decorative. Price range: $3-150; bestsellers: $5-25. Buys outright or on consignment; 35% commission. Retail price set by joint agreement. Requires exclusive area representation. Query with color transparencies or b&w prints of work. Reports in 2 weeks. Dealer pays shipping from shop and insurance on exhibited work.
Profile: "Display is in a manner most complimentary to craft, with enough space to give it individual attention." Maximum display time: 6 months. Heaviest wholesale buying time: fall; best selling time: fall-Christmas. "Located in restored, turn-of-the-century house, we are the only gallery of our kind in a town of 140,000 (in well-to-do, upper-middle-class section)." Customers, ages 20-55, interested in the arts.

THE OCTAGON ART CENTER SHOP, 232½ Main St., Ames IA 50010. (515)232-5331. Contact: Gloria Mutchmor. Considers ceramics, jewelry, needlecrafts, glass, leather, tie dye, batik, wood and toys. Price range: 50¢-$150. Buys outright or on consignment; 30% commission. Craftsman sets retail price. "We primarily feature local and area artists' work, but we also actively seek quality handcrafts from other parts of the country."

Kansas

CRAFTS INCREDIBLE, INC., 7217 Mission Rd., Prairie Village KS 66208. (913)362-9430. Contact: Irene Marsh, or Claude or Donna Adam. Estab: 1967. Represents 150 craftsmen. Considers batik, candlemaking, ceramics, dollmaking, glass art, enameling, jewelry, leatherworking, metalsmithing, needlecrafts, pottery, quilting, soft sculpture, tole painting, wall hangings, weavings and woodcrafting. Finished, one-of-a-kind and handmade production-line items OK; utilitarian and/or decorative. Price range: 15¢-$650; bestsellers: $2.50-20. Buys outright or on consignment; 40% commission. Retail price set by gallery on outright purchases; by craftsman on consignments. Requires exclusive area representation. Query with color transparencies or b&w prints of work. Reports in 2 weeks (exception: 4 weeks during Christmas peak season). Shipping to shop paid by joint agreement; artist pays in-transit insurance; dealer pays shipping from shop and insurance on exhibited work.
Profile: Stock rotated in group displays. No time limit on display duration, but 4-month trial period following initial entry to shop. Heaviest wholesale buying time: autumn. Customers are mostly 35-year-old upper-middle-class women; they buy crafts for home decor and for gifts.
Special Needs: Nonwooden items for children, Christmas-related work and small sculptures in any medium.

SIGN OF THE ACORN, 4816 E. Douglas, Wichita KS 67208. Contact: Mary Leedom or Mary Ann Ranney. Considers ceramics, sculpture, glass, weavings and wall hangings. Price range: $5-1,200. 35% commission. Craftsman sets retail price. Requires exclusive area representation. Charges commission on crafts sold in area after exclusive representation. Gallery pays shipping to craftsman and insurance for exhibited work. Items displayed 4 weeks minimum.

Kentucky

BEREA COLLEGE STUDENT CRAFT INDUSTRIES, CPO 778, Log House Sales Room, Berea KY 40403. Contact: Earl McCreary. Considers ceramics, sculpture, jewelry, metalsmithing, rugs, tapestries and leatherwork. Price range: $1-2,900 with retail price set by joint agreement. Exclusive representation in area required. "We buy outright at 50% off listed retail. Although the majority of our purchases are from artists and craftsmen within the Appalachian region, we do purchase from outside the region."

COFFEETREES GALLERY & GIFT SHOP, 416 W. Walnut St., Louisville KY 40202. (502)587-1976. Contact: Rod Beck. Estab: 1973. Represents 200+ Kentucky craftsmen. Considers batik, candlemaking, dollmaking, jewelry, leatherworking, hand-forged iron, pewter work, pottery, quilting, soft sculpture, wall hangings, weavings, woodcrafting and wooden toys. Finished, one-of-a-kind and handmade production-line items OK; utilitarian and/or decorative. Price range: 50¢-$2,500; bestsellers: $5-40. Buys outright or on consignment; 40% commission. Retail price set by joint agreement. Prefers exclusive area representation. Write. Dealer pays shipping from shop and insurance on exhibited work.

DOWNSTAIRS DOWNTOWN, 224½ W. Walnut St., Louisville KY 40202. (502)583-6202. Manager: Joann Ryan. Estab: 1973. Represents 50 craftsmen. Considers batik, oils, acrylics, candlemaking, dollmaking, glass art, jewelry, leatherworking, metalsmithing, pottery, quilting, soft sculpture, wall hangings, weavings and woodcrafting. Finished, one-of-a-kind and production-line, handmade items OK; utilitarian and/or decorative. Price range: $2.30-500; bestsellers: $2.30-150. Works on consignment; 40% commission. Craftsman sets retail price. Write. Reports in 3 weeks. Dealer pays return shipping and insurance for exhibited work.
Profile: "Crafts remain in shop until sold, unless it's more than 1 year and hasn't moved." Best selling time: Christmas and May (Derby time). "High quality shop with unusual entrance; more of a gallery atmosphere than a craft shop." Customers age 18-55 with $15,000+ income; they buy crafts for artistic value, for gifts or for originality.

EMERGENCY WORKSHOP, Box 8, Barbourville KY 40906. (606)546-3152. Contact: Liz Hollinde. Estab: 1966. Represents 40 Knox County craftsmen. Considers dollmaking, needlecrafts, quilting and woodcrafting. One-of-a-kind, primitive and finished items OK; utilitarian and/or decorative. Bestsellers: 75¢-$60. Shop gives cash advances to people needing emergency funds who are then expected to produce crafts to repay debt. Dealer pays insurance for exhibited work. Heaviest wholesale buying time: winter and spring. Customers are middle-income people who buy crafts for artistic value and to help the poor.

OWENSBORO AREA MUSEUM, 2829 S. Griffith Ave., Owensboro KY 42301. (502)684-8548. Director: Joe Ford. Estab: 1966. Considers all crafts with a natural science theme. Price range: 25¢-$150; bestsellers: $1-5. Buys outright or on consignment; 20% commission. Craftsman sets retail price. Query. Reports in 10 days.

TWIG ART GALLERY, Railroad St., Midway KY 40347. (606)846-4884. Contact: Enzina Mastrippolito. Estab: 1973. Represents 80 craftsmen. Considers batik, candlemaking, ceramics, dollmaking, pottery and soft sculpture. Primitive and finished, one-of-a-kind and handmade production-line items OK; utilitarian and/or decorative. Price range: $1.50-36; bestsellers: $1.50-7. Buys outright or on consignment; 33-1/3% commission. Retail price set by joint agreement. Write. Reports in 2 weeks. Dealer pays shipping from shop and insurance for exhibited work.
Profile: Items displayed 3-6 months. Heaviest wholesale buying time: spring and fall; best selling time: summer and winter. "This is the only gallery in central Kentucky besides the Guild Gallery to feature original contemporary crafts."

Maine

EASTERN MAINE CRAFTS CO-OP INC., Box 22, Steuben ME 04680. (207)546-2269. Contact: Peter Weil. Estab: 1973. Represents 11 Hancock and Washington counties craftsmen. Write for membership information. Considers high-quality batik, ceramics, furniture, glass art, jewelry, leatherworking, metalsmithing, pewter, pottery, soft sculpture, wall hangings, weavings and woodcrafting. Price range: $3-150; bestsellers: $5-45. For special exhibits, works on consignment; 40% commission. Craftsman sets retail price. Dealer pays insurance for exhibited work.

Profile: Member items displayed constantly; special exhibit items displayed 2-3 weeks in central location of gallery. Best selling time: June-October. Customers are tourists and summer residents; they buy crafts for artistic value.

THE ISLAND STORE, Spruce Head Island ME 04859. (207)594-7475. Contact: Erika Pilver. Estab: 1972. Represents 12-24 (prefers Maine) craftsmen. Considers candlemaking, decoupage, glass art, jewelry, leatherworking, metalsmithing and woodcrafting. Finished, handmade production-line items OK; utilitarian and/or decorative. Price range: 50¢-$125; bestsellers: 50¢-$5. Buys outright. Craftsman sets retail price. Write. Reports in 1 week in summer; 4 weeks+ in winter. Dealer pays shipping from shop and insurance for exhibited work.
Profile: Displays changed twice a season. Heaviest wholesale buying time: early spring; best selling time: July-September.

THE LUBEC CRAFTS COUNCIL, INC., The Wharf Shop, Water St., Lubec ME 04652. (207)733-4701. Contact: Robert O. Voight. Estab: 1970. Represents 30 craftsmen. Considers candlemaking, glass art, jewelry, leatherworking, metalsmithing, pottery, wall hangings, weavings and woodcrafting. Finished, one-of-a-kind items OK; utilitarian and/or decorative. Price range: $2-300; bestsellers: $5-25. Buys outright; 20% commission. Retail price set by joint agreement. Write. Reports in 4 weeks. Dealer pays shipping from shop and insurance for exhibited artwork. Best selling time: summer.

GEORGE MARSHALL STORE, 140 Lindsay Rd., York ME 03909. (207)363-4974. Director: Rachel Grieg. Estab: 1967. Represents 100 New England craftsmen. Considers batik, candlemaking, ceramics, decoupage, dollmaking, glass art, jewelry, leatherworking, metalsmithing, needlecrafts, pottery, quilting, soft sculpture, tole painting, wall hangings, weavings and woodcrafting; especially needs silk-screened notes and prints, boat and ship models, puzzles, quilts and unscented candles. Finished, one-of-a-kind and handmade production-line items OK; utilitarian and/or decorative. Price range: $2-500; bestsellers: $3-20. Works on consignment; 33 1/3% commission. Retail price set by joint agreement. Requires exclusive area representation. Query with transparencies or photos. Reports in 1 week. Dealer pays shipping from shop and insurance on exhibited work. Heaviest wholesale buying time: April; best selling time: summer and Christmas. Customers are well-to-do summer residents and tourists who buy crafts for their artistic value and as gifts.

NO TRUMPETS—NO DRUMS, Perkin's Cove, Ogunquit ME 03907 (winter address: 5 Ledge Rd., Ogunquit ME 03907). Contact: Paul W. Hagen. Considers ceramics, jewelry, metalsmithing, glass and leather. Price range: $5-150. 33 1/3% commission. Craftsman sets retail price. Though exclusive representation not required, commission charged on crafts sold in area after display. Send transparencies or photos. Items displayed 6 weeks minimum.

PLUM DANDY, RFD #2, Box 50, Wells ME 04090. (207)646-9093. Contact: Linda Haydock. Estab: 1974. Considers batik, basketweaving, candlemaking, ceramics, Christmas items, dollmaking, fiberwork, glass art, jewelry, metalsmithing, needlecrafts, silkscreening and soft sculpture; especially needs stoneware pottery with no wheel rings. "We need a potter to provide dinnerware sets and customer special orders within 6-8 weeks." Finished, one-of-a-kind and handmade production-line items OK; utilitarian and/or decorative. Price range: 15¢-$175; bestsellers: 50¢-$38. Buys outright or occasionally on consignment; 30% commission. Shop sets retail price. Requires exclusive area representation in York County. Query with transparencies or photos, price list and SASE. "We return items which don't meet our standards." Reports in 1 week (longer in July-August). Dealer pays insurance for exhibited work; negotiates payment for shipping and in-transit insurance.
Profile: Items displayed maximum 6 months (consignment). Heaviest wholesale buying time: late spring; best selling time: July-September. Shop offers largest wall hangings selection from northern Boston to Portland. Customers ages 25-50 with upper-lower to middle incomes, interested in home decoration and plants.

THE SEA CRAFTERS, Ocean Ave., Kennebunkport ME 04046. (207)967-2059. Contact: W.J. Berey. Estab: 1966. Represents 25 craftsmen. Considers ceramics, decoupage, dollmaking, glass art, jewelry, metalsmithing and woodcrafting with nautical themes. Finished, one-of-a-kind and handmade production-line items OK; utilitarian and/or decorative. Price range: $1-395; bestsellers: $15-75. Buys outright or on consignment; 33-1/3% commission. Retail price set by joint agreement. Requires exclusive area representation. Write or query with

transparencies or photos. Reports in 2 weeks. Dealer pays shipping and insurance.
Profile: New items are featured in high-traffic location and in window. Heaviest wholesale buying time: spring; best selling time: summer. "Shop is exclusively nautical, featuring traditional Early American or Colonial-type merchandise in appropriate setting of a 1785 ship's chandlery." Customers are tourists of above average education and income.

STRONG CRAFT GALLERY, Bar Harbor Rd., Ellsworth ME 04605. (207)667-2595. Contact: Roslyn Strong. Estab: 1970. Represents 150 craftsmen. Considers glass art, jewelry, metalsmithing, pottery, soft sculpture, wall hangings, weavings and woodcrafting; especially needs unusual, simple earrings, bracelets, pendants and metal and glass items at modest prices. Finished, one-of-a-kind and handmade production-line items OK; utilitarian and/or decorative. Price range: $2-500; bestsellers: $4-50. Buys outright or on consignment; 34% commission. Gallery sets retail price. Requires exclusive area representation. Write. Reports in 3 weeks. Dealer pays shipping to shop and insurance for exhibited work.
Profile: Displays are changed constantly. Heaviest wholesale buying time: spring; best selling time: summer. Customers are visitors to Acadia National Park and are interested in simple, well-made work.

WILEY'S CORNER GIFT & GALLERY, Rte. 131, St. George ME 04857. Contact: Dennis M. Tracy. Considers metal sculpture, pottery, porcelain, ceramic sculpture, rugs, blown glass and jewelry.

Maryland

APPALACHIANA, INC., 10400 Old Georgetown Rd., Bethesda MD 20014. (301)530-6770. Contact: Joan A. Farrell or Anne S. Powell. Considers ceramics, jewelry, wood, fiber, metal and prints. Price range: $2-200. Negotiates price. Buys general merchandise outright; 50% discount. Works on consignment for exhibitions; 40% commission. Send transparenies or photos. Dealer pays shipping and insurance.

APPALACHIANA, INC., 5 N. Harrison St., Easton MD 21601. (See Appalachiana, Bethesda.) Write to Bethesda shop.

CALICO CAT, 2137 Gwynn Oak Ave., Baltimore MD 21207. (301)944-2450. Contact: Bruni Obriecht. Estab: 1968. Represents 250 craftsmen. Considers candlemaking, dollmaking, glass art, jewelry, needlecrafts, pottery, quilting, tole painting and woodcrafting. Finished handmade production-line items OK; utilitarian. Price range: $1-350; bestsellers: $5-20. Buys outright or on consignment; 30% commission. Craftsman sets retail price. Reports in 2 weeks. Dealer pays shipping and insurance for exhibited work.
Profile: Consigned items displayed 6 weeks maximum. Heaviest wholesale buying time: fall. Women customers; they buy crafts for gifts.

THE MUSEUM SHOP, Baltimore Museum of Art, Art Museum Dr., Baltimore MD 21218. (301)396-6338. Considers batik, calligraphy, candlemaking, ceramics, dollmaking, glass art, jewelry, metalsmithing, mobiles, needlecrafts, pottery, soft sculpture, tole painting, wall hangings, weavings, woodcrafting and toys. Price range: $3.50-200; bestsellers: $1-25. Buys outright or on consignment; 35-65% commission. Retail price set by joint agreement. Requires exclusive area representation. Query with transparencies or photos. Items displayed 1 month minimum.

NOSTALGIA ET CETERA GALLERIES LTD., Stevenson Village Center, Stevenson MD 21153. Contact: Marvin or Leslie Wies. Considers ceramics, jewelry, metalsmithing, glass, tapestries, leather, wood, rugs, batik and tie dyeing. Prices are $5+. Buys outright or on consignment; 40% commission; 50% mark-up on outright purchases. Retail price set by joint agreement. Requires exclusive Baltimore area representation. Charges commission on crafts sold in area after show. Send transparencies or photos. Shipping costs shared. Items displayed 4 weeks minimum.

THOUGHT GALLERY, 76 East St., Annapolis MD 21401. Director: Hal McWhinnie. Estab: 1972. Represents 10 local craftsmen. Considers batik, ceramics, prints, drawings, jewelry, leatherworking, metalsmithing, needlecrafts, quilting, wall hangings and weavings; especially needs glass art and pottery. Finished one-of-a-kind items OK; utilitarian and/or decorative. Price range: $2-100; bestsellers: $2-10. Works on consignment and co-op; 25% commission.

Craftsman sets retail price. Write. Reports in 2 weeks. Dealer pays shipping from shop.
Profile: Members are professors and students from Virginia and Maryland schools and receive a show in the windows each year. Best selling time: fall. Customers are college-age.

THE TOMLINSON CRAFT COLLECTION, 711 W. 40th St., Baltimore MD 21211. (301)338-1560 or 1555. Director: Virginia Tomlinson. Estab: 1972. Represents 300 craftsmen. Considers batik, candles, ceramics, glass art, jewelry, leatherworking, metalsmithing, pottery, quilting, soft sculpture, wall hangings, weavings and woodcrafting. Finished, one-of-a-kind and handmade production-line items OK; utilitarian and/or decorative. Price range: $2-500; bestsellers: $2-25 and $30-75. Buys outright (50% commission) or on consignment (33 1/3% commission). "I'm trying to reduce the amount of consignment items (too much bookkeeping), but will introduce new or one-of-a-kind items that way." Craftsman sets retail price. Write or call for interview to show crafts. Reports in 1 week (if out-of-town it could be longer). Payment for shipping and in-transit insurance arranged; dealer pays insurance on exhibited work.
Profile: Heaviest wholesale buying time: summer and February; best selling time: November-December and April-May. "Customers are mainly city people, so I have found that large country-type pottery is slower moving than in other places. We are near Johns Hopkins University and draw from there also."

Massachusetts

ABRAHAM ARTS AND CRAFTS, 348 Boston Post Rd., Sudbury MA 01776. (617)443-6362. Contact: Ted Davison. Considers sculpture, jewelry, metalsmithing, glass and leather; 6 weeks minimum exposure. Price range: $1-300. Buys outright or on consignment; 30% commission. Exhibited work insured.

AYN'S SHUTTLE SHOP, Lake Ave., Oak Bluffs-Martha's Vineyard Island MA 02557. (617)693-0134. Contact: Ayn Chase. Estab: 1955. Represents 20-30 craftsmen. Considers batik, dollmaking, glass art, jewelry, leatherworking, metalsmithing, needlecrafts, pottery, wall hangings, weavings, woodcrafting and other current crafts. Finished handmade production-line items OK; utilitarian and/or decorative. Price range: 65¢-$75; bestsellers: $3-10 and $1.25-1.50. Works on consignment; 25% commission. Retail price set by craftsman or joint agreement. Write with color photos of work. Reports in 2 weeks. Dealer pays insurance on exhibited work. Artist receives payment for shoplifted items.
Profile: Display changed weekly on rotation basis. Heaviest wholesale buying season: spring-summer. "Only shop in area that sells only handcrafted items."
Special Needs: Enamelware, cards (notes), woodenware, buttons in any medium and items in new media. No weaving, macrame or lampshades.

THE GLASS EYE, Eastham Village Green, Rte. 6, North Eastham MA 02651. (617)255-5044. Contact: John Knight. Estab: 1971. Represents 20-24 craftsmen. Considers beadwork, enamels, glass art, jewelry, metalsmithing, pottery, scrimshaw, wall hangings, weavings and woodcrafting. Finished, one-of-a-kind and handmade production-line items OK; utilitarian and/or decorative. Price range: $1-300; bestsellers: $4-75. Buys outright. Craftsman sets retail price, "depending on wholesale price." Requires exclusive North Eastham/Eastham/Orleans/Well Fleet representation. Mail artwork. Reports in 30 days maximum. Dealer pays shipping.
Profile: Heaviest wholesale buying time: late spring; best selling time: July-December. "Our help is totally familiar with craft items and creators. Most of our customers are regulars."

THE GOLDSMITH, 5 Edgell Rd., Framingham MA 01701. (617)879-3996. Manager: Ann Frey. Estab: 1972. Represents 200 craftsmen. Considers batik, candlemaking, leatherworking, metalsmithing, pottery and woodcrafting; especially needs jewelry. Handmade production-line, primitive and finished items OK; utilitarian and/or decorative. Price range: $1-100; bestsellers: $5-25. Buys outright. Gallery sets retail price. Requires exclusive area representation. Write. Reports in 2 weeks. Gallery pays shipping to shop and insurance.
Profile: Heaviest wholesale buying time: fall. Customers are college girls and upper-middle-class women; they buy crafts for gifts.

LEATHER SHED, 199 N. Pleasant St., Amherst MA 01002. Contact: Donald W. Muller. Estab: 1965. Represents 75 craftsmen. Considers ceramics, glass art, jewelry, leatherworking, metalsmithing and pottery. Finished, one-of-a-kind and handmade production-line items OK; utilitarian and/or decorative. Price range: $10-200; bestsellers: $10-100. Buys outright. Retail price set by joint agreement. Requires exclusive area representation. Mail artwork. Reports in 2 weeks. Dealer pays shipping from shop and insurance. Best buying and selling time: fall. Customers are college students and faculty.

THE LONDON VENTURERS CO., 2 Dock Square, Box 434, Rockport MA 01966. (617)546-7161. Contact: John Manera. Estab: 1968. Represents 10 out-of-town craftsmen. Considers contemporary ceramics, pottery, wall hangings and weavings; especially needs glass art and jewelry. Finished, one-of-a-kind and handmade production-line items OK; utilitarian and/or decorative. Price range: $5-1,000. Buys outright or on consignment; 40% commission. Gallery sets retail price. Requires exclusive area representation. Write. Reports in 2 weeks. Dealer pays shipping.
Profile: Items exhibited on pedestal and shelves with spotlights. Heaviest wholesale buying time: spring and winter; best selling time: summer. Upper-middle-class customers; they buy crafts for artistic value.

MEETINGHOUSE BARN, Main St., East Orleans MA 02654. (617)255-9765. Contact: Albert M. Kaufman. Estab: 1975. Represents 12-15 craftsmen. Considers batik, ceramics, glass art, jewelry, leatherworking, metalsmithing, needlecrafts, pottery, soft sculpture, woodcrafting, printmaking and cards (handprinted). Finished, one-of-a-kind and handmade production-line items OK; utilitarian and/or decorative. Price range: 75¢-$600; bestsellers: $3-35. Buys outright or on consignment; 40% commission. Retail price set by joint agreement. Requires exclusive area representation. Query with color transparencies or b&w prints. Reports in 2 weeks. Kaufman pays shipping and insurance for exhibited work.
Profile: Best selling time: summer; heaviest wholesale buying time: winter and spring. "The Meetinghouse Barn is a large old barn which lends itself to good display areas. There are no shop windows so items are displayed throughout 2 large barn rooms." Customers are all ages "from an upper-class section of the Cape."

QUITTACUS WORKSHOP ORIGINALS, 477 Bedford St., Lakeville MA 02346. (617)947-4172. President: Arthur. Treasurer: Maureen. Estab: 1972. Represents 12 craftsmen. Considers ceramics, glass art, jewelry, metalsmithing, pottery and woodcrafting. Finished, handmade production-line items OK; utilitarian and/or decorative. Price range: $5-75; bestsellers: $12-20. Buys outright. Shop sets retail price. Write. Reports in 2 weeks. Dealer pays shipping. Best selling season: fall; heaviest wholesale buying season: spring and summer.

THE SNEAK BOX STUDIO, Box 55, Concord MA 01742. (617)369-8312. Contact: Charles F. Murphy. Represents 10 craftsmen. Considers decoys and bird carvings, but may accept any medium if subject pertains to wildfowl or birds. Finished, one-of-a-kind and handmade production-line items OK; utilitarian and/or decorative. Price range: $1-1,000; bestsellers: $20-500. Buys outright or on consignment. Artist sets his price and studio then sets retail price. Requires exclusive area representation. Write or query with transparencies or color photos. Reports in 1 week.
Profile: Consigns items for 12 weeks minimum. All items displayed and many photographed and added to mail order literature. Customers are mostly collectors.

SOUTHERN BERKSHIRE LEATHER WORKS, 9 Railroad St., Great Barrington MA 01230. Contact: Larry Newey. Considers leatherwork for exhibition. Prices are $25+. "Price is no object, but top quality work only!" 25% commission. Retail price set by joint agreement. Items exhibited 2 weeks minimum. Openings sponsored.

WONDERFUL THINGS INC., 232 Stockbridge Rd., Great Barrington MA 01230. (413)528-2473. President: William Tanguay. Estab: 1973. Considers all crafts. Finished, one-of-a-kind and handmade production-line items OK; utilitarian and/or decorative. Price range: $3-300. "Any reasonably good value craft under $15 sells in big volume — especially if it's different." Buys outright. Gallery sets retail price. Requires exclusive representation if mutually beneficial. Query with color transparencies or b&w prints. SASE. Reports in 1-4 weeks ("more when busy, well-supplied, or presentation is poor"). Dealer pays insurance for exhibited work; negotiates payment for shipping and in-transit insurance.
Profile: "Gallery-quality crafts exhibited in a very large area; other crafts in 2 side rooms." No limit on display time. Heaviest wholesale buying time: April-November; best selling time: June-December.
To Break In: "When considering crafts for our gallery we give the most complete presentations top priority. Give us samples that clearly show and represent your work."

WORCESTER ART MUSEUM, 55 Salisbury St., Worcester MA 01608. Contact: Barbara Saltiel. Gift shop buys cards, crafts and jewelry.

Michigan

LEAVES-N-WEAVES, 211 Washington, Grand Haven MI 49417. (616)846-4880. Contact: Nancy Vander Vere. Estab: 1972. Represents 10 craftsmen. Considers batik, dollmaking, glass art, macrame, soft sculpture, wall hangings and weavings. Finished, one-of-a-kind and handmade production-line items OK; utilitarian and/or decorative. Price range: $3-150; bestsellers: $3-20. Buys outright or on consignment; 33 1/3% commission. Craftsman sets retail price. Requires exclusive area representation. Write. Reports in 2 weeks. Dealer pays insurance for exhibited work.
Profile: "Items hung in the shop 6-9 months. We specialize in tropical foliage plants, which complement crafts."

ARNOLD KLEIN GALLERY (formerly Klein-Vogel), 4520 N. Woodward Ave., Royal Oak MI 48072. (313)647-7709. Director: Arnold Klein. Estab: 1971. Represents 6 craftsmen. Considers ceramics, glass art, jewelry and pottery. Finished, one-of-a-kind items OK; utilitarian and/or decorative. Price range: $30-400; bestsellers: $30-100. Buys outright or on consignment; 40% commission. Retail price set by joint agreement. Requires exclusive area representation. Write. Reports in 1 week. Dealer pays insurance for exhibited work.
Profile: Crafts are displayed periodically in cases and on tables. Customers are young and middle-aged professionals; they buy crafts for artistic value.

REEDCRAFT WEAVERS, 153 N. Michigan, Beulah MI 49617. (616)882-5575. Contact: Lewis Small. Estab: 1940. Represens 5 craftsmen. Considers candlemaking, jewelry, needlecrafts and wall hangings; especially needs woven towels, napkins and lunch cloths. Finished handmade production-line items OK; utilitarian and/or decorative. Price range: 20¢-$26; bestsellers: $1.35-26. Buys outright or on consignment; 50% commission. Shop sets retail price. Requires exclusive area representation. Write. Reports in 1 week.
Profile: Items shown in glass cases and hanging displays. Heaviest wholesale buying time: spring; best selling time: summer. Shop located in "barn"; daily handweaving demonstrations. Tourists customers with middle to upper incomes."

THE SPARROW'S NEST, 2149 Hamilton Rd., Okemos MI 48864. (517)349-1424. Contact: Jerold Grashoff. Considers ceramics, sculpture, jewelry, naturalistic and impressionistic paintings in any medium and weavings (pillows, hangings). "Our primary interest is in functional crafts and naturalistic or impressionistic fine art. We carry both original art and limited edition prints." Price range: $1-500. Works on consignment at first; 33 1/3% commission. Sometimes buys later shipments outright. Craftsman set retail price. Prefers exclusive Lansing representation. Send transparencies or photos. Gallery pays shipping on outright purchases. Items displayed till sold or returned; new work featured for 1 month.

Minnesota

ENDION STATION, 208½ W. Superior, Duluth MN 55802. (218)727-3534. Contact: Pat Spencer. Estab: 1971. Represents 12 craftsmen. Considers ceramics, glass art, jewelry, leatherworking, pottery and woodcrafting. Primitive and finished, one-of-a-kind and handmade production-line items OK; utilitarian and/or decorative. Price range: $3-250; bestsellers: $5-15. Buys outright or on consignment; 30% commission. Shop sets retail price. Write. Reports in 3 weeks. Dealer pays shipping to shop and insurance for exhibited work; negotiates payment for in-transit insurance. Prefers hand delivery.
Profile: "We prefer to buy with option to exchange for equal value after 3 months display." Heaviest wholesale buying time: fall. Women customers age 12-45 with lower to upper-middle income; they buy crafts for their usefulness and for gifts.

THE HONEYCOMB, Rte. 2, Lewiston MN 55952. (507)523-3642. Contact: Mrs. Clifford Babcock. Estab: 1973. Represents 50 craftsmen. Considers candlemaking, ceramics, decoupage, dollmaking, glass art, jewelry, needlecrafts, quilting, wall hangings, weavings and woodcrafting. Finished, one-of-a-kind and handmade production-line items OK; utilitarian and/or decorative. Price range: $1-50; bestsellers: $2-10. Works on consignment. Shop sets retail price. Write. Reports in 1 week. Dealer pays insurance for exhibited work. Best selling time: pre-Christmas season and summer. Customers are ages 30-50 with middle incomes.

STONEFLOWER, 1694 Grand Ave., St. Paul MN 55105. (612)699-0535. Contact: Nan Bolstad. Estab: 1972. Represents 40 craftsmen. Considers batik, candlemaking, nonmolded ceramics, glass art, jewelry, leatherworking, metalsmithing, pottery, wall hangings, weavings and woodcrafting. Finished, one-of-a-kind and handmade production-line items OK; utilitarian and/or decorative. Price range: 90¢-$500; bestsellers: $5-25. Buys outright or on consignment; 35-40% commission. Craftsman sets retail price. Requires exclusive Grand Avenue representation. Query with transparencies or photos. Reports in 2 weeks. Dealer pays shipping from shop and insurance for exhibited work.
Profile: Consigned items must be left for 3 months minimum. A minimum number of items per artist is set and varies with medium. Heaviest wholesale buying time: April and fall; best selling time: November-December and May-June. Customers are age 19-35 from a middle-class college community and have double incomes. They buy crafts for gifts.

Mississippi

THE WHISTLE STOP, Box 576, Ocean Springs MS 39564. Director: David S. McFalls. Considers sculpture, jewelry and metalsmithing. "The artist sets his price (from $2-2,500), and we increase it to provide a 33⅓% commission on sales." Payments made monthly. Material may be taken out at any time — no time requirements. Prefers, but does not require, exclusive representation.

Missouri

CRAFT ALLIANCE GALLERY, 6640 Delmar Blvd., St. Louis MO 63130. (314)822-2952. Director: Dorothy Farley. Estab: 1964. Represents 65 member craftsmen. Considers batik, ceramics, glass art, jewelry, metalsmithing, needlecrafts, pottery, quilting, soft sculpture, wall hangings, weavings and woodcrafting. Finished, one-of-a-kind items OK; utilitarian and/or decorative. Price range: $4-1,000's. Works on consignment. Retail price set by joint agreement. Requires exclusive area representation within 3 miles. Write. Dealer pays insurance for exhibited work. Best selling time: pre-Christmas.

SERMON-ANDERSON, INC., 10815 Winner Rd., Independence MO 64052. (816)252-9192. Contact: R.T. Sermon. Estab: 1949. Represents 25-30 craftsmen. Considers all crafts. Finished, one-of-a-kind and handmade production-line items OK; utilitarian and/or decorative. Price range: $1-3,000; bestsellers: $2-100. Buys outright or on consignment; 25% commission. Retail price set by gallery or joint agreement. Requires exclusive Independence representation. Query with transparencies or photos. Reports in 2 weeks. Dealer pays shipping from shop and insurance; negotiates payment for shipping to shop. Items displayed in furnished rooms representing primarily traditional styles and periods. Business and professional customers.

HANK SMITH GALLERY AND GIFT CENTER, 3001 Main St., Kansas City MO 64108. Contact: Hank Smith. Considers ceramics, sculpture, jewelry, metalsmithing, glass, needlecrafts, leather, rugs, tapestries, tie dyeing and batik. Price range: $5-500. 33-1/3% commission. Retail price set by joint agreement. Dealer pays insurance for exhibited work.

Montana

THE BIRD'S NEST, 929 W. Broadway, Missoula MT 59801. (406)721-1125. Manager: Betty Anderson. Estab: 1975. Represents 90-100 craftsmen. Considers needlecrafts, paintings and quilting; especially needs dollmaking and toys. Finished, one-of-a-kind and handmade production-line items OK; utilitarian and/or decorative. Price range: $2.25-300; bestsellers: $2.25-25. Works on consignment; 33⅓% commission. Retail price set by joint agreement. Write. Reports in 1 week. Dealer pays insurance for exhibited work; negotiates shipping from shop.
Profile: Items displayed in colorful settings and rotated weekly. "Our colorful, unusual and well-made dolls and toys are our drawing card."

FLATHEAD LAKE GALLERIES, Corner Lake and Grand, Box 272, Bigfork MT 59911. (406)837-6633. Contact: Richard Ettinger. Estab: 1963. Represents 20 craftsmen. Considers ceramics, jewelry, leatherworking and pottery. Finished, one-of-a-kind and handmade production-line items OK; utilitarian and/or decorative. Price range: $2-200; bestsellers: $25-50. Buys outright; 50% mark-up. Retail price set by joint agreement. Query with transparencies or photos. Reports in 3 weeks. Dealer pays shipping from shop and insurance for exhibited work. Heaviest wholesale buying time: spring; best selling time: June-September. Customers buy crafts for artistic value and for gifts.

HOCKADAY CENTER FOR THE ARTS GIFT SHOP, Box 83, Kalispell MT 59901. (406)755-5268. Director: Steve Lehmer. Considers serigraphs, lithographs, pottery, weaving, painting and watercolors. Prices are $4+. Most items taken on consignment; 25% commission. 40% discount for items purchased outright. Also sponsors annual outdoor art festival and sale. Write for more information.

Nebraska

THE PEDDLERS, 111 W. Mission, Bellevue NE 68005. Contact: Ms. M. Pastorino. Considers ceramics, sculpture, jewelry, metalsmithing, needlecrafts, macrame, glass, leather, tie dye and batik. Price range: $20-500. 33 1/3% commission. Send transparencies or photos. Items displayed 10 weeks minimum.

New Hampshire

ARTISAN'S WORKSHOP, Main St., New London NH 03257. (603)526-4227. Contact: Muffin Bushueff. Estab: 1975. Represents 40-50 craftsmen. Considers batik, glass art, jewelry, leatherworking, metalsmithing, pottery, graphics and prints. Finished, one-of-a-kind and production-line items OK; utilitarian and/or decorative. Price range: $1-175; bestsellers: $1-5 and $25-30. Buys outright or on consignment; 33 1/3% commission. Retail price set by joint agreement. Prefers exclusive area representation. Reports in 2 weeks maximum. Dealer pays shipping and insurance for items bought outright.
Profile: "All items are displayed or returned; none kept in storage. Jewelry placed in cases; paintings and prints hung or placed in print boxes." Heaviest wholesale buying time: summer-fall. "Summer brings large number of tourists. Shop located in lake region with many second homes and camps. College community."

AYOTTES' DESIGNERY, Box 287, Center Sandwich NH 03227. (603)284-6915. Contact: Robert or Roberta Ayotte. Estab: 1958. Represents 30 craftsmen. Considers candlemaking, ceramics, glass art, jewelry, leatherworking, metalsmithing, pottery and woodcrafting. Finished handmade production-line items OK; utilitarian and/or decorative. Price range: 10¢-$495; bestsellers: $14-65. Buys outright. Retail price set by joint agreement. Requires exclusive area representation. Write. Reports in 2 weeks. Dealer pays shipping to shop.
Profile: "We are handweavers and our weaving makes up 80% of our crafts." Heaviest wholesale buying time: January-May; best selling time: July-September.

BERNIER STUDIO, Rte. 25, Wentworth NH 03282. (603)764-5720. Contact: Carol Ann Bernier. Estab: 1965. Represents 75 craftsmen. Considers ceramics, dollmaking, glass art, jewelry, leatherworking, metalsmithing, pottery and woodcrafting. Finished handmade production-line items OK; utilitarian and/or decorative. Price range: $2-450; bestsellers: $5-25. Buys outright. Gallery sets retail price. Requires exclusive area representation. Query with transparencies or photos. Reports in 3 weeks. Dealer pays shipping from shop. Heaviest wholesale buying time: spring and early summer; best selling time: summer. Customers are mainly tourists, over 30 with incomes of $20,000. They buy crafts for gifts.

CHOCORUA POTTERS, Rte. 16, Chocorua NH 03817. (603)323-7939. Contact: Bob Solar. Estab: 1973. Considers hand-built or wheel-thrown ceramics and pottery; especially needs mugs and items under $4. Finished and primitive, one-of-a-kind and handmade production-line items OK; utilitarian and/or decorative. Price range: $2-200; bestsellers: $2-20. Buys outright; 50% commission with retail price set by joint agreement. Requires exclusive area representation. Write or query with color transparencies or b&w prints. Reports in 1 week.
Profile: "Chocorua Potters is a potters studio and display gallery housed in an 1840's barn. Background of wood and spot lighting creates softness and allows for emphasis of individuality of pieces." Heaviest wholesale buying time: spring and early summer.

KIRK-LAMOTHE GALLERY, Main St., Walpole NH 03608. (603)756-3234. Manager: Mrs. Paul Lamothe. Estab: 1971. Represents 30 New England craftsmen. Considers dollmaking, greeting cards, jewelry, leatherworking, metalsmithing, paintings, pottery and woodcrafting; especially needs doll house items, toys and children's clothes. Finished one-of-a-kind items OK; utilitarian and/or decorative. Price range: $1-300; bestsellers: $5-25. Buys outright or on consignment; 34% commission. Retail price set by joint agreement. Write. Artist pays shipping to shop and in-transit insurance; dealer pays shipping from shop and insurance for exhibited work.
Profile: Items displayed in a "formal living room or a cozy sitting room." Heaviest wholesale buying time: spring. Best selling time: August-December. Tourist customers; they buy crafts for artistic value and gifts.

New Jersey

THE ARTISAN'S GALLERY, 161 Main St., Ridgefield Park NJ 07660. Contact: Paul or Janet Sisko. Considers ceramics, jewelry, metalsmithing, glass, leather, enamels, wall hangings, macrame and stitchery. Price range: $1-3,000; bestsellers: up to $30. 50% mark-up on crafts bought outright. Craftsman sets retail price. Requires exclusive area representation. Send transparencies or photos. Items displayed 4 weeks minimum. Openings sponsored.

THE BEAUTIFUL THINGS FACTORY, INC., 1838 E. 2nd St., Scotch Plains NJ 07076. (201)322-1817. Contact: Paula Leighton. Estab: 1973. Represents 60 craftsmen. Considers ceramics, glass art, jewelry, leatherworking, pottery, soft sculpture, toys and cards. Finished, one-of-a-kind and handmade production-line items OK; utilitarian and/or decorative. Price range: $1-500; bestsellers: $2-40. Buys outright in shop; on consignment in gallery; 40% commission. Craftsman sets retail price. Query with transparencies or photos. Dealer pays shipping when buying outright. Heaviest wholesale buying time: fall. Customers are ages 25-40.

CABIN CREEK QUILTS, 195 Nassau St., Princeton NJ 08540. (See Cabin Creek Quilts, Cabin Creek, West Virginia.)

THE DEPOT, 217 1st St., Ho-Ho-Kus NJ 07423. (201)444-1914. Contact: Barbara Smith or Barbara Dietrich. A women's exchange and gift shop. Considers ceramics, small sculpture, jewelry, metalsmithing, needlecrafts, glass, leather, tie dye and batik. Price range: $1-300 set by joint agreement. Works on consignment; 25% commission donated to family counseling service. Send transparencies or photos. Not responsible for unsolicited merchandise. Items displayed 12 weeks minimum.

THE GARRET ART GALLERY, INC., 8 Monmouth St., Red Bank NJ 07701. (201)842-6626. Contact: Jan Gillen Voytko. Estab: 1969. Exhibits fine crafts such as glass art, jewelry, metalsmithing, needlecrafts, pottery, soft sculpture, wall hangings, weavings and woodcrafting; 8 weeks minimum exposure. Buys outright or on consignment; 40% commission. Retail price set by joint agreement. Requires exclusive area representation. Write. Gallery pays shipping from shop.

HANDMAIDS, 39 Maple St., Summit NJ 07901. (201)273-0707. Contact: Peggy McNamara. Estab: 1974. Represents 250 craftsmen. Considers batik, candlemaking, ceramics, dollmaking, glass art, jewelry, leatherworking, metalsmithing, needlecrafts, pottery, quilting, soft sculpture, wall hangings, weavings and woodcrafting. Finished, one-of-a-kind and handmade production-line items OK; utilitarian and/or decorative. Price range: 50¢-$300; bestsellers: $5-30. Buys outright or on consignment; 40% commission. Retail price set by joint agreement. Write. Reports in 2-3 weeks. Dealer pays insurance for exhibited work; shipping costs shared. Items displayed 3 months maximum. Heaviest wholesale buying time: January and June; best selling time: October-December.

HOUSE OF BERNARD, 353 Millburn Ave., Millburn NJ 07041. (201)376-8088. Contact: Berry or Shirley Bernard. Estab: 1961. Represents 60 out-of-town craftsmen. Considers batik, ceramics, jewelry, metalsmithing, pottery, wall hangings and weavings. Primitive

Emergency Workshop, Kentucky, accepts crafts only from persons in need of emergency funds. A cash advance is given to eligible persons who are then expected to produce enough crafts, that when sold, will pay off the debt. Liz Hollinde, shop coordinator, calls it "welfare with dignity." This woman is making wooden flowers to sell in the shop.

and finished, one-of-a-kind and handmade production-line items OK; utilitarian and/or decorative. Price range: $1-thousands of dollars; bestsellers: $5-50. Buys outright. Retail price set by joint agreement. Requires exclusive area representation. Write. Reports in 2 weeks. Dealer pays shipping to shop and insurance for exhibited work. Best selling time: Christmas. Customers, ages 20-50 with $20,000+ incomes, are informed about art.

KAKIE'S GOLDMINE, Church Rd., Sicklerville NJ 08081. Contact: Katharine Cusack. Estab: 1976. Represents 6 craftsmen. Considers dollmaking, glass art, metalsmithing, needlecrafts, pottery, quilting, weavings and woodcrafting; especially needs jewelry, wall hangings and unusual handbags. Finished handmade production-line items OK; utilitarian and/or decorative. Price range: 29¢-$9.95; bestsellers: 89¢-$7.95. Works on consignment; 25% commission. Retail price set by joint agreement. Write. Reports in 1 week. Dealer pays shipping from shop and insurance on exhibited work.
Profile: Rotates crafts monthly. Heaviest wholesale buying time: Christmas and May. Customers are young marrieds with $12,000-15,000 incomes and interest in home and children.

PETERS VALLEY CRAFTSMEN, Delaware Water Gap National Park, Layton NJ 07851. (201)948-5200. Director: Molly Mechem. Estab: 1969. Represents 60-80 (mainly New Jersey, New York and Pennsylvania) craftsmen. Considers batik, ceramics, glass art, jewelry, leatherworking, blacksmithing, needlecrafts, quilting, stationery graphics, wall hangings, weavings and fine woodwork; especially needs candles, soft sculpture, dolls and pottery place settings. Finished, one-of-a-kind and handmade production-line items OK; utilitarian and/or decorative. Price range: $1-1,200; bestsellers: $3.50-30 and $75-175. Occasionally buys outright; primarily works on consignment; 33 1/3% commission. Craftsman usually sets retail price; sometimes set by joint agreement. Write. Reports in 1 week. Dealer pays insurance for exhibited work; negotiates payment for shipping.
Profile: Crafts are juried "in the flesh," and displayed 90 days maximum. Heaviest wholesale buying time: April-December. Shop located in a community of professional and teaching craftsmen. Tourist customers age 30-60 with middle to upper incomes.

QUINCY HALL, CRAFTS SHOP & STUDIO, 410 Maple St., Kearney NJ 07032. Contact: J. Jorda. Considers ceramics, sculpture, jewelry, metalsmithing, rugs, tapestries, glass, leather, tie dye, batik, macrame and weaving. Buys outright (items under $100 retail) or on consignment (items over $100 retail); 25% commission; 40-50% wholesale discount. Craftsman sets retail price. Send transparencies or photos.

WILLIAM RIS GALLERIES, 9725 2nd Ave., Stone Harbor NJ 08247. (609)368-6361. Contact: Barbara Shreckengaust or Elizabeth Courson. Estab: 1966. Represents 150 craftsmen. Considers ceramics, glass art, jewelry, pottery, sculpture, wall hangings, weavings, woodcrafting, and enameled plates and plaques with birds, animals and flowers. Finished, one-of-a-kind and handmade production-line items OK; utilitarian and/or decorative. Price range: $5-500; bestsellers: $5-150. Buys outright or occasionally on consignment; 40% commission. Retail price set by gallery or joint agreement. Requires exclusive area representation. Write. Reports in 2 weeks. Dealer pays shipping.
Profile: "We feature monthly exhibitions of craftsmen's work." Heaviest wholesale buying time: spring, summer and fall. Customers age 20-55 with middle and upper incomes.

VITTI ARTISANS GALLERY, 594 Valley Rd., Upper Montclair NJ 07043. (201)746-1715. Contact: Vitti Stein. Estab: 1974. Represents 40-60 craftsmen. Considers all crafts; especially needs jewelry and glass art. Finished, one-of-a-kind and handmade production-line items OK; utilitarian and/or decorative. Price range: $4-1,600; bestsellers: $15-500. Buys outright or on consignment; 40% commission. Craftsman sets retail price. Requires exclusive city representation. Query with transparencies or photos. Reports in 3 weeks. Dealer pays insurance for exhibited work.
Profile: Heaviest wholesale buying time: fall, winter and spring. Closed during August. Upper-middle class to wealthy customers, age 20-65; they buy crafts for artistic value.

WHALE'S TALE, 312 Washington Mall, Cape May NJ 08204. (609)884-4808. Contact: Hilary Russell. Estab: 1974. Represents 20 craftsmen. Considers batik, candlemaking, ceramics, dollmaking, glass art, jewelry, pottery, soft sculpture, wall hangings, weavings and woodcrafting. Finished, one-of-a-kind and handmade production-line items OK; utilitarian and/or decorative. Price range: $2-160; bestsellers: $2-20. Buys outright or on consignment;

40% commission. Retail price set by joint agreement. Requires exclusive area representation. Query with transparencies or photos. Reports in 2 weeks. Dealer pays shipping and insurance.
Profile: "Display structures are versatile and we're able to build them around the work displayed." Most crafts displayed 1 month. Heaviest wholesale buying time: spring and summer; best selling time: summer and fall. "A large number of 25-35 year olds who appreciate the work of serious craftspeople (as opposed to hobbyists) pass through shop in summer."

THE YELLOW DOOR, 24 Washington Ave., Tenafly NJ 07670. Contact: Betty Turino. Estab: 1973. Represents 375-400 craftsmen. Considers batik, candlemaking, ceramics, glass art, jewelry, leatherworking, metalsmithing, pottery, soft sculpture, wall hangings, weavings and woodcrafting. Finished, one-of-a-kind and handmade production-line items OK; utilitarian and/or decorative. Price range: $2.50-1,500; bestsellers: $6.50-55. Buys outright or on consignment; 40% commission. Gallery sets retail price. Requires exclusive area representation. Write. Dealer pays shipping to shop and insurance on exhibited work.
Profile: Items displayed 3-4 weeks. Heaviest wholesale buying time: Christmas; best selling time: December. Customers are 30-55, urban-oriented and affluent.

New Mexico

HILL'S HANDCRAFTED FURNITURE AND CONTEMPORARY CRAFTS, 110 W. San Francisco St., Sante Fe NM 87501. (505) 982-2549. Director: Anne Schleider. Estab: 1970. Represents 20-30 craftsmen. Considers ceramics, dollmaking, furniture, glass art, pottery, soft sculpture, wall hangings and weavings. Finished one-of-a-kind items OK; utilitarian and/or decorative. Price range: $25-650; bestsellers: $25-300. Buys outright or occasionally on consignment; 40% commission. Retail price set by shop or joint agreement. Requires exclusive area representation. Query with transparencies or photos. Reports in 2 weeks. Dealer pays shipping from shop and insurance for exhibited work.
Profile: Items displayed with handcrafted furniture; displays rotated every 2-3 months. Heaviest wholesale buying time: summer. Tourist customers.

POPOVI DA INDIAN ARTS & CRAFTS, Rte. 5, Box 309, San Ildefonso Pueblo, Santa Fe NM 87501. (505)455-2456. Contact: Anita Da. Estab: 1949. Represents 100 southwestern Indian craftsmen. Considers beadwork, dollmaking, jewelry, leatherworking, metalsmithing, needlecrafts, pottery, sand painting, sculpture, wall hangings, watercolor paintings, weavings and woodcrafting. One-of-a-kind, primitive and finished items OK; utilitarian and/or decorative. Price range: $9-5,000; bestsellers: $10-200. Buys outright or rarely on consignment; 10-20% commission. Retail price set by joint agreement. Requires exclusive area representation. Call for interview. Dealer pays insurance for exhibited work. Heaviest wholesale buying time: April-September. Tourist customers; they buy crafts for artistic value and gifts.

SHALAKO SHOP, INC., Box 970, Community Center, Los Alamos NM 87544. (505)662-2539. Contact: Edward B. Grothus. Estab: 1957. Represents 2 craftsmen. Considers candlemaking, ceramics, glass art, jewelry, leatherworking, metalsmithing, needlecrafts, pottery, wall hangings, weavings, woodcrafting, works in copper, brass and tile, and ecological and futuristic crafts. Primitive and finished, one-of-a-kind and handmade production-line items OK; utilitarian and/or decorative. Price range: 50¢-$1,500; bestsellers: $50. Buys outright or occasionally on consignment; 33⅓% commission. Retail price set by joint agreement. Arrange appointment. Negotiates payment for shipping and insurance. Heaviest buying and selling time: Christmas. Customers buy crafts for gifts.

SOUTHWESTERN INDIAN ARTS, Box 1892, Taos Indian Pueblo, Taos NM 87571. Contact: Tony or Ann Reyna. Estab: Shop #1, 1950; Shop #2, 1960. Represents 25 Indian craftsmen. Considers jewelry, drums, rugs, paintings, beadwork, carvings, baskets and pottery. Finished, one-of-a-kind handmade items OK; utilitarian and/or decorative. Price range: $10-2,000; bestsellers: $10-350. Buys outright. Retail price set by joint agreement. Write. Reports in 2 weeks. Dealer pays insurance for exhibited work.
Profile: Best selling time: March-June. Shop is Indian-owned and operated. Tourist customers; they buy crafts for artistic value.

TOUCHSTONES, 1919 Old Town Rd. NW, 2 Plaza Hacienda, Albuquerque NM 87104. Contact: Betty Isslieb. Considers ceramics, jewelry, metalsmithing and crafts. Prices up to $50. Send transparencies or photos. Items displayed 12 weeks minimum.

WINONA TRADING POST, 211-213 Galisteo St., Box 324, Sante Fe NM 87501. (505)988-4811. Contact: Pierre Bovis. Estab: 1965. Represents 100+ Indian craftsmen. Considers beadwork, jewelry, pottery and quillwork. One-of-a-kind, primitive and finished items OK; utilitarian and/or decorative. Minimum price: $10. Buys outright or on consignment; 25% commission. Retail price set by joint agreement. Requires exclusive area representation. Write. Reports in 1 week. Dealer pays shipping from shop.

New York

A TOUCH OF WHIMSY, 45 E. 89th St., Apt. 28C, New York NY 10028. Contact: Joan Rowland. Considers ceramics, sculpture, jewelry, metalsmithing, needlecrafts, rugs, tapestries, glass, leather, tie dye, batik, papier mache, macrame, acrylic and other crafts. Price range: $25-2,500. 100% mark-up on crafts. Send transparencies or photos. Dealer pays insurance for exhibited work. Items displayed 1 week minimum. Openings sponsored. "Openings and shows are heavily promoted in the media."

ALL BY HAND, 7810 3rd Ave., Brooklyn NY 11209. (212)745-8904. Contact: Lou Gaita. Estab: 1976. Represents 20 craftsmen. Considers ceramics, glass art, jewelry, leatherworking, pottery and woodcrafting. Finished handmade production-line items OK; utilitarian and/or decorative. Price range: $1-250; bestsellers: $10-25. Buys outright. Shop sets retail price. Query with transparencies or photos. Reports in 2 weeks. Dealer pays shipping and insurance.
Profile: Craftsman's item(s) displayed as a unit, 4 weeks minimum. Heaviest wholesale buying time: summer; best selling time: Christmas. Customers, late 20's, with middle incomes.

THE ARTISAN, 118 E. Noyes Blvd., Sherrill NY 13461. (315)363-5151. Contact: Rosamond Bennati or Carol Weimer. Estab: 1976. Represents 80 craftsmen. Considers batik, candlemaking, dollmaking, glass art, jewelry, leatherworking, pottery, wall hangings and woodcrafting. Finished handmade production-line items OK; utilitarian and/or decorative. Price range: $1-45; bestsellers: $1-15. Buys outright. Retail price set by joint agreement. Query with transparencies or photos. Reports in 2 weeks. Dealer pays shipping to shop. Best selling time: summer and Christmas.

ARTISAN HOUSE, 80 Main St., Northport NY 11768. (516)261-3800. Contact: G. Jackier or M. Lenaerts. Estab: 1972. Represents over 400 craftsmen. Considers batik, candlemaking, dollmaking, glass art, jewelry, leatherworking, metalsmithing, pottery, soft sculpture, wall hangings, weavings, woodcrafting, handmade beads, basketry, graphics and papier mache. Primitive and finished, one-of-a-kind and handmade production-line items OK; utilitarian and/or decorative. Price range: $1-500. Buys outright or on consignment; 40% commission. Retail price set by joint agreement. Requires exclusive area representation. Write. Dealer pays insurance for exhibited work. Heaviest wholesale buying time: spring and fall; best selling time: summer and Christmas.

BALDWIN POTTERY INC., 540 La Guardia Place, New York NY 10012. (212)475-7236. President: Judith Baldwin. Estab: 1960. Represents 12 craftsmen. Primitive or finished ceramics OK; utilitarian and/or decorative. Price range: $3-150; bestsellers: $3-50. Buys outright. Craftsman sets retail price. Requires exclusive area representation. Write or call. Reports in 2 weeks. Negotiates payment for shipping and insurance.
Profile: Window and central display. "Try not to keep old merchandise (have sales or exchange these for new items)." Customers are ages 20-40, middle-class.

BENSON GALLERY, Bridgehampton NY 11932. (516)537-0598. Director: Elaine Benson. Estab: 1966. Represents 2-3 craftsmen. Considers all crafts. Price range: $25-10,000; bestsellers: up to $250. Works on consignment; 40% commission. Retail price set by gallery or joint agreement. Requires exclusive area representation. Query with transparencies or photos. Reports in 1-2 weeks. Dealer pays insurance for exhibited work. Items exhibited for 2-week periods during May-September.

WESLEY BERGEN, 65 W. 55th St., New York NY 10019. Contact: Wesley Bergen. Considers jewelry and metalsmithing. Price range: $10-5,000. Retail price set by joint agreement. Dealer pays insurance for exhibited work. Openings sponsored. Advanced designs only.

CANDLESTOCK, 16 Mill Hill Rd., Woodstock NY 12498. (914)679-8711. Contact: Barbara Moss. Estab: 1970. Represents 30-40 craftsmen. Considers anything relating to candles or

lighting. Primitive and finished, one-of-a-kind and handmade production-line items OK; utilitarian and/or decorative. Price range: 25¢-$200; bestsellers: $2-20. Buys outright or on consignment; 40% commission. Shop sets retail price. Requires exclusive area representation. Query with transparencies or photos. Reports in 2 weeks. Dealer pays insurance for exhibited work.
Profile: Each item receives personal attention. Heaviest wholesale buying time: spring and fall; best selling time: summer and Christmas. Most customers ages 20-30; they buy crafts for usefulness and gifts.

THE CLAY POT, 162 7th Ave., Brooklyn NY 11215. (212)788-6564. Contact: Bob Silberberg. Estab: 1969. Represents 40 craftsmen. Considers candlemaking, ceramics, dollmaking, glass art, jewelry, leatherworking, metalsmithing, pottery and woodcrafting. Finished, handmade production-line items OK; utilitarian. Price range: $1-300; bestsellers: $1-30. Buys outright or on consignment; 40% commission. Retail price set by joint agreement. Write or query with transparencies or photos. Reports in 4 weeks. Dealer pays shipping to shop and insurance on exhibited work. Best selling time: late spring and Christmas. Customers have $10,000-50,000 incomes.

CORNER CANDLE STORE, Depot St., Washingtonville NY 10992. (914)496-6868. Contact: Paula Spector. Estab: 1970. Represents 12-25 craftsmen. Considers candlemaking, dollmaking, glass art, jewelry, leatherworking, pottery and quilting. Primitive and finished, one-of-a-kind and handmade production-line items OK; utilitarian and/or decorative. Price range: $1-35; bestsellers: $1-15. Buys outright or on consignment; 34% commission. Retail price set by joint agreement. Write. Reports in 1 month. Dealer pays shipping and insurance for exhibited work. Heaviest wholesale buying time: summer and fall. Young married customers with middle incomes; they buy crafts for gifts.

CRAFT DESIGNS UNLIMITED, 548 La Guardia Place, New York NY 10012. (212)477-1690. Contact: Joel Waldman. Considers woven or textile crafts; especially needs woven art designs. Price range: $20-500; bestsellers: $50-250. Buys outright or on consignment; 25-50% commission. Retail price set by joint agreement. Call for interview. Reports in 1 week. Dealer pays insurance for exhibited work.
Profile: Items displayed 3 weeks minimum. Gallery also distributes wholesale woven art designs to retailers.

THE CRAFTSMAN'S GALLERY, LTD., 16 Chase Rd., Scarsdale NY 10583. (914)725-4644. Contact: Sybil Robins or John Mucciolo. Estab: 1973. Represents several hundred craftsmen. Considers batik, ceramics, glass art, jewelry, leatherworking, metalsmithing, pottery, quilting and soft sculpture; especially needs woven wall hangings and fine functional woodworks. Finished, one-of-a-kind and production-line handmade items OK; utilitarian and/or decorative. Price range: $10-2,000; bestsellers: $20-90. Works on consignment; 30-40% commission. Retail price set by joint agreement. Query with color transparencies or b&w prints. SASE. Reports in 3 weeks; dealer pays insurance for exhibited work. Crafts exhibited 4-5 weeks minimum. Best selling time: spring and winter.

CREATIVE JEWELRY (formerly Ruth Pawelka-Creative Jewelry), 107 Tinker St., Woodstock NY 12498. (914)679-9223. Contact: Gus Pawelka. Estab: 1965. Represents 35 craftsmen. Finished, one-of-a-kind and handmade production-line items OK; utilitarian and/or decorative. Price range: $5-1,000; bestsellers: $10-200. Buys outright. Shop sets retail price. Requires exclusive area representation. Write. Reports in 2 weeks. Dealer pays shipping to shop and in-transit insurance. Heaviest wholesale buying time: spring; best selling time: summer and Christmas.

DESIGNS IN SILVER, ETCETERA, 230 E. Main St., Port Jefferson NY 11777. (516)928-2037. Contact: Charles Kohn. Estab: 1976. Represents 23 craftsmen. Considers candlemaking, ceramics, glass art, jewelry, leatherworking, metalsmithing, pottery, wall hangings, weavings and woodcrafting. Primitive and finished, one-of-a-kind and handmade production-line items OK; utilitarian and/or decorative. Price range: $1.75-500; bestsellers: $1.75-300. Works on consignment; 40% commission. Retail price set by joint agreement. Requires exclusive area representation. Query with transparencies or photos. Reports as soon as inquiry is received. Dealer pays shipping from shop and insurance.
Profile: Items displayed 1 month minimum. Displays are on walls, windows, tables, pedestals

and showcases. Each craft is treated independently as required. Crafts arranged in museum-like atmosphere where everything can be viewed without distracting items surrounding them. Best selling time: Christmas and warm weather.

EARTHWORKS POTTERY, 251 W. 85th St., New York NY 10024. (212)874-8245. Contact: Clairese DesBecker. Estab: 1971. Represents 20 craftsmen. Considers candlemaking, ceramics, clay jewelry and pottery. Finished, one-of-a-kind and handmade production-line items OK; utilitarian and/or decorative. Price range: $2-200; bestsellers: $5-50. Buys outright or on consignment; 40% commission. Retail price set by joint agreement. Query with color transparencies or b&w prints. Reports in 1 week. Gallery pays insurance for exhibited work. Heaviest wholesale buying time: summer.

THE ELDER CRAFTSMEN, 850 Lexington Ave., New York NY 10021. (212)535-8030. Manager: Mrs. Alfred I. Miranda. Estab: 1955. Represents 500 age 60+ craftsmen. Considers decoupage, silver and macrame jewelry, needlecrafts and soft sculpture; especially needs copper enamel dishes, ashtrays, inlaid wood boxes, picture frames, baby toys, gifts, sweaters and quilts. Finished, one-of-a-kind and handmade production-line items OK; utilitarian and/or decorative. Price range: $4-125; bestsellers: $10-25. Works on consignment; 35% commission. Retail price set by joint agreement. Prefers exclusive area representation. Write or send transparencies or photos. Reports in 3 weeks.
Profile: Items displayed 3 months minimum. Best selling time: September-December. "We make crafts to order." Accepts work only from elderly craftsmen.

THE FAT DUCK, 94 E. Market St., Corning NY 14830. Contact: Lee F. Baldwin. Considers glass, needlecrafts, jewelry, metalsmithing, sculpture, ceramics, batik and tie dyeing. Price range: $5-300. 30% commission. Requires exclusive area representation. Charges commission on crafts sold in area after showing. Send transparencies or photos. Dealer pays insurance for exhibited work. Items displayed 12 weeks minimum. Openings sponsored. "Our biggest problem is finding the good craftsman or artist. We have work from all over the U.S."

THE GALLERY SHOP AT THE JAMAICA ARTS CENTER, 161-04 Jamaica Ave., Jamaica NY 11432. (212)658-1770. Director: Carole Joyce McCully. Estab: 1976. Represents 50 craftsmen. Considers batik, jewelry and ceramics. Primitive and finished, one-of-a-kind and handmade production-line items OK; utilitarian and/or decorative. Price range: 50¢-$300; bestsellers: $2.50-30. Buys outright or on consignment; 33⅓% commission. Craftsman sets retail price. Write. Reports in 2 weeks. Dealer pays shipping from shop and insurance for exhibited work. Work displayed in lighted cabinets, opera glass shelving and wall space. Best selling time: Christmas. Customers buy crafts for gifts.

GLASS MASTERS GUILD, 621 Avenue of the Americas, New York NY 10011. (212)929-7978. Contact: Bruce Berkman. Estab: 1970. Represents 10 craftsmen. Considers blown and stained glass. Finished one-of-a-kind items OK; utilitarian and/or decorative. Price range: $10-1,000; bestsellers: $30-60. Buys outright or on consignment; 40% commission. Craftsman sets retail price. Query with transparencies or photos. Reports in 1 month. Shipping from shop and insurance negotiated.
Profile: "Glass hung in windows or displayed in cases." Heaviest wholesale buying time: fall. Customers ages 20-50 with middle to upper incomes; they buy crafts for artistic value and gifts.

HAND OF THE CRAFTSMAN, 58 S. Broadway, Nyack NY 10960. (914)358-6622. Contact: Shel or Jan Haber. Considers ceramics, jewelry, metalsmithing, leather and original graphics. Prices are $5+. Usually buys outright; 50% commission; occasionally on consignment; 33⅓% commission. Craftsman sets retail price. Sends transparencies or photos. Never marks down merchandise or runs clearance sales. Requires exclusive representation in area. Exhibited art insured. Gallery pays shipping costs of work bought outright.

JEANNE HASTINGS GALLERY & WORKSHOP, Old Stone Schoolhouse & Middle Rd., Lake George NY 12845. Director: Jeanne Hastings. "Our business is done during July-September." Considers ceramics, jewelry, metalsmithing, leather, tie dyeing and batik. Price range: $6-800. 40% commission. Send transparencies or photos. Items displayed 3 weeks minimum.

JULIE: ARTISANS' GALLERY, 687 Madison Ave., New York NY 10021. (212)688-2345. Contact: Julie. Estab: 1973. Represents 150-200 craftsmen. Considers batik, ceramics, decoup-

age, dollmaking, glass art, jewelry, leatherworking, metalsmithing, needlecrafts, pottery, quilting, soft sculpture, wall hangings, weavings and woodcrafting. Finished, one-of-a-kind items OK; utilitarian and/or decorative. Price range: $5-2,500. Works on consignment. Gallery sets retail price. Query with color transparencies or b&w prints. Reports in 1-2 weeks. Dealer pays shipping from shop and insurance on exhibited work.
Profile: "Each piece is displayed according to its own merit. We carry only museum-quality crafts."

JUST ACCESSORIES, INC., 112 W. 34th St., New York NY 10001. (212)564-5168. Contact: R. N. Bloch. Estab: 1961. Represents 25 out-of-town craftsmen. Considers all crafts. Finished handmade production-line items OK; utilitarian and/or decorative. Buys outright. Query with color transparencies or b&w prints. Reports immediately. Dealer pays shipping to shop.

LOVE AND LET LOVE, 1278 1st Ave., New York NY 10021. Crafts Dealer: Lourie Greenblatt. Considers ceramics, sculpture, jewelry and metalsmithing. Price range: $5-200. Gallery sets retail price. Buys outright at 50% of retail price. Requires exclusive area representation. Gallery pays shipping costs.

PERFORMERS' OUTLET, 222 E. 85th St., New York NY 10028. (212)249-8435. Contact: Jerry Young. Estab: 1969. Represents 250 craftsmen. Considers candlemaking, ceramics, jewelry and pottery. Finished, one-of-a-kind and handmade production-line items OK; utilitarian and/or decorative. Price range: $1-250; bestsellers: $10-25. Buys outright or on consignment; 50% commission. Retail price set by joint agreement. Write or call. Dealer pays shipping and insurance. Heaviest wholesale buying time: fall. "We specialize in crafts by performing artists." Well-traveled, educated customers, ages 20-50; they buy crafts for artistic value and gifts.

QUASIMODO ORIGINALS, Montauk Hwy., Bridgehampton NY 11932. (516)537-1177. Contact: Henry M. Kesselman. Estab: 1972. Considers ceramics, sculpture, jewelry, metalsmithing, batik and stained glass. Price range: $5-300. Buys 90% of crafts outright, 10% on consignment; 33⅓% commission. Send description of work. Requires exclusive area representation. Prefers unique, imaginative work in moderate price range; likes to select items by personal visit when possible.

ROADS GALLERIES, 400 E. 57th St., New York NY 10022. (212)486-1441. Contact: Louis Horwin. Estab: 1975. Represents 75 craftsmen. Considers batik, metalsmithing, soft sculpture, wall hangings and weavings. Finished, one-of-a-kind and handmade production-line items OK; decorative. Price range: $50-1,000; bestsellers: $150-300. Works on consignment; 50% commission. Retail price set by joint agreement. Mail slides or photos. Reports in 4 weeks. Dealer pays shipping from gallery and insurance for exhibited work.
Profile: "We sell office decorations to corporations. We show photos or slides to the customers; if there's interest, we have the item sent to us."

1770 CRAFTS, 583 Little Britain Rd., Newburgh NY 12550. (914)564-1777. Contact: W. H. McCauley. Estab: 1975. Represents local craftsmen. Considers batik, decoupage, glass art, jewelry, leatherworking, metalsmithing and pottery. Primitive one-of-a-kind and handmade production-line items OK; utilitarian and/or decorative. Price range: 5¢-$100; bestsellers: $5. Buys outright or on consignment; 70% commission. Retail price set by joint agreement. Requires exclusive area representation. Write or query with transparencies or photos. Reports in 4 weeks. Buys and sells most crafts in fall.

THE STUDIO, INC., 15 Main St., Lake Placid NY 12946. (518)523-3589. Contact: Carter Lockwood. Estab: 1968. Represents 100-150 craftsmen. Considers non-abstract ceramics, decoupage, dollmaking, glass art, jewelry, metalsmithing, needlecrafts, paintings, pottery, quilting, tole painting, wall hangings and woodcrafting; especially needs figure skating and winter sports craft themes. Finished, one-of-a-kind and handmade production-line items OK; utilitarian and/or decorative (likes nature themes). Price range: $2-2,000; bestsellers: $2-75. Buys outright or on consignment; 33⅓% commission. Retail price set by joint agreement. Requires exclusive area representation. Call for interview or send transparencies or photos. Reports in 1 week. Dealer pays shipping from shop; negotiates shipping to shop and insurance.
Profile: Consigned items displayed 6 months maximum. Heaviest wholesale buying time: spring; best selling time: summer and fall. Tourist customers ages 18+ with middle to upper incomes; they buy crafts for artistic value.

TAPESTRY ASSOCIATES, 300 Central Park W., New York NY 10024. (212)362-4090. Director: Lee Naiman. Estab: 1970. Considers batik, quilting, wall hangings and weavings. Finished and one-of-a-kind items OK; decorative. Open price range. Bestsellers: $800-2,400. Works on consignment; 20-40% commission. Craftsman sets retail price. Write or query with professional biography and color transparencies or b&w photos. Reports in 2 weeks. Dealer pays insurance for exhibited work.
Profile: Work presented directly via slides to customers, which are mainly banks and corporations; they buy crafts for artistic and decorative value.

THE THREE CROWNS, Box 144, Pittsford NY 14534. (716)586-5160. Contact: George Gordon. Estab: 1966. Represents 50 craftsmen. Considers batik, ceramics, glass art, jewelry, metalsmithing, pottery, wall hangings, weavings, woodcrafting, copper enamel and textiles. Finished one-of-a-kind items OK; utilitarian and/or decorative. Price range: $3-250; bestsellers: $8-40. Buys outright or on consignment; 33 1/3% commission. Retail price set by craftsman. Requires exclusive area representation. Write. Reports in 1 week. Dealer pays shipping from shop and insurance for exhibited work.
Profile: "We have 1,200' square of display area plus counters, shelves and showcases. We rearrange our exhibits weekly and try to keep a representative assortment of each craftsman on display at all times." No students or self-taught craftsman's work. Most exhibitors have had 4-6 years in technical school. Customers buy crafts for their usefulness.

UNDERPASS GALLERY, 1 N. Main St., Monroe NY 10950. Contact: Tanya Laurer. Considers ceramics, sculpture, glass, jewelry, metalsmithing, needlecrafts, rugs, leather, tapestries, batik and tie dye. Retail price set by joint agreement. Buys mostly outright; 50% discount; 33 1/3% commission for consignments. Requires exclusive area representation. Charges commission on crafts sold in area after showing. Gallery pays insurance for exhibited work.

VALLEY HANDCRAFTS, Rte. 1, Box 153, Kerhonkson NY 12446. Contact: Linda Corrapo. Considers ceramics, sculpture, jewelry, metalsmithing, needlecrafts, rugs, tapestries, glass, leather, tie dye, batik and small drawings and prints. Price range: $2-100. 25% commission. Retail price set by joint agreement. Dealer pays insurance for exhibited work. Items displayed 6 weeks minimum.

VILLAGE CRAFTSMEN, 219 W. Water, Elmira NY 14801. (607)732-5472. Contact: Julius or Carol Williams. Estab: 1973. Represents 50 craftsmen. Considers batik, ceramics, glass art, leatherworking, pottery, wall hangings and weavings. Finished, one-of-a-kind and handmade production-line items OK; utilitarian. Price range: $1.50-300; bestsellers: $1.50-20. Buys outright or on consignment; 33 1/3% commission. Craftsman sets retail price. Query with transparencies or photos. Reports in 2 weeks. Dealer pays shipping from shop and insurance on exhibited work. Heaviest wholesale buying time: pre-Christmas.

THE VILLAGE SILVERSMITH, 149 Main St., Bellport NY 11713. (516)286-1660. Contact: Dwight M. Trujillo. Estab: 1971. Represents 15 craftsmen. Considers ceramics, glass art, jewelry, leatherworking and pottery. Finished handmade production-line items OK; utilitarian only. Price range: $2-500; bestsellers: $2-35. Buys outright or on consignment; 33 1/3% commission. Retail price set by joint agreement. Requires exclusive area representation. Query with color transparencies or b&w photos. Reports in 4 weeks. Dealer pays shipping from shop and insurance on exhibited work. Heaviest wholesale buying time: spring and fall; best selling time: summer and winter. Customers are upper-middle-class.

THE WHEELBARROW, 135 Main St., Cold Spring Harbor, Long Island NY 11724. Contact: Mrs. R. L. Mahan. Considers ceramics, sculpture, metalsmithing, jewelry, rugs, glass, leather, woodworking, toys, dolls, prints, letter/note paper and batik. "Nothing too conservative in design." Price range: $5-750. Works on consignment; 40% commission. Retail price set by joint agreement. Requires exclusive area representation. Charges commission on crafts sold in area after showing. Send slides or prints. Items displayed 4 weeks minimum.

WILKES GALLERY INC., 101 Main St., Northport NY 11768. (516)261-4007. Contact: Norman Wilkes. Estab: 1970. Represents 12 craftsmen. Considers ceramics, jewelry, leatherworking, metalsmithing, pottery, wall hangings, weavings and woodcrafting. Finished one-of-a-kind items OK; decorative. Price range: $2.50-50; bestsellers: $5-15. Buys outright or on consignment; 40% commission. Retail price set by joint agreement. Requires exclusive area representation. Write. Reports in 1 week. Dealer pays shipping and insurance for exhibited work.

YARN KITS, INC., 361 E. 50th St., New York NY 10022. Contact: Bob Gottlieb. Considers artwork for needlecrafts, wall hangings and weavings. Buys outright. Some finished pieces purchased; others purchased as artwork. Write and send copies, not originals. Reports in 1 month.

North Carolina

JOHN C. CAMPBELL FOLK SCHOOL, Brasstown NC 28902. (704)837-2775. Director: Esther Hyatt. Estab: 1925. Represents 50 craftsmen within commuting distance. Considers candlemaking, jewelry, leatherworking, metalsmithing, pottery, wall hangings, weavings, woodcrafting, basket weaving, caning and cornshuck dolls; especially needs woven wall hangings. Finished, one-of-a-kind and handmade production-line items OK; utilitarian and/or decorative. Price range: 75¢-$250; bestsellers: $2.50-$80. Buys outright or on consignment; 20% commission.
Profile: Items displayed 90 days. Heaviest wholesale buying time: winter; best selling time: April-October. Customers are farmers, housewives, bankers and teachers.

CAROLINA MT. ARTS & CRAFTS, Rte. 6, Box 71A, Murphy NC 28906. (704)644-5688. Contact: Barbara Sampson. Estab: 1973. Represents 150 North Carolina, Tennessee and Georgia member craftsmen. Considers candlemaking, ceramics, decoupage, dollmaking, jewelry, leatherworking, metalsmithing, needlecrafts, pottery, macrame, quilting, tole painting, wall hangings, weavings and woodcrafting. Price range: 50¢-$5; bestsellers: $3-5. Works on consignment; 40% commission. Craftsman sets retail price. Write or visit shop. Reports in 2-3 weeks. Best selling time: Easter-Thanksgiving.

CAROLISTA JEWELRY DESIGNERS, 137 E. Rosemary St., Chapel Hill NC 27514 (summer: May-September, Box 201, Nags Head NC 27959). Contact: W. G. Baum. Estab: 1962. Considers ceramics, sculpture, tapestries, woven objects, glass, miniature watercolors, tie dye and batik. Price range: $5-3,000. Work taken on consignment first year; often bought outright afterwards. 25-40% commission. Requires exclusive area representation. Send resume.

LITTLE ART GALLERY, North Hills Shopping Center, Raleigh NC 27609. Director: Ruth Green. Considers ceramics, sculpture, jewelry, metalsmithing, tapestries and paintings. Price range: $8-100 and "more on items such as bronze pieces and woven tapestries." 40% commission. Craftsman sets retail price. Send slides or b&w prints. Gallery pays shipping to gallery. Items displayed 36 weeks minimum.

MACO CRAFTS, INC., Rte. 2, Box 1345, Franklin NC 28734. (704)524-7878. Manager: Betty Jo Warstler. Represents 350 local craftsmen. Considers quilts and furniture. Finished, one-of-a-kind and handmade production-line items OK. Price range: $1-235; bestsellers: $5-235. Works on consignment; 15% commission. Retail price set by joint agreement. Write. Reports immediately. Dealer pays shipping to shop. Best selling time: summer and fall. Customers buy crafts to use as unusual gifts.

MIDLAND CRAFTERS, Box 105, Pinehurst NC 28374. (919)295-6156. Contact: Mr. or Mrs. R. F. Stearn. Estab: 1960. Represents 1,800-2,000 craftsmen. Considers batik, candlemaking, glass art, jewelry, leatherworking, metalsmithing, needlecrafts, pottery, soft sculpture, tole painting, wall hangings, weavings, woodcrafting, furniture, limited clothing, lampshades, nature crafts and noncommercial craft kits. Finished, one-of-a-kind and handmade production-line items OK; utilitarian and/or decorative. Price range: 15¢-$3,300; bestsellers: $2-30. Buys outright. Gallery sets retail price. Requires exclusive area representation. Query with color transparencies or b&w prints; or, if within driving distance, call and then visit. Reports in 1 week unless owner is out of town. Dealer pays shipping.
Profile: "We usually keep all the work of a crafter together in display, either on counter or in lighted niche. We coordinate colors and feel of items if media or crafters' work are mixed." Heaviest wholesale buying time: spring and fall. "Shop is large rambling building with carefully staged displays of handcrafts from across the U.S. Customers are mainly golfers, retired persons and housewives; but shop interests all ages."
Special Needs: Something for teenage boys and men; more handprinted (screen printed) note papers and Christmas cards. Always interested in Christmas decorations. Somewhat interested in crafts that might be catalogued for limited mailing list.

NEW MORNING GALLERY, 3½ Kitchen Place, Asheville NC 28803. (704)274-2831. Director: John Cram. Estab: 1972. Represents 200 craftsmen. Considers wall hangings, weav-

ings and soft sculpture; especially needs ceramics, glass art, jewelry and kitchen pottery. Finished one-of-a-kind items OK; utilitarian and/or decorative. Price range: $5-250; bestsellers: $5-50. Buys outright or occasionally on consignment; 40% commission. Craftsman sets retail price. Requires exclusive area representation. Write. Reports in 1 week. Dealer pays shipping from shop and insurance for exhibited work.
Profile: Glass, pottery and jewelry items displayed in oak cases. Heaviest wholesale buying time: summer-Christmas. "Artists/craftsmen from around the country display in the gallery." Customers ages 27-45. Also distributes wholesale to shops and galleries.

SOUTHERN HIGHLAND HANDICRAFT GUILD, Box 9145, Asheville NC 28805. (704)298-7928. Contact: Alex Miller. For membership, artists in Guild's 9 states must submit 5 examples of recent work to the Standards Committee. Members are permitted to sell through Guild shops and participate in the Craftsman's Fairs. Annual Asheville Fair is in July. Crafts of iron, clay, glass, wood, textiles and other materials exhibited. The Knoxville, Tennessee Fair is held in October with woodworkers, potters, jewelry fashioners, weavers, spinners, and carvers exhibiting.

WA YAH' STI INDIAN TRADITIONS, Box 130, Hollister NC 27844. (919)586-4519. Contact: Arnold and Patricia Richardson. Mail order business. Estab: 1975. Represents 2 craftsmen. Considers Indian crafts and arts; many pieces are collectors items. One-of-a-kind primitive and finished items OK; utilitarian and/or decorative. Price range: 50¢-$850; bestsellers: $4-50. Buys outright. Gallery sets retail price. Write. Reports in 2 weeks. Dealer pays shipping from shop. Heaviest wholesale buying time: winter and spring; best selling time: spring and summer. Customers buy crafts for artistic value.

WOHALI TRADERS, Box 45A, Rte. 1, Cherokee NC 28719. (704)497-9649. Contact: Lois J. deVries. Estab: 1973. Represents 25 craftsmen. Considers candlemaking, jewelry, leatherworking, metalsmithing, needlecrafts, pottery, quilting, wall hangings, weavings, woodcrafting and any authentic Indian handicrafts or original paintings; especially needs non-silver crafts made by Indian tribes from outside North Carolina. Finished, one-of-a-kind and handmade production-line items OK; utilitarian and/or decorative. Price range: 50¢-$1,000; bestsellers: $1-75. Buys outright or on consignment; 40% commission. Retail price set by joint agreement. Requires exclusive area representation. Query with transparencies or photos, or inquire at shop.
Profile: Each item is labeled with the craftsman's name. Heaviest wholesale buying time: spring and early summer; best selling time: summer and early fall.

Ohio

FRONTIERSMEN GIFT SHOP, 67 S. Main St., Centerville OH 45459. (614)433-8691. President: Anna Mae Lockard. Estab: 1972. Represents 70 craftsmen; 85% from Appalachia. Considers glass art, metalsmithing, pottery, quilting, soft sculpture, woodcrafting, doll houses, miniatures, pewter and wooden toys. Finished, one-of-a-kind and handmade production-line items OK; utilitarian and/or decorative. Price range: 50¢-$150; bestsellers: $4.50-10. Buys outright. Shop sets retail price. Requires exclusive representation within 5 miles. Write. Reports in 2 weeks. Shipping to shop paid by Lockard.
Profile: Presents items in front windows and on display tables in center of shop. Best selling time: July-August, November-December; heaviest wholesale buying time: April and October. "Customers with high incomes, average age 35, and interested in the unusual."

PEOPLES AND CULTURES SHOP-IN-THE-FLATS, 1330 Old River Rd., Cleveland OH 44113. (216)621-3749. Manager: Amparo Hernandez. Estab: 1972. Represents 150 craftsmen from the Greater Cleveland area. Considers batik, ceramics, decoupage, dollmaking, jewelry, leatherworking, metalsmithing, quilting, needlecrafts, pottery, soft sculpture, wall hangings, weavings and woodcrafting related to cultural heritage. Primitive or finished, one-of-a-kind or handmade production-line items OK; utilitarian and/or decorative. Price range: 90¢-$500; bestsellers: $1-2.50 Christmas ornaments. Works on consignment; 30% commission. Retail price set by joint agreement. Make appointment to show work to selection jury. Reports in 2 weeks.
Profile: New crafts exhibited in feature display. Best selling time: Christmas and spring. "Customers are all ages, colors, creeds, incomes — those interested in diverse cultures of Cleveland."
Special Needs: Clothing with ethnic stitchery, new culturally-related crafts, toys, games, pillows, instruments and cooking utensils.

POTPOURRI INC., 585 Dover Center, Bay Village OH 44140. (216)871-6500. Manager: Dorli Rosenzopf. Estab: 1968. Represents 50 craftsmen. Considers candlemaking, ceramics, glass art, jewelry, pottery and tole painting; especially needs woodcrafting and metal sculpture. Prefers "Early American style, nothing super modern — it doesn't sell here." Finished handmade production-line items OK; utilitarian and/or decorative. Price range: $2-250; bestsellers: $5-25. Works on consignment; 40% commission. Retail price set by joint agreement. Requires exclusive area representation. Query with transparencies or photos. Reports in 3 weeks.
Profile: Items displayed 3 months minimum. Heaviest wholesale buying time: Christmas. Customers are middle-aged housewives with middle and upper incomes; they buy crafts for gifts.

STORY BOOK CRAFTS — ALL AMERICAN GALLERY/SHOP, 6021 Dayton Rd., Springfield OH 45502. Contact: Elmo or Betty Sprigg. Represents over 250 craftsmen. Considers ceramics, sculpture, metalsmithing, jewelry, needlecrafts, glass, leather, batik, tie dyeing, rugs and tapestries. "We are working craftsmen; we have our own pottery and glass-blowing studio and jewelry and metal shop. We welcome all artists and craftsmen to visit us and make their evaluation of our shop and determine whether they would like to supply us." Price range: $5-1,500. 33 1/3% commission. Retail price set by joint agreement. Requires exclusive representation. Charges commission on crafts sold in area after showing. Gallery pays shipping. Items displayed 4 weeks minimum. Openings sponsored.

Oklahoma

WEWOKA TRADING POST, 524 S. Wewoka, Wewoka OK 74884. (405)257-5580. Contact: Idabel Bishop. Estab: 1974. Represents 25 local craftsmen. Considers dollmaking, jewelry, Seminole patchwork, wall hangings and weavings; especially needs Seminole beadwork, painting and sculpture. Finished one-of-a-kind items OK; utilitarian and/or decorative. Price range: 25¢-$250. Buys outright or on consignment; 25% commission. Retail price set by galley or joint agreement. Write.

Oregon

CONTEMPORARY CRAFTS ASSOCIATION, 3934 SW Corbett Ave., Portland OR 97201. (503)223-2654. Director: Jan de Vries. Estab: 1937. Represents 350+ Northwest craftsmen. Considers ceramics, glass art, jewelry, leatherworking, metalsmithing, quilting, soft sculpture, wall hangings, weaving and woodcrafting. Finished, one-of-a-kind and handmade production-line items OK; utilitarian and/or decorative. Price range: $5-1,500; bestsellers: $25. Works on consignment; 25% commission. Craftsman sets retail price. Write with slides of work. Reports in 3 weeks. Dealer pays insurance on exhibited work.
Profile: Best selling time: November-December. "Customers are upper and middle-class, interested in all arts activities offered in the community."

Pennsylvania

BARE WALL GALLERY, 712 Green St., Harrisburg PA 17102. (717)236-8504. Contact: Ronn Fink. Estab: 1972. Represents 50 craftsmen. Considers batik, candlemaking, jewelry, metalsmithing, needlecrafts, pottery, wall hangings, weavings, woodcrafting and wooden toys. Primitive and finished, one-of-a-kind and handmade production-line items OK; utilitarian items only. Price range: $3-100; bestsellers: $3-30. Buys outright. Craftsman sets retail price. Requires exclusive area representation. Write. Reports in 1 week. Dealer pays shipping to shop. Best wholesale buying time: June; best selling time: December.
To Break In: "Craftsmen striving to be professional need help in developing their lines and in setting up merchandising practice. The most frequent problems craftsmen seem to have are limited selection of items, fluctuating prices and little respect for order dates. When I place an order with a craftsman and he fails to produce, I'm hurt, and what is more is that another craftsman is also hurt because if I had known the items on order were never to be delivered, I would have ordered from another craftsman."

BIRD IN THE HAND, INC., 427 Broad St., Sewickley PA 15143. (412)741-8286. Contact: Katharine N. Amsler. Estab: 1969. Represents 50 craftsmen. Considers ceramics, glass art, jewelry, leatherworking, pottery, wall hangings, weavings and woodcrafting. Finished, one-of-a-kind items OK; utilitarian and/or decorative. Price range: $5-1,000. Buys outright or on consignment; 40% commission. Retail price set by joint agreement. Requires exclusive area representation. Write or query with transparencies or photos. Reports in 2 weeks. Dealer pays shipping from shop and insurance for exhibited work.

Profile: Gallery has 2 floors, each with separate shows. One-man show on lower level runs about 1 month; upper level displays artists' work on walls, boxes and cases for 6 months maximum. Heaviest wholesale buying time: Christmas season. Customers buy crafts for artistic value and usefulness.

THE COLLECTION, 5424 Walnut St., Pittsburgh PA 15232. (412)682-6668. Contact: R. F. McNeish. Considers wedding bands and engagement rings. Must be able to deliver finished goods in 2 weeks. Price range: $36-2,000; bestsellers: $300+. Works on consignment; 40% commission. Craftsman sets retail price. Requires exclusive area representation. Query with samples. Reports in 2 weeks.
Profile: Each craftsman's work displayed in its own area and labeled with name. In order to make sales, craftsman must display work in this manner.

CREATIVE HANDS SHOP, Peddlers Village, Lahaska PA 18931. (215)794-7012. Contact: Florence Kummer or Friedl Allen. Estab: 1963. Represents 8-10 craftsmen. Considers batik, candlemaking, ceramics, glass art, jewelry, metalsmithing and woodcrafting; especially needs pottery, wall hangings and weavings. Finished, one-of-a-kind and handmade production-line items OK; utilitarian and/or decorative. Price range: $1-50; bestsellers: $1-30. Buys outright or on consignment; 30% commission. Retail price set by joint agreement. Requires exclusive area representation. Query with transparencies or photos. Reports in 2 weeks. Dealer pays shipping from shop and insurance for exhibited work. Items displayed 2 months. Heaviest wholesale buying time: summer-Christmas.

HELEN DRUTT GALLERY, 1625 Spruce St., Philadelphia PA 19105. (215)735-1625. Contact: Helen Drutt. Estab: 1974. Represents 20-25 craftsmen. Considers ceramics and jewelry. One-of-a-kind items OK. Price range: $100-1,500. Works on consignment; 40% commission. Retail price set by craftsman or joint agreement. Requires exclusive area representation. Write for interview. Dealer pays shipping from shop and insurance; negotiates payment for shipping to shop. Customers buy crafts for artistic value.

THE EMPORIUM GIFT & PLANT CENTER, Heyburn Center, Baltimore Pike, Concordville PA 19331. (215)459-9200. Contact: Joan Fyk. Estab: 1972. Represents 40-100 craftsmen. Considers candlemaking, ceramics, glass art, jewelry, metalsmithing, pottery, soft sculpture, toys, wall hangings, weavings, woodcrafting and other crafts. Finished, one-of-a-kind and handmade production-line items OK; utilitarian and/or decorative. Price range: $1.25-500; bestsellers: up to $50. Buys outright or on consignment; 40% commission. Craftsman sets retail price. Prefers exclusive area representation. Call for interview. Reports in 2 weeks. Dealer pays insurance for exhibited work; negotiates payment for shipping. Heaviest wholesale buying time: late summer and early fall. Customers ages 20-40 with upper-middle incomes; they buy crafts for gifts.

EVERYDAY PEOPLE, 6th St. and Reed Ave., Monessen PA 15062. (412)684-3450. Director: Carol E. Burrows. Estab: 1974. Represents 80 local craftsmen. Considers candlemaking, ceramics, decoupage, dollmaking, jewelry, pottery, leatherworking, metalsmithing, needlecrafts (knitting and crocheting), quilting, wall hangings and weavings. Finished, one-of-a-kind and handmade production-line items OK; utilitarian and/or decorative. Price range: 25¢-$160; bestsellers: $1-15. Works on consignment. Craftsman sets retail price; gallery adds 20% commission. Stop by shop for interview; reports at that time. Dealer pays insurance on exhibited work.
Profile: Craft given prominent display for 2 months; 10% reduction after 2 and 4 months; returned to craftsman after 6 months. Best selling time: spring and fall. "Shop is designed to meet the needs of people who are just learning a craft and cannot afford to purchase more supplies until they have sold items." Deals with craftsmen of all ages with maximum income of $12,000 and 6 children, or medical disability. If handicapped, staff picks up merchandise. "Our goal is to help people who are trying to help themselves."

THE GOLDSMITH SHOP, 5600 Walnut St., Pittsburgh PA 15232. Contact: Ronald E. McNeish. Considers jewelry, metalsmithing and handmade pipes. Price range: $10-20,000. Buys outright. Retail price set by joint agreement. Requires exclusive area representation. Prefers to see samples. Dealer pays shipping from gallery and insurance for exhibited work. Items displayed 2 weeks minimum. Openings sponsored.

I & WE, 5320 Germantown Ave., Philadelphia PA 19144. Contact: Stan Levin. Considers ceramics, sculpture, jewelry, metalsmithing, needlecrafts, glass, leather, tie dye and batik. Price range: $2-250 set by joint agreement. Send transparencies or photos. Dealer pays insurance for exhibited work. Items displayed 4 weeks minimum. Openings sponsored.

LANGMAN GALLERY, 218 Old York Rd., Jenkintown PA 19046. (215)887-3500. Director: Richard Langman. Estab: 1970. Represents an average of 20 craftsmen. Considers all media. Emphasis is on one-of-a-kind, craft/art items; utilitarian and/or decorative. Price range: $20-2,500; bestsellers: $50-400. Works on consignment; 40% commission. Retail price set by joint agreement. Requires exclusive area representation. Query with transparencies or photos. SASE. Reports in 2 weeks. Dealer pays shipping from shop and insurance for exhibited work. Heaviest wholesale buying time: September and October; best selling time: December. Customers are recent college graduates, professionals and serious craft collectors who buy crafts for their artistic value.

THE OPEN DOOR, 319 Market St., Lewisburg PA 17837. (717)524-7904. Contact: Owner. Estab: 1973. Represents 250 craftsmen. Considers batik, ceramics, jewelry, leatherworking, metalsmithing, pottery, quilting, wall hangings, numbered prints, weavings and woodcrafting; especially needs items under $20. Finished one-of-a-kind and handmade production-line items OK; utilitarian and/or decorative. Price range: $2-300; bestsellers: $2-20. Buys outright. Query with color transparencies or b&w prints. Reports in 4 weeks. Dealer pays insurance on exhibited work.
Profile: Best selling time: December, May-June. Customers are mostly upper-middle-class families.

OVERLY-RAKER VILLAGE, R.D. 1, McConnellsburg PA 17233. (717)485-4705. Contact: Helen Overly. Estab: 1972. Represents 20-25 craftsmen. Considers candlemaking, dollmaking, glass art, jewelry, leatherworking, metalsmithing, pottery, quilting and woodcrafting. Finished, one-of-a-kind and handmade production-line items OK; utilitarian and/or decorative. Price range: $5-100; bestsellers; $15-40. Buys outright. Retail price set by joint agreement. Write. Reports in 2 weeks. Dealer pays shipping and insurance.
Profile: Items displayed 1 month on antique furniture and trees. Heaviest wholesale buying time: July; best selling time: October-December.

PRUDENCE AND STRICKLER, 617 South St., Philadelphia PA 19147. Contact: Prudence. Considers jewelry, metalsmithing and leather. Price range: $3-500. 30% commission. Retail price set by joint agreement. Send transparencies or photos. Dealer pays insurance for exhibited work. Items displayed 5 weeks minimum.

WILLIAM RIS GALLERIES, 2208 Market St., Camp Hill PA 17011. (717)737-8818 or 9731. Contact: Barbara Schreckengaust. Estab: 1966. Represents 150 craftsmen. Considers ceramics, glass art, jewelry, enamels, pottery, sculpture, wall hangings, wall sculpture, weavings and woodcrafting. Finished, one-of-a-kind and handmade items OK; utilitarian and/or decorative. Price range: $5-500; bestsellers: $5-150. Buys outright or occasionally on consignment; 40% commission. Retail price set by gallery or joint agreement. Requires exclusive area representation. Write. Reports in 2 weeks. Dealer pays shipping.
Profile: "We feature monthly exhibitions of craftsmen's work." Heaviest wholesale buying time: spring and fall. Customers ages 20-55 with middle and upper incomes.

WILLIAM RIS GALLERIES, Briar Barn, 939 W. Governor Rd., Hershey PA 17033. (717)534-1800. Contact: Barbara Schreckengaust. Estab: 1966. Represents 150 craftsmen. Considers ceramics, glass art, jewelry, pottery, sculpture, wall hangings, weavings, woodcrafting, and enameled plates and plaques with birds, animals and flowers. Finished, one-of-a-kind and handmade production-line items OK; utilitarian and/or decorative. Price range: $5-500; bestsellers: $5-150. Buys outright or occasionally on consignment; 40% commission. Retail price set by gallery or joint agreement. Requires exclusive area representation. Write. Reports in 2 weeks. Dealer pays shipping.
Profile: "We feature monthly exhibitions of craftsmen's work." Heaviest wholesale buying time: spring and fall. Customers ages 20-55 with middle and upper incomes.

CHARLES E. SHOOP, 5539 Walnut St., Pittsburgh PA 15232. Contact: Charles Shoop. Considers ceramics, jewelry, metalsmithing and sculpture. Price range: $3-1,000. Buys outright. "We pay shipping costs, but frown on a packing charge." Requires exclusive area representation.

THE SOURCE GALLERY, 121 S. Penna Ave., Greensburg PA 15601. (412)836-1190. Manager: Carol Pollock. Estab: 1972. Represents 100 western Pennsylvania craftsmen. Considers batik, jewelry, metalsmithing, paintings, pottery and prints; especially needs fiberwork. Finished, one-of-a-kind and handmade production-line items OK; utilitarian and/or decorative. Price range: $10-300; bestsellers: $10-75. Works on consignment; 33 1/3% commission. Retail price set by joint agreement. Requires exclusive area representation. Write. Reports in 2 weeks.
Profile: Items displayed 3 months with new items featured. Gallery holds 4 shows annually. Heaviest wholesale buying time: winter and spring. Accepts work only from western Pennsylvania craftsmen. Customers are young working professionals, college students and collectors.

THE STORE, 719 Allegheny River Blvd., Verona PA 15147. (412)828-6121. Director: Elizabeth Raphael. Estab: 1972. Represents 250 out-of-town craftsmen. Considers contemporary batik, candlemaking, ceramics, dollmaking, glass art, jewelry, leatherworking, metalsmithing, needlecrafts, pottery, quilting, wall hangings, weavings and woodcrafting. "We carry only 'designer handcrafts.' No traditional, manufactured, folk or ethnic crafts." Finished, one-of-a-kind and handmade production-line items OK; utilitarian and/or decorative. Price range: $1-3,000; bestsellers: $15-100. Buys outright. Query with transparencies or photos. Reports in 1 week, longer during Christmas. Dealer pays shipping to shop and insurance. Heaviest wholesale buying time: summer; best selling time: November-December.

THE SUN SHOP, 491 Lancaster Ave., Frazer PA 19355. (215)647-0374. Contact: Bob Frantz. Estab: 1972. Represents 15 craftsmen. Considers ceramics, glass art, jewelry, pottery and woodcrafting; especially needs planters. Finished, one-of-a-kind and handmade production-line items OK; utilitarian and/or decorative. Price range: $2-100; bestsellers: $8-25. Buys outright or on consignment (for very expensive items); 40% commission. Retail price set by joint agreement. Call for interview. Reports in 3 weeks. Dealer pays insurance; negotiates shipping cost.
Profile: Each craftsman's work displayed by itself. Purchased crafts are permanently displayed; consigned crafts by agreement. Heaviest wholesale buying time: fall and early spring; best selling time: fall. "We limit the types of crafts and offer a large variety of those particular types." Customers ages 25-40 with $25,000 incomes and fairly conservative tastes.

WINFIELD HOUSE, Rte. 15, Winfield PA 17889. (717)524-7006. Manager: Erica Burns. Estab: 1972. Represents 100+ craftsmen. Considers batik, candlemaking, dollmaking, jewelry, leatherworking, macrame, metalsmithing, pottery, stained glass, wall hangings, weavings, and stuffed and wooden toys. Finished, one-of-a-kind and handmade production-line items OK. Price range: 50¢-$525; bestsellers: $4-20. Buys outright or on consignment; 33 1/3% commission. Requires exclusive area representation. Mail artwork. Reports in 2 weeks. Dealer pays shipping and insurance for exhibited work.
Profile: Craftsman's item(s) displayed as a unit and marked with name. Heaviest wholesale buying time: late summer-early fall. Customers ages 18-45 with middle incomes.

THE WORKS CRAFT GALLERY, 319 South St., Philadelphia PA 19147. (215)922-7775. Contact: Ruth or Rick Snyderman. Estab: 1965. Represents 230 craftsmen. Considers batik, ceramics, glass art, jewelry, metalsmithing, pottery, quilting, soft sculpture, wall hangings, weavings and woodcrafting. One-of-a-kind and handmade production-line items OK; utilitarian and/or decorative. Price range: $3.50-1,800; bestsellers: $5-40. Buys outright or on consignment; 40% commission. Craftsman sets retail price. Requires exclusive center city representation. Send transparencies or photos and arrange interview. Reports in 2 weeks. Dealer pays shipping and insurance for exhibited work.
Profile: Craftsman's item(s) displayed as a unit and marked with name and medium. Items rotated weekly in gallery. Heaviest wholesale buying time: October-December.

Rhode Island

COOPER AND FRENCH, LTD., 130 Thames St., Newport RI 02840. (401)849-6512. Director: Marve H. Cooper. Estab: 1974. Represents over 150 craftsmen. Considers ceramics, glass art, jewelry, leatherworking, metalsmithing, pottery, quilting, soft sculpture, wall hangings, weavings and woodcrafting; especially needs sea subjects. Finished, handmade production-line items OK; utilitarian and/or decorative. Price range: $2-3,000; bestsellers: $5-20. Buys outright; on consignment for exhibitions. 40% commission. Craftsman sets retail price. Query with transparencies or photos, or arrange interview. Reports in 1 week. Dealer pays shipping to shop and insurance on exhibited work. Heaviest wholesale buying time: spring and fall; best selling time: summer and Christmas.

WELCOME ROOD STUDIO, S. Killingly Rd., Foster RI 02825. (401)397-3045. Contact: Elizabeth Zimmerman. Estab: 1970. Represents 6 local craftsmen. Considers primarily stoneware pottery; also candlemaking, dollmaking, glass art, metalsmithing, quilting, soft sculpture, wall hangings, weavings and woodcrafting. Finished, one-of-a-kind and production-line, handmade items OK; utilitarian and/or decorative. Price range: $3.50-100; bestsellers: $3.50-25. Works on consignment; 25% commission. Retail price set by joint agreement. Arrange interview. Reports in 4 weeks.
Profile: Crafts remain in shop until sold. All items, except wall hangings, are rearranged monthly. Best selling time: fall-Christmas. "It is primarily a salesroom for the stoneware pottery produced on the premises. Other work is an addition to this, but does not receive the same volume turnover." Customers are young married couples; they buy crafts for usefulness.

South Carolina

THE CARGO HOLD, INC., 342 King St., Charleston SC 29401. (803)722-1377. Contact: Tom Young. Estab: 1973. Represents 5 craftsmen. Considers blown glass and finely finished silver jewelry. Finished, one-of-a-kind items OK; utilitarian and/or decorative. Price range: 50¢-$95; bestsellers: $3-30. Buys outright, also "occasionally on consignment to locals"; 33 1/3% commission. Retail price set by joint agreement. Write. Reports in 3 weeks. Dealer pays insurance for exhibited work and shipping to shop if bought outright. "Can supply cabochons to jewelers; will consider trading materials for finished pieces."
Profile: "Prominently displayed according to method of purchase." Heaviest wholesale buying time: fall and spring. "Customers, ages 20-35, have great appreciation for quality art but not enough funds to pursue their tastes."

THE GALLERY, 385 S. Spring St., Spartanburg SC 29301. Contact: Curator. Considers ceramics, sculpture, glass, paintings, rugs, tapestries, jewelry and metalsmithing. Price range: $5-1,000. Works on consignment; 33 1/3% commission. Retail price set by joint agreement. Send transparencies or photos. Gallery pays insurance for exhibited work. Items displayed 4 weeks minimum. Openings sponsored.

OLD SLAVE MART MUSEUM AND GALLERY, 6 Chalmers St., Charleston SC 29401. (803)722-0079. Director: Mrs. Louise A. Graves. Museum of black heritage. Estab: 1937. Represents 100-200 black craftsmen. Considers batik, candlemaking, ceramics, decoupage, dollmaking, glass art, jewelry, leatherworking, metalsmithing, needlecrafts, pottery, quilting, soft sculpture, tole painting, wall hangings, weavings and woodcrafting. Primitive and finished, one-of-a-kind and handmade production-line items OK; utilitarian and/or decorative. Price range: 25¢-$75; bestsellers: $2-10. Buys outright or on consignment; 25% commission. Retail price set by joint agreement. Query with transparencies or photos, or arrange interview. Reports in 2-3 weeks. Dealer pays shipping from shop and insurance for exhibited work.
Profile: Items arranged in glass cases in relation to other crafts and art. Items displayed approximately 6 weeks. Heaviest wholesale buying time: fall and spring; best selling time: spring and summer. Only shop in Charleston featuring work of black artists/craftsmen. Over 35,000 visitors annually. Customers buy for artistic value and gifts.

South Dakota

PRAIRIE PEOPLES HANDICRAFT MARKET, INC., Armour SD 57313. (605)654-2370. Chairman of the Board: Barbara Beals. Estab: 1970. Represents 300-500 craftsmen. "Our consignees are mostly over 65, although no one is ever refused. We also have many handicapped people consigning." Considers all crafts. Finished handmade production-line items OK; utilitarian and/or decorative. Price range: 25¢-$100; bestsellers: $1-50. Works on consignment: 25% commission. Craftsman sets retail price. Write. Reports in 2-3 days maximum. Shop pays return shipping and insurance on exhibited work.
Profile: New items displayed in front window for 1 week, then placed on shelves or walls in the shop until sold or artist wants them returned. Best selling time: March-December. Store operated by volunteers. Customers mostly interested in useful items.

Tennessee

LADY BUG GALLERY, 208 E. Main St., Johnson City TN 37601. Contact: Sandy Joy. Considers ceramics, sculpture, jewelry, metalsmithing, needlecrafts, rugs, tapestries, glass, leather, tie dye, batik and woodcrafts. Price range: $1-500. Buys outright or on consignment; 30% commission. Retail price set by joint agreement. Requires exclusive area representation. Send transparencies or photos. Shipping costs shared. Items displayed 4 weeks minimum.

GALLERY III, 122 Stadium Dr., Hendersonville TN 37075. (615)824-7675. Contact: Pat Beaver. Estab: 1968. Represents 50-100 craftsmen. Considers basketweaving, jewelry, quilting, wall hangings, weavings and woodcrafting; especially needs functional pottery. Finished, one-of-a-kind and handmade production-line items OK; utilitarian and/or decorative. Price range: $5-400; bestsellers: $5-35. Buys outright at 50% or on consignment at 35% commission. Retail price set by joint agreement. Query with color transparencies or b&w prints. Reports in 2 weeks. Dealer pays shipping to shop and insurance for exhibited wholesale purchases. Heaviest wholesale buying time: fall and winter.

THE PLUM NELLY SHOP, 1201 Hixson Pike, Chattanooga TN 37405. (615)266-0585. Contact: Celia Marks. Estab: 1971. Represents 300 out-of-town craftsmen. Considers candlemaking, ceramics, dollmaking, metalsmithing, needlecrafts, pottery, wall hangings, weavings and woodcrafting. "We use the Southern Highland Handicrafts Guild standards in judging crafts to be bought for our shop; however, we don't limit ourselves to the crafts accepted for membership in that organization." Finished, one-of-a-kind and handmade production-line items OK; utilitarian and/or decorative. Price range: $1-200; bestsellers: $3-35. Buys outright. Retail price set by joint agreement. Requires exclusive Chattanooga representation. "We usually spot new work at craft fairs and shows, but frequently craftsmen know us by reputation and write to set up an appointment to show their work." Reports in 2 weeks. Dealer pays shipping from shop and insurance on exhibited work. "Send work by UPS; it is then automatically insured while in-transit."
Profile: "We buy with considerable discrimination and time period between purchase and sale is not of great concern to us." Heaviest wholesale buying time: spring and summer; best selling time: Christmas. Customers are young career women and male executives in their 30's.
To Break In: "I am an ex-food editor and author of 2 cookbooks and therefore am extremely practical in my approach to functional items. Those items to be used in the kitchen come in for special scrutiny (i.e., handles large enough to grasp while holding a cloth pot holder, smooth bottoms, dishwasher-safe, etc.).

RIDGEWAY GALLERY, 132 Ridgeway Center, Oak Ridge TN 37830. (615)483-6690. Manager: Mirjam Koehler. Considers ceramics, sculpture, tapestries, rugs, glass, jewelry and metalsmithing. Price range: $2-1,000. Buys outright (50% discount) or on consignment (33 1/3% commission). Craftsman sets retail price. Send transparencies or photos. Gallery pays half shipping costs and insurance for exhibited work. Items displayed 6 months minimum. Sponsors openings.

SERENDIPITY GALLERIES, 516 N. University Ave., Murfreesboro TN 37130. (615)893-5540. Contact: Mrs. Louis Rowland. Estab: 1967. Represents 40-45 craftsmen "within hand-delivery distance." Considers jewelry, metalsmithing, pottery, wall hangings, weavings and woodcrafting. Finished, one-of-a-kind items OK; utilitarian and/or decorative. Price range: 25¢-$100; bestsellers: 25¢-$12. Buys outright or occasionally on consignment; 25% commission. Gallery sets retail price. Query with color transparencies or b&w prints; or make appointment to bring work to gallery. Reports in 2 weeks. Personally deliver work; "too much damage, craftsmen don't know how to ship their own work." Dealer pays insurance on exhibited work.
Profile: "If enough is purchased, the work will be treated as an exhibit and is advertised as such for a 4-week period. Other pieces are displayed along with other items." Customers, ages 25-55, are professionals with $12,000-25,000 incomes; they buy crafts for their usefulness and individuality.

Texas

ALABAMA-COUSHATTA INDIAN ARTS & CRAFTS, Rte. 3, Box 640, Livingston TX 77351. (713)563-4391. Director: R.W. Hamilton. Estab: 1967. Represents 6 craftsmen. Considers jewelry, pottery, Indian beadwork and basketmaking. Primitive and finished, one-of-a-kind and handmade production-line items OK; utilitarian and/or decorative. Price range: $1-500; bestsellers: $1-35. Buys outright. Gallery sets retail price. Write. Reports in 2 weeks. Dealer pays shipping from shop and insurance for exhibited work.
Profile: Heaviest wholesale buying time: spring; best selling time: summer. Customers are middle-aged with middle incomes; they buy crafts for artistic value and gifts.

ARTISAN GALLERY, 317 N. Commerce, Gainesville TX 76240. Contact: Ruby Cogdell. Considers ceramics, sculpture, jewelry, metalsmithing, needlecrafts, rugs, tapestries, glass, leather, tie dye and batik. Price range: $1-400 set by joint agreement. Salability of items determines whether gallery buys wholesale or whether merchandise will be put on consignment at 25% commission. Requires exclusive area representation. Send transparencies or photos. Payment on or before end of month. Items displayed 12 weeks minimum. "Expect artist and public to meet at open house, usually held in fall."

CERAMIC HUT, 260 Walnut, Colorado City TX 79512. (915)728-3942. Contact: Johnnie Hammond. Estab: 1971. Represents 2 craftsmen. Considers ceramics, decoupage, tole painting, wall hangings and weavings; especially needs vases, 9-10" high. Finished handmade production-line items OK; utilitarian and/or decorative. Price range: $75-250; bestsellers: $30-250. Buys outright. Shop sets retail price. Requires exclusive area representation. Write first. Reports in 3 weeks. Dealer pays shipping and insurance.
Profile: Displays items 2 weeks. Heaviest wholesale buying season: November-December. Only shop in a 40-mile area. Customers ages 25-65; income of age 25 about $500 per month; they buy crafts for originality.

CRAFT INDUSTRIES, 78 Woodlake Square, Houston TX 77063. (713)789-8170. Contact: Linda Lee. Estab: 1970. Represents 20 craftsmen. Considers batik, ceramics, glass art, metalsmithing, needlecrafts, quilting, soft sculpture, wall hangings, weavings and woodcrafting; especially needs functional pottery. Primitive and finished, one-of-a-kind and handmade production-line items OK; utilitarian and/or decorative. Price range: $2.50-1,500; bestsellers: $5-350. Works on consignment; 40% commission. Retail price set by joint agreement. Requires exclusive representation in 3-mile radius. Query with transparencies or photos. Reports in 3 weeks. Dealer pays insurance for exhibited work.
Profile: Items displayed on cedar pedestals and risers. Craftsmen leave work on a 3-month basis. Most crafts are bought and sold in the fall. "We have an area of general crafts and 600 square feet of special gallery space for shows. Women customers ages 18-50 with upper incomes; they buy crafts for artistic value and gifts."

One-of-a-kind craft items are emphasized at the Langman Gallery, Pennsylvania. Richard Langman, director, says his prices range from $20-2,500. Work can be either utilitarian or decorative. Langman represents an average of 20 craftsmen.

ESTUDIOS RIO, GALLERY OF CONTEMPORARY ARTS AND CRAFTS, 518 Doherty St., Box 632, Mission TX 78572. Contact: Xavier Gorena. Considers ceramics, sculpture, glass, jewelry, metalsmithing, batik, paintings, prints and mixed media. Price range: $5-1,000. Works on consignment; 40% commission. Craftsman sets retail price. Requires exclusive area representation. Charges commission on crafts sold in area after showing. "We require resume and/or bio with transparencies or photos." Items displayed 8 weeks minimum.

JOHN KEBRLE STUDIO, Stained & Faceted Glass, 2829 Bachman Dr., Dallas TX 75220. Considers sculpture and glass. Price range: $700-20,000. 20% commission. Send transparencies or photos. Items displayed 1 week minimum.

LAGUNA GLORIA ART MUSEUM, Box 5568, Austin TX 78763. Contact: Mary Erler. Considers ceramics, jewelry, glass and weaving. "We specialize in Texas crafts, so naturally we're more interested in seeing submissions from artists in this area." Price range: $5-200. 30% commission. Craftsman sets retail price. Send transparencies or photos. Dealer pays insurance for exhibited work. Items displayed 12 weeks minimum.

THE PARLOUR, 2124 The Strand, Galveston TX 77550. (713)762-4006. Contact: Judith Copeland. Estab: 1975. Represents 200 craftsmen. Considers candlemaking, dollmaking, glass art, jewelry, leatherworking, metalsmithing, needlecrafts, pottery, quilting, wall hangings, weavings and woodcrafting. Finished, one-of-a-kind and handmade production-line items OK; utilitarian and/or decorative. Price range: $1.50-200; bestsellers: $5-30. Buys outright or on consignment; 33 1/3% commission. Retail price set by joint agreement. Requires exclusive area representation. Write. Reports in 2 weeks. Dealer pays shipping from shop and insurance for exhibited work.
Profile: Items displayed 3 months maximum; marked down after 45 days. Best selling time: summer-Christmas. Customers are tourists, local residents and medical students; they buy crafts for gifts. "This area is restored Victorian on the order of a small New Orleans."

THE SHED, INC., 1649 Blalock, Houston TX 77080. (713)467-3078. Contact: G. Murphy. Represents 50 Southwestern craftsmen. Considers basketweaving, batik, calligraphy, glass art, metalsmithing, pottery, soft sculpture, fiber wall hangings, weavings and woodcrafting. Price range: $5-1,800; bestsellers: $5-150. Works on consignment; 40% commission. Retail price set by joint agreement. Query with slides or photos. Reports in 1 month maximum. SASE. Dealer pays insurance for exhibited work. Items displayed 1-12 months.

SOUTHWEST CRAFT CENTER GALLERY, 420 Paseo De La Villita, San Antonio TX 78205. (512)222-0926. Chairman: Maggie L. Reed. Represents 50 craftsmen. Considers batik, calligraphy, ceramics, dollmaking, glass art, jewelry, leatherworking, metalsmithing, needlecrafts, pottery, prints, sculpture, soft sculpture and wall hangings. Price range: $3-250; bestsellers: $5-25. Works on consignment; 40% commission. Craftsman sets retail price. Send slides with SASE. Reports in 1 month. Dealer pays shipping from gallery and insurance for exhibited work. Items displayed 6-12 months.
Special Needs: Gallery uses art for membership literature, catalogs and public service TV announcements.

THE THUMB PRINT, 605 Lubbock Rd., Brownfield TX 79316. Contact: Vicki Simpson. Estab: 1976. Represents 3-4 craftsmen. Considers decoupage, glass art, needlecrafts, tole painting, wall hangings, weavings and woodcrafting. Primitive and finished, one-of-a-kind and handmade production-line items OK; utilitarian and/or decorative. Price range: 50¢-$250; bestsellers: $3-10. Works on consignment; 40% commission. Retail price set by joint agreement. Write. Reports in 2 weeks. Dealer pays insurance for exhibited work.
Profile: Items displayed 6 weeks with a sign naming craftsman and details of work. Buys and sells most crafts in fall. Shop takes special orders. Customers are 24-40 with upper-middle incomes.

URSULINE GALLERY, 300 Augusta St., San Antonio TX 78205. (512)224-1848. Director: Judy Cross. Represents 50 craftsmen. Considers batik, calligraphy, ceramics, dollmaking, glass art, jewelry, leatherworking, metalsmithing, needlecrafts, pottery, prints, sculpture, soft sculpture and wall hangings. Price range: 75¢-$2,000; bestsellers: $5-25. Works on consignment; 30% commission. Craftsman sets retail price. Send slides with SASE. Reports in 1

month. Dealer pays shipping from gallery and insurance for exhibited work. Items displayed 6-12 months.
Special Needs: Gallery uses art for membership literature, catalogs and public service TV announcements.

YE OLD TOWN SHOPPE, 113 E. Main, Eagle Lake TX 77434. (713)234-3911. Contact: Candy McCreary. Estab: 1976. Represents 15 craftsmen. Considers batik, candlemaking, dollmaking, needlecrafts, quilting, wall hangings, weavings and woodcrafting. Finished one-of-a-kind items OK; utilitarian and/or decorative. Price range: $5-150; bestsellers: $5-10. Works on consignment; 20% commission. Craftsman sets retail price. Write or call. Reports in 10 days.
Profile: "We display crafts in front window the first week." Best selling time: fall. "Ours is the only craft shop in town; located downtown in an old building with a player piano featured."

Vermont

EBENEZER ALLEN COUNTRY STORE & GIFT SHOP, Burlington Square Mall, Burlington VT 05401. (802)863-4215. Contact: John Luck. Estab: 1972. Represents 60 craftsmen. Considers candlemaking, ceramics, dollmaking, glass art, jewelry, leatherworking, metalsmithing, pottery, quilting and woodcrafting. Finished handmade production-line items OK; utilitarian and/or decorative. Price range: $1-400; bestsellers: $1.65-30. Buys outright or occasionally on consignment; 33 1/3% commission. Shop sets retail price. Requires exclusive area representation. Query with transparencies or photos. Reports in 3 weeks. Dealer pays shipping to shop and insurance for exhibited work. Heaviest wholesale buying time: Christmas and summer.

EBENEZER ALLEN COUNTRY STORE & GIFT SHOP, Rte. 2 and 314, South Hero VT 05486. (802)372-4619. Contact: John Luck. Estab: 1972. Represents 30 craftsmen. Considers candlemaking, ceramics, dollmaking, glass art, jewelry, leatherworking, metalsmithing, pottery, quilting and woodcrafting (furniture). Finished handmade production-line items OK; utilitarian and/or decorative. Price range: $1-800; bestsellers: $1.65-80. Buys outright or occasionally on consignment; 33 1/3% commission. Shop sets retail price. Requires exclusive area representation. Query with transparencies or photos. Reports in 3 weeks. Dealer pays shipping to shop and insurance for exhibited work. Heaviest wholesale buying time: Christmas and summer.

COLONIAL VERMONT, INC., Rte. 7, Shelburne VT 05482. (802)985-2742. Contact: M. Gazley. Estab: 1965. Represents several craftsmen. Considers metalsmithing, furniture, woodcrafting and pottery. Finished, one-of-a-kind utilitarian items OK. Prices are $3+. Buys outright or on consignment; 40% commission. Retail price set by joint agreement. Requires exclusive area representation. Write. Reports in 2 weeks. Dealer pays insurance for exhibited work.

THE FEDERAL ESTABLISHMENT, 1 Federal St., St. Albans VT 05478. (802)524-2735. Contact: Roger King-Hall. Estab: 1974. Represents 20 craftsmen. Considers batik, candlemaking, glass art, jewelry, leatherworking, metalsmithing, pottery, quilting, soft sculpture, wall hangings, weavings and woodcrafting. Finished handmade production-line items OK; utilitarian and/or purely decorative. Price range: $1-50; bestsellers: $1-18. Buys outright; 34% commission. Retail price set by joint agreement. Write. Reports in 1 month.

THE POMFRET SHOP, Old Barnard Stage Rd., South Pomfret VT 05067. (802)457-2464. Contact: Mr. or Mrs. D. Cleveland. Estab: 1972. Represents 12 craftsmen. Considers ceramics, glass art, metalsmithing, needlecrafts, pottery, quilting, wall hangings, weavings and woodcrafting; especially needs garden sculpture, plant containers, fountains, bird baths, houses, feeders and Christmas decorations. Primitive and finished, one-of-a-kind and handmade production-line items OK; utilitarian and/or decorative. Price range: $5-350; bestsellers: $5-20. Buys outright or on consignment; 33 1/3% commission. Retail price set by joint agreement. Requires exclusive area representation. Query with color transparencies or b&w prints. Reports in 2 weeks. Dealer pays shipping to shop.
Profile: "Our shop is small, but uncluttered. When we take a craft in, it is tagged with the maker's name and price and given prime location." Heaviest wholesale buying time: winter and spring; best selling time: summer and fall. "We go out of our way to handle things that others do not have; plant displays use artificial lighting; outdoor deck features container gardening."

SAMARA, Box 1115, Stowe VT 05672. (802)253-8318. Contact: Lynn W. Miles. Estab: 1972. Represents 100 craftsmen. Considers batik, candlemaking, glass art, jewelry, leatherworking, metalsmithing, pottery, quilting, soft sculpture, wall hangings, weavings and woodcrafting. Finished, one-of-a-kind and handmade production-line items OK; utilitarian and/or decorative. Price range: $1-150; bestsellers: $3-30. Primarily buys outright, some consignment; 33 1/3% commission. Craftsman sets retail price. Query with color transparencies, b&w prints or samples. Reports in 1 week. SASE.
Profile: Heaviest wholesale buying time: early summer and pre-Christmas; best selling time: summer. Typical resort area clientele; primarily skiers in winter from Boston, New York and Montreal.

SUNSHINE SNOWY DAY, R.D. 1, Box 54A, Waterbury Center VT 05077. (802)244-7546. Contact: John Hunter Wetmore. Considers ceramics, glass and wooden toys. Price range: $1-75. Buys outright. Craftsman sets retail price. Send transparencies or photos. Dealer pays shipping and insurance for exhibited work.

VERDE-MONT GIFTS, 50 Main St., Middlebury VT 05753. (802)388-6504. Contact: Bernice W. Fucile. Estab: 1967. Considers candlemaking, glass art, metalsmithing, pottery, soft sculpture, woodcrafting and nonsilver jewelry (Fucile is silversmith). Finished and primitive, one-of-a-kind and handmade production-line items OK; utilitarian and/or decorative. Price range: $1-25; bestsellers: $2.50-20. Buys outright or on consignment; 40% commission. Craftsman sets retail price. Requires exclusive area representation. Query with color transparencies or b&w prints. Reports in 2 weeks. Dealer pays shipping from shop and insurance for exhibited work.
Profile: Items displayed on shelves or behind glass. Consigned work held 2 months. Heaviest wholesale buying time: summer and pre-Christmas. Middlebury is college town. "Customers are all ages; they buy crafts for their usefulness and individuality."

Virginia

APPALACHIANA, 315 Cameron St., Alexandria VA 22314. (703)683-6100. Contact: Joan Farrell at Bethesda, Maryland shop. Estab: 1970. Represents 300 craftsmen. Considers batik, candlemaking, ceramics, jewelry, leatherworking, metalsmithing, pottery and woodcrafting. Finished, one-of-a-kind and handmade production-line items OK; utilitarian and/or decorative. Price range: $1-400; bestsellers: $15-25. Buys outright. Retail price set by joint agreement. Write or query with transparencies or photos. Reports in 2 weeks. Dealer pays shipping to shop and insurance for exhibited work. Heaviest wholesale buying time: spring and fall.

CREATIVE ARTS, Drawer Q, Williamsburg VA 23185. (804)229-8232. Contact: Mike Makulowich. Estab: 1973. Represents 25 craftsmen. Considers batik, candlemaking, ceramics, glass art, graphics, jewelry, leatherworking, metalsmithing, needlecrafts, pottery, quilting, soft sculpture, tole painting, wall hangings, weavings and woodcrafting. Primitive and/or finished, one-of-a-kind and handmade production-line items OK; utilitarian and/or decorative. Price range: $5-500; bestsellers: $5-20. Buys outright or on consignment; 66 2/3% commission. Retail price set by joint agreement. Requires exclusive area representation. Write or query with color transparencies or b&w photos. Reports in 2 weeks. Dealer pays insurance on exhibited work.
Profile: New arrivals placed in front window and listed in area magazine. Best selling time: Christmas. "We try to accompany items with graphics, home settings, furniture and table settings that appeal to decorators, readers and music lovers."

FAIRFAX COUNTY COUNCIL OF THE ARTS, Green Spring Farm Park, 4601 Green Spring Rd., Alexandria VA 22312. (703)941-6066. Gallery and display areas for pottery and crafts. Exhibits change monthly. Sponsors spring festival and summer outdoor exhibits on 16-acre grounds. Also sponsors Area Exhibition of Painting and Graphics at Northern Virginia Community College and grant programs for public schools and a Concerts-in-the-Schools program.

FIRST IMPRESSIONS, 13809 Lee Hwy., Centreville VA 22020. (703)631-9019. Contact: Barbara Sanders. Estab: 1972. Represents 300 (mostly local) craftsmen. Considers all crafts; especially needs traditional styles. Finished, one-of-a-kind and handmade production-line items OK; utilitarian and/or decorative. Price range: 75c-$50; bestsellers: $1.50-22. Works on consignment; 35% commission. Retail price set by joint agreement. Write. Reports in 2 weeks. Dealer pays "break-in" insurance for exhibited work.

Profile: Items displayed 3 months maximum among antiques. Heaviest wholesale buying time: late summer and fall; best selling time: fall and spring.

LONGHORN LEATHER, 1513 Lolley Ave., Norfolk VA 23517. Contact: Shep Saltzman. Considers ceramics, jewelry, metalsmithing and leather. Price range: $1-150. Retail price set by joint agreement. Send transparencies or photos. Shipping costs shared.

Washington

ALPHA DOUBLE PLUS, Box 98457, Des Moines WA 98457. (206)246-1570. Contact: Morton Silverbow. Estab: 1973. Represents 40 gay craftsmen. Considers batik, ceramics, glass art, jewelry, metalsmithing, needlecrafts, pottery, soft sculpture, wall hangings, weavings, woodcrafting and fine arts; especially needs figurative works. Primitive and finished, one-of-a-kind and handmade production-line items OK; utilitarian and/or decorative. Price range: $5-35; bestsellers: $5-175. Buys outright or on consignment; 50% commission. Gallery sets retail price. Query with transparencies or photos. Reports in 3 weeks. Dealer pays shipping from shop and insurance. Heaviest wholesale buying time: spring and fall. Affluent customers.

THE GAIL CHASE GALLERY, 22 103rd NE, Bellevue WA 98004. (206)454-1250. Contact: Gail Chase. Estab: 1965. Represents 90 craftsmen. Considers batik, candlemaking, ceramics, jewelry and pottery; especially needs ethnic crafts, rugs and clothing. Finished, one-of-a-kind and handmade production-line items OK; mostly utilitarian. Price range: $5-100; bestsellers: $10-25. Buys outright or on consignment; 40% commission. Gallery sets retail price. Write. Reports in 2 weeks. Negotiates shipping. Dealer pays insurance for exhibited work. Buys and sells most crafts from October-December. Customers, ages 20-45, are teachers, professors and intellectuals.

THE COUNTRY CRAFTSMEN, Rte. 1, Box 529, Long Beach WA 98631. (206)642-2644. Contact: Bonny Lowry. Estab: 1975. Represents 50 craftsmen. Considers all crafts, toys, paintings, prints, clothing, cards and gift wrap with a country-type look. Finished, one-of-a-kind and production-line, handmade items OK; utilitarian and/or decorative. Price range: 10¢-$200; bestsellers: 15¢-$15. Works on consignment; 25% commission. Craftsman sets retail price. Write or submit work in person. Reports in 2 weeks. Dealer pays shipping from shop and insurance for exhibited work.
Profile: Craftsmen notified before the 10th of each month as to whether they have made sales. Heaviest wholesale buying time: February and August; best selling time: summer. Shop, located in retirement and family tourist area, looks like a cottage. "We are strictly country-casual in a countrified setting." Customers ages 30+ with average incomes.

CROCKERY SHED, 22 103rd NE, Bellevue WA 98004. Contact: Gail Chase. Considers ceramics, jewelry, metalsmithing, ethnic crafts (which includes carpets, baskets, jewelry, clothing, tapestries) and cards. Price range: $5-1,000. Works on consignment; 40% commission. Retail price set by joint agreement. Requires exclusive Bellevue representation. Send transparencies or photos. Gallery pays shipping "if we buy" and insurance for exhibited work. Items displayed 6 weeks minimum. Sponsors openings.

EAST SHORE GALLERY, 12700 SE 32nd St., Bellevue WA 98004. Co-chairmen: Carol Wright/Pam Easley. Considers sculpture, needlecrafts, rugs and tapestries. Prices are "open," as set by craftsman. 25% commission. Items displayed 4 weeks minimum.

THE LEGACY, LTD., 71 Marion Viaduct, Seattle WA 98104. (206)624-6350. Contact: Mardonna McKillop. Considers metalsmithing, pottery, prints, sculpture and woodcrafting. Maximum size: 3x6'. Unframed prints displayed in books; prints must be framed for wall display. Specializes in Indian and Eskimo art based on traditional themes and produced by native artists. Price range: $15-500, prints; $60-1,200, sculpture; $200-3,000, woodcarvings. Bestsellers: $20-300. Buys outright or on consignment; 30-40% commission. Retail price set by joint agreement. Requires exclusive area representation. Send slides of work. SASE. Dealer pays shipping from shop and insurance for exhibited work. Items displayed 3-6 weeks.

PRINCESS ANGELINE GALLERY, 214 1st St., Seattle WA 98104. Chairman: Janice Hyde. Estab: 1976. Represents 40 local craftsmen. Considers batik, jewelry, pottery, wall hangings, weavings, original prints, sculpture and paintings. Finished one-of-a-kind items OK; utilitarian

and/or decorative. Price range: 35¢-$500; bestsellers: 35¢-$80. Works mainly on consignment; 40% commission. Craftsman sets retail price. Write or submit on or shortly before first Thursday of the month. Reports in 1 week. Dealer pays insurance for exhibited work.
Profile: Consigned items displayed 90 days maximum. Heaviest wholesale buying time: spring and fall; best selling time: summer and Christmas. Customers buy crafts for artistic value.

SUZANNE'S BOUTIQUE, 19841 1st Ave. S., Seattle WA 98148. (206)824-1441. Contact: Suzanne or Rochelle St. Charles. Estab: 1970. Represents 6-8 craftsmen. Considers wall hangings and weavings; especially needs beads, macrame and pottery. One-of-a-kind, primitive and finished items OK; utilitarian and/or decorative. Price range: $2-200; bestsellers: $2-50. Buys outright or on consignment; 30% commission. Retail price set by joint agreement. Requires exclusive area representation on some items. Write. Reports in 2 weeks.
Profile: Items displayed 1 month. Heaviest wholesale buying time: fall; best selling time: winter. Customers buy crafts for artistic value.

THE WOOD SHOP, 402 Occidental St., Seattle WA 98104. (206)624-1763. Contact: Marcia or Will Norwood. Estab: 1972. Represents 50 craftsmen. Considers batik, dollmaking, jewelry, pottery and woodcrafting. Finished, one-of-a-kind and handmade production-line items OK; utilitarian and/or decorative. Price range: up to $100; bestsellers: up to $50. Works on consignment; 33⅓% commission. Retail price set by joint agreement. Prefers exclusive area representation. Write or stop in. Reports immediately. Dealer pays insurance for exhibited work.
Profile: "We make wooden toys and dulcimers in the store." Heaviest wholesale buying time: summer and Christmas. Young customers with middle to upper incomes; they buy crafts for gifts.

Washington, D.C.

EARTHWORKS HEADSHOP, 1724 20th St. NW, Washington DC 20009. (202)332-4323. Manager: Brian Vance. Estab: 1971. Represents 35-50 craftsmen. Considers candlemaking, ceramics, glass art, jewelry, stonework and woodcrafting; especially needs "marijuana paraphernalia such as pipes, stash boxes, serving trays, clips, spoons and etched mirrors." Finished, one-of-a-kind and handmade production-line items OK; utilitarian and/or decorative. Price range: $2-200; bestsellers: $10-50. Buys outright. Retail price set by joint agreement. Write. Reports in 1 week. Dealer pays shipping from shop and insurance for exhibited work. Heaviest wholesale buying time: spring and late summer; best selling time: December. Young customers with $15,000+ incomes.

THE MIDNIGHT SUN, 1700 Pennsylvania Ave. NW, Washington DC 20006. (202)393-4769. Contact: Mrs. A. Kranish. Estab: 1964. Represents 100 craftsmen. Considers candlemaking, ceramics, glass art, jewelry, pottery and woodcrafting. Finished, one-of-a-kind and handmade production-line items OK; utilitarian and/or decorative. Price range: $5-250; bestsellers: $5-25. Buys outright. Shop sets retail price. Query with transparencies or photos. Reports as soon as possible; longer during Christmas season. Dealer pays shipping and insurance.

West Virginia

CABIN CREEK QUILTS, Box 383, Cabin Creek WV 25035. (304)595-3928. Director: Mack Miles. Assistant Director: Deena Postlethwait. Estab: 1970. Represents 125 West Virginia craftsmen. Considers needlecrafts, quilting, wall hangings, weavings, woodcrafting and silk-screened notecards with quilt pattern designs. Finished, one-of-a-kind and handmade production-line items OK; utilitarian only. Price range: $1.50-450; bestsellers: $6-250. "As a cooperative, we pay for labor and materials." Retail price set by joint agreement. West Virginia craftsmen should write. Reports in 4 weeks. Dealer pays shipping from shop and insurance.
Profile: All items receive equal treatment and window display time. "We carry only handmade crafts of top quality. "We're a specialty patchwork and quilting shop."

CABIN CREEK QUILTS, 200 Broad St., Charleston WV 25301. (See Cabin Creek Quilts, Cabin Creek).

THE CRAFT SHOP, Science and Culture Center, Capitol Complex, Charleston WV 25305. (304)348-3982. Manager: Rebecca Stelling. Estab: 1976. Represents 70 craftsmen. Considers all crafts by West Virginians. Finished, one-of-a-kind and handmade production-line items OK;

utilitarian and/or decorative. Price range: 60¢-$1,500; bestsellers: 60¢-$40. Buys outright. Retail price set by craftsman or joint agreement. Write. Reports in 2 weeks. Dealer pays shipping from shop and insurance for exhibited work; shipping cost to shop shared. Best selling time: Christmas and summer.

MOUNTAIN CRAFT SHOP, American Ridge Rd., Rte. 1, New Martinsville WV 26155. (304)455-3570. Contact: Dick Schnacke. Estab: 1965. Represents 60 West Virginia craftsmen. Considers folk toys made by needlecrafts, woodcrafting, ceramics and metalsmithing. Handmade production-line, primitive and finished items OK; utilitarian. Price range: 60¢-$40; bestsellers: $2.50-12.95. Buys outright. Shop sets retail price. Write. Reports in 1 week. Dealer pays shipping from shop. Best selling time: summer and fall. Customers buy crafts for usefulness and gifts.

SUNRISE SHOPS, 755 Myrtle Rd., Charleston WV 25314. (304)344-8035. Contact: Alma M. McMillan. Estab: 1974. Represents 10 out-of-town craftsmen. Considers batik, ceramics, jewelry, pottery, wall hangings and weavings. Works on consignment; 33 1/3% commission. Retail price set by joint agreement. Requires exclusive area representation. Query with transparencies or photos. Reports in 2 weeks. Dealer pays shipping from shop and insurance for exhibited work. Heaviest wholesale buying time: August-September; best selling time: fall and early spring. "We're a children's museum, art gallery and garden center."

Wisconsin

THE ART BARN, Rte. 1, Country Lane, Waupaca WI 54981. (715)258-2082. Contact: Delores Quimby. Estab: 1967. Represents 125 craftsmen. Considers batik, candlemaking, ceramics, decoupage, dollmaking, glass art, jewelry, leatherworking, metalsmithing, needlecrafts, paintings, pottery, quilting, soft sculpture, tole painting, wall hangings, weavings and woodcrafting; especially needs Christmas ornaments and items for children and males. Primitive and finished, one-of-a-kind and handmade production-line items OK; utilitarian and/or decorative. Price range: 25¢-$35. Works on consignment; 25% commission. Retail price set by joint agreement. Requires exclusive area representation. Prefers appointment made; or send transparencies or photos. Reports in 4 weeks.
Profile: Shop located in barn with straw and hay bales. Heaviest wholesale buying time: spring; best selling time: summer. Customers buy crafts for usefulness and artistic value.

ART INDEPENDENT GALLERY, 706 Main St., Lake Geneva WI 53147. (414)248-3612. Contact: Beatrice Herr. Estab: 1968. Represents 220 craftsmen. Considers batik, ceramics, enamel, fiberwork, glass art, furniture, jewelry, sculpture, prints, drawings and paintings. Price range: $1.50-2,000; bestsellers: $8-35 and $300-750. Works on consignment; 40% commission. Craftsman sets retail price. Requires exclusive area representation. Write, query with samples or mail artwork. Reports in 1 week. Dealer pays shipping from gallery for jewelry only.
Profile: "Work displayed for longer periods of time than in most galleries because we're established in tourist area with many clients from the East and West Coasts and Europe." Best selling time: summer and winter. "Artists own and manage gallery; have good relations with artists and clients." Customers have "medium to extremely high incomes."

COUNTRY CRAFTS, Rte. 2, Plymouth WI 53073. (414)893-8095. Contact: Rebecca Summers and Shirley Kohl. Estab: 1974. Represents 100-125 craftsmen. Considers all crafts, including Christmas decorations, paintings, small furniture and toys. Finished one-of-a-kind items OK; utilitarian and/or decorative. Price range: 50¢-$500; bestsellers: $1-25. Buys outright or on consignment; 25% commission. Retail price set by joint agreement. Requires exclusive area representation. Write. Reports in 2 weeks. Dealer pays shipping from shop and insurance for exhibited work.
Profile: Consigned items displayed 2 months minimum. Sponsors weekly shows. Best selling time: June-August. "Shop located in large barn with 2 lofts; we serve gourmet food in the tearoom."

MATHIS GALLERY, 735 Center St., Racine WI 53403. Contact: Emile Mathis II. Considers ceramics, sculpture, rugs, tapestries, glass, graphics and paintings. Prices are $5+. 20-40% commission. Retail price set by joint agreement. Send transparencies or photos. Negotiates shipping costs. Items displayed 5 weeks minimum.

RAINBOW HANDCRAFTS, Box 197, Boulder Junction WI 54512. Contact: Lynette Russell. Considers ceramics, sculpture, jewelry, metalsmithing, rugs, tapestries, glass, leather, weaving, batik, wood accessories, toys and dolls. "We're open from Memorial Day to Labor Day. We prefer crafts from Wisconsin, Minnesota and Michigan." Price range: $5-100. 33¹/₃% commission. Requires exclusive area representation. Send transparencies or photos. Items displayed 6 weeks minimum.

Wyoming

GALLERY THREE TWENTY THREE, INC., 323 S. David, Casper WY 82601. (307)234-8158. Contact: Linda Marion. Estab: 1972. Represents 60 craftsmen. Considers ceramics, leatherworking, pottery, wall hangings, weavings and woodcrafting; especially needs jewelry, fiber arts, baskets, stained glass and handcrafted furniture. Finished, one-of-a-kind and handmade production-line items OK; utilitarian and/or decorative. Price range: $1.50-1,000; bestsellers: $5-100. Will buy outright but prefers consignment; 33¹/₃% commission. Craftsman sets retail price. Write or query with transparencies or photos. Reports in 2 weeks. Dealer pays shipping from shop and insurance for exhibited work.
Profile: Items displayed 6 months. Heaviest wholesale buying time: November-December. Customers are young singles and marrieds with moderate incomes and older couples with large incomes.

GRAND TETON LODGE COMPANY, Box 250, Moran WY 83013. Contact: Mr. D.M. Ware. Estab: 1955. Represents 100 craftsmen. Considers candlemaking, ceramics, decoupage, glass art, jewelry, leatherworking, metalsmithing, pottery, wall hangings, weavings and woodcrafting. Finished, one-of-a-kind and handmade production-line items OK; utilitarian and/or decorative. Price range: $1-3,000; bestsellers: $3-75. Buys outright. Shop sets retail price. Requires exclusive area representation. Write. Reports in 3 weeks. Dealer pays shipping and in-transit insurance. Heaviest wholesale buying time: late winter and spring; best selling time: summer. Customers ages 30-50.

Exposition Space

About the easiest way for the artist to make money is to let the art buyer come to him, rather than vice-versa. But it's not quite that easy. First of all you have to find a place where it's guaranteed that art buyers will come to look your work over. That's where galleries and other exposition space comes in.

For the fine artist who is only a fine artist, the gallery is probably his second home and probably where he makes most of his money. In the last 10 years, fine artists — by selling most of their works in art galleries — have increased their incomes almost 10 times.

Almost every city has at least one respectable art gallery. And, there are other places such as restaurants, hair stylist salons and financial institutions that are anxious to show artists' work since it helps attract potential customers to the business.

To approach a gallery or institution to inquire about showing your work, it's best to go in with (or mail) a portfolio showing slides or prints of your work. Gallery and institution owners want to be sure you can produce quality work and that it's the kind they want to show.

Ed Braegelmann, of Art Depot I (New Hope, Minnesota), says artists should include the asking price with each photo or slide of their work. When pricing, remember the time you've spent on the piece, cost of materials, overhead, handling, incidental expenses and selling costs. Also consider the aesthetic value of the work, your reputation and what similar works are selling for in the area.

Any agreements you ultimately make with a gallery should be in writing. Subjects covered should include the date the agreement takes effect, provisions for termination, amount of commission on sales, territory of exclusive representation and selling price. (The retail price of your work should *not* include reproduction rights.)

Most galleries operate by charging a commission on all sales they make of exhibited work. However, many also require a commission on work sold independently by the artist during exclusive representation (for example, art the artist sells from his own studio during that period).

Other galleries charge the artist for show space. But whether the gallery gets its money through charging for space or by commission, usually part of the money received is used to promote the artist's work (for advertising, to make up brochures, refreshments for openings, etc.).

There are a few galleries that also charge the artist for promotional costs. Beware of these galleries since it can indicate the owner doesn't believe your work will sell well in his gallery or institution.

Note that being shown in a gallery or institution does not necessarily guarantee other openings in other places. Norman Miller, of Miller Gallery (Cincinnati), says past experience is of secondary importance to the work the artist wants to show. "We look first at the work. The artist's background or resume is only of secondary importance."

Bill Orovan, of The Pavilion (Scottsdale, Arizona), agrees. "Quality and craftsmanship are the first consideration. The articles must have some unique quality without being outlandish or bizarre. Value is also important; the article must look its price."

But past experience does help in the respect that many gallery owners want to know that the artist shows a consistency in quality and has the ability to produce regularly.

The following two categories — Galleries and Financial Institutions — contain listings of places open to the professional and/or beginning artist (beginner being defined as a person who already knows how to make quality art, but who is new at getting his work shown in galleries or institutions).

Miller says he shows work by both the beginner and professional. "We mix the two. We feel the established artist is definitely a solid investment, because his sales have been proven. On the other hand, we like to show the climbing artist because there's excitement in finding someone new. We experience this excitement, as does our clientele."

The *Artist's Guide to His Market* (Watson-Guptill Publications) and *Fine Arts Market Place* (R. R. Bowker Co.) are both good sources for more information and lists of names and addresses of galleries and institutions seeking art. Also, contact the Art Information Center, Inc., 189 Lexington Ave., New York City 10016.

Galleries

Alabama

GREATER BIRMINGHAM ARTS ALLIANCE, Box 3325, Birmingham AL 35205. (205)251-1228. Publicity Director: John S. Mills. Exhibits all fine art; 2-4 weeks exposure. No size restrictions. Art must be offered for sale. Works on consignment; 25-30% commission. Minimum price: $20; bestsellers: $85-200. Retail price set by joint agreement. Send slides. SASE. Gallery pays insurance for exhibited work.

CARL F. LUCKEY FINE ARTS, Lingerlost Trail, Killen AL 35645. Gallery Director: Carl F. Luckey. "We're primarily interested in paintings and sculpture of all types and media." Works on consignment; 40% commission. Send transparencies or photos. Reports in 2 weeks.
Special Needs: Uses graphic designers for announcements for opening receptions and one-man shows.

Arizona

GALLERY 3, 3819 N. 3rd St., Phoenix AZ 85012. (602)277-9540. Contact: Sherry Manorkian. Exhibits acrylics, airbrush, batik, calligraphy, ceramics, drawings, jewelry, oils, pottery, prints, sculpture, wall hangings, watercolors, weavings and woodcrafting; 2 months minimum exposure. "If we are going to represent an artist, we prefer to frame his work because it looks and sells better." Specializes in contemporary and Southwest art. Art must be offered for sale. Works on consignment; 40% commission. Price range: $25-1,000, oils and acrylics; $25-500, graphics. Bestsellers: $150-400. Retail price set by joint agreement. Requires exclusive area representation. Query with samples. SASE. Gallery pays insurance on exhibited work.

GARELICK'S GALLERY, 7145 Main St., Scottsdale AZ 85251. (602)994-3108. Contact: Robert Garelick. Exhibits drawings, oils, pastels, prints, sculpture and watercolors; 1-6 months exposure. Interested in contemporary realism. Art must be offered for sale. Works on consignment; 40% commission. Price range: $100-5,000, oils; $50-1,000, graphics; $100-750, watercolors. Retail price set by joint agreement. Requires exclusive area representation. Send slides or photos of work. SASE. Gallery pays insurance on exhibited work.

GOLD KEY GALLERY, 7086 5th Ave., Scottsdale AZ 85251. Contact: Thomas McKee. Exhibits Western sculpture, either bronze or welded metal; "permanent" exposure through advertising. Works on signed contract basis; 40% commission. Price range: $40-10,000. Retail price set by joint agreement. Requires exclusive area representation. Send transparencies or photos.

HOUSE OF BRONZE, Dewey Rte., Hwy. 69, Prescott AZ 86301. Contact: Jack and Jague Osmer. Exhibits Western and Indian traditional paintings, sculpture, prints, drawings and jewelry; 3 months exposure minimum. 33 1/3% commission. Price range: $15-10,000. Artist sets retail price. Exhibited art insured for wholesale price. Sponsors openings. "We give good exposure in the gallery, and collectors travel many miles to see the bronze foundry. Our major function is art bronze castings. We do represent artists for wholesale and collector-discounted art, though, and sculptors casting with us receive gallery display and show exhibition."

KNOX CAMPBELL GALLERIES, 3015 N. Campbell Ave., Tucson AZ 85719. (602)793-2100. Administrator: Melody Sears. Exhibits acrylics, drawings, oils, pastels, prints, watercolors and occasionally sculpture and woodcrafting; 1 month minimum exposure. No size restrictions.

Specializes in Western art, but is interested in any theme. Art must be offered for sale. Buys outright or on consignment; 40% commission. Price range: $85-500, graphics; $100-500, watercolors; $150-2,000, oils and acrylics. Bestsellers: $500-1,000. Retail price set by joint agreement. Requires exclusive area representation. Send slides of work or call or write for interview. SASE.

LA GALERIA, Box 617, Hwy. 179, Sedona AZ 86336. (602)282-3580. Contact: Ernestine Nestler. Exhibits acrylics, ceramics, drawings, oils, pastels, pottery, sculpture and watercolors; 90 days minimum exposure. Paintings must be framed; sculpture mounted on base. Specializes in Western, scenic art and portraits (Indian/Anglo children). Art must be offered for sale. Works on consignment; $33\frac{1}{3}\%$ commission. Prices: $10, miniatures; $100+, other works. Artist sets retail price. Requires exclusive area representation. Query or call for interview. SASE. Gallery pays insurance (if notified).

O'BRIEN'S ART EMPORIUM, 7122 Stetson Dr., Scottsdale AZ 85251. (602)945-1082. Managing Director: J. B. Sherwood. Exhibits drawings, oils, pastels, sculpture, watercolors and fine art; 90 days minimum exposure. Paintings must be framed. Art may be placed for "on order only." Works on consignment; 40% commission. Price range: $200+, watercolors; $500+, oils. Retail price set by joint agreement. Requires exclusive area representation. Call or write for interview, or send slides. SASE.

THE PAVILION, 7150 Main St., Scottsdale AZ 85251. (602)994-9444. Contact: Bill Orovan. Exhibits all fine art; 2 weeks minimum exposure. Maximum size: 8' tall; "also have courtyard for outdoor sculpture." Works should be prepared for display and sale; pedestals and cases supplied. Art must be offered for sale. Buys outright or on consignment; 50% commission ("or less for well-established artists in high-price bracket"). Price range: $1-10,000. Bestsellers: under $1,000. Retail price set by artist with gallery approval. Requires exclusive area representation. Send photos or slides, "or call or write for interview if you plan to be in the area (samples appreciated if possible)." Dealer pays shipping from gallery.
To Break In: "Quality and craftsmanship are first consideration. The articles must have some unique quality without being outlandish or bizarre. Value is also important; the article must look its price."

Prestige Galleries, Inc. (Skokie, Illinois) buys and consigns French Impressionistic, surrealistic, traditional romantic and representational works. Prices range from $10-10,000. The above surrealistic painting was purchased outright by Prestige from artist Tito Salomoni.

SCOTTSDALE FINE ARTS COMMISSION, Scottsdale Civic Center Gallery, 3839 Civic Center Plaza, Scottsdale AZ 85251. Visual Arts Director: Ms. Dickson Hartwell. Has year-round exhibition program in Civic Center Gallery and Scottsdale Center for the Arts; a small acquisition program, and an annual spring arts festival. (See Competitions/Exhibitions.) Works commissioned for execution when funds available. Works hang in various municipal public buildings, indoors and out, and range from monumental sculpture to ceramic pots. Matching grants sometimes solicited from Arizona Commission on the Arts and Humanities or National Endowment for the Arts. Sponsors 12-24 annual group exhibitions of artists in selected or juried shows. Art may be offered for sale. 20% commission. Painters, sculptors and craftsmen may submit published samples, slides of original work and/or list of professional credits, prizes and awards.

THE THOMPSON GALLERY, 2020 N. Central, Phoenix AZ 85004. (602)258-4412. Contact: John R. Thompson. Exhibits traditional painting, experimental artwork, prints, graphics, sculpture, pottery and jewelry; 2 weeks exposure. Works on consignment; 40% commission. Prices from $100 as set by artist. Requires exclusive area representation.

YUMA ART CENTER, Box 1471, Yuma AZ 85364. (602)782-9261. Director: Laurel Meinig. Exhibits acrylics, airbrush, batik, calligraphy, candlemaking, ceramics, drawings, glass art, jewelry, leatherworking, metalsmithing, mobiles, oils, pastels, pottery, prints, sculpture, soft sculpture, wall hangings, watercolors, weavings and woodcrafting; 1-3 months exposure. Paintings should be framed; works on paper are to be under glass. Art must be offered for sale. Works on consignment; 33 1/3% commission. Minimum price: $15; bestsellers: $25-150. Retail price set by joint agreement. Query with slides or photos. "If bringing work for consideration, advance notice of artist's arrival is essential." SASE. Dealer pays insurance.
Promotional Needs: Also uses artists for membership literature, posters and public service TV announcements. Pays $100 minimum, poster design.

Arkansas

ARKANSAS ARTS CENTER ART RENTAL-PURCHASE GALLERY, Box 2137, Little Rock AR 72203. Director: Townsend Wolfe. "Open to regional artists from Arkansas, Louisiana, Missouri, Oklahoma, Texas, Tennessee and Mississippi who have had one or more works accepted for any regional or national juried exhibition." 20% commission. Artist receives half rental fee. Submit 3 works for review.

SOUTHEAST ARKANSAS ARTS AND SCIENCE CENTER, Civic Center, Pine Bluff AR 71601. Director: Philip A. Klopfenstein. Exhibits all art and crafts. "We have a small sales gallery which includes works from 25-50 artists at any given time. We accept works on consignment based on the individual's presentation of slides for review." Slides reviewed monthly by selection committee. 20% commission.

California

BIRD'S EYE VIEW GALLERY, 3420 Via Oporto #3, Newport Beach CA 92663. (714)673-0462. Director: R. Feuerstein. Exhibits acrylics, drawings, oils, pastels, prints, sculpture, wall hangings, watercolors and weavings; 30 days minimum exposure. Maximum size: 7x7', paintings; 14x14x24", sculpture. Paintings must be framed and ready to hang. Art must be offered for sale. Works on consignment; 40% commission. Price range: $100-800, weavings; $85-800, graphics; $150-3,000, paintings. Bestsellers: $300-500. Retail price set by joint agreement. Requires exclusive area representation. Send slides of work. SASE. Gallery pays insurance for exhibited work.

BOTH-UP GALLERY, Telegraph and Haste, Berkeley CA 94704. Coordinator: Evelyn Glaubman. Exhibits acrylics, drawings, oils, prints, sculpture and soft sculpture; 5 weeks maximum exposure. Paintings must be ready to hang; sculpture should include pedestals. Artist handles own sales. Artist sets retail price. Send for membership information. Samples returned with SASE.

CATCHPENNY ART GALLERY, 18350 Ventura Blvd., Tarzana CA 91356. (212)881-3218. Contact: Charles Hecht. Submit resume and slides or photos of work. Exhibits traditional painting, sculpture and prints. Buys outright or on consignment; 30% commission. Price range: $150-10,000. Requires commission on art sold in area after exclusive representation. Exhibited art insured. Gallery pays shipping costs. Occasionally uses artists for newspaper advertising.

COLLIER ART CORP., 2051 Pontuis Ave., Los Angeles CA 90025. (213)478-0666. Contact: A. M. Gottfried. Exhibits graphics, drawings, oils and watercolors. Send resume and photos. Buys outright or on consignment. Prices are $25-10,000. Gallery sets retail price. Requires exclusive representation in area. Prefers consigned art unframed.

DEVORZON GALLERY, 744½ N. La Cienega Blvd., Los Angeles CA 90069. Contact: Barbara DeVorzon. Exhibits prints, graphics and sculpture; 2 weeks minimum exposure. Works on consignment; 40% commission. Retail price set by joint agreement. Send color slides. A promotion list for shows is mailed semiannually. Occasionally uses artists for announcement design.

DIABLO VALLEY COLLEGE ART GALLERY, 321 Golf Club Rd., Pleasent Hill CA 94523. (415)685-1230 ext. 471. Director: R. B. Ripley. Exhibits acrylics, airbrush, calligraphy, ceramics, drawings, jewelry, metalsmithing, mobiles, oils, pastels, pottery, prints, sculpture, soft sculpture and watercolors; 3-5 weeks exposure. Maximum size: 25x6x6'. Art may be offered for sale. No commission. Price range: $10-10,000, paintings/sculptures; $10-800, ceramics. Artist sets retail price. Query. SASE. Negotiates payment for shipping; dealer pays insurance on exhibited work.

THE EMERSON GALLERY, 18676 Ventura Blvd., Tarzana CA 91356. Contact: Wayne LaCom. Exhibits acrylics, batik, ceramics, glass art, mobiles, oils, pastels, prints, sculpture, wall hangings, watercolors and weavings; 3 weeks-6 months exposure. Maximum size: 48x12x30". Contemporary work only. Art must be offered for sale. Works on consignment; 40% commission. Price range: $40-1,500, paintings; bestsellers: $25-350. Requires exclusive area representation. Query with slides of work. SASE.

FINE ARTS EXCHANGE INTERNATIONAL BROKERS, Box 1768, San Francisco CA 94101. Contact: Art Director. Exhibits oils and watercolors; 90 days minimum exposure. Maximum height: 48". Art must be offered for sale. Buys outright or on consignment; 50% commission. Minimum price: $5; bestsellers: $5-500. Retail price set by joint agreement. Requires exclusive area representation. Query. SASE. Also commissions specific murals and portraiture.

FOUR CORNERS FRAMING GALLERY, 904 Kline St., La Jolla CA 92037. (714)454-1810. Contact: Rose A. Grigas. Exhibits lithographs, watercolors, oil paintings, etchings and engravings; 12 weeks minimum exposure. Works on consignment; 35% commission. Art priced from $10-300 as set by gallery. Requires exclusive area representation. Exhibited art insured.

JANE FREEMAN ART GALLERY, 7000 Saranac #12, La Mesa CA 92041. Director: Jane Freeman. Wishes to see, "by appointment only," color transparencies or b&w photos of traditional paintings and drawings. Work gets minimum 4 weeks exposure. Prices: $200-5,000, set by joint agreement. 50% commission. Exclusive representation in area required; commission on art sold in area after exclusive showing. Also represents a number of art print publishers in other cities; on receiving slides of paintings which have possibilities for publication, gallery contacts artist and publisher regarding royalty arrangements.

GALERIE DE TOURS, Box 4996, Carmel CA 93921. Contact: Robert J. Kaller. Exhibits paintings and sculpture; 4 weeks minimum exposure. "Those we represent must have some previous record. Recently, our gallery has handled works more in a historical vein." By joint agreement, prices run from $500-75,000. 40-50% commission. Exclusive local representation required; charges commission on art sold in area after exclusive representation. Exhibited art insured. Graphic artists also needed occasionally to design show promotions.

THE GALLERIE, 1051 Westwood Blvd., Los Angeles CA 90024. (213)477-5085. Manager: Bob James: Exhibits graphics; 2 weeks minimum exposure. Art must be offered for sale. Buys outright or on consignment; 50% commission. Minimum price: $40, graphics; bestsellers: $50-500. Retail price set by joint agreement. Query or call for interview. SASE. Gallery pays insurance on exhibited work.
Promotional Needs: Uses artists for literature and newspaper advertisements.

GALLERY 8, Harvard and Bonita, Claremont CA 91711. (714)624-2588. Director: Barbara Beretich. Exhibits acrylics, airbrush, ceramics, drawings, oils, pastels, prints, sculpture and watercolors; 2-8 weeks exposure. Maximum size: 48" square. Paintings must be ready to hang. Art must be offered for sale. Works on consignment; 50% commission. Price range: $20-2,500, ceramics; $100-8,000, sculpture; $100-20,000, paintings; bestsellers: $150-1,500. Artist sets retail price. Requires exclusive area representation. Query with samples of work. SASE.

GARDEN GROVE ARTISANS' GUILD, 9858 Garden Grove Blvd., Garden Grove CA 92644. Contact: Marsha Alexander or Margaret McKay. Exhibits paintings, sculpture and untraditional media. Send transparencies or photos of work. "Our gallery maintains available space for one-man shows, or themed exhibits, for 1 or 2-month periods. Artists are expected to hang their own show and prepare a mailing list (we use their list in combination with our own) and price list. Artists living too far away to make this feasible need not send their own mailing list, but must pay a $50 hanging fee. Guild provides printing and postage for standard invitations and food for opening receptions. Artist provides wine and/or punch for reception and agrees to donate 1 work of art for drawing to help defray exhibit expenses. We enjoy good coverage from the local media. Therefore, it is important that we feature only quality art and that we have sufficient time to interview and photograph the artist with his work. If person-to-person interview is not feasible, artist must send ample public relations information and 10 b&w glossy photos for newspapers 4-8 weeks prior to exhibit's opening date. All sales of exhibited work will be made through the Guild Hall cashier, with 20% retained to help defray overhead. Balance will be remitted to artist on the 10th of the following month."

GRAPHICS INTERNATIONAL, Box 13292, Station E, Oakland CA 94661. Contact: Rob R. Kral. Exhibits drawings, etchings, drypoints and lithographs. Price range: $12-8,000. 50% commission. Exclusive representation required; charges commission on art sold in area after showing. Send transparencies or photos. Exhibited art insured.

HOOVER GALLERY, 710 Sansome St., San Francisco CA 94111. (415)391-2740. Contact: Director. Exhibits acrylics, drawings, oils, pastels, sculpture, wall hangings, watercolors and weavings. No size requirements. Art must be ready for display. Specializes in representational, abstract art, impressionism and abstract impressionism. Art may be offered for sale. Buys outright or on consignment. Retail price set by joint agreement. Send slides of work. SASE. Gallery pays shipping from gallery.

INCURABLE COLLECTOR, 17203 Ventura Blvd., Encino CA 91316. (213)783-1450. Contact: Valerie Mathews. Exhibits experimental artwork, prints, drawings, graphics, sculpture and jewelry; 4 weeks minimum exposure. Works on consignment; 40-60% commission. Prices from $5-350 set by artist. Requires commission on art sold in area after show. Sponsors openings.

KLEIN ART GALLERY, 332 N. Rodeo Dr., Beverly Hills CA 90210. (213)274-8955. Contact: David Klein. Exhibits representational drawings, oils, pastels, sculpture and watercolors; 2-6 months exposure. Maximum size: 30x40". Art must be offered for sale. Buys outright or on consignment; 40% commission. Price range: $200-15,000, oils; bestsellers: $300-3,500. Retail price set by joint agreement. Sometimes requires exclusive area representation. Send photos of work or call or write for interview. SASE.

LESLI ART DEALERS, 1633 La Cienega Blvd., Los Angeles CA 90035. (213)271-4493. President: Stan Shevrin. Exhibits traditional and abstract watercolors, pastels and drawings; 26 weeks minimum exposure. Maximum size: 36x48". Prefers to receive art unframed. "We are artists' agents — we wholesale artists' works to galleries throughout the U.S. and Canada. We either accept works on consignment or purchase outright or both. We look for exceptional quality and artists who understand 'color value' in our acquisitions." Price range: $50-5,000 as set by joint agreement. 50% commission. Exclusive representation in local area required. Send transparencies or photos. Gallery pays return shipping and insurance for exhibited work. Occasionally uses artwork for show promotions.

LONGPRE GALLERY, La Canada CA 91011. (213)790-0777. Art Curator: Mrs. Mucciolo. Exhibits acrylics, drawings, glass art, jewelry, leatherworking, oils, pastels, pottery, prints, sculpture, soft sculpture, tole painting, wall hangings, watercolors and weavings; 2-8 weeks exposure. Maximum size: 48" square. "We feature special shows on a variety of themes." Art must be offered for sale. Works on consignment; 40% commission. Price range: $15-7,000;

bestsellers: $150-650. Retail price set by joint agreement. Requires exclusive area representation. Send slides or photos of work, or write or call for interview. SASE.

MENDOCINO ART CENTER, Box 36, Mendocino CA 95460. (707)937-5818. Contact: Linda Perry. Exhibits all fine art; 1 month maximum exposure. Work must be ready for hanging. Bimonthly thematic shows. Art must be offered for sale. Buys outright or on consignment; 40% commission. Price range: $5-1,500, pottery and paintings; bestsellers: $5-25. Artist sets retail price. Query with $10 membership fee. SASE. Gallery pays insurance on exhibited work. **Promotional Needs:** Uses artists for membership literature and public service TV announcements. Pays $15 minimum, spot layout and drawings.

ANN MURPHY FINE PRINTS, 707 E. Chapman Ave., Fullerton CA 92613. Contact: Ann Murphy or Mike Ripley. Exhibits primarily antique prints, but also handles sculpture and pottery; 6 weeks minimum exposure. "Original art in our gallery ranges in price from $15-400 for drawings and prints, and our commission is 33 1/3-40%. The most popular prices are items from $30-100, as our customers tend to be young marrieds." Prefers to receive unframed consignment art. Send transparencies or photos. Exhibited art insured.

OLD TOWN, Box 1537, Los Gatos CA 95030. A screening committee at this shopping village views work of artists/craftsmen. Portfolio review is by appointment or through photos submitted in advance. Art is displayed in the marketplace on a first-come basis from June-September 15 from 10 a.m.-10 p.m. daily. Rental charges vary seasonally.

ORLANDO GALLERY, 17037 Ventura Blvd., Encino CA 91316. (213)789-6012. Contact: Robert Gino. Exhibits drawings, oils, pastels, pottery, prints, sculpture, wall hangings, watercolors and weavings; 3-4 weeks exposure. No size requirements. Paintings must be ready to hang. Specializes in contemporary art. Art must be offered for sale. Works on consignment; 40% commission. Price range: $45-5,000; bestsellers: $485+. Retail price set by joint agreement. Requires exclusive area representation. Send slides or photos or call or write for interview. SASE. Gallery pays insurance for exhibited work. Uses artists for membership literature.

ORR'S GALLERY, 2222 4th Ave., San Diego CA 92101. Contact: Daniel Jacobs. Exhibits prints and drawings; 3 weeks minimum exposure. 40% commission. Price range: $100-5,000. Retail price set by joint agreement. Requires exclusive representation; commission collected on art sold locally after showing. Send transparencies or photos. Also, with artist's permission, some objects can be rented for 2-month period for nominal fee. Details on request.

PACIFIC GROVE ART CENTER, 568 Lighthouse, Pacific Grove CA 93950. Consulting Director: Jacqueline Bray. Exhibits paintings and sculpture; 4 weeks minimum exposure. 30% commission. Price range: $50-550. Retail price set by artist. Gallery works on signed contract basis with artist. Openings sponsored and promoted through regular mailing list. Exhibited art insured.

POLISH ARTS AND CULTURE FOUNDATION, 166 Geary St., San Francisco CA 94108. President: Wanda Tomczykowska-Grabianowska. "Work on Polish subjects or by artists of Polish origin" are of interest. Exhibits traditional and abstract paintings, prints, drawings and hand-woven paintings/tapestries; 4 weeks minimum exposure. 25% commission. Price range: $10-1,000. Price set by artist. Openings sponsored. Exclusive representation in area required; charges commission on art sold in area after show.

RUBICON GALLERY, 1st and Main Sts., Los Altos CA 94022. (415)984-4848. Director: Paul Klein. Exhibits acrylics, airbrush, drawings, oils, pastels, prints, sculpture and watercolors; 6-8 weeks exposure. Art may be offered for sale. Buys outright or on consignment; 40-50% commission. Price range: $100-1,500, original prints; $300-3,000, drawings/watercolors; $200-20,000, sculpture; bestsellers: $300-1,000. Retail price set by joint agreement. Prefers exclusive area representation. Send slides of work. SASE. Klein pays shipping from gallery and insurance on exhibited work.

SCHOOLHOUSE GALLERY, Box 132, Amador City CA 95601. (209)267-0012. Contact: Maxine Dalben. Exhibits acrylics, batik, calligraphy, ceramics, drawings, glass art, metalsmithing, needlecrafts, oils, pastels, pottery, prints, sculpture, wall hangings, watercolors

and weavings; 3 weeks minimum exposure. Maximum size: 24x36", paintings; 200 lbs., sculpture. Paintings must be framed and ready to hang; graphics may be matted only. Specializes in wildlife prints, contemporary paintings and California landscape. Art must be offered for sale. Occasionally buys outright, usually on consignment; 33¹/₃% commission. Price range: $50-1,200, paintings; $5-180, graphics; bestsellers: $50-250. Retail price set by artist or joint agreement. Requires exclusive area representation. SASE.
To Break In: "We are a small tourist-oriented village in the old gold mining historical area. Work with a nostalgic flavor goes well."

THE SCULPTURE GALLERY, ETC., 3030 5th Ave., San Diego CA 92103. (714)298-7000. Director: Peggy Oberlies. Exhibits acrylics, airbrush, batik, ceramics, drawings, glass art, jewelry, mobiles, oils, pastels, pottery, prints, sculpture, soft sculpture, wall hangings, watercolors, weavings and enamels; 2 months minimum exposure. Maximum size: 4' square. Paintings must be ready for hanging. Specializes in sculpture and sculptural work in all media. Art must be offered for sale. Works on consignment; 40% commission. Price range: $3.50-4, porcelain perfume bottles; $50-1,000, sculpture; bestsellers: under $100. Retail price set by joint agreement. Requires exclusive area representation. Prefers personal showing of work by appointment, but artist may send slides. SASE. Gallery pays insurance on exhibited work.
To Break In: "If an artist is going to make a living freelancing in the area of fine art, he must show a consistency of quality and must produce regularly."

SEASIDE ART COMMISSION, 1962 Mariposa St., Seaside CA 93955. Contact: C.Y. Lee. "We show artists' work in a public city hall, which is not a professional commercial art gallery. We do help sell some of the artists' work occasionally — very rarely, though. At present, we have no grants or matching funds for anything." Works with painters, sculptors, graphic designers, serigraphers, ceramists and craftsmen. Submit letter with published samples, slides of original work and a list of professional credits, prizes and awards won.

MARY PORTER SESNON ART GALLERY, College 5, University of California, Santa Cruz CA 95064. (408)429-2857. Manager: Philip Brookman. Exhibits all art; 2-6 weeks exposure. Maximum size: 15x40', disassembled; 84x60", assembled. Art may be offered for sale. "Our purpose is purely educational and not related to the sale of art." Price range: $25-50,000. Artist sets retail price. Write with a proposal for exhibit and include photos. SASE. Negotiates shipping and insurance.

SOURCE GALLERY, 1099 Folsom St., San Francisco CA 94103. (415)621-0545. Exhibits acrylics, airbrush, oils, pastels, prints, sculpture, soft sculpture, wall hangings, watercolors and weavings; 6 weeks minimum exposure. Art must be offered for sale. Works on consignment; 50% commission. Price range: $200-2,000, paintings; $500 minimum, fiberworks; $75-350, prints. Retail price set by joint agreement. Requires exclusive area representation. "Visit gallery to see if artwork is appropriate and compatible"; then, query or call for interview; if out-of-town, send resume and slides. SASE. Gallery pays insurance on exhibited work and shipping from gallery unless work is specifically requested by artist at an earlier date.

SPIEGL GALLERY, 303 3rd St., San Juan Bautista CA 95045. Contact: Bobbie Spiegl. Exhibits fine art, sculpture and crafts; 8 weeks minimum exposure. "We charge 40% commission but also purchase some work outright." Price range: $20-3,500, as set by joint agreement. Requires exclusive local representation.

DAVID STUART GALLERIES, 748 N. La Cienega (Penthouse), Los Angeles CA 90069. (213)652-7422. Contact: D. Stuart. Exhibits acrylics, airbrush, ceramics, drawings, mobiles, oils, pastels, sculpture and watercolors; 1 month exposure. Art must be ready for hanging. Specializes in contemporary painting and sculpture. Art must be offered for sale. Buys outright or on consignment; 40% commission. Minimum price: $100, drawings; $400, oil paintings. Retail price set by joint agreement. Requires exclusive area representation. Query. SASE. Dealer pays insurance on exhibited work.

SZYMANSKI GALLERY, 9510 Wilshire Blvd., Beverly Hills CA 90212. (213)276-0507. Contact: Joseph Szymanski. Considers traditional or impressionist paintings and drawings; 4 weeks minimum exposure. Price range: $500-30,000, set by joint agreement. 30-40% commission. Exclusive representation in area required; commission collected on art sold in area after show. Send transparencies or photos. SASE.

TIDEPOOL GALLERY, 22762 Pacific Coast Hwy., Malibu CA 90265. (213)456-2551. Contact: Jan Greenberg. Exhibits all ocean-related arts and crafts except calligraphy, decoupage, dollmaking, leatherworking and tole painting; 2 years maximum exposure. Maximum size: 2x4x6'. Work must be ready for exhibit. Specializes in ocean-related work. Art must be offered for sale. Buys outright or on consignment; 33 1/3% commission. Price range: $100-1,500, oil paintings; $35-450, jewelry; $25-1,750, wood sculpture; bestsellers: $50-250. Retail price set by joint agreement. Query or call for interview; send photos if out-of-town. SASE.

TRITON MUSEUM OF ART, 1505 Warburton Ave., Santa Clara CA 95050. Director: Donna Thomas. Works with painters, sculptors, graphic artists, jewelers and glass and textile artists. Features work of San Francisco Bay area and Santa Clara Valley artists, but will consider work of artists from other areas as well. 25% commission. Send resume and photos or slides. Is currently expanding its bookstore facility and welcomes inquiries regarding the sale of suitable artwork (cards, reproductions of original works, etc.).

VALLEY ART GALLERY, 1641 Locust Ave., Walnut Creek CA 94596. (415)935-4311. Director: Dorothy Magoffin. Exhibits acrylics, airbrush, batik, ceramics, glass art, jewelry, leatherworking, metalsmithing, oils, pastels, pottery, sculpture, watercolors and woodcrafting; 6 months exposure. No size requirements. Art must be offered for sale. Works on consignment; 20-25% commission. Price range: $1-75, crafts; $50-800, paintings; bestsellers: $15-25, crafts; $150-300, paintings. Artist sets retail price. Query.

VAN DOREN GALLERY, 10 Gold St., San Francisco CA 94133. (415)392-0434. Exhibits painting, prints, graphics, drawings, sketches and sculpture. Handles contemporary painting and sculpture; 3 weeks minimum exposure. Maximum size: 10x15'. 50% commission. Price range: $100-15,000 as set by joint agreement. Requires exclusive representation. Sponsors openings. Send resume and color slides. Exhibited art insured. Shipping costs shared.

ISABELLE PERCY WEST GALLERY, 5212 Broadway, Oakland CA 94618. Contact: Director. Exhibits all art and crafts except candlemaking; 3 weeks maximum exposure. Maximum size: 15x20x10'. Paintings should be ready to hang. Specializes in new contemporary work. Art may be offered for sale. Price range: $100-"several thousand," paintings, drawings, prints. Artist sets retail price. Write for interview. Gallery pays insurance on exhibited work.

BLAINE WILSON GALLERY, 1520 E. Shaw, #111, Fresno CA 93710. (209)431-3432. Contact: Don or Barbara Wilson. Exhibits traditional and abstract painting, drawings, prints, graphics and jewelry; 3-4 weeks minimum exposure. 20x24" size limit on art. Works on signed contract basis and on consignment; 40% commission. Artist and gallery set price. Requires commission on any art sold in area after exclusive representation. Send resume with color transparencies or photos. Sponsors openings.

ZARA GALLERY, 553 Pacific Ave., San Francisco CA 94133. (415)788-8696. Director: Joseph Chowning. Exhibits acrylics, airbrush, ceramics, oils, pastels, sculpture, soft sculpture and watercolors; 4-5 weeks exposure. Maximum size: 12' square. Work must be ready for exhibition. Primarily interested in figurative work. Art may be offered for sale. Works on consignment; 33 1/3-60% commission. Price range: $200-20,000, paintings; $150-30,000, sculpture; bestsellers: $500-5,000. Retail price set by joint agreement. Requires exclusive area representation. Send slides and resume. SASE. Gallery pays insurance.

Colorado

GILPIN COUNTY ARTS ASSOCIATION, Box 65, Central City CO 80427. (303)582-5952. Contact: Kay Russell. Exhibits acrylics, airbrush, batik, calligraphy, drawings, glass art, jewelry, oils, pastels, pottery, prints, sculpture, soft sculpture, watercolors, weavings, woodcrafting and enamels; 2½ months maximum exposure. Maximum size: 5' square. Paintings must be ready to hang. Art must be offered for sale. Works on consignment; 30% commission. Price range: $25-2,000; bestsellers: $50-250. Artist sets retail price. Send for entry form. SASE.

GRYPHON GALLERIES, LTD., 2440 E. 3rd Ave., Denver CO 80206. Director: Cheryl Natzmer. Exhibits acrylics, drawings, oils, pastels, graphics, sculpture and watercolors; 3 weeks minimum exposure. Paper works, if framed, must have a museum quality fit (100% ragboard backing and mat, etc.). Specializes in contemporary representational art. Art must be offered for sale. Works on consignment; 40% commission. Price range: $50-3,000, paintings/graphics; bestsellers: $200-500. Artist sets retail price. Requires exclusive area representation. Send slides or photos of work. SASE. Gallery pays shipping from gallery and insurance on exhibited work. "Send biographical information; we only represent 12 artists from across the country."

Connecticut

THE DOUGLAS GALLERY, INC., 1117 High Ridge Rd., Stamford CT 06905. (203)322-7233. Contact: Douglas Jayne. Exhibits acrylics, oils, watercolors and sculpture; 2-6 months exposure. Maximum size: 5' square. Paintings must be ready to hang and sculpture must have pedestal. Art must be offered for sale. Works on consignment; 33 1/3% commission. Price range: $100-4,000, oils; $25-800, watercolors; $25-2,000, sculpture; bestsellers: $150-800. Retail price set by joint agreement. Requires exclusive area representation. Send slides or photos of work. SASE. Gallery pays insurance for exhibited work.

GARFIELD GALLERIES, 500 Boston Post Rd., Orange CT 06477. Director: Paul G. Phelps. Exhibits acrylics, oils, prints and watercolors; 2 months maximum exposure. Maximum size: 48" square. Art must be offered for sale. Buys outright or on consignment. Minimum price: $50. Bestseller range: $75-500. Retail price set by joint agreement. Requires exclusive area representation. Send photos or write for interview. SASE.

Florida

ARNOLD'S ART CENTER, 1712 E. 7th Ave., Tampa FL 33605. (813)248-2993. Contact: Saul Arnold. Exhibits acrylics, airbrush, batik, ceramics, drawings, oils, pastels, pottery, prints and sculpture; 3-4 weeks exposure. Maximum size: 96x60". Paintings must be ready to hang. Art must be offered for sale. Works on consignment; 40% commission. Price range: $200-5,000; bestsellers: $75-2,500. Retail price set by joint agreement. Requires exclusive area representation. Query or send photos of work. SASE. Gallery pays insurance.

BACARDI ART GALLERY, 2100 Biscayne Blvd., Miami FL 33137. (305)573-8511. Director: Jose F. Castellanos. Secretary: Gladys F. Smithies. Exhibits acrylics, drawings, glass art, oils, pastels, prints, sculpture and watercolors; 2-3 weeks minimum exposure. Maximum size: 4-5'. Paintings must be ready to hang. Gallery provides average-size pedestals. Art may be offered for sale. Works on consignment; no commission. Price range: $25-3,000, paintings; bestsellers: $25-500. Artist sets retail price. Query with samples or call or write for interview. SASE. Gallery pays insurance on exhibited work.

CAVALIER GALLERY OF ART, INC., 167 Miracle Strip Pkwy., Ft. Walton Beach FL 32548. Contact: Mrs. M.B. See. Exhibits traditional and abstract painting and sculpture; 2 weeks exposure for special showings. Usually buys outright, some consignment; 40% commission. By joint agreement prices range from $2-2,000. Send color transparencies or b&w photos of work.

DELAND MUSEUM, Box 941, 449 E. New York Ave., DeLand FL 32720. (904)734-4371. Executive Director: E. Steve Estes. Artists interested in rental gallery service should send slides or original artwork to Exhibit Committee, Board of Directors. 10% commission. "We require our permanent collection to exemplify a style or period of art, and to use the universal elements of color, shape, composition, line and texture in such a way as to be timeless in their appeal." For consideration, submit slides to Acquisitions Committee, Board of Directors. Art and crafts show held by museum each fall with $1,000 in prizes.

FLORIDA STATE UNIVERSITY GALLERY, University Gallery, Fine Arts Bldg., Florida State University, Tallahassee FL 32306. Sponsors exhibition and competition in painting, sculpture, prints and drawings. Send color transparencies or b&w photos of work for possible follow-up appointment at gallery's request. Reports within 4 weeks. Graduate assistantships available to eligible persons.

HOUSE OF FINE ART, 9476 Harding Ave., Surfside FL 33154. President: Iris G. Klein. Exhibits all fine art except mobiles, needlecrafts and tole painting; 1-6 months exposure. Maximum height: 2-3'. Work must be ready for hanging. Art must be offered for sale. Works on consignment; 40% commission. Price range: $3-35, crafts; $1-150, jewelry; $15-450, paintings; $15-300, sculpture; bestsellers: $15-75. Retail price set by joint agreement. Send slides or call for interview. SASE. Also uses artists for direct mail advertising art.

HOWARD GALLERIES, LTD., 148 Pompano Fashion Square, Pompano Beach FL 33062. (305)781-9481. President: H.B. Solomon. Exhibits acrylics, oils, prints, sculpture and watercolors; 60 days minimum exposure. Maximum size: 48x36". Work should be submitted unframed. Oils should be stretched. Watercolors matted preferably. Art must be offered for sale. Buys outright or on consignment. Minimum price: $50, oils; $25, prints and sculpture; bestsellers: $100-300. Retail price set by joint agreement. Requires exclusive area representation. Write for interview or send photos of work. SASE. Gallery pays shipping from gallery and insurance on exhibited work.

MUSEUM OF ARTS AND SCIENCES, 1040 Museum Blvd., Daytona Beach FL 32014. (904)255-0285. Contact: Sharon Whempner. Museum offers rental gallery service, and members only exhibit every 2 years. No commission. Public relations department occasionally uses artists for catalogs and posters. Gift shop buys crafts outright or on consignment. Prices in shop range from $1-30. No commission. Also sponsors annual festival.

NAPLES ART GALLERY, 275 Broad Ave. S., Naples FL 33940. Exhibits traditional and abstract paintings, sculpture and prints; entire winter or summer season exposure. By joint agreement of artist and gallery, art retails for $100-12,000. Gallery takes 40% commission. Requires exclusive area representation. Send color transparencies or b&w photos.
To Break In: "The buying public is turning away from abstract and hard-edged art. Our sales are for the realistic, and impressionistic paintings and sculpture. The trend has been evident for 3 years and has developed strength this past year."

QUADRANGLE GALLERIES, INC., 1855 NE 163rd St., North Miami Beach FL 33162. (305)944-4771. President: Daniel L. Coel. Exhibits acrylics, batik, drawings, oils, pastels, prints, sculpture and watercolors; displayed until sold. Maximum size: 50x40". Prefers unframed art. Art must be offered for sale. Buys outright. Price range: $5-500. Bestsellers: $20-200. Gallery sets retail price. Send slides or photos of work. SASE. Gallery pays insurance for exhibited work and shipping to gallery.

QUADRANGLE GALLERIES, INC., 1546 S. Dixie Hwy., Coral Gables FL 33146. (See Quadrangle Galleries, North Miami Beach.)

QUADRANGLE GALLERIES, INC., 1181 N. State Road 7, Hollywood FL 33021. (See Quadrangle Galleries, North Miami Beach.)

RINGLING MUSEUMS, Box 1838, Sarasota FL 33578. (813)355-5101. Director of Information: James Bleyer. Only shows artists with national reputation and an association with Florida. No rental gallery service. Purchases art to add to or complement existing collection. Public relations department occasionally uses graphic artists for membership literature, catalogs, posters and advertising literature.

ROOFTOP GALLERY, Harbor House, 423 Front St., Key West FL 33040. Contact: Jack Doremus. Exhibits sculpture, jewelry, painting, printmaking, rugs, tapestries and wood. Price range: $5-500, as set by joint agreement. 40% commission on exclusive representation basis. Send color transparencies or b&w photos.

JOY RUBIN'S ART EMPORIUM, 101 Hollywood Fashion Center, Hollywood FL 33023. Contact: Ivan Rubin. Exhibits contemporary paintings, sculpture, drawings and prints (consisting of signed, limited lithographs, intaglios, etchings and serigraphs). 40% commission. Price range: $30-4,000. Exclusive local representation required. Gallery pays shipping and insurance for exhibited work.

SELECT GALLERY, 19108 W. Dixie Hwy., Miami FL 33160. (305)931-2264. Contact: Tina Roy. Exhibits acrylics, airbrush, calligraphy, drawings, glass art, jewelry, metalsmithing, mobiles, needlecrafts, oils, pastels, pottery, prints, sculpture, soft sculpture, wall hangings, watercolors, weavings and woodcrafting; 3 weeks maximum exposure. Maximum size: 60x48". Paintings must be ready to hang; statues should include pedestals. Art must be offered for sale. Buys outright or on consignment; 40% commission. Maximum price: $2,000, paintings/sculptures; bestsellers: $20-800. Retail price set by joint agreement. Call or write for interview or send slides or photos of work. SASE.

TAMPA BAY ART CENTER, 320 North Blvd., Tampa FL 33606. Director: James M. Bell. Exhibits paintings, prints and drawings. Working agreement with artists: 33¹/₃% on rental; 25% on purchase. Sale prices are $10+. Submit transparencies, photos, printed samples or original artwork. SASE. Reports in 3 weeks if work accepted.

Georgia

BARCLAY GALLERY, 3500 Peachtree Rd., Phipps Plaza, Atlanta GA 30326. (404)233-8712. Director: Suzanne Isla. Exhibits original prints; 90 days minimum exposure. Maximum size: 30x40". Prints must be temporarily matted and wrapped in acetate or vinyl. Do not use masking or cellophane tape to attach print to backing. Art may be offered for sale. Works on consignment; 50% commission. Price range: $10-1,000; bestsellers: $40-200. Retail price set by joint agreement. Requires exclusive area representation. Query with resume and slides of work. SASE. Gallery pays insurance for exhibited work.

PICTURE HOUSE INC., 1109 W. Peachtree NE, Atlanta GA 30309. (404)875-9341. President: George Mitchell. Sales Manager: Jim Saunders. Exhibits acrylics, airbrush, batik, calligraphy, ceramics, drawings, oils, prints, sculpture, soft sculpture, wall hangings and watercolors; 30 days minimum exposure. Maximum size: 48" square. Unframed work OK. "We appeal primarily to the interior designer market, dealing primarily in graphics, prints of all kinds." Art must be offered for sale. Buys outright or on consignment; 50% commission. Price range: $5-1,000, original graphics; $100-3,000, oils and acrylics; $25-500, sculpture; bestsellers: $50-300. Retail price set by joint agreement. Prefers exclusive area representation. Send slides of work. SASE. Also needs artists for public service TV announcements, monthly shows, openings and mailers.
To Break In: "Since we deal with interior designers and decorators, color and size are major considerations. Landscape and nature themes go best."

REGENCY GALLERY, Hyatt Regency Atlanta, 265 Peachtree St. NE, Atlanta GA 30303. (404)577-1234. Contact: Charlie G. or Penelope M. Heath. Exhibits original acrylics, drawings, metalsmithing, mobiles, oils, pottery, prints, sculpture, soft sculpture, wall hangings, water media and weavings; 6 months maximum exposure. Maximum size: 7x6'. Art must be prepared for exhibit by artist. Art must be offered for sale. Works on consignment; 50% commission. Prices: $5 minimum; $200, average painting. Bestsellers: $16-600. Retail price set by joint agreement. Prefers exclusive area representation. Query with samples or send slides. SASE.

Hawaii

THE FOUNDRY, 899 Waimann St., Honolulu HI 96813. (808)533-2609. Director: Alice Leitner. Exhibits acrylics, airbrush, batik, ceramics, drawings, glass art, jewelry, oils, pottery, prints, sculpture, soft sculpture, wall hangings, watercolors and weavings; 3 months maximum exposure. Paintings should have screw eyes — proper supports on back — frame and glass for graphics. Specializes in contemporary avant-garde. Art must be offered for sale (except conceptual environmental art). Works on consignment; 40% commission. Price range: $15-200, ceramics/crafts; $50-1,000, sculptures/wall hangings; $50-5,000, 2-dimensional/paintings; bestsellers: $50-500. Retail price set by joint agreement. Query or send slides of work. SASE. Gallery pays shipping from gallery and insurance on exhibited work.
Promotional Needs: Uses artists to design catalogs, public service TV announcements, special show announcements, press releases and art magazine coverage. Pays $250 minimum.

Illinois

AMERICAN SOCIETY OF ARTISTS, INC., 700 N. Michigan Ave., Chicago IL 60611. (312)751-2500. President: Nancy Fregin. Membership Chairman: Helen Del Valle. Exhibits acrylics, batik, drawings, glass art, jewelry, metalsmithing, mobiles, oils, pastels, pottery, prints, sculpture, soft sculpture, wall hangings, watercolors, weavings and woodcrafting. "Size and presentation requirements worked out with individual according to what is best for the work." Art may be offered for sale. Works on consignment; 25% commission. Membership fee: $30 per year plus $10 initiation fee. Price range: $10-150, enamel pieces; $5-500, engraved glass; $25-2,000, oil paintings. Retail price set by artist or joint agreement. Send for membership information. SASE. Gallery pays insurance on exhibited work. "Many times exposure results in a member being asked to lecture and/or demonstrate through our 'Lecture and Demonstration Service'."

ARTS INTERNATIONAL LTD., 58 E. Walton St., Chicago IL 60611. (312)943-1793. Sales

Manager: Frank Miya. Exhibits acrylics, oils and sculpture; 4 weeks minimum exposure. Maximum size: 48x36". Paintings must be unstretched and unframed. Art must be offered for sale. Buys outright; 50% commission. Price range: $10-1,000, acrylics/oils; $25-300, sculpture; bestsellers: $35-125. Retail price set by joint agreement. Requires exclusive area representation. Query with samples. SASE. Gallery pays shipping from gallery and insurance on exhibited art.

CONTEMPORARY ART WORKSHOP, INC., 542 W. Grant Place, Chicago IL 60614. (312)525-9624. Contact: Lynn Kearney. Exhibits acrylics, airbrush, drawings, oils, prints, sculpture and watercolors; 3-4 weeks exposure. Maximum size: 96x72". Paintings must be ready to hang. Art must be offered for sale. Works on consignment; 33 1/3% commission. Price range: $50-10,000; bestsellers: $200-900. Artist sets retail price. Query with slides of work. SASE.

CUPPS OF CHICAGO, 666 N. Lake Shore Dr., Chicago IL 60611. (312)787-7261. Contact: Dolores Cupp. Exhibits traditional painting, experimental artwork and sculpture. Specializes in abstract and traditional oil paintings. Buys art outright. Requires exclusive area representation. Send photos of work.

THE EYE CORPORATION, 214 S. Clinton St., Chicago IL 60606. (312)726-7484. President: Arthur Lipschultz. Exhibits acrylics, airbrush, calligraphy, drawings, glass art, oils, pastels, prints, sculpture, soft sculpture, wall hangings, watercolors and weavings; 1 month maximum exposure. Art may be offered for sale. Buys outright or on consignment; 25-60%. Minimum price: $50, graphics; $100, paintings; $100, sculpture; bestsellers: $100-5,000. Retail price set by joint agreement. Requires exclusive area representation. Query or send slides of work. SASE. Gallery pays insurance on work.
Promotional Needs: Uses artists to design catalogs and posters. Negotiates payment.

FINE ARTS ASSOCIATES, 1313 E. State St., Rockford IL 61108. Contact: Sally Bradley-Huffington. Exhibits architectural murals, prints, paintings, tapestries and sculpture; 60 days minimum exposure. Maximum size: 4x4'. Specializes in architectural and interior design. Art must be offered for sale. Buys outright or on consignment; 40% commission. Price range: $15-1,600; bestsellers: $35-100. Retail price set by joint agreement. Requires exclusive area representation. Query with transparencies or photos of work. SASE. Gallery pays shipping from gallery.

FOUR ARTS GALLERY, 1629 Oak Ave., Evanston IL 60201. (312)328-8834. Contact: Sidney or Rosemary Zwick. Exhibits contemporary paintings, prints, sculpture, pottery and jewelry; 4 weeks minimum exposure. Works on signed contract basis. Buys craftwork outright. Works with paintings, prints and sculpture on consignment; 40% commission. Work priced from $3-500. Send resume and color transparencies. Gallery sets price and pays shipping on purchased work; artist prices work bought on consignment and pays shipping costs.

KOEHNLINE GALLERY, 7900 Nagle, Morton Grove IL 60053. (312)967-5120 ext. 396. Contact: Bernard Krule. Estab: 1972. Primarily handles fine art photography. Exhibits experimental artwork, prints, graphics and sculpture; work on exhibit 2 weeks minimum. Maximum size: 4x6'. Works on consignment. Price range: $15-3,000. Send resume and slides or photos. Exhibited art insured. Also uses artists to design announcements. Audience of 300 receives mailing with each show.

MASTERS ART GALLERIES, F-311 Woodfield Mall, Schaumburg IL 60195. (312)882-2760. Contact: Val Ramonis. Exhibits contemporary and traditional paintings; 4 weeks minimum exposure. Price range: $25-2,000, by joint agreement. 50% commission. After exclusive representation, commission required on art sold locally. Exhibited art insured.

MERRILL CHASE GALLERIES, LTD., Box 1448, Oakbrook Center, Oakbrook IL 60521. (312)449-5100. Contact: Robert Chase. Exhibits acrylics, drawings, oils, pastels, prints, sculpture and watercolors. Art must be offered for sale. Buys outright or on consignment. Price range: $15-65,000. Retail price set by joint agreement. Requires exclusive area representation. Send slides or photos. SASE. Gallery pays shipping to gallery and insurance for exhibited work.

PRESTIGE GALLERIES INC., 3909 W. Howard St., Skokie IL 60076. (312)679-2555. Vice President: Louis Schutz. Exhibits acrylics, airbrush, drawings, glass art, metalsmithing, oils, pastels, prints, sculpture and watercolors; 3 weeks minimum exposure. Maximum size: 5' square. Specializes in traditional romantic (i.e. mother with child) and representational works. Art may be offered for sale. Buys outright or on consignment; 33 1/3% commission. Price range: $10-10,000, contemporary work; $50-5,000, sculpture; bestsellers: $500-10,000. Retail price set by joint agreement. Requires exclusive area representation. Send slides or photos of work. **Promotional Needs:** Uses artists for catalogs and posters. Pays $25 minimum catalog design; $50 minimum, poster.

TOWER PARK GALLERY, 4709 N. Prospect Rd., Peoria Heights IL 61614. (309)682-8932. Contact: Jackie Buster. Exhibits acrylics, etchings, lithography, silkscreen, drawings, oils and watercolors. Art must be offered for sale. Framed art can be rented. Price range: $20-5,000; bestsellers: $100-500. Retail price set by joint agreement. Prefers exclusive area representation. Query.

Indiana

ART CENTER, INC., 121 N. Lafayette Blvd., South Bend IN 46601. (219)233-8201. Contact: Jennifer Buck. Rental gallery service available in which selected artists are represented for a 1-year contract. 20% commission. Public relations department uses graphic artists for membership literature, catalogs and posters. Gift shop buys original art and crafts outright and on consignment for resale. Prices in shop range from $2-500 for cards, calendars, sculpture and 3-dimensional pieces. 20% commission.

Expose Yourself With Postcards

Exposure for an artist can come in sizes as small as a postcard. Artist Patricia Renick regularly gets postcards made which feature a picture(s) of her work.

"I slip my postcards into museum postcard racks, or into art books in libraries or leave them lying around at all exhibitions," says Renick. Another way to distribute your postcards, she adds, is to ask chambers of commerce and hotels/motels to pass them out. Also, gift shops and bookstores can be possible outlets.

Patricia Renick, who created "Stegowagenvolkssaurus" (which was used by the J. Walter Thompson advertising agency), uses postcards as a way to get exposure for her work. She says that about 2,000 color postcards can be obtained for under $200.

EVANSVILLE MUSEUM OF ARTS AND SCIENCE ART RENTAL AND SALES GALLERY, 411 SE Riverside Dr., Evansville IN 47713. Director: John W. Streetman III. Accepts work on consignment on rental-purchase basis. Artist-in-residence program occasionally sponsored. Affiliated Artists Guild offers members sales opportunities in other locations and exhibits in the Museum through "Art of the Month" program. Write for more information. Also sponsors art and craft shows. (See Mid-States Art Exhibition or Mid-States Craft Exhibition.)

FORT WAYNE MUSEUM OF ART, 1202 W. Wayne St., Fort Wayne IN 46804. Contact: Betty Newton. Exhibits all art; 1-6 months exposure. Maximum size: 30x40", prints; 2x2x4', 100 lbs., sculpture. Paintings must be ready to hang; prints must be framed or covered with acetate. Art must be offered for sale. Works on consignment; 25% commission. Price range: $25-300, prints; $75-700, paintings; $95-450, sculpture; bestsellers: $25-400, art; $5-40, crafts. Artist sets retail price including commission. Query or send slides or photos of work. SASE. Gallery pays insurance for exhibited work.

LAFAYETTE ART CENTER, 101 S. 9th St., Lafayette IN 47901. (317)742-4470. Director: Suzanne Stafford. Exhibits acrylics, airbrush, batik, calligraphy, ceramics, drawings, jewelry, metalsmithing, oils, pastels, pottery, prints, sculpture, soft sculpture, wall hangings, watercolors, weavings and multi-media; 1-30 days exposure. Maximum size: 8x4x8'. Paintings must be ready to hang. Art may be offered for sale. Works on consignment; 25% commission. Price range: $2-90, ceramics; $5-100, pottery; $6-500, batik; bestsellers; 5¢-$500. Retail price set by joint agreement. Query with samples. Apply 2 years in advance. SASE. Gallery pays insurance on exhibited work.

WINTHROP GALLERY, 5228 Winthrop Ave., Indianapolis IN 46220. (317)283-1147. Contact: Herman W. Kapherr. Exhibits traditional painting, prints, graphics, drawings, sketches and sculpture. Handles mainly 19th and 20th century American art. Prefers unframed art. Buys outright. Price range: $25-3,000.

Iowa

BLANDEN ART GALLERY, 920 3rd Ave. S., Fort Dodge IA 50501. (515)573-2316. Director: Stephen Rhodes. Use of rental gallery requires approval by director and shop manager. Commission is 33%; artists receive 50% of rentals, 67% of purchase price. Artist's share of rental applies to purchase. Art purchases by museum for its collection require approval by Board of Trustees. Gift shop buys original art and crafts outright or on consignment. 33% commission. Price range: $1-500.

Kansas

COHLMIA'S ART GALLERY, 6302 Marjorie Lane, Wichita KS 67208. (316)685-3411. Contact: Jim Cohlmia. Estab: 1964. Specializes in paintings. Exhibits prints, graphics and sculpture; 4 weeks minimum exposure. Buys outright or on consignment; 50% commission. Prices from $500-10,000. Gallery sets price. Requires exclusive area representation. Exhibited art insured. Gallery pays return shipping.

FREDONIA ARTS COUNCIL, INC., Box 355, Fredonia KS 66736. Contact: Director. Interested in artists exhibiting work in the Council's gallery. Works with painters, sculptors, ceramists, printmakers, weavers and other craftsmen. Submit slides of work and resume.

Louisiana

ED BLOUIN, 905 Decatur St., New Orleans LA 70116. (504)523-1477. Contact: Ed Blouin. Exhibits landscape, boats and florals; 8 weeks minimum exposure. Maximum size: 5' square. By joint agreement, art is priced from $15-1,000. Commission is 33 1/3%. Has promotion mailing list to which mailings go once a year.

COLLECTORS GALLERY, INC., 5607 Government St., Baton Rouge LA 70806. Exhibits traditional and abstract paintings, pottery and jewelry; 2 weeks minimum exposure. Specializes in Louisiana artists and scenes. Prices: $2-1,000. 40% commission. Send photos of work. Gallery pays insurance for exhibited work. Most customers are young married couples.

HARRINGTON GALLERY, 1113 Johnston St., Lafayette LA 70501. Contact: Herschel Harrington. Represents mostly Southern traditional artists. "We are interested in seeing the works of Southern artists through slides or photos." 33 1/3% commission. "Payment of shipping costs depends on each individual situation. Work receives 4-week showing. All work is properly insured by gallery."

LES ENFANTS TOWNHOUSE GALLERIES, 416 Bourbon St., New Orleans LA 70130. (504)524-8203. President: Carl Plaisance. Exhibits jewelry, oils, acrylics and watercolors. No abstracts. Art may be offered for sale. Buys outright or on consignment; 50% commission. Price range: $10-15,000. Gallery sets retail price. Requires exclusive area representation. Query with transparencies or photos. Gallery pays insurance for exhibited work. Shipping costs shared.

927 GALLERY, 927 Royal, New Orleans LA 70116. (504)525-4527. Contact: Floyd McLamb. Exhibits prints. Maximum size: 23x33". Art must be offered for sale. Buys outright. Price range: $6-500. Retail price set by joint agreement. Requires exclusive area representation. Query. SASE. Gallery pays shipping from gallery and insurance on exhibited work.

SPORTS ART, 633 Toulouse St., New Orleans LA 70130. Contact: J. Peter Eaves. Exhibits traditional painting, prints, drawing and sculpture. Specializes in wildlife, hunting and fishing themes. Price range: $20-10,000, as set by joint agreement. 30% commission. Consigned art should be sent unframed, and shipping costs depend on prior arrangements. Exhibited art insured. Mailings sent with each show. Occasionally uses graphic artists to design announcements for shows.

TAYLOR CLARK'S, INC., 2623 Government St., Baton Rouge LA 70806. (504)383-4929. Contact: Taylor Clark. Exhibits traditional paintings; 2 weeks minimum exposure. Buys outright or on consignment. Prices from $50-15,000 set by gallery. Requires commission on art sold in area after exclusive representation. Gallery provides frame. Exhibited art insured. Sponsors openings.

TYGIER-KNIGHT GALLERIES, LTD., 313 Royal St., New Orleans LA 70130. (504)523-7043. Contact: Jack Knight. Exhibits traditional paintings and drawings; 13 weeks minimum exposure. Specializes in fine art and prints. Prefers unframed art. Prefers art size be limited to 36x48". Buys outright or on consignment; 50% commission. Prices from $35-1,000. Price set by gallery and artist. Requires exclusive representation in area. Send slides or photos. Sponsors openings.

Maine

BOOTHBAY REGION ART GALLERY, Brick House, Boothbay Harbor ME 04538. Contact: Director. Exhibits acrylics, drawings, metalsmithing, mobiles, oils, pastels, prints, sculpture and watercolors; 1-2½ months exposure. Paintings must be ready to hang. Artists from Boothbay region only. Works on consignment; 25% commission. Minimum price: $2, drawings; bestsellers: $2-600. Artist sets retail price. Call or write for interview.

Maryland

ESSEX COMMUNITY COLLEGE, College Cultural Events Council, Baltimore MD 21237. Contact: Zoran Tosic. Works with painters and graphic designers. Does not take commissions or handle direct sales of work. "Should someone be interested in buying a piece, we direct the person to the artist for information and further arrangements." Send slides.

ETCHCRAFTERS ART GUILD, 8 W. 25th St., Baltimore MD 21218. (301)366-6852. Contact: Don Swann. Exhibits original etchings and oil paintings. Buys artwork outright or on consignment, Commission is 33⅓% on consignment and 50% on purchase. Prices from $1-150. Exhibited art insured. Sponsors openings. Also operates framing business.

JERRY GILDEN GALLERY, 303 Reistertown Rd., Baltimore MD 21208. Contact: Miriam Gilden. Exhibits traditional paintings, sculpture, prints and drawings; 3 months minimum exposure. Artist sets retail price. Send color transparencies or b&w photos of work. Exhibited art insured.

LAWYERS ARTSHOP, 1106 Cathedral St., Baltimore MD 21201. (301)837-0820. General Manager: Doris Pierce. Exhibits prints and sculpture. Specializes in art related to law and the legal profession (i.e., showing lawyers, judges, courts, lawyer-client scene, law offices, courtroom scenes, etc.). Buys outright. Price range: $25-100; bestsellers: $25-40. Retail price set by joint agreement. Query with samples or photos of work. SASE. Gallery pays shipping from gallery.

MODEART GALLERIES, LTD., Belair Shopping Center, Bowie MD 20715. Contact: Dorothy B. Schmier. Exhibits painting (traditional/abstract), sculpture and pottery; 6 weeks minimum exposure. Size limit is 48x48". 50% commission. Prices set by joint agreement range from $35-450. Promotion mailing list maintained, with mailings sent 4 times annually. Exclusive representation in area required.

PHOENIX-CHASE GALLERIES, LTD., 5 W. Chase St., Baltimore MD 21201. President: John Charles Butler. Exhibits traditional and abstract painting, sculpture, prints and drawings; 2 weeks minimum exposure. 40% commission. Prices from $100-2,000, as set by gallery. Since exclusive representation is required in area, commissions are collected on art sold after show. Send transparencies or photos. Sponsors openings.

THE TOMLINSON COLLECTION, 711 W. 40th St., Baltimore MD 21211. (301)338-1555. Contact: Virginia or William Tomlinson. Exhibits graphic art by old and modern masters (particularly 19th century) and by contemporary living artists. The craft shop (see Craft Dealers), run by Ginny Tomlinson, often combines with the gallery for special exhibitions of a common theme. Gallery pays insurance for exhibited work.

Massachusetts

THE AINSWORTH GALLERY, INC., 42 Bromfield St., Boston MA 02108. Director: A. Donald Conron. Exhibits prints; 52 weeks minimum exposure. Buys outright or on consignment; 40% commission. Art ranges in price from $25-2,500, set by joint agreement. Prefers to receive consigned art unframed and unmatted. Has promotion mailing list to which mailings go with each new show. Occasionally uses graphic artists to design announcements for shows.

ANDOVER GALLERY OF FINE ART, 91 N. Main St., Andover MA 01810. (617)475-7468. Contact: Howard Yezerski. Exhibits acrylics, drawings, oils, pastels, prints, sculpture and watercolors; 6 weeks minimum exposure. Maximum size: 60" square. Prefers paintings and graphics framed and ready to hang. Art must be offered for sale. Works on consignment; 33⅓% commission. Price range: $15-300, graphics; $75-2,000, paintings/drawings; $50-1,000, sculpture; bestsellers: $75-300. Retail price set by joint agreement. Requires exclusive area representation. Send slides of work. SASE. Gallery pays shipping from gallery and in-transit insurance.

BOSTON ATHENAEUM GALLERY, 10½ Beacon St., Boston MA 02108. (617)227-0270. Exhibits ceramics, decoupage, drawings, glass art, jewelry, mobiles, needlecrafts, oils, pastels, pottery, prints, sculpture, soft sculpture, wall hangings, watercolors and weavings; 1 month exposure. Paintings must be ready to hang. Art may be offered for sale. No commission. Price range: $25-10,000+. Artist sets retail price. All methods of contact OK. SASE.

BRIDGEWATER STATE COLLEGE, Student Union, Bridgewater MA 02324. Contact: Claire A. Scott. "We're a nonprofit educational institution interested in promoting the arts through exposure to our student body and college community." Interested in scheduling lecturers and artists to display work in college gallery. Send resume, published samples and/or slides.

BROCKTON ART CENTER, Oak St., Upper Porter's Pond, Brockton MA 02401. (617)588-6000. Contact: Richard Minutillo. Exhibits all arts/crafts; 2 months maximum exposure. Art may be offered for sale; 10% donation. Price range: $15-10,000, crafts; $90-15,000, paintings/sculpture; $50-10,000 prints; bestsellers: $90-200. Retail price set by joint agreement. Send slides or photos of work. SASE. Gallery pays shipping and insurance.

THE ROBERT BROOKS ART GALLERY, 762 Falmouth Rd., Hyannis MA 02601. (617)775-4149. Gallery Director: Rosalyn Brooks. Exhibits acrylics, oils and watercolors; 3 months minimum exposure. Maximum size: 45" square. Paintings must be ready to hang. Art must be offered for sale. Works on consignment; 40% commission. Price range: $75-750; bestsellers: $150-300. Artist sets retail price. Requires exclusive area representation. Send slides. SASE.

CAMBRIDGE ART ASSOCIATION, 23 Garden St., Cambridge MA 02138. Contact: Executive Director. Exhibits traditional and abstract painting, sculpture, prints, drawings, pottery, jewelry, weaving and batik; 2 weeks minimum exposure. 33⅓% commission. Price range: $5-3,000. Artist sets retail price. Membership: $20 annual fee.

CORNELL GALLERIES, 270 Maple St., Springfield MA 01105. (413)736-3609. Contact: Robert Cornell. Exhibits acrylics, airbrush, calligraphy, ceramics, drawings, glass art, jewelry, mobiles, oils, pottery, prints, sculpture, wall hangings and weavings; 45 days-4 months exposure. No size restrictions. Paintings must be ready to hang. Art must be offered for sale. Buys outright or on consignment; 33⅓-50% commission. Price range: $10-10,000, pottery/jewelry; $25-10,000, weavings/glass art; $50-10,000, framed art/sculpture; bestsellers: $100-400. Retail price set by joint agreement. Requires exclusive area representation. Send slides or photos of work. SASE. Gallery pays shipping from gallery.

COSS GALLERY, Box 991, 56 Union St., Nantucket MA 02554. (617)228-2662. Contact: Ms. C. J. Coss. Exhibits traditional and abstract painting, sculpture, pottery, jewelry, unique crafts and limited edition graphics; 2 weeks minimum exposure. Maximum size: 3x5'. Works on signed contract basis with artists. 33⅓% commission. Art ranges in price from $25-2,000. Price set by joint agreement. Requires exclusive representation in area and requires commissions on any art sold in area after showing. "Nothing is received unframed except graphics." Has a promotion mailing list and also uses graphic artists to design announcements for shows.

DODGE HOUSE ART GALLERY, 442 Main St., Chatham, Cape Cod MA 02633. Director: Mr. H. Latham Kent. "Only traditional art is handled at our gallery. Our season runs from May 15-Labor Day." Exhibits paintings, small sculpture and art photography; 8 weeks minimum exposure. "New approaches are always welcome. The most popular prices in our gallery are in the $50-250 range, but we do carry items priced from $10-1,000." Price set by joint agreement, with gallery taking 33⅓% commission. Requires exclusive area representation.

EDGARTOWN ART GALLERY, INC., S. Summer St., Edgartown MA 02539. (617)627-5991. President: Gerret D. Conover. "We exhibit only a high quality of work representing many of today's leading artists." No abstract work. Maximum size: 30x40". Usually takes work on consignment; 33⅓% commission. Prices from $200-8,000. Artist usually sets price. Requires exclusive representation in area and commission on any art sold in area after showing. Send slides of work. Gallery pays insurance for exhibited work. Sponsors openings.

DANIEL FRISHMAN GALLERY, 933 Main St., Osterville MA 02655. Contact: Daniel Frishman. Exhibits painting, prints, sculpture and pottery. Prices from $10-10,000, as set by joint agreement. 40% commission. Artist usually pays shipping; but gallery may share expenses. Exclusive representation in area required, and commission taken on any art sold locally after showing. Send transparencies or photos. Exhibited art insured. Sponsors openings.

GALLERY OF WORLD ART INC., 745 Beacon St., Newton Centre MA 02159. (617)332-1800. Art Director: Dorothea J. Mautner. Exhibits airbrush, drawings, oils, pastels, prints, sculpture and watercolors; 1-3 months exposure. Maximum size: 72" square. "Paintings or drawings must be ready to hang or have cellophane protection for bin display. All works on paper must be matted." Specializes in contemporary, realistic art. Art must be offered for sale. Works on consignment; 40% commission. Retail price set by joint agreement. Requires exclusive area representation. Arrange interview to show slides on larger work, samples on small. **To Break In:** "Any artist interested in showing work should first come to the gallery and see in his own mind if his work fits in. If that is not possible, we will make suggestions."

GRAPHICS 1 AND GRAPHICS 2, 168 Newbury St., Boston MA 02116. (617)266-2475. Contact: Lindsay Lasser/Margaret Reeve. Exhibits prints. Work should be unframed. Art must be offered for sale. Works on consignment; 50% commission. Price range: $35-2,000, prints; bestsellers: $100-400. Artist sets retail price. Requires exclusive area representation. Send slides or photos of work. SASE. Gallery pays shipping from gallery and insurance on exhibited work.

IMAGE GALLERY, Main St., Stockbridge MA 01262. (413)298-5500. Contact: Clemens Kalischer. Exhibits paintings, calligraphy, ceramics, drawings, glass art, jewelry, pottery, prints, sculpture, soft sculpture, wall hangings, watercolors and weavings; 4-6 weeks exposure. Maximum size: 8x8'. Work should be ready to hang. Art must be offered for sale. Works on consignment; 35% commission. Price range: $50-10,000, artwork; $50-500, prints; bestsellers: $300-1,000. Retail price set by joint agreement. Requires exclusive area representation. Query with photos or slides of work. SASE. Also uses artists for catalog and poster design.

PETER JOHN'S STUDIO & GALLERY OF ART ON CAPE COD, Box E, Buzzards Bay MA 02532. (617)759-7335. Director: Peter Fugere, Sr. Exhibits acrylics, oils, prints, sculpture and watercolors; 8 weeks minimum exposure. Maximum size: 4' square. Prefers paintings to be ready to hang and sculpture to have pedestals. Specializes in traditional landscapes and seascapes, abstracts and contemporary surrealism. Art must be offered for sale. Works mainly on consignment; 40% commission. Price range: $50-1,500, framed original paintings; $40-500, prints and original graphics; bestsellers: $50-600. Retail price set by joint agreement. Requires exclusive area representation in Plymouth and Barnstable counties. Query with slides or photos or samples of work. SASE. Gallery pays shipping from gallery. "Most of our business is transacted between April and December. We take a commission on any art sold in the area for 1 year because we do such an extensive promotional campaign for any artist we represent."

MUSEUM OF THE OCCULT (formerly Stage Door Studios), Rte. 2, Camelot, North Adams MA 01247. (413)663-6060. Curator: Dr. Robert M. Master, Ph.D. Nonprofit museum operated by Universal Religious Brotherhood, Inc., Temple of the Holy Grail, Inc. Exhibits candlemaking, glass art, jewelry, metalsmithing, oils, pastels, pottery, sculpture, wall hangings and watercolors; 4-12 weeks exposure. Size and hanging specifications arranged with individual. Art may be offered for sale. Specializes in the occult, witchcraft, magic, ancient civilization and awareness. Wants "rituals and ceremony scenes of 'singles' or groups. Must be skyclad per ancient pagan ways (nude). Work should express a feeling of belonging with or to nature/earth/people during ancient pagan rituals, ceremonies and of bring 'down the Powers and Forces'. Specializing subjects: ancient goddesses, priestesses such as Shakti to Bhakti." Works on consignment; 20% commission. Price range: $1-100; bestsellers: $8-16. Retail price set by joint agreement. Send slides or photos of work. SASE.

ORLEANS ART GALLERY, Box 672, Orleans MA 02653. (617)255-2676. Contact: Frank Hogan. Exhibits acrylics, calligraphy, ceramics, drawings, mobiles, oils, pastels, pottery, prints, sculpture, watercolors and woodcrafting; 6 months-1 year exposure. Traditional art only. Art must be offered for sale. Works on consignment; 40% commission. Price range: $50-1,000, paintings; bestsellers: $200-500. Artist sets retail price. Requires exclusive area representation. Query with slides of work. SASE.

PACIFICO GALLERIES, INC., European Imports, 395 Commercial St., Boston MA 02109. Contact: R. Pacifico. "Color photos only" should be submitted by artists interested in exhibiting traditional and abstract paintings and graphics. Negotiates commission. Price range: $10-2,000.

POOR RICHARD'S GALLERY, 77 Rocky Neck Ave., East Gloucester MA 01930. (617)283-6861. (Winter address: 20 King George Dr., Boxford MA 01921. (617)887-2264). Contact: Richard or Nancy Korb. Exhibits acrylics, batik, drawings, enamels, glass art, metalsmithing, mobiles, oils, pottery, prints, sculpture and watercolors; May 30-October 30 exposure. Maximum size: 2x3'. Paintings must be ready to hang and graphics must be matted and wrapped. Specializes "to some degree" in New England marine themes. Art must be offered for sale. Buys outright or on consignment; 40% commission. Price range: $75-1,000, oils/acrylics; $5-300, crafts; bestsellers: $25-400. Artist sets retail price. Requires exclusive area representation. Send slides or photos of work. SASE. Gallery pays shipping from gallery and insurance for exhibited work.

VIGNARI GALLERY, 7 Main St., Ogunquit MA 03907. (207)646-7328. Contact: John Vignari. Exhibits fine art wood or metal nautical sculpture. No large pieces. Art must be offered for sale. Works on consignment; 33 1/3% commission. Price range: $250-5,000, paintings; bestsellers: $250-700. Gallery sets retail price. Requires exclusive area representation. Query. SASE.

Michigan

JESSE BESSER MUSEUM, 491 Johnson St., Alpena MI 49707. (517)356-2202. Contact: Dennis R. Bodem. No rental gallery, but has exhibits of artists' work which are offered for sale. Commission is 15%. Purchases for museum's collection are mostly northeastern Michigan artists or graphics by known artists. Gift shop buys art and crafts outright for resale. Price range: from 20¢-$8.

BIRMINGHAM GALLERY, INC., 1025 Haynes, Birmingham MI 48011. (313)642-7455. Contact: John McKinney. Exhibits experimental artwork, prints, graphics, drawings, sketches and sculpture; 4 weeks minimum exposure. Specializes in contemporary art. Buys art outright or on consignment. 40% commission. Art priced from $50-8,000. Artist sets retail price. Gallery requires exclusive representation in area and commission on any art sold in area after showing. Send resume, slides and information on previous showings and education. Exhibited art insured. Prefers consigned art unframed. Occasionally uses artists to design announcements for shows. About 1,500-2,400 mailings are made for each new show.

DETROIT ARTISTS MARKET, 1452 Randolph St., Detroit MI 48226. Gallery Manager: Margaret Conzelman. Exhibits acrylics, airbrush, batik, ceramics, drawings, glass art, jewelry, metalsmithing, oils, pottery, prints, sculpture, soft sculpture, wall hangings, watercolors and weavings; 1 month minimum exposure. Work should be ready for exhibition; framed work equipped with wire and screw eyes, matted work covered with acetate. Art must be offered for sale. Works on consignment; 25-30% commission. Minimum price: $2.50, ceramics; bestsellers: $3-100. Artist sets retail price. Query, then submit work in person. If accepted, work is exhibited on a rotating basis.

FIELD ART STUDIO, 2646 Coolidge Ave., Berkley MI 48072. Contact: Sam Field. Exhibits traditional and abstract painting, sculpture, drawings and pottery. "We sponsor quality-controlled art shows in major shopping centers which last 4-10 days." 20% commission. Price range: $10-5,000, with artist deciding price. Send transparencies or photos. Sponsors openings.

FORSYTHE GALLERIES, 201 Nickels Arcade, Ann Arbor MI 48108. Director: Daniel L. DeGraaf. Exhibits acrylics, ceramics, drawings, glass art, oils, prints, sculpture, soft sculpture, wall hangings, watercolors and weavings; 2 months maximum exposure. Art must be offered for sale. Buys outright or on consignment. Price range: $75-10,000, paintings; $50-5,000, sculpture; $25-500, prints. Retail price set by joint agreement. Requires exclusive area representation. Query with samples. SASE.

GALLERY 22, 22 E. Long Lake Rd., Box 251, Bloomfield Hills MI 48013. (313)642-1310. Contact: Fred Nordsiek. Exhibits acrylics, ceramics, glass art, oils, prints, sculpture, wall hangings, watercolors and weavings; 2 months minimum exposure. Maximum size: 2x6x6'. Specializes in "contemporary artwork of a sophisticated nature; no landscapes or still life or figurative unless abstract." Art must be offered for sale. Works on consignment; 40% commission. Price range: $50-2,000, paintings; $20-1,500, prints; $10-1,000, other media; bestsellers: $100-400. Retail price set by joint agreement. Requires exclusive area representation. Send slides of work. SASE. Gallery pays shipping from gallery and insurance on exhibited work.

ARNOLD KLEIN GALLERY (formerly Klein-Vogel), 4520 N. Woodward Ave., Royal Oak MI 48072. (313)647-7709. Director: Arnold Klein. Exhibits acrylics, ceramics, drawings, oils, prints and watercolors; 1-12 months exposure. Maximum size: 48x12x36". Oils must be framed. Specializes in figurative art. Art must be offered for sale. Buys outright or on consignment; 40% commission. Price range: $30-1,000, prints; $300-1,000, paintings; $75-500, drawings; bestsellers: $100-300. Retail price set by joint agreement. Requires exclusive representation in Detroit's northern suburbs. Query. Send samples only on invitation. SASE. Gallery pays shipping from gallery and insurance for exhibited work. "We prefer younger and less well-known artists."

LEFT BANK ART GALLERY, 231 Water St., Saughtuck MI 49453. (616)857-8181. Contact: Joyce Stack. Exhibits oils, watercolors, acrylics, prints, ceramics, sculpture, jewelry, metalsmithing, rugs and tapestries; 12 weeks minimum exposure. One-man shows arranged. Works on consignment; 33 1/3% commission. Prices from $2-2,000. Prices set by artist. Send transparencies or photos. Sponsors openings.

PARK WEST GALLERIES, 24151 Telegraph, Southfield MI 48075. (313)354-2343. Contact: Dr. Albert Scaglione. Exhibits traditional painting, graphics and sculpture. Buys work outright. Prefers exclusive representation in area. Prefers art unframed. Gallery pays insurance on exhibited work. Occasionally uses artists for show announcement designs.

THE ROBERT THOM GALLERY, 175 W. Merrill, Birmingham MI 48011. Contact: Robert Thom. Exhibits jewelry, prints, drawings, sculpture, pottery and traditional and abstract painting; 6 weeks minimum exposure. "We prefer exclusive representation in our area." Prices in $75-1,000 range, with 40% commission. Send transparencies or photos. Sponsors openings.

Minnesota

ART DEPOT I, 4207 Winnetha N., New Hope MN 55428. (612)533-1771. Contact: Ed Braegelmann. Exhibits prints, watercolors and pen and ink; 6 months minimum exposure. Send work unframed and unglassed. Art must be offered for sale. Buys outright or on consignment; 35% commission. Price range: $10-1,200; bestsellers: $25-300. Artist sets retail price. Requires exclusive area representation. Query with samples. SASE. "Cover artwork with protective acetate for mailing."
To Break In: Develop a catalog of work and set prices.

ART DEPOT II, 5207 W. 84th St., Bloomington MN 55437. (612)835-6689. (See Art Depot I, New Hope.)

BROOKLYN CENTER COMMUNITY CENTER, 6301 Shingle Creek Pkwy., Brooklyn Center MN 55430. (612)561-5448. Contact: Kathy Flesher. Sponsors openings; minimum 2 weeks exposure. Artist sets retail price. "Our small gallery is available without charge to local artists/craftsmen. It is a small portion of a complete community center operation. We would be interested in showing traveling shows." Call or write.

JACQUES GALLERY, BELL MUSEUM OF NATURAL HISTORY, 10 Church St. SE, Minneapolis MN 55455. (612)373-3193. Contact: Julie Barrett. Gallery "provides a place for natural history artists to show their works. We cooperate with artists hoping to sell their work by providing price lists, artists' addresses and phone numbers to prospective buyers." Exhibits all media. Maximum size: 4'. Send slides or photos. Gallery pays insurance for exhibited work.

THE LUTHERAN BROTHERHOOD LUTHERAN CENTER GALLERY, 701 2nd Ave. S., Minneapolis MN 55402. (612)340-7261. Fine Arts Coordinator: Joan Sheldon. Fraternal benefit society. Exhibits all fine art except mobiles; 30 days exposure. Maximum size: 6x3'. Wire framed work; matted works need no wire. Prefers conservative works; no nudes. Art may be offered for sale. No commission. Price range: $5-25,000; bestsellers: $5-150. Artist sets retail price. Query with slide samples and resume. SASE. Gallery pays shipping and insurance.
To Break In: "Lutheran Brotherhood schedules exhibits up to a year in advance. We encourage exhibits in almost all media, and try to vary them each month. Dual exhibits (standing art and hanging art) are encouraged whenever possible."
Promotional Needs: Contact Charles Johnson, purchasing agent. Uses artists for membership literature and posters.

NORMANDALE COLLEGE GALLERY, 9700 France Ave. S., Bloomington MN 55431. (612)831-5001. Contact: J. Jack Bean. Exhibits painting, graphics, pottery, jewelry, weaving and glass enameling; 3 weeks minimum exposure. Prefers framed or matted art. Artist sets price. Prices: $15-500. Send resume and slides or photos. Gallery pays shipping.

3 ROOMS UP, 4316 Upton Ave. S., Minneapolis MN 55410. (612)926-1774. Contact: Alice Engstrom. Exhibits traditional painting, experimental artwork, prints, graphics, drawings, sketches, sculpture, pottery, jewelry, batik, wooden toys, stuffed toys, weavings and macrame; 4 weeks minimum exposure. Works on consignment; 33⅓% commission. Price range: $5-300. Artist sets price. Send resume and slides or photos. Mailings sent 2-3 times annually to promotion list of 2,000.

WINDSOR GALLERY, 5019 France Ave. S., Minneapolis MN 55410. Contact: Don J. Long. Exhibits traditional and abstract painting, sculpture, prints and drawings; 2 weeks minimum exposure. By joint agreement, prices range from $5-750. Commission is 33⅓%. Send transparencies or photos.

Missouri

ART MART INC., Harmon Galleries, 8112 Maryland Ave., St. Louis MO 63105. Contact: Jim Harmon. Exhibits traditional and abstract painting, sculpture, pottery, jewelry, prints and drawings; 2 weeks minimum exposure. Works on signed contract basis with artists. 33% commission. Price range: $20-30,000. Charges commissions on art sold in area after exclusive representation for 30 days, but exclusive representation not required. Send transparencies or photos. Exhibited art insured. Also employs graphic artists for design of show announcements.

CHRISMAN GALLERY, Highways 25 and 114, Dexter MO 63841. Contact: Tom Bowen or Joe Vinson. Has 3 other galleries located in Missouri — at Cape Girardeau, Kansas City and Sikestown. Exhibits traditional and abstract painting, sculpture, pottery, jewelry, prints, drawings and unique tables or furniture; 12 weeks minimum exposure. Also has large volume framing business, and prefers to receive art unframed. Negotiates commission. Prices: $20-5,600, as set by agreement between gallery and artist. Shipping handled by gallery. Exclusive representation in area required, and gallery works on signed contract basis with artists. Send transparencies or photos. Has a large promotion mailing list and sponsors openings.

GREENBERG GALLERY, 7526 Forsyth Blvd., Clayton MO 63105. (314)862-1640. Director: Ronald Greenberg. Exhibits acrylics, drawings, oils, prints and sculpture; 2 months maximum exposure. Maximum size: 16x9'. Specializes in post-World War II American contemporary. Art may be offered for sale. Works on consignment. Price range: $150-2,000, prints; $2,000 minimum, paintings/sculpture. Retail price set by joint agreement. Query with samples. SASE. Gallery pays insurance on exhibited work.

LAWRENCE GALLERY, 901 Westport Rd., Kansas City MO 64111. (816)531-2423. Director: Susan Lawrence. Exhibits ceramics, drawings, paintings, prints, sculpture and watercolors; 2 weeks minimum exposure. Art should be ready for display and must be offered for sale. Buys outright or on consignment; 40% commission. Price range: "$25 and up, depending on quality of work and artist." Artist sets retail price. Requires exclusive area representation. Send resume and background information with photos or slides of work. SASE. "Original prints sell best."

RAACH'S PLAZA GALLERY INC., 630 W. 50th, Kansas City MO 64112. (816)753-2047. President: F.A. Raach. Exhibits acrylics, airbrush, batik, calligraphy, ceramics, drawings, glass art, jewelry, mobiles, oils, pastels, pottery, prints, sculpture, soft sculpture, wall hangings, watercolors, weavings and woodcrafting; 1-6 months exposure. Paintings should be ready to hang; statues, include pedestals. Art must be offered for sale. Works on consignment; 33⅓% commission. Price range: $10-10,000; bestsellers: $100-500. Gallery sets retail price. Requires exclusive area representation. Query with slides of work. SASE. Also uses artists for catalog and poster art.

MARTIN SCHWEIG GALLERY, 4657 Maryland Ave., St. Louis MO 63108. (314)361-3000. Contact: Martin Schweig, Jr. or Lauretta Schumacher. Exhibits acrylics, batik, ceramics, drawings, dollmaking, glass art, jewelry, oils, pastels, pottery, prints, sculpture, soft sculpture, wall hangings, watercolors and weavings; 2 months maximum exposure. Maximum size: 6' square. Prefers paintings be ready to hang. Art must be offered for sale. 33⅓% commission. Retail price set by joint agreement. Query or call for interview. Artist must send own announcements.

Montana

MAGIC MUSHROOM GALLERIES, 211 N. Higgins, Missoula Bank Bldg., Missoula MT 59801. (406)549-9322. Contact: Kaye Johnson or Lee Morrison. Exhibits acrylics, batik, calligraphy, ceramics, drawings, glass art, jewelry, mobiles, oils, pastels, pottery, prints, sculpture, soft sculpture, watercolors, weavings and woodcrafting; 90 days exposure. Paintings should be ready to hang. Art must be offered for sale. Works on consignment; 40% commission. Minimum price: $5, paintings/original prints; $4.50, pottery; $10, jewelry; bestsellers: $5-150. Retail price set by joint agreement. Requires exclusive area representation. Query. SASE.

J. K. RALSTON MUSEUM AND ART CENTER GIFT SHOP, Box 50, Sidney MT 59270. (406)482-3500. Director: Linda K. Mann. Exhibits paintings, ink sketches, ceramics and sculpture on consignment. 25% commission. Prices from $5-200.

Nebraska

CARRIAGE HOUSE GALLERY (formerly Brownsville Fine Arts Association), 1312 Fall Creek Rd., Lincoln NE 68510. Contact: Ms. Carl H. Rohman. Works with painters, sculptors, graphic designers, muralists and other craftsmen, especially "pioneer." Artists from Nebraska, Iowa, Missouri and Kansas may submit published samples or slides of original work and a list of professional credits, prizes and/or awards. Works on consignment. Contract available on request.

LIMITED IMAGE GALLERY, 1103 Galvin Rd., Bellevue NE 68005. Contact: William Cox. Exhibits traditional and abstract paintings, prints, drawings, pottery, sculpture and jewelry; 2 weeks minimum exposure. Prices from $50-5,000, set by joint agreement. 30-50% commission. Has framing business, and prefers to receive consigned art unframed. Send transparencies or photos. Occasionally uses graphic artists to design show announcements. Maintains list to which mailings go with each show.

Nevada

GREEN APPLE GALLERY, 4800 S. Maryland Pkwy., F, Las Vegas NV 89109. (702)736-6604. Contact: Peg Bolen. Exhibits acrylics, airbrush, batik, ceramics, drawings, unusual doll-making, glass art (no stained glass), mobiles, stitchery, oils, pastels, pottery, prints, sculpture, wall hangings, watercolors, weavings and woodcrafting; 1 year minimum exposure. Paintings must be framed. Art must be offered for sale. Buys outright or on consignment; 40-50% commission. Price range: $25+; bestsellers: $25-1,000. Retail price set by joint agreement. Requires exclusive area representation. Send slides or photos of work. SASE. Gallery pays insurance for exhibited work.

New Hampshire

PLYMOUTH STATE COLLEGE ARTS GALLERY, Plymouth State College, Plymouth NH 03264. (603)536-1550 ext. 280. Director: David Batchelder. Exhibits paintings, calligraphy, ceramics, drawings, metalsmithing, mobiles, oils, pastels, pottery, prints, sculpture, wall hangings, watercolors and weavings; 3-4 weeks minimum exposure. No size requirements. All work, except sculpture, must be under glass. Art may be offered for sale. Works on consignment; no commission. Price range: $50-5,000. Artist sets retail price. Sends slides of work. SASE. Gallery pays shipping and insurance.

New Jersey

GLASSBORO STATE COLLEGE, Glassboro NJ 08028. Gallery Director: William Traves. Exhibition space available in Westby Gallery, Wilson Concert Hall lobby, Student Center and Memorial Hall for painters, sculptors, craftsmen and printmakers. "We do not sell artwork, although we do have a large exhibition program where visitors have the opportunity to purchase work."

New Mexico

BLAIR GALLERIES LTD., Box 2342, Santa Fe NM 87501. Contact: Don Blair. Exhibits traditional paintings, sculpture, prints and drawings; 2 weeks minimum exposure. Price range: $150-25,000. Artist sets price. Requires exclusive area representation; charges commission on art sold in area after show. Sponsors openings. Mailing for each new show goes to 1,500 individuals. Insurance covers exhibited art.

BRANDYWINE GALLERIES, LTD., 120 Morningside Dr. SE, Albuquerque NM 87108. (Also at: Sheraton Old Town Inn, Mercado Plaza, Albuquerque NM 87104.) Contact: Louise M. Abrums. Exhibits paintings (traditional/abstract/Western), sculpture, prints and drawings; 12 weeks minimum exposure. By joint agreement, prices are $12-50,000. 40% commission. "All art submitted for consignment is reviewed by a 6-man panel. Please allow 3 weeks for response." Send transparencies or photos. Will sponsor artists' openings "after they have been with the gallery for a year." Exclusive representation in area required; charges commission on art sold after show. Exhibited art insured and extensively advertised.

GALLERY WEST, INC., 654 Chavez Plaza, Santa Fe NM 87501. Director: James Parsons. Exhibits traditional and metaphysical paintings; 2 weeks minimum exposure. Works on a signed contract basis with artist. 40% standard commission. Art priced from $100-2,500. Price set by joint agreement. Send transparencies or photos. Exhibited art insured. The gallery has a promotion mailing list, to which mailings go with each new show. Sponsors openings.

GUIYERMO GALLERIES, 1825 San Mateo Blvd. NE, Albuquerque NM 87110. (505)265-2597. Curator: Mr. G. McDonald. Exhibits oils, lithographs, sculpture and watercolors; 1-3 months exposure. Maximum size: 48x30x48". Paintings must be ready to hang; sculpture must have pedestals. Art must be offered for sale. Works on consignment; 33⅓% commission. Price range: $50-400, oils; $25-150, watercolors; $10-150, sculpture; bestsellers: $25-250. Gallery sets retail price. Requires exclusive area representation. Send photos of work. SASE.

INSTITUTE OF AMERICAN INDIAN ARTS MUSEUM, Cerrillos Rd., Santa Fe NM 87501. (505)988-6281. Director: Charles Dailey. Exhibits acrylics, calligraphy, beadwork, ceramics, drawings, glass art, jewelry, leatherworking, metalsmithing, mobiles, oils, pastels, pottery, prints, quillwork, sculpture, wall hangings, watercolors, weavings and woodcrafting; negotiates exposure time. No size restrictions. Specializes in Indian art and crafts only. Art may be offered for sale. Works on consignment; no commission. Price range: $15-1,000, paintings; $2-500, ceramics; $5-1,000, jewelry; bestsellers: $2-100. Artist sets retail price. Query. SASE. "First priority is always to current institute students or to graduates; then other requests are evaluated."

THE LITTLE GALLERY OF TAOS, Box 362, Guadalupe Plaza, Taos NM 87571. Contact: James N. Wilson. Works with traditional painters and sculptors; 6 weeks minimum exposure. By joint agreement art is priced from $50-1,000. Commission is negotiable. Exclusive representation in local area required. Send transparencies or photos. Exhibited art insured.

NEW MEXICO ART LEAGUE, 400 Romero NW, Albuquerque NM 87104. (505)243-0398 or 293-5034. Director: Jean Rosenburg. Exhibits acrylics, airbrush, batik, calligraphy, ceramics, oils, pastels, pottery, prints, sculpture, watercolors, weavings and woodcrafting; 1 month minimum exposure. No size requirements. Art must be ready to hang. Art must be offered for sale. Works on consignment; 30% commission. Price range: $5-1,000, paintings; bestsellers: $45-125. Artist sets retail price. Call for interview. SASE. Open to artists with New Mexico addresses.

NEW MEXICO ART LEAGUE, 3401 Juan Tabo, Albuquerque NM 87111. (See above listing).

THE STUDIO GALLERY, 3529 Constitution NE, Albuquerque NM 87106. (505)262-0672. Contact: Tom W. Thomason or Bruce Howden. Exhibits all forms of fine art; 30 days minimum exposure. Paintings should be ready to hang; if special displays are needed artists should provide. Contemporary art only. Art must be offered for sale except in retrospective shows. Works on consignment; 40% commission. Price range: 50¢-$5,000; bestsellers: 50¢-$400. Retail price set by artist or joint agreement. Query with slides of work. SASE. Gallery pays shipping from gallery and insurance on exhibited work.

THE WHEELWRIGHT MUSEUM, Box 5153, Santa Fe NM 87501. (505)928-4636. Director: Steven Tremper. Museum gallery. Exhibits acrylics, ceramics, drawings, dollmaking, jewelry, metalsmithing, oils, pastels, pottery, prints, sculpture, watercolors and weavings; 1-2 months exposure. Maximum size: 6x8'. Exhibition department handles installation. Historical and contemporary Indian art only. Art may be offered for sale. Works on consignment; 20% commission. Price range: $50-1,500. Artist sets retail price. Query, send samples or call or write for interview. No samples returned. Museum pays shipping from gallery and insurance.
Promotional Needs: Uses artists for posters. Pays $50 minimum.

New York

ALONZO GALLERY, INC., 30 W. 57th St., New York NY 10019. (212)586-2500. Director: Jack Alonzo. Exhibits acrylics, drawings, oils, pastels, prints, sculpture, wall hangings, watercolors and weavings; 3-4 weeks exposure. Maximum height: 9'. Art must be ready to exhibit. Specializes in abstracts with some literal work. Art must be offered for sale. Works on consignment; 50% commission. Price range: $25-12,000; bestsellers: $50-1,000. Retail price set by joint agreement. Requires exclusive area representation. Send slides of work or call for interview. SASE.

ASSOCIATED AMERICAN ARTISTS, 663 5th Ave., New York NY 10022. (212)755-4211. President/Director: Sylvan Cole, Jr. Estab: 1934. Exhibits original prints. Works on consignment; 50% commission. Art is priced from $10-25,000. Price set by joint agreement. Gallery pays return shipping charges. Matting, cellophaning costs paid by gallery. Work should be sent unmatted and unframed. Send resume.

AVANTI GALLERIES, 145 E. 72nd St., New York NY 10021. Director: Frances Wynshaw. Exhibits painting (traditional/abstract) and sculpture; 3 weeks minimum exposure. Works on signed contract basis. 33⅓% commission. Prices set by joint agreement are $200+. Send resume and transparencies or photos. Has promotion list to which mailings go with each show.

BARNES GALLERIES, LTD., 1 Nassau Blvd., Garden City South NY 11530. (516)538-4503. Director: Mr. Liebing. Exhibits acrylics, airbrush, batik, calligraphy, drawings, metalsmithing, oils, pastels, pottery, prints, wall hangings, watercolors, weavings and woodcrafting; 3-12 weeks exposure. Maximum size: 3' square. Art must be offered for sale. Works on consignment; 30-40% commission. Price range: $30-1,200, oils; $10-400, watercolors; bestsellers: $100-400. Retail price set by joint agreement. Requires exclusive area representation. Write for interview. SASE.

THE BROWNSTONE GALLERY, 76 7th Ave., Brooklyn NY 11217. (212)636-8736. Director: J. DeMartis. Exhibits acrylics, airbrush, batik, calligraphy, drawings, oils, pastels, pottery, prints, sculpture, soft sculpture, wall hangings, watercolors and weavings; 3 weeks minimum exposure. Art may be offered for sale. Works on consignment; 20-33 1/3% commission. Price range: $5-5,000. Retail price set by joint agreement. Query. SASE. Gallery pays insurance on exhibited work.

CARAVAN HOUSE GALLERIES, 132 E. 65th St., New York NY 10021. (212)744-4793. Gallery Director: John Lally. Nonprofit organization. Exhibits acrylics, batik, ceramics, drawings, mobiles, oils, pastels, prints, sculpture, soft sculpture, wall hangings and watercolors; 3 weeks maximum exposure. Maximum size: 6x8x6'. Work should be ready to hang. Art may be offered for sale. 33 1/3% commission. Minimum price: $75, drawings; $250, paintings/sculpture; bestsellers: $250-1,500. Retail price set by joint agreement. Send slides or call for interview. SASE.

JAMES F. CARR, 227 E. 81st St., New York NY 10028. Contact: James F. Carr. Interested solely in self-portraits or portraits of other artists. These may be prints, drawings, watercolors or oils. Buys outright.

CARROLL-CONDIT GALLERIES, 210 Mamaroneck Ave., White Plains NY 10601. Director: Howard O. Carroll. "We are especially interested in traditional paintings and individualized crafts at the moment, as we already carry many excellent abstract artists from this area." Exhibits traditional and abstract painting, prints, drawings, pottery, jewelry, macrame, candles and folk art; 4 weeks minimum exposure. "Quality at reasonable prices is hard to find." Price is $5-1,000, with 33 1/3% commission. $100-300 is best selling range. Payment of shipping costs is "open, according to the individual case." Exclusive representation in area required, as well as commission on art sold in central Westchester County after showing. Send transparencies or photos. Insurance terms arranged with artist. Has general insurance on work in the galleries.

CLOVELLY LANE WORKS OF ART, 548 LaGuardia Place, New York NY 10012. (212)473-0534. Contact: Marie Tolnay. Exhibits experimental artwork, prints, graphics and contemporary paintings; 3½ weeks minimum exposure. Works on consignment; 40% commission. Art priced from $50-2,000, by joint agreement. Exhibited art insured. Send slides. Brochures sent to mailing list of 3,000 with each new show. Also uses artists to design announcements for shows.

ETCHINGS INTERNATIONAL, 200 E. 58th St., New York NY 10022. (212)752-5434. Director: Perle Goodwin. Exhibits acrylics, batik, prints, sculpture, wall hangings, watercolors and weavings; 1-2 months exposure. Specializes in abstracts and landscapes. Art must be offered for sale. Works on consignment; 40-50% commission. Minimum price: $75; bestsellers: $200-400. Retail price set by joint agreement. Requires exclusive area representation. Send slides of work. SASE. Gallery pays shipping from gallery and insurance for exhibited work. Uses artists for catalogs.

THE MARGO FEIDEN GALLERIES, 51 E. 10th St., New York NY 10003. Contact: Margo Feiden and Stanley R. Goldmark. Exhibits prints, drawings and works on paper by well-known artists; 3 weeks minimum exposure. No reproductions. Sponsors openings and publicizes exhibitions through promotion mailing list. Exclusive representation required in area, including commission on art sold in area after show. Prices set by joint agreement, range from $100-5,000. Exhibited art insured. Consigned works must be unframed, as gallery specializes in custom-made framing. Also occasionally uses graphic artists to design exhibit announcements.

EDWARD S. FRISCH, LTD., 979 3rd Ave., New York NY 10022. Contact: Edward Frisch. Exhibits traditional and abstract paintings. Prices $45-10,000, as set by gallery. Works with some artists on signed contracts. Has framing business, and prefers to receive consigned art unframed. Exhibited art insured. Sponsors openings.

GALERIE INTERNATIONALE, 1095 Madison Ave., New York NY 10028. (212)861-7877. Manager: E.M. Martin. Exhibits acrylics, airbrush, batik, calligraphy, decoupage, drawings, glass art, oils, pastels, pottery, sculpture, wall hangings and watercolors. Paintings must be ready to hang. Specializes in contemporary art. Art may be offered for sale. Buys outright or on consignment; 33$^{1}/_{3}$% commission. Price range: $500-50,000, paintings/sculpture. Retail price set by joint agreement. Send slides of work. SASE.

GALERIE PAULA INSEL, 987 3rd Ave., New York NY 10022. (212)355-5740. Director: Paula Insel. Exhibits all art; 2 weeks minimum exposure. No size requirements. Art may be offered for sale. Buys outright or on consignment; 40% commission. Price range: $10-20,000; bestsellers: $50-1,000. Retail price set by joint agreement. Requires exclusive area representation. Call or write for interview. SASE.
Promotional Needs: Uses artists for posters and public service TV announcements.

GALLERY 84 INC., 1046 Madison Ave., New York NY 10021. (212)628-4920. Director: Cecile Fine. Exhibits acrylics, calligraphy, drawings, mobiles, oils, pastels, prints, sculpture, wall hangings and watercolors; 3 weeks maximum exposure. Maximum size: 14'x54x60". Paintings must be ready to hang. Art may be offered for sale. 25% commission. Price range: $80-3,000, paintings; $35-350, prints; $25-300, drawings; bestsellers: $100-450. Artist sets retail price. Query. Artist is requested to bring 3 works to be viewed to become member. SASE.

GALLERY 124, INC., 124 Mamaroneck Ave., Mamaroneck NY 10543. (914)698-7069. Director: Herbert Berkenfeld. Exhibits oils, drawings, pastels, prints, sculpture, wall hangings and watercolors; 2-4 weeks exposure. Maximum size: 8' square. Art must be ready to display. Art must be offered for sale. Buys outright or on consignment; 33$^{1}/_{3}$% commission. Price range: $50-15,000, paintings; $25-1,500, watercolors/drawings; $25-1,000, prints; bestsellers: $25-1,000. Retail price set by joint agreement. Requires exclusive area representation. Query or write for interview. SASE.

GARDEN CITY GALLERIES, LTD., 923 Franklin Ave., Garden City NY 11530. Contact: Patrick James. Exhibits watercolors, acrylic and tratitional oil paintings; 8 weeks minimum exposure. Art should be under 48". 33$^{1}/_{3}$% commission. Price range: $25-2,000. Retail price set by joint agreement. Send transparencies or photos. Mailings go to promotion list with each show.

GILLARY GALLERY, 62 Maiden Lane, Jericho NY 11753. (516)681-2015. Director: Sylvia R. Gillary. Exhibits acrylics, ceramics, drawings, glass art, jewelry, oils, pastels, pottery, prints, sculpture and watercolors; 6 weeks maximum exposure. Maximum size: 48x36". Paintings should be wired for hanging; statues must have pedestals. Specializes in modern, contemporary, realistic, impressionistic and primitive work. Art must be offered for sale. Works on consignment; 40% commission. Price range: $150-1,000, oils; $150-2,000, sculpture; $10-500, jewelry; bestsellers: $150-300. Retail price set by joint agreement. Query or call for interview.

NECHEMIA GLEZER GALLERY, 870 Madison Ave., New York NY 10021. (212)684-0160. Contact: Mrs. Glezer. Exhibits drawings, oils, pastels, sculpture and watercolors; 10-30 days exposure. Maximum size: 30x12x40". Statues should have pedestals. Art may be offered for sale. Buys outright or on consignment; 33% commission. Price range: $1,000-10,000. Retail price set by joint agreement. Requires exclusive area representation. Send slides of work. SASE.

JOHN GORDON GALLERY, 37 W. 57th St., New York NY 10019. (212)832-2255. Director: John Gordon. Exhibits calligraphy, ceramics, oils, pottery, sculpture and watercolors. Art must be offered for sale. Buys outright or on consignment. Price range: $100-100,000. Negotiates retail price. Requires exclusive area representation. Send slides or photos. SASE. Negotiates shipping and insurance.

GRAHAM GALLERY, 1014 Madison Ave., New York NY 10021. (212)535-5767. Contact: Robert Graham or Terry Davis. Exhibits ceramics, drawings, glass art, oils, pastels, pottery,

Acrylics, oils and watercolors in the $75-750 price range is of interest to The Robert Brooks Art Gallery. Featured artwork is displayed facing the glass exterior of the building, thus attracting passersby. Work must be left at the gallery for a minimum of 3 months.

sculpture and watercolors; 2-4 weeks exposure. Art may be offered for sale. Buys outright or on consignment; 40% commission. Price range: $100-100,000; bestsellers: $500+. Retail price set by joint agreement. Requires exclusive area representation. Query with slides or samples of work. SASE.

NANCY HOFFMAN GALLERY, 429 W. Broadway, New York NY 10012. (212)966-6676. Director: Nancy Hoffman. Exhibits paintings, drawings, sculpture and prints. Specializes in contemporary art. Art may be offered for sale. Works on consignment. Retail price set by joint agreement. Requires exclusive area representation. Query with slides or samples of work. SASE.Gallery pays shipping and insurance.

LARCADA GALLERY, 23 E. 67th St., New York NY 10021. (212)249-4561. Contact: Jane Scharf. Exhibits drawings, oils, sculpture and watercolors; 3 weeks minimum exposure. No size restrictions. Art may be offered for sale. Buys outright or on consignment; 40% commission. Price range: $100-100,000. Negotiates retail price, shipping and insurance. Call or write for interview.

KARL MANN ASSOCIATES, 232 E. 59th St., New York NY 10022. Exhibits traditional and abstract paintings, prints and drawings. "We are interested in seeing slides and/or photos of work by artists capable of designing for or doing high-style decorative paintings. Terms, commissions, etc. are negotiable. All material submitted will be returned to the artist." Prefers to receive consigned art unframed.

MITCH MORSE GALLERY, INC., 305 E. 63rd St., New York NY 10021. (212)593-1812. Director: Allan Gerstle. Exhibits painting (traditional/impressionistic/realistic/figurative), prints and drawings; 2 weeks minimum exposure. Maximum size: 40x50". "We are artists' agents for paintings, and publishers and distributors of graphics. Artists working on a 'contract' basis are promoted with one-man shows throughout the country in galleries we supply." Price range: $100-1,000 as set by joint agreement. Work purchased outright. Send transparencies or photos. Shipping paid by gallery.

MUGGLETON GALLERY, 7 William St., Auburn NY 13021. Contact: Robert Muggleton. Exhibits oil paintings, original prints, watercolors, ceramics, sculpture, jewelry, metalsmithing, glass and leather; 8 weeks minimum exposure. "Our emphasis is on finer art, as our customers are profesional people ages 25-50." 40% commission. Prices are $10-3,000 as set by mutual agreement. Exclusive representation in area required. Send slides or photos.

LEE NORDNESS GALLERIES, 140 E. 81st, New York NY 10028. (212)988-4410. President: Mr. Nordness. Exhibits acrylics, batik, calligraphy, ceramics, drawings, glass art, jewelry, metalsmithing, oils, pastels, prints, sculpture, soft sculpture, wall hangings, watercolors, weavings and woodcrafting; unlimited exposure. Paintings must be ready to hang; statues must have bases. Art must be offered for sale. Buys outright or on consignment; 40% commission. Price range: $50-40,000. Retail price set by joint agreement. Send slides or photos of work. SASE.

OXFORD GALLERY, 267 Oxford St., Rochester NY 14607. (716)271-5885. Co-Directors: Edythe Sheden or Glorya Mueller. Exhibits acrylics, airbrush, drawings, oils, pastels, prints, sculpture, soft sculpture, wall hangings and watercolors; 4-6 weeks exposure. Specializes in contemporary and ethnic arts. Art must be offered for sale. Works on consignment; 40% commission. Price range: $20-500, graphics; $50-4,000, paintings; $75-10,000, sculpture; bestsellers: $100-1,000. Artist sets retail price. Requires exclusive area representation. Call for interview. "We have an important 'letter of agreement' which is not legally binding and we require an insurance release."

PACE EDITIONS INC., 32 E. 57th St., New York NY 10022. (212)421-3237. Director: Karen McCready. Exhibits prints and weavings; 4-6 weeks exposure. Maximum size: 80x90". Specializes in contemporary art. Art must be offered for sale. Buys outright or on consignment; 50% commission. Price range: $100-5,000, prints; $15-35, posters; $7,500-15,000, tapestries; bestsellers: $225-2,000. Retail price set by joint agreement. Visit gallery with proofs. No work returned.

PARK AVENUE GALLERY, 15 Armonk Rd., Mt. Kisco NY 10549. (914)666-3401. Director: J. G. Van De Vyver. Exhibits acrylics, glass art, metalsmithing, mobiles, oils, pastels, sculpture and watercolors. Art must be offered for sale. Works on consignment; 33 1/3-50% commission. Minimum price: $200, paintings; bestsellers: $300-1,500. Retail price set by joint agreement. Requires exclusive area representation. Query with samples.

PHOENIX GALLERY, 30 W. 57th St., New York NY 10019. (212)245-5095. Director: Lorraine Kelly. Exhibits acrylics, airbrush, drawings, mobiles, oils, pastels, prints, sculpture and watercolors; 3-9 weeks exposure. Maximum size: 90" long. Art must be ready to hang. Specializes in contemporary art. Art may be offered for sale. Works on consignment; 30% commission. Price range: $200-2,500, paintings; $200-5,000, sculpture; $50-400, graphics; bestsellers: $400-1,500. Retail price set by joint agreement. Query.

PINCHPENNY GALLERY, 564 Lexington Ave., Mt. Kisco NY 10549. President: B. J. Lange. Exhibits acrylics, oils, sculpture and soft sculpture; 1-3 months exposure. Maximum size: 60x54". "If paintings are of a standard size we prefer to frame them ourselves." Art must be offered for sale. Buys outright or on consignment; 40% commission. Price range: $25-4,000, framed paintings; $25-3,500, sculpture; bestsellers: $25-2,000. Retail price set by joint agreement. Requires exclusive area representation. Send photos of work. SASE.

PRINCE STREET GALLERY, 106 Prince St., New York NY 10012. (212)226-9153. Exhibits acrylics, drawings, oils, pastels, sculpture and watercolors; 3 weeks maximum exposure every 2 years. Art may be offered for sale; no commission, but each member must pay $150 membership fee and $25 monthly fee. Price range: $50-150, drawings/watercolors; $100-2,000, paintings/sculpture. Artist sets retail price. Write for interview.

RABINOVITCH & GUERRA GALLERY, 74 Grand St., New York NY 10013. (212)226-2873. This Soho gallery specializes in non-commercial sculpture and experimental painting with expressionistic overtones. Works on signed contract basis. Exhibited work displayed minimum 2½ weeks. 25% commission. Price range: $20-2,000. Artist sets price, sometimes with gallery's advice. "If art is sold within a month and directly as a result of our show, we might expect something, say 10%." Sponsors openings. 500 people receive mailings with each show.

RAMSCALE GRAPHICS, INC., 398 W. Broadway St., New York NY 10012. Director: Paul Knatz. Exhibits contemporary painting and prints. Works on signed contract basis with artists. No large out-of-doors pieces accepted. 40% commission. Prices, reached by joint agreement, range from $125-3,000. Send transparencies or photos. Exhibited art insured. Has promotion list to which mailings are sent several times annually. Charges commission on art sold after showing.

ROSENHOUSE GALLERY, 26 Greenwich Ave., New York NY 10014. Contact: Mittchell Sewall. Exhibits traditional paintings, watercolors, prints, drawings, etchings and lithographs; 4 weeks minimum exposure. "We take work on commission (50%) until such time that we find the work sells. After establishing a market, the gallery will buy work outright. Or if we find the work does not sell, we return it to the artist. The gallery frames the art and absorbs the cost." Prices from $20-500, as decided by joint agreement. Sponsors openings.

S.D. ART GUILD CO., INC., 6514 20th Ave., Brooklyn NY 11204. (212)331-6693. Contact: Sandy or Danny. "We are wholesalers out of the New York area and we buy outright. We only work on a commission basis if an artist should be put into a large print house by our connection. We are interested in paintings, lithographs and enamels." Price range: $5-1,000. Artist sets retail price. Requires exclusive representation in area and commissions on art sold locally after show. Prefers unframed art.

SAMUELS GALLERY, Box 465, Locust Valley NY 11560. (516)671-6059. Contact: Peggy or Harold Samuels. Exhibits drawings, oils, pastels and watercolors; 1 month minimum exposure. Specializes in art completed by 1950 by American and Canadian West artists. Art must be offered for sale. Buys outright. Minimum price: $100; bestsellers: $1,000-10,000. Gallery sets retail price. Write for interview.

THE RHODA SANDE GALLERY, 220 E. 60th St., New York NY 10022. (212)688-1904. Director: Rhoda Sande. Associate: David Miller. Exhibits acrylics, drawings, oils, sculpture, and watercolors; 2 months minimum exposure. Maximum size: 6x5'. Sculpture should be free-standing on a base; watercolors and drawings, unframed. Contemporary American art only. Art may be offered for sale. Works on consignment; 50% commission. Price range: $400-1,500, paintings; $300 minimum, watercolors/drawings; $500 minimum, sculpture; bestsellers: $400-1,500. Retail price set by joint agreement. Requires exclusive area representation. Call for interview (bring slides and a sample of work). Gallery pays insurance.

SHADOW BOX ART GALLERY, 213 Glen St., Glen Cove NY 11542. Director: Harlow Wohlfelder. Exhibits oil painting (traditional/impressionistic), watercolors, prints, sculpture, pottery and jewelry; 4 weeks minimum exposure. Maximum size: 30x40". Prices, from $100-1,500, set by joint agreement. 33⅓% commission. Requires exclusive area representation. Send transparencies or photos. Gallery pays insurance for exhibited work. Sponsors opening for artists. Mailings sent with each show. Occasionally uses graphic artists to design announcements for shows.

LIZA SHERMAN CORPORATE ART, 19 W. 55th St., New York NY 10019. (212)581-1638. Contact: Liza Sherman. Specializes in selling large quantities of posters and limited edition original prints to international business clients. Exhibits large, colorful abstract images or landscapes. Maximum size: 18x24". Send samples.

ELLEN SRAGOW, LTD., Fine Arts Bldg., 105 Hudson St., New York NY 10013. (212)966-6403. Director: Ellen Sragow. Exhibits drawings, pastels, works on paper, prints and sculpture; 1 month maximum exposure. Art may be offered for sale. Works on consignment; 50% commission. Price range: $125-600, prints; $200-500, sculpture; $350, drawings. Retail price set by joint agreement. Call for interview. SASE. No unsolicited material, large paintings or sculptures.

SUMMERFIELD GALLERY, 303 Broadway, Dobbs Ferry NY 10522. (914)693-3790. Contact: Grace Saionz. Exhibits painting, prints, sculpture and jewelry; 12 weeks minimum exposure. Works on consignment "till proven"; 40% commission. Prices from $10-1,000. Exclusive representation in area required. Send resume and slides or photos. Exhibited art insured. Sponsors openings. Occasionally uses artists for show announcements.

SUZUKI GALLERY, 38 E. 57th St., New York NY 10022. Director: Katsko Suzuki. Exhibits paintings, prints and watercolors; 1 month maximum exposure. Art must be offered for sale. Buys outright or on consignment: 33⅓-50% commission. Price range: $25-3,500, prints; $200-6,000, paintings; bestsellers: $100-500. Retail price set by joint agreement. Gallery pays shipping from gallery.

TERRAIN GALLERY, 141 Greene St., New York NY 10012. (212)777-4426. Contact: Carrie Wilson. Exhibits airbrush, drawings, oils, pastels, prints and watercolors; 4-5 weeks exposure. Maximum size: 8' square. Paintings must be ready to hang. Art may be offered for sale. Works on consignment; 40% commission. Price range: $10-225, prints; $20-2,000, paintings; $15-500, drawings; bestsellers: $10-200. Retail price set by joint agreement. Query, send slides of work or call or write for interview. SASE.
To Break In: "Basis for selection and exhibition of work is the Aesthetic Realism of Eli Siegel: 'All beauty is the making one of opposites.' "

THOMPSON GALLERY, 20 Cornelia St., New York NY 10014. (212)243-5610. Contact: Frank Thompson. Specializes in American Impressionists' paintings and erotic paintings and drawings. Maximum size: 20x24". Buys outright or on consignment; 33⅓% commission. Price range: $15-300. Prefers interview, but artists may send resume, slides or photos and information on education and previous showings.

VERZYL GALLERY, 377 Rte. 25A, Northport NY 11768. (516)261-8962. Director: June C. Verzyl. Exhibits acrylics, ceramics, drawings, oils, pastels, pottery, prints and sculpture; one-man show given 3 weeks exposure. Maximum size: 7' square. Paintings must be ready to hang. Art must be offered for sale. Works on consignment; 33 1/3% commission. Minimum price: $100, sculpture/paintings; bestseller range: $200-800. Artist sets retail price, but gallery will not exhibit work Verzyl feels is overpriced. "No exclusive representation, but we hope an artist will not overextend in the area. We welcome artists at any time during business hours."

WARD-NASSE GALLERY, 178 and 131 Prince St., New York NY 10012. (212)925-6951 or 475-9125. Director: Harry Nasse. Exhibits all art, "whatever the artist membership votes in"; 2 years minimum exposure. Maximum size: 16' square. Art must be ready to exhibit. Art may be offered for sale. Works on consignment; no commission. Price range: $25-1,500, paintings; $3-3,000, sculpture; bestsellers: $100-300. Artist sets retail price. Query. Gallery pays insurance for exhibited work. "This is an artist-run gallery and members vote in January and June to determine which artists are exhibited."

WESTBROADWAY GALLERY, 431 W. Broadway, New York NY 10012. (212)966-2520. Director: Robbie Ehrlich. A cooperative gallery made up of 38 member artists. Members chosen by a jury committee elected by total membership. Exhibits painting, sculpture, prints, drawings and conceptual work in prices ranging from $25-50,000. 15% commission but member artist's dues donated to gallery's expenses is $1,200 per 18-month period. Single work given 3 weeks minimum exposure. Exhibited art insured.

ROBERT AARON YOUNG, INC., 979 3rd Ave., New York NY 10022. (212)421-2440. Buyer: Mrs. Young. Exhibits acrylics, drawings, oils, pastels, prints, sculpture, wall hangings and watercolors; 2-12 weeks exposure. Maximum size: 48x64". Art must be offered for sale. Buys outright or on consignment. Price range: $90-5,000; bestsellers: $600-3,000. Gallery sets retail price. Requires exclusive area representation. Send slides or photos of work or call for interview. SASE. Gallery pays shipping from gallery and insurance for exhibited work. "Gallery deals exclusively to the decorator, architect and dealer trade."

North Carolina

ARTS COUNCIL OF WILSON, 205 Gray St., Wilson NC 27893. Executive Director: Vicky E. Bell. Exhibits all media. 25% commission. Most popular price range: $10-350. "We use a variety and will continue to do so. It is my feeling that we should provide something for everyone, and give our visitors something to think about!" Arrange interview or mail slides, biography and artist's photo, if available. Shipping costs shared. Works insured while on exhibition.

GALLERY 501, Mint Museum of Art, 501 Hempstead Place, Charlotte NC 28207. (704)334-9723. Manager: Jane Kessler. Exhibits acrylics, batik, drawings, art glass, jewelry, leatherworking, metalsmithing, oils, pottery, prints, small sculpture, wall hangings, watercolors, weavings and woodcrafting; 3-12 months exposure. Maximum size: 3' square. Paintings and drawings must be framed or matted and covered with acetate. Art must be offered for sale. Buys outright or on consignment; 30% commission (50% markup on work purchased outright). Price range: $5-50, pottery; $15-500, prints/paintings; bestsellers: $15-250. Artist sets retail price. Send resume and slides of work. SASE. Gallery pays insurance.

GOLDSBORO ART CENTER, 106 N. Lionel St., Goldsboro NC 27530. (919)736-3335. Executive Director: Pat Turlington. Exhibits acrylics, airbrush, batik, drawings, mobiles, oils, pastels, pottery, prints, sculpture, soft sculpture, wall hangings, watercolors and weavings; 3-12 months exposure. Maximum size: 80" square. Work on paper must be matted and covered with acetate; paintings must be framed and wired; statues must have pedestals. Art must be offered for sale. Works on consignment; 20% commission. Price range: $2.50-100, pottery; $25-400, sculpture; $5-400, paintings/drawings/prints/watercolors; bestsellers: $8-120. Artist sets retail price. Requires exclusive Wayne County representation. Query with samples, or write or call for interview. SASE. Gallery pays insurance on exhibited work.

McNEAL GALLERY, 1626 East Blvd., Charlotte NC 28203. (704)332-9202. Contact: Mark McNeal/Christie Taylor. Exhibits acrylics, airbrush, batik, drawings, glass art, jewelry, metalsmithing, mobiles, oils, pastels, pottery, prints, sculpture, wall hangings, watercolors, weavings and woodcrafting; 1 month minimum exposure. Art must be offered for sale. Works on consignment; 33⅓% commission. Price range: $15-1,500, watercolors; $2-175, pottery; bestsellers: $5-300. Artist sets retail price. Requires exclusive area representation. Query with samples. SASE. Gallery pays insurance on exhibited work.

SEASIDE ART GALLERY, Box 1, Nags Head NC 27954. (919)441-5418. Contact: Chester Smith. Exhibits all quality art; 3-12 months exposure. No size restrictions. Art must be ready to exhibit. Art must be offered for sale. Buys outright or on consignment; 45% commission. Price range: $5-450, watercolors; $35-5,000, oils; bestsellers: $50-150. Gallery sets retail price. Requires exclusive area representation. Send slides or photos of work. SASE.

Ohio

CHIARA GALLERIES, INC., 1250 Euclid Ave., Cleveland OH 44115. Director: Ruth Fobell. Exhibits acrylics, airbrush, batik, ceramics, drawings, oils, pastels, pottery, prints, sculpture, soft sculpture, wall hangings and watercolors; 6 months minimum exposure. Maximum size: 6' square. Prefers paintings be ready to hang. Specializes in living American artists. Art must be offered for sale. Works on consignment; 33⅓% commission. Price range: $50 minimum, paintings/sculpture; $10-300, prints; bestsellers: $50-600. Retail price set by joint agreement. Query with samples, or call for interview. SASE.

ARTHUR L. FELDMAN FINE ARTS, 53 The Arcade, Cleveland OH 44114. (216)861-3580. Contact: A.L. Feldman. Exhibits ceramics, prints and multiples. Specializes in internationally-known artists. Buys outright. Price range: $100-10,000, prints/ceramics; bestsellers: $200-500. Gallery sets retail price. Query. Gallery pays shipping to gallery.

FRENCH ART GALLERY, 530 1st Ave., Gallipolis OH 45631. (614)446-3834. Curator: Jan Thaler. Exhibits acrylics, batik, ceramics, drawings, glass art, jewelry, mobiles, oils, pastels, pottery, prints, sculpture, wall hangings, watercolors and weavings; 1 month minimum exposure. Maximum size: 4x7'. Paintings must be framed and ready to hang. Art may be offered for sale. Works on consignment; 15% commission. Price range: $80-1,500, paintings; $35-250, prints; $10-100, ceramics; bestsellers: $100-250. Artist sets retail price. Requires exclusive area representation. Query with samples. SASE. Gallery pays shipping to gallery and insurance for exhibited work.
Promotional Needs: Uses artists for membership literature and posters. Negotiates payment.

THE GALLERY ON MAIN STREET, 114½ W. Main, Circleville OH 43113. (614)474-2633. Contact: Buyer. Exhibits all art; 6 months minimum exposure. Maximum size: 4' square. Art must be offered for sale. Works on consignment; 25% commission. Price range: $5-250, paintings; bestsellers: $5-150. Retail price set by joint agreement. Send slides or photos of work. SASE.

IMAGES GALLERY, 4324 W. Central Ave., Toledo OH 43616. (419)537-1400. Director: Frederick D. Cohn. Exhibits acrylics, drawings, glass art, oils, pastels, prints, sculpture and watercolors. Art must be offered for sale. Buys outright or on consignment. Price range: $25 minimum, prints. Gallery sets retail price. Prefers exclusive area representation. Send slides or call for interview. SASE.

LINDEN GALLERY, 13010 Woodland Ave., Cleveland OH 44120. (216)791-6450. Contact L.G. Linden. Exhibits traditional painting, experimental artwork, prints, graphics, drawings, sketches, sculpture, pottery and jewelry; 4 weeks exposure. 33⅓% commission. Price range: $20-20,000. Gallery helps determine retail prices. Requires exclusive representation in area and commission on art sold locally after show. Send resume and slides or photos. Exhibited art insured and shipping from gallery paid by gallery. Sometimes needs artists for work on show announcements.

THE MASSILLON MUSEUM, 212 Lincoln Way E., Massillon OH 44646. (216)833-4061. Director: Mary M. Merwin. "We are not a gallery to promote sales, but have exhibitions to promote the artists and craftsmen who wish exposure. They must be professional." Exhibits acrylics, batik, ceramics, drawings, glass art, jewelry, metalsmithing, mobiles, oils, pastels, pottery, prints, sculpture, soft sculpture, wall hangings, watercolors and weavings; 1 month maximum exposure. Maximum size: 4x9'. Paintings should be ready to hang. Art may be offered for sale; 20% commission. Price range: $50-500, paintings; $10-50, crafts. Artist sets retail price. Send slides of work. SASE. Gallery pays shipping and insurance. "We endeavor to exhibit the work of Ohio artists and craftsmen who meet the standards."

MILLER GALLERY, 2722 Erie Ave., Cincinnati OH 45208. (513)871-4420. Contact: Norman or Barbara Miller. Exhibits oils, acrylics, prints, ceramics, glass art, jewelry, mobiles, pottery, sculpture (including kinetic), wall hangings and watercolors; 3 months minimum exposure. Maximum size: 7x6'. Paintings must be ready to hang; sculpture must have base. Interested in contemporary and traditional work; no hard edge. "We pioneered in contemporary glass art and are still doing well in it." Art must be offered for sale. Works on consignment; 40-45% commission. Price range: $15-1,000, glass art/ceramics; $50-3,000, oils/acrylics; $5-20,000, prints/drawings; $3,000 maximum, sculptures; bestsellers: $50-900. Negotiates retail price. Requires exclusive area representation. Send slides or photos of work with information and prices (artist's price and selling price). SASE.
To Break In: "Don't attach or imprint address or phone number on your work. Don't send improperly stretched, framed or mounted art."

NOT IN NEW YORK GALLERY, 314 W. 4th St., Cincinnati OH 45202. Director: Margarete Roeder. Exhibits painting, experimental artwork, prints, graphics, drawings and sculpture. 40% commission. Price range: $100-4,000. Send transparencies or photos. Sponsors openings and requires exclusive local representation.

PACKARD GALLERY, 933 W. Exchange St., Akron OH 44302. (216)836-3307. President: Ray Packard. Exhibits acrylics, airbrush, calligraphy, ceramics, oils, pottery, prints, sculpture and weavings; 90 days maximum exposure. Specializes in contemporary masters such as Calder, Dali, Vasarely. Art must be offered for sale. Works on consignment; 40% commission. Minimum price: $65, oils; $60, sculpture; bestsellers: $65. Retail price set by joint agreement. Query with samples or slides. SASE. Gallery pays insurance on exhibited work.

RALICE STUDIO, 4954 Glenway Ave., Cincinnati OH 45238. Contact: Steve de Stefano. Works with artists, sculptors, potters and graphic artists. Accepted work receives 6 weeks minimum exposure. Must be smaller than 44" framed. Prefers to receive art framed. Price range: $20-1,000. 35% commission. Price set by joint agreement. Requires exclusive representation in area. Send photos of work. Exhibited art insured.

STRONGS GALLERY, 33 Public Square, Cleveland OH 44113. (216)241-6940. Contact: Marcia Hall. Handles contemporary and wildlife subject matter. Exhibits painting, prints, graphics, drawings and sculpture; 2 weeks minimum exposure. Works on signed contract basis. Works on consignment; 40% commission. Prices from $5-5,000. Requires exclusive representation in area. Send transparencies or photos. Exhibited art insured. Sponsors openings.

ROSS WIDEN GALLERY, 5120 Mayfield Rd., Lyndhurst OH 44124. Contact: Mr. or Mrs. Widen. Exhibits acrylics, batik, ceramics, drawings, glass art, jewelry, mobiles, oils, pastels, pottery, prints, sculpture, soft sculpture, wall hangings, watercolors, weavings and woodcrafting; 1-3 weeks exposure. Maximum size: 8x4'. Work must be ready for presentation. Art must be offered for sale. Buys outright or on consignment; 40% commission. Price range: $50-5,000, paintings; $35-5,000, sculpture; $10 minimum, crafts; bestsellers: $50-400. Retail price set by joint agreement. Write with photos of work to arrange interview. SASE. Gallery pays shipping from gallery and insurance on exhibited work.

Oklahoma

CARAVAN GALLERY, LTD., 6029 S. Sheridan, Tulsa OK 74145. (918)627-7575. Contact: Mrs. William W. Haugh. Exhibits traditional and abstract painting, sculpture, drawings and jewelry. "We request a broad representation of work — 6 to 20 pieces, depending on the medium. Lately, we've been handling more contemporary, exclusively American artists. Our clientele tends to be young businessmen and middle-aged persons of upper-middle class income." Price range: $5-2,000; bestsellers: $200-500. 40% commission. Exclusive representation in the Tulsa area required, plus commission on art sold 60 days after show. Send photos or brochures of work. Sponsors openings. Exhibited art insured.

GREEN COUNTY ART CENTER (formerly Eloise J. Schellstede), 1825 E. 15th, Tulsa OK 74104. (918)932-4259. Director: R.L. Schellstede. Estab: 1967. Exhibits oils, watercolors, bronze, wood and stone sculpture; 3 weeks minimum exposure. Specializes in Western art, animals and landscapes. Works on consignment; 30% commission. Price range: $10-1,000. Retail price set by joint agreement. Send slides or photos stating size, medium, price, artist's name and address on each.

JAN MAREE GALLERIES, 6463 Avondale Dr., Nichols Hills Plaza, Oklahoma City OK 73116. (405)842-1166. Director: Rose Marie Jernigan. Exhibits acrylics, ceramics, drawings, dollmaking, glass art, jewelry, oils, pastels, pottery, prints, sculpture, watercolors and rug weavings; 1-4 weeks exposure. Paintings must be framed and ready to hang. Art may be offered for sale. Works on consignment; 40% commission. Price range: $50-5,000, paintings; $100-5,000, bronze work; $25-1,000, graphics; bestsellers: $25-200. Retail price set by joint agreement. Requires exclusive area representation for some artists. All methods of contact OK. Gallery pays shipping from gallery (on sold work) and insurance for exhibited work.

Oregon

CORVALLIS ARTS CENTER, 7th and Madison, Corvallis OR 97330. (503)752-0186. Director: Corrine Woodman. Exhibits all art; 3 months maximum exposure. Paintings must be ready to hang. Art may be offered for sale. Works on consignment; 30% commission. Price range: $2-5,000; bestsellers: $5-500. Artist sets retail price. Query or send slides. SASE. Gallery pays shipping from gallery and insurance.

FAVELL MUSEUM OF WESTERN ART & INDIAN ARTIFACTS, Box 165, Klamath Falls OR 97601. (503)882-9996. Contact: Gene Favell. Exhibits acrylics, drawings, glass art, jewelry, metalsmithing, oils, pastels, pottery, prints, sculpture, wall hangings, watercolors and woodcrafting; 1 month minimum exposure. No size requirements. Paintings must be ready to hang; sculpture must have pedestals. Specializes in Western and Indian art. Art may be offered for sale. Buys outright or on consignment; 35% commission. Price range: $27.50-5,000, paintings; $5-200, Indian crafts; $2.50-195, prints; bestsellers: $100-300. Retail price set by joint agreement or artist. Sometimes requires exclusive area representation. Query with samples or call for interview. SASE. Gallery pays insurance for exhibited work.

GALLERY WEST, 4836 SW Scholls Ferry Rd., Portland OR 97225. (503)292-6262. Contact: Joanne Perri. Exhibits acrylics, batik, ceramics, drawings, oils, pottery, prints, sculpture, wall hangings, watercolors and weavings; 6 months minimum exposure. Maximum size: 20x6x8'. Paintings must be ready to hang. Art must be offered for sale. Works on consignment; 40% commission. Price range: $20-150, prints; $50-2,700, paintings; $100 sculpture; bestsellers: $20-350. Retail price set by joint agreement. Requires exclusive area representation. Send slides or photos of work and call for interview. SASE. Gallery pays shipping from gallery and insurance.

MAUDE I. KERNS ART CENTER, 1910 E. 15th, Eugene OR 97403. (503)345-1126. Director: Callum MacColl. Administrative Assistant: Karen Johnson. Nonprofit private community art center, rental/sales gallery and gift shop. Exhibits acrylics, batik, calligraphy, ceramics, drawings, glass art, jewelry, metalsmithing, oils, pottery, prints, sculpture, wall hangings, watercolors, weavings and woodcrafting; 3 weeks minimum exposure. Art must be finished, ready for installation and offered for sale. Works on consignment: 30% commission, main gallery; 25%, gift shop. Price range: up to $2,000, fine arts; $1-100, crafts; bestsellers: $5-100. Artist sets retail price. Query with slides of work. SASE. Gallery pays insurance on exhibited work.

MILLIE'S TIFFANY SHADE GALLERY, 459 2nd St., Lake Oswego OR 97034. Contact: Millie Van Sickle. Exhibits oils, watercolors, acrylics, ceramics, sculpture, jewelry, metalsmithing and needlecrafts; 4 weeks minimum exposure. 33 1/3% commission. Price range: $2.50-350. Send transparencies or photos. Sponsors openings.

'NEATH THE WIND, Box 811, Port Ortono OR 97465. Contact: Bob Warring. Exhibits acrylics, airbrush, batik, calligraphy, drawings, jewelry, metalsmithing, oils, pastels, prints, sculpture, wall hangings, watercolors and weavings; 6-12 weeks exposure. Maximum size: 8x4x8'. Art must be ready to display. Art must be offered for sale. Works on consignment; 30% commission. Price range: $65-1,000, sculpture; $75-500, weavings/paintings; bestsellers: $15-200. Retail price set by joint agreement. Send slides of work. SASE. Gallery pays shipping from gallery and insurance for exhibited work.

Pennsylvania

FONTANA GALLERY, 307 Iona Ave., Narberth PA 19072. Director: Joy Kushner. Exhibits acrylics, jewelry, mobiles, oils and sculpture; 6 weeks minimum exposure. Especially needs primitive paintings. Maximum size: 50" square. Paintings must be framed with simple stripping. Art must be offered for sale. Works on consignment; 40% commission. Price range: $300-5,000, paintings; bestsellers: $500-3,000. Retail price set by joint agreement. Requires exclusive area representation. Send slides or photos of work. SASE.

GALLERY 500, 500 Germantown Pike, Lafayette Hill PA 19444. Exhibits traditional and abstract paintings, sculpture, prints, drawings, pottery, jewelry and crafts; 2 weeks minimum exposure. 33⅓% commission. By joint agreement, prices are $10-1,000. Exclusive representation required. Send transparencies or photos. Exhibited art insured. Sponsors openings.

GALLERY 252, 252 S. 16th St., Philadelphia PA 19102. Contact: Mrs. A. Jacobs. Exhibits paintings, sculpture, prints and pottery; 2 weeks minimum exposure. 40% commission. Price range: $20-2,000. Send slides or photos. Shipping costs shared.

GOLDEN DOOR GALLERY, Parry Barn, 52 S. Main St., New Hope PA 18938. (215)862-5529. Director: Mary Gardner. Exhibits acrylics, oils, pastels, prints, sculpture and watercolors; 2-6 months exposure. Maximum size: 3x4'. Paintings must be ready to hang. Specializes in representational art, "although we do carry a few abstracts." Art must be offered for sale. Works on consignment; 40% commission. Price range: $10-500, prints; $50-4,000, oils; $30-1,500, watercolors; $50-1,000, acrylics; $30-1,200, sculpture; bestsellers: $250-1,500. Retail price set by joint agreement. Usually requires exclusive area representation. Send photos of work. SASE. Gallery pays insurance for exhibited work.

KINGPITCHER GALLERY, 303 S. Craig, Pittsburgh PA 15213. (412)687-4343. Director: Ms. Philo A. Pitcher. Exhibits acrylics, airbrush, calligraphy, drawings, oils, pastels, prints, sculpture, soft sculpture and watercolors; 3 weeks maximum exposure. Maximum size: 9x6'. Prefers prints wrapped, works protected for convenient handling. Specializes in contemporary work. Art must be offered for sale. Works on consignment; 40% commission. Retail price set by joint agreement. Requires exclusive area representation. Send slides or photos of work. SASE. Gallery pays shipping from gallery and insurance on exhibited work.

ALMA PERLIS ART GALLERY, 1131 Hamilton St., Allentown PA 18101. Contact: Linda or Ron Chmielewski. Exhibits graphics, paintings, fiberwork, ceramics and sculpture; 1 month minimum exposure. Buys outright or on consignment; 40% commission. Maximum price: $1,500. Retail price set by joint agreement. Requires exclusive area representation. Send transparencies. Sponsors openings.

PHILADELPHIA ART ALLIANCE, 251 S. 18th St., Philadelphia PA 19103. (215)515-4302. Exhibits all fine art and crafts; 1-2½ months exposure. Maximum size: 52x52". All paintings must be framed except acrylics which are exhibited at artist's own risk; prints must be matted, framed or under plastic. Art may be offered for sale. Works on consignment: 33⅓% commission, nonmembers; 25%, members. Price range: $10-1,500, crafts; $30-5,000, paintings/prints; $100-1,000, sculpture; bestsellers: $30-500. Artist sets retail price. Query or write for interview. SASE. Gallery pays insurance on exhibited work.

THE SOURCE, 121 S. Pennsylvania Ave., Greensburg PA 15601. (412)836-1190. Contact: Carol Pollock. Exhibits ceramics, jewelry, metalsmithing, batik, prints, paintings, sculpture and watercolors; 4 weeks minimum exposure. Works on consignment; 33⅓% commission. Prices from $5-300, set jointly. Exclusive area representation required. Send transparencies or photos. Exhibits work of artists located in western Pennsylvania, West Virginia, Ohio and surrounding area. Exhibited art insured.

Puerto Rico

GALERIE PAULA INSEL, Box 131, Plaza, Ponce, Puerto Rico 00731. (809)844-8478. Director: Paula Insel. Exhibits all art; 2 weeks minimum exposure. No size requirements. Art may be offered for sale. Buys outright or on consignment; 40% commission. Price range: $10-20,000; bestsellers: $50-1,000. Retail price set by joint agreement. Requires exclusive area representation. Call or write for interview. SASE.
Promotional Needs: Uses artists for posters and public service TV announcements.

Rhode Island

LENORE GRAY GALLERY, INC., 15 Meeting St., Providence RI 02903. Director: Lenore Gray. Exhibits acrylics, drawings, oils, prints (signed limited editions), sculpture, soft sculpture, wall hangings, watercolors and weavings; 4 weeks maximum exposure. Paintings must be ready to hang; sculpture must have stand. Specializes in contemporary art. Most art must be offered for sale. Works on consignment; negotiates commission. Retail price set by joint agreement. Requires exclusive area representation. Send slides. SASE. Gallery pays insurance on exhibited work.

South Dakota

DAKOTA ART GALLERIES, Dahl Fine Art Center, 713 7th St., Rapid City SD 57701. Exhibits traditional, abstract and Western paintings in any media; 60 days minimum exposure. Works on consignment (6 months minimum); 33 1/3% commission. Art submitted for consignment reviewed by jury or by executive board of the gallery. Send transparencies or photos.

Tennessee

OATES GALLERY, 97 N. Tillman, Memphis TN 38111. (901)323-5659. Director: Rena Dewey. Exhibits acrylics, airbrush, drawings, glass art, oils, pastels, sculpture and watercolors; 2-4 weeks exposure. Art must be offered for sale; however, artist may display some works that are not for sale during exhibition. Buys outright or on consignment; 45% commission. Price range: $200-20,000, oil paintings; bestsellers: $300-1,500. Retail price set by joint agreement. Requires exclusive area representation. Send photos; if gallery is interested, will arrange interview. SASE. Gallery pays insurance on exhibited work and may pay shipping and in-transit insurance.
Promotional Needs: Uses artists to design catalogs. Pays $1,200 minimum with 3 color sheets.

Texas

ART DIMENSIONS GALLERY, 808 Montana, El Paso TX 79902. Contact: Lynne Tomor. Exhibits graphics, experimental art, paintings, prints, pottery, sculpture and weavings. No size restrictions. Art may be offered for sale. Works on consignment; 40% commission. Price range: $15-400. Gallery sets retail price. Send resume and slides or photos of work. Gallery pays shipping from gallery and insurance for exhibited work.

ART DIMENSIONS GALLERY, 5823 N. Mesa, El Paso TX 79902. (See above listing.)

BRADFORD UPSTAIRS GALLERY, 401 Guadalupe, Austin TX 78701. (512)478-6426. Director: Marie McKinney. Exhibits acrylics, airbrush, batik, ceramics, drawings, jewelry, metalsmithing, mobiles, oils, pastels, pottery, prints, sculpture, wall hangings, watercolors and weavings; 6 months maximum exposure. Maximum size: 60" square; sculpture: 4x3'. Prefers paintings be ready to hang, statues with pedestals. Art must be offered for sale. Buys outright or on consignment; 30% commission. Minimum price: $30, original graphics; $100, paintings; $50, sculpture; bestseller range: $100-300. Retail price set by joint agreement. Requires exclusive area representation. Call or write for interview. SASE. Gallery pays insurance on exhibited work.

CONTEMPORARY GALLERY, 2425 Cedar Springs, Dallas TX 75201. (214)747-0141. Director: R.H. Kahn. Exhibits acrylics, calligraphy, ceramics, drawings, glass art, jewelry, mobiles, oils, pastels, graphics, sculpture, soft sculpture, wall hangings, watercolors and weavings; 6 weeks exposure for one-man shows. Paintings must be ready to hang; sculptures must have pedestals. Contemporary work only. Art must be offered for sale. Buys outright or on consignment; 40-50% commission. Price range: $10-50,000; bestsellers: $150-1,000. Retail price set by joint agreement. Requires exclusive area representation. Query with slides or photos of work. SASE. Gallery pays insurance.

CROW'S NEST ART GALLERY, 230 Jefferson, La Porte TX 77571. (713)471-4371. Contact: Fern Yung. Exhibits acrylics, batik, drawings, blown glass, Indian jewelry, metalsmithing, mobiles, oils, pastels, pottery, prints, sculpture, wall hangings, watercolors, weavings and woodcrafting. No size restrictions. Paintings must be ready to hang. Art must be offered for sale. Works on consignment; 30% commission. Price range: $30-500, watercolors; $35-1,800, acrylics/oils; $5-2,400, jewelry; bestsellers: $35-700. Retail price set by joint agreement. Send slides or photos of work. SASE. Gallery pays shipping from gallery and insurance for exhibited work. "We specialize in promoting unknown artists."

FAIRMOUNT GALLERY, 6040 Sherry Lane, Dallas TX 75225. (214)369-5636. Director: Carolyn Conner. Exhibits acrylics, airbrush, batik, ceramics, drawings, oils, pastels, pottery, sculpture, wall hangings and watercolors; 1 month minimum exposure. Maximum size: 4½x3½x4. Paintings must be ready to hang. Art must be offered for sale. Works on consignment; 40% commission. Price range: $75-1,500, paintings; $15-200, ceramics; bestsellers: $150-450. Retail price set by joint agreement. Requires exclusive area representation. Query with samples or send slides or photos of work. SASE. Gallery pays insurance on exhibited work.

THE FRAMERY GALLERY, 1645 S. Voss, Houston TX 77057. (713)782-6000. Contact: Marvel Galloway. Exhibits acrylics, batik, drawings, glass art, oils, pastels, pottery, prints, sculpture, wall hangings, watercolors and woodcrafting; 2 months minimum exposure. Maximum size: 40x50". Paintings must be ready to hang; sculpture must have pedestal. Art must be offered for sale. Works on consignment; 40% commission. Price range: $5-600, paintings; bestsellers: $100-400. Retail price set by joint agreement. Requires exclusive representation in immediate area. Query with slides or samples of work. SASE. Gallery pays shipping from gallery and insurance for exhibited work. Payment shared for shipping to gallery.

RAUL GUTIERREZ FINE ARTS GALLERY, 8940 Wurzbach Rd., San Antonio TX 78240. (512)696-5356. Gallery Manager: G.E. Smiley. Exhibits acrylics, batik, drawings, jewelry, oils, pottery, sculpture, watercolors, weavings, woodcrafting and bronzes; 30-90 days exposure. Maximum size: 24x30". Specializes in wildlife and Western art. Art must be offered for sale. Works on consignment ("sometimes outright if the price is right"); 40% commission. Price range: $60-10,000; bestsellers: $60-450. Artist sets retail price. Requires exclusive area representation. Call for interview or send photos. SASE. Gallery pays shipping from gallery and insurance on exhibited work.

HELGA'S OF ROCKPORT GALLERIES, INC., 409 Austin St. S., Rockport TX 78382. (512)729-7155. Contact: Jane Goodrich. Exhibits acrylics, batik, drawings, oils, pastels, pottery, prints, sculpture and watercolors; 2 weeks-1 year exposure. No size restrictions. Specializes in art related to shells, birds, wildlife and seascapes. Art must be offered for sale. Buys outright or on consignment; 33⅓% commission (50% mark-up on outright purchases). Price range: $20-1,800; bestsellers: $50-100. Retail price set by joint agreement. Prefers exclusive area representation. Query with slides or samples of work. SASE. Gallery pays shipping from gallery and insurance for exhibited work.

HOUSE OF FRAMES AND PICTURES (formerly Green-Field Galleries & The Framery), 1131 E. Yandell Dr., El Paso TX 79902. (915)533-5690. Managing Director: Edgar Schnadig. Exhibits acrylics, airbrush, batik, calligraphy, ceramics, decoupage, drawings, glass art, metalsmithing, mobiles, oils, pastels, pottery, prints, sculpture, soft sculpture, wall hangings, watercolors, weavings and woodcrafting; 90-180 days exposure. Gallery does framing. Art must be offered for sale. Buys outright or on consignment; 40% commission. Minimum price: $5; bestseller range: $25-65. Gallery sets retail price on items bought outright; set by joint agreement for consigned art. Query. SASE. Gallery pays shipping from gallery.

MARJORIE KAUFFMAN GRAPHICS, 5015 Westheimer, Houston TX 77056. (713)622-6001. Contact: Richard Kauffman. Exhibits original limited edition weavings, graphics and tapestries. Prefers art unframed. Sells art to architects and designers for public and office interiors. Commission depends on work. Price set by artist and gallery. Requires exclusive representation in area. Send resume and samples. Exhibited art insured.

PATIO GALLERY, 3416 Camp Bowie Blvd., Fort Worth TX 76107. (817)336-3404. Contact: Pat Mohler. Exhibits acrylics, oils, pastels, pottery, sculpture, soft sculpture, watercolors and weavings; 1 month minimum exposure. Maximum size: 7x9'. Paintings must be ready to hang. Art must be offered for sale. Works on consignment; 40% commission. Price range: $5-5,000, paintings; $20-1,000, sculpture; $2-150, pottery; bestsellers: $5-250. Retail price set by artist. Requires exclusive area representation. Query with samples. SASE.
To Break In: Supply 50 copies of simple, 1-page biography and list of credits.

SIMPATICO GALLERY, 1 Allen Center, Houston TX 77002. (713)658-9544. Director: Ms. Billie Fant. Exhibits acrylics, jewelry, oils, pastels, prints, sculpture (wood/terra cotta/bronze) and weavings; 1-12 months exposure. Maximum size: 6x6x8'. Prefers paintings be ready to hang. Specializes in sculpture, portraiture and monumental work. Art must be offered for sale. Works on consignment; 40% commission. Price range: $25-750, jewelry; $150+, sculpture; $150-3,500, paintings; bestsellers: $150-600. Retail price set by joint agreement. Requires exclusive area representation. Send photos of work. SASE.

THE SKETCH BOX, 1011 W. 5th Ave., Corsicana TX 75110. (214)874-8845. Contact: Betty Graham or Peggy Drain. Exhibits acrylics, batik, calligraphy, drawings, glass art, jewelry, mobiles, oils, pastels, pottery, prints, sculpture, tole paintings, wall hangings, watercolors, weavings and woodcrafting; 3-6 weeks exposure. Maximum size: 5x4'. Watercolors must be matted and wrapped with acetate; oils/acrylics must be framed and ready to hang. Specializes in Southwestern landscapes, Indian and Western art. Art must be offered for sale. Works on consignment; 30% commission. Price range: $10-95, tole paintings; $25-250, watercolors; $20-500, oils; bestsellers: $50-200. Retail price set by joint agreement. Requires exclusive area representation. Query with slides or photos. SASE.

Robert Cornell, owner of Cornell Galleries, considers slides or photos of work for future exhibitions of fine art, jewelry, glass art, mobiles, pottery and weavings. This woodcut, by Leonard Baskin, is just one example of the many types of art handled by Cornell.

SOL DEL RIO, 1020 Townsend, San Antonio TX 78212. (512)828-5555. Contact: Dorothy Katz. Exhibits acrylics, airbrush, batik, ceramics, drawings, glass art, jewelry, oils, pastels, pottery, prints, sculpture, wall hangings, watercolors and weavings; 2-12 months exposure. No size restrictions. Specializes in contemporary art. Art must be offered for sale. Works on consignment; 40% commission. Price range: $20-4,250, drawings; bestsellers: $20-500. Retail price set by joint agreement or artist. Requires exclusive San Antonio representation. Send slides of work or write or call for interview. SASE. Gallery pays shipping from gallery and insurance for exhibited work.

SPORTSMAN'S GALLERY, 5015 Westheimer, Houston TX 77056. Manager: Ron Tulbert. Specializes in wildlife, Western art and sculpture, nautical paintings and antiques; 8 weeks minimum exposure. Openings sometimes sponsored. Exhibited art insured.

TEXAS ART GALLERY, 1400 Main St., Dallas TX 75202. (214)747-8159. Contact: Tony Altermann or Miriam Ross. Exhibits acrylics, drawings, oils, pastels, porcelain, prints, sculpture and watercolors; 6 months minimum exposure. Specializes in Americana, landscapes, florals and contemporary work with emphasis on Western art. Art must be offered for sale. Works on consignment; 33 1/3-60% commission. Price range: $175-25,000, oils; $150-10,000, sculpture; $125-4,600, acrylics; bestsellers: $150-7,000. Retail price set by joint agreement. Requires exclusive area representation. Query, send slides or photos of work or call for interview. SASE. Gallery pays shipping from gallery and insurance.

TWO TWENTY TWO GALLERY, 6006 N. Mesa, #1007, El Paso TX 79912. Contact: Mrs. E.P. Schuster. Exhibits painting, sculpture, prints and drawings. 40% commission. Price range: $25-2,000 by mutual agreement. Send transparencies or photos. Exhibited art insured. Sponsors openings.

VISUAL ART GALLERY, 6333 Gaston Ave., Dallas TX 75214. (214)821-1616. President: K. Niven. Exhibits acrylics, batik, oils, prints, wall hangings, weavings and watercolors; 1-4 weeks exposure. Maximum size: 4' square. Specializes in realistics and impressionism. Art must be offered for sale. Works on consignment; 33 1/3% commission plus advertising expenses. Price range: $10-100, graphics; $25 minimum, oils; bestsellers: $100-1,000. Retail price set by joint agreement. Query or send slides or photos of work. SASE. Also uses artists to design catalogs and posters.

Utah

BRIGHAM CITY MUSEUM-GALLERY, 24 N. 3rd W., Brigham City UT 84302. Director: Phyllis K. Owen. Exhibits oils, watercolors, acrylics, ceramics, sculpture, jewelry, metalsmithing, needlecrafts, rugs, tapestries, glass, leather, tie dye and batik; 3½ weeks minimum exposure. 20% commission. Range in price from $5-150. Retail price set by artist. Requires exclusive area representation. Send transparencies or photos. Sponsors openings. Shipping paid by artist; however, "we have paid expense one-way if not too prohibitive."

Vermont

ROBERT HULL FLEMING MUSEUM, University of Vermont, Colchester Ave., Burlington VT 05401. (802)656-2090. Curator: Nina Parris. Exhibits all art and crafts. Art may be offered for sale. Buys outright (rarely) or on consignment; 10-30% commission. Bestsellers: $2-25. Retail price set by joint agreement. Send photos of work or write for interview. Gallery pays insurance on exhibited work.

Virginia

THE AMERICAN ART SOCIETY, Box 1031, Warwick Station, Newport News VA 23601. Contact: W.W. Wool. Supplies member galleries with original art. Artists wishing to be represented should send 3 color slides with biography.

ANDERSON GALLERY, Virginia Commonwealth University, 907½ W. Franklin St., Richmond VA 23220. (804)770-6910. Director: Bruce Koplin. Exhibits acrylics, airbrush, ceramics, drawings, glass art, jewelry, metalsmithing, mobiles, oils, pastels, pottery, prints, sculpture, soft sculpture, watercolors, weavings and woodcrafting; 2-6 weeks exposure. Maximum size: 10x5x8'. Drawings and prints should be framed behind glass. Specializes in contemporary art of experimental nature. Art may be offered for sale. Charges 25% commission. Price range: $200-2,000, paintings; $35-300, prints; $50-200, ceramics;

bestsellers: $50-300. Artist sets retail price. Send slides and resume stating educational background and exhibitions. "Requests must be reviewed by the university's exhibitions committee." Gallery pays insurance for exhibited work.
Promotional Needs: Buys artwork for catalogs, posters and public service TV announcements.

FAIRFAX COUNTY COUNCIL OF THE ARTS. Green Spring Farm Park, 4601 Green Spring Rd., Alexandria VA 22312. (703)941-6066. Gallery and display areas for pottery and crafts. Displays change monthly. Sponsors spring festival, summer outdoor exhibits. International Children's Festival, Area Exhibition of Painting and Graphics, and grant programs for public schools.

FIRST IMPRESSIONS, LTD., 13809 Lee Hwy., Centreville VA 22020. (703)631-9738. Contact: Barbara Sanders. Exhibits all art; 90 days minimum exposure. Maximum size: 24x30". Paintings must be framed and ready to hang. Specializes in traditionalism. Art must be offered for sale. Works on consignment; 35% commission. Price range: $10-25, miniature oils; $35-250, large paintings; bestsellers: $5-15. Retail price set by joint agreement. Requires exclusive area representation. Query with samples or photos of work. SASE. Gallery pays insurance for exhibited work.

STUCKEY'S ART MALL, 954 N. Monroe St., Arlington VA 22201. Contact: Anne Stuckey. Exhibits traditional abstract, Western and Indian painting, sculpture, prints, drawings and pottery; 8 weeks minimum exposure. "I would especially like to make contact with a good Western painter." 33 1/3% commission. Retail prices, set by artist or joint agreement, range from $10-1,000, with $100-300 preferable. Stuckey's pays return of all accepted works. Requires exclusive representation in northern Virginia, and may require commissions on art sold after show. Send transparencies or photos. Sometimes sponsors openings.

UNIVERSITY ART GALLERY, VPI & SU, 20 Owens Hall, Blacksburg VA 24061. (703)951-5935. Curator: Kathy Douglass. Exhibits all art; 2-4 weeks exposure (3 months in summer sometimes). Maximum length: 18'. Paintings must be ready to hang. Art may be offered for sale. "We rarely buy since funds are limited." Minimum price: $10, student paintings/crafts; $20, student sculpture; bestseller range: $5-200. Artists sets retail price. Query. SASE.

Washington

BURIEN ARTS GALLERY, 421 SW 146th Ave., Seattle WA 98166. (206)244-7808. Contact: Director. Exhibits acrylics, batik, calligraphy, candlemaking, ceramics, decoupage, drawings, glass art, jewelry, leatherworking, metalsmithing, mobiles, needlecrafts, oils, pastels, pottery, prints, sculpture, tole painting, wall hangings, watercolors, weavings and woodcrafting; 1 month exposure (items kept longer will be brought out periodically). Maximum size: 6' square. Paintings should be wired and ready to hang; sculptures, have pedestals when needed. Art must be offered for sale. Works on consignment; 33 1/3% commission. Price range: $1.25-2,000; bestseller: $10 pottery. Artist sets retail price. Query with photos of work. SASE.

DAVIDSON GALLERIES, 702 1st Ave., Seattle WA 98104. (206)624-7684. Director: Sam Davidson. Exhibits original etchings, woodcuts, lithographs, silkscreens and other multiple edition prints. Art must be offered for sale. Buys outright (occasionally on consignment); 60% commission, except where otherwise negotiated. Price range: $5-10,000. Retail price set by joint agreement. Requires exclusive area representation. Send photos of work. SASE. Gallery pays shipping from gallery and insurance.

FIFTH AVENUE GALLERY, 1312 5th Ave., Seattle WA 98101. (206)682-8520 or 624-3233. Contact: Carl Brecht. Exhibits acrylics, airbush, drawings, leatherworking, needlecrafts, oils, pastels, prints, sculpture, wall hangings, watercolors, weavings and woodcrafting; 4-8 weeks exposure. No size restrictions. Art may be offered for sale. Buys outright or on consignment; 33-50% commission. Price range: $20-60,000; bestsellers: $50-1,500. Retail price set by joint agreement. Requires exclusive area representation. Query with slides or photos of work or call or write for interview. Gallery pays shipping from gallery and insurance for exhibited work.
Promotional Needs: Uses artists for membership literature, catalogs and public service TV/radio announcements.

OLDE MAIN GALLERY, INC., 10025 Main St., Bellevue WA 98004. (206)454-1818. Director: Mr. Kowalyk. Exhibits acrylics and oils; 3 months maximum exposure. Maximum size:

4' square. Specializes in realism through impressionism. Art must be offered for sale. Works on consignment; 45% commission. Price range: $300-7,500; bestsellers: $300-2,500. Retail price set by joint agreement. Send slides or photos of work. SASE.

Washington, D.C.

BENCSIK GALLERY, 5012 Connecticut Ave. NW, Washington DC 20008. President: R.H. Kornemann. Exhibits acrylics, airbrush, batik, ceramics, drawings, mobiles, needlecrafts, oils, pastels, pottery, prints, sculpture, wall hangings and watercolors; 2 weeks minimum exposure. Maximum size: 6' square. Art must be offered for sale. Works on consignment; 40% commission. Minimum price: $20, serigraphs/etchings; bestseller range: $100-350. Retail price set by joint agreement. Requires exclusive area representation. Query with samples or photos of work. SASE. "Framed pieces look and sell better."

CORCORAN GALLERY OF ART, 17th St. and New York Ave. NW, Washington DC 20006. (202)638-3211. Contact: Chief Curator. Exhibits acrylics, airbrush, drawings, oils, prints, sculpture and watercolors; 4-6 weeks exposure. "Art not sold through the Gallery. The Corcoran Gallery of Art does not exhibit 'arts and crafts.' Some 'arts and crafts' are on sale in the Gallery Shop. Contact Cathy Windus.

FISHER GALLERIES, 1509-11 Connecticut Ave. NW, Washington DC 20036. (202)265-6255. Contact: P.H. Fisher. Exhibits oils, pastels, sculpture and watercolors; 6 months minimum exposure. Maximum size: 30x40". Paintings must be ready to hang; statues should include pedestals. Art must be offered for sale. Works on consignment; 50% commission. Minimum price: $200; bestseller range: $500-10,000. Gallery sets retail price. Requires exclusive area representation. Call for interview or query with non-returnable samples; no slides or photos of work. Gallery pays insurance on exhibited work.

GALLERIA CLELIA, 2111 K St. NW, Washington DC 20037. (See Gallery 19.)

GALLERY 19, 924 19th St. NW, Washington DC 20037. Director: Clelia Higgins. Exhibits traditional and abstract paintings and prints. By joint agreement, work is priced from $50-1,500. 40% commission. "We usually hold paintings for 3 months," but other accepted work will receive at least 1 year exposure. Send transparencies or photos.

GALLERY NUKI, 1321 4th St. SW, Washington DC 20024. (202)554-5330. Director: Thomas N. Snyder. Consultant: Daniel Millsaps. Exhibits acrylics, drawings, oils, pastels, prints, sculpture, soft sculpture and watercolors. Art should be ready for showing and must be offered for sale. Works on consignment; 40% commission. Minimum price: $100, fine art; bestseller range: $150-2,500. Retail price set by joint agreement. Send slides or photos of work. SASE. Gallery pays insurance on exhibited work.
Promotional Needs: "We do a series of 'Postcards for Collectors' reproducing work of artists whose work we handle, sharing cost of production with artist (usually in large numbers and artist gets a proportion of the printing for his own distribution). We, as a gallery, distribute the rest as promotion for the artist. There are no money returns for artist except that sales are promoted and he gets his share this way."

GALLERY 10 LTD., 1519 Connecticut Ave. NW, Washington DC 20036. (202)232-3326. Exhibits contemporary fine art in all media; 4 weeks exposure. Maximum size: 6x9'. Work must be ready to install. Art must be offered for sale. 40% commission. Price range: $65-1,000. Retail price set by joint agreement. Query. Send slides or photos if in Eastern region.

INDIAN ARTS AND CRAFTS DEVELOPMENT PROGRAM, Indian Arts and Crafts Board, Dept. of the Interior, Washington DC 20240. Contact: General Manager. The Board operates 3 museums: Museum of the Plains Indian and Crafts Center, Browning, Montana; Southern Plains Indian Museum and Crafts Center, Anadarko, Oklahoma; and Sioux Indian Museum and Crafts Center, Rapids City, South Dakota. One-man and comprehensive traveling exhibitions are presented, some of which are toured in collaboration with state arts agencies.

LAMBDA RISING, 1724 20th St. NW, Washington DC 20009. (202)462-6969. Manager: Rich McGinnis. Gay book and gift shop. Exhibits all fine art; held until sold. Paintings should be ready to hang. "We will only accept work which reflects a gay (male or lesbian) theme or has been completed by a gay artist." Art must be offered for sale. Works on consignment; 25% commission. Minimum price: $5; bestseller range: $5-80. Artist sets retail price. Query with samples. SASE. Shop pays insurance on exhibited work.

MICKELSON GALLERY, 707 G St. NW, Washington DC 20001. (202)628-1735. Director: Jean Gulyas. Exhibits acrylics, oils, pastels, prints, sculpture and watercolors; 1-6 months exposure. Maximum size: 5' square. Art must be offered for sale. Works on consignment; 40% commission. Price range: $25-350, graphics; $100-1,500, paintings; $150-2,500, sculpture; bestsellers: $75-800. Artists sets retail price. Requires exclusive area representation. Query, send slides of work or write for interview. SASE. Gallery pays insurance for exhibited work.

SMITH-MASON GALLERY MUSEUM, 1207 Rhode Island Ave. NW, Washington DC 20005. (202)462-6323. Director: Helen S. Mason. Exhibits acrylics, batik, ceramics, drawings, glass art, jewelry, metalsmithing, oils, pastels, pottery, prints, sculpture and watercolors; 6 weeks maximum exposure. Paintings must be ready to hang. Specializes in contemporary art. Art may be offered for sale. Works on consignment; 40% commission. Price range: $50-500, paintings/sculpture; $50-1,000, prints. Artist sets retail price. Query with samples or send slides or photos of work. SASE. Gallery pays insurance on exhibited work.

VENABLE-NESLAGE GALLERIES, 1742 Connecticut Ave. NW, Washington DC 20009. (202)462-1800. Exhibits acrylics, drawings, oils, pastels, prints, sculpture and watercolors; 6 works receive 6 months exposure. Maximum size: 4x6'. Art must be offered for sale. Works on consignment; 40% commission. Price range: $100-5,000, paintings; $60-300, drawings; $35-1,500, prints; bestsellers: $100-300. Retail price set by joint agreement. Requires exclusive area representation. Send slides of work.

Wisconsin

ART CENTER, Prospect Mall, 2233 N. Prospect Ave., Milwaukee WI 53202. (414)271-9600. Contact: Peter J. Kondos. Exhibits all arts/crafts. Maximum size: standard framing. Art must be offered for sale. Buys outright and on consignment. Specializes in traditional art. Minimum price: $15+. Retail price set by gallery. Requires exclusive area representation. Query first with slides and/or photos. SASE.

GALLERY 853, 853 Williamson St., Madison WI 53703. (608)257-6984. Visual Arts Coordinator: Perry Nesbitt. Exhibits acrylics, airbrush, batik, calligraphy, ceramics, drawings, glass art, jewelry, oils, pastels, pottery, prints, sculpture, soft sculpture, tole painting, wall hangings, watercolors, weavings and woodcrafting; 3 weeks maximum exposure. Maximum size: 10' square. Artist must hang work. Art may be offered for sale. 25% commission. Minimum price: $75, paintings; $100, sculpture. Artist sets retail price. Write for interview or send slides or photos of work. SASE. Uses artists to design membership literature and catalogs.

PETER J. KONDOS ART GALLERIES, 700 N. Water, Milwaukee WI 53202. (414)271-8000. Contact: Peter Kondos. Exhibits fine traditional paintings and sculpture; 2 weeks-1 month exposure. Maximum height: 6'. Art must be offered for sale. Buys outright or on consignment; negotiates commission. Price range: $15-2,000; bestsellers: $75-250. Gallery sets retail price. Requires exclusive area representation. Query with slides or photos of work. SASE.

MADISON ART CENTER, INC., 720 E. Gorham St., Madison WI 53703. (608)257-0158. Contact: Jane Liska. Write with slides or photos. Photos must be fully insured and representative of artist's work. Biographical information also helpful. 10% commission. Insurance and all transportation handled by gallery.

MILWAUKEE ART CENTER WISCONSIN GALLERY, 750 N. Lincoln Memorial Dr., Milwaukee WI 53202. (414)271-9508. Contact: Barbara Coffman or Judith Porter. Exhibits experimental art, prints, drawings and sculpture. Size limited to 4x4'. 30% commission. Artist sets price. Prices from $50-100. Prefers framed work. Open to Wisconsin artists. Send resume and slides. 2,500 members notified of spring and fall collections and special openings.

THE WHIFFERDILL, Rte. 1, Trempealeau WI 54661. (608)534-6271. Contact: Jeanette Sasgen. Exhibits acrylics, airbrush, batik, candlemaking, ceramics, drawings, glass art, jewelry, leatherworking, metalsmithing, oils, pottery, prints, sculpture, tole paintings, wall hangings, watercolors, weavings and woodcrafting; 1-8 months exposure. Maximum size: 36" square.

Paintings must be ready to hang. Specializes in wildlife themes. Art must be offered for sale. Works on consignment; 25% commission. Price range: $2.50-35, pottery; $7.50-200, oils; $10-500, woodcarvings; bestsellers: $5-30. Artist sets retail price. Call or write for interview. SASE. Gallery pays insurance for exhibited work.

Wyoming

RUSTIC RELECTIONS GALLERY, 436 Greybull Ave., Greybull WY 82426. (307)765-4258. Contact: Gloria Champine or Allen Pugh. Exhibits acrylics, airbrush, calligraphy, drawings, oils, pastels, pottery, prints, sculpture, soft sculpture, tole painting, wall hangings, watercolors and woodcarving; 3-12 months exposure. Maximum size: 4' square. "Paintings must be ready to hang or include agreement to assume framing expense." Specializes in Western and traditional art. Many rustic and nostalgic themes. Art must be offered for sale, except for special showings. Buys outright or on consignment; 25% commission. Price range: $20-1,000, paintings; bestsellers: $75-200. Retail price set by joint agreement. Call or write for interview to show slides or photos of work. SASE. Gallery pays shipping from shop and insurance on displayed work.

Canada

GALERIE L'ART FRANCAIS, 370 Ouest Laurier, Montreal Canada H2V 2K7. (514)277-2179. Contact: Jean-Pierre Valentin. Has exhibited traditional paintings for 42 years. Primarily handles figurative works; 3 weeks minimum exposure. Works on signed contract basis. Work bought outright or on consignment. Commission: 40% on works under $1,000; 25% on works over $1,000. Art prices $150-25,000 set by joint agreement. Requires exclusive representation in area and commission on art sold in area after show. Exhibited art insured. Gallery pays return shipping. Mailing sent with each show to list 2,500. Occasionally uses artists to design announcements.

HERITAGE GALLERIES LTD., 905 Heritage Dr. SW, Calgary, Alberta Canada T2V 2W8. (403)255-6233. Contact: Diana Gonsalves. Exhibits oils, sculpture and watercolors. Maximum size: 36x24". No abstracts. Art must be offered for sale. Buys outright or on consignment; 33 1/3% commission. Price range: $150-2,000, oils; bestsellers: $300-800. Artist sets retail price. Write for interview.

KAR GALLERY OF FINE ART, 131 Bloor St. W., Toronto Canada M5S 1R1. (416)921-3077. Director: E. Karniol. Exhibits acrylics, drawings, oils, pastels, prints, sculpture and watercolors; 14-20 days exposure. Maximum size: 48x60". Paintings must be ready to hang. Art must be offered for sale. Buys outright or on consignment; commission arranged. Minimum price: $200; bestseller range: $200-10,000. Price set by joint agreement. Requires exclusive area representation. Send slides or photos and biography. Gallery pays insurance on exhibited work. Also uses artists for catalog art.

PYRAMID ART GALLERY, Box 640, Jasper, Alberta Canada T0E 1E0. (403)852-4902. Contact: Sandy Robinson. Exhibits acrylics, ceramics, decoupage, drawings, oils, pastels, pottery, prints, sculpture, watercolors and woodcrafting; 2-8 weeks exposure. Maximum size: 40" square. Art must be offered for sale. Works on consignment; 33 1/3% commission. Price range: $6-1,000, prints; bestsellers: $50-100. Retail price set by joint agreement. Requires exclusive area representation. Query or send slides or photos of work. SASE. Gallery pays insurance for exhibited work. "Local Rocky Mountains scenes and smaller sizes best." Uses artists for advertising and show invitations.

Financial Institutions

EAST-WEST FEDERAL SAVINGS AND LOAN ASSOCIATION, 935 N. Broadway, Los Angeles CA 90012. (213)489-5300. President: F.C. Chan. Exhibits Chinese art and watercolors. Works on consignment; occasionally buys outright. Artist must handle sales. Savings and loan provides publicity. Send resume and slides.
Special Needs: Occasionally needs commercial artists for promotional layouts and design.

FIRST NATIONAL BANK, Box 709, White Sulphur Springs MT 59645. (406)547-3331. Contact: Marlene Teague. Exhibits all art; 2 months maximum exposure. Paintings must be ready to hang. Art may be offered for sale. Minimum price: $5, paintings; bestseller range: $15-125. Artist sets retail price. Gallery acts as sales agent. Requires exclusive area representation. Call or write for interview. SASE. Gallery pays insurance for exhibited work.

FIRST NATIONAL BANK OF PLATTEVILLE, Box 264, Platteville WI 53818. (608)348-9541. President: R.J. Roesler. Exhibits all fine art; 2-4 weeks exposure. Paintings must be ready for hanging; statues, include pedestals. Art may be offered for sale. Buys outright or on consignment. Price range: $2+; bestsellers: $5-25. Retail price set by joint agreement. Requires exclusive area representation. Query. SASE.

FIRST SECURITY BANK, 9th at Idaho Sts., Boise ID 83730. (208)384-6877. Vice President: Glenn Lungren. Exhibits acrylics, drawings, oils, prints, wall hangings and watercolors; 30 days exposure. Paintings must be ready for hanging. Art may be offered for sale. Buys outright or occasionally on consignment; no commission. Minimum price: $50; bestsellers: $75-1,000. Artist sets retail price. Gallery acts as sales agent. Query with photos. SASE. Gallery pays shipping from gallery and insurance on exhibited work.

HOME BUILDING AND LOAN ASSOCIATION, Box 112, Mountain Grove MO 65711. Contact: Steve Romines. Headquarters and branch offices offer exhibition space to artists who must handle sales.

HOPKINS SAVINGS AND LOAN ASSOCIATION, 7901 W. Burleigh St., Milwaukee WI 53222. (414)873-5555. Contact: Terrence Cleary or Jerry Beyersdorff. Exhibits art and sculpture. Gallery acts as sales agent "if prices are marked." Arrange to show portfolio.

NORTHERN FEDERAL SAVINGS AND LOAN, 6th & Wabasha, St. Paul MN 55082. (612)222-7771. Vice President/Director: C.J. Kabis. Artist must handle sales. Send slides and resume.

THE PIERRE NATIONAL BANK, Box 998, Pierre SD 57501. (605)224-7391. Assistant Vice President, Marketing: Comet Haraldson. Exhibits any art that is "readily displayable in a bank lobby"; 2-3 weeks exposure. Provides some flats and 6 light-duty wooden easels. Art may be offered for sale (no commission), but prefers no prices posted. Minimum price: $10. Artist sets retail price and handles sales. Query with samples or call or write for interview.

SECURITY SAVINGS AND LOAN ASSOCIATION, Platte Ave. & Union Blvd., Colorado Springs CO 80909. (303)473-7600. Contact: Constance R. Smith. Shows art in 3 offices as community service to Colorado artists/craftsmen. Acts as sales agent when prices are shown, but no commission requested. Occasionally buys work. Call for interview.

STATE SAVINGS & LOAN ASSOCIATION, 3258 S. Topeka, Topeka KS 66611. (913)267-3247. Treasurer: M. Janelle McMahan. Exhibits acrylics, airbrush, batik, calligraphy, drawings, oils, pastels, prints, tole painting, wall hangings, watercolors and weavings; 1-2 months exposure. Paintings should be ready for hanging. Art may be offered for sale. Maximum price: $1,500. Artists sets retail price. Call for interview.

Fashion-Related Firms

Being an artist in the fashion world today requires two major attributes: talent and imagination. Without both, the competition gets even tougher than it already is. Today there are more than 1.4 million persons employed in the fashion business, including illustrators, designers and retail advertising directors.

There's a third attribute that's not necessary, but helpful — living in either California or New York. These are the country's most active fashion centers. But then every state has apparel manufacturing plants, and every city its retail clothing outlets and department stores. Most need fashion art.

The following listings are firms interested in looking at fashion designs and illustrations. Some require that you stop in for an interview and show your portfolio; others will let you send samples. Study each listing carefully to determine proper submission methods.

If you're more interested in getting a regular job in fashion rather than freelancing designs here and there, Larry Bell, vice president of merchandising and sales at Ambe Division of Charter Oak Industries, says there are three methods of getting in.

"First, if you graduated from a design school, you might be able to get a job through the reputation of your alma mater." The most prestigious fashion schools are Parson's, the Fashion Institute of Technology and Pratt. A survey taken by Parson's School of Design showed that 75 percent of the working designers in eight major garment center buildings received formal academic training. This compares with 41 percent in 1963.

"Secondly, look under 'Help Wanted' or 'Services Offered' in the *California Apparel News, Fashion Week* and *Women's Wear Daily.*" These publications report on fashion trends and advertise openings. (But, a word to the wise: these publications are not a good market for fashion illustrators. More and more fashion magazines are turning to photography to illustrate styles.)

"And thirdly, apply directly to manufacturers." If you decide to do this, be sure to research the company prior to your interview. They'll want you to know who they sell to, what materials they work in, and have some idea of what their present line consists of.

Artists should watch fashion trends and develop an original offshoot of current styles, says Jeff Elden, art director of Angelique Jewelry. This is particularly good advice for the fashion illustrator who has not yet had a design assignment.

In addition to designing clothing, there are also markets for fashion illustrators and advertising directors. These positions can be found with retail stores and manufacturers.

Most stores prefer to use illustrations rather than photographs for their advertising because it lets them convey an easily-recognized image through their ads. It's hard to improve on an unexciting outfit through photography, but with a drawing you can. Also, by consistently using one style of art (sketchy, or highly stylized), the store shows the potential customer it is his ad — even before the customer sees the store's name in print.

Assignments in fashion illustration can be very lucrative. Top artists can earn as high as $300 per figure for illustrations. One illustrator, working for an elite New York City store, says he earns close to $100,000 annually.

In addition to reading American fashion magazines, keep abreast of the total fashion scene by reading France's *L'Officiel* and *Femme Chic* and Italy's *E'Moda* and *Eleganza.*

ACT YOUNG IMPORTS, INC., 49 W. 37th St., New York NY 10018. Contact: Joe Hafif. Specializes in accessories and clothing for women and children. Uses artists for fashion design of infants' wear, sales promotion/advertising layouts and package design. Send samples of work.

AFRICAN FABRIC PRINTS/AFRICAN GARMENTS, INC., 303 W. 42nd St., New York NY 10036. Art Buyer: Vince Jordan. 3 divisions: African Fabric Prints, African Garments, Inc., and Africa Card Co., Inc. Uses artists for fashion and textile design and ready-to-wear patterns. Pays $50 minimum. Mail tearsheets of previously published works, original artwork or design ideas. Reports in 5-6 weeks.

AMBE DIVISION OF CHARTER OAK INDUSTRIES, 1407 Park St., Hartford CT 06106. (203)524-0801. Vice President, Merchandising: Larry Bell. Estab: 1967. Produces women's outerwear in leather and cloth for better department and specialty stores. Buyers are contemporary young women. Products carry the Ambe label. Uses artists for fashion design and advertising mailers. Buys 75+ designs annually. Pays $50-100 per sketch; negotiates collection price. Send resume. Reports in 1 week. SASE.
To Break In: "It's important to have a working knowledge of the company's market. Design school and experience with a fashion firm is preferable. For us, you should have designs of women's coats in your portfolio."
Special Needs: Predicts a need for feminine clothes with intrinsic value in the future.

ANGELIQUE JEWELRY, 8400 Magnolia, Suite G, Santee CA 92071. (714)449-6050. Art Director: Jeff Elden. Estab: 1969. Specializes in porcelain, floral and feather jewelry for Casual Corner, Macy's and Bloomingdale's. Buyers are young women. Products carry the Angelique label. Uses artists for product design and illustration. Buys 50-100 designs annually. Pays $10-25 for pendant designs. Query with color drawings. Reports in 1 week. SASE.
To Break In: "Prepare a series based on one theme. Look for fashion trends and develop an original off-shoot."

ARKAY OUTERWEAR, Division of Arkay Pants Co., Box 588, Fall River MA 02722. (617)677-9325. (New York office: 358 5th Ave., Rm. 304. (212)244-7326.) Contact: Harold G. Katzman. Uses artists for fashion design of boys' and men's outerwear. Pays $100 for folio of sketches (approximately 100 interpretations); $200 each for full creative design, sample and paper. Mail samples.

AVON GLOVE CORP., 10 E. 38th, New York NY 10016. Contact: Mr. D. Schwartz. Specializes in gloves, mittens and head-wear. Uses artists for sales promotion/advertising layouts and direct mail brochures. Prefers artists in the New York City area. Arrange interview.

BATIK IMPORTS, A. R. Lawrence & Associates, Box 4096, Fullerton CA 92634. (714)525-7069. Contact: A. Robert Lawrence. Specializes in original and hand-printed batik fabrics. Uses artists for fashion design of men's sport shirts, women's blouses, sales promotion layouts, direct mail brochures, hand tags and inserts. Negotiates payment. Call for interview or mail 8x10" samples.

LARRY BERMAN, 8004 Bustleton Ave., Philadelphia PA 19152. Contact: Lorraine Berman. This retail apparel shop uses artists for men's fashion design, package design, shopping bag art and window displays.

SAM BOBMAN DEPARTMENT STORE, 2877 Kensington Ave., Philadelphia PA 19134. Contact: Sam Bobman. Uses artists for newspaper advertising layout in strong b&w or reverse design, billboard advertising, bags and window display. Arrange interview to show portfolio.

BONNIE DOON, 11 E. 36th St., New York NY 10016. Contact: Jerry Loren. This hosiery manufacturer uses artists for fashion design of apparel and package design. Prefers local artists. Arrange interview.

BOUTIQUE SPORTSWEAR, 10 W. 33rd St., New York NY 10001. President: Mike Weber. Specializes in men's shirts and sweaters. Uses artists for fashion design. Pays $50 minimum for sweater design.

Sell Your Art in Style

"It's not enough just to know how to do free-life sketching when you're looking for work as a fashion illustrator. An artist needs to be able to draw fabric textures so customers can look at the drawing and know what fabric the piece is made from," says David Liebschutz of Martin's Town and Country Fashions.

Liebschutz advises artists to study the advertisements for stores they're interested in working with, because each store has a distinct style preference. "There are several newspapers that are particularly good to read if you're concerned with studying fashion illustration and the styles used by various stores. Naturally, the best one is the *New York Times.* But other cities with several specialty shops also have papers with a great deal of fashion illustration. These include the *Pittsburgh Press, Seattle Times, Chicago Sun* and Dallas papers."

Daily newspapers, not the fashion magazines, are the best source for learning what styles are preferred by various stores, says David Liebschutz of Martin's Town and Country Fashions (Hamilton, Ohio). Illustrations, such as this fashion drawing by Helen Gelke, appear in the *Cincinnati Enquirer* as examples of Martin's style.

THE BUGATTI, 222 3rd St., Cambridge MA 02142. Contact: Terry Scheller. Uses artists for fashion design of leather handbags, luggage and sales promotion layouts. Pays $25 minimum for fashion design. Other monies contingent on sales. Send samples.
To Break In: "Know construction and detail — design programs not just discrete items."

CALIFORNIA SPORTSWEAR COMPANY, 1024 S. Maple Ave., Los Angeles CA 90015. Contact: Leonard W. Jaffee. Produces men's and women's fashions in leathers and suedes. Uses artists for fashion design. Send resume.

MIKE CARUSO, 335 Wilshire Blvd., Santa Monica CA 90402. Art Buyer: Dick Caruso. Retail store dealing in better men's clothing, sportswear, furnishings and shoes. Uses artists for container design (for bags and boxes), fashion design and newspaper advertising layouts (software).

CHATTANOOGA CHOO-CHOO, 2354 Hunters Woods Plaza, Reston VA 22091. Art Buyer: Reza. This retail store uses artists for art renderings, building interiors, fashion design, newspaper advertising layouts, sales promotion art, shopping bags and window displays.

CLOTHESHORSE INC., 319 W. 16th St., New York NY 10011. Contact: Anthony Calardo. Specializes in sportswear and women's and girl's clothing. Uses artists for fashion design of apparel, sales promotion/advertising layouts and package design. Prefers artists in the New York City area. Arrange interview.

COOPER SPORTSWEAR CO., INC., 390 5th Ave., New York NY 10018. Contact: R. D. Benedetto. Produces sportswear, men's outerwear and boys' wear. Uses artists for fashion design, direct mail brochures and hang tags. Send samples.

COOPERMAN PANTS CO., 308 W. Erie, Chicago IL 60610. Contact: Ed Kooperman. Produces men's ethnic suits and slacks. Uses artists for fashion design of apparel and direct mail brochures.

CROWN WATERPROOF AND CLOTHING CO., 9600 St. Lawrence Blvd., Rm. 401, Montreal, Quebec Canada H2N 1R2. Contact: Samuel Epstein. Would like to hear from local artists experienced in men's and young men's sportswear, outerwear and leather design. Arrange interview to show samples. Advises designers to know European trends.

J. M. DYER CO., Box 620, Coriscana TX 75110. Art Buyer: Bob Cathey. This department store uses artists for art renderings, building interiors, fashion design, graphic design, newspaper advertising layouts, posters and window displays.

FAMOUS NECKWEAR CO., 104 W. 29th St., New York NY 10001. Contact: David Eisdorfer. Produces boys' wear and men's neckwear. "We are manufacturers of men's bow ties and neckwear — both long ties and ready-tied neckwear, plus Apaches and scarves." Write for future assignments.

FISHER'S MEN'S SHOP, INC., 269 E. Paces Ferry Rd., Atlanta GA 30305. Uses artists for newspaper advertising layouts, shopping bags, signs, letterheads, catalogs and window displays. Write for assignments.

GIBSON DESIGN STUDIO, 77 N. Washington St., Boston MA 02114. (617)723-3607. President/Art Director: Mark Gibson. Estab: 1975. Produces screen-printed fabrics, tote bags, aprons and clothes in cotton and polyester for Bloomingdale's, Saks Fifth Ave., boutiques and gift stores. Products carry the Gibson label. Uses artists for fashion and fabric design. Buys 50 designs annually. Pays $50-300 per sketch or first pattern. Send sketches or slides. Reports in 1 week. SASE.

GINGER-PEACHY, 112 W. 34th St., New York NY 10001. Contact: Mr. L. Stieglitz. Specializes in girls' wear. Uses artists for fashion design of apparel, package design, hang tags and inserts. Prefers local artists.

I. GOLDBERG ARMY-NAVY, 902 Chestnut St., Philadelphia PA 19107. (215)928-0979. Advertising Director: Susan Shore. Estab: 1919. Markets outerwear, underwear, footwear, sweatclothes, military surplus, fashion clothing and camping clothes and gear. Carries Sebago, BVD, Oshkosh, Levi, Lee, Wrangler and Timberland labels among others. Uses local artists for advertising, catalog covers, mechanicals, direct mail brochures and fashion illustration. Buys approximately 100 designs annually. Pays $8-15, spot illustration; $15-20, mechanicals; $6-25, newspaper ad; $175-200, catalog cover; $25-50, bag ad design. Call or send sketches. Reports as needs arise. No work returned.

HANG TEN INTERNATIONAL, 751 7th Ave., San Diego CA 92101. Contact: Bill Gabriel. Produces apparel, sportswear and sports products (with the 2 little feet). Uses local artists for sales promotion/advertising layouts, package design and direct mail brochures.

HOUSE OF JACQUES BOUTIQUE, 3072 Dixie Hwy., Erlanger KY 41018. Contact: Lola Muhlberger. Specializes in women's ready-to-wear and accessories. Uses artists for newspaper/yellow page ads and window and in-store display.

J & J MANUFACTURING CO., 130 W. 34th St., New York NY 10001. Contact: Arthur Sippel. Produces girls' wear. Uses artists for fashion design of girl's sportswear and pants, sizes 4-6x and 7-14. Mail samples.

JODY-TOOTIGUE, 1380 W. Washington Blvd., Los Angeles CA 90007. Contact: J. Hoggert. This junior wear fashion firm reviews fashion designers' resumes. Reports in 1 week.

JOSEPH & FEISS, 1290 Avenue of the Americas, New York NY 10019. Contact: Susan Smyth. Produces men's wear under the Cricketeer label. Uses artists for design of men's suits, sports coats and slacks. Pays $100 minimum for illustrations. Prefers artists in the New York area.

JUST ACCESSORIES, INC., 112 W. 34th St., New York NY 10001. Contact: Richard N. Bloch. Specializes in accessories. Uses artists for fashion accessory design, package design, insertions, direct mail brochures and T-shirt artwork. Mail samples.

KAYSER ROTH HOSIERY CO., INC., 1221 Avenue of the Americas, New York NY 10021. (212)764-4335. Regional Sales Manager: Robert M. Lieberman. Estab: 1958. Produces socks in cotton, nylon and orlon for department stores, supermarkets and mass merchandisers. Buyers are "everyone with feet!" Products carry the Fruit of the Loom, Esquire and Perma-Pair labels. Uses artists for advertising/catalog layouts, direct mail brochures, inserts, package design and window display. Send resume or sketches or call for interview. Reports in 1 week.

KLOPMAN MILLS, 7 Link Dr., Rockleigh NJ 07647. (201)564-7000 ext. 563. Contact: Tom Langan. Produces textile and fabric designs. Uses artists for fashion design, sales promotion/ad layouts, package design, direct mail brochures, window display, hang tags and inserts. Prefers local artists.

LAMOUREUX DESIGNS, 191 NW 71st St., Miami FL 33150. Contact: Ermagaard Lamoureux. Firm specializing in soft and hard lines of fashion retailing business. Uses artists for fashion design for men, women and children, package design and T-shirt artwork. Write for more information.

LEE CO., Division of Lee Byron Corp., Empire State Bldg., Suite 4619, New York NY 10001. Contact: Dan L. Lieberfarb. Produces accessories and boy's wear. Uses artists for fashion design of men's and boys' belts, sales promotion/ad layouts, package design and direct mail brochures. Prefers artists in New York City area. Mail samples or call for interview.

MADEMOISELLE PROMOTIONS LTD., 350 7th Ave., New York NY 10001. Art Buyer: Fred Schwartz. Uses line illustrations made from photos of female sportswear 5 times annually and corporate logos made into textile patterns year-round. Pays $10 minimum per figure for line illustration. Pays on acceptance of finished work. Buys all rights. "We prefer to have constant contact with any artist who is doing work for us, so the artist would have to be available locally."

MARTIN'S TOWN AND COUNTRY FASHIONS, 239 High St., Hamilton OH 45011. Contact: Mr. D. Liebschutz. This retail women's apparel shop uses artists for fashion design, newspaper advertising layouts, lettering and art renderings.

HARRY MATSIL AND SONS, 10 W. 33rd St., New York NY 10001. Contact: Irving Matsil. Specializes in boys' and men's robes. Uses artists for fashion design of apparel, package design and direct mail brochures. Prefers artists in the New York City area. Mail samples or arrange interview.

MIGNON FAGET, 710 Dublin St., New Orleans LA 70118. Contact: Charlotte Norman. Designs and makes fine jewelry and accessories. Uses artists for jewelry, belt buckles and other fashion accessories used in medallic art. Query with resume and samples. SASE.

MISS BOUTIQUE IMPORTS INC., 112 W. 34th St., New York NY 10001. (212)564-5169. Contact: Richard Block. Estab: 1973. Specializes in children's wear. Products carry the Miss Boutique label. Uses artists for catalog layouts, fashion and package design. Buys 50 designs annually. Pays $75 minimum. Send sketches or call for interview. Reports in 1 week. SASE.

MOBILE SOX CORP., 366 5th Ave., New York NY 10001. Contact: Stanley Kreinik. Specializes in anklets and knee-hi socks for all ages. "We're also interested in screen prints (i.e. comics) on socks." Uses artists for sales promotion/ad layouts, package design and direct mail brochures.

NATIONAL ASSOCIATION OF HOSIERY MANUFACTURERS, Box 4314, Charlotte NC 28204. President: S. M. Berry. Estab: 1905. Produces hosiery. Uses artists for fashion design, advertising/catalog layouts and direct mail brochures. Negotiates payment. Send resume. No work returned.

PALM BEACH CO., 1290 Avenue of the Americas, New York NY 10019. Advertising Director: Hal De Bona. Specializes in men's tailored clothing and sportswear. Uses artists for sales promotion/ad layouts and fashion illustration. Pays $275 minimum for 4-color fashion art. Prefers artists in the New York City area. Call for interview.

PENN OUTERWEAR CO., 625 Broadway, New York NY 10012. Contact: M. B. Friedman. Specializes in boys' wear, sportswear and outerwear. Uses artists for fashion design of apparel and direct mail brochures.

PENNBROOK CO., INC., 119-20 Merrick Blvd., St. Albans NY 11434. Contact: Abe Ehrlich. Specializes in children's wear and women's and misses' apparel and sportswear. Uses artists for fashion design of sportswear, T-shirt artwork and direct mail brochures. Arrange interview to show work.

PLAYTIME HEADWEAR INC., 244 W. 27th St., New York NY 11714. Contact: Richard Miller. Specializes in women's and misses' headwear. Uses artists for headwear (novelty) fashion design. Prefers artists in the New York City area. Mail samples or arrange interview.

POUND STERLING, 7979 Reading Rd., Cincinnati OH 45237. Contact: Ross Riley. This men's clothing and accessories firm uses local artists for fashion design of apparel and advertising layouts. Arrange interview.

QUARTET SALES INC., 236 5th Ave., New York NY 10001. (212)686-8911. Contact: Bob Zakarin. Uses artists for direct mail brochures and T-shirt artwork. "We are just beginners in the decorating of T-shirts (hot wax transfers mainly . . . but also some plastisol-plastic transfers) . . . and our needs are small but growing. Our runs are not large, so we can't pay large fees to well established and costly artists. We are seeking artists who are in similar positions in their field . . . willing to work on small order jobs for a small fee to get started with us, and help us start." Prefers artists in the New York City area, but will work with out-of-town artist if convenient. Arrange interview or send samples.

SILVIL CORP., 34 W. 33rd St., New York NY 10001. Contact: Sy Silverberg. Produces boy's robes and pajamas. Uses artists to design boys' pajamas — screen prints. Mail samples.

STRETCH & SEW, INC., Box 185, Eugene OR 97401. (503)686-9961. Contact: Carol Pica. Estab: 1966. Sells knit fabrics, patterns and notions and gives sewing classes. Assigns 200 freelance jobs annually. Uses artists for pattern envelopes/instructions, catalog covers/layouts, direct mail/publicity brochures, newspaper ad layouts, packaging, posters and company publications. Payment determined by number of illustrations. Pays $30-50 for fashion illustration. Buys all rights. Query with samples. Reports in 2 weeks. SASE. Recently assigned artist swimsuit illustrations. "Use realistic figures, not too high-fashion, in your portfolio."

I. Goldberg Army-Navy Stores uses approximately 100 artists annually for mechanicals, direct mail brochures, catalogs and fashion illustration. This 1977 camping catalog cover earned artist Tom Herbert $200.

To Break In: Have the ability to follow instructions accurately; have some understanding of sewing; work fast; be able to use ink/washes well; and be able to portray specific garments accurately.

E. J. TOWLE CO., 406 Dexter Ave. N., Seattle WA 98109. (206)624-0013. President: W. G. Lefort. Estab: 1895. Produces jewelry in Alaskan and Hawaiian motifs for gift and jewelry stores. Uses artists for jewelry design. Buys 10-20 designs annually. Pays $25-75 for jewelry design. Query. Reports in 2 weeks.

TRIBORO QUILT MANUFACTURING CORP., 451 Broadway, New York NY 10013. (212)966-2662. Sales Manager: Alvin Kaplan. Estab: 1935. Produces infant's wear for chain stores. Products carry the Triboro label. Uses artists for advertising/catalog layouts, direct mail brochures, fabric and fashion design, hang tags, inserts, iron-ons and package design. Call for interview. Reports in 1 week. SASE.

TROPIX TOGS INC., 333 NW 22 Lane, Miami FL 33127. Contact: Sam Kantor. Specializes in children's wear, junior wear, sportswear, polo shirts and sweatshirts. Uses artists for advertising layouts, artwork for polo shirts and direct mail brochures. Call for interview.

WESTERN ART MFG. CO., INC., 38 E. 5th Ave., Denver CO 80203. President: Robert Hilb. Specializes in children's wear, junior wear and men's wear. Uses artists for T-shirt and sweatshirt art. Mail samples.

WHITE SEWING MACHINE CO., 11750 Berea Rd., Cleveland OH 44111. Contact: Mrs. B. Gold. Uses artists for sales promotion/ad layouts. Prints leaflets illustrating sewing machines as well as booklets on sewing tips, such as "Stitching the Kits." Prefers artists in Cleveland area. Arrange appointment.

Fine Art Publishers & Distributors

The fine artist who is able to sell his work so it can be made into prints is doing good business these days. Total sales figures on art prints were in the neighborhood of $25 million in 1973, as compared to $1 million in 1963.

All over the country — especially in the West and Midwest — fine art publishers and distributors are reporting large increases in the demand for art prints. Prices are ranging from $5 to $100,000.

The most important factor in getting accepted on the print bandwagon is to have good artistic abilities. "Competition is very keen. The key to selling to a company such as ours is that the art be decorative. Also, we are interested in new concepts which make the subject submitted different than the general run of paintings which many artists show us so often," says Frank Tornabene, executive vice president of Scafa-Tornabene Art Publishing Company.

Opinions vary on the way to approach art print publishers/distributors. Robert A. Hill, president of Hedgerow House Publishing Co., Inc., advises artists to send a letter to the publisher or distributor which includes background, a resume and information on general experience (i.e. gallery showings and other professional art credits).

Don Wright, art director of Ocular Bazaar, puts less merit on past experience and more on the work itself. "Forget the professional qualifications. Just submit tearsheets of previously published work or slides and prints of current work for consideration," says Wright.

The listings in this section are interested in buying serigraphs, oil paintings, watercolors, woodcuts, etchings, lithographs, drawings and other reproducible art.

Watercolors and bright, boldly executed work are selling exceptionally well today, according to Tornabene. Subject matter needed varies from firm to firm, with publishers considering everything from florals to art of children.

Each publisher is in the print publishing business as a commercial venture, and will choose only the artwork he feels will sell well. In return he pays the artist by royalties, a fixed fee for rights to a limited edition or a combination of royalties and a fixed fee. Working with a printer allows you wide exposure without the cost of having the work reproduced and distributed yourself.

Get all agreements with a publishing company in writing. Work should be copyrighted by the publisher to protect you from piracy by other firms or individuals.

Although prints by old masters such as Picasso increase most rapidly in value, a good-selling piece by a contemporary artist, such as yourself, will also increase in value and can demand top prices. Most prints are now increasing in value by more than 10% annually.

More print publishers and distributors for your artwork can be found by reading the ads in *Art Dealer & Framer* and *Decor,* publications for the framing industry.

AARON ASHLEY, INC., 230 5th Ave., New York NY 10001. (212)532-9277. Contact: Aaron Ginsburg or Ashley L. Leavitt. Estab: 1928. Publisher and distributor. Clients are wholesale frame manufacturers, art dealers and educational institutions. Media bought include paintings and watercolors. Pays flat fee or royalties. Query with samples. Samples should be small color photos or transparencies. Reports in 2 weeks. SASE.

ALVA MUSEUM REPLICAS, INC., 140 Greenwich Ave., Greenwich CT 06830. (203)661-2400. Contact: Eleanore David. Estab: 1944. Publisher and distributor. Clients are museum shops, department stores, libraries and universities. Media bought include sculpture and jewelry. Mail samples. Samples should be slides or photos stating size, medium and showing all views. Reports in 4 weeks. SASE.

AMERICAN MASTERS FOUNDATIONS, INC., 303 Jackson Hill, Suite 110, Houston TX 77007. President: Randy Best. Publisher and distributor. Specializes in landscapes, wildlife, florals and other representational art for art dealers, galleries and frame shops. Media bought include acrylics, oils, pastels, prints and watercolors. Send slides or photos of work. Reports in 2-4 weeks. SASE.

THE ARIZONA TURQUOISE & SILVER COMPANY LTD., 7086 5th Ave., Scottsdale AZ 85251. (602)945-2118. Contact: Tom McKee. Estab: 1965. Fine arts distributor. Specializes in western art and sculpture for wholesale and retail. Media bought include sculpture and paintings. Works on consignment. Query. SASE.

HERBERT ARNOT, INC., 250 W. 57th St., New York NY 10019. Contact: Peter Arnot. "We have over 700 artists working for us on a full-time basis with wholesale prices from $50-5,000. We have an inventory of 20,000 paintings and sales representatives covering every state of the country and Canada. We pay on delivery to our artists. We always look for new artists."

ART RESOURCES EDITIONS LTD./ART RESOURCES TREASURY LTD., 129 W. 29th St., New York NY 10001. (212)564-8677. President: Eunice Lowell. Estab: 1974. Fine arts distributor. Specializes in contemporary, realistic and expressionistic art for galleries. Media bought include original limited edition serigraphs. Pays $100 minimum. Query, mail samples or call for interview. "We try to answer immediately." SASE.

JOHN BARTON ASSOCIATES, INC., 915 Broadway, New York NY 10010. Vice President: Leonard S. Barton. Specializes in "original hand-signed and numbered fine art graphic editions: contemporary hard edge, landscapes, still lifes — no 'portraits.' " Media bought include silkscreens, woodcuts, etchings and lithographs. No photo mechanical processes are acceptable. "We are looking for salable art that has strong individuality. Biographical resumes are not a strong factor — but professionalism has to be prime. We do not print editions for artists. We purchase complete editions only. The average edition size is 120 numbered graphics plus 20 artist proofs. After completion of edition, we must get all canceled plates or proof that edition can't be run again." Send resume and proof of original graphic editions.

BERMOND ART LTD., 3000 Marcus Ave., Lake Success NY 11040. (516)328-3550. Contact: Raymond Kay or Bernice Weiss. Estab: 1952. Publisher and distributor. Clients are art galleries and interior designers. Media bought include original signed and numbered etchings, lithographs and serigraphs. Negotiates payment. Query and send sample proofs with all information. Reports in 1 week. SASE.

CIRCLE GALLERY LTD., 108 S. Michigan Ave., Chicago IL 60603. (312)726-2226. President: Jack Solomon, Jr. Estab: 1969. Publisher and distributor. Clients are general public, art galleries and interior decorators. Buys all media. Pays $500 for lithographs. Mail unframed samples. Reports in 3 weeks. SASE.

H. S. CROCKER CO., 1000 San Mateo Ave., San Bruno CA 94066. Contact: Al Trice. Specializes in posters, fine art prints, postcards, catalogs and fine art books for restaurants, distributors and fund raisers. Negotiates rates; some work bought directly; some pays up to 20%. Send resume and slides.

DONALD ART CO. INC., Donald Art Bldg., Port Chester NY 10574. President: Donald M. Bonnist. Media bought include paintings and color lithographs in all subject matter. 10% royalty from net billing price with $150-250 advance per subject. "Decorator colors nature scenes" is 1 kind of art hard to locate; and in the last 5 years, customers seem to prefer more Americana nostalgic subjects, as well as modern, but not abstract, art. All kinds of paintings — oil, watercolor, tempera — are used and sizes range from 6x8" to 24x48". Also reproduces paintings on table place mats, hot pads and related items and is a specialist in premiums, promotions and business gifts. Send color slides or photos before submitting painting.

EDITIONS PRESS, 621 Minna St., San Francisco CA 94103. Contact: Walter Maibaum. Prints, wholesales and exports lithographs from hand-inked stones and plates.

EMROSE ART CORPORATION OF FLORIDA, 5181 NE 12th Ave., Fort Lauderdale FL 33334. (305)772-1386. Contact: Mr. M. Rosenbaum. Specializes in traditional and abstract paintings and sculpture. "We buy artwork for cash." Retail price set by gallery. Send transparencies or photos.

FABULOUS FORGERIES LTD., 230 Central Park S., New York NY 10019. Contact: Ted Marshall. Specializes in traditional, contemporary and realistic art. "Our technique utilizes both lithography and photography combining either with an acrylic to form a true mixed media; finished product usually on canvas or wood. Some consider this a new art form." Payment: usually 10% of wholesale price; set by publisher. Submit resume and slides. Slides should be 4x5" or 8x10" transparencies or 35mm if quality is excellent.

FINE ARTS, Wheaton Plaza, Wheaton MD 20902. President: R. H. Kornemann. Estab: 1970. Fine arts distributor. Clients are department stores, card shops, gift shops and galleries. Media bought include contemporary original graphics by artists such as Neiman, Moore, Dali, Picasso, Moti, Boulanger and Kornemann. Works on consignment. Mail samples. Reports in 4 weeks. SASE.

FINE ARTS RESOURCE, INC., 60 E. 42nd St., New York NY 10017. Contact: Murry Hirsch. Publishers and distributors of limited edition, hand-signed original graphics. Media bought include screen prints, lithographs and etchings. Payment determined by artist's standing, nature of work, size of edition and projected retail price. Buys all or reproduction rights. Send resume and brief description of work and subject matter.

GALLERIE RABINDRA, 2720 S. La Cienega Blvd., Los Angeles CA 90034. Art Director: David Holden. Estab: 1972. Fine arts publisher. Specializes in wildlife art for wholesale

"Original, hand-signed and numbered, limited edition etchings, lithographs and screenprints" are sought by Original Print Collectors Group, Ltd. (New York City). A promise of salability prompted Original to buy this print — for a limited edition of 125 etchings — from Fernando Torm.

framers, galleries and department stores. Media bought include graphics and paintings. Pays royalties. Query with 35mm slides of work. Reports in 4 weeks. SASE.

GEMINI G E L, Graphics Editions Ltd., 8365 Melrose Ave., Los Angeles CA 90069. Contact: Sidney B. Felsen or Stanley Grinstein. Publishes screen, lithograph and intaglio prints.

GLASSERS ART GALLERY, 2121 N. Main, San Antonio TX 78212. (512)732-1121. Contact: C. W. Knight. Estab: 1902. Publisher and distributor. Specializes in limited edition western, wildlife and representational art for frame shops and art galleries. Pays royalties. Query with samples or photos. Reports in 4 weeks. No work returned.

GOES LITHOGRAPHING COMPANY, 42 W. 61st St., Chicago IL 60621. Contact: Walter J. Goes. Estab: 1878. Fine arts publisher. Specializes in floral, children's, landscape and wildlife art. Buys paintings. Pays flat fee. Mail samples. Buys all rights. SASE.

GRAPHICS EDITIONS, 2312 Divisadero St., San Francisco CA 94115. Contact: Mr. R. Strauss. Specializes in hand-printed, limited edition fine art. Send resume and educational background before sending slides, photos or reproductions. SASE.

H. S. GRAPHICS LTD., Box 243, Keasbey NJ 08832. Director: M. S. Milco. Estab: 1965. Fine arts publisher. Specializes in florals and landscapes for galleries. Media bought include woodcuts and stone. Pays $500-1,000, lithographs, etchings and woodcuts. Pays flat fee. Query. Samples should be 35mm slides. Reports in 1 week. SASE.

HADDAD'S FINE ARTS INC., Box 3016-C, Anaheim CA 92803. (714)996-2100. President: James Haddad. Estab: 1959. Publisher and distributor. Clients are galleries, art shops, framers and bookstores. Method of reproduction: HPAPHP YHSH. Mail 35mm slides or small transparencies. Do not send original art unless requested. Buys all rights. Reports in 60 days. SASE.

HEDGEROW HOUSE PUBLISHING CO., INC., 225 5th Ave., New York NY 10010. (212)679-2532. President: Robert A. Hill. Publisher and distributor. Estab: 1971. Specializes in impressionistic and realistic landscapes, florals, and original graphics (lithographs, etchings) for national framers, jobbers, frame shop dealers, galleries and department stores. Considers "top-selling artists in the original graphic field and promising new artists in acrylics and watercolors (tempera)." Method of reproduction: 4 or 6-color offset lithography. Pays $250-500 for reproduction rights. Pays flat fee or regular royalties based on 10% selling price. Arrange interview; do not send samples or art without permission. Requested samples should be color transparencies or 8x10" color glossies. "We require exclusive reproduction rights." Reports in 2 weeks. SASE.
To Break In: "Initial query can be on phone; however, it is more helpful if written request is made submitting background and resume, as well as general experience (i.e., gallery showings, etc.). We are very anxious to meet all new and promising artists; however, in order to screen out unprofessional applicants, we prefer written application for appointment which will be acknowledged promptly."

INTERNATIONAL ART COMPANY, 1644 NE 123rd St., North Miami FL 33181. (305)891-4182. Contact: Sidney Litwin. Estab: 1970. Publisher and distributor. Specializes in all art except abstracts for galleries, picture framers, department stores and gift shops. Media bought include oil paintings, watercolors and lithographs. Method of reproduction: serigraphy and lithography. Pays royalties. Mail photos or slides of work. Reports in 3 weeks. SASE.

JAMIN EDITIONS, INC., 16140 Valerio St., Van Nuys CA 91406. Contact: Kenneth Benjamin. Specializes in graphics: lithogaphs, etchings, serigraphs and watercolors. Art must fit standard frame size: 20x24", 24x30", 16x20", etc. Negotiates payment. Send resume and slides.

LESLI ART DEALERS, 8730 W. 3rd St., Los Angeles CA 90048. (213)271-4493. Contact: Stan Shevrin. Estab: 1965. Publisher and distributor. Specializes in impressionistic and super-realistic art for galleries. Buys outright or on consignment. Query with samples. Samples should include size, medium and wholesale price range. Reports in 1 week. SASE.

PHYLLIS LUCAS GALLERY (CAMILLA LUCAS INC. PUBLISHING), 981 2nd Ave., New York NY 10022. Contact: Phyllis Lucas. "We specialize in original signed graphics (publish Dali, etc.). We buy outright editions signed." Arrange interview to show samples.

Selling Your Art to the Masses

The secret to selling to most fine art publishers is to present them with something that will sell to the masses, says Fred Merida, owner of Merida Gallery, Inc. (Louisville, Kentucky). "There is no set rule as to what is salable, but if an artist will scout the market he can get a pretty good idea of what sells best."

Subjects dealing with elements people can personally identify with are particularly good sellers, says Merida. "People like things such as bright dasies in a milk can, because the subjects are something most people can relate to and they bring back fond memories of flowers in fields. Along these same lines, bright purple poppies probably won't sell because most people feel these flowers are overpowering in color and smell."

Fred Merida

CARL F. LUCKEY FINE ARTS, 226 N. Court St., Florence AL 35630. Contact: Carl F. Luckey. Estab: 1970. Fine arts distributor. Clients are individuals and firms. Media bought include original prints, paintings and sculpture. Works on consignment. Mail 35mm slides or color photos. Reports within 30 days. SASE.

MERIDA GALLERY INC., 4156 Westport Rd., Louisville KY 40207. (502)896-2331. Contact: Fred Merida. Estab: 1966. Fine arts distributor. Clients are frame shops, banks, institutions and private businesses. Media bought include complete edition woodcuts and paintings. Pays $2 minimum woodcuts/lithographs/etchings; $100 minimum, posters. Pays flat fee or royalties. Query or mail samples. Reports in 3 weeks. SASE.

MITCH MORSE GALLERY, INC., 305 E. 63rd St., New York NY 10021. (212)593-1812. Vice President, Sales: Allan Gerstle. Fine arts publisher. Clients are frame shops, interior designers, architects and contract specifiers. Media bought include acrylics, airbrush, drawings, oils, pastels, prints and watercolors. Negotiates payment. Call for interview. Reports in 1 week. **Special Needs:** Uses artwork for porcelain collector plates. Pays "minimum guarantee plus royalties."

NATURE HOUSE INC., Box 222AM, Griggsville IL 62340. Contact: Art Director. Specializes in detailed nature art; particularly interested in watercolor landscape art featuring animals or birds. Art must be 22x28". Send resume and slides or 8x10" glossies.

NEW YORK GRAPHIC SOCIETY, 140 Greenwich Ave., Greenwich CT 06830. (203)661-2400. Contact: Tina Liverakos. Estab: 1925. Publisher and distributor. Clients are print shops, department stores, libraries and universities. Media bought include paintings and original graphics. Pays royalties or flat fee. Mail slides or color photos. Reports in 3 weeks. SASE.

OCULAR BAZAAR, c/o Apocalypse Press, Box 1821, Topeka KS 66601. Art Director: Dan Wright. This mail-order gallery deals directly with collectors of fine art prints and lithographic reproductions. "Submit tearsheets of previously published work or slides and/or prints of current work for consideration. We are looking for artists' editions of woodcuts, lithographs, etchings, silkscreen and photo-mechanical process artwork." 30% commission. Originals accepted produced for resale at 50% commission. Signed, limited editions only, with proof of destroyed masters required. "We are now oriented toward science fiction artwork, but will look at anything you may have as samples."

OESTREICHER'S PRINTS INC., 43 W. 46th St., New York NY 10036. Contact: Edward Gultz. Interested in original lithographs, etchings and prints.

ORIGINAL PRINT COLLECTORS GROUP, LTD., 120 E. 56th St., New York NY 10022. Contact: Marjorie Katzenstein/Bruce Whyte. Specializes in representational and semi-abstract art. Media bought include original, hand-signed and numbered, limited edition etchings, lithographs and screenprints. "Artist must have printmaking expertise. It is preferred, although not required, that artists pull their own prints." Send resume and slides.

PACE EDITIONS INC., 32 E. 57th St., New York NY 10011. (212)421-3237. Director: Karen McCready. Estab: 1969. Fine arts publisher. Specializes in abstract, hard edge work for individuals, designers and corporations. Media bought include screenprints, lithographs, etchings, intaglio prints and relief engravings. Call for interview to show prints in portfolio. Work on consignment. Reports in 1 week. SASE.

PHOENIX GALLERY, 30 W. 57th St., New York NY 10019. Director: Lorraine Kelly. Estab: 1961. Fine arts distributor. Specializes in contemporary art for consultants, decorators, architects, art purchasers and collectors. Works on consignment; 30% commission. Query or call for interview to show slides or photos, resume and 2-3 actual works. Reports in 1 month. SASE.

PORTAL PUBLICATIONS LTD., Box 659, Corte Madera CA 94925. Art Director: Cathleen Casey. Clients are retail outlets, galleries, department stores, picture framers and individuals. Prefers written contracts. Rates: $500 for each piece or flat rate for a series (produces everything in a theme-related series). Prints 10,000 minimum. Send resume and slides.

POSTER PLUS, 2906 N. Broadway, Chicago IL 60657. (312)549-2822. President: Gartler. Estab: 1969. Fine arts distributor. Clients are galleries and museum shops. Media bought include lithographs and silkscreen prints. "We purchase remaining stocks of posters done for exhibitions or self-promotion". Pays $1-10 for posters. Mail samples. Reports in 2 weeks. SASE.

ARTHUR ROTHMANN FINE ARTS, 1123 Broadway, New York NY 10010. Editor: Arthur Rothmann. Estab: 1947. Publisher and distributor. Specializes in figurative and representational art for galleries and museums. Media bought include graphics, etchings, drawings, engravings, lithographs and woodcuts. Pays $100-1,000. Query with samples or write for interview. Samples should be 8x10"-24x36". Reports in 2 weeks. SASE.
To Break In: "Work must have a humanistic appeal and say something with meaning that has universal appeal."

RAE ROY & COMPANY, 300 Tampico, Irving TX 75062. (214)255-4600. Contact: Mrs. Rae Roy Anderson. Estab: 1958. Publisher and distributor. Specializes in representational and modern art for picture frame manufacturers, galleries, print shops and decoupage distributors. Media bought include paintings, pastels and pen and ink. Method of reproduction: lithography. Pays 5% royalty. Query with slides of work. Buys all rights. Reports in 4-5 weeks. SASE.

SCAFA-TORNABENE ART PUBLISHING COMPANY INC., 100 Snake Hill Rd., West Nyack NY 10994. (914)358-7600. Executive Vice President: Frank Tornabene. Estab: 1970. Publisher and distributor. Specializes in full range of decorative art for manufacturers of frames, plaques, trays, puzzles and premiums. Media bought include drawings and paintings. Method of reproduction: offset. Pays $50-250. Pays flat fee, occasionally royalties after artist is established with company. Query with color photos or slides. Insure originals and send unframed. Reports in approximately 2 weeks. SASE.
To Break In: Artist should have unique approach, decorative composition, professional execution, flexibility, market understanding and be receptive and responsive to direction.

SELECT GALLERIES, 19108 W. Dixie Hwy., Miami FL 33160. (350)931-2264. Contact: Tina Roy. Estab: 1974. Fine arts distributor. Specializes in landscapes, abstracts and impressionistic art for collectors and retailers. Media bought include paintings and sculpture. Pays $10-2,000. Buys outright or on consignment. Call for interview. Reports in 2-3 weeks. SASE.

SHIP LORE LTD., 655 Madison Ave., New York NY 10021. (212)759-1175. Specializes in limited and general edition prints of maritime subjects for frame markets, galleries and specialty stores. Usually buys all rights. Also represents artists with regard to locating commissions and showing original work. Reports in 2 weeks. "The more you can show us the style and variety of your work, the better we are able to determine our ability to adequately represent you."

NATHAN SILBERBERG FINE ARTS, 507 5th Ave., New York NY 10017. (212)661-3665. Estab: 1972. Publisher and distributor. Specializes in 20th century masters and "school of Paris" art for fine arts galleries. Media bought include silkscreen and paintings. Call or write for interview.

VANGUARD STUDIOS, INC., Subsidiary of Kirsch Co., 9185 Kelvin St., Chatsworth CA 91311. Vice President/Art Director: Thomas Piszczek. Designer and producer of framed paintings and manufacturer of wall decor, including framed reproductions, limited edition prints, posters, decorative mirrors and sculpture. Uses all media. Buys original art and exclusive reproduction rights usually through outright purchase or royalties. Pays $100 minimum, outright purchase; negotiates royalties. Arrange interview or send slides.

Institutions, Associations, Businesses & Bureaus

Art needed by institutions, associations, businesses and bureaus is very similar. Assignments include brochure design, posters, signs, ads, logos, POP displays, cartoons, annual reports and special tie-in products. Regardless of your area of interest, J. C. Hunt, marketing manager of Letraset Consumer Products Ltd., suggests the artist show originality, quality and a knowledge of the market for which he'll be working. The local librarian should be consulted for a list of what trade publications can help the artist learn more about his fields of interest.

Knowledge of the processes involved in art is important, too. "Hang around a printing office to learn the necessity of sharp, square layouts so you can learn the importance of the bottom line being parallel with the first line. And a learn to spell and proofread your work," says R. C. Dinsmore, president of Dinsmore Instrument Company. Other important elements of becoming a good artist include the ability to produce camera-ready copy, meeting deadlines and keeping up with today's trends.

Payment for assignments in this section vary from a low of $3 for a label design to $10,000 for a 32-page color brochure. Certainly, no one would scoff at $10,000 payments; but, likewise, lower paying markets are valuable as leads to future work.

There are five categories within this section: Amusement-Related Firms, Associations, Businesses & Manufacturers, Educational Institutions, and Chambers of Commerce & Convention Bureaus.

Amusement-Related Firms covers a $1-billion industry including amusement/mass entertainment facilities such as auditoriums, amusement parks, arenas, stadiums, grandstands and tourist attractions. Art buyers for these firms need artwork for posters, signs, brochures, advertising, tie-in products (such as T-shirts and bumper stickers), portraits, costume designs, calligraphy and other projects. To keep abreast of trends and developments in this industry, read *Amusement Business,* a weekly Billboard publication.

Associations, museums, churches and philantropic organizations that require art services for promotion are listed in the Association category. Payment here ranges from $5 for cover art to $1,200 for a brochure. Associations granting aid to artists are included in the Aid section, while those offering show space are listed in the Exposition Space section, under Galleries.

Businesses & Manufacturers have work for both artists and craftsmen. Among the listings are manufacturers of craft kits that buy craft designs for their lines. For more information on craft kit manufacturers, write the National Hand Knitting Association, 230 Fifth Avenue, New York City 10003. Other companies in this section range from Blue Cross and Blue Shield of Michigan to manufacturers of metallic products. Assignments include promotional work, illustrations for company publications and product design.

Colleges, universities, foreign exchange programs, military schools, and libraries are all listed under Educational Institutions. Assignments in this area include work for sports departments, recruitment offices and college publications. Beause some schools are government subsidized, some jobs in this area require that bids be submitted (check with your local or state government officials for the correct procedure on bidding).

Robert E. Simanski, editor at The Catholic University of America, advises artists who want to find jobs on educational publications to "Get a staff job in a publications office and become familiar with all stages in the development of a publication from initial planning through story development, layout and printing. Learn to expediate the production process."

For the names of additional colleges, check *Lovejoy's College Guide,* published by Simon & Schuster, Inc. There were 3,075 colleges and universities in the U.S. in 1977 — an excellent freelance market.

Just as businesses are good markets for your work, so are the organizations that traditionally promote them — specifically, chambers of commerce and convention bureaus. A complete list of chambers of commerce can be found in *Johnson's World Wide Chamber of Commerce Directory.* In addition to hiring artists, many chamber of commerce publish booklets listing firms, galleries, publications and other businesses in their area. These could be an added source of markets for your work.

Amusement-Related Firms

ADVENTURELAND, Box 199, North Webster IN 46555. Contact: F. Edward Herron. Uses artists for direct mail brochures, posters, newspaper ads, tie-in products (such as T-shirts) and signs. Send photos or tearsheets of past work.

AFRICAN LION SAFARI, Box 326, Port Clinton OH 43452. Contact: S. K. Mohan. Uses artists for posters and signs. Pays $10 minimum for signs. Query with resume and photos or tearsheets to arrange interview.

ART SHOPPE-GEAUGA LAKE PARK, 1541 Bell Rd., Chagrin Falls OH 44022. (216)338-3015. Contact: Richard Kaman. Interested in portrait artists for 5 minute sketches. Query with resume and arrange interview to show portfolio.

EIGHT FLAGS, MARINE LIFE, 150 Debuys Rd., Biloxi MS 39531. Contact: Michael S. Liebaert. Uses artists for design and illustration of posters, signs and bumper stickers. Send photos, tearsheets or photocopies of past work.

EVANSTON DEPARTMENT OF PARKS, RECREATION AND FORESTRY, 1802 Maple Ave., Evanston IL 60201. Community Relations Director: Mary Jane Gauen. Uses graphic artists for direct mail brochures, annual reports and occasional posters. Gauen says their budget is limited, but "usually we can compensate to some degree by planning in advance so our projects can be fitted into slack time of artist's schedule, if any."

FUNNI-FRITE, INC., 3770 E. Livingston Ave., Columbus OH 43227. General Manager: Don Gibson. Manufacturer of dark rides and walk-through fun houses, both portable and park models. All material supplied; all work is inside. Pays $5-10 per hour. Send resume.

INDIANA BEACH, INC., 306 Indiana Beach Dr., Monticello IN 47960. Contact: T. E. Spackman. Uses artists for direct mail brochures, newspaper releases, costume design, exhibits, displays, signs and public relations. Submit samples.

INTERNATIONAL FINALS RODEO, Box 615, Pauls Valley OK 73075. (405)238-6488. President: Bob Ink. Office Manager: Dianna Beason. This is the World Series of rodeo for the top 15 contestants in the 7 International Rodeo Association championship events. Uses artists for direct mail brochures, posters, programs, advertising, costume design, exhibits, displays, signs, bumper stickers, and tie-in products such as T-shirts, toys, posters, ashtrays, lighters, glasses and buttons. Submit photos or tearsheets.

LAKEVIEW PARK, Rte. 16, Mendon MA 01756. Contact: William Green. Also features Flame & Sword Restaurant and Lakeview Ballroom. Uses artists for newspaper ads and posters. Submit photos or tearsheets of published work.

LONG BRANCH AMUSEMENT PIER, Ocean Ave., Long Branch NJ 07740. (201)222-2624. Contact: Matthew Sowul. Promotes a summer antique car show, sand castle contest and fishing facility. Uses artists for posters and newspaper ads. Pays $100, posters; $15, newspaper ads. Prefers artists bring samples of work in person.

LONGHORN WORLD CHAMPIONSHIP RODEO INC., Box 8280, Nashville TN 37207. (615)226-1120. President: W. Bruce Lehrke. Editor: Marty Martins. Estab: 1965. Produces and promotes major league rodeos/rodeo publications. Assigns 24 jobs annually. Uses artists for catalog covers and layouts, magazine ads, direct mail and publicity brochures, displays, exhibit designs, newspaper ad layouts, lettering, packaging, POP displays, posters, signage, trademarks, logos and company publications. Pays $100-250 for rodeo program covers. Query with samples. Reports in 4 weeks. SASE.
To Break In: Have perseverance and knowledge of rodeo, cowboys, horses, cattle and related items so art is authentic in every way.

LOS ANGELES MEMORIAL COLISEUM AND SPORTS ARENA, 3939 S. Figueroa, Los Angeles CA 90037. Public Relations Director: Glenn E. Mon. Uses artists from January-June at Arena, August-December at Coliseum. Average interview.

NATURELAND'S FANTASY FARM, Rte. 3, Lincoln NH 03251. Contact: Donald E. Mitchell. Uses artists for direct mail brochures, exhibits, displays, costume design and bumper stickers. Submit photos or tearsheets of past work.

OLD TOWNE MALL, 19800 Hawthorne Blvd., Box 137, Torrance CA 90503. General Manager: Richard Pink. Turn-of-the-century shopping mall featuring double-decker Venetian Carousel, daily puppet shows, bumper cars and other rides. Uses artists for posters, ads, costume design, exhibits, displays and signs. Send photos or tearsheets of past work.

PERA'S AMUSEMENT PARK, Lake Rd., Geneva on the Lake OH 44043. (513)466-8659 or 8650. Contact: Martha Woodward. Locations provided for artists to do sketches and portraits for public. Areas may be rented or arrangements made for percentage on works sold.

PLEASANT VALLEY INVESTMENTS, 754 Boardwalk, Ocean City NJ 08226. (609)398-6059. Contact: Roger Jakubowski. Amusement pier including restaurants. Uses artists/designers for posters, exhibits, displays and portraits. Query with resume and arrange interview to show portfolio.

ROCKY POINT PARK, Warwick RI 02889. President/General Manager: Conrad Ferla. Uses artists for direct mail brochures, programs, trade magazines ads and bumper stickers. Submit photos or tearsheets of past work.

SANTA FE PARK SPEEDWAY, 9100 S. Wolf Rd., Hinsdale IL 60521. Contact: Howard Tiedt. Stock car speedway. Uses artists for programs, ads, costume design, bumper stickers and signs. Submit photos or tearsheets of past work.

SCOLLON PRODUCTIONS, INC., 3619 Walton Ave., Cleveland OH 44113. Contact: E. W. Scollon. Uses artists to create and build costumed cartoon characters and marionette shows for amusement parks and other attractions. Sample cartoon characters produced include: The Flintstones, Yogi Bear and the Banana Splits. Pays $25 for designs. Submit resume and photos of work.

SEA BREEZE PARK, 4600 Culver Rd., Rochester NY 14622. Contact: Robert Norris. Uses artists for posters, signs, exhibits, displays, costumes, newspaper ads, interiors and exteriors of rides, special effects, light shows and projections. Submit photos, tearsheets or photocopies of past work.

STORYBOOK GARDENS, Rte. 1, 134A, Wisconsin Dells WI 53965. Contact: Thomas G. Egan. Amusement park. Uses artists for posters, newspaper ads, direct mail brochures, costume design, exhibits, displays, signs and bumper stickers. Submit photos or tearsheets of past work.

STORYLAND VALLEY ZOO, c/o 10th Floor, CN Tower, Edmonton, Alberta Canada T5J OK1. Contact: C. Vanderpolder. Amusement park. Uses artists for exhibits, displays, signs, bumper stickers, brochures, pennants and postcards.

THUMB FUN, INC., Box 128 HY 42, Fish Creek WI 54212. (414)868-3418. Contact: Doug Butchart. Uses artists for direct mail brochures, posters, newspaper ads, costume design, signs, bumper stickers, contemporary designs for T-shirt printing and tie-in products. Send samples.

VENICE AMUSEMENT CORP., Casino Pier, Seaside Heights NY 08751. Contact: Kenneth Wynne. Seashore resort/amusement park. Uses artists for direct mail brochures, ads, exhibits, displays, signs, bumper stickers and painting rides. Submit photos or tearsheets of past work.

Artists with a genuine knowledge of rodeo are used by Longhorn World Championship Rodeo Inc. for promotional purposes. Longhorn Rodeo souvenir program covers, such as this one designed by Carolyn Sloan, can earn the artist anywhere from $100-250. Payment is determined by merit.

Associations

ALABAMA EDUCATION ASSOCIATION, Box 4177, Montgomery AL 36101. Director of Publications/Public Relations: A. Synne Brammer. "We don't require sophisticated artwork. Educational cartoons are of primary interest with us." Artwork should be suitable for newsprint reproduction. Pays on acceptance. Previously published work OK. Reports in 2 weeks.

AMERICAN OPTOMETRIC ASSOCIATION PUBLIC INFORMATION DIVISION, 7000 Chippewa St., St. Louis MO 63119. Art Buyer: R. W. Malmer. Produces large variety of public information materials on vision and vision care subjects. Uses artists for direct mail promotion brochures, pamphlets, booklets and educational illustrations. Query, then send photocopies or transparencies.

AMERICAN SURFING ASSOCIATION, Box 342, Huntington Beach CA 92648. (714)644-5357. Contact: Gary F. R. Filosa II. Uses artists for membership recruitment literature, public information brochures and magazine graphics. Pays $500 for brochure designs. Buys all rights. Write.

AUTOMOTIVE AFFILIATED REPRESENTATIVES, 625 N. Michigan Ave., Suite 1525, Chicago IL 60611. (312)751-2114. Executive Director: Judy Neel. Uses artists for membership recruitment literature, public information brochures, annual reports, annual roster, trade show exhibits, convention and seminar literature and a newsletter. Payment determined by project. Buys one-time rights. Arrange interview and submit ideas or sketches.

BUREAU OF ALCOHOL, TOBACCO AND FIREARMS, Public Affairs, Room 4406, Washington DC 20226. Contact: Howard D. Criswell, Jr. Administers and enforces laws on alcoholic beverages, tobacco, firearms and explosives. Uses artists for information booklets; illustrations for printed material; slides, filmstrips and other audiovisual materials, displays; dioramas; and special exhibitions. Artists working with the Bureau would in some way be involved in these programs. Query.

CEDAR RAPIDS COMMUNITY CONCERTS ASSOCIATION/CZECH FINE ARTS ASSOCIATION, 1455 Parkview Dr., Marion IA 52302. Contact: Ronald L. Raim. Works with performing artists. All arts related to Czech ethnic heritage. Uses artists for direct mail brochures. Pays $30-200.

CENTRAL ILLINOIS CULTURAL AFFAIRS CONSORTIUM, 1501 W. Bradley Ave., Peoria IL 61625. (309)674-7355. Contact: Norma Murphy. Works with performing artists. Uses artists for direct mail brochures, programs and local artist registry. Also offers artist-in-residence program. Send resume and list of prizes won.

CLEVELAND AREA ARTS COUNCIL, 108 The Arcade, Cleveland OH 44114. (216)781-0045. Contact: Nina Gibans. Uses artists for direct mail brochures, posters, ads, bumper stickers and programs. Send resume and list of prizes or awards won.

COMPUTER & BUSINESS EQUIPMENT MANUFACTURERS ASSOCIATION, 1828 L St. NW, Washington DC 20036. (202)466-2288. Communications Director: Timothy G. Donovan. Estab: 1916. Uses artists for annual reports, lettering, publicity brochures, signage, technical charts/illustrations, trade magazine ads, trademarks, logos and company publications. Pays $50, covers; $10, inside line art. Buys all U.S. rights. Query with samples. Reports in 4 weeks. SASE. Recently assigned artist graphic design of a series of special coordinated mailings. Portfolio should include examples of association work, especially work for clients in the business world, and be issue-oriented.
To Break In: "Have patience and creativity, don't just copy the style from successful multinational's advertising spots, etc."

CYSTIC FIBROSIS FOUNDATION, 3379 Peachtree Rd. NE, Atlanta GA 30326. Director of Public Relations: Ann B. Watson. Uses artists for brochures, annual reports, public service TV and educational films.

DENVER ART MUSEUM, 100 W. 14th Avenue Pkwy., Denver CO 80204. (303)297-2793. Director of Public Relations: Patricia Stocker. Publications department uses graphic artists.

FIRST BAPTIST CHURCH, 1707 San Jacinto, Dallas TX 75021. Assistant Director/Public Relations: Eloise Wright. Interested in using graphic artists for direct mail brochures, newspapers and interchurch bulletins. Prefers local artists.

GENERAL SERVICES ADMINISTRATION, Bldg. 41, Denver Federal Center, Denver CO 80225. Uses artists in its task of maintaining "an economical and efficient system for the management of government property and records." Professionals interested in being considered for assignment should write for appropriate application forms.

GIRL SCOUTS OF THE U.S.A., 830 3rd Ave., New York NY 10022. Executive Art Director: Michael Chanwick. Uses New York City area artists for direct mail brochures, annual reports, promotions, publications, exhibits, catalogs and posters. Submit printed samples.

GOODWILL INDUSTRIES OF GREATER NEW YORK, 4-21 27th Ave., Astoria, Queens NY 11102. Public Relations Director: Thomas C. Brenker. Uses New York artists for brochure design.

HUDSON COUNTY OFFICE OF CULTURAL & HERITAGE AFFAIRS, Suite 503A, County Administration Bldg., 595 Newark Ave., Jersey City NJ 07306. Director: Charles K. Robinson. Uses artists for direct mail brochures, posters, programs, magazine and newspaper ads, bumper stickers and special projects. Submit resume and published samples.

INTERNATIONAL ASSOCIATION OF INDEPENDENT PRODUCERS, Box 2801, Washington DC 20013. Uses graphic designers for art which pertains to motion pictures, TV, records, tapes, advertising and book/record cover illustrations. Submit tearsheets, photostats or transparencies. Payment by job. Usually buys all future rights.

INTERNATIONAL FENCE INDUSTRY ASSOCIATION, Box 426, Mineral Wells TX 76067. Contact: L. Gordon Nelson. Uses artists for advertising art/design, animated cartoons, convention exhibits, direct mail brochures, graphic design, magazine covers, newspaper advertising layouts (software), newspaper editorial cartoons, sales promotion art (exhibit booths, membership) and signs. Submit rough or finished art samples. Pays $100-500, advertising magazine layout; $400-1,200, brochures. Negotiates rights.

LIVING ARTS MANAGEMENT, 240 E. 76th St., Suite 9F, New York NY 10021. Contact: Peter Klein. Uses artists for direct mail brochures and programs. Mail resume and published samples.

MAINE STATE COMMISSION ON THE ARTS AND HUMANITIES, State House, Augusta ME 04333. Executive Director: Alden C. Wilson. Uses artists for direct mail brochures and posters. Send resume and samples.

MIDDLESEX COUNTY ARTS COUNCIL, 37 Oakwood Ave., Edison NJ 08817. Director: Estelle Hasenberg. Uses artists for programs, posters and direct mail brochures.

THE MONTREAL MUSEUM OF FINE ARTS, 3400 Avenue du Musee, Montreal, Quebec Canada H3G 1K3. Public Relations Counsel: Bill Bantey. Uses local artists for direct mail brochures, posters, annual reports, interior designs, billboards and public service TV spots.

NATIONAL-AMERICAN WHOLESALE GROCERS' ASSOCIATION (NAWGA), 51 Madison Ave., Rm. 1810, New York NY 10010. Editor: Ellen Lusk. Uses artists for membership recruitment literature, public information brochures, operations manuals, training guides, invitations and Educational Exposition announcements. Buys all rights. Query with resume.

NATIONAL BICYCLE DEALERS ASSOCIATION, INC., 29023 Euclid Ave., Wickliffe OH 44092. Contact: Tom K. Sayler. Uses artists for membership recruitment literature, public information brochures, trade show exhibits and magazine graphics. Write.

NATIONAL DRIVE-IN FAST FOOD & SOFT ICE CREAM ASSOCIATION, 14627 Watt Rd., Novelty OH 44072. Contact: Harry J. Kimpel. Uses artists for membership recruitment literature, trade show exhibits, magazine graphics and public information brochures. Query.

NATIONAL EMPLOYMENT ASSOCIATION, 1835 K St. NW, Suite 910, Washington DC 20006. (202)331-8040. Contact: Kenneth Fisher. Uses artists for public information brochures, public service TV spots and trade show exhibits. Pays $30 for TV spot graphics. Buys one-time rights. Mail samples and fees.

NATIONAL INSTITUTE FOR AUTOMOTIVE SERVICE EXCELLENCE, 1825 K St. NW, Suite 515, Washington DC 20006. Contact: Barry McNulty. Uses artists for magazine graphics, audiovisual materials, recruitment literature and public information brochures. Minimum payment: $100, brochure design; $300, cartoon strip. Buys all rights. Call or write.

NATIONAL TELEPHONE COOPERATIVE ASSOCIATION, 2626 Pennsylvania Ave., Washington DC 20037. (202)833-2113. Contact: Suzanne Stack. For rural telephone cooperatives. Uses artists for annual reports, magazine graphics and covers for special publications. Pays $150 for brochure design. Buys all rights. Arrange interview to show portfolio.

PROVINCETOWN ART ASSOCIATION, 460 Commercial St., Provincetown MA 02657. (617)487-1750. Director: Sheila Miles. Uses graphic artists for membership literature, catalogs and posters.

J. B. SPEED ART MUSEUM, 2035 S. 3rd St., Louisville KY 40208. (502)636-2893. Contact: Caroline B. Cavett. Uses artists for membership literature, catalogs, posters, brochures and public service TV spots.

TOPEKA ARTS COUNCIL, INC., 216 W. 7th, Topeka KS 66603. (913)357-7119. Contact: Susan Ellis. Public Relations Department uses artists for membership literature, catalogs, posters, public service TV spots, other promotion services and membership drives.

UNION OF AMERICAN HEBREW CONGREGATIONS, 838 5th Ave., New York NY 10021. (212)249-0100. Director of Publications: Ralph Davis. Estab: 1873. Produces books, filmstrips and cassettes for Jewish school children. Uses artists for book covers and illustrations. Pays $50-200 for illustrations. Payment determined by job. Mail samples or write for interview. Material copyrighted. Reports in 3 weeks. SASE. Free catalog.

U.S. DEPARTMENT OF INTERIOR, Bureau of Land Management, c/o General Services Administration, Federal Supply Schedule, Bldg. 41, Industrial Group 899, Lakewood CO 80225. Contact: Mary Gaylord. Uses artists for exhibits, displays, graphics and illustrations. Payment arranged through Purchase Requisition before work begins. Query with samples.

U.S. DEPARTMENT OF LABOR, Division of Graphics Services, 200 Constitution Ave. NW, Washington DC 20210. Contact: Donald Berry. Uses artists for information booklet design, illustrations, slides or other audiovisual materials, documentary films and displays. Query.

U.S. ENVIRONMENT PROTECTION AGENCY, Region V, 230 S. Dearborn, Chicago IL 60604. Chief, Graphics Arts Section: M. G. Neumann. Uses artists to prepare badges, books, pamphlets, decals, exhibits, displays, illustrations, periodicals and posters. "Payment specified at time of employment." Query with samples.

U.S. INFORMATION AGENCY, 1776 Pennsylvania Ave. NW, Rm. 523, Washington DC 20547. Contact: Chief, Contract and Procurement Division. Seeks to "promote a better understanding of the U.S. in other countries." Uses artists for architectural and engineering services, books, pamphlets, exhibits, displays, films, graphics, periodicals, posters and printing. Employment on a contractual basis. Submit resume and samples.

U.S. POSTAL SERVICE, Bidder's Mailing List Application (PS Forms 7429 and 7424A). Write to nearest U.S. Postal Service Region, Contracts and Supply Management Branch: New York NY 10098; Philadelphia PA 19101; Memphis TN 38166; Chicago IL 60694; or San Bruno CA 94099. Indicate service or commodity of interest and geographical marketing area preferences. Applicants placed on mailing list to receive appropriate solicitations for bids, proposals or quotations. Some services included are exhibit/display designs, sales promotion, advertising/training films and instructional material. Also of interest to bidders is Department of Commerce publications, *Commerce Business Daily* which publicizes federal government proposed procurements. Available by subscription from Superintendent of Documents, Government Printing Office, Washington DC 20402, and can be examined at Small Business Administration offices and most government purchasing activities. The SBA publication *U.S. Government Purchasing and Sales Directory,* a guide to selling or buying in the government market, is also available from the Superintendent of Documents and may be examined at SBA offices.

Businesses and Manufacturers

A & A TROPHY MANUFACTURERS, 11523 Harry Hines, Dallas TX 75229. (214)241-3211. Contact: William P. Hess. Manufactures trophies, plaques and tools for working light and decorative metal. Uses artists for sales literature, in-house publications, catalog covers, trophies and employee handbooks. Pays $10,000 for 32-page color catalog. Query with 3x5" transparencies.

ACHIEVEMENT PRODUCTS, INC., 64 Franklin St., East Orange NJ 07017. Contact: Philip Van Rooyen, Jr. Specializes in the production of emblematic jewelry, plaques, mementos, advertising specialties, badges, gifts, awards, trophies and Lucite embedments. Query.

ADVANCED R&D, INC., Box 7600, Orlando FL 32804. Personnel Administrator: Ruth Byron. Acts as "broker" between client companies and technical illustrators desiring temporary assignments in various localities. Pays negotiated hourly rate determined by nature and complexity of job. "A resume of experience is the best initial contact with us. We have recently paid $7 per hour for technical illustrations, and need technical art from time to time for catalog covers, internal/external publications and technical charts, manuals, IPB's."

ALGOMA NET COMPANY (formerly Goshen Mfg. Co.), 310 4th St., Algoma WI 54201. Contact: Jim Westrich. Manufactures porch, patio and yard furnishings. Designer should submit resume and transparencies of sample designs.

THE ALL AMERICAN CO., 15 Bergen Blvd., Fairview NJ 07022. (201)945-0234. Contact: C. Schneider. Manufactures embroidered emblems, heat transfer litho prints and heat transfer sublimation prints. "We deal in trends: CB radios, motorcycles, novelty, fashion and children's designs." Uses artists for original art for emblems and prints. Pays up to $250.

ALLCRAFT COMPANY, 306 S. Edinburgh Ave., Los Angeles CA 90048. (213)653-0819. Contact: Alfred Laszloffy. Designs and makes custom planters, pedestals and restores antique furniture. Uses local artists for catalog covers/layouts and direct mail brochures. Query.

THE ALLEN COMPANY, Box 528, Broomfield CO 80020. Advertising Manager: George Cavanaugh. Manufactures gun cases, archery cases and accessories. Uses artists for sales literature and annual catalogs. Query.

R. C. ALLEN, INC., 678 Front Ave. NW, Grand Rapids MI 49501. Vice President: Jan Hjelm. Business machines firm. Uses artists for sales literature, public service newspaper ads, catalog covers/illustrations, exhibit designs, technical charts/illustrations, company logos and labels. Query with samples.

ALLYEAR FUND RAISING, INC., 1462 Erie Blvd., Schenectady NY 12305. Contact: D. Joseph Fay. Uses artists for layout, paste-up, retouching and lettering for direct mail; design ideas for custom memo pads, stationery, inspirational and gag signs; marketable ideas to print and sell by mail. Submit samples. SASE.

AMERICAN AIR FILTER COMPANY, INC., 215 Central Ave., Louisville KY 40207. (502)637-0295. Manager: Robert C. Braverman. Estab: 1925. Develops, manufactures and sells equipment and systems to improve and control air quality. Uses artists for annual reports, catalog covers/layouts, direct mail/publicity brochures, displays, exhibit designs, posters, recruitment literature, technical charts/illustrations and company publications. Negotiates payment. Buys all rights. Write for interview.

AMERICAN PHOTO & MODELS, 19400 Collins Ave., Miami Beach FL 33160. Uses artists for sales literature, public service newspaper ads, in-house publications, recruitment literature, catalog covers/illustrations and displays. Prefers local artists. Query with published samples.

AMERICAN SILVER EDITIONS, 1140 Bloomfield Ave., West Caldwell NJ 07006. Contact: David P. Pearson. "We at times commission artists and sculptors to create our programs and ideas." Negotiates payment. Buys all rights. Sometimes buys reprint rights to non-exclusive designs. Send photos or transparencies of previously produced work.

ARROW HANDICRAFT CORPORATION, 900 W. 45th St., Chicago IL 60609. (312)927-2000. Director of Product Development: Kenneth S. Caplan. Manufactures children's craft hobby kits. Submit idea(s) in writing only. Company provides a form for product design disclosure. Pays 2-3% royalties. December-June is best time for new product review.

ARTISAN'S & CRAFTSMEN, (Division of Environmental Educators, Inc.), 2100 M St. NW, Washington DC 20037. (202)466-3055. Creative Director: B. Brooke Dyer. Estab: 1972. Publishes mail order catalogs of art crafts. Uses artists for catalog covers/layouts, direct mail brochures and advertising. Pays $100 minimum for brochures. Negotiates payment. Buys exclusive rights. Query. Reports in 3 weeks. SASE. Portfolio should include successful direct mail/mail order experience.

ATLAS SUPPLY COMPANY, 11 Diamond Rd., Springfield NJ 07081. (201)379-0550. Art Director: Joseph Batich. Estab: 1929. Carries tires, batteries and auto accessories. Uses artists for filmstrip animation, catalog covers/layouts, packaging, POP displays and technical charts/illustrations. Call for interview. Reports in 2 weeks.

AVERY LABEL, 777 E. Foothill Blvd., Azusa CA 91702. (213)969-3311. Contact: Bob Cardinali. Estab: 1935. Manufactures pressure-sensitive labels/labeling equipment. Assigns 100 freelance jobs annually. Uses local artists for catalog layouts and packaging. Pays $3-25 per hour for label designs. Buys all rights. Call for interview. Reports in 1-2 weeks.

BARON PUTTERS INC., 156 W. Providencia, Burbank CA 91502. (213)846-9113. Contact: Roberta Bailey. Manufactures golf putters. Uses artists for sales literature, catalog covers, displays and ads. Arrange interview to show portfolio.

ED BENJAMIN & SONS, 516 East St., San Diego CA 92101. Art Buyer: Ed Benjamin. Mail artwork or design ideas for jewelry. Will also review tearsheets, photo copies or transparencies of previous work.

BEROL USA, Berol Corporation, Eagle Rd., Danbury CT 06810. (203)744-0000. Sales Promotion Manager: Marvin Zimmerman. Estab: 1856. Manufactures writing instruments. Assigns 6 freelance jobs annually. Uses artists for catalog covers/layouts, magazine ads, direct mail/publicity brochures, displays, newspaper ad layouts, packaging, POP displays and posters. Payment determined by number of illustrations. Query with samples.

BLONDER-TONGUE LABORATORIES, INC., 1 Jake Brown Rd., Old Bridge NJ 08857. Director of Communications: George Bahue. Manufactures TV signal distribution equipment for schools, hotels, hospitals and communities. Uses artists for catalog cover designs, spec sheet layouts, POP display designs and direct mail brochures. Buys all rights. Pays $10, line drawings; "up to several thousand dollars," catalog layout, POP display. Submit resume. Reports in 2 weeks.

BLUE CROSS AND BLUE SHIELD OF MICHIGAN, 600 Lafayette E., Detroit MI 48226. Art and Production Manager: Robert H. Jones. Uses Detroit artists to prepare designs for annual reports, posters, brochures and related items. Query with printed samples.

BOBBY G, 112 W. 34th St., New York NY 10001. (212)736-8977. Contact: Bob Gershin. Manufactures accessories and toy novelties. Uses artists to design stuffed animals, dolls, children's shoe bags and pajama bags. Pays $3-4 minimum for finished samples with patterns. Mail samples.

THE BOFFER CORPORATION, 111 8th Ave., New York NY 10011. Art Buyer: John Bifano. Uses New York artists for direct mail promotion. Mail samples. SASE. Reports in 2 weeks.

BRINE SPORTS LTD., 1450 Highland Ave., Needham MA 02192. (617)444-9200. Contact: Ed Merritt. Manufactures soccer and lacrosse equipment. Uses artists for sales literature, catalog covers, athletic clothing and displays. Send photos or transparencies.

BROCKWAY GLASS COMPANY, Glassware Division, 30 Evergreen Place, East Orange NJ 07018. (201)672-0600. Director of Design: Raymond H. Van Blargan. Manufactures glass tableware. Assigns 200-300 freelance jobs annually. Uses artists for design of decorations on glassware (tumblers for drinking). Pays $100-250 for color sketches on acetate and finished art. Buys all rights. Query or call for interview. Reports in 3 weeks. SASE.

Cartoon illustrations for heat transfers and embroidered emblems bring artists up to $250 from The All American Co. This heat transfer was purchased from artist Nancy Lloyd on the basis of its uniqueness, originality and humorous subject matter.

BUSINESS CONSULTANTS OF AMERICA, Box 4098, Waterbury CT 06704. Vice President, Advertising/Sales Promotion Manager: William J. Nolan. Uses artists for sales literature and catalog covers/illustrations. All media accepted. Negotiates payment. Sample payment: $20 per hour.

CADLYN'S INC., 10250 N. 19th Ave., Phoenix AZ 85021. (602)944-9649. President: Dan Cain. Estab: 1971. Manufacturers coats of arms and personalized items. Assigns 6-12 freelance jobs annually. Uses artists for catalog covers/layouts, consumer magazine ads, direct mail brochures and lettering. Negotiates payment. Pays $10 minimum. Buys exclusive rights. Query with samples. Reports in 2 weeks.

CENNEX, Box "G", St. Paul MN 55165. (612)451-5151. Contact: Robert W. Trevis. Estab: 1931. Regional farm supply cooperative. Assigns 2-20 freelance jobs annually. Uses local artists for filmstrip animation, annual reports, direct mail brochures, employee handbooks, POP displays, posters, trade magazine ads and company publications. Payment determined by bids. Pays $20-35 per hour, layout and design; $15-25 per hour, keylining; $25-50 per hour, illustrations. Buys one-time rights. Query. Reports in 2 weeks. SASE. Recently assigned artist layout, design, keyline of financial services book, Christmas items, newspaper insert, products and prices.

CENTRAL ENGRAVING CO., CENTRAL LABEL CO., 394 Atlantic Ave., Boston MA 02210. Contact: James McEwan. Photo engraving firm. Uses local artists mostly at Christmastime for layout, technical art, paste-up, lettering and retouching. Send resume before calling for interview.

CHAMPION BUILDING PRODUCTS (formerly U.S. Plywood), 1 Landmark Square, Stamford CT 06921. Contact: Louis A. Scelta. Manufactures and sells wood products. Uses artists for sales literature, catalog covers, exhibit designs, displays and employee handbooks. Prefers local artists.

CHESSIE SYSTEM, 4100 Terminal Tower, Cleveland OH 44101. (216)623-2353. Director Visual Media/Design: Franklyn J. Carr. Uses artists for covers and illustrations, exhibit designs, handbooks and technical charts. Also interested in railroad-related fine art and sculpture. Mail resume and samples.

CLIMB HIGH, INC., 227 Main St., Burlington VT 05401. (802)864-4122. Advertising/Sales Promotion Manager: Bob Olsen. Wholesale/retail manufacturer of backpacking gear and outdoor clothing. Uses artists for sales literature, catalog covers and illustrations. Mail samples or arrange interview.

COAST FEDERAL SAVINGS, 855 S. Hill St., Los Angeles CA 90014. (213)623-1351. Contact: Shirley Berger. Buys art for offices through interior design firm. Artist must handle sales. Send resume and slides. Occasionally needs commercial artists.

COASTAL STATES LIFE INSURANCE CO., Box 56189, Atlanta GA 30343. Director: Max Busbee. Uses artists for sales materials and annual reports. Arrange interview to show work.

COCO JOE'S PRODUCTS, 45-552 D Kam Hwy., Kaneohe HI 96744. President: Don Gallacher. Estab: 1961. Manufactures jewelry and curio items. Uses artists for catalog covers/layouts, direct mail brochures, displays, employee handbooks, exhibit designs, packaging, POP displays and product design. Buys 20 designs annually. Pays $75-300. Call for interview. Reports in 2 weeks. SASE.

CONSO PRODUCTS COMPANY, 261 5th Ave., New York NY 10016. Contact: Ed Goodman. Trimmings manufacturing firm. Uses local designers for creation of new decorative trim styles.

CORNELL INDUSTRIES INC., 6909 Eton Ave., Canoga Park CA 91303. (213)883-9166. Contact: Bill C. Cornwell. Manufactures iron-on heat transfers and die-cut flock letters and numbers. Uses artists for sales literature, in-house publications, catalog covers, exhibit designs, lettering and cartoon designs. Prefers local artists. Query with samples.

CREATIVE AWARDS BY LANE, Suite 1567-75, Elmhurst Rd., Elmhurst Village, Elk Grove Village IL 60007. (312)593-7700. Art Buyer: Don Thompson. Manufactures plaques, trophies, loving cups, jewelry and advertising specialties. "Our needs are not excessive, but we're always looking for creative award ideas." Uses artists for design of creative jewelry, awards and logotypes. Pays $50 minimum for award idea.

CROVATTO MOSAICS INC., 1085 Yonkers Ave., Yonkers NY 10704. (914)237-6210. Contact: Costante Crovatto. Executes all types of murals for public buildings, churches and synagogues. "We generally recommend the artist to our client in need of a mosaic mural. Our firm, for ethical reasons, does not submit color renderings." Query with artwork or design ideas.

CUNNINGHAM ART PRODUCTS, INC., 1422 Kelton Dr., Stone Mountain GA 30083. (404)296-0333. Vice President: William Bromley. Manufactures adult hobby crafts. Uses local artists for catalog covers/layouts, magazine ads, direct mail brochures and product designs. Buys all rights. Query with samples. Reports in 2 weeks. SASE.

CURTISS CAMPERS, INC., Curtiss WI 54422. (715)223-4478. Manufactures folding tent campers. Uses artists for sales literature.

DAIWA CORPORATION, 14011 S. Normandie Ave., Gardena CA 90249. Contact: James W. Redfield. Manufactures and distributes complete line of sport-fishing rods and reels. We are "only interested in new or unusual techniques that lend themselves to highly effective printed materials." Prefers local artists.

DELTONA CORP., 3250 SW 3rd Ave., Miami FL 33129. Contact: Bill Gentry. Community builder. Works with artists in Florida on posters and b&w and color art for publications.

DINSMORE INSTRUMENT COMPANY, 1814 Remell St., Flint MI 48503. (313)744-1330. President: R.C. Dinsmore. Estab: 1927. Designs, develops and engineers custom products in the instrument, electronics, mechanical and pneumatics fields. Assigns 20-30 freelance jobs annually. Uses artists for catalog layouts, direct mail brochures, displays, packaging, design of instrument cases/product exteriors, signage, trade magazine ads, trademarks and logos. Payment determined by time spent. Pays $10-500. Buys all rights. Query. Reports in 2 weeks. SASE. Recently assigned artist reverse rotation of series of highly accurate special dials; design mailing piece for new product; design label; line drawing of new product from blueprints. Portfolio should include accurate mechanical art with costs and/or list of satisfied customers.
To Break In: "Learn how to do what you are trying to sell. Be capable of making camera-ready copy. Keep to an agreed deadline. Hang around a printing office to learn the necessity of sharp, square layouts so you can learn the importance of the bottom line being parellel with the first line. Learn to spell and proofread your work. Keep up with today's trends!"

DOCUTEL CORPORATION, Box 22306, Dallas TX 75222. Publications Manager: P.W. Orlebeke. Estab: 1967. Manufactures automated teller machines for financial institutions. Assigns 10 freelance jobs annually. Uses artists for annual reports, publicity brochures, technical charts/illustrations, trade magazine ads, trademarks and logos. Pays $10-15 per hour. Buys all rights. Submit tearsheets or photos. Reports in 2 weeks. SASE. Recently assigned artist brochure design for new product.

DUOFOLD, INC., Drawer A, Mohawk NY 13407. (315)866-4000. Contact: Douglas J. Pirnie. Manufactures tennis and golf shirts, tennis shorts and underwear. Query with samples.

THE E. T. GROUP, LTD., 230 5th Ave., Rm. 808, New York NY 10001. (212)889-5959. Contact: Carole Hibel. Estab: 1976. Sales and merchandising organization. Assigns 200 freelance jobs annually. Uses artists for product design of needlepoint and crewel. Payment determined by design salability. Query with samples. Reports in 4-6 weeks.

EINSON FREEMAN DETROY BERGEN CORPORATION, 1801 Pollitt Dr., Fairlawn NJ 07410. (202)797-8000. Executive Creative Director: Robert C. Jennee. Firm deals in POP display and sales promotion. Uses artists for catalog covers, annual reports and liquor display art. Art varies from industrial to cosmetic subject matter.

ELDER MANUFACTURING CO., Box 273, St. Louis MO 63166. Contact: Mick Zoll. Manufactures sportswear and men's and boys' wear. Uses artists for sales promotion/ad layouts and direct mail brochures. Prefers local artists. Arrange interview.

ELKA TOYS, 200 5th Ave., Suite 524, New York NY 10010. Contact: Irving Kwasnik. Manufactures infant toys such as "Klutch Me", Trixie, Chubbies and Cuddle Cat. Uses artists to design ideas for stuffed toys. Payment on completion. Reports in 1 week.

EVLOW PRODUCTS COMPANY, 1015 Chestnut St., Philadelphia PA 19107. Contact: John F. Slack. Manufactures pharmaceutical capsules. Uses artists for advertising art, catalog design, trademarks and package design.

FISHER'S GATEWAY SUPPLY, 1725 E. 4th St., Sioux City IA 51101. Contact: Henry H. Fisher. Wholesale gift firm. Seeks design ideas for giftware and party goods. Submit rough ideas and "asked price" for finished art. Buys exclusive rights. Reports within 10 days.

A.L. GARBER CO., 600 N. Union St., Ashland OH 44805. Contact: D.R. Foster. Uses artists for advertising art, catalog illustrations/covers, direct mail packages, folding carton design, premiums and direct response items. Write for interview. SASE. Reports in 2 weeks.

GENERAL MOTORS CORPORATION, 3044 W. Grand Blvd., Detroit MI 48202. (313)556-2017. Contact: Art Director. Estab: 1908. Manufactures cars and trucks. Uses local artists for annual reports, direct mail/publicity brochures, employee/student handbooks, lettering, posters, technical charts/illustrations, trademarks, logos and company publications. Payment determined by time spent for photo retouching, degree of difficulty for illustrations, where work will appear and reputation of artist. Call for interview or mail samples that can be filed for future reference (slides, printed pieces) along with price information. Buys all rights. SASE.

GENERAL STONE & MATERIALS CORPORATION, Box 1198, Roanoke VA 24006. Art Buyer: L. Donald Repass. Manufactures wholesale crushed marble, stone and building marbles, landscape aggregates and imported Italian marbles. Pays $50-150 for cartoons and brochure design. Pays on acceptance. Query with resume. Will then consider artwork, design ideas and cartoons (related to construction) submitted by mail, and will also look at samples of style in the form of tearsheets of previously published work, photocopies or transparencies. Submissions should be in ink. Reports in 1 month.

GEORGIA-PACIFIC CORPORATION, 900 SW 5th Ave., Portland OR 97204. Creative Services Director: Ted Haines. Manufactures building products, pulp, paper and chemicals. Uses artists for direct mail brochures, annual reports, billboards, interior design, posters, catalogs, spec sheets and print collateral. Prefers local artists. Sample payment: $25-30 per hour, design; $20-25 per hour, finish. Query with resume and printed samples.

GOLDEN STATE BOX FACTORY, 810 S. Kohler St., Los Angeles CA 90021. (213)627-9807. President: C. Romick. Estab: 1966. Publishes gift and decorative wood novelty boxes. Uses artists for packaging and product design. Buys 50 annually. Pays $25-250, lettering; $25-550, original art; $25-200, adaptive art from other media. Buys all rights. Query with samples. SASE. Reports in 3 weeks. Recently assigned artist to create a line of index and recipe cards for recipe box line.
To Break In: "Be current with the times. Try to anticipate new trends before the public is aware of them — i.e. the craze for Art Nouveau."

GUARANTEE RESERVE LIFE INSURANCE CO., 128 State St., Hammond IN 46320. Vice President: Richard C. Nevins. Uses artists for direct mail brochures, graphic designs and insurance sales promotion art. Query with resume and samples and arrange interview. Reports in 30 days.

HARRIS CORPORATION, Computer Systems Division, 1200 Gateway Dr., Fort Lauderdale FL 33309. Advertising Manager: David Soule. Uses local artists for sales literature and employee handbooks. Payment determined by time spent or job.

HELENOR TRADING CORPORATION, 60 Marbledale Rd., Tuckahoe NY 10707. (914)337-7373. Contact: Norm Ament. Specializes in sewing notions and writing instruments.

Uses artists for sales promotion/advertising, layouts, package design and direct mail brochures. Arrange interview to show portfolio.

HERITAGE MINT, 527 Ceres Ave., Los Angeles CA 90013. President: F.A. Meyers. Uses designers/sculptors for coins, medallic jewelry and medallions on contract for commercial design use or commemorative use. Also looking for medallic sculptors who can model and carve out master plaster or epoxy patterns from designated artwork. Payment determined by whether work is original or rendered from detailed instructions. Buys exclusive rights. Query with photos or transparencies.

HIGH POINT GLASS & DECORATIVE COMPANY, Box 101, High Point NC 27261. President: A.W. Klemme, Jr. Manufactures church/memorial windows and ecclesiastical craft work (stained glass windows, bevel plate set in zinc, clear leaded glass, leaded art glass and imported and domestic glass). Uses artists for window designs and stained glass painting. Submit pen and ink, line and wash art, or photos or color transparencies. Previously used work OK.

HOLLYWOOD PRESBYTERIAN MEDICAL CENTER, 1300 N. Vermont, Los Angeles CA 90027. Contact: Susan Piper. Uses artists for catalogs, layouts, lettering and public relations art. Pays on acceptance. Prefers to deal directly with artists. Query with resume before sending samples.

GEORGE C. INNES & ASSOCIATES, 517 Broad St., Elyria OH 44035. (216)323-4526. President: George C. Innes. Estab: 1960. Provides complete advertising services for accounts — art, writing and printing. Assigns 25-50 freelance jobs annually. Uses artists for annual reports, catalog covers/layouts, magazine ads, direct mail/publicity brochures, displays, employee handbooks, exhibit designs, layouts for newspaper ads, product design (marine boat products/travel trailer industry), technical charts/illustrations, trademarks, logos and company publications. Payment determined by time spent for keyline/line illustrations. Pays $4-10 per hour, keyline/line illustrations; $4-12 per hour, continuous-tone illustrations; $8-250, paintings. Query with samples. Buys limited reproduction rights. Reports in 2 weeks. SASE. Recently assigned artist 6 illustrations for 4-color brochure.

INTER-AMERICAN FOUNDATION, 1515 Wilson Blvd., Rosslyn VA 22209. Contact: Mel Asterken. Agency seeks artists with both writing and design backgrounds for information booklet design and other illustrations for printed material. Call or write.

JENSRISON DESIGN, INC., (Williams Hudson America, Inc.), 505 Park Ave., New York NY 10022. Advertising Manager: Ingrid S. Olsen. Uses local artists for sales literature, public service newspaper ads, in-house publications and technical charts. Query.

HOWARD JOHNSON COMPANY, 222 Forbes, Braintree MA 02184. Graphics/Design Manager: Robert C. Downing. Uses artists for sales promotion literature, menu design, children's menu (entertainment) design, annual reports, catalog covers/illustrations, exhibit designs and displays. Prefers local artists. Fees are usually daily, hourly or by job. Query with samples.

JOULE TECHNICAL CORPORATION, Rte. 22 W., Union NJ 07083. Contact: E.N. Logothetis. Engineering firm. Uses artists for advertising gimmicks, graphic sales promotion, audiovisual presentations and exhibit equipment. Pays $300 average for camera-ready art.

KCL CORPORATION, Hodell & Prospect, Shelbyville IN 46176. (317)392-2521. Director: Timothy Lee Deatm. Estab: 1912. Packaging manufacturer. Assigns 5-10 freelance jobs annually. Uses artists for slide animation, industrial magazine ads, direct mail/publicity brochures, displays, exhibit designs and packaging. Negotiates payment. Pays $25-70, bag design art; $100-400, brochures/line art/design; $5-45, slides. Query with samples. Reports in 1 week. SASE. Recently assigned artist to design descriptive bag.

LA HAYE BRONZE (formerly A.J. Bayer Company), 14060 Gannet St., Suite 101, Santa Fe Springs CA 90670. (213)921-9436. Manager: Les Skinner. Art metal manufacturing firm; specializes in corporate identification. Works in bronze, aluminum, nickel-silver, brass and stainless steel. Produces plaques, tablets, symbols, letters, signs and sculptured castings. Uses artists for lettering, trademarks and exhibit design. Mail samples. Reports in 30 days.

LANELLO RESERVES, INC., Box 1227, Santa Barbara CA 93102. Vice President: Murray L. Steinman. "We are looking for original art creations, interesting unusual and beautiful fine art objects." Buys all rights. Submit ideas or photos or transparencies.

LE FEBURE CORPORATION, Box 2028, Cedar Rapids IA 52406. Manager, Advertising/Sales Promotion: William R. Needham. Specializes in bank equipment-security systems. Uses artists for in-house publications material, exhibit designs, displays and sales literature. Prefers working by mail.

LEISURE LEARNING PRODUCTS, INC., 50 Greenwich Ave., Greenwich CT 06830. (203)661-2777. Advertising/Sales Promotion Manager: R. Bendett. Manufactures educational products. Uses artists for sales literature, in-house publications, recruitment literature, catalog covers/illustrations, exhibit designs and displays. Pays $10-25, minimum for product illustration. Query with photocopies, designs and line drawings.

LETRASET CONSUMER PRODUCTS LTD., Wotton Rd., Ashford, Kent England TN23 2JU. 0233-24421. Marketing Manager: J.C. Hunt. Manufactures dry rub down transfers and craft kits. Assigns 100 freelance jobs annually. Uses artists for displays, exhibit designs, artwork for transfers, trade magazine ads, trademarks, logos and newspaper ad layouts. Negotiates payment. Pays $25-50 for 7x5' decoupage illustrations. Buys all rights. Query. Reports in 1 week. SASE.

LINCOLN MINT, 1 S. Wacker Dr., Chicago IL 60606. Manufactures commemorative medallic coins, tokens and medals. Submit photos or transparencies of previously produced work. Pays $500-1,200 for 12" bas-relief design produced to specs. Buys exclusive minted product rights.

LOMBARDO MINT, Box 525, Derby Line VT 05830. President: O.N. Lombardo. Designers of commemorative medals. "We would appreciate receiving information concerning fees charged, or royalties usually received, along with information on other medal designs they have worked on previously." Negotiates payment. Buys exclusive rights. Submit photos.

The Whole Kit & Kaboodle Co., Inc., a craft manufacturing company, uses local artists for product designs and illustrations. This floral stencil design by Tom Burgio was purchased for $75. Minimum payment for a design is $25.

McCLOSKEY & CO., BUILDERS, Box 16098, Philadelphia PA 19114. Public Relations Director: James A. O'Donnell. Uses local artists for direct mail brochures and interior design. Pays $200 minimum per page for direct mail brochures. Mail samples.

THE MARKET PLACE, Shops at Glen Lochen, 39 New London Turnpike, Glastonbury CT 06033. (203)633-8391. Promotion Director: Gretchen Fairweather. Estab: 1974. Shopping center. Assigns 50+ freelance jobs annually. Uses artists for consumer magazine ads, direct mail/publicity brochures, displays, newspaper ad layouts and posters. Negotiates payment. Pays $15-1,000, series of newspaper ads; $10-35, posters; $100-3,000, decorating material. Buys all rights. Query with samples. Reports in 2 weeks. SASE. Recently assigned artist to do series of Christmas ads and costume designs.

FRANK MARTINEAU, INC., 7204 Clarendon Rd., Washington DC 20014. Art Buyer: Jill M. Wettrich. Uses artists for advertising art/design, book jacket design, calendar art, calligraphy, cartoons, catalog illustrations/covers, convention exhibits, decorative spots, graphic design, letterheads, lettering, magazine covers/editorial illustrations/layouts, newspaper advertising layouts (software), posters, books, services sales promotion art, signs, theater programs/posters and TV commercials. "We are association managers, operating a number of national organizations. Our needs are not regular except in the case of the weekly, biweekly, monthly and bimonthly magazines and annual directories that we publish for our client associations." (These include: *Association Trends Weekly* and publications for Public Relations Society, National Association of Government Communicators and other professional groups.) An idea sketch is initially preferred. SASE.

MEDALLIC ART COMPANY, Old Ridgebury Rd., Danbury CT 06810. Contact: Carol Cipot. Will offer commissions to those who qualify for constant needs. Pays $500-1,000 per 12" model. Send photos of bas-relief sculpture.

MERRIBEE NEEDLECRAFT CO., 2904 W. Lancaster, Fort Worth TX 76107. Buyer: Betsy Vance. Manufactures needlecraft designs. Purchase price of $25-125 includes finished model, scale drawing of design for stencil, complete instructions on color and stitch codes and any necessary diagrams. Buys all rights. Submit resume before sending original art.

METRO TV SALES, 485 Lexington Ave., New York NY 10017. Director of Research and Promotions: Mel Harris. Assistant, Promotion: Joanne Salvia. Metromedia company and broadcast time sales representative. Uses artists for sales literature, in-house publications, annual reports, catalog covers/illustration, displays and technical charts.

MIKASA (AMERICAN COMMERCIAL, INC.), 25 Enterprise Ave., Secaucus NJ 07094. Director, Product Development: Alfio Maugeri. Manufactures dinnerware and gift boxes. Submit original art for 10" dinner plate during September-October and January-February. Pays $50 minimum for dinnerware pattern design. Reports in 2 weeks.

GORDON B. MILLER AND CO., 100 E. 8th St., Cincinnati OH 45202. Contact: J.C. Miller. Manufactures custom-designed business awards, emblems, jewelry, rings, plaques and trophies. Uses artists for product design. Query with resume and samples.

MYERS-SUZIO, INC., Box 888, Wallingford CT 06492. (203)269-4424. Vice President: Robert P. Suzio. Estab: 1951. Manufactures and sells gifts, figurines, awards and jewelry. Assigns 12 freelance jobs annually. Uses artists for product design. Payment determined by degree of difficulty. Pays $50, b&w line drawings; $350-1,500, metal or clay models. Buys exclusive rights. Query with samples. SASE. Recently assigned artist to design bust for award coin and eagle pewter statue.

NORTH-SOUTH ARTS, Box 10273, Winston-Salem NC 27108. Contact: Mary Nordstrom. Booking and advertising service for performing artists, principally in the college and prep school market. Uses artists for newspaper and trade magazine ads, brochures, programs and posters. Query by mail.

OPEN BOOK MARKETING CORPORATION, 2966 Biddle, Wyandotte MI 48192. Vice President: David Sucher. Estab: 1973. Book store franchise; provides in-store promotional aids and POP displays. Assigns 25-50 freelance jobs annually. Uses artists for displays, exhibit designs, lettering, POP displays and newspaper ad layouts. Pays $5-15 per hour, signs/displays; $500-1,000, sales brochures. Query. Reports in 2 weeks. SASE.

OPEN DOOR ENTERPRISES, INC. (formerly Open Door Company), 1201 Comstock St., Santa Clara CA 95050. Contact: Fred Fortune. Manufactures string, wire, doodle and mosaic art. Uses artists for kit and color-in poster designs. Write for color brochure illustrating designs. Payment for exclusive rights to new designs from $50-300. Reports in 2 weeks.

PENNWAX WORKS, INC., 5200 Unruh Ave., Philadelphia PA 19135. Art Buyer: James Beales. Candle designs (wax-filled glass) should be submitted before May 1. Sizes restricted to 4¼x9¼" and 8¾x9¼". Submit full-color illustrations (color-separated art), a series of 6 designs, watercolor, paint and color media. Previously published work OK if used for different purpose. Sample rates: $60, design idea or full-color art; $100-200, 6-design series. Reports as soon as possible.

PLASTICS MANUFACTURING CO., 2700 S. Westmoreland, Dallas TX 75224. Contact:

Richard Cone. Manufactures dinnerware. Pays $300-350 for dinner plate design. Submit finished art within a 10" circle. "No royalties or guaranteed purchases. We pay flat price. Requirements may be 4 or 5 designs per year up to 25. The purchased designs become our property."

PRG INC., 3914 W. Market St., Akron OH 44313. President: Donald C. Nelson. Estab: 1958. Mail order firm for recreation equipment and supplies. Uses out-of-town artists for catalog covers/layouts, direct mail brochures, employee handbooks and packaging. Pays $10 per hour for illustrations. Query. Reports in 2 weeks. SASE.

PROCON INCORPORATED, 30 UOP Plaza, Algonquin and Mt. Prospect Rds., Des Plaines IL 60016. Public Relations Director: Fred Pfeifer. International engineering and construction company. Uses local artists for direct mail brochures, capabilities literature and publicity releases. Query with resume.

PROFESSIONAL TRAINING AIDS, 38 W. Bethune, Detroit MI 48202. Art Buyer: H. Hook. Produces direct mail sales and motivation programs for businesses. Uses artists for envelope inserts, comics, wall posters and meeting guides. Submit spot drawings, cartoons, tearsheets or photocopies as examples of style. Previously published work OK. Pays $25 on acceptance for spot drawing. Reports in 10 days.

QUALITY INDUSTRIES, 2293 Amber Dr., Hatfield PA 19044. (215)822-0125. Art Director: John Harrison, Jr. Estab: 1912. Manufactures woven bookmarks and wall hangers. Assigns 30 freelance jobs annually. Uses artists for advertising art, product design and illustrations. Pays $25 maximum for advertising and design. Buys all rights. Mail artwork. Reports in 2 weeks. SASE.

R&D CREATIONS, 20722 S. Belshaw, Carson CA 90746. (213)537-0993. Contact: Ralph Dyer. Specializes in needlepoint, crewel and rug designs. Accepts 8x10" acrylic 8-color designs on paper. Rug designs should be on 24x26" or 20x27" graph paper. All colors must match company yarn — samples provided on request. Minimum payment: $20 per 8x10" design; $35 per rug design. Arrange interview to show work.

RAYMOR/RICHARDS, MORGENTHAU, INC., 734 Grand Ave., Ridgefield NJ 07657. (201)941-0220. "Though we are manufacturers, our main use of designers and artists are for other manufacturers who we represent as a sales and marketing arm. We select the design person they will work with. Normal compensation is mutually agreed to advance against a royalty of 3%, negotiable depending upon the items designed." Send resume and transparencies. Reports in 2-3 weeks.

RED BARN SYSTEM, 6845 Elm St., McLean VA 22101. (703)893-2111. Public Relations Director: Sherry More. Estab: 1961. Fast food restaurants. Assigns "dozens" of freelance jobs annually. Uses artists for filmstrip animation, catalog covers/layouts, direct mail/publicity brochures, displays, employee handbooks, exhibit designs, newspaper ad layouts, packaging, POP displays, recruitment literature, signage, student handbooks, technical charts/illustrations and company publications. Query.

RED COACH GRILLS, 222 Forbes Rd., Braintree MA 02184. Contact: Laurance A. Read. Uses local artists for sales literature and in-house publications. Arrange interview to show portfolio.

REVCO DRUGSTORES, INC., 1925 Enterprise Pkwy., Twinsburg OH 44087. Assistant Vice President/Corporate Relations: Charles R. Dehaven. Uses artists for annual reports. Pays $20 per hour minimum. Prefers local artists. Mail samples of printed work.

RUEBRO MANUFACTURING, 1002 Grand St., Brooklyn NY 11211. (212)782-6885. President: Jack Goldstein. Estab: 1955. Produces buckles and jewelry. Uses artists for direct mail brochures, newspaper ad layouts and ring/buckle design. Buys 1,000 designs annually. Pays $10-15 for ring/buckle designs. Query with samples or call for interview.

SMART STYLE INDUSTRIES, 112 W. 34th St., New York NY 10001. (212)564-0760. Contact: Howard Feigelman. Specializes in boys' wear. Uses artists for direct mail brochures. Prefers local artists. Interested in seeing samples of work from inception to completion.

Serious subjects such as illustrations of endangered species, fruit and other decorative designs are of interest to Brockway Glass Company, a glass tableware manufacturer. Brockway assigns 200-300 designs annually, including this "Flower-of-the-Month" collector's series designed by Leo Art Studio. Payment ranges from $100-250.

SOLOMSON PRODUCTS, 4 Beacham St., Everett MA 02149. Contact: Nathan Solomson. Manufactures place mats. Uses artists for 4x5" color transparencies for place mats, preferably scenes from the eastern U.S., rural/ocean scenes and good animal pictures, including pedigree dogs and cats. Pays $50 minimum on acceptance. Submit tearsheets. SASE. Reports in 1-2 weeks.

THE SOUTHLAND CORPORATION, 2828 N. Haskell Ave., Box 719, Dallas TX 75221. Director Corporate Design: Hans A. Streich. Food retailer, dairy products processor, fast food manufacturer and truck lessor. Uses artists for direct mail brochures, annual reports, package design and store interior design. Prefers local artists but will work by mail. Query with resume and samples of printed work.

SPERBER ASSOCIATES, INC., 79 Pleasant Ave., East Bridgewater MA 02333. Contact: Joseph C. Nadolny. Uses artists for direct mail brochures, annual reports, billboards, posters, public service TV spots and interior designs. Query with samples.

SYSTEMA CORPORATION, 150 N. Wacker Dr., Chicago IL 60606. Contact: Jack Snader or Steve Knapp. Uses artists for direct mail promotion, audiovisuals, package design and sales promotion art for technical product and technical/medical illustrations. Query with resume and samples and arrange interview. SASE. Reports in 4 weeks.

SYSTEMS EXCHANGE, INC., 5101 W. St. Charles Rd., Suite E, Bellwood IL 60104. President/Art Buyer: Louis J. Klufetos. Sells new and reconditioned data processing machines. Uses artists for sales literature/brochures, graphic design, greeting card art, animated cartoons, lettering, letterheads, magazine editorial illustrations/layouts, newspaper advertising layouts (software and hardware) and posters. Previously published work OK. Artwork may be rough. Query with resume before sending tearsheets, photocopies or transparencies.

T.J.B. ASSOCIATES, INC., 555 White Plains Rd., Tarrytown NY 10591. (212)931-4300. Advertising/Sales Promotion Manager: Jerry Wolk. Insurance agency and brokerage selling insurance. Uses artists for sales literature, lettering, advertising, direct mail brochures, greeting cards and posters. Query with samples.

3P INDUSTRIES, INC., Box 242, Oakland NJ 07436. Contact: Ben Walker. Wall accessories firm. Interested in design ideas for wall plaques in sizes 9½x23¾"; 9x12"; 8x10"; 4x5"; or 5x7". Uses artists for graphic design, posters, calendars and advertising art. Will look at artwork relevant to the following subjects: children, bathrooms, whimsy, portraits of people, animals, pets, landscapes and cartoons. Submit samples of published work.

TILBURY FABRICS INC., 261 5th Ave., New York NY 10016. Contact: Al Hazen or Alan Weisberg. Produces printed fabrics, bedspreads, draperies, slipcovers and upholstery. Interested in buying designs as needed. Designers in New York City area may write for interview.

2 NEEDLES LTD., 1283 Madison, New York NY 10028. Contact: W. Johnson or P. Chaarte. Uses artists for needlepoint design. Previously published work OK. Sample payment: $100, 14x14" design for 10/14 gauge. Royalty arrangements considered. Buys sole rights. Submit original art or photocopies. Reports in 2 weeks-1 month.

U.S. POSTAL SERVICE, Bidder's Mailing List Application (PS Forms 7429 and 7424A). Write to nearest U.S. Postal Region. Contracts and Supply Management Branch: New York NY 10098; Philadelphia PA 19101; Memphis TN 38166; Chicago IL 60694; or San Bruno CA 94099. Indicate service or commodity of interest and geographical marketing area preferences. Applicants placed on mailing list to receive appropriate solicitations for bids, proposals or quotations. Some services included are exhibits/display designs, sales promotion, advertising/training films and instructional material. Also of interest to bidders is Department of Commerce publications, *Commerce Business Daily,* which publicizes federal government proposed procurement. Available by subscription from Superintendent of Documents, Government Printing Office, Washington DC 20402, and can be examined at Small Business Administration offices and most government purchasing activities. The SBA publication *U.S. Government Purchasing and Sales Directory,* a guide to selling or buying in the government market, is also available from the Superintendent of Documents and may be examined at SBA offices.

UNITED ARTS, RHODE ISLAND, 45 The Arcade, Providence RI 02903. Contact: John B. Briley. Service bureau for art organizations in Rhode Island; also conducts United Arts Fund drive for the state. Works with graphic designers.

UTA FRENCH AIRLINES, Tishman Airport Center, 9841 Airport Blvd., Rm. 1000, Los Angeles CA 90045. Public Relations Manager: Liliane Brassine. Uses artists for sales literature, catalog covers/illustrations, public service newspaper ads and multimedia slide presentations.

VOGART CRAFTS CORPORATION, 230 5th Ave., New York NY 10001. Contact: Nancy

Edwards. Produces needlework items. Uses artists for product design. Pays $40 minimum. Mail samples or call for interview.

WALLACH MANUFACTURING, 8834 National Blvd., Culver City CA 90230. Contact: Don Davis. Wholesale jeweler. "We need someone to do line drawings for ad mats. We supply the product and need an illustration of same."

THE WHOLE KIT & KABOODLE CO., INC., 8 W. 19th St., New York NY 10011. (212)675-8892. Art Directors: James Fobel/James Boleach. Estab: 1974. Manufactures craft kits. Uses local artists for product design and illustrations. Payment determined by job. Pays $25 minimum. Buys all rights. Call or write for interview. Reports in 1 week. SASE.

WILTON CORPORATION, 2400 E. Devon Ave., Des Plaines IL 60018. Advertising Manager: Randy Bartow. Industrial machinery company. Uses artists to prepare sales literature and catalog covers/illustrations. Prefers local talent. Payment determined by job. Query with samples.

WILLIAM E. WRIGHT CO., 1 Penn Plaza, New York NY 10001. Contact: Edward Bogosian. Produces apparel/decorator trimmings, tapes and accessories for the home sewing market and manufacturers; decorative packaging; and art needlework. Uses artists for needlework and crewel designs. Pays $25-250. Mail resume and samples. Reports in 3 weeks.

WYANDOTTE GENERAL HOSPITAL, 2333 Biddle Ave., Wyandotte MI 48192. (313)282-2400. Community Relations Director: Mike Jenkins. Estab: 1926. Assigns 40-100 freelance jobs annually. Uses artists for annual reports, direct mail brochures, displays, employee handbooks, newspaper ad layouts, posters and company publications. Payment determined by time spent, degree of difficulty or number of illustrations. Pays $25-100 for illustrations for publications and brochures. Buys all rights. Query or call for interview. Reports in 2 weeks. SASE.
Portfolio: Include samples of human response, persons reacting to situations and events.

Educational Institutions

ADELPHI UNIVERSITY, Garden City NY 11530. Public Relations Director: Ron Cannava. Uses local graphic designers skilled in publications, advertising and promotion art with ability to carry project through from design to camera-ready art. Sample payment: $25 per 3 hours. "No drop-in visits, please!"

ARKANSAS STATE UNIVERSITY ATHLETIC DEPARTMENT, Box 1000, State University AR 72467. (501)972-2077. Sports Information Director: Jerry Schaeffer. Estab: 1950. Promotes and publicizes all phases of athletic program. Assigns 5-10 freelance jobs annually. Uses artists for catalog covers/layouts, direct mail/publicity brochures, displays, posters, recruitment literature, trademarks and logos. Pays $50-100, publicity brochure cover; $50-100, posters with athletic schedule; $10-35, cartoons/caricatures. Query with samples. SASE. Reports in 1 week. Recently assigned artist to complete series of logos with mascot involved in 6 different sports.
To Break In: Study the designs of athletic publicity brochures, posters and pamphlets.

BRIAR CLIFF COLLEGE, 3303 Rebecca St., Sioux City IA 51104. Publicity and Publications Director: Doug Smith. Uses artists on limited basis for direct mail brochures and posters. Pays $50 minimum. Query with samples.

BROWARD COMMUNITY COLLEGE, 225 E. Las Olas Blvd., Ft. Lauderdale FL 33301. Contact: Dr. Ellen Chandler. Uses artists for promotion for performing arts activities. Query with resume, awards won and published samples.

CALIFORNIA BAPTIST COLLEGE, 8432 Magnolia Ave., Riverside CA 92504. (714)689-5771. News Bureau Director: Carmen Sandoval. Estab: 1950. Promotes Christian higher education. Assigns 10-15 freelance jobs annually. Uses local artists for annual reports, catalog covers/layouts, direct mail/publicity brochures, displays, newspaper ad layouts, lettering, recruitment literature and company publications. Payment determined by time spent. Query with samples. Reports in 3 weeks. SASE.

CALIFORNIA INSTITUTE OF TECHNOLOGY, Ramo Auditorium, Office of Public Events (332-92), Pasadena CA 91125. Contact: Joe Farmer. Buys designs for brochures from October-June. Artwork may be rough or finished 10x14" art. Pays $10 per hour minimum. Query with resume. On approval, send tearsheets, photocopies or transparencies.

THE CATHOLIC UNIVERSITY OF AMERICA, Office of Public Relations, Washington DC 20064. (202)635-5600. Editor: Robert E. Simanski. Estab: 1887. Emphasis on graduate studies in liberal arts and 9 professional schools. Uses artists for catalog covers/layouts, direct mail/publicity brochures, recruitment literature, student handbooks and college publications. Negotiates payment. Pays $25, illustrations; $10-15 per page, tabloid page layout and design. Query with samples and call or write for interview. SASE. Reports in 1 week. Recently assigned artist design of development brochure, redesign of in-house newsletter, format design for new magazine and revised design for alumni tabloid.
Portfolio: "Include samples of work done for other educational institutions, particularly line art, which we use frequently."
To Break In: Get a staff job in a publications office — become familiar with all stages in the development of a publication from initial planning through story development, layout and printing. Learn to expedite the production process.

CHAMPLAIN COLLEGE, 232 S. Willard St., Burlington VT 05401. (802)658-0800. Editor: Steve Harris. Estab: 1878. Private junior college oriented towards career education. Uses local artists for posters, publicity brochures and college magazine. Query. SASE. Reports in 3 weeks. Recently assigned artist to illustrate article about 1 of the last rides on the Orient Express in Europe.

CHAPMAN COLLEGE, 333 N. Glassell St., Orange CA 92666. (714)633-8821. Director of Publications: Chrystal Kopf. "Our office seeks the person best qualified to develop a specific project in terms of skills, availability, reliability and price. In general, most of the job is done by the office staff with the freelancer contributing illustration or layout ideas." Uses local artists for direct mail brochures, annual reports, posters, catalogs, viewbooks and slide shows. "We often work with advanced students and pay less than the usual commercial rates." Query with samples of printed work.

CHATTANOOGA STATE TECHNICAL COMMUNITY COLLEGE, 4501 Amnicola Hwy., Chattanooga TN 37406. Public Relations Director: Mary Ann Carter. Uses artists for posters, public service TV spots and letterhead logo. "We are a state institution and must obtain at least 3 bids on jobs over $50." Send printed samples.

CLAREMORE JUNIOR COLLEGE, College Hill, Claremore OK 74017. Dean of Information/Development: Larry Fowler. Uses artists for direct mail brochures, posters and public service TV spots. Sample minimum rates: $5, cartoons; $26, graphics for TV spot. Send printed samples.

COLLEGE OF ST. FRANCIS, 500 Wilcox, Joliet IL 60435. Public Relations Director: Mariene W. Stubler. Uses local artists for annual reports and public service TV spots.

COPPIN STATE COLLEGE, 2500 W. North Ave., Baltimore MD 21216. Contact: Ruth N. Cole. Urban state college with coed enrollment of 2,218. Query. Will work by mail if necessary.

DREXEL UNIVERSITY, Philadelphia PA 19104. Director of Public Relations: James M. Wilson. Uses local artists for direct mail brochures and posters.

D'YOUVILLE COLLEGE, 320 Porter Ave., Buffalo NY 14201. Public Relations Director: James J. Zolczer. Uses artists for posters and admissions department publications. Alumni department also uses artists. Query Rosetta Rico.

THE EXPERIMENT IN INTERNATIONAL LIVING, 13 Kipling Rd., Brattleboro VT 05301. (802)257-7751. Public Relations Director: Richard Friedman. Estab: 1932. Promotes mutual understanding. Assigns 30 freelance jobs annually. Uses artists for catalog covers/layouts, consumer magazine ads, direct mail/publicity brochures, newspaper ad layouts, lettering, POP displays and company publications. Payment determined by time spent, degree of difficulty, number of illustrations, where work will appear and reputation of artist. Pays $250-1,000, catalog layout; $15-100, sketch for newsletter; $200-500, posters. Buys exclusive rights. Query with samples. Reports in 1-2 weeks. SASE.

FINDLAY COLLEGE, 1000 N. Main St., Findlay OH 45840. Public Relations Director: Vicki W. Shirden. Uses local artists for annual reports, posters, catalog cover design, student recruitment literature and TV spots. Write.

FORT VALLEY STATE, State College Dr., Fort Valley GA 31030. College/Community Relations Director: J. C. Hill, Jr. "Most work has been done through printing companies or from services rendered on campus or by campus art department." Uses local artists for direct mail brochures, posters, public service TV spots and postcard transparencies. Pays $30-115. Query with resume and/or printed samples.

GALVESTON COMMUNITY COLLEGE, 4015 Avenue Q, Galveston TX 77550. Contact: Susannah Moore. Uses local artists. Typical assignment is direct mail brochure design for which minimum pay is $20.

GODDARD COLLEGE, Plainfield VT 05667. Contact: Janet Kotler. Uses artists for direct mail brochures, posters, newspaper ads, press releases and feature stories. Negotiates payment. Send samples.

GREENVILLE COUNTY LIBRARY, 300 College St., Greenville SC 29601. Public Relations Director: Verena L. Bryson. Uses local artists for posters, direct mail brochures, interior design, billboards, annual reports and public service TV spots.

HAMILTON COLLEGE, Clinton NY 13323. Public Relations Director: George Newman. "We deal almost entirely in b&w. Spring and fall are the best times to query. We rarely hire artists for more than 2 or 3 jobs a year." Local artists should send samples of work on annual reports, direct mail brochures, catalog and other publications. Average payment: $120, catalog picture layout; $1,200, fund-raising brochure.

ILLINOIS WESLEYAN UNIVERSITY, 210 E. University, Bloomington IL 61701. Public Relations Director: Jerry D. Bidle. Coed Methodist college. Uses local artists for direct mail brochures, annual reports, posters and artwork for slides. Pays $5-7 per hour minimum.

JEFFERSON PARISH LIBRARY, Box 7490, Metairie LA 70010. Public Relations Director: Maurice D. Walsh, Jr. Uses local artists for direct mail brochures, annual reports and posters. "Most material has to be suitable for reproduction by mimeograph." Pays $25 maximum for poster design or annual report. Has paid $250 for oil portrait.

LE MOYNE COLLEGE, Le Moyne Heights, Syracuse NY 13214. (315)-446-2882. Undergraduate liberal arts college. Uses artists for catalog covers, lettering, publicity brochures, student handbooks and college publications. Payment determined by degree of difficulty and number of illustrations. Pays $25, cover art; $15, line drawings. Query with samples. SASE. Reports in 4 weeks. Recently assigned artist to design catalogs and Christmas card.

MEHARRY MEDICAL COLLEGE, 1005 18th Ave. N., Nashville TN 37208. Director of Public Relations: Jean Morton. Interested in hearing from artists with experience in graphic design, illustrations and TV commercials.

MIDDLE TENNESSEE STATE UNIVERSITY, Box 58, Murfreesboro TN 37132. Contact: Paul Keckley. "Our outside work is done on bid basis only." Uses local artists. For information on freelance work for alumni department, contact Dr. Homer Pittard, director, alumni affairs.

MUNCIE PUBLIC LIBRARY, 301 E. Jackson St., Muncie IN 47305. Public Relations Director: Karen Crane. Uses local artists for posters and small light-weight sculptures made of unbreakable material.

OHIO NORTHERN UNIVERSITY, Ada OH 45810. Public Relations Director: Karen Winget. Methodist university located in rural setting with enrollment of 2,700. Offers degrees in liberal arts, engineering, law and pharmacy. Uses local artists for direct mail brochures, posters, annual reports, catalogs and recruitment brochures. Sample payment: $150, cover design for 2-part catalog; $30, poster.

OKLAHOMA CITY UNIVERSITY, 2501 N. Blackwelder, Oklahoma City OK 73106. (405)521-5348. Public Relations Director: David Graham. Estab: 1904. Liberal arts college. Offers graduate degrees in business, education, criminal justice, music and law. Assigns 40 freelance jobs annually. Uses local artists for catalog covers, consumer magazine ads, direct mail/publicity brochures, employee/student handbooks, newspaper layout ads, POP displays, recruitment literature, technical charts/illustrations and company publications. Payment determined by degree of difficulty. Pays $5-25 per hour for design and layout. Buys first and subsequent rights. Call for interview. SASE. Reports in 2 weeks. Recently assigned artist to design law school placement bulletin.

PFEIFFER COLLEGE, Box D, Misenheimer NC 28109. Public Relations Director: William S. Reasonover. Artists in the Charlotte/Greensboro/Winston-Salem, North Carolina area should submit samples of work, especially for student recruiting brochures. Pays $100-1,200.

PIKEVILLE COLLEGE, Sycamore St., Pikeville KY 41501. Public Relations Director: E. David Clevinger. Work is seasonal. Samples may be held for 8 months. Uses artists for direct mail brochures, posters and public service TV spots. Send printed samples.

QUINCY COLLEGE, Quincy IL 62301. Public Relations Director: Donald Werr. Uses artists for direct mail brochures and annual reports.

QUINIPIAC COLLEGE, Mt. Carmel Ave., Hamden CT 06518. Public Relations Director: Pierre Masse. Uses artists for direct mail brochures and publications. Pays $150 for catalog cover design and mechanicals. Query and arrange interview.

LUTHER RICE SEMINARY, 1050 Hendricks Ave., Jacksonville FL 32207. Contact: Dr. Hollis L. Green. Uses artists for direct mail brochures, posters, annual reports and interior designs. "Our needs are now limited, but we plan to expand." Query with samples.

RIPON COLLEGE, Ripon WI 54971. Public Relations Director: Kenneth Lay. Uses artists within 200-mile radius for brochures, direct mail, annual reports and posters.

ROCKFORD COLLEGE, 5050 E. State St., Rockford IL 61101. Sports Information Director: Walter H. Wells, Jr. Uses artists for direct mail brochures and posters related to campus sports activities. Query with resume and printed samples.

ROCKHURST COLLEGE, 5225 Troost Ave., Kansas City MO 64110. (816)363-4010. Director of News and Publications: Allie Patrick. Estab: 1910. Liberal arts, coed Jesuit college with masters program in business administration. Assigns 4-20 freelance jobs annually. Uses local artists for catalog covers, direct mail brochures, newspaper ad layouts and technical charts/illustrations; especially needs graphs and life-like sketches of people. Pays $25-250, poster design; $25-100, catalog cover. "We buy the right to use any piece of artwork as much as we wish for any purpose we wish." Call or write for interview. Reports in 2 weeks. Recently assigned artist to design total catalog cover and maps to guide people to campus. Portfolios should include cover displays, graphs and several line drawings.
To Break In: "It is important that the artist has imagination and an accurate sense of detail with the ability to work well when limited to 1 or 2-color art."

ROCKY MOUNTAIN COLLEGE, 1511 Poly Dr., Billings MT 59102. Contact: Public Relations Director. Uses local graphic artists for advertising design, publication illustrations, direct mail brochures and public service TV spots. Send samples.

OSCAR ROSE JUNIOR COLLEGE, 6420 SE 15th St., Midwest City OK 73110. Contact: Coordinator, Public Information Office. Uses local artists for direct mail brochures, billboard art, posters and public service TV spot art. Negotiates payment. Send resume.

Snowball Your Way to Success

The secret to success in art is to choose a large field needing art, but one that isn't supplied by professional artists, says Ted Watts, one of the nation's most successful freelance sports artists.

Watts began his career by selling sports art to colleges and universities. "I didn't know one professional artist trying to sell to them fulltime. Most (schools) relied on student art for covers for press guides, programs, sports facts books, portraits and other needs," says Watt.

After finding 2,000 schools with athletic programs, Watts developed brochures containing a series of action sports sketches detailing his services and mailed them to 150 schools. Fifteen replied favorably. Then he visited four nearby colleges and universities for meetings with sports information directors. "I took samples and got work from three schools," recalls Watts.

Ted Watts' wife told him, "All you do is talk about having your own studio — so start one!" Watts did and now he sells his sports illustrations to 65 colleges and universities coast to coast.

"When you select a field like this, you'll find it has a snowballing effect. Soon it does its own selling. That first year I spent 90% of my time selling myself and my art. Today, I work 95% of my time, supplying 65 colleges and universities coast to coast."

What other fields are lucrative for freelance artists? According to Watts, country and western stars and political organizations are possibilities. For the latter, "Start by contacting state representatives, senators, and the governor in your state. Paint campaign material. I thought seriously of entering this field. It would have a snowballing effect too."

And don't wait. "I was always talking about freelancing. Finally my wife told me, 'All you do is talk about having your own studio — so start one! Otherwise you'll still be talking about it when you're 50.' If you plan it out, you can make it big now."

— *Ben Townsend*

ST. AUGUSTINE'S COLLEGE, Oakwood Ave., Raleigh NC 27601. Public Relations Director: Ron H. Phillips. Uses local artists for direct mail brochures, annual reports and posters at this coed Episcopal college.

SAINT JOSEPH'S COLLEGE, Rensselaer IN 47978. Contact: Public Relations Director. Graphic artists interested in assignments at this coed Catholic college should query with printed samples.

ST. LAWRENCE UNIVERSITY, Canton NY 13617. Assistant Director of Public Relations: Robert A. Clark. Uses local artists in preparing brochures and mailers. Send printed samples.

SAINT MARY'S COLLEGE OF CALIFORNIA, Moraga CA 94575. Public Relations Director: Michael R. Vernetti. Uses local artists for direct mail brochures, posters and newspaper art. Pays $20 minimum for newspaper illustration. Query with printed samples.

ST. PAUL BIBLE COLLEGE, Bible College MN 55375. Assistant to President: John C. Briggs. "We've done most of our own work on a limited budget, and used artwork of our printers, but we would consider $50-75 fees." Uses artists for direct mail brochures, posters and magazine ads. Send printed samples.

ST. THOMAS AQUINAS COLLEGE, Rte. 340, Sparkill NY 10976. Director of College Relations: L. John Durney III. Needs artists during late spring, as most publications are sent to press by May 1. "I must insist on honoring only mail contacts, whether local or not. Further contact will be initiated from this office." Uses artists for descriptive literature design (cover and interior), advertising mechanicals, logo design and posters.

THE SCHOOL FOR INTERNATIONAL TRAINING, Kipling Rd., Brattleboro VT 05301. (802)257-7751. Public Relations Director: Richard Friedman. Estab: 1932. Assigns 50 freelance jobs annually. Uses artists for annual reports, catalog covers/layouts, consumer magazine ads, direct mail/publicity brochures, exhibit designs, recruitment literature and company publications. Payment determined by degree of difficulty, number of illustrations and where work will appear. Pays $10-1,000. Buys exclusive rights. Query. Reports in 3 weeks. SASE. Recently assigned artist to illustrate newsletter.

ELIZABETH SETON COLLEGE, 1061 N. Broadway, Yonkers NY 10701. Public Relations Director: Mary McGilvray. Private coed college. Uses local artists for direct mail brochures, posters and advertising art.

SHASTA COLLEGE, 1065 N. Old Oregon Trail, Redding CA 96001. (916)241-3523. Contact: Craig O. Thompson. Uses artists for direct mail brochures, annual reports, billboards, posters, public service TV spots and event programs. Work should be b&w line drawings or color separations. Sample payment: $10-20, event program designs; $50, direct mail brochures. Query with resume, published samples and slides.

SIENA COLLEGE, McGuire Hall, Loudonville NY 12211. Public Relations Director: Joseph P. Orzechowski. "We rely on freelance graphic artists exclusively." Uses artists for direct mail brochures, alumni magazines/reports, billboards, airport displays, posters, admissions brochures and capital fund major publications. Pays $15 per hour. "Last year we produced 90 college publications and 141 other jobs." Artists in the state should send samples or arrange interview.

SPARTANBURG METHODIST COLLEGE, Powell Mill Rd., Spartanburg SC 29301. (803)576-3911. Public Information and Publications Director: Pam Nix. Estab: 1911. Uses local artists for filmstrip animation, annual reports, catalog covers/layouts, direct mail brochures, displays, exhibit designs, newspaper ad layouts, lettering, posters, recruitment literature, student handbooks and alumni newsletter. Negotiates payment. Buys rights to use artwork at later date. Query with samples. SASE. Recently assigned artist to produce ad, including concept, copy and typesetting.

SUBURBAN LIBRARY SYSTEM, 125 Tower Dr., Burr Ridge IL 60521. Chief Consultant: Joanne Klene. "Our system provides offset printing services to member libraries. Each library orders its own materials and asks for the names of artists to help design special brochures, letterheads, etc. Also, as a system, we produce many printed items — newsletters, workshop announcements, bookmarks, posters and others — and often need artistic assistance." Uses local artists to design direct mail brochures, annual reports, posters, logos, letterheads and bookmarks. Pays $5-35 per hour, depending on project's complexity. Query with resume and printed samples.

TEMPLE UNIVERSITY, Publications Dept., Room 602, University Services Bldg., Broad and Oxford Sts., Philadelphia PA 19122. Contact: Gail Smith. Uses local artists for direct mail, annual reports and posters. Send 1 piece of representative work to be kept on file. If artist has several good styles, send sample of each. No samples should be larger than 8½x11". Alumni department also uses artists. Contact Rich Wescott at the *Alumni Review*, c/o the above address.

TENNESSEE STATE UNIVERSITY, 3500 Centennial Blvd., Nashville TN 37203. Public Relations Director: Mabel Crooks Boddie. Uses local artists for direct mail brochures, annual reports, fund raising folders and recruiting brochures. Assignments issued on bid basis. Query with printed samples.

THIEL COLLEGE, College Ave., Greenville PA 16125. Public Relations Director: Gerald L. Rasa. Uses artists for direct mail brochures, public service TV spots, interior design, annual reports and posters. Payment determined by job. Send photocopies or samples.

U.S. MERCHANT MARINE ACADEMY, Steamboat Rd., Kings Point NY 11024. Public Relations Director: Martin Skrocki. Uses artists for direct mail brochures and publications. Aluminum department also uses artists. Contact Frank Sinnott.

UNIVERSITY OF IDAHO, Moscow ID 83843. Creative Director: Leo Ames. "The majority of art is straight line-work which can be printed inexpensively. The artwork can be general, rather typical university student-faculty material. I would be interested in seeing art that could be used on a large poster, suitable for high school juniors. We will not place ourselves under any obligation to any outside artist without careful evaluation of his capabilities and our needs." Uses artists for direct mail brochures, annual reports and "promotional pieces for the university or its departments encouraging students to enroll." Payment determined by time spent and/or project. Prefers Idaho artists. Query with resume and printed samples.

UNIVERSITY OF PITTSBURGH AT JOHNSTOWN, Johnstown PA 15904. Coordinator of Information Services: William A. Gillin. Uses local artists for direct mail brochures, posters and public service TV spots. Query with resume.

UNIVERSITY OF UTAH, Lectures and Concerts, Box 200, Salt Lake City UT 84110. Contact: Paul Cracroft. Uses artists for direct mail brochures, posters and newspaper ads. "We are essentially a booking and promoting office for the performing arts. As such, we occasionally need promotional assistance from freelancers. Much of our work is done with artists agencies or management offices, who provide promotional materials which we adapt." Sample payment: $50-85, posters; $60-120, direct mail brochure design. Payment determined by complexity of job and artist's experience. Mail resume, published samples and/or slides.

UNIVERSITY OF WISCONSIN-WHITEWATER, 800 W. Main St., Whitewater WI 53190. University Relations Director: W. E. Zastrow. Uses local artists for direct mail brochures and alumni magazine.

WAUKESHA COUNTY TECHNICAL INSTITUTE, 800 Main St., Pewaukee WI 53072. Manager, Community Relations Dept: William J. Moylan. Uses local artists for direct mail brochures, annual reports, posters and catalogs.Send printed samples.

WAYLAND ACADEMY, Beaver Dam WI 53916. (414)885-3373. Assigns up to 50 freelance jobs annually. Uses local artists for annual reports, catalog covers/layouts, direct mail/publicity brochures, displays, posters, recruitment literature, student handbooks, trademarks, logos and newspaper ad layouts. Pays $10-20 per hour. Buys all rights. Query with samples. SASE. Reports in 1-2 weeks.
Portfolio: Include samples showing style, graphic designs and educational materials done in the past.

WESTMINSTER COLLEGE, 1840 S. 13th E., Salt Lake City UT 84105. Public Relations Director: Lee Douglas. Uses artists for posters and publications. Query with resume or printed samples.

GEORGE WILLIAMS COLLEGE, 555 31st, Downers Grove IL 60515. Public Relations Director: K. Abbott. Uses artists for direct mail brochures, posters and public service TV spots. Query with resume and samples.

Chambers of Commerce & Convention Bureaus

CHICO CHAMBER OF COMMERCE, Box 3038, Chico CA 95926. Contact: Jim Lynch. Uses local artists for preparing brochures.

FERRIDAY CHAMBER OF COMMERCE, Box 11, Ferriday LA 71334. (318)757-2771. Contact: Manager. Estab: 1952. Promotes Ferriday to businesses and vacationers. Uses local artists for publicity brochures. Payment determined by number of copies for lithography. Query.

GADSDEN COUNTY CHAMBER OF COMMERCE, Box 389, Quincy FL 32351. (904)627-9231. Executive Director: Jack P. Strickland. Estab: 1946. Promotes Gadsden County. Assigns 10 freelance jobs annually. Uses artists for direct mail/publicity brochures, newspaper ad layouts, trade magazine ads and publications. Negotiates payment; determined by design, material and printing. Call or write for interview or mail artwork. Reports in 1 month. SASE. Recently assigned artist to design front page for newsletter.

GEORGETOWN CHAMBER OF COMMERCE, Box 655, Georgetown CO 80444. Contact: Dee Barrom. Uses artists for brochures. "We are a very small town and most picturesque. Town calls itself 'Silver Queen of the Rockies'." Query.

GOLIAD COUNTY CHAMBER OF COMMERCE, Box 606, Goliad TX 77963. (512)645-3563. Contact: Directors. Promotes area for purposes of business, industry and tourism. Uses artists for magazine ads, direct mail brochures, newspaper layout ads, posters, publicity brochures, signage, trademarks, logos and publications. Payment determined by project. Query. Reports in 2 weeks. SASE.

GREATER COLUMBIA CHAMBER OF COMMERCE, Box 1360, Columbia SC 29202. Contact: Mike Gibson. Uses local artists for brochures, annual reports, slide film presentations and public service TV spots. Arrange interview to show portfolio.

GREATER HARTFORD CHAMBER OF COMMERCE, 250 Constitution Plaza, Hartford CT 06103. Communications Manager: Charles Robert Hogen, Jr. Uses artists for direct mail brochures, annual reports and 3-screen slide presentations. Pays $50 minimum for brochure design.

McALLEN CHAMBER OF COMMERCE, Box 790, McAllen TX 78501. Publicity Director: Jack McNally. Uses artists for brochures, annual reports, billboards, posters, 16mm films, magazine artwork and bumper stickers. Prefers local artists. Send resume or arrange interview to show portfolio.

METROPOLITAN EVANSVILLE CHAMBER OF COMMERCE, 329 Main St., Evansville IN 47708. (812)425-8147. Director: Joyce Donaldson. Estab: 1887. Assigns approximately 12 freelance jobs annually. Uses local artists for direct mail/publicity brochures, displays, newspaper layout ads, lettering, signage, trademarks, logos and company publications. Buys reproduction rights. Query. Reports in 1 week. SASE. Recently assigned artist to design cardboard modular display.

MIAMI CONVENTION BUREAU, 499 Biscayne Blvd., Miami FL 33132. (305)579-6341. Works with local artists on signs. Query.

OZARKS CHAMBER OF COMMERCE, Box 1, Silver Dollar City MO 65616. (417)338-8210. Manager: Don Richardson. 1870-style colony of Ozark handcraftsmen. Uses artists for sales literature. Will work by mail. Negotiates payment.

ROCKING HORSE, Box 306, Highland NY 12528. Contact: "Bucky" Turk. Convention center. Uses artists for descriptive brochures, exhibits, signs and meeting room decorations. Send samples of published work.

ST. BONIFACE CHAMBER OF COMMERCE (La Chambre de Commerce de St. Boniface), Box 37, Norwood Grove P.O., St. Boniface, Manitoba Canada R2H 3B8. Uses local artists for assignments in Winnipeg area.

SAN MATEO COUNTY CONVENTION & VISITORS BUREAU, 888 Airport Blvd., Burlingame CA 94010. Contact: John G. Steen. Uses local artists for descriptive brochures, exhibits, signs and displays.

SHREVEPORT-BOSSIER CONVENTION-TOURIST BUREAU, Box 1761, Shreveport LA 71166. (318)222-9391. Estab: 1971. Promotes area to tourists. Assigns 10 freelance jobs annually. Uses local artists for catalog covers/layouts, consumer magazine ads, direct mail/publicity brochures, newspaper ad layouts, lettering and posters. Negotiates payment. Call for interview. Reports in 1 week. SASE.

TRI-COMMUNITY AREA CHAMBER OF COMMERCE, 348 Main St., Southbridge MA 01550. Contact: John S. Frykenberg. Tri-Community is made up of Southbridge, a primarily industrial community; Sturbridge, a restored historical village and tourist mecca; and Charlton, an agricultural community. Pays $500 for brochure design. Prefers local artists. Call for interview to show portfolio.

The names of graphic artists are kept on file by the Greater Hartford Chamber of Commerce for future assignments. Mailed samples can lead to assignments such as this illustration by Richard Welling, one of many in a brochure he designed. Brochure assignments usually bring a minimum of $50.

Paper Products

The last birthday card that you received was more than likely designed by a freelance artist. As was probably the gift wrapping that covered the gift that accompanied the card and the paper table settings for the birthday party.

And, to go on. Stationery, postcards, announcements, wall decor, diplomas, playing cards, notebooks and matchbooks are all products of the paper products industry.

Greeting cards are the biggest staple of the industry. It's a $1 billion business with more than 3 billion cards sold annually. Subject matter runs from X-rated to religious. If you're interested in designing greeting cards but don't know what subjects will sell, it's helpful to know that greeting cards reflect the times. When streaking was popular, there were cards based on streaking; when CB sales were booming, so were CB-related cards. But, if you still don't feel you're sure what subjects paper product companies are interested in, there are several other ways to learn what the market is buying.

The most important is to study the market by visiting as many gift and card stores as possible. Or, as Hans Baumgarten, art director of Baumgarten's, advises, "Attend all gift and stationery trade shows and spend some time in the china and gift departments of better gift, jewelry or department stores." Read *Greetings Magazine,* a monthly for the gift and stationery industry, for the latest information in the field.

It's not enough just to have an interesting subject to sell a greeting card design, says Lew Fifield of Creative Papers Inc. "Cultivate and become highly skilled at your own personal style of technique. Be capable of working within deadlines," he advises. In addition, it is important to send as many ideas as possible with a maximum variety of styles. But, regardless of what your style is, you should be familiar with the type and style required by the publisher.

Once you begin studying your potential market, you'll find that greeting cards are primarily vertically proportioned, with space for the title at the top of the folder or card. When designing gift wrapping, note that it may be sold on a roll and should be simple and look good on this type of merchandising device. Most giftwrapping design is based on a repeated pattern.

Although studio cards are extremely popular, you'll find that traditional cards are also in demand by some publishers. So, in addition to cartoon sketches for studio cards, party plates and giftwrapping, fine artists will also find a market for their work here (particularly if they have knowledge of the production process). One company will pay as high as $2,000 for a drawing or oil painting.

Greeting card and paper product companies generally work well in advance to fulfill seasonal needs. Check the Seasonal Needs subheads in the following listings to see how far in advance seasonal ideas must be turned in.

More greeting card markets — names and addresses only — can be found by writing *Greetings Magazine* at 95 Madison Avenue, New York City 10016 and asking about its annual directory of greeting card companies and related firms. And, in addition to working with established paper product firms, check into publishing a few of your own cards for sale to gift shops, boutiques and other specialty shops.

AA SALES, INC., 9600 Stone Ave. N., Seattle WA 98103. Art Director: Gail Gastfield. In business for 25+ years. Publishes posters. "Our needs change from time to time so it would be best to inquire first before sending us art. Then, since the original artwork is usually bulky, heavy and difficult to package for shipment, we suggest that you either submit a sketch or photograph of the artwork for our preview. If we like what we see, we could then make arrangements with you to see the original artwork. In either event you will hear from us within two weeks of receipt of your material. We will return the unwanted materials by first class mail. If you want them returned by airmail or insured, then please include extra postage. Also, if you do submit the full size original artwork, then please include postage for return." Payment varies "depending on the stage the work is in and how much work is required to translate it into a finished product."

ABBEY PRESS, St. Meinrad IN 47577. Creative Director: Gerald Knoll. Estab: 1876. Publishes calendars, stationery, greeting cards and posters. "In trying to reach a general and ecumenical audience, we emphasize aesthetic, educational and religious subjects that are basically Christian without being sectarian." Uses artists for product design and illustration. Buys 200 designs annually. Pays $85 for finished art. Query with samples. No previously published, photocopied or simultaneous submissions. Buys exclusive rights. SASE. Reports in 2 weeks. Submit Christmas cards by October 1. Artist spec sheet available.

ACME GREETING CARD CO., INC., 201 3rd Ave. SW, Cedar Rapids IA 52406. (319)364-0233. Art Director: S. Richardson. Estab: 1928. Publishes funeral director paper specialties; scenes, religious, floral OK. Uses artists for product design and illustration. Buys 5 designs annually. Pays $30 minimum for single color. Query with samples. Line drawings or washes OK; color or b&w. Previously published, photocopied and simultaneous submissions OK. Buys complete rights. SASE. Reports in 1 week.

AFRICA CARD CO., INC., 303 W. 42nd St., New York NY 10036. (212)582-2930. President: Vince Jordan. Estab: 1967. Publishes and uses artists for greeting cards and posters. Buys 25 designs annually. Pays $50 minimum. Mail artwork or call or write for interview. Buys all rights. Reports in 4 weeks. SASE.

AMBERLEY GREETING CARD COMPANY, Box 37902, Cincinnati OH 45237. Art Buyer: Herb Crown. Publishes humorous novelty and studio greeting cards, including risque and non-risque types. Considers the following themes: birthday, illness, hospital, friendship, anniversary, congratulations, please write, miss you, travel cards, thank you, retirement, apology, goodbye, promotion, new home, new car and expectant parents. Uses artists for greeting cards, mottos and bumper stickers. Buys all rights. Reports in 30 days.

AMERICAN CALENDAR COMPANY, Box 69, Greeneville TN 37743. Contact: John H. Kilday III. Uses artists for calendars from March-November. Submit rough or finished inks, line and wash, acrylics or oils. Buys calendar rights.

AMERICAN GREETINGS CORPORATION, 10500 American Rd., Cleveland OH 44144. Director of Recruitment/Creative: Tony Byrd. Publishes seasonal cards, studio cards, figurines, puzzles, calendars, books and games. Buys full reproduction rights. Pays on acceptance. Query with resume, then mail ideas, samples or portfolio.

ANTIOCH BOOKPLATE COMPANY, 888 Dayton St., Yellow Springs OH 45387. Art Director: Ann S. Harris. Estab: 1926. Publishes calendars, bookplates and bookmarks. Specializes in book-oriented, religious, humorous and inspirational art. Uses artists for illustrations. Buys 100-150 designs annually. Pays $50-150, art; $25, bookmark ideas. Mail artwork. Previously published and simultaneous submissions OK. Buys some complete or partial promotional rights. SASE.
To Break In: "Look at our merchandise in a book store; be clever, don't just rework what we have."
Seasonal Needs: Submit calendars 14 months prior to January of that calendar year.

RJR ARCHER INC., Box 3306, Greeneville TN 37743. (615)639-2161. Art Director: Robert T. Casteel. Estab: 1966. Publishes gift boxes and Christmas giftwrapping. Specializes in traditional, high-style and juvenile Christmas designs. Uses artists for product design and illustrations. Buys 23-30 designs annually. Pays $100-200 for gift wrap designs. Mail 10x10" color artwork in February-May. No previously published work. Photocopied and simultaneous submissions OK. SASE. Reports in 2 weeks.

BARKER GREETING CARD CO., DIVISION OF RUST CRAFT GREETING CARDS, INC., Rust Craft Park, Dedham MA 02026. Art Director: Bonnie Zacherle. Publishes studio greeting cards. All designs done on assignment. Pays $60 minimum for complete job (design, blackline key with lettering and hand-separated color overlays). Query with color line drawings or washes. Previously published, photocopied and simultaneous submissions OK only as samples. Buys all rights. SASE. Reports in 4 weeks.

BARNARD ROBERTS & CO., INC., 6655 Amberton Dr., Baltimore MD 21227. Art Buyer: Charles S. Roberts. Publishes greeting cards and stationery primarily for the Catholic religious field — certificates, mass cards, priest Christmas cards, etc. Buys design ideas. Art previously published considered "only if exclusive in our field." Submit seasonal and occasional ideas 6 months-1 year in advance. Sample payment: $75, design idea; $100, color transparency; and $150, full-color art. Buys all rights. Reports in 2-3 weeks.

BARTON-COTTON, INC., 1405 Parker Rd., Baltimore MD 21227. (301)247-4800. Art Director: A. Robert Nohe. Estab: 1928. Publishes religious calendars, stationery and greeting cards. Uses artists for product design and illustrations. Buys 50-60 designs annually. Pays $100-250 for illustrations. Query with samples or artwork. Accepts previously published and simultaneous submissions. Buys all rights. SASE. Reports in 4 weeks.

BAUMGARTEN'S, 1190-A N. Highland Ave. NE, Atlanta GA 30306. (404)874-7675. Art Director: Hans Baumgarten. Estab: 1949. Publishes rice paper tableware and napkin products. Specializes in floral designs similar to expensive Chinese patterns. Uses artists for product design. Buys 12 designs annually. Pays $25-50. Query with sample napkins. Designs must be drawn on 7x7" rice paper napkins (available on request). No previously published, photocopied or simultaneous submissions. Buys all rights. SASE. Reports in 4 weeks.

Antioch Bookplate Company is on the lookout for 100 to 150 designs annually for bookmarks, bookplates and calendars. Payment for a design ranges from $50-150. Calendars should be submitted 14 months prior to when the calendar year begins. This calendar cover was submitted to Antioch by freelance artist Mikki Lippe.

To Break In: "Attend gift or stationery trade shows; spend some time in china and gift departments of better gift, jewelry or department stores."

BEACH PRODUCTS, 2001 Fulford St., Kalamazoo MI 49001. (616)349-2626. Art Director: Virginia Lefkes. Estab: 1941. Publishes paper tableware products. Specializes in general, birthday, special occasion and seasonal subjects. Uses artists for product design and illustration. Buys 75-100 designs annually. Pays $50 minimum for color sketch. Mail color artwork. Accepts previously published submissions. No photocopied or simultaneous submissions. Buys designs outright. No work returned. Reports in 6-8 weeks. July deadline for everyday designs; October for seasonal designs.
To Break In: "A catalog illustrating current line sent on request to show types of designs used. Study current market — not only in paper tableware but other houseware items (giftwrapping, textiles for color trends and type of best selling designs)."

BEN-MONT CORPORATION, Benmont Ave., Bennington VT 05201. Art Buyer: F. Karakaya. Produces giftwrapping. Pays $50 minimum. Previously published work OK. Buys exclusive rights. Mail artwork or design ideas. Reports in 2 weeks.

BIRTH-O-GRAM COMPANY, 1720 Ponce de Leon Blvd., Coral Gables FL 33134. Contact: Melvin M. Schwartz. Specializes in birth announcements. Reprints designs of current cards every 24 months. Might consider new designs before reprinting. Artwork is key-color black with overlays to produce pink, blue and yellow colors and tones. Buys all rights. "Query to see if we're considering new designs."

BRILLIANT ENTERPRISES, 117 W. Valerio St., Santa Barbara CA 93101. Art Director: Ashleigh Brilliant. Estab: 1967. Publishes postcards. All subjects OK. Uses artists for product design and illustrations. Buys up to 200 designs annually. Pays $25 minimum for complete camera-ready word-and-picture design. "Since our approach is very off-beat, it is essential that freelancers first study our line. We supply a catalog and sample set of cards for $1." Submit 5½x3½" horizontal b&w line drawings only. No previously published, photocopied or simultaneous submissions. Buys all rights. SASE. Reports in 1 week.

SIDNEY J. BURGOYNE & SONS, INC., 2120 W. Allegheny Ave., Philadelphia PA 19132. Art Director: Paul F. Montgomery. Estab: 1907. Publishes greeting cards. Specializes in religious and Christmas subjects. Uses artists for product design and illustration for Christmas cards only from September-March. Buys 40-50 designs annually. Mail artwork. No previously published or photocopied submission. Simultaneous submissions OK. Buys all rights. SASE. Reports in 2 weeks.

CELEBRATION CARDS, Box 2052, Falls Church VA 22042. (703)532-8899. Art Director: Linda Spivak. Estab: 1975. Publishes calendars, stationery, note cards and greeting cards. Uses artists for calligraphy, product design and illustration. Buys 36-48 designs annually. Pays $30-75 or royalties for greeting card designs. Query with samples. Submit 4¾x6¾" line drawings. No previously published, photocopied or simultaneous submissions. Buys all rights. SASE. Reports in 3 weeks.

CHAMPION PAPERS, Knightsbridge Dr., Hamilton OH 45020. Art Buyer: John Hildenbiddle. Manufactures fine quality giftwrapping and box wrap papers. All occasion line consisting of geometrics, stripes and abstracts; special occasion line consisting of nautical, patriotic, children, floral, masculine, birthday and wedding patterns; Christmas specialties line. Artwork should conform to 5¼" system of repeat or multiples. Designs considered which will reduce or enlarge slightly to fit this repeat. Each piece of art should be identified with a number or name applicable to the design, and name and address of artist. Pays $75-300. Pays on publication. Buys exclusive rights. Mail original art or design ideas. Reports in 2-4 weeks.

CHARLEY'S CHUCKLE CARDS, Box 45040, Tulsa OK 74145. Art Buyer: Ray Price. Publishes studio greeting cards. Rough ideas may be submitted for 4x9" cards. Pays $25 for finished art. Buys all rights. Reports in 2 weeks.

CHARM CRAFT PUBLISHERS, INC., 34-34th St., Brooklyn NY 11232. Contact: Robert K. Edelmann. Publishes greeting cards and giftwrapping. Interested in designs for all seasons and events. Pays $75-150 depending on size and subject. Buys all rights. Payment on acceptance. Query before submitting samples. Reports in 2 weeks.

COLORTYPE, 4388 E. LaPalma Ave., Anaheim CA 92807. (714)524-9130. Art Director: Mike Gribble. Estab: 1968. Publishes humorous greeting cards and posters. No previously published, photocopied or simultaneous submissions. Buys all rights. SASE. Reports in 30 days.

COLUMBIA MATCH COMPANY, 8500 Station St., Mentor OH 44060. Contact: J. H. Weaver III. "Only on occasion are sketches required at which time we contact a local artist for services." Creative artist's sketches used in multiple colors.

CORONET GENERAL CORPORATION, 151 W. 26th St., New York NY 10001. Art Director: Richard Spitz. Estab: 1956. Publishes calendars, stationery, postcards, invitations and pad items. "We need a chic, classy look." Uses artists for calligraphy, product design and illustrations. Buys 50-100 designs annually. Pays $50-100 for rough art. Query or call for interview. Submit 8x10" b&w drawings. No previously published work. Photocopied and simultaneous submissions OK. Buys exclusive rights. SASE. Reports in 2 weeks.

CPS INDUSTRIES, Columbia Hwy., Franklin TN 37064. Art Buyer: James Blackburn. Publishes giftwrapping. Buys designs for Christmas line and everyday line. Everyday line is comprised of wedding, shower, baby, floral, masculine, abstract, juvenile and birthday category designs. Christmas line uses topical themes such as wreaths, snowmen, Santa Claus, bells, etc. "We prefer a comprehensive sketch at least partially complete, with a layout of the repeat pattern." Prints in 4-color rotogravure. Repeats must be an even division of 18" such as 9", 6", 4½" or 3". Reports usually within 2-4 weeks.

CREATIVE PAPERS, INC., 41 Main St., Jaffrey NH 03452. (603)532-8736. Art Director: Lew Fifield. Estab: 1976. Publishes calendars, stationery, note paper, postcards, greeting cards and posters. Considers all styles and techniques of good quality art; contemporary and traditional. Uses artists for calligraphy, product design and illustrations. Buys 200-300 designs annually. Negotiates payment. Query or write or call for interview. "We will send artist a registration form with letter explaining Creative Papers." Submit 35mm slides or 8½x11" color prints. Accepts previously published, photocopied or simultaneous submissions if they have not been published as cards and the artist has previous publisher's permission. Buys exclusive reproduction rights, reproduction rights for a specified product or the original art and exclusive reproduction rights. SASE. Reports in 3 weeks.
Seasonal Needs: Christmas designs should be in by January or February.
Special Needs: "We are interested in artwork or ideas for 2- or 3-dimensional paper products."
To Break In: " Cultivate and become highly skilled at your own personal style or technique. Be capable of working within deadlines."

CROCKETT COLLECTIONS, Gilfeather Rd., Warsboro VT 05355. (802)896-2821. Art Director: J. L. Anderson. Estab: 1952. Publishes traditional postcards and greeting cards. Uses artists for product design and illustrations. Buys 150 designs annually. Pays $25 minimum for finished art design. Mail artwork. No fine line or airbrush. No previously published submissions. Buys all rights. SASE. Reports in 4 weeks. Submit Christmas designs by March 1.

ELLIOTT CALENDAR CO., 1148 Walnut St., Coshocton OH 43812. (614)622-3113. Art Director: Tom Eaton. Interested in innovative approaches to calendar illustration, technique and unusual subject material. Query before sending tearsheets, photocopies or slides. Transparencies for 4-color reproduction must be of highest quality, technically and aesthetically. Color work should be carefully isolated in protective sleeves. Sizes preferred are 2¼x2¼"; 4x5"; 5x7"; and 8x10". Brief description of locale should be included. Horizontal format only. Buys 1 year exclusive rights to original. Work returned after production run. Reports in 2 weeks. Payment determined by quality of material and use in year published. Calendar producers work 2 years ahead; therefore, careful consideration should be given to subject material that will still be in vogue in 2 years.

ERBE PUBLISHERS, 220 Tyrone Circle, Baltimore MD 21212. Contact: Theodore H. Erbe. Publishes calendars and cards. uses artists for ideas, calendar art, greeting card art, letterheads, lettering and stamp designs. Payment determined by project. Query before sending samples. "It helps if you are a stamp collector."

EUREKA, Box 160, Dunmore PA 18512. Marketing Manager: John A. Yourishen. Manufactures decorations and school and stationery supplies. Uses artists for party decorations, package design, greeting cards and lettering. Pays for finished art on acceptance. Send samples. Reports within 30 days.

THE EVERGREEN PRESS, Box 4971, Walnut Creek CA 94596. (415)825-7850. Art Director: M. K. Nielsen. Estab: 1944. Publishes stationery, postcards, greeting cards, Christmas cards and giftwrapping. Specializes in sophisticated art, humor and unusual Christmas cards. Uses artists for product design and illustration. Buys 150-200 designs annually. Most work paid for on a royalty basis with a downpayment against the royalty. Query or mail artwork. Write for specifications. Previously published, photocopied and simultaneous submissions OK. Buys rights for domestic publication. SASE. Reports in 2 weeks.

FOOTHILLS DISTRIBUTING COMPANY, 1295 Ithaca, Boulder CO 80303. Publishes humorous books and postcards. Uses artists for advertising art and layout. Buys 3-4 designs annually. Pays $5-250. Query with samples. Line drawings and color separations OK. Previously published, photocopied and simultaneous submissions OK.

D. FORER & COMPANY, 511 E. 72nd St., New York NY 10021. Art Director: D. Forer. Interested in sample designs for Christmas and everyday lines for "Cutie Pies" cards. Christmas cards are 6x9" and 4½x6"; everyday cards are 4¾x6½". Pays $40+ for finished art. Buys exclusive rights. Reports in 2 weeks.

FRAN MAR GREETING CARDS LTD., Box 1057, Mt. Vernon NY 10550. (914)664-5060. Art Director: Stan Cohen. Estab: 1957. Produces stationery, gift boxes, greeting cards and canvas bags. No religious themes. Uses artists for product design and illustration. Buys 150-200 designs annually. Pays $45-300. Mail color samples (no larger than 10x12"). Line drawings, washes or color separations OK. No previously published, simultaneous or photocopied submissions. Buys all rights. SASE. Reports in 2 weeks.

FRAVESSI-LAMONT, INC., 11 Edison Place, Springfield NJ 07081. Art Director: Helen M. Monahan. Publishes humorous and juvenile greeting cards. Uses artists for calligraphy, product design and illustrations. Pays $50 minimum. Query. No previously published, photocopied or simultaneous submissions. Buys all rights. No work returned. Reports in 2 weeks.

FREEDOM GREETINGS, Box 715, Bristol PA 19007. (215)785-4042. Art Director: Jerome Wolk. Estab: 1969. Publishes greeting cards. Specializes in subjects depicting people. Uses artists for calligraphy, product design and illustrations. Buys 200 designs annually. Pays $70-125 for greeting cards.

Studio cards, relating to all occasions from birthdays to thank yous, are the specialty of Amberley Greeting Card Company. This particular card was illustrated by Peggy Ward.

Submit 5x7", 10x14" or 9x12" color artwork. Line drawings, washes, and color separations OK. No previously published, photocopied or simultaneous submissions. Buys all rights. SASE. Reports in 1 week. "Be able to draw black people well."
Seasonal Needs: Wants Christmas designs in August; Valentine's Day in December; Mother's and Father's Day in June.

GEME' ART GALLERY, 6234 NE Glisan, Portland OR 97213. (503)236-6678. Art Director: Merilee Will. Estab: 1966. Publishes stationery, postcards, greeting cards, art prints and reproductions. Specializes in publishing artwork and books for use in the craft and stationery industries. Uses artists for calligraphy, product design and illustrations. Buys 35-300 designs annually. Pays $25 minimum for original artwork. Query with color samples. Previously published and simultaneous submissions OK. Photocopies OK only for calligraphy. Buys all rights. SASE. Reports in 4 weeks.

THE C. R. GIBSON COMPANY, 32 Knight St., Norwalk CT 06856. Art Director: Gary E. Carpenter. Estab: 1870. Publishes stationery. Specializes in religious, floral and general notes. Uses artists for calligraphy, product design and illustration. Buys 200 designs annually. Pays $75-125 for full-color note designs. Query with samples. Buys all rights. No work returned. Reports in 4 weeks.

GIBSON GREETING CARDS, INC., 2100 Section Rd., Cincinnati OH 45237. Company is completely art-staff produced and/or deals with a select list of outside artists.

GRAND RAPIDS CALENDAR CO., 906 S. Division Ave., Grand Rapids MI 49507. (616)243-1732. Art Director: Rob Van Sledright. Estab: 1911. Publishes calendars and greeting cards. Specializes in pharmacy, medical and family subjects. Uses artists for advertising art and line drawings. Buys approximately 15 designs annually. Pays $10 minimum. Query with b&w drawings. Previously published, photocopied and simultaneous submissions OK. Material not copyrighted. SASE. Reports in 1 week.

THE GRAPHIC ARTISAN, LTD., 8 Roosevelt Ave., Spring Valley NY 10977. (914)352-3113. Art Director: Peter A. Aron. Estab: 1967. Publishes calendars, stationery, greeting cards, invitations, diplomas, certificates and posters. Specializes in general, romantic and biblical. Uses artists for calligraphy and illustrations. Buys 50-100 designs annually. Pays $10-100, calligraphy; $15-500, illustrations. Mail samples or write or call for interview. Previously published or simultaneous submissions OK. Photocopies OK for submission purposes, not for purchase. Buys all rights. SASE. Reports in 1 week.
Seasonal Needs: Submit Christmas and Jewish New Year's designs 9 months in advance.

GRAPHIC IDEAS, 3108 5th Ave., San Diego CA 92103. Art Director: Jill Timm. Estab: 1971. Publishes general and juvenile calendars, postcards, greeting cards and posters. Uses artists for product design and illustrations. Buys 25-60 designs annually. Pays $50-100, b&w illustrations; $50-500, product ideas; $150-350, color illustrations. Query with samples. No previously published, simultaneous or photocopied submissions. Buys all rights. SASE. Reports in 4 weeks.

GREENTREE PUBLISHERS, INC., 14-16 Greenbaum St., Boston MA 02127. (617)426-0707. Art Buyer: Martin H. Slobodkin. Publishes Christmas cards. Buys U.S. rights. Mail full-color watercolors. Reports in 2 days.

HALLMARK CARDS, INC., 25th and McGee, Kansas City MO 64141. Art Director: Robert Harr. Firm has sufficient art staff and outside contacts to handle present art needs.

HOUSE OF GEMINI, INC., 12775 Lyndon Ave., Detroit MI 48227. Art Director: Jill Knight. Estab: 1973. Publishes calendars, stationery, gift boxes, and greeting cards. Specializes in minority themes. Uses artists for calligraphy, product design and illustrations. Buys 50 designs annually. Pays $25 minimum for finished art. Query with samples. Submit 8¼x11¾" or 5½x7½" line drawings or washes. No previously published or photocopied submissions. Buys all rights. SASE. Reports in 3 weeks.

HOUSE OF HARI INC., 228 Sherman St., Perth Amboy NJ 08861. Art Director: Mr. Paul. Estab: 1970. Publishes calendars, greeting cards, postcards and graphics. Uses artists for product designs and illustrations. Pays $200-2,000, drawings and oil paintings; $150-1,000, watercolors. Query. Submit 8x10" color photos or 35mm slides. No previously published, photocopied or simultaneous submissions. Buys all rights. SASE. Reports in 1 week.

I.T.K. PLASTICS, INC., 49 Congress, Salem MA 01970. (617)744-5787. Art Buyer: I. Kutai. Publishes posters, stationery, plaques, greeting scrolls and album covers. Uses artists for b&w designs. Pencil sketches acceptable. Should have caption or verse. Pays $20-50 for 7x9" design. Payment on acceptance. Reports in 1 week.

KALAN INC., 7002 Woodbine Ave., Philadelphia PA 19151. Art Director: Marty Kalan. Estab: 1963. Publishes greeting cards and posters. Specializes in humorous and "X-rated humorous" subjects. Uses artists for ideas. Buys 100-200 designs annually. Pays $10-20. Query with ideas. SASE. Reports in 1 week.

LAFF MASTERS STUDIOS INC., Drawer T, Merrick NY 11566. Art Director: Sean S. McMahon. Estab: 1956. Publishes humorous greeting cards. Uses artists "for full-color dummies from our ideas. We work with professionals only; must have complete technical experience in greeting card art." Pays $32.50 minimum. "Never submit completed artwork. Query as to our needs and include a few samples of published work — at least 1 in full color, may photocopy the rest. Submit 4x9" pencil or pen and ink sketches on assignment only. If we approve sketch, we will assign dummy for it." No previously published, photocopied or simultaneous submissions. Buys all rights. SASE. Reports in 1 week.

THE LEMON TREE, 118 Forest Dr., Jericho NY 11753. Art Buyer: I. Mendelsohn. Publishes greeting cards and stationery. Floral designs and whimsical styles needed for novelty stationery, informal notes and party invitations. Uses artists for b&w line drawings, line and wash drawings and full-color illustrations (media open). Buys all rights. Sample rates: $25+, design idea; $50+, full-color art; some payments on royalty basis. Previously published work OK. Mail design ideas or artwork. SASE. Reports in 2-3 weeks.

LILAC HEDGES CORPORATION, Box 1046, Santa Barbara CA 93102. (805)965-7061. Art Director: George Conk. Estab: 1958. Publishes stationery, greeting cards, invitations and notes. Specializes in cute designs, formal borders and scenes. Uses artists for product design and illustrations. Buys 75 designs annually. Pays $75-100 for full-color art design. Mail samples. Submit 5x7" or 7⅛x9⅜" designs. No previously published, photocopied or simultaneous submissions. Buys designs outright. SASE. Reports in 2 weeks.

LITTLE CREATURES COMPANY, 7370 N. Iroquois Rd., Milwaukee WI 53217. (414)351-0181. Art Director: Dianne Spector. Estab: 1971. Manufactures framed and matted pictures. Specializes in whimsical styles that appeal to all ages. Uses artists for product design and illustration. Buys 24 designs annually. Pays $25+. Mail 5x7", 8x10", 11x14" or 16x20" line drawings or color work. No previously published, photocopied or simultaneous submissions. Buys all rights. SASE. Reports in 1 week.

ALFRED MAINZER, INC., 39-33 29th St., Long Island NY 11101. (212)786-6840. Art Director: Arwed H. Baenisch. Publishes traditional calendars, postcards and greeting cards. Mail artwork. No previously published or simultaneous submissions. Buys all rights. SASE. Reports in 1-2 weeks.

MAKEPEACE COLONY PRESS, Box 111, Stevens Point WI 54481. (715)344-2636. Art Director: James L. Murat. Estab: 1967. Publishes stationery, greeting cards and posters. Uses artists for calligraphy and art. Buys 30-"several hundred" designs annually. Pays $25+. Query. Previously published work OK. Rights purchased vary. SASE. Reports in 3-4 weeks.

MARK I INC., 1700 W. Irving Park Rd., Chicago IL 60613. (312)281-1111. Art Director: Alex H. Cohen. Estab: 1969. Publishes stationery, greeting cards, wall plaques, puzzles, posters and books. Specializes in humor, tenderness and sensitivity. Uses artists for calligraphy, product design, illustrations and finished artwork. Assigns 300 projects annually. Pays $50-150 for artwork. Mail artwork. Buys exclusive rights on stationery products. SASE. Reports in 2 weeks.

MECHANICAL MIRROR WORKS, INC., 661 Edgecombe Ave., New York NY 10032. (212)795-2100. Art Director: J. Bezzy. Estab: 1942. Publishes greeting cards, posters and mirror graphics. Uses artists for product design and illustrations. Buys 50-100 designs annually.

Pays $30 minimum, product design ideas; $200 minimum, full-color illustrations. Mail artwork if no larger than 8½x11". Color and b&w, line drawings, washes and color separations OK. Submit artwork in transparent plastic sheets for mirror graphics. Accepts previously published, photocopied and simultaneous submissions. Buys American and world rights. SASE. Reports in 3-4 weeks.

MERRY THOUGHTS INC., Bedford Hills NY 10507. Specializes in stationery decoration and design of paperware. Send transparencies or photocopies. SASE.

MESSENGER CORPORATION, 318 E. 7th St., Auburn IN 46706. (219)925-1700. Contact: Fred A. Simon. Uses artists for full-color artwork, art on religious subjects and Bible illustrations. Acceptable media include ink, line and wash, acrylics, oils, scratchboard, woodcuts and sculpture. Sample payment: $750, full-color calendar cover art; $500, monthly full-color illustrations. Query with slides.

Calendars, stationery, note paper, postcards, greeting cards and posters are all of interest to Creative Papers, Inc. This marker illustration was purchased from freelancer Les Morrill for use on a card. "Les is very skilled and dependable. That dependability has become a very important factor in our decision to work with a particular artist."

METROPOLITAN ARTIST, 33046 Calle Aviador, San Juan Capistrano CA 92675. Art Director: Duncan McIntosh. Estab: 1965. Publishes stationery and Christmas cards. Specializes in general, whimsical and religious cards. Uses artists for product design and illustrations. Buys 200 designs annually. Pays $100 minimum for full-color (with words) finished art. Write for specifications. Requests finished art in full color with acetate overlays for bronze or leafing areas. No previously published, photocopied or simultaneous submissions. Buys exclusive greeting card reproduction rights. Reports in 1 week. SASE. Solid-pack deadline: September 15; personalized greetings deadline: January 15.

MICHEL & COMPANY, 1952 Selby Ave., Los Angeles CA 90025. (213)475-5381. Art Director: Dan Neuhar. Estab: 1971. Publishes juvenile and fine/graphic art greeting cards. Uses artists for layout, product design and illustrations. Buys 50 designs annually. Pays $25-50 for designs and illustrations. Mail samples or call for interview. Submit 5x7" b&w or color art. No previously published, photocopied or simultaneous submissions. Buys exclusive rights. SASE. Reports in 2 weeks.

MILLER DESIGNS, INC., 9 Ackerman Ave., Emerson NJ 07630. (201)265-7133. Contact: W. McDermot. Greeting card firm. Interested in seeing designs for both Christmas and everyday cards — birthday, anniversary, get well, Valentines and friendship. Payment determined by design and finished color separations. Reports in 1-2 weeks.

MISTER B GREETING CARD CO., 3500 NW 52nd St., Miami FL 33142. Contact: Al Barker. Interested in greeting cards and stationery designs in actual, preferably miniature, size. No landscapes or still lifes. Pays $25-100 for design idea. Buys all rights. Reports in 4 weeks.

MONOGRAM OF CALIFORNIA, 500 Hampshire St., San Francisco CA 94010. Contact: Susie Barker. Uses artists for paper napkins, placemats, towels and some Christmas designs. Query with resume before sending samples.

MONY-X, INC., Box 45040, Tulsa OK 74145. Contact: Ray Price. Greeting card firm. Specializes in 4x9" studio cards in humorous and soft-touch types. Uses artists for illustration and lettering. Pays $25 minimum. Mail samples.

J.T. MURPHY CO., 200 W. Fisher Ave., Philadelphia PA 19120. Contact: Jack Murphy. Publishes social stationery and greeting cards. Uses artists for invitations, thank you notes, stationery and decorative notes. Sample minimum rates: $30 for stationery designs and decorative notes with finished drawings. Mail actual size samples.

NICHOLAS PRESS, 132 Nassau St., New York NY 10038. Art Director: Mr. A. Goldson. Publishes stationery, greeting cards and posters. Specializes in conventional and studio black greeting cards. Uses artists for calligraphy. Pays $15-25, studio card ideas; $50-75, studio card finished art. Query with samples. Submit 4x9" or 5x7" line art or color washes. No previously published, photocopied or simultaneous submissions. Buys all rights, SASE. Reports in 4 weeks. **To Break In:** "Study our market seriously and visit as many gift and card stores as possible."

NORCROSS, INC., 950 Airport Rd., West Chester PA 19380. (215)436-8000. Contact: Nancy Lee Fuller. Publishes calendars, stationery, giftwrapping and greeting cards. Uses artists for product design and illustrations. Pays $85 minimum for greeting card design. Mail artwork. Submission requirements available. No previously published, photocopied or simultaneous submissions. Buys exclusive greeting card rights. SASE. Reports in 3 weeks.

NU-ART, INC., 6247 W. 74th St., Chicago IL 60638. Art Director, Christmas Cards: Gil Gaw. Art Director, Wedding Invitations: Leo J. LaVela. Submissions should be in proportion to these sizes: 4x5¼"; 4⅝x6½"; 5x7⅛"; 5⅝x7⅞"; 6x8"; 3⅝x7⅞"; and 4⅜x8¼". Personalized cards sold in multiples of 25 from books or albums in better gift, stationery and/or department stores from September-December. Pays $20-30, roughs of good ideas; $30-45, finished sketches (dummies, comps); $45-100, final art. Buys exclusive rights. Reports in 1 week; may hold art 2-6 weeks for final decision.

PAKWELL PAPER PRODUCTS, Box 800, Wilsonville OR 97070. (503)638-9833. Art Director: Anna Bijan. Estab: 1946. Publishes gift boxes, Christmas giftwrapping and paper bags. Specializes in holiday items. Uses artists for product design and illustrations. Buys 100 designs annually. Pays $30 minimum for giftwrapping design. Mail 8½x11" artwork; prefers line art. No previously published, photocopied or simultaneous submissions. Buys all rights. SASE. Reports in 2 weeks.

PAPERCRAFT CORPORATION, Papercraft Park, Pittsburgh PA 15238. (412)362-8000. Art Director: Ralph F. Marmo, Jr. Estab: 1945. Publishes greeting cards and giftwrapping. Specializes in traditional Christmas subjects. Uses artists for greeting card and giftwrapping illustrations. Buys 150 designs annually. Pays approximately $100 for finished art. Mail artwork. Size specifications for finished full color: 3½x8"; 4¼x6¾"; 4¾x6¾"; 4x8½"; 6x7¼"; or 4½x9½". Previously published and photocopied submissions OK. Buys all rights. SASE. Reports in 2-3 weeks.

THE PARAMOUNT LINE, INC., 400 Pine St., Pawtucket RI 02863. Art Director: Walter A. Jones. Estab: 1925. Publishes greeting cards. Specializes in general, religious, floral, cutes and "studio" humor. Uses artists for product design and illustrations. Pays $75-100 for cover illustration. Query with samples. Any size in approximate proportion to 2x3" color OK. No previously published, photocopied or simultaneous submissions. Buys all greeting card rights. SASE. Reports in 2 weeks.

PATTIES PRINTS, INC., Box 341601, Coral Gables FL 33134. Art Director: Robert Shea. Estab: 1975. Publishes greeting cards, notes and invitations. Specializes in whimsical subjects, short verse for everyday and seasonal ideas and sophisticated graphic designs for notes and invitations. Uses artists for product design and illustrations. Pays $10-15 for whimsical new ideas, sophisticated graphic design, and juvenile subjects. Query with samples. No previously published, photocopied or simultaneous submissions. Buys all rights. SASE. Reports in 4 weeks. Submit seasonal ideas 6 months in advance.

PECK INC., 516 Lafayette Rd., St. Paul MN 55101. (612)222-1731. Art Director: Richard Wells. Estab: 1947. Publishes gift boxes, Christmas tags and holiday cutouts. Specializes in

juvenile greeting card type artwork. Uses artists for product design and illustrations. Buys 12 tags and 32 packages annually. Pays $30-75, tags; $50-500, cutouts. Query with samples. Preliminary submissions, pencil; finished art, color separations. No previously published, photocopied or simultaneous submissions. Reports in 4 weeks. SASE.
Seasonal Needs: Submit Halloween cutouts, Christmas cutouts and tags in early spring.

PIONEER PRODUCTS, INC., Box 279, Ocala FL 32670. (904)622-3134. Art Director: Kenneth Heller. Estab: 1957. Publishes paper tableware products and cake decorations. Specializes in birthday party subjects. Uses artists for advertising art, layout, product design and illustrations. Buys 200+ designs annually. Pays $150-300, 4-color, camera-ready cartoon-type illustration; $300-400, camera-ready paper product design; $25-40, product design and cake decoration rough. Query with samples or write or call for interview. No previously published work. Photocopied and simultaneous submissions OK. SASE. Reports in 4 weeks.

RECYCLED PAPER PRODUCTS, INC., 3325 N. Lincoln Ave., Chicago IL 60657. Art Directors: Michael Keiser/Philip Friedmann. Estab: 1971. Publishes Christmas and everyday greeting cards. Uses artists for product design and illustrations. Buys 1,200 designs annually. Pays $100 for reflective and color-separated art. Query with samples. Submit 5x7" or 7½x10½" b&w or color sketches. No previously published, photocopied or simultaneous submissions. Buys all rights. SASE. Reports in 4 weeks.
To Break In: "Send as many ideas with maximum variety of styles demonstrated, including roughs. The more we see, the easier to evaluate."

REED STARLINE CARD COMPANY, 3331 Sunset Blvd., Los Angeles CA 90026. Greeting card firm. Produces everyday and seasonal cards in regular and studio formats. Submission deadlines for seasonal ideas are: March 31 for Valentine's Day, St. Patrick's; August 1 for Easter, Mother's Day, Father's Day, Graduation; January 1 for Halloween, Thanksgiving, Hanukkah, Christmas.

REGENCY GREETINGS, DESIGN DIVISION, 15041 Calvert St., Van Nuys CA 91409. (213)785-1488. Art Director: David Cuthbertson. Estab: 1930. Publishes Christmas greeting cards. Uses artists for calligraphy, product design and illustrations. Buys 300 designs annually. Pays $75-150 for finished art. Query and mail color or b&w drawings. Previously published work OK (if prior publication not for Christmas cards). No photocopied or simultaneous submissions. Buys all reproduction rights as Christmas cards. SASE. Reports in 4 weeks. Submit designs from April-June.
To Break In: "Keep to traditional subjects and styles. However, I am looking for mock-ups of unique finished designs such as flocked, hot stamped, engraved, etc."

REPRODUCTA COMPANY, INC., 11 E. 26th St., New York NY 10010. Art Director: Ronald M. Schulhof. Estab: 1935. Publishes stationery, postcards and greeting cards. Specializes in religious and general subjects; especially needs Easter, Christmas and everyday items. Uses artists for calligraphy, illustrations and drawings. Buys 750 designs annually. Pays $50-200. Mail artwork. No previously published, photocopied or simultaneous submissions. Buys all rights. SASE.

ROTH GREETING CARDS, 7900 Deering Ave., Canoga Park CA 91304. Contact: Charles Roth. Uses artists for full-color studio and "cute" everyday greeting cards. "We supply gags and copy, and we're only interested in hearing from experienced artists." Buys exclusive rights.

ROUSANA CARDS, 28 Sager Place, Hillside NJ 07205. (201)373-1000. Art Director: Robert K. Edelmann. Estab: 1938. Publishes greeting cards. Uses artists for calligraphy, product design and illustration. Buys 500-750 designs annually. Pays $65-85, color finishes; $2-2.50, caption; $1-1.25, line of lettering. Query with color samples. No previously published, photocopied or simultaneous submissions. Buys world rights. SASE. Reports in 4 weeks.

ROYAL STATIONERY COMPANY, 13010 County Road 6 at Highway 55, Minneapolis Industrial Park, Minneapolis MN 55441. (612)559-3671. Art Director: Randi L. Van Brocklin. Estab: 1960. Produces calendars, stationery, postcards, notecards, mugs, key chains and soaps. Specializes in floral, scenic, animal, children and novelty items. Uses artists for product design and illustrations. Buys 50 designs annually. Pays $25 minimum, camera-ready designs. Mail artwork. Color, or b&w line drawings, washes and color breaks OK. No previously published, photocopied or simultaneous submissions. Buys all rights. All work returned. Reports in 2 weeks.

RUNNING STUDIO, INC., 1020 Park St., Paso Robles CA 93446. (805)238-2232. Contact: John or Dennis Running. Publishes greeting cards for birthday, anniversary, get well, wedding, friendship, Valentine's, Easter, Mother's and Father's Day and Christmas gift enclosures. Cards are "cute and whimiscal to elegant — all in good taste. No strictly funny cards." Uses artists for 1 to 4-color designs in vertical format suitable for silkscreen. Sample payment for full-color art, $60-80. Buys all rights. Mail samples. Reports in 1-2 weeks maximum.

RUST CRAFT GREETING CARDS, INC., Rust Craft Rd., Dedham MA 02026. Vice President/Creative Director: James Plesh. Produces full line of conventional, humorous, studio, juvenile cards, special promotions and other gift-product lines. Query with resume before sending samples.

THE RYTEX COMPANY, 432 N. Capitol Ave., Indianapolis IN 46206. Art Buyer: Thomas Payne. Manufactures personal stationery. Uses artists for product design, counter display ideas and advertising flyers. Pays $100 minimum. Reports in 30-60 days.

ST. CLAIR MANUFACTURING CORP., 120 25th Ave., Bellwood IL 60104. (312)547-7500. Graphic Arts Director: Larry Vincent. Design Art Director: Elaine Brochocki. Estab: 1932. Publishes gift boxes, giftwrapping and graphic packaging. Uses artists for calligraphy, custom logos, gift and package design. Buys 50-150 designs annually. Pays $25-150, sketch; $75-250, finished art. Query. No previously published, photocopied or simultaneous submissions. Buys all rights. SASE. Reports in 3 weeks.
To Break In: Giftwrapping designs should lend themselves to continuous repeat printing. We can print color process (rotogravure) or flat line work (flexographic).

SANGAMON, Rte. 48 W. Taylorville IL 62568. Art Director: Gary DeCourcy. Estab: 1930. Publishes calendars, stationery, greeting cards and giftwrapping. Specializes in religious, juvenile, floral, landscape and humorous subjects. Uses artists for product design and illustrations. "Payment will be discussed with the artist after we have reviewed his work. We pay competitive rates with other publishers." Query with samples. Submit giftwrapping, 10x10"; stationery, 6x8"; color greeting cards, 4⅜x7", 4¾x7½", 5½x8¼" or 6x9⅛". Watercolor only. No previously published, photocopied or simultaneous submissions. Buys all rights. SASE. Reports in 2 weeks.
Seasonal Needs: Submit work at the same time the season is on display in the stores.
To Break In: "Be aware of current trends, techniques and subject matter on the market today."

B. SHACKMAN & COMPANY, 85 5th Ave., New York NY 10003. (212)989-5162. Art Director: Mike Goodwin. Estab: 1898. Produces calendars, stationery, postcards, puzzles, games, toys, greeting cards and posters. Specializes in nostalgic and juvenile subjects. Uses artists for advertising art, product design and illustrations. Pays $25-50 for design ideas. Query with samples or write for interview. Previously published work and photocopies OK. SASE. Reports in 2 weeks.

SHAW-BARTON, INC., 545 Walnut St., Coshocton OH 43812. Art Buyer: W. L. Tallichet. Produces greeting cards, advertising calendars and specialties. Uses artists for Thanksgiving and Christmas subjects. Submit in January. Interested in finished art or comps that will scale to sizes 5½x7½" and 3⅞x8¾". Full color in any art medium OK. Pays $50 minimum for finished art. Reports in 1 month.

SMALL WORLD GREETINGS, 319 Richmond St., El Segundo CA 90245. Art Director: Jack Shaw. Estab: 1969. Publishes calendars, stationery and greeting cards. Specializes in "charming little animals, flowers and children." Uses artists for product design and illustrations. Buys 150-200 designs annually. Payment determined by assignment size and time spent. Mail artwork; "we prefer printed samples or color photos so we may file them for immediate or future contact." Previously published work OK "only to see if artist's basic style is adaptable to our line." No photocopied or simultaneous submissions. Buys exclusive rights. SASE. Reports usually in 2 weeks. Will contact artist concerning seasonal needs.
To Break In: "Consult with card shop owners to determine perpetual best selling subjects and ideas. Subjects must be commercial."

STANCRAFT PRODUCTS, 1621 E. Hennepin Ave., Minneapolis MN 55414. (612)331-8910 ext. 46. Director of Art and Design: M. Michael R. Battis. Reviews playing card designs in mid-summer and first half of year. Produces playing cards and calendar line. Interested in fresh, colorful, current design. Sample fee: $75-200 per design for exclusive playing card rights. "We produce 12 calendars annually and purchase about 100 playing card designs from around the world." Query.

STAR CITY, INC., 16134 Valerio St., Van Nuys CA 91406. (213)782-0500. Art Director: Hal Tupler. Estab: 1960. Publishes humorous posters and scrolls. Uses artists for product design and illustration. Pays $25 minimum. Query with samples. Color or b&w OK. Previously published and simultaneous submissions OK. No photocopies. Buys all rights. SASE. Reports in 2 weeks.

STRAND ENTERPRISES, 1809½ N. Orangethorpe Park, Anaheim CA 92801. (714)871-4744. Art Director: S.S. Waltzman. Estab: 1967. Publishes stationery, greeting cards, posters, notecards and memo board novelties. Specializes in scenic, inspirational, humorous, nature and animal subjects. Uses artists for calligraphy, art prints, product design and illustrations. Buys 50-100 designs annually. Pays $25 minimum for prints and notecards. Query with samples. Submit 8½x11" illustrations; pen and ink, acrylic or watercolor OK. No previously published, photocopied or simultaneous submissions. Buys all rights. SASE. Reports in 2 weeks.

SUNRISE PUBLICATIONS, INC., 637 S. Walker St., Bloomington IN 47401. (812)336-9900. Art Buyer: Gustavo Polit. Publishes greeting cards, posters and art prints. Seeks well-executed, finely drawn illustrations. Specializes in landscapes, children, nostalgic or fantasy scenes without being overly sentimental or cute. Accepts b&w drawings, line, line and wash and full-color illustrations in ink, watercolor, oils or collage. Work should be scaled to 5x7" unless design can be successfully cropped. Submit seasonal ideas 18 months in advance. Previously published work OK. Submit tearsheets or photocopies. Pays $50, color transparencies; $100, full-color art. Buys second rights for unbound formats. Reports in 30-60 days. SASE.

SUNSHINE ART STUDIOS, INC., 45 Warwick St., Springfield MA 01101. Art Director: W.S. Robbins. Publishes calendars, stationery, postcards and greeting cards. Specializes in religious and humorous subjects. Uses artists for calligraphy, product design and illustrations. Buys 300 designs annually. Pays $75-150 for drawings. Mail artwork. Submit 5x7" color drawings. No previously published, photocopied or simultaneous submissions. Buys exclusive rights. SASE. Reports in 1 week. Submit Christmas designs in May.

UNITED STATES PLAYING CARD COMPANY, Beech and Park Ave., Cincinnati OH 45212. Art Director: Jim O'Brien. One of the largest playing card manufacturers in the U.S. Uses artists for Congress full-color card (including gold or silver) design. "Generally speaking, we prefer to see comps which leave little to the imagination. Artists whose work we ask to see will be asked to submit pairs of original sketches in vertical playing card proportion. Finished art may be requested." Pays $600 for Congress finished full-color pair involving 2 original designs. Payment on acceptance. Buys world rights on designs for playing cards and score pads adapted from them. Previously published work OK, if right-of-use clearance documented. Mail design ideas or samples. Usually reports in 1 month; good material often held longer.

UNIVERSAL MATCH, 400 Paul St., Ferguson MO 63135. Contact: Russell J. Fahning. Uses artists to design and letter matchbook covers, actual size, in opaque watercolor. Work may be 1 to multi-color. Summer months are the busiest. Sample payment: $25 per design on acceptance. Buys matchbook cover reproduction rights.

VAGABOND CREATIONS, 2560 Lance Dr., Dayton OH 45409. (513)298-1124. Art Director: George F. Stanley, Jr. Estab: 1957. Publishes stationery, postcards, greeting cards, posters and spiral notebook covers. Specializes in contemporary humor. Uses artists for product design and illustration. Buys 750+ designs annually. Pays $10-25 for product design. Query. Submit any size drawing; prefers it fits in #10 envelope. Line drawings, washes and color separations as assigned OK. No previously published, photocopied or simultaneous submissions. Buys outright. SASE. Reports in 2 weeks.
To Break In: "It is important that freelancers determine exactly the type and style of product required by publisher. Product should be studied through purchase at retail outlets."

WESTERN GRAPHICS CORPORATION, Box 10728, Eugene OR 97401. (503)686-2200.

Art Director: D.W. Berlin Jr. Estab: 1968. Publishes calendars, greeting cards, posters, craft and hobby products. Specializes in humorous, sensitive, animals, cartoon and nature subjects. Uses artists for product design, illustrations and paintings. Buys 180 designs annually. Pays $100 minimum, color transparencies; $150 minimum, hand-rendered pieces. Mail artwork. Previously published, photocopied and simultaneous submissions OK. Buys all rights. SASE. Reports in 2 weeks.

WESTERN PUBLISHING CO., INC., 1220 Mound Ave., Racine WI 53404. Art Director: John Zierten. Estab: 1907. Publishes playing cards. Specializes in subjects suitable for mass market distribution and acceptable to average consumer tastes. Uses artists for product design and illustrations. Pays $75-200 for full-color illustration. Query. Submit 2¼x3½" color drawings in related pairs. Previously published and simultaneous submissions OK. No photocopies. Buys all reproduction rights. SASE. Reports in 4 weeks.

WESTVACO, C.A. REED DIVISION, 99 Chestnut St., Williamsport PA 17701. Art Director: Gene Sortman. Estab: 1923. Publishes paper tableware products. Specializes in birthday, everyday, seasonal and holiday subjects. Uses artists for product design and illustrations. Buys 150-200 designs annually. Pays $50-100 for product designs. Query with samples. Submit 5½" square, 4-color line drawings. No previously published work. Photocopied and simultaneous submissions OK. "Buys all rights within our field of publication." SASE. Reports in 3 weeks. **To Break In:** "Previous experience as staff artist is invaluable. Any experience in similar field would help."

WILLIAMHOUSE-REGENCY, INC., 28 W. 23rd St., 4th Floor, New York NY 10010. Creative Director: Diane Carol Brandt. Publishes social, wedding and commercial invitations, announcements and stationery. Send art, lettering designs or transparencies.

Performing Arts

Performing artists, just like you, are artists — but with talent based on action rather than the visual media. And, just as is often true with visual arts organizations, performing arts groups must rely heavily on federal appropriations for their working funds. Therefore, payment for artwork is generally less than high here. The potential is from $15 for a newspaper layout to $1,500 for complete costume design.

Work needed by performing arts groups includes animation art; set, light and costume design; direct mail brochures and advertising. Promotional assignments are similar to those given by advertising and public relations firms, and include graphics, layout and illustration.

There are three categories in this Performing Arts section: Music-Related Groups, Theater and Radio & TV. Among music-related groups are schools, opera companies, music festivals and orchestras; theater includes a variety of groups from repertory to musical comedies; and radio and TV stations encompass television production groups and cable TV, as well as other stations.

Artists interested in working on lighting, costume or set design need a technical knowledge of the subject as well as an artistic background. Frequently directors say artists who have theater backgrounds work best in these areas because they have a good knowledge of the subject they're working with. It is also helpful to know how to do research and have some construction ability, says Jim Jester of Concord Community Arts. "Not always will the artist be asked to do the actual constructing, but he should have a knowledge of what can be constructed and what cannot. In other cases he will be asked to do the actual construction and should be able to do so.

"Almost anyone can design a set, but you need the technical knowledge of how it goes together. If it can't be built, it doesn't do hoot. Also it's important to have an idea of what your design will cost to produce."

Developing a portfolio for stage, costume and lighting design is a little more complicated than for other art areas. For stage and set design you can present illustrations or photos of your design. But, for lighting design you'll need to have photos of sets you've worked on or a scale (light plot) of lights, adds Jester. A list of references and an outline of past experience should be included in the portfolio.

For ideas on what trends are vogue in dance costume design, check the ads in *Dance Magazine* (Danad Publishing Company, Inc.). The same publisher also sells *Dance Magazine Annual*, published each December. In 1977, the annual contained more than 11,500 entries, including dance companies, solo attractions and choreographers.

Artists who want to work in radio and television should contact department heads at each of the various networks, says Richard H. Roffman, president of Richard H. Roffman Associates. "I can't speak for everyone in New York, but I believe they all accept some freelance art, even though they have staffs of their own."

Roffman suggests artists wanting to work with the electronic media register with stations for future assignments. "New people have as much chance of getting a job as recognized people because these companies are always looking for new talent," he says.

Other performing arts publications you'll find helpful include *The Artist's Directory* (Sar-Les Music, Inc.) and *Musical America, International Directory of the Performing Arts* (ABC Leisure Magazines Inc.).

Music-Related Groups

AFRICAN HERITAGE DANCERS & DRUMMERS, 2146 Georgia Ave. NW, Washington DC 20001. (202)347-5589. Managing Director: Melvin Deal. Estab: 1968. Specializes in traditional African dance. Assigns 6 freelance jobs annually for flyers and posters in late winter/early spring. Local artists only. Payment determined by job and degree of difficulty. Pays $50-100, layouts/design. Write for interview with photos, portfolio or slides. Reports in 2-4 weeks. SASE.

ALLNATIONS DANCE COMPANY, 500 Riverside Dr., New York NY 10027. Contact: Herman Rottenberg. Ethnic dance company. Uses artists for direct mail brochures, trade magazine ads, programs, posters and bumper stickers. Submit photos or tearsheets.

BALLET FOLK OF MOSCOW INC., University of Idaho, Ridenbaugh Hall, Moscow ID 83843. Contact: Carl J. Petrick. Uses artists for poster and program designs. Send samples.

ZINA BETHUNE & COMPANY, 3096 Lake Hollywood Dr., Hollywood CA 90068. Contact: Lois Scotts. Dance company specializing in contemporary, classical, dramatic and multi-media dance. Uses artists for direct mail brochures, posters, programs and trade magazine ads. Send photos or tearsheets.

BRANNIGAN-EISLER PERFORMING ARTS INTERNATIONAL, 1501 Broadway, Suite 1504, New York NY 10036. Contact: Charles Eisler. Uses artists for posters, newspaper ads and programs.

CHICAGO CONTEMPORARY DANCE THEATRE, 2261 N. Lincoln Ave., Chicago IL 60614. (312)871-5386. Director: Maggie Kast. Estab: 1963. Specializes in modern dance. Assigns 6-10 freelance jobs annually for costume design, advertising design/layout, direct mail brochures, flyers, graphic design, newspaper ads, paste-up, posters, programs, technical charts/illustrations and theatrical lighting design. Local artists only. Payment determined by time spent. Call or write. Reports in 2 weeks. SASE.

CLEVELAND BALLET, 1375 Euclid, Suite 110, Cleveland OH 44115. Contact: Gerald Ketelaar. Uses artists for direct mail brochures, posters, programs and newspaper/trade magazine ads. Send samples.

CLEVELAND STATE UNIVERSITY MODERN DANCE COMPANY, 2451 Euclid Ave., Cleveland OH 44115. (216)687-4883. Director: Gretchen Moran. Estab: 1973. Assigns approximately 4 freelance jobs annually for direct mail brochures, flyers, graphic design, posters, programs and set/theatrical lighting design. Local artists only. Payment determined by time spent, job, degree of difficulty and availability of funds. Pays $2.30-$6 per hour. Query or mail illustrations. Reports in 2 weeks. SASE. Recently assigned artist to design flyer announcing auditions for company membership.

CONCORD PAVILION, Box 6166, Concord CA 94524. (415)798-3315. Public Relations Manager: Jay Bedecarre. Estab: 1975. Specializes in dance, rock, pop music, jazz, symphonies, sports and boat shows. Assigns 5-10 freelance jobs annually in January-September for advertising design/layout, billboards, bumper stickers, direct mail brochures, flyers, graphic design, trade magazine/newspaper ads, posters, programs, set design, set/stage design painters, technical charts/illustrations and theatrical lighting design. Payment determined by job. Pays $150-500, poster design/paste-up; $50-200, newspaper ads. Query with photos, tearsheets or portfolio. Reports in 4 weeks. SASE. Recently assigned artist to design poster and ad for recreation-sports-boat show.

DANCE CIRCLE OF BOSTON, INC., 11 Garden St., Cambridge MA 02138. (617)354-2162. Contact: Administrator. Estab: 1954. Specializes in offering the best modern dance training in the Boston area. Classes for professionals as well as beginners. Assigns approximately 30 freelance jobs annually for advertising design/layout, set/costume design, direct mail brochures, exhibit/graphic design, flyers, newspaper ads, posters and programs. Local artists only. Payment determined by job. Query with photos or samples of graphic design work. Reports in 3 weeks. SASE.

FUSION DANCE COMPANY, INC., 4542 SW 75th Ave., Miami FL 33155. Contact: William Lord. Dance company specializing in modern, ballet and dance theatre. Uses artists for trade magazine/newspaper ads, posters, direct mail brochures and programs. Minimum payment: $50, ads; $150, programs.

GRAND RAPIDS SYMPHONY ORCHESTRA, 5th Floor, Exhibitors Bldg., Grand Rapids MI 49503. Manager: Ned Crouch. Artist should send samples of previous work for assignments in direct mail brochures, posters, newspaper ads, bumper stickers and programs.

HONOLULU SYMPHONY SOCIETY & OPERA THEATRE, 1000 Bishop St., Suite 303, Honolulu HI 96813. Public Relations Director: Cliff Coleman. Uses artists for newspaper ads, direct mail brochures, posters, public service TV spots, annual reports, billboards, bus signs, interior design for symphony orchestra, and opera season promotions. "Please contact us on speculation with samples of your work. We are in constant need of new designs and print media art." Sample rates: $100, annual report; $150, direct mail brochure; $350, season tickets prospectus.

HOUSTON GRAND OPERA, 615 Louisiana, Houston TX 77002. Contact: Martha Munro. Opera company using strong marketing techniques. Uses artists for direct mail brochures, posters, bumper stickers and trade magazine/newspaper ads. Send samples.

THE INNER CITY CULTURAL CENTER, 1308 S. New Hampshire Ave., Los Angeles CA 90006. (213)387-1161. Executive Director: C. Bernard Jackson. Estab: 1966. Cultural arts organization specializing in theater, dance activities, music and educational programming. Assigns freelance jobs in October-June for advertising design/layout, billboards, bumper stickers, costume design, direct mail brochures, exhibit/graphic design, flyers, newspaper/trade magazine ads, paste-up, posters, programs, set design painters, stage/set design, technical charts/illustrations and theatrical lighting design. Payment determined by time spent, job and degree of difficulty. Mail samples with mugshot and resume. Reports in 4 weeks. SASE.

JACKSON SYMPHONY ASSOCIATION, Box 3098, Jackson TN 38301. Music Director/Conductor: James Petty. Uses artists for direct mail brochures, posters, newspaper ads, bumper stickers and programs. Send samples.

JACOBS LADDER DANCE COMPANY, 39 A Gramercy Park N., New York NY 10010. (212)254-4397. Contact: Judith Jacobs. Uses artists for logo design, direct mail brochures, posters, newspaper ads, bumper stickers and programs. Submit photos or tearsheets.

LEXINGTON PHILHARMONIC ORCHESTRA, Box 838, Lexington KY 40501. Managing Director: George Benson. Uses artists for direct mail brochures, newspaper ads, posters and bumper stickers. Submit photos or tearsheets.

MEADOW BROOK MUSIC FESTIVAL, Oakland University, Rochester MI 48063. Contact: Leon Petrus. Uses artists for direct mail brochures, posters and newspaper ads. Submit photos or tearsheets.

MILWAUKEE FLORENTINE OPERA CO., 750 N. Lincoln Memorial Dr., Milwaukee WI 53202. Contact: Alan J. Bellamente. Uses artists for direct mail brochures, posters, bumper stickers, programs, and newspaper/trade magazine ads.

MILWAUKEE SYMPHONY ORCHESTRA, 929 N. Water St., Milwaukee WI 53202. (414)273-5592. Development/Promotion Director: D. Andrew Moquin. Uses artists for programs, newspaper ads, posters and direct mail brochures.

MINNESOTA DANCE THEATRE, 107 SE 4th St., Minneapolis MN 55414. (612)335-7808. Promotional Director: Diane Fridley. Estab: 1962. Specializes in contemporary and classical ballet. Assigns 15 freelance jobs annually for graphic design, newspaper ads, posters, programs, set/stage design and theatrical lighting design. Local artists only. Pays $20, poster design; $50, brochures. Mail photos or tearsheets. Reports in 1 week. SASE.

MONADNOCK MUSIC, Francestown NH 03043. (603)547-6809. Director: James Bolle. Estab: 1966. Specializes in free concerts in the Monadnock region from July-September. Considering using artists for fliers and posters. Write or call for more information.

THE NEW YORK HARP ENSEMBLE, 140 W. End Ave., New York NY 10023. Director: Dr. Aristid von Wurtzler. Concert group which tours the U.S., Europe and the Near East. Uses artists for direct mail brochures, posters, programs and layouts for record covers. Local artists only. Submit samples.

NORTH CAROLINA SYMPHONY, Box 28026, Raleigh NC 27611. Public Relations Director: Elissa Josephsohn. Uses artists/graphic designers for ticket sales promotional materials, posters, development/general information brochures and special educational publications for children's concerts and displays. Buys all reproduction rights. Pays $25-100. "Because the North Carolina Symphony is such a unique organization in that it performs in the metropolitan areas of the state as well as in very small, rural communities, it must strive for printed matter that is appealing both to the sophisticated taste and the traditional supporter. Extensive performance schedule requires massive printings, especially of membership materials for ticket sales. For example: ticket flyer printed in quantity of 180,000 and distributed throughout the state." Offers 250 educational and evening performances each season statewide.

OMAHA OPERA COMPANY, 1200 City National Bank Bldg., Omaha NE 68102. Contact: Jonathan Dudley. Uses artists for direct mail brochures, posters, newspaper ads, bumper stickers and programs. Submit tearsheets.

PENTACLE MANAGEMENT, 200 W. 72nd St., Suite 20, New York NY 10023. Contact: Ivan Sygoda. Modern dance companies need artists for direct mail brochures and posters. Negotiates payment. Submit samples.

PERFORMING ARTSERVICES, 463 West St., New York NY 10014. Contact: Margaret Wood. Uses artists for direct mail brochures and posters. Call or write.

PHILHARMONIC SOCIETY OF NORTHEASTERN PENNSYLVANIA, Box 71, Avoca PA 18641. General Manager: Sally Preate. Uses graphic artists for direct mail brochures, programs, posters and public service TV spots. Query with resume.

SAINT PAUL CHAMBER ORCHESTRA, 302 St. Paul Bldg., St. Paul MN 55102. (612)222-2779. Contact: Joanne Schlattman. Estab: 1968. Specializes in orchestral ensemble, recital performances, educational services and residency programs. Assigns 2 freelance jobs annually for program notes, commercial art and keylining. Local artists only. Negotiates payment; determined by job. Query. Reports in 1 week-1 year. SASE.

SALT LAKE SYMPHONIC CHOIR, Box 45, Salt Lake City UT 84110. Contact: Richard M. Taggart. Uses artists for direct mail brochures, posters, newspaper ads and programs. Send samples. SASE.

JUDITH SCOTT DANCE THEATRE, 205 W. 95th St., New York NY 10025. Contact: Judith Scott. Dance improvisation group. Uses artists for programs, posters, newspaper ads and direct mail brochures. Artist may exchange services for dance classes. Submit samples.

STATE UNIVERSITY AT ALBANY, Performing Arts Center, Albany NY 12222. (518)457-8608. Specializes in educational programming. Assigns 1 freelance job annually for costume design, flyers, set/stage design, set design painters and theatrical lighting design. Payment determined by job. Pays $100-250 per week. Send resume and write for interview. Reports if needed. SASE.

STRAWBERY BANKE CHAMBER MUSIC FESTIVAL, Box 1529, Portsmouth NH 03801. Contact: Jeanne W. Lappen. Resident piano quartet. Uses artists for posters, programs and newspaper ad services. Write for more information. SASE.

TRANSCENDPROVISATION, 1505 4th Ave., Tuscaloosa AL 35401. (205)758-0145. Director: LaDonna Smith. Estab: 1975. Specializes in compositional, improvised music. Assigns 3-6 freelance jobs annually for advertising design/layout, newspaper ads, posters and programs. Local artists only Payment determined by job and degree of difficulty. Pays $20, poster layout/paste-up/printing. Query with photos or tearsheets. Reports in 3 weeks. SASE.

MARUJA VARGAS AND COMPANIA DEL ORO (formerly Maruja Vargas and Robin Brown), 509 W. 15th St., Tempe AZ 85281. (602)966-5995. Artistic Director: Vargas. Estab: 1975. Dance company specializing in Spanish classical dance. Assigns 3 freelance jobs annually for flyers, graphic design, paste-up, posters and/or theatrical lighting design. Payment determined by job. Pays $300, master design. Query. Reports in 2 weeks. SASE. Recently assigned artist to design logo, type design and layout.

WISCONSIN ARTS QUINTET, University of Wisconsin, Stevens Point WI 54481. Contact: Julius Erlenbach. Uses artists for promoting woodwind quintet performances with newspaper ads, programs, posters and direct mail brochures. Submit photos or tearsheets.

WORCESTER COMMUNITY CONCERT ASSOCIATION, Box 1141, Worcester MA 01613. Public Relations Chairman: Joseph O. Lupien. Presents series of artistic programs. Uses artists for direct mail brochures, posters, newspaper ads, bumper stickers, programs and brochure layouts. Submit samples.

THE ANNA WYMAN DANCE THEATRE, 656 15th St., West Vancouver, BC Canada V7T 2S7. General Manager: Helene Dostaler. Uses graphic designers for brochures, programs, newspaper/trade magazine ads and posters. Query with published samples.

Theater

BIGFORK SUMMER PLAYHOUSE, Box 456, Bigfork MT 59911. (406)837-4886. Producer: Donald Thomson. Estab: 1960. Repertory theatre — musical comedies. Assigns 5 freelance jobs annually for designer-in-residence, set design painters and costume/set/stage/graphic/theatrical lighting design in June-August. Payment determined by job. Pays $150-250, set design; $150-250, costume design. Query with portfolio or write for interview. Reports in 3 weeks. SASE. Apply before March for summer season.

BROWN UNIVERSITY, RITES AND REASON, Box 1148, Providence RI 02912. (401)863-4177. Contact: Rita Campbell. Afro-American performing arts organization. Uses artists for brochures, posters, graphics, scenic design and general theatrical arts. Query with resume.

CALIFORNIA STATE POLYTECHNIC UNIVERSITY, 3801 Temple Ave., Pomona CA 91768. (714)598-4549. Uses artists for poster design, mailers and paste-up. Sample payment for poster design is $50.

CANDLELIGHT PLAYHOUSE, 5620 S. Harlem Ave., Summit IL 60501. Producer: William Pullinsi. Interested in receiving resumes from designers whose services are used on year-round basis.

CECILWOOD THEATRE, (Equity), Box 56, Fishkill NY 12524. Producer: James Glass. Employs designer and/or costumer from mid-June to Labor Day. Negotiates salary. 16 apprentices, no salary.

CHATEAU DE VILLE PRODUCTIONS INC., 161 Highland Ave., Needham Heights MA 02194. Art Buyer: Jeremy Shaw. Theater production company. Uses artists for billboard art, graphic design, letterheads, set/stage design, programs and posters. Query with resume.

CIRCLE REPERTORY COMPANY, 186 W. 4th St., New York NY 10014. (212)691-3210. Artistic Director: Marshall W. Mason. Contact: Daniel Irvine or Steven Gomer. Uses artists for graphics and scenic design. Season runs September-July. Pays $25 minimum for poster/program design and newspaper ad layout. Program credits given. Call for interview to show portfolio.

CONCORD COMMUNITY ARTS, 1950 Parkside Dr., Concord CA 94519. (415)671-3065. Contact: Jim Jester. Estab: 1974. Specializes in musicals, comedy, drama and ballet. Assigns 3-10 freelance jobs annually for costume design, flyers, graphic/set design, posters, programs and theatrical lighting design, primarily September-May. Payment determined by job, degree of difficulty and budget. Pays $250-700, set/lighting design; $100-1,500, costume design/construction; $250-700, artistic director. Query, then mail photos, portfolio or slides. No work returned.

EAST CAROLINA PLAYHOUSE, Box 2712, East Carolina University, Greenville NC 27834. General Manager: Albert Pertalion. Uses artists for posters and brochures. Hires set designer usually for September-May season. Pays $50 average for posters and brochures.

Mastery of Techniques Secret to Freelance Animation

There's more to producing technical animation than good illustrations, says E. Raymond Arn of Film Associates, Inc. "The biggest fault most artists looking for work in this field have is that they haven't learned the techniques involved."

California production firms, such as Hanna Barbera, are excellent places to gain the necessary technical experience, says Arn. Work with these firms would primarily involve figure (cartoon) animation, but from there Arn says the transition is simple. "It's difficult drawing people, while technical animation involves easier drawings such as bars, charts, wheels turning and other less complicated drawings."

"The biggest fault most artists looking for work in this field (animation) have is that they haven't learned the techniques involved," says Raymond Arn.

The technical knowledge you'll gain while working on figure animation includes a knowledge of how to produce art on acetate cells, put color on the artwork and make something move fluently from frame to frame. "As far as background goes, there isn't much of a problem, because they are produced on regular card stock."

It's important to be able to do other types of art, in addition to animation, says Arn. "Animation assignments are only occasional. Most freelance technical animation artists also do a little set design, straight graphics for magazines and other work."

EASTERN OPERA THEATRE, 530 E. 89th St., New York NY 10028. Contact: Donald Westwood. Does fully-staged operatic and musical productions. Uses artists for direct mail brochures, posters and programs. Submit samples.

GOODSPEED OPERA HOUSE, Box A, East Haddam CT 06423. Contact: Kay McGrath. Uses artists for theater programs, posters, direct mail and set/stage design. Submit samples. Reports in 6 weeks.

HERITAGEFEST, Box 461, New Ulm MN 56073. (507)354-5893. Chairman: Leo H. Berg. Community festival reflecting on the past. Estab: 1975. Uses artists for costume/set/stage and lighting design, and set design painting. Assigns 2-3 freelance jobs each summer. Pays $50-1,000 for technical direction. Payment determined by degree of difficulty. Write for interview. Reports within 10 days. Looks for artists with overall knowledge and enthusiasm for project.

WILLIAM HUNT PRODUCTIONS, 801 W. End Ave., Apt. 10C, New York NY 10025. Contact: William Hunt. Uses artists for advertising art/design, direct mail brochures, film titles, graphic design, lettering, posters, programs, signs and set/stage design. Query with rough art sample. Artist will be contacted for interview.

KANSAS CITY LYRIC THEATER, 1029 Central, Kansas City MO 64105. Contact: Ms. Bobbi Wedlan. Musical organization presenting the only repertory season of opera in a 6-state region. Uses artists for direct mail brochures, posters, newspaper ads, bumper stickers and programs. Sample payment: $500 for production of season art. Submit photos or tearsheets.

MICHIGAN OPERA THEATRE, 350 Madison Ave., Detroit MI 48226. (313)963-3717. Contact: Phyllis Snow. Professional opera company producing 4 works (October-February) and a 7-week tour in Michigan. Uses artists for direct mail brochures, posters, newspaper/trade magazine ads, bumper stickers and programs. Submit samples.

MICHIGAN STAR THEATRES, INC., Box 1, Hartford OH 44424. (313)239-1465. Contact: Frank Kenley. Interested in scenic artists for staff position June-August; salary of $300 per week. Submit resume.

MILLBROOK PLAYHOUSE, Mill Hall PA 17751. (717)748-8083. Contact: Producer. Estab: 1962. Specializes in summer stock. Assigns freelance jobs for designer-in-residence and set/costume/theatrical lighting design in the summer. Pays room, board and spending money for set/costume/lighting designers. Query. Send photos or slides on request.

NATIONAL CENTER OF AFRO AMERICANS THEATRE CO., 122 Elm Hill Ave. S., Boston MA 02124. Producer: Vernon F. Blackman. Interested in designers/artists during May, June and August. Designer-in-residence usually hired each season. Submit resume or fact sheet and photo.

OGUNQUIT PLAYHOUSE, Ogunquit ME 03907. Contact: John Lane. June-September theater. Uses artists for set/stage designers and painters. Query with resume.

OPERA THEATRE OF SYRACUSE, INC., Civic Center, Suite 60, Syracuse NY 13202. Contact: Robert B. Driver, Jr. Uses artists for direct mail brochures, posters, newspaper/trade magazine ads, bumper stickers and programs.

PACKAGE PUBLICITY SERVICE, INC., 1501 Broadway, New York NY 10036. Contact: Bernard Simon. Supplies posters and advertising logotypes on plays and musicals to performing arts organizations. Usually has own ideas of design and special lettering. Uses artists for b&w art with overlay for 2-color reproduction. Submit 8x10" or 11x14" work maximum. Pays $60-80 for all rights. Query with resume.

PARK SQUARE THEATRE, 400 Sibley St., St. Paul MN 55101. (612)291-7005. Managing Director: Paul Mathey. Estab: 1974. Classical theater. Assigns 2-3 freelance jobs annually for bumper stickers, flyers, posters and programs. Local artists only. Payment determined by job and degree of difficulty. Pays $20-25, poster design; $15-25, flyer design. Query with tearsheets. Reports in 3 weeks. SASE. Recently assigned artist to design season brochure.

PIONEER PLAYHOUSE, Danville KY 41422. (606)236-2747. Producer: Col. Eben Henson. Estab: 1950. Outdoor educational theater. Hires artists in summer for designer-in-residence and set/stage/costume/theatrical lighting design.

SCORPIO RISING THEATRE, 426 N. Hoover St., Los Angeles CA 90004. Artistic Director: Alistair Hunter. Uses artists for set/costume/program/lighting/graphic design. Services required year-round. Negotiates payment. Designer-in-residence sometimes hired. Write.

SENECA THEATRE CENTRE, 1750 Finch Ave. E., Willowdale, Ontario Canada. Contact: Darrell Calvin or Kathleen Young. Uses artists for direct mail brochures, posters and newspaper ads. Submit slides or published samples.

SHASTA COLLEGE THEATRE, Shasta College, Redding CA 96001. (916)241-3523. General Director: Cecil O. Johnson. Interested in being contacted by designers in January. "We present a Summer Festival of Arts which is built during June-July and presented in repertory during July-August. We also engage designers during the academic year for single productions. The qualification for a California Teaching Credential for the Community College is helpful. (MA or MFA fills this requirement.)" Pays $1,000 per season; room included. Submit portfolio.

TACONIC THEATRE COMPANY (formerly Taconic Project, Inc.), Arnolfini Arts Center, Rhinebeck NY 12572. Director: Michael T. Sheehan. Estab: 1973. Specializes in producing and presenting theater and dance. Assigns 5-8 freelance jobs annually for designer-in-residence, direct mail brochures, flyers, set design painters, technical charts/illustrations and set/stage/costume/exhibit/theatrical lighting design in spring and summer. Payment determined by time spent, job, degree of difficulty and level of production. Pays $50-300, theater design;

$50, graphics. Query, write for interview or send resume. Reports in 2 weeks. SASE. Recently assigned artist to design for traveling theater production.

THEATRE DE LYS, 121 Christopher St., New York NY 10014. (212)924-8782. Uses non-union artists/designers. Season runs September-June. Pays $200 minimum for poster design.

UNIVERSAL MOVEMENT THEATRE REPERTORY, Box 774 Times Square Station, New York NY 10036. Contact: Mark Hall Amitin. Uses artists for direct mail brochures, posters, programs and trade magazine ads. Submit published samples.

VERMONT OPERA THEATRE, Box 181, Johnson VT 05656. Contact: Barbara Owens. Uses artists for direct mail brochures and posters.

Radio/ TV

ALBUQUERQUE CABLE TV, Box 3460, Albuquerque NM 87110. Manager: Norma Manson, APR. Uses local artists for direct mail brochures, annual reports, billboards, posters and public service TV spots. Write to arrange interview.

AMERICAN CABLE NETWORK, 701 Airport Rd., Traverse City MI 49684. General Manager: Ross Biederman. Supplier of program material to cable TV systems. Uses artists to prepare documentaries and industrial films. Payment determined by job. Buys all rights. Query before arranging interview to show samples.

BERGMAN FILM ASSOCIATION, INC., 212 E. 48th St., New York NY 10017. (212)751-4143. Contact: Walter Bergman. Uses artists for animation art and graphic design. Payment determined by job. Query with resume.

JOHN BLAIR & COMPANY, 717 5th Ave., New York NY 10022. Vice President, Communications: Josef B. Rosenberg. Director of Promotion, Blair Graphics Division: Martin J. Maloney. Broadcast time sales representative and graphic arts service firm. Uses local artists for technical charts, annual reports, sales literature and exhibit designs. Payment determined by job.

CANADIAN BROADCASTING CORPORATION, 1840 McIntyre St., Regina, Saskatchewan Canada. Public Relations Director: Doug Chase. Uses artists for animation art and graphic/exhibit/set design. Payment determined by job. Buys all rights. Query with resume.

CENTURY 21 PRODUCTIONS, INC., 2825 Valley View Lane, Suite 221, Dallas TX 75234. Contact: Dick Starr. Radio production company; interested in contemporary pop/rock art and lettering. Heavily involved in promotion for client stations who utilize freelance art services through the firm. Submit samples of finished album covers, ads or stats of layouts. Typical payment: $20 minimum, album design; $25-200, finished album art; $15-75, sales promotion flyers/bulletins. Buys all reproduction rights. Reports in 5 days.

Art that is sophisticated and appealing to the North Carolina Symphony's traditional supporter is sought by the symphony for promotional materials, posters and other literature. Illustrations such as this, designed by Kathy Lester Talansky, may be distributed to as many as 180,000 people if used on ticket flyers.

CHANNEL 13, Drawer E, Corpus Christi TX 78408. Contact: H. A. Steward. Uses artists for graphic/set design. Buys all rights. Arrange interview to show work.

CONCEPT PRODUCTIONS, Suite 535, Fresno Towne House, Fresno CA 93721. (209)486-5294. Contact: Frank Frasher. "We do design, layout and finished art for radio clients throughout the country." Uses artists for radio program promotion folders, posters, billboards and newspaper ad layouts. Arrange interview.

FILM ASSOCIATES, INC., 4600 S. Dixie Hwy., Dayton OH 45439. (513)293-2164. Contact: E. Raymond Arn. TV producer teaches animation to cartoon or technical artists. Artists experienced in animation art should query with resume. Usually pays $15 per hour.

FORREST BROADCASTING CORPORATION (KDON-KSBW-KZOZ), 933 N. Main St., Salinas CA 93901. Creative Director: George Bryant. Uses graphic artists for program promotion folders, posters and trade magazine ads. Sample fee: $200 for poster art. Send resume. No calls.

GAYLE GARY ASSOCIATES, 1212 5th Ave., New York NY 10029. (212)876-6503. Contact: Gayle Gary. Radio TV consultants. Uses artists for direct mail brochures, posters, public service TV spots and other assignments. Query with printed samples.

INDIANA CABLEVISION CORPORATION (formerly Valley Cablevision Corporation), 815 E. Pennsylvania Ave., South Bend IN 46618. Contact: Gary L. Stephenson. Uses artists for video presentations. "We will schedule programs available on a 'free-loan' basis. We are always interested in exploring new sources for programming and we are willing to cablecast shows of appropriate subject and length without cost to the producer."

KAAL, Box 577, Austin MN 55912. Contact: Terry Dolan. Uses artists for graphic/set design. Query with resume.

KAET-TV, Arizona State University, Tempe AZ 85281. Art Director: Rob Covey. Uses artists for animation art and graphic/set design. Buys all rights. Submit resume.

KCAL-FM, Box 390, Redlands CA 92373. Contact: Jim James. Uses artists for newspaper ad layouts and posters. "We desire freelancer to design radio station sigs for variety radio (nostalgia-oriented) FM stereo station. Also progressive rock sig for same station." Buys all rights.

KCFW-TV, Box 857, Kalispell MT 59901. Contact: Mike Stocklin. Uses artists for animation art and graphic/set design. Payment determined by job. Query. Samples presented at interview. Slides must be horizontals.

KECC-TV, Box 29, El Centro CA 92243. Contact: Dick Sampson. Uses artists for graphic design. Payment by job or $8 per hour. Sample fee: $155, 15x20" identification cards; $110, graphics for commercial accounts. Buys all rights. Query with resume.

KENTUCKY EDUCATIONAL TV, 600 Cooper Dr., Lexington KY 40502. Contact: Sid Webb. Uses artists for animation art and graphic/set design. Work submitted can be video tape (all formats), 8/16/35mm film or slide projection. Negotiates payment. Buys all rights. Query with resume.

KFME/CHANNEL 13, 4500 S. University Dr., Fargo ND 58102. Contact: Dan Hart. Uses artists for animation art and graphic/set design. Payment determined by job. Arrange interview to show samples.

KFYE-FM 94, Rodeway Inn, Suite 535, Fresno CA 93721. Contact: Promotion Director. Uses artists for posters, billboards, newspaper ad layouts and sales sheets. Arrange interview to show samples.

KGVO-TV, Drawer M, Missoula MT 59801. Director of Production and Promotion: K.H.

LaCasse. Uses artists for animation art and graphic/exhibit/set design. Payment determined by job. Query with resume. Samples shown at interview.

KPLR-TV, 4935 Lindell Blvd., St. Louis MO 63108. (314)367-7211. Contact: Jerry Cappa. Uses artists for animation art, graphic/set design and TV graphics. Sample payment: $25-65, individual job; $75, color caricatures. Buys all rights. Query with resume and slides or printed material.

KREX-TV, Box 789, Grand Junction CO 81501. Production Director: Harley Terrill. Uses artists for set design, audiovisuals, film titles and TV commercials. Submit slides. SASE.

KRON-TV, Box 3412, San Francisco CA 94119. (415)441-4444. Advertising Director: Bill Row. Estab: 1949. NBC-TV affiliate carrying standard commercial programming. Assigns approximately 50 freelance jobs annually for advertising design/layout, animation art, flyers, graphic/exhibit design, paste-up and newspaper/trade magazine ads. Payment determined by job. Call for interview.

KUSD-TV, Vermillion SD 57069. Contact: Jim Cherry. Uses artists for graphic and set design. Negotiates payment. Pays $2.10 per hour; or $40, set design; $1 per slide. Query with resume.

KUSP, Box 423, Santa Cruz CA 95061. Contact: David M. Freedman. Radio station. Uses artists for program promotion folders, posters and newspaper ad layouts. Sample fee: $50, poster design; $75, promotional package design. Prefers to see samples after phone interview.

KVCR-TV/FM RADIO, 701 S. Mount Vernon Ave., San Bernardino CA 92403. Program Director: Lew Warren. Estab: 1953. Specializes in public and educational radio/TV. Assigns 1-10 freelance jobs annually for graphic/set design, set design painters and camera-ready cards. Payment determined by job. Pays $15-25, camera-ready cards. Query, mail photos or slides. Reports in 2 weeks. SASE.

KVON, CABLE TV-6, 1124 Foster Rd., Napa CA 94558. Contact: Tom Young or Mike Piper. Uses artists for program promotion folders, posters and TV graphics. Negotiates payment; determined by job. Query with resume.

LEMORANDE PRODUCTION COMPANY, 205 E. Wisconsin Ave., Milwaukee WI 53202. (414)271-3358. Contact: William Lemorande. TV producer/production house. Uses artists for animation art and graphic/set design. Pays $5-30 per hour, depending on job. Arrange interview to show samples.

LEWIS BROADCASTING CORPORATION, Box 13646, Savannah GA 31406. Public Relations Director: C.A. Barbieri. Uses artists for direct mail brochures, billboards, posters and public service TV spots. Query with resume and printed samples.

MISSISSIPPI EDUCATIONAL TV NETWORK, Box 1101, Jackson MS 39205. Contact: Jane Puryear. TV production center specializing in educational and public TV production. Also executes designs for print support in advertising and teaching materials. Uses artists for animation art, graphic/set design and illustration for TV and print. Suggests 35mm slide; 16mm film or Sony cassette for animation for interview portfolio viewing. Pays $6.35 per hour. Sample fee: $6 per hour, mechanicals/paste-up; $35 per hour, creative concept and execution of animation for video tape. Query with resume.

LOUISA MORITZ COMMERCIAL CAPERS, 1709 N. Fuller, Suite 31, Hollywood CA 90046. Contact: Tilly Tiffany. Uses artists for graphic design and lettering. Looking for "imaginative and different lettering and/or ad ideas." Sample payment: $50 for hand-lettering on 1 ad. Send photocopies before arranging interview.

NBC TV NETWORK, 30 Rockefeller Plaza, New York NY 10020. Contact: Bob Greenwell. Uses artists for audiovisual and graphic design projects produced for advertisers and agencies. Payments generally above average. Arrange interview to submit resume and/or portfolio. Ability to meet short deadlines essential.

NEW YORK FILM AND VIDEOTAPE, 450 N. Narberth Ave., Narberth PA 19072.

(215)667-0787. Contact: Bill DuPertuis. Uses artists for set design and storyboards. Payment determined by job. Query with resume.

NORTHERN LIGHTS CABLE CORPORATION, Box 224, Presque Isle WI 54557. Contact: Thomas J. Forster. Uses artists for animation art, graphics and set design; especially needs educational TV layouts. Buys all rights. Query with samples.

ORBIT RADIO, Box 1644, Louisville KY 40201. (502)584-5535. Contact: S.A. Cisler. Uses artists for work on broadcast equipment, program/market promotion folders, posters and trade magazine ads. Submit 8½x11" work. Buys area rights. Write.

RICHARD H. ROFFMAN ASSOCIATES, 697 West End Ave., Suite 6A, New York NY 10025. (212)749-3647. President: Richard H. Roffman. Estab: 1956. Specializes in public affairs programming. Assigns approximately 12 freelance jobs annually for advertising design/layout, posters, programs and trade magazine ads. Local artists only. Pays "the going rate." Call or write for interview. Reports in 1 week. SASE.

RPM RADIO PROGRAMMING AND MANAGEMENT, INC., 25140 Lanser Rd., Suite 232, Southfield MI 48075. (313)358-1040. President: Thomas M. Krikorian. Estab: 1970. Music programming for radio. Assigns 5-10 freelance jobs annually for advertising design/layout, billboards, bumper stickers, direct mail brochures and trade magazine ads. Payment determined by degree of difficulty. Pays $50-100, trade ads; $20-100, logo design. Mail photos or tearsheets. Reports as services are needed. SASE. Recently assigned artist to design nationwide mailer and trade ad.

STUDIO WEST, 5929 Tiber Dr., Anaheim CA 92807. (714)637-8349. Contact: Jim Meeker. Uses artists for program promotion folders, posters, newspaper ad layouts and trade magazine ads. "We are looking for clever ideas depicting the formats we program on radio stations." Arrange interview to show samples.

TV PRODUCTION CENTER, 445 Melwood St., Pittsburgh PA 15213. (412)682-2300. Contact: Craig Perry. Produces commercial, institutional and industrial video tape presentations. Uses artists for graphic and set design. Payment determined by job experience. Query with resume.

WGBY-TV, 1 Armory Square, Springfield MA 01105. (617)781-2801. Contact: Sandy Gran. Uses artists for animation art, slides and graphic/set design. "Channel 57 is a young, small public TV station in search of beginning artists seeking experience and exposure who are willing to donate their services."

WGR-TV, 259 Delaware Ave., Buffalo NY 14202. Art Director: Marcel Lissek. Uses artists for animated art and graphic/exhibit/set design. Payment determined by job. Buys all rights. Query with resume.

WITI-TV 6, 5445 N. 27th St., Milwaukee WI 53209. Contact: Tim Truesdell. Uses artists for animation art and graphic/set design. Negotiates payment. Sample minimum payment: $10 each, pastel or opaque watercolors for TV slides. Query with resume before sending samples.

WLTV-23, 695 NW 199th St., Miami FL 33169. Contact: A. Mieres. Spanish international network. Uses artists for TV graphic arts. Submit letter, indicating fees for various services, before mailing any samples.

WXII-TV, Box 11847, 700 Coliseum Dr., Winston-Salem NC 27106. Contact: Douglas Bales. Uses artists for animation art, graphic/exhibit/set design and illustrations. Arrange interview to show samples.

WXON-TV 20, Box 2020, Southfield MI 48075. (313)355-2902. Contact: Janis Neal. Uses artists for animation art. Query with resume.

Periodicals

The *National Enquirer* buys 540 cartoons a year; *Changing Times,* 50; *Cartoons,* 150 pages worth; *Better Homes and Gardens,* 30. In all there are more than 800 periodicals listed in this section buying thousands of freelance illustrations and cartoons annually. They pay from a rock-bottom $10 to more than $1,000.

Freelancing for periodicals varies greatly when compared to trying to freelance for other firms and places listed in *Art & Crafts Market.* The main difference is that few publications require any past experience or in-person appointments, and that rarely do you have to present a portfolio to be considered. In most cases all the artist has to do is read sample copies of the publication before submitting, study the style used, and then check out the submission requirements in this book. If these guidelines are followed, the freelance artist who has never sold a cartoon or illustration has as much chance of getting accepted as the artist who sells his work regularly.

Smaller publications are often understaffed and have no art director. Particularly in these cases, you should submit finished artwork because there won't be an art staff to smooth out your roughs. Also, this saves the publication the overhead of touching up your work.

The competition for acceptance is naturally heavier on the better-known publications. Not only is the artist competing against other freelancers, but possibly against a staff artist, syndicates, clip art firms and public relations outlets.

All work you plan to submit to publications should be accompanied by a *typewritten* cover letter and SASE. Many smaller publications prefer that you include the payment — in your letter — that you'd like for your artwork, while other larger publications prefer to set payment themselves. When in doubt, omit the price and allow the publication to bring up the subject. The Cartoonist Guild, Inc. (156 W. 72nd St., New York City 10023) can provide additional information on pricing; while illustrators can learn more by reading *Pricing & Ethical Guidelines* (Graphic Artists Guild, Box 3928, Grand Central Station, New York City 10017).

When a magazine says to query first, don't waste their time and yours by sending submissions. Many publications only buy illustrations and cartoons on specific themes for upcoming or special issues and have no need for off-the-cuff submissions — no matter how good they may be.

Sheldon Wax, managing editor of *Playboy Magazine*, suggests artists should always include their name on all samples submitted — do *not* send original work — and to send all work by registered mail. Many editors are leery of the U.S. Postal Service and suggest sending work by U.P.S., Postal Express or by other private firms.

It is best to affix a copyright symbol to submitted work. Work is automatically copyrighted after creation according to the new copyright law, but having a copyright symbol attached to the art gives it added legal protection. Later, the work should then be registered with the U.S. Copyright Office (see "The New Copyright Law: What You Need to Know"). When you work with an uncopyrighted publication you should particularly keep these suggestions in mind.

One of the biggest mistakes artists can make when submitting work for publication (other than presenting unprofessional art) is to send a cartoon or illustration that reeks of cliché (that is, an idea that has been submitted or an object drawn in the same way time and time again). Another problem with clichés arises when the artist tries to do work in an area he knows nothing about and creates a piece of work that is essentially the uninformed public's idea of what the field is like. For example, Nels Winkless of *Personal Computing* has this problem: "It's almost impossible to discourage artists from drawing computers with tape reels on them, and this isn't the way most computers look. Unfortunately, this is the impression moviemakers have given the public. We need to get away from these clichés and show the equipment as it really is to our readers who are using them. There are 250 computer stores in this country where people can buy computers on a retail basis. Artists close to a store such as this should check these out, rather than relying on what they've seen in movies."

For additional names and addresses of publications, consult *Editor & Publisher Year Book, Ayer Directory of Publications* and *Gebbie House Magazine Directory.*

Magazines

AB BOOKMAN PUBLICATIONS, Box AB, Clifton NJ 07015. Art Buyer: Jacob L. Chernofsky. Publishing company specializes in magazines for book dealers. Offset. Buys cartoons on bookselling, books, libraries or book collecting. Also uses artists for ad layouts and mechanical paste-ups. Query with resume.

ABC AMERICAN ROOFER AND BUILDING IMPROVEMENT CONTRACTOR, Shelter Publications, Inc., 915 Burlington St., Downer's Grove IL 60515. (312)964-6200. Editor-in-Chief: J. C. Gudas. Monthly; 8⅛x11"; 32 pages. Offset. Estab: 1911. Circ: 29,220. For owners of roofing businesses. Buys all rights. Pays on publication. No previously published, photocopied or simultaneous submissions. Query. SASE. Free sample copy. "We want only that which is pertinent to our field, which is roofing and exterior improvements, not general construction or interior home improvement. Usually, we get a lot of material that is totally irrelevant. Also, I received nearly 50 illustrations last year, but was unable to use all but 15 of them because of poor quality."
Cartoons: Buys themes on the roofing industry. Single panel OK. Submit finished art. Line drawings only. Pays $5-25. Buys 2-3 cartoons annually. Reports in 1 week.
Illustrations: Buys cover art and article illustrations on the industry. Submit roughs. Cover: b&w line drawings and color OK; "must be really unusual with a different perspective." Inside: b&w line drawings and veloxes OK. Pays $5+. Buys 15 illustrations annually. Reports in 1 week.

ABUNDANT LIFE (formerly Oral Roberts Association), Box 2187, Tulsa OK 74102. Art Buyer: Paul Davidson. Monthly. Pays $15-25 per hour, artwork; $12-18 per hour, production. Buys all rights. Submit resume and samples. Reports in 10 days.

ACCENT ON LIVING, Box 700, Bloomington IL 61701. Editor: Ray Cheever. For the physically handicapped. Emphasis on success and ideas for better living for physically handicapped. Will look at samples of previously published work as examples of artist's style. Pays on acceptance. Buys all rights. Pays $15 for cartoons. Reports in 2 weeks. Sample copy $1.

ACCENT ON YOUTH, 201 8th Ave. S., Nashville TN 37202. Editor: Margaret L. Barnhart. "Leisure reading for ages 12-14 in the United Methodist and United Presbyterian churches." Monthly. Uses 2 and 3-color illustrations, full-color cover illustrations, cartoons and cover designs, on assignment. Sample payment for a cover design in 4 colors is $75. Buys all rights. Buys reprint rights on cartoons. Pays on acceptance. Previously published work OK. Query with resume before sending samples.

ACTION!, Greater Hartford Chamber of Commerce, 250 Constitution Plaza, Hartford CT 06103. Editor: Jamie E. Haines. For community readers. Buys cover designs.

ADULT BIBLE TEACHER/STUDENT, Dept. of Church Schools, 6401 The Paseo, Kansas City MO 64131. (816)333-7000. Editor: John B. Nielson. Estab: about 1908. Circ: 225,000. Quarterly; 8¼x11". Primarily interests are full-color illustrations. Seasonal needs are for religious holidays, Thanksgiving and patriotic themes. Not copyrighted. Pays $15-25, spot drawings; $50-100, full-color illustration; $75-125, cover designs; $6-10, cartoons. Mail ideas. Reports in 1 month. Sample copy $1.

ADVENTURE, 127 9th Ave. N., Nashville TN 37234. Editor: Ginny Davis. Juvenile 4-color publication issued monthly in weekly parts for ages 8-11 in Southern Baptist churches. Works on assignment with Sunday school curriculum artists.

AFTER DARK, 10 Columbus Circle, New York NY 10019. Editor-in-Chief: William Como. Monthly. For those interested in the entertainment scene, including theater, films, TV, dance, opera, music, happenings and travel. Buys exclusive rights. Pays on publication. Previously published work occasionally OK. Query. Reports in 1-3 weeks. Sample copy $1.25.

AGENCY SALES, Manufacturers' Agents National Association, Box 16878, Irvine CA 92713. Art buyer: Linda Hamner. Monthly. For independent, commissioned industrial salesmen. Uses pen and ink, finished art. "We have never done covers by mail. We do pay $70, however, for camera-ready art that we use in black plus another color (with white paper as background). Payment for spot drawings is $10-15." Uses cartoons about business, marketing and industry. Pays $10. Buys all or first rights. Pays on publication. Previously published work OK. Query with resume. Reports in 30-60 days.

AIM, Box 20554, Chicago IL 60620. Editor-in-Chief: Ruth Apilado. Managing Editors: Dr. Myron Apilado/Al Jones. Bimonthly; 8½x11"; 44 pages. Offset. Estab: 1974. Circ: 5,500. For general audience, including grammar and high school students. Not copyrighted. Pays on publication. Previously published work and photocopies OK. Mail artwork. SASE. Sample copy $1. "We are interested in unknown individuals who are making a contribution to social progress in their communities."
Cartoons: Buys all themes; anything promoting racial harmony. Submit finished art. B&w only. Pays $5-15. Buys 18 cartoons annually. Reports in 2-3 weeks.
Illustrations: Buys cover art, article illustrations and spot drawings on material of social significance; not too academic. Submit finished art. B&w line drawings OK. Pays $15-25, cover; $5-15, inside. Buys 30 illustrations annually. Reports in 3 weeks.

AIR LINE PILOT, 1625 Massachusetts Ave. NW, Washington DC 20036. Editor: C. V. Glines. Pays $25 for cartoons and gag lines. Buys all rights. Pays on publication. Reports in 4 weeks.

AIR PROGRESS, 7950 Deering Ave., Canoga Park CA 91352. Art Buyer: Keith Connes. Buys all rights.
Cartoons: Buys themes on "general aviation — covering businss and personal flying, sport aviation, military, personal travel. No airlines." Submit finished art. Negotiates payment. Pays $25 minimum 6-8 weeks after publication.

THE ALBUQUERQUEAN, Jaymar Publications, Box 25024, Albuquerque NM 87125. Editorial Coordinator: Greg Lay. For those interested in city life and government. Buys illustrations and cartoons. Pays $4-12, fairly simple work; $13-50, more elaborate work. Pays on publication. Negotiates special projects.

ALEPH MAGAZINE, 7319 Willow Ave., Takoma Park MD 20012. (301)270-5754. Editors: M. Raff/L. R. Fox. Quarterly. Circ: 500. Readers are college educated, intellectual, in all occupations. Uses b&w line, line and wash drawings and cover designs. Pays contributor's copies. Buys all rights. Mail artwork or design ideas. Reports in 2-4 weeks. Sample copy $1.50.

ALFRED HITCHCOCK MYSTERY MAGAZINE, Davis Publications, 229 Park Ave. S., New York NY 10003. Contact: Irving Bernstein. Pays $20 minimum, line drawings; $400 maximum, full-color cover design. Pays on acceptance. Buys first rights. Reports in 1 week.

ALGOL MAGAZINE, Box 4175, New York NY 10017. Editor: Andrew Porter. Published semiannually. For the science fiction reader interested in behind-the-scenes workings of the field. Publishes articles, interviews and essays by and about award-winning authors. Pays on acceptance. Mail art or design ideas. SASE. Reports in 2-5 weeks. Sample copy $1.95. "Unless the artist is well-versed in SF, and genuinely loves the field, we advise he not submit. High standards are set here."
Cartoons: Submit finished art. Pays $10 per page.
Illustrations: Buys fantasy and science fiction themes. No horror or supernatural work. B&w line drawings, and line and wash OK. Pays $10 per page, spot art; $50, full-color illustration.

ALIVE!, Christian Board of Publication, Box 179, St. Louis MO 63166. Editor: Darrell Faires. Denominational monthly for junior high students. Buys one-time rights. No previously published work.
Cartoons: Buys themes on life and teenage problems. Pays $6-8. Buys 8 cartoons annually.

Illustrations: Works on assignment. Submit finished inks, line drawings or washes. Pays $20-40 on acceptance. Send tearsheets.

ALLEGHENY FLIGHTIME, East-West Network, Inc., 5900 Wilshire Blvd., #300, Los Angeles CA 90036. (213)937-5810. Editor: James Clark. Senior Art Director: Chris Mossman. Monthly. Buys all rights. Query with resume. Sample copy $1.
Illustrations: Buys cover art and spot drawings on assignment. Pays $25 minimum, spot art; $400, full-color cover. Reports in 4 weeks.

AMA NEWS, American Motorcyclist Association, Box 141, Westerville OH 43081. (614)891-2425. Editor-in-Chief: Jeff John. Art Director: Bob Pluckebaum. Monthly; 8½x11"; 40 pages. Offset. Estab: 1947. Circ: 130,000. Buys first and reprint rights. Pays on publication. Previously published work OK. No photocopied or simultaneous submissions. Query with samples. SASE. Free sample copy.
Cartoons: Buys motorcycling themes. Single panel OK. Submit roughs. B&w washes OK. Pays $10 minimum. Buys 36 cartoons annually. Reports in 3 weeks.
Illustrations: Buys cover art, article illustrations and spot drawings on motorcycling. Submit roughs. Cover: color-separated and reflective art OK. Inside: all media OK. Pays $50 minimum, color cover; $15-50, inside. Buys 24 illustrations annually. Reports in 3 weeks.

AMATEUR ARCHAEOLOGIST, Rte. 1, Norfolk NE 68701. Editor-in-Chief: Daniel J. Vap. Quarterly; 8½x11"; 52 pages. Offset. Estab: 1976. Circ: 3,000. For students, members of archaeological societies and professional archaeologists. Buys all rights, but may reassign rights to artist after publication. Pays on publication. Previously published, photocopied and simultaneous submissions OK. Query with samples. SASE. Sample copy $2.
Cartoons: Buys themes on archaeology. All formats OK. Submit finished art. Line drawings only. Pays $15 minimum. Buys 4-12 cartoons annually. Reports in 2 weeks.

AMAZING SCIENCE FICTION, Ultimate Publishing Company, 69-62 230th St., Bayside, Queens NY 11364. Art Buyers: J. Edwards/Sol Cohen. Buys first rights. Payment on acceptance. Submit published samples or rough or finished original art.
Illustrations: Buys fantasy and science fiction themes. Pays $10, half-page editorial illustration/spot drawing; $50, 4-color cover design. Reports in 90 days.

THE AMERICAN ATHEIST, Box 2117, Austin TX 78768. (512)458-1244. Editor: Madalyn M. O'Hair. Monthly. Circ: 10,000. For atheists, agnostics, materialists and realists. Uses b&w drawings, cover designs, and various sizes of cartoons. Especially interested in 4-seasons artwork. Not copyrighted. Pays on acceptance. Previously published work OK. Pays $10, spot drawings; $100, cover designs; $10, cartoons. Sample copy $1.

AMERICAN FAMILY PHYSICIAN, 1740 W. 92nd St., Kansas City MO 64114. Publisher: Walter H. Kemp. Buys all rights.
Cartoons: Buys finished cartoons to run with articles dealing with everything from scientific to legislative information of interest to doctors. Pays $25 on acceptance. Buys 12-24 cartoons annually. Reports in 2 weeks.

THE AMERICAN FIELD, 222 W. Adams St., Chicago IL 60606. (312)372-1383. Editor-in-Chief: William Brown. Managing Editor: Bernard Matthys. Weekly; 12x14"; 37-38 pages. Letterpress. Estab: 1874. Circ: 25,000. For well-to-do hunters who work with pointing breeds. Not copyrighted. Pays on acceptance. Previously published work OK. Query. SASE. Free sample copy.
Cartoons: Buys outdoor hunting themes. Pays $5 minimum. Reports in 2 weeks.
Illustrations: Buys article illustrations on outdoor hunting with pointing dogs. B&w art OK. Pays $5 minimum. Reports in 2 weeks.

AMERICAN HOROLOGIST AND JEWELER, 2403 Champa St., Denver CO 80205. (303)572-1777. Managing Editor: Kathleen Egan. Monthly; 8½x11"; 80 pages. Offset. Estab: 1936. Circ: 13,000. For retail jewelers and watch repair people, some manufacturers, wholesalers, students, hobbyists and collectors. Buys first rights. Pays on publication. Previously published work and photocopies OK. No simultaneous submissions. Query with samples. SASE. Free sample copy.
Cartoons: "We have received none, but will consider them."

Illustrations: Patricia Barker, editor. "We seldom accept inside art and, generally, we like an accompanying story. We will consider, however, any appropriate art." Buys cover art and article illustrations on jewelry, watches, clocks or store management. Submit roughs. Cover: washes and color-separated art OK. Inside: b&w line drawings and veloxes OK. Pays $100-150, color cover; $20-50, inside color; $10-25, inside b&w. Reports in 3 weeks.

AMERICAN HUMANE MAGAZINE (formerly *National Humane Review*), 5351 S. Roslyn St., Englewood CO 80110. Editor: Anne Brennan. Monthly. Previously published work OK. Pays $30, color cover. Buys one-time rights. Payment on publication. Previously published work OK. Mail artwork. Reports in 3 months. Sample copy 50¢.

THE AMERICAN HUNTER, 1600 Rhode Island Ave. NW, Washington DC 20036. (202)783-6505. Associate Editor: Earl Shelsby. Published monthly for sports hunters. Circ: 140,000. Buys all rights. Pays on acceptance. No previously published work. Sample copy available.
Illustrations: Buys finished drawings of game animals. Pays $30-75, spot drawings; $100-200, full-color illustrations. Reports in 2 weeks.

AMERICAN JEWISH TIMES-OUTLOOK, 1400 W. Independence Blvd., Charlotte NC 28234. (704)372-3296. Editor-in-Chief: Ron Unger. Monthly; 8¼x11"; 48 pages. Offset. Estab: 1934. Circ: 5,000. For Jewish readers interested in world affairs, politics, sports, entertainment and literature. Buys all rights. Pays on publication. Previously published and simultaneous submissions OK. No photocopies. Mail artwork. SASE. Free sample copy.
Cartoons: Buys all themes. All formats OK. Submit finished art. B&w art OK. Pays $5-10. Buys 12 cartoons annually. Reports in 4 weeks.
Illustrations: Jean Stromberg-Unger, editor. Buys cover art, article illustrations and spot drawings relating to Judaism. Submit finished art. Cover: watercolors, acrylics and oils OK. Inside: b&w line drawings OK. Pays $5-10, b&w cover and inside; $5 minimum, color cover. Buys 12 illustrations annually. Reports in 4 weeks.

AMERICAN JOURNAL OF NURSING, 10 Columbus Circle, New York NY 10019. (212)582-8820. Editor-in-Chief: Thelma Schorr. Managing Editor: Gretchen Gerds. Art Director: Forbes Linkhorn. Monthly; 8⅛x11"; 230 pages. Offset. Estab: 1900. Circ: 350,000. For nursing professionals. Buys first rights. Pays on acceptance, cartoons; on publication, illustrations. No previously published, photocopied or simultaneous submissions. Mail cartoons. Arrange interview for illustration assignments. SASE. Free sample copy, "but we prefer they look in the library for our magazine."
Cartoons: Buys cartoons on nursing. All formats OK. Submit finished art. Line drawings, halftones and washes OK. Pays $20-50. Buys 36 cartoons annually. Reports in 4 weeks. "Please keep cartoons tasteful; no nudes, buxom nurses, or sexual connotations. Do not show nurses as receptionists."
Illustrations: B&w line drawings, duatones and washes OK. Pays $75-300. Buys 300 illustrations annually.
To Break In: "Go to hospitals to study nurses in their natural habitat. Try to get real inside humor, not just nurses vs. doctors, or nurses as receptionists, etc."

THE AMERICAN LEGION MAGAZINE, 1608 K St. NW, Washington DC 20006. Contact: Cartoon Editor. Buys first rights. Pays on acceptance.
Cartoons: "Generally interested in cartoons with a broad, mass appeal. Prefers action in the drawing, rather than the illustrated joke-type gag. Those which have a beguiling character or ludicrous situation that attract the reader and lead him to read the caption rate the highest attention. No-caption gags purchased only occasionally. Because of the tight space problem, we're not in the market for the spread-type or multi-panel cartoon. Themes should be home life, business, sports and everyday Americana. Cartoons which pertain only to 1 branch of the service are too restricted for this magazine. The service-type gag should be recognized and appreciated by any ex-serviceman or woman. Cartoons in bad taste, off-color or which may offend the reader not accepted. Liquor, sex, religion and racial differences are taboo. Ink roughs not necessary, but are desirable. Finish: line, Ben-Day." Pays $50-100.

AMERICAN LIBRARIES, ALA Association, 50 E. Huron, Chicago IL 60611. Editor: Art Plotnik. Commissions artwork or design ideas for covers and feature illustration. Portfolios welcome and may include tearsheets, photocopies or transparencies. Buys first rights. Pays on acceptance.

THE AMERICAN RIFLEMAN, 1600 Rhode Island Ave. NW, Washington DC 20036. (202)783-6505. Editor: Ken Warner. Monthly; 8⅛x10⅞"; 84 pages. Offset. Estab: 1906. Circ: 1 million. For National Rifle Association members with interests in hunting, competitive shooting, conservation, legislation, hunter safety, gunsmithing and anything technical pertaining to firearms. Buys first North American serial rights. Pays on acceptance. No previously published, photocopied or simultaneous submissions. Query. SASE. Free sample copy.
Cartoons: Buys themes on shooting sports. Single panel OK. Submit finished art. Washes OK. Pays $50 minimum, b&w. Buys 12-15 cartoons annually. Reports in 2 weeks.
Illustrations: Buys article illustrations and spot drawings on shooting sports. Submit finished art. B&w line drawings and washes OK. Pays $50 minimum, b&w. Buys 8-9 illustrations annually. Reports in 2 weeks.

AMERICAN SHOEMAKING, Shoe Trades Publication Co., 15 East St., Boston MA 02111. Contact: John Moynihan. Buys advertising art. Pays on publication. Submit samples.

AMERICAN SQUAREDANCE, Box 788, Sandusky OH 44870. Editors: Stan and Cathie Burdick. Monthly; 8½x5½"; 100 pages. Offset. Estab: 1945. Circ: 12,500. For squaredancers. Buys all rights. Pays on publication. Photocopies OK. No previously published or simultaneous submissions. Mail artwork. SASE. Free sample copy.
Cartoons: Buys square/round dancing cartoons. Single panel only. Submit finished art. Halftones and washes OK. Pays $5-15. Buys 6 cartoons annually. Reports in 1 week.
Illustrations: Buys cover art and spot drawings on square/round folk dancers. Submit finished art. Cover: b&w line drawings, washes and color-separated art OK. Inside: b&w line drawings and washes OK. Pays $10-25, cover; $5-15, b&w inside. Buys 6-10 illustrations annually. Reports in 1 week.

THE AMERICAN SURFER, Box 342, Huntington Beach CA 92648. Buys cartoons. Single panel OK. Copyrighted.

ANIMAL KINGDOM, New York Zoological Society, Bronx NY 10460. (212)220-5121. Editor: Eugene J. Walter, Jr. Bimonthly. Devoted to wildlife and conservation. For well-educated audience. Buys one-time rights. Pays on acceptance. Previously published work OK. Sample copy $1.25.
Illustrations: Works mainly on assignment. B&w line drawings, line and wash, and full-color illustrations OK. Pays $40-50, b&w; $100-150, full-color. Reports in 4-6 weeks.
Special Needs: Art for issues on wildlife and habitat in India, the Galapagos and the Serengeti.

ANIMALS, 350 S. Huntington Ave., Boston MA 02130. Editor-in-Chief: Deborah Salem. Bimonthly; 8¼x11"; 40 pages. Offset. Estab: 1868. Circ: 20,000. For members of 3 affiliated humane organizations primarily in the Northeast. Not copyrighted. Pays on publication. No previously published, photocopied or simultaneous submissions. Query with samples. SASE. Sample copy 75¢ (include 8½x11" SASE).
Illustrations: Buys cover art and article illustrations on wild and domestic animals outside "commercial" settings. "We most often buy good, representational artwork to accompany specific pieces, particularly of hard-to-photograph species like marine animals, exotic and endangered species." Submit finished art. Cover: washes and color-separated art OK. Inside: b&w line drawings, washes and color-separated art OK. Minimum payment: $30, color cover; $25, inside color; $15, inside b&w. Buys 25-30 illustrations annually. Reports in 2 weeks.
To Break In: "Almost all artwork is commissioned, so we seldom purchase or use finished art as is. Sample art would be most effective."

THE ANNALS OF ST. ANNE DE BEAUPRE, Basilique St. Anne, Quebec Canada G0A 1C0. (418)827-4538. Editor-in-Chief: Eugene LeFebre. Managing Editor: J.C. Nadeau. Monthly; 8½x11"; 32 pages. Offset. Estab: 1876. Circ: 74,000. For family readers. Buys first North American serial rights. Pays on acceptance. No previously published, photocopied or simultaneous submissions. Query. SASE. Free sample copy.
Cartoons: Buys educational, family life, humor through youth and religious themes. Single panel

OK. Submit finished art. Halftones OK. Pays $5-10. Buys 3 cartoons per issue. Reports in 3 weeks.
Illustrations: Buys article illustrations on education, family life, social issues and human interest. Submit finished art. B&w line drawings OK. Pays $30 minimum. Buys 2 illustrations per issue. Reports in 3 weeks.

THE ANTIQUES DEALER, 1115 Clifton Ave., Clifton NJ 07013. (201)779-1600 or (212)947-9270. Editor: Stella Hall. Monthly; 8¼x11¼"; 65 pages. Letterpress. Estab: 1949. Circ: 10,000. For antiques dealers. Buys all rights. Pays on publication. Photocopies OK. No previously published or simultaneous submissions. Query or mail artwork. SASE. Free sample copy.
Cartoons: Buys antiques themes. Single panel OK. Submit roughs or finished art. Line drawings, washes and halftones OK. Pays $5, b&w. Buys 2-3 cartoons annually. Reports in 4 weeks.
Illustrations: Buys cover art, article illustrations and spot drawings on antiques themes. Submit roughs or finished art. B&w line drawings, washes and veloxes OK. Pays $5-15, b&w cover; $5-10, inside b&w. Buys 2-3 illustrations annually. Reports in 4 weeks.

APPALACHIA BULLETIN, 5 Joy St., Boston MA 02108. Contact: Communications Director. Published by oldest mountaineering/conservation group in U.S. Monthly. Pays $15 for pen and ink sketches or cuts. "We offer superb exposure to East Coast business and academic markets."

APPALACHIA JOURNAL, 5 Joy St., Boston MA 02108. Contact: Communications Director. Published by oldest mountaineering/conservation group in U.S. Published semiannually. Pays $15 for pen and ink sketches or cuts. "We offer superb exposure to East Coast business and academic markets."

APPLE, A JOURNAL OF WOMEN'S SEXUALITY AND EROTICA, 100 NE 56th, Seattle WA 98105. (206)522-8588. Editor-in-Chief: Jessica Amanda Salmonson. Managing Editor: Jan London. Quarterly; 8½x11"; 50 pages. Offset. Estab: 1976. Circ: 1,000. Buys all rights, but may reassign rights to artist after publication. Previously published, photocopied and simultaneous submissions OK. Mail artwork. SASE. Sample copy $2. "Published by a nonprofit, tax-exempt organization. Contributions are tax-deductible if the artist is professional."
Illustrations: Buys cover art, article illustrations and spot drawings on women's sexuality. "We want erotica, not pornography. We want nothing from men and nothing degrading to women or exploitive of women's sexuality." Submit finished art. Cover: b&w line drawings OK. Inside: b&w line drawings, washes and reflective art OK. Pays contributor's copies. Buys 60 illustrations annually. Reports in 4 weeks.

APPLIANCE SERVICE NEWS, 5841 W. Montrose Ave., Chicago IL 60634. Editor/Publisher: J. J. Charous. Monthly. For owners/managers of service firms, service divisions of sales organizations, electric/gas appliance service shops, and repairmen of home laundry equipment, ranges, refrigerators, sewing machines, vacuum cleaners, and other small appliances (no TV or radio). Buys all rights.
Cartoons: Prefers roughs. Pays $7.50 on acceptance. Buys 25-30 cartoons annually. Reports in 30 days.

APPLIED RADIOLOGY, Brentwood Publishing Corporation, 825 S. Barrington Ave., Los Angeles CA 90049. Contact: Clay Camburn. Buys b&w spot drawings and full-color paintings. Pays $30, spot art; $175, full-color cover. Buys all rights. Pays on acceptance. Submit published samples. Reports in 30 days.

AQUARIAN AGENT, 127 Madison Ave., New York NY 10016. (212)679-5676. Editor: H. Weingarten. Quarterly. Circ: 1,750. For astrology students. Interested in b&w drawings and cartoons. Copyrighted. Previously published work OK. Pays on publication. Work must be astrologically related. Mail artwork. Reports in 1 month.

AQUATIC WORLD, World Publications, Box 366, Mt. View CA 94040. Art Buyer: Bob Anderson. Buys cover designs, soft drawings and cartoons. "Our readers are participants and we try to use material that shows insight into sports that we cover." Pays $10+. Buys reprint rights. Pays on publication. Reports in 1 week.

ARDIS, 2901 Heatherway, Ann Arbor MI 48104. Contact: E. Proffer. Published 3 times annually. Interested in artwork related to Russian letters and arts. Payment for drawings from $10-20; for cover design in finished art, $100. Pays on publication for one-time rights. Reports in 1 month.

ARIZONA, Box 1950, Phoenix AZ 85016. Editor: Bud DeWald. Sunday rotogravure magazine. Previously published work OK. Pays on publication. Pays $25 minimum, spot drawings; $13, cartoons. Submit published samples. Reports in 3 months.

ARMY MAGAZINE, 1529 18th St. NW, Washington DC 20036. Contact: Michael Dunbar. Copyrighted. 95,000 circulation. Estab: 1956. Monthly. "Professional journal devoted to the advancement of the military arts and sciences." Uses b&w drawings for inside. Pays on publication. Pays $10. Send samples. Reports in 6 weeks.

ART AND LITERARY DIGEST, Madoc-Tweed Art Centre, Tweed, Ontario Canada K0K 3J0 (summer); 1109 N. Betty Lane, Clearwater FL 33515 (winter). Editor: Roy Cadwell. Quarterly; 5½x8½". Estab: 1969. Circ: 1,000. Offset. For those interested in music, art, poetry and literature. Buys first rights. Pays on publication. Previously published work OK if release obtained. Mail samples or design ideas. Reports in 30 days. Sample copy $1.
Illustrations: Buys cover designs and spot drawings. B&w line drawings OK. Pays $5, spot art.

THE ARTS OBJECTIVELY, Box 15716, Philadelphia PA 19103. Editor-in-Chief: Frederic C. Kaplan. Quarterly; 8½x11"; 30-40 pages. Offset. Estab: 1975. Circ: 1,000. For professionals interested in art, music, literature, philosophy, politics and economics. Buys first rights. Pays on publication. No photocopies. Previously published and simultaneous submissions OK. Query with samples. SASE. Sample copy $1.50 (made payable to Podium II).
Cartoons: Buys current event, education, politics, art, music, communications and philosophy themes. "Work should be handled simply, with minimum of line. Subjects preferred are cerebral. Avoid rubber figures, infantile drawings." Single and double panel OK. Finished line drawings OK. Pays $5-10. Buys 1 cartoon per issue. Reports in 6-8 weeks.
Illustrations: Buys cover art, article illustrations and spot drawings on anything relating to the arts and communication; "only clean, crisp illustrations, preferably with figures." Submit roughs. B&w line drawings and veloxes OK. Pays $10-25, b&w cover; $5-10, inside b&w; $2.50-$5, spots. Buys 3-15 illustrations per issue. Reports in 3 weeks.
Special Needs: Pays $25 per 2 pages, mechanicals/layout.
To Break In: "Do not try to create a masterwork; just be competent and strive for a professional look: clean, sharp, crisp."

ASSEMBLY ENGINEERING, Hitchcock Publishing Co., Hitchcock Bldg., Wheaton IL 60137. Editor-in-Chief: Robert T. Kelly. Managing Editor: Richard D. Holtz. Monthly; 8¼x11¼"; 88 pages. Offset. Estab: 1958. Circ: 73,000. For design and manufacturing engineers and managers. Buys all rights, but may reassign rights to artist after publication. Pays on acceptance. No previously published or simultaneous submissions. Photocopies OK but "original required if accepted." Mail artwork. SASE. Free sample copy.
Cartoons: Buys themes on product assembly, design and conversion to metrics. "Metric conversion is increasingly important in our field; we need cartoons on that subject. Send roughs of suggested cartoon series. Such cartoons should refer to the humorous side of conversion, not the difficulties. Fine detail may be lost in printing; artwork should thus be relatively simple." Single panel OK. Line drawings only. Pays $15 minimum. Buys 15+ cartoons annually. Reports in 3 weeks.
To Break In: "If you don't have an engineering or manufacturing background, bounce your ideas off some engineers you know, and then send us samples."

ASSOCIATION AND SOCIETY MANAGER, Brentwood Publishing Corporation, 825 S. Barrington Ave., Los Angeles CA 90049. Contact: Clay Camburn. Buys spot drawings and full-color paintings. Pays $30, spot art; $175, full-color cover. Buys all rights. Pays on acceptance. Submit published samples. Reports in 30 days.

ASTROLOGY 78, 127 Madison Ave., New York NY 10016. Editor-in-Chief: Henry Weingarten. Quarterly; 6x9"; 64 pages. Offset. Estab: 1969. Circ: 2,500. For serious students of astrology. Buys first rights. Pays on publication. Previously published, photocopied and simultaneous submissions OK. Query with samples. SASE. Artists "must be into astrology and the

universe, and must live in the New York area." Also pays $5-100 for book jackets and paste-up.
Cartoons: Buys astrology themes. Submit finished art. Line drawings only. Pays $2 minimum. Reports in 4 weeks.
Illustrations: Buys spot drawings on astrology. Submit finished art. Pays $2 minimum. Reports in 4 weeks.

THE ATLANTIC ADVOCATE, Phoenix Square, Fredericton, New Brunswick Canada E3B 5A2. Editors: J. D. Morrison/H. P. Wood. Monthly. For professional men and women on matters concerning the Atlantic provinces. Buys first North American serial rights. Pays about $5 on publication for finished cartoons. Sample copy 75¢.

AUDIO, 401 N. Broad St., Philadelphia PA 19108. Editor: Gene Pitts. For those interested in stereo and high fidelity products. "Most artwork purchased is submitted with specific articles or columns. I prefer to assign each piece but would like to get together a group of artists of various styles to freelance." Pays $15 minimum for spot drawings. Buys all rights. Pays on publication. Reports in 1 month.

AUTO & FLAT GLASS JOURNAL, 1929 Royce Ave., Beloit WI 53511. (608)365-9416. Editor: David Benjamin. Published monthly for auto glass and flat glass replacement specialists. Estab: 1952. Circ: 2,300. "We're a small publication with a tight budget, but we are willing to pay acceptable rates to artists who fill our rather specialized need for illustrations and cartoons. If an artist can meet our needs, we will use him whenever possible." Art showing automobiles, focusing on auto glass, and illustrating service shops for auto glass, business management and retail salesmanship is needed. Sample payment: $15-30 for spot drawing. Buys one-time rights. Pays on acceptance. Mail artwork. Reports in 60 days. Sample copy available.

AUTO TRIM NEWS, 129 Broadway, Lynbrook NY 11563. Art Buyer: Nat Danas. Copyrighted. Pays on publication. Query. Reports in 30 days.
Illustrations: Uses spot drawings and cover designs. Prefers pen and ink. Pays $5 for spot drawings; $25-50 for cover design.

AUTOMATION, Penton Plaza, Cleveland OH 44114. (216)696-7000. Editor: Larry Boulden. Published monthly for production engineers. Circ: 90,000. Wants 3x4" cartoons. Sample payment: $15 for cartoons. Buys all rights. Copy sent on request.

AUTOMOTIVE AGE/KELLEY BLUE BOOK REPORTER, 6931 Van Nuys Blvd., Van Nuys CA 91405. (213)873-1320. Editor: Art Spinella. Assistant Editor: John Pashdag. Monthly; 8½x11"; 80-90 pages. Offset. Estab: 1966. Circ: 47,000. For college-educated owners and management personnel of new car dealerships. Buys first rights. Pays on publication. No previously published work or photocopies. Simultaneous submissions OK if accompanied by list of other publications receiving same or very similar material. Query with samples. SASE. Free sample copy. Prefers material which "reflects the magazine's aim of treating the auto dealership owner as a successful businessman and an individual with a private nonbusiness life." Also assigns artists to do promotion mailers and display booth graphics.
Cartoons: Buys themes on current events, environment, politics, golf, boating, and retail auto sales and management. Single and double panel OK. Submit roughs. Halftones and washes OK. Pays $15 minimum, b&w; $25 minimum, color. Cartoons are new addition to format, so no annual purchase figure available. Reports in 2 weeks.
Illustrations: Buys cover art, article illustrations and spot drawings for regular columns on Detroit, Washington, security, promotion beat, ad line, leasing and statistics. Submit roughs. Cover: washes and color-separated art OK. Inside: b&w line drawings, washes, color-separated and reflective art OK. Pays $100 minimum, color cover; $85 minimum, inside color; $70 minimum, inside b&w. Illustrations are new addition to format, so no annual purchase figure available. Reports in 3 weeks.

AVIATION QUARTERLY, 3613 Blossom Trail, Plano TX 75074. Art Buyer: B. Bierman. Features past, present and future in aviation. Will consider large original aircraft-related drawings submitted by mail. Negotiates payment. Reports in 180 days.

AWAY, 888 Worcester St., Wellesley MA 02181. Editor: Gerard J. Gagnon. Quarterly; 8⅛x10¾"; 32 pages. Offset. Circ: 230,000. For New England members of the Automobile Legal Association Auto & Travel Club, interested in their autos and in travel. Slanted to

Cover, article and spot illustrations on assigned themes are purchased by *Bucks County Panorama*. This drawing, by Larry Snyder, was purchased as an introductory illustration to catch the reader's eye and get him to read the accompanying article. Payment for the drawing was $15.

seasons. Buys one-time rights. Previously published work OK. Reports as soon as possible. Sample copy available.

AXIOM-ATLANTIC CANADA'S MAGAZINE, Box 1525, Halifax, Nova Scotia Canada B3J 3C6. (902)422-6797. Publisher: D.T. (Pat) Murphy. Bimonthly; 8x11"; 64 pages. Offset. Estab: 1974. Circ: 42,000. For professionals, university people and consumers interested in literature, art and sports. Buys first North American serial rights, and all rights but may reassign rights to artist after publication. Pays on publication. No previously published, photocopied or simultaneous submissions. Query with samples. SASE. Free sample copy.
Cartoons: Buys themes on current events, education, environment, family life and politics. Single panel OK. Submit finished art. Line drawings, halftones and washes OK. Pays $10-25. Buys 12 cartoons annually. Reports in 4 weeks. No nudes.
Illustrations: Buys cover art, article illustrations and spot drawings on anything but erotica and ethnics. Submit finished art. Cover: color-separated art OK. Inside: b&w line drawings, washes, color-separated and reflective art and veloxes OK. Pays $50-500, color cover; $50-200, inside color; $25-150, inside b&w. Buys 90 illustrations annually. Reports in 4 weeks.

B.C. BUSINESS, 200-1520 Alberni St., Vancouver, BC Canada V6G 1A3. (604)685-2376. Editor-in-Chief: J.R. Martin. Monthly; 8¼x11"; 48-64 pages. Offset. Estab: 1973. Circ: 18,000. For business and professional men and women. Buys first rights. Pays on acceptance. Previously published, photocopied and simultaneous submissions OK. Query. SASE. Free sample copy.
Cartoons: Buys environment, political, business and management-oriented themes. Single panel OK. Submit finished art. Washes OK. Pays $10-25, b&w. Buys 12 cartoons annually. Reports in 3 weeks.
Illustrations: Buys cover art, article illustrations and spot drawings on assignment. Pays $200-400, color cover; $10-50, inside b&w. Buys 6 illustrations annually.

B.C. HORSEMAN, # 212, 20216 Fraser Hwy., Langley, BC Canada V3A 4E6. (604)533-1281. Editor-in-Chief: Lynn MacDonald. Published 9 times annually; 8½x11"; 32 pages. Offset. Estab: 1971. Circ: 7,500. Buys first rights. Pays on acceptance. Previously published and simultaneous submissions OK. No photocopies. Query with samples. SASE. Free sample copy.
Cartoons: "We would like to develop a cartoon character with episodes to run each issue." Buys themes on the environment, humor through youth and horses. Single panel OK. Submit finished art. Line drawings only. Pays $25 minimum. Reports in 2 weeks.

BABY CARE, 52 Vanderbilt Ave., New York NY 10017. (212)685-4400. Quarterly; 7½x5⅜"; 58 pages. Offset. Estab: 1970. Circ: 850,000. For new parents. Buys all rights. Pays on acceptance. Previously published and simultaneous submissions OK. No photocopies. Query. SASE. Free sample copy. "I discuss each issue's needs with the artist, who then submits work."
Cartoons: Evelyn Podsiadlo, editor. Buys themes on family life. Single panel OK. Submit finished art. Line drawings only. Pays $25 minimum. Reports in 3 months.
Illustrations: Ruth Kitaif, editor. Buys cover art and article illustrations of babies up to 1-year-old with or without parents. Washes OK. Pays $250 maximum, inside color. Reports in 3 months.

BACHY, c/o Papa Bach Bookstore, 11317 Santa Monica Blvd., Los Angeles CA 90025. (213)478-2374. Editor-in-Chief: John Harris. Published 3 times annually; 8½x11"; 108 pages. Offset. Estab: 1972. Circ: 800. For literature and poetry-oriented writers and artists. Photocopied and simultaneous submissions OK. Mail artwork. SASE.
Illustrations: Beverly Pasternack, editor. Buys cover art, article illustrations and spot drawings. Uses b&w line drawings and collages that reflect contemporary themes. "The art slant in *Bachy* is fine art — looking for work with not only technical excellence but also work that communicates something fresh and relevant; social commentary, unusual media." Pays contributor's copies.

BAROID NEWS BULLETIN, Box 1675, Houston TX 77001. Editor: Kit van Cleave. Circ: 18,000. For those in petroleum-related fields. Artwork usually purchased with an article between 1,500 and 3,000 words on general interest subject. Recent articles include "Railroad to the Moon" (in the Peruvian Andes Mountains); "The Upside Down Country" (Australia); "Annie Palmer and Rose Hall" (the famous Jamaican mansion). Pays up to $25 per illustration. Buys first rights. Pays on acceptance. Reports in 2 weeks.

BATH PRODUCTS MERCHANDISING, Patio Bldg., 76 SE 5th Ave., Delray Beach FL 33344. Editor: William Dogan. Quarterly. For those interested in bath products/accessories, linens, domestics, bath remodeling and allied fields. Articles deal with merchandising, buying, promotion, management assistance, personnel, new products, sales efficiency and show coverage. Freelance material used on speculation only. Query.

BEAVER, 235 Park Ave. S., New York NY 10003. Editor-in-Chief: Jayson Rollands. Managing Editor: Gilda Duncan. Bimonthly; 8½x11"; 80 pages. Offset. Estab: 1976. Circ: 200,000. For ages 18-40 with high school education, interested in pretty women and sex. Buys first North American serial rights. Pays on acceptance. No previously published or simultaneous submissions. Photocopies OK. Mail artwork. SASE. Sample copy $2.
Cartoons: Buys erotic themes. All formats OK. Submit finished art. Line drawings, halftones and washes OK. Pays $50, b&w; $100, color. Buys 180 cartoons annually. Reports in 4 weeks.
Illustrations: Ben Harvey, editor. Buys article illustrations on assignment. B&w line drawings and washes OK. Pays $50-400. Buys 24 illustrations annually. Reports in 4 weeks.

THE BEEHIVE, 201 8th Ave. S., Nashville TN 37203. Editor-in-Chief: Martha Wagner. Weekly; 5x8½"; 8 pages. Estab: 1964. Circ: 250,000. For ages 9-11 in church school. Buys all rights. Pays on acceptance. No previously published, photocopied or simultaneous submissions. Mail artwork. SASE. Free sample copy.
Cartoons: Dave Dawson, editor. Buys themes on children doing things and nature. Doesn't want "swearing, off-color, smoking/drinking, adult-type" themes. Single panel OK. Submit finished art. Line drawings, halftones and washes OK. Minimum payment: $7.50, b&w; $35, color. Buys 52 cartoons annually. Reports in 4 weeks.

BEER WHOLESALER, Patio Bldg., 76 SE 5th Ave., Delray Beach FL 33344. Editor: William Dogan. Quarterly. For those in the beer distribution field, including owners, general managers, advertising/sales promotion managers and salesmen. Buys themes on sales promotions, conventions and management. Freelance material used on speculation only. Query before submitting art.

BEND OF THE RIVER, Box 239, Perrysburg OH 43551. (419)874-1691. Editors-in-Chief: Lee Raizk/Christine Alexander. Monthly; 8½x11"; 24 pages. Offset. Estab: 1972. Circ: 2,000. For well-educated, ages 40+ readers. Pays on publication. Previously published work OK. No photocopied or simultaneous submissions. Mail artwork. SASE. Sample copy 25¢.
Illustrations: Buys cover art, article illustrations and spot drawings on history and antiques. Submit finished art. B&w line drawings OK. Pays $3-5, cover; $2-5, inside. Buys 2 illustrations per issue. Reports in 2 months.
Special Needs: Any seasonal work considered. Also occasionally needs brochures: pays $5 per sketch.

BEST WISHES, Box 8, Station C, Toronto, Ontario Canada M6J 3M8. Contact: Mrs. K. Applegate. Given to new mothers. Quarterly. Buys spot drawings, cartoons and cover designs. Pays $10, drawings. Previously published work OK. Lifetime rights bought but not exclusively. Pays on acceptance. Mail artwork. Reports in 1 month.

BETTER HOMES AND GARDENS, 1716 Locust, Des Moines IA 50336. Cartoon Editor: Gerry Knox. Published monthly for husbands and wives who have a serious interest in home and family as the focal point in their lives. Buys all rights.
Cartoons: About 30 cartoons purchased yearly. Pays $150-200. Prefers 8x10" finished work, but will review roughs. "Good taste and originality are our chief requirements." Reports in 2 weeks.

BEYOND REALITY, 303 W. 42nd St., New York NY 10036. Contact: Harry Belil. For those interested in the occult. Interested in spot drawings submitted in 8½x11" size. Buys all rights. Pays on acceptance. Payment: $15-20, spot drawings; $35-50, half page editorial illustration. Reports in 30 days.

BIG FARMER, INC., 131 Lincoln Hwy., Frankfort IL 60423. Cartoon Editor: Robert Moraczewski. For farm executives who manage, own and/or operate large food factories or family farms. Designed to assist them in making more intelligent decisions as they organize their money, men and materials. Pays on acceptance.
Cartoons: Uses 18-20 cartoons per year. Prefers finished art, single panel. Pays $15-25. Reports in 2-6 weeks.

BIG MAGAZINE, Box 13208, Phoenix AZ 85002. Editor: Frederick H. Kling. Published 3 times annually. For Goodyear earthmover tire buyers, including contractors and personnel who work on highways, airports, dams, and in open-pit mines, quarries, sand and gravel operations. Buys first and reprint rights.
Cartoons: Will look at roughs or finished art. Vehicles shown must be rubber-tired, not steel track. Pays $25-40 for finished art, on acceptance. Reports in 2-3 weeks.

BIKE WORLD, Box 366, Mt. View CA 94040. Editor: John Potter. Monthly. For participant bike tourists and racers of high level of sophistication. Will send sample copy to artists "if they have history of cycling work." Buys all rights. Pays on publication. Previously published work occasionally OK. Submit art. Reports in 1 week.
Illustrations: Uses b&w drawings, line and line and wash. Pays $2.50, spot art; $100-200, 8½x11" or larger, color-separated cover designs.

BIRMINGHAM MAGAZINE, 1914 6th Ave. N., Birmingham AL 35203. Art Buyer: Donald Brown. Buys one-time rights.
Illustrations: "We use simple, clean work — 'non-cartoonish'." Prefers finished art 8x10", any medium. Pays $25, spot drawings; $50, half-page editorial illustration. Reports in 2 weeks.

BLACK AMERICAN LITERATURE FORUM (formerly *Negro American Literature Forum),* Indiana State University, Terre Haute IN 47809. Editor: Joseph Weixlmann. Quarterly. Mainly uses articles on black American literature, primarily aimed at high school and college teachers. Buys one-time rights. Previously published work OK. Pays on acceptance. Mail artwork. SASE. Sample copy 25¢.
Illustrations: Uses b&w line drawings and line and washes. Pays $15. Reports in 8 weeks.

BLACK BELT, 1845 W. Empire Ave., Burbank CA 91504. Contact: Pam Barrett. Monthly. For martial artists of all ages. Uses b&w line drawings, line and wash, cover designs (on assignment), full-color illustrations with color separations and cartoons. Buys all rights. No previously published work. Pays on publication. Artwork must relate to the martial arts. Query. Reports in 2 weeks. Sample copy available.

BLACK BUSINESS DIGEST, 3133 N. Broad St., Philadelphia PA 19132. Editor: Vincent Capozzi. Monthly. For college-educated professionals interested in international business news as it relates to the developing black nations in Africa, the Caribbean, South and Central America. Buys all rights. Pays on publication. Mail artwork. Reports in 8 weeks. Sample copy available.
Illustrations: Uses cover designs and full-color illustrations. Negotiates payment.

THE BLACK COLLEGIAN, 3217 Melpomene Ave., New Orleans LA 70125. Editor: Kalama ya Salaam. Bimonthly during academic year. For black college students. "If artists query in advance, we can tell them what articles we need illustrated and they can thereby submit material to meet our needs." Buys serial and first serial rights. Pays on publication. Previously published work OK. Sample copy available.
Illustrations: Uses b&w drawings, full-color illustrations (color separations required). Pays $5-10, spot drawing; $10-15, full-color illustration; $50, cover design in color.
Cartoons: Roughs or finished art. Pays $5.
Seasonal Needs: Artwork for these issues: September — careers; November — black history; January — travel and women; March — jobs; May — women.

BLACK MARIA, 815 W. Wrightwood, Chicago IL 60614. Contact: Editors. Quarterly. "We are involved with the women's movement and our content reflects this. We are a women's publication; we only publish women." In addition to material intended specifically for this magazine, will also look at examples of artist's style in tearsheets or photocopies. Buys one-time rights. Previously published work OK. Reports in 3 months.
Illustrations: Uses spot drawings, 6x9 maximum; pen and ink, line and wash. Pays contributor's copies and a subscription.

BLACK SPORTS, 31 E. 28th St., New York NY 10016. Editor: Les Carson. Art Director: Ollie Johnson. Monthly. "Our audience is adult males from 18-35, blue and white collar workers. We primarily use art to illustrate our stories which deal with all phases of the sports world that would be of interest to the black consumer." Buys one-time rights. Previously published work OK. Pays on publication. Query with resume. Reports in 4 weeks; sometimes longer on "holds." Sample copy 75¢. Buys some cartoons.
Illustrations: Buys cover designs. B&w line drawings, line and wash, and full-color illustrations OK. Pays $200-400, 4-color cover design.

BLACK WRITERS NEWS, 4019 S. Vincennes Ave., Chicago IL 60653. (312)624-3184. Editor-in-Chief: Alice C. Browning. Managing Editor: Roma L. Jones. Quarterly; 8½x11"; 100 pages. Offset. Estab: 1970. Circ: 20,000. Buys first rights. Pays on publication. Previously published work OK. No photocopied or simultaneous submissions. Query with samples. SASE. Sample copy $1.75.
Cartoons: Buys current events, education, environment, sports and entertainment themes. Double panel OK. Submit roughs. Line drawings only. Pays $5. Reports in 2 months.
Illustrations: Charles Arnold, editor. Buys cover art, article illustrations and spot drawings. Submit roughs. Pays $5, b&w. Buys 40 illustrations annually. Reports in 2 months.

THE BLADE SUNDAY MAGAZINE, 541 Superior St., Toledo OH 43660. Editor-in-Chief: Mike Tressler. Weekly; 11x13"; 32 pages. Rotogravure. Circ: 210,000. For newspaper-reading audience. Buys one-time rights. Pays on publication. Previously published and simultaneous submissions OK. No photocopies. Query. SASE. Free sample copy.
Illustrations: Buys cover art and article illustrations on local or regional themes. "Most of our original artwork is done by staff artists or Toledo-area people. We currently use very little outside freelance illustration since it is hard to illustrate a Toledo story with work from a New York artist." Submit finished art. Cover: washes and color-separated art OK. Inside: b&w line drawings OK. Pays $30-75, color cover; $35-50, inside color; $20-30, inside b&w. Buys 6-12 illustrations annually. Reports in 3 weeks.

BLUEGRASS UNLIMITED, Box 111, Broad Run VA 22014. Art Buyer: Peter V. Kuykendall. Interested in spot drawings or cartoons in pen and ink relating to country music, whether bluegrass, old-time or traditional. Pays $10-20 on publication. Buys all rights, but sometimes returns rights on artist's request, after publication.

BOAT BUILDERS, Davis Publications, 229 Park Ave. S., New York NY 10003. Contact: Irving Bernstein. Pays $20 minimum, line drawings; $400 maximum, full-color cover design. Buys first rights. Pays on acceptance. Reports in 1 week.

BOWHUNTER MAGAZINE, Box 5377, Fort Wayne IN 46805. (219)432-5772. Editor-in-Chief: M. R. James. Bimonthly; 8½x11"; 72 pages. Offset. Estab: 1971. Circ: 80,000. For those who hunt with bow and arrow. Buys all rights, but may reassign rights to artist after publication.

Pays on acceptance. No previously published, photocopied or simultaneous submissions. Query. SASE. Free sample copy.
Cartoons: Buys themes on archery and bowhunting. Single panel OK. Submit finished art. Line drawings OK. Pays $15-25. Buys 6-12 cartoons annually. Reports in 4 weeks. No unsafe or dangerous hunting situations.
Illustrations: Buys cover art and article illustrations on outdoor scenes, bow and arrow hunting and wildlife. Inside: b&w line drawings and washes OK. Pays $50-150, color cover; $25-100, inside b&w. Reports in 4 weeks.

BOWLERS JOURNAL, 875 N. Michigan Ave., Chicago IL 60611. Art Buyer: Mort Luby. 16,500 circulation. Buys first North American rights. Buys cartoons, line drawings, wash drawings or caricatures of bowlers or billiard players in the news. Minimum payment for spot drawing is $25. Mail artwork. Reports in 2 weeks.

BOY'S LIFE, North Brunswick NJ 08902. Cartoon Editor: Jon Halter. 2 million circulation. Estab: 1911. Monthly. For boys ages 8-14. Buys first North American serial rights. Pays on acceptance. Query. Reports in 2 weeks.
Cartoons: Uses 4-6 sports or general interest cartoons per issue. Pays $75. "No cute stuff." Prefers 8x10" roughs.
Illustrations: Assigns b&w line drawings, line and wash, and full-color illustrations.

BRANCHING OUT, Box 4098, Edmonton, Alberta Canada T6E 4S8. (403)433-4021. Editor: Sharon Batt. Bimonthly. For Canadian women. 4,000 circulation. Buys cover designs, cartoons and drawings. Interested in work by Canadian women only. Each issue features a series of drawings or prints. Interested in themes concerning women. Buys first North American serial rights. Rates negotiable. Pays on publication. Query. Reports in 4-6 weeks. Sample copy $1.

BREAD, Church of the Nazarene, 6401 The Paseo, Kansas City MO 64131. Editor: Dan Ketchum. Monthly. 60,000 circulation. Estab: 1946. For junior and senior high students. Uses creative and candid close-ups of junior and senior high students. Buys b&w line drawings, cartoons and cover designs. Buys one-time rights. Pays on acceptance. Previously published work OK. Mail artwork. Reports in 2 weeks. Sample copy available.

BRIGADE LEADER, Christian Service Brigade, Box 150, Wheaton IL 60187. (312)665-0630. Editor: Paul Heidebrecht. For Christian laymen and adult male leaders of boys enrolled in the Brigade's 3 man-boy programs. "Our magazine seeks to promote consciousness, acceptance of and personal commitment to Jesus Christ." Buys finished b&w drawings and cartoons. Maximum size: 8½x11". "We use 1 cartoon per issue. Editors assign cartoon strips or stories to artists." Pays on publication of artwork; acceptance of cartoons. Pays $20-30, spot drawings; $7.50-15, cartoons; $50-80, full-page b&w or 2-color illustrations. Buys one-time rights. Send samples. Reports in 6 weeks. Sample copy 50¢.

BROADCASTING ENGINEERING, 1014 Wyandotte, Kansas City MO 64105. Art Buyer: Ron Merrell. For the broadcast/communications industry. Needs "material in good taste that is seasonal from a communications and broadcasting point of view, including conventions." Tearsheets, photocopies or transparencies, as well as original art, considered. "We are an unusual magazine. While we communicate with management, technical broadcast and cable people on business and technical subjects, we take an over-the-backyard-fence approach to our readers. We try to serve our industry and nudge it forward." Pays on acceptance. Minimum rate for spot drawing is $10. Buys all rights. Mail drawings and cartoons. Reports in 2 weeks.

BROILER BUSINESS, Watt Publishing Co., Mount Morris IL 61054. Editor: Bernard E. Heffernan. For businessmen engaged in the production, processing and marketing of broilers. Buys all rights.
Cartoons: Buys cartoons with slant on broilers and turkeys. Pays $8-10 on acceptance. Uses 2-3 cartoons per month.

BROMOS CON PIMIENTA, 6360 NE 4th Court, Miami FL 33138. (305)751-1181. Editor: W. A. Sandler. Bimonthly, adult, Spanish, sex-oriented humor publication. Interested in b&w drawings, line art, cartoons (5x7" or 8x10") or cartoon strips of full-page length or more. Finished art only. Buys one-time and reprint rights. Previously published work in languages other than Spanish considered. Pays on acceptance. Sample payment: $1-5, cartoons; $10-25, comic strips. "No puns in captions!" Captions should be translatable into Spanish. Mail art. SASE. Reports in 30 days. Sample copy 75¢.

BRONZE THRILLS, 1220 Harding St., Box 2257, Ft. Worth TX 76101. Monthly. Buys all rights. Free sample copy. For ages 18-45, in middle and lower income families.
Cartoons: Buys about 100 cartoons a year. Cartoons must be funny and geared to blacks. Not interested in over-used sex. Finished art only, 5x7", in any format. Pays $7.50 on acceptance. Reports in 90 days.

BROTHERHOOD OF MAINTENANCE OF WAY EMPLOYEES JOURNAL, 12050 Woodward Ave., Detroit MI 48203. Editor-in-Chief: R. J. Williamson. Monthly; 7x10"; 32 pages. Offset and letterpress. Estab: 1891. Circ: 150,000. For members of international railroad maintenance workers' union, who build, repair and maintain tracks, buildings and bridges. Buys simultaneous rights. Pays on publication. Previously published, photocopied and simultaneous submissions OK. Mail artwork. SASE. Free sample copy.
Cartoons: Buys humorous themes about railroads. Single panel OK. Submit roughs. Line drawings only. Pays $5-15. Reports in 2 weeks.

BUCKS COUNTY PANORAMA, 57 W. Court St., Doylestown PA 18901. (215)348-9505. Editor-in-Chief: Gerry Wallerstein. Monthly; 8½x11"; 56 pages. Offset. Estab: 1959. Circ: 8,000. For educated, affluent families interested in area history, issues, people, ecology, environment, antiques, horses and gardening. Buys all rights. Pays on publication. No previously published, photocopied or simultaneous submissions. Query with samples. SASE. Sample copy $1.25.
Illustrations: Jeanne E. Stock, editor. Assigns cover art, article illustrations and spot drawings on local architecture, history, and holiday and seasonal themes. Submit roughs. Cover: b&w line drawings, color-separated and reflective art OK. Inside: b&w line drawings OK. Pays $25 maximum, cover; $10-15, inside. Buys 30-40 illustrations annually. Reports in 2 weeks.

THE BUF SWINGER, 303 W. 42nd St., New York NY 10036. Editor: Will Martin. For young men. Bimonthly. Uses b&w drawings in line and wash and 7x10" rough cartoons. Pays $35-40 for wash drawing. "Because of time element, it is difficult to work with artists not in, or close to, New York." Buys all rights. Previously published work OK. Mail artwork. SASE.

BURROUGHS CLEARING HOUSE, Box 418, Detroit MI 48232. Monthly. For bank and financial officers. Buys all rights. Sample copy available.
Cartoons: Buys themes on loans, investments, personnel, systems and public relations. These accompany articles offering information on specific bank problems. Sample rate: $15 on acceptance. Reports as soon as possible.

BUSINESS & COMMERCIAL AVIATION, Hangar C-1, Westchester City Airport, White Plains NY 10604. Monthly; 8¼x11⅛"; 120 pages. Offset. Estab: 1958. Circ: 55,000. Technical publication for corporate pilots; mostly male, ages 35-55. Buys all rights, but may reassign rights to artist after publication. Pays on acceptance. No previously published or simultaneous submissions. Photocopies OK. Query with samples. SASE. Free sample copy.
Illustrations: Elaine Jones, art director. Buys cover art and article illustrations on aviation themes. "We generally only use artists with a fairly realistic style. This is a serious business publication — graphically conservative." Submit roughs. Cover: color-separated art OK. Inside: b&w line drawings, washes and color-separated art OK. Pays $350-1,100, color cover; $100-500, inside color; $50-300, inside b&w. Buys 15-20 illustrations annually. Reports in 4 weeks.
Special Needs: Pays $5 per hour minimum for paste-up/mechanicals; local artists only. Pays $100 minimum for portraits of editors for monthly columns, printed size, 2⅛x3".

BUSINESS ON WHEELS, Box 13208, Phoenix AZ 85002. Contact: Frederick H. Kling. For Goodyear fleet truck tire buyers. Buys first and reprint rights.
Cartoons: Interested in themes about truck companies and private companies with truck fleets (manufacturers, processors, distributors, retailers, etc.). May be submitted rough or finished. Payment: $25-40, finished art on acceptance. Reports in 2-3 weeks.

BUSINESS TODAY, Green Hall Annex, Princeton NJ 08540. Buys cartoons and color-separated art on student/faculty/business relationships. Prefers cartoons be 3½x4" in pen and ink. Pays $10, cartoon; $20, color separation for cover use. Will consider buying reprint rights to previously published material. Pays on publication for one-time rights. Reports in 1-2 months.

BUSINESS WEEK, 1221 Avenue of the Americas, New York NY 10020. Art Director: John R. Vogler. "Most art is commissioned but we welcome samples from artists who are in easy reach of New York City. Pays $75 for spot illustrations. Buys one-time rights. Send non-returnable samples.

CALIFORNIA BUILDER & ENGINEER, Box 10070, Palo Alto CA 94303. Editor: Mahlon Fisher. Published bimonthly for heavy construction contractors and equipment manufacturers. Estab: 1893. 15,000 circulation. Needs material relating to heavy construction in California. Previously published work OK. Payment made on publication. Mail artwork. Reports as soon as possible.
Cartoons: Pays $8 for 3x5" finished art.
Illustrations: Buys b&w line, and line and wash drawings. Pays $10, spot art; $100-200, 4-color cover design.
Special Needs: Artwork for these issues: January — forecast; February — equipment directory; July — materials directory; September — water.

CALIFORNIA JOURNAL, 1617 10th St., Sacramento CA 95814. (916)444-2840. Editor: Ed Salzman. Published monthly. 14,000 circulation. Copyrighted. Buys cartoons, line, line and wash drawings and cover designs. Pays $20-40, spot drawings; $10-25, cartoons. California artists should send resume. Sample copy available.

CAMPING INDUSTRY, 225 E. Michigan, Milwaukee WI 53202. (414)276-6600. Editor-in-Chief: Connie Howes. Published 7 times annually; 8¼x11¼"; 48 pages. Offset. Estab: 1966. Circ: 13,800. For camping equipment manufacturers, distributors, wholesalers and retailers. Not copyrighted. Pays on acceptance. Photocopied and simultaneous submissions (if exclusive in circulation area) OK. Query with samples. SASE. Free sample copy.
Cartoons: Buys themes on environment, camping and retail sales. Single panel OK. Submit roughs or finished art. Line drawings, halftones and washes OK. Pays $10-25, b&w. Buys 1-2 cartoons annually. Reports in 3 weeks.

CAMPUS, Jaymar Publications, Box 25024, Albuquerque NM 87125. Editorial Coordinator: Greg Lay. For high school students. Buys illustrations and cartoons on school themes. Pays $4-12, fairly simple work; $13-50, more elaborate work. Pays on publication. Negotiates special projects.

CAMPUS LIFE, Box 419, Wheaton IL 60187. (312)668-6600. Editor-in-Chief: Philip Yancey. Managing Editor: Tim Stafford. Monthly; 8½x11"; 80 pages. Offset. Circ: 200,000. For high school students. Buys first and simultaneous rights. Pays on acceptance. Previously published, photocopied and simultaneous submissions OK. Submit portfolio. SASE. Free sample copy. Also pays $100 minimum for promotional material.
Cartoons: Buys education, environment, family life, humor through youth, political and religious themes. Prefers single panel. Submit finished art. Halftones and washes OK. Pays $40 minimum, b&w. Buys 50 cartoons annually. Reports in 3 weeks.
Illustrations: Joan Nickerson, editor. Buys article illustrations on assignment. Pays $150-250, color; $125-200, b&w. Buys 25 illustrations annually.

THE CANADIAN FICTION MAGAZINE, Box 46422 Station G, Vancouver, BC Canada V6R 4G7. Editor: Geoffrey Hancock. Anthology devoted exclusively to contemporary Canadian fiction. Quarterly. Copyrighted. Buys b&w line drawings. Pays $5 per printed page; $20, cover. Normal format includes 4-8 pages of art. Only publishes work of artists residing in Canada and Canadians living abroad. Mail artwork. SASE. Reports in 4-6 weeks. Sample copy $3.

THE CANADIAN FORUM, 3 Church St., #40, Toronto, Ontario Canada M5E 1M2. Editor: Denis Smith. Monthly. Estab: 1920. 12,000 circulation. For students and professional people. Publishes Canadian nonfiction, political and literary commentary, experimental and mainstream fiction, poetry and verse. Buys b&w line drawings, cover designs and cartoons. Pays $15. Buys one-time rights. Previously published work OK. Query. Reports in 2 months. Sample copy $1.25.

CANADIAN LIBRARY JOURNAL, Canadian Library Association, 151 Sparks St., Ottawa, Ontario Canada K1P 5E3. Art Buyer: Barbara Crate. Buys pen and ink, rough. Pays on acceptance. Buys first Canadian publishing rights or one-time use. Previously published work OK. Query. Reports in 4 weeks, earlier if possible.

CANADIAN PRINTER & PUBLISHER, Maclean-Hunter Publications, 481 University Ave., Toronto, Ontario Canada M5W 1A7. Editor/Publisher: William B. Forbes. Buys pen and ink and line and wash cartoons and illustrations. Submit finished art. Pays $15, spot art; $15-35, cartoons. Buys all rights. Pays on acceptance. Previously published work OK. Reports in 2 weeks.

THE CANADIAN REVIEW, 251 Cooper St., Cooper House, Ottawa, Ontario Canada. (613)234-1594. Editor: E. Graydon Carter. Monthly. Buys first serial rights on cartoons. Mail b&w finished drawings. Pays up to $25 on acceptance. Reports immediately. Sample copy $1.

THE CAPE ROCK, English Dept., Southeast Missouri State University, Cape Girardeau MO 63701. Editor-in-Chief: R.A. Burns. Published semiannually; 5½x11"; 64 pages. Offset. Estab: 1964. Circ: 500. For general audience, academicians and libraries. Buys first rights. No previously published, photocopied or simultaneous submissions. Query with samples. SASE. Free sample copy "if you indicate you're an artist."
Illustrations: Buys inside graphics. B&w art only. Pays contributor's copies. Buys 15-20 photos/graphics per issue. Reports in 1-4 months.

CAR CRAFT MAGAZINE, 8490 Sunset Blvd., Los Angeles CA 90069. (213)657-5100. Editor-in-Chief: Rick Voegelin. Managing Editor: Don Evans. Monthly; 8x11"; 120 pages. Offset. Estab: 1952. Circ: 305,000. For individuals with high school education, interested in drag racing and high-performance autos. Buys first North American serial rights. Pays on publication. No previously published, photocopied or simultaneous submissions. Query with samples. SASE. Free sample copy.
Illustrations: Charlie Hayward, editor. Buys article illustrations and spot drawings on race and

Drawings by
Ray Billingsley

Breezy, funny material, not subtleties, are preferred by *Current Consumer*, a magazine for junior and senior high school students. *Current Consumer* buys approximately 15 cartoons and 15 illustrations annually. This cartoon, by Ray Billingsley, was purchased to accompany an article on taxes.

street cars. Submit roughs. All media OK. Pays $50 minimum, b&w; $150, color. Buys 13 illustrations annually. Reports in 2 weeks.

CAREER WORLD, 501 Lake Forest Ave., Highwood IL 60040. (312)432-2700. Editor: Whayne Dillehay. Associate Editor: Jan Farrington. Published 9 times annually; 8³/₁₆x10⁷/₈"; 32 pages. Offset. Estab: 1972. Circ: 130,000. For junior and senior high school students. Buys all rights, but may reassign rights to artists after publication. Pays on publication. Previously published and simultaneous submissions OK. Query with samples. SASE. Free sample copy.
Cartoons: Buys themes on education and jobs for young people. "Funny cartoons on job hunting are good. But, don't demean a job or insult a worker." All formats OK. Submit finished art. Line drawings OK. Pays $10 minimum. Buys 9-18 cartoons annually. Reports in 2 weeks.
Illustrations: Buys cover art, article illustrations and spot drawings on assignment. Query for topic. Submit roughs. Cover: color-separated and reflective art OK. Inside: b&w line drawings OK. Minimum payment: $25, color cover; $10, inside. Buys "up to 20" illustrations annually. Reports in 4 weeks.
Special Needs: Pays $5 minimum, keyline and paste-up.
To Break In: "Be simple and realize that our kids are not fond of subtleties. This is an excellent opportunity for beginners to get started in print."

CAROLINA COOPERATOR, 125 E. Davie St., Raleigh NC 27601. (919)828-4411. Editor-in-Chief: Robert J. Wachs. Managing Editor: Ken Ramey. Monthly; 8⅜x10⅞"; 40 pages. Offset. Estab: 1922. Circ: 60,000. For farm families in North and South Carolina. Not copyrighted. Pays on acceptance. Previously published work OK. No photocopied or simultaneous submissions. Query with samples. SASE. Free sample copy.
Cartoons: Buys themes on farming, outdoor/current events, education and humor through youth. Single panel OK. Submit finished art. Line drawings OK. Pays $5 minimum. Reports in 2 weeks.

CAROLINA COUNTRY, Box 27306, Raleigh NC 27611. Editor: Owen Bishop. Cartoon Editor: Marge Howell. General interest, monthly, family magazine. Buys first rights. "We do not know from 1 month to the next what artwork we might need, and when we do need it, the subject matter is specific and must be received promptly. We have a tight deadline." Buys 1-2 cartoons per issue. Pays $5 on acceptance. Submit published samples.

CARTOONS, 8490 Sunset Blvd., Los Angeles CA 90069. Contact: Dennis Ellefson. Buys 150 pages of cartoon stories annually and 60 single panel cartoons for male youths who like cars and bikes. Pays $75 minimum per page and $15 per single panel for all rights on acceptance. Cartoons should be well drawn, identifiable, detailed cars. Also uses spot drawings; $15. Prefers roughs. Reports in 2 weeks.

CASTLE OF FRANKENSTEIN, 509 5th Ave., New York NY 10017. Editor: Calvin T. Beck. Bimonthly. Readership is primarily youth to college level.
Cartoons: Uses 40-60 cartoons a year; any size. Roughs OK for unusual work, but not one-panel jobs. Pays $4 and up on publication for spots. Buys all rights. Reports in 8-12 weeks. "We like the style of Charles Addams and Gahan Wilson and any cartoonist who follows in their footsteps; especially needs cartooning in advanced 'sick' and psychedelic categories. We're also using comic strips and pay $20 minimum per page (including art, story and lettering). A comic strip usually runs 5-10 pages (sometimes longer if we're thoroughly convinced it's worth the space) in the adult horror comic book tradition. Wash and halftone style preferred if artist has good knowledge of reproduction (otherwise wash and halftone fade badly). Good idea if material is relevant and cerebral since our readership is strongly 'head' and 'now' oriented."

CATS, Box 557, Washington PA 15301. (412)225-3753. Editor-in-Chief: Jean Laux. Co-Editor: Patrick L. Oliver. Monthly; 7¾x10½"; 56 pages. Offset. Estab: 1945. Circ: 65,000. For cat lovers and breeders, mostly women. Buys first rights. Pays on publication. No previously published, photocopied or simultaneous submissions. Query. SASE. Free sample copy.
Cartoons: Buys cat themes. "No talking cats or dressed-up cats please." Single panel OK. Submit roughs. Halftones OK. Pays $25 minimum. Buys 6 cartoons annually. Reports in 4 weeks.
Illustrations: Buys cover art and article illustrations on cats. Submit roughs. Cover: color-separated and reflective art OK. Inside: b&w art OK. Minimum payment: $100, color cover; $25, inside. Buys 3-4 illustrations annually. Reports in 4 weeks.

CATTLEMEN, 1760 Ellice Ave., Winnipeg, Manitoba Canada R2W 0Y3. (204)774-1861. Editor-in-Chief: Harold Dodds. Monthly; 8¼x11"; 80 pages. Offset. Estab: 1936. Circ: 50,000. For cattle producers and related trades; oriented toward production. Buys Canadian rights. Pays on acceptance. Previously published work OK. Query with samples. SASE. Free sample copy.
Cartoons: Buys themes on current events, environment, family life, politics, retirement and beef production. Nothing unrelated to beef or not Canadian in content. Single panel OK. Submit roughs or finished art. Halftones and washes OK. Pays $5 minimum, b&w. Buys 30-40 cartoons annually. Reports in 2 weeks.
Illustrations: Ken Armistead, editor. Buys cover art and article illustrations on beef production and marketing. Submit roughs or finished art. Cover art: reflective art OK. Inside art: b&w line drawings, washes and veloxes OK. Pays $50 minimum. Buys 5-10 illustrations annually. Reports in 2 weeks.
Special Needs: Artwork for animal health, forage and transportation issues.

CAVALIER, Dugent Publishing Company, 316 Aragon Ave., Coral Gables FL 33134. Editor/Publisher: Douglas Allen. Managing Editor: Nye Wilden. For men. Buys first time rights.
Cartoons: Buys "funny, somewhat 'sick' humor and sexual themes." Submit finished art. B&w OK. Pays $50 per spot drawing; $100 per page. Mail cartoons.
Illustrations: Works on assignment. Pays $150, b&w; $250, color. Buys 3-4 illustrations per issue. "Submit samples of work for our files."

CB, 531 N. Ann Arbor, Oklahoma City OK 73127. (405)947-5731. Editor-in-Chief: Leo G. Sands. Managing Editor: Edward K. Minderman. Art Director: Donald M. Clark. Monthly; 8⅛x10⅞"; 96 pages. Offset. Estab: 1961. Circ: 308,000. For CB owners. Buys all rights, but may reassign rights to artist after publication. Pays on publication. Previously published work, and photocopies OK. No simultaneous submissions. Query with samples. SASE. Free sample copy.
Cartoons: Buys themes on current events, humor through youth and CB radios. All formats OK. Submit finished art. Line drawings and halftones OK. Pays $10 minimum, b&w. Buys 6 cartoons per issue. Reports in 1 month.
Illustrations: Buys article illustrations and spot drawings on CB's, sports, adventure and life. Submit finished art. B&w line drawings and reflective art OK. Buys 1 illustration per issue. Reports in 4 weeks.

CGA, #700, 535 Thurlow St., Vancouver, BC Canada V6E 3L2. Editor-in-Chief: Merrilee Davey. Published 9 times annually; 8¼x11¼"; 44 pages. Offset. Estab: 1967. Circ: 21,984. For accounting students, accountants, auditors, and other business and financial executives. Not copyrighted. Pays on acceptance. No previously published or simultaneous submissions. Photocopies OK. Mail artwork. SASE. Free sample copy.
Cartoons: Buys accounting, current event and political themes. Single panel OK. Submit finished art. Line drawings OK. Pays $25 minimum. Buys 36 cartoons annually. Reports in 4 weeks.

CHANGE MAGAZINE, NBW Tower, New Rochelle NY 10801. Contact: Art Director. Buys art on higher education. "We give assignments based on samples we've seen." Payment: $25-100 for spot drawing or illustration; $100 for 2-color finished art for cover. Payment on acceptance. Buys all rights. Reports in 2 weeks. Sample copy available.

CHANGING TIMES, 1729 H St. NW, Washington DC 20006. Editorial Director: Robert A. Marshall. Monthly.
Cartoons: Buys themes on shopping, home budgeting, family cars and taxes. Line only with tone or color overlay. Uses about 4 cartoons each issue. Pays $150 on acceptance. Reports in 3 weeks.

CHATTERLEY, 15 Bedford Rd., Toronto, Ontario Canada M5R 2J7. (416)923-2409. Managing Editor: Patrick Withrow. Bimonthly; 8³⁄₁₆x10⁷⁄₈"; 84 pages. Offset. Estab: 1973. Circ: 80,000. For women. Buys all rights, but may reassign rights to artist after publication. Pays on publication. No previously published or simultaneous submissions. Photocopies OK. Query with samples or arrange interview. SASE. Free sample copy.
Cartoons: Buys themes on working women. Single and double panel OK. Submit finished art. B&w art OK. Pays $25-50. Reports in 1-2 weeks.
Illustrations: Valya Pavluk, art director. Buys article illustrations and spot drawings on beauty

products, fashion and poetry. Submit roughs. B&w line drawings and washes OK. Pays $25-100 per page. Buys 2 pages of art per issue. Reports in 1 week.

CHEMICAL PROCESSING, 430 N. Michigan, Chicago IL 60202. Editor-in-Chief: Gordon Weyermuller. Monthly; 8½x11"; 140 pages. Offset. Circ: 77,000. For plant engineers and operating plant management in the chemical processing industry. Buys first rights. Pays on acceptance. No previously published or simultaneous submissions. Photocopies OK. Mail artwork. SASE. Free sample copy.
Cartoons: Laurie Lawlor, editor. Buys themes on chemical plant work. "If you haven't been in a plant situation, it's a good idea to visit one. Humor should be directed at man in plant operations and his responsibilities." Single panel OK. Submit finished art. Washes OK. Pays $10 minimum, b&w. Buys 5 cartoons annually. Reports in 3 weeks. No sexist cartoons.

CHEVRON USA, Box 6227, San Jose CA 95150. (408)296-1060. Editor: Marian E. May. Quarterly. Circ: 225,000. For members of Chevron Travel Club, Standard Oil of California. Pays $50 for cartoons on acceptance. Buys 10+ cartoons annually. Buys one-time rights. Reports in 2-4 weeks.

CHIC, Larry Flynt Publications, 1888 Century Park E., Los Angeles CA 90067. (213)556-2521. Editor-in-Chief: Peter Brennan. Monthly; 9x12"; 102 pages. Estab: 1976. Circ: 800,000. For well-educated men, ages 18-34, who are active and acquisitive. Buys all rights. Pays 3 months prior to publication. No previously published, photocopied or simultaneous submissions. Call collect or mail artwork. SASE.
Cartoons: Forrest Plesko, editor. "I would like to see work dealing with lifestyles, current trends and general feelings of the 70s. Cartoons do not have to be exclusively sex-oriented, but must be humorous, well-drawn and sophisticated. Am particularly interested in seeing color work." Single panel OK. Submit finished art. Washes OK. Pays $50 minimum, b&w; $100-200, color; negotiates breakaways. Buys 15-20 cartoons per issue. Reports in 3 weeks; "a little longer on holds."
Illustrations: Paul Bruhwiler, art director. Buys art on assignment. Query.

CHICAGO, 500 N. Michigan Ave., Chicago IL 60611. (312)751-7168. Editor-in-Chief: Allen H. Kelson. Editor: John Fink. Art Editor: Jack Lund. Monthly; 8½x11"; 240 pages. Offset and letterpress. Estab: 1975. Circ: 175,000. For active, well-educated, high-income residents of Chicago's metropolitan area concerned with quality of life and seeking insight or guidance into diverse aspects of urban/suburban life. Buys first rights. Pays on publication. No previously published, photocopied or simultaneous submissions. Arrange interview. SASE.
Cartoons: Buys Chicago-oriented humor, suitable for family audience. Single panel OK. Might consider multi-panel. Submit finished art. Halftones and washes OK. Minimum payment: $25, b&w; $35, color. Buys 10-12 cartoons annually. Reports in 2 weeks.
Illustrations: Buys cover art, article illustrations and spot drawings on assignment. Submit roughs. Cover: color-separated and reflective art OK. Inside: b&w line drawings, veloxes, washes, color-separated and reflective art OK. Minimum payment: $200, color cover; $75, inside color; $35, inside b&w. Buys 85 illustrations annually. Reports in 2 weeks.
Special Needs: Pays $50 minimum for advertisements, brochures and car card spots.

CHICAGO REVIEW, Box C, Faculty Exchange, University of Chicago, Chicago IL 60637. (312)753-3571. Editors-in-Chief: Mary Ellis Gibson/David Shields. Quarterly; 9x6"; 200 pages. Offset. Estab: 1946. Circ: 3,000. For college-educated readers interested in cultural affairs, fine arts and the experimental. Buys all rights. No previously published or simultaneous submissions. Mail artwork. SASE. "We prefer submissions close to our format size so that reduction won't diminish the clarity of the original. We are extremely sympathetic to unsolicited over-the-counter graphic material. We publish from 8-35 pages of art per issue."
Illustrations: Lee Lordeaux, editor. Buys cover art, article illustrations and spot drawings. "We publish art for its artistic value." Submit finished art. Cover: b&w line drawings, washes and color-separated art OK. Inside: b&w line drawings, washes and veloxes OK. Pays $50 minimum, color cover; contributor's copies for other art. Reports in 4 weeks. Prefers not to see sentimental treatment of subjects.

CHICAGOLAND, Itasca IL 60143. (312)595-2800. Editor-in-Chief: Edwin G. Schwenn Biweekly; 8½x11"; 32 pages. Offset. Estab: 1973. Circ: 15,000. For travelers, suburbanites and city condominium dwellers. Buys first rights. Pays on publication. No photocopied or simul-

taneous submissions. Mail artwork. SASE. Free sample copy.
Cartoons: E. George/Muriel White, editors. Buys themes on current events, dining out and traveling by plane. Single and double panel OK. Submit finished art; washes OK. Pays $10 minimum, b&w. Reports in 4 weeks.

CHICAGOLAND SNOWMOBILER, 222 W. Adams, Chicago IL 60606. (312)236-5550. Editor-in-Chief: Paul Hertzberg. Managing Editor: Denis Schmidlin. Published 6 times annually, September-February; 10x15"; 32 pages. Offset. Estab: 1972. Circ: 15,000. Buys all rights, but may reassign rights to artist after publication. No previously published work or photocopies. Simultaneous submissions OK. Query with samples. SASE. Free sample copy.
Cartoons: Buys snowmobiling themes. All formats OK. Submit roughs. Line drawings and halftones OK. Pays $10 minimum. Buys 1-2 cartoons per issue. Reports in 3 weeks.

CHICAGO'S ELITE, 7001 N. Clark, Chicago IL 60626. (312)338-7600. Editor-in-Chief: Mary Marvin. Managing Editor: Tom McNulty. Bimonthly; 8½x11"; 66 pages. Offset. Estab: 1976. Circ: 26,000. For affluent people, ages 30-50, interested in Chicago families, history, business, travel, leisure, restaurants, school and culture. Usually buys all rights. Pays on acceptance. Previously published and simultaneous submissions OK. No photocopies. Query with samples. SASE. Free sample copy.
Illustrations: Milo Savich, editor. Buys article illustrations on assignment. Submit roughs. B&w line drawings, color-separated art and veloxes OK. Pays $15 minimum, inside b&w; $20 minimum, inside color. "We haven't bought any illustrations yet." Reports in 3-4 weeks.
Special Needs: Uses artists for brochures. Pays $15 minimum, b&w; $20 minimum, color.

CHILD LIFE, Box 567B, Indianapolis IN 46206. (317)634-1100. Editorial Director: Beth Wood Thomas. Editor: Peg Rogers. Art Director: Paul Sharp. Monthly; 6½x9¼"; 48 pages. Offset. For children up to ages 14. Pays on publication. Previously published, photocopied and simultaneous submissions OK. Mail artwork or query with samples. SASE. Sample copy sent if artist's work might be used.
Cartoons: Buys themes on science fiction and mystery. Single panel OK. Submit finished art. Halftones and washes OK. Pays $5 minimum, b&w. Buys 8-10 annually. Reports in 2 weeks.
Illustrations: Buys cover art, article and story illustrations on science fiction or mystery. Submit roughs. Cover: Color-separated and reflective art OK. Inside: b&w line drawings, washes, color separated and reflective art OK. Pays $135, color cover; $20-40, inside b&w and 2-color; $40-60, inside full-color. Reports in 2 weeks.

CHILDREN'S DIGEST, 52 Vanderbilt Ave., New York NY 11201. Contact: Arline Campbell. For ages 8-12. Works with artists on assignment. Query with resume.

CHILDREN'S HOUSE, Box 111, Caldwell NJ 07006. (201)239-3442. Editor: Ken Edelson. Bimonthly. Circ: 50,000. Uses b&w line drawings. Buys all rights. Pays on publication. Reports in 1 month. Sample copy $1.

CHILDREN'S PLAYCRAFT, 52 Vanderbilt Ave., New York NY 10017. (212)685-4400. Art Editor: Joseph A. Carrara. Monthly. For ages 6-12. 378,000 circulation. Uses b&w drawings, 2-color illustrations and craft ideas. Pays $25-35 for spot drawing. Buys all rights. Pays on acceptance. Previously published work OK. Submit samples. Reports as soon as possible.

CHILDREN'S PLAYMATE, Box 567B, Indianapolis IN 46206. (317)634-1100. Editorial Director: Beth Wood Thomas. Monthly; 6½x9¼; 48-64 pages. Offset. For ages 3-8. Buys all rights. Pays on publication. Previously published work OK. Query with samples. SASE. Sample copy sent if artist's work might be used.
Illustrations: Andrea Eberbach, art director. Buys cover art, article illustrations and spot drawings on people and animals. Submit finished art or reproductions. Considers full-color art, b&w line drawings and color-separated 2-color art. Minimum payment: $135, color cover; $20-40 per page, inside 2-color and b&w; $35-50 per pages, inside full-color. Buys approximately 15 illustrations per issue.

THE CHRISTIAN ATHLETE, 1125 Grand Ave., Kansas City MO 64106. (816)842-3908. Editor-in-Chief: Gary Warner. Managing Editor: Julian Dyke. Published 9 times annually; 9x6"; 32 pages. Offset. Estab: 1959. Circ: 40,000. For high school and college male and female athletes, and parents and coaches who are seeking to bridge the faith. Not copyrighted. Pays on

publication. Previously published and simultaneous submissions OK. No photocopies. Query with samples. SASE. Free sample copy.
Cartoons: Buys themes on sports with humorous or serious Christian angle or perspective. Single and multi-panel OK. Submit roughs. Line drawings only. Pays $25 maximum. Reports in 1 week.

CHRISTIANITY TODAY, 465 Gundersen Dr., Carol Stream IL 60187. Editors: Harold Lindsell/David Singer. Biweekly; 8⅜x11"; 44-92 pages. Offset. Estab: 1956. Circ: 140,000. For evangelical Protestant readers, average age 43, many with post-graduate degrees. Buys first rights. Pays on acceptance. Previously published work OK. No photocopied or simultaneous submissions. Query with samples. Free sample copy.
Cartoons: Buys religious themes. Double panel OK. Submit roughs. Washes OK. Pays $50-200, b&w; $75-300, color. Reports in 3 weeks.
Illustrations: Buys cover art, article illustrations and spot drawings. Submit roughs. Inside: b&w line drawings, washes and veloxes OK. Cover: color-separated and reflective art OK. Pays $175-300, cover; $50-200, inside b&w. Reports in 3 weeks.
Special Needs: Artists for preparation of in-house ads and direct mail promotional packages. Payment based on current market values.

THE CHURCH HERALD, 1324 Lake Dr. SE, Grand Rapids MI 49506. Editor: John Stapert. The official magazine of the Reformed Church in America. Biweekly. Buys all or first rights. Previously published work OK. Reports in 2 weeks. Sample copy available.
Cartoons: Uses 40-50 cartoons per year. Finished art preferred. Pays $3-10 on acceptance.

THE CHURCHMAN, 1074 23rd Ave. N., St. Petersburg FL 33704. (813)894-0097. Editor: Edna Ruth Johnson. Estab: 1804. Published 9 times annually. 10,000 circulation. Buys small b&w drawings. Pays $5 on acceptance. Mail artwork. Reports in 1 week. Sample copy available.

CINCINNATI ENQUIRER SUNDAY MAGAZINE, 617 Vine St., Cincinnati OH 45201. (513)721-2700. Editor: Graydon DeCamp. Weekly; 11x12½"; 52 pages. Rotogravure. Circ: 288,000. Usually buys all rights. Pays on publication. Previously published, photocopied and simultaneous submissions OK. Arrange interview. SASE. Free sample copy.
Illustrations: Ron Huff, art director. Buys cover art and article illustrations on assignment. "We rarely, if ever, use unsolicited freelance art. The usual procedure is for the artist to show a portfolio. If we like the work, we'll give the artist a manuscript to illustrate." Cover: washes OK. Inside: b&w line drawings and washes OK. Pays $25-100. Buys 35 illustrations annually. Reports in 1-4 weeks.

CINCINNATI MAGAZINE, 120 W. 5th St., Cincinnati OH 45202. (513)721-3300. Editor: Leslie Major. Art Director: Theo Kouvatsos. Monthly; 8½x11"; 80 pages. Offset. Circ: 13,500. For college-educated, ages 35+ with $35,000 incomes. Buys all rights. Pays on acceptance. Previously published and simultaneous submissions OK. No photocopies. Arrange interview. SASE. Free sample copy.
Cartoons: Buys themes on current events, education and politics. Single panel OK. Submit finished art. Washes OK. Pays $25-75, b&w. Buys 1 cartoon per issue. Reports in 2 weeks.
Illustrations: Buys cover art and article illustrations on assignment. Submit roughs or finished art. Cover: washes, color-separated and reflective art OK. Inside: b&w line drawings, washes, reflective art and veloxes OK. Pays $100-250, cover; $50-200, inside color; $50-150, inside b&w. Buys 30-60 illustrations per issue. Reports in 2 weeks.

CLAVIER, 1418 Lake St., Evanston IL 60204. Editor: Dorothy Packard. Published 9 times annually for teachers and students of keyboard (musical) instruments. Buys all rights. Sample copy available.
Cartoons: Buys 20 cartoons per year — all on music, mostly on keyboard music. Pays $6 on acceptance.

COASTLINE, Box 914, Culver City CA 90230. (213)839-7847. Editor/Publisher: Robert M. Benn. Bimonthly. Estab: 1973. Buys approximately 15 pieces of freelance work per year in the area of b&w drawings (line and line and wash), cover designs, 4x4" cartoons and layout services. Rights are negotiable. Will consider using work previously published. Payment: $25, full page spot drawings; $75+, cover designs in 2 colors; $15, cartoons; $50+, special design consultations. Query. Sample copy $1.

COED, 50 W. 44th St., New York NY 10017. (212)867-7700. Editor: Kathy Gogick. For teenagers. Monthly. Circ: 1 million. Pays $25 for b&w line drawings. Buys all rights. Pays on publication. Arrange interview to show portfolio.

COLLEGE PRESS REVIEW, Dept. of Journalism, Bradley University, Peoria IL 61625. (309)633-3185. Editor-in-Chief: John Windhauser. Quarterly; 8½x11"; 32-40 pages. Offset. Estab: 1956. Circ: 1,000. For journalism teachers, college publications advisers and general managers of student publications. Owns all rights, but may reassign rights to artist after publication. No previously published, photocopied or simultaneous submissions. Mail artwork. SASE. Free sample copy.
Illustrations: Needs cover art, article illustrations and spot drawings on collegiate press. Submit finished art. All media OK. No payment. Uses 2 illustrations annually. Reports in 4 weeks.

COLUMBIA JOURNALISM REVIEW, 700 Journalism Bldg., Columbia University, New York NY 10027. Editor: Kenneth M. Pierce. Art Director: Christian von Rosenvinge. Bimonthly. Readers are professional journalists, government leaders and students. 40,000 circulation. "All illustrations are intended to advance the editorial point of individual articles and are therefore planned in close consultation with the art director." Over $5,000 in freelance art/photography sought annually. Buys one-time and first serial rights. Previously published work OK. Pays on publication. Query with resume. Sample copy available.
Illustrations: Uses b&w line drawings and washes; full-color illustrations for covers only (8½x11"). Pays $50-100 for spot drawings; $300 for 4-color cover designs.

COLUMBIA MAGAZINE, Drawer 1670, New Haven CT 06507. (203)772-2130 ext. 263-64. Editor: Elmer Von Felt. Monthly. 1,200,000 circulation. Fraternal magazine of the Knights of Columbus. Themes include family life, social problems, education, current events and apostolic activities as seen from the Catholic viewpoint. Buys all rights. Pays on acceptance. Sample copy available.
Cartoons: Interested in pungent, captionless humor. Pays $25.
Illustrations: Pays $50-100, spot drawing; $250, 2-color illustration; up to $650, full-color cover design.

COMMERCIAL CAR JOURNAL, Chilton Way, Radnor PA 19089. Editor: James D. Winsor. Monthly. Buys themes on management, maintenance, and operating phases of truck, bus, and passenger car fleet operations. Pays $10 for cartoons on acceptance.

COMMODITIES, 219 Parkade, Cedar Falls IA 50613. Editor: Darrell Jobman. Devoted strictly to fundamental and technical aspects of trading commodity futures and stock options. Monthly. Buys cartoons relating to agriculture and finance. "The artist should understand commodities, markets or stock options to know what sort of humor in illustrations is appropriate to match our editorial comment." Payment on publication. Sample payment: $25-50, spot drawings; $15, cartoons (28x30 picas). Buys all rights. Will consider previously published material, depending on subject. Query. Sample copy available.

COMMUNICATIONS WORLD, Davis Publications, 229 Park Ave. S., New York NY 10003. Contact: Irving Bernstein. Pays $20 minimum, line drawings; $400 maximum, full-color cover design. Buys first rights. Pays on acceptance. Reports in 1 week.

CONFRONTATION/CHANGE REVIEW, 32 College St., Dayton OH 45407. (513)275-8637. Editor-in-Chief: Frederick Finney. Quarterly; 8½x11"; 80-124 pages. Offset. Estab: 1976. Circ: 2,000. Primarily for college and university faculty and students. Buys all rights, but may reassign rights to artist after publication. Pays on publication. Previously published, photocopied and simultaneous submissions OK. Query with samples. SASE. Free sample copy. "We are looking particularly for black artists. Will not accept work that adversely reflects on minority groups."
Cartoons: Buys themes on current events, education, politics, law and black history. All formats OK. Submit finished art. Line drawings only. Pays $5-50. Buys 8-24 cartoons annually. Reports in 2 weeks.
Illustrations: Milton DePage, editor. Buys cover art and article illustrations on fiction, poetry, current events, politics, economics and black history. Submit roughs. Cover: all media OK. Inside: b&w line drawings OK. Pays $10-50, b&w cover; $25-75, color cover; $5-50, inside b&w. Buys 16 illustrations annually. Reports in 4 weeks.

CONNECTICUT FIRESIDE, Box 5293, Hamden CT 06518. (203)248-1023. Editor-in-Chief: Albert Callan. Quarterly; 7x9½"; 96 pages. Offset. Estab: 1972. Circ: 1,500. For intelligent people interested in writing, Connecticut history, people and alternative lifestyles. Buys first North American serial rights. Previously published, photocopied and simultaneous submissions OK. Query with samples. SASE. Sample copy $1.50.
Cartoons: Buys all themes. Single panel OK. Submit roughs or finished art. All media OK. Pays contributor's copies. Buys 5-6 cartoons annually. Reports in 2 weeks.
Illustrations: Buys cover art, article illustrations and spot drawings. "We need pen and ink drawings for our cover vignette — something in line with our literary theme or a country scene like the vignettes on the British magazine *Countrymen*." Submit finished art. Cover: b&w line drawings OK. Inside: b&w line drawings and washes OK. Pays contributor's copies. Buys 4 cover vignettes annually. Reports in 2 weeks.

CONSTRUCTION EQUIPMENT OPERATION AND MAINTENANCE, Construction Publications, Inc., Box 1689, Cedar Rapids IA 52406. (319)366-1597. Editor-in-Chief: C.K. Parks. Bimonthly; 8¼x11"; 28 pages. Offset. Estab: 1948. Circ: 68,300. For people interested in heavy construction and industrial equipment, including management, machine operators, mechanics and local government officials. Buys all rights, but may reassign rights to artist after publication. Pays on acceptance. No previously published work or photocopies. Simultaneous submissions OK. Mail artwork. SASE. Free sample copy.
Cartoons: Buys themes related to heavy construction industry and equipment. Multi-panel OK. Submit finished art. Halftones OK. Pays $7.50, b&w. Buys 60 cartoons annually. Reports in 3 weeks.
Illustrations: Buys cover art on Christmas themes. Submit roughs or finished art. Color-separated and reflective art OK. Pays $80-125. Buys 10 illustrations annually. Reports in 3 weeks.

CONSTRUCTIONEER, 1 Bond St., Chatham NJ 07928. (201)635-6450. Editor: Ken Hanan. Art Director: Richard E. Stevancsecz. Biweekly for contractors, public officials, distributors and producers. Buys cartoons mostly for April directory issue. Pays $5-10. Not copyrighted. Payment on publication. Previously published work OK. Mail cartoons. Reports in 30 days.

CONSUMERS' RESEARCH MAGAZINE, Washington NJ 07882. Managing Editor: Angelita M. Hinek. Monthly. Buys cartoons of special interest to consumers. Pays $10 each on acceptance. Buys 10 annually.

CONTACT, 302 Lake St., Box 650 Huntington IN 46750. (219)356-2312. Editor: Stanley Peters. Assistant Editor: Dennis Miller. Weekly; 5½x7"; 8 pages. Offset. Circ: 6,500. For conservative, evangelical Christians. Buys first, reprint and simultaneous rights. Pays on acceptance. Previously published, photocopied and simultaneous submissions OK. Mail artwork. SASE. Free sample copy and guidelines.
Cartoons: Buys themes on education, environment, family life, religion and retirement. Single panel OK. Submit finished art. Halftones OK. Pays $2 minimum. Reports in 6 weeks.
Illustrations: Buys cover art and article illustrations. Submit finished art. Cover: b&w line drawings OK. Pays $6.50 minimum. Reports in 6 weeks.

CONTACTS, Box 407, North Chatham NY 12132. Editor: Joseph Strack. Published bimonthly for dental laboratories. 1,000 circulation. Uses 2-3 cartoons per issue. Buys first serial rights. Pays $17.50 on acceptance. Mail cartoon ideas dealing with dental laboratory industry. Reports in 1 week.

CONTINENTAL FLIGHTIME, East-West Network, Inc., 5900 Wilshire Blvd., #300, Los Angeles CA 90036. (213)937-5810. Editor: James Clark. Senior Art Director: Chris Mossman. Monthly. Buys all rights. Query with resume. Sample copy $1.
Illustrations: Buys cover art and spot drawings on assignment. Pays $25 minimum, spot art; $400, full-color cover. Reports in 4 weeks.

CONTINUING EDUCATION, 3100 Broadway, Suite 1111, Kansas City MO 64111. Publisher: Mac F. Cahal. Monthly. For physicians in general or family practice.
Illustrations: "All art is on commission basis, though the staff welcomes professional credits and examples of work from established medical illustrators. Determination of assignments may be based on this information." Tearsheets of previously published work submitted as example of

style only. Uses finished art only of slightly larger than reproduction size. Pays on publication. Pays $50 minimum, spot drawings; $150-250, finished 4-color art. Buys all rights. Query. Reports in 2 weeks. Sample copy $1.50.

CONTRACT, 1515 Broadway, New York NY 10036. (212)869-1300. Editor: Len Corlin. Managing Editor: Anne Fallucchi. Monthly; 8½x11"; 100 pages. Offset. Circ: 30,000. For interior architects, designers and specifiers. Buys first, reprint and all rights, but may reassign rights to artist after publication. Pays on acceptance. No previously published, photocopied or simultaneous submissions. Query. No work returned.
Illustrations: Buys article illustrations and spot drawings on assignment. Submit roughs. B&w line drawings OK. Pays $25-50. Reports in 1 week.

CONVENIENCE STORE MERCHANDISER, 101 Park Ave., Suite 1838, New York NY 10017. (212)689-5111. Editor-in-Chief: Michael Ball. Managing Editor: Joan Benjamin. Monthly; 9x12"; 80 pages. Offset. Estab: 1973. Circ: 28,000. For claim executives and store managers. Buys first and reprint rights. Pays on publication. Previously published and simultaneous submissions (to noncompeting publications) OK. No photocopies. Query with samples. SASE. Free sample copy.
Cartoons: Buys retailing themes. All formats OK. Submit finished art. Line drawings and halftones OK. Pays $20-50. Buys 6 cartoons annually. Reports in 2 weeks.
Illustrations: Buys cover art and article illustrations. Ask for editorial calendar. Submit finished art. Cover: washes and color-separated art OK. Inside: b&w line drawings, color-separated art and veloxes OK. Minimum payment: $25, b&w cover; $50, color cover; $10, inside b&w. Buys 12 illustrations annually. Reports in 2 weeks.

CO-OP GROWER (formerly Farmland Industries), 3715 N. Oak Traffic Way, Kansas City MO 64116. Art Buyer: K. Reif. Pays $10-100 for illustrations; $25-300, cover designs. Pays on publication. Not copyrighted. Submit samples. Reports in 1 month.

Fifty-two illustrations are assigned annually by *Glad*, a magazine for young adult Christians. Editor-in-chief Judy Trotter pays $40 for b&w cover artwork and $35 for inside b&w artwork. The above clown drawing was purchased from Kathryn Hutton.

THE COOPERATOR, 8570 Wilshire Blvd., Beverly Hills CA 90211. (213)652-3674. Editor-in-Chief: Lou Acheson. Published annually; 11x14"; 225 pages. Offset. Circ: 8,000. For "people interested in nontraditional new ways of thinking on art, science and religion." Buys all rights. Pays on publication. No previously published or simultaneous submissions. Photocopies OK. Query with samples or arrange interview. SASE. Sample copy $2.
Illustrations: Wilma Sadeghin, editor. Buys cover art, article illustrations and spot drawings on assignment. Submit finished art. B&w line drawings, color-separated and reflective art OK. Reports in 2 months. "If you have an illustration that is indicative of universality — oneness of life — or the unification of our planet, send it."

CORE MAGAZINE, 200 W. 135th St., New York NY 10030. (212)368-8104. Editor: Denise Mitchell. Monthly. Accepts 5x7" or 8x10" cover designs, color-separated illustrations and cartoons. No previously published work. Query with resume. Sample copy available.

COSMOPOLITAN, 959 8th Ave., New York NY 10019. Cartoon Editor: Francine Lancaster. Works only with extensive present list of cartoonists.

COUNTERFORCE MAGAZINE, 4039 Cole Ave., Dallas TX 75204. (214)526-9699. Editor-in-Chief: Frank W. Taggart. Managing Editor: Hugh G. Aynesworth. Monthly "intelligence report on terrorism"; 8½x11"; 16 pages. Offset. Estab: 1977. Circ: 2,500. For executives, security directors, and other personnel in industry, business and government. Buys first rights. Pays on acceptance. Previously published, photocopied and simultaneous submissions OK. Query with samples. SASE. Free sample copy.
Cartoons: Buys material on any aspect of terrorism. Single panel OK. Submit finished art. Prefers b&w art. Pays $15-35. Buys 24 cartoons annually. Reports in 2 weeks.
Illustrations: Buys article illustrations and spot drawings on any aspect of terrorism. Submit finished art. B&w line drawings, washes and veloxes OK. Pays $15-35, b&w. Buys 24 illustrations annually. Reports in 2 weeks.

THE COUNTRY GENTLEMAN, 1100 Waterway Blvd., Indianapolis IN 46202. Art Editor: Starkey Flytle, Jr. Quarterly. Readership in rural and suburban (good life). Estab: 1851. 150,000 circulation. "We are interested in seeing samples, color transparencies, of artists' work. We like illustrations in a representational vein but we can use abstractions too." Buys all rights. No previously published work. Pays on publication. Query with resume. Reports in 2 weeks.
Cartoons: Pays $75-200 for 8½x11½" finished art.
Illustrations: Buys b&w line drawings, line and wash and full-color illustrations. Pays $50, spot art; $150-750, full-color art; up to $1,000, finished cover design.
Special Needs: Artwork for these issues: September — TV; October/November — automobile and football; December — Christmas.

COUNTRY GUIDE, 1760 Ellice Ave., Winnipeg, Manitoba Canada R3H 086. (204)774-1861. Editor: Dave Wreford. Monthly; 7x10"; 60 pages. Offset. Estab: 1883. Circ: 252,000. For operating farmers. Buys first rights. Pays on acceptance. Previously published and simultaneous submissions OK. No photocopies. Mail artwork. SASE. Free sample copy.
Cartoons: Buys themes on politics and farming. Single panel OK. Submit finished art. Line drawings only. Pays $20 minimum. Buys 40-60 cartoons annually. Reports in 2 weeks. "We like cartoons which depict politicians as con men, fools, etc."

COUNTRY STYLE, 11058 W. Addison, Franklin Park IL 60131. Editor-in-Chief: Vince Sorren. Biweekly; 10x12"; 48 pages. Offset. Estab: 1976. Circ: 450,000. Buys all rights, but may reassign rights to artist after publication. Pays on acceptance. Previously published work and photocopies OK. No simultaneous submissions. Mail artwork or query with samples. SASE. Sample copy for $1.
Cartoons: Ray Bachar, managing editor. Buys themes on country lifestyle/music. All formats OK. Submit finished art. Line drawings, halftones and washes OK. Pays $15-50, b&w; $30-100, color. Reports in 3 weeks.
Illustrations: Mike Ryan, layout editor. Buys cover art, article illustrations and spot drawings. Submit finished art. Inside: b&w line drawings, washes and color-separated art OK. Cover: color-separated art OK. Pays $200, color cover; $20, inside b&w; $40, inside color. Reports in 3 weeks.

COUNTRY WORLD, Box 1770, Tulsa OK 74102. (918)583-2161. Editor-in-Chief: Herb Karner. Monthly tabloid; 16-20 pages. Letterpress. Estab: 1950. Circ: 210,000. For general audience. Not copyrighted. Pays on publication. No previously published, photocopied or simultaneous submissions. Query. SASE.
Cartoons: Buys themes on family life, agriculture and ranching. Single panel OK. Submit roughs. Line drawings only. Pays $7.50 minimum. Buys 10-12 cartoons annually. Reports in 2 weeks.

THE COVENANT COMPANION, 5101 N. Francisco Ave., Chicago IL 60625. (312)784-3000. Editor: James R. Hawkinson. Biweekly. 28,500 circulation. For religious-oriented readers of all ages and occupations. Estab: 1924. Interested in material for Advent, Christmas, Lent and Easter. Buys b&w drawings. Pays on publication. Buys first or all rights. Work should be submitted 10 weeks in advance. Write. Replies immediately. Sample copy available.

CREATIVE COMPUTING, Box 789-M, Morristown NJ 07960. Editor-in-Chief: Steve Gray. Managing Editor: Burchenal Green. Bimonthly; 8½x11"; 96 pages. Offset. Estab: 1974. Circ: 30,000. For computer hobbyists. Buys all rights, but may reassign rights to artist after publication. Pays on acceptance. Previously published work OK. No photocopied or simultaneous submissions. Mail artwork. SASE. Sample copy $1.50.

Cartoons: Buys themes on home computers, calculators, robots, data processing, and computers in unusual applications (i.e. music, horticulture). Single and multi-panel OK. Submit finished art. Line drawings and halftones OK. Pays $10-20. Buys 30-40 cartoons annually. Reports in 2 weeks.
Illustrations: Buys cover art, article illustrations and spot drawings on assignment. "Artist should send us (non-returnable) portfolio, which may include photocopies." Cover: color-separated and reflective art OK. Inside: b&w line drawings, color-separated art and veloxes OK. Pays $75-200, color cover; $20-100, inside color; $10-75, inside b&w. Buys 50-60 illustrations annually. Reports in 2 weeks.
Special Needs: Uses artists for layout. Payment varies by complexity; $2-10 per page. "We don't do this by mail; artist must be in New York metro area or northern New Jersey." Pays $10-25 for schematic diagrams; "we furnish rough — artist lays out and inks final."

CREATIVE WORLD MAGAZINE, 1012 S. Robertson, Los Angeles CA 90035. Contact: Audree Coke. Uses artists for original jazz-related art for the cover. Buys all rights. Reports in 15 days. Write for sample copy.

CREEM, Box P-1064, Birmingham MI 48012. Art Director: Charles Auringer. Monthly, for rock and roll music fans. 550,000 circulation. Buys all and one-time rights on illustrations. Pays on publication. Will consider previously published work. Reports in 60-90 days. Pays $25 for cartoons.
Illustrations: Submit finished art. Minimum payment: $25, spot drawing; $100, full-color illustration.

THE CRITICAL LIST, 32 Sullivan St., Toronto, Ontario Canada M5T 1B9. (416)923-0716. Publisher: Dr. Jerry Green. Quarterly. Concerned with issues in health and the illness business as related to consumers and professionals. 12,000 circulation. Seeks approximately 20 pieces of freelance artwork annually. Accepts b&w drawings, cartoons, cover designs and design ideas. Buys one-time rights. Pays $5-10 for spot drawings/cartoons; $15 for 1-color cover design. Payment on publication. Query with resume. Reports in 3 months. Free sample copy. "We're interested in expose artwork critical of establishment medicine and that deals with alternative forms of health care."

CROPS & SOILS MAGAZINE, 677 Segoe Rd., Madison WI 53711. Editor: William R. Luellen. Published 9 times annually. For farmers, seedgrowers, agribusiness executives, salesmen, county agents, researchers and vo-ag teachers. About 85% of editorial content relates to crop production and soil management. Buys one-time rights. Will consider previously published work. Reports in 1 week.
Cartoons: Pays $5 on acceptance. Uses about 50 per year. Submissions should run no larger than 8½x11.

CRUSADER, Box 7244, Grand Rapids MI 49510. (616)241-5616. Editor: M.R. McGervey. Published 7 times a year by the Calvinist Cadet Corps for boys ages 10-14. Sample copy sent on request. Previously published work OK. Submit resume. Reports in 6 weeks.
Cartoons: Minimum payment: $5, single panel; $10, double panel; $15, full page.
Illustrations: Uses b&w line, and line and wash drawings. Illustrations of seasonal sports needed 4 months before publication date.

CS JOURNAL, 818 Roeder Rd., Suite 302, Silver Spring MD 20910. (301)588-7896. Editor-in-Chief: Rita Sublett Hawkins. Monthly; 8½x11"; 56 pages. Letterpress. Estab: 1976. For Christians and potential Christians. Buys all rights, but may reassign rights to artist after publication. Previously published work OK. No photocopied or simultaneous submissions. Mail artwork. SASE. Sample copy $2. Sometimes considers illustrations.
Cartoons: Buys themes on current events, education, environment, family life, humor through youth, politics, religion and retirement. All formats OK. Submit rough or finished art. Reports in 4-6 weeks.

CURRENT CONSUMER, 501 Lake Forest Ave., Highwood IL 60040. (312)432-2700. Editor: Whayne Dillehay. Monthly, September-May; 8³⁄₁₆x10⅞"; 32 pages. Offset. Estab: 1976. Circ: 50,000. For junior and senior high school students. Buys all rights. Pays on publication. Previously published and simultaneous submissions OK. No photocopies. Query with samples. SASE. Free sample copy. "Be simple. Realize that our kids are not fond of subtleties. Breezy, funny material suits them best."

Cartoons: Buys themes on current events, education, the environment and problems faced by young consumers. All formats OK. Submit finished art. Line drawings and halftones OK. Pays $10 minimum. Buys up to 15 cartoons annually. Reports in 2 weeks.
Illustrations: Buys cover art, article illustrations and spot drawings on assignment. Submit roughs. Cover: color-separated and reflective art OK. Inside: b&w line drawings OK. Pays $25 minimum, color cover; $10 minimum, inside. Buys up to 15 illustrations annually. Reports in 4 weeks.
Special Needs: Uses artists for keyline and paste-up. Pays $4+ per hour.

CURRENT HEALTH, 501 Lake Forest Ave., Highwood IL 60040. (312)432-2700. Managing Editor: Laura Ruekberg. Published 9 times annually; 8³/₁₆x10⅞"; 32 pages. Offset. Estab: 1974. Circ: 150,000. For junior and senior high school students. Buys first, reprint and simultaneous rights. Pays on publication. Previously published, photocopied and simultaneous submissions OK. Query with samples. SASE. Free sample copy.
Cartoons: Buys environment, family life, humor through youth and health themes. All formats OK. Submit finished art. Line drawings OK. Pays $10 minimum. Reports in 4 weeks.
Illustrations: Buys cover art and article illustrations on assignment. Query. Submit roughs; submit finished art for previously published work. Cover: color-separated and reflective art OK. "Cover art should be 4-color, lively and dramatic without being negatively sensational." Inside: b&w line drawings, color-separated art and veloxes OK. Minimum payment: $25, cover; $10, inside b&w. Reports in 4 weeks.

CYCLE, 780-A Lakefield Rd., Westlake Village CA 91361. Editor: Cook Neilson. Monthly. Covers wide variety of motorcycle-oriented activities and products. Buys finished cartoons, pen and ink, line and wash, and full-color illustrations. Payment on publication. Buys first rights. Pays $25-50, spot drawing; $250+, full-color illustration. Reports in 10 days. Sample copy on request.

CYCLE GUIDE, 1440 W. Walnut, Compton CA 90220. Editor: Paul Dean. Buys filler drawings of motorcycles. May be creative, interpretive or straightforward. Pays $20 on publication. Copyrighted. Reports immediately. Sample copy on request.

CYCLE TIMES, 222 W. Adams, Chicago IL 60606. (312)236-5550. Editor-in-Chief: Paul Hertzberg. Managing Editor: Denis Schmidlin. Monthly; 10x15"; 32+ pages. Offset. Estab: 1975. Circ: 40,000. For competitive dirt bike riders, who may own street bikes. Buys all rights, but may reassign rights to artist after publication. Pays on publication. No previously published work or photocopies. Simultaneous submissions OK. Query with samples. SASE. Free sample copy. Needs art for "Helmet Moss" motorcycle satire column.
Cartoons: Buys themes on motorcycling. All formats OK. Submit roughs. Line drawings and halftones OK. Pays $10 minimum. Buys 1-2 cartoons per issue. Reports in 3 weeks.

DAILY BLESSING (formerly Oral Roberts Association), Box 2187, Tulsa OK 74102. Art Buyer: Paul Davidson. Quarterly. Pays $15-25 per hour, artwork; $12-18 per hour, production. Buys all rights. Submit resume and samples. Reports in 10 days.

DAILY COMMERCIAL NEWS, 34 St. Patrick St., Toronto, Ontario Canada M5T 1V2. Editor: T. McAuliffe. For architects, engineers, construction men, building officials, municipal and government officials. Buys first Canadian rights on cartoons. Pays on publication.

THE DAKOTA FARMER, Box 1950, Aberdeen SD 57401. Publications Manager: Don Evashenko. Issued monthly for farm and ranch families in North and South Dakota. Considers reprint rights on previously published work. Pays on publication. Query. Reports in 2-3 weeks.
Cartoons: Should slant toward agricultural progress of North and South Dakota. Prefers 8x10" finished art. Pays $10. Buys 95 annually.
Illustrations: Pen and ink or line and wash OK. Submit roughs or finished art. Pays $10, spot drawing; $50, 4-color finished cover design.

DANCE MAGAZINE, 10 Columbus Circle, New York NY 10019. Editor-in-Chief: William Como. Monthly. Buys exclusive rights. Sometimes considers previously published work. Payment on publication. Query. Reports in 1-3 weeks. Sample copy $1.50.

DARK TOWER, University Center 7, Cleveland State University, Cleveland OH 44115. Managing Editor: Linda Unger. Published annually; 6x9"; 100-150 pages. Letterpress. Estab:

1972. Circ: 1,500. For college students and local poets. Buys first North American serial rights. Pays on publication. No previously published work. Photocopied and simultaneous submissions OK. Mail artwork. SASE. Sample copy $1.50.

Illustrations: Buys cover art and spot drawings on "reflective people." Submit finished art. Cover: b&w line drawings and reflective art OK. Inside: reflective art OK. Pays $5 minimum, b&w. Reports in 4 weeks.

DASH, Box 150, Wheaton IL 60187. Cartoon Editor: Rick Mould. For church-oriented middle-class boys, 8-12. Published by Christian Service Brigade. Buys cartoons and illustrations. Should have "general humor involving home and school situations common to boys." No suggestive themes, ethnic humor or questionable language. Finished art only. Will accept line drawings with or without ink wash. Pays $7.50-20. Buys 12-16 cartoons and illustrations annually. Buys first North American serial rights. Pays on publication. SASE. Sample copy 50¢.

DAVKA MAGAZINE, 900 Hilgard Ave., Los Angeles CA 90049. (213)474-7717. Editor-in-Chief: Neil Reisner. Managing Editor: Jeremy Alk. Quarterly; 8½x11"; 60 pages. Offset. Estab: 1970. Circ: 3,500. For ages 18-40, active in the Jewish community; many students, young professionals, rabbis and others active in exploring Jewish identity. Buys all rights, but may reassign rights to artist after publication. Previously published, photocopied and simultaneous submissions OK. Query with samples. Sample copy $1.40. "Davka is a small, struggling magazine that has gained some reputation in the Jewish community. We are theme-oriented. Some recent and upcoming themes: the convert, the Jewish child, the Jewish woman, the Jew and the media, Israel/Diaspora relations."

Cartoons: Buys themes on current events, education, humor through youth, politics and religion. All formats OK. Submit roughs. Halftones and washes OK. Pays 3 contributor's copies. Buys 5-7 cartoons per issue. Reports in 4 weeks.

Illustrations: Ellen Lampert, editor. Buys cover art, article illustrations and spot drawings on assignment. Submit roughs. B&w line drawings, washes, color-separated and reflective art and veloxes OK. Pays 3 contributor's copies. Buys 2-3 illustrations per issue. Reports in 4 weeks.

DC COMICS, 75 Rockefeller Plaza, New York NY 10019. Managing Editor: Joe Orlando. Published 35 times monthly; 6½x10"; 32-80 pages. Lithography. For comic book readers, average age 14. Buys all rights. Pays on acceptance. No previously published, photocopied or simultaneous submissions. Arrange interview. SASE.

Cartoons: Assigns comic book art. Negotiates payment. "Samples might get you in the door, but comic books are done strictly on assignment, generally using established characters owned and controlled by DC Comics, Inc. If you don't know what a superhero comic is like, you aren't likely to be qualified for work."

THE DEAF CANADIAN, Box 1016, Calgary, Alberta Canada T2P 2K4. Editor: Lynette Burnett. Art Editor: David Burnett. Bimonthly; 8½x11"; 24 pages. Offset. Estab: 1975. Circ: 125,000. For teachers, professionals and the deaf. "Although we're copyrighted, we don't buy any rights." Pays on publication. No previously published, photocopied or simultaneous submissions. Query or mail artwork. Free sample copy.

Cartoons: Buys themes on the deaf. Single panel OK. Submit finished art. Line drawings only. Pays $5 minimum. Buys 16 cartoons annually. Reports in 4 months.

Illustrations: Buys cover art, article illustrations and spot drawings on the deaf. Submit finished art. Cover: washes OK. Inside: b&w line drawings OK. Pays $25 minimum, color cover; $5 minimum, inside b&w. Buys 30 illustrations annually. Reports in 4 months.

DECEMBER MAGAZINE, 4 E. Huron, Chicago IL 60611. Editor: Curt Johnson. Literary magazine, published irregularly. Uses b&w drawings. Pays 2 contributor's copies. Buys all rights. No previously published work. Sample copy $2.

DEKALB LITERARY ARTS JOURNAL, 555 Indian Creek Dr., Clarkston GA 30021. Editor-in-Chief: W.S. Newman. Quarterly; 6x9"; 100 pages. Offset. Estab: 1966. Circ: 5,000. For ages 20-50, college-educated, interested in humanities. Buys first serial rights. No previously published, photocopied or simultaneous submissions. Mail artwork. SASE. Sample copy $1.40.

Cartoons: Single panel OK. Submit finished art. Halftones and washes OK. Pays contributor's copies. Reports in 2-3 months.

Illustrations: Submit finished art. Inside: b&w line drawings, washes, color-separated and reflective art and veloxes OK. Buys 20-30 illustrations annually. Reports in 2-3 months.

DELTA SKY, East-West Network, Inc., 5900 Wilshire Blvd., #300, Los Angeles CA 90036. (213)937-5810. Editor: James Clark. Senior Art Director: Chris Mossman. Monthly. Buys all rights. Query with resume. Sample copy $1.
Illustrations: Buys cover art and spot drawings on assignment. Pays $25 minimum, spot art; $400, full-color cover. Reports in 4 weeks.

DENVER, 8000 E. Girard Ave., Suite 210, Denver CO 80231. (305)755-1295. Editor-in-Chief: Jan Golab. Editor: Bill Ballas. Monthly; 10⅞x8⅜"; 76 pages. Offset. Estab: 1972. Circ: 27,000. For college-educated, middle-class readers, ages 25-49. Buys all rights, but may reassign rights to artist after publication. Pays on publication. No previously published, photocopied or simultaneous submissions. All methods of contact OK. SASE. "We are looking for artists with their fingers on the pulse of our city and with an awareness of national interests. We don't accept only local work, but anything of interest to the American people."
Cartoons: Buys all themes and "anything pertaining to the Denver experience or national events of interest." All formats OK. Submit finished art. Halftones and washes OK. Pays $5-50, b&w; $10-50, color-separated art; $10-100, 4-color art. Buys 60-70 cartoons annually. Reports in 4 weeks.
Illustrations: Buys article illustrations and spot drawings on all themes, particularly those relevant to Denver. Submit finished art. B&w line drawings, washes, color-separated and reflective art and veloxes OK. Pays $5-50, inside b&w; $5-50, color-separated art; $10-100, 4-color inside art. Buys 35-45 illustrations annually. Reports in 4 weeks.
Special Needs: Uses local graphic artists for ad layout. Pays $5-50 per illustration. Also needs artwork for the following interests: investments, psychic phenomena, health, modern living, wine, food, music, drama, movies and literature.

DESERT, Box 1318, Palm Desert CA 92260. (714)346-8144. Editor-in-Chief: William Knyvett. Monthly; 8½x11"; 48 pages. Offset. Estab: 1937. Circ: 40,000. For backpackers, hikers and those who love the outdoors. Buys first rights. Pays on publication. Previously published work OK. No simultaneous submissions. Mail artwork. SASE. Free sample copy.
Illustrations: George Braga, editor. Buys cover art and article illustrations on the desert. Submit finished art. All color media OK. Submit 4x5" transparencies for covers. Pays $35-50, cover; $25-35, inside. Buys 12 covers and 36 inside illustrations annually. Reports in 4 weeks.

DETROIT ENGINEER (formerly Detroit Publications Consultants), 18226 Mack, Grosse Pointe Farms MI 48236. Contact: Jack Grenard. Sample copy on request.
Illustrations: Interested in spot illustrations on the following subjects: transportation, automation, construction, metrication, energy, noise abatement, computers, solid waste, pollution control, management and new materials. Drawings should be in ink. Reports in 2 weeks. Pays $5-15 for first North American serial rights, on acceptance.

DIRT BIKE MAGAZINE, 16200 Ventura Blvd., Encino CA 91436. Editor: Bruce Woods. Monthly; 8½x11". 150,000 circulation. Buys all rights. Will consider previously published material. Buys b&w line and wash illustrations. Query with resume. Reports within 2 weeks.

THE DISCIPLE, Christian Board of Publication, Disciples of Christ, Box 179, St. Louis MO 63166. Editor/Art Buyer: James L. Merrell. Biweekly. Buys 8x10" cover art and cartoons. Pays $25-50, cover art; $1-5 cartoons. "Since this journal goes entirely to members of our denomination, cartoons should be sharp humor without offensive implications." Buys exclusive rights. Pays on acceptance. Artwork published elsewhere considered. Sample copy 25c. Query. Reports in 3 weeks. Sample copy 25¢.

DISPENSING OPTICIAN, 1250 Connecticut Ave. NW, Washington DC 20036. Editor: James H. McCormick. Published 11 times yearly. Circ: 5,500. Buys all rights; will release for use not competing with Opticians Association of America. Pays on publication. Query. Sample copy sent "if initial query is close to target. We can't stress too strongly the need to tie to current editorial needs (which we don't really know in advance) and interests of the dispensing optician." Pays $5-10 for cartoons.
Illustrations: Uses b&w drawings and full-color art. Pays $10-20 for spot drawing. Other rates depend on job.

DOLL WORLD, Box 338, Chester MA 01011. Editor: Barbara Hall Pedersen. Bimonthly; 64 pages. Offset. Estab: 1977. For doll lovers. Buys all rights. Pays on acceptance. No photocopied or simultaneous submissions. Query. SASE. Free sample copy. Needs original doll designs for Christmas issue.
Cartoons: Buys doll-related themes. Single panel OK. Submit finished art. Line drawings OK. Pays $15. Buys 6-12 cartoons annually. Reports in 8 weeks.
Illustrations: Carol Pedersen, art director. Buys article illustrations on assignment. "Artists should send samples that can be kept on file."

DOMESTIC ENGINEERING (formerly *D/E Journal*), 110 N. York Rd., Elmhurst IL 60126. Contact: Editor. Business magazine aimed at mechanical contractors in plumbing, heating and air conditioning. Pays $10 minimum for drawings on publication. Buys all rights. Reports in 2 weeks.

DOWN RIVER, World Publications, Box 366, Mt. View CA 94040. Art Buyer: Bob Anderson. Buys cover designs, spot drawings and cartoons. "Our readers are participants and we try to use material that shows insight into the sports that we cover." Pays $10+. Buys reprint rights. Pays on publication. Reports in 1 week.

THE DRAGON, Box 756, Lake Geneva WI 53147. Editor-in-Chief: Timothy Kask. Published 8 times annually; 8½x11"; 32 pages. Offset. Estab: 1976. Circ: 5,000. For well-read and educated fans of fantasy, sorcery and science fiction gaming. Buys all rights, but may reassign rights to artist after publication. Pays on publication. No previously published or simultaneous submissions. Query with samples (photocopies OK). SASE. Sample copy $1.
Cartoons: Buys themes on wargaming and game playing. All formats OK. Submit roughs. Halftones and washes OK. Minimum payment: $5, b&w; $20, color. Buys 8-20 cartoons annually. Reports in 6 weeks maximum.
Illustrations: Buys cover art, article illustrations and spot drawings on fantasy, science fiction, sorcery and game playing. Submit roughs or finished art. All media OK. Minimum payment: $5, inside b&w; $20, inside color; $25, b&w cover; $50, color cover. Buys 100-125 illustrations annually. Reports in 6 weeks maximum.

DRAMATICS, College Hill Station, Box E, Cincinnati OH 45224. Editor: S. Ezra Goldstein. Educational magazine for students, teachers and directors of theater arts. Published in September, November, January, March and May by International Thespian Society. 50,000 circulation. Estab: 1929. Buys first serial rights. Pays on acceptance. Prefers to see finished product, but will welcome and respond to query letters. SASE. Reports in 3 months.
Illustrations: Buys b&w line drawings, line and wash, cover designs and cartoons in finished art. Pays $5-20 and contributor's copies.

DRAMATIKA, 390 Riverside Dr., New York NY 10025. (212)749-5092. Editor: J. Pyros. Published semiannually. Estab: 1968. Copyrighted. Pays on acceptance. Prefers unpublished work. Pays $15, b&w cover design; $5, b&w line drawing. Mail artwork. Reports in 1 month. Sample copy $1.

DRUG TOPICS, 680 Kinderkamack Rd., Oradell NJ 07649. Cartoon Editor: Ralph M. Thurlow. Biweekly. Buys all rights. For pharmacists, small store owners and chain executives. Pays on acceptance. Usually reports in 2 weeks. Sample copy available.
Cartoons: Buys single panel b&w cartoons "on any aspect of pharmacy at the retail level, customers, the drug or medication industry, pharmacists. Some cartoons we buy deal with other pharmacy areas — hospitals, pharmacy school — and we use some general cartoons. No doctor cartoons used." Submit finished art; color cartoons by arrangement. Pays $25-30. Usually buys 4-5 cartoons per issue.

DUDE, Dugent Publishing Company, 316 Aragon Ave., Coral Gables FL 33134. Editor/Publisher: Douglas Allen. Managing Editor: Nye Wilden. For men. Buys first time rights.
Cartoons: Buys "funny, somewhat 'sick' humor and sexual themes." Submit finished art. B&w OK. Pays $15 per spot drawing; $100 per page. Mail cartoons.
Illustrations: Works on assignment. Pays $50-75, b&w. Buys 3-4 illustrations per issue. "Submit samples of work for our files."

EARLY AMERICAN LIFE MAGAZINE, Box 1831, Harrisburg PA 17105. Managing Editor: Fran Carnahan. Buys one-time rights. Pays on acceptance. Reports in 1 month. Sample copy available.
Illustrations: "We are always anxious to consider well-organized sequence drawings which tell the story of a craft, historic site, or which inform our readers how to achieve Early American style in architecture or home furnishing." Looks for early style primitive paintings especially for cover use. Payment is $10 for spot drawing; $100 for cover design in 4 colors, finished art.

EARNSHAW'S REVIEW, 393 7th Ave., New York NY 10001. (212)563-2742. Editor-in-Chief: Thomas Hudson. Managing Editor: Warren Shoulberg. Monthly; 8½x11½"; 80 pages. 4-color offset and letterpress. Estab: 1917. Circ: 10,000. For designers, manufacturers, buyers and retailers in the children's fashion industry. Buys all rights. Pays on publication. No photocopied or simultaneous submissions. Arrange interview. SASE.
Illustrations: Lorrie R. Messinger, editor. Buys illustrations and occasional cover art on fashion (infants to pre-teenagers). Submit finished art or cover roughs. Cover: b&w line drawings, washes, color-separated and reflective art OK. Inside: b&w line drawings and washes OK. Pays $50-100, color cover; $50 minimum, b&w cover; $20-30, inside color figure; $15-20, inside b&w figure. Buys 180 illustrations annually. Reports in 1 week.
Special Needs: Pays $20-25 per color or b&w advertisement figure.
To Break In: "Artist must have at least 4 child fashion illustrations in his portfolio. He must work quickly and accurately and know the difference between the figures of a 3 and 6-year-old."

EARTH'S DAUGHTERS, 944 Kensington Ave., Buffalo NY 14215. Contact: Editors. Published 2-3 times annually. Offset. Estab: 1971. Circ: 1,000. For feminists. Buys first rights. Mail artwork. SASE.
Illustrations: Buys cover art, article illustrations and spot drawings on feminist themes. Submit finished art. B&w line drawings, washes and veloxes OK. Pays 6 contributor's copies. Reports in 4 weeks.

EAST WEST JOURNAL, 233 Harvard St., Brookline MA 02146. (617)738-7760. Editor-in-Chief: Sherman Goldman. Managing Editor: Alex Jack. Art Editor: Peter Harris. Monthly; 8½x11"; 96 pages. Offset. Estab: 1971. Circ: 31,000. For men and women, average age 30, with all interests and pursuing alternative and natural lifestyles. Buys all rights, but may reassign rights to artist after publication. Pays on publication. Previously published, photocopied and simultaneous submissions OK. Query with samples. SASE. Free sample copy.
Cartoons: Buys themes on alternative energy sources, ecology and philosophy. All formats OK. Submit finished art. Line drawings, halftones and washes OK. Pays $15 minimum, b&w. Reports in 4 weeks.
Illustrations: Buys cover art and article illustrations on commission; information available on request. Submit finished art. Cover: color-separated art OK. Inside: b&w line drawings and washes OK. Pays $125, color cover; $10 minimum, inside b&w. Buys 24 illustrations annually. Reports in 4 weeks.

EASTERN REVIEW, East-West Network, Inc., 5900 Wilshire Blvd., #300, Los Angeles CA 90036. (213)937-5810. Editor: James Clark. Senior Art Director: Chris Mossman. Monthly. Buys all rights. Query with resume. Sample copy $1.
Illustrations: Buys cover art and spot drawings on assignment. Pays $25 minimum, spot art; $400, full-color cover. Reports in 4 weeks.

EASYRIDERS, Box 52, Malibu CA 90265. Art Director: Art Honcho. Published 8 times a year. For adult bikers. Looking for art cartoons, or scenes with choppers in them, sexy women — in other words, "bikes, booze and broads," or scenes depicting the good times derived from owning a Harley-Davidson (if a cycle is illustrated)." Buys all rights. Pays on acceptance. Reports in 2 weeks.
Cartoons: Pays $25, small b&w gags; $100, full-page b&w.
Illustrations: "We prefer to buy good art related to our subject and hold it for possible use. We're only interested in finished art. Price depends on space and use. A spot drawing pays minimum $25; a full-page b&w pays $100-150; full-color pays about $250. Subject matter more important than the medium. We use more b&w than color."

Cover art, article illustrations and spot drawings are all assigned to freelancers by Don Nelson, designer of *Notre Dame Magazine*. John Twohey was commissioned by the magazine to create a cover for this politically-oriented issue. *Notre Dame* pays $75-100 on publication of a b&w cover.

EBONY JR!, 820 S. Michigan, Chicago IL 60605. (312)786-7726. Editor: Constance VanBrunt Johnson. For ages 6-14. Published monthly; bimonthly during summer months. 150,000 circulation. Previously published work not considered. Buys all rights. Pays $35 for b&w drawing; $15-50 for 8x10 cartoon; $50-100, complete color-separated ink/acetate illustrations. Mail samples. Reports in 6-12 weeks. Sample copy available. Also needs art for Kwanza's and Martin Luther King's birthdays.

THE EDGE, 6401 The Paseo, Kansas City MO 64131. Editor: Melton Wienecke. Quarterly for church school workers, Christian education directors and pastors. 45,000 circulation. Buys b&w drawings, 4-color cover designs and 5x7" 2-color cartoons. Payment: spot drawing, $25-50; full-color illustration, $75-100; 4-color cover design, $100; cartoon, $25-35. Buys all rights.

Pays on acceptance. Previously published work OK. Mail artwork. Sample copy available. Reports in 6 weeks.

EDUCATION BROADCASTING (formerly Brentwood Publishing Corporation), 825 S. Barrington Ave., Los Angeles CA 90049. Contact: Clay Camburn. Buys spot drawings and full-color paintings. Pays $30, spot art; $175, full-color cover. Buys all rights. Pays on acceptance. Submit published samples. Reports in 30 days.

18 ALMANAC, 1005 Maryville Pike, Knoxville TN 37920. Editor: Phillip W. Moffitt. Annual publication gives practical information for high school seniors. Buys b&w line drawings, line and wash, full-color illustrations and cartoons in rough or finished art. Pays $15 for spot drawings; $125 for full-color illustration; $200 for cover design in 4 colors. Pays on publication. Mail artwork. Reports in 6 weeks. Sample copy available.

THE EL PASO TIMES SUNDIAL, Drawer 20, El Paso TX 79999. (915)747-6765. Editor: Stan Russell. Weekly 11½x13¾"; 30 pages. Letterpress. Estab: 1960. Circ: 95,000. For general Sunday newspaper readership. Not copyrighted. Pays on publication. Previously published, photocopied and simultaneous submissions OK. Mail artwork. SASE.
Cartoons: Buys all themes. Single panel OK. Submit finished art. Halftones OK. Pays $5 minimum. Reports in 2 weeks.
Illustrations: Buys cover art, article illustrations and spot drawings on all themes. Submit finished art. Cover: washes, color-separated art and veloxes OK. Inside: b&w line drawings OK. Minimum payment: $35, color cover; $25, b&w cover; $10, inside color; $5, inside b&w. Reports in 3 weeks.

ELECTRICAL APPARATUS, Barks Publications, Inc., 400 N. Michigan, Chicago IL 60611. Art Buyer: Elsie Dickson. Query with resume.

ELECTRICAL INFORMATION PUBLICATIONS, Box 1648, Madison WI 53701. Editor: Donald J. Jonovic. Buys all rights. Pays on acceptance. Reports in 1 week. Sample copy available.
Cartoons: Buys themes related to school administrators, principals, superintendents, builders, architects and electrical contractors. Should be in ink, finished, in size 5x7". Pays $10-15.

ELECTROMECHANICAL BENCH REFERENCE, Barks Publications, Inc., 400 N. Michigan, Chicago IL 60611. Art Buyer: Elsie Dickson. Query with resume.

ELECTRONIC TECHNICIAN/DEALER, 1 E. 1st St., Duluth MN 55812. Editor: J. W. Phipps. For TV/radio, hi-fi, and communications service dealers and technicians.
Cartoons: Pays $7.50 for cartoons providing good image of radio/TV electronic technician and service dealer. Prefers 8½x11" submissions.

ELECTRONICS, McGraw-Hill Publishing Co., 1221 Avenue of the Americas, New York NY 10020. (212)997-2430. Biweekly; 8¼x11⅛"; 190 pages. Offset. Estab: 1930. Circ: 100,000. For college graduates, electronics engineers, marketing people and executives. Buys all rights. Pays on acceptance. No previously published work. Photocopied and simultaneous submissions OK. Arrange interview to show portfolio. SASE.
Illustrations: Fred Sklenar, art director. Buys cover art, occasional article illustrations and spot drawings. "All art used is on assignment. Any unsolicited art will not be published. It is desirable that all art submitted go on file for future reference." Submit roughs or finished art. Cover: washes, color-separated and reflective art, collage and montage OK. Inside: b&w line drawings, washes, color-separated and reflective art OK. Pays $300 minimum, color cover; $30-300, inside. Buys 26 covers annually.

ELECTRONICS HOBBYIST, Davis Publications, 229 Park Ave. S., New York NY 10003. Contact: Irving Bernstein. Pays $20 minimum, line drawings; $400 maximum, full-color cover design. Buys first rights. Pays on acceptance. Reports in 1 week.

ELEMENTARY ELECTRONICS, Davis Publications, 229 Park Ave. S., New York NY 10003. Contact: Irving Bernstein. Pays $20 minimum, line drawings; $400 maximum, full-color cover design. Buys first rights. Pays on acceptance. Reports in 1 week.

ELITE, 606 Avenue Rd., Suite 404, Toronto, Ontario Canada M4V 2K9. Editor-in-Chief: David Wells. Bimonthly; 8⅛x10⅞"; 100 pages. Offset. Estab: 1975. Circ: 200,000. For men, ages 18-33, interested in modern lifestyles. Buys first rights. Pays on publication. No previously published or simultaneous submissions. Photocopies OK. Query. SASE.
Cartoons: Chris Curl, editor. Buys themes on current events and erotica. Single panel OK. Submit finished art. All media OK. Pays $25-30, b&w; $40-50, color. Buys 84 cartoons annually. Reports in 4 weeks.
Illustrations: Anne Englebright, editor. Buys article illustrations. Submit roughs. All media OK. Minimum payment: $75 b&w; $150, color. Buys 24 illustrations annually. Reports in 4 weeks.

THE ELKS MAGAZINE, 425 W. Diversey Pkwy., Chicago IL 60614. Managing Editor: Jeffrey Ball. Monthly; 8¼x11"; 56 pages. Letterpress. Circ: 1,600,000. For members of the Elks. Buys first and North American serial rights. Pays on acceptance. No previously published, photocopied or simultaneous submissions. Mail artwork. SASE. Free sample copy.
Cartoons: Buys all themes in good taste. "Cartoons must have family appeal." Single panel OK. Submit finished art. Line drawings OK. Pays $50 minimum. Buys 12-36 cartoons annually. Reports in 2 weeks.

ELLERY QUEEN'S MYSTERY MAGAZINE, Davis Publications, 229 Park Ave. S., New York NY 10003. Contact: Irving Bernstein. Pays $20 minimum, line drawings; $400 maximum, full-color cover design. Buys first rights. Pays on acceptance. Reports in 1 week.

EMERGENCY PRODUCT NEWS, Box 159, Carlsbad CA 92008. (714)438-3456. Managing Editor: Linda Olander. Bimonthly; 8⅜x10⅞"; 96 pages. Offset. Estab: 1968. Circ: 35,000. For emergency medical technicians, paramedics, doctors, nurses and rescue squads. Buys all rights, but may reassign rights to artist after publication. Pays on publication. No previously published, photocopied or simultaneous submissions. Query with samples. SASE. Free sample copy.
Cartoons: Buys emergency medicine themes. All formats OK. Submit roughs or finished art. Line drawings, halftones and washes OK. Pays $35 minimum, b&w. Buys 30 cartoons annually. Reports in 1 week.
Illustrations: Buys cover art and article illustrations on assignment. Submit roughs. Cover: washes, color-separated and reflective art OK. Inside: b&w line drawings and veloxes OK. Minimum payment: $75, color; $25, inside b&w. Buys 30 illustrations annually. Reports in 1 week.

THE EMISSARY, Box 328, Loveland CO 80537. (303)667-0599. Editor-in-Chief: Robert Moore. Managing Editor: Theodore Black. Monthly; 6x9"; 48 pages. Offset. Estab: 1975. Circ: 2,500. For all ages, backgrounds, with a basic interest in the art of living. Buys first rights. Previously published, photocopied and simultaneous submissions OK. Request free sample copy, then query with samples. SASE.
Illustrations: Buys life-oriented cover art and article illustrations. Submit finished art. B&w line drawing, washes and color-separated art OK. Pays contributor's copies. Reports in 4 weeks.

EMPIRE MAGAZINE, c/o *Denver Post,* 650 15th St., Denver CO 80202. (303)297-1687. Editor-in-Chief: Carl Skiff. Weekly. Rotogravure. Circ: 375,000. Buys first rights. Pays on acceptance. No previously published, photocopied or simultaneous submissions. Mail artwork. SASE.
Cartoons: Jack Flemming, art director. Buys themes on family life. Single panel OK. Submit finished art. Halftones and washes OK. Pays $10 minimum, b&w.

EN PASSANT POETRY QUARTERLY, 1906 Brant Rd., Wilmington DE 19810. Editor-in-Chief: James A. Costello. Quarterly; 8½x5½"; 40 pages. Offset. Estab: 1975. Circ: 500. For people who like poetry. Buys first rights and "shares remaining rights." No previously published, photocopied or simultaneous submissions. Query with samples. SASE.
Illustrations: Buys cover art and "any pen and inks that are strong enough to carry a page." Submit finished art. Prefers b&w line drawings. Pays 3 contributor's copies. Buys 12-16 illustrations annually. Reports in 1 week. "I like drawings from which it is clear that the artist has at least as much drawing talent as imagination."

ENGINEERING AND CONTRACT RECORD, 1450 Don Mills Rd., Don Mills, Ontario Canada M3B 2X7. Editor: B. Jones.
Cartoons: "We use 3-4 cartoons per issue relating to heavy construction themes — equipment,

labor, safety, roadbuilding, sewer construction, general business management — and we prefer winter settings in winter months. We will look at original pen and ink cartoons or clean photocopies of cartoons previously published in nonCanadian magazines. Any construction theme applicable except house building. We also can use cartoons on general business themes." Annual issue features government at all levels as it affects construction and contractors. Pays $10 minimum on publication for first and second Canadian rights.

THE ENTHUSIAST, 3700 W. Juneau, Milwaukee WI 53201. Editor: Robert H. Klein. Published by Harley-Davidson Motor Co., Inc. for "motorcycle riders of all ages, education and professions." Estab: 1920. Quarterly. Circ: 150,000. Not copyrighted. Buys b&w line drawings and cartoons in finished art. Cartoons should be about motorcycles, of Harley-Davidson design or of no recognizable brand. Pays $15 for spot drawing. Previously published work OK. Pays on publication. Mail artwork. Reports in 30 days. Sample copy available.

ENVIRONMENT MAGAZINE, 560 Trinity Ave., St. Louis MO 63130. (314)863-6560. Contact: Julian McCaull, Sheldon Novick or K. P. Shea. Published monthly except January/February and July/August issues. Estab: 1958. Circ: 24,000. Buys finished cartoons on environmental subjects: air and water pollution. Pays $35. Will consider reprint rights on previously published material. Send published samples. Reports in 2 weeks. Will send sample copy and editorial guide.

THE EQUESTRIAN IMAGE, Rte. 5, Foss Rd., Fenwick, Ontario Canada L0S 1C0. (416)892-2222. Editor: Ms. Pat Mellen. Readers are horsemen, breeders and trainers. Monthly; 8¼x10½". 3,500 circulation. Needs cover designs, full-color illustrations (color-separated) and 7x9½" maximum cartoons. All work should pertain to horses. Pays $100 for full-color illustrations with separations; $50 for cover designs in 2 colors; $3 for cartoons. Pays on publication. Buys one-time rights. Mail artwork. Reports in 1 month. Sample copy on request.

ERBE PUBLISHERS, 220 Tyrone Circle, Baltimore MD 21212. Contact: Theodore H. Erbe. Publishes philatelic magazine. Uses artists for covers, illustrations and layout. Payment determined by project. Query. "It helps if you are a stamp collector."

ESQUIRE, 488 Madison Ave., New York NY 10022. Art Director: Michael Gross. Pays $100-150 for b&w page; $200-250 for full-color page. Arrange interview to show portfolio.

THE EVANGELICAL FRIEND, Box 232, Newberg OR 97132. Managing Editor: Harlow Ankeny. Monthly. Buys art and editorial cartoons. Payment: $10 for spot drawing; $35 for 2-color cover art. Payment on publication. Not copyrighted. Send samples. Sample copy available. Reports in 15-20 days.

EVENT, Box 2503, New Westminster, BC Canada V3L 5B2. (604)588-4411. Editor-in-Chief: John Levin. Managing Editor: Mary Pat Wasmuth. Semiannually; 6x9"; 135 pages. Offset. Estab: 1971. Circ: 800. Pays on publication. Previously published work and photocopies OK. Mail artwork. SASE. Sample copy $2.50
Illustrations: Ken Hughes, editor. Buys cover art and article illustrations. Submit finished art. B&w line drawings and lithographs OK. Pays $5 minimum. Reports in 8 weeks.

EXECUTIVE REVIEW PUBLISHERS, 224 S. Michigan Ave., Chicago IL 60604. Contact: Editor. Monthly; 5½x7½". Estab: 1954. Most art published is freelance. Particularly interested in layout services. Buys one-time rights on cartoons. Artwork previously published considered. Payment on publication. Mail artwork. Reports as soon as possible. Sample copy available.

EXPECTING, 52 Vanderbilt Ave., New York NY 10017. (212)685-4400. Quarterly; 7½x5⅜"; 58 pages. Offset. Estab: 1967. Circ: 850,000. For expectant parents. Buys all rights. Pays on acceptance. Previously published and simultaneous submissions OK. No photocopies. Query. SASE. Free sample copy. "I discuss each issue's needs with the artist, who then submits work."
Cartoons: Evelyn Podsiadlo, editor. Buys themes on family life. Single panel OK. Submit finished art. Line drawings only. Pays $25 minimum. Reports in 3 months.

EXPLORING, Boy Scouts of America, Rte. 1, North Brunswick NJ 08902. (201)249-6000. Editor: Dick Pryce. Published bimonthly for coed teenage members of Explorers. 390,000 circulation. Pays $50-800 for art. Buys first rights. Pays on acceptance. Query with resume. Sample copy available.

FAMILY CIRCLE, 488 Madison Ave., New York NY 10022. Art Director: John Bradford. Circ: 8,200,000. Supermarket-distributed publication for women/homemakers. Submit portfolios on "portfolio days" every other Wednesday. Will look at submissions by mail of preceded by letter of inquiry detailing experience.

FAMILY FOOD GARDEN, Box 1014, Grass Valley CA 95945. (916)273-3354. Editor-in-Chief: George S. Wells. Published 10 times annually; 11x14½"; 32 pages. Offset. Estab: 1973. Circ: 250,000. For middle-income, home food gardeners, all ages; some raise small stock such as rabbits and goats. Buys all rights, but may reassign rights to artist after publication. Pays on acceptance. Previously published work OK. No simultaneous submissions. Mail artwork. SASE. Free sample copy.
Cartoons: Buys home food gardening themes. Single panel OK. Submit finished art. Pen and ink OK. Pays $10 minimum. Buys 10 cartoons annually. Reports as soon as possible.

FAMILY LIFE TODAY, 110 W. Broadway, Glendale CA 91204. Art Director: Joyce Thimsen. Monthly. Buys all rights. Pays 3 weeks after acceptance. Prefers to see general portfolio. Reports in 2 weeks - 1 month.
Illustrations: "We have all kinds of needs: cover designs, line drawings, 4-color and tone art. Nearly all the art we use contains people and children. All work on assignment. We prepare the roughs and buy the finished art from freelancers." Pays $5-80, spot drawings; $200-300, 4-color cover design including paste-up of covers 1 and 4.

FAMILY PET, Box 22964, Tampa FL 33622. Editor-in-Chief: M. Linda Sabella. Quarterly; 16 pages. Estab: 1971. Circ: 3,000. For Florida pet owners. Buys one-time rights. Pays on acceptance. Previously published work OK. No photocopied or simultaneous submissions. Mail artwork. SASE. Free sample copy.
Cartoons: Buys pet themes. Single panel OK. Submit finished art. Line drawings only. Pays $5. Buys 4 cartoons annually. Reports in 3 weeks.
Illustrations: Buys cover art and article illustrations on pets and pets with people. Submit finished art. B&w line drawing OK. Pays $5-20, cover; $3-10, inside. Buys 4-8 illustrations annually. Reports in 3 weeks.

FANTASTIC STORIES, 69-62 230th St., Bayside, Queens NY 11364. Art Buyer: Sol Cohen. For science fiction buffs. Pays $10 for line drawing; $50 for full-color cover art. Payment on acceptance for first rights. Also buys reprint rights to previously published work. Submit published samples. Reports in 60 days.

FANTASY AND TERROR, Box 89517, Zenith WA 98188. Editor: Jessica Amanda Salmonson. Offset. "Deals with adult fantasy, a genre of literature distinct from science fiction, having its origins in mythologies such as Homer's *Illiad,* with more modern forms being *Lord of the Rings,* Robert Howard's *Canon,* the writings of Lord Dunsany, etc." Semiannually. Buys all rights, but may reassign to artist after publication. Mail artwork. Reports in 1 month. Sample copy $1.50.
Illustrations: Buys b&w line drawings, cover designs and story illustrations. Pays $10 per full-page story illustration done on assignment. Pays in copies, subscriptions and honorariums for spot drawings.

FARM SUPPLIER, Watt Publishing Co., Mount Morris IL 61054. Editor: Ray Bates. Buys all rights.
Cartoons: Buys themes on situations in retail farm supply stores or related to outside sales and services by representatives of such local firms. Pays $5-10 on acceptance. Uses 1-2 cartoons per month. Interested in seeing spot cartoons also.

THE FAULT, 33513 6th St., Union City CA 94587. (415)487-1383. Editor-in-Chief: Terrence Ames. Associate Editor: Rustie Cook. Semiannually; 8½x6½"; 150 pages. Offset and letterpress. Estab: 1971. Circ: 500. For small press afficionados. Copyrighted. Pays on receipt of grant (usually 1 year after publication). Previously published work and photocopies OK. No simultaneous submissions. Query with samples. SASE. Sample copy $1. "Any images of contemporary art will fit a particular issue. Selection based on quality rather than topic."

Cartoons: Buys surreal and Dada themes. All formats OK. Submit finished art. Washes OK. Pays $5-10. Buys 40 cartoons annually. Reports in 2 weeks.
Illustrations: Buys cover and full-page art. "I select work from portfolios, rather than have artists conceive for a publication. Their work is placed alongside parallel themes from writers." Submit finished art. B&w line drawings, washes and litho prints OK. Pays $5-10. Buys 40 illustrations annually. Reports in 2 weeks.
To Break In: "We judge work upon the quality of reproduction; a good 5x7" photo of the original is probably the best way to submit."

FAVORITE CROSSWORD PUZZLES & QUALITY CROSSWORD PUZZLES, 855 S. Federal Hwy., Boca Raton FL 33432. Editor: J. L. Quinn. Bimonthly. Sample copy 50¢. Buys all rights. No previously published work.
Cartoons: Buys digest-size cartoons. Pays $25 on acceptance. Submit rough pencil idea; pen or brush finished art. Reports in 2 weeks.

FDA CONSUMER, Food and Drug Administration, 5600 Fishers Lane, Rockville MD 20852. Art Buyer: Jesse R. Nichols. Published 10 times annually. 40 pages. For consumers. Not copyrighted. Deals with areas regulated by FDA, such as foods, medicines, cosmetics and medical devices. Buys spot drawings, cartoons and cover designs. Prefers roughs. Will look at photocopies or tearsheets but uses only original art. Pays on acceptance. Minimum payment: $100 for spot drawing; cover design in 2 colors, finished art, $250. Most freelance work done on assignment. Artist must be on schedule of General Services Administration.

FEED/BACK, THE JOURNALISM REPORT & REVIEW FOR NORTHERN CALIFORNIA, 1600 Holloway, San Francisco CA 94132. (415)469-2086. Managing Editor: David Cole. Art Director: Tim Porter. Quarterly; 8x10¾"; 60 pages. Offset. Estab: 1974. Circ: 1,750. Buys first rights. Previously published, photocopied and simultaneous submissions OK. All methods of contact OK. SASE. Sample copy $1.
Cartoons: Buys themes on journalism — the press "biz." All formats OK. Submit roughs. Washes OK. Pays 5 contributor's copies and 1 year's subscription. Buys 4 cartoons annually. Reports in 2 weeks. "The cartoonist that can come up with funnies about the inner workings of the press, and about reporters specifically, will get published."
Illustrations: Buys cover art, article illustrations and spot drawings on journalism themes. Submit roughs. All media OK. Pays 5 contributor's copies and 1 year's subscription. Buys 4 illustrations annually. Reports in 2 weeks. "Most illustrations don't run alone, but with stories we have already planned. So contact us."

FICTION, 339 Newbury St., Boston MA 02115. (617)266-7746. Contact: Vincent McCaffrey. Buys first rights. Pays on publication. Send samples. Reports in 1 month. Sample copy $1.50.
Illustrations: "Art must have some relevancy to a storytelling magazine (i.e., conform to a theme of an issue, or tell a story within itself). We use general artwork illustrating the seasons; themes such as children, men, women, poetry, science fiction, mystery and westerns. No avant-garde art please." Pays $5 for spot drawing/cover art.

FIELD & STREAM, 383 Madison Ave., New York NY 10017. Art Director: Victor J. Closi. Monthly. "Our editorial content ranges from very basic 'how to' stories that tell in pictures or words how an outdoor technique is done or device is made, to feature articles of penetrating depth about national conservation, game/resource management and recreational development problems. Between these 2 ranges we carry many articles on hunting, fishing, camping, travel, nature, backpacking, photography, equipment, snowmobiling, fish and game cooking, and other family-oriented activities allied to the outdoors. But the key word for most of our articles is service. The 'me and Joe' story is about dead, with the exception of adventure articles." Buys all rights. Pays on acceptance.
Cartoons: Submit 8x10" b&w sketches, any medium. Pays $50. Reports in 15-30 days.

THE FIGHTER'S HOME, 202 Lucerne Ave., Lake Worth FL 33460. Art Buyer: Daniel Gorham. Uses b&w line drawings, line and wash, cover designs (on assignment), full-color illustrations with color separations and cartoons. "We prefer that the artist set his own rates with us so we can be fair, and also see if we can afford him." Not copyrighted. Query. Reports in 3 months.

FIGHTING STARS, 1845 W. Empire Ave., Burbank CA 91504. Editor: Charles Lucas. Published every 3 months. Features personality pieces on media stars involved with martial arts.

Buys cover design in 4 colors. Pays average of $100. Buys all rights. Pays on publication. Previously published work OK. Mail artwork. Reports in 30 days. Sample copy available.

FINISHERS' MANAGEMENT, 22 S. Park St., Montclair NJ 07042. (201)746-8936. Editor-in-Chief: James D. O'Donnell. Monthly; 8x11"; 50 pages. Offset. Estab: 1950. Circ: 8,000. For college-educated, average age 55, owners and managers of metal finishing shops who enjoy leisure sports. Buys first rights. Pays on publication. Simultaneous submissions OK. No previously published work. Query or arrange interview. SASE. Free sample copy.
Cartoons: Buys themes on current events, environment, retirement, golf and tennis. Single panel OK. Submit finished art. Line drawings only. Pays $10-50. Reports in 4 weeks.
Illustrations: Don Canter, art director. Buys cover art and article illustrations. Submit roughs. Color and b&w OK. Pays $50-100. Reports in 4 weeks.
Special Needs: Uses artists for brochures and layout of articles. Pays approximately $25 per page.
To Break In: "The freelancer must know the industry. Should be familiar with set-up and gear his cartoons to management vs. employees."

FIRELANDS ARTS REVIEW, c/o Firelands Campus, Huron OH 44839. Executive Editor: Joel Rudinger. Annually; 8½x5½"; 72 pages. Offset. Estab: 1972. Circ: 1,000. For those generally educated in the arts. Buys first rights. No previously published work or photocopies. Simultaneous submissions OK. Mail artwork. SASE. Sample copy $2.20.
Illustrations: Julius T. Kosan, editor. Buys cover art and spot drawings on general themes. Submit finished art. Cover: b&w line drawings, washes and color-separated art OK. Inside: b&w line drawings OK. Pays contributor's copies. Buys 12-20 illustrations per issue. Reports in 4 weeks.

FISH & GAME SPORTSMAN MAGAZINE, Box 737, Regina, Saskatchewan Canada S4P 3A8. (306)523-8384. Editor-in-Chief: J. B. (Red) Wilkinson. Quarterly; 8½x11"; average 96 pages. Offset. Estab: 1969. Circ: 15,000. For people interested in the outdoors: fishermen, hunters, campers, snowmobilers and conservationists. Buys first and reprint rights. Pays on acceptance. Previously published, photocopied and simultaneous submissions OK. Mail artwork. SASE.
Cartoons: Buys themes on fishing, hunting, camping and outdoor recreation. All formats OK. Submit finished art. Halftones and washes OK. Pays $7, minimum, b&w. Buys 40-60 cartoons annually. Reports in 3 weeks.
Illustrations: Buys article illustrations and spot drawings on outdoor sports. Submit finished art. B&w line drawings, washes and veloxes OK. Pays $25-150, b&w. Buys 8 illustrations annually. Reports in 3 weeks.

FLEA MARKET QUARTERLY, Box 243, Bend OR 97701. Contact: Kenneth Asher. Buys art and cartoons. "In addition to flea market coverage, we also feature items on changing lifestyles, ecology, money-making ideas and money-saving tips." Pays $5, drawing; $30, cover art. Payment on acceptance. Buys all rights. Reports in 6 weeks.

FLING, 1485 Bayshore Blvd., San Francisco CA 94124. Bimonthly. Buys first rights. Query. Reports in 3 weeks. Sample copy (with editorial guidelines) $2.
Cartoons: Wants sophisticated male slant cartoons. Approximately 10 cartoons printed each issue. Any medium OK. Pays $20-50 on acceptance. Looking for double-page spread ideas and multipanel gags. Sometimes will buy idea for cartoon spreads; roughs to be farmed out to regulars. Spreads pay $50-100.
To Break In: Best chance to sell to *Fling* is by having unusual, slick, stylized technique.

FLORAFACTS, Box 9, Leachville AR 72438. (501)539-6320. Editor: Debbie Gamblin. Readers of this monthly are florists, florists wholesalers and suppliers. Estab: 1960. 13,000 circulation. Needs b&w drawings, full-color illustrations (color-separated) and finished art. Seasonal editions require special material related to Christmas, Mother's Day, Easter and other occasions. First serial rights are bought. Mail artwork. Reports in 1 month. Sample copy available.

FLORAFACTS, Box 45745, Tulsa OK 74145. (918)622-8415. Editor-in-Chief: Angela H. Caruso. Assistant Editor: Elaine Simpson. Monthly 8½x11"; 60 pages. Offset. Estab: 1961. Circ: 22,500-25,000. For retail florists. Buys all rights, but may reassign rights to artist after

publication. Pays on acceptance. Previously published work OK. No photocopied or simultaneous submissions. Mail artwork. SASE. Free sample copy with letter. Pays $25 for ad brochures and special projects.
Cartoons: Buys themes on florists or floral industry. "Should be of a fun nature, depicting customer and/or everyday problems in the floral trade. Avoid mention of any wire service." All formats OK. Submit finished art. Line drawings, halftones and washes OK. Pays $10-30, color; $5-25, b&w. Buys 10-20 cartoons annually. Reports in 6 weeks.
Illustrations: Buys cover art, article illustrations and spot drawings on flowers. Submit finished art. Cover: color-separated art OK. Inside: b&w line drawings, washes, reflective art and veloxes OK. Minimum payment: $35, color cover; $25, b&w cover and inside color; $10, inside b&w. Buys 5-15 illustrations annually. Reports in 6 weeks.

FLORIDA ELECTRIC COOPERATIVE NEWS, Box 590, Tallahassee FL 32302. Art Buyer: Johnna Cannon. Monthly. For consumer members of Florida's rural electric cooperatives. Interested in "anything related to 'energy crisis' or energy-related; also agricultural-oriented." Buys finished pen and inks. Negotiates payment. Pays on publication. Not copyrighted. Previously published work OK; "would like to know what other publications work has appeared in." Send published samples. Reports in 2-3 months.

FLORIDA QUARTERLY, 300 Rietz Union, University of Florida, Gainesville FL 32601. Editor: Loren v. Michals. Published 3 times annually. Literary publication. Buys spot drawings, "preferably b&w and not larger than 10x12". Pays contributor's copies. Buys all rights. Previously published work OK. Send original art or published samples.

FOCUS: A JOURNAL FOR GAY WOMEN, 419 Boylston St., Boston MA 02116. Monthly. Requires drawings and cartoons about women and feminist/gay issues. Female artists only. Buys b&w line drawings and finished quarter-page cartoons. Political slant not necessary. Pays contributor's copies. Buys one-time and first serial rights. Mail artwork. Reports in 2 months. Sample copy 60¢.

FOCUS: CHICAGO, Facets Multimedia, Inc., 555 W. Belden Ave., Chicago IL 60614. (312)281-9075. Editor: W. H. Johnson. Art Director: Luke McGuff. For those interested in film. Uses work related to major seasonal events in film in Chicago, nationally or internationally. Buys b&w line, line and wash drawings and cover designs. Rough art only. Buys first serial rights. Pays on publication. Payment: spot drawings, $25; 1-color cover design, $50. Will consider previously published work. Mail artwork. Reports in 3-4 weeks. Sample copy 50¢.

FOOD MARKETER, 2700 Cumberland Pkwy., Suite 500, Atlanta GA 30339. Editor: Beth Souther. For food retailers and wholesalers. Published semiannually. Pays $25-150 for artwork or design ideas. Buys first rights. Pays on publication. Previously published work OK. Mail artwork. Sample copy available.

FOOD PROCESSING, 430 N. Michigan Ave., Chicago IL 60611. Editor: Roy G. Hlavacek. Monthly. For executives and operating management in food processing industries. Buys all rights.
Cartoons: Pays $10 on acceptance for humorous situations relating to processing, distribution, inspection and packaging of food and beverage products, including beer and wine but not hard liquor. No sexiness unless handled with humor and taste and with a point to be made. 8x11" roughs acceptable. Uses 5-6 cartoons each issue. Line reproduction. Reports in 1 week.

FORE, Southern California Golf Association, 3740 Cahuenga Blvd., North Hollywood CA 91604. Editor: Will Hertzberg. Quarterly. Previously published work OK. Buys b&w drawings in line or line and wash and cartoons. Pays $35-50 for spot drawings. Buys one-time rights. Pays on publication. Query. Reports in 2 weeks. Sample copy available.

THE FOREMAN'S LETTER, National Foremen's Institute, 24 Rope Ferry Rd., Waterford CT 06386. Editor: Frank Berkowitz. For industrial supervisors. Buys all rights. Sample copy 75¢.
Cartoons: Buys single panel cartoons, sight or with caption, on industrial supervisory themes emphasizing foreman-worker relationships. Uses about 30 cartoons annually. Pays $10 on acceptance.

FORET ET PAPIER, 625 President Kennedy Ave., Montreal, Quebec Canada H3A 1K5. (514)845-5141. Editor-in-Chief: Paul Saint-Pierre. Quarterly; 8¼x11¼; 50 pages. Offset. Estab: 1975. Circ: 6,500. For engineers and foremen in paper mills and woodlands operations. Buys all rights, but may reassign rights to artist after publication. Pays on acceptance. No previously published, photocopied or simultaneous submissions. Query with samples. SASE. Free sample copy.

Illustrations: Buys cover art on paper mills, papermaking machines, men at work and tree harvesting. Submit roughs. 4-color drawings OK. Pays $125-175. Buys 4 illustrations annually. Reports in 2 weeks.

FORM, National Business Forms Association, 433 E. Monroe Ave., Alexandria VA 22301. Managing Editor: E. C. Raleigh. Continuing need for magazine cover ideas appropriate to

"Its very difficult for an artist to satisfy an editor in a field as technical as sporting dogs when a fault in the artwork conformation-wise or coloration-wise would be apparent to our astute readers," says George Quigley, publisher of *Hunting Dog*. An accurate portrayal of the hunting beagle is what prompted Quigley to pay $35 for this illustration by Ellen Recknor.

business forms design and construction and illustrations of interior construction of business forms. Uses artists for advertising art/design, syndicate cartoons, decorative spots, direct mail brochures, magazine covers/editorial illustrations and technical illustrations. Requires submission of layouts or idea sketches, then finished art. Pays $20-50, illustrations; $50-100; covers. "We usually provide artists with copy and rough sketch of what we want to illustrate. We expect artist to refine and revise into best possible artistic and graphic presentation." Query with resume.

FOUR WHEELER, Box 978, North Hollywood CA 91603. Contact: Michael F. Grout. Off-road magazine for 4-wheel drive consumers. Buys art and cartoons. Pays $15, inside drawings on publication. Buys first rights. Reports in 2 months. SASE.

FOUR ZOAS PRESS, RFD Ware, Hardwick MA 01082. (413)967-9735. Editors: M. Gordon/P. Daniels. Estab: 1971. Circ: 1,000. Quarterly. For students, poetry readers and artists. Needs cover designs and type-high etching blocks and woodcuts. Artwork of political or poetic inclination is of special interest. Pays contributor's copies. Copyrighted. Query with resume. Reports in 3-6 weeks. Sample copy $2.

FREELANCE PHOTO NEWS, National Free Lance Photographer's Association, 4 E. State St., Doylestown PA 18901. Buys cartoons about photographers, their clients and photography in general. Minimum 5x7". Pen and ink OK. Pays $5 for all rights.

FREELANCE PHOTOGRAPHY, National Free Lance Photographer's Association, 4 E. State St., Doylestown PA 18901. Buys cartoons about photographers, their clients and photography in general. Size: minimum 5x7" in pen and ink. Payment $5 for all rights.

THE FRIEND MAGAZINE, 50 E. North Temple, Salt Lake City UT 84150. Art Director: Richard D. Brown. Children's publication of the Church of Jesus Christ of Latter-day Saints. Pays on acceptance. Usually buys all rights.
Illustrations: "Generally our magazine is of a reserved nature because of our religious orientation. Yet we favor art of excellent merit that is freshly developed and designed. We can span a vast range of styles and techniques." Seeks art dealing with ages 1-12. Covers often emphasize seasons and holidays. Art can be any media and size. Uses b&w, 2-color and 4-color art. Payment is $50-250. Reports in 30 days.

FRONT LINE, Merck Sharp & Dohme, West Point PA 19486. (215)699-5311. Editor: William P. Pearre. Bimonthly; 5x7½"; 28 pages. Offset. Estab: 1966. Circ: 1,500. For Merck Sharp & Dohme field representatives. Buys first rights. Pays on publication. No previously published, photocopied or simultaneous submissions. Mail artwork. SASE. Free sample copy.
Cartoons: Buys themes on medicine or selling to the medical/pharmacy professions. "Prefers not to see cartoons that poke fun at patients." Single panel OK. Submit finished art. Washes OK. Pays $60, b&w. Buys 24 cartoons annually. Reports in 2 weeks.

FRONT PAGE DETECTIVE, Detective Publications, 1 Dag Hammarskjold Plaza, New York NY 10017. Editor: James W. Bowser. Monthly. For mature adults — law enforcement officials, professional investigators, criminology buffs and interested laymen. Pays $15 on acceptance for finished cartoons. Must have crime theme. Buys North American serial rights. Reports in 10 days. Sample copy available.

FRONTIER TIMES, Western Publications, Inc., Box 3338, Austin TX 78704. Publisher: Joe Austell Small. Editor: Pat Wagner. For those interested in 1840-1910 western Americana nonfiction. Buys one-time rights. Pays on acceptance. Previously published work OK "depending on where it appeared." Sample copy 60¢.
Illustrations: Buys cover art in 4-color oils. "We prefer a color snapshot or transparency for evaluation of the artist's style. We also prefer vertical paintings because the use of bands above and below a horizontal gives issues a look of sameness. We also have to pass up good paintings at times because our titles would cover some vital element or because the painting has no space left for story titles. We like to leave the artist's work as uncluttered as possible, but a certain amount of type is required. Often, the artist doesn't take this into account." Pays $100. Reports in 2-3 weeks.

FRONTIERS, Academy of Natural Sciences of Philadelphia, 19th and The Parkway, Philadelphia PA 19103. (215)567-3700. Editor-in-Chief: Vi Dodge. Quarterly; 8½x11"; 44 pages. Offset. Estab: 1936. Circ: 6,000. For those interested in the natural sciences. Buys all rights, but may reassign rights to artist after publication. Pays on publication. No previously published or simultaneous submissions. Photocopies OK. Mail artwork. SASE. Sample copy $1.50.
Illustrations: Buys cover art, article illustrations and spot drawings on natural science. Submit finished art. B&w line drawings, washes and reflective art OK. Minimum payment: $100, 2-tone color and b&w cover and inside color; $50, inside b&w. Buys 20-25 illustrations annually. Reports in 4 weeks.

FUR-FISH-GAME, 2878 E. Main St., Columbus OH 43209. Editor-in-Chief: A. R. Harding. Monthly; 8x11"; 64 pages. Offset. Estab: 1925. Circ: 190,000. For outdoorsmen, all ages. Buys all rights, but may reassign rights to artist after publication. Pays on acceptance. Previously

published work OK. No photocopied or simultaneous submissions. Mail slides or color snapshots of art as proofs. SASE. Sample copy 50¢.
Illustrations: Buys cover art and article illustrations on all outdoor subjects. "No salt-water fishing. The cover subject is usually large and stands out; should show action of some kind." Submit finished art. Cover: reflective art OK. Inside: b&w line drawings and washes OK. Pays $50-75, color cover; $25-75, b&w illustrations with ms. Buys 25 illustrations per issue. Reports in 4 weeks.

GALAXY, Universal Publishing & Distributing Corporation, 235 E. 45th St., New York NY 10017. Editor: James Baen. Estab: 1950. Circ: 65,000. Interested in artwork on science fiction themes. Payment is $30 for b&w illustrations; $200 for 4-color cover in finished art. Covers bought for inventory are $150. Buys first serial rights. No previously published work. SASE. Reports in 1-3 weeks. Sample copy available.

GALLIMAUFRY, 3208 N. 19th Rd., Arlington VA 22201. Editor: Mary MacArthur. Published semiannually. Uses 1 freelance artist (preferably in Washington DC area) for each issue. Uses collages and drawings not previously published. Pays $25 for 1-color cover. Buys one-time rights. Send samples. Reports in 3 months. SASE. Sample copy $1.25.

GAS DIGEST, Box 35819, Houston TX 77035. Editor: Ken Kridner. Monthly; 8¼x11; 40-60 pages. Offset. Estab: 1975. Circ: 10,000. For the college-educated, ages 35-40, in the gas industry. Buys all rights, but may reassign rights to artist after publication. Pays on acceptance. No previously published, photocopied or simultaneous submissions. Query. SASE. Sample copy $2. Also buys art for tabloid supplement.
Cartoons: Buys b&w cartoons on the gas industry. Single panel only. Submit roughs. Line drawings only. Pays $10 minimum. Reports in 1 week.
Illustrations: Buys article illustrations. Submit roughs. B&w line drawings OK. Pays $10 minimum. Reports in 1 week.

GEM, 303 W. 42nd St., New York NY 10036. Editor: Will Martin. Bimonthly. For young men. Buys b&w line drawings, washes and 7x10" rough cartoons. Pays $35-40 for wash drawing. Prefers local artists. Buys all rights. Previously published work OK. Mail artwork. SASE.

GENT, Dugent Publishing Company, 316 Aragon Ave., Coral Gables FL 33134. Editor/Publisher: Douglas Allen. Managing Editor: Nye Wilden. For men. Buys first time rights.
Cartoons: Buys "funny, somewhat 'sick' humor and sexual themes." Submit finished art. B&w OK. Pays $15 per spot drawing; $100 per page. Mail cartoons.
Illustrations: Works on assignment. Pays $50-75, b&w. Buys 3-4 illustrations per issue. "Submit samples of work for our files."

GEORGIA STRAIGHT, Georgia Straight Publishing Ltd., 2110 W. 4th Ave., Vancouver, BC Canada V6K 1N6. Art Buyer: Dan McLeod. Alternative press. Uses spot drawings, cover designs (including seasonal). Cover art: 7x7" print size, 3-4 colors. Pays $4 for spot drawing; $25-50 for cover art. Buys one-time rights. Pays on acceptance. "Invoice must be submitted before payment made." Submit photocopies or photos of art aimed at the publication. SASE (with Canadian stamps). Reports in 2 weeks.

GHOST DANCE: THE INTERNATIONAL QUARTERLY OF EXPERIMENTAL POETRY, 526 Forest, East Lansing MI 48823. Editor-in-Chief: Hugh Fox. Managing Editor: N. W. Werner. Quarterly; 8½x5½"; 32-36 pages. Offset. Estab: 1968. Circ: 300-400. For avant-garde poets in the U.S., United Kingdom, Australia and New Zealand. Buys first rights. Pays contributor's copys. Photocopies OK. No previously published or simultaneous submissions. Mail artwork. SASE.

GIG MAGAZINE, 415 Lexington Ave., New York NY 10017. (212)661-6790. Editor: Jean-Charles Costa. Monthly; 11x14"; 72 pages. Offset. Estab: 1974. Circ: 100,000. For those with musical interests, ages 16-30. Buys first and reprint rights. Pays on publication. Previously published work OK. No photocopied or simultaneous submissions. Arrange interview. SASE. Free sample copy.
Illustrations: Michael Todd, art director. Buys cover art, article illustrations and "mostly spot drawings with a cartoonish feel" on rock music artists. Submit finished art. Cover: color-separated art OK. Inside: b&w line drawings, washes and veloxes OK. Pays $200-500, color

cover; $50 minimum, inside color; $75-150, b&w cover; $25 minimum, inside b&w. Buys 80 illustrations annually. Reports in 4 weeks.

GLAD (formerly *Days of Youth*), 8121 Hamilton Ave., Cincinnati OH 45231. (513)931-4050. Editor-in-Chief: Judy Trotter. Published quarterly in weekly parts; 5½x8¼; 8 pages. Offset. "*Glad* to begin September 4, 1977 and is a continuation of *Days of Youth* and other publications started in 1902." Circ: 70,000. For young Christian adults. Buys first rights on cartoons and all rights on art. Pays on acceptance. Accepts previously published cartoons but not illustrations. Query. SASE. Free sample copy. "Not open to art that puts questionable activities in an accepted light — no smoking, drinking, dancing, revealing clothes."
Cartoons: Buys themes on current events, education, humor through youth, religion and teenagers. Single panel OK. Submit finished art. Line drawings only. Pays $10. Reports in 2-4 weeks.
Illustrations: Buys article illustrations on assignment. Pays $40, b&w cover; $35, inside b&w. Buys 52 illustrations annually. Reports in 2-4 weeks.
To Break In: "We are willing to work with beginners. Be flexible and agreeable to work with."

GLAMOUR, 350 Madison Ave., New York NY 10017. Art Director: George Hartman. Women's fashion magazine. Pays $225 per page. Query with resume and arrange interview to show portfolio. "We don't buy work from portfolio. All work done here is freelance."

GLASS DIGEST, 15 E. 40th St., New York NY 10016. Editor: Oscar S. Glasberg. For management in the distribution, merchandising, and installation phases of the flat glass, architectural metal, and allied products industry (including stained, art glass and mirrors). Buys all rights. Free sample copy. Reports as soon as possible.
Cartoons: Buys finished themes related to storefront and curtain wall construction and automotive glass industry. Pays $5 on acceptance. Accepts roughs, gag lines with descriptions, or finished line work ready for engraving camera.

GOLF, 380 Madison Ave., New York NY 10017. (212)687-3000. Editor-in-Chief: John M. Ross. Managing Editor: Vincent J. Pastena. Monthly; 8½x11". 100 pages. Estab: 1959. Circ: 650,000. For recreational golfers. Buys all rights. Pays on acceptance. No previously published, photocopied or simultaneous submissions. Query with samples. SASE. Free sample copy.
Cartoons: Buys golf themes. Single panel OK. Submit finished art. Pays $75 minimum. Buys 6-12 cartoons annually. Reports in 4 weeks.
Illustrations: Robert Bode, art director. Assigns illustrations. Pays $25, b&w; $50 minimum, color.

GOLF BUSINESS (formerly *Golfdom),* 9800 Detroit Ave., Cleveland OH 44102. Editor-in-Chief: David Slaybaugh. Managing Editor: Nick Romano. Monthly; 9½x13"; 64 pages. Offset. Estab: 1976. Circ: 30,000. For golf course management personnel. Buys all rights. Pays on publication. No previously published or simultaneous submissions. Photocopies OK. Query with samples. SASE. Free sample copy.
Illustrations: Buys cover art and article illustrations on club food and beverage service, golf course design and maintenance, golf cars, pro shop, lessons and management. Cover: washes and reflective art OK. Inside: b&w line drawings, washes and reflective art OK. Pays $100-300, color cover; $25-150, inside b&w; $50-200, inside color. Buys 12-15 illustrations annually. Reports in 4 weeks.

GOLF DIGEST, 495 Westport Ave., Norwalk CT 06856. Art Director: John Newcomb. "Although we usually commission artwork for our publication, we are always interested in submitted materials specifically on golf or golf-related subjects." Pays $200 per page for full-color illustration; $100 per page for b&w. Buys first rights. Pays on acceptance of finished art. Query with resume. Usually reports in 2 weeks.

GOLF SHOP OPERATIONS, 495 Westport Ave., Norwalk CT 06856. (203)847-5811. Editor: James McAfee. Published 6 times annually; 10x13½; 32 pages. Letterpress. Circ: 11,000. For golf pros. Buys all rights, but may reassign rights to artist after publication. Pays on publication. Mail artwork. SASE. Free sample copy.
Cartoons: Buys themes relating to golf pros. Single panel OK. Submit finished art. Line drawings OK. Pays $10-25. Buys 10 cartoons annually. Reports in 4 weeks.
Illustrations: Buys cover art and article illustrations on golf fashion; for example: the sunny

outlook for sales after rainy spring. Submit finished art. Cover: b&w line drawings and color-separated art OK. Inside: b&w line drawings OK. Pays $50-100, color cover; $25-50, b&w cover; $15-25, inside. Buys 5 illustrations annually. Reports in 4 weeks.

GOOD HOUSEKEEPING, 959 8th Ave., New York NY 10019. Art Director: Herb Bleiweiss. For women. Uses b&w and full-color art on assigned projects. Query with resume or call to arrange interview.

GOOD NEWS BROADCASTER, Box 82808, Lincoln NE 68501. Managing Editor: Thomas Piper. Monthly. 44-page organizational religious magazine. Circ. 215,000. Buys illustrations. Previously published work OK. Prefers all rights; but, will buy one-time rights. Pays on acceptance. Query with resume or send samples. Free sample copy.

GOOD OLD DAYS, c/o Tower Press, Inc., Box 428, Seabrook NH 03874. Editor: Edward Kutlowski. Nostalgic magazine depicting life 40-70 years ago. Buys nostalgic material only. Monthly. Uses b&w drawings, full-color cover designs and cartoons. Buys all rights. Payment on acceptance. Pays $250-500 for cover design in 4 colors; $100-150, full-page b&w drawings. Always looking for new and original nostalgic cartoon features. Submit Christmas material in June-July. Reports in 10-30 days.

GRAFICA, 705 N. Windsor Blvd., Los Angeles CA 90038. Contact: A. del Moral. Spanish bimonthly. Buys spot drawings oriented toward Hispanic and Mexican American persons, their problems and progress. Pays $2+ on acceptance. Reports in 14 days.

GRAPHIC ARTS MONTHLY, 222 S. Riverside Plaza, Chicago IL 60606. (312)648-5911. Editor: Bertram D. Chapman. Managing Editor: Donald Curda. Monthly; 8⅛x10¾"; 160 pages. Offset. Estab: 1929. Circ: 74,523. For management and production personnel in commercial and specialty printing plants and allied crafts. Buys first rights. Pays on acceptance. No previously published, photocopied or simultaneous submissions. Mail artwork. SASE. Sample copy $1.50.
Cartoons: Buys themes on printing, layout, paste-up, typesetting and proofreading. Single panel OK. Submit finished art. Halftones OK. Pays $15. Buys 40 cartoons annually. Reports in 3 weeks.

GREAT LAKES GAZETTE, Box 47, Grand Marais MI 49839. Editor-in-Chief: Rose Mary Marshall. Managing Editor: Thomas M. Scaife. Monthly; 8½x11"; 20 pages. Offset. Estab: 1971. Circ: 1,500. Buys first and simultaneous rights. Mail artwork. SASE. Free sample copy.
Cartoons: Buys current event, education, environment, family life, humor through youth, retirement, outdoors, Great Lakes and regional themes. All formats OK. Submit finished art. Line drawings OK. Pays contributor's copies. Buys 2 cartoons per issue. Reports in 4 weeks.

GREAT LAKES PRESS, 3750 Nixon Rd., Ann Arbor MI 48105. Copyrighted maritime publication. Buys spot drawings. Pays $10-25 minimum. Prefers 2¼x2¼" or 4x5". Previously published work OK. Submit tearsheets or photocopies. Reports in 2 weeks.

GREEN PAGES, 641 W. Fairbanks, Winter Park FL 32789. (305)644-6326. Editor-in-Chief: John Erving. Quarterly; 8½x11", 80-100 pages. Offset. Estab: 1975. Circ: 25,000. For the disabled and professionals in the rehabilitation industry. Buys first rights. Pays on publication. Previously published, photocopied and simultaneous submissions OK. Query with samples. SASE. Free sample copy.
Cartoons: Buys themes having anything to do with disability, even "sick" humor. "Don't pull punches. Disabled people can relate to falling out of wheelchairs, being blown over by a slight breeze, off-beat humor." All formats OK. Submit roughs or finished art. Line drawings only. Pays $7.50-$15. Buys 4-6 cartoons per issue. Reports in 30-45 days.
Illustrations: Buys cover art on article themes. Submit roughs. B&w line drawings, washes and color-separated art OK. Pays $25, b&w cover. Reports in 3 months.

GREEN REVOLUTION (formerly School of Living), Box 3233, York PA 17402. (717)755-1561. Editor-in-Chief: Jubal. Managing Editor: Kyla. Monthly; 8½x11"; 36 pages. Offset. Estab: 1943. Circ: 1,500. For those interested in "back to the land." Not copyrighted. Pays on publication. Previously published, photocopied and simultaneous submissions OK. Write. SASE. Sample copy $1.

Illustrations: Buys cover art on landscapes. Submit finished art. Pen and ink OK. Pays $10 minimum. Buys up to 10 illustrations annually. Reports in 4 weeks.

GROCERY COMMUNICATIONS MAGAZINE, Box 8268, Van Nuys CA 91409. Editor: Linda Callen. Monthly. "Readership includes executives, supervisors, buyers, and management in the grocery industry as well as allied trades such as food brokers, wholesalers and manufacturers." Not copyrighted. Buys art and cartoons. Pays $10 for cartoons on publication. Prefers cartoons be 4x5". No previously published work. Mail artwork. Reports immediately on rejections; on publication if used.

GROUND WATER AGE, 110 N. York Rd., Elmhurst IL 60126. (312)833-6540. Editor-in-Chief: Gene Adams. Monthly; 8½x11½"; 64 pages. Offset. Estab: 1965. Circ: 15,000. For water well drilling contractors and water systems specialists. Buys all rights, but may reassign rights to artist after publication. Pays on acceptance. Previously published and simultaneous submissions OK. Mail artwork. SASE. Free sample copy.
Cartoons: All formats OK. Submit roughs or finished art. Halftones and washes OK. Pays $10-12, b&w. Buys 48 cartoons annually. Reports in 2 weeks.
Illustrations: Buys article illustrations and spot drawings. Submit roughs. B&w line drawings, washes, color-separated and reflective art and veloxes OK. Pays $10-100, b&w; $20-100, color. Buys 24 illustrations annually. Reports in 2 weeks.
Special Needs: Uses artists for promotional material and ads. Pays $10.

GROUP MAGAZINE, Box 481, Loveland CO 80537. (303)669-3836. Editor-in-Chief: Thom Schultz. Monthly; 11x17"; 24 pages. Offset. Estab: 1974. Circ: 10,000. For members and leaders of high school Christian youth groups. Buys all rights. Pays on publication. No photocopies. Previously published and simultaneous submissions OK. Query. SASE. Free sample copy.
Illustrations: Buys cover art, article illustrations and spot drawings on assignment. Submit roughs. B&w line drawings and washes OK. Pays $10-30. Buys 6 illustrations per issue. Reports in 3 weeks.

GRUB STREET, Box 91, Bellmore NY 11710. (212)733-3922. Art Editor: Russel Lockwood. Published semiannually. Circ: 1,000-2,000. Buys b&w drawings, cover art and cartoons. Negotiates payment and rights purchased. Reports in 3-6 weeks. Sample copy $1.

GUIDEPOSTS, 747 3rd Ave., New York NY 10012. Art Director: Jessica M. Weber. Monthly interfaith publication. Buys all rights. Pays on acceptance. Mail artwork. Reports immediately. Free sample copy.
Illustrations: Buys cover designs, full-color illustrations, b&w line drawings and line and washes. Pays $100-175, spot art; $500, full-color illustration.

GUN WORLD, Box HH, Capistrano Beach CA 92624. Editorial Director: Jack Lewis. Managing Editor: Dean A. Grennell. Monthly; 8⅛x10⅜"; 72 pages. Offset. Estab: 1960. Circ: 126,000. For shooters and hunters. Buys all rights, but may reassign rights to artist after publication. Pays on acceptance. No previously published, photocopied or simultaneous submissions. Mail artwork. SASE. Free sample copy. "No anti-gun or anti-hunting art." Buys illustrations on assignment.
Cartoons: Buys shooting and hunting themes. All formats OK. Submit finished art. Halftones OK. Pays $7.50-$12. Buys 3-4 cartoons per issue. Reports in 3 weeks.

GYMNASTICS WORLD, World Publications, Box 366, Mt. View CA 94040. Art Buyer: Bob Anderson. Buys cover designs, spot drawings and cartoons. "Our readers are participants and we try to use material that shows insight into the sports that we cover." Pays $10+. Buys reprints rights. Pays on publication. Reports in 1 week.

HAM RADIO, Greenville NH 03048. (603)878-1441. Editor-in-Chief: James Fisk. Monthly; 8x11"; 128 pages. Offset. Estab: 1968. Circ: 57,000. For licensed amateur radio operators, ages 18+. Buys all rights. Pays on acceptance. No previously published, photocopied or simultaneous submissions. Query with samples. SASE. Free sample copy.
Cartoons: Buys amateur radio communications themes (no CB). Single panel OK. Submit finished art. Line drawings and halftones OK. Pays $10-15. Buys 12-15 cartoons annually. Reports in 2 weeks.

Illustrations: Buys cover art, article illustrations and spot drawings on amateur radio and electronics. Submit roughs. Cover: color-separated and reflective art OK. Inside: b&w line drawings OK. Minimum payment: $80, b&w cover; $100, color cover; $25, inside b&w. Buys 15-20 illustrations annually. Reports in 2 weeks.
Special Needs: Artwork for May's "Antennas" and October's "Receivers" issues. Also uses local artists for advertising layouts and finished art. Negotiates payment.

HAM RADIO HORIZONS, Greenville NH 03048. (603)878-1441. Editor-in-Chief: James Fisk. Managing Editor: Thomas McMullen, Jr. Monthly; 8x11"; 96 pages. Offset. Estab: 1977. Circ: 40,000. For amateur radio operators and those interested in becoming amateurs, ages 13+. Buys all rights. Pays on acceptance. No previously published, photocopied or simultaneous submissions. Query with samples. SASE. Free sample copy.
Cartoons: Buys amateur radio communications themes (no CB). Single panel OK. Submit finished art. Halftones OK. Pays $10-15. Buys 30 cartoons annually. Reports in 2 weeks.
Illustrations: Buys cover art, article illustrations and spot drawings on amateur radio and electronics. Submit roughs. Cover: color-separated and reflective art OK. Inside: b&w line drawings OK. Minimum payment: $80, b&w cover; $100, color cover; $25, inside b&w. Buys 36-50 illustrations annually. Reports in 2 weeks.
Special Needs: Artwork for June's "Antennas" issue. Also uses local artists for advertising layouts and finished art. Negotiates payment.

HARPER'S, 2 Park Ave., New York NY 10016. Contact Sheila Berger. Monthly. For well-educated, socially concerned, widely-read men, women and college students active in community and political affairs. Prefers art portfolio be left for at least half day or overnight for review.

HARVARD ADVOCATE, 21 South St. Cambridge MA 02138. (617)495-2764. Editors: Paul Rowe/Douglas McIntyre. Estab: 1866. Quarterly literary and arts magazine. Buys b&w line drawings, line and wash and finished cartoons. Negotiates payment. Buys all rights. Previously published work OK. Query. Reports in 2-4 weeks. Sample copy $1.

HEALTHWAYS, 2200 Grand Ave., Des Moines IA 50312. Editor-in-Chief: Maryann Smith. Published 6 times annually; 7½x5⅛"; 50 pages. Offset and letterpress. Estab: 1946. Circ: 115,000. "For those interested in staying healthy in the most natural way, with minimal use of drugs, surgery, etc." Not copyrighted. Pays on publication. Previously published and simultaneous submissions OK "if we are told." No photocopies. Query with samples. SASE. Free sample copy. "The artists whose work we've used were contacted in visits to art shows, galleries or through seeing their work advertised."
Illustrations: Buys cover art and spot drawings on outdoor themes. Submit roughs. B&w line drawings and color-separated art OK. Pays $15-25, b&w cover; $15-50, color cover; $5 minimum, inside b&w. Reports in 3 weeks.

HEIGHTS, Le Moyne College, Le Moyne Heights, Syracuse NY 13214. (315)446-2882.
Illustrations: Buys cover art and inside illustrations. Payment determined by degree of difficulty and number of illustrations. Pays $25, cover art; $15, line drawings. Query with samples. SASE. Reports in 4 weeks.

HEIRS MAGAZINE INTERNATIONAL, 657 Mission St., San Francisco CA 94105. Multi-cultural magazine in the vein of international art publications. Publishes major articles in English, Spanish and Chinese. Buys rough or finished art. Write for payment. Pays on publication. Buys first rights. Submit art. Reports in 30-60 days. Sample copy $3.

HICALL, 1445 Boonville Ave., Springfield MO 65802. (417)862-2781. Editor-in-Chief: Dr. Charles W. Ford. Managing Editor: Kenneth D. Barney. Weekly; 5½x9"; 8 pages. Offset. Estab: 1954. Circ: 160,000. For junior high and high school students. Not copyrighted. Pays on acceptance. Previously published and simultaneous submissions OK. No photocopies. Send portfolio. "Portfolio of cartoons may be b&w. Illustration portfolio should be color if possible. Originals returned. Assignments made according to talent displayed in portfolios." SASE. Free sample copy.
Cartoons: Buys all youth-oriented themes in good taste. All formats OK. Submit finished art. Halftones and washes OK. Pays $3 minimum, b&w. Buys 25 cartoons annually. Reports in 3 weeks.

Illustrations: Buys cover art and article illustrations on assignment. Submit finished art. Cover: color-separated and reflective art OK. Inside: b&w line drawings, washes, color-separated and reflective art OK. Pays $100, color cover; $11-37, inside b&w. Buys 200 illustrations annually. Reports in 3-4 weeks.

HIGH FIDELITY, Publishing House, Great Barrington MA 01230. (413)528-1300. Graphics Editor: Roy Lindstrom. Monthly. Circ: 300,000. Buys all rights. Previously published work OK. Query. Reports in 1 week. Sample copy available.
Illustrations: Buys drawings and cover designs. Pays $15 for spot drawing; $300 for cover design.

HIGH FIDELITY TRADE NEWS, 6 E. 43rd St., New York NY 10017. Editor: Ronald Marin. Buys all rights. "We're primarily looking for portrait artists who can do various handlings of people working from photos. Also looking for cover artists. All work by assignment." Pays $35-100 on acceptance.

HIGHLIGHTS FOR CHILDREN, 803 Church St., Honesdale PA 18431. Editor: Walter B. Barbe, Ph.D. Managing Editor: Mrs. Garry C. Myers. Monthly; bimonthly in June/July and August/September; biweekly in December. 11½x9"; 42 pages. Estab: 1946. Circ: 1,300,000. For ages 2-12. Buys all rights. Pays on acceptance. No previously published, photocopied or simultaneous submissions. Query with samples. SASE.
Cartoons: Buys themes on family life and humor through youth. Single panel OK. Submit finished art. Line drawings only. Pays $20-25. Reports in 4-6 weeks. "No nudes, war, crime, violence or anything which makes fun of parents or teachers."

HOCKEY ILLUSTRATED (formerly Gambi Publications), 333 Johnson Ave., Brooklyn NY 11206. Contact: Joseph Mauro. Buys b&w line drawings and washes with 2-color overlays. Prefers 11x6". Pays $200, 2-color art. Pays on publication. Buys first North American serial rights. SASE. Reports in 1 month. Sample copy available.

HOLIDAY, 1100 Waterway Blvd., Indianapolis IN 46202. Editor-in-Chief: Henry O. Dormann. Managing Editor: Kathryn Klassen. Bimonthly; 80 pages. Offset. Estab: 1946. Circ: 450,000. For mature, sophisticated travelers, average age 40. Buys first, all and first North American serial rights. Pays on publication. No previously published simultaneous submissions. Photocopies OK. Query. SASE. Sample copy 50¢.
Cartoons: Buys themes related to travel, entertainment, dining, skiing, golf, tennis, cooking and reading. Single panel OK. Submit roughs. Halftones and washes OK. Pays $25 minimum, b&w; $50 minimum, color. Buys 6-10 cartoons annually. Reports in 4 weeks.
Illustrations: Dean Eller, design director. Buys cover art, article illustrations and spot drawings on travel, places and modes of transportation. Submit finished art. Cover: color-separated art OK. Inside: b&w line drawings, washes, color-separated and reflective art and veloxes OK. Pays $100-500, cover and inside color; $100-400, inside b&w. Buys 10-25 illustrations annually. Reports in 4 weeks.

"Don't just stand there, Frimly. Ask him what he knows about dichlorotetrafluoroacetone acids!"

If you haven't worked in a plant, Laurie Lawlor, cartoon editor of *Chemical Processing,* suggests you visit one before submitting cartoons to her specialized publication. Five cartoons, such as this one by Walt Miller, are purchased annually at a minimum of $10 for use in this trade publication.

HOLIDAY INN COMPANION, East-West Network, Inc., 5900 Wilshire Blvd., #300, Los Angeles CA 90036. (213)937-5810. Editor: James Clark. Senior Art Director: Chris Mossman. Monthly. Buys all rights. Query with resume. Sample copy $1.
Illustrations: Buys cover art and spot drawings on assignment. Pays $25 minimum,

spot art; $400, full-color cover. Reports in 4 weeks.

HOME LIFE, 127 9th Ave., N., Nashville TN 37234. Editor: George W. Knight. Monthly. Buys all rights.
Cartoons: Pays $15-25 on acceptance for cartoons on humorous family life situations. Particularly interested in cartoons on marriage. Sex is the only taboo. Any size roughs acceptable. Uses 2 cartoons per issue. Line and halftone reproduction. Reports in 45 days or less. Vertical composition only for 1 column.

HOME REPAIR, Davis Publications, 229 Park Ave. S., New York NY 10003. Contact: Irving Bernstein. Pays $20 minimum, line drawings; $400 maximum, full-color cover design. Buys first rights. Pays on acceptance. Reports in 1 week.

HOME WORKSHOP, Davis Publications, 229 Park Ave. S., New York NY 10003. Contact: Irving Bernstein. Pays $20 minimum, line drawings; $400 maximum, full-color cover design. Buys first rights. Pays on acceptance. Reports in 1 week.

HOOSIER FARMER, Indiana Farm Bureau, Inc., 130 E. Washington St., Indianapolis IN 46204. Managing Editor: Tom Asher. Monthly. Buys first rights.
Cartoons: Pays $5 on acceptance for cartoons which portray the modern farmer, problems and/or situations pertaining to agriculture. Uses 1-2 cartoons per issue. Roughs in pen and ink acceptable. Reports in 6 weeks.

HORSE AND HORSEMAN, Box HH, Capistrano Beach CA 92624. (714)493-2101. Editor/Publisher: Jack Lewis. Managing Editor: Mark Thiffault. Monthly; 8⅜x11"; 74 pages. Offset. Estab: 1973. Circ: 94,000. For pleasure horse owners, mostly women, ages 13-30. Buys all rights, but may reassign rights to artist after publication. Pays on acceptance. No previously published, photocopied or simultaneous submissions. Query. SASE. Free sample copy.
Cartoons: Buys themes on the environment, family life, humor through youth, horseback riding and stables. Single or double panel OK. Submit finished art. Line drawings only. Pays $5-7.50. Buys 15-20 cartoons annually. Reports in 2 weeks.
Illustrations: Buys cover art and article illustrations on assignment. Cover: transparencies of paintings OK. Pays $15 minimum for illustrations.

HORSE, OF COURSE, Temple NH 03084. Editor/Publisher: R. A. Greene. Pays on acceptance. Sample copy $1. Pays $4 per panel for cartoons.
Illustrations: Uses "simple line drawings, preferably realistic in style, depicting horses in action." 5x7" minimum. Pays $4-50 for all rights. Average payment is $20.

HOSPITAL FINANCIAL MANAGEMENT, 666 N. Lake Shore Dr., Chicago IL 60611. (317)787-3876. Contact: Hellena Smejda/Patricia Rummer. Deals with financial, accounting, management, personnel and related topics in health care. Buys pen and inks, and single or panel cartoons. Rights and payments negotiable. Mail samples or arrange interview. Reports in 60 days.

HOUSE PLANTS & PORCH GARDENS, 355 Lancaster Ave., Haverford PA 19041. (215)527-5100. Editor-in-Chief: Peter Tobey. Managing Editor: Kim MacLeod. Monthly; 8¼x10¾"; 96 pages. Web offset. Estab: 1976. Circ: 250,000. For all ages interested in gardening, particularly indoor. Most readers are college-educated. Buys all rights. Pays on acceptance. No previously published or simultaneous submissions. Photocopies OK only as samples, not for assigned work. Query with samples marked "freelance artwork." SASE. Sample copy $1.25.
Cartoons: Buys humorous themes relating to plants. Single panel OK. "They will be only a quarter page at most; rarely use larger cartoons." Submit finished art. Line drawings only. Pays $15-25. Buys 10 cartoons annually. Reports in 3 weeks.
Illustrations: Buys article illustrations and spot drawings on plant subjects and some people, but only if accompanied by plants. "I prefer realistic renderings, but not those done in fine detail that are very large. Reduction in size often loses very fine lines." Submit finished art. B&w line drawings, washes and color-separated art OK. Pays $20-100, color; $10-50, b&w. Buys 240 illustrations annually. Reports in 3 weeks.

HUGHES WEST SUNDANCER, East-West Network, Inc., 5900 Wilshire Blvd. , #300, Los Angeles CA 90036. (213)937-5810. Editor: James Clark. Senior Art Director: Chris Mossman. Monthly. Buys all rights. Query with resume. Sample copy $1.

Illustrations: Buys cover art and spot drawings on assignment. Pays $25 minimum, spot art; $400, full-color cover. Reports in 4 weeks.

THE HUMANIST, 923 Kensington Ave., Buffalo NY 14221. Editor: Paul Kurtz. Journal of humanist and ethical concern. Published 6 times annually. 52 pages. "Intellectual content." Buys one-time rights. Pays on publication. Previously published work OK. Send published samples. SASE. Reports in 1 month.
Illustrations: Buys pen and ink, line and wash rough or finished art. Pays $15, spot art; $50, 2-color finished cover design.

HUMPTY DUMPTY'S MAGAZINE, 52 Vanderbilt Ave., New York NY 10017. Art Editor: Duncan Morrison. Works with local artists on assignment. Query with resume.

HUNTING DOG, 9714 Montgomery Rd., Cincinnati OH 45242. Editor: George R. Quigley. Monthly. Buys b&w line drawings and line and wash. Buys all and one-time rights. Minimum of $5 for b&w. Previously published work OK. Query. Reports in 2-3 weeks. Sample copy 50¢.

HUSTLER MAGAZINE, 40 W. Gay St., Columbus OH 43215. (614)464-2068. Cartoon and Humor Editor: Susan Tinsley. Monthly. For men. Buys all rights. Pays on acceptance. Mail samples. Reports in 2 weeks.
Illustrations: Buys b&w drawings and full-color illustrations.
Cartoons: Primarily interested in cartoons dealing with sex and social issues. Pays $300 for full-color page; $150 for ¼ color page; $100 for ¼ b&w page.

ICONOCLAST, 3507 Cedar Springs, Dallas TX 75219. (214)528-4031. Editor: Douglas Baker. For those interested in Dallas news and entertainment. Estab: 1970. Circ: 25,000. Weekly. Buys b&w line drawings, cover designs (local interest only) and cartoons. Pays $30-60, 2-color cover design; $10+ for local and national editorial cartoons. Buys all rights. Pays on publication. Previously published work OK. Mail artwork. Reports in 1 week. Sample copy available.

IDEALS, Box 1101, Milwaukee WI 53201. Managing Editor: Ralph Luedtke. Issues 6 editions annually. Three editions are Christmas, Easter and Autumn issues. The other 3 issues devoted to inspirational and informative topics with emphasis on seasonal subjects.
Illustrations: Interested in realistic treatment of subjects in the following media: pencil, pen and ink, line and wash, watercolor, designer's colors, pastels, acrylic and charcoal. "Most of our artwork is 1-color, but we do review 4-color artwork. For initial submissions we like to see a rough sketch showing enough detail for good impression. In the case of proposed 4-color artwork, colors should be indicated on the sketch. Final artwork should be on appropriate material such as white illustration board or paper mounted on heavy backing, with protective overlay. We look at original samples as well as tearsheets or photocopies of published work." Payment for 4-color illustrations ranges from $25-300. Vignette art for 1 page brings $50. Detailed illustration for double-page spread ranges from $150-200. If Luedtke decides to hold art for future issues, payment not made until publication. In most cases, buys work outright with the right to future re-use without additional payment. Assignments guaranteed. Reports in 1-3 weeks.

IF, 235 E. 45th St., New York NY 10017. Editor: James Baen. Estab: 1950. Circ: 65,000. Interested in artwork on science fiction themes. Pays $30, b&w illustrations; $200, 4-color finished cover; $150, inventory covers. Buys first serial rights. No previously published work. SASE. Reports in 1-3 weeks. Sample copy available.

ILLINOIS MASTER PLUMBER, 140 S. Dearborn, Chicago IL 60603. Monthly. Deals with plumbing trade at the contractor level. Buys spot drawings, cartoons and cover designs relative to the plumbing industry. Tearsheets, photocopies or transparencies of previously published work considered. Not copyrighted. Pays on acceptance of final work. Minimum payment for spot drawing is $7.50. Mail artwork. Reports in 30 days.

IN A NUTSHELL, Box 22248, Sacramento CA 95822. (916)428-2766. Editor-in-Chief: Margaret Wensrich. Quarterly; 5½x8½"; 40 pages. Offset. Estab: 1975. Circ: 5,000. For people who like to read and enjoy art. Buys first rights. Pays on publication. No previously published, photocopied or simultaneous submissions. Mail artwork. SASE. Sample copy $1.

Cartoons: Buys themes on current events, education, environment, family life and humor through youth. All formats OK. Submit finished art. Line drawings only. Pays $5 minimum. Buys 8 cartoons annually. Reports in 2 weeks.
Illustrations: "We assign illustrators for our stories and poems." Buys 12-18 illustrations annually.
Special Needs: Uses series of 4 pictures for illustrating a theme. Pays $20 minimum. Past themes: "San Francisco," "Derelicts," and "Victoriana."

INCENTIVE TRAVEL MANAGER (formerly Brentwood Publishing Corporation), 825 S. Barrington Ave., Los Angeles CA 90049. Contact: Clay Camburn. Buys b&w spot drawings and full-color paintings. Pays $30, spot art; $175, full-color cover. Pays on acceptance. Buys all rights. Submit published samples. Reports in 30 days.

INCOME OPPORTUNITIES, Davis Publications, 229 Park Ave. S., New York NY 10003. Irving Bernstein. Pays $20 minimum, line drawings; $400, maximum, full-color cover design. Buys first rights. Pays on acceptance. Reports in 1 week.

INDIANA GENERAL NEWS, General Telephone Company of Indiana, 8001 U.S. 24 W., Fort Wayne IN 46805. Editor-in-Chief: Deborah Sutton. Monthly; 11½x14¼"; 8 pages. Offset. Circ: 6,400. For General Telephone employees. Not copyrighted. Pays on publication. Previously published and simultaneous submissions OK. No photocopies. Query. SASE. Free sample copy. "Include resume and rates."
Cartoons: Buys themes on the environment, retirement, communications industry, safety, productivity and economics. Single panel OK. Submit finished art. Line drawings and halftones OK. Minimum payment: $1, b&w; $1.50, color. Buys 2-3 cartoons annually. Reports in 4 weeks.
Illustrations: Buys cover art, article illustrations and spot drawings on safety, economics and the communications industry. Submit finished art. Cover: b&w line drawings and color-separated art OK. Inside: b&w line drawings, washes and color-separated art OK. Pays $5-50, b&w cover; $10-100, color cover; $2-5, inside b&w; $2.50-$10, inside color. Buys 2-3 illustrations annually. Reports in 4 weeks.
Special Needs: Uses artists for brochure and booklet art. Pays $10-100.

INDUSTRIAL ENGINEERING, 25 Technology Park/Atlanta, Norcross GA 30092. (404)449-0460. Editor-in-Chief: Lee Miller. Monthly; 8⅛x11"; 70 pages. Offset. Estab: 1968. Circ: 32,000. For industrial engineering and management people interested in productivity improvement. Buys all rights. Pays on acceptance. No previously published or simultaneous submissions. Photocopies OK. Query. SASE. Sample copy $3.
Cartoons: Buys current events, education, environment, family life and industrial engineering themes. Single panel OK. Submit finished art. Halftones and washes OK. Pays $10 minimum, b&w. Buys 12 cartoons annually. Reports in 4 weeks.
Illustrations: Buys cover art and article illustrations on industrial engineering. Submit finished art. Cover: color-separated art OK. Inside: b&w line drawings, washes, color-separated art and veloxes OK. Minimum payment: $20, b&w cover and inside color; $25, color cover; $15, inside b&w. Reports in 4 weeks.

INDUSTRIAL LAUNDERER, 1730 M St. NW, Washington DC 20036. (202)296-6744. Editor: Jim Roberts. Monthly. Circ: 3,000. Uses b&w line drawings, line and wash, and cartoons in rough and finished forms. Negotiates payment. Pays on publication. Buys first North American rights. No previously published work. Submit resume. Reports as soon as possible. Sample copy available.

INDUSTRIAL MACHINERY NEWS CORPORATION, 29516 Southfield Rd., C.S. #5002, Southfield MI 48037. (313)557-0100. Contact: Ms. Lucky D. Slate. For those in the metalworking industry responsible for manufacturing, purchasing and engineering. Interested in line ink cartoons about metalworking or personal relationships. Pays $5 on publication. Buys one-time rights.

INDUSTRIAL PROGRESS, Box 13208, Phoenix AZ 85002. Cartoon Editor: Frederick H. Kling. For research and development men, production men, maintenance supervisors, purchasing directors in all types of industry — a sophisticated audience. Buys first and reprint rights. Sample copy available.

Cartoons: Must have a good situation involving research, new-product development, testing, purchasing, engineering, drafting or shop scenes. Pays $25-40.

INFOTRAIL, Box 158, Brandon SD 57005. (605)582-6013. For antiques dealers and collectors. Annually. If informed in advance, previously published work considered. Buys cover designs, cartoons, b&w drawings in finished art and design ideas. Buys all rights. Pays on publication. Reports promptly.

INLAND PRINTER/AMERICAN LITHOGRAPHER, 300 W. Adams St., Chicago IL 60606. Editor: R.H. Green. Printing, publishing, graphic arts industry magazine. Issued monthly to help owners, executives, managers, production managers, and department heads operate more efficiently and at a greater profit. Buys all rights. Send samples. Reports in 30-60 days. Pays on acceptance. "We only require that artwork not be sold to competing publications — it can be used again in other sectors without bothering us."
Cartoons: Especially needs general cartoon characters. Uses 40-48 cartoons annually. Must relate to printing industry. Pays $10 on publication for finished art.
Illustrations: "Particularly need good line work for all articles. We need someone who can do good industrial line work from photos."

INSIDE DETECTIVE, Detective Publications, 1 Dag Hammarskjold Plaza, New York NY 10017. Editor: James W. Bowser. Monthly. For mature adults — law enforcement officials, professional investigators, criminology buffs and interested laymen. Pays $15 on acceptance for finished cartoons. Must have crime theme. Buys North American serial rights. Reports in 10 days. Sample copy available.

INSIGHT, Box 7244, Grand Rapids MI 49510. Editor-in-Chief: Rev. James C. Lont. Art Editor: Chris Cook. Monthly (except June, August); 8½x11"; 32 pages. Offset. Estab: 1925. Circ: 22,000. For Christian youth, ages 14-19. Buys first rights. Pays on publication. No previously published work. Photocopied and simultaneous submissions OK. Query. SASE. Free sample copy.
Cartoons: Buys themes on current events, humor through youth and religion. "Our favorites are the ones that speak for themselves, no caption." Single panel OK. Sumit finished art. Line drawings, halftones and washes OK. Minimum payment: $15, b&w; $30, color. Buys 6 cartoons annually. Reports in 2 weeks.
Illustrations: Buys article illustrations and spot drawings with religious themes applied to current events. Submit finished art. B&w line drawings and washes OK. Pays $10 minimum. Buys 3 illustrations annually. Reports in 2 weeks.

INSTRUCTOR PUBLICATIONS, INC., Instructor Park, Dansville NY 14437. Editor: Ernest Hilton. Published 9 times a year for elementary school teachers. Buys cartoons about elementary children and school situations. Pays on acceptance. Buys all rights. Reports in several weeks. Write for sample copy.

THE INSTRUMENTALIST, 1418 Lake St., Evanston IL 60204. Editor: K.L. Neidig. School-instrumental music magazine. Buys original art and cartoons in pen and ink and line and wash. Copyrighted. Pays on publication. Minimum payment: $6, cartoons. Mail artwork.

INTELLECT, 1860 Broadway, New York NY 10023. (212)265-6680. Editor-in-Chief: Stanley Lehrer. Managing Editor: Bob Rothenberg. Monthly; 8⅜x11"; 68 pages. Letterpress. Estab: 1914. Circ: 10,000. For intellectual college graduates with wide range of interests. Buys all rights. Pays on publication. No previously published, photocopied or simultaneous submissions. Query with samples. SASE. Free sample copy.
Illustrations: Buys cover art, article illustrations and spot drawings on assignment. "Send samples of work for our files. We make assignments according to styles in our files." Submit finished art "in most cases, except cover." Cover: color-separated art OK. Inside: b&w line drawings OK. Pays $75-100, color cover; $15-50, inside. Buys 70-80 illustrations annually. Reports in 1 week.

INTERLUDE, Box 6680, Vancouver, BC Canada V6B 4L4. (604)732-1371. Editor-in-Chief:-W.J.B. Mayrs. Bimonthly; 8½x11"; 32 pages. Offset. Estab: 1976. Circ: 50,000. Buys first rights. Pays on publication. No previously published, photocopied or simultaneous submissions. Query with samples. SASE. Free sample copy.

Cartoons: Buys themes on current events, environment, family life, humor through youth, retirement and any Western-oriented hobbies or businesses. Single panel OK. Submit finished art. Line drawings only. Pays $15 minimum. Reports in 4 weeks. Nothing controversial, no, airplane crashes or racial themes.
Illustrations: Buys article illustrations and spot drawings. Submit finished art. B&w line drawings and color-separated art OK. Pays $35-75, b&w; $100-200, color. Reports in 4 weeks.

INTERMEDIA, 2431 Echo Park Ave., Los Angeles CA 90026. Editor-in-Chief: Harley W. Lond. Published 3 times annually; 8½x11"; 48 pages. Offset. Estab: 1974. Circ: 2,000. For college-educated artists, ages 18-45, interested in experimental and avante-garde art. Buys all rights, but may reassign rights to artist after publication. Previously published, photocopied and simultaneous submissions OK. Query. SASE.
Illustrations: "All artwork considered on its own merits. We don't use artwork as 'illustration,' but focus on the artwork." Buys art for cover and article illustrations. Submit finished art. B&w line drawings, washes and veloxes OK. Pays 2 contribution's copies. Buys 15-30 illustrations annually. Reports in 4 weeks.

THE INTERNAL AUDITOR, 249 Maitland Ave., Altamonte Springs FL 32701. Contact: Don Anders. Uses illustrations representative of various industries. Buys cartoons, covers, illustrations and layout. Pays $15-150, spot line drawings, cartoons and charts; $40-150, covers. Submit rough or finished ink or line and wash art. Reports in 2 weeks.
Special Needs: Uses artists for advertising art/design, animation, book jacket design/illustration, catalog illustration/covers, decorative spots and direct mail brochures.

IOWA MUNICIPALITIES, 444 Insurance Exchange, Des Moines IA 50309. Editor: Frank Bowers. Monthly; 8½x11". For Iowa city officials. Not copyrighted. Buys cover art and cartoons. Pays $35 on acceptance for cover design in 1 or 2 colors. Previously published work OK. Query. Reports in 60 days. Sample copy available.

JACK AND JILL, 1100 Waterway Blvd., Indianapolis IN 46206. (317)634-1100. Editor: William Wagner. Published 10 times annually; 6½x9¼"; 48 pages. Offset. For ages 5-12. Buys all rights. Pays on publication. Previously published, photocopied and simultaneous submissions OK. Query with samples. SASE. Sample copy 50¢.
Illustrations: Edward F. Cortese, art director. Buys cover art, article illustrations and spot drawings on assignment. Submit roughs. Cover: reflective art OK. Inside: b&w line drawings, washes, color-separated and reflective art OK. Pays $135, color cover; $30-80, inside color; $25-35, inside b&w. Buys 200 illustrations annually. Reports in 1-3 weeks.

JACKSONVILLE, 604 N. Hogan St., Jacksonville FL 32202. Editor: Lee Sinoff. For the business community. Circ: 8,000-10,000. Estab: 1963. Bimonthly. Buys one-time and all rights. Pays on publication. Query with resume or send samples. Must relate to the city and its environs, or articles in the magazine. Reports in 2 weeks. Write for sample copy.
Cartoons: Submit roughs or finished art. Pays $25-50.
Illustrations: Buys b&w line drawings, line and wash, full-color illustrations, design ideas and layout services. Submit roughs or finished art. Pays $25-50, spot art; $50-75, full-color illustration; $100, 4-color cover design.

JAPANOPHILE, Box 223, Okemos MI 48864. Editor-in-Chief: Earl R. Snodgrass. Quarterly; 8¾x5¾"; 50 pages. Offset. Estab: 1974. Circ: 500. For those interested in Japan. Buys first North American serial and all rights, but may reassign rights to artist after publication. Pays on acceptance. Previously published, photocopied and simultaneous submissions OK. Query. SASE. Sample copy $1.75. "We especially like Japanese art forms such as sumi-e and woodblock prints."
Cartoons: Buys themes on Japan and its culture anywhere. All formats OK. Submit finished art. Line drawings and halftones OK. Pays $5-7. Buys up to 8 cartoons annually. Reports in 4 weeks.
Illustrations: Robert Copland, editor. Buys cover art and article illustrations on Japanese scenes or subjects anywhere in the world; especially needs covers to suggest 1 of the 4 seasons. Submit finished art. Cover: b&w line drawings, color-separated and reflective art OK. Inside: b&w line drawings OK. Pays $10-15, b&w cover; $5-7, inside. Buys up to 30 illustrations annually. Reports in 4 weeks.

JET CADET, 8121 Hamilton Ave., Cincinnati OH 45231. Editor: Dana Eynon. For ages 8-12. Buys first and, occasionally, second rights. Send samples. Reports in 4-6 weeks.
Cartoons: Pays $10-$15 on acceptance for finished art. Popular subjects are outer space, animals, school and sports. Buys 12-15 cartoons annually.
Illustrations: "Art that accompanies nature or handcraft articles may be purchased, but most everything is assigned. Pays $10, spot drawings; $40, cover line drawing in several colors.

JEWELERS' CIRCULAR-KEYSTONE, Chilton Way, Radnor PA 19089. Editor: George Holmes. For retail jewelers. Buys all rights. Reports immediately.
Cartoons: Uses 30 cartoons annually with jewelry store environment themes. "Avoid theft gags, please. Crime is unfunny to jewelers."

JEWISH CURRENT EVENTS, 403 Keller Ave., Elmont NY 11003. Editor: S. Deutsch. Biweekly for Jewish adults and children, distributed through Jewish schools. Interested in a cartoon strip and drawings with Jewish content or flavor. Previously published work OK.

JEWISH LIFE, 116 E. 27th St., New York NY 10016. (212)725-3405. Editor: Yaakov Jacobs. Religious family quarterly. Features fiction, nonfiction and poetry about Orthodox Jewish living. Buys one-time rights. Previously published work OK. Pays on publication. Sample copy available.
Illustrations: Buys religious b&w drawings, line art and roughs. Negotiates payment. Reports in 3-4 weeks.

JOBBER TOPICS, 7300 N. Cicero Ave., Lincolnwood IL 60646. News Editor: Gerry Dawson. Monthly. For automotive parts and supplies wholesalers. Aimed at owners, managers and salesmen. Buys finished cartoons, preferably on automotive subjects. Buys all rights. Pays on acceptance.

"JOINT" CONFERENCE, Box 19332, Washington DC 20036. Editor-in-Chief: Kathryn E. King. Quarterly; 6x9"; 60-64 pages. Offset. Estab: 1974. Circ: 500-600. For prison inmates and people interested in inmate writing. Buys all rights, but may reassign rights to artist after publication. Pays on acceptance. No previously published work. Photocopied and simultaneous submissions OK. Mail artwork. SASE. Free sample copy. "I use material only from inmates in correctional institutions. I'd like to see some work from female inmates. I do not like to see drawings in pencil or pornography."
Cartoons: Buys themes on current events, education, environment, family life, politics and prison life. Single panel OK. Submit finished art. Line drawings OK. Pays $5-25. Buys 8-10 cartoons annually. Reports in 4 weeks.
Illustrations: Buys cover art and spot drawings on prison life. Submit finished art. B&w line drawings and veloxes OK. Pays $10-25, b&w cover; $5-25, inside b&w. Buys 16-25 illustrations annually. Reports in 4 weeks.

JOURNAL OF CARDIOVASCULAR AND PULMONARY TECHNOLOGY, (formerly Brentwood Publishing Corporation), 825 S. Barrington Ave., Los Angeles CA 90049. Contact: Clay Camburn. Buys b&w spot drawings and full-color paintings. Pays $30, spot art; $175, full-color cover. Buys all rights. Pays on acceptance. Submit published samples. Reports in 30 days.

JOURNAL OF FRESHWATER, 2500 Shadywood Rd., Box 90, Navarre MN 55392. (612)471-7467 or 8407. Editor: Richard A. Hughes. Quarterly; 8½x11". Offset. Estab: 1977. For the educated, concerned about the environment and interested in a scientific approach to solving freshwater problems. Buys all rights, but may reassign rights to artist after publication. Pays on acceptance. No previously published, photocopied or simultaneous submissions. Query with samples. SASE. Sample copy $3.
Cartoons: Buys freshwater-oriented themes. "Freshwater is more than just lakes, rivers and streams. Water is everywhere." All formats OK. Submit finished art. Line drawings, halftones and washes OK. Minimum payment: $20, color; $10, b&w. Reports in 2-3 weeks.
Illustrations: Buys cover art, article illustrations and spot drawings on freshwater environments. "Look for different approaches to water as the 'elixir of life' and 'universal solvent.' " Submit finished art. All media OK. Pays $50 minimum, inside. Reports in 2-3 weeks.

JOURNAL OF INTERNATIONAL PHYSICIANS, 1030 N. Kings Hwy., Suite 213, Cherry Hill NJ 08034. (609)667-7526. Editor-in-Chief: A.E. Woolley. Monthly; 8¼x11"; 28 pages.

Offset. Estab: 1976. Circ: 26,500. For physicians who received their basic M.D. degree outside the U.S. Buys first rights. Pays on acceptance. Previously published work OK. Arrange interview. SASE. Sample copy $2.
Illustrations: Dale Artis, editor. Buys cover art and article illustrations on assignment. Submit roughs. B&w line drawings, washes, color-separated and reflective art OK. Pays $200-300, color cover; $150-200, inside color and b&w cover; $100-150, inside b&w. Buys 10-20 illustrations annually. Reports in 2 weeks.

JUDICATURE, 200 W. Monroe, Suite 1606, Chicago IL 60606. Contact: Esther Lerner. Journal of the American Judicature Society. Assigns illustrations related to court improvement. Negotiates payment. Payment for unsolicited cartoon is $20.

JUVENILE MERCHANDISING, 370 Lexington Ave., New York NY 10017. Editor: Lee Clarke Neumeyer. Juvenile products industry monthly. Previously published work OK. Buys one-time rights. Pays on publication. Previously published work OK. Mail artwork. Reports immediately. Will send sample copy on request.

KANSAS QUARTERLY, Denison Hall, Kansas State University, Manhattan KS 66506. (913)532-6716. Editors: Harold Schneider/Ben Nyberg. For academic and general readership. Copyrighted. Circ: 1,500. Uses b&w drawings. Pays in copies. Reports in 3 months. Sample copy $2.50.

KARATE ILLUSTRATED, 1845 W. Empire Ave., Burbank CA 91504. Contact: Ben Kalb. Monthly. Buys cover designs, inside illustrations and cartoons on the martial arts. Inside: b&w line drawings and line and wash OK. Payment depends on quality, need and use. Pays on publication. No previously published work. Query. Reports in 2 weeks. Sample copy available.

KENTUCKY FOLKLORE RECORD, Box U-169, Western Kentucky University, Bowling Green KY 42101. Editor: Charles S. Guthrie. For libraries and individuals having an interest in folklore as a learned discipline. Estab: 1955. Quarterly. Circ: 400. Buys cover designs and b&w drawings. Buys all rights. Pays in copies. Previously published work OK. Mail artwork. Reports in 4-12 weeks. Sample copy $1.25.

KEY TO CHRISTIAN EDUCATION, 8121 Hamilton Ave., Cincinnati OH 45231. (513)931-4050. Editor-in-Chief: Marjorie Miller. Quarterly; 8⅜x11"; 48 pages. Estab: 1962. Circ: 60,000. For Sunday school teachers, leaders, ministers and superintendents. Buys first rights. Pays on acceptance. Previously published work and photocopies OK. No simultaneous submissions. Query with samples. SASE. Free sample copy.
Illustrations: Buys cover art, article illustrations and spot drawings on Christian education themes. Submit roughs or finished art. Cover: b&w line drawings and color-separated art OK. Inside: b&w line drawings OK. Pays $50-100, b&w cover; $10, inside b&w. Buys 100-160 illustrations annually. Reports in 3 weeks.
Special Needs: Artwork related to TV, multimedia, the blind, the deaf, recreation, church socials, sports teams, singing groups, field trips, teacher recruitment, training and conservation.

KILOBAUD, Peterborough NH 03458. Publisher: Wayne Green. For computer hobbyists. Buys all rights. Pays on acceptance. Sample copy $2.
Illustrations: Buys cover art and inside illustrations on hobby computer themes. Submit rough line drawings for assignment as oil, watercolor or pastel covers. Pays $5-20, spot art; $75 per page, finished art. Reports in 2 weeks.

THE KINDERGARTNER, 201 8th Ave., S., Nashville TN 37202. Editor: Arba O. Herr. Weekly; 8½x11"; 4 pages. Estab: 1964. Circ: 168,154. For kindergartners. Buys all rights. Pays on acceptance. No previously published, photocopied or simultaneous submissions. Query with samples. SASE. Free sample copy. Prefers not to receive "anything that does not have a wholesome quality in harmony with the best Christian standards of thought, feeling and action. Avoid reference to drinking or smoking in ways that suggest approval or acceptance."
Cartoons: Buys current event, education, environment, family life and humor through youth themes. Single panel OK. Submit finished art. Line drawings OK. Pays $12-15. Buys 3 cartoons annually. Reports in 4 weeks.
Illustrations: David Dawson, art director. Buys article illustrations and spot drawings on

assignment. Submit finished art. B&w line drawings and color-separated art OK. Pays $40, color; $30, b&w. Buys 30 illustrations annually. Reports in 4 weeks.

THE KIWANIS MAGAZINE, 101 E. Erie St., Chicago IL 60611. Editor: David B. Williams. For business and professional men. Published 10 times annually. Stresses civic and social betterment, business, education, religion and domestic affairs. Pays on acceptance. Reports in 2 weeks.
Cartoons: Buys finished art. Pays $35. Buys first rights.
Illustrations: Jane Bushwaller, art/design coordinator. "Many of our articles are illustrated by art, but on assignment only. Artists must be available to appear when needed in our office to work with art and production people on designs, rought and finished work." Spot drawings pay $50-75; full-color illustrations $180-250; full-color covers $200-300.

KNIFE DIGEST, Knife Digest Publishing Co., Box 4310, Berkeley CA 94704. Art Buyer: Shari Berne. Annually; 8½x11"; 320-400 pages. For well-educated sportsmen, outdoorsmen and collectors. Buys all rights. Pays on publication. Mail artwork. SASE. Reports in 6 weeks-6 months. Sample copy $5.95 plus 75¢ postage.
Illustrations: "We are particularly seeking good technical illustrators for current titles and titles in production. Must be polished, professional, ready-to-go. We can always use spot art of old swords, locks, knives, etc." Artwork should be pen and ink, finished, submitted on Crescent 201 illustration board with tissue overlays, or reproduction quality photocopies only. Pays $10-25 for spot drawing; $50-100 for half-page editorial illustration.

LADIES' HOME JOURNAL, 641 Lexington Ave., New York NY 10022. Art Director: Donald A. Adamec. Query with resume and arrange interview. SASE.

LADY'S CIRCLE, 21 W. 26th St., New York NY 10010. (212)689-3933. Editor-in-Chief: Shirley Howard. Managing Editor: Connie Barbara. Monthly; 8x11"; 72 pages. Offset. Circ: 500,000. Buys all rights. Pays on publication. SASE.
Cartoons: Buys themes on current events, education, environment, family life and humor through youth. Single and double panel OK. Submit finished art. Line drawings, halftones and washes OK. Pays $20 minimum, b&w.

THE LAKE SUPERIOR REVIEW, Box 724, Ironwood MI 49938. Editors-in-Chief: Faye Korpi/Lee Merrill/Cynthia Willoughby. Published 3 times annually; 8½x5½"; 48 pages. Offset. Estab: 1970. Circ: 500. For those interested in contemporary literature. Buys first rights. Pays contributor's copies. No previously published, photocopied or simultaneous submissions. Mail artwork. SASE. Sample copy $1.50.
Cartoons: Dail Willoughby, editor. Buys current event, education, environment, erotica and political themes. Single panel OK. Submit finished art. Line drawings only. Reports in 6-10 weeks.
Illustrations: Buys cover art and will match art to poems and short stories or use separately. Submit finished art. B&w line drawings OK. Reports in 6-10 weeks.

LE BUREAU, 625 President Kennedy Ave., Montreal, Quebec Canada H3A 1K5. (514)845-5141. Editor-in-Chief: Paul Saint-Pierre. Bimonthly; 8¼x11¼"; 52 pages. Offset. Estab: 1965. Circ: 7,500. For office managers, electronic data processing experts and systems analysists. Buys all rights, but may reassign rights to artists after publication. Pays on acceptance. No previously published, photocopied or simultaneous submissions. Query with samples. SASE. Free sample copy if artist sends samples.
Illustrations: Buys cover art on calculators, small computers, in-plant printing and word processing. "We appreciate humor in good taste." Submit roughs. Color-separated art, veloxes and color drawings OK. Pays $125-200. Buys 12 illustrations annually. Reports in 2 weeks.

LEARNING MAGAZINE, 530 University Ave., Palo Alto CA 94301. Art Buyers: Mike Shenon/David Hale/Bob Bryant. Monthly during the school year. For teachers of kindergarten-8th grade. Buys cover art. Pays $500 maximum. Buys one-time rights. Pays on acceptance. Send tearsheets or photocopies. "Don't send anything valuable or that must be returned."

LEATHERNECK, Magazine of the Marines, Box 1918, Quantico VA 22134. Art Director: James Hopewell. Buys all rights.
Cartoons: Must be of Marines in action — sports, leave, liberty, barracks life, rifle range —

everyday military life. Buys 25-50 cartoons per year. Prefers rough, single panel, sport drawings. Not larger than 8x10" for single panel or spot. Pays $10-$20. Reports in 30 days.

LEGAL ECONOMICS, Box 11418, Columbia SC 29211. (803)771-8964. Editor: Robert P. Wilkins. Quarterly. Circ: 18,000. Accepts b&w drawings, cover designs and full-color illustrations. Primarily interested in cartoons relating to the economics of law practice. Usually buys all rights. Will consider previously published work. Negotiates payment. Pays on publication. Query with resume. Reports in 90 days.

LEGION, 359 Kent St., Ottawa Ontario Canada K2P 0R6. (613)235-8741. Editor-in-Chief: Jane Dewar. Monthly; 8¼x11"; 64 pages. Offset. Circ: 500,000. For Royal Canadian Legion members. Not copyrighted. Pays on publication. No previously published, photocopied or simultaneous submissions. Query with samples. SASE. Free sample copy.
Illustrations: Dick Logan, editor. Buys cover art, article illustrations and spot drawings on assignment. Submit roughs. Cover: reflective art OK. Inside: all media OK. Pays $200-1,200, color cover; $20-1,200, inside b&w; $40-1,200, inside color. Buys 120 illustrations annually. Report in 1-2 weeks.

LEISURE HOME LIVING, 13 Evergreen Rd., Hampton NH 03842. Editor: Richard Livingstone. Buys art on any subject concerning second or vacation homes, such as exteriors, interiors and leisure home communities. Pays $10+, drawings; $100, 4-color covers. Buys one time rights. Reports in 2 weeks. Sample copy $1.50.

LEISUREWHEELS, Box 40, Irricana, Alberta Canada T0M 1B0. (403)935-4688. Editor-in-Chief: Gladys Taylor. Art Editor: Paul Boisvert. Monthly; 8½x11"; 56 pages. Offset. Estab: 1969. Circ: 20,000. For campers. Buys all rights. Pays on publication. Previously published work and photocopies OK. No simultaneous submissions. Query with samples. SASE. Free sample copy.
Cartoons: Buys camping themes. Single panel OK. Submit finished art. Line drawings OK. Pays $10 minimum. Buys 20 cartoons annually. Reports in 4 weeks.
Illustrations: Buys spot drawings on camping themes. Submit finished art. B&w line drawings and color-separated art OK. Buys 6 illustrations annually. Reports in 4 weeks.

LEMMING, 3585 Central Ave., San Diego CA 92105. Editor: Rex Burwell. Poetry quarterly. For all ages, though most appealing to college-age readers. Previously published work OK. Submit tearsheets or original art. Reports in 1 month maximum.
Illustrations: Buys pen and ink drawings only, 8½x5½", finished art. "Artists interested in doing covers invited to submit." Pays contributor's copies.

THE LESBIAN TIDE, 8855 Cattaraguas, Los Angeles CA 90034. (213)839-7254. Contact: Jeanne Cordova. Bimonthly; 8½x11"; 40 pages. Offset. Estab: 1970. Circ: 6,000. For lesbians, feminists, women and political radicals. Not copyrighted. Pays on publication. Previously published, photocopied and simultaneous submissions OK. Mail artwork. SASE. Sample copy $1. "We do not accept work from men."
Cartoons: Buys current events, education, environment, erotica and political themes. Prefers not to receive male or heterosexual humor. All formats OK. Submit finished art. Line drawings OK. Pays $3. Buys 6 cartoons annually. Reports in 4 weeks.
Illustrations: Buys cover art, article illustrations and spot drawings on "women in activities and women with other women." No heterosexual, sexist or racist themes. Submit finished art. B&w line drawings OK. Pays $3. Buys 30 illustrations annually. Reports in 4 weeks.

LIBERTY MAGAZINE, 6840 Eastern Ave. NW, Washington DC 20012. Editor: R. R. Hegstad. Deals with subjects related to religious freedom and church-state separation-parochial aid, federal involvement in church activities, Sunday laws. Buys spot drawings, cartoons and cover designs. Minimum size: 4x5" in pen and ink and line and wash, rough or finished art. All, first, or U.S. rights purchased, depending on circumstances. Previously published work OK. Pays for final work on acceptance and final work when used if reprinted from another publication. Minimum payment: spot drawing is $10-25; cover design in 4 colors, finished art $150. Query. Reports in 7-10 days. Sample copy and guidelines available.

Spot drawings, cartoons and cover designs are all of interest to *Best Wishes*, a magazine for new mothers. Payment for a spot drawing is around $10. This cover design was purchased from Richard Chretien.

LIFE & HEALTH, Washington DC 20012. (202)723-3700. Editor: Don Hawley. Monthly. Circ: 100,000. Estab: 1884. For laymen interested in nonfaddish programs of good health. Pays $15-30, spot drawings; $40-80, 2-color illustrations; $100-150, color illustration; $15-25, cartoons. Work should be about health topics. "Will consider almost any style art. Subject matter rather conservative. 4-color work for cover only — inside pages are b&w with second color." Buys all rights. Uses 10-12 freelance items per issue. Previously published work OK. Mail or deliver samples. Reports in 2 weeks. Sample copy 50¢.

LIGHT: A POETRY REVIEW, Box 1105, Stuyvesant, New York NY 10009. Editor: Roberta C. Gould. Annually. Buys b&w drawings. "We need more submissions from women." Buys 50 illustrations/photos annually. Buys first serial rights. Pays contributor's copies. Previously published work OK. No photocopies. Mail artwork. Reports in 1-3 months. Sample copy $1.25.

THE LION, York and Cermak Rds., Oak Brook IL 60521. Senior Editor: Robert Kleinfelder. Published 11 times annually for members of Lions clubs. Buys all rights. Will send free sample copy on request. Reports in 10 days.
Cartoons: Pays $30 on acceptance for finished art. Subjects generally limited to humanitarianism, community betterment and self-improvement. Uses 11 cartoons annually. Taboos include politics, consumption of liquor, tobacco, sex and marital infidelity.

LISTEN MAGAZINE, 6830 Laurel St. NW, Washington DC 20012. Editor: Francis A. Soper. Concerns prevention of alcoholism and drug addiction in youth. Buys artwork to illustrate articles. Payment determined by size and complexity. Also buys 4x5" minimum cartoons. Pays $15. Pays on acceptance. Submit samples. Reports in 2-4 weeks.

THE LITTLE FLOWER MAGAZINE, Rte. 4, Box 1150, Little Rock AR 72206. Contact: Father John Michael. Religious magazine. Especially needs "drawings of St. Therese of Liseux, or anything that looks like a nun." Drawings can be ink, line and wash or etchings. Most art donated but has paid $10 maximum for sketches, on acceptance. Buys first rights, but will look at previously published art for possible reprinting. Reports in 3 weeks.

LITTLE WARS, Box 756, Lake Geneva WI 53147. Editor-in-Chief: Timothy Kask. Quarterly; 8½x11"; 40 pages. Offset. Estab: 1976. Circ: 2,500. For well-educated military buffs, historians and simulations players. Buys all rights, but may reassign rights to artist after publication. Pays on publication. Photocopies as samples OK. No simultaneous submissions. Query with samples. SASE. Sample copy $1.
Cartoons: Buys history and wargaming themes. All formats OK. Submit roughs. Halftones and washes OK. Minimum payment: $5, b&w; $20, color. Buys 12-25 cartoons annually. Reports in 6 weeks maximum.
Illustrations: Buys cover art, article illustrations and spot drawings on military and history themes. Submit roughs or finished art. All media OK. Minimum payment: $5, inside b&w; $20, inside color; $25, b&w cover; $50, color cover. Buys 40-80 illustrations annually. Reports in 6 weeks maximum.

LLEWELLYN PUBLICATIONS, Box 3383, St. Paul MN 55765. Art Editor: Jackie Urbanovic. Buys b&w drawings to accompany occult-oriented astrology and witchcraft magazine articles. Pays $5-$20. Previously published work OK. Reports in 8 weeks.

LONG TIME COMING, Box 128, Station G, Montreal, Quebec Canada. (416)842-4781. Editor-in-Chief: J. Manthorne. Art Editor: Judith Carsion. Bimonthly; 8x11½"; 35 pages. Mimeograph. Estab: 1973. Circ: 2,000. For lesbians and feminists. Pays on acceptance. Previously published, photocopied and simultaneous submissions OK. Mail artwork. SASE. Free sample copy.
Cartoons: Buys themes on lesbians and feminists. Single panel OK. Submit finished art. Halftones OK. Pays $2-5. Reports in 3 weeks.
Illustrations: Buys article illustrations. Submit finished art. B&w line drawings and reflective art OK. Pays $2-5, b&w. Reports in 3 weeks.

THE LOOK AROUND, Box 2491, Denver CO 80201. General Sales Manager: Mickey Jones. Published 4-11 times annually for construction equipment buyers (International, Galion, Cedarapids equipment). Uses about 40 cartoons annually. Pays on publication for finished art. Buys first North American serial rights.

THE LOOKOUT, Seamen's Church Institute of New York, 15 State St., New York NY 10004. Editor: Carlyle Windley. Estab: 1909. Published 10 times annually. Uses b&w drawings, line and wash, cover designs and cartoons. Will consider previously published work. Buys one-time rights. Pays on publication. Query. Reports in 4 weeks. Sample copy available. "The basic purpose of the publication is to engender interest in the work of the Institute and to encourage monetary gifts in support of its work with merchant seamen."

THE LOOKOUT, 8121 Hamilton Ave., Cincinnati OH 45231. (513)931-4050. Editor-in-Chief: Mark A. Taylor. Weekly; 8⅜x10¾"; 16 pages. Offset. Estab: 1888. Circ: 160,000. For Christian churches. Buys all rights. Pays on acceptance. No previously published photocopied or simultaneous submissions. Send portfolio or arrange interview. SASE. Free sample copy.
Illustrations: "All our illustration is on assignment, although many freelancers work for us." Buys cover art and article illustrations on Christian themes. Submit finished art. B&w line drawings OK. Pays $50-100. Buys 2-3 illustrations per issue.

LOPEZ PUBLICATIONS, 21 W. 26th St., New York NY 10010. Contact: Leonard Kabatsky. Publishes men's "girly" magazines. Buys cartoons, and editorial illustrations for fiction. Minimum payment for cartoon is $15; $80 for editorial illustration. Query.

LOST TREASURE, John H. Latham Publications, Box 328, Conroe TX 77301. Contact: John Latham. Buys illustrations for articles, but they must fit the "very specialized style of the magazine." Monthly. Buys all rights. Pays on acceptance. Submit sample drawings in magazine's style. Reports in 3-4 weeks.
Illustrations: Work must be in line or dry brush. Pays $10 minimum, spot drawings; $25 minimum, half-page editorial illustrations; $100, cover designs in 4-colors.

LOUISVILLE, 300 W. Liberty, Louisville KY 40202. Art Director: Stephen Hall. Buys one-time rights. Query with samples.
Illustrations: Buys cover art, inside illustrations and layout services. Pays $150, cover; $35, spot art.

LOVE, 770 Lexington Ave., New York NY 10021. Editor: Sherry Armstrong. Managing Editor: Marsha Parker Cox. Bimonthly; 5⅝x8½"; 100 pages. Offset. Estab: 1976. Circ: 300,000. For young women, ages 18-30. Buys all rights. Pays on publication.
Illustrations: John Wilton, art director. Buys article illustrations and spot drawings on assignment. Submit roughs. B&w line drawings, washes and reflective art OK. Pays $125 maximum, b&w. Buys 60 illustrations annually.

THE LUTHERAN, 2900 Queen Lane, Philadelphia PA 19129. (215)848-6800. Editor-in-Chief: Albert Stauderman. Associate Editor: Edgar Trexler. Biweekly; monthly in July and August; 8½x11"; 36 pages. Offset. Circ: 570,000. Buys first rights. Pays on publication. Previously published work OK. No photocopied or simultaneous submissions. Query. SASE. Free sample copy.
Cartoons: Carl Uehling, editor. Buys environmental, family life and religious themes. Single panel OK. Submit finished art. Line drawings and washes OK. Pays $10-50, b&w. Buys 22 cartoons annually. Reports in 4 weeks.
Illustrations: Bernhard Sperl, editor. Buys article illustrations on assignment. B&w line drawings, washes and color-separated art OK. Pays $10-50, b&w. Buys 30-40 illustrations annually. Reports in 4 weeks.

THE LUTHERAN JOURNAL, 7317 Cahill Rd., Edina MN 55435. Contact: J.W. Leykom. Uses seasonal artwork related to Christmas, Easter, fall and winter. Uses 1-2 color flap art. Submit rough or finished pieces stating price desired. Previously published work OK. Pays on publication. Buys one-time rights. Sample copy sent on request.

THE LUTHERAN STANDARD, 426 S. 5th St., Minneapolis MN 55415. (612)332-4561. Editor-in-Chief: George H. Muedeking. Managing Editor: Lowell G. Almen. Biweekly; 7¾x10¾"; 32 pages. Offset. Circ: 520,000. For members of the American Lutheran Church. Buys first and simultaneous rights. Pays on acceptance. Previously published, photocopied and simultaneous submissions OK. Mail artwork. SASE. Free sample copy.
Cartoons: Buys current events, education, family life, humor through youth and religious themes. All formats OK. Submit finished art. Line drawings and washes OK. Pays $7.50-10, b&w. Reports in 4 weeks.
Illustrations: Buys spot drawings. Submit rough or finished art. B&w line drawings and washes OK. Pays $10-20, b&w. Reports in 4 weeks.

McCALL'S, 230 Park Ave., New York NY 10017. Art Director: Alvin Grossman. Leave portfolio with art department for review.

MADEMOISELLE, 350 Madison Ave., New York NY 10017. Art Director: Roger Schoening. Monthly. For college-educated women, ages 18-25. Bring portfolio on a Wednesday or query with resume.

MAGAZINE OF FLOWERS, Box 23505, Fort Lauderdale FL 33307. Associate Editor: L. Hinton. Buys North American serial rights. Reports in 2-4 weeks.
Cartoons: Uses about 30 cartoons annually on flowers. Wholesome, family cartoons also wanted. Pays $5 on acceptance. Sizes up to 8½x11"; finished b&w art.

MAKARA, 1011 Commercial Dr., Vancouver, BC Canada V5L 3X1. (604)253-8931. Editors: Nora D. Randall/Saeko Usukawa. Bimonthly; 8½x11"; 48 pages. Offset. Estab: 1975. Circ: 5,000. For Canadian women, ages 20-40, with children; employed in education and community work, interested in alternatives. Buys first North American serial rights. Pays on publication. Previously published, photocopied and simultaneous submissions OK. Arrange interview. SASE. Sample copy $1.25. "We are searching for alternative ways of living, thinking and working in Canada; artwork should reflect this. Canadian artists given preference. Don't send original artwork."
Cartoons: Buys all themes, except sexism and racism. All formats OK. Submit finished art. Line drawings, halftones and washes OK. Pays $15-30, b&w; $25-30, color. Buys 2 cartoons annually. Reports in 8 weeks.
Illustrations: Buys cover art, article illustrations and spot drawings on all themes. Submit finished art. Pays $15-30, inside; $25-30, cover. Buys 60 illustrations annually. Reports in 8 weeks.

MAKE IT WITH LEATHER, 201 W. 1st, Fort Worth TX 76101. (817)335-8500. Editor-in-Chief: Earl F. Warren. Bimonthly; 8¼x10¾"; 68 pages. Offset. Estab: 1956. Circ: 60,000. Buys all rights. Pays on publication. Previously published, photocopied and, occasionally, simultaneous submissions OK. Query. SASE. Free sample copy.
Illustrations: Buys illustrations and spot drawings on assignment. Interested in leathercraft illustrations. "We are how-to-do-it oriented." Submit finished art. B&w line drawings, washes, reflective art and veloxes OK. Pays $10-100. Reports in 4 weeks.

MANAGEMENT ACCOUNTING, 919 3rd Ave., New York NY 10022. (212)754-9700. Managing Editor: Erwin S. Koval. Monthly; 8¼x11¼"; 64 pages. Offset. Circ: 80,000.
Cartoons: Robert F. Randall, editor. Buys themes on accounting, finance and corporate offices. Single panel OK. Submit finished art. Line drawings only. Pays $10 minimum. Buys 10 cartoons annually. Reports in 2 weeks.

MARATHON WORLD, Marathon Oil Co., 539 S. Main St., Findlay OH 45840. (419)422-2121. Editor-in-Chief: Robert Ostermann. Quarterly; 11⅛x9¾"; 30 pages. Offset. Estab: 1964. Circ: 70,000. For Marathon employees, shareholders, executives, customers and suppliers. Not copyrighted. Pays on acceptance. No previously published, photocopied or simultaneous submissions. "We normally work through artists' agents." SASE. Free sample copy. "We're not a market for beginning artists. We usually use illustrators with a national reputation and/or a track record of work in publications like *Esquire, Time* and *Fortune*."
Illustrations: Stan Corfman, editor. Buys article illustrations on assignment. Submit roughs. Media determined by subject. Pays $200-800, b&w; $400-1,000, color. Buys 10-15 illustrations per issue. Reports in 1 week.

MASTER DETECTIVE, Reese Publishing Co., 235 Park Ave. S., New York NY 10003. Managing Editor: Walter Jackson. Monthly. Buys all rights. Pays on acceptance. Reports in 2 weeks. Sample copy 60¢.
Cartoons: "Avoid overemphasizing cliche situations such as 2 convicts in cell. No horror. Cute, mild sex." Buys about 100 cartoons annually. Submit roughs. Single panel. Pays $25.

THE MASTER'S WORK, Convent of the Holy Spirit, Techny IL 60082. (312)272-5930. Editor: Terisse Zosso. For those interested in helping underdeveloped people. Quarterly. Circ: 8,000. Buys b&w drawings. Subjects for art should include "mission, underdeveloped areas and their cultures, human interest." Not copyrighted. Previously published work OK. Query with resume. Reports in 1 month. Write for sample copy.

MATURE YEARS, 201 8th Ave. S., Nashville TN 37215. Editor-in-Chief: Ewart Watts. Quarterly; 8½x11"; 64 pages. Letterpress. Circ: 106,000. For people ages 60+. Buys all rights, but may reassign rights to artists after publication. Pays on acceptance. No previously published work. Mail artwork. SASE.
Cartoons: Daisy Warren, editor. Buys family and retirement themes. "Nothing saccharine or that pokes fun at older adults." Single panel OK. Submit roughs. Halftones OK. Pays $8 minimum. Buys 4 cartoons annually. Reports in 4 weeks.

MBA COMMUNICATION, 730 3rd Ave., New York NY 10017. (212)557-9240. Art Director: John C. Jay. Publishes 4 monthly magazines. For medical, law, business and engineering professions. Accepts drawings, color illustrations and cover designs. Occasional need for layout services. Buys one-time rights. No previously published work. Pays on publication. Mail artwork. Reports in 30 days.

MEAT PLANT MAGAZINE, 8678 Olive Blvd., St. Louis MO 63132. Editor: A. Todoroff. Bimonthly business magazine for meat plants, locker plants and frozen food provisioners. Not copyrighted. Previously published work OK. Pays on acceptance. Send published samples. Reports in 10 days-2 weeks.
Cartoons: Submit roughs. Pays $5.
Illustrations: Submit roughs. Pays $20, spot drawing; $100, finished, 2-color cover design.

MEDICAL ECONOMICS, Litton Publications, 680 Kinderkamack Rd., Oradell NJ 07649. Biweekly. Buys all rights. Guidelines sent on request. Wants spot drawings and cartoons concerning the world of medicine, the home life of physicians, and general areas of everyday life. All formats OK. Prefers 9x8½ or 4x7 roughs. Pays $80 minimum on acceptance. Reports in 2-3 weeks. Sample copy $2.

MEDICAL TIMES, 80 Shore Rd., Port Washington NY 11050. Art Buyer: Michael Shipman. Monthly. "We are interested in medical scenes — doctors, nurses, patients, hospitals. "Prefer original material but will look at samples of previously published material. Buys all rights. Pays on acceptance. Reports in 1 month. Pays $15 for cartoons.
Illustrations: Buys cover art and spot drawings. Prefers pen and ink or line and wash, 8x10" roughs. Pays $20-40, spot art. Negotiates payment for finished color covers.

THE MENNONITE, 600 Shaftsbury Blvd., Winnipeg, Manitoba Canada R3P 0M4. (204)888-6781. Editor-in-Chief: Bernie Wiebe. Weekly; 8½x11"; 16 pages. Offset. Estab: 1885. Circ: 17,000. For middle-class Mennonite families, somewhat agrarian-oriented. Not copyrighted. Pays on publication. Previously published, photocopied and simultaneous submissions OK. Query with samples. SASE. Free sample copy.
Cartoons: Buys all themes in good taste. Single panel OK. Submit finished art. Line drawings and halftones OK. Pays $10-25. Buys 25 cartoons annually.
Illustrations: Buys cover art and article illustrations on topics related to family, current issues and everyday life; especially needs artwork for education and children's issues. Submit finished art. B&w line drawings OK. Pays $10-25, cover; $5-20, inside. Buys 25 illustrations annually.

MERCHANDISING 2-WAY RADIO, 200 Park Ave. S., New York NY 10003. (212)777-6400. Editor: Eric Ian Mathison. Monthly; 64 pages. Offset. Estab: 1975. Circ: 33,000. For wholesale and retail managers, owners and buyers. Buys all rights, but may reassign rights to artist after publication. Pays 2 weeks before publication. Previously published, photocopied and simultaneous submissions OK. Mail artwork. SASE.
Cartoons: Buys themes on retailing CB and marine radios. Single panel OK. Submit finished art. Line drawings only. Pays $15-25. Buys 1 cartoon per issue. Reports in 2 weeks.
Illustrations: Buys article illustrations and spot drawings on assignment. Submit roughs. B&w line drawings OK. Pays $15-25. Buys 2-3 illustrations per issue. Reports in 1 week.

MERLIN PAPERS (formerly *Open Cell*), Box 5602, San Jose CA 95150. Editor-in-Chief: Milton Loventhal. Managing Editor: Jennifer McDowell. Published annually; 18x11½". Offset. Estab: 1969. Circ: 1,000. For ages 20-45, college-educated with intellectual and cultural interests. Buys all rights, but may reassign rights to artist after publication. Pays on publication. No previously published work. Photocopied and simultaneous submissions OK. Mail artwork. SASE. Sample copy 50¢.
Illustrations: Daniel Marlin, editor. Buys cover art, article illustrations and spot drawings on cultural or nature themes. "We are interested in any work that accurately renders the relationship between the individual and society." Submit finished art. B&w line drawings OK. Pays contributor's copies. Buys 10 illustrations annually. Reports in 2 months.

METLFAX, 5821 Harper Rd., Solon OH 44139. (216)248-1125. Editor-in-Chief: Thomas H. Dreher. Monthly; 5⅝x4⅛"; 225 pages. Offset. Estab: 1956. Circ: 102,000. For those in the metalworking field. Buys all rights. Pays on acceptance. No previously published, photocopied or simultaneous submissions. Mail artwork. SASE. Free sample copy.

Cartoons: Buys themes on the metalworking industry. Single panel OK. Submit finished art. Line drawings only. Pays $15 maximum. Buys 18 cartoons annually. Reports in 2 weeks.

METRO, THE MAGAZINE OF SOUTHEASTERN VIRGINIA (formerly *Metro, Hampton Roads),* Box 7088, Norfolk VA 23501. Publisher: Paul G. Katabian. Editor-in-Chief: St. Leger Joynes. Monthly. Estab: 1970. Circ: 20,000. Readers have above-average income and education. "Content is regionalized. Issues planned 3-4 months prior to cover date. Typical special issues are Economic Forecast, Wine Guide, Ski Guide and Condominium Guide." Buys all rights on art; buys first serial and reprint rights for cartoons. Will consider previously published work. Reports in 1 week. Sample copy available.
Cartoons: Prefers roughs. Pays $5-15 on publication.
Illustrations: Buys b&w line drawings and full-color illustrations. All media, 8½x11", OK. Requires color separations. Pays on acceptance: $20, spot drawing; $100, full-color art/4-color cover design; $50-100, advertising assignment.

METROPOLIS, Flour Exchange Bldg., 310 4th Ave. S., Minneapolis MN 55415. Editor: Scott Kaufer. Art Director: Patrick J. B. Flynn. Weekly; 11x17"; 32 pages. Offset. Estab: 1976. Circ: 30,000. For Twin Cities readers, ages 18-40. Buys all rights, but may reassign rights to artist after publication. Pays on publication. No previously published work or photocopies. Simultaneous submissions OK "only if we are aware of them." Query with tearsheets. SASE. Free sample copy. "All work submitted should be ready for print."
Cartoons: Buys all themes. All formats OK. Submit finished art. Line drawings, halftones and washes OK. Pays $20-50, b&w. Buys 50 cartoons annually. Reports in 4 weeks.
Illustrations: Buys cover art and article illustrations on assignment. Cover: b&w line drawings, washes and color-separated art OK. Inside: b&w line drawings, washes, color-separated and reflective art and veloxes OK. Minimum payment: $50, cover; $20, inside. Buys 300 illustrations annually. Reports in 4 weeks.

MICHIGAN OUT OF DOORS, Box 30235, Lansing MI 48909. Contact: Kenneth S. Lowe. "Following the various hunting and fishing seasons we sometimes have a need for illustration material but we consider submissions 3-5 months in advance to help us fit art to our editorial needs. "Not copyrighted. Uses pen and ink illustrations in a vertical treatment. Pays $10 on publication. Reports as soon as possible. Sample copy 25¢.

MICROFORM REVIEW, Box 1297, Weston CT 06880. Contact: Alan Meckler. Buys cartoons dealing with microforms in the library (microfilm, microfiche) and pays $5 minimum for all rights. Sample copy available.

MILITARY COLLECTORS NEWS, Box 7582, Tulsa OK 74105. Editor-in-Chief: Jack Britton. Monthly; 8½x7"; 30 pages. Offset. Estab: 1967. Circ: 10,000. For collectors of all types of military items. Buys all rights. Pays on publication. No previously published, photocopied or simultaneous submissions. Mail artwork. SASE. Free sample copy.
Cartoons: "Should relate to medals, badges, uniforms and insignia." Single panel OK. Submit finished art. Line drawings only. Pays $1-5. Reports in 4 weeks. Medals and uniforms should look authentic. Buys 12-24 cartoons annually.
Illustrations: Buys cover art and article illustrations. "We prefer artist who collects military items so he will be able to send exact art." Submit finished art. B&w line drawings OK. Pays $1-15, cover; $1-10, inside. Reports in 4 weeks. Buys 12-24 illustrations annually.

MILITARY MEDIA REVIEW, Public Affairs Office, Defense Information School, Ft. Benjamin Harrison IN 46216. Editor: Connie McKean. Quarterly. For and about information people. Concerns information techniques — including articles, fillers, artwork, photos and cartoons on the following: print and broadcast journalism, oral communication, public relations, internal information programs and problems, media relationships and new directions in communicative arts — especially with application to military information and public affairs. Buys rough or finished line drawings and cartoons. Pays contributor's copies; also, wide exposure to all service information offices and many federal agencies guaranteed, as well as to commanders in the field and several schools of journalism. Query. Indicate if material should be returned. SASE not required.

MINNESOTA AAA MOTORIST, 7 Travelers Trail, Burnsville MN 55337. Editor: Ron Johnson. Features travel, motoring, car care, safety, historical, humor and related articles. Pays

$20 on acceptance for cartoons. Buys North American serial rights. Reports in 2 weeks. Sample copy available.

MODEL RETAILER, Clifton House, Clifton VA 22024. (703)830-1000. Editor-in-Chief: David Ritchey. Monthly; 8½x11"; 100 pages. Offset. Circ: 4,000. For hobby store owners. Buys all rights. Pays on publication. Previously published and simultaneous submissions ("must be notified") OK. No photocopies. Query. SASE. Sample copy $1.
Cartoons: Buys themes relating to operation of hobby store. Double panel OK. Submit finished art. Line drawings only. Pays $10 minimum. Buys 220 cartoons annually. Reports in 4 weeks.

MODERN BULK TRANSPORTER, 4801 Montgomery Lane, Washington DC 20014. (301)654-8802. Editor-in-Chief: C. R. Don Sutherland. Monthly; 8⅛x10⅞"; 40 pages. Offset. Estab: 1937. Circ: 10,000. For tank truck industry executives in petroleum, gases, chemicals and milk and bulk foods. Buys first rights. Pays on acceptance. No previously published, photocopied or simultaneous submissions. Query with samples. SASE. Free sample copy.
Cartoons: Buys themes on tank truck operation. "Must be favorable to company management operating trucks." Single panel OK. Submit finished art. Line drawings OK. Pays $7 minimum. Buys 5 cartoons annually. Reports in 2 weeks.

MODERN DRUMMER MAGAZINE, 47 Harrison St., Nutley NJ 07110. (201)667-2211. Editor-in-Chief: Ronald Spagnardi. Quarterly; 8¼x10⅝"; 32 pages. Offset. Estab: 1976. Circ: 5,000. For drummers, all ages and levels of playing ability with varied interests within the field of drumming. Buys first rights. Pays on publication. Previously published work OK. No photocopied or simultaneous submissions. Mail artwork. SASE. Free sample copy.
Cartoons: Buys drumming themes. Single and double panel OK. Submit finished art. Halftones OK. Pays $5-15. Buys 12-20 cartoons annually. Reports in 4 weeks. "We want strictly drummer-oriented gags."
Illustrations: Buys cover art, article illustrations and spot drawings about drummers. Submit finished art. Cover: color-separated art and veloxes OK. Inside: all media OK. Pays $35-75, b&w cover; $10-25, inside b&w; $50-125, color cover; $10-30, inside color. Buys 20-60 illustrations annually. Reports in 4 weeks.

MODERN HAIKU, 260 Vista Marina, San Clemente CA 92672. (714)498-3652. Editor-in-Chief: Kay Titus Mormino. Quarterly; 5½x8½"; 48 pages. Letterpress. Estab: 1969. Circ: 500. Buys first rights. Pays on acceptance. No previously published, photocopied or simultaneous submissions. Mail artwork. SASE. Free sample copy.
Illustrations: Buys cover and inside art on sume-i and nature; especially needs seasonal art. Submit finished art. B&w line drawings OK. Pays $5 minimum. Buys approximately 40 illustrations annually. Reports in 3 months.

MODERN LITURGY (formerly *Folk Mass and Modern Liturgy),* Box 444, Saratoga CA 95070. Editor-in-Chief: William Burns. Published 8 times annually; 8½x11"; 36 pages. Offset. Estab: 1973. Circ: 10,000. For religious artists, musicians and planners of worship services to Catholic and Protestant liturgical traditions. Buys all rights, but may reassign rights to artist after publication. Pays on publication. No previously published, photocopied or simultaneous submissions. Query with samples. SASE. Sample copy $2.
Cartoons: Buys themes on "situations depicting humorous or other aspects of contemporary religious celebrations." All formats OK. Submit roughs. Halftones OK. Pays $10-25. "We'd like to buy 8 cartoons annually." Reports in 4-6 weeks.
Illustrations: George F. Collopy, editor. Buys article illustrations on assigned themes. Submit roughs. Color-separated art OK. Pays $25-50. Buys 4 illustrations annually. Reports in 4-6 weeks.
Special Needs: Artwork for tentative articles: saints and seasons, liturgy and community, the aging, the body at prayer, paraliturgy, celebrating special events, Christmas and visual religious arts.

MODERN MATURITY, 215 Long Beach Blvd., Long Beach CA 90801. Editor: Hubert C. Pryor. Bimonthly. Published for members of American Association of Retired Persons. Buys spot drawings and 8x10 finished cartoons. Pays $35. Sample copy available on request. Material must be slanted to retiree. Buys one-time and first serial rights. Previously published work OK. Mail artwork.

MODERN SECRETARY, Box 23505, Fort Lauderdale FL 33307. Associate Editor: M. Stilkind. Buys North American serial rights only. Reports in 2-4 weeks.
Cartoons: Pays $5 on acceptance. Prefers finished art. Uses about 30 cartoons annually on secretaries in offices. No sexy jokes. 8½x11" maximum. B&w OK.

MODERN TIRE DEALER MAGAZINE, 77 N. Miller Rd., Akron OH 44313. (216)867-4401. Editor: Stephen LaFerre. Estab: 1919. Circ: 34,000. For owners-operators of independent retail/wholesale tire shops. Typical seasonal need would be its July undercar services issue — using line drawings of men performing services on tires, brakes, shocks and mufflers. Uses pen and ink with wash. Pays $20 for inside drawings; $50-100 for color covers; $25 for 8x10 cartoons. Payment on publication for all rights.

MODERN VETERINARY PRACTICE, Drawer KK, Santa Barbara CA 93111. (805)966-6523. Editor: P. F. Rubsam. Monthly. 15,500 circulation. Uses drawings, full-color illustrations and cartoons to accompany articles. Pays $5-50 on publication. Copyrighted. Query with resume. Reports in 2 weeks.

MONTREAL SCENE, 245 St. James St. W., Montreal, Quebec Canada. (514)282-2954. Editor: Brian Moore. Weekly; 8¼x11"; 32-36 pages. Offset. Estab: 1973. Circ: 225,000. For all ages, especially TV viewers, as it includes weekly TV listings. Buys first rights. Pays on acceptance. No previously published, photocopied or simultaneous submissions. Free sample copy.
Illustrations: Maxine McLaren, art director. Buys cover art and article illustrations on Montreal restaurants, buildings, parks, grocery stores, monuments, historical sites and people. "Any artist we would consider would almost have to be living in Montreal. For the cover, I would have to see a finished work of a Montreal scene." Submit finished art. Cover: reflective art OK. Inside: b&w line drawings and reflective art OK. Pays $100, color cover; $75-100, inside color; $50 minimum, inside b&w. Buys 52 covers and 20 illustrations annually. Reports in 4 weeks.

MONUMENT IN CANTOS AND ESSAYS, 4508 Mexico Gravel Rd., Columbia MO 65201. Editor: Victor Myers. Poetry journal appears irregularly — usually once a year. Buys first rights. Previously published work OK "if exceptional." Send samples. SASE. Reports in 3 months. Sample copy $1.50. Prefers "natural images (from nature) which are evocative, startling in their simplicity."
Illustrations: Will consider spot drawings, cover designs, b&w line drawings and pen and ink. Submit finished art, photo reproducible, maximum 4½x7½. Pays 2 contributor's copies.

MOONS AND LIONS TAILES, Box 8434, Lake Street Station, Minneapolis MN 55408. (612)377-4384. Managing Editor: H. Schjotz-Christensen. Quarterly; 5¼x8¼"; 100 pages. Offset. Estab: 1974. Circ: 1,500. For college students, teachers and professional people with an interest in contemporary literature. Buys first rights. Pays on publication. Photocopies OK. No previously published or simultaneous submissions. Query with samples. Sample copy $1.75. Pays $25 minimum, ad illustration.
Illustrations: Buys cover art, article illustrations and spot drawings of contemporary writers. Submit roughs. Cover: b&w line drawings and color-separated art OK. Inside: b&w line drawings OK. Pays $100-150, color cover; $25-50, b&w cover; $25, inside. Buys 20-25 illustrations annually. Reports in 2-3 weeks. "We're particularly interested in poignant graphic art: wood/linoleum cuts with dramatic impact."

MOTHER JONES, 607 Market St., San Francisco CA 94105. (415)495-6326. Editor-in-Chief: Jeffrey Klein. Art Editor: Louise Kollenbaum. 8½x11"; 64 pages. Offset. Estab: 1976. Circ: 150,000. Buys first rights. Pays on acceptance. No previously published or simultaneous submissions. Query with samples, mail artwork or arrange interview. SASE. Free sample copy.
Cartoons: Buys current events, education, environment and political themes. All formats OK. Submit finished art. All media OK. Pays $15 minimum. Buys 5-10 cartoons per issue. Reports in 4 weeks.
Illustrations: Buys cover art, article illustrations and spot drawings. Submit roughs. Cover: color-separated and reflective art OK. Inside: b&w line drawings, washes and veloxes OK. Pays $100-375, cover; $25-250, inside b&w; $15-250, inside color. Buys 15-20 illustrations per issue. Reports in 4 weeks.

MOTHERS' MANUAL, 176 Cleveland Dr., Croton-on-Hudson NY 10520. (914)271-8415 or 8926. Editor-in-Chief: Beth Waterfall. Bimonthly; 8½x11"; 52 pages. Offset. Estab: 1965. Circ:

Cover, article and spot drawings centering around people and animals earn artists from $20-135 from *Children's Playmate*. This illustration was bought for $35 from Ellen Appleby because of its cartoon style and good portrayal of story characters. Artists wanting to break in to this publication should submit samples of artwork — for possible later assignment — that cater to young children.

900,000. Buys one-time rights. Pays on publication. No previously published, photocopied or simultaneous submissions. Mail artwork. SASE. Sample copy 50¢.

Cartoons: Buys family life themes. "Especially interested in pregnancy and parenting through age 6. Would like to see truly funny cartoons in good taste reflecting the joys and sorrows of child-rearing." Submit finished art. Halftones and washes OK. Pays $10-25, b&w. Reports in 4 weeks.

Illustrations: Kenneth McMullen, art editor. Buys article illustrations and spot drawings on family life with children under age 6. Submit finished art. B&w line drawings and washes OK. Pays $10-25, b&w. Reports in 4 weeks.

MOTORLAND, 150 Van Ness Ave., San Francisco CA 94101. (415)565-2464. Editor/Manager: William C. Ellis. Bimonthly; 8½x11"; 48 pages. Offset. Estab: 1915. Circ: 1 million. Travel magazine for California Automobile Association members. Buys all rights. Pays on acceptance. Previously published work OK. Query with samples. SASE. Free sample copy.

Illustrations: Al Davidson, art director. Buys cover art, article illustrations and spot drawings on travel and leisure activities on assignment. Submit roughs. B&w line drawings, washes, color-separated and reflective art OK. Pays $150-500, color cover; $100-300, b&w cover. Reports in 2 weeks.

MOUNTAIN REVIEW, Box 660, Whitesburg KY 41858. (606)633-4811. Managing Editor: Peter Carey. Quarterly literary/cultural journal; 8½x11"; 48 pages. Offset. Estab: 1974. Circ: 1,800. For Appalachians and those interested in Appalachian culture. Buys all rights, but may reasign rights to artist after publication. Previously published, photocopied and simultaneous submissions OK. Mail artwork. SASE. Free sample copy.
Illustrations: Buys cover art, article illustrations and spot drawings on Appalachian life and culture. Submit finished art. Cover: washes and color-separated art OK. Inside: b&w line drawings, washes and veloxes OK. No payment. Uses 48 illustrations annually. Reports in 4 months.

MOVING OUT, 4866 3rd, Wayne State University, Detroit MI 48202. (313)577-3355. Contact: Editor. Published semiannually; 8½x11"; 50 pages. Offset. Estab: 1971. Circ: 1,000. For college-age women, writers and feminists interested in the women's aesthetic as reflected in creative writing and graphics. Buys first rights. Pays on publication. No previously published work or photocopies. Simultaneous submissions OK "if we are the first to publish." Mail artwork. SASE. Sample copy $1.25. "Work should be high contrast so that grays and very light lines will not be lost in the printing process. Also, to cut down on reduction costs, work should not be larger than our page."
Illustrations: Buys article illustrations, cover art and spot drawings related to women, and some abstract work. Submit finished art. B&w line drawings and washes OK. Pays contributor's copies. Buys 10-20 illustrations annually. Reports in 2-3 months. Prefers not to see art offensive or degrading to women.

MR., MAN TO MAN, SIR!, 280 Madison Ave., New York NY 10016. Cartoon Editor: Everett Meyers. Published 12 times annually. For men. Buys all rights. Reports in 2 weeks maximum.
Cartoons: Interested in sex-oriented themes. Buys hundreds annually. Prefers finished art unless established in the market. Single panel. Page proportions preferred; 8x10 maximum size. Pays $15.

MUSCLE MAGAZINE INTERNATIONAL, Unit 1, 270 Rutherford Rd. S., Brampton, Ontario Canada L6W 3K7. (416)457-3030. Editor-in-Chief: Robert Kennedy. Quarterly; 8x11"; 110 pages. Offset. Estab: 1974. Circ: 110,000. Buys all rights. Pays on acceptance. Previously published work OK. No photocopied or simultaneous submissions. Mail artwork. SASE. Sample copy $1.50.
Cartoons: Buys weight lifting and body building themes. Single panel OK. Submit finished art. Halftones and washes OK. Pays $15-25, color; $10-20, b&w. Buys 6 cartoons per issue. Reports in 2 weeks.
Illustrations: Buys cover art, article illustrations and spot drawings on body building personalities. Submit finished art. B&w line drawings, washes, color-separated and reflective art OK. Minimum payment: $80, inside color; $50, color cover and inside b&w. Buys 2 illustrations per issue. Reports in 2 weeks.

NATIONAL BOWLER'S JOURNAL AND BILLIARD REVIEW, 875 N. Michigan Ave., Chicago IL 60611. (312)266-7171. Editor: Jim Dressel. Monthly. Estab: 1913. Circ: 16,000. Buys one-time rights. Reports in 2-3 weeks. Sample copy available.
Cartoons: Cartoons can be business or consumer slanted; must concern bowling or billiards. Pays $5 on acceptance.
Special Needs: Buys line drawings of top 10 bowlers for annual issue.

NATIONAL FIRE PROTECTION ASSOCIATION, 470 Atlantic Ave., Boston MA 02210. Contact: Lee Liberman. Publishes comic books and other material teaching fire prevention. Buys illustrations, comic book art and graphic design from Boston and New York City artists. Initial submissions can be tearsheets of previously published work, photostats, transparencies, or pen and ink rough art. Buys all rights. Pays on acceptance. Reports in 1 month.

NATIONAL 4H NEWS, 150 N. Wacker Dr., Chicago IL 60606. Editor: Bonnie B. Sarkett. Buys one-time rights. Pays on acceptance. Reports in 1 month.
Illustrations: "Send tearsheets or photostats. We'll file these to keep a record of the artist's techniques and when we need a particular style for an article, we'll contact the artist and

discuss our needs. Artwork may be any type b&w technique, watercolor, charcoal sketch, scratchboard, pen and ink or woodcuts. Use artwork only when its effect is more appropriate than photos. Art should suggest rather than show literal detail. Whatever form, art must show evidence of technique, plus good craftsmanship, composition and content." Pays $10-50.

THE NATIONAL FUTURE FARMER, Box 15130, Alexandria VA 22309. (703)360-3600. Editor: Wilson Carnes. Bimonthly. 500,000 circulation. For ages 14-21. Estab: 1952. All drawings, except cartoons, must relate to Future Farmers of America. Buys all rights. No previously published work. Pays on acceptance. Pays $7.50, cartoon. Sample copy available. Illustration usually must accompany article. Reports in 2 weeks.

NATIONAL GEOGRAPHIC, 17th and M Sts. NW, Washington DC 20036. (202)857-7000. Editor-in-Chief: Melville B. Grosvenor. Editor: Gilbert M. Grosvenor. Monthly; 6⅞x10"; 150 pages. Offset, letterpress and rotogravure. Estab: 1888. Circ: 10 million. Buys all rights. Pays on acceptance. No previously published, photocopied or simultaneous submissions. Query with samples and arrange interview. SASE.
Illustrations: Andrew H. Poggenpohl, editor. Buys article illustrations on natural history, science and archaeology. "No art purchased for simply decorative reasons. All art must be related to specific needs in a scientific or historical article, and must be researched with utmost accuracy. All work must be prepared under the supervision of the art editor." Submit roughs. Reflective art OK. Minimum payment: $1,000, color; $200, b&w. Buys 20 illustrations annually. Reports in 3 weeks.

THE NATIONAL GUARDSMAN, 1 Massachusetts Ave. NW, Washington DC 20001. Interested in cartoons and spot drawings about military topics in good taste and in finished form. Uniforms must be technically correct. Requires pen and ink on 8½x11" bond. "No balloons emerging from mouths of subjects!" Items selected for future use held in file until publication. Pays $10. Send artwork. SASE.

NATIONAL HOBBYIST, 805 N. 1st St., McGehee AR 71654. Editor: Win Farrell. Monthly; 8½x11". Circ: 2,000. For readers of all ages, middle-income families and coin collectors. Needs b&w drawings, cover designs and layout services. Not copyrighted. Pays $4 for cover design in 2 colors. Each issue contains an article on a state. Query with resume. Reports in 2 months. Sample copy 25¢.

NATIONAL JOURNAL, 1730 M St. NW, Washington DC 20036. (202)833-8000. Weekly. Estab: 1969. 3,000 circulation. For those interested in federal policymaking: government officials, corporate executives, lobbyists and political scientists. Pays $35 for cartoons. Query with resume. Sample copy $6.

NATIONAL LAMPOON, 635 Madison Ave., New York NY 10022. Art Buyer: Peter Kleinman. Humor magazine for general audience. Payment averages $50+ for first North American serial rights on acceptance. Will consider buying reprint rights on previously published material. Comic illustrators should submit published samples. SASE. Reports in 3 weeks.

NATIONAL PARKS AND CONSERVATION MAGAZINE, National Parks and Conservation Association, 1701 18th St. NW, Washington DC 20009. Editor: Eugenia Horstman Connally. Copyrighted. Monthly. For well-educated, environmentally conscious audience. "We use spot drawings of animals, plants, and landscapes as fillers in our news section; and we will also consider cartoons on environmental topics. Also uses full-color illustrations. Pays $15, spot art. Pays on acceptance. Previously published work OK. Query with description of proposed subject matter. Reports in 1 month. Sample copy $1.50.

NATIONAL REVIEW MAGAZINE, 150 E. 35th St., New York NY 10016. Contact: Anna Lieber. "We need seasonal and decorative spot drawings for our book review section, caricatures or portraits of American and foreign political figures, and cartoons of a political nature (readers are politically conservative). We consider b&w line drawings, washes or halftones." Pays $10 for spot drawings; $35 for editorial art. Payment on acceptance. Copyrighted. Reports in 2 weeks.

NATIONAL RURAL LETTER CARRIER, Suite 1204, 1750 Pennsylvania Ave. NW, Washington DC 20006. (202)298-9260. Editor: Clifford Edwards. Managing Editor: Melissa

Messner. Weekly; 8½x11"; 16 pages. Offset. Estab: 1903. Circ: 58,000. For rural letter carriers and family-oriented, middle-Americans; many are part time teachers and businessmen. Buys first rights. Pays on publication. Previously published, photocopied and simultaneous submissions OK. Mail artwork. SASE. Sample copy 24¢.
Cartoons: "Have not had suitable cartoons submitted so have not published any."
Illustrations: Buys cover art on rural scenes, views of rural mail boxes and animal sketches. Submit roughs or finished art. B&w OK. Pays $20-30. Buys 4 illustrations annually. Reports in 3 weeks. "Absolutely no nudes or other offensive material. We rarely have used people as cover material; usually serene scenes of rural America."
Special Needs: Artwork for convention issue from Indianapolis, Indiana; substitute carrier issue; covers depicting Christ for Easter and Christmas issues.

NATIONAL SOCIETY OF PUBLIC ACCOUNTANTS, 1717 Pennsylvania Ave. NW, Suite 1200, Washingon DC 20006. Managing Editor: Linda Hemphill.
Illustrations: Artists work on assignment only. Buys line drawings and color-separated art. Subject matter is of accounting/business/financial/taxation/economic nature. Pays $25 minimum, line drawings. Send samples.

NATIONAL WILDLIFE, 225 E. Michigan, Milwaukee WI 53202. (414)273-2486. Contact: Karen Altpeter. Bimonthly. Readership is interested in the environment, outdoor activities and wildlife. Wants b&w drawings and cartoons. Subjects of interest are mammals, birds, fish, reptiles and insects, flowers and plant life, scenics, ecological series, and man — how he lives. Mail artwork. Reports promptly.

NEBRASKALAND, Box 30370, Lincoln NE 68503. (402)464-0641. Editor-in-Chief: Lowell Johnson. Monthly; 8½x11"; 52 pages. Offset. Estab: 1926. Circ: 54,000. For hunters, anglers, campers, hikers and history buffs. Buys first rights. Pays on acceptance. Previously published, photocopied and simultaneous submissions OK. Mail artwork. SASE. Free sample copy.
Cartoons: Buys environment, hunting, fishing, camping and outdoor recreational themes. Single panel OK. Submit finished art. Halftones OK. Pays $5 minimum. Buys 30 cartoons annually. Reports in 2 weeks.

NEW COVENANT, Box 617, Ann Arbor MI 48107. Editor-in-Chief: Bert Ghezzi. Managing Editor: Randall Cirner. Monthly; 8½x11"; 36 pages. Offset. Estab: 1971. Circ: 70,000. For college-educated Christians, interested in furthering Christian growth. Buys all rights, but may reassign rights to artist after publication. Pays on acceptance. Previously published, photocopied and simultaneous submissions OK. "We prefer to see samples from an artist, get to know him, and then contact him about a particular job." SASE. Free sample copy.
Illustrations: John B. Leidy, design director. Buys cover art and article illustrations on contemporary Christian themes. Submit finished art. B&w line drawings, washes and reflective art OK. Pays $100-400, b&w cover; $20-400, inside b&w. Buys 50-60 illustrations annually. Reports in 3 weeks.

NEW EARTH REVIEW, Box 83, Murfreesboro NC 27855. (919)398-3341. Editor-in-Chief: Robert Mulder. Managing Editor: Rex Mitchell. Quarterly; 8½x11"; 24 pages. Offset. Estab: 1975. Circ: 750-900. For poetry lovers, mostly older women. Not copyrighted. Pays on acceptance. Previously published work and photocopies OK. Mail artwork. SASE. Sample copy $1.
Cartoons: Buys themes on writing, current events, education, family life, humor through youth and religion. Double panel OK. Submit finished art. Line drawings OK. Pays $5-10. Buys 10 cartoons annually. Reports in 2 weeks.
Illustrations: Anne K. Hunt, editor. Buys spot drawings for poems. Submit finished art. B&w line drawings OK. Pays $5-10. Buys 30 illustrations annually. Reports in 2 weeks.

THE NEW ERA, 50 E. North Temple, Salt Lake City UT 84150. (801)531-2951. Editor: Brian K. Kelly. Monthly. For ages 12-18 of the Church of Jesus Christ of Latter-day Saints. 160,000 circulation. Pays $25-125 for spot drawings; $100-250 for full-color illustrations; $150-400 for full-color cover designs; $20-25 for cartoons. Buys all rights. No previously published work. Mail samples. SASE. Reports in 30-60 days.

NEW GUARD, Woodland Rd., Sterling VA 22015. Editor: David Boaz. Conservative magazine of Young Americans for Freedom. Submit samples, or original pen and ink finished art of subject matter related to courts, politics, Washington, education, big government and defense. Pays $10+ for illustrations on publication. Reports immediately.

THE NEW INFINITY REVIEW, Box 412, South Point OH 45680. Art Buyer: James R. Pack. Quarterly literary magazine. Buys North American serial rights. Pays on publication. Previously published work OK. Mail original art or published samples. SASE. Reports in 4 weeks.
Illustrations: "Art should have 'distance' as well as surface content; we are highly critical of abstract art. We look to the visionary; no imitations; our tastes run toward Blake, Dadd, Durer, Dali, Chagall." Cover designs (maximum size 9x12) and line drawings used; also woodcut, serial sketches and silkscreen prints. Rough or finished art. Pays $5+, spot drawing; $10+, cover art.

NEW LETTERS, 5346 Charlotte, Kansas City MO 64110. Art Buyer: Judy Ray. Buys camera-ready spot drawings, cartoons and cover designs. Submit roughs. B&w, pen and ink, and line and wash OK. Pays $5-10. Buys all rights. Reports in 2-8 weeks. Sample copy $2.

NEW MEXICO SPORTS MAGAZINE, Jaymar Publications, Box 25024, Albuquerque NM 87125. Editorial Coordinator: Greg Lay. For those interested in team sports and outdoor activities. Buys illustrations and cartoons. Pays $4-12, fairly simple work; $13-50, more elaborate work. Pays on publication. Negotiates special projects.

NEW MEXICO STOCKMAN, Box 7127, Albuquerque NM 87104. (505)247-8492. Editor: Chuck Stocks. Monthly; 8½x11". 10,500 circulation. Readers are ranchers, farmers, horsemen, ranch wives and youngsters. Buys b&w line drawings, washes and cover designs. Not copyrighted. Will consider work previously published. Reports in 60 days. Complimentary copy available.

NEW MEXICO WILDLIFE, New Mexico Dept. of Game and Fish, State Capitol, Santa Fe NM 87501. (505)827-2586. Editor-in-Chief: John Crenshaw. Managing Editor: Sandi Doughton. Bimonthly; 8½x11"; 32 pages. Offset. Estab: 1961. Circ: 14,000. For hunters, fishermen and conservationists. Not copyrighted. Payment "on completion of processing invoice and contract through state government channels." Previously published work and photocopies OK. No simultaneous submissions. Query with samples. SASE. Free sample copy.
Illustrations: Buys cover art, article illustrations and spot drawings on hunting, fishing, conservation officers at work and wildlife. Submit finished art. Cover: color-separated art OK. Inside: b&w line drawings OK. Pays $50-100, color cover; $5-40, inside. Buys 20 illustrations annually. Reports in 3 weeks.

NEW ORLEANS MAGAZINE, 6666 Morrison Rd., New Orleans LA 70126. (504)246-2700. Editor: Joe Manguno. Monthly. 50,000 circulation. Readers have upper-level income and education. Estab: 1966. Needs approximately 250 pieces of freelance work annually. Interested in b&w drawings, cover designs, full-color illustrations (color-separated) and cartoons. Buys first serial rights. Will consider artwork previously published. Payment on publication. Typical payment: $40-100 for spot drawings; $200 for full-color illustration/cover designs; $25 for cartoons. Reports immediately. Sample copy $1.50.

NEW ORLEANS REVIEW, Loyola University, New Orleans LA 70118. Editor: Marcus Smith. Quarterly journal of literature and culture. Uses full-color cover designs, and b&w drawings as decorative additions. Pays $10, spot drawing; $75, portfolio of 6-8 pages of art. Payment on publication. Buys all rights, but will reassign rights to artist after publication. Reports in 2-8 weeks. Sample copy $1.50.

NEW YORK MAGAZINE, 755 2nd Ave., New York NY 10017. Contact: Tom Tarnowsky or Nina Subin. Circ: 355,000. Will examine portfolios for future assignments. Arrange interview or leave portfolio overnight.

NEW YORK TIMES BOOK REVIEW, 229 W. 43rd St., New York NY 10036. Picture Editor: Margaret Berkvist. Sunday supplement. Buys first rights. Pays on acceptance.
Illustrations: Buys spot drawings about books, publishers, authors, the literary life in general, crime (for "Criminals at Large" column), science fiction and letters-to-the-editor, preferably humorous. Good drawing, subtle ideas. Fairly finished, legible sketches preferred. Line and halftone OK. Pays $50-$85. Reports in 2-3 weeks.

THE NEW YORKER, 25 W. 43rd St., New York NY 10036. Contact: Cartoon Editor. Buys cartoons, spots and cover designs. Strict standards regarding style, technique, plausibility of drawing. Pays $250 minimum for cartoons. Top rates for spots and cover designs. Submit by mail or deliver sketches each Wednesday.
To Break In: Roughs get preference in gag buying, and many cartoonists get started by first selling gag ideas.

NICA OUTLOOK, National Insulation Contractors Association, 1120 19th St. NW, Suite 405, Washington DC 20036. (202)223-4406. Monthly. Uses spot drawings and cover designs related to the insulation field. Copyrighted. Write.

NITTY-GRITTY, 331 W. Bonneville, Pasco WA 99301. (509)547-5525. Editor-in-Chief: W. R. "Bill" Wilkins. Quarterly; 8½x11"; 100 pages. Offset. Estab: 1976. Circ: 3,000. Buys all rights, but may reassign rights to artist after publication. Pays on acceptance. No previously published or simultaneous submissions. Photocopies OK. Mail artwork. SASE. Free sample copy. Submissions maximum size 7x9".
Cartoons: Buys current event, erotica, humor through youth and political themes related to the issue's "tool-theme." All formats OK. Submit finished art. Line drawings OK. Pays $2-25. Buys 6 cartoons per issue. Reports in 4 weeks.
Illustrations: Buys cover art, article illustrations and spot drawings on the issue's "tool-theme." Submit finished art. Cover: color-separated art OK. Inside: b&w line drawings OK. Pays $25-50, color cover; $2-10, inside. Buys 20 illustrations per issue. Reports in 4 weeks.

NJEA REVIEW, 180 W. State St., Trenton NJ 08608. Editor-in-Chief: George M. Adams. Monthly; 8½x11"; 56-64 pages. Offset. Estab: 1922. Circ: 105,000. For New Jersey teachers and administrators. Buys all rights. Pays on acceptance. Previously published work OK. No photocopied or simultaneous submissions. Query with samples. SASE. Free sample copy.
Cartoons: Buys educational themes. Single panel OK. Submit finished art. Line drawings, halftones and washes OK. Pays $5 minimum, b&w. Cartoons should have positive image of teachers. Buys 10-15 cartoons annually.
Illustrations: Buys illustrations to accompany articles. Submit finished art. B&w line drawings and washes OK. Pays $15-25, b&w.

NORDEN NEWS, Norden Laboratories, 601 W. Cornhusker Hwy., Lincoln NE 68521. (402)475-4541. Editor-in-Chief: Pat Pike. Quarterly; 8½x11"; 36 pages. Offset. Circ: 28,000-30,000. For veterinary clinicians and students in veterinary colleges. Buys first and reprint rights. Pays on acceptance. No photocopies. Previously published and simultaneous submissions OK. Query with samples. SASE. Free sample copy.
Cartoons: Buys veterinary medicine themes. Single panel OK. Submit roughs. Line drawings OK. Pays $5-10. Buys 4 cartoons annually. Reports in 2 weeks.

NORDIC WORLD, World Publications, Box 366, Mt. View CA 94040. Art Buyer: Bob Anderson. Buys cover designs, spot drawings and cartoons. "Our readers are participants and we try to use material that shows insight into the sports that we cover." Pays $10+. Buys reprint rights. Pays on publication. Reports in 1 week.

NORTH AMERICAN MENTOR, Drawer 69, Fennimore WI 53809. (608)822-6237. Editor-in-Chief: John Westburg. Managing Editor: Mildred Westburg. Quarterly; 8½x11"; 60 pages. Offset. Estab: 1964. Circ: 400. For professional people, half of whom are ages 60+. Buys all rights. Pays on publication. Previously published, photocopied and simultaneous submissions OK. Query with samples. SASE. Sample copy $1.25.
Illustrations: Buys cover art and article illustrations on all themes. Submit finished art. B&w line drawings OK. Pays $25 minimum. Buys 1-4 illustrations annually. Reports in 6 months.

NORTHERN LIGHT, 605 Fletcher Argue Bldg., University of Manitoba, Winnipeg, Manitoba Canada R3T 2N2. Editor: George Amabile. Publishes contemporary Canadian poetry and reviews of recent poetry books. Buys b&w line drawings and washes. Subject matter of graphics depends on poems. Human interest, landscape, dramatic effects of light and texture — all are possible. Pays contributor's copies. No previously published work. Reports in 6 weeks. Sample copy $1.50.

NORTHERN VIRGINIAN, Box 334, Vienna VA 22180. Monthly; 48 pages. Offset. 4-color cover plus 7 pages inside full-color. Audience similar to most city magazines. Wants regional or

state material. Always needs line art to illustrate articles; uses some cartoons. Will consider art previously published. "The regional nature of our market should not discourage artists from other parts of the country. We do publish topical and issue pieces which are not specific to northern Virginia. Also, article illustrations, if assigned far enough in advance could (in many cases) be done anywhere. This is a good publication for young artists looking to develop a portfolio." Buys b&w line drawings; 34x14" or 28 picas. Submit roughs. Buys various rights. Pays on publication. Pays $5 minimum for spot drawings. Query. Will send guidelines, then sample copy. Reports in 6 weeks.
To Break In: Team up with a writer and illustrate an article for submission; the art supports the copy and vice versa.

NORTH/NORD, 110 O'Connor St., Ottawa, Ontario Canada K1A 0H4. (613)995-9371. Editor-in-Chief: Robert Shannon. Bimonthly; 8¼x11"; 64 pages. Offset. Estab: 1959. Circ: 16,000. For high school, college students and professionals. Buys all rights, but may reassign rights to artist after publication. No previously published, photocopied or simultaneous submissions. Query. Work returned with or without SASE. Free sample copy. Also pays $150 for brochure design.
Illustrations: Morton Baslaw, editor. Buys cover art and article illustrations about the Arctic. Submit roughs, then finished art. All media OK. Pays $100-250, b&w cover; $250-300, color cover; $25-150, inside b&w; $50-200, inside color; $100-300, full-story illustration. Buys 12-24 illustrations annually. Reports in 8 weeks.

NORTHWEST CHESS, Box 1631, Yakima WA 98907. (206)753-3841. Editor-in-Chief: Kennedy Poyser. Art Editor: Victoria Poyser. Monthly; 7x11"; 32 pages. Offset. Estab: 1947. Circ: 1,000, mostly in Oregon, Washington and British Columbia. For Northwest audience of diverse background; chess bums to systems analysts; most readers have above-average intelligence and abiding interest in board games and science fiction. Not copyrighted. Pays on acceptance. Previously published work OK. No photocopied or simultaneous submissions. Query. Guidelines available. Sample copy 50¢.
Cartoons: Buys themes on chess. Single panel OK. "Original limited by our layout grids to 4⅝x8". Submit finished art. We prefer line drawings depicting foibles of chess players. Caricatures acceptable." Halftones OK. Pays contributor's copies or $5. Buys 12 cartoons annually. Reports in 2 weeks. Prefers not to receive erotica: "I might like it, but I can't publish it."
Illustrations: Buys cover art and article illustrations on chess. "Inside illustrations usually accompany fiction; needed most for March, June, September and December (especially science fiction) issues. If necessary, will send photocopy of ms. More latitude for cover art subject, but it must be striking." Submit roughs. Cover: prefers 10x10" b&w line drawings. Inside: b&w line drawings and veloxes OK. Pays $20 maximum, cover; $5 maximum, inside b&w. Buys 6 illustrations annually. Reports in 2 weeks.
Special Needs: For editor's page, 1 irreverent or whimsical 4⅝x6" drawing. Pays $50 maximum for new design for cover, contents page and department sections; will send complete information, requirements and sample copies. Needs advertising brochure for prospective clients.
To Break In: "Do line drawings with Rapidograph on 'repro paper'; use cross-hatching or Zipatone for shading; the screens we use aren't very kind to the subtle nuances of shadow. Martin Taylor of *Chess Voice* (California) and Jim Riopolle of *Michigan Chess* do the kind of art we're interested in. Get addresses from U.S. Chess Federation or write Cleveland Public Library for photocopied samples."

NORTHWEST REVIEW, 369 PLC, University of Oregon, Eugene OR 97403. (503)686-3957. Editor: Michael Strelow. Published 3 times annually. Commissions work after reviewing portfolios. Uses b&w line drawings and cover designs. Buys one-time rights. May hold art for future issue. Pays on publication. No previously published work. Reports immediately. Sample copy $1.50.

THE NOTEBOOK AND OTHER REVIEWS, Box 180, Birmingham MI 48012. Editor-in-Chief: Michael G. O'Neill. Published 10 times annually; 5½x8½"; 28-36 pages. Offset. Estab: 1976. Circ: 300. For well-educated, literate general audience. Buys all rights, but may reassign rights to artist after publication. Pays on acceptance. No previously published or simultaneous submissions. Photocopies OK. "We prefer samples of artist's work, not original material that requires a lot of fuss regarding packaging." SASE. Sample copy 75¢.
Cartoons: Buys themes on current events, education, politics, writing and literature. Single panel OK. Submit roughs. Line drawings only. Pays $5-10. Buys 2-3 cartoons per issue. Reports

Approximately 120-180 illustrations appealing to preteens are assigned to artists annually by *Young World*. Werner Willis earned $40 with this illustration that accompanied an article on lady pirates. Artists interested in similar assignments should query with samples.

in 1 week.
Illustrations: Buys cover art and spot drawings on all themes. Submit roughs. B&w line drawings and veloxes OK. Pays $10-25, b&w cover; $5-10, inside b&w. Buys 2-3 illustrations per issue. Reports in 1 week.
Special Needs: Uses artists for book illustration, advertising and layout needs. Negotiates payment.
To Break In: "Query me personally and ask what you can do for me. I am more than willing to help beginners."

NOTRE DAME MAGAZINE, 415 Administration Bldg., University of Notre Dame, Notre Dame IN 46556. Editor-in-Chief: Ronald Parent. Published 5 times annually; 9x12"; 64 pages. Offset. Circ: 80,000. For alumni. Buys one-time rights. Pays on publication. Previously published work OK. No photocopied or simultaneous submissions. Query with samples. SASE. Free sample copy.
Illustrations: Don Nelson, designer. Buys cover art, article illustrations and spot drawings on assignment. Recent article topics: architecture, politics and the press, and world hunger. Submit roughs. B&w line drawings, washes and color-separated art OK. Pays $75-150, b&w cover; $10-40, inside b&w. Buys 5-10 illustrations annually.

NPN, 1221 Avenue of the Americas, New York NY 10020. (212)997-2361. Editor: Frank Breese. Monthly; 8x11. 20,000 circulation. Readers interested in petroleum marketing. Estab: 1909. Pays $10 on acceptance for spot drawings. Buys all rights. Will consider work previously published. Contact art director for work on special issues. Sample copy available. Reports promptly.

NRTA JOURNAL, 215 Long Beach Blvd., Long Beach CA 90801. Editor: Hubert C. Pryor. Publication of the National Retired Teachers Association. Bimonthly. Buys b&w spot drawings and 8x10 finished cartoons. Buys one-time and first serial rights. Pays $35+ on acceptance. Reports in 2-4 weeks. Sample copy available.

NUGGET, Dugent Publishing Company, 316 Aragon Ave., Coral Gables FL 33134. Editor/Publisher: Douglas Allen. Managing Editor: Nye Wilden. For men. Buys first time rights.
Cartoons: Buys "funny, somewhat 'sick' humor and sexual themes." Submit finished art. B&w OK. Pays $15 per spot drawing; $100 per page. Mail cartoons.
Illustrations: Works on assignment. Pays $50-75, b&w. Buys 3-4 illustrations per issue. "Submit samples of work for our files."

THE NUMISMATIST, Box 2366, Colorado Springs CO 80901. Editor-in-Chief: N. Neil Harris. Monthly; 6x9"; 224 pages. Offset. Estab: 1888. Circ: 34,000. For collectors of coins, medals, tokens and paper money. Buys all rights, but may reassign rights to artist after publication. Pays on acceptance. Photocopies OK. No previously published or simultaneous submissions. Query with samples. SASE. Free sample copy.
Cartoons: Single panel OK. Submit roughs. Washes OK. Rates to be announced. Reports in 3 weeks.
Illustrations: Buys article illustrations and spot drawings. Submit roughs. B&w drawings and washes OK. Rates to be announced. Reports in 3 weeks.

NURSERY DAYS, 201 8th Ave. S., Nashville TN 37202. Editor: Doris Willis. Published weekly for ages 2-4. Contact: Art Dept. Should cover things of interest to children — church, family, nature, friends, God. Must have religious significance. Deadline 18 months before publication. Takes b&w drawings and cover designs in finished art. Pays $45, full-color illustration; $40, 3-color art. Buys all rights. Will consider previously published work. Pays on acceptance. Query. SASE. Sample copy available.

NURSING CARE, 75 E. 55th St., New York NY 10022. (212)688-7110. Editor-in-Chief: Serena Stockwell. Monthly; 8½x11"; 36 pages. Offset. Circ: 70,000. For licensed practical and vocational nurses. Buys various rights. Pays on acceptance. Previously published, photocopied and simultaneous submissions OK. All methods of contact OK. SASE. Free sample copy. Pays $25-100, promotional artwork.
Cartoons: Buys medical themes. Single panel OK. Submit roughs or finished art. Line drawings OK. Pays $10-50. Reports in 2 weeks.
Illustrations: Buys cover art, article illustrations and spot drawings on hospitals, nurses and health care. Submit roughs or finished art. Cover: color-separated art OK. Inside: b&w line

drawings OK. Pays $50-100, color cover; $10-75, inside. Buys 10-20 illustrations annually. Reports in 2 weeks.

O.S.S.T.F. FORUM, 60 Mobile Dr., Toronto, Ontario Canada M4A 2P3. Art Buyer: M. Crawford. For high school teachers. Buys pen and ink, line and wash roughs. Previously published work OK as examples of artist's style. Minimum rate for spot drawing, $20. Payment on acceptance. Buys first rights. Reports in 30 days.

OCCULT TRADE JOURNAL, 2274 Como Ave., St. Paul MN 55108. Contact: Editor. Uses sketches and cartoons on astrology, parapsychology and related occult subjects. Pays $5-25. Submit samples for files for future assignment. Buys all rights but may release other rights on request. Reports in 90 days.

OCEANS, 240 Fort Mason, San Francisco CA 94123. (415)441-1104. Editor-in-Chief: Keith K. Howell. Bimonthly; 8½x11"; 72 pages. Offset. Estab: 1969. Circ: 50,000. For the middle-aged, well-educated who enjoy science and are concerned about the environment. Buys first rights. Pays on publication. No previously published work. Photocopied and simultaneous submissions OK. Query with samples. SASE. Sample copy 50¢.
Illustrations: Buys article illustrations on assignment. Submit finished art. All media OK. Pays $30-100, color; $20-60, b&w. Buys 36 illustrations annually. Reports in 4 weeks.

OFF DUTY, Tak Yan Commercial Bldg., 10th Floor, Hong Kong. Editor-in-Chief: Jim Shaw. Monthly; 8⅜x11"; 60 pages. Offset. Circ: 235,000. For U.S. military and their dependents around the world. Buys reprint rights. Pays on publication. Previously published, photocopied and simultaneous submissions OK. Query with samples. SASE. Free sample copy if qualified.
Illustrations: L. Iwase, associate editor. Buys article illustrations and spot drawings on assignment. B&w line drawings, washes and color-separated art OK. Pays $10-30, b&w; $15-50, color. Reports in 4 weeks.
Special Needs: Often needs illustrations that depict areas and countries.

OFFICIAL DETECTIVE STORIES, 235 Park Ave. S., New York NY 10003. Editor: Albert P. Govoni. Monthly. For readers of factual crime stories. Buys all rights. Pays on acceptance.
Cartoons: Buys crime genre themes. Avoid cliche situations such as 2 convicts conversing in cell; cute, mild sex. Submit single panel roughs. Pays $25. Reports in 2 weeks.

OFFSHORE, 1200 S. Post Oak, Houston TX 77056. (713)621-9720. Presentation Editor: Nancy Teinert. Monthly. For offshore drilling, production and all supporting business readership. 18,000 circulation. Uses cover designs, full-color illustrations, b&w drawings and logos. Will consider previously published work. Rights and payments negotiable. Pays $5-250. Pays on publication. Query with resume. Reports in 2 weeks. Sample copy available.

OHIO FARMER, 1350 W. 5th Ave., Columbus OH 43212. Editor: Andrew L. Stevens. Biweekly. Aims to interpret current findings of science and agricultural business in terms of practical farm application.
Cartoons: Pays $3 per finished art on publication. Buys 40-50 cartoons annually. Reports in several days.

THE OKLAHOMA FARMER-STOCKMAN, Box 25125, Oklahoma City OK 73125. Aimed at aiding rural families to grow better crops, improve their livestock, enjoy modern equipment, and achieve finer living. Buys all rights. Sample copy available.
Cartoons: Pays $10 on acceptance for finished art dealing with farm and ranch situations or the people with whom farmers do business. Uses 25 cartoons annually. Reports in 1 week.

OKLAHOMA LP GAS ASSOCIATION, 2910 N. Walnut, Suite 114A, Oklahoma City OK 73105. Contact: John E. Orr. "We have a monthly trade publication that can utilize some artwork and we'd like to hear from artists with samples of their work." Pays $5 minimum. Reports in 2 weeks.

OLD BOTTLE MAGAZINE, Box 243, Bend OR 97701. Contact: Kenneth Asher. Buys cartoons about old bottles. Pays $5. Payment on acceptance. Buys all rights. Reports in 6 weeks.

OLD WEST, Western Publications, Inc., Box 3338, Austin TX 78704. Publisher: Joe Austell Small. Editor: Pat Wagner. For those interested in Western Americana, 1840-1910, nonfiction.

Buys one-time rights. Pays on acceptance. Previously published work OK "depending on where it appeared." Sample copy 60¢.
Illustrations: Buys cover art in 4-color oils. "We prefer a color snapshot or transparency for evaluation of the artist's style. We also prefer vertical paintings because the use of bands above and below a horizontal gives issues a look of sameness. We also have to pass up good paintings at times because our titles would cover some vital element or because the painting has no space left for story titles. We like to leave the artist's work as uncluttered as possible, but a certain amount of type is required. Often, the artist doesn't take this into account." Pays $100. Reports in 2-3 weeks.

OPEN ROAD AND THE PROFESSIONAL DRIVER, 1015 Florence, Ft. Worth TX 76102. (817)336-5837. Editor-in-Chief: Chris Lackey. Monthly; 8½x11"; 48 pages. Offset. Estab: 1967. Circ: 30,112. For truckers interested in safety, driving habits, equipment and community service. Buys various rights. Pays on publication. No previously published work. Mail artwork. SASE. Free sample copy.
Cartoons: Buys trucking themes. Single panel OK. Submit finished art. Line drawings OK. Pays "on a case by case basis."

OPINION, Box 1885, Rockford IL 61110. Contact: J. Kurtz. "We are a philosophical, sociological and theological journal. Artwork should be easily understood — not abstract. We like to find and promote new talent." Uses b&w line art. Artist retains all rights to work.

ORAL IMPLANTOLOGY, 469 Washington St., Abington MA 02351. Editor-in-Chief: Dr. Isaih Lew. Quarterly; 6x9"; 160 pages. Offset. Estab: 1970. Circ: 2,000. For dentists. Pays on publication. Previously published work OK. No photocopied or simultaneous submissions. Query with samples. SASE. Free sample copy.
Cartoons: Buys themes on dentistry. Single panel OK. Submit finished art. Line drawings, halftones and washes OK. Negotiates payment. Reports in 6 months.
Illustrations: Buys cover art and article illustrations. Submit finished art. B&w line drawings, washes, color-separated and reflective art OK. Reports in 6 months.
Special Needs: Uses artists to touch-up poor artwork submitted, and to do new layouts and ad designs.

OUI, 919 N. Michigan Ave., Chicago IL 60611. Art Director: Michael Brock. "For the man of the world." Buys all rights. Interested in seeing portfolio for future assignments.

OUR FAMILY, Box 249, Battleford, Saskatchewan Canada S0M 0E0. (306)937-2131. Editor-in-Chief: A.J. Reb Materi. Monthly; 8¼x10¾"; 32 pages. Offset. Estab: 1949. Circ: 10,791. For the average family man and woman with high school and early college education. Buys various rights. Pays on acceptance. Previously published and simultaneous submissions OK. Photocopies OK, but "we do not like a great number of these submitted in 1 packet." Query with samples. SASE. Sample copy 25¢. Non-Canadian artists: "Please include Canadian stamps or some other return postage. U.S. and foreign stamps cannot be used in Canada."
Cartoons: Buys themes on education, family life, humor through youth and religion. Single panel OK. Submit finished art. Halftones and washes OK. Pays $4-10, b&w. Buys 1 or more cartoons per issue. Reports in 2-4 weeks.
Illustrations: Buys article illustrations and spot drawings on assignment. Submit finished art. B&w line drawings and washes OK. Pays $10-100, b&w. Buys 1-4 illustrations per issue. Reports in 2-4 weeks.

OZARK FLIGHTIME, East-West Network, Inc., 5900 Wilshire Blvd., #300, Los Angeles CA 90036. (213)937-5810. Editor: James Clark. Senior Art Director: Chris Mossman. Monthly. Buys all rights. Query with resume. Sample copy $1.
Illustrations: Buys cover art and spot drawings on assignment. Pays $25 minimum, spot art; $400, full-color cover. Reports in 4 weeks.

PACIFIC, Box 1578, Newport Beach CA 92660. Editor: D. Morrison. Monthly. 50,000 circulation. Travel and business magazine oriented to the Pacific Basin area. Buys one-time rights. Pays on publication. No previously published work. Mail artwork.
Illustrations: Buys b&w drawings and full-color illustrations. Periodically needs special projects on island drawings. Pays $100, 4-color cover design (color-separated). Reports in 10 days.

PACIFIC PRINTERS PILOT, 583 Monterey Pass Rd., Monterey Park CA 91754. (213)576-

1538. Editor-in-Chief: Patrick Totty. Monthly; 7x10"; 48 pages. Estab: 1959. Circ: 10,500. For graphic artists and related tradesmen in 10 western states; education varies but all are familiar with printing equipment, techniques and jargon; approximately 1/3 are women. Not copyrighted. Pays on publication. Previously published work OK. No photocopied or simultaneous submissions. Mail artwork. SASE. Free sample copy.
Cartoons: Buys graphic arts themes. All formats OK. Halftones OK. Pays $10-30. Buys 5-10 cartoons annually. "Cartoons can vary from abstract concepts (alphabet letters talking to each other) to comments on the business world with graphic arts slant."
To Break In: "Cartoonists can keep their foot in the door by staying in touch. One submission might not be what it takes. Those who submit will be given a critique when their artwork is returned if we like the style, but not the gags."

PACIFIC SKIPPER MAGAZINE, 300 N. Newport Blvd., Suite G, Newport Beach CA 92663. Art Director: Blossom Siegel. Monthly; 8⅜x10⅞. For those interested in family cruising, sail and power. Buys art and cartoons. B&w line drawings, washes and full-color illustrations OK. These should be of boating scenes with people (close-up) size 1-1 on light paper or tissue ready to paste down — no illustration board. Pays $100, cover; $20, inside color; $25, full-page b&w drawing; $12.50, half page; $10, spot drawing. Payment on publication. Buys all rights. Previously published work in noncompeting publications OK. Mail artwork.

PACIFIC TRAFFIC, Box 2000, Napa CA 94558. Art Buyer: J. P. Eichorn. For transportation/traffic field (all modes). Of special interest is material on air cargo, shipping (steamship companies, ships), rail and truck. Buys art and cartoons. Buys finished pen and ink, line and wash drawings, 4x5 or larger. Sample payment: drawings, $10+; 4-color cover design, $50+. Material previously published considered. Not copyrighted. Pays on publication. Reports in 2 weeks.

PAMPHLETEER MONTHLY, 55 E. 86th St., New York NY 10028. Editor-in-Chief: Paul Busby. Art Editor: Albert Botwich. Monthly, September-June; 6x9"; 32-48 pages. Letterpress. Estab: 1940. Circ: 6,200. For school, public, college, university and special libraries. Buys all rights. Pays on assignment. Previously published, photocopied and simultaneous submissions OK. Query. SASE.
Illustrations: Buys spot drawings on assignment. B&w line drawings and washes OK. Pays $25 minimum.

PAN AM CLIPPER, East-West Network, Inc., 5900 Wilshire Blvd., #300, Los Angeles CA 90036. (213)937-5810. Editor: James Clark. Senior Art Director: Chris Mossman. Monthly. Buys all rights. Query with resume. Sample copy $1.
Illustrations: Buys cover art and spot drawings on assignment. Pays $25 minimum, spot art; $400, full-color cover. Reports in 4 weeks.

PANORAMA MAGAZINE, Greer Bldg., Morgantown WV 26505. Editor: Sarah Stevenson. For southwestern Pennsylvania and northern West Virginia with emphasis on the arts, history and lifestyle of Appalachians. Weekly. Buys b&w drawings in line and line and wash, and cartoons usually on assignment. Pays $5, spot drawing; $15, full-color illustration. No previously published work. Payment on publication. Query. Reports in 2 weeks. Sample copy available.
Special Needs: Artwork for issues on garden, travel, regional progress, coal, mountain cookbook, basketall, football and Buckwheat Festival.

PARADE, 248 Mt. Joy Ave., Freeport NY 11520. Sunday newspaper magazine. Circ: 19 million +. Buys first North American serial rights. Pays on acceptance. Mail artwork.
Cartoons: Lawrence Lariar, editor. Wants topical and human interest themes. An open market for captionless single panels and pantomimes (2-5 boxes). Line and halftone OK. Single panels 8½x11 roughs preferred, inked, and ready to be printed. Pays $60 for single panels; $110 for multipanels. Reports in 2 weeks.

PARKING, 1101 17th St. NW, Washington DC 20036. (202)296-4336. Editor-in-Chief: Norene Dann Martin. Associate Editor: David L. Ivey. Quarterly; 8⅛x11⅛"; 50 pages. Offset. Estab: 1953. Circ: 5,500. For members of National Parking Association — trade organization of the commercial offstreet parking industry — architects, engineers, traffic planners and city officials. Buys one-time rights. Pays on acceptance. No photocopies. Previously published and

simultaneous submisions OK. Query. SASE. Free sample copy. "Though restricted by a fairly tight budget, we're open to submissions."
Cartoons: Buys themes on environment, parking, engineering, construction and transportation. Submit finished art. Halftones and washes OK. Pays $15 minimum. Reports in 1 week.
Illustrations: Buys cover art, article illustrations and spot drawings on parking themes; "would especially like to see a particularly dramatic rendering of attactive parking garage or lot." Submit finished art. Cover: color-separated art OK. Inside: b&w line drawings, washes and veloxes OK. Minimum payment: $35, color cover; $20, b&w cover; $10, inside. Reports in 1 week.

PARTS PUPS, Box 54066, Atlanta GA 30308. Editor-in-Chief: Don Kite. Monthly; 8½x11"; 8 pages. Offset and letterpress. Estab: 1932. Circ: 185,000. For automotive repairmen. Not copyrighted. Pays on acceptance. No previously published work or photocopies. Simultaneous submissions OK. Mail artwork. SASE. Free sample copy.
Cartoons: Buys themes on erotica and auto repairmen. Single panel OK. Submit finished art. Halftones and b&w washes OK. Pays $15. Buys 120 cartoons annually. Reports in 4 weeks.

PASSAGES PRESS GAZETTE, Box 14, Evanston IL 60204. (312)492-1288. Editor-in-Chief: John Fluent. Managing Editor: Bobette Berg. Monthly; 8½x11"; 16 pages. Offset. Estab: 1976. Circ: 800. For freelance writers, poets, cartoonists and photojournalists. Buys all rights, but may reassign rights to artist after publication. Pays on acceptance. No previously published, photocopied or simultaneous submissions. Query with samples. SASE. Free sample copy.
Cartoons: Buys themes on freelancing. "We need cartoons dealing with humorous aspects of writing and poetry." Single panel OK. Submit finished art. Line drawings only. Pays $10 minimum. Buys 2 cartoons per issue. Reports in 2 weeks.
Illustrations: F. Jacks, editor. Buys cover art and article illustrations on writing, poetry and photography; especially needs artwork for Christmas issue. No eroticism. Submit finished art. B&w line drawings and veloxes OK. Pays $10, b&w. Buys 2 illustrations per issue. Reports in 2 weeks.

PATHFINDERS, Box 81005, San Diego CA 92138. Contact: Arnold Senterfitt. "We are a highly diversified book and periodical publisher with an emphasis in — but not dealing exclusively in aviation — family-owned and flown aircraft. We're always interested in good spot art and aviation-oriented cartoons. We'll even suggest ideas for cartoons once we get an idea of the artist's style." Pays $5-25.
Special Needs: Pays $100, 6x18" 1-color bumper sticker; $150, 8½x10½" 1-color ad layout/design.

PENNSYLVANIA ILLUSTRATED, Box 246, 17 S. 19th St., Camp Hill PA 17011. (717)761-6605. Editor-in-Chief: Albert Holliday. Editor: Robert Hillegas. Bimonthly; 7⅜x11"; 60 pages. Offset. Estab: 1976. Circ: 20,000. For college-educated readers, ages 35-50, interested in self-improvement, history, and civic and state affairs. Buys first North American serial rights. Pays on publication. Previously published, photocopied and simultaneous submissions OK. Query with samples. SASE. Free sample copy.
Cartoons: Buys themes on history. Single panel OK. Submit roughs. Line drawings OK. Minimum payment: $15, b&w; $25, color. Buys 6 cartoons annually. Reports in 3 weeks.
Illustrations: Buys cover art, article illustrations and spot drawings on history-related themes. Submit roughs. Cover: color-separated and reflective art OK. Inside: b&w line drawings and washes OK. Minimum payment: $30, inside b&w; $45, b&w cover; $55, inside color; $70, color cover. Buys 12 illustrations annually. Reports in 3 weeks.

PERSONAL COMPUTING, 401 Louisiana SE, Suite "G," Albuquerque NM 87108. Editor-in-Chief: David Bunnell. Managing Editor: Nels Winkles. Bimonthly; 8½x11"; 120 pages. Web offset. Estab: 1976. Circ: 50,000. For people interested in computers for their own personal use, whether at home, school or business; well-educated, upper-middle income, wide spectrum of professions and interests. Buys all rights. Pays on acceptance. No previously published or simultaneous submissions. Photocopies OK. Query with samples. SASE. Free sample copy.
Cartoons: Buys humorous themes that apply to computers and the people using them. Does not want to see "sophomoric artwork, cartoons depicting computers as gods or monsters." All formats OK. Submit roughs. Halftones and washes OK. Minimum payment: $25, b&w; $35, color. Buys 1-5 cartoons per issue. Reports in 2 weeks.
Illustrations: Buys cover art, article illustrations and spot drawings on personal computers.

Submit roughs or finished art. Cover: washes, color-separated and reflective art and veloxes OK. Inside: b&w line drawings, washes, color-separated and reflective art and veloxes OK. Pays $25-150, inside b&w; $50-250, inside color; $150-500, color cover. Buys 10-15 illustrations per issue. Reports in 2 weeks.

PETROLEUM TODAY, 2101 L St. NW, Washington DC 20037. Editor: Patricia M. Markun. Published 4 times annually for the general public. Buys article illustrations. Query with resume. Sample copy available.

PHI DELTA KAPPAN, Box 789, 8th and Union, Bloomington IN 47401. Design Director: Victoria Voelker. Monthly, September-June. Circ: 120,000+. "Phi Delta Kappa is an international organization of educators, mostly on the higher education level. As the largest monthly magazine in the field, we have frequent reprint requests which help to make up to artists the relatively low rates we pay." All material must be education-oriented. Buys art and cartoons in any medium reproducible by offset. Submit finished art, unless commissioned. Pays $100, cover design in full color; $15-25, cartoons. "Our purchases are for one-time rights. Artists may resell as they wish and our cartoonists find that reprint requests are frequent and profitable. All reprint fees go to artists and we request (but cannot require) reprinters to give us credit as well as the artist. Will consider reprint rights on previously published material, but previous publication must be indicated and, if possible, tearsheet enclosed; our specialized audience makes it feasible to use art from other field publications, but we have to know where it has appeared before." Pays on acceptance. Query. Reports in 1-4 weeks. Sample copy $1.25.

PHILADELPHIA, 1500 Walnut St., Philadelphia PA 19102. Art Director: Pat Kiesling. "We're a metropolitan magazine and winner of many awards. We consider only professional work and we've used some of the country's finest illustrators. Terrific forum for young illustrators just starting out if they're top talent, but this is no place for beginners. We don't use art just to dress up a page. As far as we're concerned, the art treatment is the backdrop, the stage — and the words are the actors." Pays $10 minimum, spots; $175 maximum, full-page illustration. Pays on acceptance. Buys all rights. Send published samples to be kept on file.

PHOEBE, 4400 University Dr., Fairfax VA 22030. (703)323-2287. Editor-in-Chief: Samuel O'Neal, Jr. Quarterly; 8½x11"; 64 pages. Offset. Estab: 1971. Circ: 4,000. For university-oriented readers, including writers and artists. Buys one-time rights. No previously published or simultaneous submissions. Photocopies OK. Send resume and artwork. SASE. Sample copy $2.
Cartoons: Buys all themes. All formats OK. Submit finished art. B&w art OK. Pays contributor's copies. Reports in 2 months.
Illustrations: Buys cover art, article illustrations and spot drawings on all themes. Submit finished art. B&w art OK. Pays contributor's copies. Reports in 2 months.

THE PHOENIX, Morning Star Press, RFD Haydenville MA 01039. Art Buyer: James Cooney. Literary journal of radical resistance and reconciliation — "for those who can understand, its anarchist radical aspects are essentially Promethean." Quarterly. Buys first rights. Previously published work OK. Send published samples or original art. SASE.
Illustrations: Buys woodcuts and line drawings, primarily — suitable for letterpress b&w reproduction. Pays 12 contributor's copies and a subscription.

PHONE CALL, 2626 Pennsylvania Ave., Washington DC 20037. (202)833-2113. Editor: S. J. Stack. Monthly publication of National Telephone Cooperative Association. For rural telephone cooperatives. Includes information on equipment, conventions, other telephone aspects. Buys cover designs and spot drawings. Finished pen and ink, or line and wash OK. Pays $50 minimum, spot art; $120, 2-color cover. Not copyrighted. Arrange interview to show portfolio.

PIGIRON MAGAZINE, Box 237, Youngstown OH 44501. (216)744-2258. Editor-in-Chief: Jim Villani. Published 1-3 times annually; 8½x11"; 100 pages. Offset. Estab: 1975. Circ: 1,000. Readers are university students and young adults. Buys first North American serial rights. Pays on acceptance. Previously published work and photocopies OK. No simultaneous submissions. Mail veloxes or slides. SASE. Sample copy $2.
Cartoons: Buys themes on current events, education, environment, erotica and politics; especially interested in fine art cartoons. Multi-panel OK. Submit finished art. Halftones and washes OK. Pays $2 minimum, b&w. Buys 5-50 cartoons annually. Reports in 3 weeks-3 months.
Illustrations: Buys cover art and spot drawings. Submit finished art. B&w line drawings, washes,

reflective art and veloxes OK. Minimum payment: $4, b&w cover; $2, inside b&w. Buys 5-50 illustrations annually. Reports in 3 weeks-3 months.
Special Needs: Artwork for "Fascia," "a fast-paced, broad-based editorial that explores and accentuates the creative aspect of magazine publishing and the expression of the creative process in art and culture."

PLACEMENT AGE, National Employment Assocation, 1835 K St. NW, Suite 910, Washington DC 20006. (202)331-8040. Contact: Kenneth Fisher. Buys pen and ink finished art and single panel cartoons. Buys one-time rights. Mail samples and fees.

PLAN AND PRINT, 10116 Franklin Ave., Franklin Park IL 60131. Editor: James C. Vebeck. Issued 12 times annually. For blueprint, photocopy, offset, microfilm, diazo and allied reproduction firms; dealers in architects', engineers', and draftsmen's supplies and equipment; in-plant reproduction department supervisors, design/drafting specialists and architects. Buys all rights. Pays on acceptance. Reports in 2 weeks.
Cartoons: Buys blueprint, photocopy and print themes. Pays $7.50. Buys approximately 60 cartoons annually.
Illustrations: Uses spot drawings related to industry. Finished art, pen and ink, line and wash, scratchboard OK. Pays $5.

PLANE & PILOT MAGAZINE, Box 1136, Santa Monica CA 90406. (213)451-1423. Editor-in-Chief: Don Werner. Monthly; 8½x11"; 76 pages. Offset. Estab: 1965. Circ: 90,000. For general aviation pilots. Buys all rights. Pays on publication. No previously published, photocopied or simultaneous submissions. Mail artwork. SASE. Free sample copy.
Cartoons: "We need cartoons that appeal to general aviation pilots, but we're laughing with them, not at them, so avoid satire." Single panel OK. Submit finished art. Line drawings only. Pays $10 minimum. Buys 36 cartoons annually. Reports in 4 weeks.

PLAYBOY, 919 Michigan Ave., Chicago IL 60611. Art Director: Arthur Paul. Generally all artwork done on assignment. Buys all rights. Submit samples. Reports in 2-4 weeks.
Cartoons: Buys satirical, sophisticated drawings, girlie and other situations. Must be slanted toward young, urban male market. Style and technique very important. Submit roughs with 1 finished drawing included. Must deal with sex ideas. Pays $350, b&w; $600, full-page color reproduction. Buys about 35 cartoons a month.
Illustrations: Buys illustrations and spot drawings. Pays $800 per page or $1,200 per spread, illustrations; $200-250, spot art.

PLAYERS MAGAZINE, 8060 Melrose Ave., Los Angeles CA 90046. Editor/Art Buyer: Michael St. John. Black men's sex-oriented magazine. Buys cartoons, and illustrations on assignment. Payment is $50-75, b&w; $150, full-color. "We have a preference for art aimed at black readership, but will consider other." Buys all rights. Pays on publication. Pays one-half first rights rate on material previously published. Reports in 4 weeks.

PLAYGIRL, 1801 Century Park E., Suite 2300, Los Angeles CA 90067. "For ages 18-34, 70% career oriented; extremely interested in beauty, fashion, health, sports, politics, the environment, the world around her; she is aware of her sexuality and response to erotica." Buys one-time rights. Pays on acceptance. Reports in 2-4 weeks.
Cartoons: Kathe Klopp, editor. Buys general humor and sex gags, but no sexist material. "We are in the market for more illustrative, fully drawn cartoons. We need 7⅜x9⅝" (for color)." Pays $250, full-page color; $125, b&w.
Illustrations: Michael Parish, art director. "All art bought on assignment with the artist given the ms and instructions for illustrations."

POETCARD SERIES, Box 33512, San Diego CA 92103. Editor-in-Chief: Richard Soos, Jr. Weekly; 2x3"; 1 page. Letterpress. Estab: 1977. Circ: 300. For college graduate poets and artists. Buys first rights. No previously published, simultaneous or photocopied submissions. Mail artwork. SASE. Free sample copy. "Be creative and a little nutsy. Nothing larger than 2x2½"."
Cartoons: Buys current event, education, environment, politics, poetry and writing themes. Single panel OK. Submit finished art. Line drawings only. Pays contributor's copies and 1¢ royalty per card sold. Buys 2-10 cartoons annually. Reports in 2 weeks.
Illustrations: Buys cover art on all themes. Submit finished art. B&w line drawings OK. Pays contributor's copies and 1¢ royalty per card sold. Buys 2-10 illustrations annually. Reports in 2 weeks.

POETRY/PEOPLE, Box 264, Menomonee Falls WI 53051. Editor: S. P. Stavrakis. Published semiannually; 5½x8½"; 100-200 pages. Poetry and short stories anthology. Estab: 1973. Circ: 500-2,000. Buys b&w drawings, cover designs and rough cartoons. Buys more than half of material used. Payment is in cash and prizes to top artists. Exact terms specified to artist prior to publication. Buys one-time, first serial and reprint rights. Previously published work OK. Query. Reports in 2-3 months. Sample copy $5.

POLLUTION CONTROL JOURNAL, 144 N. 12th Ave., Denver CO 80204. (303)222-7734. Editor: Lou Thomas. Quarterly. Buys b&w drawings, cover designs and 4x6" cartoons. Pays $5-75, illustrations. Buys one-time rights on art; for cartoons, first serial, reprint or simultaneous rights. Pays on publication. Pays less for previously published work. Submit artwork. Reports in 60 days. Sample copy $1.

POOL NEWS, 3923 W. 6th St., Los Angeles CA 90020. Contact: J. Field. Interested in cartoons that relate to swimming pools and swimming pool industry. Payment is $10 for all rights. Payment on acceptance. Buys reprint rights to work previously published. Reports immediately.

POPULAR ELECTRONICS MAGAZINE, 1 Park Ave., New York NY 10016. Contact: Ed Buxbaum. Buys artwork and cartoons on electronics, test instruments, experimenters, hi-fi, TV service and CB/ham radios. Usually uses pen and ink or line and wash. Pays $35-70, art; $15-25, cartoons. Buys all rights. Pays on acceptance. Call or send resume. Reports in 2 weeks.

Science fiction and mystery themes appropriate for children age 14 and younger are the basis for cartoons and illustrations for *Child Life* magazine. This article illustration was purchased from George Sears for $50 because of its good strong composition, attractive color and style. The magazine also buys 8-10 cartoons annually.

POPULAR HANDICRAFT HOBBIES, Tower Press, Inc., Box 428, Seabrook NH 03874. Editor-in-Chief: Karen P. Sherrer. Bimonthly; 8x11"; 72 pages. Offset. Estab: 1964. Circ: 140,000. For amateur hobbyists and crafters, mostly women. "Our readers are interested in easy-to-do crafts, which require a minimum of expensive materials and tools." Buys all rights. Pays on acceptance. No previously published, photocopied or simultaneous submissions. Mail artwork. SASE. Free sample copy.
Cartoons: Buys themes related to crafts or hobbies. "Sex, sin and liquor are taboo. Show women in a favorable light; we're very square, no sick humor." Single panel OK. Submit finished art. Washes OK. Pays $20 minimum, b&w. Buys 12 cartoons annually. Reports in 6-8 weeks.

POPULAR SCIENCE MAGAZINE, Times Mirror Magazines, Inc., 380 Madison Ave., New York NY 10017. Art Director: Herbert Anthony. "We do not publish unsolicited art. We would like to see samples of artwork, however, in the scientific and technological fields for future assignments." Buys first rights on acceptance. Submit tearsheets. Reports in several days.

PORTS O'CALL, Society of Wireless Pioneers, Box 530, Santa Rosa CA 95402. Editor: William A. Breniman. For active and retired radio-telegraph men who handle(d) communications with ships and at shore stations; included are military, commercial, aeronautical and governmental communications personnel. "Since many have earned their living aboard ships as 'Sparks,' we like to bring a nautical flavor to our pages." Buys b&w line drawings and cartoons. Pays $5+, drawings; rates open, cartoons. Pays on acceptance. Buys reprints.

POWDER, Box 1028, Dana Point CA 92629. (714)496-5922. Editor: David Moe. Circ: 100,000. "We're interested in all aspects of the ski experience, especially deep powder skiing. Material should be submitted by early June." Publishes 5 issues in the fall. Considers spot drawings, cartoons and cover designs. Rough or finished, pen and ink or line and wash OK. Pays $30, spots/cartoons; $100-200, 4-color cover design. Query, except for cartoons. SASE. Will consider submissions published elsewhere. Reports in 3 weeks. Pays on acceptance. Sample copy 50¢.

THE PRACTICING FAMILY LAWYER, 3711 Long Beach Blvd., Suite 718, Long Beach CA 90807. (213)426-0425. Editor-in-Chief: James E. Sutherland. Quarterly; 6x9"; 40 pages. Offset. Estab: 1977. Circ: 2,000. For attorneys and judges handling divorces, adoptions, child custody and visitation, and community property rights. Buys all rights, but may reassign rights to artist after publication. Pays on acceptance. Previously published, photocopied and simultaneous submissions OK. Mail artwork. SASE. Free sample copy.
Cartoons: Buys themes on lawyers, judges, marital problems and divorce. Single panel OK. Submit roughs. Halftones OK. Pays $35-70. "We want lawyers to take their work seriously, but not themselves, and to see the humor in situations where clients are often seen at their worst." Buys 10-12 cartoons annually. Reports in 4 weeks.

PRESBYTERIAN SURVEY, 341 Ponce de Leon Ave. NE, Atlanta GA 30308. (404)873-1531 ext. 405. Editor: John Allen Templeton. Monthly. 126,000 circulation. Buys one-time rights. Pays on acceptance. Sample copy available.
Illustrations: Buys cover art and inside illustrations on religious themes. Submit roughs or finished art. B&w line drawings and washes OK. Pays $25, spot art; $50-100, cover design. Buys several illustrations per issue.

PRESENT TENSE, c/o CBS, 51 W. 52nd St., Rm. 2719, New York NY 10019. Quarterly magazine of journalism and good writing concerning Jewish affairs. Contact: Ira Teichberg. Buys b&w line drawings, washes and graphic art. Pays $25-75, spot art. Buys all rights. Payment on publication. Query. Reports in 4-6 weeks. Sample copy $2.50.

PRIMAVERA, 1212 E. 59th St., University of Chicago, Chicago IL 60637. (312)684-3189. Editor-in-Chief: Janet Heller. Managing Editor: Arlene Zide. Published annually; 8½x11"; 90 pages. Offset. Estab: 1975. Circ: 800. For those interested in the work of women writers and artists. Buys first North American serial rights. No previously published or simultaneous submissions. Mail artwork. SASE. Sample copy $3.50. "We accept work only from women."
Illustrations: Judith Fildes, editor. Buys cover art, article illustrations and spot drawings on women, nature, children and abstract themes. Submit finished art. B&w line drawings, washes, reflective art and veloxes OK. Pays 2 contributor's copies. Buys 15 illustrations per issue. Reports in 3 weeks.

PROFESSIONAL MEDICAL ASSISTANT, 1 E. Wacker Dr., Chicago IL 60601. Editor: Susan S. Croy. Bimonthly. For medical office personnel. 17,500 circulation. Considers medical office-oriented cartoons submitted by mail. Pays $7.50 on acceptance. Buys all rights. Will consider previously published work. Reports in 1 month. Sample copy available.

PROFITABLE CRAFT MERCHANDISING, PJS Publications, Inc., News Plaza, Peoria IL 61061. Contact: Wayne Mathison. For craft retailers. Buys cartoons and illustrations on assignment. Pays $10-200. Buys all rights. Pays on acceptance. Send samples. Reports in 3-4 weeks.

THE PROGRESSIVE FARMER, 820 Shades Creek Pkwy., Birmingham AL 35202. Art Director: Al Ellis. Concentrates on agricultural interests of the South and Southwest. Buys all rights.
Cartoons: Roughs acceptable. "Would like to see more cartoons about actual farming operations, use of farm machinery, cattle. We use quite a few around-the-home, family, recreation, school and church activities gags; also hunting and fishing gags." Pays $30 minimum on acceptance. Buys approximately 75 cartoons annually. Reports in 1 week.

PROPERTY MANAGEMENT JOURNAL, Box 853, Temple City CA 91780. Editor-in-Chief: Gladys Dickholtz. Monthly; 11x14"; 12-16 pages. Offset. Estab: 1971. Circ: 7,000. For real estate people, owners of rental property, resident managers and property management

companies in California. Pays on acceptance. Previously published and simultaneous submissions OK. Query with samples. SASE. Sample copy $1.
Cartoons: Buys themes related to problems or topics common to landlord/tenant/manager relationships. Submit finished art. Line drawings only. Pays $10-15, b&w. Buys 12 cartoons annually. Reports in 4 weeks.

PSA CALIFORNIA, East-West Network, Inc., 5900 Wilshire Blvd., #300, Los Angeles CA 90036. (213)937-5810. Editor: James Clark. Senior Art Director: Chris Mossman. Monthly. Buys all rights. Query with resume. Sample copy $1.
Illustrations: Buys cover art and spot drawings on assignment. Pays $25 minimum, spot art; $400, full-color cover. Reports in 4 weeks.

PSYCHOLOGY TODAY, 1 Park Ave., New York NY 10016. (212)725-7530. Editor: Jack Nessel. Art Director: Carveth Kramer. Monthly; 8⅜x10⅞"; 100 pages. Offset. Estab: 1967. Circ: 1,100,000. For laymen interested in social science and the human condition. Buys first, all and one-time rights. Pays on acceptance. No previously published, photocopied or simultaneous submissions. Arrange interview, submit artwork by mail or deliver portfolio. SASE.
Cartoons: Submit finished art. Line drawings and washes OK. Pays $250 minimum, b&w. Buys 24 cartoons annually. Reports in 4 weeks.
Illustrations: Buys article illustrations and spot drawings on assignment. B&w line drawings and color-separated art OK. Pays $600 minimum, inside color; $100-300, inside b&w. Buys 120 illustrations annually.

PUBLICATIONS CO., 1220 Maple Ave., Los Angeles CA 90015. Contact: George Dubow. House organ syndicate. Buys all rights. Pays on acceptance. Previously published work OK. Reports in 2 weeks.
Cartoons: Buys general and political themes. Pays $5-10. Buys 8-10 cartoons per month.
Illustrations: Buys spot drawings. Line drawings, and pen and ink OK. Pays $5-10.

THE QUARTER HORSE OF THE PACIFIC COAST, Box 254822, Sacramento CA 95825. Editor-in-Chief: Jill Scopinich. Monthly; 8½x11"; 150 pages. Offset. Estab: 1963. Circ: 7,800. For horse breeders, trainers and owners interested in performance, racing and showing; quarter horses only. Buys first, reprint, all and simultaneous rights. Pays on acceptance. Previously published and simultaneous submissions OK "if we are notified of this." No photocopies. Query with samples. SASE.
Cartoons: Buys themes on horses. Single panel OK. Submit finished art. Washes OK. Pays $5-10. Buys 12 cartoons annually. Reports in 4 weeks.

THE QUILL, 35 E. Wacker Dr., Chicago IL 60601. Contact: Charles Long. "Magazine for journalists about the practice of journalism — newspapers, radio/TV news, magazines, freelance writing and journalism education and the campus press." Pays on publication. Query with tearsheets or original ink drawings. Sample copy available.
Illustrations: Buys cover art, spot drawings and inside illustrations on assignment. Pays $25+. Reports in 5 days.

QUILT WORLD, Box 338, Chester MA 01011. Editor: Barbara Hall Pedersen. Bimonthly; 64 pages. Offset. Estab: 1976. Circ: 100,000. For those interested in patchwork and quiltmaking. Buys all rights. Pays on publication. Previously published work OK. No photocopied or simultaneous submissions. Query with samples. SASE. Free sample copy.
Cartoons: Buys quilt-related themes. Single panel OK. Submit finished art. Line drawings OK. Pays $15. Buys 12 cartoons annually. Reports in 8 weeks.
Illustrations: Carol Pedersen, art director. Buys original quilt designs, patterns drafted from antique quilts and some illustrations. B&w line drawings OK. Pays $5 minimum. Buys 12 designs annually. Reports in 8 weeks.
Special Needs: Christmas-related designs, cartoons and illustrations featuring quilts for Christmas issue.

RADIO-ELECTRONICS, 200 Park Ave. S., New York NY 10003. (212)777-6400. Editor-in-Chief: Larry Steckler. Managing Editor: Arthur Kleiman. Monthly; 8½x13"; 124 pages. Offset. Circ: 176,000. Buys first and all rights. Pays on acceptance. Previously published work OK. No photocopied or simultaneous submissions. Mail artwork. SASE. Free sample copy.

Cartoons: Buys themes on electronics, service hi-fi, computers and TV games. Single panel OK. Submit finished art. Washes OK. Pays $15 minimum, b&w. Buys 2 cartoons per issue. Reports in 1 week.

RAILROAD MODEL CRAFTSMAN, Box 700, Newton NJ 07860. (201)383-3355. Editor: Tony Koester. Monthly. Interested in 5x7 or larger cartoons, rough art and b&w drawings. Buys all rights. Inquire about rates. Uses line drawings of railroad equipment and model railroad layouts requiring extensive firsthand knowledge of real/scale model railroading. Occasionally uses oil paintings of railroad subjects as tie-in with feature material.

RAILWAY JOURNAL, Brotherhood of Maintenance of Way Employees, 12050 Woodward Ave., Detroit MI 48203. Art Buyer: R.J. Williamson. Monthly. Not copyrighted. Buys spot drawings, any medium, rough. Pays $5 minimum on acceptance. Will consider previously published work. Send samples. Reports in 6-8 weeks.

RAMADA REFLECTIONS, East-West Network, Inc., 5900 Wilshire Blvd., #300, Los Angeles CA 90036. (213)937-5810. Editor: James Clark. Senior Art Director: Chris Mossman. Monthly. Buys all rights. Query with resume. Sample copy $1.
Illustrations: Buys cover art and spot drawings on assignment. Pays $25 minimum, spot art; $400, full-color cover. Reports in 4 weeks.

THE RANGEFINDER, Rangefinder Publishing Company, Box 66925, Los Angeles CA 90066. Contact: Janet Marshall Victor. Monthly. Trade magazine for professional photographers. Readership includes commercial, editorial, advertising, industrial, portrait, scientific and freelance photographers. Buys cartoons on photography. Uses b&w line art for 1-column (2¼ wide) format. Pay is $5 for first serial rights. Will consider cartoons previously published. Reports in 2 weeks. Sample copy $1.

REACH OUT POETRY QUARTERLY, 204 Rome-Hilliard Rd., Columbus OH 43228. Editor: R. Lee Rader. "Encourages unknowns." Uses soft touch type material generally. Buys spot drawings, 4x6 maximum, pen and ink, finished art. Pays contributor's copies. Buys first rights. Previously published work OK. Query. Reports in 2-4 weeks. Sample copy $1.

READER'S DIGEST, 200 Park Ave., New York NY 10017. Corporate Art Director: Ken Stuart. Buys cover art and spot drawings. Pays $1,000 cover; $50, spot art. Buys all rights. Query with proofs or samples. SASE. Also buys artwork for books and record albums.

REDBOOK, 230 Park Ave., New York NY 10017. Assigns illustrations.

THE REMINGTON REVIEW, 505 Westfield Ave., Elizabeth NJ 07208. Contact: Art Editor. Semiannual poetry and fiction magazine. Buys first serial rights. Prefers original art. SASE. Reports in 2-3 months. Sample copy $1.
Illustrations: Buys line art for offset reproduction; must be finished. "Would like to see art similar to that used in publications like *Poetry, Kansas Quarterly* and *American Review.*" Pays 2 contributor's copies.

RESIDENT AND STAFF PHYSICIAN, 80 Shore Rd., Port Washington NY 11050. Cartoon Editor: James F. McCarthy. Monthly. For hospital physicians. Pays $15 for cartoons on acceptance. Roughs acceptable. Uses 4-6 per issue on "inside" medical themes. Also buys spots; pays $10-50. Buys all rights. Reports in 2 weeks.

RESPIRATORY THERAPY, Brentwood Publishing Corporation, 825 S. Barrington Ave., Los Angeles CA 90049. Contact: Clay Camburn. Buys b&w spot drawings and full-color paintings. Pays $30, spot art; $175, full-color cover. Pays on acceptance. Buys all rights. Submit published samples. Reports in 30 days.

RETIREMENT LIVING, 150 E. 58th St., New York NY 10022. Editor: Roy Hemming. Associate Editor: Helen Alpert. Monthly. For retirees and pre-retirees, with news and features on financial planning, health, consumerism, housing, living environments, hobbies, crafts, travel and leisure; also personality interviews and how-to features. Buys b&w line drawings, washes and full-color illustrations, color-separated. Rough cartoons acceptable initially. Pays

$10-50 for spot drawing. Pays on publication. Buys all, one-time and first serial rights. Query. Reports in 30 days. Sample copy 93¢.

RIVERSIDE QUARTERLY, Box 14451, University Station, Gainesville FL 32604. Editor-in-Chief: Leland Sapiro. 8½x5½"; 76 pages. Offset. Estab: 1964. Circ: 1,500. For educated audience interested in science fiction and fantasy. Buys all rights, but may reassign rights to artist after publication. Mail artwork. SASE.
Illustrations: Buys cover art, article illustrations and spot drawings on fantasy and science fiction. Submit finished art. India ink, charcoal, block print and pencil OK. Pays contributor's copies. Buys 20 illustrations annually. Reports in 1 week.

ROAD RIDER, Box 678, South Laguna CA 92677. Editor-in-Chief: Roger Hull. Managing Editor: R.L. Carpenter. Monthly; 8½x11"; 96 pages. Offset. Estab: 1969. Circ: 35,000. For cross-section of touring motorcyclists. Buys all rights, but may reassign rights to artist after publication. Pays on publication. No previously published, photocopied or simultaneous submissions. Query with samples. SASE. Free sample copy. Buys illustrations on assignment.
Cartoons: Scott Simpson, editorial assistant. Buys themes on street-touring motorcycling. "Our audience is sophisticated, hence our cartoons must represent motorcycling insights which are virtually impossible to achieve without riding knowledge." Single panel OK. Other formats by assignment only. Submit roughs. Prefers line drawings. Pays $15 minimum. Buys 12-16 cartoons annually. Reports in 3 weeks.
To Break In: Must be knowledgeable, active motorcyclists. Most freelancers will have trouble hitting this market without background experience. "To date, only 1 cartoonist who was not also a rider has been successful here. It should be added that she now owns and rides a bike as a result of our relationship through the magazine."

THE ROCKIES, Box 762, Provo UT 84601. (801)377-0294. Editor: Jim Dangerfield. Readers interested in sports, travel and recreation in the Rocky Mountain area. Needs b&w drawings, cover designs and full-color illustrations (color-separated). Also has special interest in summer vacation and Christmas material. Rates of payment: $5 for spot drawings; $50 for full-color illustration; $100 for cover designs in 4 colors. Buys one-time rights. Previously published work OK. Send resume and samples. Reports in 6-8 weeks. Sample copy $1.

RODEO NEWS, Box 8160, Nashville TN 37207. Managing Editor: Marty Martins. Monthly; 8⅜x11"; 48 pages. Offset. Estab: 1961. Circ: 13,000. For rodeo fans and participants. Buys all rights, but may reassign rights to artist after publication. Pays on acceptance. No previously published, photocopied or simultaneous submissions. Mail artwork. SASE. Free sample copy. Prefers not to reveive "off-color works which would offend a family audience."
Cartoons: Buys rodeo and ranching themes. Single panel OK. Submit finished art. Line drawings and washes OK. Pays $3.50 minimum, b&w. Buys 36 cartoons annually. Reports in 3 weeks.
Illustrations: Buys article illustrations and spot drawings on rodeo action and candid cowboy scenes. B&w line drawings and washes OK. Pays $5 minimum, b&w. Buys 12 illustrations annually. Reports in 3 weeks.

RODEO SPORTS NEWS, 2929 W. 19th Ave., Denver CO 80204. (303)477-5895. Editor-in-Chief: Randy Witte. Published annually; 8¼x10⅞"; 160 pages. Offset. Estab: 1952. Circ: 45,000. For rodeo contestants, fans, producers and past and present members of the Professional Rodeo Cowboys Association. Buys reprint rights. Pays on acceptance. No previously published, photocopied or simultaneous submissions. Mail artwork. SASE. Free sample copy. Also buys advertising art.
Illustrations: Carriellen DeMuth, editor. Buys cover art and inside illustration, rodeo and Western themes. Submit finished art. Cover: color-separated art OK. Inside: b&w line drawings, reflective art and veloxes OK. Minimum payment: $100, color cover; $50, b&w cover; $10, inside b&w. Buys 12 illustrations annually. Reports in 2 weeks.

ROLLING STONE, 78 E. 5th St., New York NY 10022. Art Director: Roger Black. Biweekly tabloid. Focus is American music and culture. Coverage includes music, film, social issues, investigative reporting, books and new lifestyles. Submit samples of spot drawings and illustrations for assignment.

ROSICRUCIAN DIGEST, Rosicrucian Park, San Jose CA 95191. Philosophical journal which features articles on mysticism, science and the arts. Buys drawings. Payment on acceptance (at rates depending on the requirement and work involved). Reports in 3 weeks.

THE ROTARIAN, 1600 Ridge Ave., Evanston IL 60201. Editor: Willmon L. White. Monthly. For business and professional men. Buys all rights. Pays on acceptance. Query. Sample copy available.
Cartoons: Uses 4-5 general situation cartoons per issue. Roughs or finished art. "Avoid sex, national origin, politics." Pays $50 each. Reports in 2-4 weeks.

ROTOR AND WING, PJS Publications, Inc., News Plaza, Peoria IL 61061. Contact: Wayne Mathison. Business helicopter magazine. Buys cartoons and illustrations on assignment. Pays $10-200. Buys all rights. Pays on acceptance. Send samples. Reports in 3-4 weeks.

ROUGH NOTES, 1200 N. Meridian, Indianapolis IN 46204. Managing Editor: Tom McCoy. Monthly. Buys all rights.
Cartoons: Pays $7.50-10 on acceptance for property and casualty insurance, some life insurance and general humor themes. Risque material taboo. Prefers 5x8 or 8x10 finished art. Uses 2-3 cartoons per issue. Mostly line reproduction, some halftone. Reports in 1 week if received during first week of the month.

THE ROYAL NEIGHBOR, Royal Neighbors of America, 230 16th St., Rock Island IL 61201. Editor: Priscilla Ann Curtis. Fraternal, benefit insurance society publication. Considers artwork submitted by mail. Buys one-time rights. Considers previously published work. Sample copy available.

RUDDER, 1515 Broadway, New York NY 10036. Editor: Martin Luray. Monthly for active yachtsmen with all sizes and types of boats. Pays $25-100 on acceptance for finished cartoons. Buys all rights. Reports in 3 weeks.

RUNNER'S WORLD, World Publications, Box 366, Mt. View CA 94040. Art Buyer: Bob Anderson. Buys spot drawings, cartoons and cover designs. "Our readers are participants and we try to use material that shows insight into the sports we cover." Pays $10+. Buys reprint rights. Pays on publication. Reports in 1 week.

RURAL KENTUCKIAN, 4515 Bishop Lane, Louisville KY 40218. Monthly. Published by Kentucky Association of Electric Cooperatives. Buys first rights.
Cartoons: Pays $5 on acceptance for farm, satirical do-it-yourself electrical projects and general themes. Uses about 2 cartoons per issue. Line reproduction. Reports monthly.

SAGA, Gambi Publications, 333 Johnson Ave., Brooklyn NY 11206. (212)456-8600. Editor-in-Chief: David Elrich. Monthly; 8½x11"; 80 pages. Offset. Estab: 1950. Circ: 300,000. Buys all rights, but may reassign rights to artist after publication. Pays on acceptance. No previously published, photocopied or simultaneous submissions. Query with samples or arrange interview. SASE.
Cartoons: Buys themes on current events, environment, family life and politics. Single panel OK. Submit roughs. Halftones and washes OK. Pays $25-50, b&w; $35, 2-color. Buys 25 cartoons annually. Reports in 3 weeks.
Illustrations: Michael Aldinger, art director. Buys cover art, article illustrations and spot drawings. Submit roughs. Cover: color-separated art OK. Inside: b&w line drawings, washes, color-separated and reflective art and veloxes OK. Minimum payment: $250, color cover; $200, inside color. Buys 2 illustrations per issue. Reports in 3 weeks.

SAIL, 38 Commercial Wharf, Boston MA 02110. (617)227-0888. Editor-in-Chief: Keith Taylor. Managing Editor: Patience Wales. Monthly; 8½x11"; 206 pages. Offset. Estab: (present format) 1970. Circ: 141,289. For those interested in sailing. Buys first North American serial rights. Prefers to pay on publication. No previously published or simultaneous submissions. Photocopies OK. Query with samples. SASE. Free sample copy.
Illustrations: Buys article illustrations and spot drawings "usually to go with articles already purchased" on sailing themes. Submit roughs. B&w line drawings and washes OK. Pays $25-150, b&w. Buys 12-20 illustrations annually. Reports in 4 weeks.

SAILING MAGAZINE, 125 E. Main St., Port Washington WI 53074. (414)284-2626. Editor: William P. Schanen III. Monthly. Estab: 1966. 24,000 circulation. Pays $50+, color cover. Buys one-time rights. Previously published work OK. Mail artwork. Reports in 2-3 weeks. Sample copy $1.75.

ST. JOSEPH'S MESSENGER AND ADVOCATE OF THE BLIND, Box 288, Jersey City NJ 07303. Editor-in-Chief: Sister Ursula Maphet. Quarterly; 6x8"; 30 pages. Estab: 1900. Circ: 71,000. For older Catholics, interested in the blind. Buys all rights, but may reassign rights to artists after publication. Pays on acceptance. No photocopies. Previously published and simultaneous submissions OK. Query. SASE. Free sample copy.
Illustrations: Buys cover art and spot drawings on "people situations." Submit finished art. B&w line drawings OK. Pays $20-30, cover. Buys up to 12 illustrations annually. Reports in 3 weeks.

SALES AND MARKETING MANAGEMENT, 633 3rd Ave., New York NY 10017. (212)986-4800. Art Editor: Tom Loria. Biweekly; 8x10⅞; 92 pages. Offset. Estab: 1925. Circ: 45,000. For sales managers. Buys all rights, but may reassign rights to artist after publication. Pays on acceptance. Simultaneous submissions OK. No previously published work or photocopies. Mail artwork. SASE.
Cartoons: Buys themes on sales management and selling. Single panel OK. Submit finished art. Halftones and washes OK. Pays $30-45, b&w. Buys 36 cartoons annually. Reports in 1 week.
Illustrations: Buys spot drawings. Submit finished art. B&w line drawings OK. Pays $10-20. Buys 5 illustrations annually. Reports in 1 week.
Special Needs: Cartoons/illustrations for "On the Road" department on travel tips, restaurant, hotel and resort information for sales managers. Pays $20 per spot; 2 spots per issue.

SALESMAN'S OPPORTUNITY MAGAZINE, 1460 John Hancock Center, Chicago IL 60611. Managing Editor: Jack Weissman. Monthly. For independent salesmen, agents, jobbers, distributors, sales managers, franchise seekers, route salesmen, wagon jobbers, and people seeking an opportunity to make money full or part time. Provides information about direct selling opportunities and business-of-your-own programs. Buys all rights.
Cartoons: Particularly interested in cartoons dealing with sales situations. Pays $5 on publication. Roughs preferred. Reports in 4 weeks.

SALT LICK, Box 1064, Quincy IL 62301. Editor: James Haining. Limited edition literary/art magazine. Buys illustrations and rough cartoons in b&w line drawings and washes. Buys first serial rights. Previously published work OK. Mail artwork. Reports in 2 weeks. Sample copy $1.50. "We are a small press that appears whenever we have the money and material. I suggest anyone interested in submitting work write the editor for a quick state of the press report."

SAMISDAT, Box 1534, San Jose CA 95109. Editor-in Chief: Merritt Clifton. Managing Editor: June Kemp. Monthly; 8½x5½"; 60 pages. Offset. Estab: 1973. Circ: 500. For writers, teachers and anarchists — hard-core literati. Buys first North American serial rights. Pays on publication. Previously published work OK. No photocopied or simultaneous submissions. Query with samples. SASE. Sample copy $1.
Illustrations: Buys cover art, spot drawings and illustrations to accompany fiction and poems. "We prefer high contrast b&w pencil or pen and ink drawings. Art must be easily cut and easy to paste over. Maximum size: 8½x5½". Must be camera-ready." Submit finished art. Pays contributor's copies. Buys 20 illustrations annually. Reports in 2 weeks.

SAN GABRIEL VALLEY MAGAZINE, 835 W. Santa Anita, San Gabriel CA 91776. (213)284-7607. Editor-in-Chief: Joseph Miller. Managing Editor: Theresa Miller. Bimonthly; 5¼x7½"; 48 pages. Offset. Estab: 1976. Circ: 3,000. For upper-middle-class people who dine out often. Buys all rights, but may reassign rights to artist after publication. Pays on publication. Previously published and simultaneous submissions OK. Query with samples. SASE. Free sample copy.
Illustrations: Buys cover art and article illustrations on success themes. Submit roughs. B&w line drawings and veloxes OK. Pays $25-50. Buys 2 illustrations per issue. Reports in 3 weeks.
Special Needs: Uses illustrators for parent organization, Miller Books (success and school textbooks).

SAN JOSE STUDIES, San Jose State University, San Jose CA 95192. (408)277-3460. Editor-in-Chief: Arlene N. Okerlund. Managing Editor: O. C. Williams. Published 3 times annually;

6x9"; 112 pages. Offset. Estab: 1975. Circ: 500. For the college-educated with interdisciplinary interests. Buys first rights. Pays on publication. No previously published, photocopied or simultaneous submissions. Mail artwork. SASE. Sample copy $3.50.
Cartoons: Buys all themes except juvenile in good taste. Single panel OK. Submit finished art. Line drawings and halftones OK. Pays 2 contributor's copies. Buys 6-9 cartoons annually. Reports in 4 weeks.
Illustrations: Buys article illustrations and spot drawings on "anything that engages the intellectual mind." Submit finished art. B&w line drawings OK. Pays 2 contributor's copies. Buys 6-9 illustrations annually. Reports in 4 weeks.

SANDAL PRINTS, 1820 Mt. Elliott Ave., Detroit MI 48207. Editor: Rev. Allen Gruenke. Bimonthly. For people interested in the work of the Capuchins religious order. Contracts individually for b&w drawings. Not copyrighted. Previously published work OK. "Please do not query unless you know the publication's purpose." Pays on acceptance. Reports as soon as possible.

THE SATURDAY EVENING POST, Box 567B, Indianapolis IN 46206. Buys all rights. Pays on publication. Reports in 1 week.
Cartoons: Linda Daniel, cartoon buyer. Buys single and multi-panel cartoons that are "good humor without ethnic slants. We're tired of wives wrecking cars in the garage and psychiatric patients; will look at anything else." Submit finished art in 8½x11 size. Pays $25-200.
Illustrations: Contact: Edward Cortese. Buys cover art and illustrations on assignment. Pays $400-2,000, cover. Submit original art or published samples. SASE.

SATURDAY REVIEW, 1290 Avenue of the Americas, New York NY 10019. Art Buyer: J. Adel. Biweekly. Magazine on international affairs, the arts, science, education and literary matters. Buys first rights. Pays on publication. Reports in 4 weeks.
Cartoons: Dorothy Re, editor. Uses cartoons on subtle, timely, topical ideas. Line or halftone. No panels or series. Pays $100.
Illustrations: Buys inside illustrations and spot drawings. Pays $75-150, illustration; $25, spot drawing.

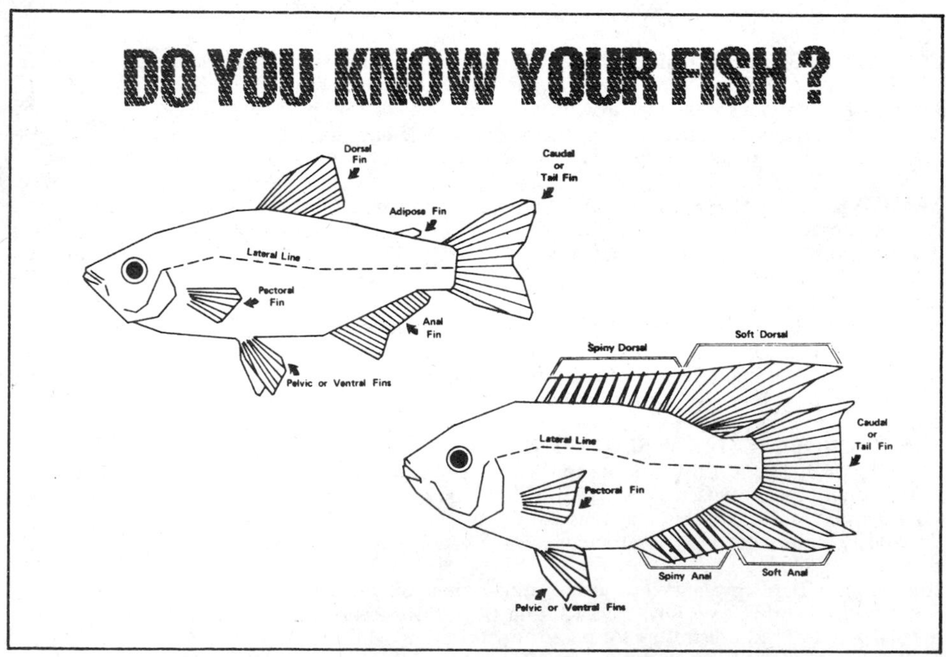

Approximately 40 illustrations, such as this line drawing by Robert Christenson, are purchased annually by *Aquarium News*. Payment for b&w illustrations ranges from $25-40; while hobby-related aquarium cartoons pay $15-25.

SCANDINAVIAN REVIEW, 127 E. 73rd St., New York NY 10021. Editor-in-Chief: Howard E. Sandum. Quarterly; 6¾x9½"; 112 pages. Offset. Estab: 1913. Circ: 6,500. For people of Scandinavian descent or interested in contemporary Sandinavia. Negotiates rights purchased. Pays on publication. Photocopied and simultaneous submissions OK. Prefers unpublished, translated work. Mail artwork SASE.
Cartoons: Should relate to contemporary Scandinavian life, history or literature. All formats OK. Submit finished art. Halftones OK. Negotiates payment. Reports in 4 weeks.
Illustrations: Buys cover art and article illustrations. Submit finished art. Cover: color-separated art OK. Inside: b&w line drawings and color-separated art OK. Negotiates payment. Reports in 4 weeks.

SCHOLASTIC EDITOR, 720 Washington Ave. SE, University of Minnesota, Minneapolis MN 55414. Editor: Jeanne Buckeye. Published 8 times annually. Contains "how-to articles for student staffs and faculty advisers of high school and college student publications (yearbooks, newspapers and magazines)." Summer Workshop issue published in April. Submit seasonal material 3 months in advance. Buys all rights, but will reassign rights to artist after publication. Will look at tearsheets or photostats as examples of style. Sample copy available.
Illustrations: Buys rough spot drawings and cover designs. "If we are interested, an article will be assigned, with a rough sketch due by a certain date and final art due later." Artist receives byline, mugshot and bio if available. Pays 5 contributor's copies. Reports in 3 weeks.

THE SCHOOL MUSICIAN DIRECTOR AND TEACHER, c/o The School Musician, Inc., Box 245, Joliet IL 60434. Editor/Publisher: Forrest L. McAllister. Educational school music magazine. Published 10 times annually. "We like to have an artist put a price on his material when sending it to us for consideration. We are only interested in material that has a musical motif." Rough or finished art (cover design in 2 colors), pen and ink, line and wash and cartoons OK. Pays $3-5 on acceptance for cartoons. Has departments on instruments, music/book reviews, audiovisual aids, choirs, "Smart Ideas" (new products), and "They are Making America Musical" (salute to an outstanding conductor). Buys all rights. Reports in 30 days.

SCIENCE AND CHILDREN, National Science Teachers Association, 1742 Connecticut Ave. NW, Washington DC 20009. (202)265-4150. Editor-in-Chief: Phyllis Marcuccio. Published 8 times annually; 8½x11"; 40 pages. Offset. Estab: 1963. Circ: 23,000. For elementary science teachers, teacher educators, administrators and other elementary school personnel. Buys all rights. No previously published or simultaneous submissions. Photocopies OK. Query with samples. SASE. Free sample copy.
Cartoons: Buys educational and environmental themes. Single panel OK. Submit finished art. Halftones and washes OK. Pays $10-100, b&w; $15-150, color. Buys 2-3 cartoons annually. Reports in 1 week.
Illustrations: Buys article illustrations and spot drawings. Submit roughs. B&w line drawings, washes and color-separated art OK. Minimum payment: $100, b&w cover; $150, color cover; $15, inside b&w; $25, inside color. Buys 90-100 illustrations annually. Reports in 2 weeks.

THE SCIENCE TEACHER, 1742 Connecticut Ave. NW, Washington DC 20009. Editor-in-Chief: Rosemary Amidei. Managing Editor: Molly Ruzicka. Published 9 times annually; 8½x11"; 64 pages. Offset. Estab: 1933. Circ: 20,000. For high school science teachers. Buys all rights, but may reassign rights to artist after publication. Pays on acceptance. No previously published, photocopied or simultaneous submissions. Query with samples. SASE.
Cartoons: Buys themes on education, the environment and humor through youth. Single or double panel OK. Submit finished art. Halftones OK. Pays $10-15. Buys 1 cartoon per issue. Reports in 4 weeks.
Illustrations: Buys cover art, article illustrations and spot drawings on science and education. Submit roughs. Cover: b&w line drawings, washes and color-separated art OK. Inside: b&w line drawings and reflective art OK. Pays $35-75, b&w cover; $50-100, color cover; $15-50, inside b&w; $25-50, inside color. Buys 3 illustrations per issue. Reports in 4 weeks.

SEA MAGAZINE, 1499 Monrovia Ave., Newport Beach CA 92663. Editor-in-Chief: Chris Caswell. Monthly; 8⅛x10¾"; 180 pages. Offset. Estab: 1907. Circ: 160,000. For well-educated pleasure boating (power and sail) enthusiasts. Buys first North American serial rights. Pays on publication. No previously published, photocopied or simultaneous submissions. Query. SASE. Free sample copy.

Illustrations: Buys article illustrations and spot drawings on boating, cruising and racing; also needs technical and cutaway drawings. "We need good technical artists as well as illustrators who can work backwards from an ms to produce artwork." Submit roughs. B&w line drawings, washes, color-separated and reflective art OK. Pays $100 minimum, color; $15-500, b&w. Buys 20-30 illustrations annually. Reports in 3 weeks.
Special Needs: Pays $10 per hour for brochure design, sales tools and advertising rate cards.

SEA POWER, 818 18th St. NW, Washington DC 20006. (202)298-9282. Editor: James D. Hessman. Monthly. For naval personnel and civilians. Copyrighted. Accepts drawings and 8x10 color illustrations. Will consider previously published work. Does not pay for most illustrations. Query with resume. Sample copy available.

SEARCH & RESCUE, Box 153, Montrose CA 91020. Managing Editor: Mike Sweeney. Quarterly; 8½x11"; 32 pages. Offset. Estab: 1973. Circ: 21,000. For adventurers of all ages. Buys one-time rights. Pays on publication. Previously published, photocopied and simultaneous submissions OK. Query with samples. SASE. Sample copy $2.25.
Cartoons: Buys current event, environment and safety outdoors themes. Single panel OK. Submit roughs. Line drawings OK. Minimum payment: $20, b&w; $30, color. Buys 8 cartoons annually. Reports in 2 weeks.
Illustrations: Buys cover art and article illustrations on survival, search and rescue. Submit roughs. All media OK. Minimum payment: $30, inside; $20, cover. Buys 16 illustrations annually. Reports in 2 weeks.

SEATTLE TIMES MAGAZINE, Box 70, Seattle WA 98111. (206)622-0300. Editor: Larry Anderson. Weekly; tabloid; 16 pages. Letterpress. Estab: 1902. Circ: 310,000. For readers with above-average incomes and education. Buys first rights. Pays on publication. Previously published work OK. No photocopied or simultaneous submissions. Query with samples. SASE. Free sample copy.
Illustrations: Buys cover art and article illustrations on Pacific Northwest subjects. Submit roughs. Cover: color-separated art OK. Inside: pen and ink OK. Minimum payment: $125, color cover; $20-30, inside b&w. Buys 20-30 illustrations, "mainly covers," annually. Reports in 1 week.

THE SECOND WAVE, Box 344, Cambridge A, Cambridge MA 02139. Contact: Editors. Quarterly; 8½x11"; 48 pages. Offset. Estab: 1971. Circ: 3,000-5,000. For radical feminists. Buys all rights. Previously published, photocopied and simultaneous submissions OK. Mail artwork. SASE. Sample copy $1.25.
Cartoons: Buys themes on women's lives, needs and experiences. "Show honesty and humor within feminist context." Single panel OK. Submit finished art. Line drawings and halftones OK. Pays contributor's copies. Buys 2 cartoons annually. Reports in 2 months.
Illustrations: Buys cover art, article illustrations and spot drawings on women and their lives. Submit finished art. B&w line drawings OK. Pays contributor's copies. Buys 30 illustrations annually. Reports in 2 months.

SECURITY MANAGEMENT, 2000 K St. NW, Suite 651, Washington DC 20006. (202)331-7887. Editor-in-Chief: Shari Mendelson. Bimonthly; 8½x11"; 48-56 pages. Offset. Estab: 1957. Circ: 10,000. For security managers who protect assets, personnel and information of organizations. Buys all rights, but may reassign rights to artist after publication. Previously published and simultaneous submissions OK. No photocopies. Query with samples or mail artwork. SASE. Sample copy $2. Pays $25 minimum for workshop brochures.
Cartoons: Buys themes on security, safety, fire prevention and management. All formats OK. Submit finished art. Halftones and washes OK. Pays $5 minimum, b&w. Reports in 3 weeks.
Illustrations: Buys cover art, article illustrations and spot drawings on security, fire protection, safety and management. Submit roughs. All media OK. Minimum payment: $50, b&w cover or inside color; $75, color cover; $20, inside b&w. Reports in 3 weeks.

SELF-DEFENSE WORLD, World Publications, Box 366, Mt. View CA 94040. Art Buyer: Bob Anderson. Buys cover designs, spot drawings and cartoons. "Our readers are participants and we try to use material that shows insight into the sports that we cover." Pays $10+. Buys reprint rights. Pays on publication. Reports in 1 week.

SERVICE SHOP, 1715 Expo Lane, Indianapolis IN 46224. Editor-in-Chief: Steve Bernard. Monthly; 8½x11"; 24 pages. Offset. Estab: 1975. Circ: 8,000. For owners and managers of consumer electronics sales and service firms. Buys first rights. Pays on acceptance. No previously published, photocopied or simultaneous submissions. Mail artwork. SASE. Free sample copy.
Cartoons: Buys themes on electronic sales and service. Single panel OK. Submit finished art. Line drawings only. Pays $10 maximum. Reports in 2 weeks. "Interested in cartoons that focus on the foibles and fallacies of the TV business — anything that helps our readers laugh at and with themselves and see their problems as common to everyone in the industry." Must have captions.
Illustrations: Buys cover art, article illustrations and spot drawings on assignment. Submit finished art. B&w line drawings OK. Pays $30-60, cover; $10-15, inside. Reports in 2 weeks.

SEVEN STARS, Box 33512, San Diego CA 92103. Editor-in-Chief: Richard A. Soos, Jr. Monthly; 6x9"; 40 pages. Offset. Estab: 1975. Circ: 800-1,000. For poets and poetry readers. Buys first and reprint rights. Pays on acceptance. No previously published or simultaneous submissions. Photocopies OK. Query with samples. SASE. Sample copy $1.50. "Don't be afraid to send anything, no matter how crazy it looks."
Cartoons: Buys current event and poetry themes. All formats OK. Submit roughs. Line drawings OK. Pays $1-5. Reports in 2 weeks.
Illustrations: Buys cover art and spot drawings on themes of the artist's preference, with exception of holiday themes. Submit finished art. B&w line drawings OK. Pays $1-5, cover; 50¢-$2, inside. Buys 1-2 illustrations per issue. Reports in 2 weeks.

73 MAGAZINE, Peterborough NH 03458. Publisher: Wayne Green. For amateur radio operators and experimenters. Buys all rights. Pays on acceptance. Sample copy $2.
Illustrations: Buys cover art and inside illustrations on amateur radio themes. Submit rough line drawings for assignment as oil, watercolor or pastel covers. Pays $5-20, spot art; $75 per page, finished art. Reports in 2 weeks.

SEX ON SEX, c/o Monarch Publications, Inc., Box 5334, Houston TX 77012. (713)641-0851. Editor-in-Chief: Rick McMilen. Managing Editor: Reg Manner. Monthly; 8⅛x10⅞"; 100 pages. Offset. Estab: 1973. Circ: 60,000. Buys all rights. Pays on acceptance. No previously published, photocopied or simultaneous submissions. SASE. "Art must be funny, sexy and naughty. We're not a market for the beginner, but we'll pay $5 for poorly drawn good gags, and finish them in shop."
Cartoons: Buys erotic themes. All formats OK. Submit roughs or finished art. All media OK. Pays $5-15 per page, b&w; $20-50 per page, b&w comic strip. Buys 100 cartoons per issue. Mail cartoons. Reports in 2 weeks.
Illustrations: Buys cover art, article illustrations and spot drawings on erotica. Submit roughs or finished art. Cover: oils, airbrush and line drawings OK. Inside: b&w line drawings and washes OK. Pays $5-50, inside b&w. Buys 72 illustrations annually. Query with ideas. Reports in 2 weeks.

SHOOTING TIMES, PJS Publications, Inc., News Plaza, Peoria IL 61061. Contact: Wayne Mathison. For those interested in guns, hunting, ammunition, reloading and ballistics. Buys cartoons and illustrations on assignment. Pays $10-200. Buys all rights. Pays on acceptance. Send samples. Reports in 3-4 weeks.

SHOPPING CENTER WORLD, 461 8th Ave., New York NY 10001. Editor: Eric Peterson. "We cover all aspects of the retail chain and shopping center industry. For those in the industry or suppliers to it." Monthly. Buys b&w line drawings and 8x10" cartoons. Prefers rough cartoons. Pays $25, spot drawings. Pays on acceptance. Buys all rights; first serial rights for cartoons. Will consider work previously published. Mail artwork. Sample copy available. Reports as soon as possible.

SIGNATURE, 260 Madison Ave., New York NY 10016. Art Director: David Stech. Executive Editor: Josh Eppinger. Monthly. For Diners Club members — urban, affluent, traveled businessmen. Prefers New York area artists. Payment is $50-100, spot drawings; $350-500, full-color illustrations. Copyrighted. Payment on acceptance. Query with resume and arrange interview to show portfolio. Reports in 2 weeks. Sample copy available.

SIMMENTAL SCENE, Suite 120, 310 9th Ave. SW, Calgary, Alberta Canada T2P 1K5. Editor-in-Chief: Sandy Sharp. Monthly; 8⅜x10¾; 60-72 pages. Offset. Estab: 1973. Circ: 6,000. For cattle producers and farmers; education limited in older readers; younger readers usually agricultural college graduates. Not copyrighted. Pays on publication. No previously published, photocopied or simultaneous submissions. Query with samples. SASE. Free sample copy.
Illustrations: Keith J. Wilson, editor. Buys cover art, article illustrations, and spot drawings on "rural and cattle scenes to accompany animal health and research articles." Submit finished art. Cover: b&w line drawings and color-separated art OK. Inside: b&w line drawings OK. Pays $100-150, b&w cover; $150-250, color cover; $10-100, inside b&w. "We haven't bought any illustrations in the past, but we are open to new artists and materials now." Reports in 4 weeks.
Special Needs: Artwork for animal health, herd management and farm machinery issues. Also employs artists for designing small ads and full-color brochures.
To Break In: "Read old issues and show us how you would improve on the work we have done. If you have good ideas and are talented, we'll look for places to use you."

SKATING, Sears Crescent, Suite 500, City Hall Plaza, Boston MA 02108. Editor-in-Chief: Gregory R. Smith. Art Editor: Valerie Bessette. Monthly, November-June; 6x9"; 56 pages. Offset. Estab: 1923. Circ: 30,000. For members of United States Figure Skating Association. Buys all rights, but may reassign rights to artist after publication. Pays on publication. Previously published work OK. No photocopies or simultaneous submissions. Mail artwork. SASE. Free sample copy.
Cartoons: Buys ice skating themes. Single panel OK. Submit finished art; line drawings only. Pays $10-25. Buys 4 cartoons annually. Reports in 3 weeks.
Illustrations: Buys cover art, article illustrations and spot drawings on figure skating and skaters. Submit finished art. B&w line drawings OK. Pays $10-25. Buys 8 illustrations annually. Reports in 3 weeks.

SKI MAGAZINE, 380 Madison Ave., New York NY 10017. Editor: Richard Needham. Published 7 times annually. For new and expert skiers. Buys b&w line drawings, washes and 8x10" cartoons. Submit roughs. Artwork usually assigned. Cartoons should be ski-related. Pays $10-15, spot art; $15-300, full-color art. Buys one-time rights; first serial rights for cartoons. Will consider material previously published "so long as material has not appeared in similar or competing publications and we're notified as to prior publication." Pays on acceptance for artwork; on publication for cartoons. Mail artwork. Reports immediately. Sample copy available.

SKIER, 22 High St., Brattleboro VT 05301. Contact: Editor. Issued 8 times annually, November-April, and July and September. For members of the Eastern Ski Association. Publishes articles dealing with snow skiing. Buys first rights. Pays on publication. Sample copy available.
Cartoons: Pays up to $15 for skiing themes. Avoid injuries as subject. Rough minimum 2x5" OK. Offset reproduction. Reports in 2 weeks.

SKIING, 1 Park Ave., New York NY 10016. Editor-in-Chief: Alfred Greenberg. Published 7 times annually; 8¼x10⅞"; 200-250 pages. Letterpress. Circ: 467,000. Buys all rights. Pays on acceptance. Arrange interview. Free sample copy.
Cartoons: Marie Hickman, editor. Buys skiing themes. Single panel OK. Submit finished art. Halftones and washes OK. Buys 35 cartoons annually. Reports in 4 weeks.
Illustrations: Ed Sobel, editor. Buys article illustrations and spot drawings on skiing. Submit roughs. B&w line drawings and washes OK. Pays $50-350. Buys 3-4 illustrations per issue. Reports in 1 week.

SKIN DIVER MAGAZINE, 8490 Sunset Blvd., Los Angeles CA 90069. Art Director: Art Smith. Monthly. Copyrighted. 150,000 circulation. Buys drawings, sketches, charts, maps, paintings and cartoons related to skin diving, equipment and personalities. Will consider previously published work. Mail artwork. Payment on publication. Reports in 1-4 weeks.

SMALL POND, 10 Overland Dr., Stratford CT 06497. Editor-in-Chief: Napoleon St. Cyr. Published 3 times annually; 5½x8"; 38 pages. Offset. Estab: 1964. Circ: 300. Primarily for college students and graduates interested in poetry. Buys all rights, but may reassign rights to artist after publication. Pays on publication. No previously published or simultaneous submissions. Query. SASE. Sample copy $1.25.

Illustrations: Buys cover art and spot drawings featuring life/nature in and around small ponds. Submit finished art. B&w line drawings and washes OK. Pays 2 contributor's copies. Buys 6-12 illustrations annually. Reports in 1 week.

SMALL WORLD, Volkswagen of America, Englewood Cliffs NJ 07632. (201)894-6314. Editor: Burton Unger. Quarterly; 6x9"; 24 pages. Offset. Estab: 1962. Circ: 400,000. For Volkswagen owners. Buys all rights. Pays on acceptance. Previously published work and photocopies OK. No simultaneous submissions. Query with samples. SASE. Free sample copy.
Cartoons: Buys themes on Volkswagens and their owners. All formats OK. Submit roughs. Halftones and washes OK. Pays $15 minimum. Buys 10 cartoons annually. Reports in 6 weeks.
Illustrations: Buys cover art and article illustrations to accompany articles. Submit finished art. Cover: color-separated art OK. Inside: b&w line drawings and color-separated art OK. Minimum payment: $250, color cover; $15, inside. Buys 120 illustrations annually. Reports in 6 weeks.

SNOTRACK MAGAZINE, 225 E. Michigan Ave., Milwaukee WI 53202. Editor: Bill Vint. Published 6 times during the winter. Buys first-time rights. Pays on acceptance. Guidelines and sample copy available.
Cartoons: "Official publication of United States Snowmobile Association, so use of USSA in cartoons is sometimes a good idea. Racing themes are best, but other topics are welcome. Our taboos are drinking, reckless conduct, anything that degrades a sport we're trying to upgrade. Our audience frowns on poking at serious problems. Understanding the problems and finding the real humor in snowmobiling (there is a lot of it) takes a definite touch." Prefers pen and ink drawings. Pays $15-25. Reports in 30 days.

SOARING, Soaring Society of America, Box 66071, Los Angeles CA 90066. Editor: Doug Lamont. Monthly. 17,000 circulation. "We are a low-budget magazine and depend on Society members for art, but I'd like to have the names of some artists to whom I could send an ms and description of what we need and figure on getting the work back in time for the next month's issue." Buys one-time rights. Pays on publication. Previously published work OK. Send published samples. Sample copy $1.10.
Illustrations: "Interested mostly in custom illustrations for articles. Readership is nuts and bolts oriented. We are leery of nonrepresentational art, though not adamant. We receive many flight stories which call for illustration. Humorous articles offer opportunity for quick sketch or cartoon type treatment. Technical cutaway drawing for display of aircraft very desirable." Pen and ink, line and wash art, rough or finished OK. Payment for inside illustrations negotiable; $40+ for cover. Reports immediately.

SOCCER AMERICA, Box 9393, Berkeley CA 94709. (415)549-1414. Publisher: Clay Berling. Editor-in-Chief: Lynn Berling. Weekly; 8½x11"; 32 pages. Offset. Estab: 1971. Circ: 4,000. For soccer fans of all ages including players, coaches, managers and referees. Buys first rights. Pays on publication. Previously published work and simultaneous submissions OK. No photocopies. Query with samples. SASE. Free sample copy.
Cartoons: Buys soccer themes. All formats OK. Submit finished art. Halftones and washes OK. Pays $5, inside b&w; $15, b&w cover. Buys 50 cartoons annually. Reports in 4 weeks.
Illustrations: Buys cover art, article illustrations, spot drawings and "editorial statements" on soccer. Submit finished art. Cover: b&w line drawings, washes, reflective art and veloxes OK. Inside: b&w line drawings and veloxes OK. Pays $5, inside b&w; $15, b&w cover. Buys 100 illustrations annually. Reports in 4 weeks.
Special Needs: Artwork for issues on: pro-season preview — March; camp directories — April; gifts and equipment — October; and the holidays — December.

SOCCER CORNER, 16200 Ventura Blvd., Encino CA 91436. (213)981-2317. Managing Editor: Grahame Jones. Art Editor: Maurice Goldman. Monthly; 8⅜x10⅞"; 64 pages. Offset. Estab: 1977. For all levels of soccer enthusiast, from professional, collegiate, olympic, to youth soccer organizations. Buys all rights. Pays on publication. No previously published or simultaneous submissions. Photocopies OK. Query with samples. SASE. Free sample copy.
Cartoons: Buys soccer themes. Single and double panel OK. Submit finished art. Halftones and washes OK. Pays $25-50, color; $6-10, b&w. Buys 7 cartoons annually. Reports in 3 weeks.
Illustrations: Buys cover art and article illustrations on soccer. Submit finished art. Cover: color-separated and reflective art OK. Inside: b&w line drawings, washes, color-separated and

reflective art OK. Pays $50, cover; $25-50, inside color; $6-10, inside b&w. Buys 7 illustrations annually. Reports in 3 weeks.

SOCCER WORLD, World Publications, Box 366, Mt. View CA 94040. Art Buyer: Bob Anderson. Buys cover designs, spot drawings and cartoons. "Our readers are participants and we try to use material that shows insight into the sports that we cover." Pays $10+. Buys reprint rights. Pays on publication. Reports in 1 week.

SOLDIERS, Building 2, Door 11, Cameron Station, Alexandria VA 22314. Contact: Editor. U.S. Army publication aimed at the under-30 soldier. Not copyrighted. Circ: 216,000. Uses pen and ink drawings, cartoons and full-color covers. Pays $10, drawings; covers, $100-250. Cover designs should not be submitted without prior coordination. Acknowledges submissions immediately, but may hold them 30-60 days. Payment on acceptance. Sample copy and artist's guide available.

SOLID WASTES MANAGEMENT, 461 8th Ave., New York NY 10001. (212)239-6200. Editor: Kevin Lynd. Monthly; 8½x11". 22,000 circulation. For refuse industry operators, municipal officials and consulting engineers. Cartoons may be submitted by mail. Pays $10. Buys all rights. Reports immediately. Sample copy $1.

SOUTH CAROLINA WILDLIFE, Box 167, Columbia SC 29202. Editor: John Culler. Published bimonthly by South Carolina Wildlife and Marine Resources Dept. Deals with wildlife, outdoor recreation, natural history and environmental concerns. Not copyrighted. Particularly interested in wildlife art. Buys b&w line drawings, washes, full-color illustrations and finished cartoons. Pays on acceptance. Will consider previously published work. Mail artwork. Reports in 2 weeks. Sample copy available.

SOUTHWESTERN MUSICIAN, Box 9908, Houston TX 77015. Editor: J. F. Lenzo. Monthly, August-May. For music educators in Texas. Buys all rights. Pays on acceptance. Reports in 30 days.
Cartoons: Buys music themes. Pays $5-10 for finished b&w art with caption.
Illustrations: Buys cover art and spot drawings. Submit roughs or finished art. "Finished art must be camera-ready; 2-, 3-, or 4-color designs OK." Pays $5, spot drawing; $50, cover design.

SOYBEAN DIGEST, Box 158, Hudson IA 50643. (319)988-3295. Editor: James Bramblett. Primarily for soybean farmers but includes entire soybean industry. Buys b&w line drawings, washes, cover designs and full-color illustrations. 8½x11" minimum size. Monthly. Buys all rights and pays on acceptance. Query. Reports as soon as possible. Sample copy available.

SPAFASWAP, 1070 Ahern, La Puente CA 91746. Editor: Lois J. Long. Poetry magazine. Bimonthly. Buys b&w drawings, cover designs and cartoons; 5½x8½". Pays contributor's copies. Previously published work OK. Query. Sample copy available.

SPARKS, Society of Wireless Pioneers, Box 530, Santa Rosa CA 95402. Editor: William A. Breniman. For active and retired radio-telegraph men who handle(d) communications with ships and at shore stations; included are military, commercial, aeronautical and governmental communications personnel. "Since many have earned their living aboard ships as 'Sparks,' we like to bring a nautical flavor to our pages." Buys b&w line drawings and cartoons. pays $5+, drawings; rates open, cartoons. Pays on acceptance. Buys reprints.

SPEAK OUT MAGAZINE, Box 737, Stamford CT 06904. (203)357-9591. Editor: Agnes D'Ottavio. Poetry publication; "an unveiling of social and moral injustice." Buys finished line drawings, cover designs and 2x3" or 3x4" cartoons on ecology, modern city vs. old city theme, ghetto scenes, the aged and infirm, poverty, prisons and mental institutions. No color work. Pays in copies. Copyrighted. Query for topic ideas. SASE. Reports in 12 weeks.

SPECIALTY SALESMAN AND BUSINESS OPPORTUNITIES MAGAZINE, 307 N. Michigan Ave., Chicago IL 60601. Editor: J.S. Taylor. Subject matter should deal with "direct customer-salesperson sales situations." Buys pen and ink finished art and cartoons. Pays $5, cartoons. Buys all rights. Previously published work OK. Reports in 3-4 weeks. Sample copy available.

SPERRY NEW HOLLAND NEWS, Sperry New Holland Division, Sperry Rand Corporation, New Holland PA 17557. Editor: Michael A. Balas. Issued 10 times annually. For dairy and beef farmers and others interested in grassland farmino.
Cartoons: Pays on publication. Humorous situations must not be cynical or touch on farmer's problems or differences from his city cousin. Pen and ink OK. Reports in 2 weeks.

THE SPIRIT, 601 Market St., Ste. Genevieve MO 63670. Art Buyer: Bob Hammack. Official publication of the Charles A. Lindbergh Association. Buys all rights, but will reassign to artist if requested. Pays on publication. Reports in 4-6 weeks.
Illustrations: "We use mostly material from unpublished sources, but would like to see composite art for cover work. We also need designs for envelopes commemorating anniversaries related to the career of Charles A. Lindbergh. As many as 10 designs (or more) per year chosen from submitted material. Artist eligible for plaque for best original design appearing in the magazine during the year. We also work to assist artists interested in selling to small businesses in the area." Pays $5 for pen and ink spot drawings; $10+ for cover design in 2 colors.

"SPIRIT OF 375", Seagram & Sons, Inc., 800 3rd Ave., New York NY 10022. Editor: Irving Babbitt. Quarterly for employees. Not copyrighted. Sample copy available.
Cartoons: Pays $10 on acceptance for office-oriented cartoons. Uses 4 finished cartoons annually.

STAG, 575 Madison Ave., New York NY 10022. Editor-in-Chief: Noah Sarlat. Managing Editor: Halsey Munson. Monthly; 8x11"; 96 pages. Offset. Estab: 1945. Circ: 175,000. For blue-collar readers. Buys all rights, but may reassign rights to artist after publication. Pays on acceptance. Previously published work OK. No photocopied or simultaneous submissions. SASE.
Cartoons: Buys themes on current events, erotica, politics, sports and popular hobbies. Single panel OK; verticals to run 3x2¼"; horizontals to run 2½-4½x4⅝". Submit finished art. Line drawings, halftones and washes OK. Pays $15 minimum, b&w. Buys 150 cartoons annually. Mail cartoons. Reports in 1 month. "Avoid over-detailing and techniques which limit the ways and sizes in which a cartoon can be used."
Illustrations: Irwin Linker, art director. Buys article illustrations, stylized line art and full-color paintings on assignment. Pays $200-300, b&w; $300-400, color. Assigns 30 illustrations annually. Arrange interview.

THE STAMP WHOLESALER, Box 529, Burlington VT 05401. Editor: Lucius Jackson. Buys cartoons on stamp collecting, stamp dealing and postal service. Pays $10 minimum for all rights. Payment on acceptance. Sample copy available.

STATE & COUNTY ADMINISTRATOR, Box 272, Culver City CA 90230. (213)836-5000. Art Director: Hal Bigman. Monthly. For state and county government elected and appointed officials. Circ: 32,000. Buys drawings, full-color illustrations and cartoons. First serial rights bought. Art previously published considered. Payment on publication. Pays $5-10, cartoon. Query. Sample copy available.

STITCH 'N SEW, Box 338, Chester MA 01011. Editor-in-Chief: Barbara Hall Pedersen. Managing Editor: Edward Kutlowski. Bimonthly; 64 pages. Offset. Estab: 1968. Circ: 158,900. For women who like to sew. Buys all rights. Pays on publication "if unsolicited; on completion of assignment, if assigned." No photocopied or simultaneous submissions. Query with samples. SASE. Free sample copy.
Cartoons: Buys sewing themes. Single panel OK. Submit finished art. Line drawings OK. Pays $15-20. Buys 6 cartoons annually. Reports in 8-10 weeks.
Illustrations: Carol Pederson, editor. Buys article illustrations on sewing. Submit finished art. B&w line drawings OK. Pays $5 minimum. Buys 10 illustrations annually. Reports in 8-10 weeks.
Special Needs: For Christmas Bazaar, toy and doll special, needs doll and toy designs, original designs for novel items to make for gifts and bazaar sales. Designer must supply patterns and illustrations or photos. "We have a constant need for original needlecraft designs."
To Break In: "Be prompt, reliable and don't bug the editor. Response to unsolicited material is apt to be slow. We're understaffed, but we do keep our commitments. It would also be helpful to know how quickly an artist can complete an assignment and return it."

STOCK CAR RACING, 1420 Prince St., Alexandria VA 22314. (703)835-5881. Editor-in-Chief: Richard S. Benyo. Managing Editor: Neil Britt. Monthly; 7½x11"; 80 pages. Offset. Estab: 1966. Circ: 100,000. For blue-collar workers interested in autos and auto racing. Buys all rights. Pays on publication. No previously published work. Photocopied and simultaneous submissions OK. Mail artwork. SASE. Sample copy $1.
Cartoons: Buys auto racing themes. All formats OK. Submit roughs or finished art. Line drawings only. Pays $15-50. Buys 36 cartoons annually. Reports in 3 weeks.
Illustrations: Buys article illustrations and spot drawings on auto racing. Submit roughs or finished art. B&w line drawings OK. Pays $15-50. Buys 60 illustrations annually. Reports in 3 weeks.

STONE COUNTRY, 20 Lorraine Rd., Madison NJ 07940. Editor-in-Chief: Judith Neeld. Published 3 times annually; 8½x5½"; 40 pages. Offset. Estab: 1974. Circ: 500. For serious poets and poetry supporters. Buys first North American serial rights. Pays on publication. Previously published work OK. No photocopied or simultaneous submissions. Mail artwork. SASE. Sample copy $1.50.
Illustrations: Pat McCormick, editor. Buys cover art and spot drawings. Must be camera-ready. Cover design can be 8½x5½" or wrap-around 8½x11"; inside drawings no larger than 3x4". "We are interested in abstract as well as representational work. Art students welcome." Submit finished art. B&w line drawings and veloxes OK. Pays $5-10, b&w cover; 1 contributor's copy, inside b&w. Buys 3 covers and up to 20 inside illustrations annually. Reports in 4 weeks.

STORE CHAT, Strawbridge & Clothier, 801 Market St., Philadelphia PA 19105. Editor-in-Chief: Caroline J. Yeager. Monthly; 8½x11"; 16-20 pages. Offset. Estab: 1906. Circ: 10,000. For department store personnel. Not copyrighted. Pays on acceptance. No previously published work or photocopies. Simultaneous submissions OK. Mail artwork. SASE. Free sample copy.
Cartoons: Buys themes on department stores, customers, employees and usual business topics. Single panel OK. Submit finished art. Line drawings OK. Pays $7.50-10. Buys 5-10 cartoons annually. Reports in 2 weeks.

STRAIGHT, 8121 Hamilton Ave., Cincinnati OH 45231. (513)931-4050 ext. 163. Editor: Judy Trotter. Weekly. For Christian teenagers. Estab: 1950. Circ: 142,000. Over 200 pieces of freelance art used each year. Buys b&w line drawings, cover designs and cartoons. Cartoons should feature teenagers as main characters. Assignments made to illustrate stories. Payments are $35, spot drawing; $40, 2-color cover design; $10, cartoon. Buys one-time rights. Pays on acceptance. No previously published work. Query. Reports in 2 weeks. Sample copy available.

STREET CRIES MAGAZINE, 33 Edi Ave., Plainview NY 11803. Editor: Robbie Woliver/Pat Velazquez. Literary and art magazine published 2-3 times annually. Circ: 5,000. Interested in artwork usually passed over by more traditional magazines. Accepts b&w drawings and cover designs. Will consider previously published work. All rights revert to artist. Pays on publication. Query. Reports in 2-4 weeks.

SUCCESS UNLIMITED, 6355 N. Broadway, Chicago IL 60660. Executive Editor: Diana Maxwell. Monthly; digest size; 112 pages. Offset. Estab: 1954. Circ: 180,000. Publishes self-help, motivational material for men and women working in a professional, sales or managerial capacity. Buys all rights, but may reassign rights to artist after publication. Pays on acceptance. Previously published work OK. No photocopied or simultaneous submissions. Mail artwork. SASE. Free sample copy.
Cartoons: Buys success themes. Single panel OK. Submit finished art. Halftones and washes OK. Pays $15-25, b&w. Buys 1 cartoon per issue.

THE SUGARBEET GROWER, 503 Broadway, Fargo ND 58102. Contact: A. Bloomquist. For the sugar industry, particularly the beet sugar industry — agriculture, processing. Buys pen and ink drawings. Pays $25. Not copyrighted. Payment on acceptance. Reports in 10 days. Sample copy available.

THE SUN, Box 4383, Albuquerque NM 87106. Art Buyer: Skip Whitson. Publishes themes on metaphysics, alternative lifestyles, "new age" cooking, natural foods, Oriental philosophy and earth changes. Buys spot drawings, 2½", 5", 7½" or 10" wide, pen and ink. Submit rough or finished art. Previously published work OK. Payment on acceptance. Copyrighted. Send published samples or original art. Reports in 2-3 months.

SUNRISE, Box 271, Macomb IL 61455. Editor: Bill Knight. Monthly. Estab: 1972. Circ: 20,000. For students interested in music and progressive politics. Buys b&w line drawings. Buys first serial rights. Previously published material considered. Pays on publication. Write. Sample copy $1.

SUNWAY PUBLICATION, 21335 Roscoe Blvd., Canoga Park CA 91304. (213)999-4100. Contact: H. Straubing. Bimonthly. For men. Buys all rights to cartoons. No previously published work. Pays $15 on acceptance. Write. Reports in 2 weeks.

SUPER STOCK & DRAG ILLUSTRATED, 1420 Prince St., Alexandria VA 22314. (703)835-5881. Editor-in-Chief: Richard S. Benyo. Managing Editor: Neil Britt. Monthly; 7½x11"; 80

Twelve to 16 cartoons and article illustrations are bought each year by *Dash*, a magazine for church-oriented middle class boys. This illustration, purchased from George Werth, was assigned to accompany an article written by Rick Mould, editor.

pages. Offset. Estab: 1964. Circ: 120,000. For blue-collar workers interested in autos and auto racing. Buys all rights. Pays on publication. No previously published work. Photocopied and simultaneous submissions OK. Mail artwork. SASE. Sample copy $1.
Illustrations: Buys article illustrations and spot drawings on auto racing. Submit roughs or finished art. B&w line drawings OK. Pays $15-50. Buys 48 illustrations annually. Reports in 3 weeks.

SURGICAL BUSINESS, 2009 Morris Ave., Union NJ 07083. Contact: Sid Frier. For manufacturers, distributors and dealers in medical-surgical products. Pays $100-150, 2-color cover; $10, cartoons. Submit original art. Sample copy available.

SWIMMING WORLD, 8622 Bellanca Ave., Los Angeles CA 90045. Editor: Albert Schoenfield. Monthly. For competitors, parents, coaches, administrators and others involved in swimming, diving and water polo. Buys all rights. Reports in 30 days. Sample copy available. Query on illustrations. Pays up to $5 on publication.
Cartoons: Buys themes on diet, body conditioning, medicine as it applies to competitive swimming, nutrition, stroke and diving techniques; developments in pool purification. Uses about 12 cartoons per year. Pays up to $6.

TALES, Box 24226, St. Louis MO 63130. Editors-in-Chief: Barry Glassner/Jonathan Moreno. Quarterly; tabloid; 16 pages. Offset. Estab: 1970. Circ: 10,000. For college students. Not copyrighted. Pays on publication. Previously published work and photocopies OK. No simultaneous submissions. Query with samples. SASE. Sample copy $1. Pays $20 minimum advertising art.
Illustrations: Tina Richter, editor. Buys cover art and article illustrations for short stories. Submit finished art. B&w line drawings OK. Pays contributor's copies. Buys 15 illustrations annually. Reports in 2 months.

TALK MAGAZINE (formerly *Girl Talk*), 380 Madison Ave., New York NY 10017. Cartoon Editor: Faith Garrett. For affluent women in beauty salons. Buys all rights. Pays $20 on publication for cartoons. Finished art preferred. Can be any kind of cartoon that would be found in general women's consumer magazine. Reports in 6-8 weeks. Sample copy available.

TATTOO, Goldenrod Publications, Box 1397, Smyrna GA 30080. Publisher: Scott Goldenrod. Quarterly. For those interested in tattooing. Buys finished art. Pays $10 per page. Pays on publication. Previously published work OK. Query with published samples or original art.

TEENS AND BOYS MAGAZINE, 71 W. 35th St., New York NY 10001. Fashion Editor: Nina Sklansky. Trade magazine.
Illustrations: "Our needs are spontaneous, when they occur from month to month, requiring the services of a fashion illustrator, specializing in teens and boys, ages 5-20. We do not have illustrations every month, but we do prepare ads which require illustrations." Prefers pen and ink, line and wash in 9x12 sizes. Send samples of previously printed work to be kept on file for assignments. Payment on acceptance. Pays $10-25 for spot drawing.

TEENS TODAY, 6401 The Paseo, Kansas City MO 64131. (816)333-7000. Managing Editor: Roy F. Lynn. Weekly; 5½x8¼"; 16 pages. Circ: 67,000. For high school students who attend Church of the Nazarene. Buys all rights. Pays on acceptance. Previously published, photocopied and simultaneous submissions OK. Mail artwork. SASE. Free sample copy. Prefers not to receive artwork with nudes, drugs, or offensive material directed at parents and other adults.
Cartoons: Buys current event, education, environment, family life, humor through youth and religious themes. All formats OK. Submit finished art. Halftones and washes OK. Pays $5-10, b&w. Buys 52 cartoons annually. Reports in 4 weeks.
Illustrations: Buys cover art, article illustrations and spot drawings to accompany articles. Submit finished art. Cover: b&w line drawings, washes and color-separated art OK. Inside: b&w line drawings and washes OK. Pays $15-75, color cover; $10-25, b&w. Buys 52-75 illustrations annually. Reports in 4 weeks.

TELEFLORA SPIRIT, 2400 Compton Blvd., Redondo Beach CA 90278. (213)973-2501. Editor: Jorian Clair. Monthly; 8½x11"; 176 pages. Offset. Estab: 1935. Circ: 14,561. For those in flower shop management. Buys all rights. Pays on acceptance. No previously published or

simultaneous submissions. Photocopies OK as samples. Arrange interview. SASE. Free sample copy.
Illustrations: Carol McDonnell, art director. Buys article illustrations and spot drawings on the flower business and instructive or decorative themes. Submit finished art. B&w line drawings, washes and color-separated art OK. Pays $15-30, inside; $15-75, full page of spot illustrations. Buys 36 illustrations annually. Reports in 1 week.
Special Needs: Uses artists for layout, advertising and brochures. Pays $15 minimum. Contact Miranda Pong.

TENNIS, 495 Westport Ave., Norwalk CT 06856. (203)847-5811. Editor: Shepherd Campbell. Managing Editor: Jeffrey N. Bairstow. Monthly; 120 pages. Offset. Estab: 1965. Circ: 360,000. For young, affluent tennis players. Buys all rights. Pays on acceptance. No previously published, photocopied or simultaneous submissions. Mail artwork. SASE. Buys illustrations on assignment.
Cartoons: Buys tennis themes. Single panel OK. Submit finished art. Line drawings OK. Pays $25 minimum. Buys 12-24 cartoons annually.

TEXAS FARMER-STOCKMAN, Box 31368. Dallas TX 75231. Concerned with helping rural families grow better crops and improve their livestock. Buys all rights. Reports in 1 week. Sample copy available.
Cartoons: Pays $10 on acceptance. Finished cartoons should deal with farm and ranch situations or people they do business with. Uses about 25 annually.

THE TEXAS MUSIC EDUCATOR, Box 9908, Houston TX 77015. Editor: J.F. Lenzo. Monthly, August-May. For music educators in Texas. Buys all rights. Pays on acceptance. Reports in 30 days.
Cartoons: Buys music themes. Pays $5-10, finished b&w art with caption.
Illustrations: Buys cover art and spot drawings. Submit roughs or finished art. "Finished art must be camera-ready; 2-, 3-, or 4-color designs OK." Pays $5, spot drawing; $50, cover design.

TEXAS OUTDOOR GUIDE, Box 55573, Houston TX 77055. (713)682-5180. Editor-in-Chief: Stan Slaten. Bimonthly; 8½x11"; 84 pages. Offset. Estab: 1968. Circ: 100,000. For fans of outdoor sports and recreation. Buys first rights. Pays on publication. Previously published work OK. No photocopied or simultaneous submissions. Query. SASE. Free sample copy.
Illustrations: Mark Fore, editor. Buys spot drawings on sports. Submit roughs. B&w line drawings, washes and veloxes OK. Pays $20 minimum, b&w. Buys 60 illustrations quarterly. Reports in 4 weeks.
Special Needs: Employs artists on hourly or contract basis for mail promotional material.

TEXAS TOWN AND CITY MAGAZINE, 1020 Southwest Tower, Austin TX 78701. Contact: Erin Morrison. "For municipal government officials. Our needs in artwork are usually directed toward specific topics, such as law enforcement, workmen's compensation, the legislature, etc." Payment is $10 for spot drawing; $35 minimum for black plus 2 other colors cover design. Payment on publication for all rights. Send published samples. Sample copy available.

TEXTILE DIRECTIONS, 1440 Broadway, New York NY 10018. Art Buyer: R. Geer. Concerns fabrics for apparel. Interested in cover design in 4 colors, finished art. Pays $120 on publication. Buys all rights. Query with resume. Reports in 3 months.

THESE TIMES, Box 59, Nashville TN 37202. Art Editor: Gail R. Hunt. Interdenominational journal published by Seventh-day Adventist Church. "The goal is to bring Christianity to the reader in a believable, readable and usable way." Buys all or one-time rights. Pays on publication. Send published samples. SASE. Guidelines and sample copy available.
Illustrations: Does not publish 'say-nothing' artwork such as portraits, still lifes of Bibles, candles and the like; pretty vacation-like scenics, clip-art style or anything similar. "We cover subject matter involved with current issues (drugs, crime, ecology); Biblical subjects; health, family and home topics; science and nature; church history and current events in the world of religion." Pays $100-350 for covers in full color; $75-200 for inside full-page color illustrations; $30-75 for line drawings and 2-color illustrations.

THIRD EYE, 250 Mill St., Williamsville NY 14221. (716)634-2735. Editor-in-Chief: Patrick Lally. Quarterly; 8x11½"; 50 pages. Offset. Estab: 1976. Circ: 300. For poetry-oriented, very

literate audience. Buys reprint rights. Pays on publication. No previously published work or photocopies. Simultaneous submissions OK. Mail artwork. SASE. Free sample copy.
Illustrations: Nancy Wall, editor. Buys cover art and inside illustrations on poetic themes. Submit finished art. B&w line drawings and washes OK. No color. Pays $5 and contributor's copies for cover; $4 and contributor's copies for inside. Buys 12 illustrations annually. Reports in 4 weeks.

TIC MAGAZINE, Box 407, North Chatham NY 12132. Editor: Joseph Strack. For dentists. Pays on acceptance. Reports in 10 days.
Cartoons: "Remember, it's for dentists, not patients — so no pain gags, please." Pen and ink or line and wash OK. Pays $20 for exclusive dental publication use.

TIE LINES, 1365 Cass Ave., Rm. 1812, Detroit MI 48226. (313)223-7250. Editor-in-Chief: Helen Franklin. Biweekly; 14½x11"; 8-16 pages. Web offset. Estab: 1966. Circ: 36,000. For Michigan Bell Telephone employees, retirees and media representatives. Not copyrighted. Pays on acceptance. Previously published, photocopied and simultaneous submissions OK. Query. SASE. Free sample copy.
Cartoons: Buys themes on telephone people, their customers and telecommunications. "Most of our material is produced in-house. We do buy freelance art, but it's usually ordered on very short notice." Single panel OK. Submit finished art. Line drawings, halftones and washes OK. Pays $25 minimum. Reports in 2 weeks.

TODAY'S ANIMAL HEALTH/ANIMAL CAVALCADE, 8338 Rosemaead Blvd., Pico Rivera CA 90660. (213)682-3080. Editor-in-Chief: Richard Glassberg, D.V.M. Managing Editor: Norene Harris. Bimonthly; 8⅜x11⅞"; 32-40 pages. Offset. Estab: 1970. Circ: 27,000. For animal owners. Buys all rights. Pays on publication. Previously published, photocopied and simultaneous submissions OK. Mail artwork. SASE. Free sample copy. "Since our magazine is published by the nonprofit, charity Animal Health Foundation, we like donations. Therefore, the best way to get into our magazine is to donate material. We only buy material when we can't get good material donated."
Cartoons: Buys animal health-related themes. Single panel OK. Submit finished art. Line drawings and all color media OK. Pays $5-25. Buys 1-2 cartoons annually. Reports in 2 months.
Illustrations: Pat Taketa, editor. Buys cover art and article illustrations on animals. Submit finished art. Cover: color-separated art OK. Inside: b&w line drawings and color-separated art OK. Pays $25-50, color cover; $5-25, inside color and b&w cover; $5-15, inside b&w. Buys up to 5 illustrations annually. Reports in 2 months.

TODAY'S CHRISTIAN PARENT (formerly *Today's Christian Mother*), 8121 Hamilton Ave., Cincinnati OH 45231. Editor: Wilma L. Shaffer. Buys 4-6 religious cartoons annually. Buys first rights. Payment on acceptance. Reports in 1 month. Sample copy available.

TODAY'S EDUCATION, 1201 16th St. NW, Washington DC 20036. Cartoon Editor: Walter Graves. Quarterly. Published by National Education Association. Buys one-time rights.
Cartoons: Pays $10 on acceptance for themes on school situations. Prefers finished 8½x11. No caricatures of teachers. Uses 4 cartoons per issue. Line reproduction. Reports in 3 weeks.

TODAY'S SECRETARY, McGraw-Hill Inc., 1221 Avenue of the Americas, New York NY 10020. Editor: Lauren Bahr. Published 8 times annually; 8¼x10¾"; 32 pages. Offset. Circ: 65,000. For young secretarial students in high school, college and business schools nationwide. Buys all rights, but may reassign rights to artist after publication. Pays on acceptance. No previously published, photocopied or simultaneous submissions. Arrange interview to show portfolio. SASE. Free sample copy.
Illustrations: Barbara H. Devine, art director. Buys cover art, article illustrations and spot drawings on secretarial scenes on assignment. "I prefer to see concepts, not just renderings. I like cartoony techniques." Submit roughs. Pays $150, color cover; $125, b&w cover; $40-75, inside color; $30-50, inside b&w. Buys 25-30 illustrations annually. Reports in 2 weeks.
Special Needs: Pays $35 for 3 spots for "What's New" page. Needs 7x1" illustration depicting consumer problem for consumer column. Pays $7-8 per hour for mechanicals.
To Break In: Have a business card printed with your artwork shown on it.

TOGETHER (formerly *Sexology*), 200 Park Ave. S., New York NY 10003. Contact: Bruce Cohen. Buys all rights. Pays on acceptance. Send published samples.
Illustrations: "We look for well-drawn illustrations of all sexual subjects — not pornographic — in all styles with a contemporary look. Subjects include love-making, nudes, child molestation, prostitution, homosexuality, perversions." Prefers rough art, 5x8". Pays $50 per page, b&w art. Reports in 2 weeks.

TOWN & COUNTRY, 717 5th Ave., New York NY 10022. Editor-in-Chief: Frank Zachary. Managing Editor: Jean Barkhorn. Monthly; 8¼x11"; 160 pages. Offset. Estab: 1846. Circ: 160,000. For high-income, well-educated, adults interested in sophisticated travel, fashion, food, beauty and society. Buys all rights, but may reassign rights to artist after publication. Pays on acceptance. Previously published work OK. Query with portfolio. No work returned.
Illustrations: Linda Stillman, art director. Buys article illustrations on assignment. "We use only very sophisticated artwork, preferably b&w line." Pays $100-150 minimum per page.

TRANSACTION INC., Rutgers University, New Brunswick NJ 08903. Art Buyer: Barbara Ciletti. Social science publication. Interested in cover art. Pays $100. Payment on publication. Buys one-time rights. Submit published samples. Reports in 4 months.

TRANSITION, 537 NE Lincoln St., Hillsboro OR 97123. Editor-in-Chief: Steven Dimeo Ph.D. Managing Editor: James Kerr. Published semiannually; 8x11½"; 36 pages. Offset. Estab: 1977. Circ: 1,000. For college students, professors and those interested in the humanities. Buys all rights. Pays on publication. No previously published, photocopied or simultaneous submissions. Query with samples and 3-5 sentence biographical statement. SASE. Sample copy $1.25. "We are most in need of art accompanying poems and short stories and, while we publish unrelated drawings if exceptional, we encourage artists to submit samples of their best work in the interest of doing a specific drawing later."
Cartoons: "We are primarily looking for witty, intelligent, satirical editorial cartoons that show the timelessness of human folly." Buys current event, education, politics, religious, writing, publishing and current "fads" themes. Single panel OK. Submit finished art. Prefers line drawings. Pays $2.50-$5. Buys 2-5 cartoons per issue. Reports in 2-3 months.
Illustrations: "We like drawings that deal uncommonly with the common, landscapes more of the mind that could include nudes, evocative portraits or unnatural nature." Buys cover art, article illustrations and spot drawings. Submit finished art. B&w line drawings and washes OK. Pays $2.50-$5. Buys 5-10 illustrations per issue. Reports in 2-3 months.
Special Needs: May use artists for author caricatures for film and book review sections. Pays $2.50-$5.

TRENTON MAGAZINE, Box 4533, Trenton NJ 08611. Editor: Patrick J. Sweeney. Monthly. "About the only unsolicited artwork we use is cartoons; however, we have a constant need for artists, preferably living in this area, to work with us illustrating stories. We occasionally use 2-page art spreads." Not copyrighted. Pays from $7.50 for a spot drawing to $75 for finished art, 4-color cover. Payment on publication. Reports in 6 weeks.

TRIP & TOUR, Box 23505, Fort Lauderdale FL 33307. Associate Editor: M. Stilkind. Buys North American serial rights.
Cartoons: Pays $5 on acceptance. Prefers finished b&w art. Uses about 30 cartoons annually on travel. Sizes up to 8½x11" OK. Reports in 2-4 weeks.

TROPIC, 1 Herald Plaza, Miami FL 33101. Editor: John Parkyn. *Miami Herald* Sunday magazine. Inside illustrations pay $50-200. Payment on publication for first Florida rights. Previously published work OK. Reports in 4 weeks.

TRUE DETECTIVE, 235 Park Ave. S., New York NY 10003. Managing Editor: Walter Jackson. For middle-aged fact crime readers. Monthly. Buys all rights. Pays on acceptance.
Cartoons: Interested in crime themes. "Avoid cliche situations such as 2 convicts conversing in cell. No horror. Slant toward male audience. Cute, mild sex. Police image must be good." Buys about 100 cartoons annually. Submit roughs, single panel. Pays $25. Drawings reproduced in line and halftone. Wednesday is "look day" for local artists. Reports in 1 week.

TRUE WEST, Western Publications, Inc., Box 3338, Austin TX 78704. Publisher: Joe Austell Small. Editor: Pat Wagner. For those interested in 1840-1910 Western Americana nonfiction.

Buys one-time rights. Pays on acceptance. Previously published work OK "depending on where it appeared." Sample copy 60¢.
Illustrations: Buys cover art in 4-color oils. "We prefer a color snapshot or transparency for evaluation of the artist's style. We also prefer vertical paintings because the use of bands above and below a horizontal gives issues a look of sameness. We also have to pass up good paintings at times because our titles would cover some vital element or because the painting has no space left for story titles. We like to leave the artist's work as uncluttered as possible, but a certain amount of type is required. Often, the artist doesn't take this into account." Pays $100. Reports in 2-3 weeks.

TRUTH ON FIRE!, Box 223, Postal Station A, Vancouver, BC Canada V6C 2M3. Editor: Wesley H. Wakefield, evangelist. Publication of the Bible Holiness Movement. Bimonthly; 32 pages. Estab: 1949. Circ: 5,000. Buys all and one-time rights. Previously published work OK. Query. Sample copy available.
Illustrations: Buys cover designs and b&w drawings "with a message on racism, worship, education, war-peace, labor, drug addiction or alcoholism." Pays $15-30, 1-color cover design. Reports in 2 weeks.

TULSA, 616 S. Boston Ave., Tulsa OK 74119. (918)585-1201. Editor: Larry Silvey. Monthly. 5,100 circulation. 75% of art purchased is freelance. Uses b&w line drawings, cover designs and full-color illustrations. Payment on publication. Pays $50-75, spot drawing; $75-100, cover design, full-color illustration. No previously published work. Query. Sample copy $1.

TURF AND SPORT DIGEST, 511-513 Oakland Ave., Baltimore MD 21212. Editor: Sean McCormick. Buys humorous cartoons on horse racing. Pays $10 on publication.

TV GUIDE, Radnor PA 19088. Assistant Managing Editor: William Marsano. Weekly. Buys all rights. Pays on acceptance.
Cartoons: Jerry Alten, art director. Interested in line and halftone cartoons relating to TV. Rates are $125, single cartoon; $400, 3 cartoons used as full-page feature. Also uses cartoon illustrations for editorial features. Fees negotiable upon assignment. Query. Reports in 2 weeks.

UFO REPORT, Gambi Publications, 333 Johnson Ave., Brooklyn NY 11206. Contact: Joseph Mauro. Buys b&w line drawings and washes with 2-color overlays. Prefers 11x6". Pays $200, 2-color art. Buys first North American serial rights. Pays on publication. SASE. Reports in 1 month. Sample copy available.

UNION GOSPEL PRESS, Box 6059, Cleveland OH 44109. Contact: T.T. Musselman, Jr. "We've been in business since 1902 and publish 31 periodicals. We buy an average of 2,200 pieces of editorial artwork annually." Would like to see tearsheets for assignments. Will return samples after review. Pays $15 for b&w and $25 for illustrations in full color in lots of 26. Payment on acceptance for first and exclusive rights.

UNIROYAL WORLD, Management and Research Center, Benson Rd., Middlebury CT 06749. Editor: Ray Anderson. Published 8 times annually for employees. Pays $50-75 for cartoons, full-color illustrations, b&w line drawings and washes. Buys one-time rights. Pays on acceptance. Previously published work OK. Mail artwork. Reports in 2 weeks. Sample copy available.

UNITED EVANGELICAL ACTION, Box 28, Wheaton IL 60187. (312)665-0500. Quarterly; 8½x11". For pastors, key church workers and lay leaders. Interested in art featuring small group interaction, concern and counseling. Needs artwork for special issues on such topics as creative worship, the family, science and creation, and the Church in witness and missions. Buys b&w line drawings, washes and cartoons. Payment on publication. Copyrighted. Will consider art previously published. Query. Reports in 2 weeks.

UNITED MAINLINER, East-West Network, Inc., 5900 Wilshire Blvd., #300, Los Angeles CA 90036. (213)937-5810. Editor: James Clark. Senior Art Director: Chris Mossman. Monthly. Buys all rights. Query with resume. Sample copy $1.
Illustrations: Buys cover art and spot drawings on assignment. Pays $25 minimum, spot art; $400, full-color cover. Reports in 4 weeks.

UNIVERSAL MAGAZINE, Box 1537, Palm Desert CA 92260. Editors-in-Chief: Dr. Paul von Johl/Mae von Johl. Published 8 times annually; 5½x8½"; 16-32 pages. Offset. Estab: 1976. Circ: 1,200. For people who want to improve themselves. Buys all rights. Pays on publication; holiday material on acceptance. No previously published, photocopied or simultaneous submissions. Query with samples. SASE. Sample copy 14¢.
Cartoons: Buys themes on family life, humor through youth and religion. All formats OK; maximum size 5x5". Submit finished art. Line drawings only. Pays $5 minimum. Buys up to 8 cartoons annually. Reports in 3 weeks.
Illustrations: Buys cover art and article illustrations to accompany articles. B&w line drawings OK. Minimum payment: $15, cover; $10, inside. Buys 8 illustrations annually. Reports in 1 week.
Special Needs: Pays $25 minimum for book illustrations and $5 for brochure illustrations.

THE UNSPEAKABLE VISIONS OF THE INDIVIDUAL, Box 439, California PA 15419. Editors-in-Chief: Arthur and Kit Knight. Published annually; 8½x11"; 176 pages. Offset. Estab: 1971. Circ: 2,000. For people with a better-than-average education interested in "beat" literature. Buys first rights. Pays on publication. Previously published work occasionally OK. No photocopied or simultaneous submissions. Query. SASE. "Work without SASE will be destroyed." Sample copy $2.
Illustrations: Buys cover art and article illustrations on "beat-related" material, such as writers Jack Kerouac, William S. Burroughs, Allen Ginsberg, Gary Snyder and Diane di Prima. Submit finished art. B&w line drawings OK. Pays 2 contributor's copies, minimum; $10 maximum. Buys 6 illustrations annually. Reports in 4 weeks.

VALLEY LIFE, Box 8268, Van Nuys CA 91409. (213)892-4381. Editor-in-Chief: Sue Endo. Monthly; 8½x11"; 72 pages. Offset. Estab: 1976. Circ: 20,000. For middle and upper-middle-income suburban college-educated readers. Pays on publication. Previously published work OK. No photocopied or simultaneous submissions. Query with samples. SASE. Free sample copy.
Cartoons: Buys current event, education, environment, family life and political themes. Single panel OK. Submit finished art. Line drawings OK. Pays $10 minimum. Reports in 3 weeks.
Special Needs: Pays $5 per illustration for columns on consumerism, sports, entertainment, home/garden, people, dining out, travel, fashion and health/nutrition.

VAN WORLD (formerly *RV Van World*), 16200 Ventura Blvd., Encino CA 91436. Editor: Chris Hosford. Monthly. For custom van owners. 80,000 circulation. Buys line or wash illustrations. Buys all rights. Query with resume. Reports in 2 weeks. Editorial guidelines available. Sample copy $1.50.

VANGUARD, 229 College St., Toronto, Ontario Canada M5T 1R4. Editor: Bonnie M. Greene. Bimonthly. "An idea magazine for radical Christians interested in socio-economic, political, educational, and cultural questions." Will supply summary of articles and needs for artwork on request. Buys cover designs, b&w line drawings, washes and finished cartoons. Pays $10, spot drawings. Rights shared with artist. Previously published work OK "if not in a magazine with overlapping readership." Pays on publication. Query. Reports in 3-4 weeks. Sample copy 50¢.

VEGETARIAN TIMES, Box A3104, Chicago IL 60690. (312)262-8918. Art Buyer: Paul Obis, Jr. Estab: 1974. 6,000 circulation. Bimonthly. Will consider spot drawings, cartoons and cover designs of nature, animals, fresh food and farming. Rates are $5 for spot drawing; $25 for cover design in 1 color, finished art. Query with published samples. SASE. Reports in 6 weeks.

VENTURE, Christian Service Brigade, Box 150, Wheaton IL 60187. (312)665-0630. Editor: Paul Heidebrecht. Size: 8½x11". Estab: 1959. Circ: 22,500. For boys, ages 12-18. "We seek to promote consciousness, acceptance of and personal commitment to Jesus Christ." Buys finished b&w drawings and cartoons. Maximum size: 8½x11". "We use 1 cartoon per issue. Editors assign cartoons strips or stories to artists." Pays on publication of artwork; acceptance of cartoons. Pays $20-30, spot drawings; $7.50-15, cartoons; $50-80, full-page b&w or 2-color illustrations. Buys one-time rights. Send samples. Reports in 6 weeks. Sample copy 50¢.

VICTIMOLOGY: AN INTERNATIONAL JOURNAL, Box 39045, Washington DC 20016. (202)686-5302. Editor-in-Chief: Emilio Viano. Quarterly; 7½x4½"; 200 pages. Offset. Estab: 1976. Circ: 2,500. For professionals, lawyers, criminologists, medical personnel and others helping child/spouse abuse programs, hotlines, rape crisis centers and other victim programs. Buys all rights. Pays on publication. Query with samples. SASE. Sample copy $5. "We prefer that the artist contact us, and ask about forthcoming articles and special issues so that the work will be in consonance with the issue's content. By 'victim,' we mean not only those victimized by crime, but by earthquakes, the environment, accidents, pollution and the state." Pays $50 minimum for brochure art.
Illustrations: Buys cover art and article illustrations on victimization. "We like to see illustrations on what is done in behalf of the victim." Submit roughs or finished art. Cover: b&w line drawings, color-separated art and veloxes OK. Inside: b&w line drawings and veloxes OK. Minimum payment: $50, b&w cover; $75, color cover; $20, inside b&w. Buys 6 illustrations annually. Reports in 4 weeks.

THE VINE, 201 8th Ave. S., Nashville TN 37202. Editor: Betty M. Buerki. Weekly. Story paper for boys and girls in grades 3 and 4 in United Methodist and United Presbyterian churches. Buys cartoons, full-color illustrations (color-separated), b&w drawings and cover designs. Pays $40 for full-color illustration and cover design in 4 colors. Buys one-time and first serial rights. Pays on acceptance. Mail artwork. Reports in 1 month. Sample copy available.

VIRGINIA WILDLIFE, Virginia Game Commission, Box 11104, Richmond VA 23230. Contact: Harry L. Gillam. Pays on acceptance. Buys one-time with reprint rights. Sample copy available.
Illustrations: "We get more submissions than we can use because we need full-color art and technically-accurate detail for our covers." Also needs color-separated animal life history panels and nature/conservation facts for back covers. Submit 8½x11" art with 3½x2½" open space in left hand corner for logo. Pays $75-100, 4-color front cover; $25-50, 2-color back cover.

VISTA, The Wesley Press, Box 2000, Marion IN 46952. Monthly in weekly parts. For adults. Not copyrighted. Will consider artwork previously published. Pays on acceptance. Send original art or samples. Reports in 30 days.
Illustrations: Buys cover art and spot drawings on assignment. Line and wash finished art OK. Ms and size requirements provided. Minimum payment:15, spot art; $25-30, 2-color cover.

VIVA, 909 3rd Ave., New York NY 10022. Editor: Kathy Keeton. Monthly; 8½x11". For women, ages 18-34. 600,000 circulation. Seeks $160,000 worth of freelance work annually. Major needs are b&w drawings, full-color illustrations and cartoons. Pays $85 for spot drawings; $400 for full-color illustration. Buys all rights. Mail artwork. Reports immediately.

VOGUE, 350 Madison Ave., New York NY 10017. Art Director: Rochelle Udell. Will review portfolio of artist who writes and sends resume. Works primarily with New York area artists. Artist should provide photocopies to leave for referral.

VOICES INTERNATIONAL, 6804 Cloverdale Dr., Little Rock AR 72209. (501)565-6305. Editor-in-Chief: Clovita Rice. Quarterly; 9x6"; 32 pages. Offset. Estab: 1968. Circ: 500. For poets and poetry readers. Buys all rights. Pays on acceptance. No previously published, photocopied or simultaneous submissions. Mail artwork. SASE. Sample copy $2.
Illustrations: Buys cover art on all themes. Submit finished art. B&w line drawings OK. Pays 5 contributor's copies. Buys 4 illustrations annually. Reports in 3 weeks.

WALLS & CEILINGS, 14006 Ventura Blvd., Sherman Oaks CA 91423. Editor: Robert F. Welch. Monthly. Not copyrighted. Sample copy available.
Cartoons: Pays $3-5 on publication. Uses 25 plastering and drywall cartoons annually. Prefers roughs. Reports in 30 days.

WASHINGTON DOSSIER, 3301 New Mexico Ave., Washington DC 20016. (202)362-5894. Editor-in-Chief: Sonia Adler. Managing Editor: Susan Wille. Monthly; 8½x11"; 68 pages. Offset. Estab: 1975. Circ: 35,000. For Washington's powerful wealthy. Buys all rights. Pays on publication. No previously published work. Photocopied and simultaneous submissions OK.

Mail artwork. No work returned.
Cartoons: Buys current event and political themes. Single panel OK. Submit finished art. Line drawings OK. Pays $25-100. Reports in 4 weeks.
Illustrations: Andy Bornstien, editor. Buys cover art and article illustrations. Submit roughs. All media OK. Pays $25-250, cover; $25-100, inside. Reports in 4 weeks.

WASHINGTONIAN, 1828 L St. NW, Suite 700, Washington DC 20036. Editor: Laughlin Phillips. Monthly. Buys North American serial rights. Pays on acceptance.
Cartoons: Uses 50 cartoons a year on "any subject, if sophisticated." Submit finished art. Pays $25-35. Reports in 1 month.

THE WATER SKIER, Box 191, Winter Haven FL 33880. Editor: Tom C. Hardman. Aims to encourage the safe enjoyment of water skiing as a primary means of family recreation. Published 7 times annually. Buys North American serial rights. Sample copy available.
Cartoons: Pays $12.50 on acceptance. Wants water skiing themes. Prefers roughs. Buys 6 cartoons annually. Reports in 10 days.

WAY, 109 Golden Gate Ave., San Francisco CA 94102. Editor-in-Chief: Simon Scanlon. Published 10 times annually; 5x8"; 64 pages. Offset. Estab: 1944. Circ: 10,000. For middle-aged readers. Buys first North American serial rights. Pays on publication. Previously published work OK. No photocopied or simultaneous submissions. Query with samples. SASE. Free sample copy.
Cartoons: Buys themes on current events, education, environment, family life, politics and religion. Single panel OK. Submit finished art. Line drawings only. Pays $10 minimum. Reports in 4 weeks.
Illustrations: Ron Sugiyama, editor. Buys cover art and article illustrations on "social landscapes." Submit finished art. B&w line drawings OK. Pays $10 minimum. Buys 4 illustrations per issue. Reports in 4 weeks.

Jack and Jill **children's magazine is an annual market for 200 illustrations. Payment ranging from $25 for inside b&w work to $135 for a color cover is given for art based on assigned themes. Edward F. Cortese, art director, bought this color article illustration from Phil Smith for $80 because of the "aesthetic quality of the art and the artist's ability to create the character and mood of the story so well."**

WEE WISDOM, Unity Village MO 64065. Contact: Jim Leftwich. For boys and girls at a third grade reading level. Buys all rights. Pays on acceptance.
Illustrations: Buys cover art, inside illustrations and puzzles. "We wish all artwork to be imaginative and innovative. The illustration or puzzle must expand a child's concept of the world and of himself." Puzzles and inside art must be black plus 1 color. Covers always 4-color. Prefers rough illustrations 9⅝x13¼ (to be increased ⅓). Pays $25-45, puzzles; up to $200, covers.

THE WEEKENDER, Box 337, Salem IL 62881. Editor: L. Shuler. Published annually; 6x9"; 256 pages. Buys first or exclusive rights. Buys spot drawings, cartoons and cover designs. Needs travel and recreational material of people doing things. Pen and ink, line and wash OK. Cartoons, single panel. Pays $25, spot drawing; $300, display artwork and full-page color illustration; $500, cover design in 3 colors.

WEEKLY BIBLE READER, Standard Publishing, 8121 Hamilton Ave., Cincinnati OH 45231. Editor: Barbara Curie. For ages 6 and 7. Quarterly in weekly parts; 4 es. Estab: 1965. 72,000 circulation. Buys b&w drawings, cartoons and simple puzzles. Pays $5-35 for spot drawing. Pays on acceptance. Buys first and one-time rights. Mail artwork. Reports in 1 month. Sample copy available.

WEIGHT WATCHERS, 635 Madison Ave., New York NY 10022. Editor-in-Chief: Bernadette Carr. Art Editor: K. Cunningham. Monthly; 64 pages. Offset. Circ: 780,000. For those interested in weight-control, proper nutrition and self-improvement. Buys all rights. Pays on acceptance. No previously published or simultaneous submissions. Photocopies OK. Query with samples. SASE. Sample copy 75¢.
Cartoons: Buys positive, weight-related themes. Single and double panel OK. Submit finished art. Line drawings and halftones OK. Pays $35-50. Buys 5-10 cartoons annually. Reports in 1-3 weeks.
Illustrations: Buys article illustrations and spot drawings with "sympathetic treatment of someone on a weight-loss program." Submit finished art. B&w line drawings, washes and color-separated art OK. Buys 1-2 illustrations per issue. Reports in 1-4 weeks.

WEIRDBOOK, Box 35, Amherst Branch, Buffalo NY 14226. Editor-in-Chief: W. Paul Ganley. Published semiannually; 8½x11"; 64 pages. Offset. Estab: 1968. Circ: 700. For those interested in fantasy, science fiction and horror. Buys first and all rights. Pays on publication. No previously published or simultaneous submissions. Photocopies OK. Mail artwork. SASE. Sample copy $2.50.
Illustrations: Buys weird, macabre, supernatural and fantastic themes. "Illustrate scenes from famous weird writers like Bradbury, Lovecraft, Poe, etc." Submit finished art. B&w line drawings and washes OK. Pays $5.50, b&w cover; $1-5, inside b&w. Buys 20-40 illustrations annually. "Reports in a few weeks for submissions received in December, early January, May, June or July."

THE WELDING DISTRIBUTOR, c/o Industrial Publishing Co., 614 Superior Ave. W., Cleveland OH 44113. Editor: Ted B. Jefferson. Bimonthly. For wholesale, retail distributors and sales staffs of welding equipment and safety supplies. Buys all rights.
Cartoons: Pays $5 on acceptance. Depict sales situations in the office and shop, if tied in with welding or allied safety equipment. Typical cartoon shows a welding distributor company boss talking to an employee.

WEST COAST REVIEW OF BOOKS, 6311 Yucca St., Hollywood CA 90028. Editor-in-Chief: D. David Dreis. Managing Editor: Crane Jackson. Bimonthly; 8½x11"; 72 pages. Offset. Estab: 1974. Circ: 76,000. For book customers. Buys all rights. Pays on publication. No previously published, photocopied or simultaneous submissions. Query with samples. SASE. Sample copy $1.25.
Cartoons: Henry Zorich, editor. Buys themes on bestseller book reading. Prefers single panel. Submit finished art. Line drawings, halftones and washes OK. Pays $50 b&w/$75 color minimum per 3 illustrations. Buys 36 cartoons annually. Reports in 4 weeks.
Illustrations: Bonita Montano, editor. Buys cover art and article illustrations on assignment. Submit roughs. Cover: color-separated and reflective art OK. Inside: b&w line drawings and washes OK. Minimum payment: $100, color cover; $75, inside color; $50, 3 inside b&w illustrations. Buys 24 illustrations annually. Reports in 4 weeks.

THE WESTERN HORSEMAN, Box 7980, Colorado Springs CO 80933. (303)633-5524. Editor: Chan Bergen. Monthly. For professional horsemen, pleasure riders, ranchers and cowboys. 198,000 circulation. Buys one-time rights. Pays on acceptance. Sample copy $1.
Illustrations: Requires 36 paintings annually for covers and inside. Also interested in full-color illustrations and 4x5" transparencies of cowboy art. Pays $100, full-color illustration.

WESTERN HUMANITIES REVIEW, University of Utah, Salt Lake City UT 84112. (801)581-7438. Editor: Jack Garlington. Quarterly. "Highly educated and literarily sophisticated" readership. 1,100 circulation. Uses cover designs and line drawings. Buys all rights. Will release rights on demand. Typical rates are $35 for spot drawings and $100 for cover designs. Reports in 1-3 months. Sample copy $1.50.

THE WESTERN PRODUCER, Box 2500, Saskatoon, Saskatchewan Canada S7K 2C4. (306)242-7651. Contact: Magazine Editor. Weekly; 15½x11½"; 8 pages. Offset. Circ: 150,000. For farm families in western Canada. Not copyrighted. Pays on acceptance. Mail artwork. SASE.
Illustrations: Buys article illustrations on rural life in western Canada. Submit finished art. B&w line drawings OK. Pays $10-100. Buys 10 illustrations annually. Reports in 2 weeks.

WESTWAYS MAGAZINE, Box 2890 Terminal Annex, Los Angeles CA 90051. (213)746-4410. Editor: Frances Ring. Art Director: Elin Waite. Monthly. 450,000 circulation. Uses themes on travel, history, and arts in the West. Artwork by assignment only. Buys all rights. Pays on acceptance. Pays $150 for drawings; $300 for full-color illustration; $500 for cover design. Send resume and arrange interview. Old copies available.

WESTWORLD, Box 6680, Vancouver, BC Canada V6B 4L4. (604)732-1371. Editor: Bill Mayrs. Bimonthly. 185,000 circulation. Concentrates on travel, leisure and living in western Canada. Buys cover art, illustrations and cartoons. B&w line drawings and washes OK. Payment: spot drawing, $35; full-color illustration, $75-100; full-color cover design, $125-150; cartoons, $15. Buys one-time rights. Payment on publication. No previously published work. Send resume. Sample copy available. Reports in 3-5 weeks.

WHISPERS, Box 904, Chapel Hill NC 27514. Editor-in-Chief: Stuart Schiff. Published 2-3 times annually; 5½x8½"; 68 or 132 pages. Offset. Estab: 1973. Circ: 3,000. For college-educated adults interested in literate fantasy, horror art and fiction. Buys first rights. Pays on publication. No previously published or simultaneous submissions. Photocopies OK. Mail artwork. SASE. Sample copy $1.25.
Illustrations: Buys cover art, article illustrations and spot drawings on monsters, dragons, skeletons, haunted houses and on themes from Poe, Lovecraft, Dunsany, Bradbury and others. "Please do not mix up fantasy and horror with science fiction. I do not want pictures of rocket ships, space creatures, robots or things of that ilk." Submit finished art. B&w line drawings, washes and veloxes OK. Pays $10-35 for retained original artwork; pays contributor's copies otherwise. Buys 10-15 illustrations annually. Reports in 8 weeks.

THE WHOLESALER, 110 N. York Rd., Elmhurst IL 60126. (312)833-6540. Estab: 1946. Monthly. For plumbing, heating and air conditioning and refrigeration wholesalers. 22,000 circulation. Interested in cartoons pertaining to the industry, especially for use in a calendar in the December issue. Pays $10 per cartoon; $7.50 each if more than 5 bought. Buys first serial rights. Payment on acceptance.

WINNING (formerly *Gambling Quarterly*), Box 412, Station F, Toronto, Ontario Canada. (416)366-9701. Editor-in-Chief: Don Valliere. Bimonthly; 8½x11¼"; 64 pages. Offset. Estab: 1974. Circ: 35,000. For racing fans, casino gamblers and those who enjoy social gambling. Buys all rights. Pays on publication. Previously published work OK. No photocopied or simultaneous submissions. Query with samples. SASE. Free sample copy.
Cartoons: Buys gambling themes. All formats OK. Submit roughs or finished art. Line drawings, halftones and washes OK. Minimum payment: $20, b&w; $25, color. Buys 1-2 cartoons per issue. Reports in 1 week.
Illustrations: Buys cover art and spot drawings on gambling. Submit roughs. Negotiates payment. Reports in 1 week.

THE WIRELESS JOURNAL QUARTERLY, Society of Wireless Pioneers, Box 530, Santa Rosa CA 95402. Editor: William A. Breniman. For active and retired radio-telegraph men who handle(d) communications with ships and at shore stations; included are military, commercial, aeronautical and governmental communications personnel. "Since many have earned their living aboard ships as 'Sparks,' we like to bring a nautical flavor to our pages." Buys b&w line drawings and cartoons. Pays $5+, drawings; rates open, cartoons. Pays on acceptance. Buys reprints.

WISCONSIN TRAILS, Box 5650, Madison WI 53705. (608)238-5564. Managing Editor: Jill Dean. Quarterly; 9x12"; 44 pages. Offset. Estab: 1960. Circ: 25,000. For those interested in the outdoors, ecology, conservation, history, industry and personalities in Wisconsin. Buys one-time rights. Pays on publication. Previously published, photocopied and simultaneous submissions OK. Query. SASE. Free sample copy.
Illustrations: Buys article illustrations and spot drawings on Wisconsin-related themes. Submit finished art. All media OK; uses mostly b&w. Pays $25, b&w; $50, color. Buys 40 illustrations annually. Reports in 3 weeks.
Special Needs: Uses artists for design/layout of sales pages, ads and brochures. Payment determined by job. Usually, artist submits a bid for the job. Send samples of graphic design and layout work to Sandra Booth.

WITCHCRAFT DIGEST, 153 W. 80th St., New York NY 10024. Contact: Dr. Leo Louis Martello. Buys first rights. Pays on publication. Sample copy $1.
Illustrations: "Artists who do illustrations for our magazine must have a feel for the old ways, Mother Earth, Mother Nature, paganism, ancient gods and goddesses, and be familiar with the symbolisms used by modern witches. Artists unfamiliar with the Old Religion, and who think that true witchcraft is the same as Satanism, or who retain Judeo-Christian stereotyped images of the witch, are wasting their time. We are a very limited market and not interested in the comic book horror and fantasy artist." Submit black pen and ink illustrations for offset reproduction. Pays $5-10.

WOMAN'S ALMANAC, 12 HOW-TO HANDBOOKS IN ONE, 14430 Massachusetts Ave., Cambridge MA 02138. Designer: Holly McLellan. A practical approach to women's needs, in sections on: The Health Advisor; The Psychological Advisor; The Sex Advisor; The Childcare Book; Education; Working; Your Own Business; The Money Manager; The Legal Advisor; Handywoman; Simple Pleasures; Woman's Directory (national, state, and local listings of resources and services). Published annually. Buys b&w line drawings, washes and rough cartoons. Pays $10, spot drawing. Buys various rights. Previously published work OK. Pays on publication. Send resume. Reports in 2-3 weeks.

WOMAN'S DAY, 1515 Broadway, New York NY 10036. Art Director: Joe Sapinsky. Monthly. 8 million circulation. Sold in supermarkets, drug and variety stores. Leave portfolio overnight for review.

WOMEN: A JOURNAL OF LIBERATION, 3028 Greenmount Ave., Baltimore MD 21218. (301)235-5245. Contact: Staff. Published 3 times annually; 8½x11"; 64 pages. Offset. Estab: 1969. Circ: 15,000. For feminists, socialists and lesbians. Photocopied and simultaneous submissions OK. Previously published work receives low priority. Mail artwork. SASE. Sample copy $1.25.
Cartoons: Buys themes on feminism and lesbianism. Submit finished art. Line drawings OK. Pays 1 contributor's copy. Reports in 6 months.
Illustrations: Buys cover art and article illustrations. Submit finished art. B&w line drawings OK. Pays 1 contributor's copy. Reports in 6 months.
Special Needs: Artwork for features on women alone and women loving women.

WOMEN IN BUSINESS, 9100 Ward Pkwy., Kansas City MO 64114. (816)361-6621. Editor: Rita R. Rousseau. Art Director: Cheri Wright. Published 9 times annually; 8⅜x10⅞"; 24 pages. Offset. Estab: 1949. Circ: 95,000. For businesswomen, all levels in all fields. Buys all rights, but may reassign rights to artist after publication. Pays on acceptance. No previously published or simultaneous submissions. Query with samples. SASE. Free sample copy. "No working women in stereotyped roles."
Cartoons: Buys themes on current events, education, retirement and businesswomen. Single and double panel OK. Submit roughs or finished art. Halftones OK. Pays $25, b&w. Buys 6-10

cartoons annually. Reports in 4 weeks.
Illustrations: Buys cover art and article illustrations on assignment. Submit roughs. Cover: color-separated art OK. Inside: b&w line drawings OK. Pays $50-100, b&w cover; $75-125, color cover; $25-50, inside. Reports in 4 weeks.

WOMEN'S CIRCLE HOME COOKING, Box 338, Chester MA 01011. Editor: Barbara Hall Pedersen. Women who enjoy cooking read this monthly. Circ: 225,000. Buys b&w drawings and cartoons. Submit seasonal work 7-8 months in advance. Buys all rights. Will consider work previously published. Pays $5-10 for spot drawings; $20 for cartoons. Reports in 2-8 weeks. Send envelope and postage for sample copy.

WOODALL'S TRAILER & RV TRAVEL, 500 Hyacinth Place, Highland Park IL 60035. (312)433-4550. Editor-in-Chief: Kirk Landers. Art Editor: Paul Casper. Monthly; 10⅞x8¼"; 175 pages. Offset. Circ: 300,000. For those involved with recreational vehicles and camping. Buys first rights. Pays on acceptance. No previously published, photocopied or simultaneous submissions. Query. SASE.
Cartoons: Buys themes on recreational vehicles and camping. Single and multi-panel OK. Submit finished art. Halftones and washes OK. Pays $20-45, b&w. Buys 30 cartoons annually. Reports in 2 weeks.
Illustrations: Buys cover art (usually on assignment), article illustrations and spot drawings on all themes. Submit finished art. Cover: reflective art OK. Inside: b&w line drawings, washes and reflective art OK. Pays $300-500, color cover; $100-500, inside color; $25-300, inside b&w. Buys 50 illustrations annually. Reports in 2 weeks.

WOODENBOAT MAGAZINE, Box 268, Brooksville ME 04617. Editor-in-Chief: Jonathan A. Wilson. Managing Editor: Jacqueline Michand. Bimonthly; 8¼x11"; 100 pages. Offset. Estab: 1974. Circ: 25,000. For people interested in wooden boats. Buys first North American serial rights. Pays on publication. Previously published work OK. No photocopied or simultaneous submissions. Query with samples. SASE. Sample copy $2.
Illustrations: Buys cover art, article illustrations and spot drawings on wooden boats or related items. Submit roughs. Cover: washes OK. Inside: b&w line drawings, color-separated and reflective art and veloxes OK. Pays $50 minimum, color cover; $10, inside b&w; $15, inside color. Buys 48 illustrations annually. Reports in 1-2 months.
Special Needs: "We are always in need of high quality technical drawings. Most are redrawn from roughs." Also needs advertising art. Pays $10 minimum.

WOODMEN OF THE WORLD, 1700 Farnam St., Omaha NE 68102. (402)342-1890. Editor-in-Chief: Leland A. Larson. Monthly; 8⅜x11⅜"; 44 pages. Offset. Estab: 1891. Circ: 456,000. For family readers. Not copyrighted. Pays on acceptance. No photocopies. Previously published work OK. Mail artwork. SASE. Free sample copy.
Cartoons: Buys current event, education, environment, family life and humor through youth themes. Single panel OK. Submit finished art. Line drawings, washes and halftones OK. Pays $10, b&w. Buys 30 cartoons annually. Reports in 2 weeks.
Illustrations: Buys cover art and article illustrations on lodge activities, seasonal, humorous and human interest themes. Submit finished art. Cover: color-separated art OK. Inside: washes OK. Pays $60-150, color cover; $50-150, b&w cover; $40-100, inside color; $20-80, inside b&w. Buys 12 illustrations annually. Reports in 2 weeks.

WORKBENCH MAGAZINE, 4251 Pennsylvania, Kansas City MO 64111. Editor: Jay W. Hedden. Bimonthly. For the home owner and "do-it-yourselfer." Buys cartoons. Pays $15 on acceptance. Buys all rights, but reassigns rights to artist after publication. Previously published work OK.

THE WORKING CRAFTSMAN, Box 42, 1500 Shermer, 226-E, Northbrook IL 60062. (312)498-2250. Editor-in-Chief: Marilyn Heise. Published 5 times annually; 8½x11"; 42 pages. Offset. Estab: 1971. Circ: 7,000. For craftsmen. Buys all rights. Pays on publication. Query. SASE. Free sample copy.
Illustrations: Buys cover art, article illustrations and spot drawings on crafts. Submit finished art. B&w line drawings OK. Pays $5 minimum. Buys 8 illustrations annually. Reports in 4 weeks.

WORLD CONSTRUCTION, 666 5th Ave., New York NY 10019. Contact: Henry Mozdzer. Technical trade magazine for English-speaking engineers, contractors and government officials in the eastern hemisphere and Latin America. Pays $15 for b&w; $25 for color; $100 for cover art. "We need definitive captions — about 100 words — with artwork." Pays on publication. Buys exclusive and reprint rights. Reports in 1 month. Sample copy available.

WRITER'S DIGEST, 9933 Alliance Rd., Cincinnati OH 45242. Editor: John Brady.
Cartoons: "Submissions must be related to the agonies and ecstasies of the writing life. No general humor — and no poorly-drawn submissions. We're most interested in discovering new and energetic cartoonists. Our rates are not kingly, but we can offer national exposure to bright talent." Pays $25-50 on acceptance. Buys first rights. Uses up to 5 cartoons per month. Will consider roughs, "but not too rough."
Illustrations: Article illustrations assigned. "If a cartoonist consistently turns out distinctive cartoons on spec, we may assign him spot illustrations." Send samples of work (good photocopies fine), with brief resume and phone number. Uses b&w only. Pays $20-50 per spot, $100-150 for series of 3-4 spots; $200 for cover art. SASE.

XANADU, 1704 Auburn Rd., Wantagh NY 11793. Art Editor: Coco Gordon. Published semi-annually. Circ: 1,000. Buys finished art, cover designs and b&w drawings. Buys one-time rights. Sample payment: $25 for 2-color cover design. Sample copy $1.50.

YACHTING, 50 W. 44th St., New York NY 10036. (212)391-1000. Editor-in-Chief: William W. Robinson. Managing Editor: Marcia Wiley. Monthly; 8³/₁₆x11"; 200 pages. Offset. Estab: 1907. Circ: 125,000. For top-level participants in boating in all its forms, power and sail. Buys first North American serial rights. Pays on acceptance or publication "depending on material." No previously published, photocopied or simultaneous submissions. Query. SASE.
Cartoons: Buys boating themes. Single panel OK. Submit finished art. Line drawings, any media OK. Pays $50. Buys 30 cartoons annually. Reports in 2 weeks "or more at busy seasons."
Illustrations: Buys cover art, article illustrations and spot drawings on boating themes. Submit finished art. Cover: color-separated art OK. Inside: all media OK. Pays $300, color cover; $25-300, inside color; $15-150, inside b&w. Buys 100 illustrations annually. Reports in 3 weeks.

YOUNG FAMILY, Box 8, Station C, Toronto, Ontario Canada M6J 3M8. Contact: Mrs. K. Applegate, Production Dept. For parents of children under age 7. Quarterly. Buys b&w line drawings, washes, cover designs, full-color illustrations and finished cartoons. Buys various rights. Previously published work in non-Canadian magazines OK. Mail artwork. Reports in 1 month. Payment on acceptance. Sample copy available.

YOUNG JUDAEAN, 817 Broadway, New York NY 10003. Editor: Barbara Gingold. Official publication of the Hadassah Zionist Youth Commission. For members of Young Judaeans, ages 8-13. Monthly, November-June. Buys b&w line drawings, washes, cover designs and finished cartoons. Needs artwork for Jewish and Israeli holiday issues. Payment on publication. Pays $2 for spot drawings; $10 for cover design in b&w. Buys first rights. Previously published work OK. "Artists should send samples of work and payment requirements and we will send material for illustration or specific requests for art. All work submitted is on speculation." Reports in 1-3 months. Sample copy 35¢.

YOUNG MISS, 52 Vanderbilt Ave., New York NY 10017. Contact: Joe Carrara. For girls, ages 10-14. "Artists should call for an interview and bring portfolios with original art samples and tearsheets of published work. All art done on assignment. We do not buy over-the-transom art, but we do use freelance artists." Prefers local artists. Pays $80-200 for editorial illustrations. Buys all rights. Sample copy $1.

YOUNG WORLD, Box 567-B, Indianapolis IN 46206. (317)634-1100. Editor-in-Chief: Beth W. Thomas. Managing Editor: Julie Plopper. Published 10 times annually; 6½x9¼"; 48 pages. Offset. For preteens. Buys all rights. Pays on publication. Previously published, photocopied and simultaneous submissions OK. Query with samples. SASE. Free sample copy.
Illustrations: Lawrence Simmons, art director. Buys cover art, article illustrations and spot drawings on assingment. Submit roughs. Cover: 4-color reflective art OK. Inside: b&w line drawings, washes, 2-color/color-separated and 4-color reflective art OK. Pays $135, color cover; $40-50 per page, inside color; $20-35 per page, inside b&w. Buys 120-180 illustrations annually. Reports in 2-3 weeks.

Newspapers & Newsletters

ACTION IN KENTUCKY, 200 W. Chestnut St., Louisville KY 40202. (502)587-0769. Editor-in-Chief: Frank R. Dornheim. Biweekly newspaper; 11½x17"; 8 pages. Offset. Estab: 1959. Circ: 5,000. For conservative businessmen in Kentucky and the Southeast. Not copyrighted. Pays on publication. Previously published work and photocopies OK. Query. SASE. Free sample copy.
Cartoons: Buys current event, education, environment and retirement themes pertaining to business and industry. Single panel OK. Submit finished art. Line drawings OK. Pays $5 minimum. Buys 12 cartoons annually. Reports in 2 weeks.

THE ADVOCATES, New Mass Media, Inc., Box 851, Amherst MA 01002. Art Buyer: Linda Matys. Publishes 3 alternative-style weeklies serving western Massachusetts and Connecticut. Offices also in Hartford and New Haven, Connecticut. Includes seasonal, entertainment, travel and outdoor sections. Uses pen and ink or line and wash art. Pays $3 minimum for spot drawings; usually $5-7. Buys all rights but may reassign rights to artist on request. Pays on publication. Previously published work OK. Send published samples or original art. SASE. Reports in 1-2 months.

ALFA OWNER, 1206 Temple Gardens, Baltimore MD 21217. (301)728-7373. Editor-in-Chief: Evan Wilson. Monthly newsletter; 8½x11"; 12 pages. Offset. Estab: 1958. Circ: 4,000. For Alfa Romeo owners. Buys first rights. Pays on acceptance. Query with samples. SASE.
Illustrations: Buys cover art, article illustrations and spot drawings. Submit finished art. Considers b&w line drawings, washes, color-separated and reflective art and inside veloxes. Minimum payment: $10, b&w cover; $15, color cover; $5, inside b&w; $8, inside color. Reports in 2 weeks.

ALFANTICS, 414 E. Alexandria Ave., Alexandria VA 22301. (703)683-5419. Contact: John D. Kidd. Newsletter of Capital Chapter of Alfa Romeo Owners Club. Not copyrighted. "Imaginative composition is preferred over straight journalism. Graphics can be as far-out or conservative as the artist wants." Buys drawings, cover designs, line (wash sometimes) and finished art. Sample minimum payment: spot drawing, $5; cover design (1-color)/finished art, $10. Rarely considers previously published material. Payment on publication. Prefers to see original art. Reports as soon as possible.

AMERICAN BOATING ILLUSTRATED, 2019 Clement Ave., Alameda CA 94501. (415)865-7500. Editor-in-Chief: Michael Dobrin. Monthly newspaper; 11x14½"; 50 pages. Offset. Circ: 26,000. For middle-aged, upper-middle-class recreational boaters. Buys all rights. Pays on publication. Previously published, photocopied and simultaneous submissions OK. Mail artwork. SASE. Free sample copy.
Illustrations: Buys technical illustrations for how-to stories. Submit roughs or finished art. B&w line drawings and veloxes OK. Pays $5 minimum. Buys 125-160 illustrations annually. Reports in 1 month.

AMERICAN COLLECTOR, Real Resources Group, Box A, Reno NV 89506. Antiques and collector tabloid of mostly feature material. Buys spot drawings and cartoons. Pays $10. Prefers art smaller than half-page. Query or mail original art.

AMERICAN MEDICAL NEWS, 535 N. Dearborn St., Chicago IL 60610. (312)751-6633. Editor-in-Chief: Larry Boston. Senior Editor: Barbara Bolsen. Weekly newspaper; 11x15"; 24-32 pages. Offset. Estab: 1958. Circ: 270,000. For physicians. Buys all rights. Pays on acceptance. No previously published work. Photocopied and simultaneous submissions OK. Mail cartoons. Query on illustrations. SASE. Free sample copy.
Cartoons: Buys current event, education and medical themes. Single panel OK. Submit finished art. All media OK. Pays $60, b&w. Buys 50-100 cartoons annually. Reports in 3 weeks.
Illustrations: Buys article illustrations and spot drawings on assigned themes. Submit roughs. B&w line drawings, washes and color-separated art OK. Pays $50-150, b&w. Buys 10-20 illustrations annually. Reports in 3 weeks.

AQUARIUM INDUSTRY, Toadtown, Magalia CA 95954. (916)872-1200. Editor-in-Chief: Robert Behme. Monthly newspaper; 9¾x13½"; 24 pages. Offset. Estab: 1973. Circ: 15,000. For those in the aquarium trade — manufacturers, wholesalers, retailers, and livestock breeders and farmers. Not copyrighted. Pays on acceptance. No previously published, photocopied or simultaneous submissions. Query. SASE. Free sample copy. Also uses artists for layout and book artwork.
Cartoons: Buys aquarium-related themes. Single panel OK. Submit roughs or finished art. Line drawings and halftones OK. Pays $15-25, b&w. Buys 1 cartoon per issue. Reports in 3 weeks.
Illustrations: Buys cover art on assignment. Submit roughs or finished art. B&w line drawings, washes, color-separated art and veloxes OK. Pays $40, color; $25-40, b&w. Buys 20 illustrations annually. Reports in 3 weeks.

AQUARIUM NEWS, Toadtown, Magalia CA 95954. (916)872-1200. Editor-in-Chief: Robert L. Behme. Managing Editor: Frederick J. Kerr. Monthly newspaper; 9¾x13½"; 24 pages. Offset. Estab: 1976. Circ: 51,000. For aquarium hobbyists, average age late 20s. Not copyrighted. Pays on acceptance. No previously published, photocopied or simultaneous submissions. Query with samples. SASE. Free sample copy. Also uses artists for layout and book artwork.
Cartoons: Buys hobby-related themes on aquariums. Single and double panel OK. Submit roughs or finished art. Line drawings and halftones OK. Pays $15-25, b&w. Buys 1 cartoon per issue. Reports in 3 weeks.
Illustrations: Buys cover art on assignment. Submit roughs or finished art. B&w line drawings, washes, color-separated art and veloxes OK. Pays $40, color; $25-40, b&w. Buys 40 illustrations annually. Reports in 3 weeks.

ART & ARCHAEOLOGY NEWSLETTER, 243 E. 39th St., New York NY 10016. Editor: Otto F. Reiss. For persons interested in archaeology of the Old World and ancient mythology. Quarterly; 5½x8½. Circ: 2,000. Buys cartoons. Does not want to see cartoons about archaeologists who wear pith helments. "A cartoonist who is steeped in Graeco-Roman lore could come up with usable cartoons. He would have to have an excellent background in mythology and classical history." Buys one-time rights. Sample copy $1.30 in 13¢ stamps.

THE ASIA MAIL, Box 1044, Alexandria VA 22313. Editor-in-Chief: Edward Neilan. Monthly tabloids; 24 pages. Offset. Estab: 1976. Circ: 30,000. For those interested in Asia. Buys first North American serial rights. Pays on publication. Query. SASE. Free sample copy.
Cartoons: Donna Gays, associate editor. Buys Asian, U.S.-Asian themes, from politics to terrorism. Submit roughs. Line drawings OK. Pays $25 minimum. Buys 23 cartoons per issue. Reports in 2 weeks.
Illustrations: Buys cover art, article illustrations and spot drawings on Asian themes, from politics to terrorism. Submit roughs. B&w line drawings OK. Pays $50 minimum. Buys 2-3 illustrations per issue. Reports in 2 weeks.

AUTOWEEK, Box A, Reno NV 89506. (702)972-0721. Editor: Cory Farley. Weekly newspaper. Circ: 75,000. Estab: 1958. Readers are young, generally well-educated car enthusiasts. Buys b&w line drawings and cartoons. Almost whole paper done by freelance work. Pays $5-10. "Cartoons used primarily as fillers but we use quite a few." Query with resume.

BAJA BUSH PILOTS NEWSLETTER, Drawer 81005, San Diego CA 92138. Editor-in-Chief: Arnold Senterfitt. Bimonthly newsletter; 8½x11"; 8-12 pages. Offset. Estab: 1970. Buys all rights, but may reassign rights to artists after publication. Pays on acceptance. Previously published work OK. Query with samples. SASE. "Keep everything light-hearted; no heavy editorializing. Absolutely nothing ethnic."
Cartoons: Buys themes on aviation and small planes. "Simpler cartoons are best if technique is good." Single panel OK. Submit finished art. Pays $10-25, b&w. Buys 20-40 cartoons annually. Reports in 1 week.
Illustrations: Buys spot drawings on Latin American scenes and aviation. Submit finished art. B&w line drawings OK. Pays $5-10. Reports in 1 week.
Special Needs: "We do books and maps and are always ready to help someone who can learn. Continual need for spot art for all our publications."

BERKELEY BARB, Box 1247, Berkeley CA 94701. Editor: Ray Riegert. Weekly newspaper; tabloid; 24 pages. Estab: 1965. Circ: 20,000. For those interested in leftist politics, avante-garde artists and the counter culture. Pays $15-25, drawings; $70, b&w cover. Reports in 1 month. Free sample copy.

BICYCLE DEALERS NEWSLETTER, National Bicycle Dealers Association, Inc., 29023 Euclid Ave., Wickliffe OH 44092. Contact: Tom K. Sayler. Bimonthly. For retail servicing dealers. Not copyrighed. Buys spot drawings and cartoons. Submit rough art; single panel cartoons.

BOTH SIDES NOW — FREE PEOPLE PRESS, 1232 Laura St., Jacksonville FL 32206. Contact: Editors. Monthly newspaper; tabloid. For "persons involved actively or as spectators in counter-culture movements, politics, contemporary art, music, cinema, organic living, religion. Readership is general and not necessarily young — many students, but also many middle-aged progressives." Buys camera-ready b&w art. Pays contributor's copies. Will consider material of "counter-cultural interest: political, satirical, psychedelic, comics, ornamental to accompany poetry. We want the right to use artwork in any publication by our press. All other rights remain with artist. Members of Alternative Press Syndicate may reprint work." Previously published work OK. Submit original art or published samples. SASE. Reports in 1 month.

THE BREAD RAPPER, 1110 Michigan, Evanston IL 60202. Editor-in-Chief: Laurie Lawlor. Bimonthly newsletter; 5½x7"; 4 pages. Offset. Estab: 1975. Circ: 13,000-16,000. For middle and lower-class (mostly black) savings and checking account holders and other bank customers. Buys all rights, but may reassign rights to artists after publication. Pays on publication. Photocopies OK. No previously published or simultaneous submissions. Mail artwork. SASE. Free sample copy. "We need artwork that reflects day-to-day operations in a bank (i.e. customer taking a loan, making a deposit, at safety deposit). Should be funny and immediately understood. Avoid ridiculing banking practices, minority groups."
Cartoons: Buys banking themes. Single panel OK. Submit finished art. Line drawings and washes OK. Pays $20 minimum, b&w. Buys 1 cartoon per issue. Reports in 3-4 weeks.
Illustrations: Buys spot drawings on banking themes. Submit finished art. B&w line drawings and washes OK. Pays $20 minimum. Buys 1 illustration per issue. Reports in 3-4 weeks.
To Break In: "The artist is already the customer he is trying to reach. Ask yourself — what do you think would be a humorous situation regarding your bank?"

BREAK!, Big Country 10-5 News, Inc., Box 12181, Denver CO 80212. Contact: Rose Harper. Newspaper for 2-way radio users expressing the user's and dealer's viewpoint. Buys illustrations or cartoons on CB radios. Seasonal art must be submitted 6 months in advance. Submit art from September-March. Prefers finished art, camera-ready; 3x4", b&w only. Pays $5 minimum; occasionally $10 for 5½x7" illustration for front page. Also pays $5 for unusual collages relating to radio, TV and communication fields. Collages may be fantasized.

THE CAMERABUG, 4507 Adrian St., Rockville MD 20853. Art Buyer: Milton T. Cohen. Photo service publication. Prefers finished pen and ink submissions. SASE. Pays up to $50 for finished art. Previously published work sometimes OK. Query. Reports in 30 days.

CAMPUS NEWS (formerly *Anthelion Press),* Box 614, Corte Madera CA 94925. Editor: William Whitney. Biweekly newspaper aimed at the university student. Buys b&w line drawings, full-color illustrations (color separations required) and cartoons. Pays $5-15, spot drawings; $25-100, full-color illustration; $50-75, cover design in 2 colors. Maximum size: 8x10", illustrations; 5x7", cartoons. Pays on publication. Buys one-time rights. Will consider work previously published. Mail artwork. Reports in 2-3 weeks. Sample copy $1.

THE CANADIAN INDIA TIMES, 161 Dalhousie St., Ottawa, Ontario Canada K1H 6T6. (613)235-2554. Editor: Mrs. T. J. Samuel. Biweekly. For people interested in India and Indian community in North America. Circ: 4,000. Uses b&w drawings and cartoons. Not copyrighted. Previously published work OK. Mail artwork. Reports in 1-2 weeks. Write for sample copy.

CAPPER'S WEEKLY, 616 Jefferson, Topeka KS 66607. Editor: Dorothy Harvey. A human interest and news weekly for families in small towns and rural areas. Buys finished b&w line drawings and 1-2 farm-related cartoons in each issue. Pays $5 for cartoons. Buys one-time and first serial rights. Pays on acceptance. Reports in 2 weeks. Sample copy 35¢.

CHARLOTTE OBSERVER & CHARLOTTE NEWS, Box 2138, Charlotte NC 28233. Contact: Allen Rhodes. Uses artists for newspaper ad layouts, sales promotion art and hardware/software advertising art. Query with resume.

CHICAGO READER, Box 11101, Chicago IL 60611. (312)828-0350. Editor: Robert A. Roth. Weekly newspaper; 10x16"; 60 pages. Offset. Estab: 1971. Circ: 76,000. For young adults in Chicago's lakefront neighborhoods. Buys all rights. Pays "by the 15th of the month following publication." Query with nonreturnable photocopies.
Illustrations: Robert E. McCamant, art director. Buys cover art, article illustrations and spot drawings on assignment. Pays $15-60, b&w. Buys 150 illustrations annually. Reports if interested.

THE CHRISTIAN SCIENCE MONITOR, 1 Norway St., Boston MA 02115. Daily newspaper except Saturdays, Sundays and holidays. Buys all rights. Pays on acceptance. Send original art or published samples. SASE.
Cartoons: Buys family-type cartoons. Submit to: People Page Editor. Finished pen and ink, line and wash OK. Pays $50. Reports in 2 weeks.
Special Needs: Artwork for issues on travel, vacations, cruises, fashion (February/September) and food (June/October). Submit seasonal material 1-2 months in advance.

THE COLORADO ALUMNUS, Koenig Alumni Center, University of Colorado, Boulder CO 80309. (303)492-8484. Editor-in-Chief: Ronald A. James. Monthly (except July); 11½x15½"; 12 pages. Offset. Estab: 1910. Circ: 78,000. For University administrators, alumni, librarians and legislators. Not copyrighted. Pays on acceptance. Previously published work and simultaneous submissions OK. No photocopies. Mail artwork. SASE. Free sample copy.
Cartoons: Buys sports, humor through youth, environment, campus and problems in higher education themes. All formats OK. Submit finished art. Line drawings and halftones OK. Pays $10 minimum. Buys 1 cartoon per issue. Reports in 2 weeks.
Illustrations: Buys cover art and article illustrations on sports, campus and higher education, "from Women's Lib to student activism." Submit roughs. Cover: b&w line drawing or occasionally color OK. Inside: b&w line drawings and veloxes OK. Pays $15 minimum, b&w cover and inside. Buys 1 illustration per issue. Reports in 2 weeks.

COMMUNICATIONS NEWS, 402 W. Liberty Dr., Wheaton IL 60187. (312)653-4040. Editor: Bruce Howat. Monthly tabloid. Harcourt Brace Jovanovich publication. For managers of communications systems — including telephone companies, broadcasting stations and all large communication systems. Estab: 1964. "Always on the lookout for good cartoons on subject of communications systems management." Pays on publication. Pays $10, spot drawings and cartoons. Buys all rights. Previously published work OK. Mail artwork. Reports in 3 weeks. Sample copy $1.

CROSS COUNTRY NEWS, Meacham Field, Fort Worth TX 76106. (817)624-3600. Editor-in-Chief: Tony Page. Newspaper published every 3 weeks; tabloid; 12 pages. Offset. Estab: 1945. Circ: 12,000. "For private/business plane owner pilots." Not copyrighted. Pays on acceptance. No previously published, photocopied or simultaneous submissions. Mail artwork. SASE. Free sample copy. "Be sure the artwork has some cheese cake, if possible."
Cartoons: Buys themes on aviation/UFO's. Single panel OK. Submit finished art. Line drawings only. Pays $10 minimum. Buys 36 cartoons annually. Reports in 1 week.

CYCLE NEWS, 2201 Cherry Ave., Long Beach CA 90801. Editor: John D. Ulrich. Weekly motorcycle newspaper for the enthusiast/racer. Circ: 100,000. Estab: 1965. Uses b&w line drawings, cover designs and cartoons. 9x12" maximum. Buys all rights. Pays on publication. Pays $3-5 for spot drawings/cartoons; $25 for cover. Previously published work OK. Mail artwork. Free sample copy.

CYCLE NEWS, EAST, Box 805, Tucker GA 30084. (404)934-7850. Editor-in-Chief: Jack Mangus. Weekly newspaper; tabloid; 56 pages. Offset. Estab: 1964. Circ: 60,000. For motorcycle competition enthusiasts. Buys all rights, but may reassign rights to artists after publication. Pays on publication. No previously published, photocopied or simultaneous submissions. Mail artwork. SASE. "Artist must have a familiarity with the subject. Unfamiliar submissions will be turned down because there are enough submitting artists who are very familiar with the subject."
Cartoons: Buys motorcycle-related themes on current events, education, environment and

politics; on the hobby and profession of motorcycling. All formats OK. Submit finished art. Line drawings, halftones and washes OK. Pays $5 minimum, b&w. Buys 100 cartoons annually. Reports "as soon as requested if SASE enclosed."
Illustrations: Buys cover art, article illustrations and spot drawings on racing motorcycles. Submit finished art. B&w line drawings OK. Pays $25 minimum. Buys 100 illustrations annually. Reports "as soon as requested if SASE enclosed."

DOCTORS' NURSE BULLETIN, 9600 Colesville Rd., Silver Spring MD 20901. Cartoon Editor: Bob Bickford. Quarterly newsletter. Pays $5 on publication for medical cartoons. Reports in 3-5 days.

THE DRUMMER/DAILY PLANET, 4221 Germantown Ave., Philadelphia PA 19140. Art Buyer: Bruce Buschel. Weekly underground alternative newspaper. For educated audience, ages 18-45, interested in politics, arts, manifestation of current reality and progressive social change. Appeal to Philadelphia audience important. Buys political cartoons. Pays $10+. Copyrighted. Pays on publication. Previously published work OK. Submit original art or published samples. Reports in 2-3 weeks.

DRYCLEANERS NEWS, 95 N. Main St., Waterbury CT 06702. (203)757-8731. Contact: John Florian. Trade tabloid sent monthly to drycleaners in the Northeast. Uses 1 cartoon each month. Cartoon should be for drycleaning plant owners; about an aspect of their business. Pays $10 on acceptance. Submit artwork. Free sample copy.

EARTH/SPACE NEWS, 4151 Middlefield, Palo Alto CA 94303. Editor-in-Chief: Paul L. Siegler. Managing Editor: Mark Frazier. Bimonthly; 8½x11"; 8-16 pages. Offset. Estab: 1975. Circ: 1,000. For space enthusiasts, libraries of major corporations, all those interested in exploring space. Buys all rights, but may reassign rights to artist after publication. Pays on acceptance. Previously published work and simultaneous submissions OK. No photocopies. Query with samples. SASE. Free sample copy.
Cartoons: Buys themes on current events, erotica, family life and politics; all with outer space angle. All formats OK. Submit roughs or finished art. Line drawings OK. Pays $10-50. Buys 5-10 cartoons annually. Reports in 4 weeks.
Illustrations: Buys spot drawings on space vehicles, living quarters/habitats and near-earth orbit views of satellites and earth. Submit roughs or finished art. B&w line drawings and veloxes OK. Pays $10-50. Buys 5-10 illustrations annually. Reports in 4 weeks.
Special Needs: Uses graphics and drawings for promotional purposes, including vehicle/launch site renderings for display.
To Break In: "It might be to your advantage to submit a rough the first few times through, since the subject area of commercial space exploitation is so new . . . not well understood."

FAMILY FOOD GARDEN, Box 1014, Grass Valley CA 95945. (916)273-3354. Editor: George S. Wells. "Magapaper" (tabloid format). Published 10 times annually. Circ: 250,000. For home gardeners. Assignments include cartoons and rough and finished art. At present, major need is for cartoons dealing with fruit and vegetable growing or raising of fowl and animals. Pays $10 for cartoons. Buys all rights, but will reassign rights on request of artist. Will consider work previously published. Query with resume. SASE. Usually reports in 2 weeks. Sample copy available.

FILLERS FOR PUBLICATIONS, 1220 Maple Ave., Los Angeles CA 90015. Editor-in-Chief: John Raydell. Managing Editor: Dean Bowie. Monthly; 8½x11"; 8 pages plus cartoon supplement. Offset. Estab: 1959. For editors. Buys all rights, but may reassign rights to artist after publication. Pays on acceptance. Previously published work and simultaneous submissions OK. No photocopies. Mail artwork. SASE. Free sample copy.
Cartoons: Buys themes on current events, education, family life, retirement and offices. Single panel OK. Submit finished art. Line drawings OK. Pays $5-10. Buys 72 cartoons annually. Reports in 2 weeks.

FIRE TIMES (formerly *National Police & Fire Journal),* 1100 NE 125th St., North Miami FL 33161. Editor: Tom Moore. Tabloid distributed to firefighters nationwide. Bimonthly. Buys b&w drawings. Buys all rights but will consider artwork previously published. Pays on publication. Mail artwork. Reports in 6 weeks. Sample copy 25¢.

FIRESTONE NON-SKID NEWSPAPER, Firestone Tire & Rubber Company, 1200 Firestone Pkwy., Akron OH 44317. Contact: R. Dean English. Biweekly, offset, tabloid for employees. Not copyrighted. Buys pen and ink drawings, no color. Payment negotible. Pays on acceptance. No cartoons. Previously published work OK. Query with resume. Reports in 2 weeks.

FISHING AND HUNTING NEWS, Box C-19000, Seattle WA 98109. Managing Editor: Vence Malernee. Art Editor: Fay Ainsworth. Weekly; 11½x17½"; 12-16 pages. Offset. Circ: 110,000. For outdoorsmen. Buys one-time and all rights. Pays on publication. Previously published, photocopied and simultaneous submissions OK. All methods of contact OK. Send 9x12 SASE for free sample copy.
Cartoons: Buys themes on fishing, hunting, boating, camping and outdoor activities. "No sexist, racist or slob hunter stereotypes. No young Disney-like animals, or scenes showing overkill or hunting of protected species. Include common sense safety concerns." All formats OK. Submit finished art. Line drawings and washes OK. Pays $15-50, color; $5-10, b&w. Buys up to 52 cartoons annually. Reports in 3 weeks.
Illustrations: Buys cover art, article illustrations and spot drawings on outdoor recreation; how-to diagrams; technical illustrations of boats and recreational vehicles; and maps. "Subject should portray the excitement of the hunt, the nobility of the elusive wildlife or a fighting fish that just might 'get away.'" Submit roughs if commissioned, finished art if on speculation. Cover: b&w line drawings, washes, color-separated and reflective art OK. Inside: b&w line drawings, color-separated art and veloxes OK. Minimum payment: $25, color cover and inside; $10, b&w cover; $5, inside b&w. Buys minimum of 24 illustrations annually. Reports in 3 weeks.
Special Needs: Pays minimum of $5-10 per b&w spot illustration for advertising, promotional material and brochures.

FROM THE KENNELS, Box 1369, Vancouver WA 98660. Uses spot drawings and cartoons. Not copyrighted. Submit roughs. Reports in 2-4 weeks. Sample copy 50¢.

GAY SUNSHINE JOURNAL, Box 40397, San Francisco CA 94140. (415)824-3184. Editor-in-Chief: Winston Leyland. Quarterly newspaper; 17½x11½"; 32-36 pages. Estab: 1970. Circ: 10,000. For gay people and those interested in gay literature and culture. Buys first rights. Pays on publication. Previously published work OK. Photocopies OK as samples only. No simultaneous submissions. Query with samples. SASE. Sample copy $1.
Illustrations: Buys cover art, article and poetry illustrations on gay themes. Submit finished art. B&w line drawings OK. Pays contributor's copies or negotiates payment. Buys 20 illustrations annually. Reports in 4 weeks.

GENERAL AVIATION BUSINESS, Box 1094, Snyder TX 79549. Editor: M. Gene Dow. Monthly newspaper for the aviation business. Estab: 1972. Circ: 13,000. Uses freelance material applicable to general aviation business and service categories; "no airline or military, however interesting. Really need to see copy before submitting anything except humorous cartoons." Buys b&w line drawings, washes, cover designs and cartoons. Pays $5+. Buys all rights. Will possibly consider previously published material. Query with resume. Reports in several days. Sample copy $1.

GENERAL AVIATION NEWS, Box 1094, Snyder TX 79549. Editor: M. Gene Dow. Biweekly newspaper for aircraft owners. Circ: 34,000+. Estab: 1945. Buys cartoons. B&w line drawings and washes OK. "We cover only general aviation — no military or airline, however interesting it might be. Wrong subject is our biggest reason for rejects." Pays on acceptance. Previously published work considered. Query with resume. Reports in several days. Sample copy $1.

GEORGIA FARMER, Box 13449, Atlanta GA 30324. Monthly tabloid newspaper. Uses b&w line drawings and full-color illustrations. Minimum payment: $10 color, $5 b&w. Not copyrighted. Pays on publication. Mail artwork. Reports immediately. Sample copy available.

GLENDALE NEWS-PRESS, 111 N. Isabel, Glendale CA 91206. Art Director: Frank Rietta. Newspaper. Arrange interview to show samples of ad/promotional art, illustrations and other freelance work. Must have skills required for newspaper work.

Newspaper Work is Good Start

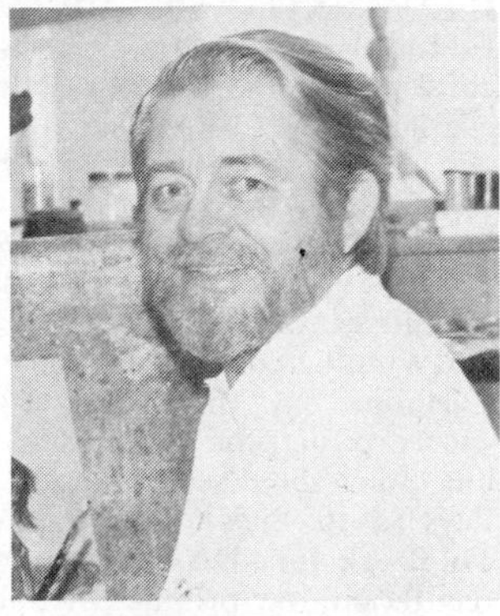
Eugene Shortridge

Though most periodicals have turned more to emphasizing photography over illustrations, Eugene Shortridge, who devotes 60 percent of his time working for magazines such as *Old West, Frontier Times* and *Lost Treasure*, insists new artists can still make regular sales. But, to break in to the field, it may be necessary to take other employment and build up freelance sales on the side.

"One of the best places to work, gain experience and make a living at the same time is a newspaper," says Shortridge. "There you will do all kinds of artwork, primarily black-and-white. The artist will deal constantly with layout and typography, and will learn to work rapidly."

About the only thing to be avoided by potential freelancers is letting rejections of your early work bother you, he adds. "Study constantly, even though from time-to-time it is necessary to be employed in other fields. All experience is valuable and can be made to work for you in your art. Try to do something related to your art each day."

— *Ben Townsend*

THE GUILD REPORTER, 1125 15th St. NW, Washington DC 20005. Art Buyer: James M. Cesnik. Published by the Newspaper Guild. Biweekly; monthly in June and December. Not copyrighted. "Our interests are almost exclusively in areas related directly to activities of The Newspaper Guild." Buys pen and ink, finished art. Pays $25 minimum, spot drawings and newspaper-related cartoons. Previously published work OK. Pays on acceptance. Query with resume. Reports in 2 weeks.

HOBBY ARTIST NEWS, Rte. 2, Box 210, Fort Atkinson IA 32144. Editor-in-Chief: Ray Gillem. Bimonthly; 8½x11"; 12+ pages. Offset. Estab: 1971. Circ: 400. For artists, authors, songwriters and craftsmen. Not copyrighted. Pays on acceptance. Previously published work OK. No photocopied or simultaneous submissions. Mail artwork. SASE. Sample copy 75¢.
Cartoons: Buys current event and family life themes. Single panel OK. Submit finished art. Line drawings only. Pays in subscription or ad space. Buys 3 cartoons per issue. Reports in 4 weeks.
Illustrations: Buys cover art and spot drawings on people, outdoor scenes and animals — life in general. Submit finished art. B&w line drawings OK. Pays in subscription or ad space. Buys 3 illustrations per issue. Reports in 4 weeks.

HOME SEWING TRADE NEWS, 129 Broadway, Lynbrook NY 11563. Editor: Nat Danas. Monthly tabloid. Uses b&w drawings and 8x10" cartoons. Pays $5-10. Buys all rights. Query. Reports after publication. Sample copy 50¢.

HOUSTON BUSINESS JOURNAL, 5314 Bingle, Houston TX 77092. (713)688-8811. Editor-in-Chief: Mike Weingart. Managing Editor: Bill Schadewald. Weekly; tabloid; 32 pages. Offset. Estab: 1971. Circ: 15,000. For highly-educated business executives, average age 40. Buys all rights. Pays on acceptance. Previously published work OK. No photocopied or simultaneous submissions. Mail artwork. SASE. Free sample copy.
Cartoons: Buys business-oriented themes. Single panel OK. Submit finished art. Line drawings OK. Pays $7.50 minimum. Buys 50 cartoons annually. Reports in 2 weeks.

HUNTER SAFETY NEWS, Box C-1900, Seattle WA 98109. Art Editor: Fay Ainsworth. Bimonthly tabloid. Circ: 20,000. For instructors of hunter safety education programs. Needs b&w drawings, cover designs, color illustrations and cartoons, rough and finished art. Pays $5-15 for spot drawings; $20 minimum for full-color illustrations; $50 for cover designs; $5-10 for cartoons. Buys various rights. Previously published work OK. Mail artwork. Reports in 2-4 weeks.

ILLINOIS WILDLIFE, Box 116, Blue Island IL 60406. (312)388-3995. Editor: Ace Extrom. Monthly tabloid for sportsmen and conservationists. Buys b&w line drawings and cartoons.

Pays $5-10, drawings; $5, cartoons. Pays on publication. Buys one-time rights. Will consider previously published work if not used in an "overlapping" publication. Sample copy 50¢.

ILLUSTRATED SPEEDWAY NEWS, 83 Grand Ave., Massapequa NY 11758. Executive Editor: Jack Schwartz. Weekly for auto racing fans. Uses b&w line drawings and 3-column cartoons. Pays $15 for cartoons. Buys all rights. Pays on acceptance. Mail artwork. Sample copy available.

INDUSTRIAL NEWS, Box 3631, Los Angeles CA 90051. (213)737-6820. Editor-in-Chief: Larry Liebman. Publishes 1 weekly, 3 monthly newspapers; 24 pages. Offset. Estab: 1947. Circ: 50,000. For factory owners, purchasing agents, engineers, small businessmen and aerospace executives. Buys simultaneous rights. Pays on acceptance. Previously published, photocopied and simultaneous submissions OK. Mail artwork. SASE. Free sample copy.
Cartoons: Buys themes relating to industrial scenes only (production problems and problems caused by detrimental legislation). "Cartoons must relate to today's factory or business; no big-bust jokes about secretaries." Single panel OK. Submit finished art. Halftones and washes OK. Pays $5-10. Buys 52 cartoons annually. Reports immediately.
To Break In: "Do cartoon on some topical industrial problem; i.e. product liability, over-regulation, low-productivity, absenteeism, foreign competition, etc."

THE JOURNAL, 33 Russell St., Toronto, Ontario Canada M5S 2S1. (416)595-6053. Editor: Anne MacLennan. Monthly. For professionals and general public interested in drug and alcohol research, treatment and education. Circ: 16,000. Artwork must apply to editorial content. Buys b&w line drawings, washes and cartoons. Pays $25+, cartoons. Minimum 3x5". Copyrighted. Pays on publication. Will consider work previously published. Mail artwork. Free sample copy.

LAS VEGAS SUN, 121 S. Highland, Las Vegas NV 89106. Art Director: Catherine Collins. Uses artists for ad layout and hardware/software advertising art. Send slides, photos or tearsheets.

LOS ANGELES FREE PRESS, 5850 Hollywood Blvd., Los Angeles CA 90028. Editor: Michael Parrish. Weekly. Circ: 50,000. Pays $5 for spot drawings; $2 for b&w illustration; $10-25 for cover art. Buys first serial rights. Pays on publication. Previously published work OK. Write. Reports in 2 weeks.

M.S. FOR MEDICAL SECRETARIES, 24 Rope Ferry Rd., Waterford CT 06386. Editor: Pamela Constantine. Educational, how-to, biweekly publication; 8 pages. "Cartoons should revolve around the medical secretary, either directly or by obvious implication. This is fertile ground for gags — dead-beat patients, no-shows, hypochondriacs, prospective parents, old folks, wonder drugs, emergencies (real or imagined) in the dead of night, now-you-see-'em, now-you-don't doctors. Most of our readers work in small offices; a few, however, in hospitals." Pays $10 for finished pen and ink on acceptance. Buys all rights. Reports in 2-3 weeks.

MFC NEWS, Box 449, Jackson MS 39205. Editor: Jim Cleveland. "Our publication is distributed to nearly 42,000 farm homes each month with news of importance to the farmer, with articles of special interest to the farm wife. We are always in the market for farm pictures or illustrations." Buys cover designs, line drawings and washes. Negotiates payment. Will consider previously published work. Pays on publication. Also uses design ideas and layout services. Submit samples. Sample copy available.

MILWAUKEE JOURNAL, Newspapers, Inc., 333 W. State, Milwaukee WI 53201. (414)414-2600. Editor-in-Chief: R. Leonard. Managing Editor: Joe Shoquist. Daily; 90 pages. Letterpress and rotogravure. Circ: 350,000. Buys all rights. No previously published, photocopied or simultaneous submissions. Query with samples. SASE.
Cartoons: George Lockwood, editor. Buys all themes acceptable to family readership. Single panel OK. Washes OK. Pays $15 minimum. Reports in 2 weeks.
Illustrations: Mel Kishner, art director. Buys article illustrations and spot drawings on all themes acceptable to family readership. Submit roughs. All media OK. Pays $10 minimum. Reports in 2 weeks.

MILWAUKEE SENTINEL, Newspapers, Inc., 333 W. State, Milwaukee WI 53201. (414)414-

2600. Editor-in-Chief: R. Wills. Managing Editor: H. Sonneborn. Daily; 60 pages. Letterpress and rotogravure. Circ: 70,000. Buys all rights. No previously published, photocopied or simultaneous submissions. Query with samples. SASE.
Cartoons: May Nelson, editor. Buys all themes acceptable to family readership. Single panel OK. Washes OK. Pays $15 minimum. Reports in 2 weeks.
Illustrations: Mel Kishner, art director. Buys article illustrations and spot drawings on all themes acceptable to family readership. Submit roughs. All media OK. Pays $10 minimum. Reports in 2 weeks.

NATIONAL ENQUIRER, Lantana FL 33464. Editor-in-Chief: Iain Calder. Weekly, tabloid; 64 pages. Letterpress. Estab: 1926. Circ: 5 million. For family readers. Buys first rights. Pays on acceptance. Previously published work and photocopies OK. No simultaneous submissions. Mail artwork. SASE. Free sample copy.
Cartoons: Cathy Brown, editor. Buys "all subjects the family reader can relate to. We like cartoons with lots of visual impact;" especially needs Christmas cartoon spread (submit 2 months in advance). All formats OK. Submit finished art. Line drawings, halftones and washes OK. Pays $210 maximum, b&w single panel; every panel thereafter, $25. Buys 540 cartoons annually. Reports in 1 week.

NATION'S RESTAURANT NEWS, 2 Park Ave., New York NY 10036. Editor: Charles Bernstein. Biweekly. Uses b&w line drawings and cartoons. Mostly needs detailed interior scenes of new, interesting restaurants. Mail artwork.

NEW ENGLAND OFFSHORE, 572 Washington St., Wellesley MA 02181. Contact: Herbert Gliick. Monthly newspaper for boating enthusiastics. Sample copy available.
Cartoons: Must be on subject of boating or water-oriented activity. Prefers roughs. Single panel, double panel and spot drawings acceptable. Will consider any size if the subject matter warrants. Pays $10-20. Reports immediately.

NEW UNITY, Box 891, Springfield MA 01101. Monthly worker-oriented tabloid. "Continuing needs relating to strikes, demonstrations, people's strengths, people in motion, people's daily lives." Not copyrighted. Prefers original material aimed at this publication. Previously published work OK.
Illustrations: Uses finished 8½x11 maximum (prefers 6½" wide maximum) pen and ink or line and wash art. No color.

NEW YORK ANTIQUE ALMANAC, Box 335, Lawrence NY 11559. (516)371-3300. Editor-in-Chief: Carol Nadel. Managing Editor: Lola Richter. Monthly newspaper; 11x16"; 24 pages. Offset. Estab: 1975. Circ: 18,000. For art, antique and nostalgia collectors/investors. Buys all rights, but may reassign rights to artist after publication. Pays on publication. Previously published work OK. Query or mail artwork. SASE. Free sample copy.
Cartoons: Buys themes on the environment, antiques, art, nostalgia, investment, money and "any potent, wry comment on our times." All formats OK. Submit roughs or finished art. All media OK. Pays $5-20. Buys 12-20 cartoons annually. Reports in 2 weeks.
Illustrations: Buys cover art, article illustrations and spot drawings on collecting and investing. B&w art OK. Pays $5 minimum. Buys 24+ illustrations annually. Reports in 2 weeks.

NEW YORK ARTS JOURNAL, 560 Riverside Dr., New York NY 10027. (212)663-2245. Editors-in-Chief: Richard Burgin/Holland Cotter. Quarterly newspaper; 15x11½"; 40 pages. Estab: 1976. Circ: 15,000. For people interested in fiction, poetry, dance, music and the visual arts. Buys first rights. Pays on publication. Previously published, photocopied and simultaneous submissions OK. Mail artwork. SASE. Sample copy $1.
Illustrations: Buys article illustrations and spot drawings. "If it's good, we'll print it, regardless of subject matter." Submit finished art. B&w line drawings, washes, reflective art and veloxes OK. Pays $10-25. Buys 5 illustrations per issue. Reports in 4 weeks.

NEW YORK CITY STAR, 149 Hester St., New York NY 10002. (212)966-0697. "We are a radical, monthly newspaper about New York City. People interested in contributing to the paper are invited to send for a free sample copy. We reach a lot of people, and treat work with respect and care." Drawings should be camera-ready. "Artists are free to send stuff printed in the *City Star* anywhere else they please. We are copyrighted, but we give movement publications permission to use whatever they like." Pays in copies. "We have an experienced staff of photo and graphics people who can 'help you along.' " Query. Reports in 1 month.

NEW YORK CULTURE REVIEW, 1807 60th St., Brooklyn NY 11204. Editor-in-Chief: Daniel M.J. Stokes. Monthly newsletter; 8½x11"; 14 pages. Offset. Estab: 1974. Circ: 2,000. For poets and New York City people, most with extensive education, interested in literature, art, dance and publishing. Buys first rights. Pays on publication. No previously published or simultaneous submissions. Photocopies OK. Mail artwork. No work returned. Sample copy $1.
Cartoons: Buys political, literary and publishing themes. "Please save us from *Playboy*-type cartoons." Single panel OK. Submit finished art. Line drawings only. Pays $5-15. Buys 12 cartoons annually. Reports in 1 week.
Illustrations: Buys cover art. "We're open to almost anything; a recent cover showed New York City as it would look while sinking; something to catch the eye in the bookstore." Submit roughs. B&W line drawings OK. Pays $5-15. Buys 12 illustrations annually. Reports in 1 week.

THE NEW YORK LAWYER, 230 Park Ave., New York NY 10017. (212)685-6562. Editor: Brian Stokes. Published bimonthly for lawyers, law students and paraprofessionals. Circ: 20,000. About 75% of newspaper is done by freelancers. Uses b&w drawings, cartoons and design ideas. Buys all rights. Will consider work previously published. Pays on publication. Mail artwork. Reports in 4 weeks. Sample copy $1.

NORTHEAST OUTDOORS, 95 N. Main St., Waterbury CT 06702. Editor: John Florian. Tabloid. "We use cartoons on outdoor life and camping in New England, New York and New Jersey." Pays $7.50 on publication. Buys all rights. Reports in 2 weeks.

NORTHEAST VAN, 95 N. Main St., Waterbury CT 06702. (203)757-8731. Editor: John Florian. Monthly newspaper for van enthusiasts. About 50% of paper's needs handled by freelancers. Pays $10, cartoons; $40, cover design. Buys first serial rights. Pays on publication. Mail artwork. Reports in 2 weeks. Sample copy available.

THE NORTHERN STAR, Campbell Hall, 535-2 Lucinda, DeKalb IL 60115. Art Buyer: Marcia Stepanek. Student newspaper. Circ: 24,000. Buys spot drawings, topical cartoons, cover designs for supplements, and art illustrations for advertising. Prefers pen and ink artwork; columns are 2¼" wide, total page size is 10x5. Topical work should focus on student issues. Pays $5 for spot drawings; $10 for b&w cover design, finished art. Not copyrighted. Pays on publication. Previously published work OK. Submit original art or published samples. Reports in 5 days.

NUTRITION HEALTH REVIEW, Box 221, Haverford PA 19041. Editor-in-Chief: F.R. Rifkin. Quarterly; tabloid; 24 pages. Offset. Estab: 1976. Circ: 125,000. For those interested in health. Buys first rights. Pays on publication. Previously published work OK "if identified as such." No simultaneous submissions. Mail artwork. SASE. Sample copy 50¢.
Cartoons: Buys themes on medicine, doctors, nutrition, food purveyors and restaurants. Single panel OK. Submit finished art. Line drawings OK. Pays $10 minimum. Buys 40-50 cartoons annually. Reports in 4 weeks.
Illustrations: Buys cover art, article illustrations and spot drawings on nutrition, health and food. Submit finished art. B&w line drawings OK. Pays $50 minimum, cover art. Buys 40-50 illustrations annually. Reports in 4 weeks.

OFFICE SUPERVISOR'S BULLETIN, 681 5th Ave., New York NY 10022. Editor: Harriet Zang. Wants cartoons that re-emphasize points in articles published relating to management of people. For first and second-line office supervisors. Buys all rights. Send SASE for sample issue and requirements.
Cartoons: "Please spare me cartoons about dumb or sexy secretaries, cringing Dagwoods, demanding wives, any situation that assumes employees are basically dishonest or inherently lazier than you or I. Also, be up-to-date. If the basic faces and hair-dos in your cartoons look like you haven't been in an office since 1950, visit a few large offices. Remember that there are many women supervisors. Perhaps a third of them supervise men as well as women. In the background are sophisticated office machines and desks arranged in cubicles or landscape fashion. I like to see cartoons that look like real offices. Cartoons on topics of current interest to managers have a better chance than general situations." Pays $10 on acceptance. Prefers

vertical cartoons in 8x10 or 5x7 ink or line and wash, "but no good gag loses out because it's horizontal."

OFFICE WORLD NEWS, 645 Stewart Ave., Garden City NY 14530. Editor-in-Chief: Robert R. Mueller. Managing Editor: Alec W. Shapiro. Biweekly newspaper; 10x14"; 24 pages. Offset. Estab: 1970. Circ: 16,000. For dealers and distributors of office supplies, furniture and machines. Buys all rights, but may reassign rights to artist after publication. Pays on publication. No previously published work or photocopies. Simultaneous submissions OK. Query with samples. SASE. Free sample copy.
Cartoons: Buys themes on office supplies, furniture and machines. Single panel OK. Submit finished art. Halftones and washes OK. Pays $10-20, b&w. Reports in 2 weeks. "We will not even consider cartoons on general office situations (Miss Jones and JB at the water cooler, etc.). Ours is a trade paper."
To Break In: "To appeal to a trade audience, a cartoonist should take time to find out a little about the trade."

OHIO MOTORIST, Box 6150, Cleveland OH 44101. Editor-in-Chief: A.K. Murway, Jr. Published 10 times annually; tabloid; 16 pages. Offset. Estab: 1909. Circ: 230,000. For members of AAA-Cleveland. Not copyrighted. Pays on acceptance. No photocopies. Previously published work and simultaneous submissions OK. SASE. Free sample copy.
Cartoons: Buys current event, environment, travel and automotive themes. "For editorial page, we need strong visual comments on safety matters, poor driving, big trucks, roadbuilding delays and potholes." Single panel OK. Submit finished art. Line drawings OK. Pays $8-15 spot cartoons; $25-50, editorial page cartoons. Buys 50 cartoons annually. Reports in 2 weeks.

P.S. FOR PRIVATE SECRETARIES, 24 Rope Ferry Rd., Waterford CT 06386. Editor: Pamela Constantine. Wants "cartoons about the secretary-businesswoman and the problems she faces moving up in the business world. Also wants cartoons concerning the problems she faces in the daily grind of getting her work done (i.e., pacifying irate callers or visitors who must wait to see her boss, juggling work for 2 or more bosses, dealing with her boss's idiosyncrasies)." Pays $10 for pen and ink finished art on acceptance. Buys all rights. Reports in 2-3 weeks.

THE PATRIOT, 243 W. Main St., Kutztown PA 19530. (215)683-7343. Editor-in-Chief: A. R. Floreen. Weekly newspaper; 11x14"; 24 pages. Offset. Estab: 1874. Circ: 5,000. For general audience. Buys newspaper ad layouts and sales promotion art. Pays $5-10 per sketch. Arrange interview.

PICTURE, 8th and Locust, Des Moines IA 50304. Editor: Charles Nettles. Weekly newspaper using general subjects with hard Iowa slant. Buys art for rural/urban emphasis articles. Minimum payment: $20, b&w; $35, inside color; $60, cover. Copyrighted. Query.

PRO PUBLICATION, Box 5400, Detroit MI 48067. (313)871-1200. Editor-in-Chief: James Keating. Monthly newspaper; 14x11"; 20-24 pages. Estab: 1976. Circ: 135,000. For General Motors upper, top management; Chevrolet Division sales department management; dealers and dealer management; and retail sales and service personnel. Buys first rights. Pays on acceptance. Previously published work (with release) and photocopies OK. No simultaneous submissions. Query with samples. SASE. Free sample copy.
Illustrations: "We believe the American automobile salesman and serviceman is a frequently and erroneously maligned member of our society. We know him to be honest and hard-working in an activity of great importance to millions of people. We are interested in seeing him depicted in this way. Show a positive attitude. Sarcasm, negativism and cynicism don't get it in this industry." Assigns illustrations on auto merchandising, its people and processes. B&w line drawings and reflective art OK. Pays $100 minimum.

PROLOG, 104 N. St. Mary, Dallas TX 75214. (214)827-7734. Managing Editor: Mike Firth. Quarterly newsletter; 8½x11"; 8-10 pages. Offset. Estab: 1973. Circ: 200. For playwrights. Not copyrighted. Pays on acceptance. Previously published, photocopied and simultaneous submissions OK. Query. SASE. Sample copy 50¢.
Cartoons: Buys themes on writing and theater. Single panel OK. Submit finished art; "may be informal. Prefers line drawings showing humor in either writing for theater or working in amateur theater." Pays $5 minimum. Buys 1-2 cartoons per issue. Reports in 4 weeks.

PULP, 720 Greenwich St., Apt. 4H, New York NY 10014. (212)989-0190. Editors-in-Chief: Howard Sage/Regina Vogel. Quarterly newspaper; 8x11½"; 12 pages. Offset. Estab: 1975. Circ: 2,000. For those interested in poetry and fiction. Buys first rights. Pays on publication. No previously published, photocopied or simultaneous submissions. Mail artwork. SASE. Free sample copy.
Cartoons: Buys cartoons on literature. All formats OK. Submit finished art. Line drawings only. Pays $2. Buys 4 cartoons annually. Reports in 4 weeks.
Illustrations: Buys cover art, article illustrations and spot drawings on eclectic themes. Submit finished art. B&w line drawings, reflective art and veloxes OK. Pays $2. Buys 12 illustrations annually. Reports in 4 weeks.

QUILTER'S NEWSLETTER/MAGAZINE, Box 394, Wheatridge CO 80033. Editor: Bonnie Leman. Buys quilt design ideas. Pays $2-3 for simple drawings and up to $20 or more for more complex ideas. "The subject matter must be quilts, quiltmaking, quilters or quilt patterns and we do need good camera-ready artwork on these subjects." Buys first or second rights. Usually pays on acceptance. Reports in 2 weeks.

SALINAS CALIFORNIAN, Box 1091, Salinas CA 93901. Advertising Director: Jack Rogers. Newspaper. Buys art renderings (interior and exterior), furniture design, layouts, and especially fashion design on a continuing or seasonal basis. Of interest are b&w halftones and washes, original art, maximum size 29x38"; color original art, maximum size 13⅝x21¼". Pays $15 minimum for drawing or layout. Buys all rights. Pays on acceptance. Previously published work OK. Mail artwork. Reports in 1 week-10 days.

SCREW MAGAZINE, 116 W. 14th St., New York NY 10011. Contact: Milton Zelman. Sex tabloid newspaper. "We like the artist's imagination and creativity to run wild. Sexual cliches are of no interest to us." Would like to see rough drawings and/or published samples of artist's style. Pays $50-100 for inside illustrations in b&w and $125 for color covers (flat with overlays) on publication. Buys one-time rights.

SHUTTERBUG ADS, Box 730, 3910 S. Washington Ave., Titusville FL 32780. Art Buyer: Glenn Patch. Newsprint photography publication. Buys spot drawings and photographic cartoons. Pays $5 for spot drawing. Pays on publication. Previously published work OK. Query with resume.

THE SIGNPOST, 16812 36th Ave. W., Lynnwood WA 98036. (206)743-3947. Publisher: Louise Marshall. Editor: Barb Diltz-Siler. Monthly; 24 pages. Offset. Estab: 1966. Circ: 5,000. For Pacific Northwest hikers who have additional outdoor hobbies and interests. Buys first rights. Previously published, photocopied and simultaneous submissions OK. Query. SASE. Sample copy available.
Cartoons: Buys outdoor themes. Single panel OK. Pays contributor's copies or subscription. Reports in 3 weeks.
Illustrations: Buys article illustrations and spot drawings on hiking primarily, some other outdoor themes. Pen and ink only. Pays contributor's copies or subscription. Reports in 3 weeks.

SIPAPU, Rte. 1, Box 216, Winters CA 95694. Co-Editor/Publisher: Noel Peattie. Published semiannually; 8½x11"; 24 pages. Offset. Newsletter for librarians, editors, collectors and others interested in Third World studies, the counter culture and the free press. Buys pen and ink drawings for the margins or centers on the pages. One artist does the complete publication. Copyrighted. Pays $50.

THE SOAP BOX, Box 1129, Manassas VA 22110. (703)361-4848. Editor: Vickie Pollock Murphy. Monthly newspaper; 32 pages. Offset. Estab: 1975. Circ: 50,000-75,000. For soap opera fans. Buys all rights. Pays on publication. No previously published or simultaneous submissions. Photocopies OK. Query with samples. SASE. Free sample copy.
Cartoons: Buys soap opera themes. Single and double panel OK. Submit finished art. Halftones and washes OK. Pays $5 minimum, b&w. Reports in 3 months.

SOLAR ENERGY DIGEST, Box 17776, San Diego CA 92117. Editor-in-Chief: William B. Edmondson. Monthly newsletter; 8½x11"; 12 pages. Offset. Estab: 1973. Circ: 1,600. For scientists, engineers, technicians and others interested in solar energy conversion. Buys all

rights, but may reassign rights to artist after publication. Pays on publication. No previously published work. Mail artwork. SASE. Sample copy $1. Pays $5 minimum per hour, advertising art/layout.
Cartoons: Buys themes on solar energy conversion. Single panel OK. Submit finished art. Line drawings OK. Pays $5 minimum. Reports in 2 weeks.
Illustrations: Buys article illustrations on solar energy conversion. Submit finished art. B&w line drawings OK. Pays $5 minimum. Reports in 2 weeks.

SOUL NEWSPAPER, 8271 Melrose Ave., Suite 208, Los Angeles CA 90046. (213)653-7775. Editor-in-Chief: Regina Jones. Managing Editor: Connie Johnson. Biweekly; 15x10¼"; 20 pages. Offset. Estab: 1966. Circ: 175,000. For blacks interested in the black entertainment scene, fashion, dancing and black progress in show business. Buys first rights. Pays on publication. Simultaneous submissions OK. No previously published work or photocopies. Query with samples. SASE. Free sample copy.
Cartoons: Buys themes on current events, environment, humor through youth, politics and entertainment. Single panel OK. Submit finished art. Halftones and washes OK. Pays $10 minimum. Reports in 4 weeks.
Illustrations: Buys cover art and article illustrations. B&w line drawings, washes and veloxes OK. Pays $25 minimum, b&w cover; $15, inside b&w. Reports in 4 weeks.
Special Needs: Uses artists for layout, advertising, brochures, logos, symbols and stationery. Pays $25 minimum.

SOUNDS INFORMATIVE, 332 E. Camelback Rd., Phoenix AZ 85012. (602)265-4830. Editor-in-Chief: William Niblick. Managing Editor: Bart Bull. Monthly; tabloid; 20-24 pages. Offset. Estab: 1973. Circ: 25,000. For music listeners, audiophiles and musicians ages 18-35. Buys all rights, but may reassign rights to artist after publication. Pays on acceptance. Previously published, photocopied and simultaneous submissions OK. Query. SASE. Sample copy 50¢. "Since we operate on a limited budget, we offer starting artists the opportunity to have work published. We invite queries from anyone more interested in having work published than cash payment. Local artists often paid with record albums and concert tickets."
Cartoons: Bill Drummond, editor. Buys themes on music and entertainment. Single panel OK. Submit roughs or finished art. Line drawings only. Pays $25 maximum. Buys 1-5 cartoons annually. Reports in 3 weeks.
Illustrations: Buys cover art, article illustrations and spot drawings on stereo equipment, music, entertainment, musicians and performing arts. Submit roughs or finished art. Cover: 2-color, color-separated art OK. Inside: b&w line drawings and washes OK. Pays $75 maximum, color cover; $25 maximum, inside b&w. Buys 1-10 illustrations annually. Reports in 3 weeks.

SOUTH CAROLINA FARMER-GROWER, Box 13755, Atlanta GA 30326. Editor: June Brotherton. Monthly taboid newspaper containing general farm information. Uses b&w line drawings and full-color illustrations. Minimum payment: $10 color; $5 b&w. Not copyrighted. Pays on publication. Mail artwork. Reports immediately. Sample copy available.

STAR WEST & S.B. GAZETTE, Box 731, Sausalito CA 94965. Editor: Leon Spiro. Quarterly. Interested in b&w drawings, 4x5 cartoons and rough and finished art. Not copyrighted. Will consider artwork previously published. Pays contributor's copies. Mail artwork. Sample copy $1.

STREET/ALTERNATIVE PAPER, Star Publishing Inc., Box 5680, Cleveland OH 44101. Contact: G. Finder. Biweekly. Uses pen and ink, line and wash, rough or finished art. For inside editorial art, no larger than 5x7"; cover art 9x12". Pays $25 for cover design in 2 colors, finished art. Buys all rights. Pays on publication. Previously published work OK. Send published samples or original art. Reports in 30 days.

TELEBRIEFS, Illinois Bell Telephone Co., 225 W. Randolph, Chicago IL 60606. Editor-in-Chief: Bill Kuhs. Monthly newsletter; 5¾x6¾"; 4 pages. Offset. Estab: 1938. Circ: 3½ million. For telephone customers. Not copyrighted. Pays on acceptance. No previously published or simultaneous submissions. Photocopies OK. Mail artwork. SASE. Free sample copy.
Cartoons: Buys telephone industry related themes. "No ethnic humor. We reduce cartoons to 1x1½" so we need few elements and drawn very boldly. Prefer strong visual with caption of 10 or fewer words." Single panel only. Submit finished art. Line drawings, Zipatone shading OK. Pays $40. Buys 20 cartoons annually. Reports in 2 weeks.

TELEVISIONS MAGAZINE, Box 21068, Washington DC 20009. Managing Editor: Larry Kirkman. Quarterly newspaper; 15x10"; 24 pages. Offset. Estab: 1975. Circ: 20,000. For video and TV producers, educators, librarians, media activists, TV viewers, journalists, broadcast and cable executives, social service administrators, and others interested in new communications. Buys first rights. Pays on publication. Previously published work and simultaneous submissions OK. No photocopies. Query with samples. SASE. Free sample copy.
Cartoons: Buys cartoons on TV and video communications. Single and multi-panel OK. Submit finished art. Line drawings and halftones OK. Pays $5 minimum, b&w. Buys 4-10 cartoons annually. Reports in 4 weeks.
Illustrations: Nick DeMartino, editor. Buys cover art, article illustrations and spot drawings. Illustrations on assignment. Also interested in random, creative illustrations dealing with the role of TV in American life, the activities of independent video producers and flimmakers, and visions of technology. Submit roughs for commissioned work; finished art for spot drawings. Cover: b&w line drawings, washes and color-separated art OK. Inside: b&w line drawings, color-separated art and veloxes OK. Pays $10 minimum. Buys 4-10 illustrations annually. Reports in 4 weeks.
Special Needs: Artwork for these issues: February 15, video aesthetics/criticism; May 1, building a library of media books; September 1, distributing independent video; November 15, annual hardware review and using video in community context. Also uses designers for editorial layouts; local artists should include layout sample with query.
To Break In: "Be tuned into the video world; understand the issues and concepts that appeal to our readers."

TEXAS TRAVELER, 2205AA Echols St., Bryan TX 77801. Editor: Josephine Payne. For amateur poets, writers and collectors/hobbyists. Not copyrighted. Published semiannually, in June and December. Previously published work OK. Send published samples or original art. SASE. Reports in 2 weeks.
Illustrations: Publication "is mimeographed and can only consider line drawings in black ink. Any line drawings have to be not more than an inch or two high (3 at the most) or wide, and clear enough for tracing on a mimeo stencil. No shadings wanted." Artwork should be "eye-catching little doodads that dress up the publication." Pays 1 contributor's copy.

THEATER ACROSS AMERICA, 104 N. St. Mary, Dallas TX 75214. (214)827-7734. Managing Editor: Mike Firth. Published 5 times annually; 8½x11"; 8-10 pages. Offset. Estab: 1975. Circ: 100. For people active in community theater. Buys first North American serial rights. Pays on acceptance. Previously published, photocopied and simultaneous submissions OK. Query. SASE. Sample copy $1.
Cartoons: Buys themes on writing and theater. Single panel OK. Submit finished art, but "may be informal." Prefers line drawings showing humor in writing for or working in amateur theater." Pays $5 minimum. Buys 1-2 cartoons per issue. Reports in 4 weeks.

TRI-STATE TRADER, Box 90, Knightstown IN 46148. Managing Editor: Kevin Tanzillo. Weekly tabloid newspaper. For persons interested in antiques, collectibles, local history and genealogy. Circ: 30,000. Estab: 1968. Always interested in seasonal material for Christmas, Thanksgiving, Easter, Halloween, July 4th, Valentine's Day; issues that express the appropriate greetings in an antique-related manner. Seasonal material required 2-4 months in advance. Also buys cover art. Not copyrighted. Will consider previously published material if not exposed to this readership. Pays on publication. Reports in 1-2 weeks.

THE UNIVERSITY OF MICHIGAN PAPERS IN WOMEN'S STUDIES, 1058 L, S & A Bldg., University of Michigan, Ann Arbor MI 48104. (313)763-2047. Monthly; 9x11"; 150-200 pages. Estab: 1974. Circ: 500. For feminist academicians. Buys cartoons on feminist themes. Pays contributor's copies. Previously published and photocopied work OK. Mail artwork.

VEGETARIAN WORLD, Suite 216, 8235 Santa Monica Blvd., Los Angeles CA 90046. Editor-in-Chief: William Blanchard. Managing Editor: Scott S. Smith. Quarterly; 11x17"; 32 pages. Offset. Estab: 1974. Circ: 30,000. For "well-read persons interested in good health and moral and humanist aspects of vegetarianism." Buys all rights. Pays on publication. Query with samples. SASE for rejection returns. Free sample copy.
Cartoons: Buys themes on vegetarianism. All formats OK. Submit roughs. Widths of 2,4,6,8 or 10" OK (8 and 10" for multi-panel only); 16" maximum depth. Line drawings only. Pays $10-

25. Buys 24-48 cartoons annually. Reports in 3 weeks. "Cartoons about so-called 'food animals' with a humane-vegetarian twist are especially sought."

THE VINEYARD, 202 Lucerne Ave., Lake Worth FL 33460. (305)588-5136. Editor-in-Chief: Daniel John Gorham. Biweekly newspaper; 26x105"; 4-8 pages. Offset. Estab: 1967. Circ: 4,500. For those college-educated persons interested in religion. Not copyrighted. Pays on publication. Previously published, photocopied and simultaneous submissions OK. Mail artwork. SASE. Free sample copy.
Cartoons: Buys themes on education, religion, and international language such as Esperanto. Submit finished art. Line drawings and washes OK. Minimum payment: $5, b&w; $10, color. Buys 48-86 cartoons annually. Reports in 4 weeks.
Illustrations: Buys cover art and spot drawings that "make 'em think." Submit roughs or finished art. B&w line drawings and washes OK. Minimum payment: $5, b&w; $15, color. Buys 48-86 illustrations annually. Reports in 4 weeks.
Special Needs: "Would like to see some religious Ikon artwork for a special on the subject, and for use throughout the year." Also uses artists for layout. Pays $200 minimum.

THE W.E.S. BULLETIN, Box 457, Henniker NH 03242. Editor: Thomas J. Watman. For educators and administrators. Monthly; 8½x11". Circ: 1,500. Needs b&w drawings, cover designs, cartoons and rough art. Pays $10-15 for spot drawings/cover designs; $5-15 for cartoons. Buys all rights. Previously published work OK. Submit resume. Reports in 2 weeks. Free sample copy.

WESTERN CANADA OUTDOORS (formerly Alberta Fish & Game Association), Box 430, North Battleford, Saskatchewan Canada S9A 2Y5. (306)445-4401. Editor-in-Chief: C. Irwin McIntosh. Bimonthly newspaper; 10x15"; 16 pages. Offset. Estab: 1977. Circ: 35,000. For hunting, fishing and outdoor families. Not copyrighted. Pays on acceptance. Previously published work OK. Mail artwork. SASE. Free sample copy.
Cartoons: Buys outdoor themes. Single panel OK. Submit finished art. Halftones OK. Pays $5-10. Buys 12 cartoons annually. Reports in 4 weeks.

WOMEN ARTISTS NEWSLETTER, Box 3304, Grand Central Station, New York NY 10017 (212)666-6990. Editor-in-Chief: Cynthia Navaretta. Monthly newsletter; 8½x11"; 8 pages. Offset. Estab: 1975. Circ: 4,500. For artists, art teachers/students, women's studies teachers/students, art writers/historians, museum curators and gallery directors. Buys all rights, but may reassign rights to artist after publication. Pays on publication. Previously published work and photocopies OK. Mail artwork. SASE. Free sample copy.
Cartoons: Judy Seigel, editor. Buys themes on art and artists. Double panel OK. Submit finished art. Washes OK. Pays $5-7.50, b&w. Reports in 2 weeks.
Illustrations: Susan Schwalb, editor. Buys article illustrations on art and artists. Submit finished art. Cover: b&w line drawings and veloxes OK. Inside: b&w line drawings, washes and veloxes OK. Pays $5-7.50, b&w. Reports in 2 weeks.
Special Needs: Employs artists on regular basis for layouts and brochures.
To Break In: Artist needs "a familiarity with the current fine art scene, what is news and what is being talked about."

Syndicates & Clip Art Services

Talent, being in the right place at the right time and professionalism in presentation are the keys to getting your work accepted by syndicates and clip art firms. Clip art firms buy thousands of illustrations annually, while each of the major syndicates buys only two or three strips a year.

Artists with a package of illustrations on one or more themes will find clip art firms a good market for their work. Submissions should include a series of illustrations (preferably on one theme) that lend themselves well to reproduction in newspapers or other publications that use clip art as their main source for illustrations.

Selling to a syndicate is a little more involved. The competition is greater and the artist has to be able to prove that he can produce quality material day after day.

The best way to approach a syndicate about your work is to have ready a list of central characters or themes that will carry your work through. Then go ahead and create several weeks worth of finished material which includes the central characters, an identity of the world they live in and a hint at what direction their lives will take.

When developing these strips, keep story lines, the illustration's quality, ruling and lettering in mind. Your cartoon should be drawn two or three times larger than 14x44 picas (the standard size of a daily strip). So remember that your lettering should be large enough that it is readible when reduced.

According to Tom Batiuk (creator of "Funky Winkerbean") and other successful cartoonists, you'll get the same consideration from syndicates whether you submit your cartoons by mail or in person. In either case, pay special attention to your presentation. If you are personally presenting your work, be neat and businesslike and have your presentation well-planned. If you're working by mail, take care to package your work neatly and include a *typewritten* cover letter.

Before sending your work to a syndicate or before trying to syndicate the material yourself, be sure to obtain a copyright on the title of the strip and on the characters. Otherwise you open yourself up to copying from other artists (see "The New Copyright Law: What You Need to Know").

And remember, even the pros know what a rejection slip looks like, so don't get discouraged if they come. "Don't give up or allow discouragement to change your objectives," says David Brown (creator of "Today's World"). "It takes a lot of time to learn to do anything well, especially cartooning. I think it best that the novice should get himself as many of the 'how to do it' books available on the subject of cartooning as he can."

But if too many rejection slips do get you down, consider teaming up with an artist who is already syndicated, says Richard Sherry, editor of Field Newspaper Syndicate. "There might be occasional freelance work with our already-established comic strip artists who are looking for assistants. If cartoonists have styles which might be close to one of those already drawing our features, they could submit samples and we would pass them along to the syndicated comic artist. If interested, the artists would then decide on any working and monetary arrangements between themselves," says Sherry.

The Cartoonists Guild (156 W. 72nd St., New York City 10023) publishes a guide — write for information on how to obtain it — outlining how to break in to the syndicate market entitled *CG Syndicate Survival Kit*. And a list of more syndicates can be found by checking the *Syndicate Directory* (Editor & Publisher).

ALLIED FEATURES SYNDICATE, 520 Citizens Bldg., Cleveland OH 44114. Contact: Jerome Langell. Syndicate. Clients are newspapers. "We are interested in material to be submitted to daily newspapers on a continuing basis, not a one-time sale. 50% commission. Submit artwork.

AUTO NEWS SYNDICATE, 8530 Canfield Dr., Dearborn Heights MI 48127. Contact: Donald E. O'Reilly. Syndicate. Clients are newspapers and magazines. Interested in cartoons and editorial illustrations relating to the automotive field. Pays $10 for stock-item line drawings. Custom work rates negotiated in advance. Query.

BANKER & BRISEBOIS CO., 3300 Book Tower, Detroit MI 48226. Contact: Harry Gilmore. Clip art service. Uses artists for illustrations of furniture for newspaper ad layouts. Artists must be skilled in perspective drawing from photos. Send samples or clips of work.

CHICAGO TRIBUNE-NEW YORK NEWS SYNDICATE, INC., 220 E. 42nd St., New York NY 10017. Editor: Don Michel. Estab: 1919. Syndicate. Considers comic strips and panel themes. Clients are newspapers. Query. Buys all rights. Submit photocopies. SASE. "We do not buy 1-shot articles or cartoons."

COLLEGE PRESS SERVICE, 1764 Gilpin St., Denver CO 80218. (303)388-1608. Contact: Thomas Tredford. Clip art and news service for college newspapers. "We have continuing need for graphic and editorial art dealing with current affairs, politics and news events. "Publishes semiweekly releases of 9 pages; 2 pages (8½x14") devoted to graphic editorial art, advertising art, editorial cartoons, line drawings and filler sketches. Has subscribing papers in 47 states with readership of more than 1.5 million. Buys individual sketches, cartoons and cartoons strips, but usually not a series. No sexist, racist or pro-war graphics. "We're especially looking for art dealing with student rights, environmental protection, feminism and consumerism. No advertising art of individual products — cans of soup, bars of soap." Pays $5-14. Maximum size of work: 4x5. "We usually run uncopyrighted art for reproduction by our subscribers. However, we will consider, in special cases, purchasing first or second rights." Submit camera-ready art. SASE. Reports in 3 weeks.

COMMUNITY AND SUBURBAN PRESS SERVICE, Box 639, Frankfort KY 40601. (502)223-1621. Managing Editor: Michael Bennett. Syndicate. Clients are 500 weekly newspapers. Considers humorous cartoons. Pays $15. Reports in 7-10 days.

CONTEMPORARY FEATURES SYNDICATE, INC., Box 1258, Jackson TN 38391. Editor: Lloyd Russell. Estab: 1974. Clients are "several dozen" newspapers and magazines. Considers all themes. Single panel cartoons OK. On outright purchases, pays $5 minimum; otherwise, 50% commission. Pays on publication. Buys various rights. Mail finished b&w originals. SASE. Reports in 4-6 weeks.

CREATIVE CARTOON SERVICES (R), 3109 W. Schubert Ave., Chicago IL 60647. Contact: Peter Vaszilson. Clip art service. "We are seeking work from cartoonists and gagwriters." Query. SASE.

DYNAMIC GRAPHICS, INC., 6707 N. Sheridan Rd., Peoria IL 61614. (309)691-0428. Vice President: John L. Rush. Clip art service. Interested in seeing all styles of illustrations, stylized art and decorative spots in line or wash. Interested primarily in b&w but will consider some 2 and full-color. "We like to purchase a series of 3 or 4 illustrations at a time on a wide variety of subjects such as: business, sports, vacations, men, women, communication or industry. We are looking for artists who can consistently produce top-quality art." Payment on acceptance for finished art. Rates negotiable. Buys all rights. Buys 1,000+ illustrations annually. Submit original art. Reports in 2-3 weeks.

MILTON FEINBERG, International Marketing, 444 E. 86th St., Suite 20E, New York NY 10028. (212)628-2353. Contact: Milton Feinberg. Uses artists for new comic strip properties suitable for books and newspapers. Worldwide market.

FIELD NEWSPAPER SYNDICATE, 401 N. Wabash Ave., Chicago IL 60611. (312)321-3093. Editor: Richard Sherry. Distributes features and comics to newspapers in the U.S. "The easiest way to submit material as far as mechanical specifications are concerned is to find the published format you wish to follow and do that twice the size. Pen or brush on 2- or 3-ply Strathmore makes good sense. As a syndicate we deal mostly in comic strips, panel cartoons and editorial cartoons. We will look at almost any kind of reproduction sample that is easily readable but we should always receive 2 week's worth of finished material so that we know how it would look. For a daily feature, that would be 6 samples. There might also be occasional freelance work with our established comic strip artists looking for assistants. If cartoonists have styles which are close to 1 of those drawing our features, they could submit samples and we would pass them along to the syndicated comic artist. If interested, the artists would then decide on any working and monetary arrangements between themselves." Remuneration varies from a price per piece arrangement to a share in the revenue of the feature on a continuing strip. Mail artwork. Submissions held from a few days to months. Usually buys all rights. Some comic features currently distributed: "Andy Capp," "Mary Worth" and "Dennis The Menace."

FILLERS FOR PUBLICATIONS, 1220 Maple Ave., Los Angeles CA 90015. Contact: John Raydell. Publishes pick-up ideas and cartoons for magazine editors. Considers general interest cartoons, finished art in line and/or Zipatone for reduction to 3½x4". Pays $5 on acceptance for all rights. Reports in 2 weeks.

FOUR STAR FEATURES/CARICATURE CLIP ART, Box 8643, Philadelphia PA 19101. General Manager: John Prinkey. Estab: 1970. Clip art service and syndicate; 37 newspapers and magazine subscribers. Considers humorous and political single-panel and caricature cartoons. Pays $35 minimum, b&w. Pays on publication. Buys various rights. Mail photocopies. SASE. Reports in 3 weeks.

FULLER ENTERPRISES, 1737 York Ave., 4N, New York NY 10028. (212)737-3082. Editor/Publisher: Harold F. Fuller. Estab: 1971. Syndicate; 106 newspaper, radio and TV publications subscribers. Considers artwork on recorded music. Pays on publication. Query. SASE. Reports in 30-90 days.

HARRIS & ASSOCIATES PUBLISHING DIVISION, 247 S. 800 East, Logan UT 84321. (801)753-3587. Contact: Dick Harris. Estab: 1970. Syndicate; 200 newspaper subscribers. Considers humorous, golf, tennis and family cartoons. All formats OK. Buys 10-12 freelance works annually. Pays $5-25, b&w. Pays on acceptance. Buys all rights. Query with photocopies or roughs. SASE. Reports in 2 weeks.

HUMORAMA, INC., 100 N. Village Ave., Rockville Centre NY 11570. Editor: Ernest N. Devver. Humorama includes *Popular Jokes, Joker, Cartoon Fun & Comedy* and *Popular Cartoons.* Considers erotic but tasteful cartoons for adults; topical, risque and visually identifiable. No porno or blatant obscenity. Wants parody on any popular subject. Pen and ink roughs, or finish for offset litho, 4-panel OK. Pays $12. Pays 15 days after acceptance. Buys all rights. SASE.

KAMP STOOL FEATURES SYNDICATE, 3001 Henderson Dr., Suite K, Cheyenne WY 82001. President: Joseph F. Prunty. Syndicate; 168 daily and weekly newspaper subscribers. 50% commission.

KING FEATURES SYNDICATE, INC., 235 E. 45th St., New York NY 10017.

KNOWLEDGE NEWS & FEATURES SYNDICATE, Kenilworth IL 60043. Executive Editor: Dr. Whitt N. Schultz. Estab: 1960. Syndicate; subscribers are dailies, weeklies and monthlies. Considers humorous, business, communications, family and political cartoons. All formats OK. Pays $5 minimum. Pays on publication. Buys exclusive rights. Query with photocopies. SASE. Reports in 2 weeks.

LOS ANGELES TIMES SYNDICATE, Times-Mirror Square, Los Angeles CA 90053. Editor: Thomas B. Dorsey. Clients are 1,500 newspapers and others. Pays for publication and translation into foreign language for foreign markets. 50% commission. Query with resume.

LYNN ENTERPRISES, Mail Trace Rd., Lagro IN 46941. (219)782-2345. Editor: R. J. Lynn. Estab: 1974. Syndicate; 250 newspaper subscribers. Considers single-panel and cartoon strips appealing to mass audience. 50% commission. Pays on publication. Buys all rights. Mail rough samples. SASE. Reports in 2 weeks.

McNAUGHT SYNDICATE, 60 E. 42nd St., New York NY 10017. Contact: Cartoon Editor. Buys about 10 cartoons weekly for newspaper feature, "This Funny World." Pays $25 each. Buys all rights. Pays on acceptance. Submit square, single panels, drawn in line, no Ben-Day. Reports in 2 weeks.

MANSON WESTERN SYNDICATE, 12031 Wilshire Blvd., Los Angeles CA 90025. (213)478-2061. Editor: Patrick McHugh. Estab: 1975. Syndicate. Clients are newspapers. Considers continuing-strip or panel features. 50% commission. Pays on publication. Buys all rights. Mail samples. SASE. Reports in 3 weeks.

MID-CONTINENT FEATURE SYNDICATE, Box 1662, Pittsburgh PA 15230. Editor: John Paulus. Distributes cartoons, strips and other features to 600 daily newspapers. Considers single panel, multi-panel cartoon strips and newspaper editorial cartoons. Ideas for new art-illustrated features for syndication welcome. Submit published samples. SASE. Reports in 7 days.

MINORITY FEATURE SYNDICATE, Box 421, Farrell PA 16121. (412)981-3751. President: Bill Murray. Estab: 1975. Syndicate; 40 newspaper and magazine subscribers. Considers humor through youth and family themes for single-panel, strips and multi-panel cartoons. Also needs ideas for "Candy Man" comic feature. Buys 300+ freelance works annually. 50% commission. Pays on acceptance. Buys all rights. Write for material slant. SASE. Reports in 2 weeks.

NC NEWS SERVICE, 1312 Massachusetts Ave. NW, Washington DC 20005. Director/Editor-in-Chief: Richard W. Daw. "NC is a service for the Catholic religious press and any artwork sent in should have some kind of religious connection or moral commentary. Usually our work is commissioned with an artist in this area, but there is occasional possibility for outside use." Interested in editorial cartoons for newspapers and religious art. Submit finished art, 8x10" b&w ink drawings only. Payment is $15-18 for original illustration for religious education series, as commissioned; $5-10 for cartoons. Buys first or second rights. Pays on acceptance. Query. Reports in 2 weeks.

NEW YORK TIMES CO., SPECIAL FEATURES, SYNDICATE DIVISION, 229 W. 43rd St., New York NY 10036. Manager: John Osenenko. Clients are worldwide newspapers and periodicals. Interested in cartoons, art and line drawings. Pays for publication and translation for foreign markets. 50% commission.

NEWSPAPER ENTERPRISE ASSOCIATION, INC., 230 Park Ave., New York NY 10017. (212)679-3600. Editorial Director: Robert Cochnar. Syndicate; 750 newspaper and other subscribers. Especially interested in comic strip ideas, editorial cartoons and comic panels. If used in NEA Daily Service, artist generally gets flat fee. If used in Enterprise Features, syndicate division, 50% commission.

NORTH AMERICAN PRECIS SYNDICATE, INC., 220 W. 42nd St., New York NY 10036. Vice President: Carol Torres. Considers illustrations and cartoons for TV and newspaper clients.

OCEANIC PRESS SERVICE, Box 4158, North Hollywood CA 91607. (213)980-6600. Manager: John R. West. Syndicate; 200 newspaper and magazine subscribers. Considers illustrations (including romantic), cartoons and book covers. All cartoon formats OK. Buys several hundred freelance works annually. 50% commission. Pays on publication. Buys all rights. Query with finished samples. SASE. Reports in 4 weeks.

THE REGISTER AND TRIBUNE SYNDICATE, INC., 715 Locust St., Des Moines IA 50304. President: Dennis R. Allen. Clients are 1,000 newspapers and others. Pays for publication and translation into foreign languages. Comic strips should reduce to about 40 picas, 2-column panels to approximately 20 picas. Commission split arranged by contract.

REPORTER, YOUR EDITORIAL ASSISTANT, 1220 Maple Ave., Los Angeles CA 90015. (213)747-6542. Editor: George Dubow. Estab: 1961. Clip art service. Single panel cartoons OK. Buys 50 freelance works annually. Pays $5-10. Buys all rights. Mail artwork. SASE. Reports in 2 weeks.

SAWYER PRESS, Box 46-578, Los Angeles CA 90046. (213)656-5481. Art Buyer: Eric Matlen. Feature syndicate. Considers cartoons, artwork, design ideas, cover design, editorial illustration, layout, lettering, spot drawings, typography for adult magazine market, such as *Oui, Penthouse.* Prefers finished art. Looking for quality realistic drawings — pin ups (line or wash) of women — "foxy ladies, glamour girls, erotic, sensual (no hardcore sex) — partially (kinky) clothed, mini-skirts, far-out clothing, costumes a la 'Barbarella,' high heels (chunky or spike), stockings. Must be tasteful. No explicit genitalia, no sex acts. Assignment may be guaranteed or on speculation, "depending on how certain we are of getting exactly what we can use in magazines." Prefers to deal directly with artist. Spot drawings pay about $15-35; full-color illustrations, $50+. Buys all rights. Pays on acceptance. Mail artwork. Reports in 1-2 weeks.

BP SINGER FEATURES, INC., 3164 W. Tyler Ave., Anaheim CA 92801. (714)527-5650. Director: Eldon Maynard. Estab: 1940. Syndicate: 300+ newspaper, magazine, book publisher, textile company and advertising subscribers. Considers jacket covers, family and sex cartoons. All cartoon formats OK. 50% commission. Pays on collection. Buys all rights. Mail "ready-made" submissions. SASE. Reports in 3 weeks. No unpublished artists.

TAGUMI FEATURES SYNDICATE AND PUBLISHING, Box 275, El Cerrito CA 94530. Contact: John C. Dvorak. Clients are 48 newspapers. Looking for fine art for jacket illustrations and single panel cartoons. Pays $10 for cartoons. Fees for fine art negotiable. "Anyone having rejected art may submit it to us (preferably a copy, initially). We may find a use for it for future works or for our gallery. We pay $20-200." Query. Reports in 30 days.

TRANS-WORLD NEWS SERVICE, Box 2801, Washington DC 20013. (202)638-5568. Bureau Chief: G. Richard Ward. Estab: 1924. Syndicate; 400 newspaper, magazine and newsletter subscribers. Considers all themes except erotica. All formats OK for cartoons. Buys 300-400 freelance works annually. Pays $7.50-$50, b&w illustrations; $10-75, 2-color; $35-100, full-color; or 50% commission. Buys all rights. Mail photocopies or roughs. SASE. Reports in 4 weeks.

U-B NEWSPAPER SYNDICATE, Box 2383, Van Nuys CA 91409. Columnist: Steve Ellingson. Interested in designs for craft and art projects for syndicated column; especially interested in advertising art, animated cartoons, architectural renderings, catalog illustrations/covers, Christmas projects, furniture and industrial designs. Ellingson is the originator of a variety of projects designed for the home handyman — woodworking projects, craft items and leatherworking. Average payment: $100 minimum. Payment on acceptance. Query with resume. SASE. Reports in 1 week.

UNIVERSAL PRESS SYNDICATE, 6700 Squibb Rd., Mission KS 66202. Editor: James F. Andrews. Wants panels and strips for daily syndication. Payment according to contract. Buys syndication rights. Reports usually in 4 weeks.

WILLIAMS NEWSPAPER FEATURES SYNDICATE, INC., Box 8005, Charlottesville VA 22906. (804)293-4706. President: G. Walton Lindsay. Estab: 1939. Syndicate; 1,200 newspaper subscribers. Produces weekly advertising features for newspaper church pages. Considers religious illustrations. Pays $60-75, b&w. Pays on acceptance. Buys all rights. Query or write for interview. SASE. Reports in 3 weeks.

WORLD NEWS SYNDICATE, LTD., 6223 Selma Ave., Hollywood CA 90028. Executive Editor: Bill Lane. Query or submit ideas or samples. 50% commission.

Helpful Aids

Agents

Art & Crafts Market is designed so that the artist and/or craftsman can use it to find places where he can try to sell his work — which is a very time consuming task. The alternative is to try to find somebody who will do the selling for you. You might need an agent.

But getting an agent is easier said than done. Since part of the agent's income depends on how much work of yours he can sell, he will accept only the best work available. In effect, you don't hire an agent; he employs you.

Agent services are not free. An agent will usually take from 25 to 33 percent commission on the selling price.

If you do decide to try to get an agent to represent you, get all agreements in writing. You'll want to include the following in a contract: What is the precise commission the representative will receive? Will it vary according to assignment? If the agent gets you one job with an agency or firm, will a commission be paid to him for future assignments from that account? Will the agent get a fee for every job regardless of who obtains the assignment? Leave nothing undiscussed, and don't sign anything you're not completely satisfied with.

Never jump trustingly into an agent's arms. Check him out — he'll be doing the same to you. Try to learn who his clients are, then contact them. Ask them how well he has sold their work. Look for a representative who has been with the same clients for several years, not one who has jumped from artist to artist.

In some cities, such as New York City, firms and agencies prefer to work with agents. According to one successful Atlanta advertising artist, who found the going rough in New York City, it's almost impossible to get a job in Manhattan without an agent (except with book and magazine publishers who generally prefer to deal in-person with the artist).

Before you seriously start thinking about getting an agent, try to build up your sales and reputation on your own. The best way to do that is by making the most of the markets in this book. Chances are the agent you'll be working with tomorrow is using *Art & Crafts Market* to find potential customers.

ARTHUR'S, Box 9191, Marina Del Rey CA 90291. Contact: M. C. Arthur. Estab: 1957. Represents contemporary artists to galleries in California. Buys outright and on commission. Mail resume with photos of work.
To Break In: "Present an original style or presentation combined with good workmanship and

visual reality, whether subject matter is in this world or fantasy. We want quality workmanship and not speed painting."

ARTIST, ETC., 3225 Lemmon, Suite 360, Dallas TX 75204. (214)528-7260. Contact: C. Seibert. Represents local artists to advertising agencies, printers, book publishers, art studios and film producers. Works on 15% commission.

ARTISTS INTERNATIONAL, 9 Jane St., New York NY 10014. (212)929-5840. Contact: Michael G. Brodie. Estab: 1970. Represents 70 artists to advertising agencies and book and magazine publishers in the U.S., U.K., France, Canada, Switzerland and Germany. Works on 25% commission. Query with resume. SASE.

SAM BRODY, 17 E. 48th St., New York NY 10017. (212)758-0640. Contact: Sam Brody. Represents New York City area artists in the film and multimedia industries to advertising agencies, film producers and magazine publishers. Send resume. A subsequent phone call should be made before submitting samples. Works on 25% commission in New York City; 30% out of New York City.

PEMA BROWNE LTD., 185 E. 85th St., New York NY 10028. (212)369-1925. Contact: Pema or Perry Browne. Estab: 1966. Represents 12 artists/craftsmen to advertising agencies, book publishers, film producers and magazine publishers in New York, New England, Philadelphia, Chicago and Texas. Works on 25-30% commission. Portfolio should have "uniqueness in style from humor to realism. Call or write for interview.

COULTHURST DAY, 1A Ferney, Dursley, Goucestershire England GL11 5AB. 0453-3159. Contact: E. G. Day. Estab: 1953. Represents 20 artists to the stationery trade in England. Works on 20% commission. Mail samples. SASE. Work remains artist's property until sold or return is requested.
To Break In: "Use good quality drawing paper, not board, and remember the cost of postage. Produce work of general stationery size."

BARBARA GORDON ASSOCIATES, 165 E. 32nd St., New York NY 10016. (212)686-3514. Represents artists to ad agencies, film producers and magazine publishers. Works on 25% commission. Mail nonreturnable work or slides. SASE. "We prefer to represent local artists, but make exceptions for out-of-towners with a specialty, i.e. medical illustration, or mechanical."

LINDA A. GOULD, 71 Park Ave., New York NY 10016. Contact: Linda Gould. Estab: 1969. Represents 4 local artists to advertising agencies and magazine publishers in the New York metropolitan area. Works on 25% commission. Portfolio should contain printed ads or magazine work with viable style. Mail nonreturnable samples.
To Break In: "Presentation is a major consideration. Pride in one's work as demonstrated by neat, clean, straight-edged, uniformly-sized presentation is essential for me to consider anyone's work. Stylistic consistency is also important. I can accept an artist having more than one style, but there must be enough samples in that style to make a complete statement."

INTERNATIONAL ARTISTS ALLIANCE, Box 131, Springfield VA 22150. (703)451-1404. Contact: Ernesto Farago. Represents artists to Springfield area art studios and concert performers. Works on 15% commission. Query with resume.

JOAN JEDELL, 370 E. 76, New York NY 10021. (212)861-7861. Represents artists to ad agencies and book and magazine publishers. Works on 25-33% commission. Query with resume and nonreturnable samples.

JEMET, INC., 115 W. 30th St., New York NY 10001. President: Jerry Eislen. Represents artists to New York City advertising agencies and manufacturers, particularly for men's fashion artwork. Works on 25% commission. Mail samples.

JERRY LEFF COMPANY, 342 Madison Ave., New York NY 10017. (212)697-8525. Contact: Jerry Leff. Estab: 1972. Represents 8 artists to advertising agencies, art studios, film producers and magazine and book publishers in the New York metropolitan area. Works on 25% commission. Query with resume. SASE.

To Break In: "A majority of the firms we do business with require full-color, tight and realistic illustrations, primarily of people."

JULIA LENTO PHOTOGRAPHY, 101 Ocean Pkwy., Brooklyn NY 11218. (212)233-8989. Represents local artists to ad agencies, retail stores and magazine publishers. Works on 25-40% commission. Query with resume and samples. All submissions become property of agency.

PERFORMING ARTIST ASSOCIATES OF NEW ENGLAND, 23 Kenwood St., Brookline MA 02146. (617)277-4535. Contact: Joan Lettvin. Estab: 1974. Represents 60 regional artists/musicians to classical and jazz concert offices in the New England states. Portfolio should contain samples of marketed products, simplicity of design and breath of experience. Query and call or write for interview. SASE.

S. J. L. MANAGEMENT, 111 W. 57th St., New York NY 10019. Contact: Count Joseph Lodato. Represents artists to New York area advertising agencies, film producers and book and magazine publishers. Works on 10-30% commission. Query with resume.

THOMAS SCHLUECK, Drostestrasse 41, 3000 Hannover, Germany. Contact: Thomas Schlueck. Estab: 1970. Represents artists to book and magazine publishers in Germany and European countries. Works on 25% commission. Query with resume.

RITASUE SIEGEL AGENCY, 60 W. 55th St., New York NY 10019. (212)586-4750. Contact: Ritasue Siegel. Estab: 1969. Represents 400 employers to doll manufacturers and toy, silver and china companies in the U.S., England, France, Brussels, Canada and Middle East. Fees paid by employers of artists; no agency fee. Mail resume and 20 nonreturnable cardboard-mounted 35mm slides of work.
Special Needs: Especially interested in stuffed toy/doll designers; traditional designs for silver, tableware, dinnerware, graphic and 3-D; contemporary decorative designs for casual china and housewares; sculptors of doll faces and caricatures; toy sculptors for clays and waxes; and glass and ceramic designers, modelmakers and sculptors.
To Break In: "Be flexible and able to meet deadlines; have a realistic appraisal of time. Show sketches as well as finished art. Be able to pick up at a moments notice and be comfortable working in a strange environment when necessary. Clients like neat down to earth nice people."

ELEANORA WALKER, 229 E. 51st St., New York NY 10022. (212)751-4860. Contact: Eleanora Walker. Estab: 1961. Represents 2 local artists to advertising agencies and book and magazine publishers in the New York metropolitan area. Works on 25% commission. Portfolio should contain good, clean, live, realistic style with a flow to it. Query with resume. SASE.

Aid

The term "starving artist" has been repeatedly tagged on artists and craftsmen who are trying to earn a living at their work. So, we've included this section in *Art & Crafts Market* that lists places willing to consider helping artists make ends meet.

Aid is more than just monetary assistance. There are also listings here for groups providing legal counseling, marketing advice, artists-in-the-schools programs and educational assistance.

One of the toughest types of aid for any artist to get is a foundation grant. Here you have to "sell yourself" to get accepted. Come up with a goal of what you want to do and stick with it.

Once you've set your goal, you'll probably need to write a proposal and cover letter. Get to the point quickly; tell why your project is significant; learn the foundation's special interests and point out the tie between your work and that interest; give exact costs; reveal other funding sources you might have; and be concrete and objective. Also, make certain everything is neatly *typewritten.* An excellent book on how to get grants is *The Art of Winning Foundation Grants* (The Vanguard Press). Listings of available grants are included in *The National Directory of Grants and Aid to Individuals in the Arts* (Washington International Arts Letter).

When you are looking for help of any sort, it's often wise to become a member of an art-related organization, such as the American Crafts Council (44 W. 53 St., New York City 10019) or the Associated Councils of the Arts (570 7th Ave., New York City 10018). Write to these associations for membership information or to learn where the nearest art or craft council is in your area.

ACADEMY OF ART COLLEGE, 625 Sutter St., San Francisco CA 94102. (415)673-4200. Registrars: J. Schroeder/D. Haight. Provides Artists-in-Schools programs, grants and scholarships to artists/craftsmen. Offers $500 Western Association grant, five $875 merit scholarships, $33,500 summer grants and work-study programs to sculptors, potters, painters, muralists, graphic designers and illustrators. Available to full-time or incoming Academy students.

ALABAMA STATE COUNCIL ON THE ARTS & HUMANITIES, 449 S. McDonough St., Montgomery AL 36130. (205)832-6758. Programs Coordinator: Cherie Kelly. Provides Artists-in-Schools programs and grants to arts/crafts organizations and schools. Offers $6,000 (matched by schools to $12,000) Artists-in-Schools and up to $1,000 Artists-in-Residence programs to sculptors, potters, painters, muralists and graphic designers. Available to professional artists. Application deadline: March 1. Work judged by 10 slides.

ALASKA STATE COUNCIL ON THE ARTS, 619 Warehouse Ave., Anchorage AK 99501. (907)279-8808. Executive Director: Roy Helms. Provides Artists-in-Schools programs and Art in Public Places commissions to artists/craftsmen. Offers $1,300 monthly stipend for Artists-in-Schools programs and 1% commission for Art in Public Places. Submit resume and portfolio. No application deadline.
Special Needs: Uses artists for programs, posters and workshop instruction. No payment.

AMERICAN WATERCOLOR SOCIETY, INC., 1083 5th Ave., New York NY 10028. Contact: Scholarship Chairman. Offers grants to be used as scholarship stipends for watercolor students. Available to schools authorized to accept tax-deductible donations and which demonstrate their capability to contribute to watercolor painting advancement. Amount of grants and selection of school recipients determined by AWS.

AMERICAN-SCANDINAVIAN FOUNDATION, 127 E. 73rd St., New York NY 10021. Contact: Exchange Division. Provides fellowships, grants-in-aid and/or awards ranging from $500-4,000 for graduate-level study at the native-language institutions of Denmark, Finland, Iceland, Norway or Sweden. With few exceptions, there are no restrictions by field. Available to U.S. residents who have completed their undergraduate education. A working knowledge of the language of the country in which the applicant wishes to study is usually required. Preference given to candidates who are at the pre-doctoral level of study and who have not previously lived or studied in Scandinavia. Query.

ARIZONA COMMISSION ON THE ARTS AND HUMANITIES, 6330 N. 7th St., Phoenix AZ 85014. Executive Director: Louise C. Tester. Provides grants to institutions, which fund painters, sculptors, photographers, muralists, designers and craftsmen on various arts programs and projects. Query with program or project proposal.

ARKANSAS STATE ARTS AND HUMANITIES, 500 Continental Bldg., Markham and Main Sts., Little Rock AR 72201. (501)371-2539. Executive Director: Sandra Perry. Provides Artists-in-Schools programs and grants to arts/crafts organizations which fund sponsored painters, sculptors, potters and craftsmen. Available to artists/craftsmen sponsored by organizations.

ARTS & CRAFTS DIVISION, Science & Culture Center, State Capitol, Charleston WV 25305. (304)348-3736. Director: Donald Page. Provides marketing information and technical assistance to artists/craftsmen and crafts organizations. Available to West Virginia residents.

ARTS COUNCIL OF ROCHESTER, INC., Hutchinson House, 930 East Ave., Rochester NY 14607. (716)442-0570. Office Manager: A. Valerie Zapf. Provides legal counseling (Volunteer Lawyers for the Arts) and publications for artists/craftsmen and organizations.

ARTS EXTENSION SERVICE, Hills North, University of Massachusetts, Amherst MA 01003. (413)545-2013. Contact: Robert Lynch. Provides legal counseling, marketing information, booking services, directory listing, community arts consulting and lawyer referals to artists/craftsmen and organizations.

ARTS, INC., Box 32382, Washington DC 20007. (202)333-0223. Director: Janet Fling. Provides job referral services to artists/craftsmen.

BROCKPORT FINE ARTS ACTIVITY BOARD, Fine Arts Bldg., State University College, Brockport NY 14420. (716)395-2543. Faculty Advisor: Peg Brokenshire. Division of Student Government. University sometimes provides funding to painters and sculptors. Also occasionally uses artists for posters.

BRONX COUNCIL ON THE ARTS, 57 E. 184th St., Bronx NY 10468. (212)733-2100. Assistant Director: Ellen Mintzer. Provides grants and technical assistance to Bronx-based arts/crafts organizations. Offers up to $3,000 in grants to sculptors, painters, potters, muralists and graphic designers. Available to artists/craftsmen sponsored by organizations. Also uses artists for poster design.

BROOKLYN ARTS AND CULTURE ASSOCIATION, INC., 200 Eastern Pkwy. Brooklyn NY 11203. Assists painters, sculptors, graphic designers, muralists and other artists. For assistance on a project, request application form. Submit published samples and/or slides with resume and list of prizes and/or awards won. Also sponsors art shows.

BUSH FOUNDATION FELLOWSHIP FOR ARTISTS, W-962 First National Bank, St. Paul MN 55101. (612)227-0891. Provides up to $10,000 for 12-18 month period for painters, sculptors or graphic artists to complete projects or to advance careers. Offers 8 awards. Applicants must be at least 25 years old, and have resided in Minnesota at least 1 year prior to filing application. Must also present evidence of professional accomplishment through publication, exhibition and examples of recent work.

CALIFORNIA STATE COLLEGE, STANISLAUS, 800 Monte Vista Ave., Turlock CA 95380. (209)632-2431. Art Department Chairman: Winston McGee. Provides scholarships and work-study programs to artists/craftsmen. Offers full tuition scholarships to sculptors, painters, potters and printmakers. Apply to registrar's office.

THE CANADA COUNCIL, Box 1047, Ottawa, Ontario Canada K1P 5V8. (613)237-3400. Chief, Information Services: Mario Lavoie. Provides Artists-in-Residence programs and grants to sculptors, painters, architects, graphic artists, administrators, illustrators and organizations.

Available to Canadian citizens or landed immigrants. Write, outlining field of interest and assistance required.

CENTRALIA COMMUNITY COLLEGE, Box 639, Centralia WA 98531. (206)736-9391. Financial Aid Director: Joseph Beaulieu. Provides grants and scholarships to artists. Offers $250,000 in Basic Educational Opportunity Grants to potters, painters and other artists. Application deadline: April 1.

CINTAS FELLOWSHIP PROGRAM, Institute of International Education, 809 United Nations Plaza, New York NY 10017. Secretary: Robert F. Morris. Provides fellowships to professional artists. Offers six $4,000 fellowships to architects, painters, sculptors and printmakers. Available to artists with Cuban citizenship or lineage. Receives applications from January 1-April 1.

CITIZEN'S COUNCIL FOR THE ARTS, Box 901, Coeur d'Alene ID 83814. Contact: Opal Brooten. Interested in painters, sculptors, graphic designers, muralists and craftsmen. Send slides.

CLEVELAND AREA ARTS COUNCIL, 108 The Arcade, Cleveland OH 44114. (216)781-0045. Contact: Nina Gibans. Provides grants outright or through matching funds from the State Council. Recently presented $1,000 grant for sculptural design.

COLORADO COUNCIL ON THE ARTS AND HUMANITIES, 770 Pennsylvania St., Denver CO 80203. Artists' Services Coordinator: Joanne Marks. Provides Artists-in-Schools programs, Chautauqua touring program, grants and technical assistance to artists/craftsmen and organizations. Offers $100-7,500 in grants to nonprofit, tax-exempt organizations. Write for deadline information.

COMMISSION OF ARTS AND HUMANITIES, 400 E. Grace St., 1st Floor, Richmond VA 23219. (804)786-4492. Executive Director: Terry Haynie. Provides Artists-in-Schools programs and grants to artists/craftsmen and organizations. Offers $10,800 9-month stipends for Artists-in-Schools and $100-5,000 in arts expansion/public service projects grants. Available to professional artists/craftsmen and nonprofit, tax-exempt organizations. To apply for AIS, send resume, slides and brief letter describing "your method of operation in working with school children." Write or call for information.

CRAFTSMEN'S GUILD OF MISSISSIPPI INC., Box 1341, Jackson MS 39205. (601)354-8884. Executive Director: Dan Overly. Provides Craftsmen-in-Residence programs, grants, legal counseling, marketing information and scholarships to potters, glass blowers, fiberworkers, sculptors, leatherworkers and arts/crafts organizations. Available to Mississippi residents. Also uses graphic designers at marketing events.

CREATIVE ARTISTS PUBLIC SERVICE PROGRAM, (CAPS), 250 W. 57th St., New York NY 10019. (212)247-6303. Contact: Henry Murphy. Provides assistance to graphic/mixed media artists, painters and sculptors. Available to "artists who are not matriculated students as of June and are state residents." Submit samples.

D.C. COMMISSION ON THE ARTS & HUMANITIES, 1329 E St. NW, Washington DC 20004. (202)737-5334. Special Projects Coordinator: Ms. Rickie Orchin. Provides Artists-in-Schools programs, grants and technical assistance workshops to artists/craftsmen and organizations.

DEPARTMENT OF STATE, Washington DC 20520. Contact: Director, Office of Press, Broadcasting and Public Affairs, Bureau of Educational and Cultural Affairs. Provides grants. Query.

EASTERN NEW MEXICO UNIVERSITY, Station 19, Art Dept., Portales NM 88130. (505)562-2652. Director: Chris Gikas. Provides fellowships, grants, grants-in-aid and scholarships to artists/craftsmen. Offers $100 minimum in grants, scholarships and work-study fellowships; $100-400, grants-in-aid to painters, sculptors, potters, commercial artists and art educators. Available to full-time students. Write the Financial Aid Office. Application deadlines: April and October.

EVANSVILLE ARTS & EDUCATION COUNCIL, 10600 Old State Rd., Evansville IN 47711. Executive Director: Ellen M. Snyder. Receives grants to work with painters, sculptors, muralists and graphic designers. Also works with Hospital Audiences, Inc., and hires artists and instructors on a one-time basis. Awards or grants administered to high school students only. "We can help artists apply to Indiana Arts Commission or National Endowment for the Arts."

FLORIDA STATE UNIVERSITY DEPARTMENT OF CRAFT DESIGN, School of Visual Arts, Florida State University, Tallahassee FL 32306. (904)644-5473. Chairman: Ivan Johnson. Provides fellowships, scholarships and marketing information to craftsmen and organizations. Offers $4,000 in fellowships and $3,500 in teaching assistantships to potters, jewelers, enamelists, fiber artists and wood designers. Available to craftsmen with B.A. or B.F.A. and 3.5 grade point average. Application deadline: February 1.

FONDATION DES ESTATS-UNIS, 15, Boulevard Jourdan, 75690 — Paris-Cedex 14 France. Contact: Director. Offers 4 Harriet Hale Woolley Scholarships annually for the study of art and music in Paris. Each grant carries a stipend of $2,200 for October-June. Additional $300 given to artists to cover the higher cost for a studio. Information concerning travel grant available from the Institute of International Education, 809 United Nations Plaza, New York NY 10017. Artists expected to participate in the foundation's cultural and social activities. They should also have a keen interest in contributing to the ideal of mutual exchange of ideas through contacts with persons of other nationalities. Eligibility requirements: (1) American citizenship; (2) Graduation with high academic standing from an American college, university, or professional school of recognized standing. Preference given to mature students who have already done graduate study; (3) Capacity for study on graduate level; (4) Artistic accomplishment; (5) Good working knowledge of French; (6) Good moral character, personality and adaptability; (7) Good health; (8) Age limit, 21-34 years. Application deadline: January 31.

THE FORD FOUNDATION, 320 E. 43rd St., New York NY 10017. No general fellowship program for visual artists at the present time.

GEORGIA COUNCIL FOR THE ARTS AND HUMANITIES, 225 Peachtree St. NE, Suite 1610, Atlanta GA 30303. (404)656-3990. Director: John Bitterman. Grants made to local sponsors on matching-funds basis and are used to aid painters, sculptors, graphic designers and muralists. Also co-sponsors workshops, exhibits and competitions.

GLASSBORO STATE COLLEGE, Division of Fine & Performing Arts, Art Dept., Glassboro NJ 08028. Contact: Daniel Chard. Provides awards and grants to painters, sculptors, craftsmen and printmakers through department of art.

GRANTS FOR GRADUATE STUDY ABROAD, Institute of International Education, 809 United Nations Plaza, New York NY 10017. (212)883-8270. Program Administrator: Arthur Tackman. Provides fellowships and scholarships "based on the cost of living in countries" to artists/craftsmen.

GREATER SAN JOSE AREA COUNCIL OF ARTS, 123 S. 3rd St., Suite 103, San Jose CA 95113. Contact: Val Ramsay. Provides awards and grants to painters, sculptors and architects. Coordinating Arts Council publishes calendar of events, expanded newsletter and arts directory (local-Santa Clara Valley).

GREENSHIELDS FOUNDATION, 1814 Sherbrooke St. W., Montreal, Quebec Canada H3H 1E4. Grants available to young painters and sculptors in the field of traditional art. Write for application form.

GREENWICH HOUSE POTTERY, 16 Jones St., New York NY 10014. (212)242-4106. Director: Jane Hartsook. Provides scholarships to potters. Offers five $100 Madeline Sadin Scholarships per semester; $100 Madeline Sadin Award; $200 Frances Simches Scholarship. Available to students. Send resume and letter stating need. Application deadline: September 1.

HUDSON COUNTY OFFICE OF CULTURAL & HERITAGE AFFAIRS, Suite 503A, County Administration Bldg., 595 Newark Ave., Jersey City NJ 07306. Director: Charles K. Robinson. Provides Artists-in-Schools programs, grants and awards to federal and state agencies; serves as a clearinghouse for services on cultural and heritage affairs; provides consultation on fundraising, professionalism, contracts, legal services, tax matters and markets.

INDIAN ARTS & CRAFTS DEVELOPMENT PROGRAM, Indian Arts and Crafts Board, Department of the Interior, Washington DC 20240. Contact: General Manager. Provides an informational, promotional, coordinating and advisory clearinghouse for matters pertaining to the development of Indian, Eskimo and Aleut art and crafts. Demonstration workshops designed to upgrade skills of craftsmen conducted in cooperation with various state and private organizations which provide funding and instructors.

INDIANA ARTS COMMISSION, 155 E. Market St., Suite 614, Indianapolis IN 46204. (317)633-5649. Executive Director: Janet I. Harris. Provides Artists-in-Schools programs and funds to artists in all disciplines and nonprofit organizations. Available to Indiana residents.

KANSAS ARTS COMMISSION, 117 W. 10th, Suite 100, Topeka KS 66612. Arts Program Coordinator: Robert Richards. Provides Artists-in-Schools programs and grants to arts/crafts organizations which sponsor painters, sculptors, graphic designers and craftsmen. Query with resume.

KENTUCKY ARTS COMMISSION, 100 W. Main St., Frankfort KY 40601. (502)564-3757. Information Officer: J. Julian. Provides Artists-in-Schools programs, grants, advice and counseling to artists/craftsmen and organizations. Offer $700,000 in grants. Available to artists/craftsmen sponsored by organizations. Application deadline: spring.

KENTUCKY GUILD OF ARTISTS & CRAFTSMEN, INC., Box 291, Berea KY 40403. (606)986-3192. Executive Director: Garry Barker. Provides marketing information to Kentucky artists/craftsmen.

KATE NEAL KINLEY MEMORIAL FELLOWSHIP, 110 Architecture Bldg., University of Illinois, Urbana IL 61801. (217)333-1662. Contact: Jeanette Lytle. Provides one $2,500 fellowship annually to an artist, architect, musician or craftsman. Application deadline: April.

KOSCUISZKO FOUNDATION, 15 E. 65th St., New York NY 10021. (212)734-2130. Contact: Scholarship Committee. Provides grants-in-aid and scholarships to artists/craftsmen. Offers grants to study in Poland, $1,000 scholarships and $300-500 in grants to those in plastic arts. Write for application. Application deadline: January 15.

LINFIELD COLLEGE, McMinnville OR 97128. (503)472-4121. Art Department Chairman: Steven Karatzas. Provides scholarships and grants to individual artists. Offers $800-1,200 scholarships and work-study programs to students. Available to art majors, including printers, with required grade point average. Write for application. Applications available on first come, first served basis.

LORAIN COUNTY ARTS COUNCIL, INC., 120 Middle Ave., Elyria OH 44035. (216)323-6694 or 233-7667. Contact: Constance Mateer. Represents 17 active arts-oriented organizations. Provides grants to painters, sculptors and graphic designers. In 1975, made grant applications of more than $1,000. Available to Lorain County artists. Write for forms.

MAINE STATE COMMISSION ON THE ARTS AND HUMANITIES, State House, Augusta ME 04333. Executive Director: Alden C. Wilson. Provides Artists-in-Schools program and grants to sponsors who hire painters, sculptors, graphic designers and muralists. Recently, $13,000, state and federal, was granted to the Portland Vocational School for a sculptor-in-residence, a component of the Artists-in-Schools program. Sculptor was in residence for academic year. Also occasionally uses artists for direct mail brochures and posters.

MASSACHUSETTS ARTS AND HUMANITIES FOUNDATION, INC., 14 Beacon St., Boston MA 02108. (617)723-3851. Executive Director: Richard S. Linzer. Provides Artists Fellowship, Artists-in-Residence and Lawyers for the Arts programs. Offers 55 $3,000 Artists Fellowships programs to painters, printmakers, sculptors and other visual and performing artists. Available to Massachusetts residents, ages 18+, who are not students. Lawyers for the Arts program refers artists with art-related problems to participating attorneys.

METROPOLITAN ARTS COMMISSION, 1220 SW 5th, City Hall, Rm. 412, Portland OR 97204. Contact: Emily Carpenter. Presently funds local painters, sculptors, graphic designers and muralists for projects that take place within Multnomah County or the City of Portland. "We encourage artists and organizations to seek additional funds, but grants are not contingent on matching funds." Query for application form.

MICHIGAN COUNCIL FOR THE ARTS, 1200 6th Ave., Detroit MI 48226. Contact: Jim Crawford. Works through professional, nonprofit organizations and institutions, which offer employment to artists for programming, commissions, fellowships and scholarships. Program is currently being developed to include artists working independently of established institutions. Open to Michigan artists. Send name and address to: Support to Individual Artists Program. It is anticipated that this program will include 1) direct grants; 2) an exposure component — which will develop new audiences and marketplaces for individual artists; 3) a service component — which may include legal assistance, equipment pools, or an 'ombudsman' to help solve artists' problems.

MIDDLESEX COUNTY ARTS COUNCIL, 37 Oakwood Ave., Edison NJ 08817. Director: Estelle Hasenberg. Most grants made on matching fund basis to painters, graphic designers and sculptors. Seeks highly professional New Jersey artists who have exhibited in the State Museum, juried state level shows, banks, public libraries, hospitals or municipal buildings in Middlesex County. Submit published samples or slides, resume and list of prizes and/or awards won. Occasionally uses artists for programs, posters and direct mail brochures.

MINNESOTA STATE ARTS BOARD, 314 Clifton Ave., Minneapolis MN 55403. (612)874-1335. Visual Arts Coordinator: Peder Sulerud. Provides Artists-in-Schools programs, fellowships and grants to artists/craftsmen and nonprofit, tax-exempt organizations. Direct grants available to Minnesota residents.

MISSISSIPPI UNIVERSITY FOR WOMEN ART DEPARTMENT, Box W-70, Columbus MS 39701. Chairman: Charles Ambrose. Provides scholarships to artists. Offers $250 Paula Robertson Art Scholarship. Available to students. Send portfolio and credits/transcripts.

MISSOURI ARTS COUNCIL, 111 S. Bemiston, Suite 410, St. Louis MO 63105. (314)721-1672. Program Coordinator: John Amberg. Provides Artists-in-Schools, Artists-in-Residence programs and matching grants to artists/craftsmen and organizations. Offers $500-12,000 in grants to nonprofit crafts organizations. Available to Missouri residents, ages 18+. Write for information.

MONTANA ARTS COUNCIL, 235 E. Pine St., Missoula MT 59801. (406)243-4883 or 543-8286. Contact: Patricia K. Simmons. Participates in the Artists-in-Schools program for painters, sculptors and graphic designers. All grants made on matching funds basis. Application deadline: April 1. Query with resume, awards and published samples. Occasionally uses artists for direct mail brochures.

NATIONAL ENDOWMENT FOR THE ARTS, Washington DC 20506. Chairman: Nancy Hanks. Independent agency of the federal government through which grants are made to organizations and individuals concerned with the arts. Grants to individuals generally require no matching funds. Provides assistance through programs on architecture/environmental arts, crafts, museums, education (Artists-in-Schools) and visual arts. *A Guide to Programs* is issued by the Endowment each August and may be obtained by contacting the Program Information Office. Booklet gives details on all programs available, eligibility requirements, calendar of application deadlines, and addresses of state arts agencies.

NEBRASKA ARTS COUNCIL, 8448 W. Center Rd., Omaha NE 68124. (402)554-2122. Director: Bob Pierle. Provides Artists-in-Schools programs, grants and advice to individual artists and nonprofit Nebraska organizations. Offers up to $500 in mini-grants, up to $20,000 in major grants and Artists-in-Schools grants to artists sponsored by nonprofit organizations. Write for application. Application deadline: February 1; 1 month before event for mini-grants.

NEVADA STATE COUNCIL ON THE ARTS, 560 Mill St., Reno NV 89502. (702)784-6231. Contact: Program Director. Provides Artists-in-Schools programs to artists/craftsmen through nonprofit organizations. Offers $1,200 monthly stipend for Artists-in-Schools program to painters, muralists, sculptors, potters, graphic designers and craftsmen. Available to Western artists.

NEW JERSEY STATE COUNCIL ON THE ARTS, 24 W. State St., Trenton NJ 08625. (609)292-6130. Executive Director: Al Kochka. Provides Artists-in-Schools programs, fellowships and grants to artists/craftsmen and organizations. Offers $3,000 in fellowships to architects, jewelers, sculptors, painters, potters, muralists, graphic designers and weavers. Available to New Jersey residents. Application deadline: February 1.

NEW MEXICO ART COMMISSION, Lew Wallace Bldg., State Capitol, Santa Fe NM 87503. Contact: Bernard B. Lopez. Artists wishing to apply for grants for projects should write and send resume.

NORTH CAROLINA ARTS COUNCIL, Dept. of Cultural Resources, Raleigh NC 27611. (919)733-7897 or 5896. Provides grants, grants-in-aid, Summer Intern Programs and Visiting Artist Programs to artists/craftsmen and nonprofit organizations. Offers $10,000 minimum annually for Visiting Artist Program; $500 monthly for 3-month Summer Intern Program; $1,000-3,000 in various grants. Application deadlines: March 1 for programs; April 1 for grants.

NORTHERN ARIZONA UNIVERSITY, Flagstaff AZ 86011. (602)523-4612. Contact: Ellery Gibson. Provides work-study programs and graduate assistantships to sculptors, potters, painters, graphic designers, fabric and jewelry craftsmen. Application deadline: spring.

OHIO ARTS COUNCIL, 50 W. Broad St., Columbus OH 43215. (614)466-2613. Visual Arts Coordinator: Jeffrey Alexander. Provides Artists-in-Schools programs and grants to artists/craftsmen and organizations. Offers Artists-in-Schools $10,800 long-term residency stipends, varying short-term residency stipends and $2-3 million in grants. Available to artists/craftsmen sponsored by organizations. Application deadlines: March 15 and September 15.

OKLAHOMA ARTS & HUMANITIES COUNCIL, 640 Jim Thorpe Bldg., Oklahoma City OK 73105. (405)521-2931. Community Services Assistant: Cheryl Alters. Provides Artists-in-Residence programs and grants to nonprofit organizations. Offers $1,000 monthly stipends for Artists-in-Residence to artists/craftsmen; $5,000 in grants to organizations. Prefers professional artists/craftsmen who have exhibited and given workshops. Application deadline: May 1.

OREGON ARTS COMMISSION, 494 State St., Salem OR 97301. Director: Peter Hero. All funds made on matching funds basis. Craftsmen, muralists, sculptors, painters and graphic designers should write for application.

ORGANIZATION OF AMERICAN STATES, Office of Direct Service Operations, Secretariat for Technical Cooperation, 1735 "I" St., NW, Washington DC 20006. Provides fellowships for study at a South American University or in the U.S. Open to persons with a university degree, or who have demonstrated ability to pursue advanced studies in their particular field of the visual arts. Candidate may not apply for a fellowship at a university in the country of which he is a citizen or maintains a permanent residence. Must have knowledge of the language of the country in which he wishes to study.

OTIS ART INSTITUTE, 2401 Wilshire Blvd., Los Angeles CA 90057. (213)387-5288. Financial Aid Officer: Judith Lymburner. Provides financial assistance to students who would be unable to pursue their education without such help. Offers grants-in-aid, Basic Educational Opportunity Grants, work-study programs, federally-insured student loans and Supplemental Educational Opportunity Grants.

PENNSYLVANIA COUNCIL ON THE ARTS, #3 Shore Drive Office Center, 2001 N. Front St., Harrisburg PA 17102. (717)787-6883. Coordinators: Jim Scaltz/Alice Eakin. Provides Artists-in-Schools programs and grants to nonprofit Pennsylvania arts/crafts organizations. Available to artists/craftsmen sponsored by an organization.

PIMA COUNTY PARKS & RECREATION DEPT., Arts Section, 1204 W. Silverlake Rd., Tucson AZ 85713. Contact: John Zeeb. Works with all visual artists. "The department acts as grant writer and grant distribution agency of the Arizona Commission on the Arts & Humanities, and of the National Endowment for the Arts. Grants to individuals are handled as salary, outright." Recent grants include a Comprehensive Employment Training Act salary grant to a metal sculptor to teach metal sculpture, construct civic metal sculpture for parks and schools, and to locate similar artists and other people interested in the arts; also an NEA grant to organize a Pima County Arts Council. Query with resume, slides and program proposal.

PROGRAMA FOMENTO ARTES POPULARES, Instituto De Cultura Puertorriquena, Apt. 4184, San Juan PR 00905. (809)724-6250. Director: Anibal Rodriguez Vera. Provides Artists-in-Schools programs, fellowships and marketing information to craftsmen and crafts organizations. Offers $1,000 monthly stipend for Artists-in-Schools programs and $60,000 in fellowships. Available to Puerto Rican craftsmen living in Puerto Rico.

RHODE ISLAND STATE COUNCIL ON THE ARTS, 4365 Post Rd., Greenwich RI 02840. (401)884-6410. Craftsman-in-Residence: George Van Duinwyk. Provides Artists-in-Schools programs, grants, grants-in-aid and marketing information to artists/craftsmen and organizations. Offers $3,000 grant to each craftsman. Grants-in-aid available to Rhode Island residents. Application deadline: February 18.

THE EDWARD C. AND ANN T. ROBERTS FOUNDATION, Box 437, Bloomfield CT 06002. Contact: Marshall Davenson. Provides scholarships and grants-in-aid to accredited schools, universities or arts organizations located in the Greater Hartford, Connecticut area. Offers funds to student visual artists; preference to disadvantaged youths. Application by letter from the school or organization, addressed as above, stating student's name, circumstances, abilities, cost and type of scholarship or grant should be made.

ROME PRIZE FELLOWSHIP, American Academy in Rome, 41 E. 65th St., New York NY 10021. Executive Secretary: Ruth D. Green. Provides fellowships to individual artists. Offers 1-year residency at Academy in Rome, $300 monthly stipend and $1,300 travel allowance to sculptors and painters. Write for application. Application deadline: November 15.

SANTE FE WORKSHOPS OF CONTEMPORARY ART, Box 1344, Santa Fe NM 87501. (505)983-5573. Advisory Director: Geraldine Price. Offers half tuition scholarships to painters, sculptors, printmakers and weavers. Application deadline: May 30 for 8-week summer session.

SCHOOL OF THE ART INSTITUTE OF CHICAGO, Jackson Blvd. at Columbus Dr., Chicago IL 60604. (312)443-3700. Contact: Dawn Burke Heffernan. Provides scholarships to art students. Write the Financial Aid Office.

SOUTH CAROLINA ARTS COMMISSION, 829 Richland St., Columbia SC 29201. (803)758-3442. Executive Director: Rick George. Provides Artists-in-Schools programs, fellowships, grants-in-aid, marketing information and various employment programs to artists/craftsmen and organizations. Offers individual $2,500 fellowships. Available to professional South Carolina artists/craftsmen ages 18+, who remain residents at least during the fellowship year. Write for information to Grants Coordinator. "We employ about 150-200 artists annually for short periods and 20 artists/craftsmen for 8 months+."

SOUTH DAKOTA ARTS COUNCIL, 108 W. 11th St., Sioux Falls SD 57102. Program Director: Dennis Holub. Provides Artists-in-Schools programs, fellowships and grants to artists/craftsmen and organizations. Offers $100 per day, short-term AIS residency; $10,800 for 10 month AIS residency; up to $1,000 in fellowships. Available to South Dakota residents. Application deadline: March 15.

JOHN F. AND ANNA LEE STACEY SCHOLARSHIP FUND, Box 2, Quemado NM 87829. Offers up to $4,000 annually for artists working in the conservative tradition. Available to artists ages 18-35. Application deadline: November 1. Write for application form.

TENNESSEE ARTS COMMISSION, Rm. 222, Capitol Hill Bldg., Nashville TN 37219. (615)741-1701. Contact: Director, Arts Programs. Provides Artists-in-Schools programs, grants, grants-in-aid and marketing information to arts/crafts organizations. Offers up to $5,000 in community assistance grants to organizations which employ artists/craftsmen. Application deadline: February 1. "Crafts Program operates sizable marketing and training services for craftsmen throughout the state."

TEXAS COMMISSION ON THE ARTS AND HUMANITIES, Box 13406, Capitol Station, Austin TX 78711. (512)475-6593. Contact: State/Community Division. Provides Artists-in-Schools programs, financial and technical assistance to nonprofit, tax-exempt arts/crafts organizations. Application deadlines: September and February.

U.S. CIVIL SERVICE COMMISSION, Arts-Related Federal Employment. Contact: Federal Job Information Center in area where employment is sought. Most arts-related jobs do not require a written test, but some do require the Professional and Administrative Career Exam (PACE), a written test given between fall and spring on a limited basis. Applications accepted from students who complete the courses necessary to meet examination requirements within 9 months. Following are some arts-related job classifications: art specialist, audiovisual production specialist, exhibits specialist, illustrator, interior designer, museum curator, museum specialist, visual information specialist, graphic designer, architect, landscape architect.

UPPER CATSKILL COMMUNITY COUNCIL OF THE ARTS, Rm. 101A, Old Milne Library, State University College, Oneonta NY 13820. (607)432-2070. Co-Executive Director: Leonard Ryndas. Provides grants and legal counseling to artists/craftsmen and organizations. Available to regional artists, ages 18+.

VIRGIN ISLANDS COUNCIL ON THE ARTS, Caravelle Arcade, Christiansted VI 00820. (809)773-3075. Executive Director: Stephen Bostic. Provides Artists-in-Schools programs, grants and scholarships to artists/craftsmen and organizations. Application deadline: June.
To Break In: "Potential applicants should discuss proposal with Council staff before submitting formal requests."

VIRGINIA MUSEUM, Boulevard and Grove Ave., Richmond VA 23221. (804)786-6324. Programs Director Secretary: Norine Ellwood. Provides fellowships to artists/craftsmen. Offers $1,500 student, $3,600 graduate and $2,400 professional fellowships to painters, sculptors, craftsmen, architects and designers. Available to 5-year (at least) Virginia residents or those born in the state. Write for application. Application deadline: April 1.

WASHINGTON STATE ARTS COMMISSION, Olympia WA 98504. (206)753-3860. Contact: James L. Haseltine. Offers grants-in-aid, grants and awards to sculptors, painters, graphic artists, mosaic artists, calligraphers, mixed media artists and craftsmen.

WEST VIRGINIA ARTS AND HUMANITIES COUNCIL, Science and Cultural Capitol Complex, Charleston WV 25305. (304)348-3711. Contact: Executive Director. Awards 9-month Artists-in-Residence grants to sculptors, painters and craftsmen. Grants made on matching funds basis. Submit resume and awards won. Resumes forwarded to communities applying for artist residencies.

WISCONSIN ARTS BOARD, 123 W. Washington Ave., Madison WI 53702. (608)266-0190. Executive Director: Jerrold Rouby. Provides Artists-in-Schools programs, fellowships, grants, grants-in-aid, legal referrals and scholarships to artists/craftsmen and organizations. Offers 5 $2,000 fellowships to visual artists. Available to Wisconsin residents with minimal exhibition record. No students. Application deadlines: September 15 for fellowships; March 1, June 15 and November 1 for other aid.

WYOMING COUNCIL ON THE ARTS, Cheyenne WY 82002. (307)777-7742. Contact: Executive Director. Request application forms for a specific project through a nonprofit organization. All grants made on matching funds basis. Grants to art association usually provide fees for painters, sculptors, muralists, graphic designers and craftsmen doing workshops or demonstrations, and for commissioning works of art. Submit resume, slides and awards won.

Art Colonies

Fewer than two dozen art colonies exist in the US today, but the need for more is great. According to Paul Pollaro of the MacDowell Colony, the few existing colonies are swamped with applicants.

For artists who show promise in their artistic endeavors, the art colony is an excellent place to find the right atmosphere for doing creative work, since they are far from the hectic rush of day-to-day living. In addition to working space, many of the colonies offer fellowships and other financial assistance. Read each listing to find information about where to apply, requirements and available facilities.

FINE ARTS WORK CENTER, Box 565, 24 Pearl St., Provincetown MA 02657. (617)487-9960. Director: Martha Fowlkes Egloff. Provides studio and living space and $100-200 monthly stipends to 10 painters and sculptors. Offers 7-month residencies from October 1-May 1. No fee. "Though there is no age limit, the Center aims to aid young candidates of outstanding promise."

THE MacDOWELL COLONY, 145 W. 58th St., #12C, New York NY 10019. Contact: Admissions Secretary. Located in Peterborough, New Hampshire. Provides room, board and exclusive use of studios equipped for art to 32 sculptors, printmakers and painters during the summer; 20 during other seasons. Average length of stay. 2 months. Only criterion for admission is "talent." Artists should file applications at least 6 months in advance. Fee: $7 per day. Fellowships available.

MILLAY COLONY FOR THE ARTS, Steepletop, Austerlitz NY 12017. (518)392-3103. Director: Ann-Ellen Lesser. Provides room, board and studio space to visual artists. Offers up to 2 months residencies during the winter; 1 month in summer. Write for application.

VIRGINIA CENTER FOR THE CREATIVE ARTS, Sweet Briar College, Sweet Briar VA 24595. (804)381-5693. Director: William Smart. Provides room, board, studio space and fee abatement if needed to 4 painters, sculptors and potters. Offers 1-3 month residencies year-round. Fee: $10 daily.

THE HELENE WURLITZER FOUNDATION OF NEW MEXICO, Box 545, Taos NM 87571. Executive Director: Henry A. Sauerwein, Jr. Provides 12 separate studio-apartments, completely furnished, to artists in all media: painting, sculpture and allied fields. Offers 3-month residencies with extensions up to 1 year. Open year-round. Studios are rent and utilities free, but residents must purchase, cook and serve their own meals, and take care of their apartments. No provisions for travel to and from Taos, stipends for living expenses or direct grants. Spouses and children may not live in foundation during residency. Write for application.

YADDO, Box 395, Saratoga Springs NY 12866. (518)584-0746. Director: Curtis Harnack. Provides room, board and studio space to 30 painters, photographers and sculptors. Offers up to 2-month residencies for 7 artists in summer, 3 in winter. No fee. For professionals who have had at least 1 show beyond student work. Write for application forms before February 1.

Publications of Interest

The listings in this book and introductory materials have been designed to help the artist/craftsman sell his work. But, it would be impossible for them to cover every market and every marketing technique. New ideas and outlets pop up every day. The listings in this section are here to help steer you to additional sources of markets and for more in-depth information on art and crafts. Included are magazines, newsletters, books and publishing sources.

AMERICAN ARTIST, Billboard Publications, 1 Astor Plaza, New York NY 10036. 100-page monthly magazine. Deals with all aspects of practicing art. Contains marketing information, book reviews, technical information, announcements of upcoming exhibitions and articles on successful artists.

AMERICAN ARTIST BUSINESS LETTER, Billboard Publications, 2160 Patterson St., Cincinnati OH 45214. 8-page newsletter published monthly except July and August. Deals with all aspects of practicing art. Frequently an entire issue will be devoted to one subject. Sample topics include financial institutions offering exhibit space, contracts, taxes and recordkeeping.

ART & THE LAW, Volunteer Lawyers for the Arts, 36 W. 44th St., New York NY 10036. 8-page newsletter. Deals with legislation of interest to artists. Subscription available through contribution.

THE ART OF WINNING FOUNDATION GRANTS, The Vanguard Press, 424 Madison Ave., New York NY 10017. Authors: Howard Hillman/Karin Abarbanel. 104-page book. Deals with choosing and applying to a foundation for a grant.

ART WORKERS NEWS, Foundation for the Community of Artists, 32 Union Square E., New York NY 10003. Bimonthly 8-page tabloid. Deals with marketing, legislation related to the arts, interviews with successful individuals and groups, hazards on the job and other valuable topics.

ARTISTS EQUITY ASSOCIATION, 2813 Albemarle St. NW, Washington DC 20008. Write for artist-gallery or artist-architect contract forms.

THE ARTIST'S GUIDE TO HIS MARKET, Watson-Guptill Publications, 1 Astor Plaza, New York NY 10036. Author: Betty Chamberlain (member of the Board of Directors of the Art Information Center, Inc. in New York City). 176-page book for painters, sculptors and printmakers who are looking for gallery space. Deals with shopping for a gallery, business terms and agreements, where to find legal advice and grants, and sample contracts, bills of sale and receipts. (Note: the copyright information in Chamberlain's book was written before passage of the 1976 copyright law.)

THE ARTIST'S HANDBOOK OF MATERIALS AND TECHNIQUES, The Viking Press, Inc., 625 Madison Ave., New York NY 10022. Editor: Ralph Mayer. 750-page reference book. Deals with synthetic resins, luminescent pigments, printmaking, collages, rubbings, preparing a canvas or wall, and other information of value to practicing artists.

ARTWEEK, 1305 Franklin St., Oakland CA 94612. Weekly 20-page tabloid. Deals mainly with gallery happenings.

THE CARTOONIST, National Cartoonist Society, 281 Bayberry Lane, Westport CT 06880. Newsletter dealing with happenings in the cartoon field and related areas.

COMMERCIAL ARTIST'S HANDBOOK, Watson-Guptill Publications, 1 Astor Plaza, New York NY 10036. Author: John Snyder. 264-page reference book for artists who must prepare material for reproduction by a printer. Describes more than 400 materials.

CONTEMPORARY CRAFTS MARKET PLACE, R. R. Bowker Co., 1180 Avenue of the Americas, New York NY 10036. Compiled by the American Crafts Council. Annual crafts directory containing listings of craft dealers, organizations, courses, audiovisual materials, suppliers, packers, shipping companies, insurers and publications.

THE CRAFTS BUSINESS ENCYCLOPEDIA, Harcourt Brace Jovanovich, Inc., 757 3rd Ave., New York NY 10017. Author: Michael Scott (editor of *The Crafts Report,* author of a weekly newspaper column and president of the International Guild of Craft Journalists, Authors and Photographers). 320-page handbook for anyone who makes crafts for sale. Organized in alphabetical order, it discusses everything from accounting to zoning, including necessities such as balance sheets, consignment sales, overhead and portfolios. Also included are basic business know-hows such as finance, insurance, marketing, bookkeeping, credit, taxes, and sales promotion.

THE CRAFTS REPORT, 1529 E. 19th St., Brooklyn NY 11230. Monthly 8-page tabloid. Deals with marketing and managing crafts. Regular features include a list of galleries seeking crafts, book reviews, upcoming fairs and teaching opportunities.

CRAFTSMEN IN BUSINESS: A GUIDE TO FINANCIAL MANAGEMENT & TAXES, American Crafts Council, 44 W. 53rd St., New York NY 10019. Author: Howard W. Connaughton, C.P.A. 73-page book. Deals with the financial aspects of running a crafts business, from accounting to taxes. Both artists and craftsmen will find this book helpful.

FARMER COOPERATIVE INFORMATION, Room 1474, South Building, U.S. Department of Agriculture, Washington DC 20250. Write for a list of their publications on starting a craft cooperative.

FINE ARTS MARKET PLACE, R. R. Bowker Co., 1180 Avenue of the Americas, New York NY 10036. Annual directory listing art buyers, services, suppliers, art organizations and exhibitions.

HOW TO MAKE MONEY WITH YOUR CRAFTS, William Morrow and Company, Inc., 105 Madison Ave., New York NY 10016. Author: Leta Clark. 240-page book on selling crafts. Deals with financing, bookkeeping, legal problems, advertising, mail order and other marketing subjects.

HOW TO SELL YOUR ART AND CRAFTS, Charles Scribner's Sons, 597 5th Ave., New York NY 10017. Author: Loretta Holz. 267-page book. Deals with ways to sell work and the advantages of each; legal obligations of partnerships; employer-employee arrangements; tax returns; handling public relations; and how to set up a business.

INTERNATIONAL GUILD OF CRAFT JOURNALISTS, AUTHORS & PHOTOGRAPHERS, 1529 E. 19th St., Brooklyn NY 11230. For writers and photographers of crafts. Members receive a periodical newsletter.

LEGAL GUIDE FOR THE VISUAL ARTIST, Hawthorn Books, Inc., 260 Madison Ave., New York NY 10016. Author: Tad Crawford (New York lawyer and lecturer at the School of Visual Arts on "Law and the Visual Artist"). 257-page book. Deals with the new copyright law, artist's rights, reproduction rights, publishing and dealer contracts, donations and estate planning.

MARKETING ART: A HANDBOOK FOR THE ARTIST AND ART DEALER, Gee Tee Bee, 11901 Sunset Blvd., #102, Los Angeles CA 90049. Author: Calvin Goodman. 318-page book. Deals with promotion, marketing, pricing, artist-dealer relationships and other aspects of marketing art.

THE NATIONAL DIRECTORY OF GRANTS AND AID TO INDIVIDUALS IN THE ARTS, Washington International Arts Letter, Box 9005, Washington DC 20003. Annual directory listing most grants, prizes and awards for professional work in the U.S. and abroad, and information about universities and schools that offer special aid to students.

PHOTOGRAPHING CRAFTS, American Crafts Council, 44 W. 53rd St., New York NY 10019. 66-page book. Deals with photographing your arts and crafts to their best advantage.

PHOTOGRAPHY FOR ARTISTS AND CRAFTSMEN, Van Nostrand Reinhold Co., 450 W. 33rd St., New York NY 10001. Author: Claus-Peter Schmid. Deals with amateur photography pertaining specifically to artists and craftsmen who want to photograph their work.

SELLING YOUR ART WORK: A MARKETING GUIDE FOR FINE AND COMMERCIAL ARTISTS, A.S. Barnes and Company, Inc., Forsgate Dr. Canbury NJ 08512. Author: Milton K. Berlye. 272-page book for the beginning artist. Deals with the background needed and the type of jobs available in the art field.

U.S. SMALL BUSINESS ADMINISTRATION, Room 3100, 26 Federal Plaza, New York NY 10007. Write for a full list of their publications on management assistance.

WASHINGTON INTERNATIONAL ARTS LETTER, 1321 4th St., SW, Washington DC 20024. Monthly 8-page newsletter. Deals with governmental happenings, support programs and reading of interest to artists.

THE WORKING CRAFTSMAN, Box 42, Northbrook IL 60062. 50-page magazine published 5 times annually. Regular features include a marketing column, book reviews, fiber news, and announcements of show openings, upcoming shows and exhibits.

Glossary

Acetate. Sheet of clear plastic film fastened over the front of artwork for protection.

Airbrush. Small pressure gun, shaped like a pencil, that sprays watercolor pigment by means of compressed air.

Animation. The creation of motion by filming still-art sequences one frame at a time.

Artists-in-Schools Program. Funded by the National Endowment for the Arts and administered by individual states, the program offers visual and performing artists salaried residencies at colleges and universities.

Batik. Method of decorating fabrics in which the parts not to be colored are covered with wax before dyeing. The wax is removed by boiling and the process repeated for each color used.

Ben-Day. An artificial process of shading line illustrations, named after its inventor.

Biennial. Every two years.

Bimonthly. Every two months.

Biweekly. Every two weeks.

Blueprint. A. Detailed outline or plan. B. Photographic reproduction, usually of architectural or engineering plans, in white on a blue background.

Calligraphy. The art of fine handwriting.

Caption. The words printed, usually directly beneath, a cartoon.

Cartography. The production of maps, including construction of projections, designs, compilation, drafting and reproduction.

Casein: Water-soluble synthetic paint derived from milk.

Color Separation. Process of preparing artwork for the printer by separating one color from another by using overlays of black or color negatives for each color.

Commission. Percentage of retail price taken by a sponsor/salesman on work sold.

Comp. See Comprehensive.

Comprehensive. Complete sketch of layout showing how a finished illustration will look when printed.

Consignment. Arrangement in which the artist/craftsman leaves his work in a shop/gallery and does not get paid for the work until it is sold.

Decoupage. Arrangement of paper cutouts into a composition on a surface, then usually varnished.

Delineator. Artist who does sketches or traces outlines, usually of buildings or sites for architectural purposes.

Diorama. A. Picture painted on a set of transparent cloth curtains and viewed through a small opening. B. Scenic representation in which sculptured figures and life-like details are displayed so as to blend with a realistic painted background.

Direct Mail Package. Sales or promotional material that is distributed by mail. Usually, it consists of an outer envelope, a cover letter, a brochure or flyer, and a postpaid reply card or order form with business reply envelope.

Engraving. Designs or letters cut into wood, metal, linoleum, etc., often for the purpose of making reproductions, i.e. engraving copper or zinc plates for letterpress printing.

Etching. Designs cut into metal or glass by means of acid.

Exclusive Representation: Requirement that an artist/craftsman's work appear in only one gallery/shop within a defined geographical area.

First Rights. The artist gives the purchaser the right to reproduce the work once in one publication, and the artist agrees not to permit any prior publication of the work elsewhere for a specified amount of time.

Flap Art. Artwork with the basic color done on one surface with a transparent overlay or flap containing the second color indication.

Gag. Amusing remark, joke or funny situation conveyed into visual form.

Graphic Arts. A. General term for the arts connected with engraving and printing. B. Art, such as drawing, which is linear in character.

Halftone. Reproduction of a continuous tone illustration with the image formed by dots produced by a camera lens screen.

Keyline. Identification, through signs and symbols, of the positions of illustrations and copy for the printer.

Layout. Arrangement of photographs, illustrations, text and headlines for printed material.

Letterhead. The name, address, etc., of a firm or organization printed as a heading on letter paper.

Letterpress. Printing process in which ink is collected on raised surfaces on the printing plate and transferred directly to the paper.

Line Drawing. Illustration done with pencil or ink using no wash or other shading.

Lithography. The process of printing from a stone or metal surface on which the image to be printed is ink-receptive and the blank area ink-repellent.

Logos. See Logotype.

Logotype. Name or design of a company or product used as a trademark in advertising.

Mechanicals. Paste-up or preparation of work for printing.

Mural. A picture, especially a large one, painted on a wall or ceiling.

Muslin. Made of muslin, a sample created to show how a final garment will appear.

NFS. Not for sale.

Offset. Printing process in which a flat printing plate is treated to be ink-receptive in image areas and ink-repellent in non-image areas. Ink is transferred from the printing plate to a rubber plate, and then to the paper.

One-time Rights. The artist sells the right to use his artwork one-time in any copyrighted media. The rights transfer back to the artist on his request after the artwork's use.

Overlay. Transparent cover over copy, where instructions, corrections or color location directions are given.

Panel. In cartooning, refers to the number of boxed-in illustrations, i.e. single panel, double panel or multi-panel.

Paste-up. Procedure involving coating the backside of art, type, photostats, etc., with rubber cement or wax and adhering them on the proper positions on the mechanical board. The boards are then used as finished art by the printer.

Photocopy. Inexpensive photographic reproduction process.

Point-of-Purchase. Display device or structure located with the product in or at the retail outlet; it advertises the product and is intended to increase sales of the product.

POR. Price on request.

Price on Request. A work's price is not immediately available to the retail customer and must be requested from the director or artist.

Prospectus. Preliminary statement describing a competition or exhibition.

Purchase Prize. Awarded for an entry which has been purchased by the sponsors of a competition.

Reproductions. Mechanically-made copies of original work.

Retouching. Adding new details or touches to art or photographs for correction or improvement.

Rotogravure. Printing process in which ink is collected in depressions on the printing plate and transferred directly to the paper.

Royalty. An agreed percentage paid by the salesman to the artist for each copy of his work sold.

Second (Reprint) Rights. The artist (or owner of the art's rights) sells the right to reprint an already published artwork.

Serigraph. Print made by the silkscreen process.

Semiannual. Two times yearly.

Semimonthly. Two times monthly.

Serial Rights. The artist sells the right to use his work in a periodical. Rights usually transfer back to the artist on his request after the artwork's use.

Simultaneous Rights. The artist sells the right to use his work simultaneously to more than one party.

Simultaneous Submissions. Submission of the same artwork to more than one potential buyer at the same time.

Speculation. Creating artwork with no assurance that the buyer will purchase it or reimburse expenses in any way, as opposed to creating artwork on assignment.

Spot Drawing. Small illustration used to decorate or enhance a page of type, or to serve as a column ending.

Storyboard. Series of panels which illustrates a progressive sequence of graphics and story copy for a TV commercial, film or filmstrip. Serves as a guide for the eventual finished product.

Syndicate. Corporation which distributes comic strips, cartoons and other features to publications. Usually, the syndicate takes a 25-50% commission.

Tabloid. Newspaper that is about half the page size of an ordinary newspaper and which often contains news in condensed form and many photographs.

Tearsheet. Published page containing an artist's illustration, cartoon, design or photograph of work.

Technical Art. The drawing of machines and structures. Also known as mechanical drawing.

Tempera. Painting medium in which pigment is mixed with water-soluble materials such as egg yolk or a gelatin substance.

Terrazzo. Mosaic flooring using small pieces of marble or granite embedded in mortar and polished.

Tole Painting. Decorative painting on tin or other metal, especially on trays, lamps or boxes.

Transparency. Color film with positive image.

Type Spec. Determination of the size and style of type to be used in a layout.

Velox. Photoprint of a continuous tone subject that has been transformed into line art by means of a halftone screen.

Wash. Thin application of transparent color, or watercolor black, for a pastel or gray tone effect.

Woodcut. Design produced on wood by removing the layers surrounding the drawn image. Prints are made by inking the image which is then pressed against paper.

Index